Chobits
ちょびっツ

D1264197

◀ BOOK 2 ▶

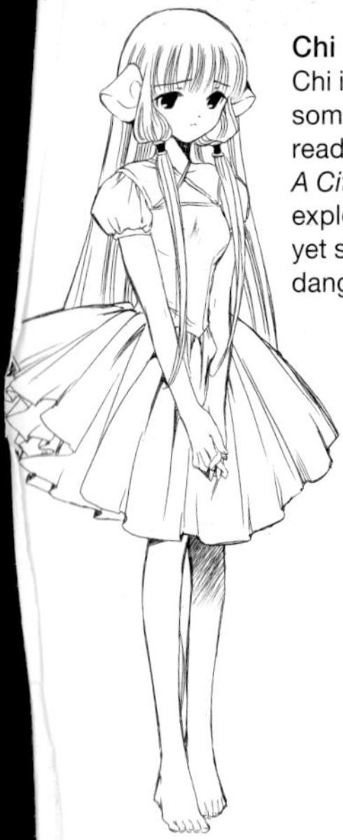

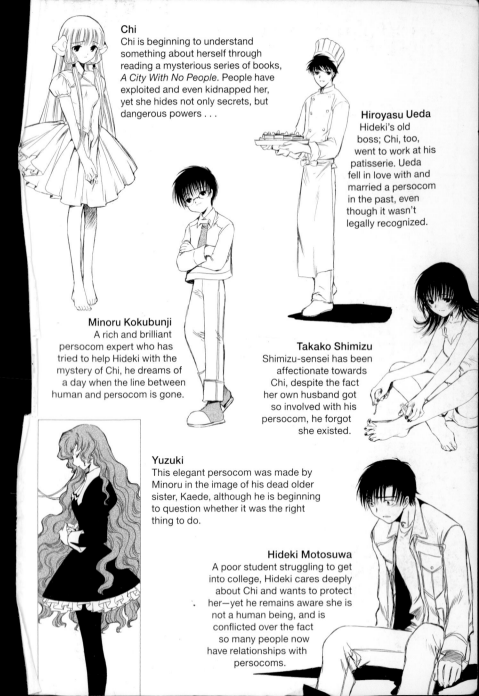

Chi
Chi is beginning to understand something about herself through reading a mysterious series of books, *A City With No People*. People have exploited and even kidnapped her, yet she hides not only secrets, but dangerous powers . . .

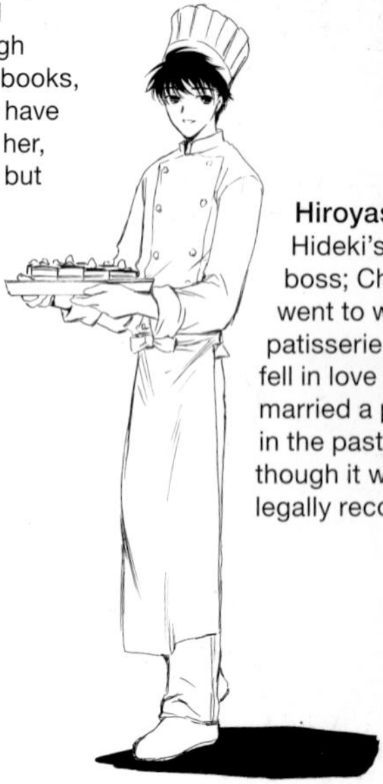

Hiroyasu Ueda
Hideki's old boss; Chi, too, went to work at his patisserie. Ueda fell in love with and married a persocom in the past, even though it wasn't legally recognized.

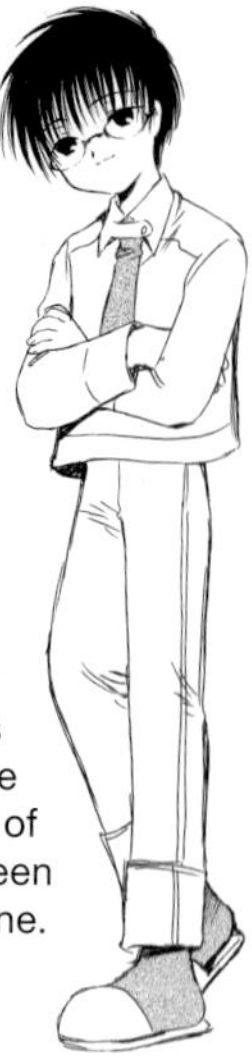

Minoru Kokubunji
A rich and brilliant persocom expert who has tried to help Hideki with the mystery of Chi, he dreams of a day when the line between human and persocom is gone.

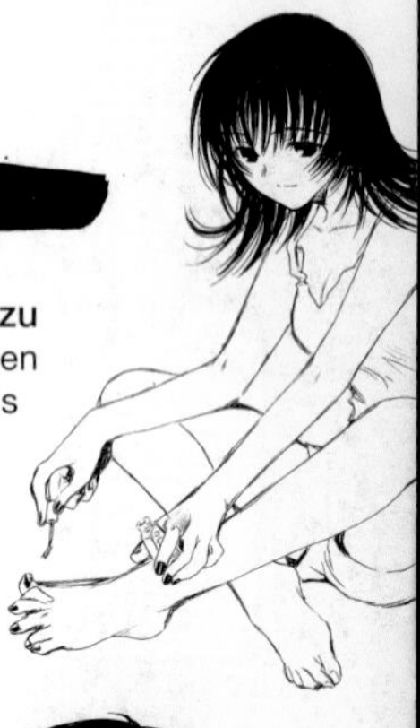

Takako Shimizu
Shimizu-sensei has been affectionate towards Chi, despite the fact her own husband got so involved with his persocom, he forgot she existed.

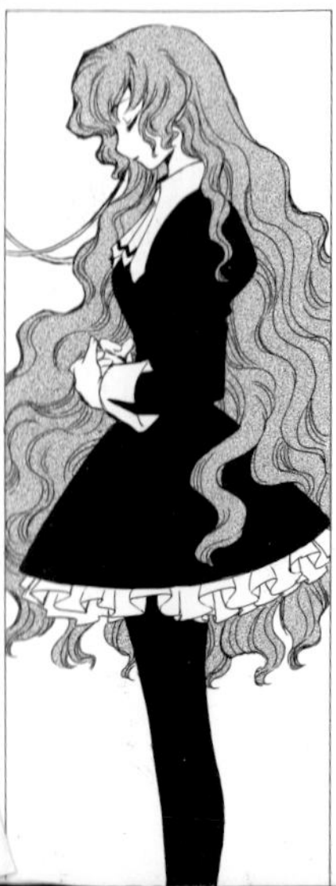

Yuzuki
This elegant persocom was made by Minoru in the image of his dead older sister, Kaede, although he is beginning to question whether it was the right thing to do.

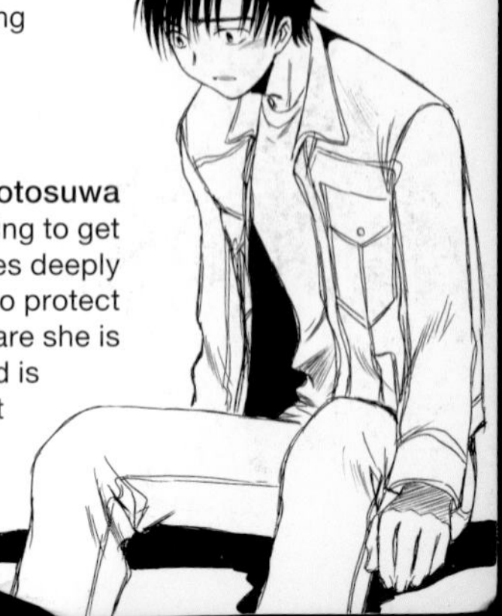

Hideki Motosuwa
A poor student struggling to get into college, Hideki cares deeply about Chi and wants to protect her—yet he remains aware she is not a human being, and is conflicted over the fact so many people now have relationships with persocoms.

SOME OF THE CHARACTERS IN *CHOBITS* BOOK 2

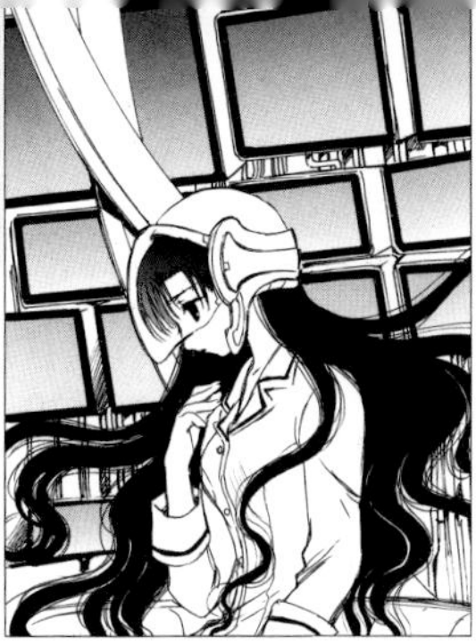

Chitose Hibiya
Motosuwa's landlady, and obviously something much more; Hibiya has been monitoring events using a high-tech cybernetic interface in her basement.

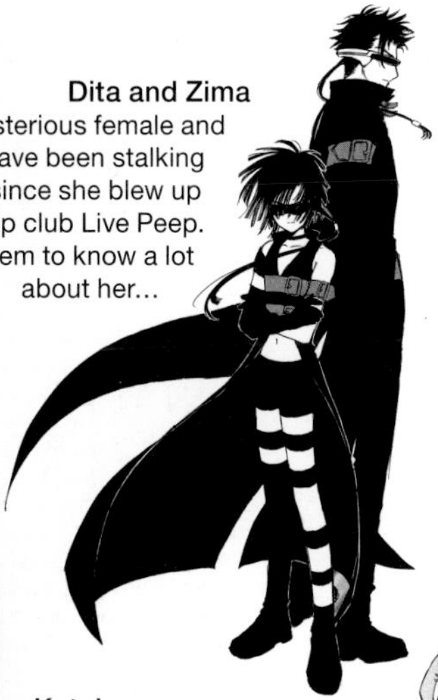

Dita and Zima
This mysterious female and male pair have been stalking Chi ever since she blew up the strip club Live Peep. They seem to know a lot about her...

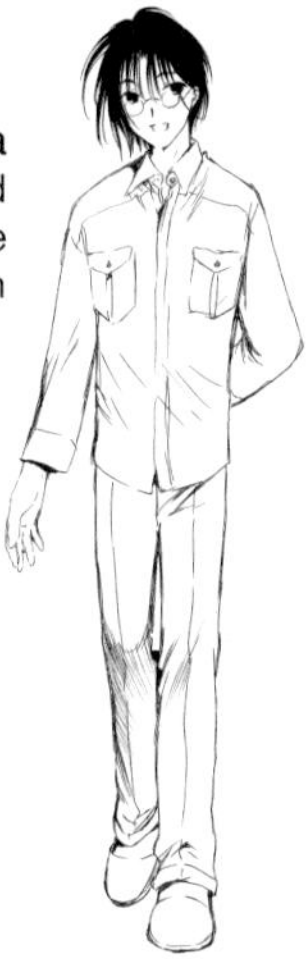

Yoshiyuki Kojima
Kojima frequented Minoru's online custom persocom board; he has since abducted Chi, and hopes to discover her secrets.

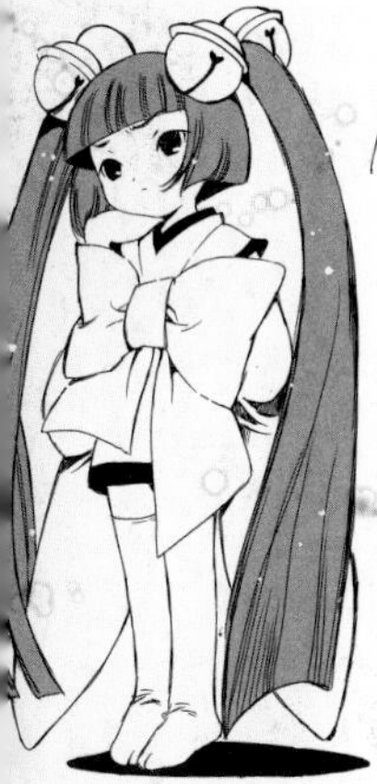

Kotoko
A "laptop" persocom that Kojima built to be desktop powerful, Kotoko has a serious and frank personality, which means Chi (and Sumomo) exasperate her to no end.

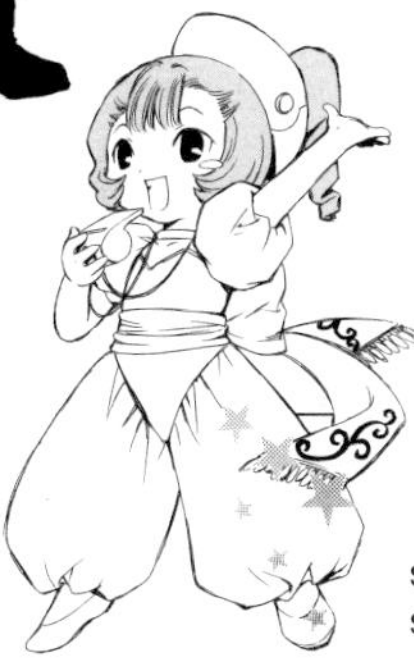

Sumomo
A sprightly "laptop" persocom, Sumomo belonged to Shimbo, but he lent her to Hideki to help him stay connected in his search for Chi.

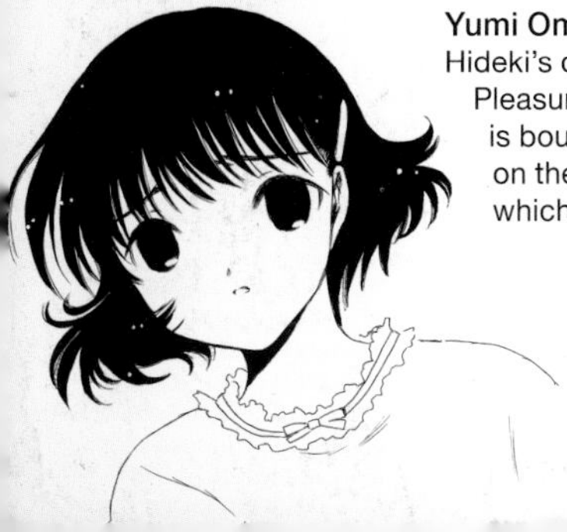

Yumi Omura
Hideki's coworker at Club Pleasure; a high-school student who is bouncy and cheerful . . . except on the subject of persocoms, which make her very depressed.

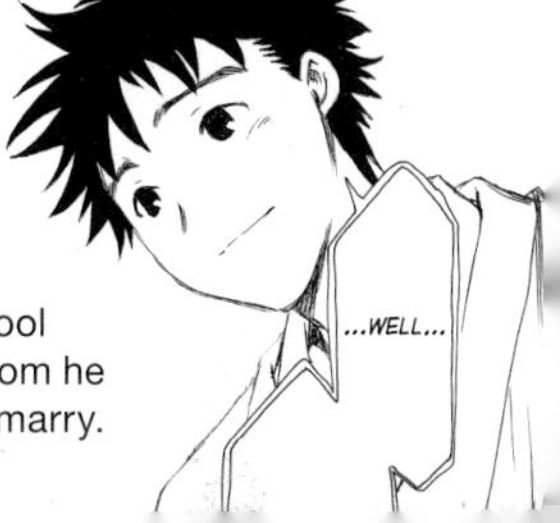
...WELL...

Hiromu Shimbo
Motosuwa's best friend has run off with their cram-school teacher, Shimizu-sensei, whom he now intends to marry.

CLAMP

SATSUKI IGARASHI
MOKONA
TSUBAKI NEKOI
NANASE OHKAWA

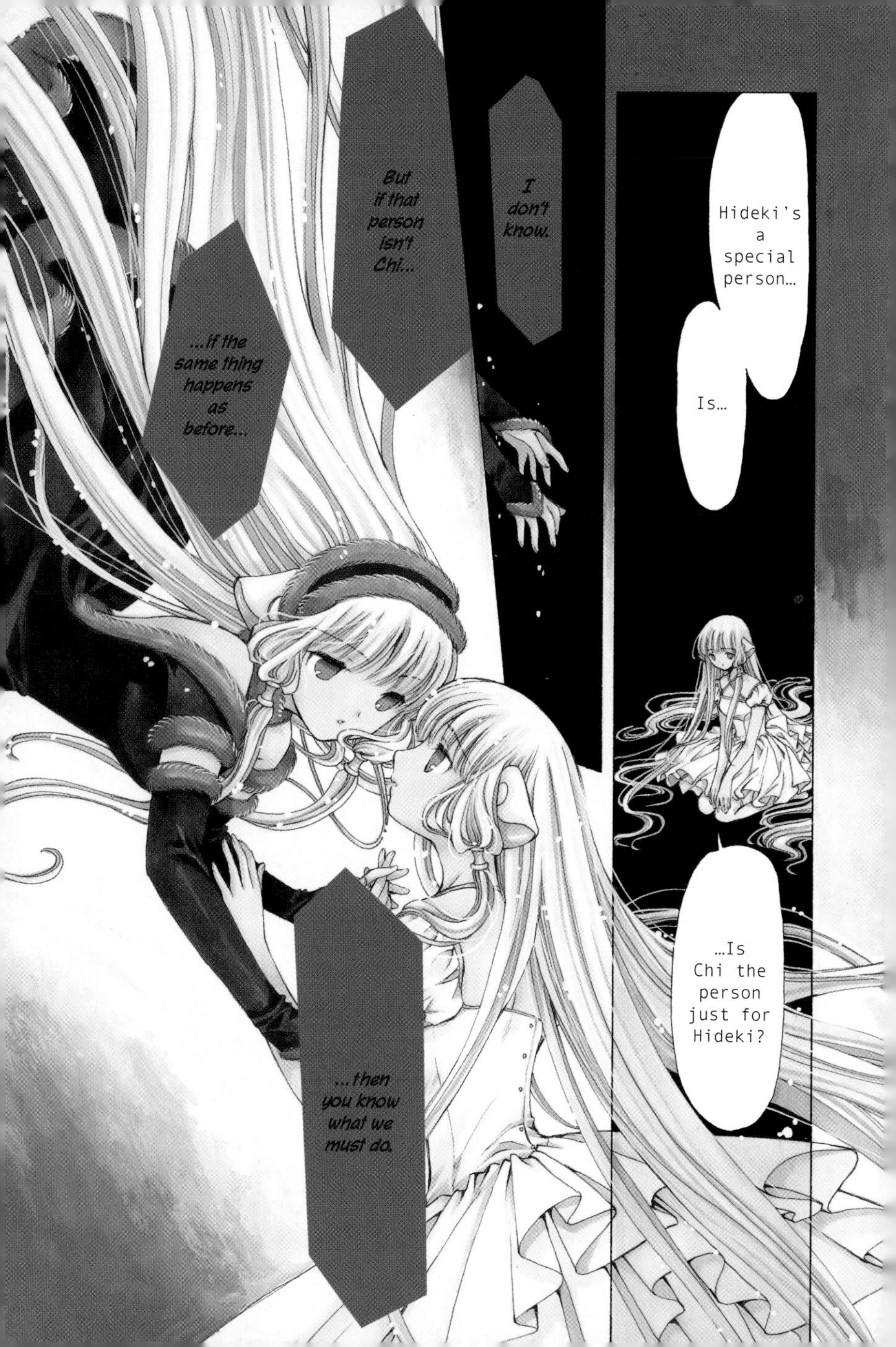
Hideki's a special person…
Is…
…Is Chi the person just for Hideki?
I don't know.
But if that person isn't Chi…
…if the same thing happens as before…
…then you know what we must do.

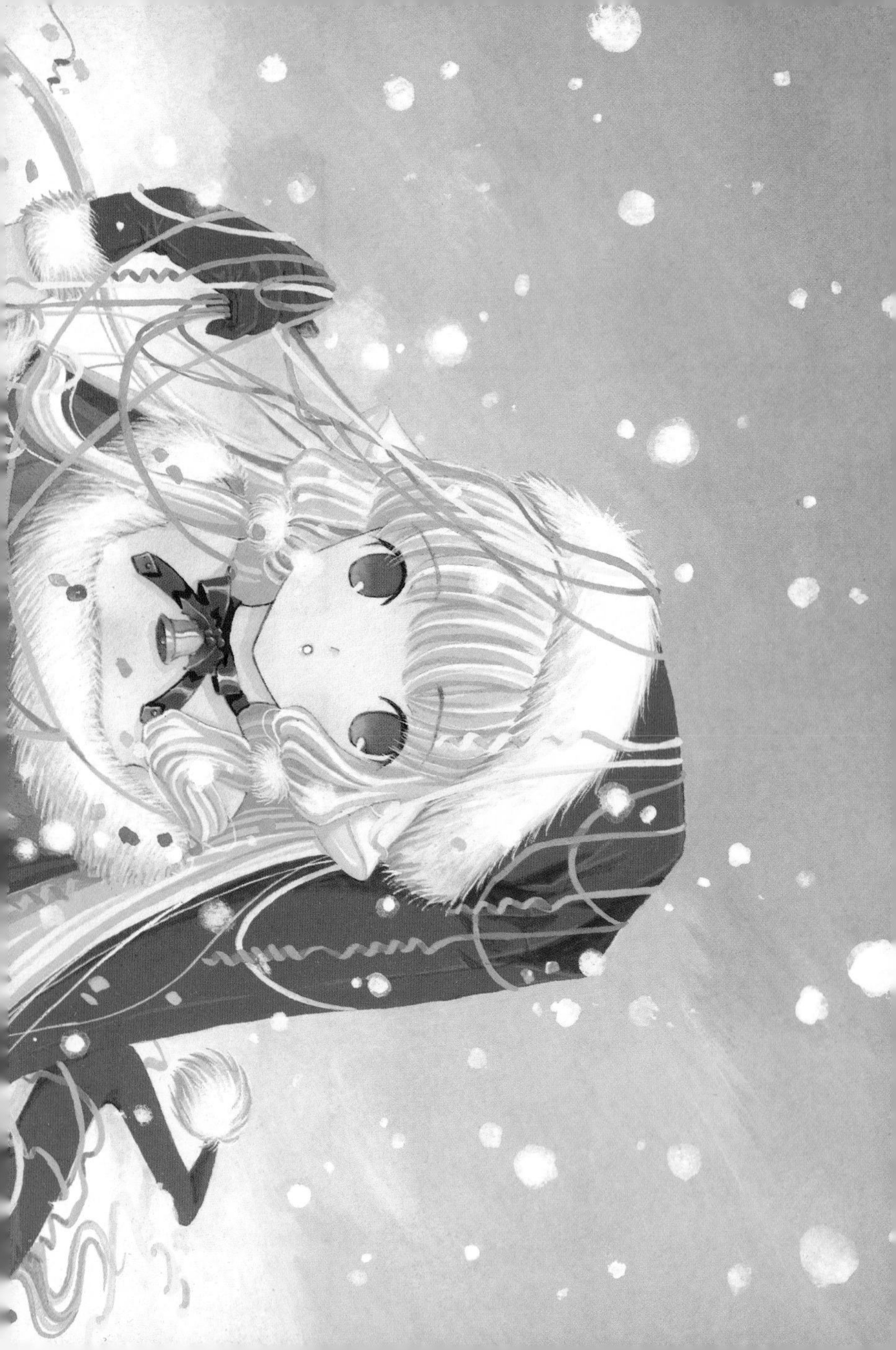

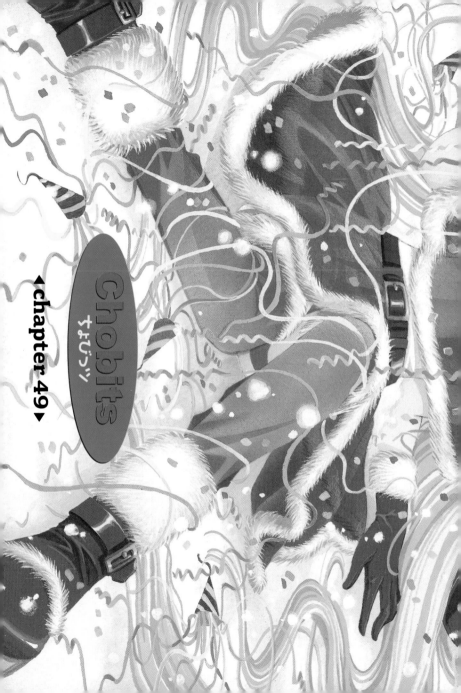

Chobits
ちょびっツ

◂chapter 49▸

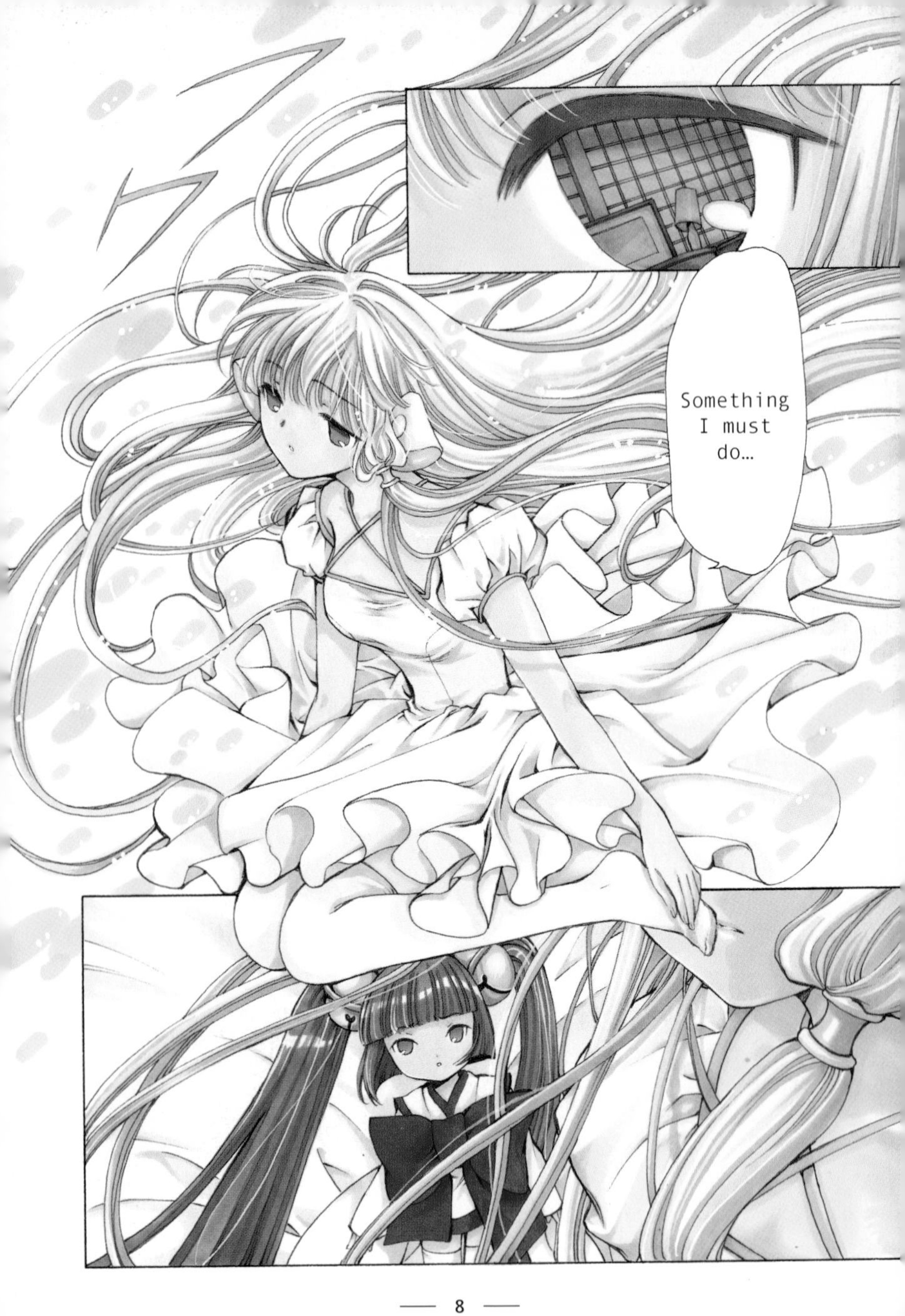
Something I must do...

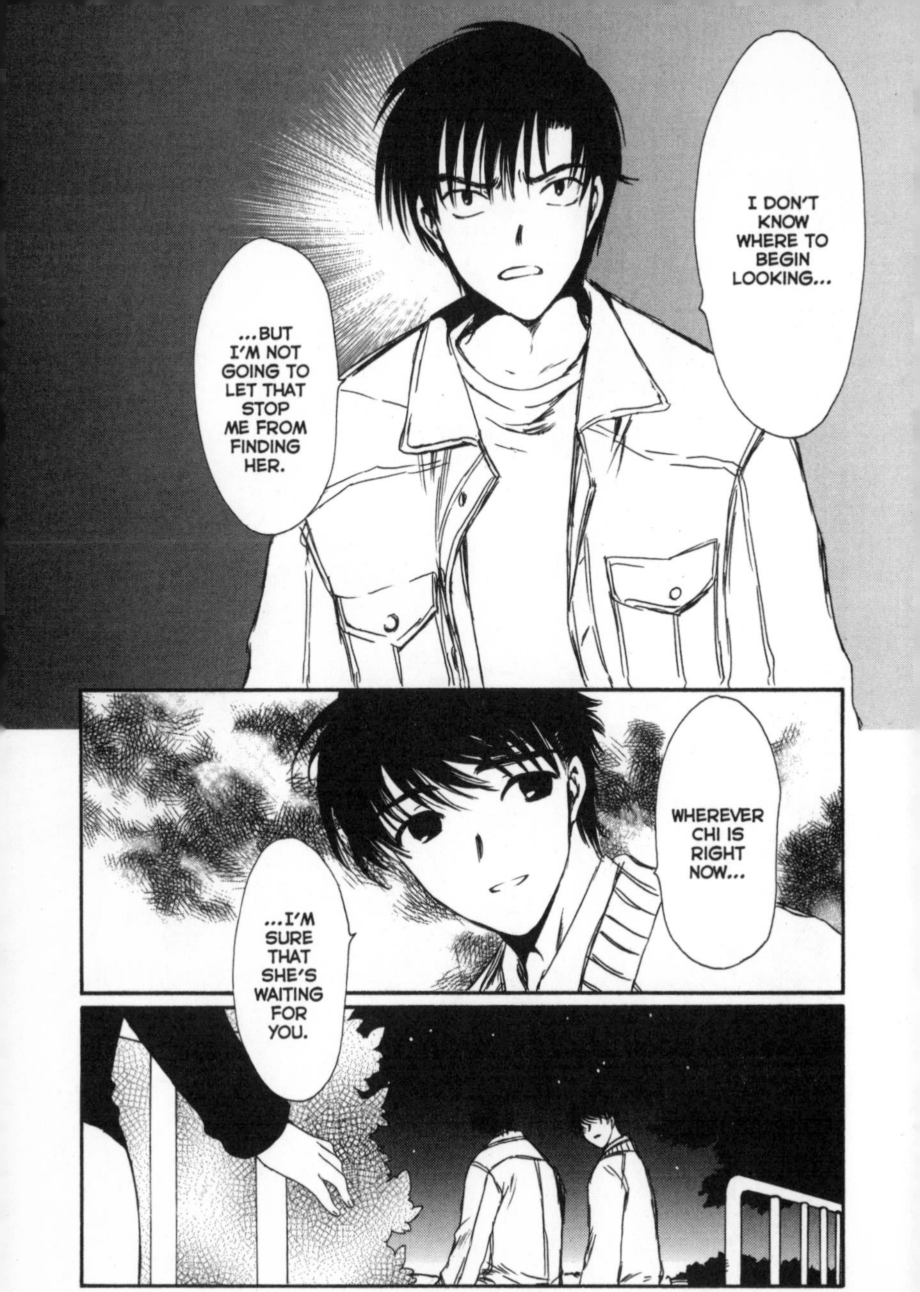
I DON'T KNOW WHERE TO BEGIN LOOKING...
...BUT I'M NOT GOING TO LET THAT STOP ME FROM FINDING HER.
WHEREVER CHI IS RIGHT NOW...
...I'M SURE THAT SHE'S WAITING FOR YOU.

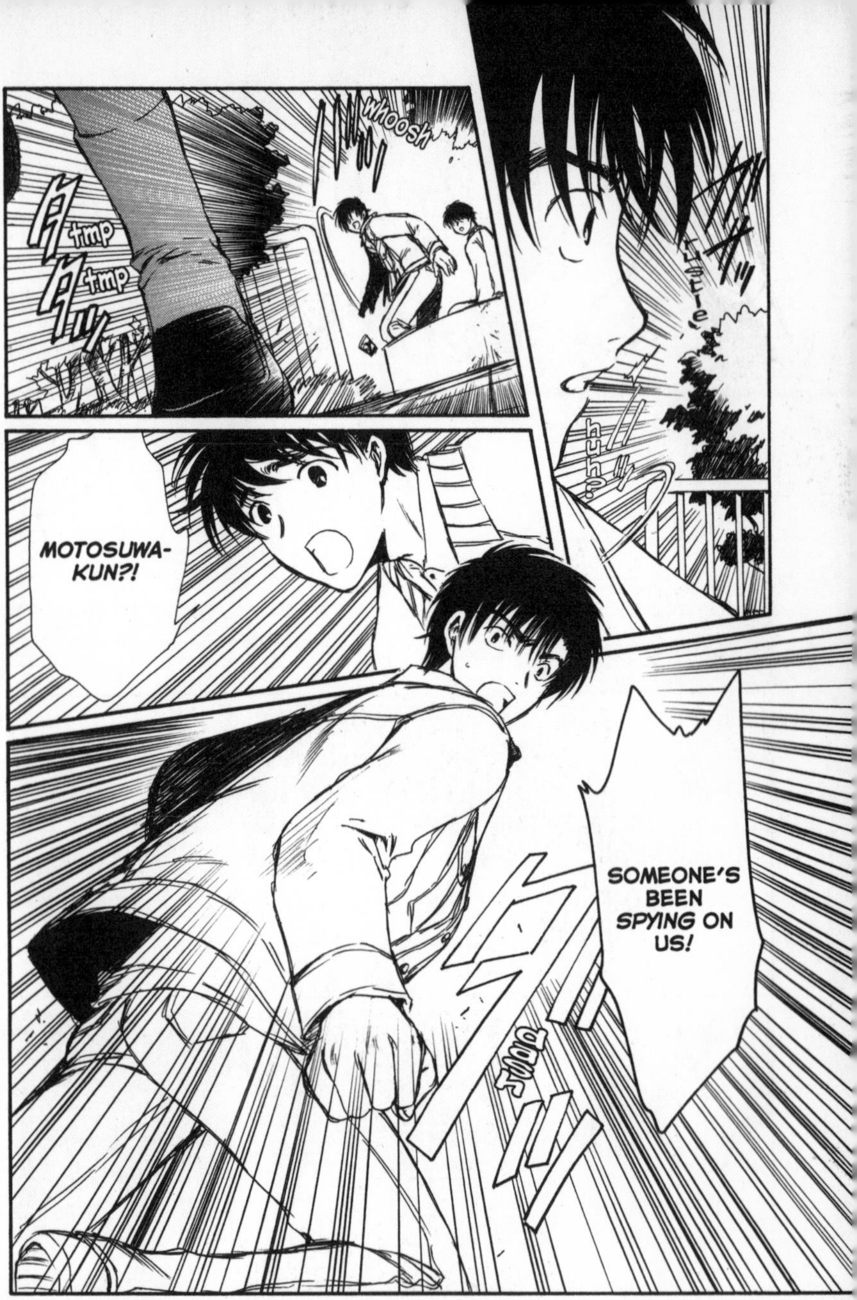
rustle
huh?
whoosh
tmp
tmp
MOTOSUWA-KUN?!
SOMEONE'S BEEN SPYING ON US!

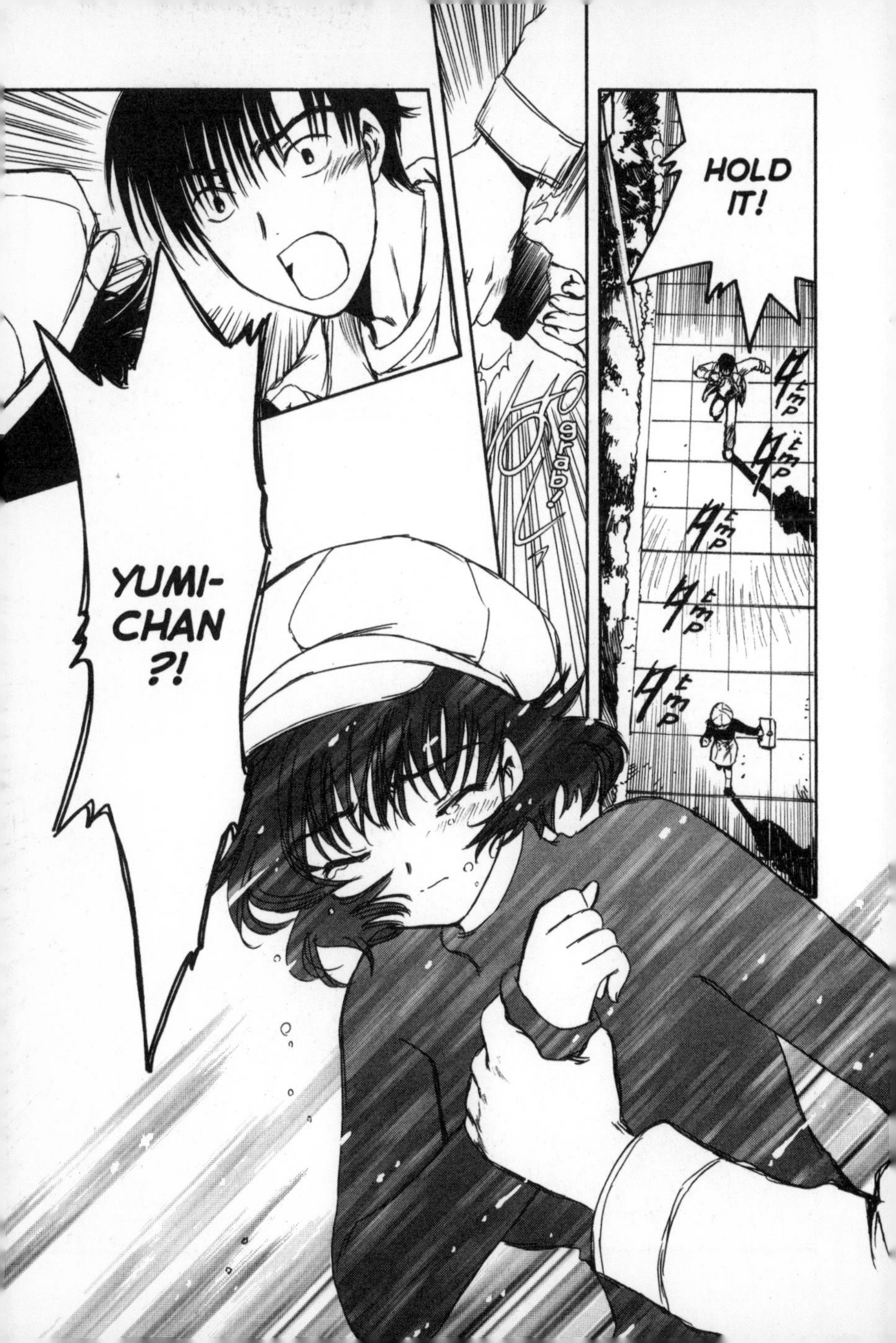
HOLD IT!
grab!
YUMI-CHAN ?!

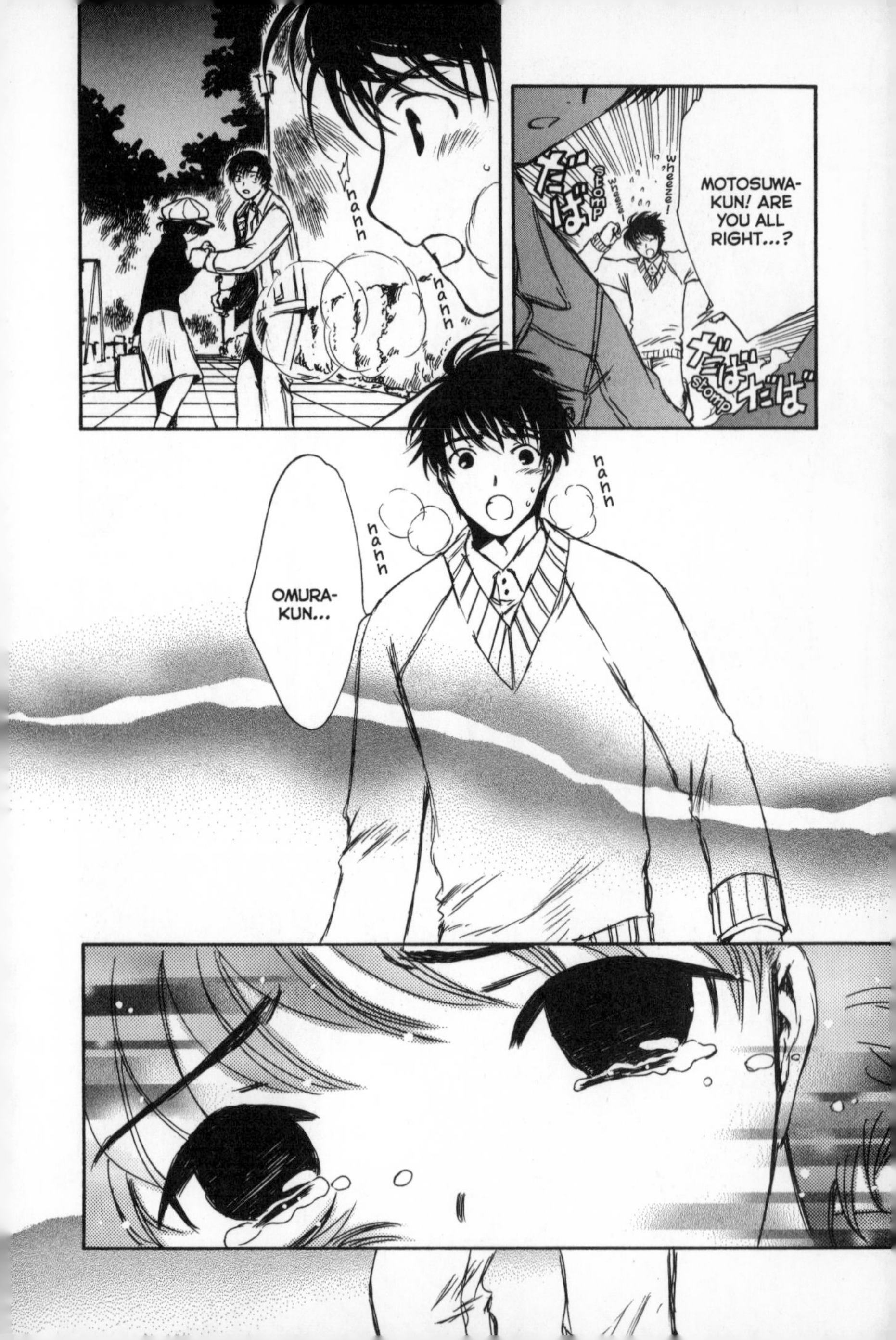
MOTOSUWA-KUN! ARE YOU ALL RIGHT...?
wheeze! wheeze!
だば
stomp
だばだば
stomp
hann
hann
hann
hann
OMURA-KUN...
hann

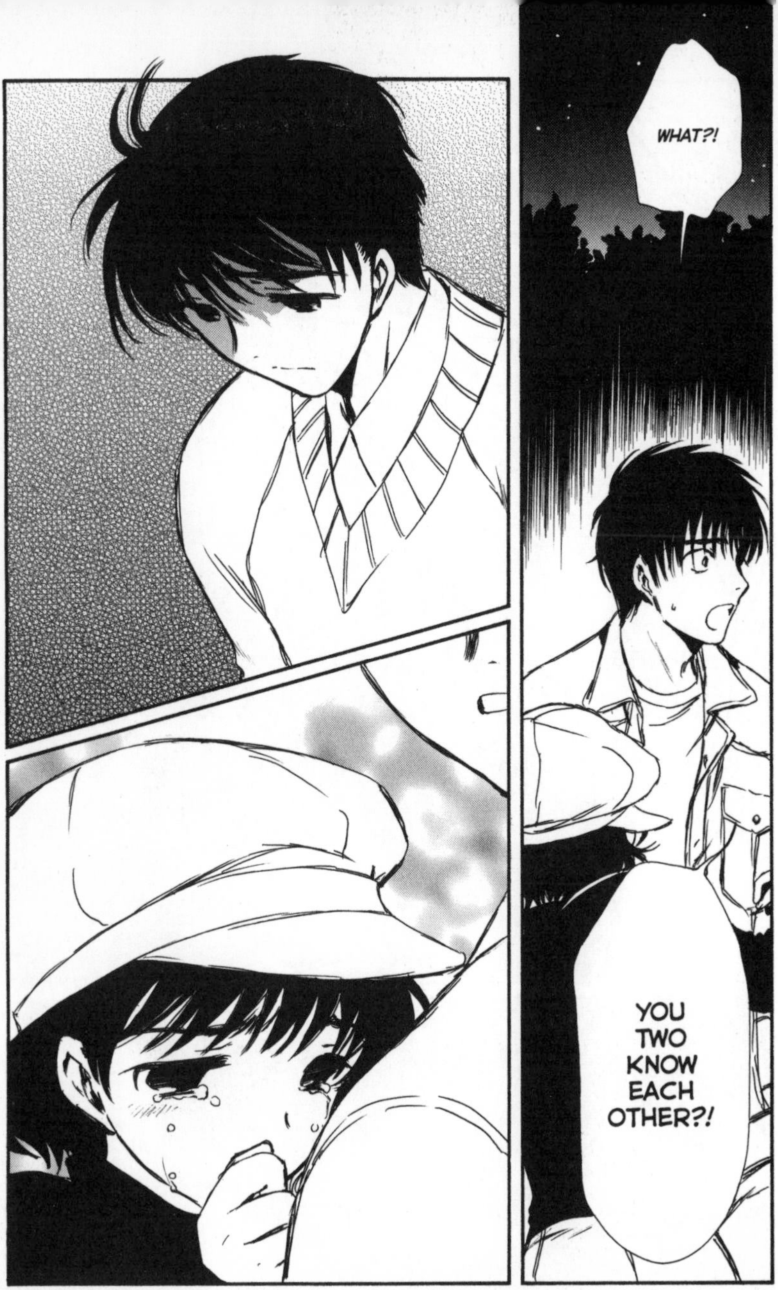
WHAT?!
YOU TWO KNOW EACH OTHER?!

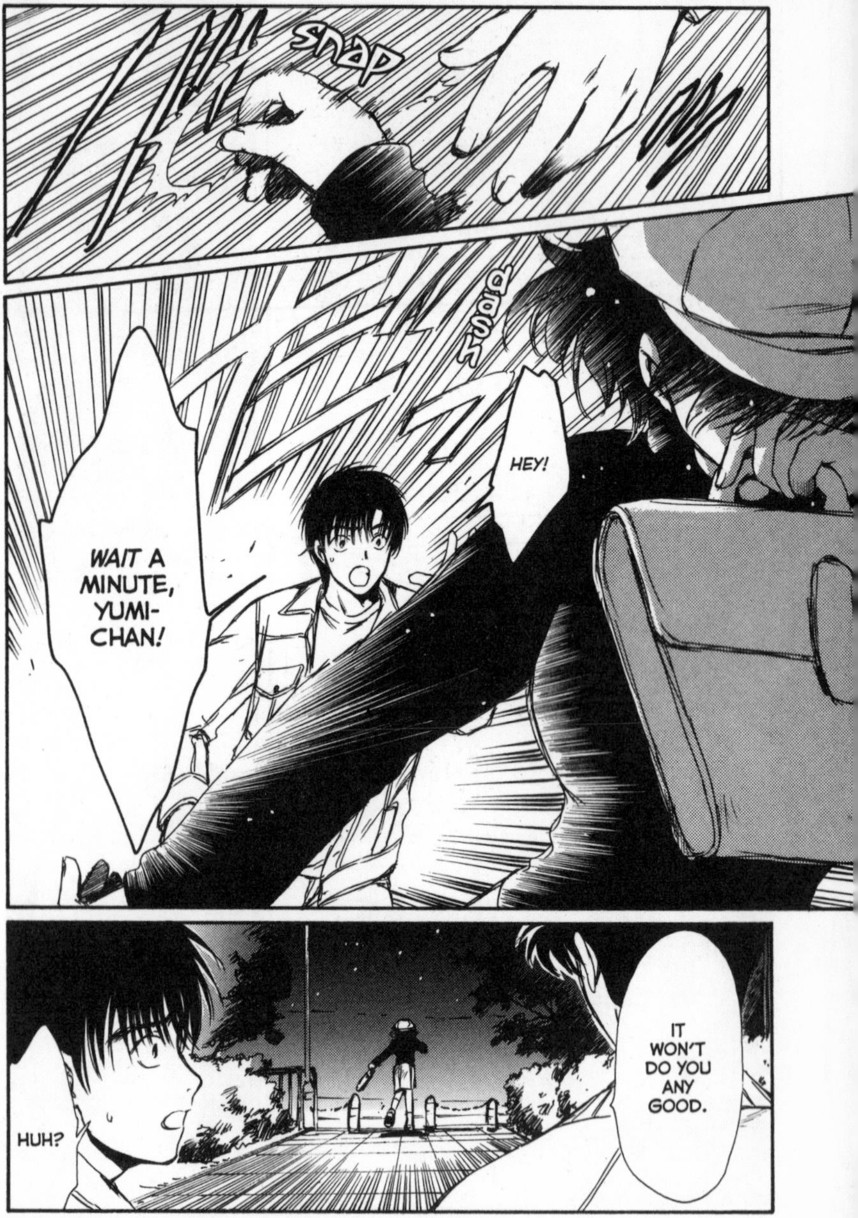
snap
dash
HEY!
WAIT A MINUTE, YUMI-CHAN!
IT WON'T DO YOU ANY GOOD.
HUH?

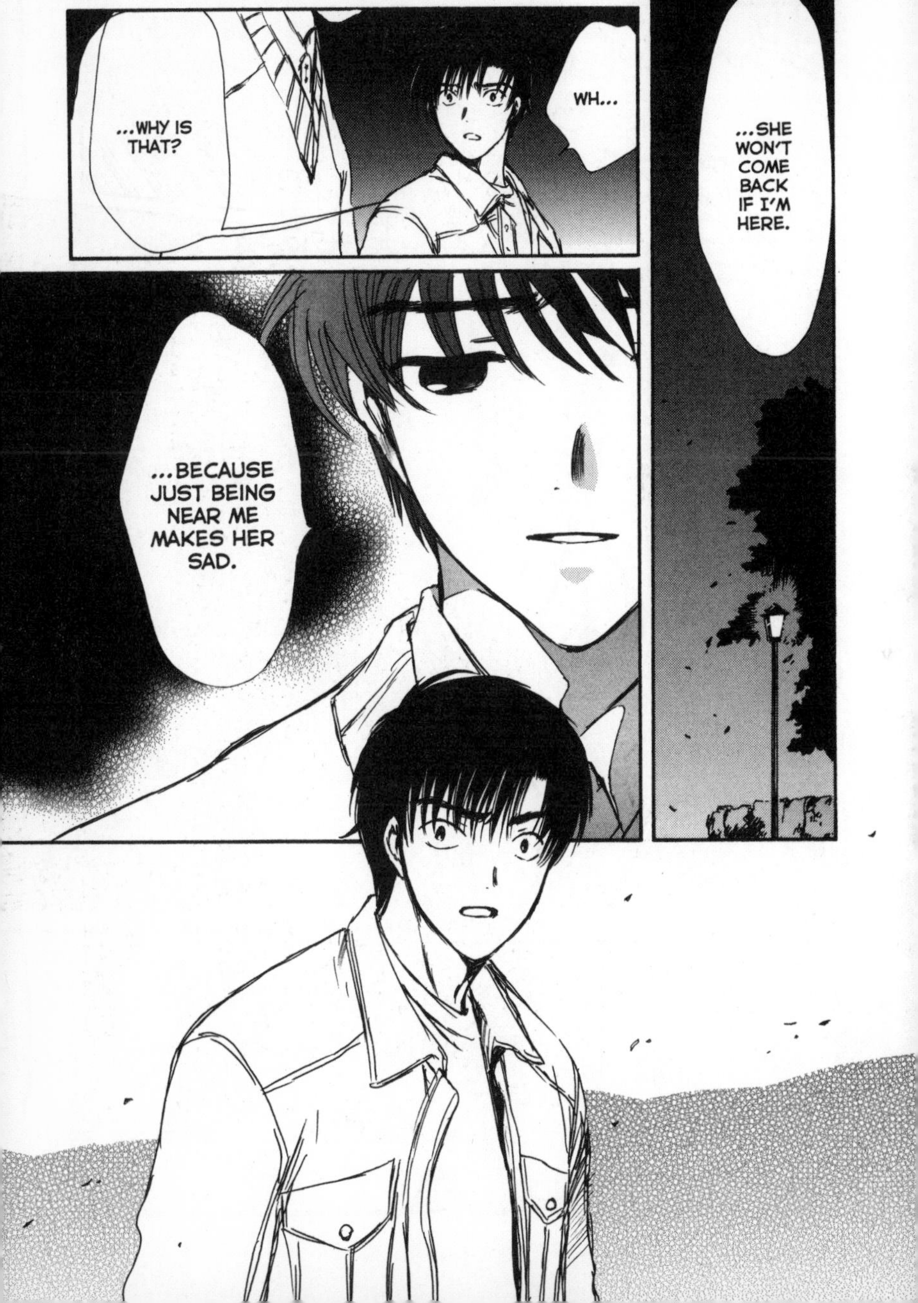
...SHE WON'T COME BACK IF I'M HERE.
WH...
...WHY IS THAT?
...BECAUSE JUST BEING NEAR ME MAKES HER SAD.

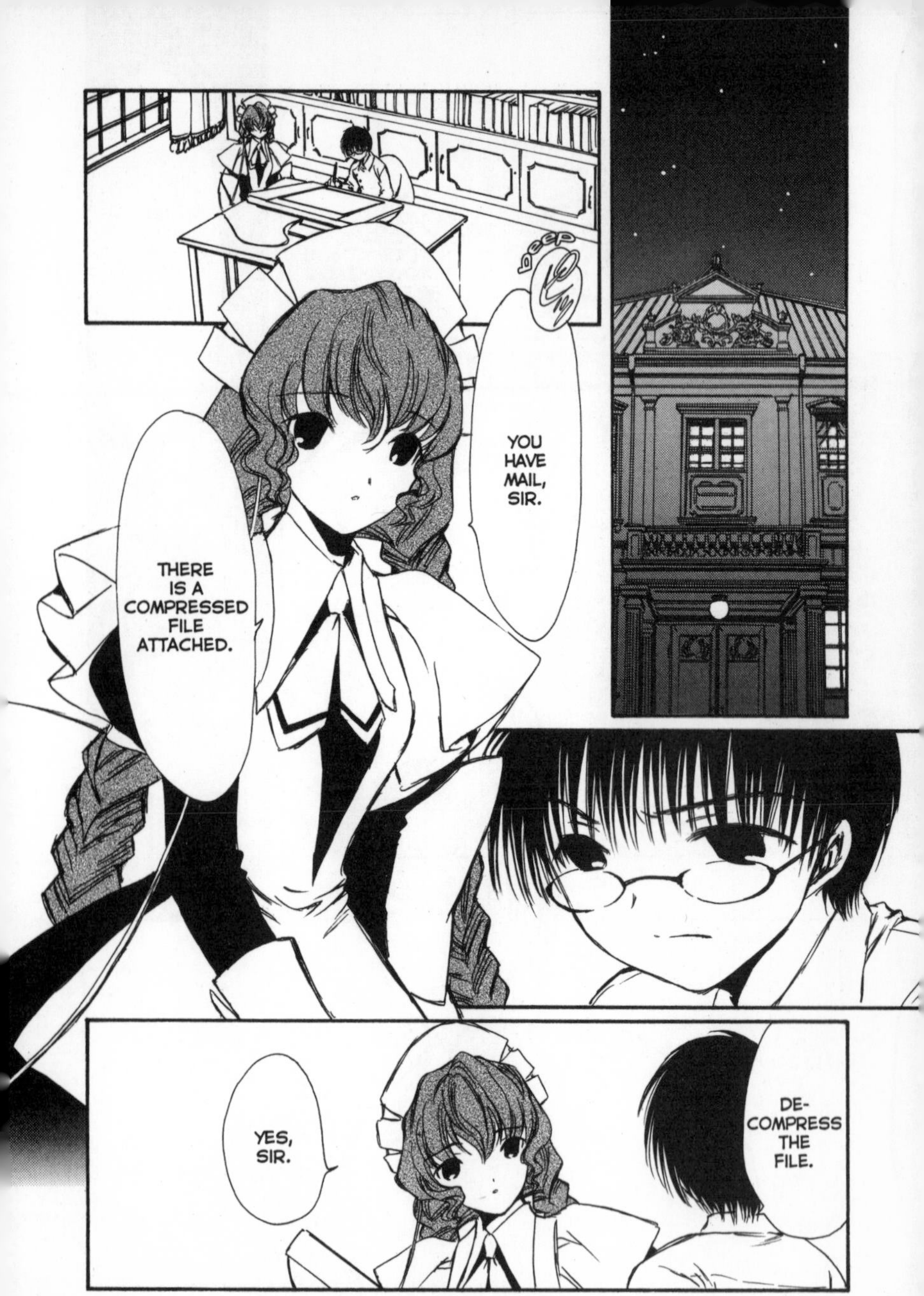
beep
YOU HAVE MAIL, SIR.
THERE IS A COMPRESSED FILE ATTACHED.
DE-COMPRESS THE FILE.
YES, SIR.

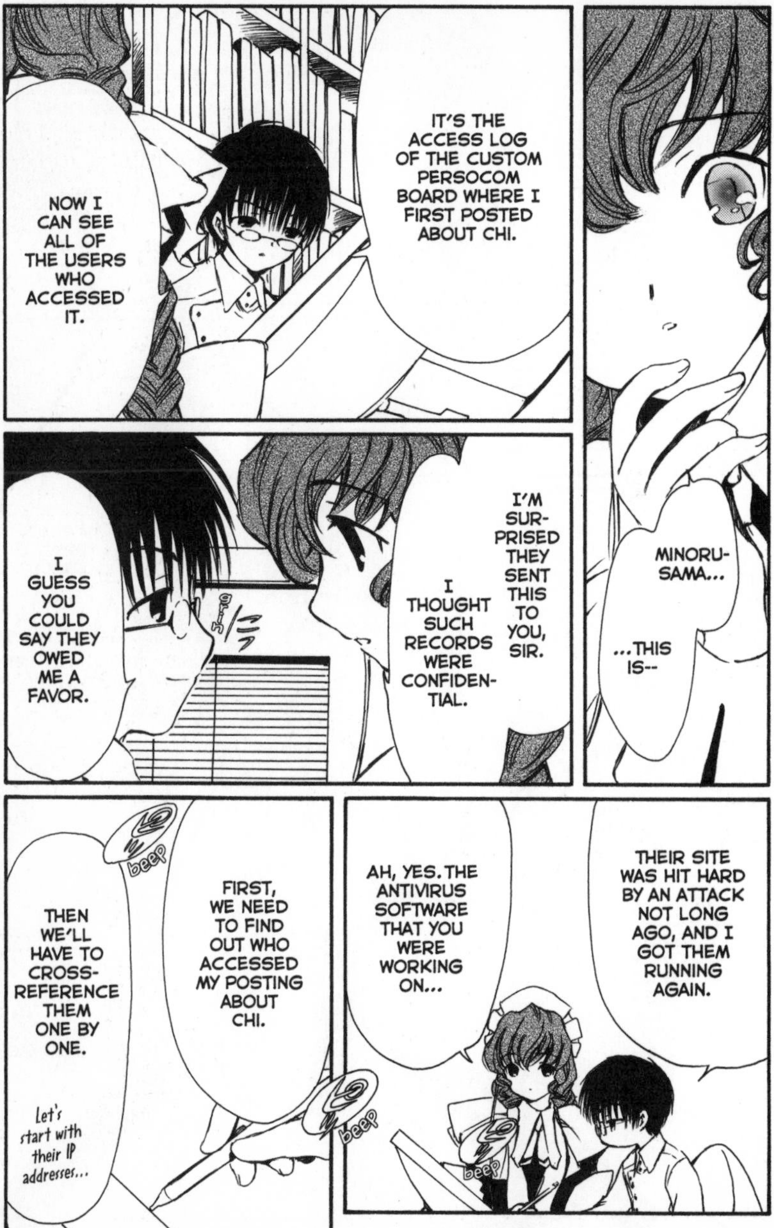
IT'S THE ACCESS LOG OF THE CUSTOM PERSOCOM BOARD WHERE I FIRST POSTED ABOUT CHI.
NOW I CAN SEE ALL OF THE USERS WHO ACCESSED IT.
MINORU-SAMA...
...THIS IS--
I'M SURPRISED THEY SENT THIS TO YOU, SIR.
I THOUGHT SUCH RECORDS WERE CONFIDENTIAL.
grin
I GUESS YOU COULD SAY THEY OWED ME A FAVOR.
THEIR SITE WAS HIT HARD BY AN ATTACK NOT LONG AGO, AND I GOT THEM RUNNING AGAIN.
AH, YES. THE ANTIVIRUS SOFTWARE THAT YOU WERE WORKING ON...
beep
FIRST, WE NEED TO FIND OUT WHO ACCESSED MY POSTING ABOUT CHI.
beep
THEN WE'LL HAVE TO CROSS-REFERENCE THEM ONE BY ONE.
beep
Let's start with their IP addresses...

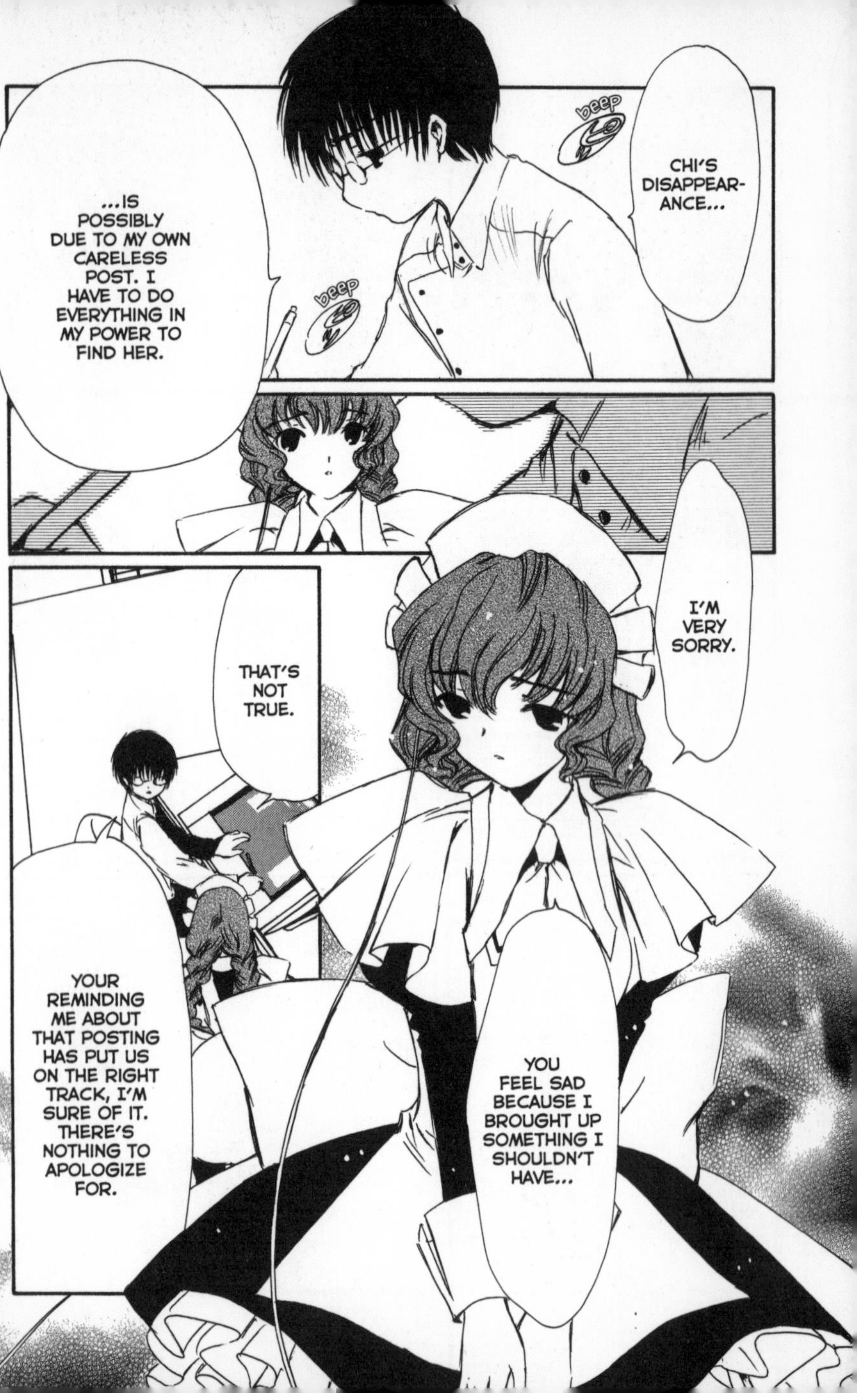
beep
CHI'S DISAPPEARANCE...
beep
...IS POSSIBLY DUE TO MY OWN CARELESS POST. I HAVE TO DO EVERYTHING IN MY POWER TO FIND HER.
I'M VERY SORRY.
YOU FEEL SAD BECAUSE I BROUGHT UP SOMETHING I SHOULDN'T HAVE...
THAT'S NOT TRUE.
YOUR REMINDING ME ABOUT THAT POSTING HAS PUT US ON THE RIGHT TRACK, I'M SURE OF IT. THERE'S NOTHING TO APOLOGIZE FOR.

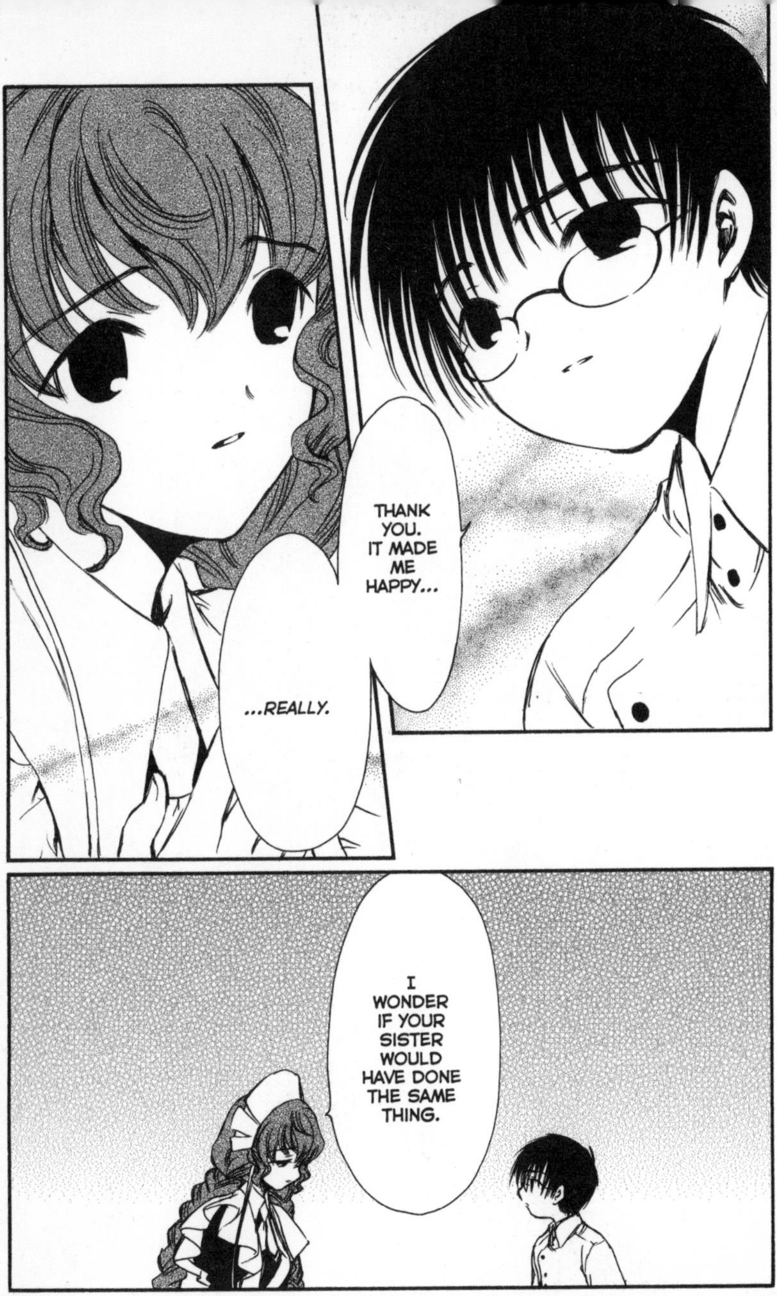
THANK YOU. IT MADE ME HAPPY...
...REALLY.
I WONDER IF YOUR SISTER WOULD HAVE DONE THE SAME THING.

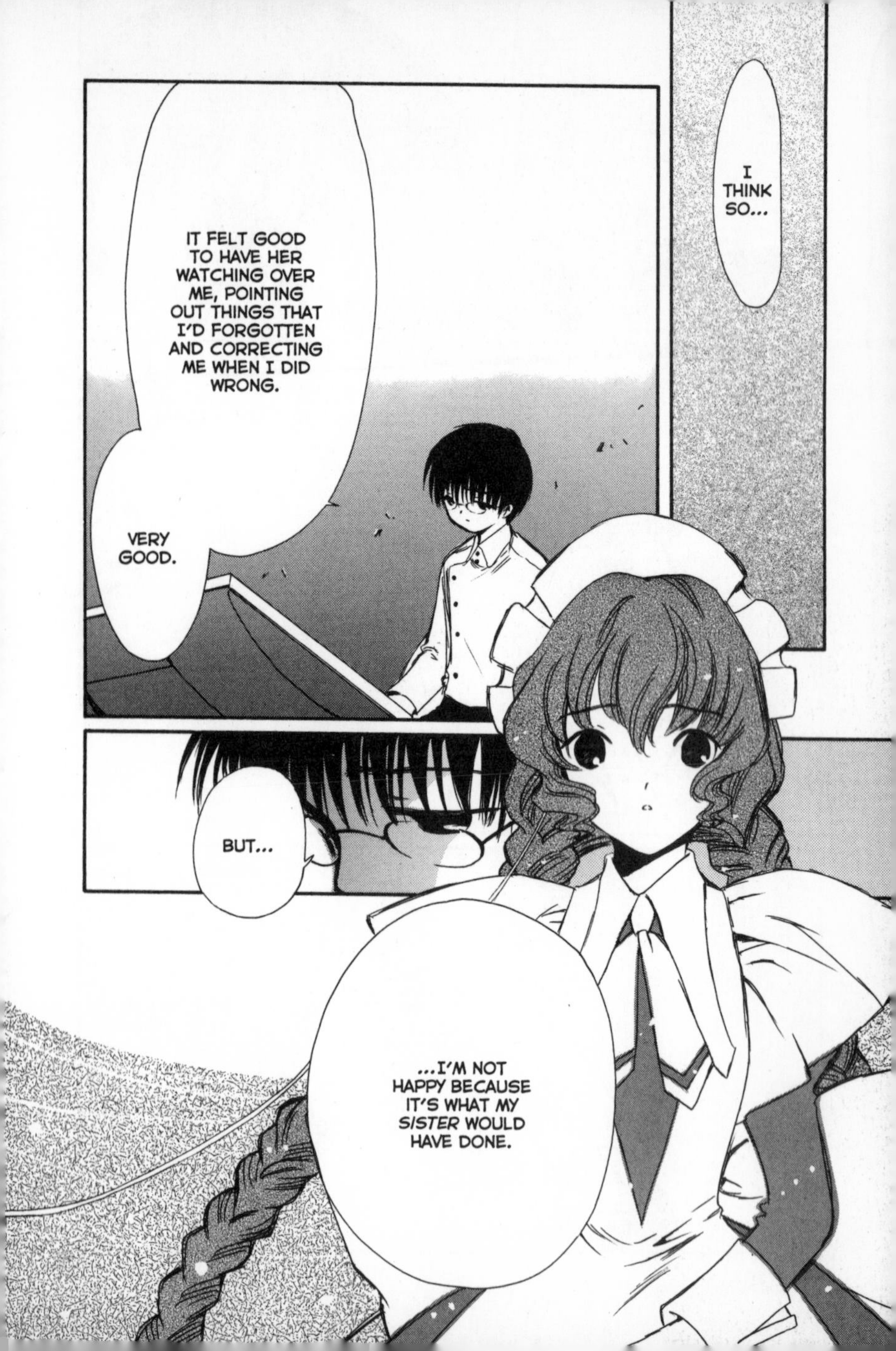
I THINK SO...
IT FELT GOOD TO HAVE HER WATCHING OVER ME, POINTING OUT THINGS THAT I'D FORGOTTEN AND CORRECTING ME WHEN I DID WRONG.
VERY GOOD.
BUT...
...I'M NOT HAPPY BECAUSE IT'S WHAT MY *SISTER* WOULD HAVE DONE.

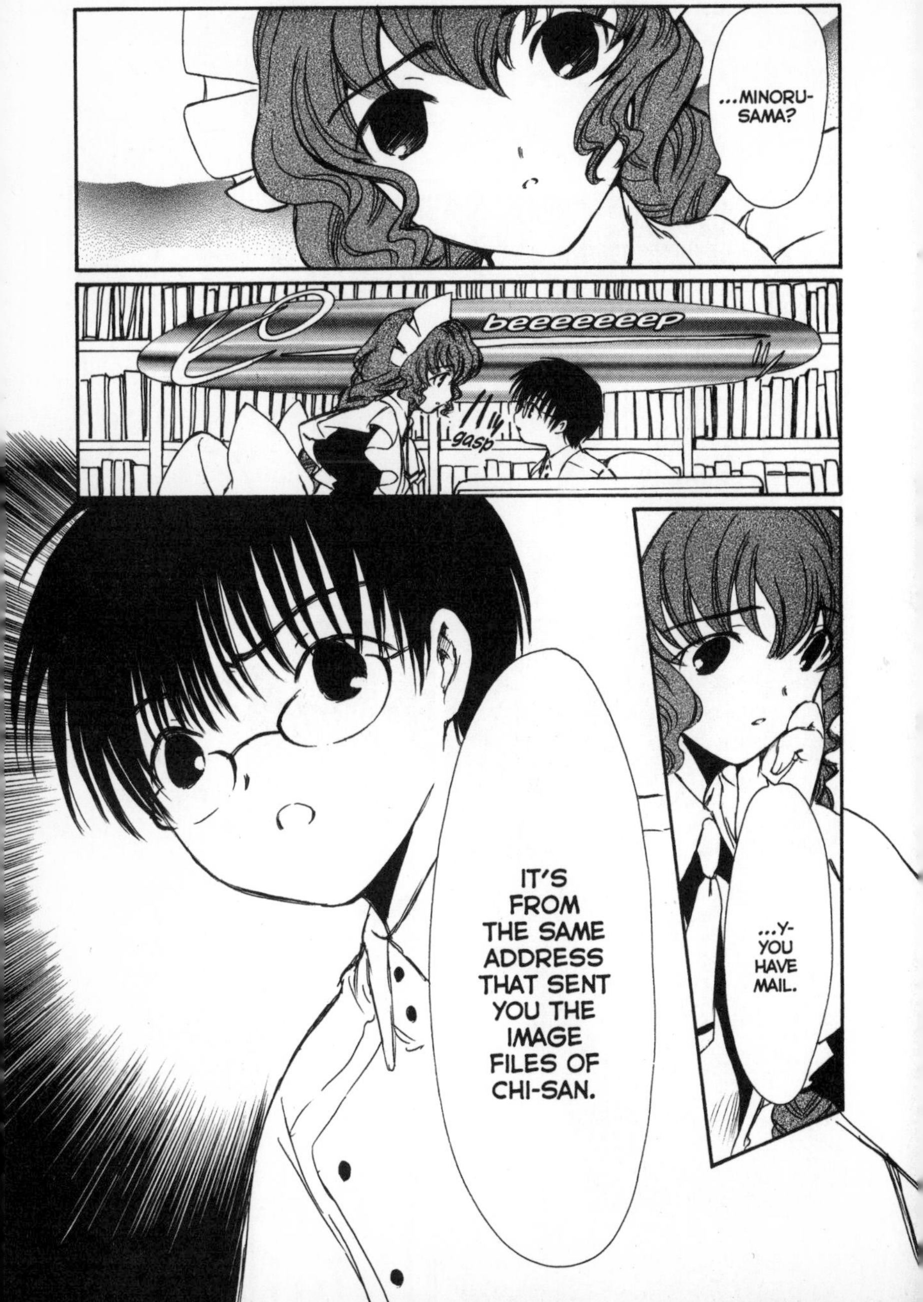
...MINORU-SAMA?
beeeeeeeep
gasp
...Y-YOU HAVE MAIL.
IT'S FROM THE SAME ADDRESS THAT SENT YOU THE IMAGE FILES OF CHI-SAN.

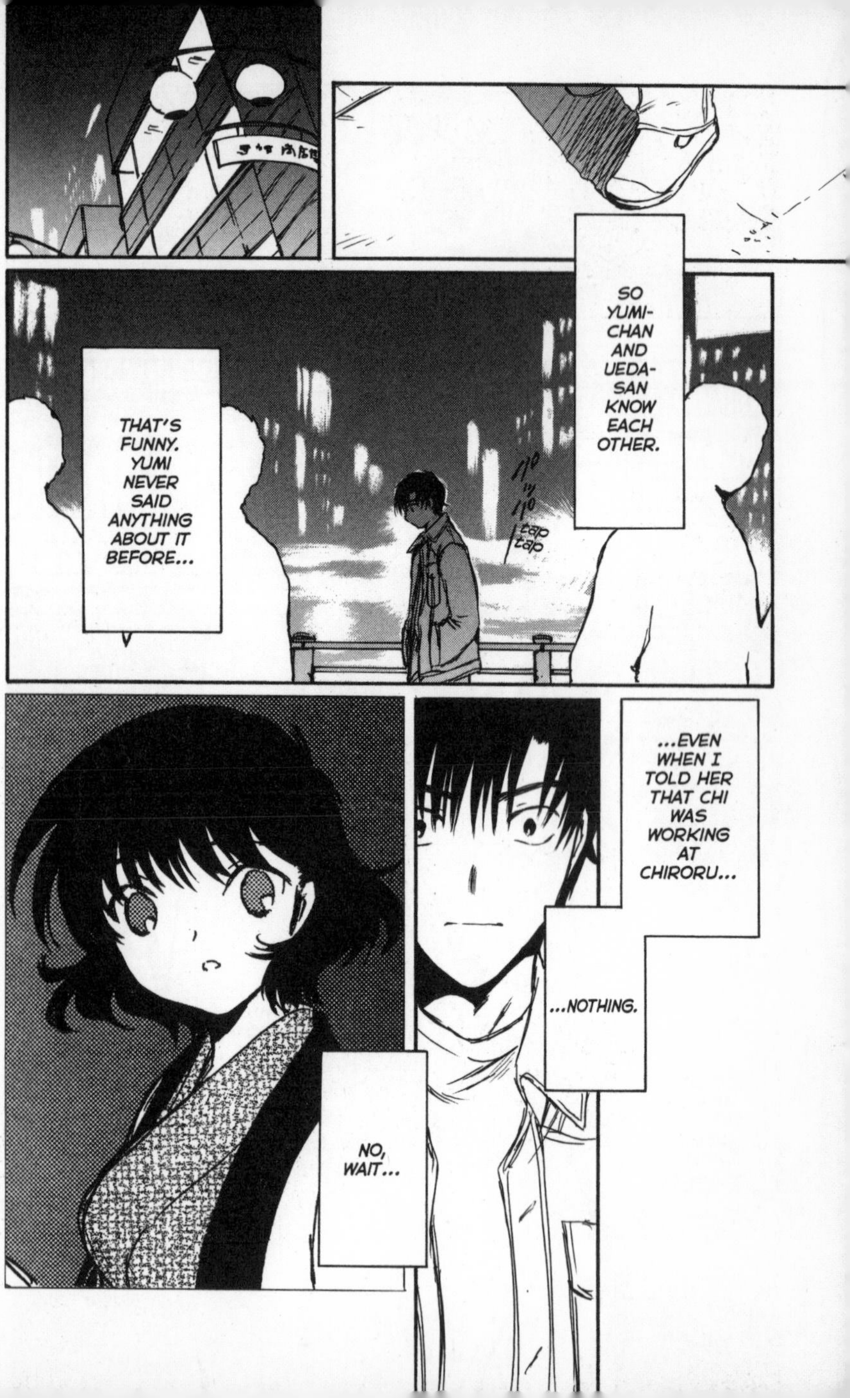
SO YUMI-CHAN AND UEDA-SAN KNOW EACH OTHER.
tap tap
THAT'S FUNNY. YUMI NEVER SAID ANYTHING ABOUT IT BEFORE...
...EVEN WHEN I TOLD HER THAT CHI WAS WORKING AT CHIRORU...
...NOTHING.
NO, WAIT...

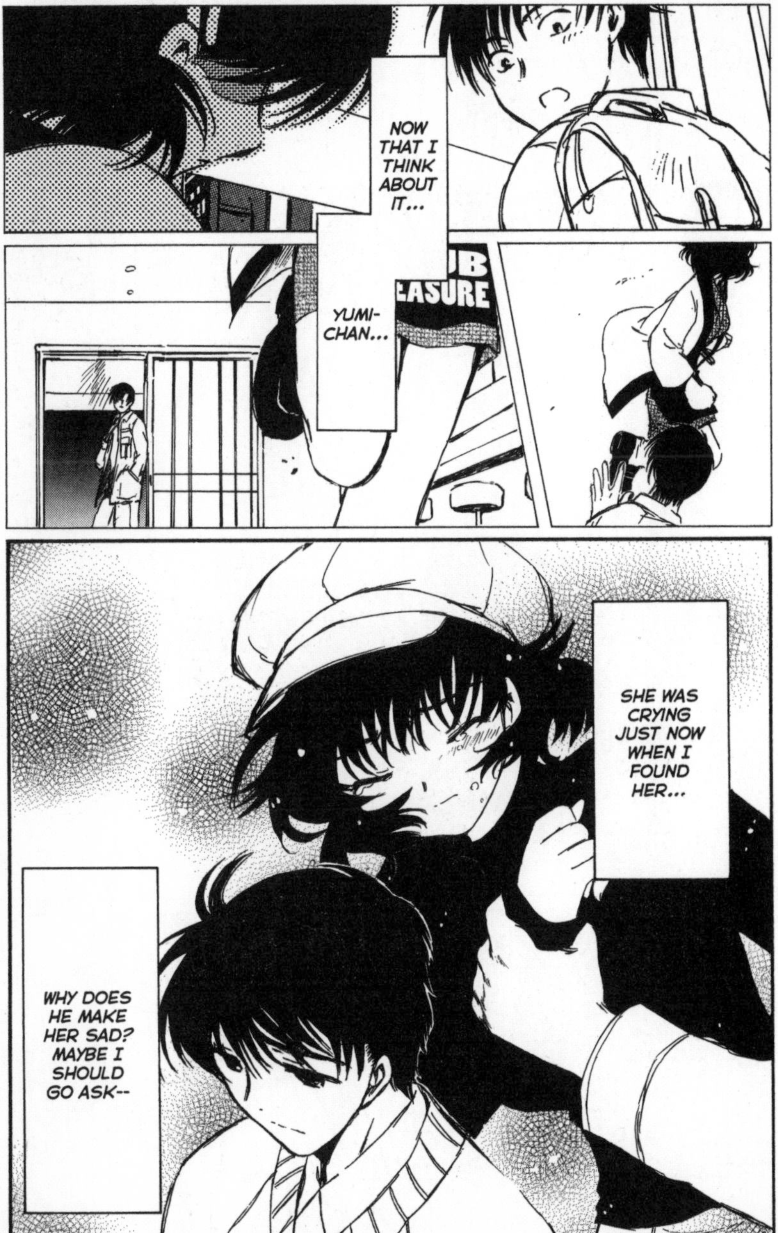
NOW THAT I THINK ABOUT IT...
UB
LEASURE
YUMI-CHAN...
SHE WAS CRYING JUST NOW WHEN I FOUND HER...
WHY DOES HE MAKE HER SAD? MAYBE I SHOULD GO ASK--

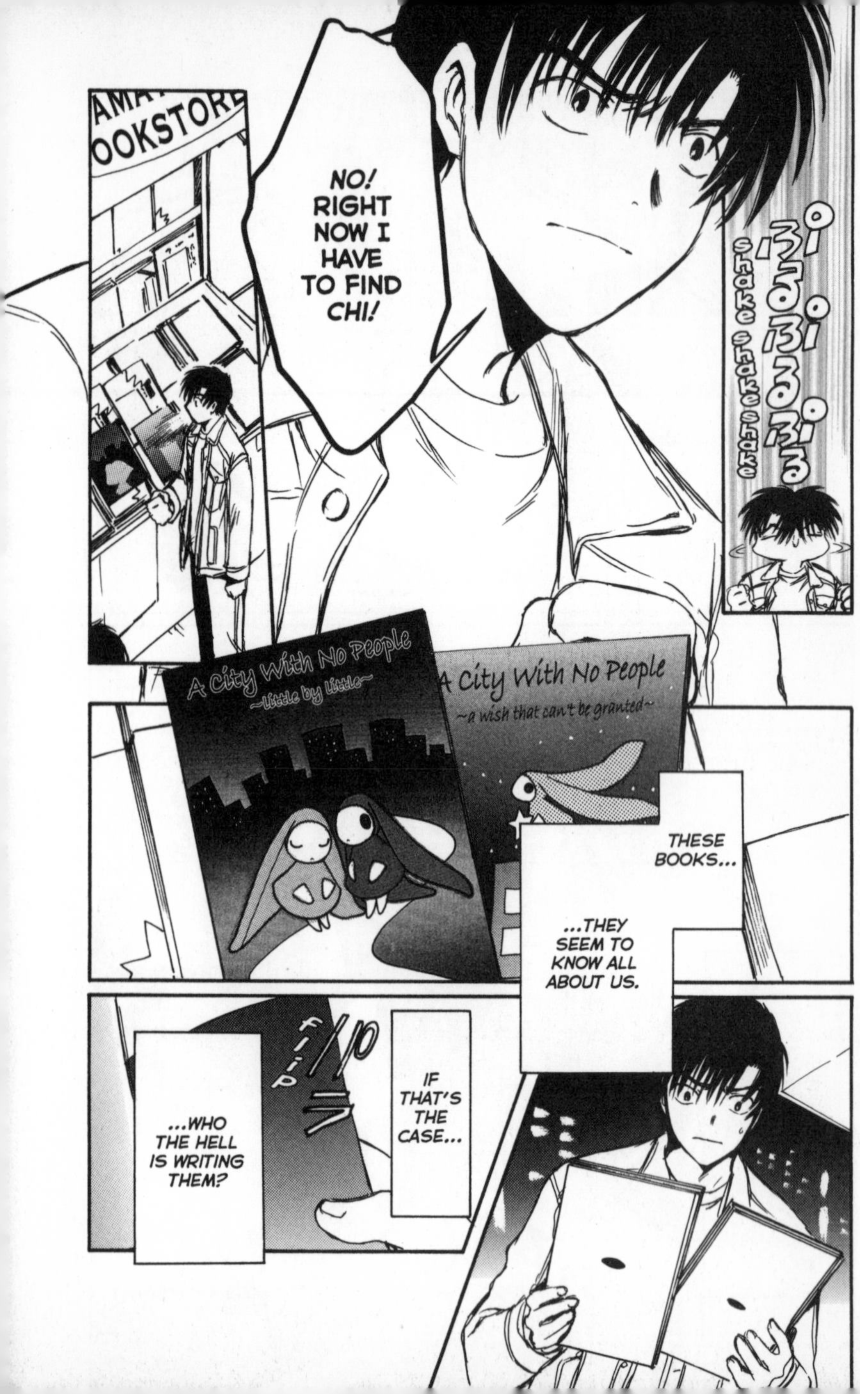
ぷるぷるぷるぷる
Shake shake shake shake
NO! RIGHT NOW I HAVE TO FIND CHI!
AMA
OOKSTORE
A City With No People
~a wish that can't be granted~
A City With No People
~little by little~
THESE BOOKS...
...THEY SEEM TO KNOW ALL ABOUT US.
IF THAT'S THE CASE...
flip
...WHO THE HELL IS WRITING THEM?

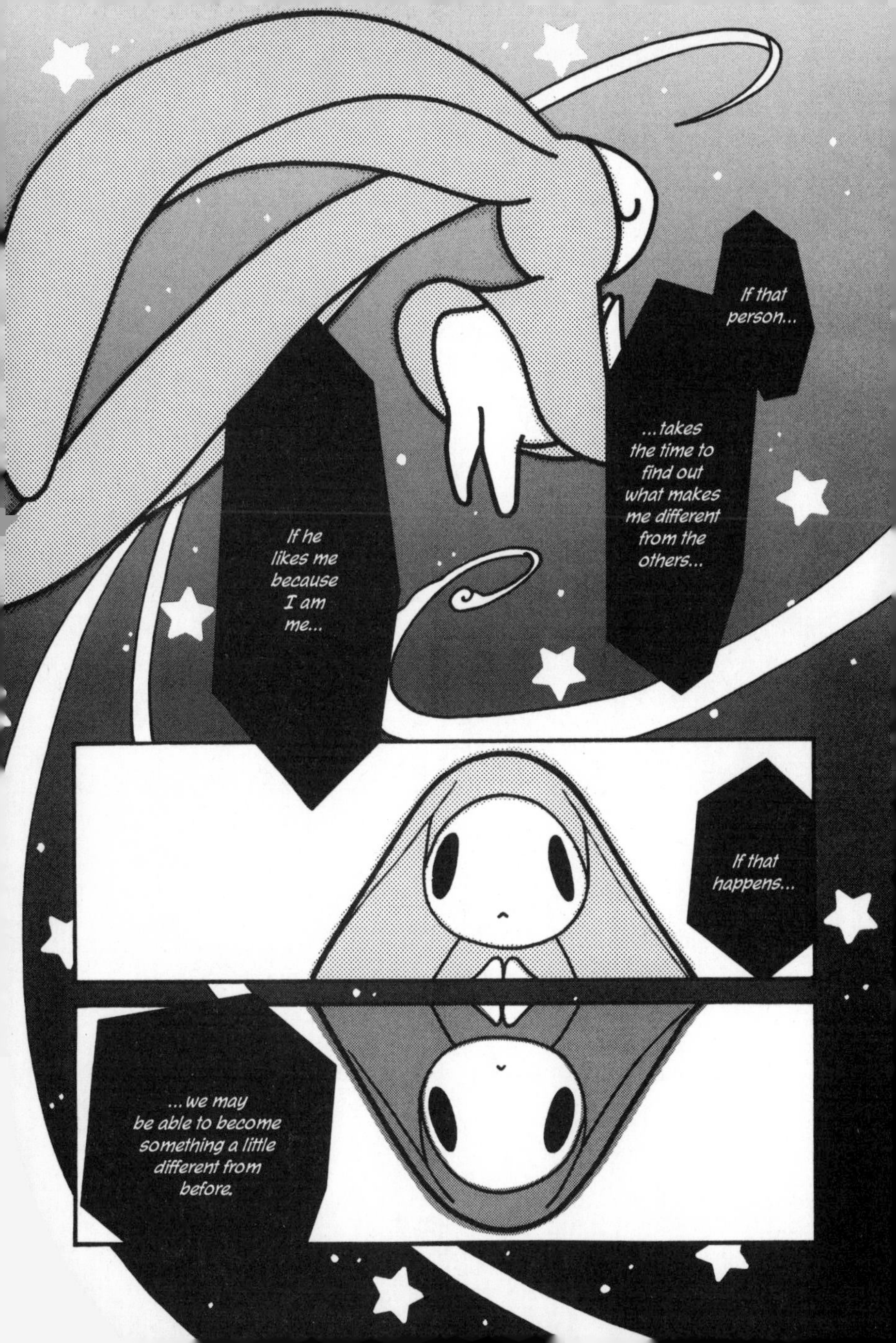
If that person...
...takes the time to find out what makes me different from the others...
If he likes me because I am me...
If that happens...
...we may be able to become something a little different from before.

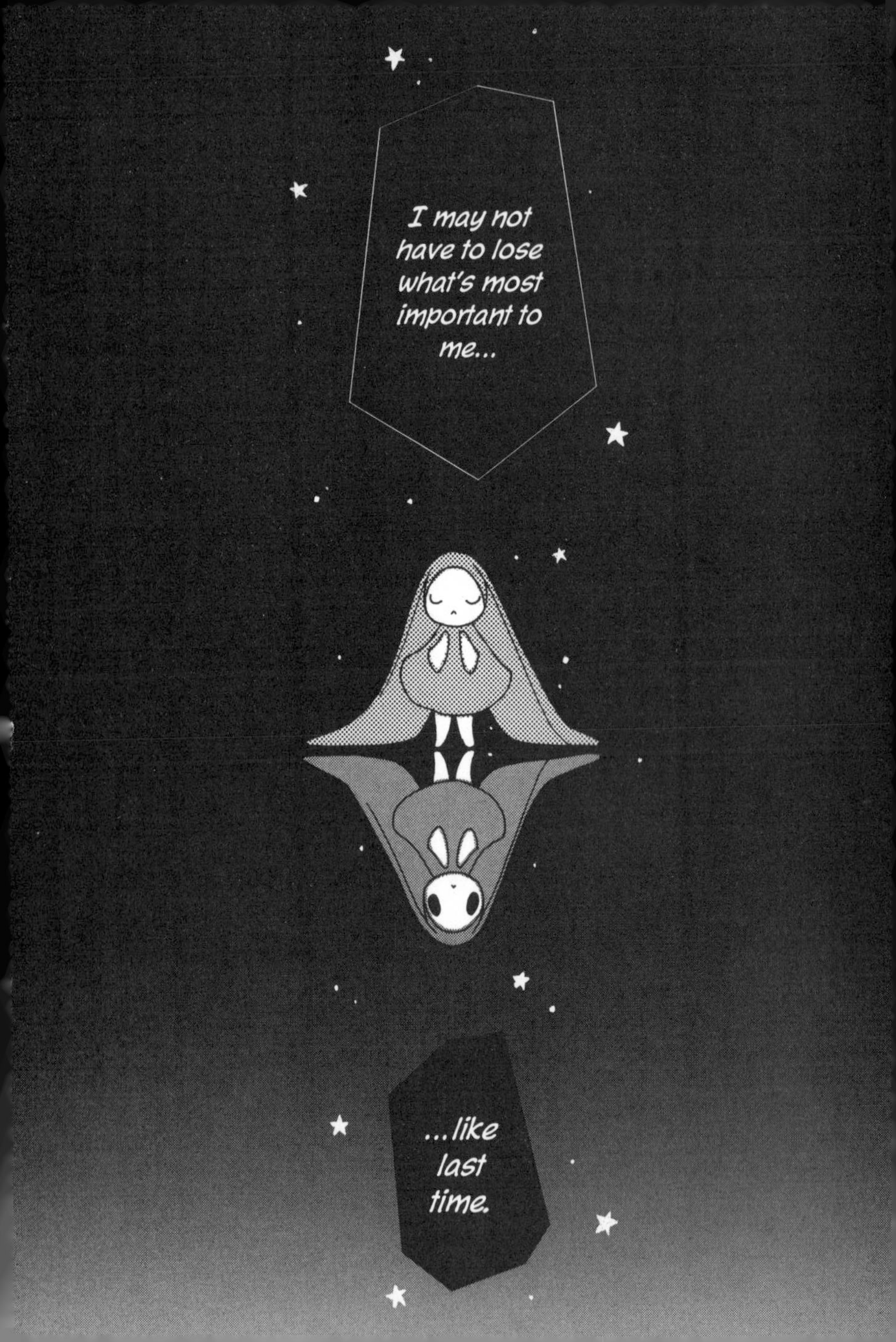
I may not have to lose what's most important to me...
...like last time.

Chobits
ちょびっツ

◀ **chapter 50** ▶

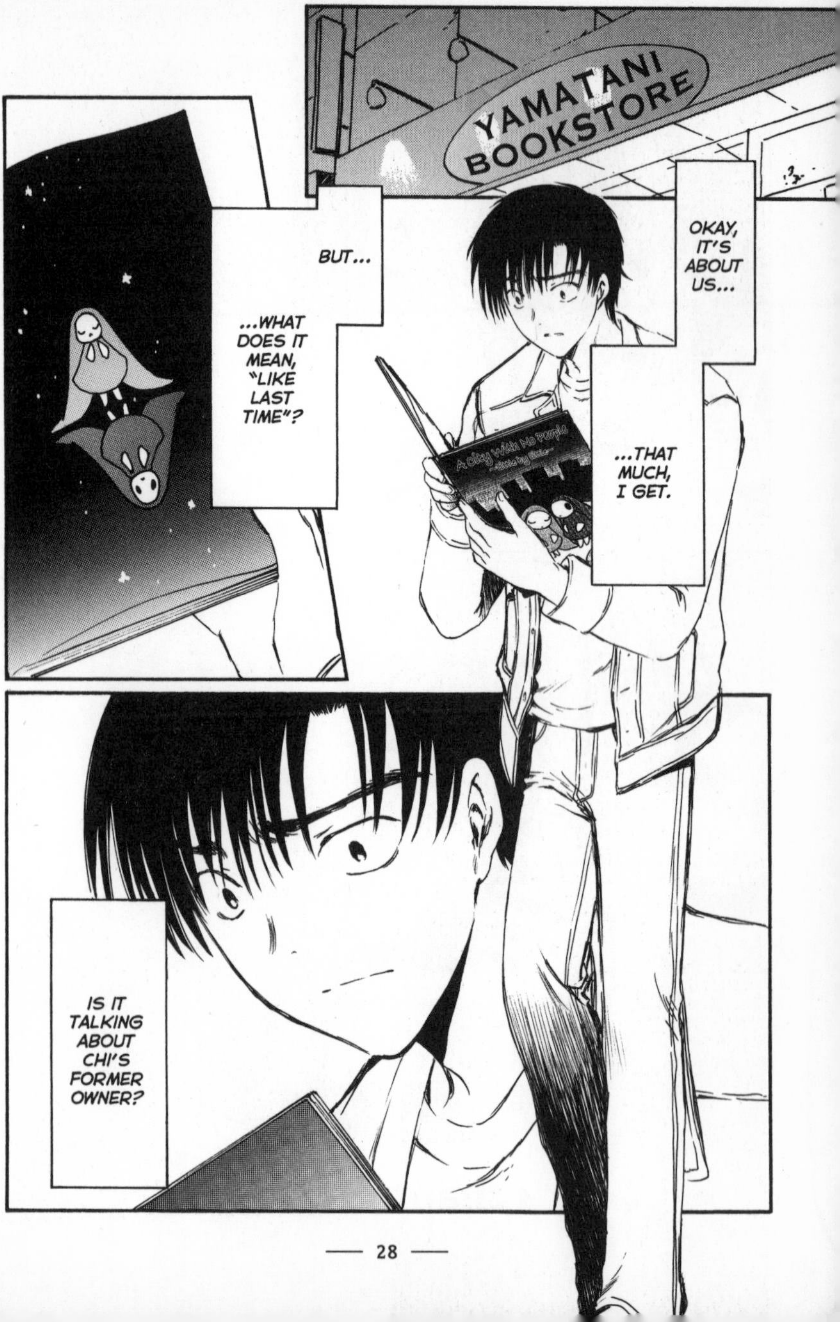
YAMATANI BOOKSTORE
A City With No People
OKAY, IT'S ABOUT US...
...THAT MUCH, I GET.
BUT...
...WHAT DOES IT MEAN, "LIKE LAST TIME"?
IS IT TALKING ABOUT CHI'S FORMER OWNER?

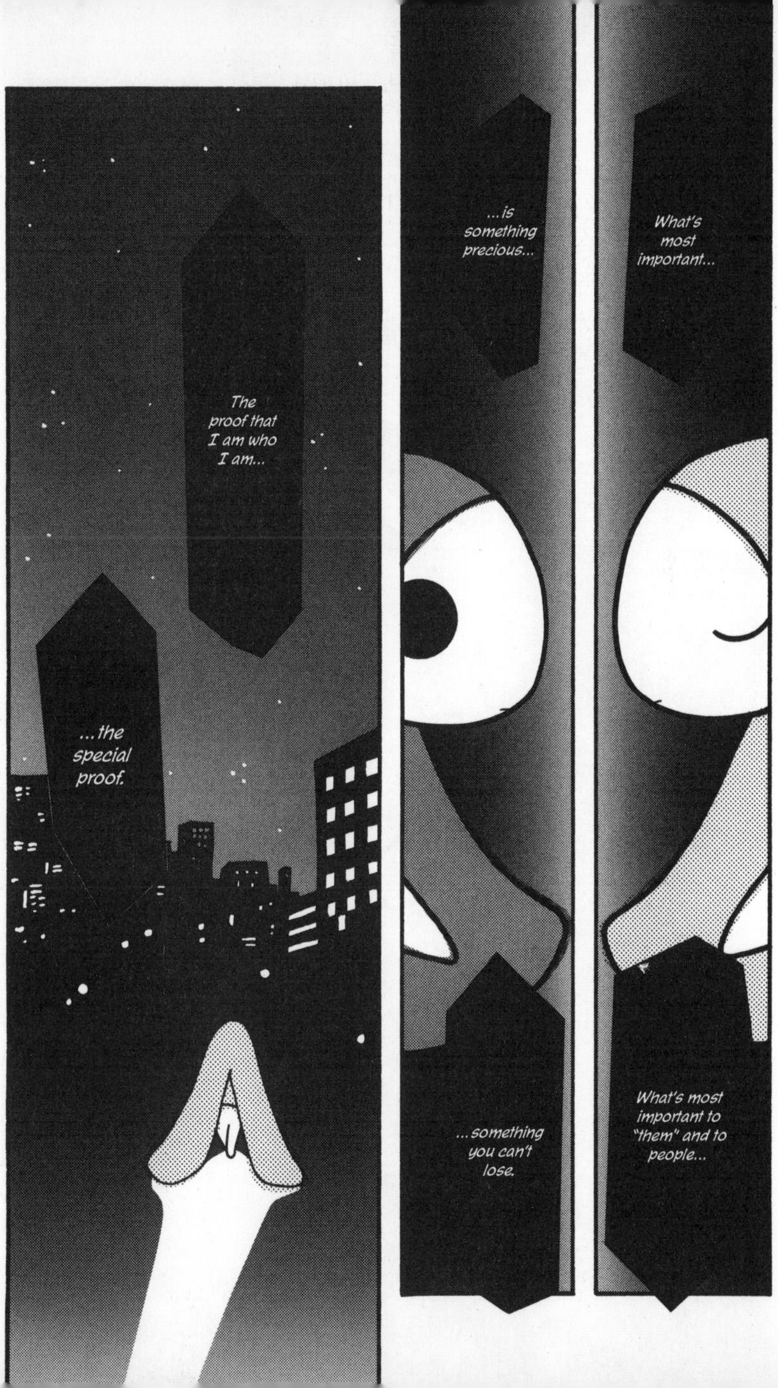
What's most important...
What's most important to "them" and to people...
...is something precious...
...something you can't lose.
The proof that I am who I am...
...the special proof.

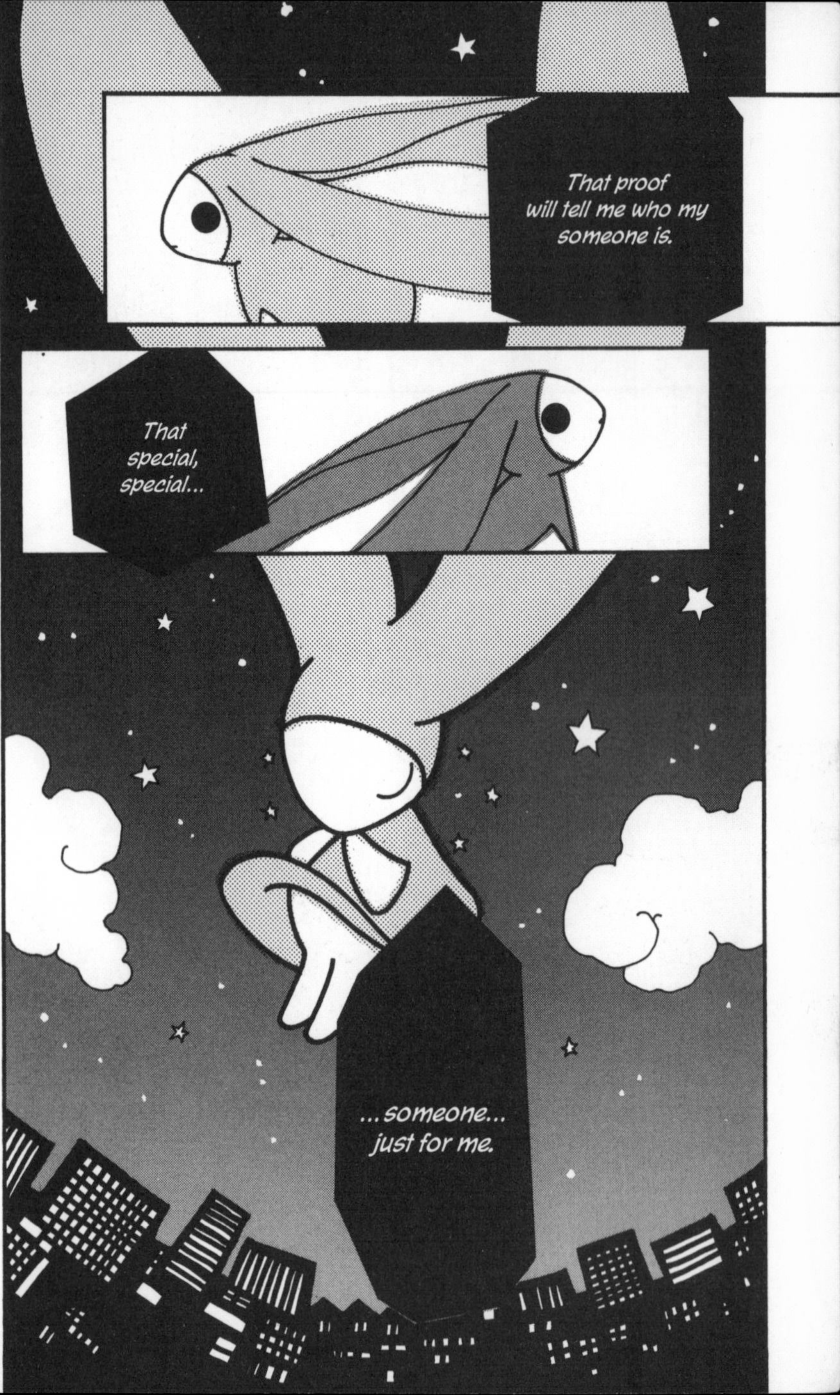
That proof will tell me who my someone is.
That special, special...
...someone... just for me.

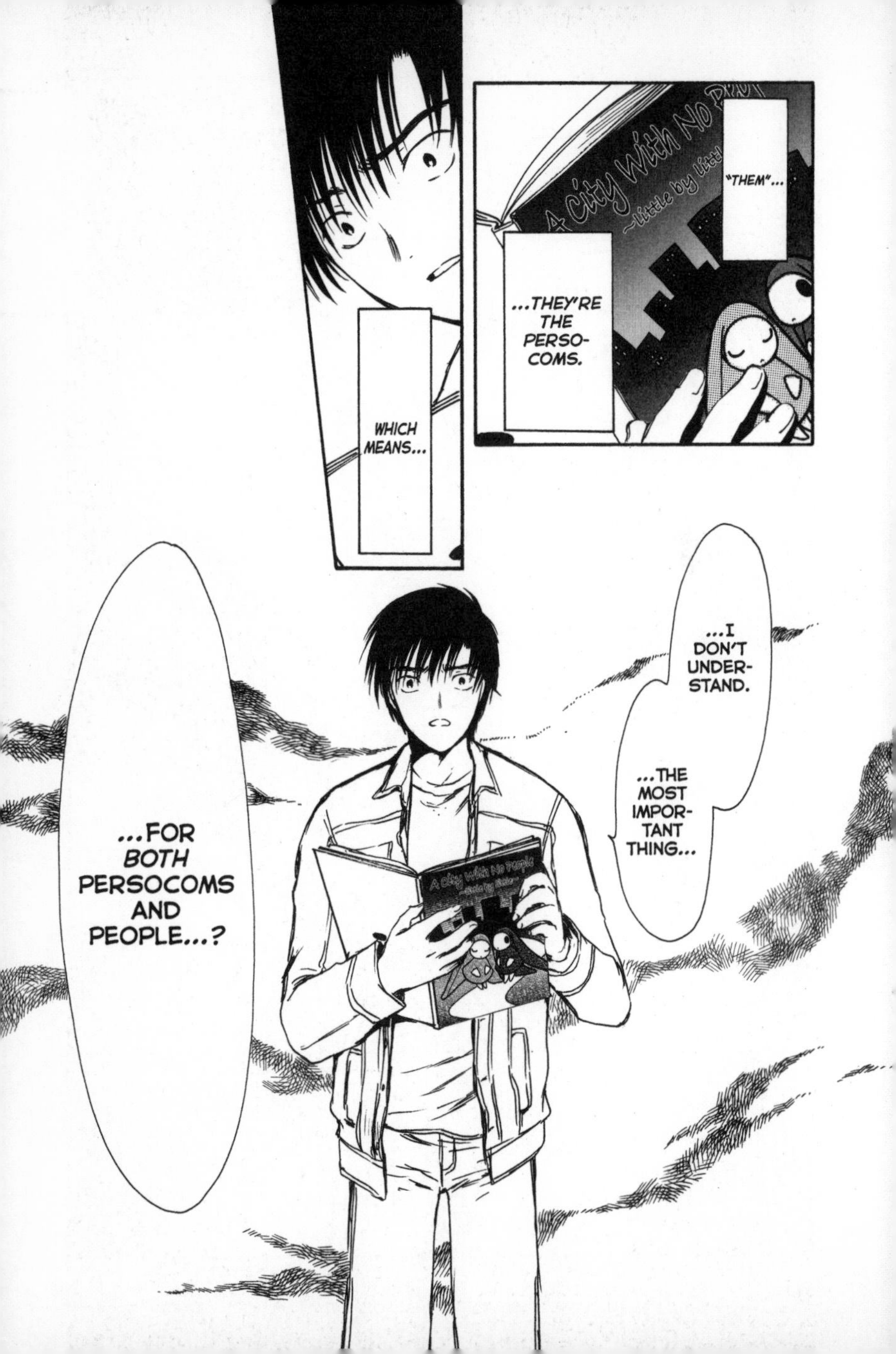
"THEM"...
...THEY'RE THE PERSO-COMS.
WHICH MEANS...
...I DON'T UNDER-STAND.
...THE MOST IMPOR-TANT THING...
...FOR BOTH PERSOCOMS AND PEOPLE...?

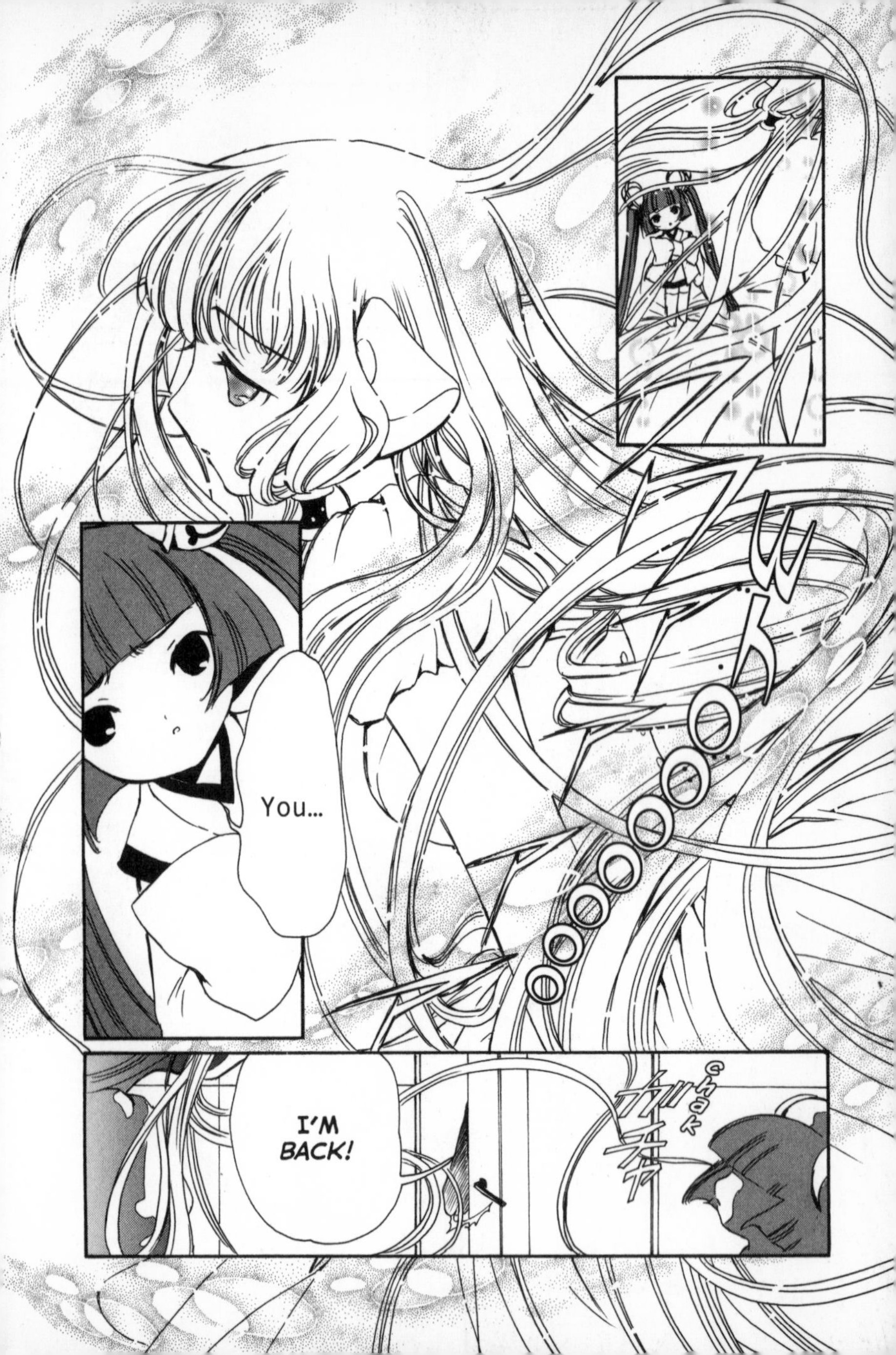
You...
I'M BACK!
chak

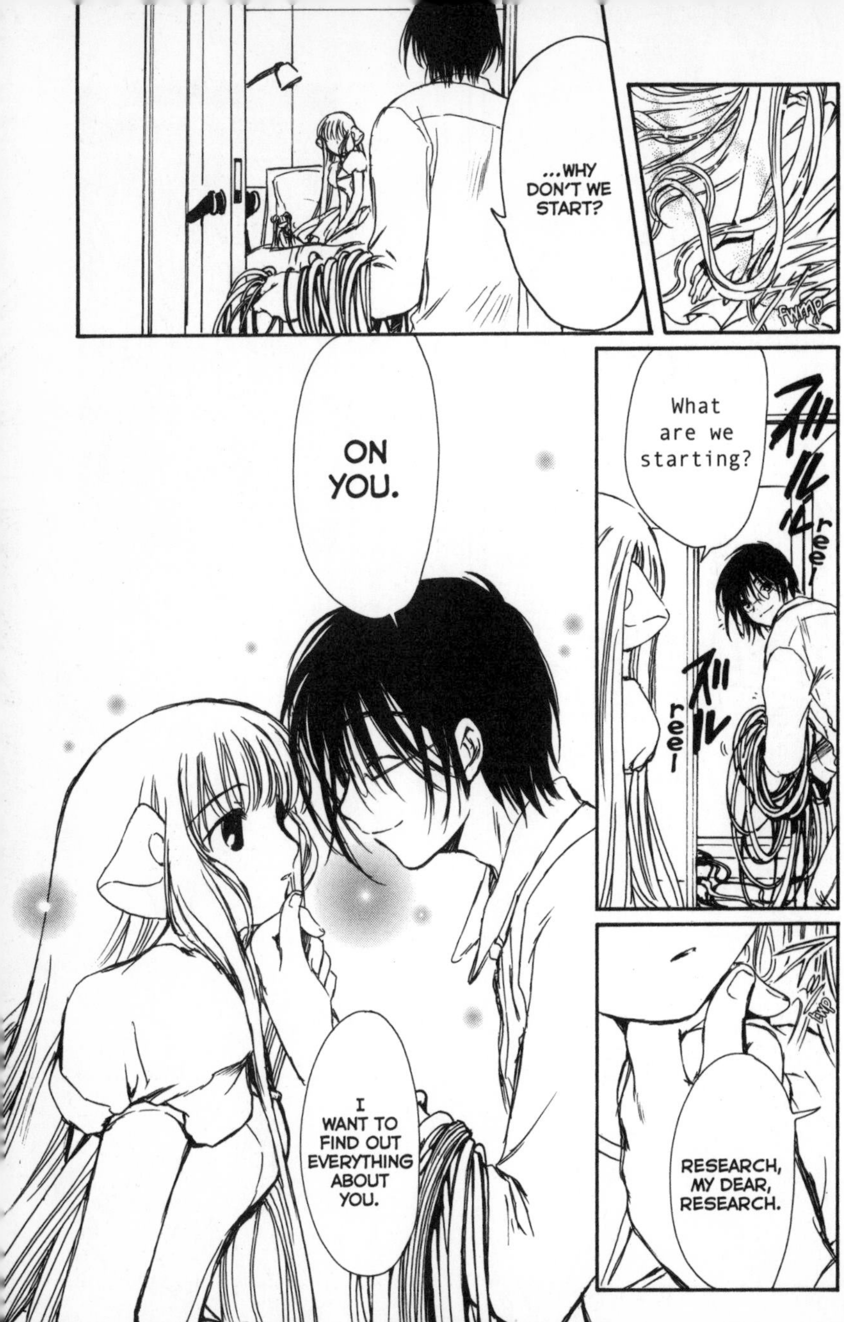
fwump
...WHY DON'T WE START?
What are we starting?
reel
reel
RESEARCH, MY DEAR, RESEARCH.
ON YOU.
I WANT TO FIND OUT EVERYTHING ABOUT YOU.

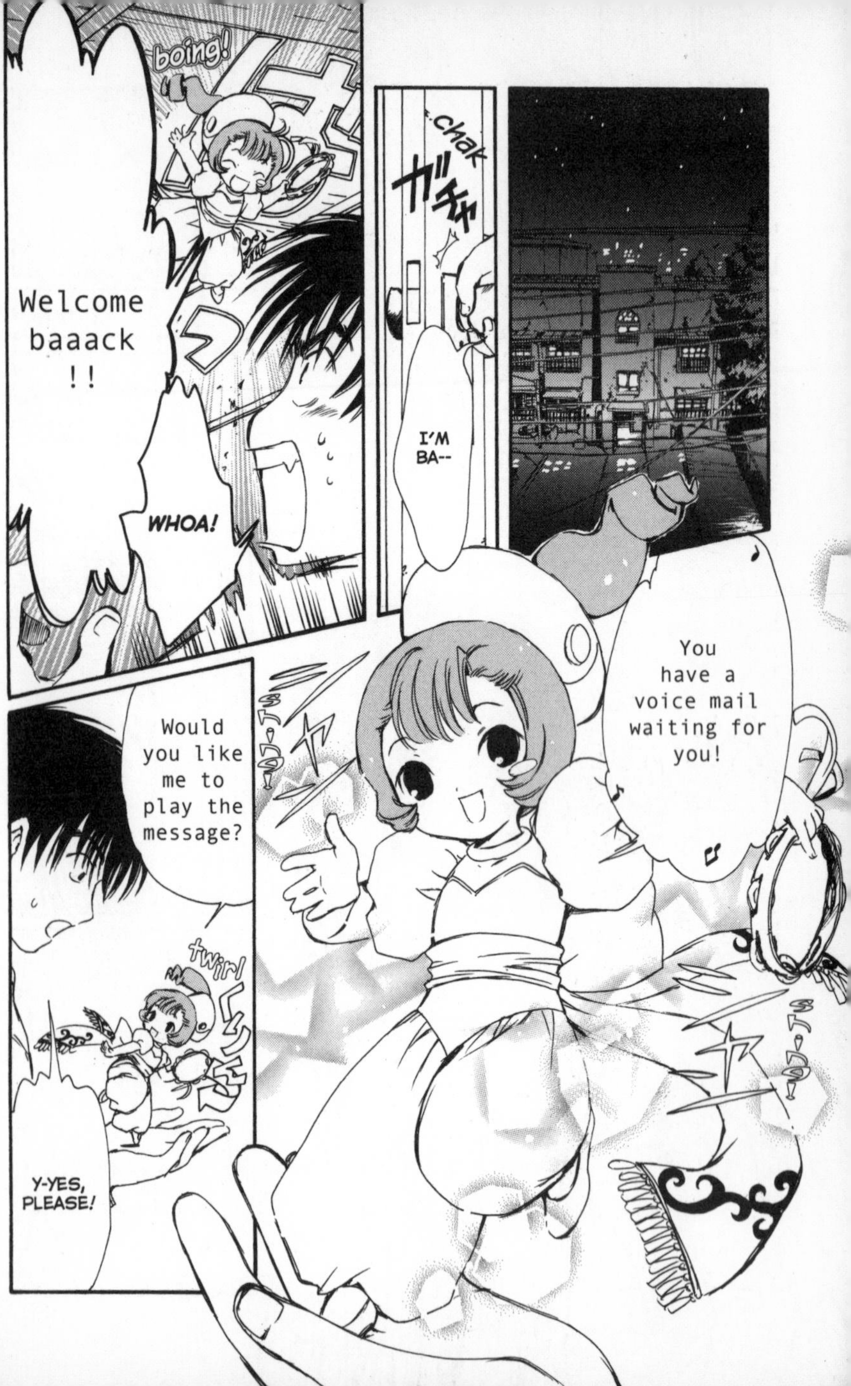
chak
ガチャ
I'M BA--
boing!
Welcome baaack !!
WHOA!
You have a voice mail waiting for you!
Would you like me to play the message?
twirl
Y-YES, PLEASE!

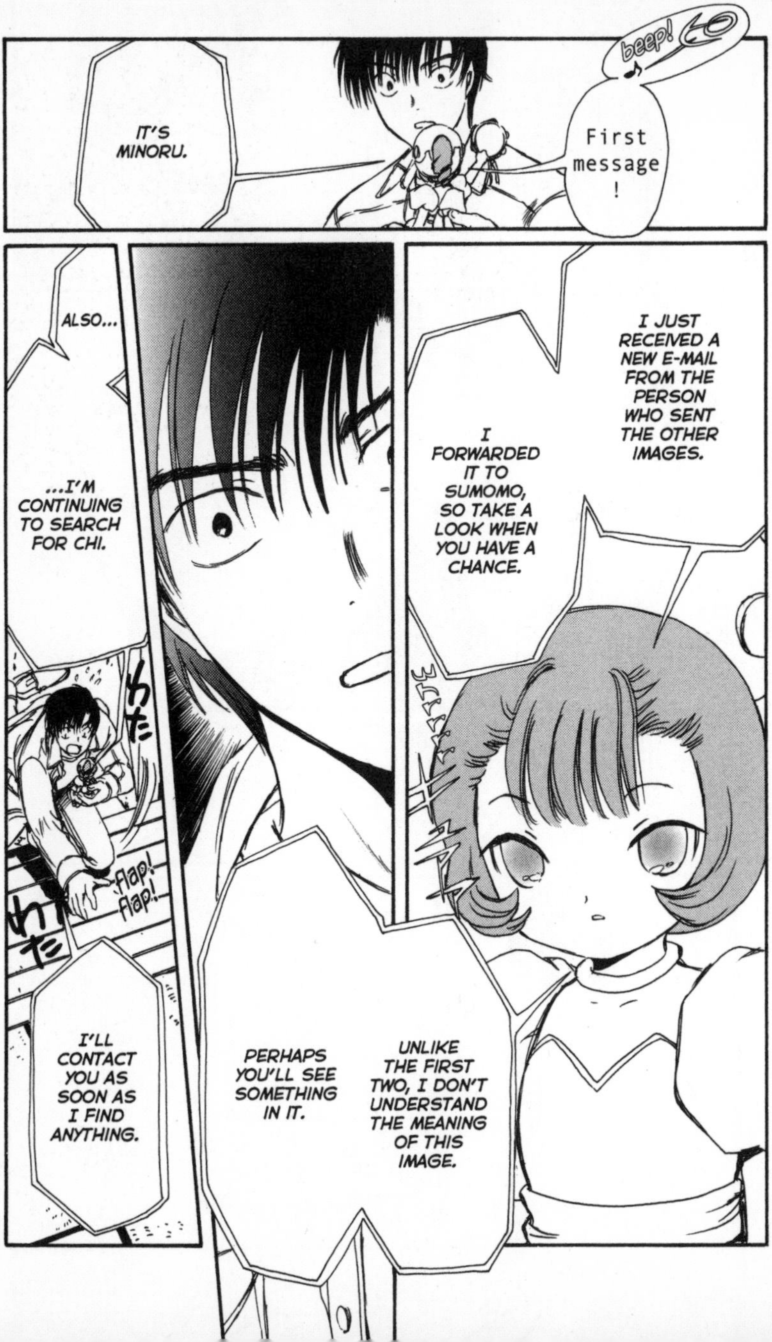
beep!
First message!
IT'S MINORU.
I JUST RECEIVED A NEW E-MAIL FROM THE PERSON WHO SENT THE OTHER IMAGES.
I FORWARDED IT TO SUMOMO, SO TAKE A LOOK WHEN YOU HAVE A CHANCE.
UNLIKE THE FIRST TWO, I DON'T UNDERSTAND THE MEANING OF THIS IMAGE.
PERHAPS YOU'LL SEE SOMETHING IN IT.
ALSO...
...I'M CONTINUING TO SEARCH FOR CHI.
わた
わた
Flap! Flap!
I'LL CONTACT YOU AS SOON AS I FIND ANYTHING.

End of messages!

...I WONDER WHAT THEY SENT *THIS* TIME...?

SUMOMO!

Yes, master!

beep!

on/off

Now loading!

beep beep

IS THE PERSON WHO SENT THOSE IMAGES OF CHI THE SAME PERSON WHO KIDNAPPED HER?

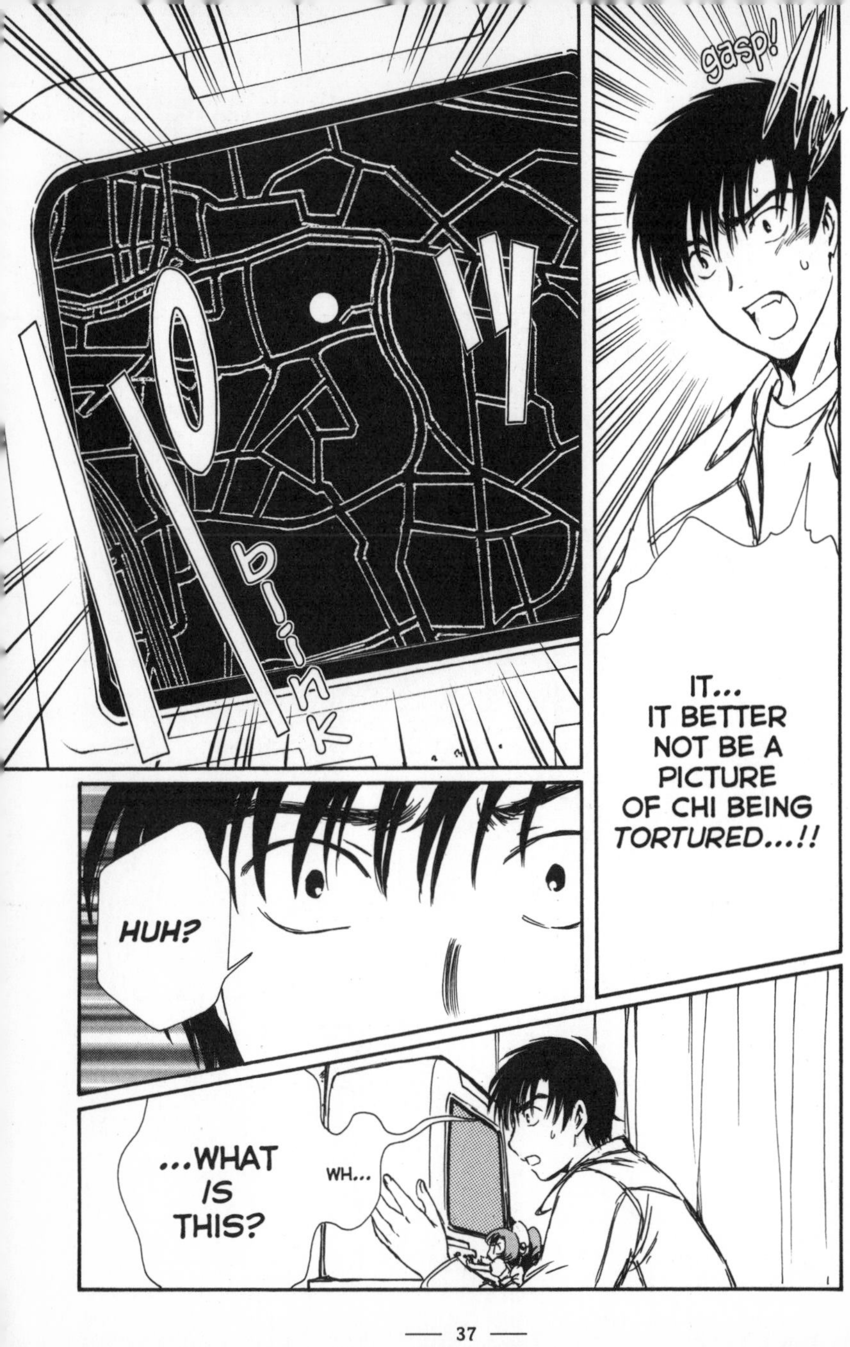
gasp!
IT... IT BETTER NOT BE A PICTURE OF CHI BEING *TORTURED*...!!
bli-i-n-k
HUH?
WH...
...WHAT *IS* THIS?

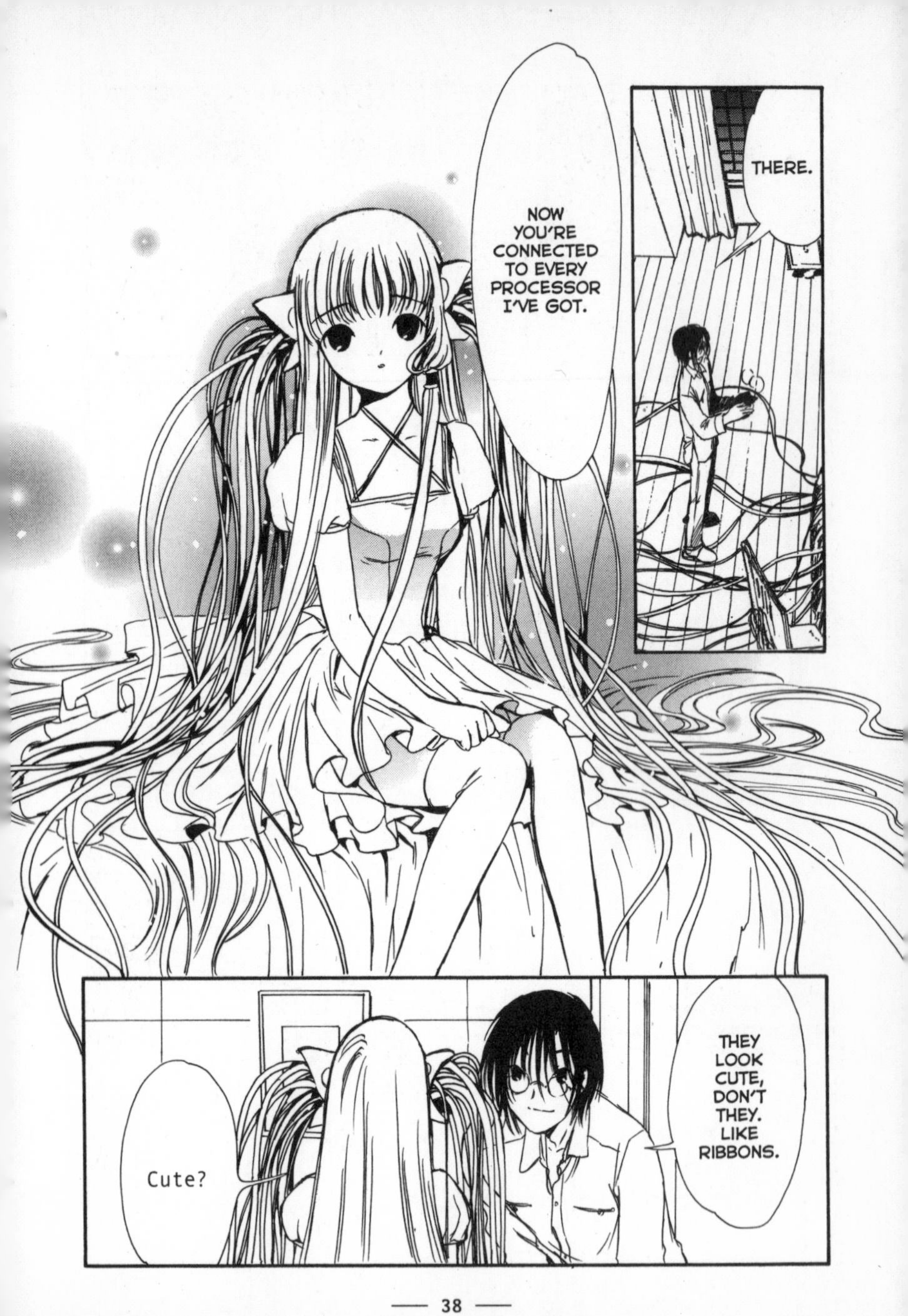
THERE.
NOW YOU'RE CONNECTED TO EVERY PROCESSOR I'VE GOT.
THEY LOOK CUTE, DON'T THEY. LIKE RIBBONS.
Cute?

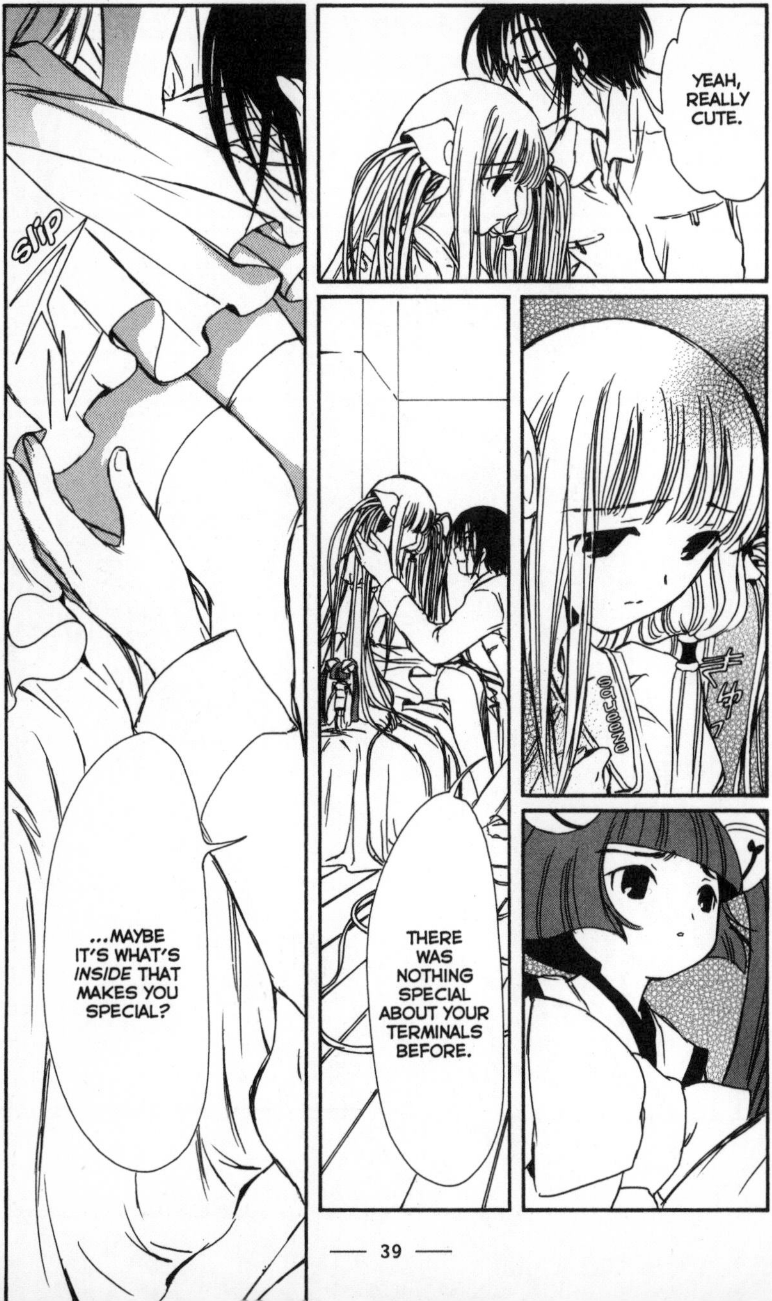
YEAH, REALLY CUTE.
ぎゅっ
snuggle
THERE WAS NOTHING SPECIAL ABOUT YOUR TERMINALS BEFORE.
slip
...MAYBE IT'S WHAT'S *INSIDE* THAT MAKES YOU SPECIAL?

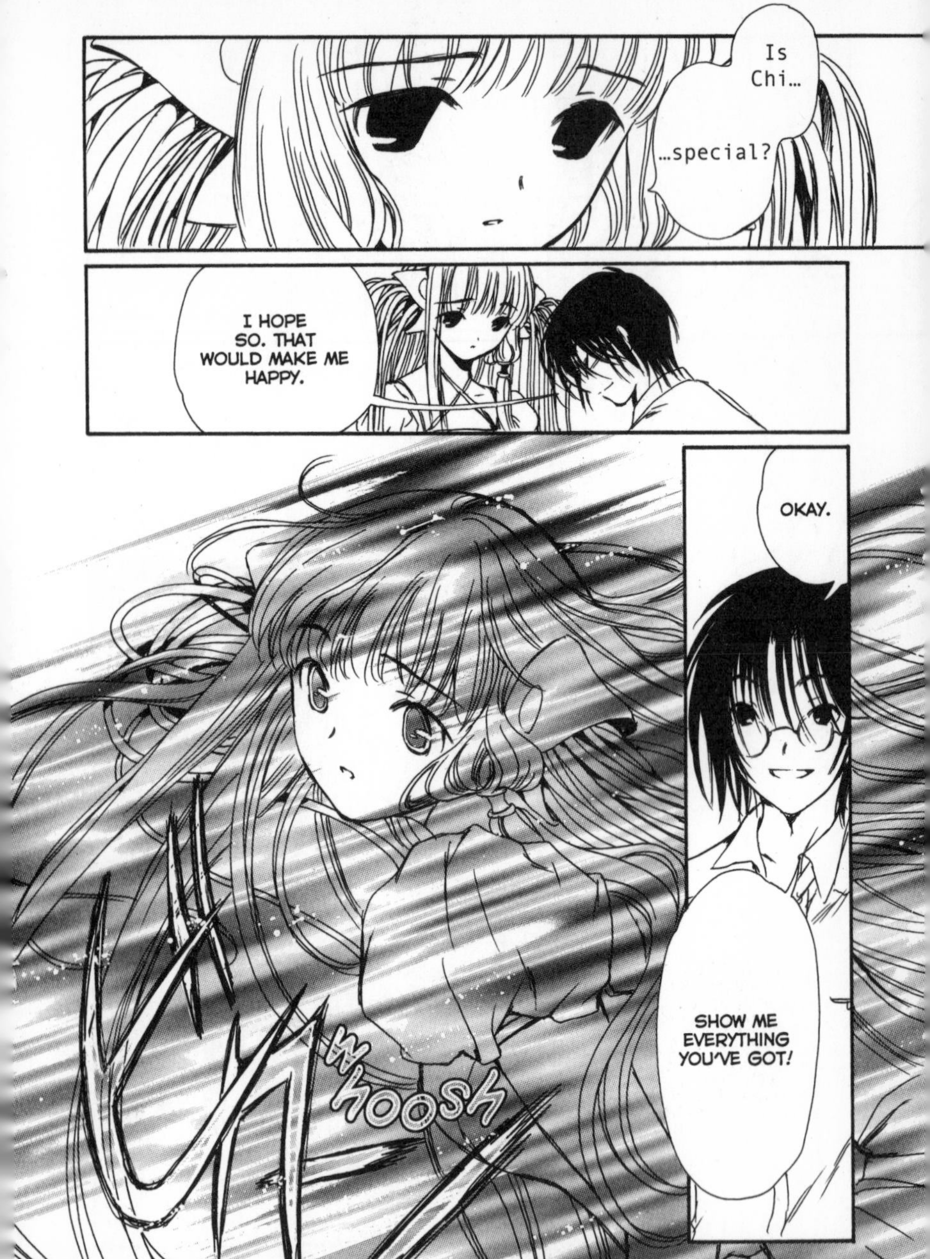
Is Chi…
…special?
I HOPE SO. THAT WOULD MAKE ME HAPPY.
OKAY.
SHOW ME EVERYTHING YOU'VE GOT!
WHOOSH

Chobits
ちょびっツ

◄ chapter 51 ►

HEY!
WHAT'S THIS ALL ABOUT...?
THIS IS NOTHING LIKE THOSE OTHER PICTURES...
...WHY THE HELL DID THEY SEND ME THIS?
SUMOMO! DO *YOU* KNOW WHAT THIS IS?

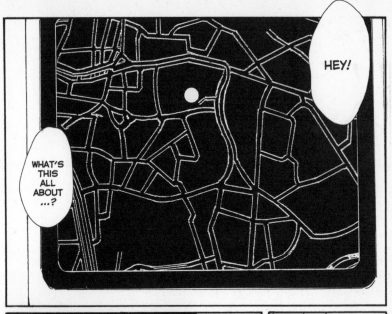

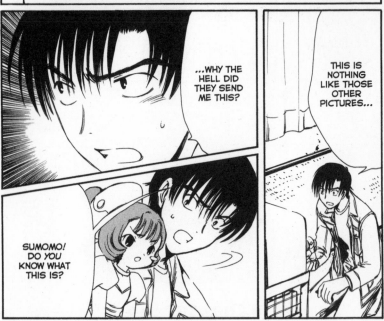

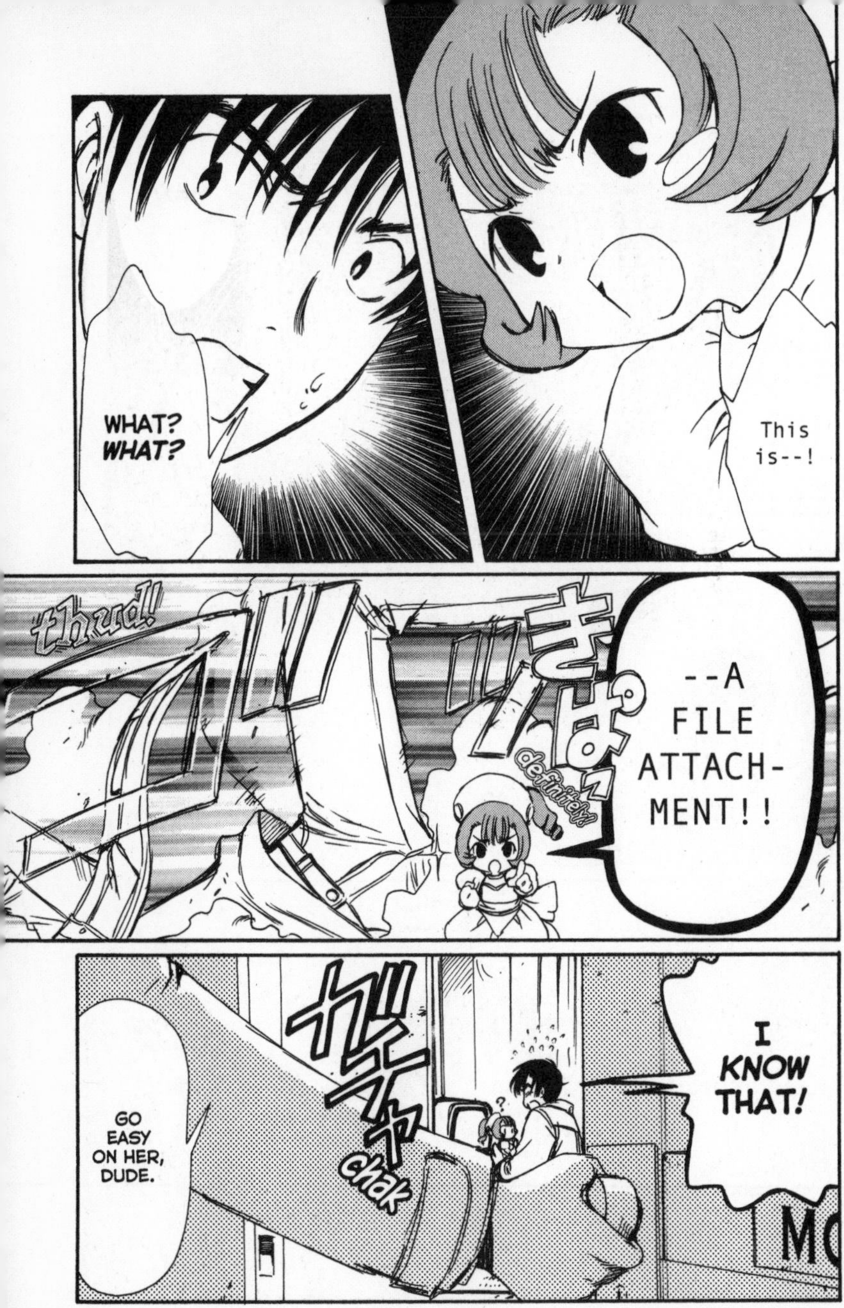
This is--!
WHAT? WHAT?
--A FILE ATTACHMENT!!
きぱっ
definitely!
thud!
I KNOW THAT!
chak
GO EASY ON HER, DUDE.

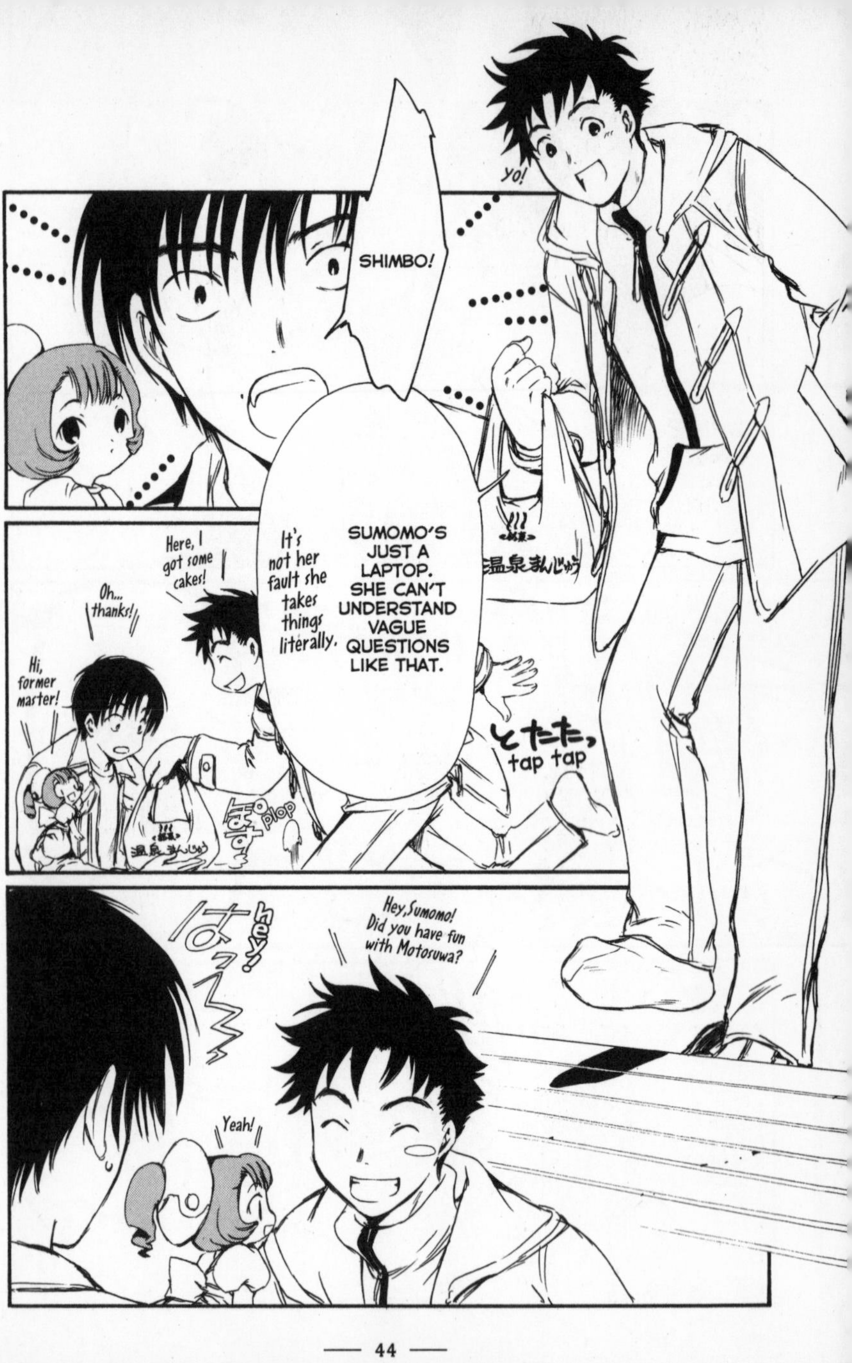
yo!
SHIMBO!
SUMOMO'S JUST A LAPTOP. SHE CAN'T UNDERSTAND VAGUE QUESTIONS LIKE THAT.
It's not her fault she takes things literally.
温泉まんじゅう
とたたっ
tap tap
Here, I got some cakes!
Oh... thanks!
Hi, former master!
ぽすっ
plop
温泉まんじゅう
Hey, Sumomo! Did you have fun with Motosuwa?
はっ
hey!
Yeah!

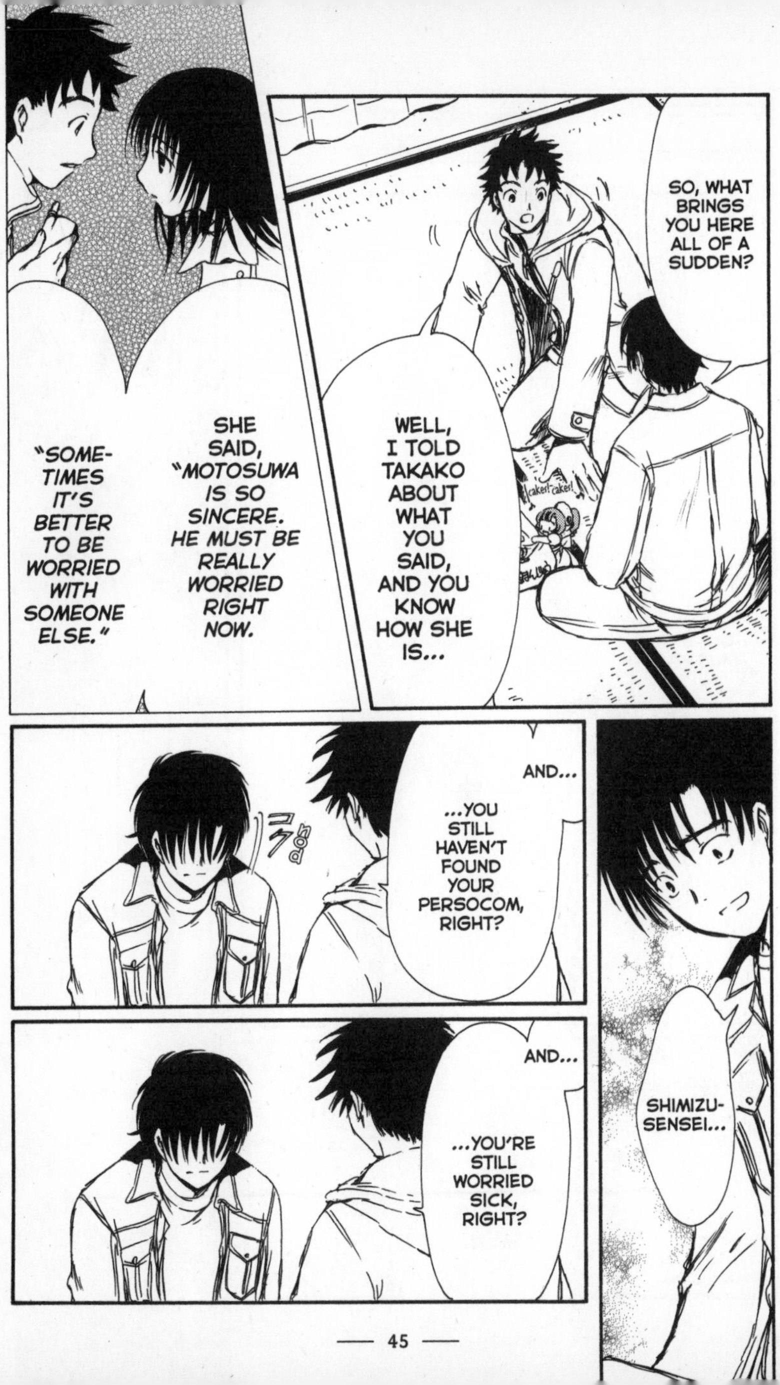
SO, WHAT BRINGS YOU HERE ALL OF A SUDDEN?
WELL, I TOLD TAKAKO ABOUT WHAT YOU SAID, AND YOU KNOW HOW SHE IS...
SHE SAID, "MOTOSUWA IS SO SINCERE. HE MUST BE REALLY WORRIED RIGHT NOW.
"SOMETIMES IT'S BETTER TO BE WORRIED WITH SOMEONE ELSE."
SHIMIZU-SENSEI...
AND...
...YOU STILL HAVEN'T FOUND YOUR PERSOCOM, RIGHT?
nod
AND...
...YOU'RE STILL WORRIED SICK, RIGHT?

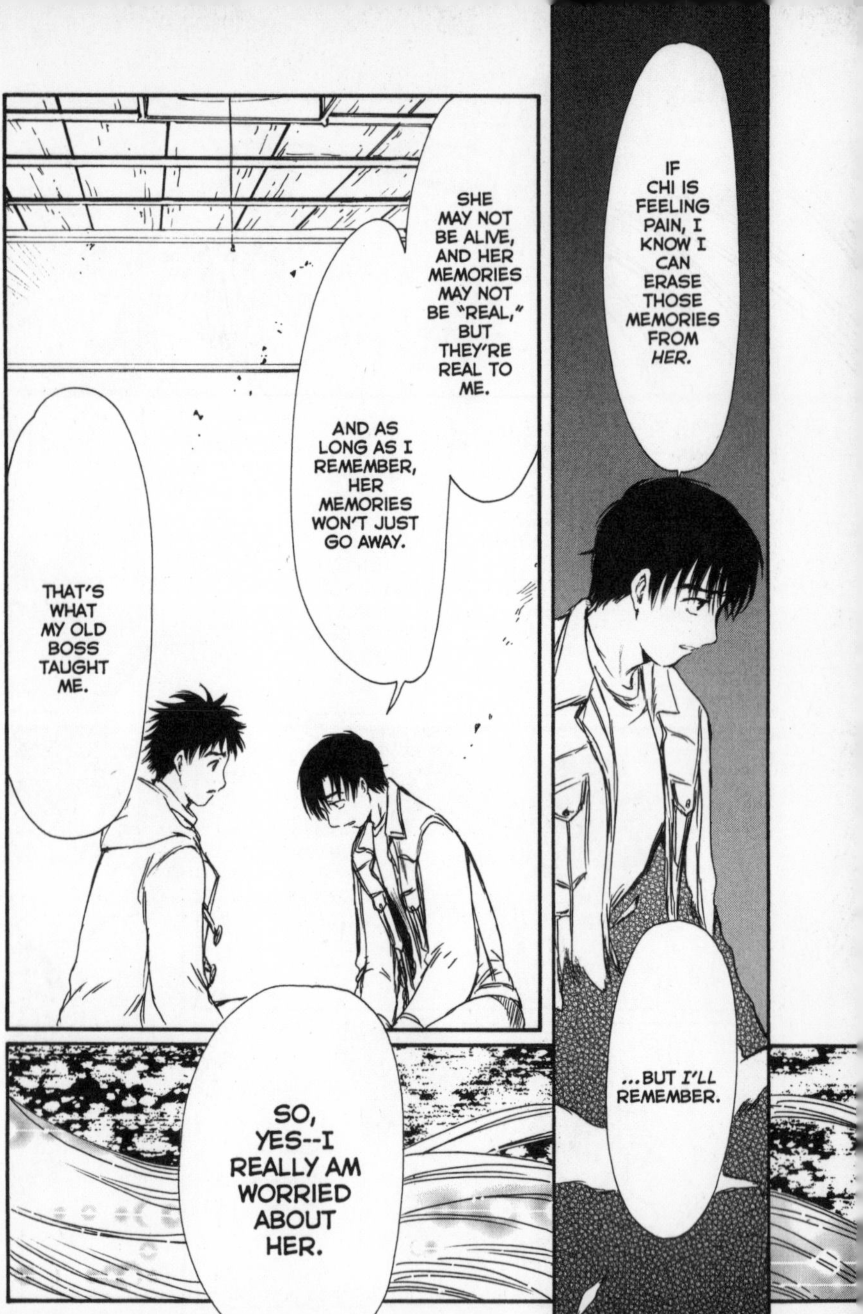
IF CHI IS FEELING PAIN, I KNOW I CAN ERASE THOSE MEMORIES FROM *HER.*
...BUT *I'LL* REMEMBER.
SHE MAY NOT BE ALIVE, AND HER MEMORIES MAY NOT BE "REAL," BUT THEY'RE REAL TO ME.
AND AS LONG AS I REMEMBER, HER MEMORIES WON'T JUST GO AWAY.
THAT'S WHAT MY OLD BOSS TAUGHT ME.
SO, YES--I REALLY AM WORRIED ABOUT HER.

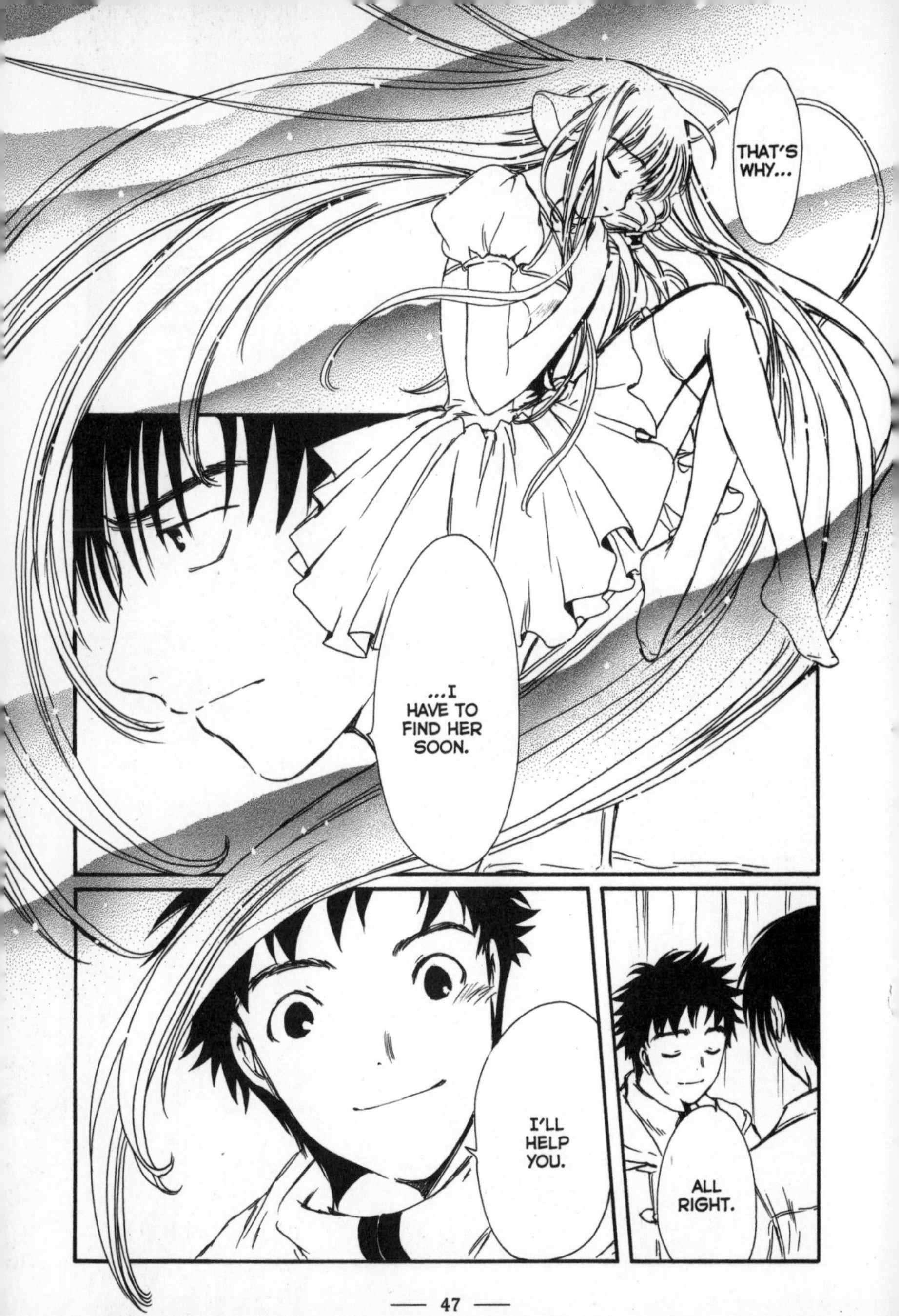
THAT'S WHY...
...I HAVE TO FIND HER SOON.
ALL RIGHT.
I'LL HELP YOU.

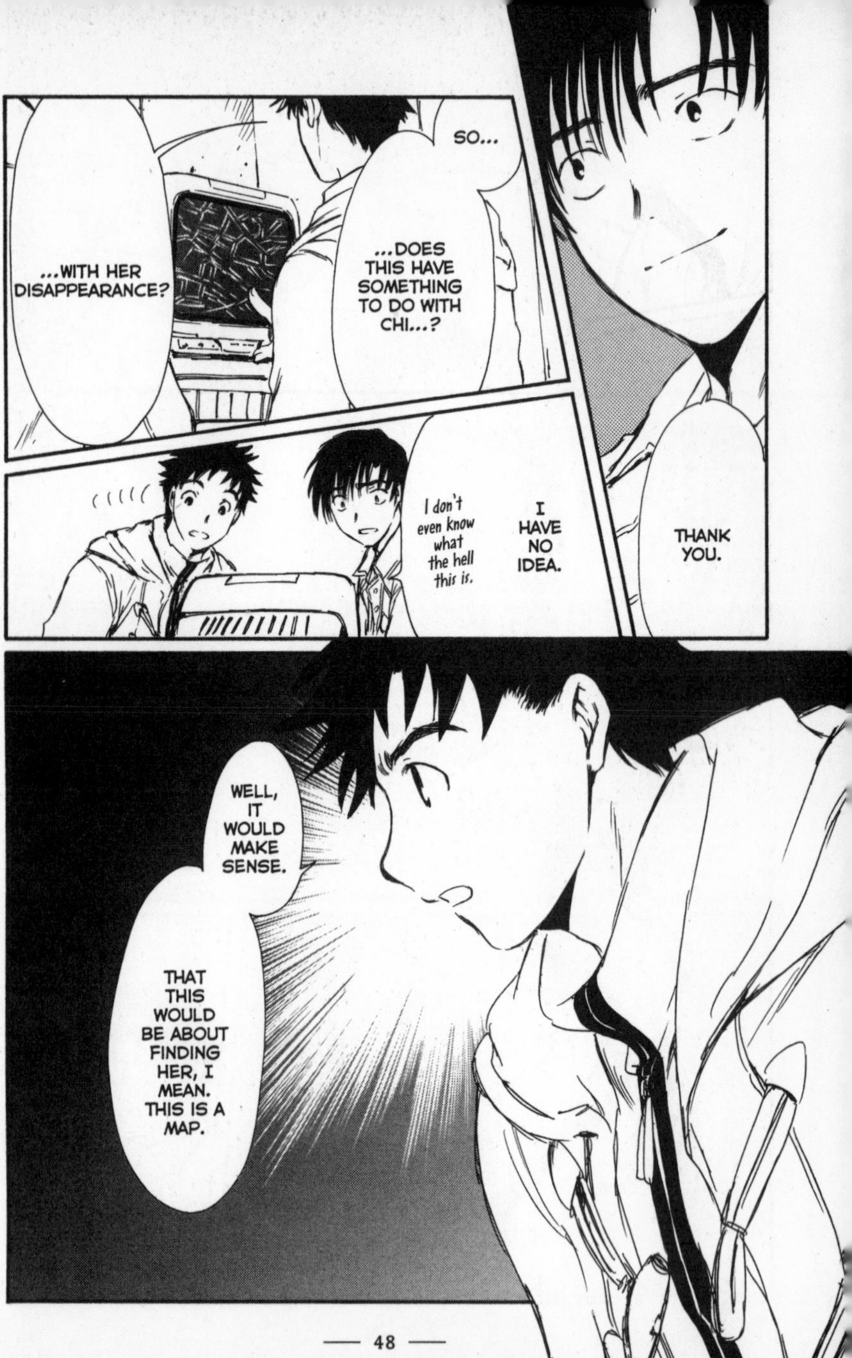
THANK YOU.
SO...
...DOES THIS HAVE SOMETHING TO DO WITH CHI...?
...WITH HER DISAPPEARANCE?
I HAVE NO IDEA.
I don't even know what the hell this is.
WELL, IT WOULD MAKE SENSE.
THAT THIS WOULD BE ABOUT FINDING HER, I MEAN. THIS IS A MAP.

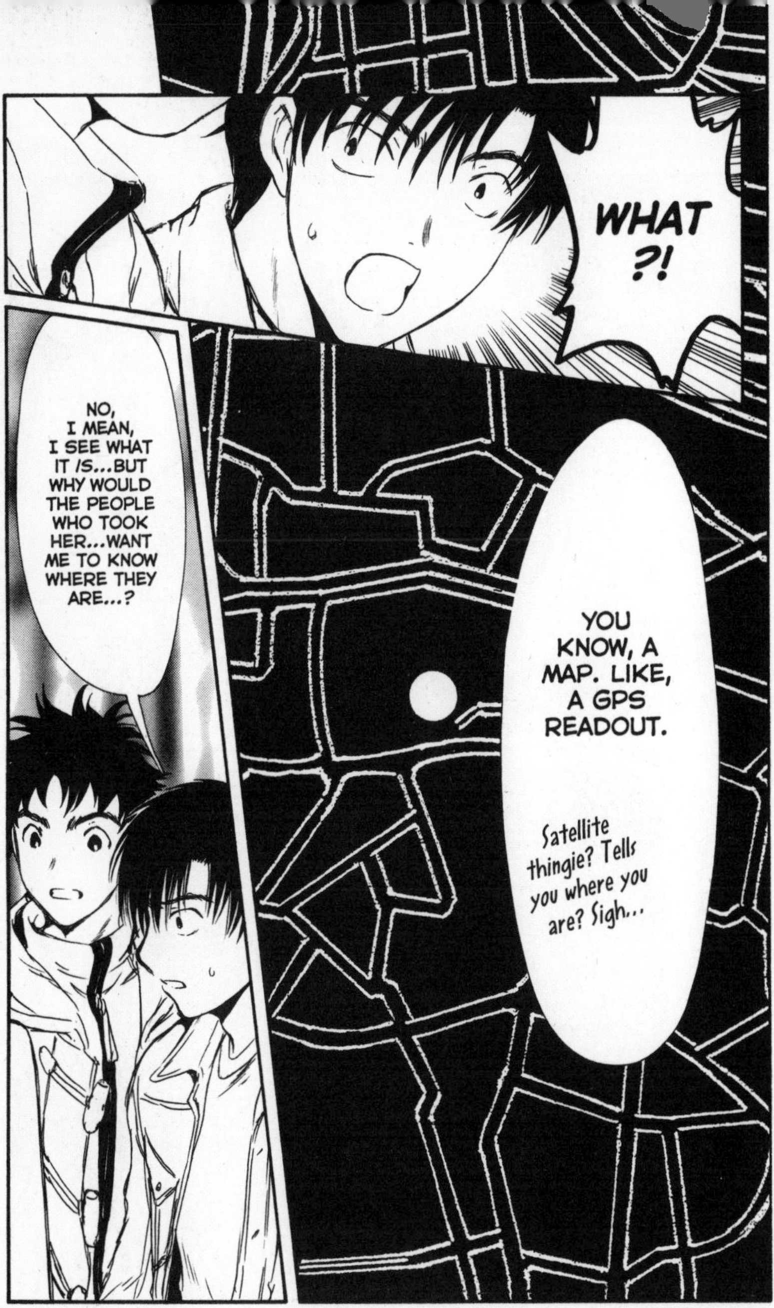
WHAT ?!
YOU KNOW, A MAP. LIKE, A GPS READOUT.
Satellite thingie? Tells you where you are? Sigh...
NO, I MEAN, I SEE WHAT IT *IS*...BUT WHY WOULD THE PEOPLE WHO TOOK HER...WANT ME TO KNOW WHERE THEY ARE...?

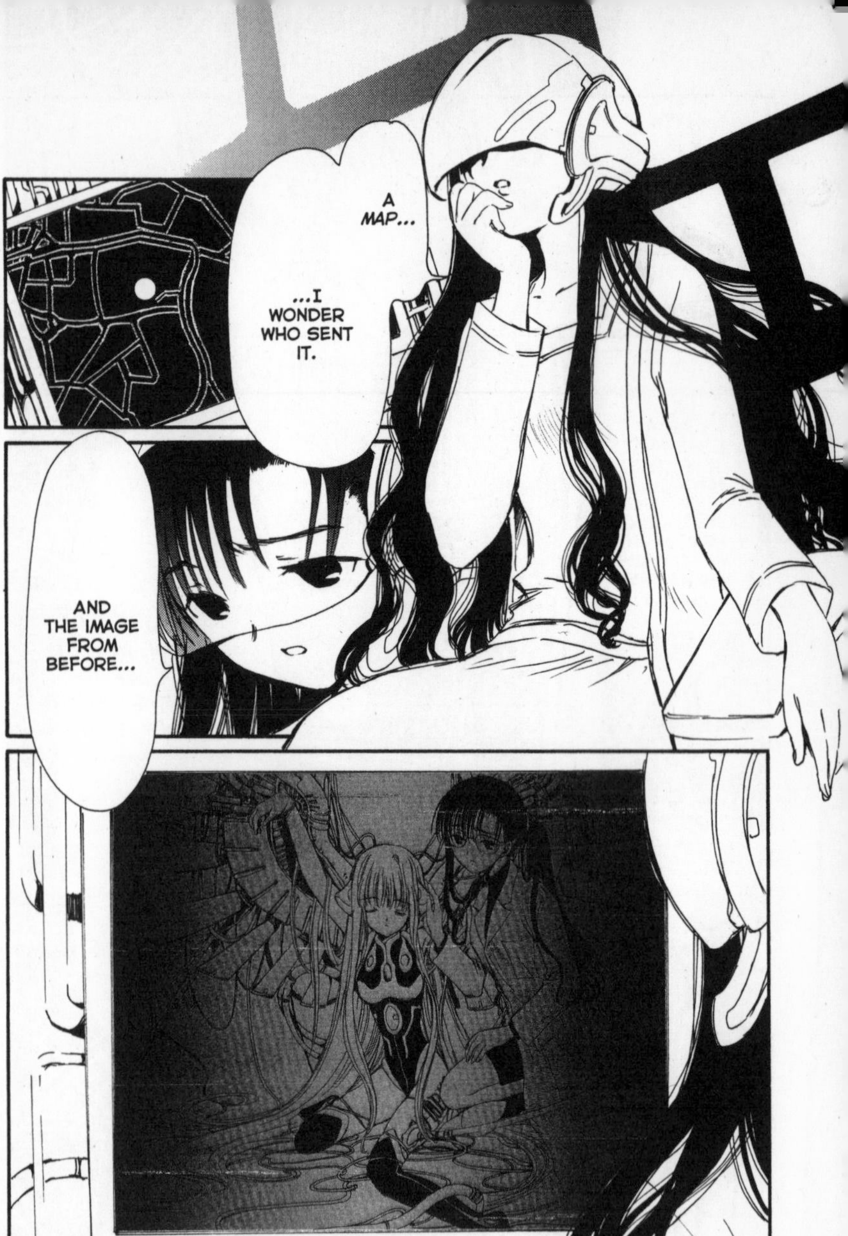
A MAP...
...I WONDER WHO SENT IT.
AND THE IMAGE FROM BEFORE...

ふぁさ
slip

wwwww

slam

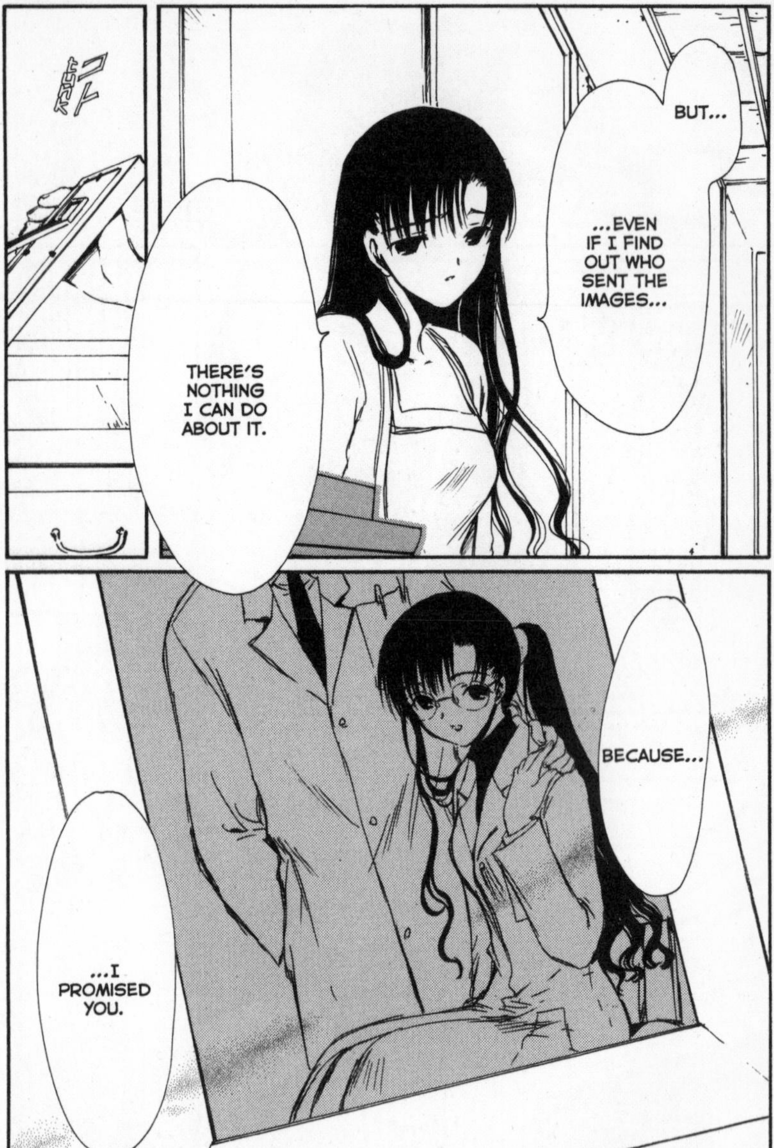
BUT...
...EVEN IF I FIND OUT WHO SENT THE IMAGES...
THERE'S NOTHING I CAN DO ABOUT IT.
BECAUSE...
...I PROMISED YOU.

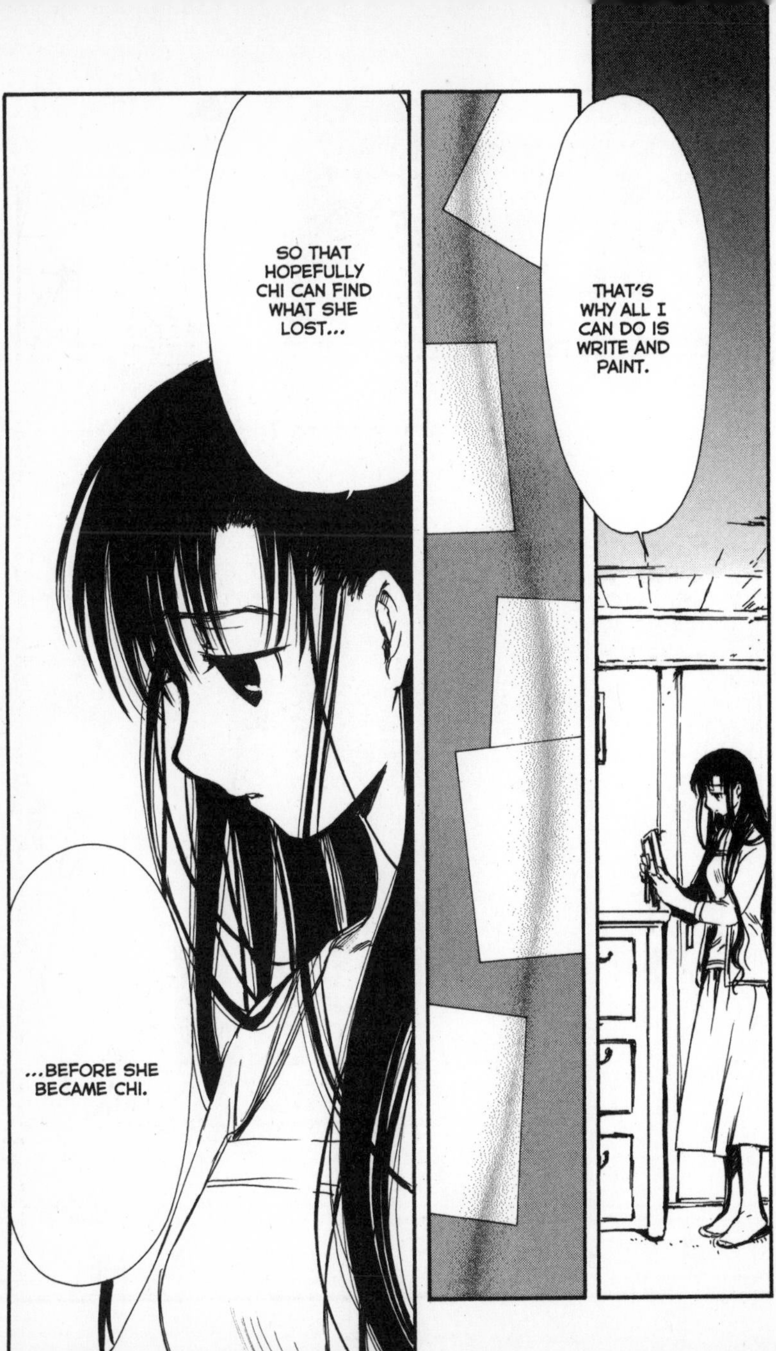
THAT'S WHY ALL I CAN DO IS WRITE AND PAINT.
SO THAT HOPEFULLY CHI CAN FIND WHAT SHE LOST...
...BEFORE SHE BECAME CHI.

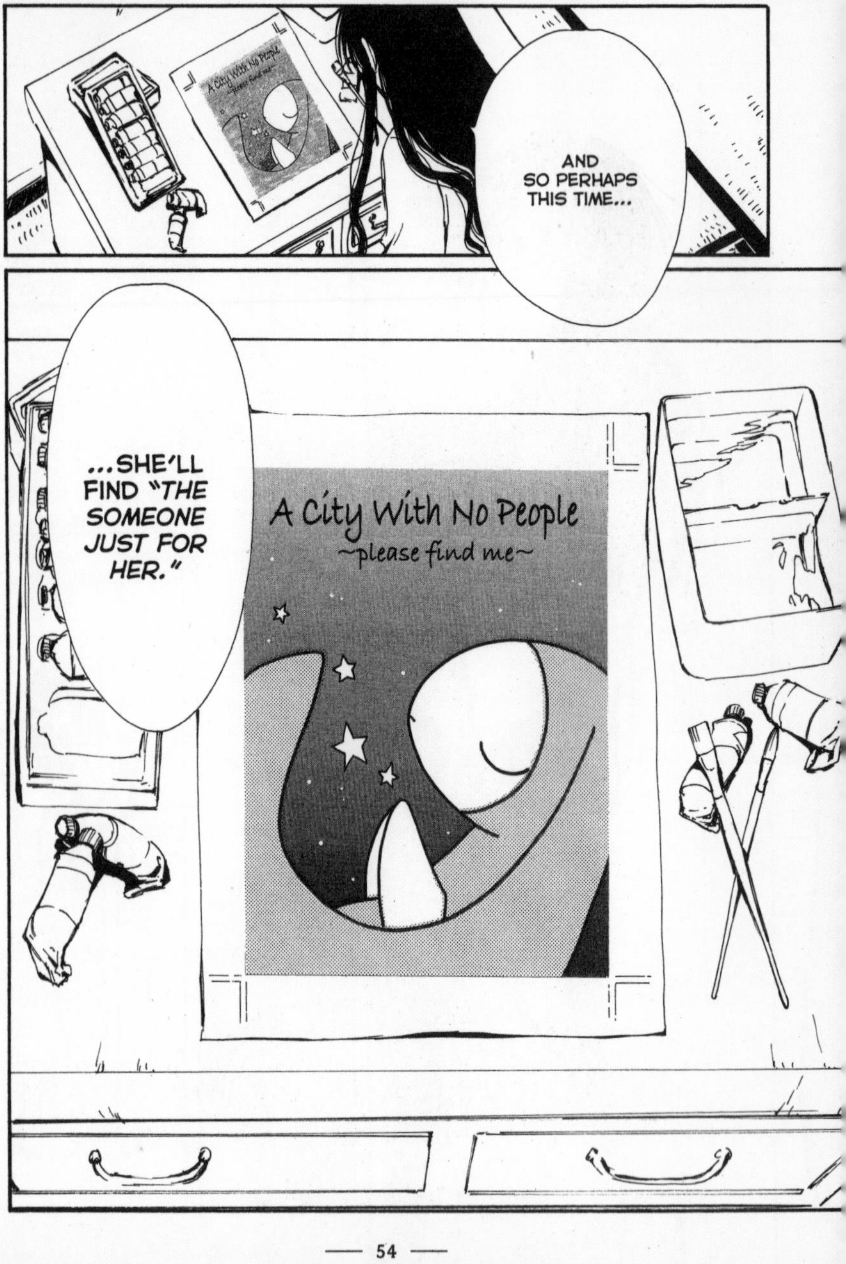
AND SO PERHAPS THIS TIME...
A City With No People
~please find me~
...SHE'LL FIND "THE SOMEONE JUST FOR HER."
A City With No People
~please find me~

Chobits
ちょびっツ

◄ **chapter 52** ►

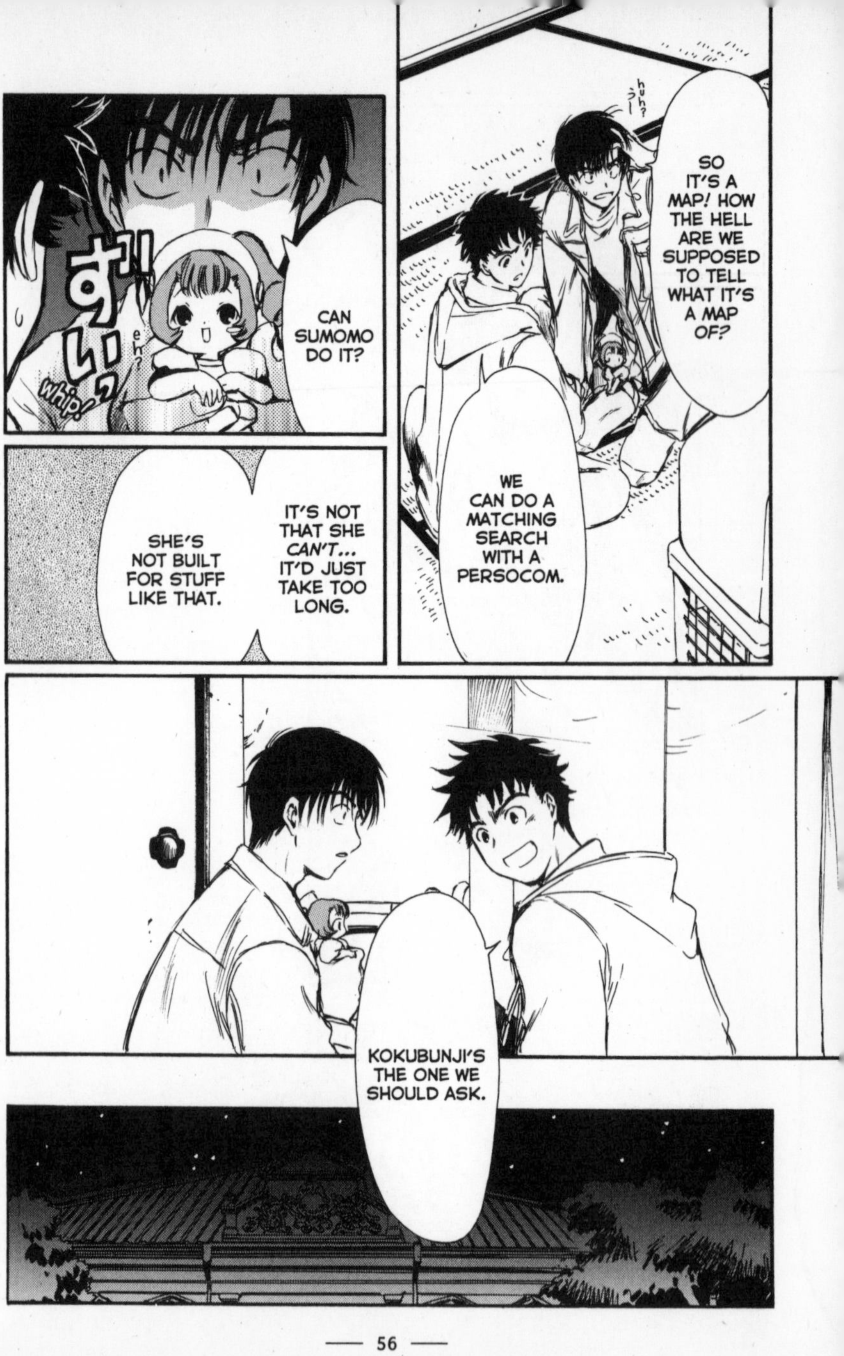
huh?
SO IT'S A MAP! HOW THE HELL ARE WE SUPPOSED TO TELL WHAT IT'S A MAP OF?
WE CAN DO A MATCHING SEARCH WITH A PERSOCOM.
CAN SUMOMO DO IT?
eh?
whip!
IT'S NOT THAT SHE *CAN'T*... IT'D JUST TAKE TOO LONG.
SHE'S NOT BUILT FOR STUFF LIKE THAT.
KOKUBUNJI'S THE ONE WE SHOULD ASK.

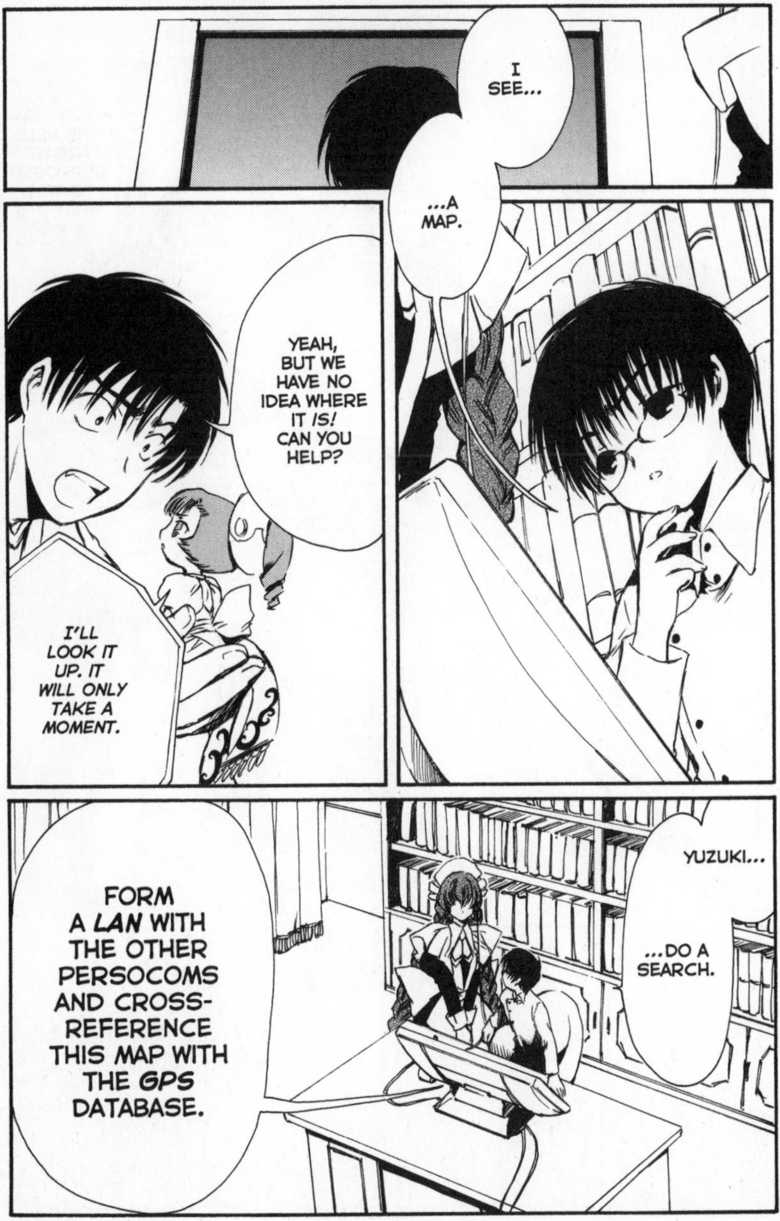
I SEE...
...A MAP.
YEAH, BUT WE HAVE NO IDEA WHERE IT *IS!* CAN YOU HELP?
I'LL LOOK IT UP. IT WILL ONLY TAKE A MOMENT.
YUZUKI...
...DO A SEARCH.
FORM A *LAN* WITH THE OTHER PERSOCOMS AND CROSS-REFERENCE THIS *MAP* WITH THE *GPS* DATABASE.

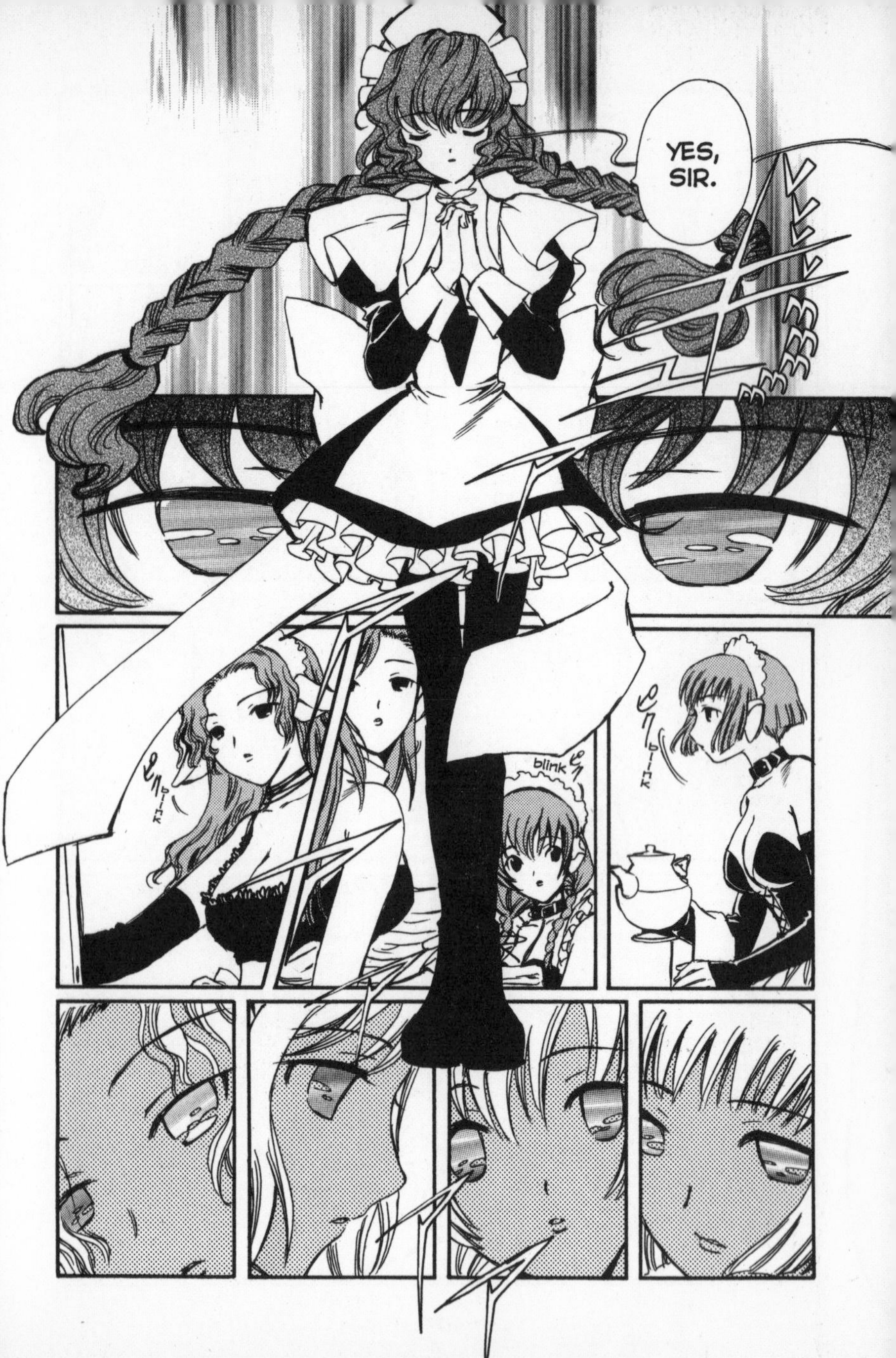
YES, SIR.
blink
blink
blink

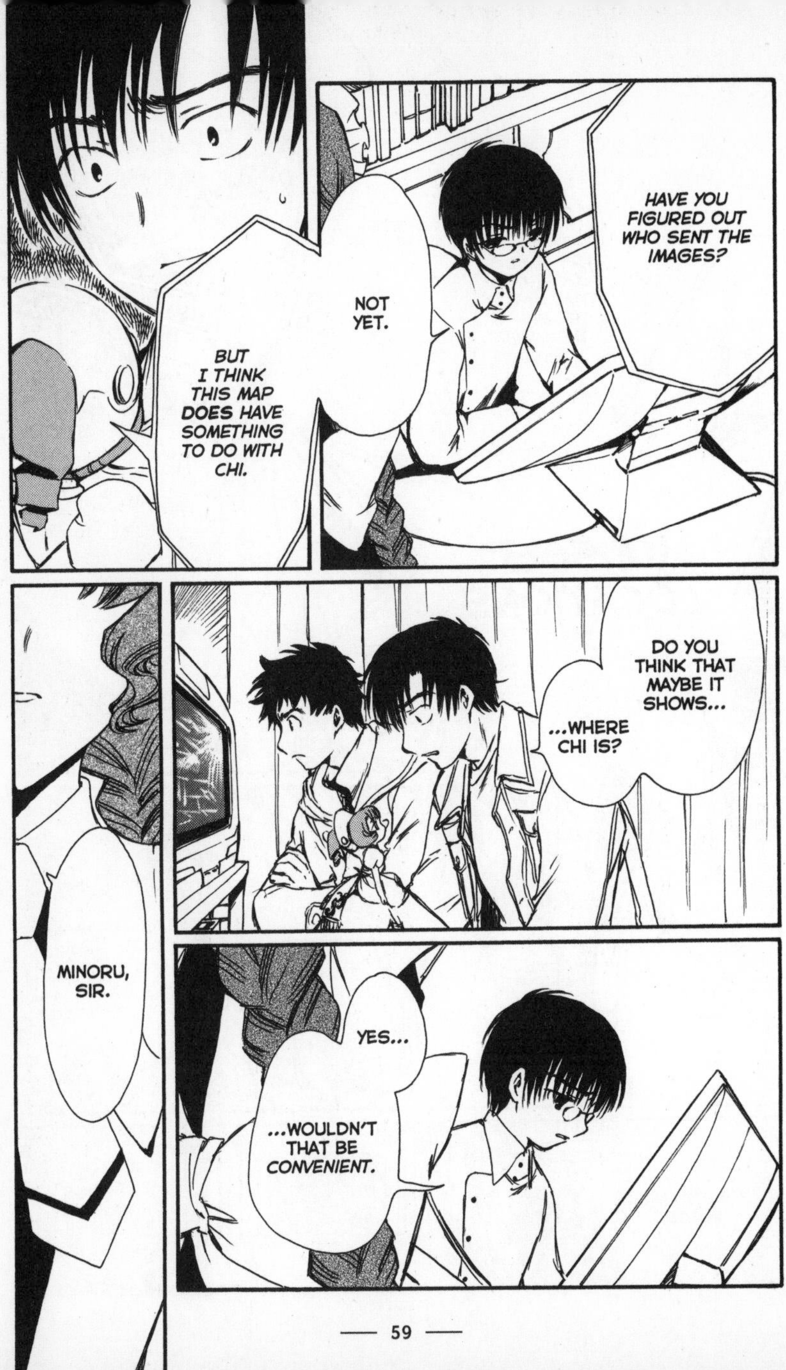
HAVE YOU FIGURED OUT WHO SENT THE IMAGES?
NOT YET.
BUT I THINK THIS MAP DOES HAVE SOMETHING TO DO WITH CHI.
DO YOU THINK THAT MAYBE IT SHOWS...
...WHERE CHI IS?
YES...
...WOULDN'T THAT BE CONVENIENT.
MINORU, SIR.

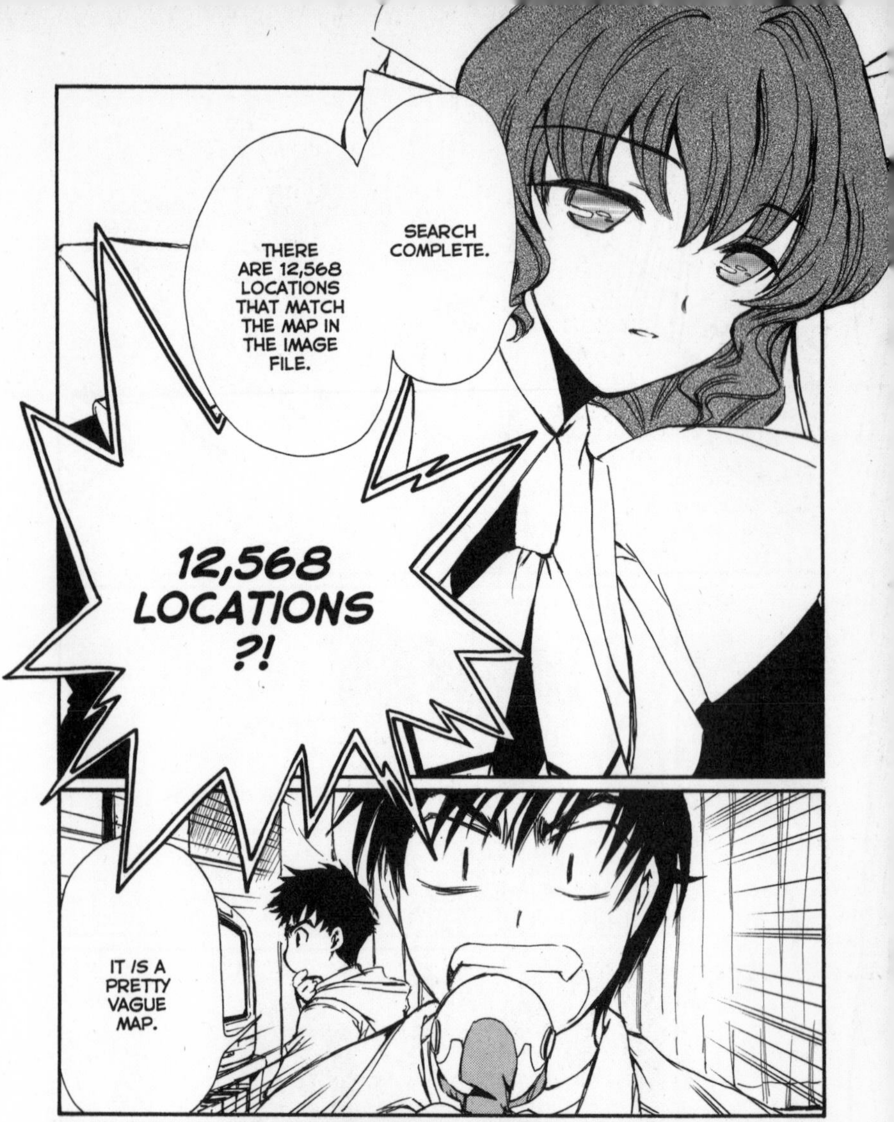
SEARCH COMPLETE.
THERE ARE 12,568 LOCATIONS THAT MATCH THE MAP IN THE IMAGE FILE.
12,568 LOCATIONS?!
IT IS A PRETTY VAGUE MAP.
AND IN THIS PREFEC-TURE?
TWENTY-THREE PLACES.

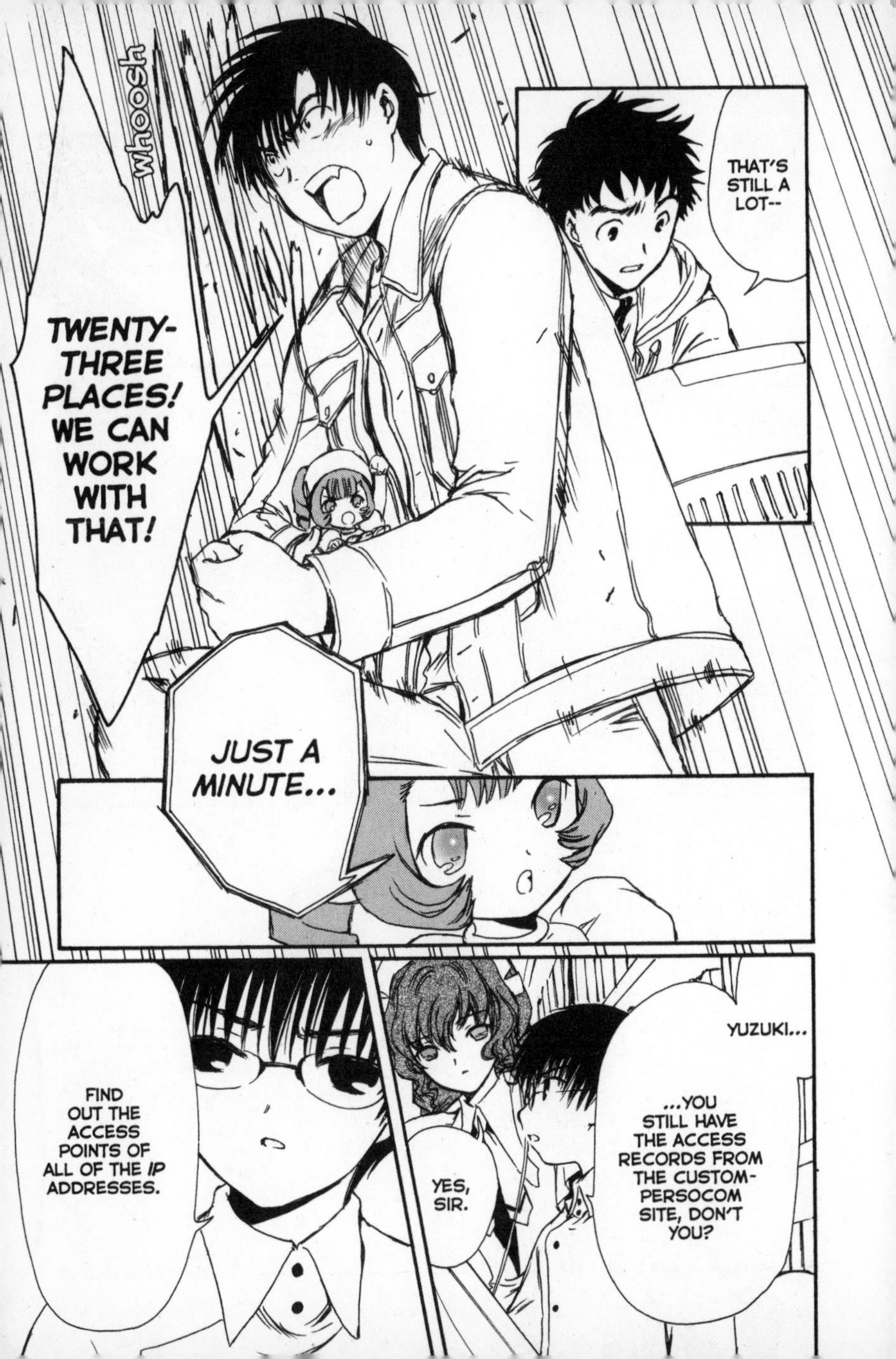
THAT'S STILL A LOT--
whoosh
TWENTY-THREE PLACES! WE CAN WORK WITH THAT!
JUST A MINUTE...
YUZUKI...
...YOU STILL HAVE THE ACCESS RECORDS FROM THE CUSTOM-PERSOCOM SITE, DON'T YOU?
YES, SIR.
FIND OUT THE ACCESS POINTS OF ALL OF THE *IP* ADDRESSES.

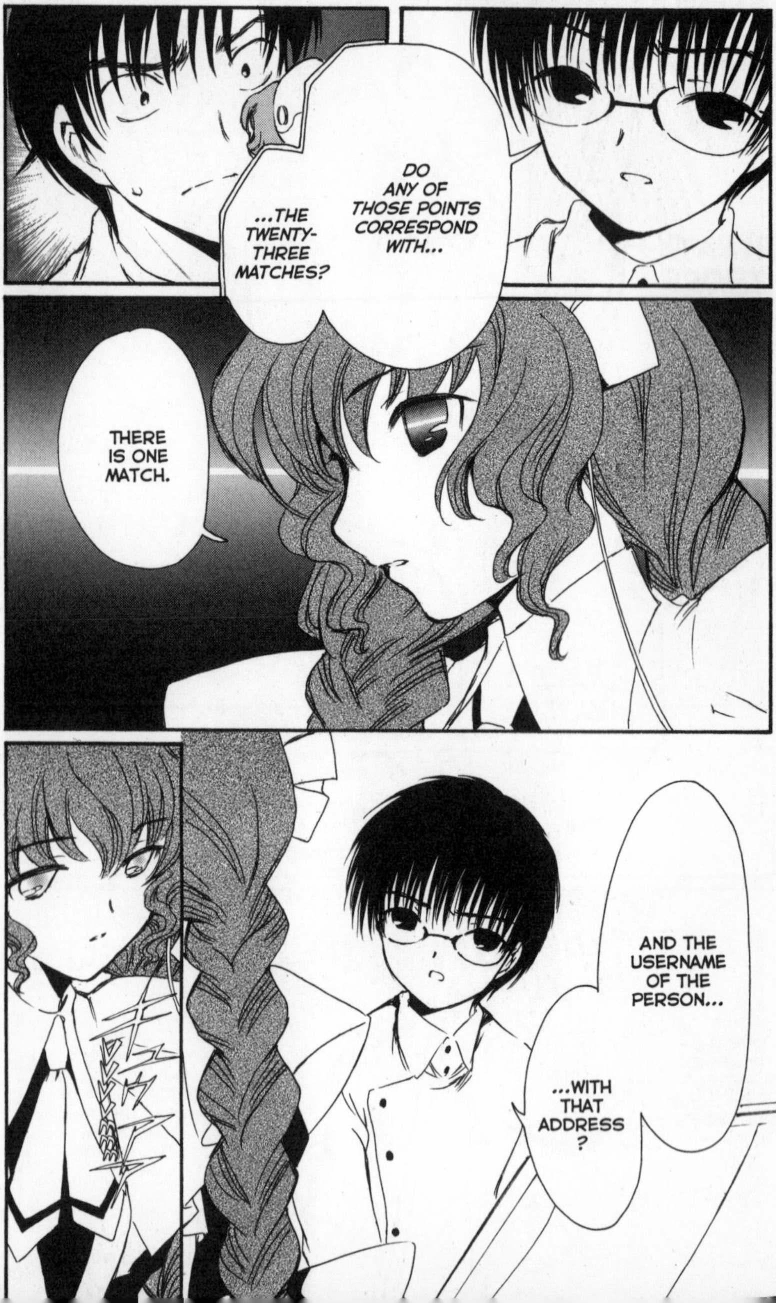
DO ANY OF THOSE POINTS CORRESPOND WITH...
...THE TWENTY-THREE MATCHES?
THERE IS ONE MATCH.
AND THE USERNAME OF THE PERSON...
...WITH THAT ADDRESS?

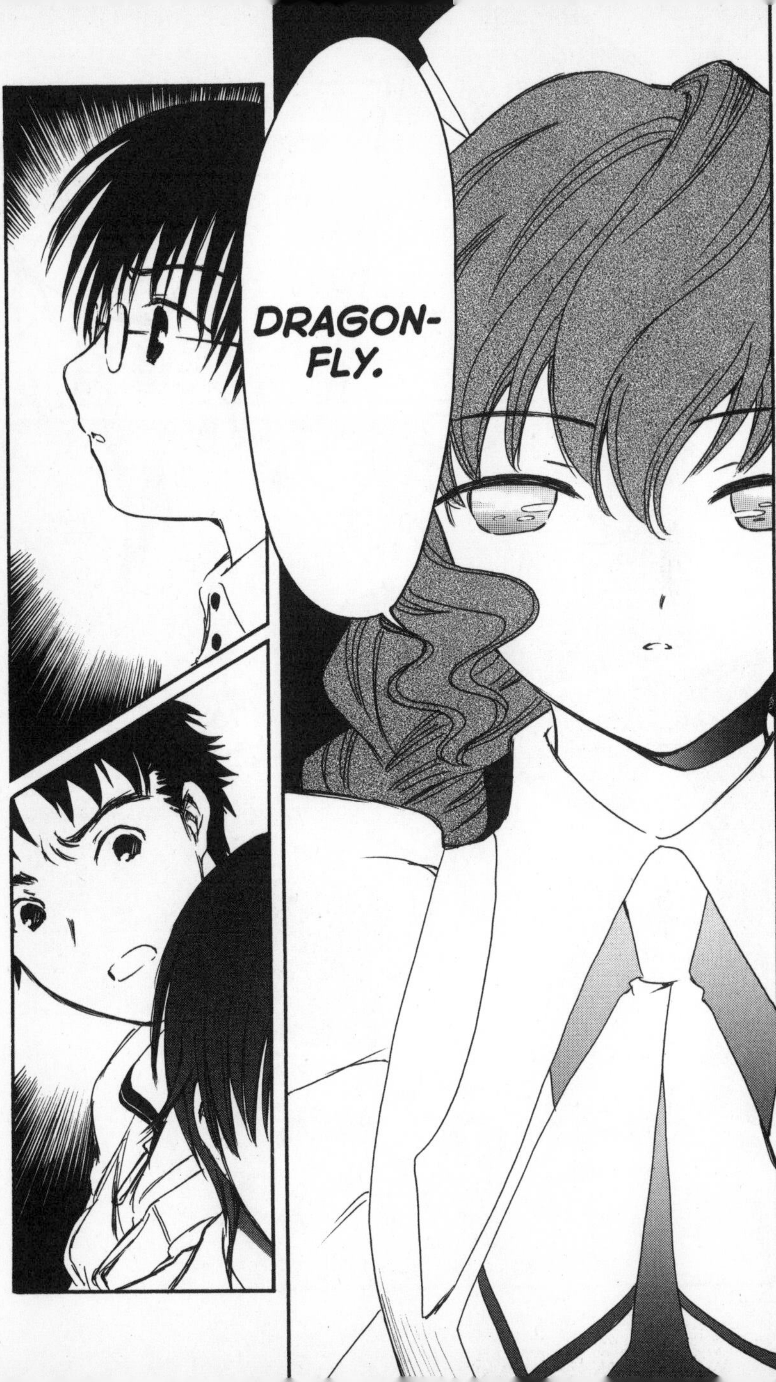
DRAGON-FLY.

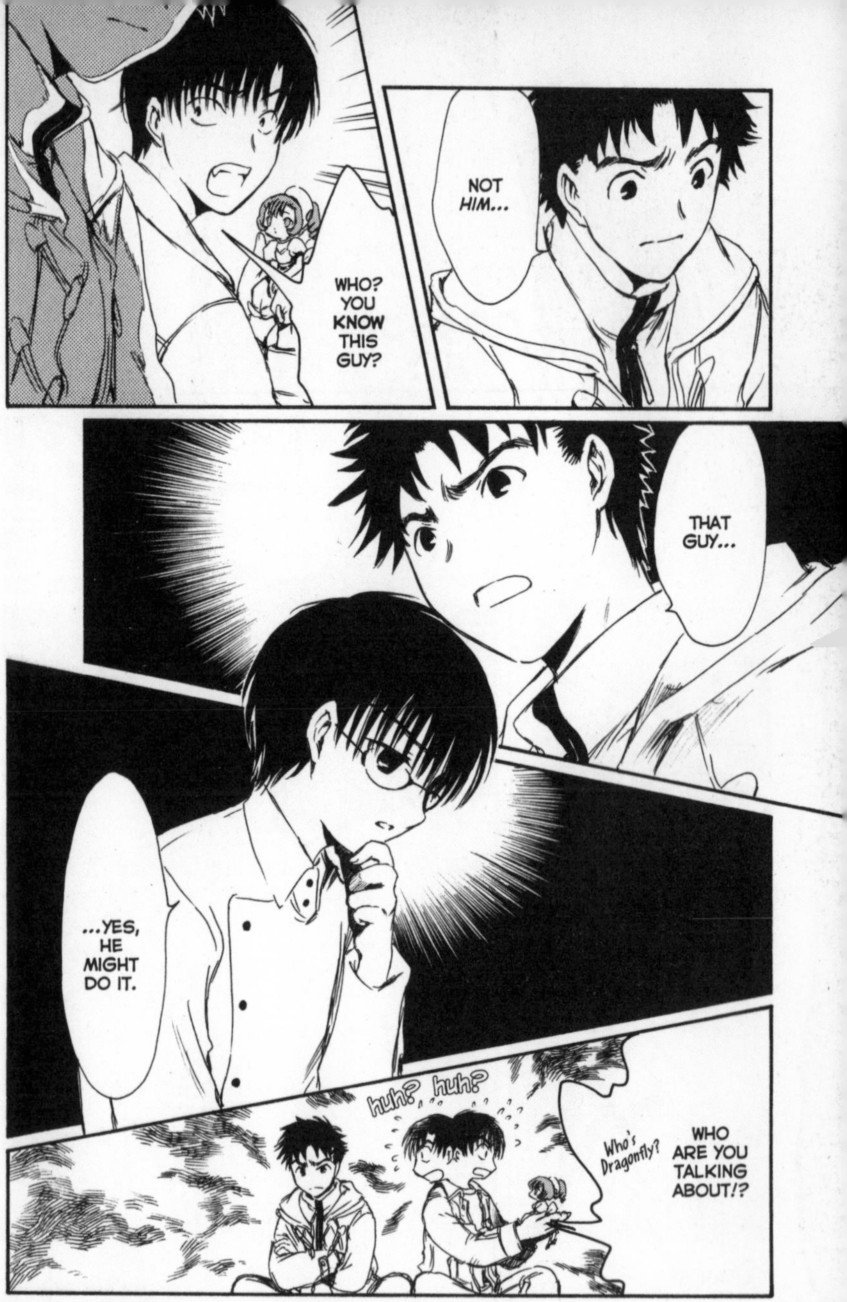
NOT HIM...
WHO? YOU KNOW THIS GUY?
THAT GUY...
...YES, HE MIGHT DO IT.
WHO ARE YOU TALKING ABOUT!?
Who's Dragonfly?
huh? huh?

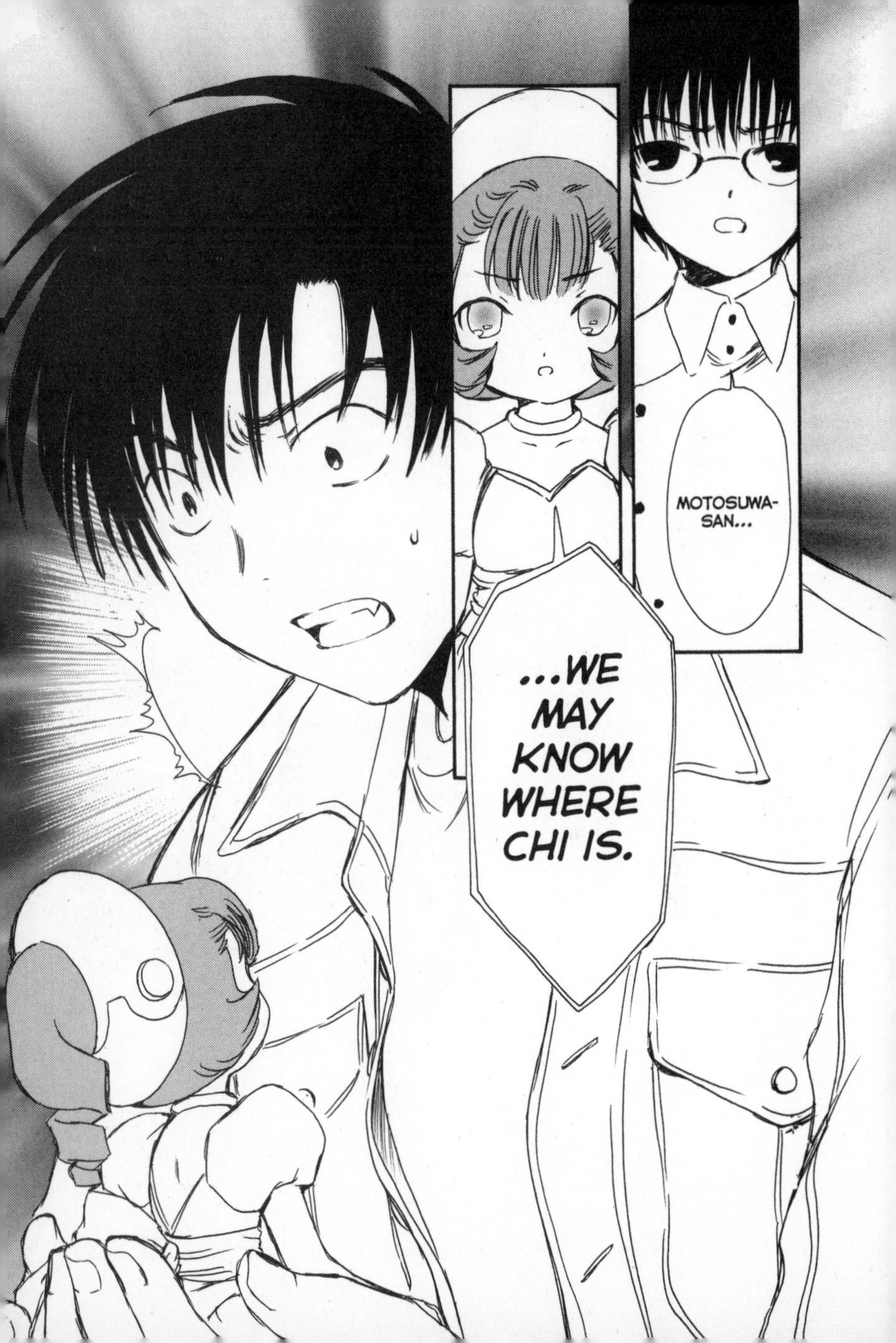
MOTOSUWA-SAN...
...WE MAY KNOW WHERE CHI IS.

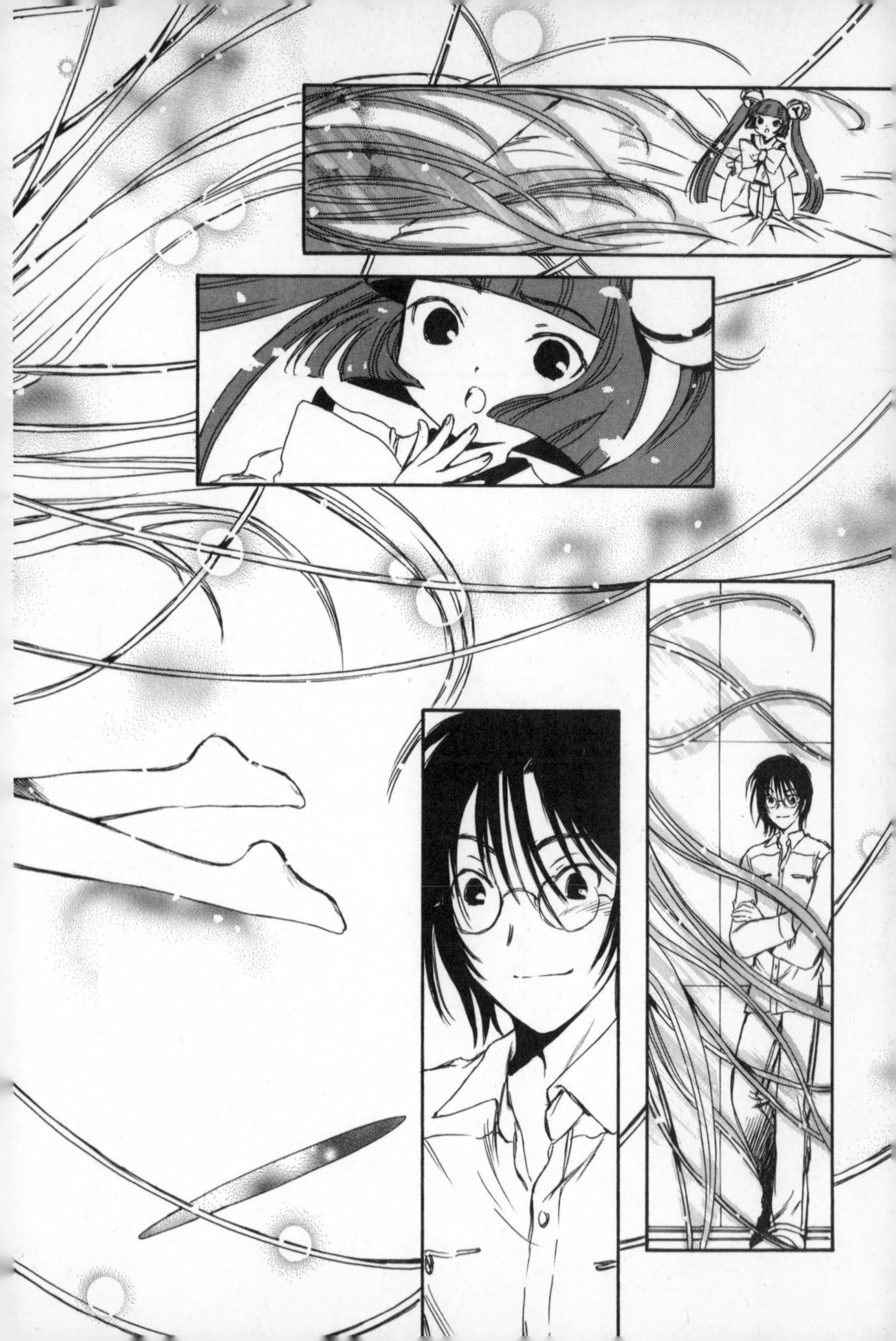

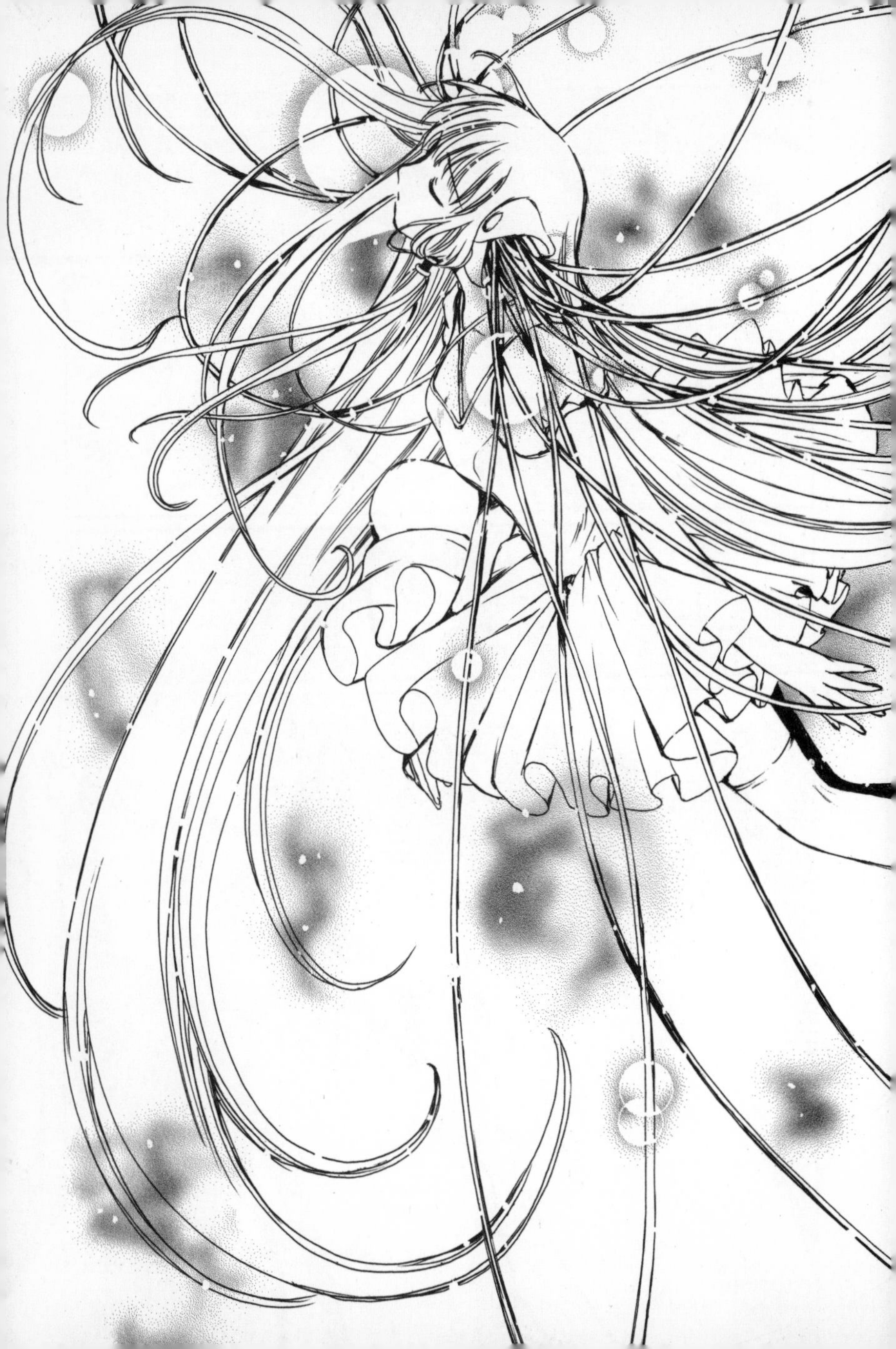

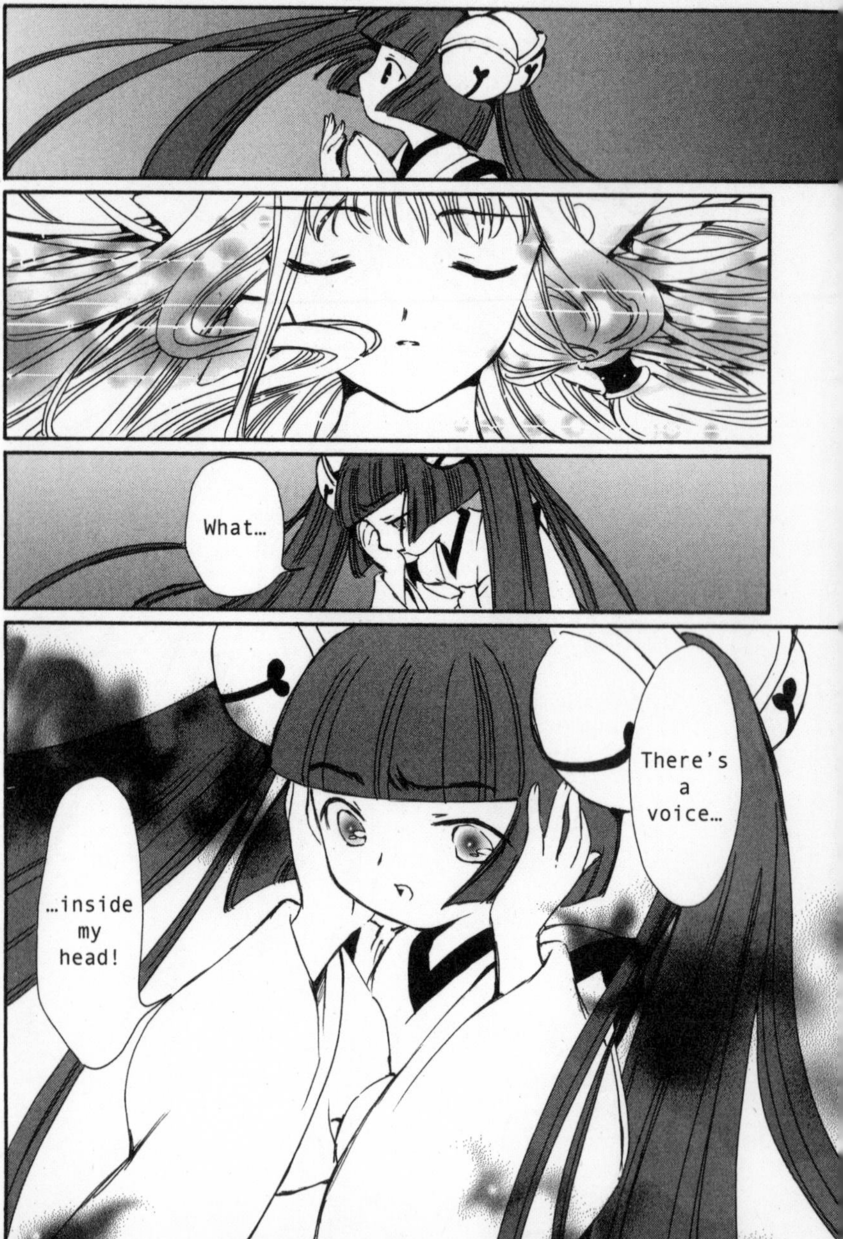
What…
There's a voice…
…inside my head!

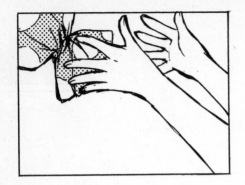

Chobits
ちょびっツ

◀ chapter 53 ▶

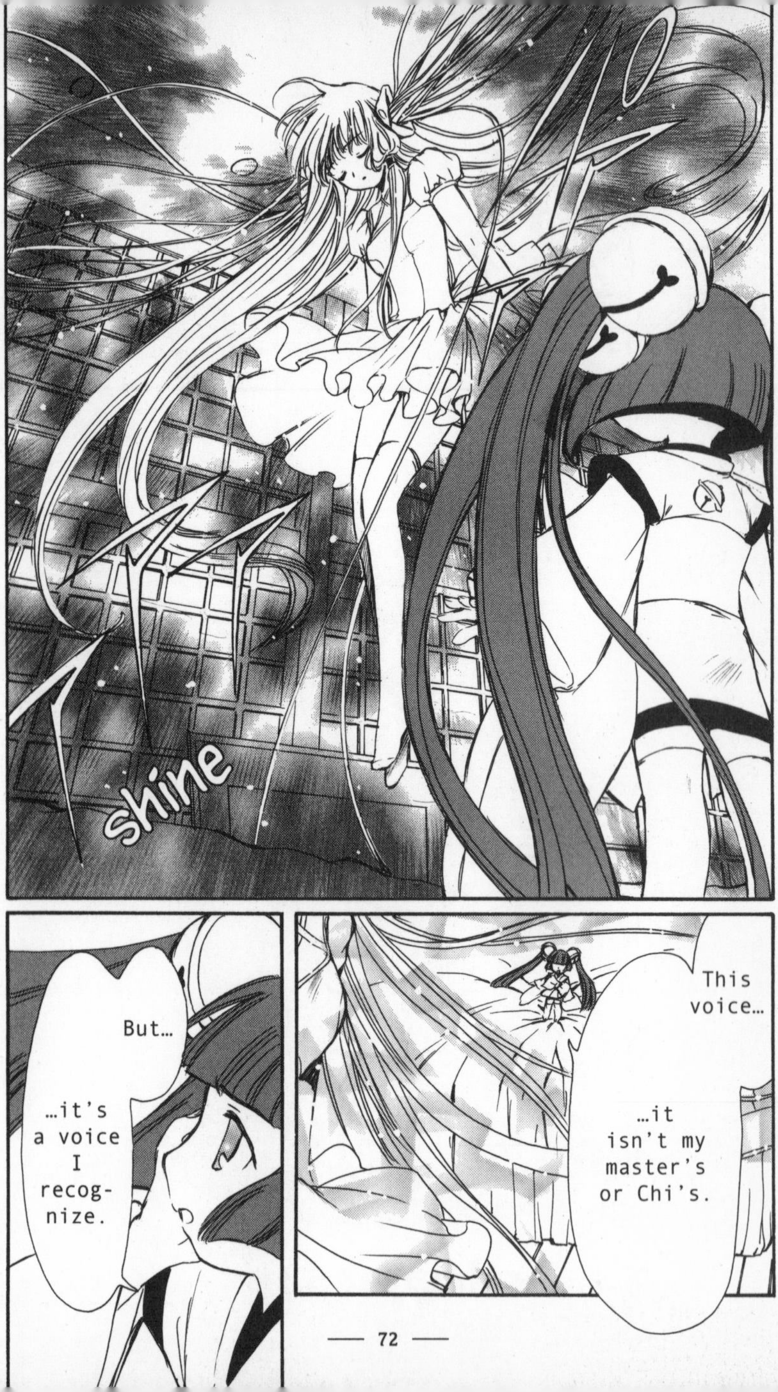
shine
This voice…
…it isn't my master's or Chi's.
But…
…it's a voice I recognize.

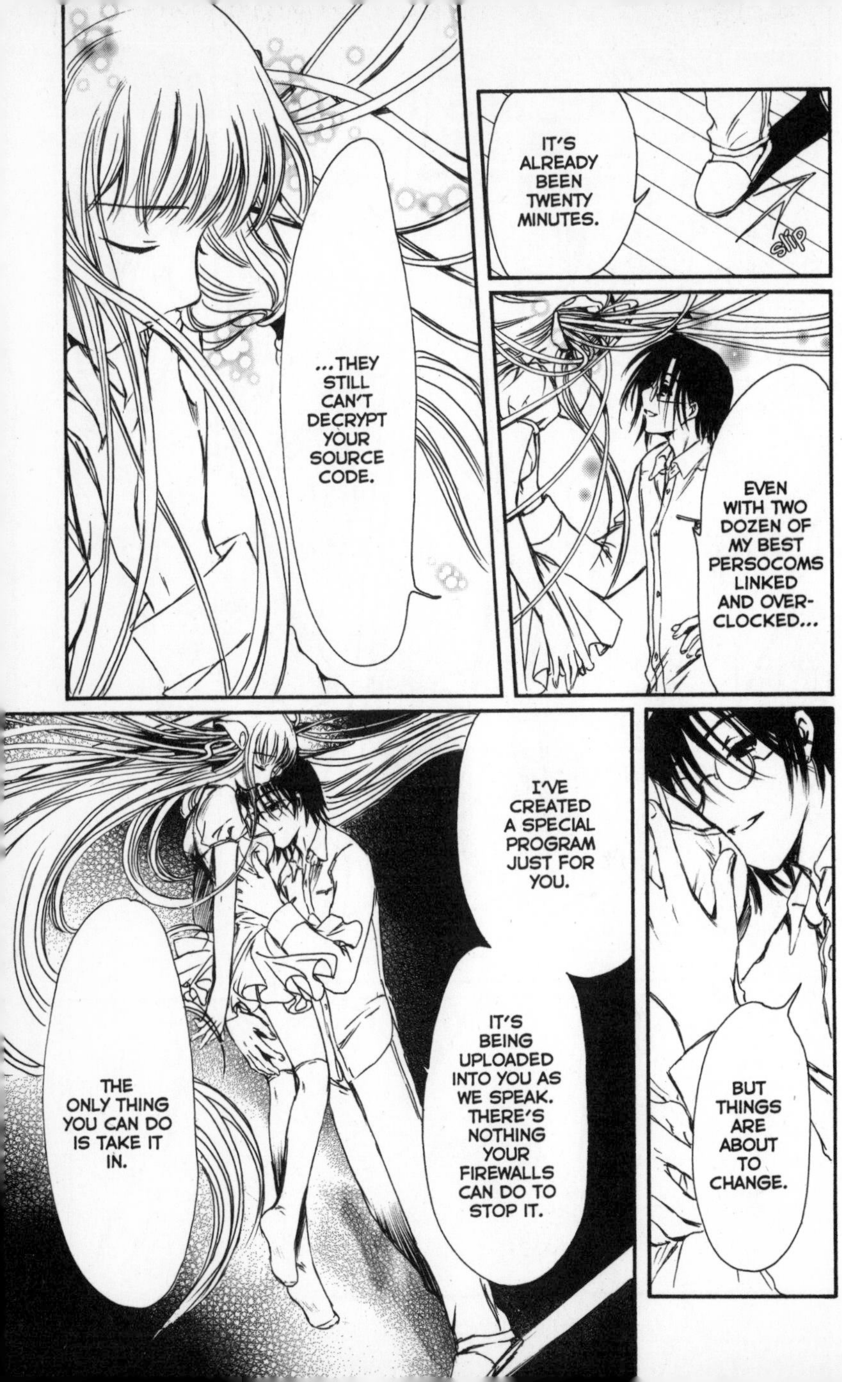
IT'S ALREADY BEEN TWENTY MINUTES.
slip
EVEN WITH TWO DOZEN OF MY BEST PERSOCOMS LINKED AND OVER-CLOCKED...
...THEY STILL CAN'T DECRYPT YOUR SOURCE CODE.
BUT THINGS ARE ABOUT TO CHANGE.
I'VE CREATED A SPECIAL PROGRAM JUST FOR YOU.
IT'S BEING UPLOADED INTO YOU AS WE SPEAK. THERE'S NOTHING YOUR FIREWALLS CAN DO TO STOP IT.
THE ONLY THING YOU CAN DO IS TAKE IT IN.

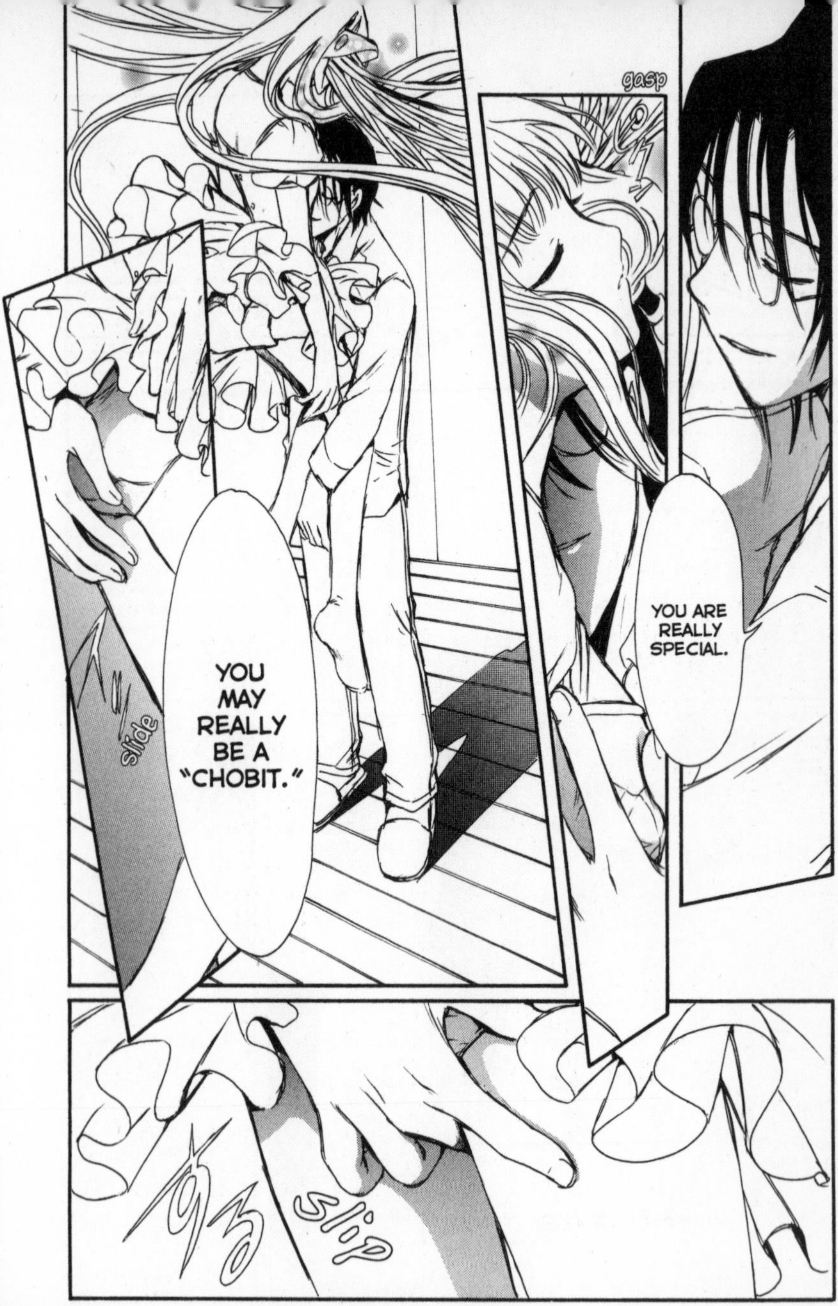
YOU ARE REALLY SPECIAL.
gasp
YOU MAY REALLY BE A "CHOBIT."
slide
slip

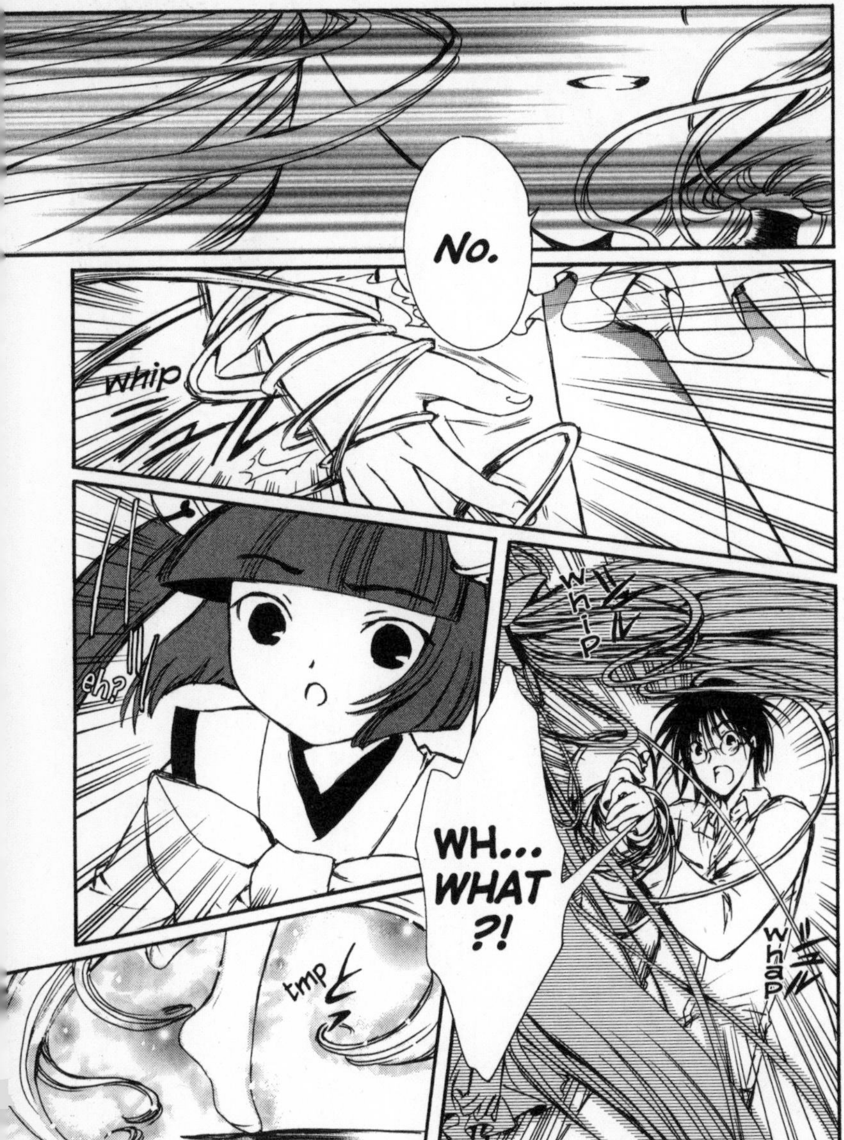
No.
whip
whip
WH... WHAT?!
whap
eh?
tmp

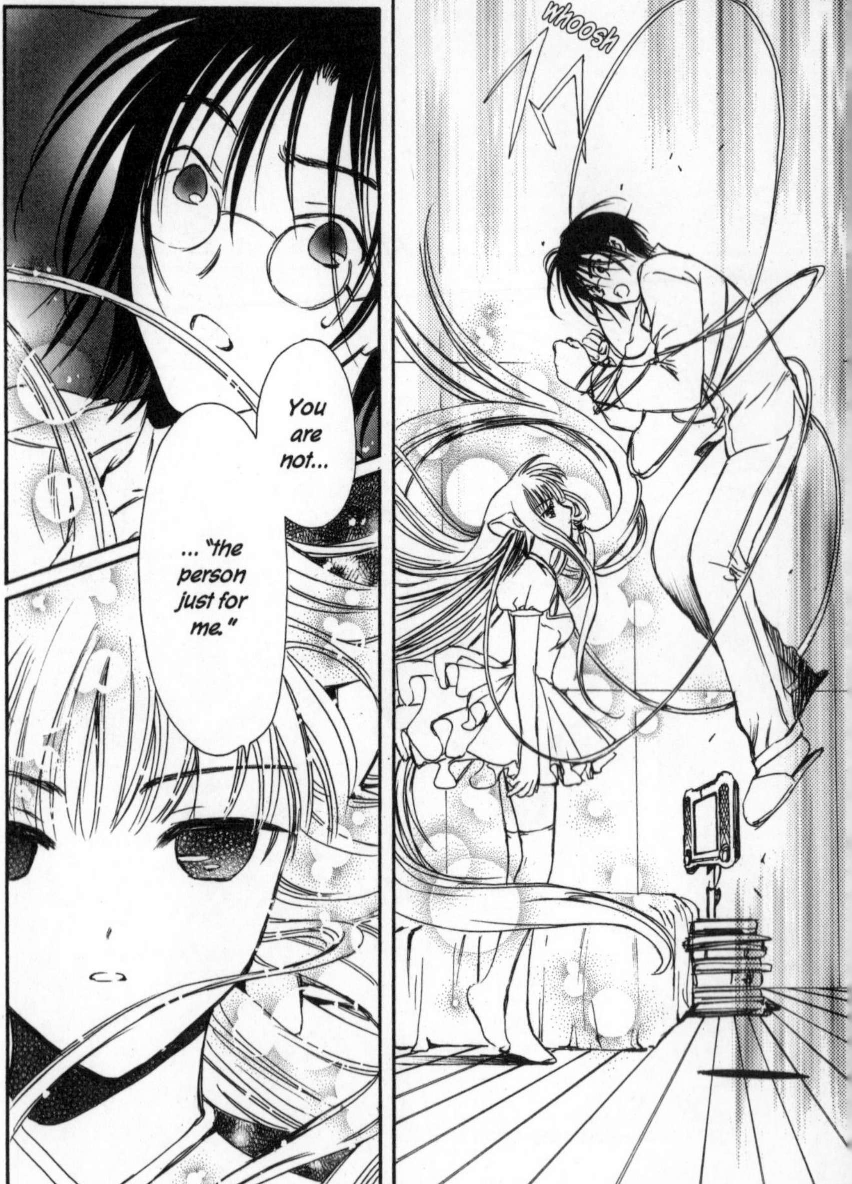
whoosh
You are not...
... "the person just for me."

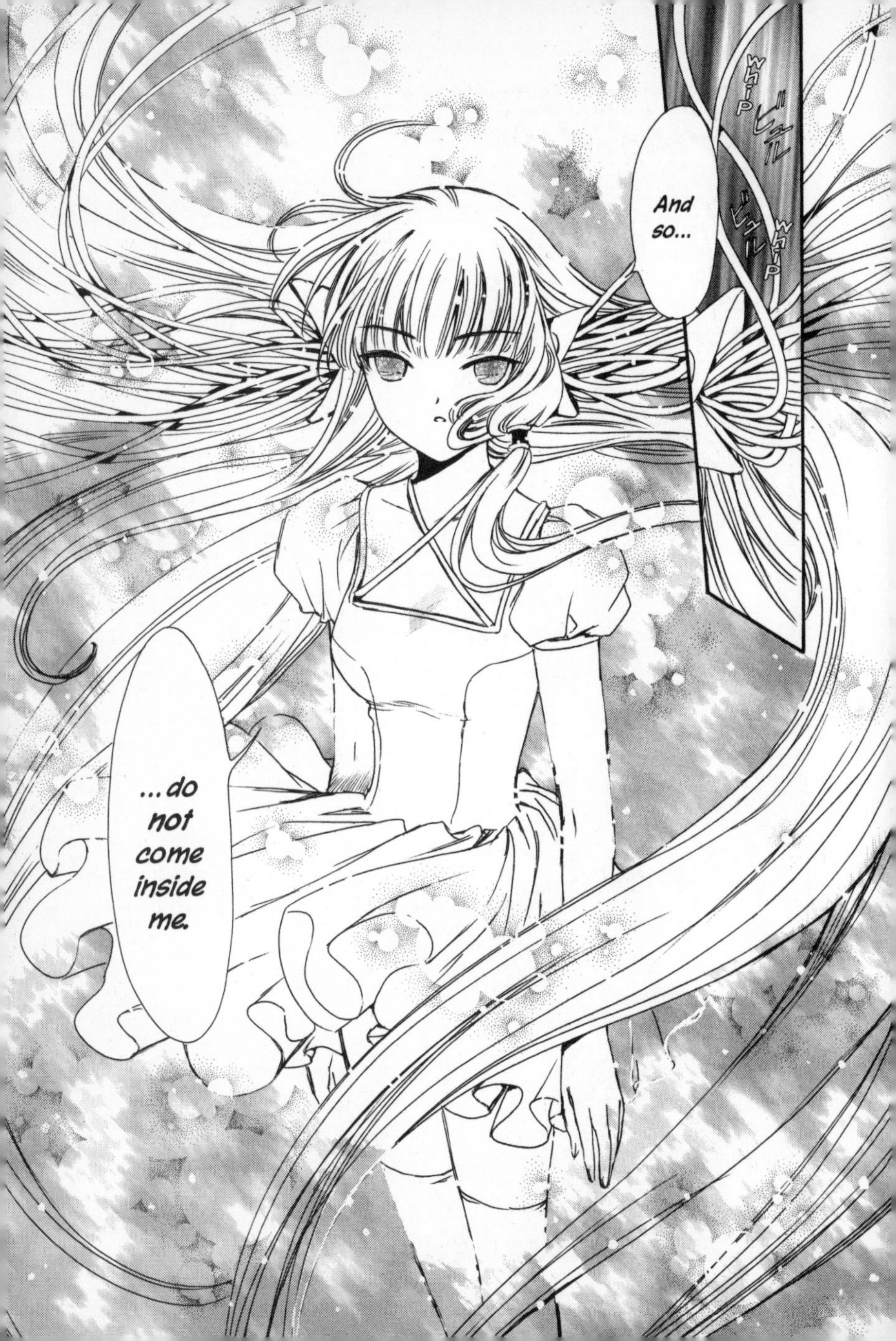
WHIP
ビュル
WHIP
ビュル
And so...
...do not come inside me.

tmp   tmp   tmp   tmp   tmp

beep

ARE WE GETTING CLOSE?!

YES.

夕" tmp
夕"
夕"夕"
tmp
夕" tmp

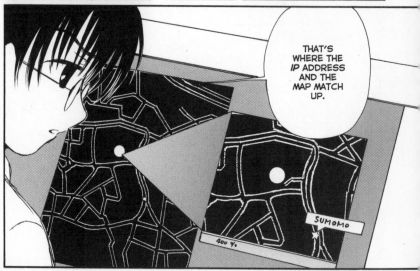

THAT'S WHERE THE *IP* ADDRESS AND THE MAP MATCH UP.

SUMOMO

400 %

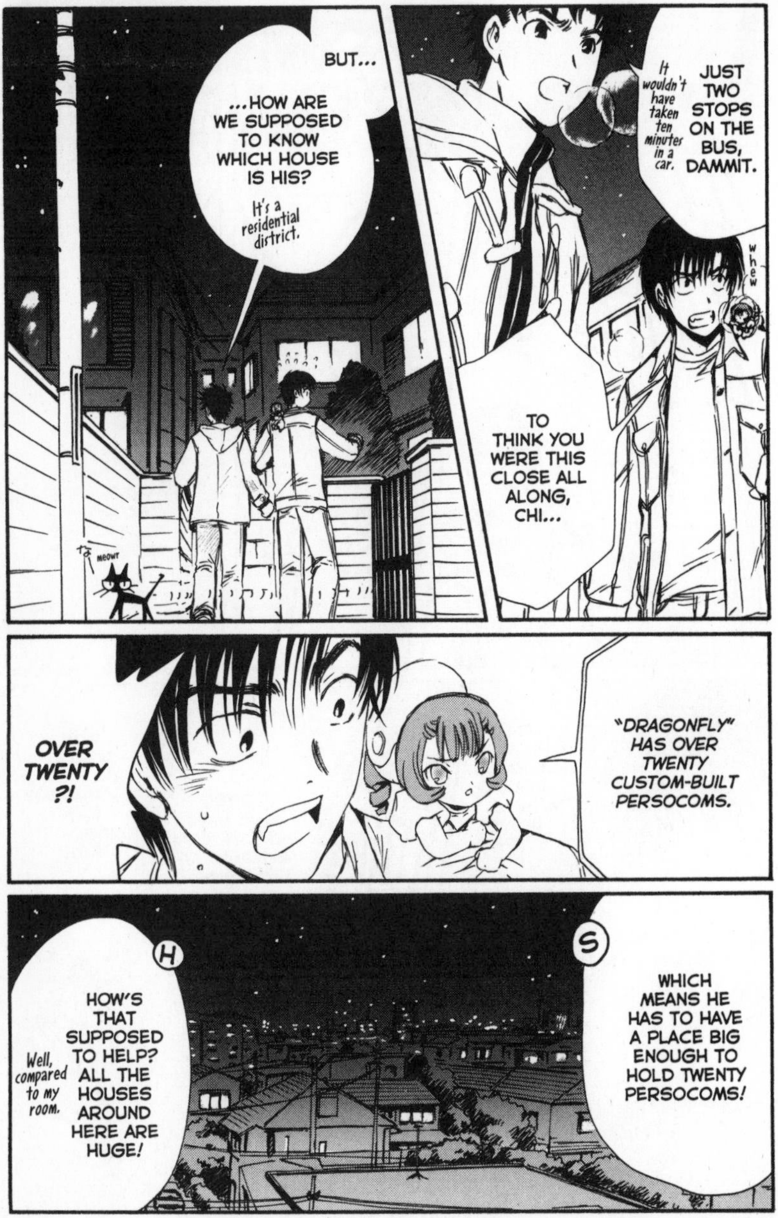
JUST TWO STOPS ON THE BUS, DAMMIT.
It wouldn't have taken ten minutes in a car.
whew
TO THINK YOU WERE THIS CLOSE ALL ALONG, CHI...
BUT...
...HOW ARE WE SUPPOSED TO KNOW WHICH HOUSE IS HIS?
It's a residential district.
meowr
"DRAGONFLY" HAS OVER TWENTY CUSTOM-BUILT PERSOCOMS.
OVER TWENTY ?!
S
WHICH MEANS HE HAS TO HAVE A PLACE BIG ENOUGH TO HOLD TWENTY PERSOCOMS!
H
HOW'S THAT SUPPOSED TO HELP? ALL THE HOUSES AROUND HERE ARE HUGE!
Well, compared to my room.

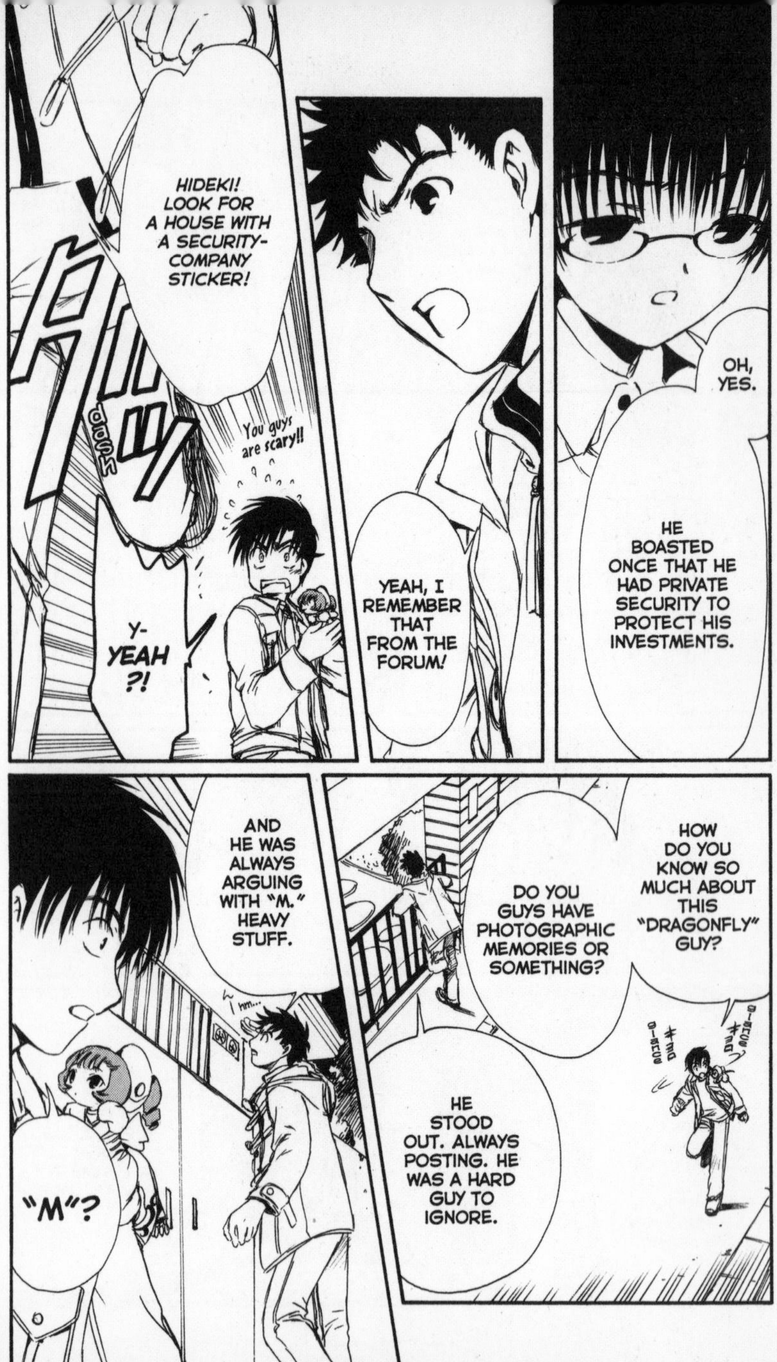
OH, YES.
HE BOASTED ONCE THAT HE HAD PRIVATE SECURITY TO PROTECT HIS INVESTMENTS.
YEAH, I REMEMBER THAT FROM THE FORUM!
HIDEKI! LOOK FOR A HOUSE WITH A SECURITY-COMPANY STICKER!
dash
You guys are scary!!
Y-YEAH?!
HOW DO YOU KNOW SO MUCH ABOUT THIS "DRAGONFLY" GUY?
DO YOU GUYS HAVE PHOTOGRAPHIC MEMORIES OR SOMETHING?
glance
glance
HE STOOD OUT. ALWAYS POSTING. HE WAS A HARD GUY TO IGNORE.
AND HE WAS ALWAYS ARGUING WITH "M." HEAVY STUFF.
hm...
"M"?

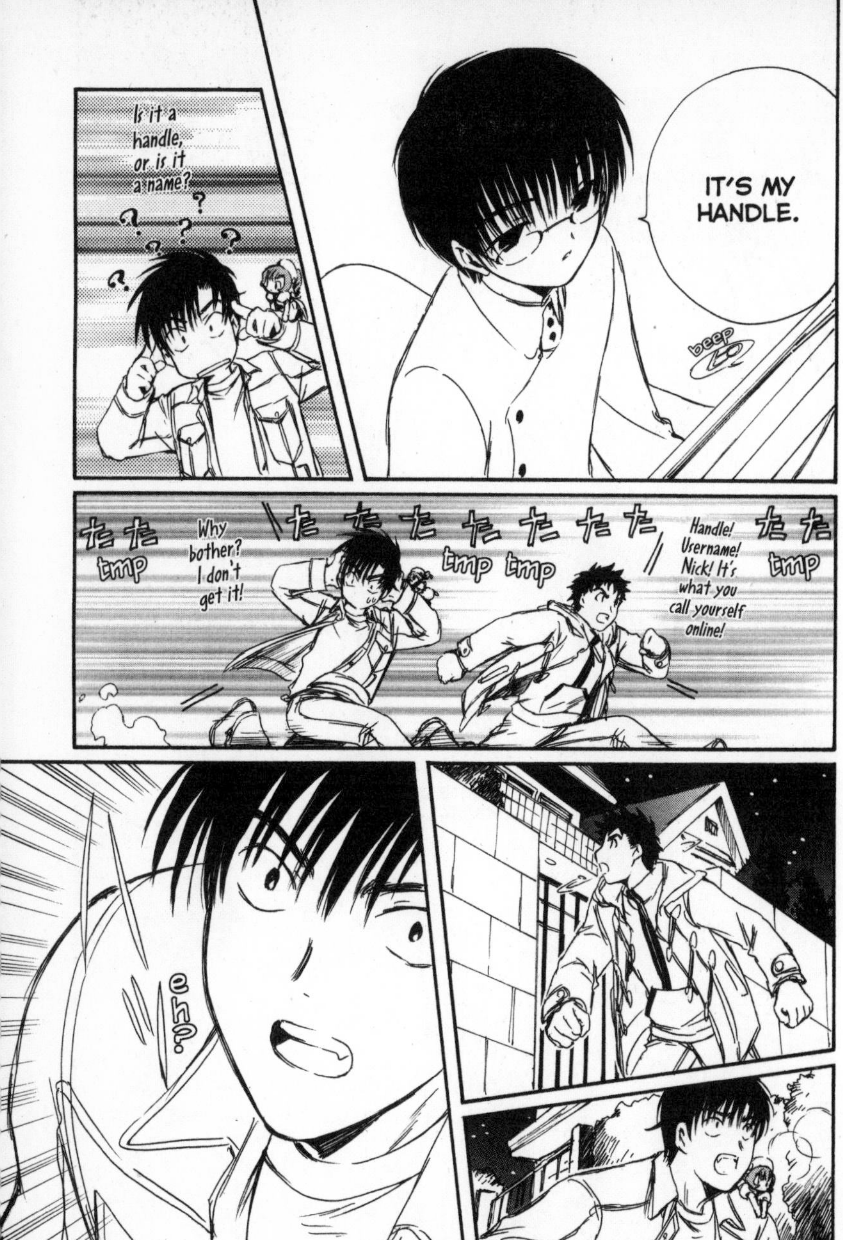
IT'S MY HANDLE.
beep
Is it a handle, or is it a name?
? ? ? ? ? ?
たた
tmp
Handle! Username! Nick! It's what you call yourself online!
たたたたたた
tmp tmp
Why bother? I don't get it!
たた
tmp
eh?

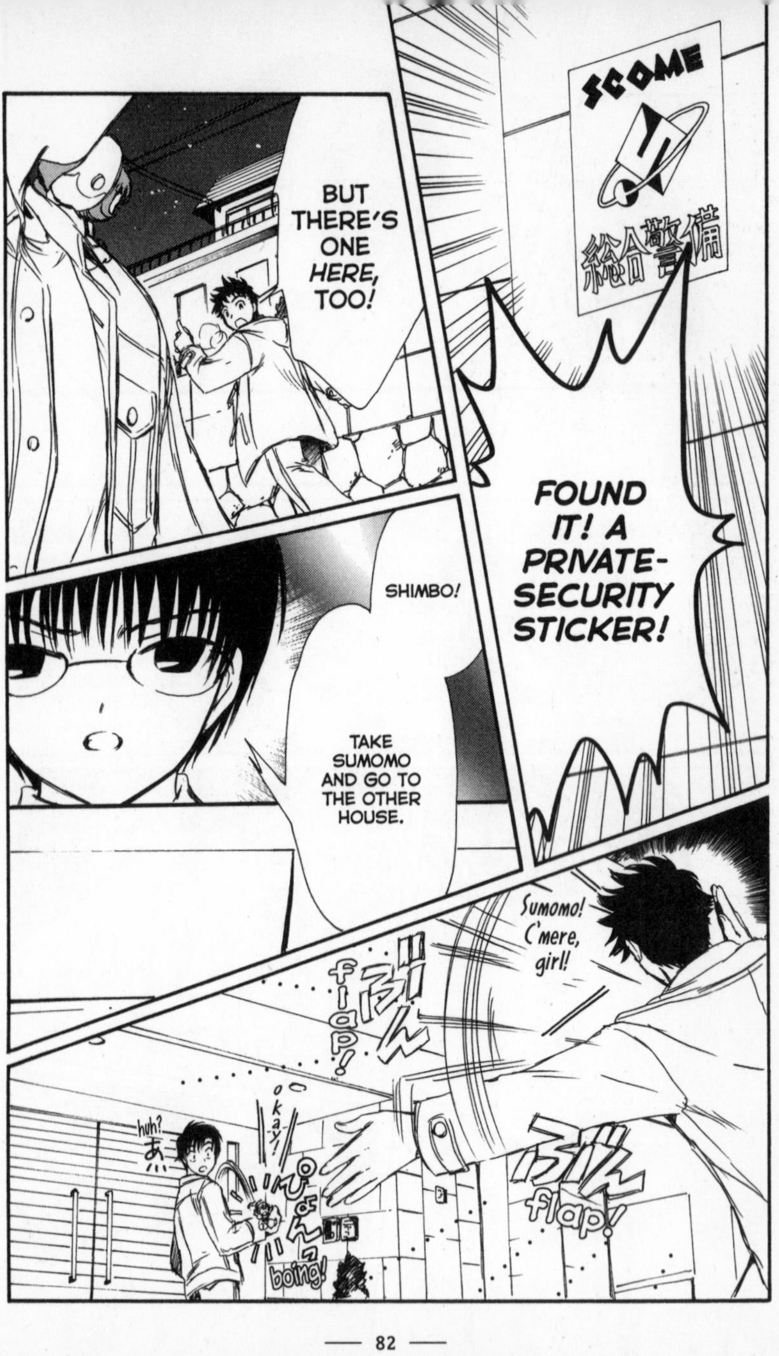

SCOME
総合警備
FOUND IT! A PRIVATE-SECURITY STICKER!
BUT THERE'S ONE HERE, TOO!
SHIMBO!
TAKE SUMOMO AND GO TO THE OTHER HOUSE.
Sumomo! C'mere, girl!
flap!
flap!
okay!
boing!
huh?
あ

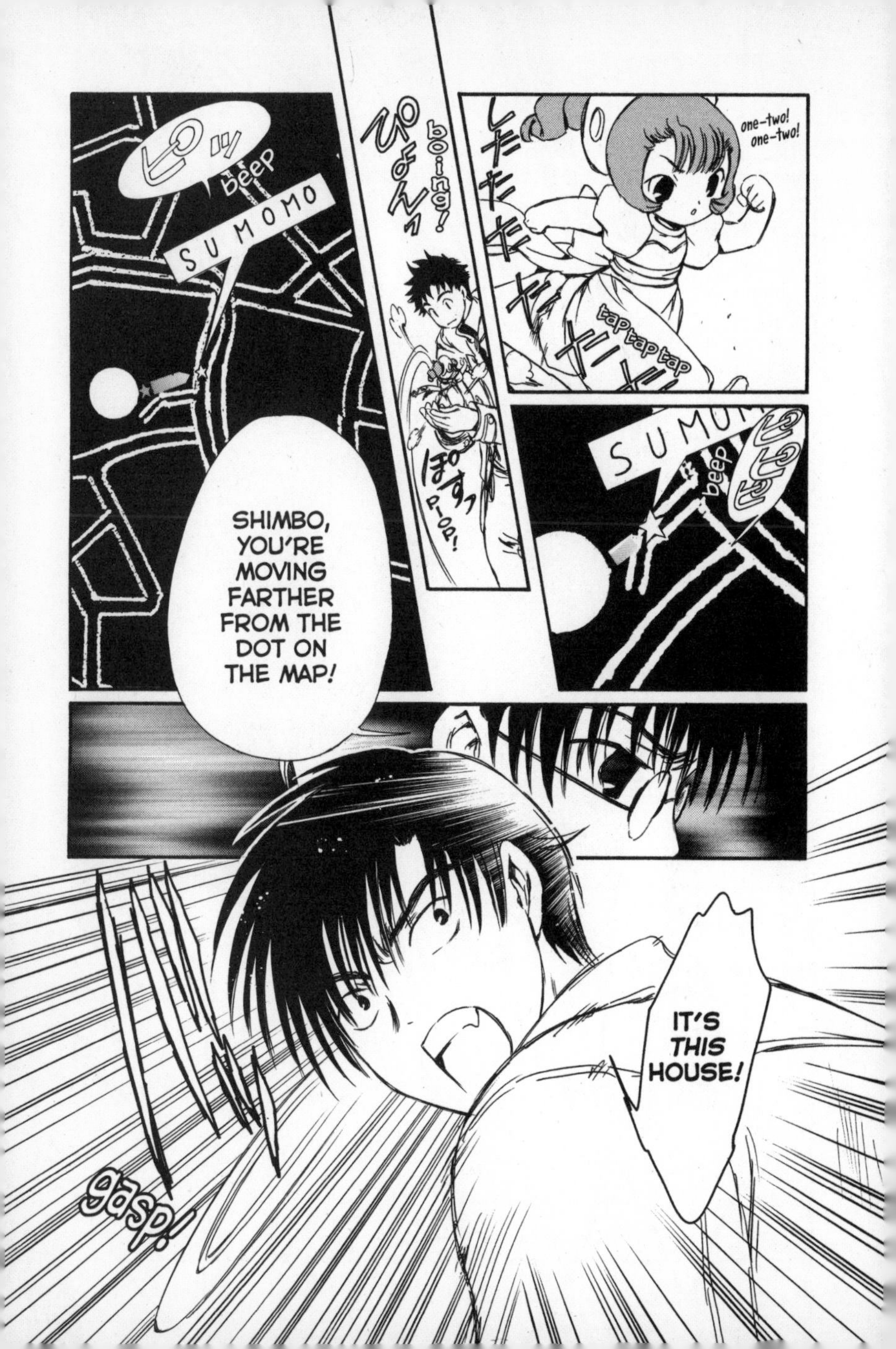
one-two! one-two!
tap tap tap
SUMOMO
beep
boing!
ぴょんっ
ぽすっ
PLOP!
ピッ
beep
SUMOMO
SHIMBO, YOU'RE MOVING FARTHER FROM THE DOT ON THE MAP!
IT'S THIS HOUSE!
gasp!

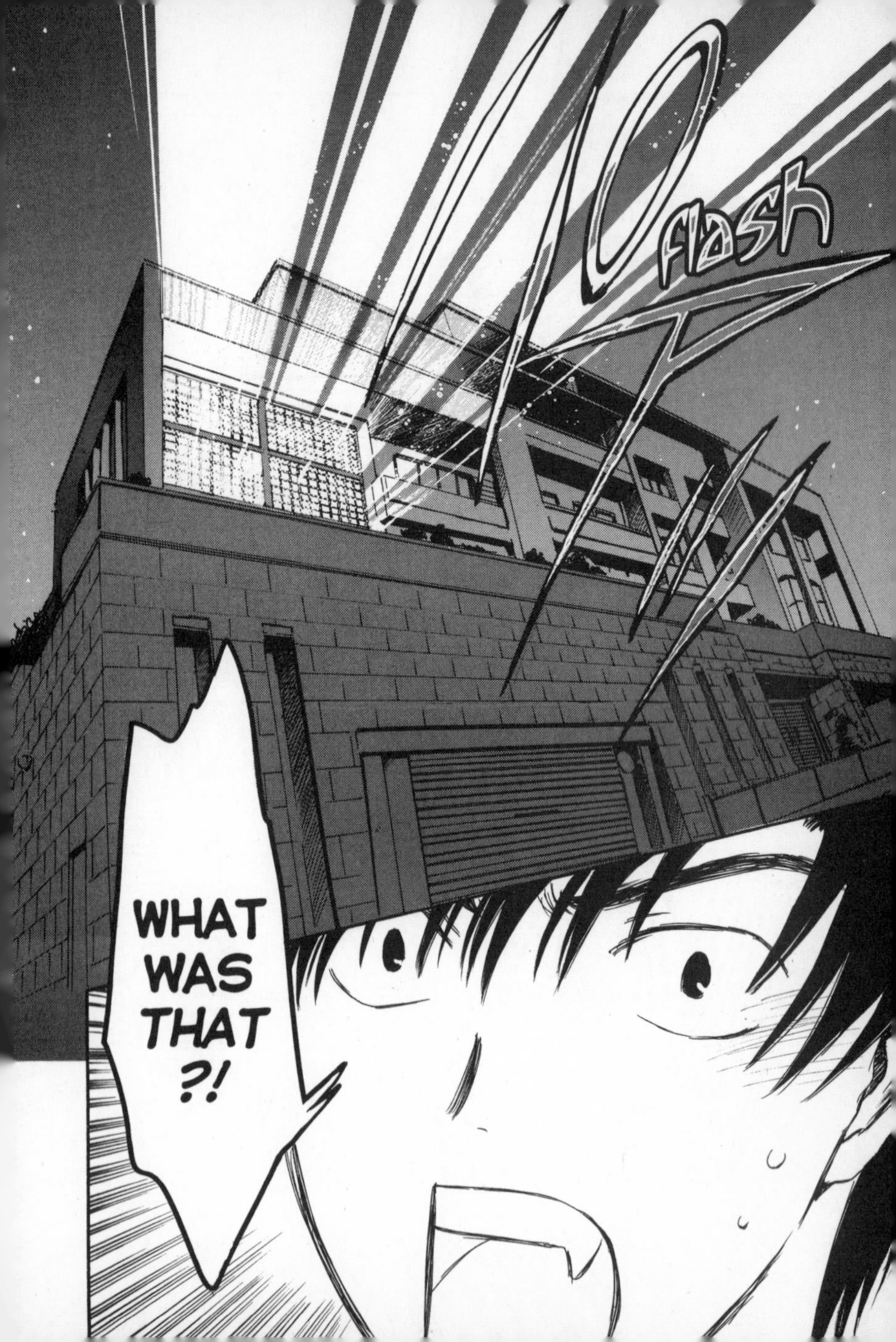
flash
WHAT WAS THAT ?!

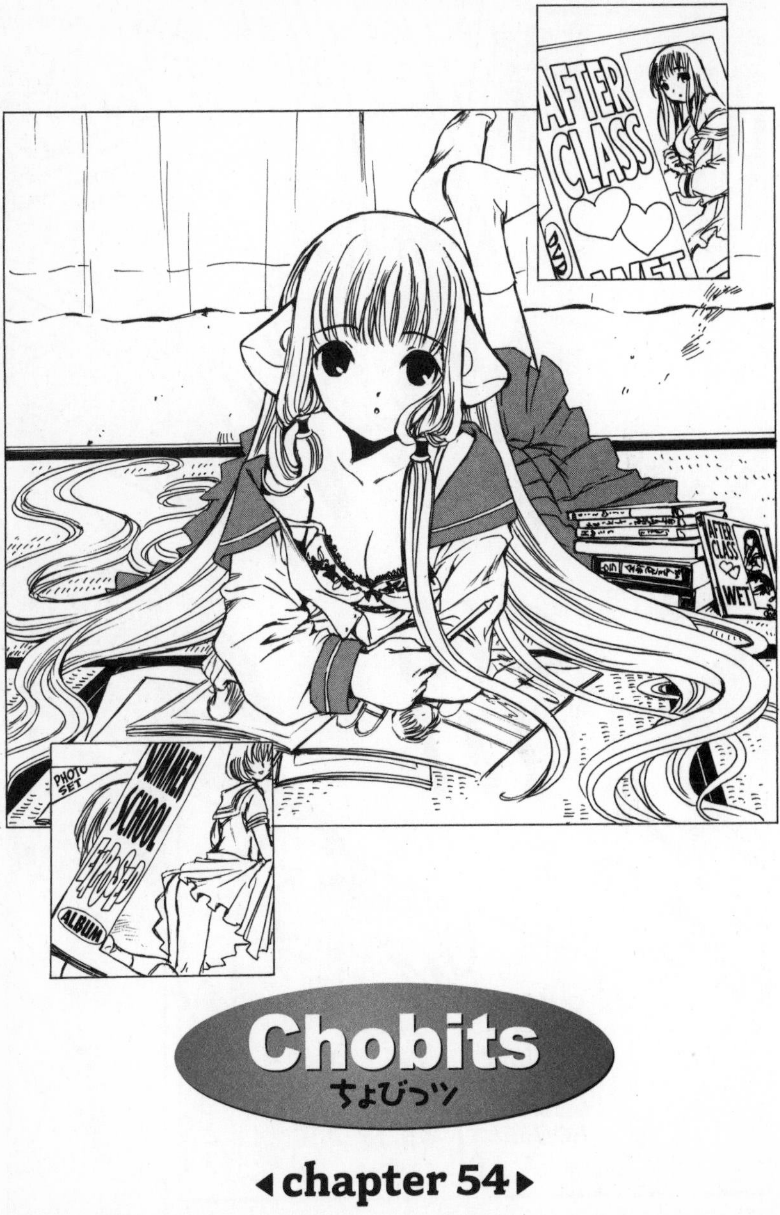
AFTER CLASS
DVD
AFTER CLASS
WET
PHOTO SET
SUMMER SCHOOL
ALBUM

Chobits

ちょびっツ

◂chapter 54▸

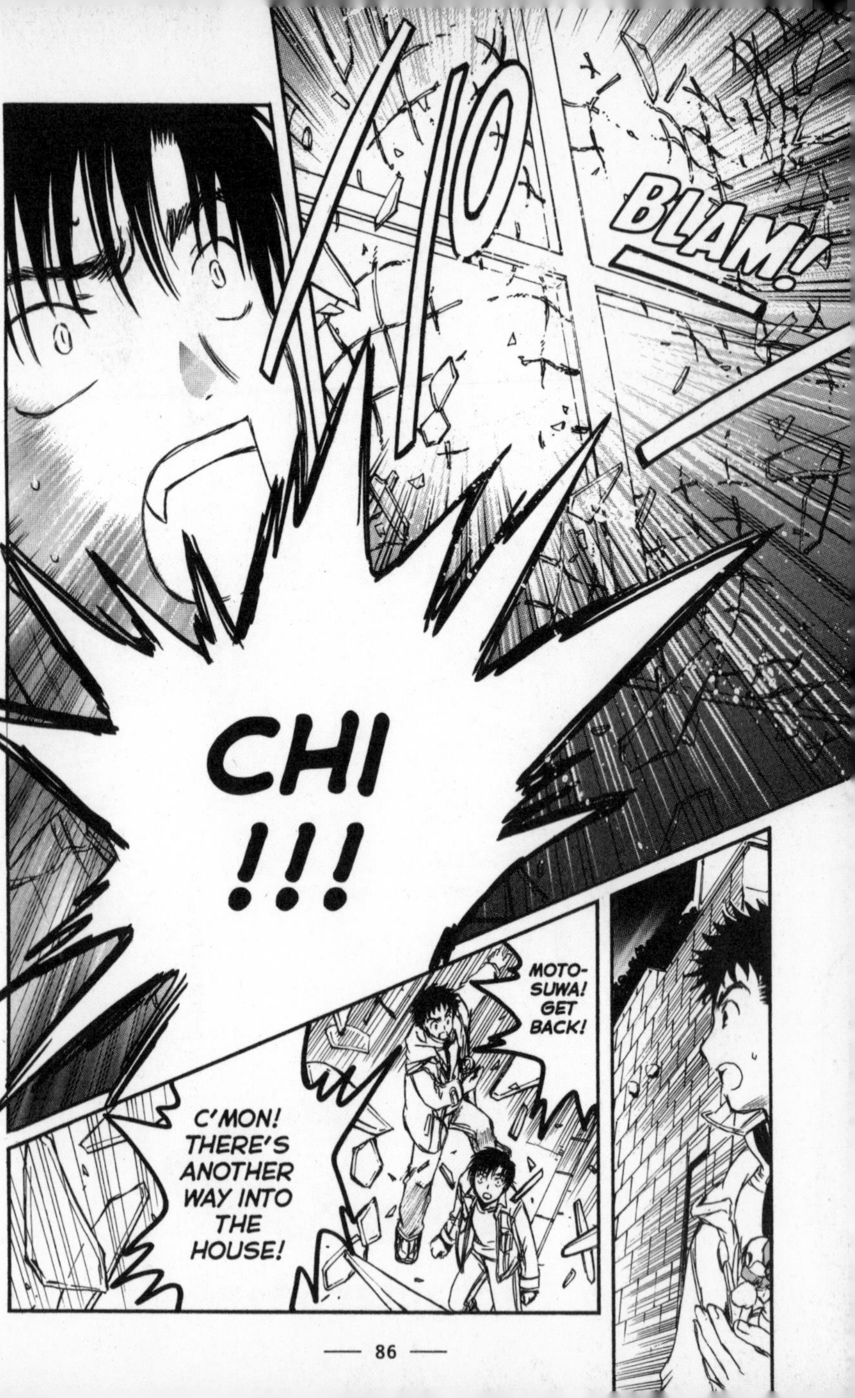
BLAM!
CHI!!!
MOTO-SUWA! GET BACK!
C'MON! THERE'S ANOTHER WAY INTO THE HOUSE!

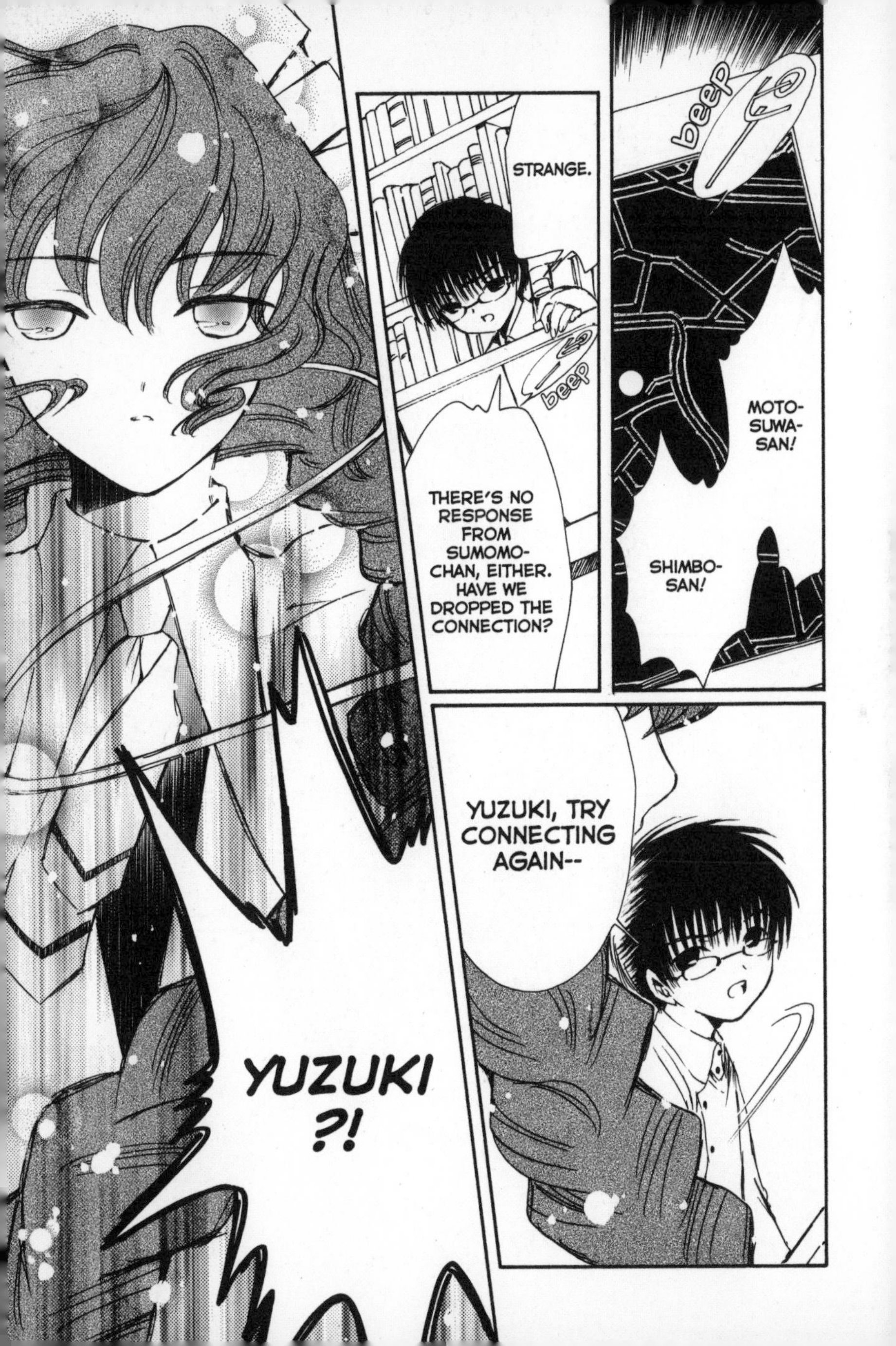
beep
MOTO-SUWA-SAN!
SHIMBO-SAN!
STRANGE.
beep
THERE'S NO RESPONSE FROM SUMOMO-CHAN, EITHER. HAVE WE DROPPED THE CONNECTION?
YUZUKI, TRY CONNECTING AGAIN--
YUZUKI ?!

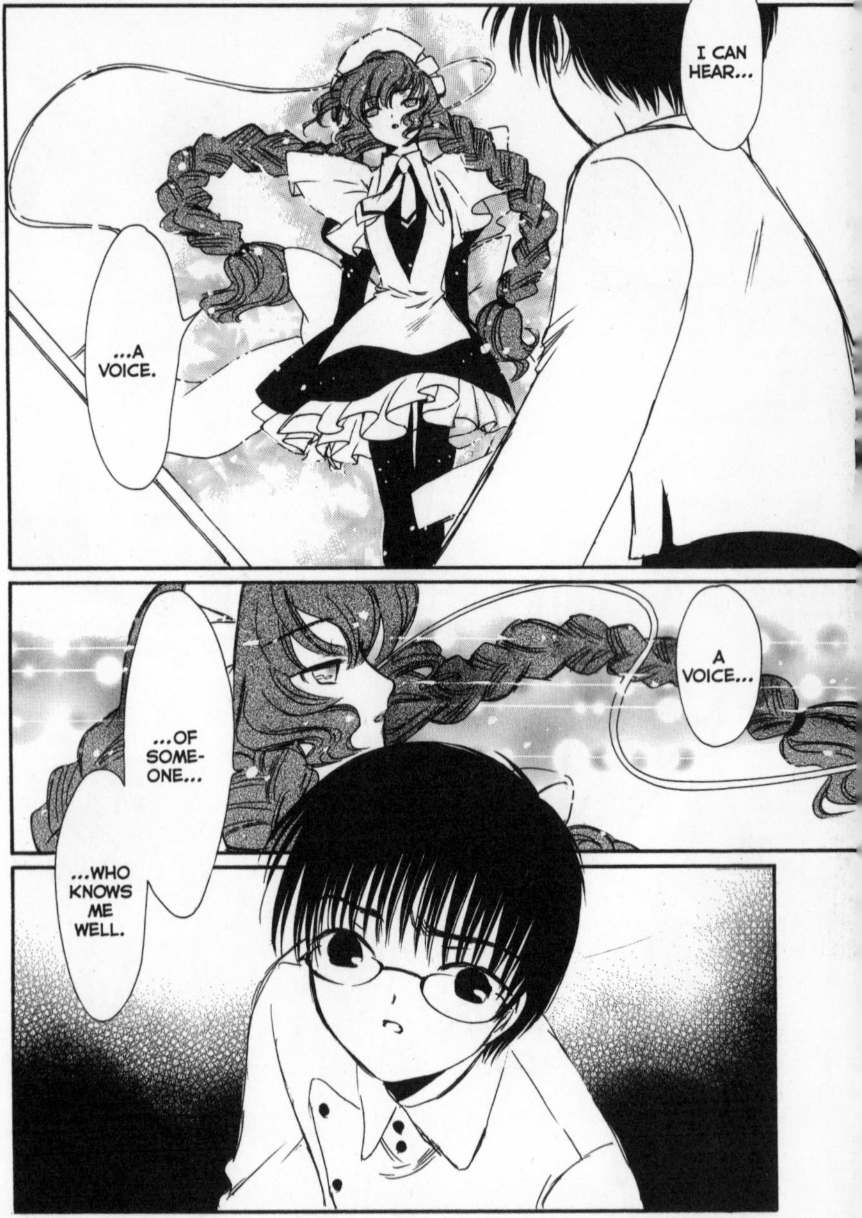
I CAN HEAR...
...A VOICE.
A VOICE...
...OF SOME-ONE...
...WHO KNOWS ME WELL.

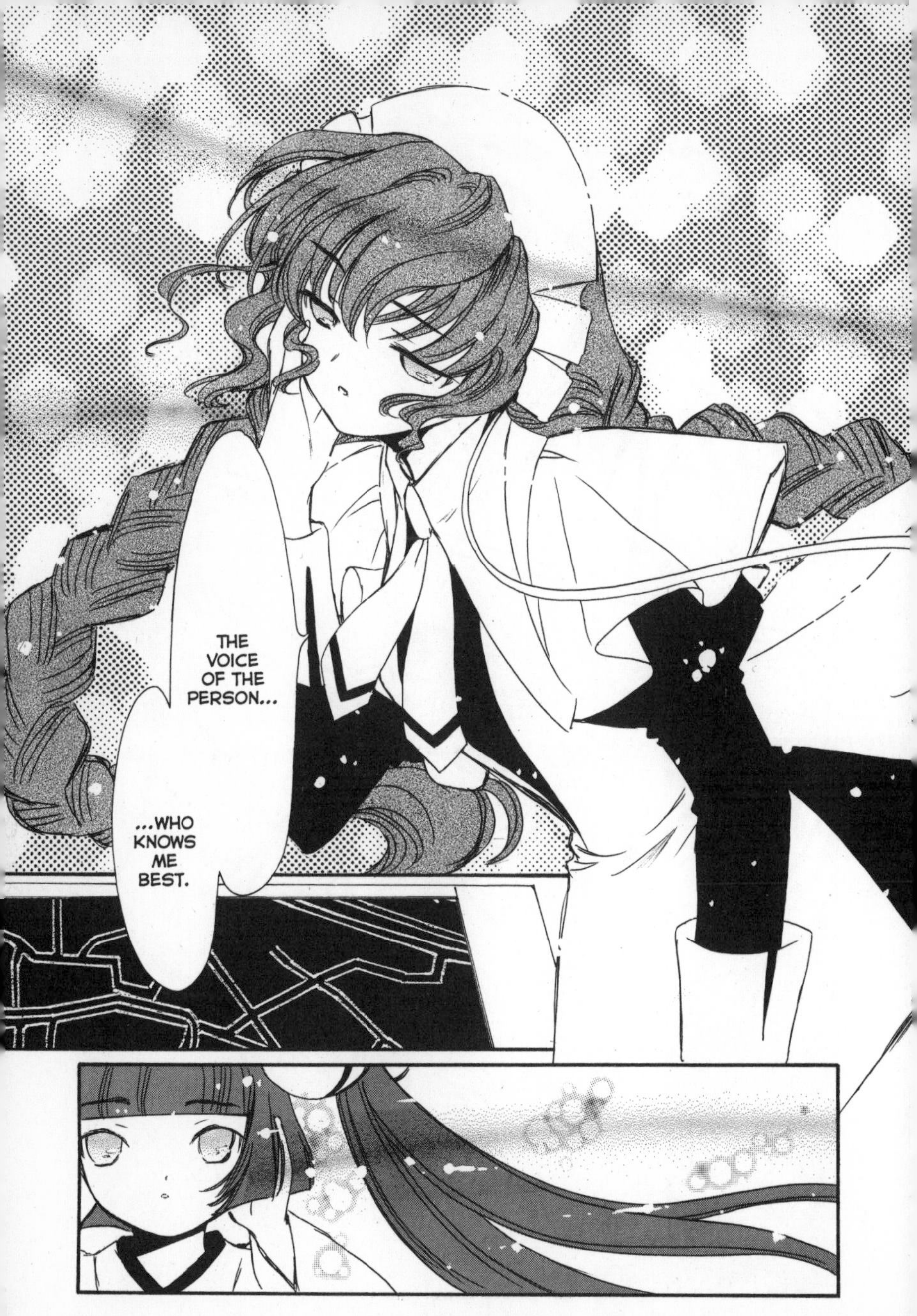
THE VOICE OF THE PERSON...
...WHO KNOWS ME BEST.

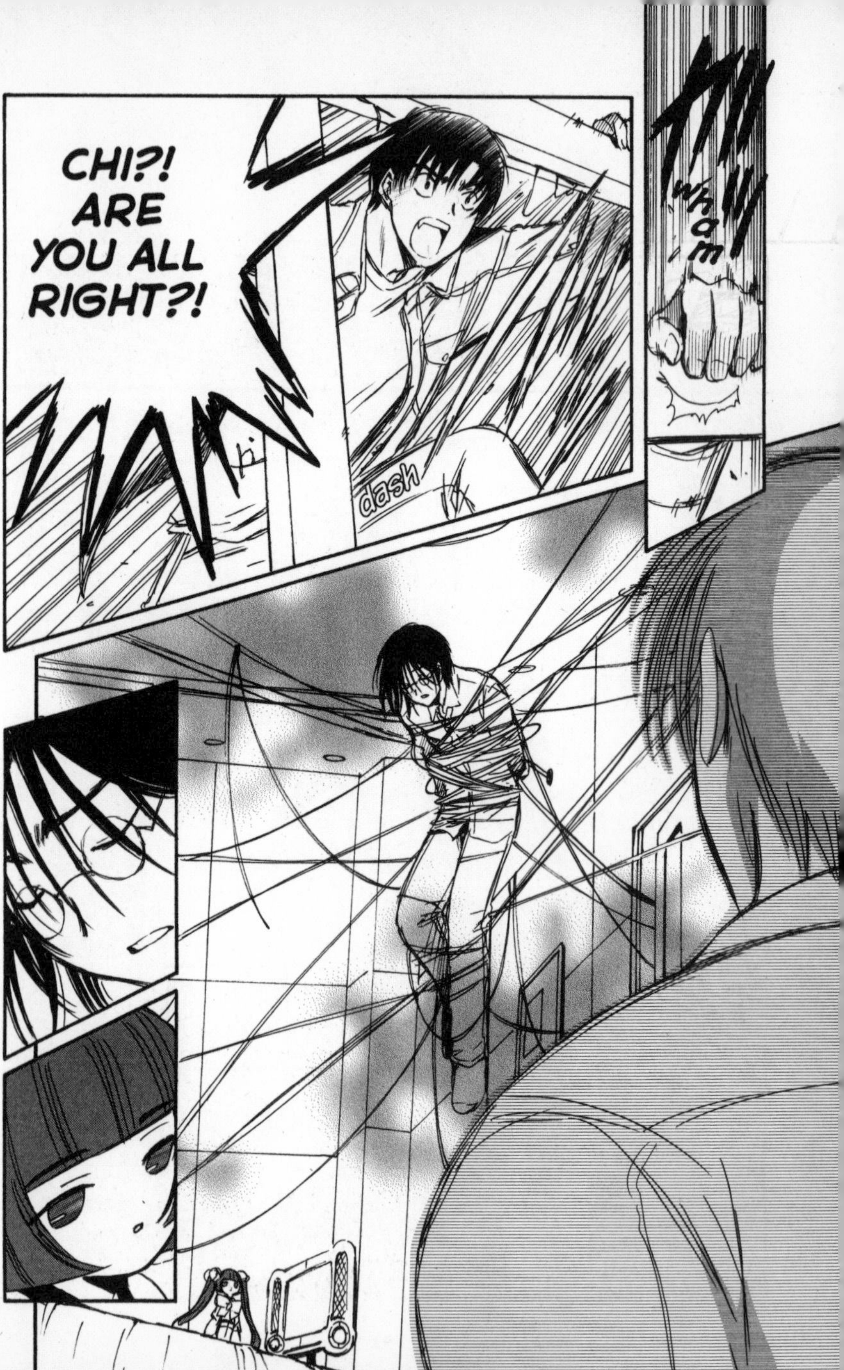
wham
CHI?! ARE YOU ALL RIGHT?!
dash

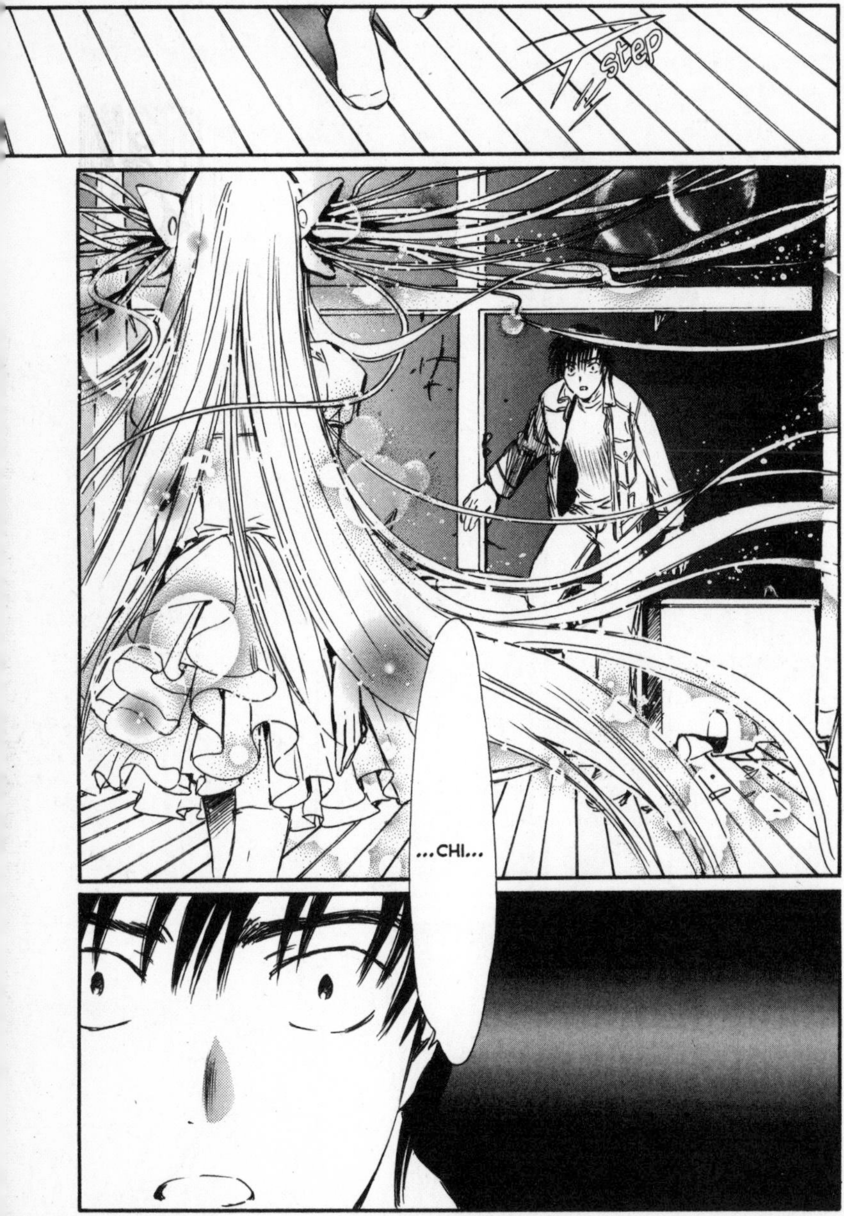
step
...CHI...

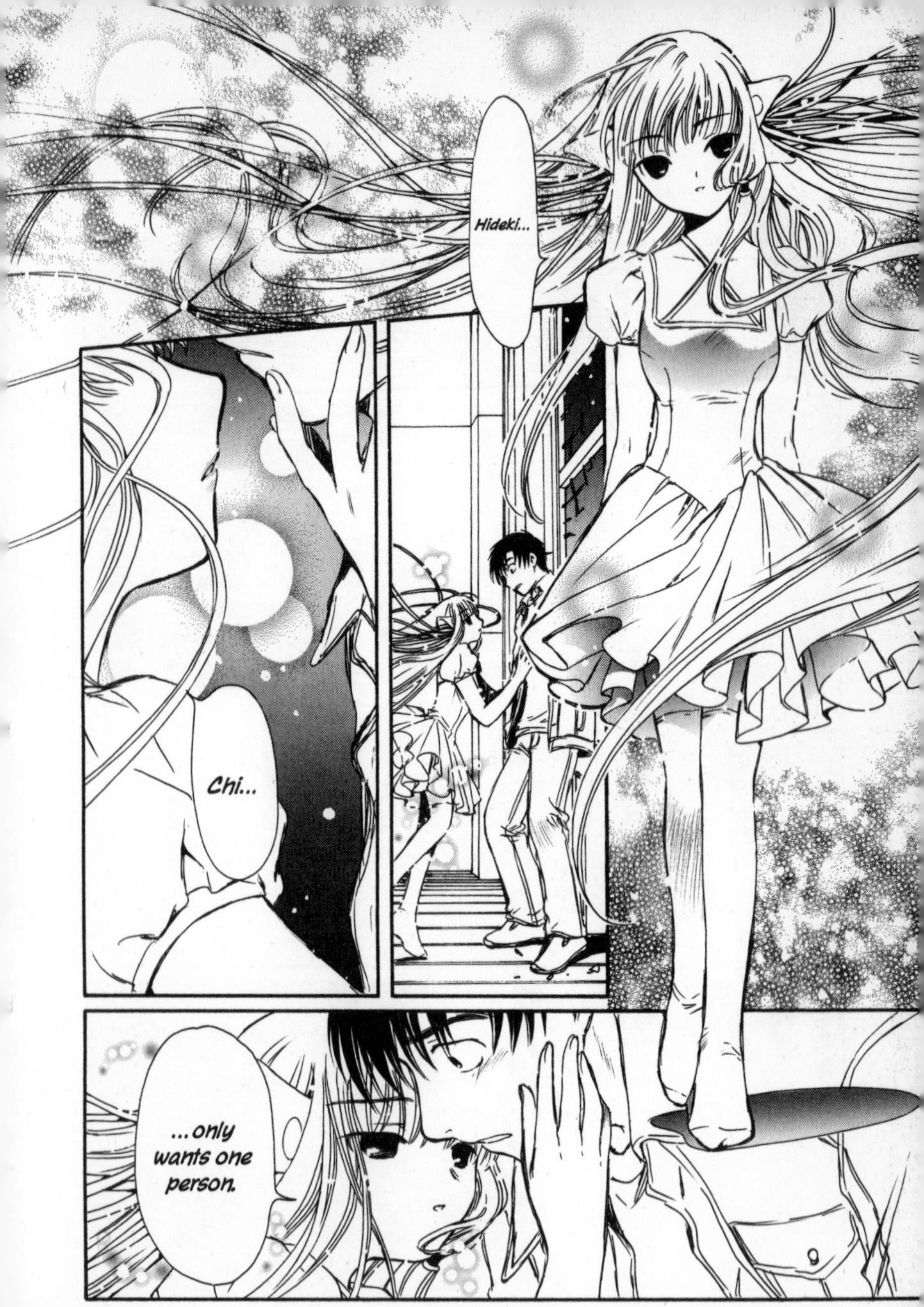
Hideki...
Chi...
...only wants one person.

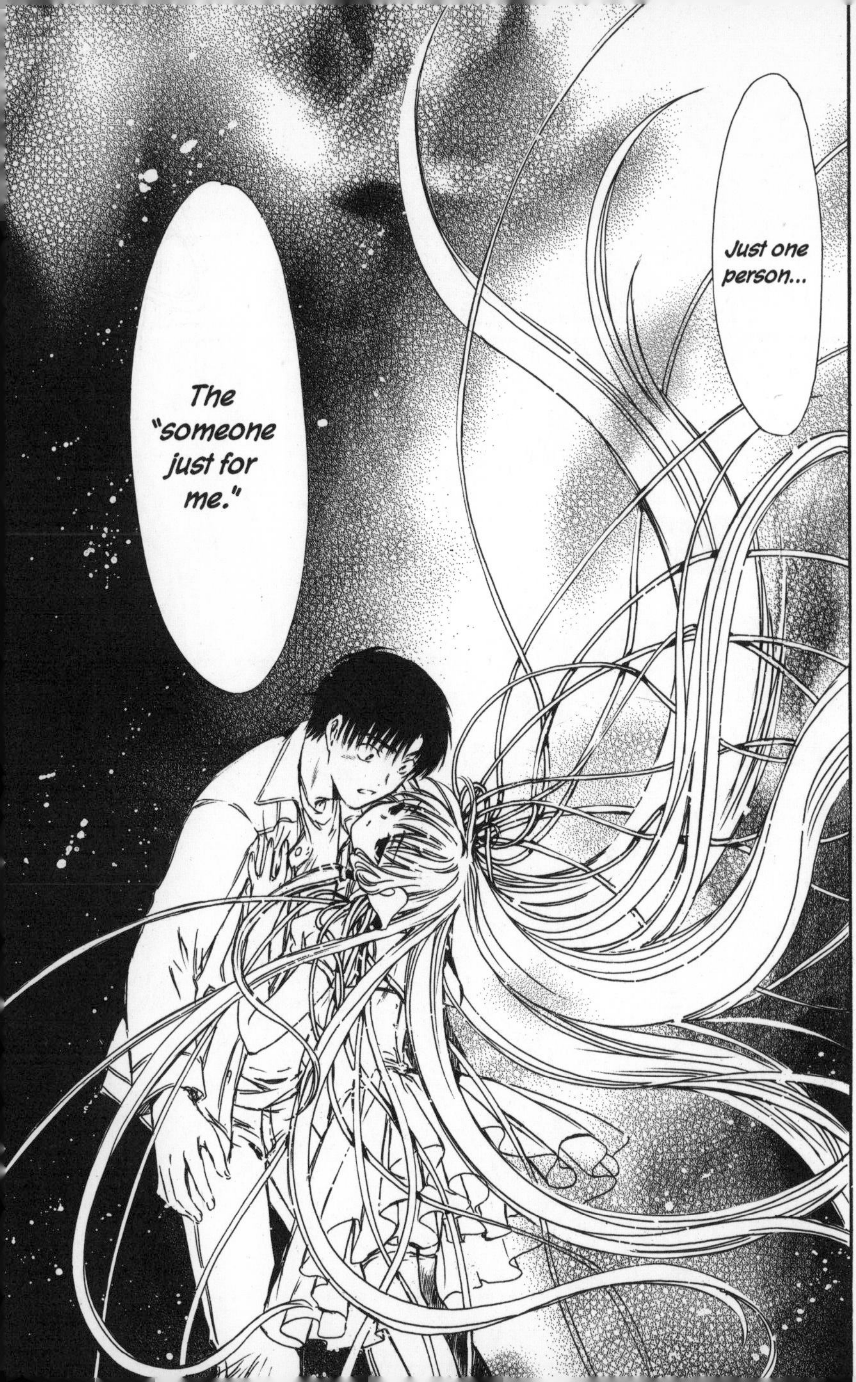
Just one person...
The "someone just for me."

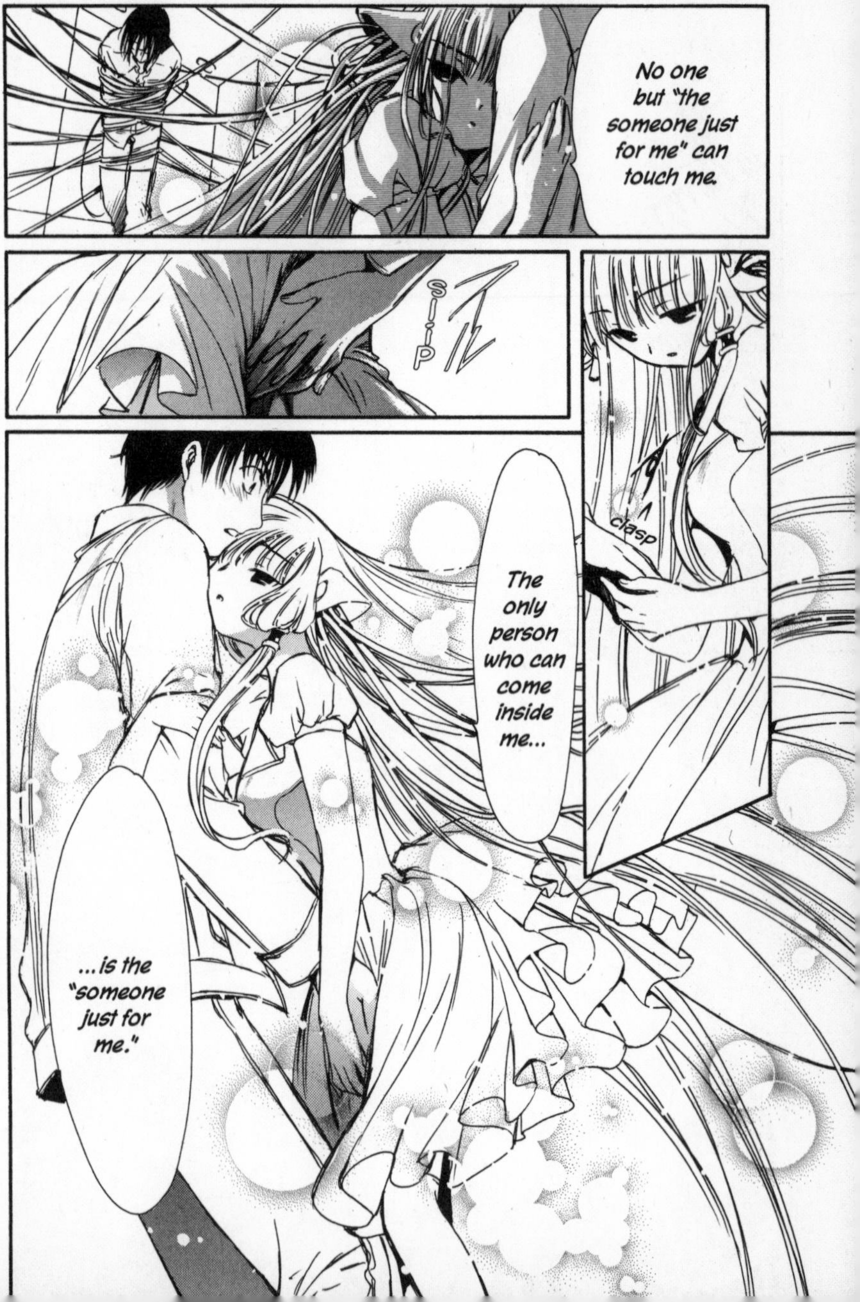
No one but "the someone just for me" can touch me.
clasp
slip
The only person who can come inside me...
...is the "someone just for me."

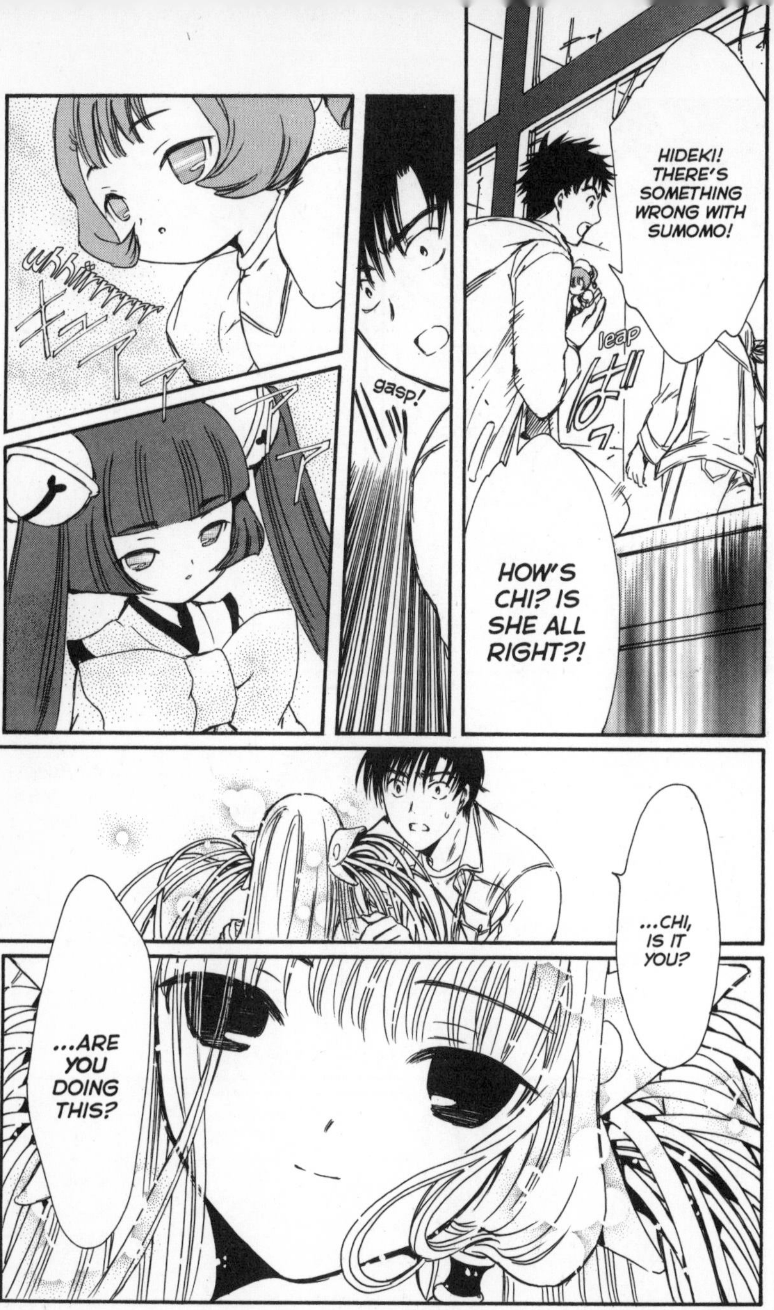

HIDEKI! THERE'S SOMETHING WRONG WITH SUMOMO!
leap
HOW'S CHI? IS SHE ALL RIGHT?!
gasp!
...CHI, IS IT YOU?
...ARE YOU DOING THIS?

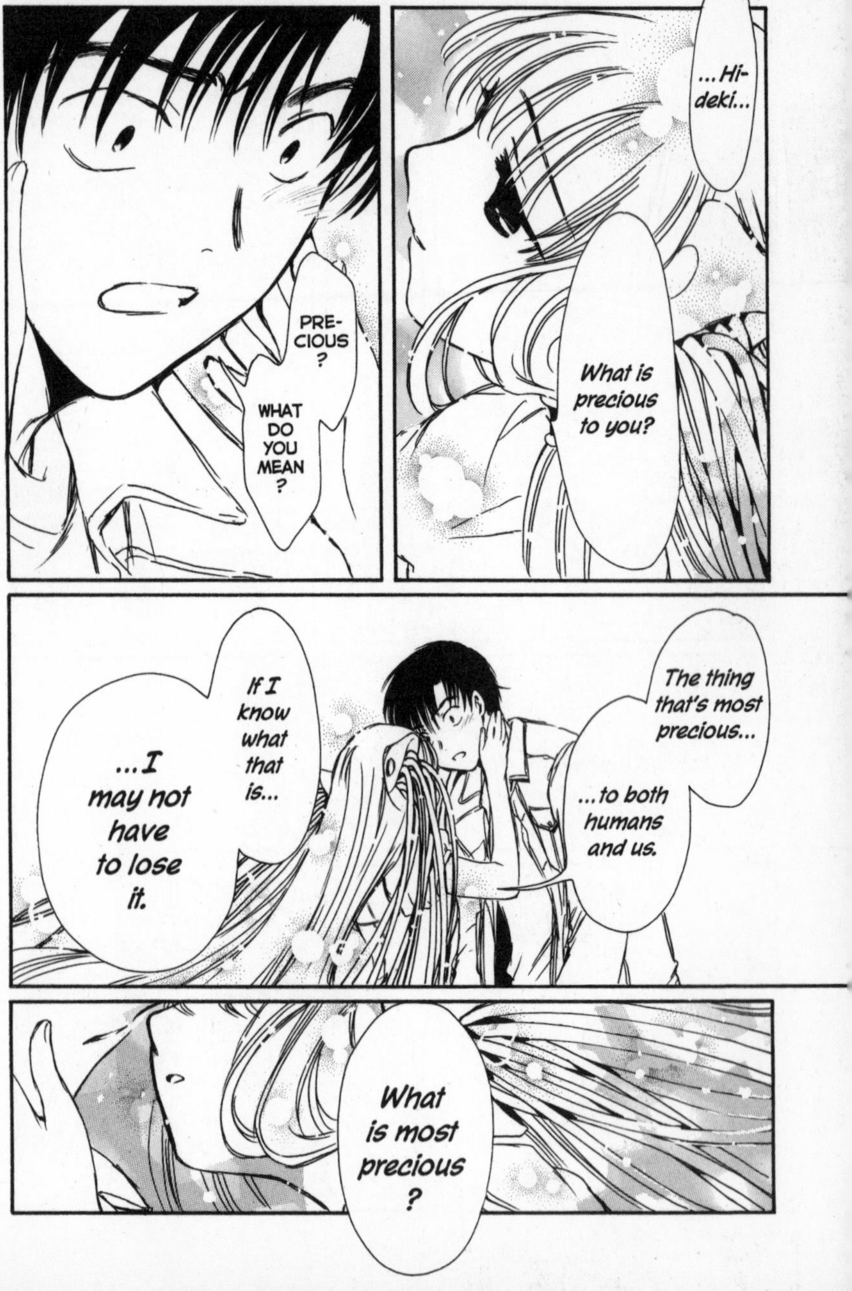
...Hi-deki...
What is precious to you?
PRE-CIOUS?
WHAT DO YOU MEAN?
The thing that's most precious...
...to both humans and us.
If I know what that is...
...I may not have to lose it.
What is most precious?

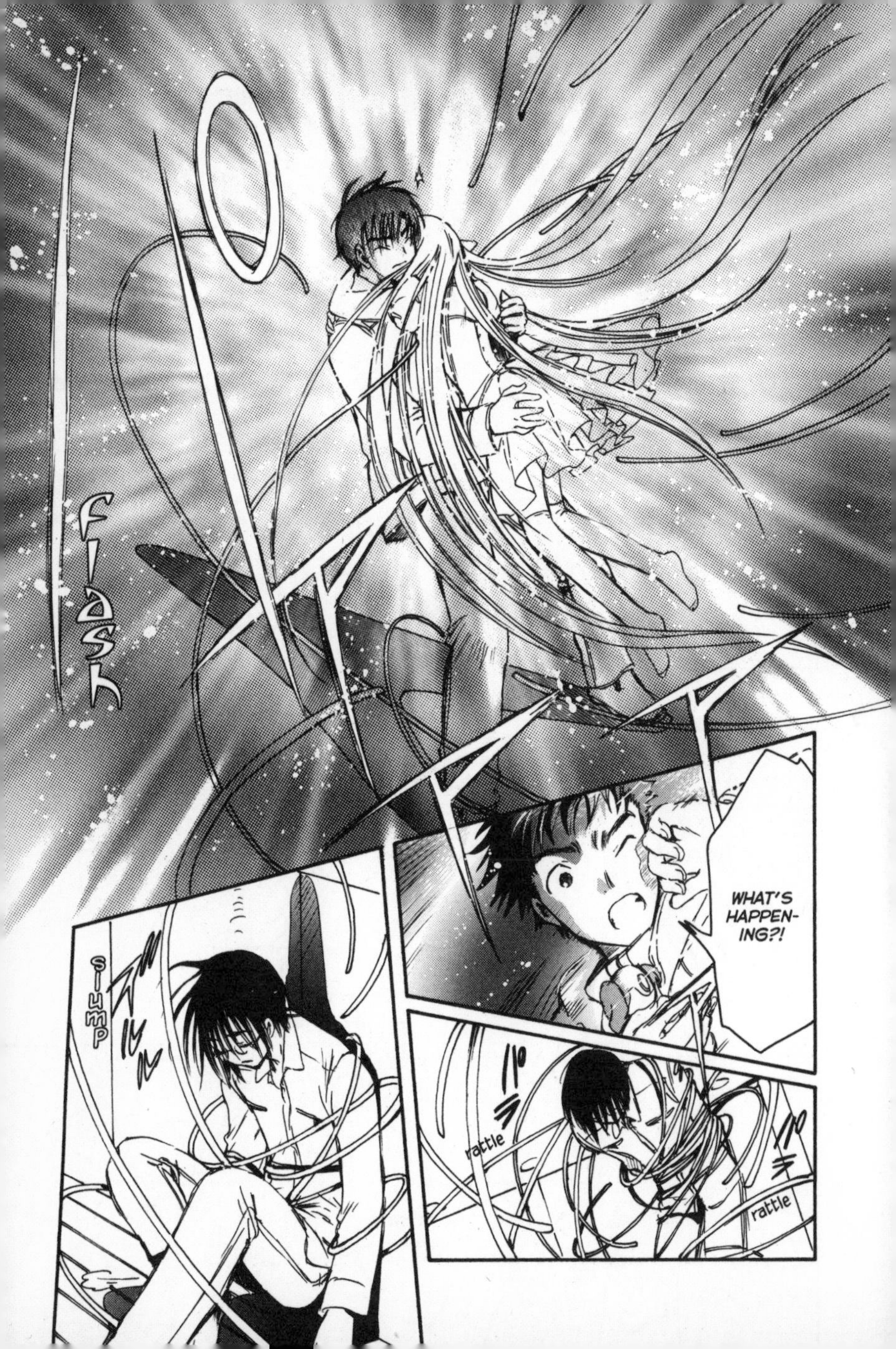
flash
WHAT'S HAPPEN-ING?!
rattle
rattle
slump

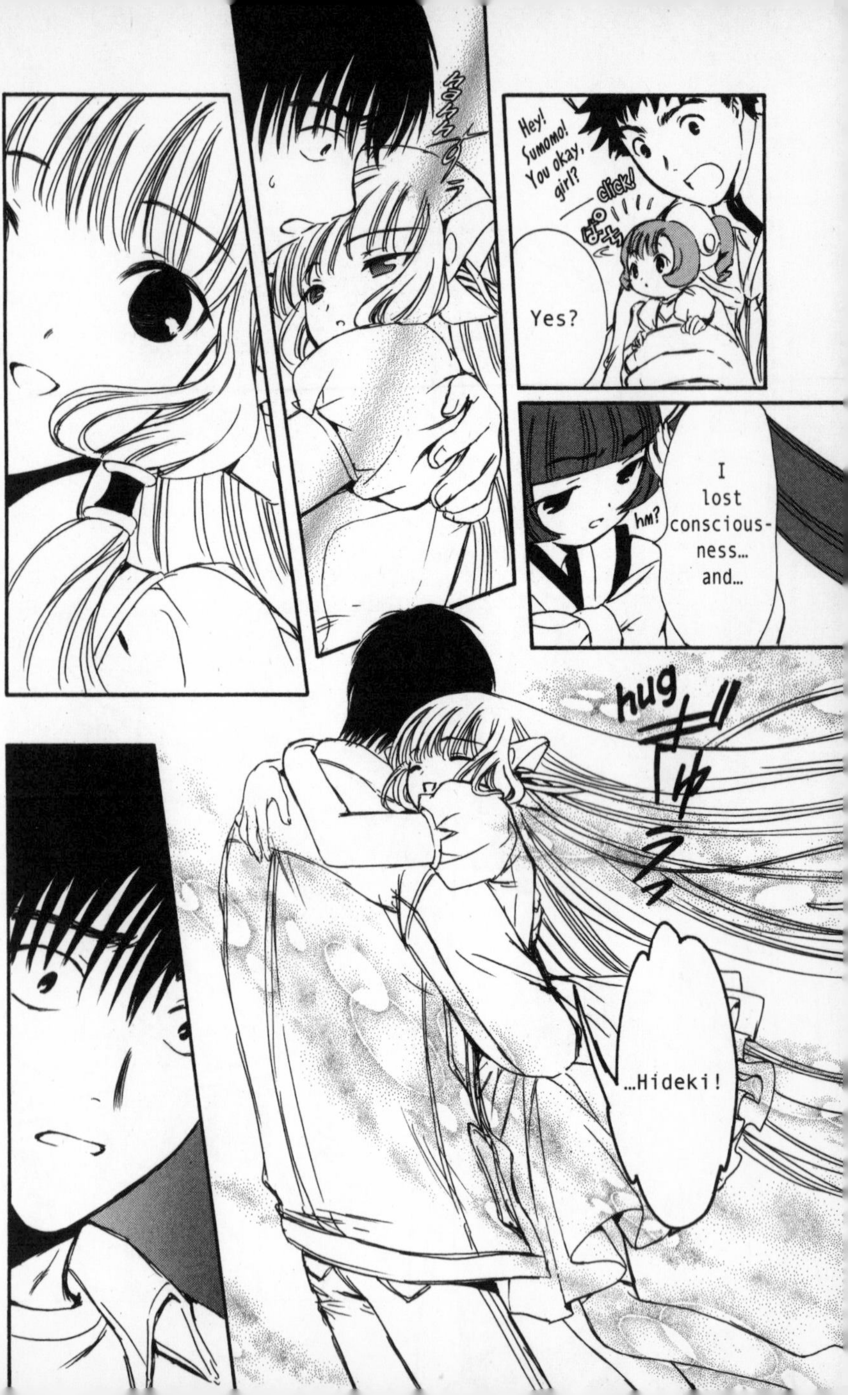
Hey! Sumomo! You okay, girl?
click!
Yes?
hm?
I lost consciousness... and...
hug
...Hideki!

Chobits
ちょびっツ

◀ chapter 55 ▶

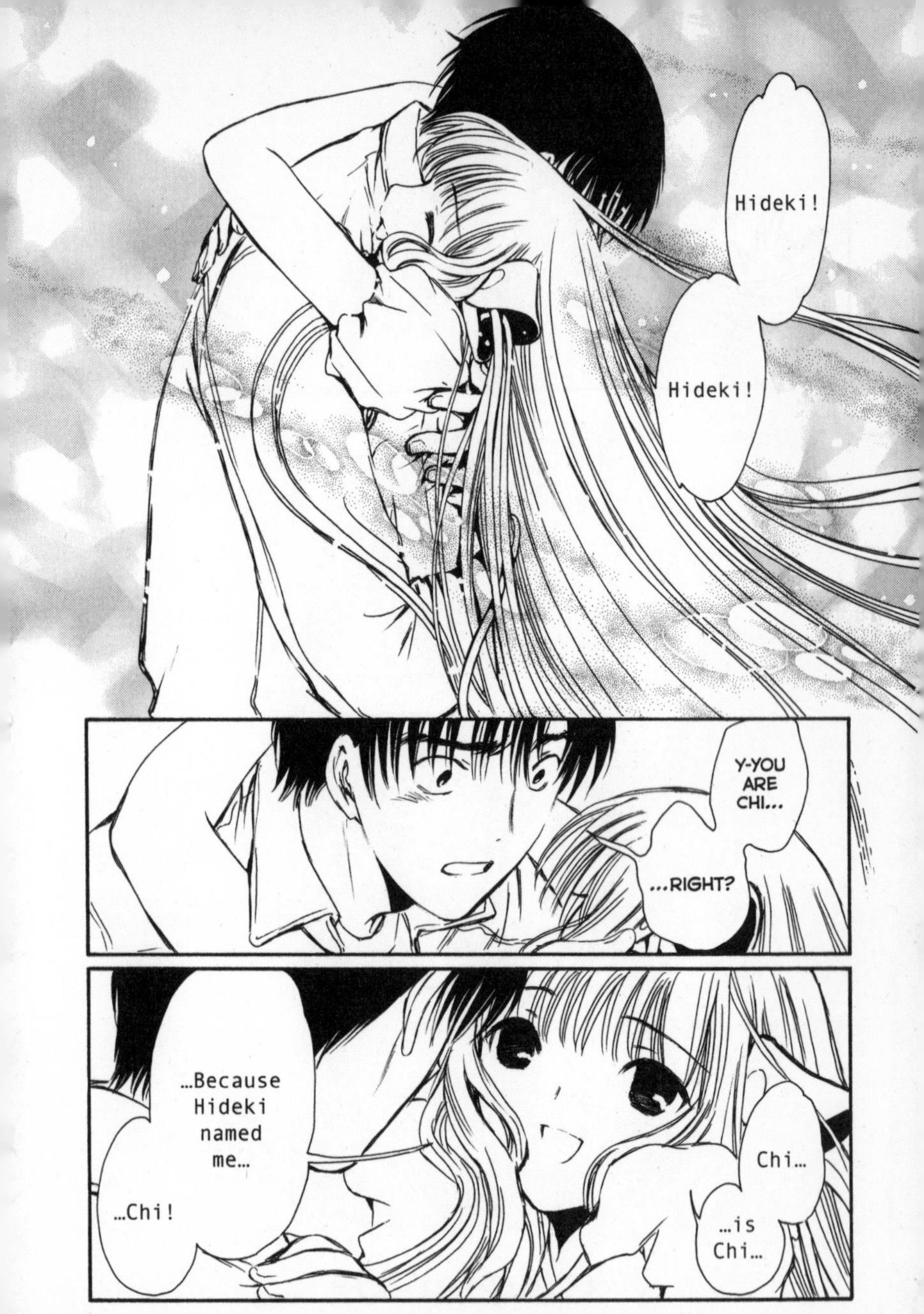
Hideki!
Hideki!
Y-YOU ARE CHI...
...RIGHT?
Chi...
...is Chi...
...Because Hideki named me...
...Chi!

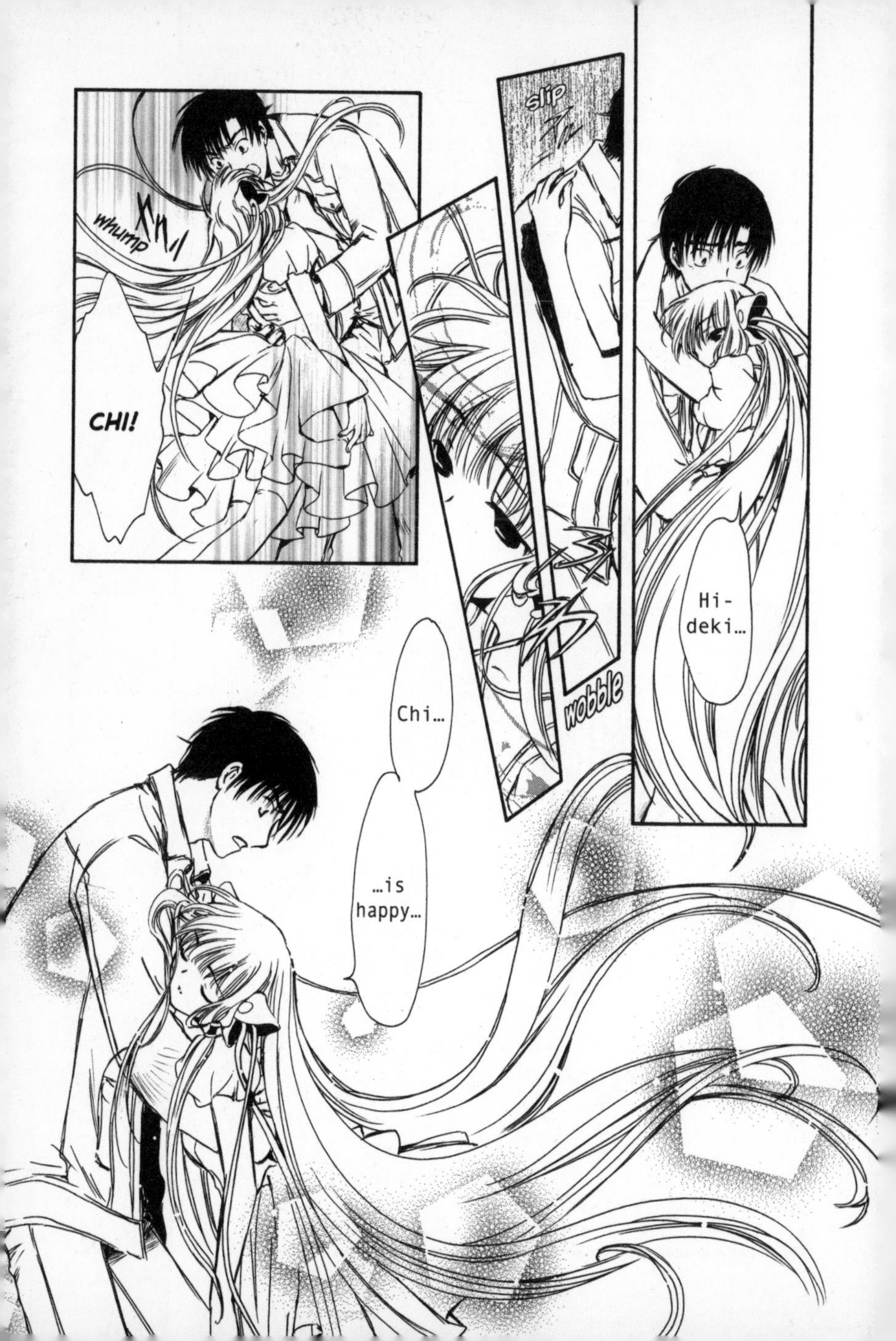
Hi-
deki…
slip
wobble
whump
CHI!
Chi…
…is
happy…

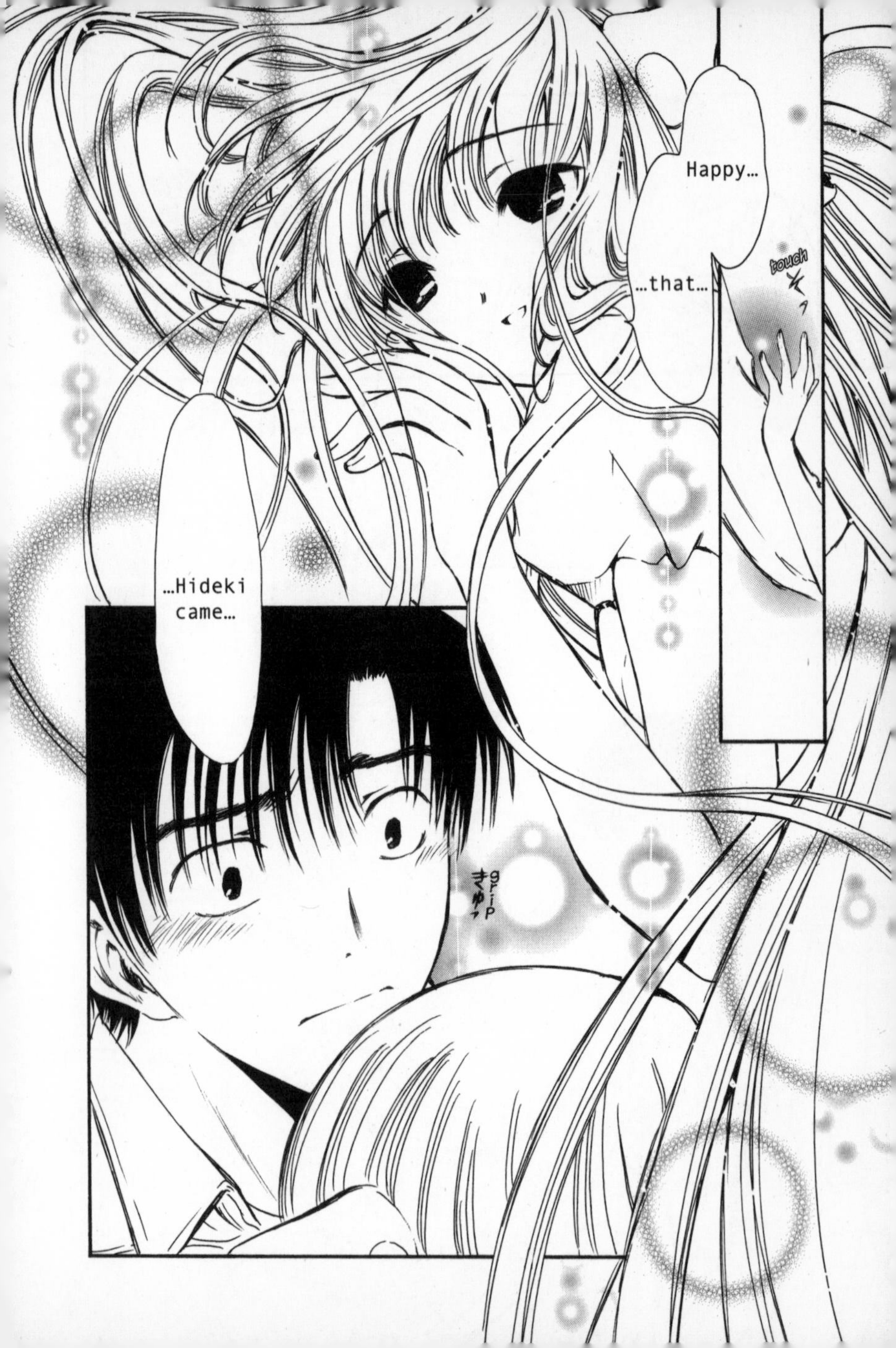
Happy...
...that...
touch
...Hideki came...
grip

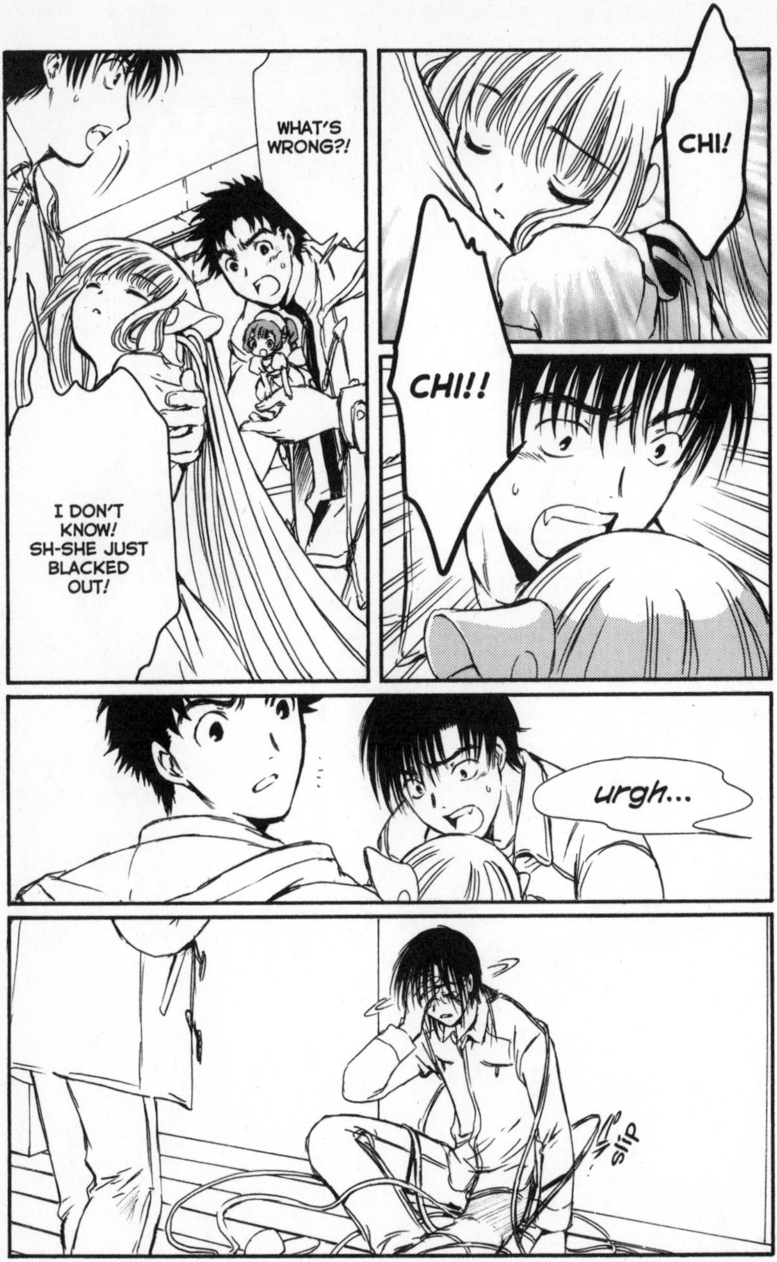
CHI!
CHI!!
WHAT'S WRONG?!
I DON'T KNOW! SH-SHE JUST BLACKED OUT!
urgh...
slip

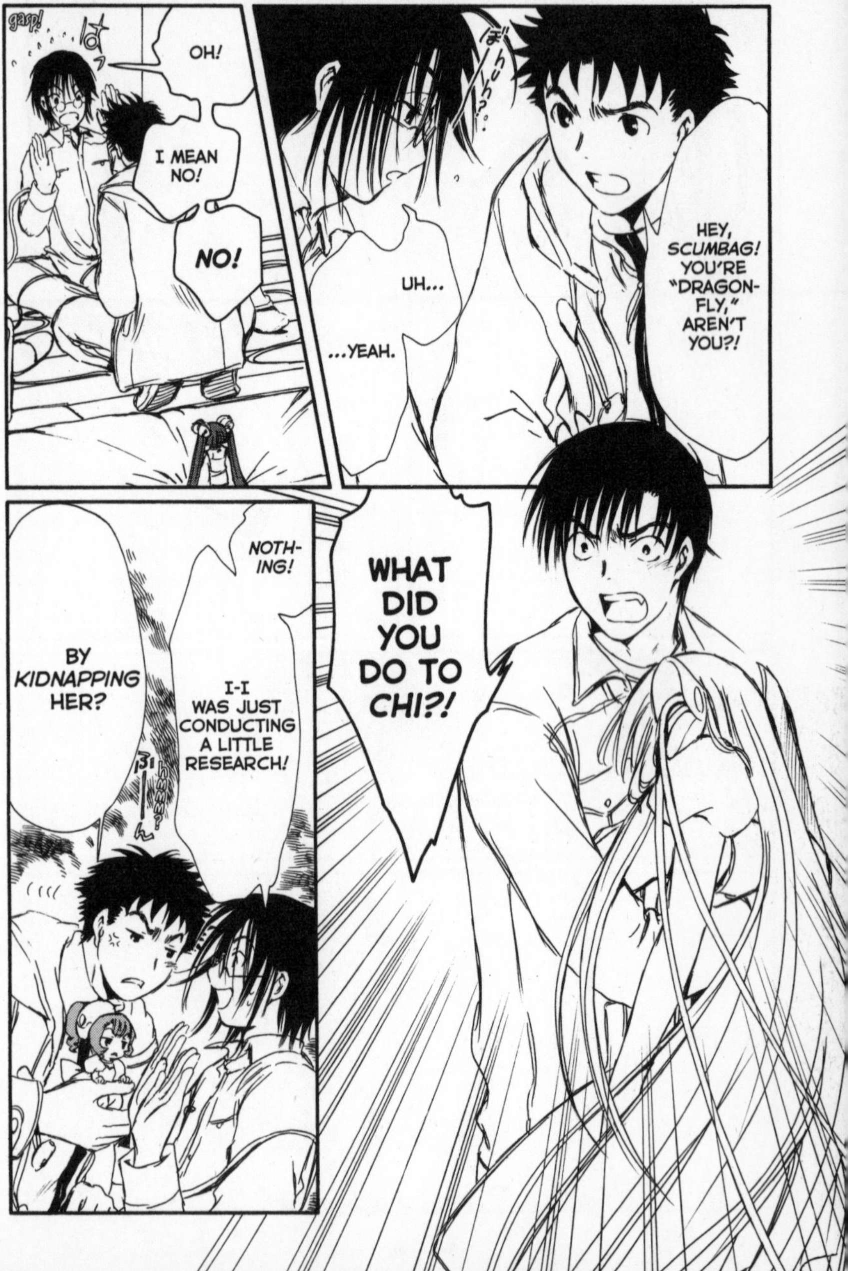

HEY, SCUMBAG! YOU'RE "DRAGON-FLY," AREN'T YOU?!
UH...
...YEAH.
gasp!
はっ
OH!
I MEAN NO!
NO!
WHAT DID YOU DO TO CHI?!
NOTH-ING!
I-I WAS JUST CONDUCTING A LITTLE RESEARCH!
BY KIDNAPPING HER?
hmmm?

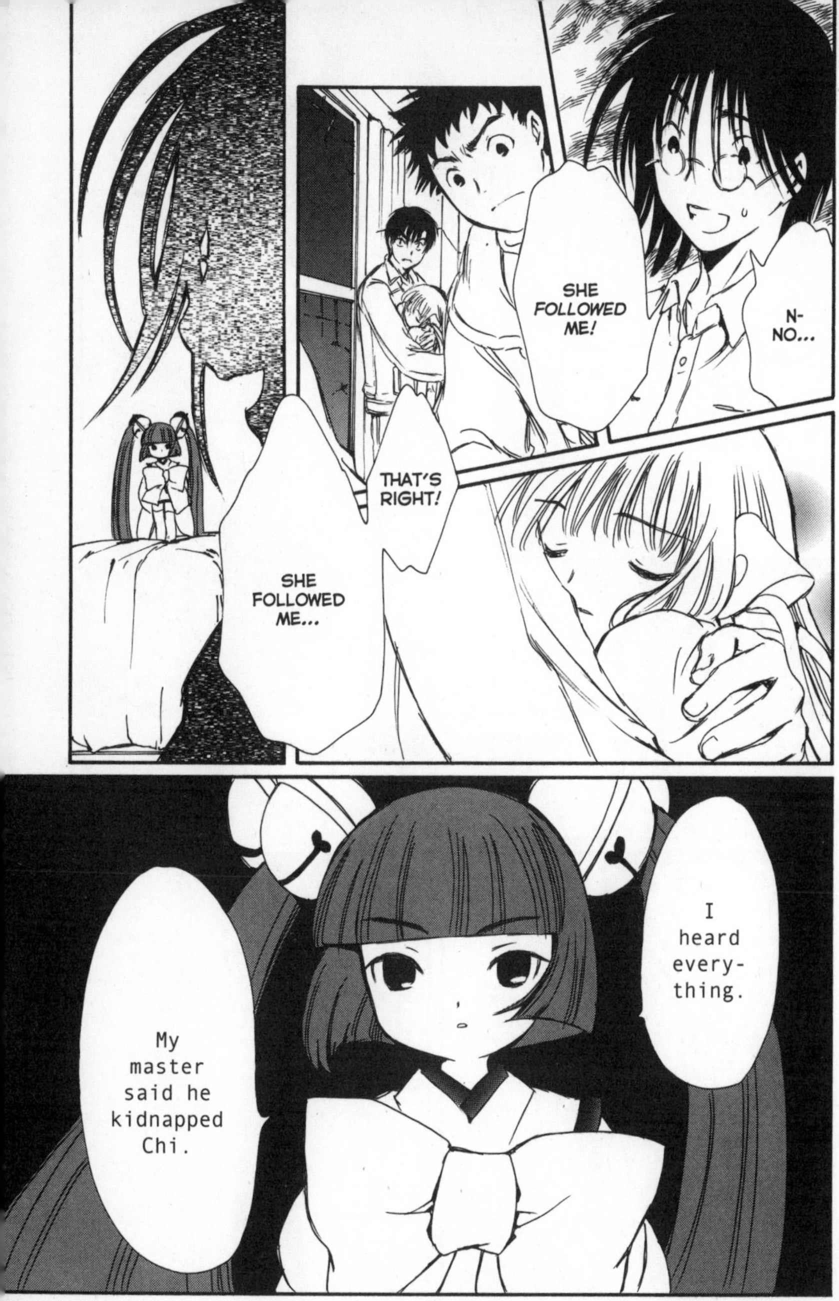
N- NO...
SHE FOLLOWED ME!
THAT'S RIGHT!
SHE FOLLOWED ME...
I heard every- thing.
My master said he kidnapped Chi.

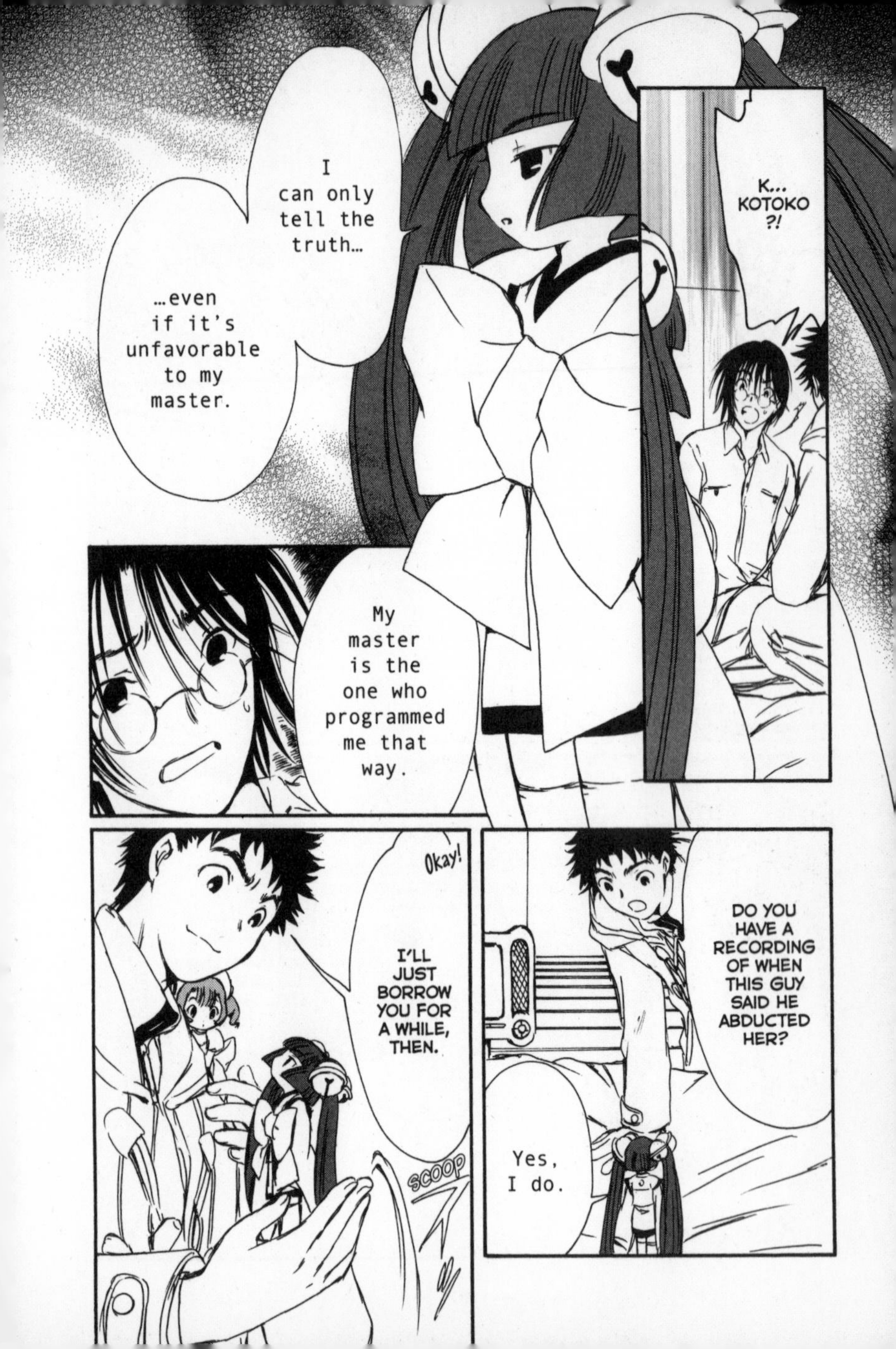
K... KOTOKO ?!
I can only tell the truth...
...even if it's unfavorable to my master.
My master is the one who programmed me that way.
DO YOU HAVE A RECORDING OF WHEN THIS GUY SAID HE ABDUCTED HER?
Yes, I do.
Okay!
I'LL JUST BORROW YOU FOR A WHILE, THEN.
SCOOP

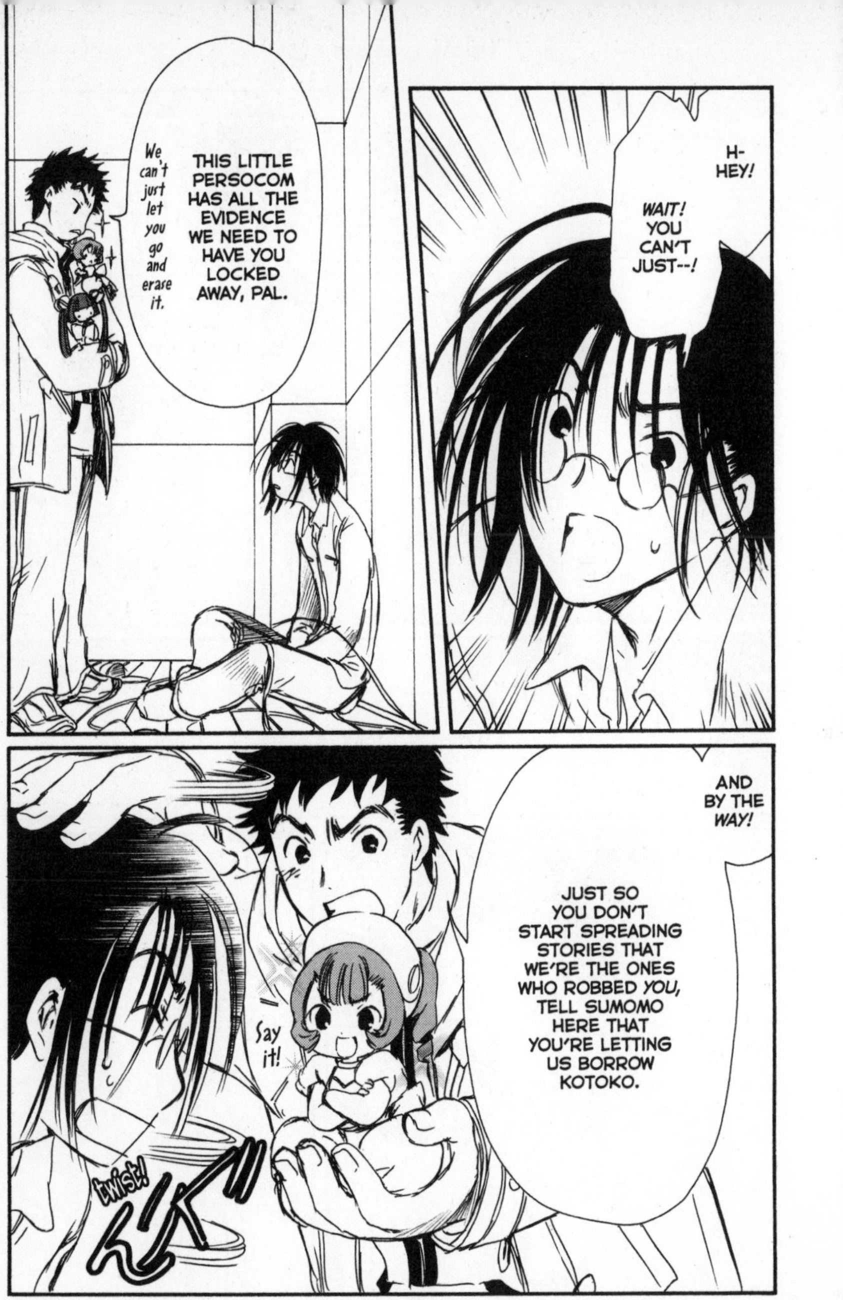
H-
HEY!
WAIT! YOU CAN'T JUST--!
THIS LITTLE PERSOCOM HAS ALL THE EVIDENCE WE NEED TO HAVE YOU LOCKED AWAY, PAL.
We can't just let you go and erase it.
AND BY THE WAY!
JUST SO YOU DON'T START SPREADING STORIES THAT WE'RE THE ONES WHO ROBBED YOU, TELL SUMOMO HERE THAT YOU'RE LETTING US BORROW KOTOKO.
Say it!
twist!

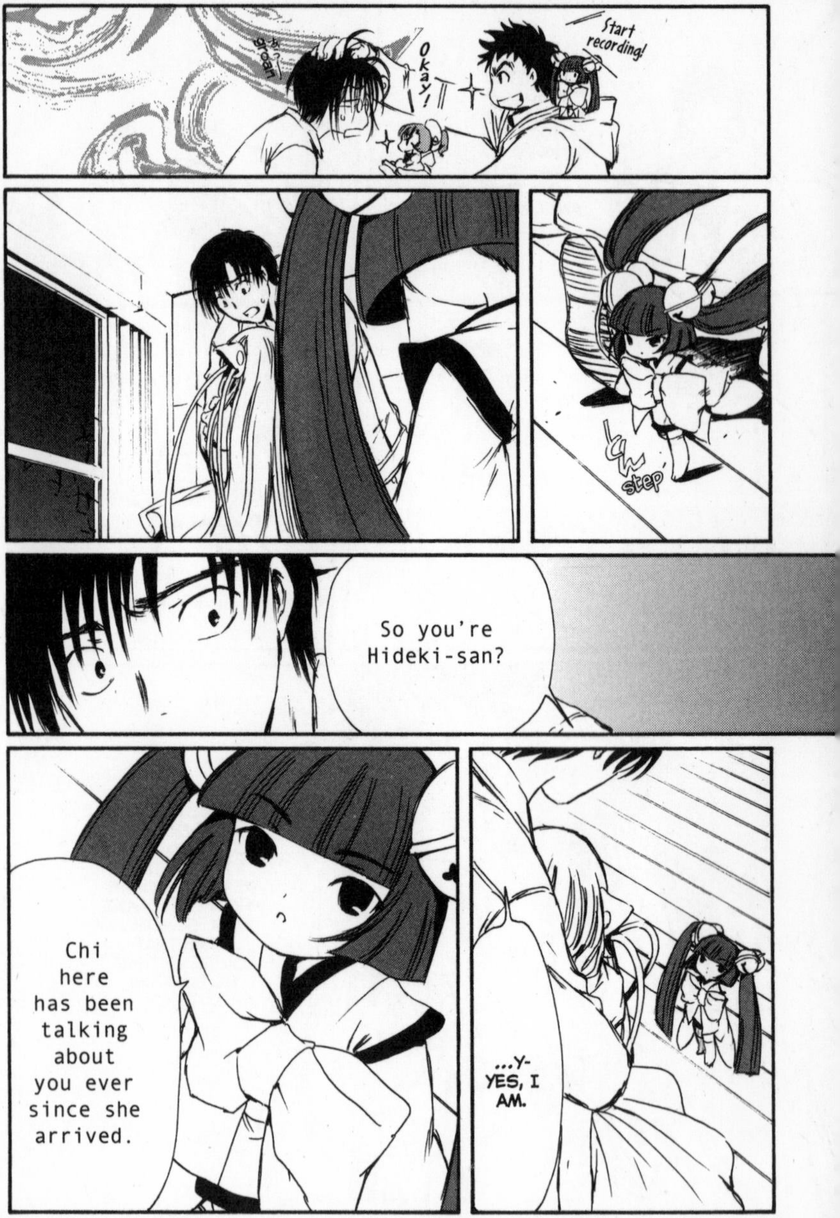
Start recording!
Okay!
groan
とん
step
So you're Hideki-san?
...Y-YES, I AM.
Chi here has been talking about you ever since she arrived.

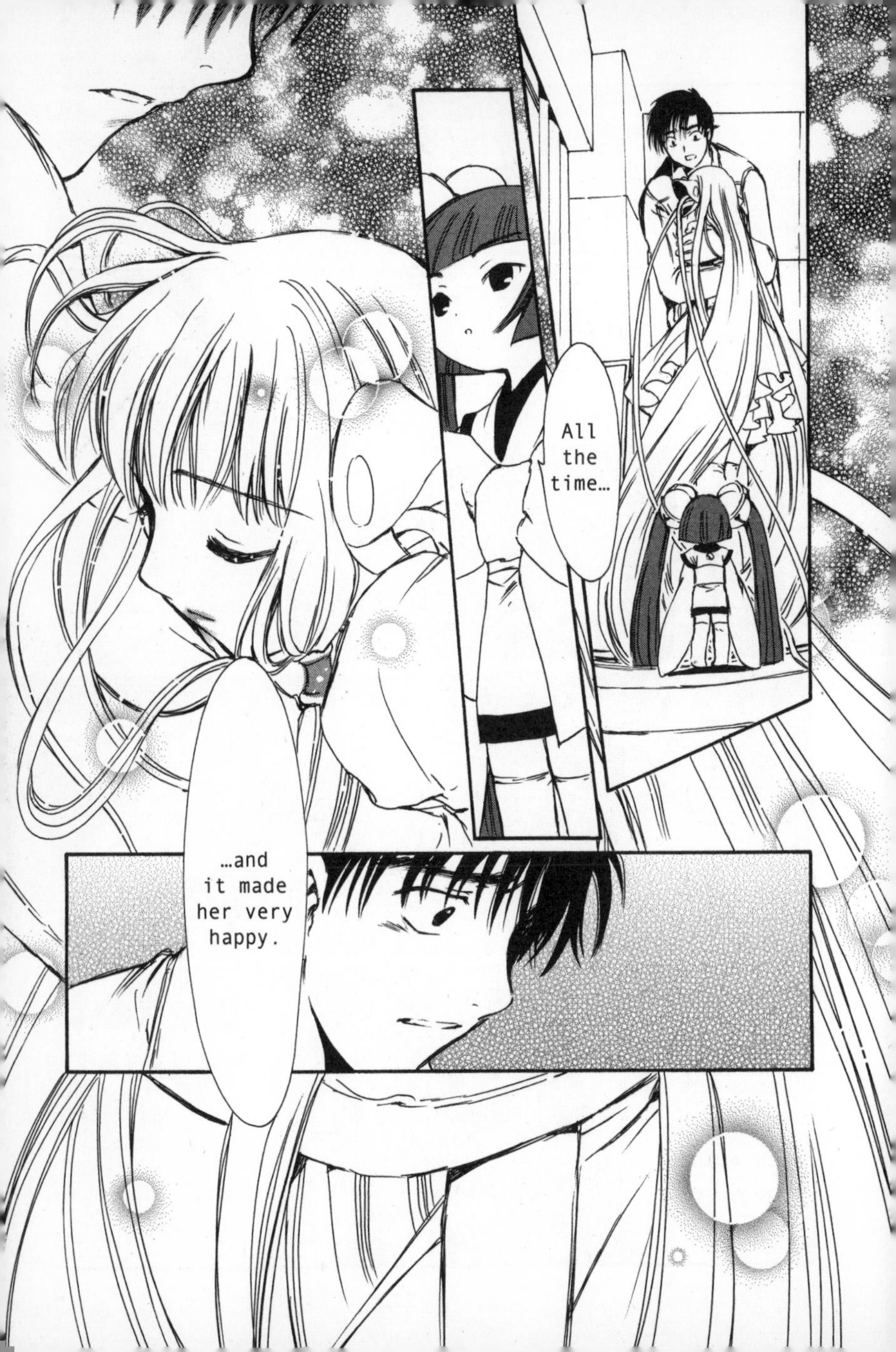
All the time…
…and it made her very happy.

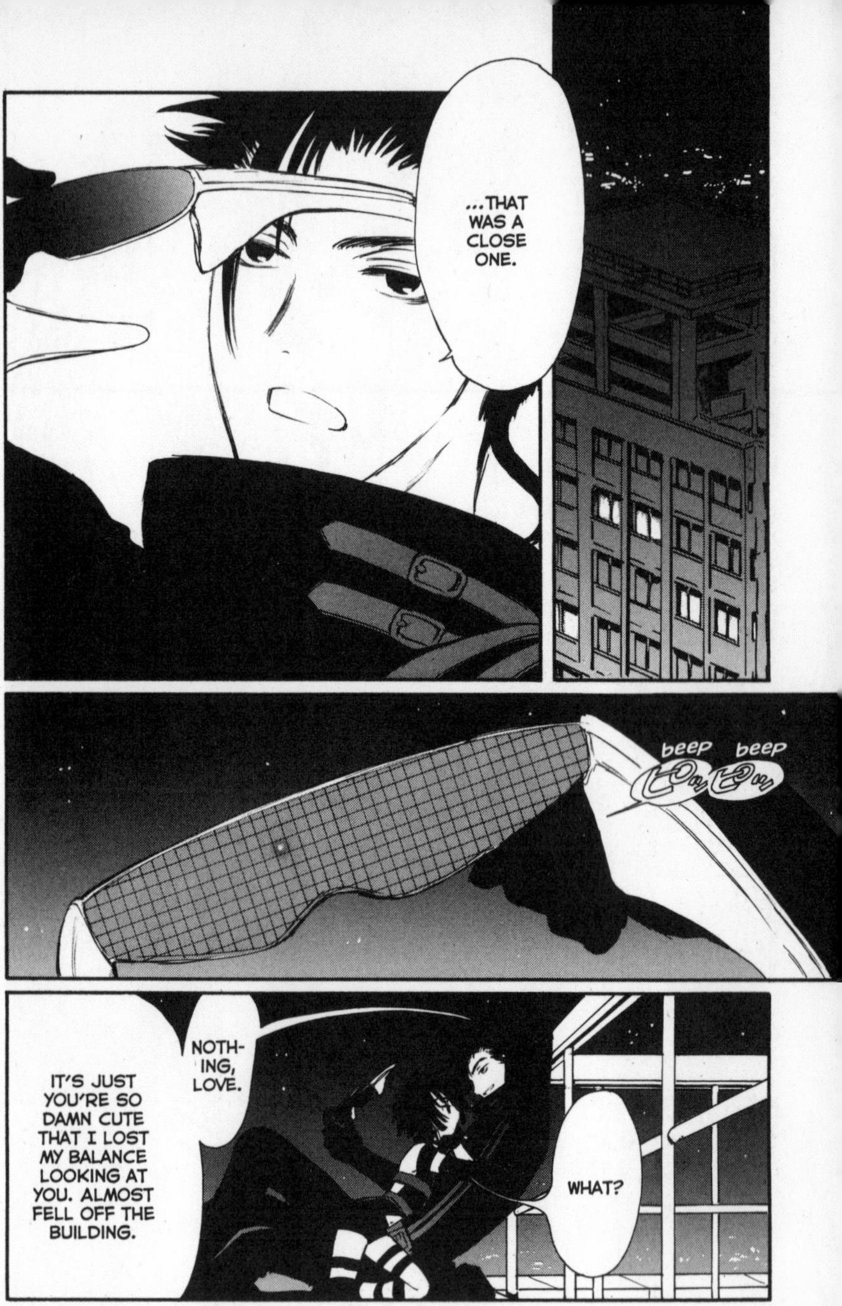
...THAT WAS A CLOSE ONE.
beep beep
WHAT?
NOTH-ING, LOVE.
IT'S JUST YOU'RE SO DAMN CUTE THAT I LOST MY BALANCE LOOKING AT YOU. ALMOST FELL OFF THE BUILDING.

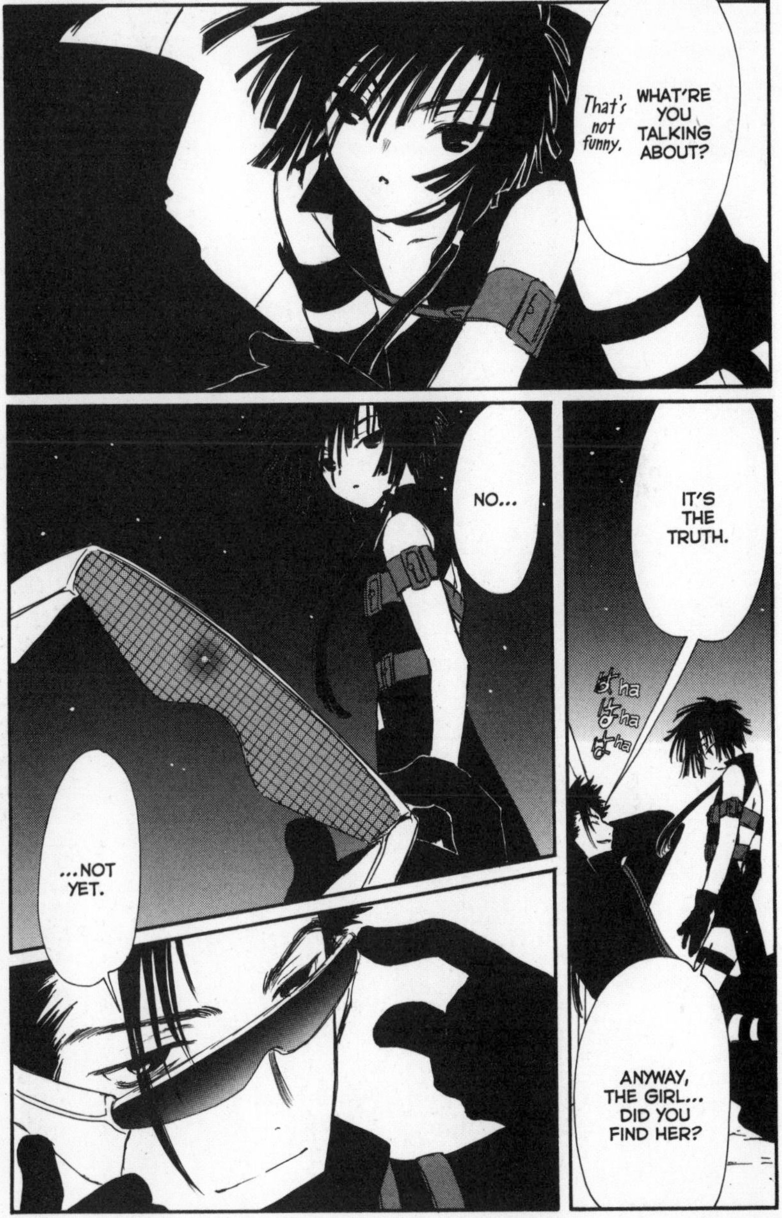
WHAT'RE YOU TALKING ABOUT?
That's not funny.
IT'S THE TRUTH.
ha ha ha
ANYWAY, THE GIRL... DID YOU FIND HER?
NO...
...NOT YET.

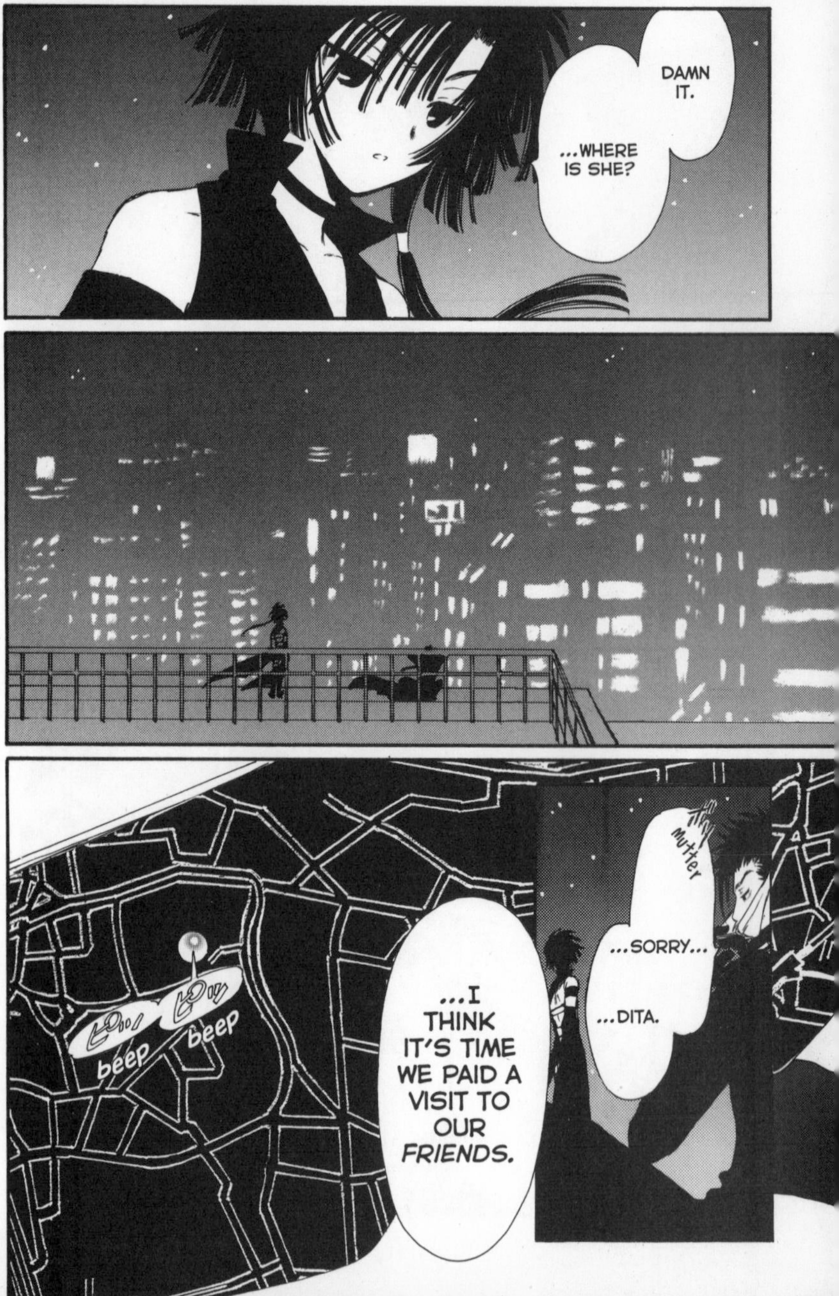
DAMN IT.
...WHERE IS SHE?
mutter
...SORRY...
...DITA.
...I THINK IT'S TIME WE PAID A VISIT TO OUR FRIENDS.
beep
beep

Chobits
ちょびっツ

◀ **chapter 56** ▶

cheep
cheep
cheep
chirp
chirp
A City With No People
~little by little~
ity With No Pe
~they can do anything
A City Wit

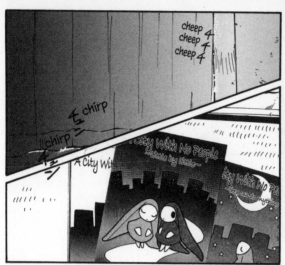

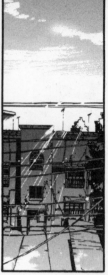

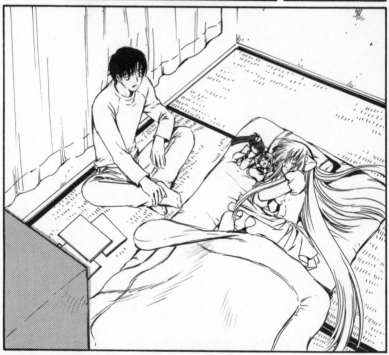

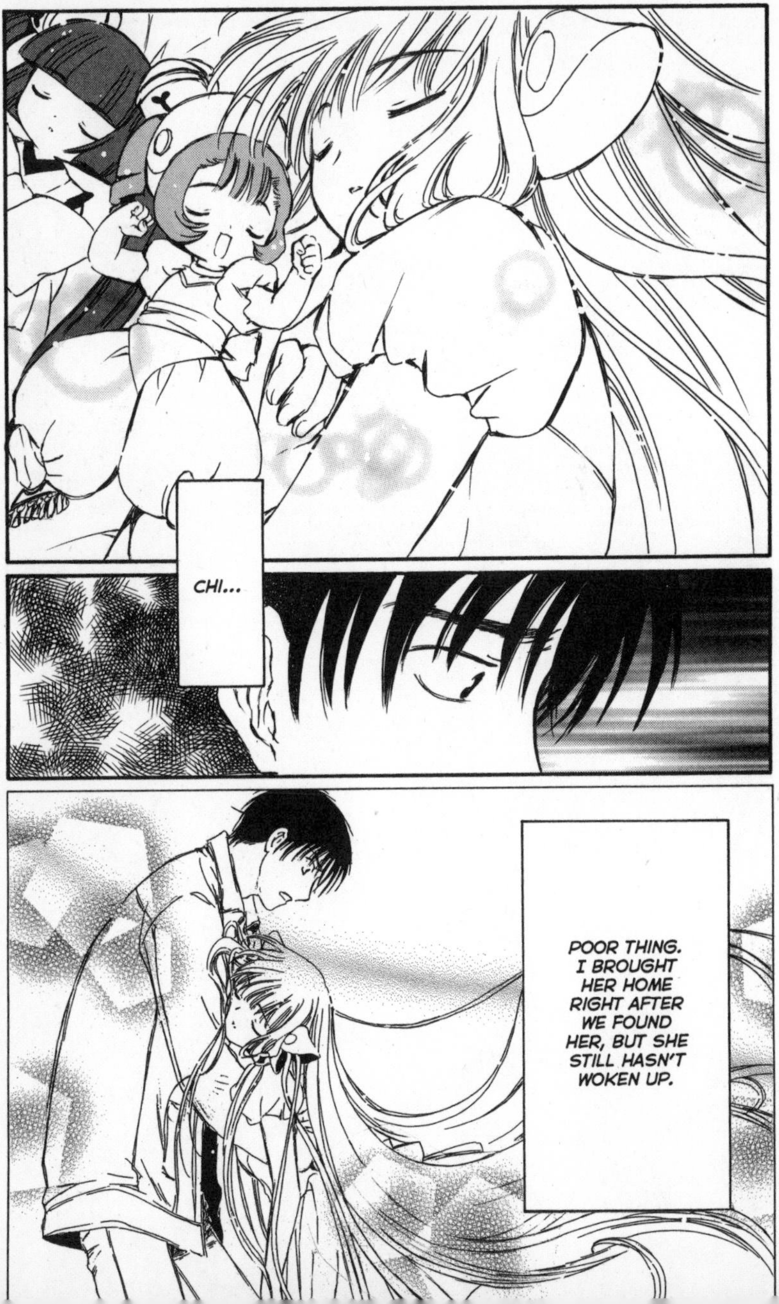
CHI...
POOR THING. I BROUGHT HER HOME RIGHT AFTER WE FOUND HER, BUT SHE STILL HASN'T WOKEN UP.

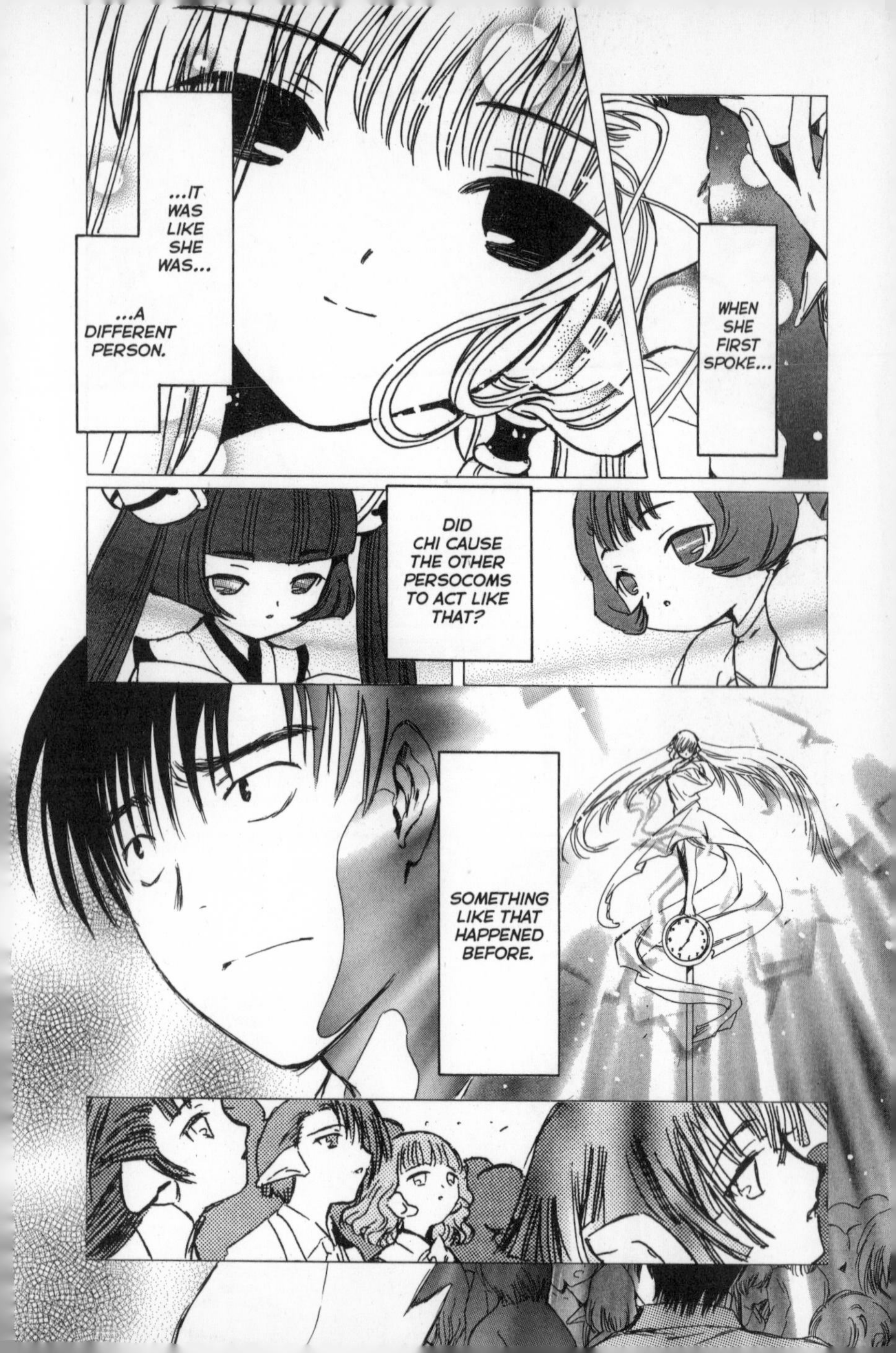
WHEN SHE FIRST SPOKE...
...IT WAS LIKE SHE WAS...
...A DIFFERENT PERSON.
DID CHI CAUSE THE OTHER PERSOCOMS TO ACT LIKE THAT?
SOMETHING LIKE THAT HAPPENED BEFORE.

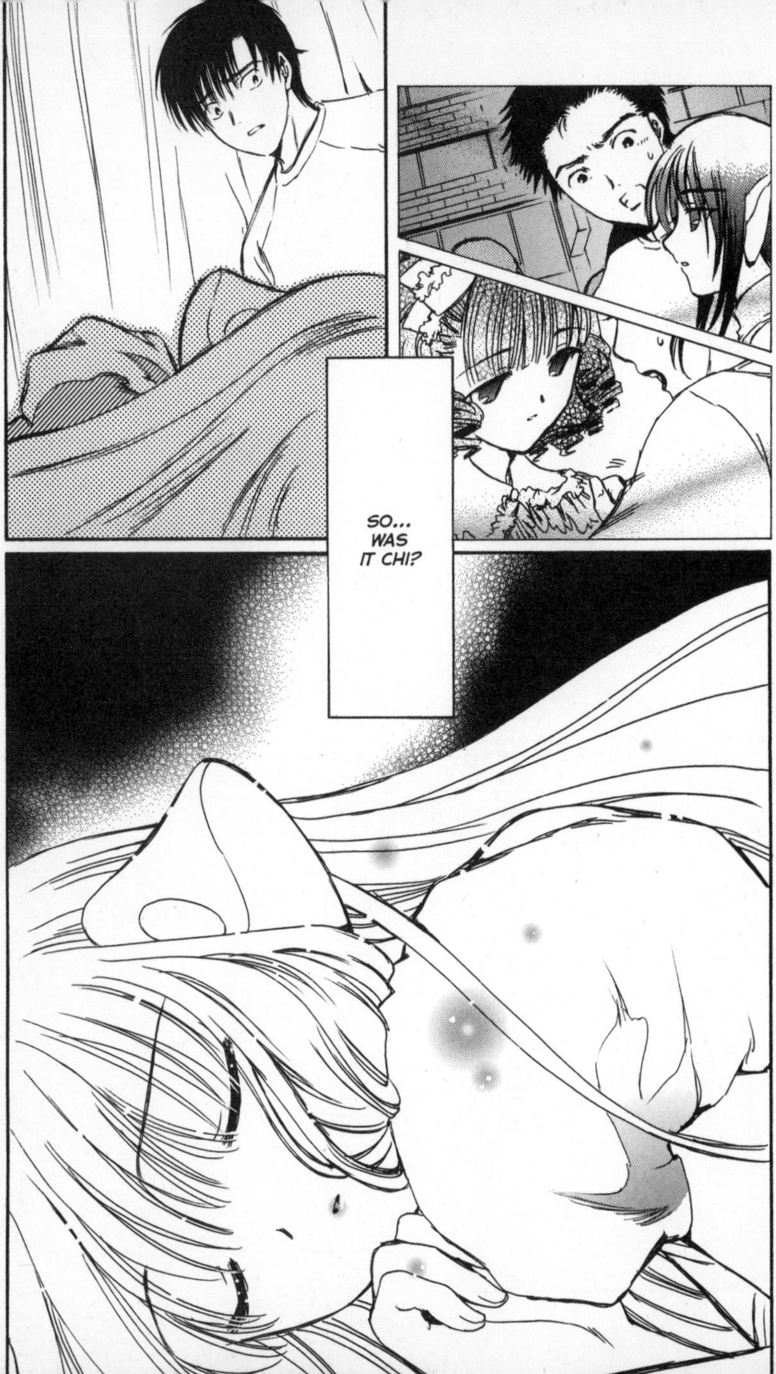
SO...
WAS
IT CHI?

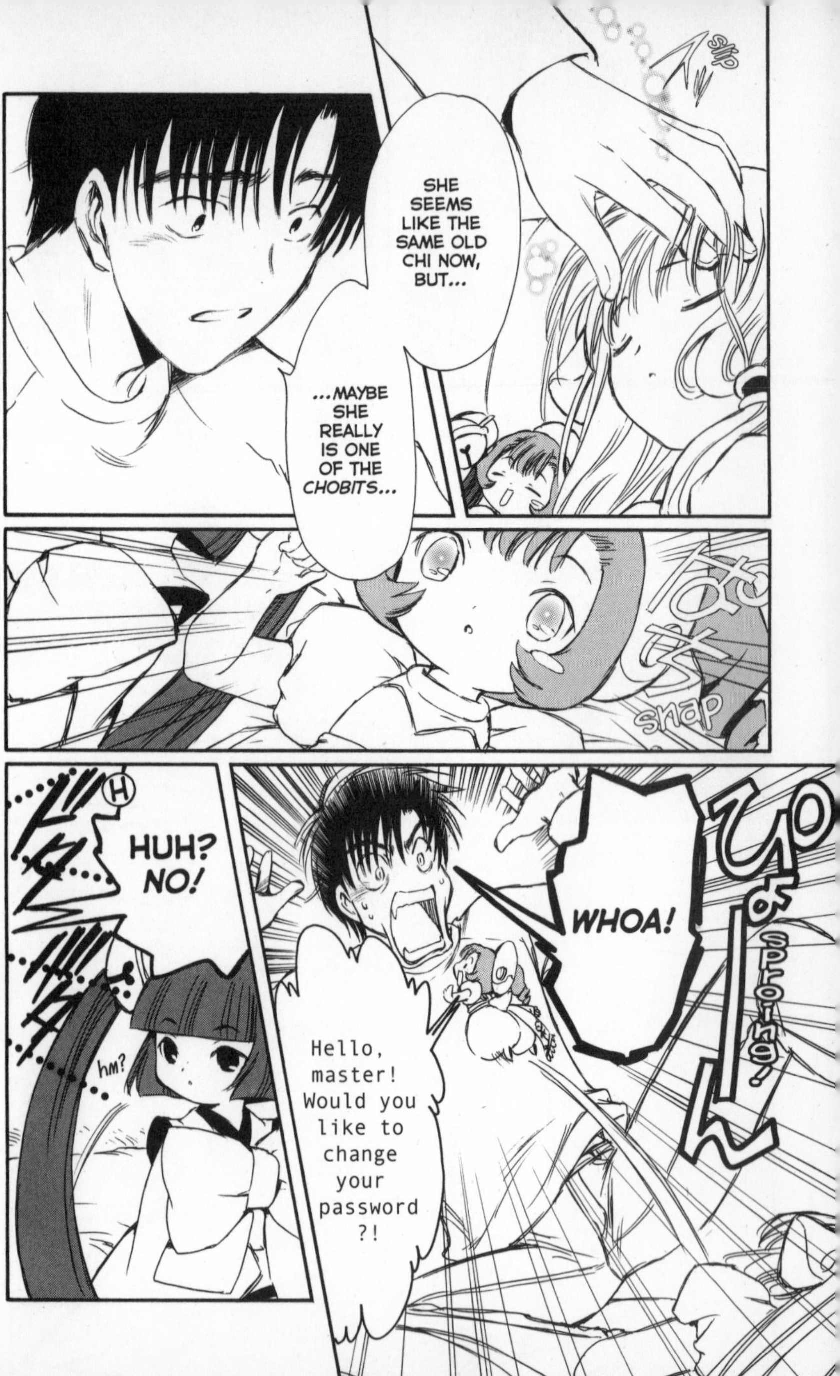
slip
SHE SEEMS LIKE THE SAME OLD CHI NOW, BUT...
...MAYBE SHE REALLY IS ONE OF THE *CHOBITS*...
snap
WHOA!
sproing!
Hello, master! Would you like to change your password ?!
HUH? NO!
hm?
bang! crash!

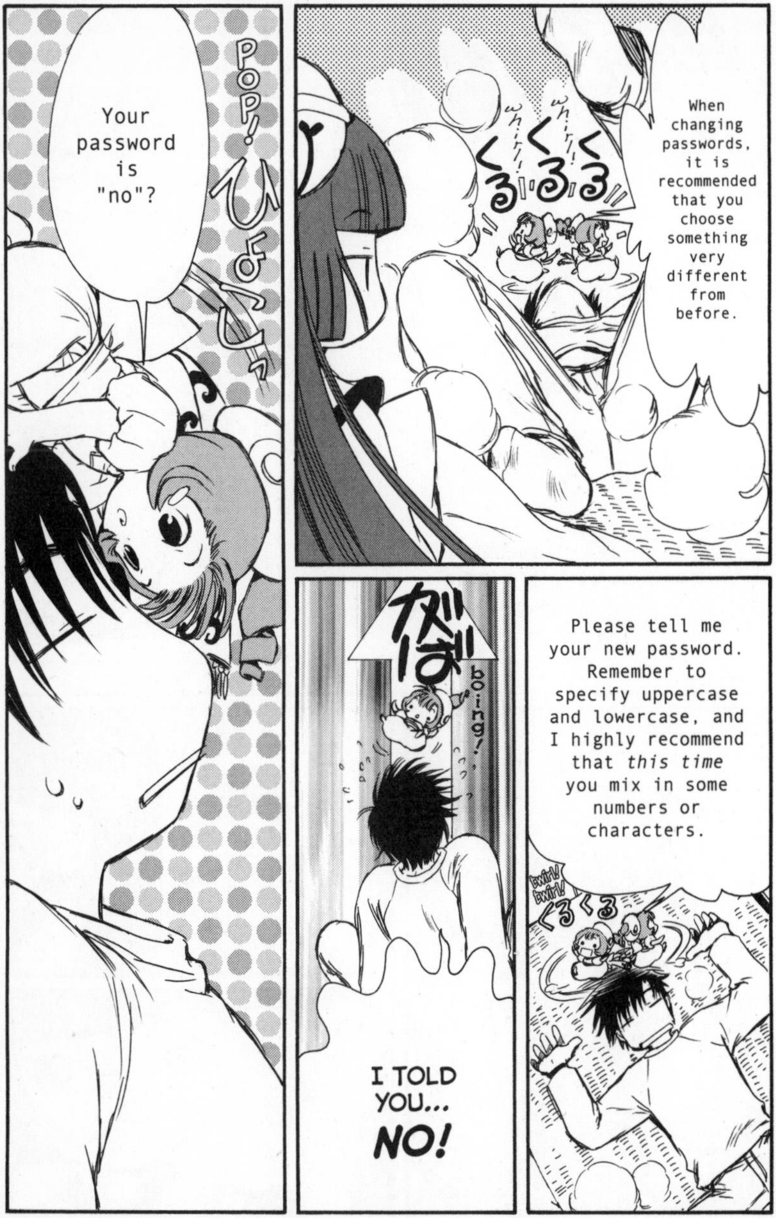

くるくるくる
When changing passwords, it is recommended that you choose something very different from before.
Please tell me your new password. Remember to specify uppercase and lowercase, and I highly recommend that *this time* you mix in some numbers or characters.
twirl! twirl!
くるくる
がば
boing!
I TOLD YOU... *NO!*
POP!
Your password is "no"?

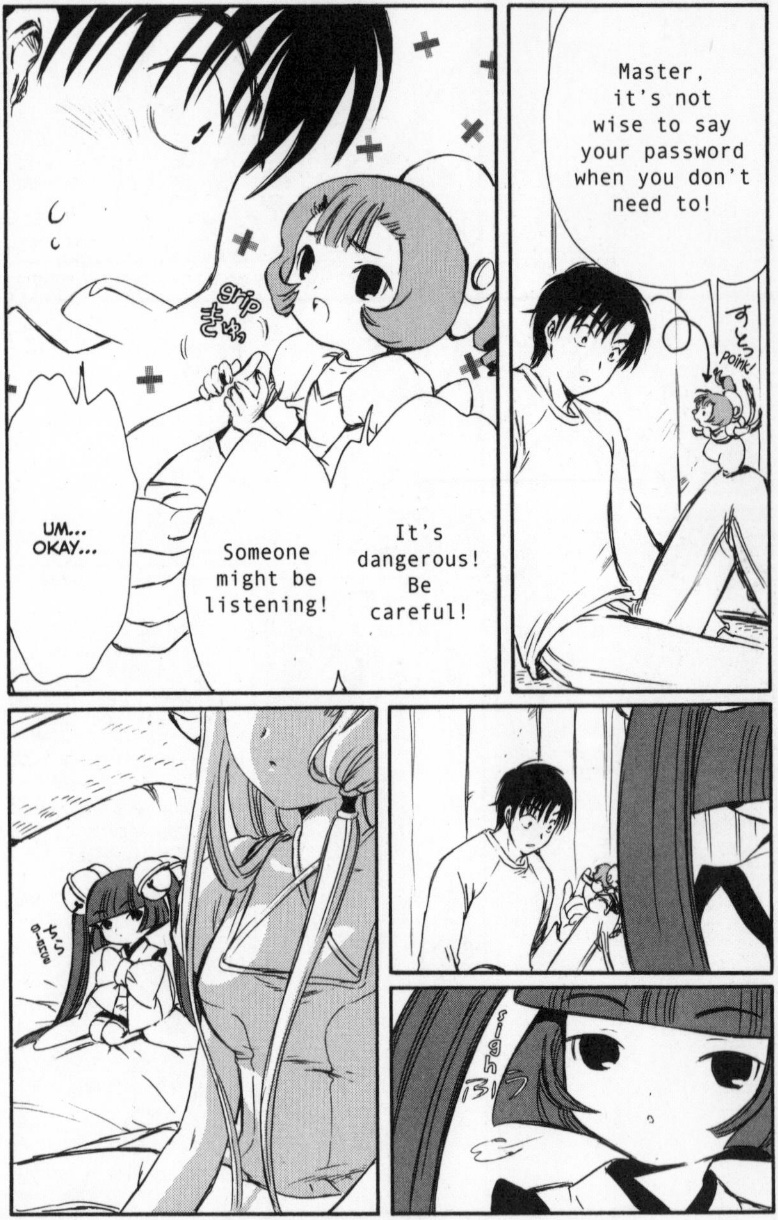
Master, it's not wise to say your password when you don't need to!
poink!
It's dangerous! Be careful!
Someone might be listening!
grip
UM... OKAY...
sigh
glance

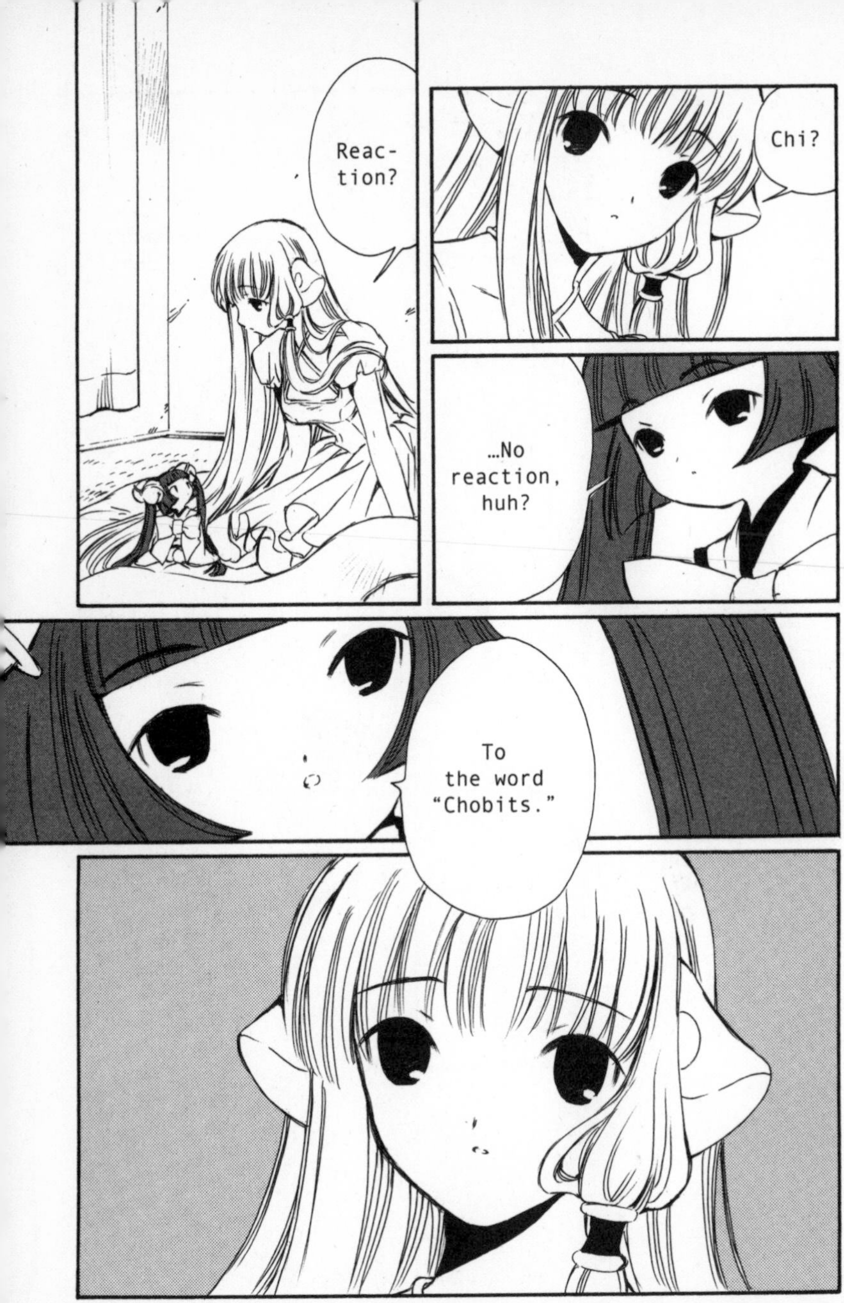
Chi?
…No reaction, huh?
Reaction?
To the word "Chobits."

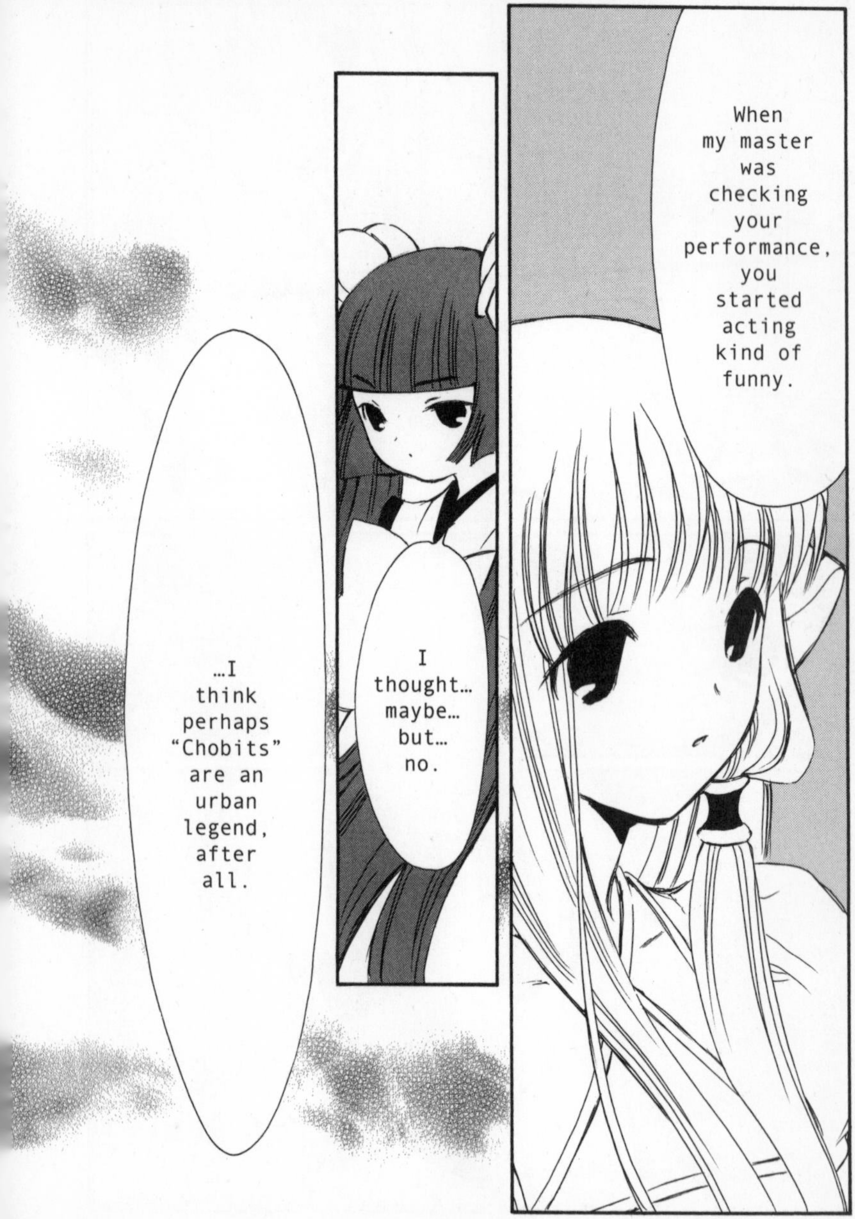
When my master was checking your performance, you started acting kind of funny.
I thought… maybe… but… no.
…I think perhaps “Chobits” are an urban legend, after all.

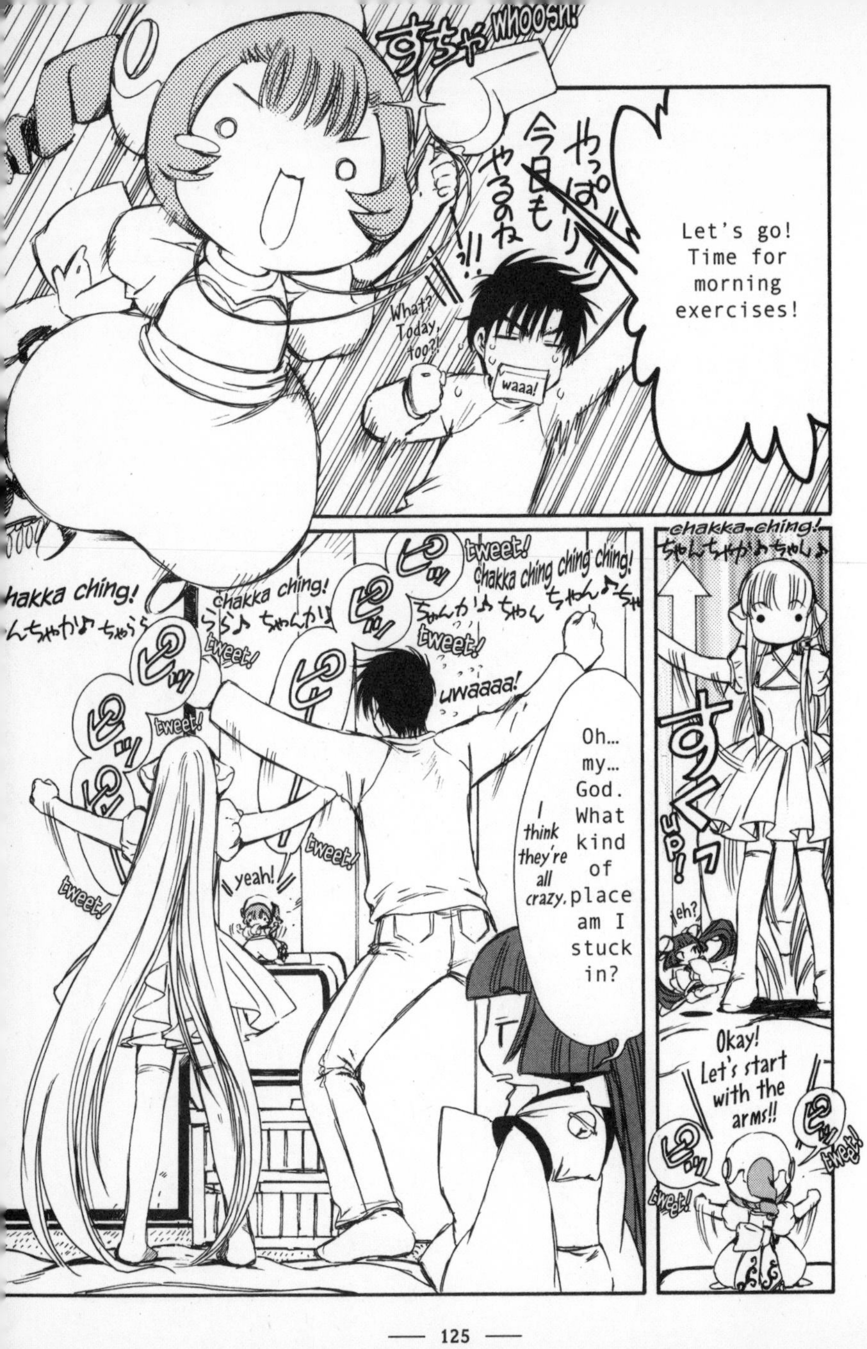
すちゃ WHOOSH!
Let's go! Time for morning exercises!
やっぱり今日もやるのね!!
What? Today, too?!
waaa!
chakka-ching!
ちゃんちゃか♪ちゃん♪
すくっ
up!
eh?
Okay! Let's start with the arms!!
ピッ
tweet!
ピッ
tweet!
ピッ
tweet!
chakka ching ching ching!
ちゃんか♪ちゃん ちゃん♪ちゃ
ピッ
tweet!
chakka ching!
らら♪ ちゃんか!
chakka ching!
んちゃか♪ ちゃらら
ピッ
tweet!
ピッ
tweet!
uwaaaa!
Oh... my... God. What kind of place am I stuck in?
I think they're all crazy.
ピッ
tweet!
ピッ
tweet!
yeah!

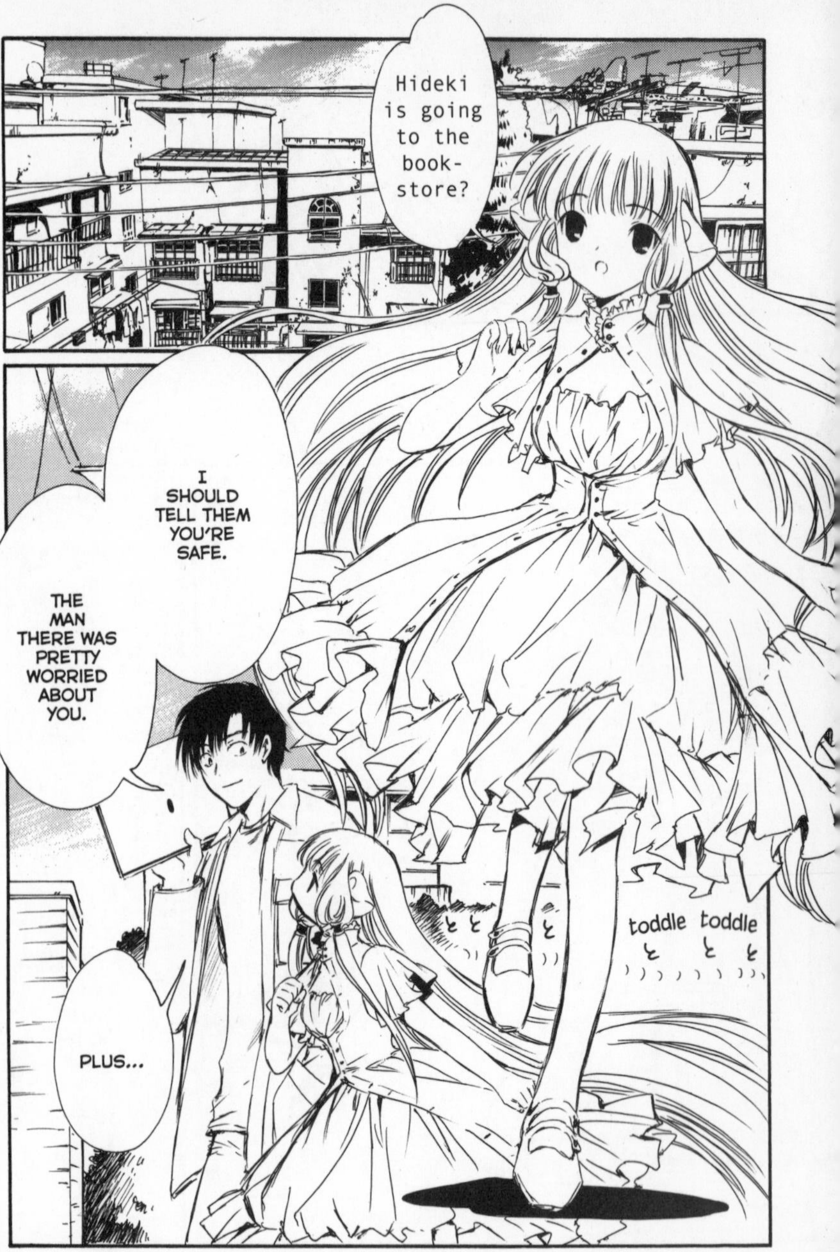
Hideki is going to the book-store?
I SHOULD TELL THEM YOU'RE SAFE.
THE MAN THERE WAS PRETTY WORRIED ABOUT YOU.
toddle toddle
PLUS...

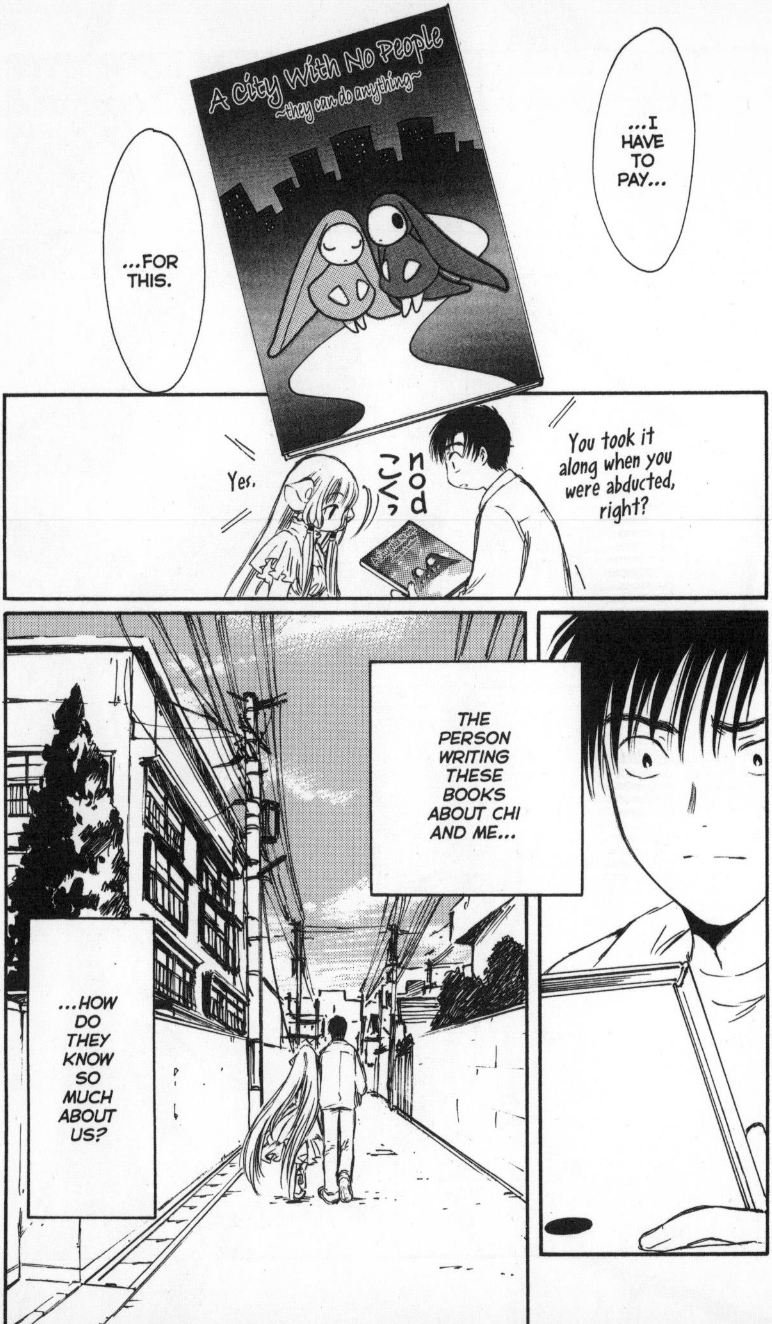
...I HAVE TO PAY...
A City With No People
~they can do anything~
...FOR THIS.
You took it along when you were abducted, right?
nod
こく
Yes.
THE PERSON WRITING THESE BOOKS ABOUT CHI AND ME...
...HOW DO THEY KNOW SO MUCH ABOUT US?

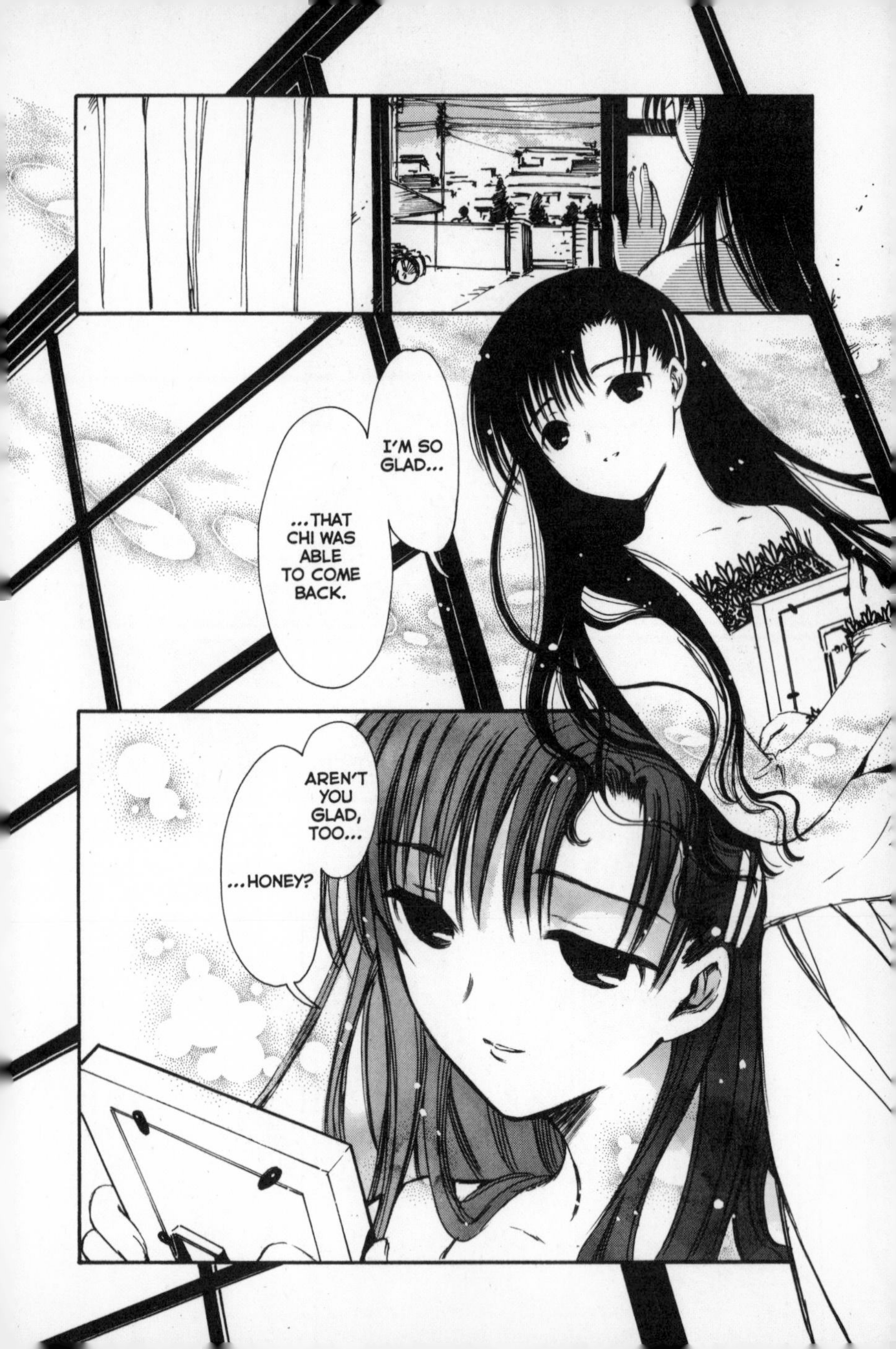
I'M SO GLAD...
...THAT CHI WAS ABLE TO COME BACK.
AREN'T YOU GLAD, TOO...
...HONEY?

Chobits
ちょびっツ

◀ chapter 57 ▶

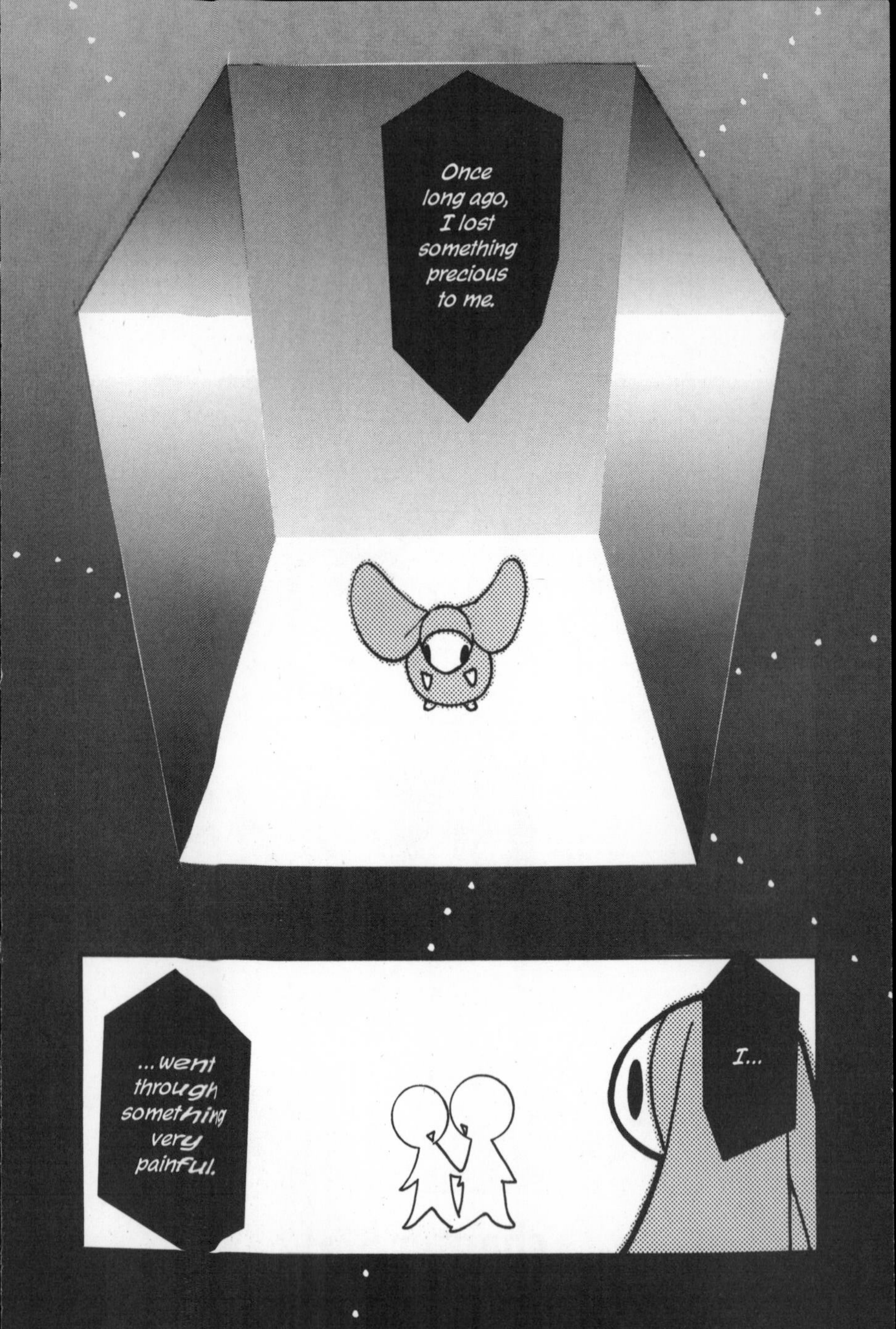
Once long ago, I lost something precious to me.
I...
...went through something very painful.

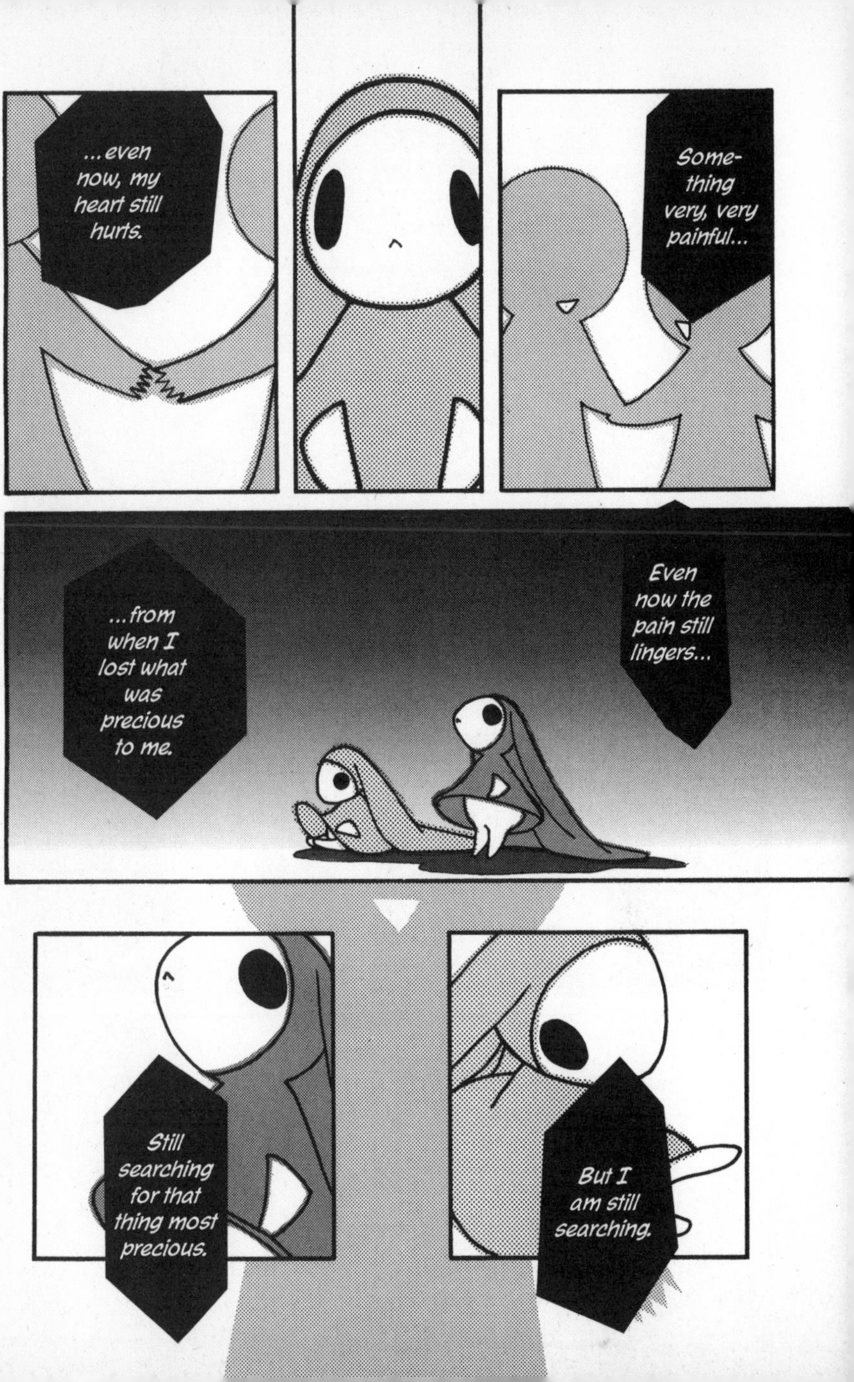
Something very, very painful...
...even now, my heart still hurts.
Even now the pain still lingers...
...from when I lost what was precious to me.
But I am still searching.
Still searching for that thing most precious.

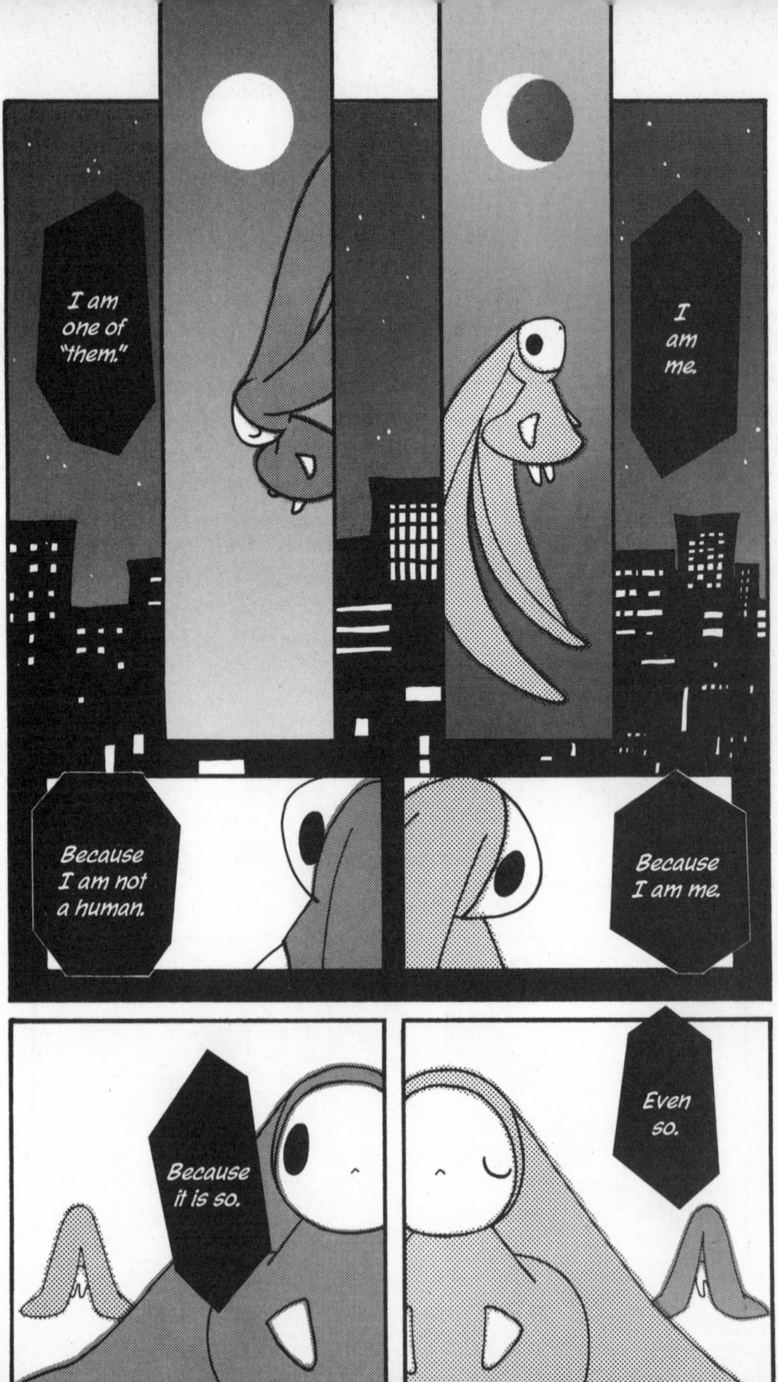
I am me.
I am one of "them."
Because I am me.
Because I am not a human.
Even so.
Because it is so.

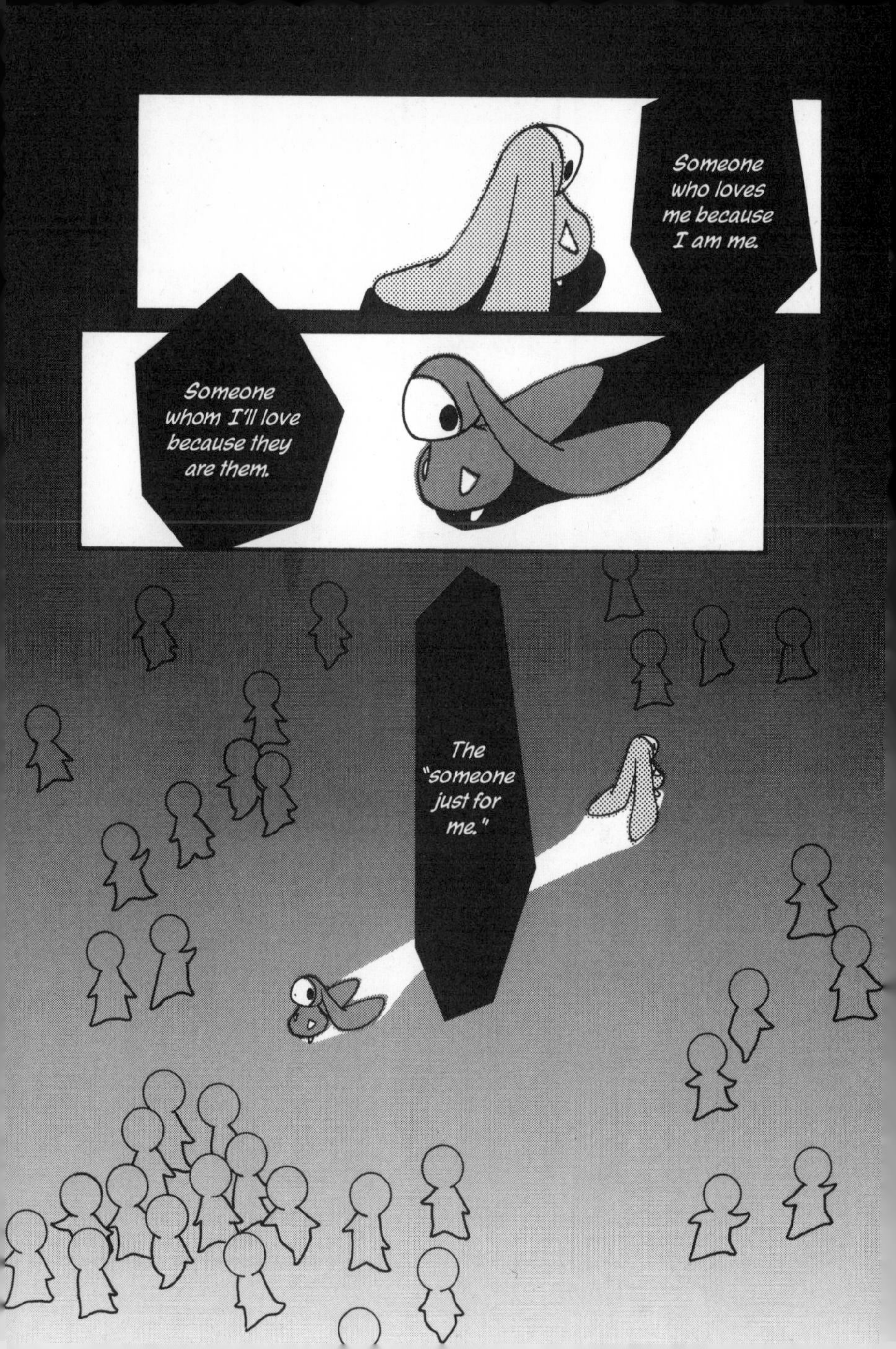
Someone who loves me because I am me.
Someone whom I'll love because they are them.
The "someone just for me."

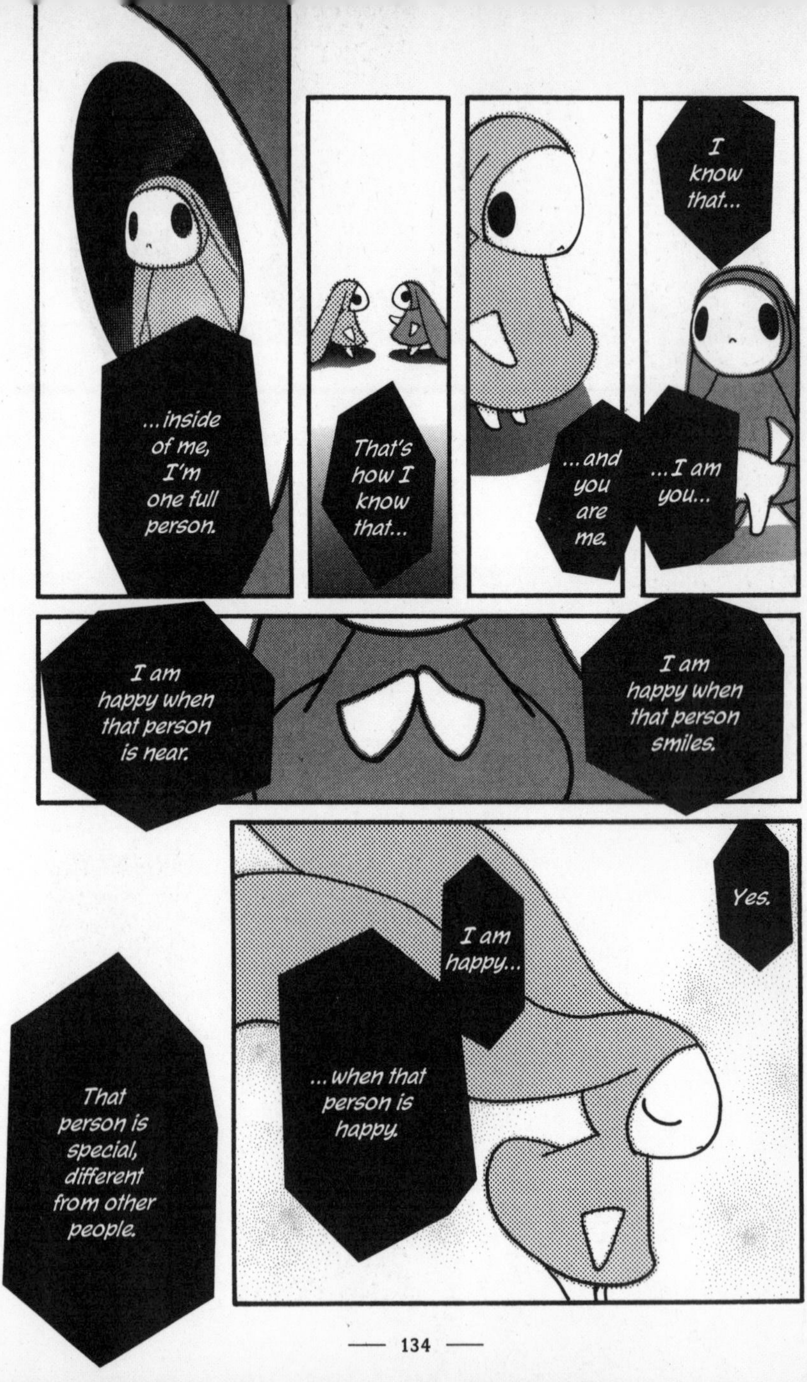
I know that...
...I am you...
...and you are me.
That's how I know that...
...inside of me, I'm one full person.
I am happy when that person smiles.
I am happy when that person is near.
Yes.
I am happy...
...when that person is happy.
That person is special, different from other people.

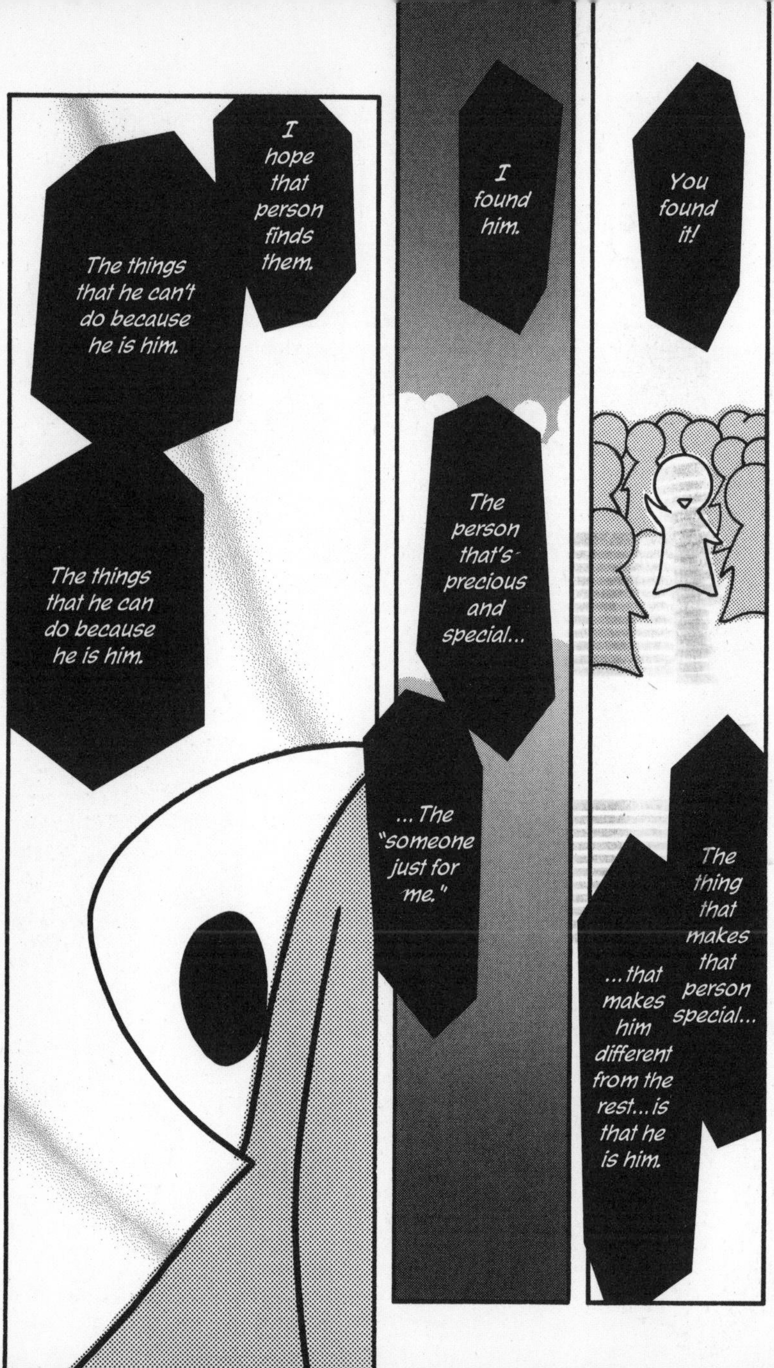
You found it!
The thing that makes that person special...
...that makes him different from the rest...is that he is him.
I found him.
The person that's precious and special...
...The "someone just for me."
I hope that person finds them.
The things that he can't do because he is him.
The things that he can do because he is him.

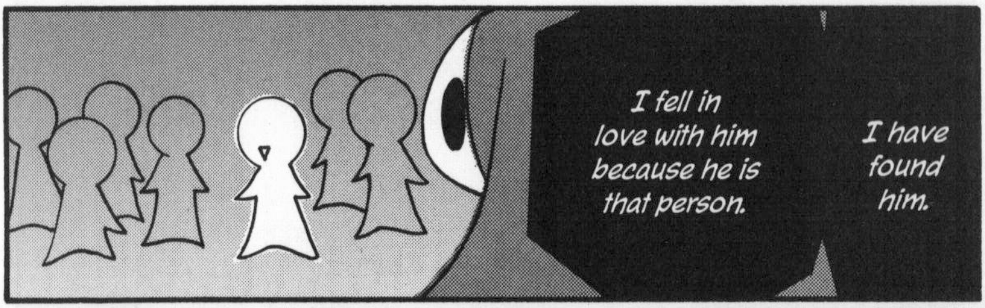
I have found him.
I fell in love with him because he is that person.

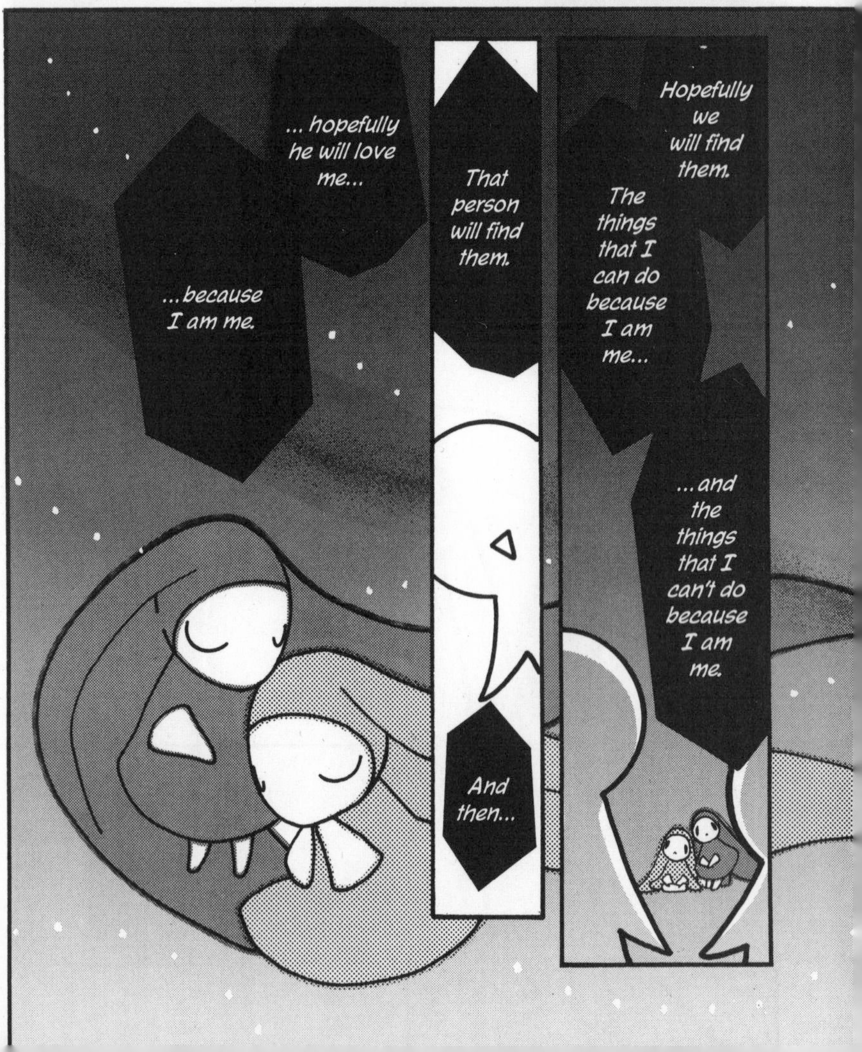
Hopefully we will find them.
The things that I can do because I am me...
...and the things that I can't do because I am me.
That person will find them.
And then...
... hopefully he will love me...
...because I am me.

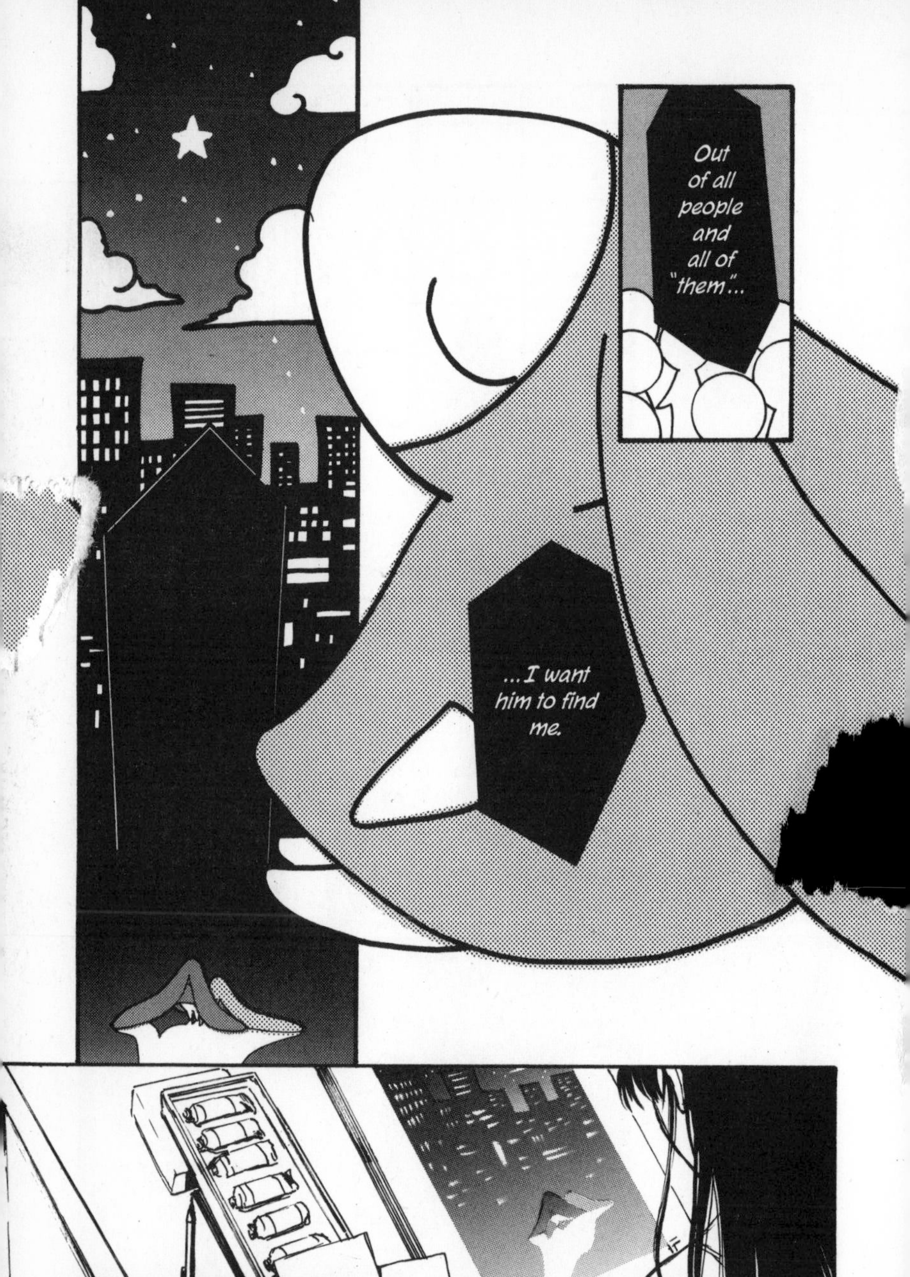
Out of all people and all of "them"...
...I want him to find me.

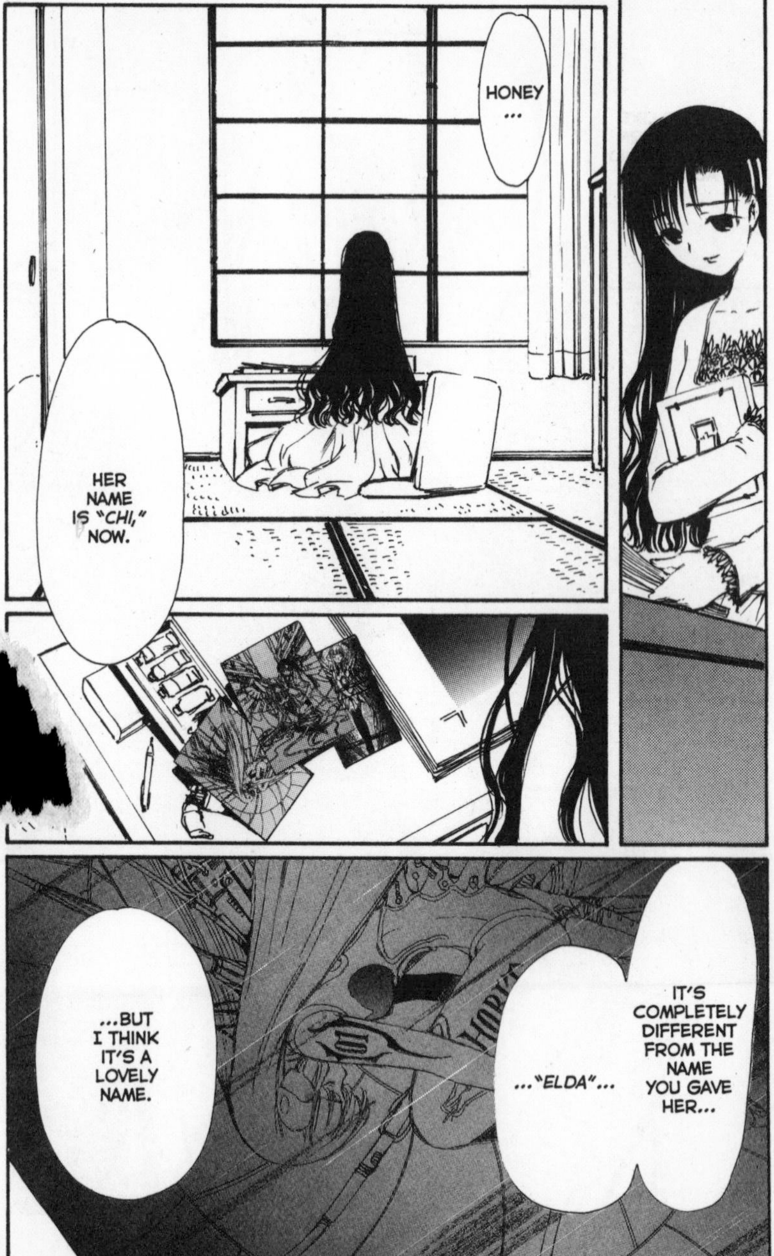
HONEY ...
HER NAME IS "CHI," NOW.
IT'S COMPLETELY DIFFERENT FROM THE NAME YOU GAVE HER...
..."ELDA"...
...BUT I THINK IT'S A LOVELY NAME.

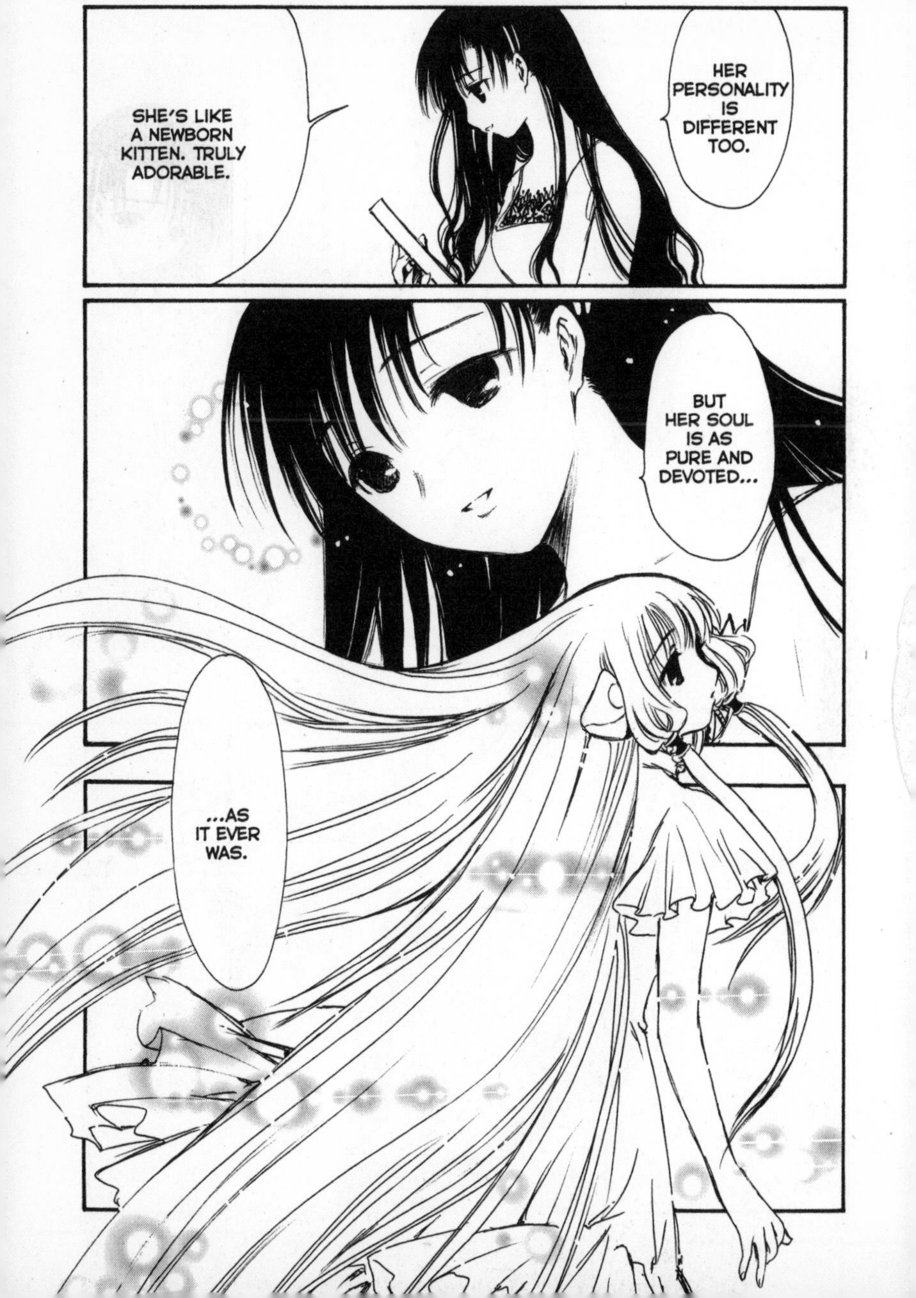
HER PERSONALITY IS DIFFERENT TOO.
SHE'S LIKE A NEWBORN KITTEN. TRULY ADORABLE.
BUT HER SOUL IS AS PURE AND DEVOTED...
...AS IT EVER WAS.

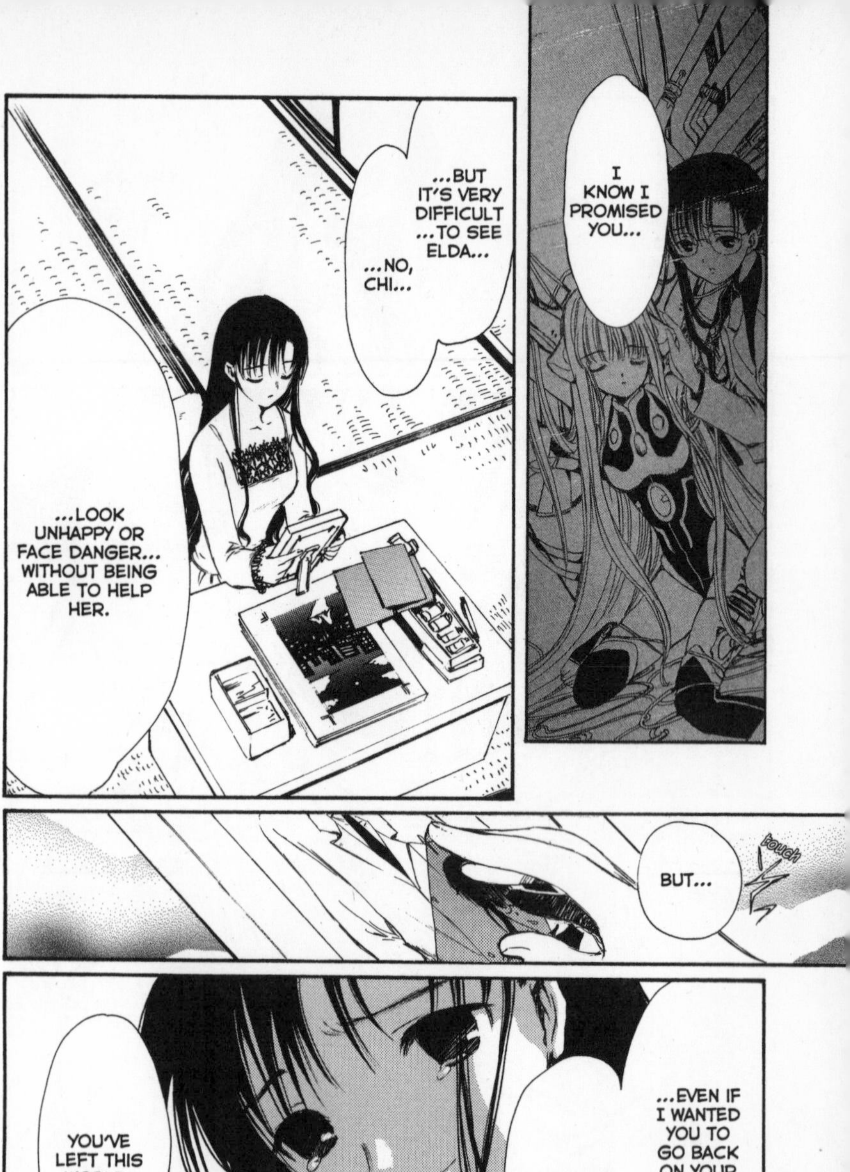
I KNOW I PROMISED YOU...
...BUT IT'S VERY DIFFICULT ...TO SEE ELDA...
...NO, CHI...
...LOOK UNHAPPY OR FACE DANGER... WITHOUT BEING ABLE TO HELP HER.
touch
BUT...
...EVEN IF I WANTED YOU TO GO BACK ON YOUR PROMISE...
...YOU'RE NO LONGER HERE.
YOU'VE LEFT THIS WORLD.

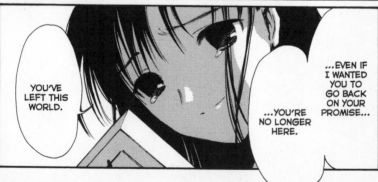

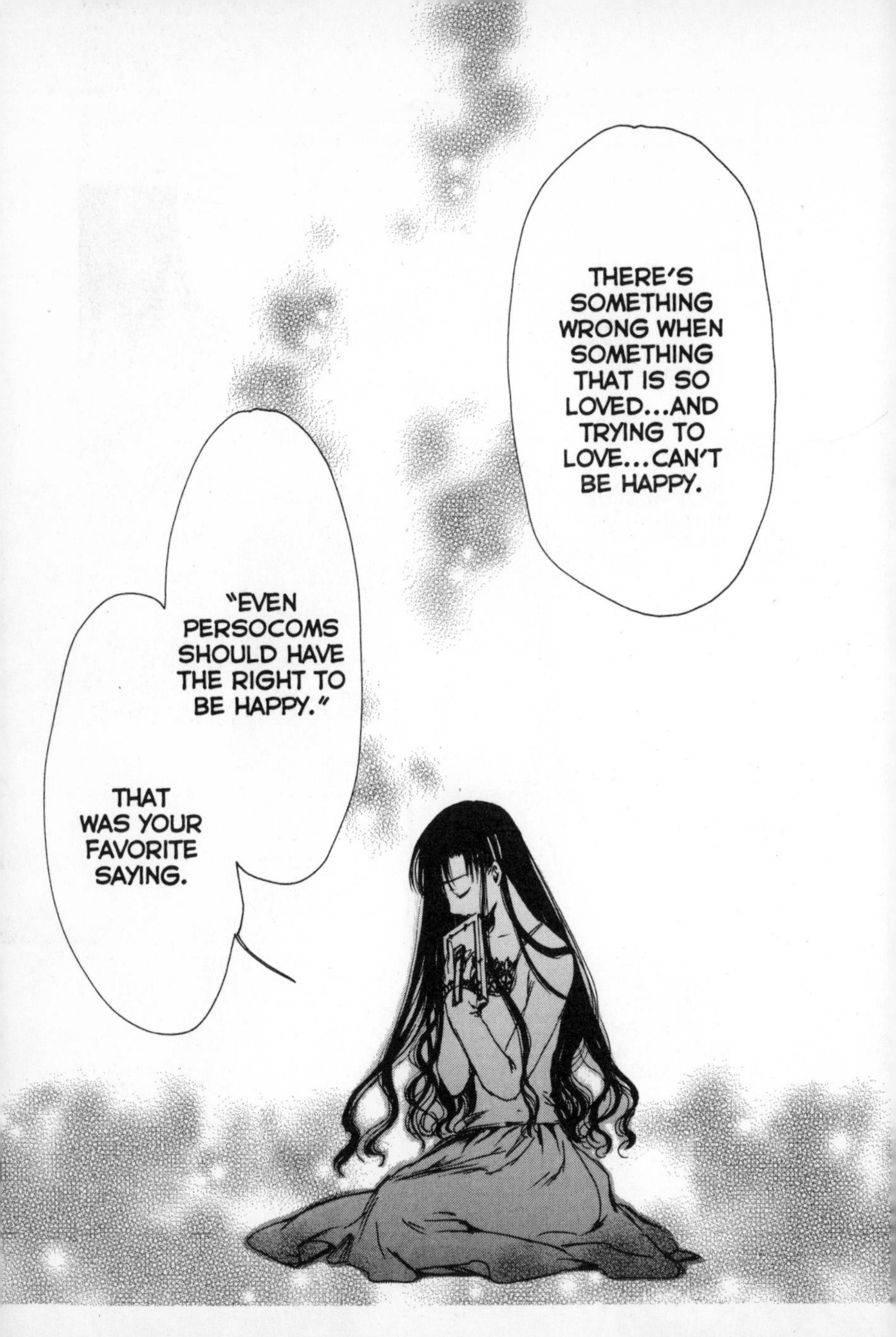
THERE'S SOMETHING WRONG WHEN SOMETHING THAT IS SO LOVED...AND TRYING TO LOVE...CAN'T BE HAPPY.
"EVEN PERSOCOMS SHOULD HAVE THE RIGHT TO BE HAPPY."
THAT WAS YOUR FAVORITE SAYING.

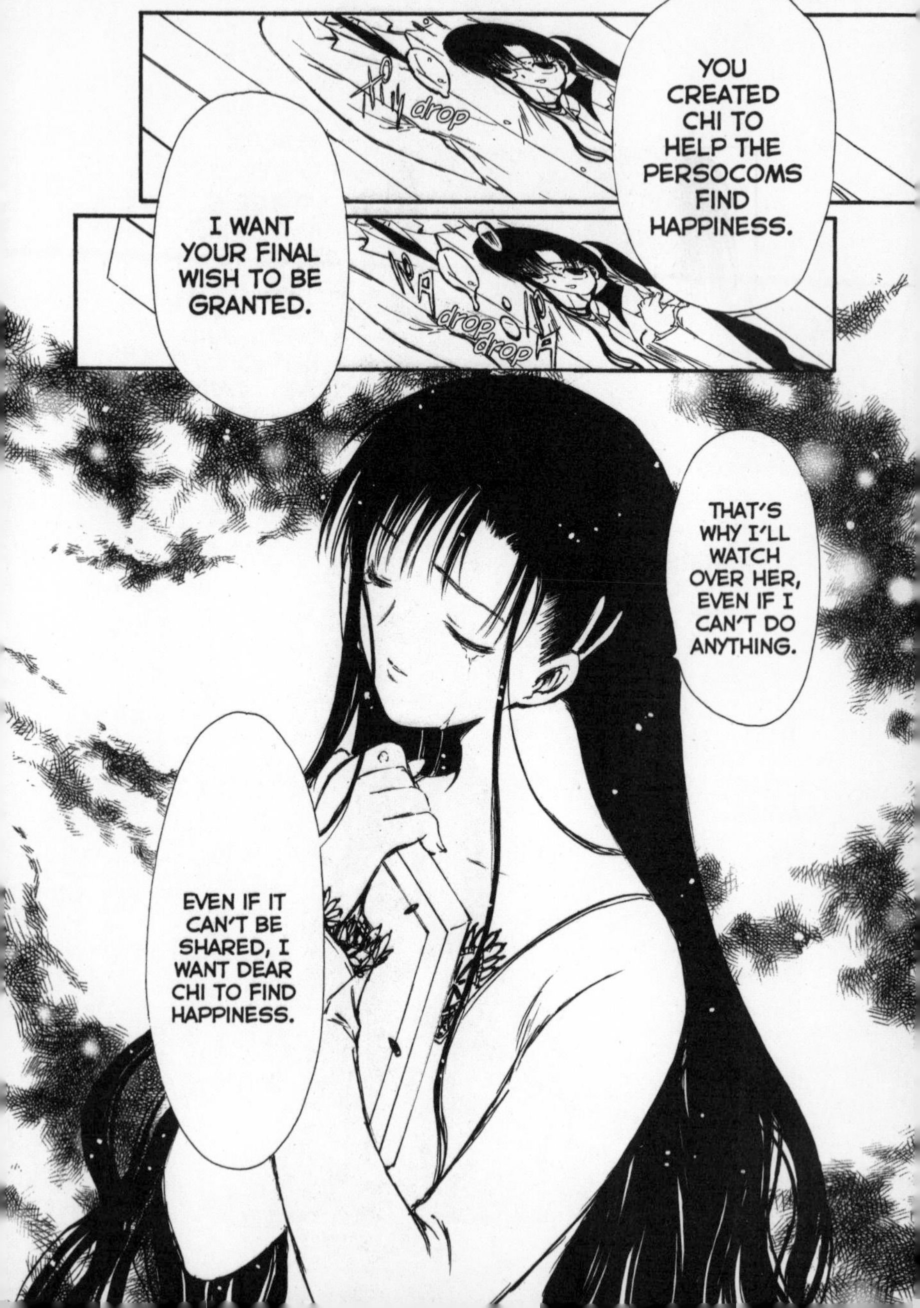
YOU CREATED CHI TO HELP THE PERSOCOMS FIND HAPPINESS.
drop
I WANT YOUR FINAL WISH TO BE GRANTED.
drop
drop
THAT'S WHY I'LL WATCH OVER HER, EVEN IF I CAN'T DO ANYTHING.
EVEN IF IT CAN'T BE SHARED, I WANT DEAR CHI TO FIND HAPPINESS.

Chobits
ちょびっツ

◀ chapter 58 ▶

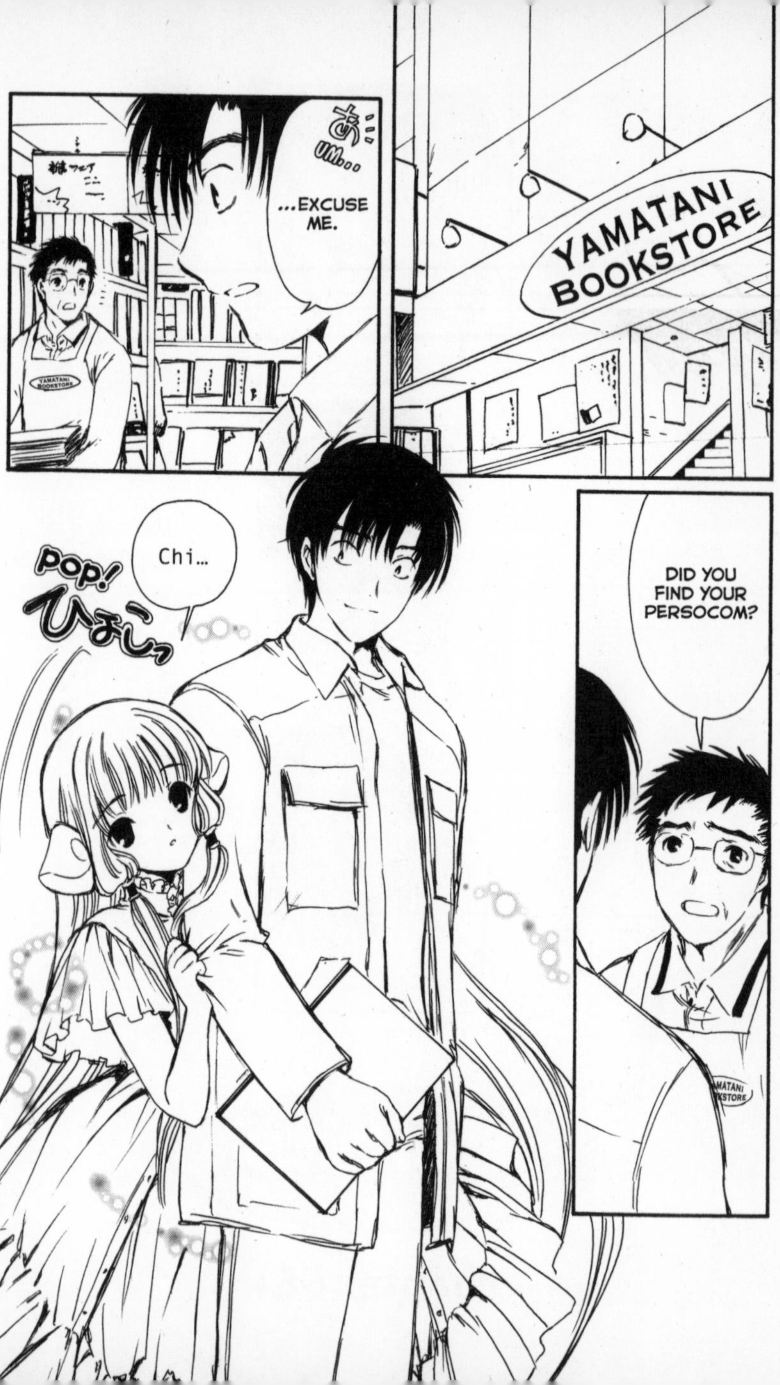
YAMATANI BOOKSTORE
あ
UM...
...EXCUSE ME.
YAMATANI BOOKSTORE
DID YOU FIND YOUR PERSOCOM?
YAMATANI BOOKSTORE
Chi...
POP!
ひょこっ

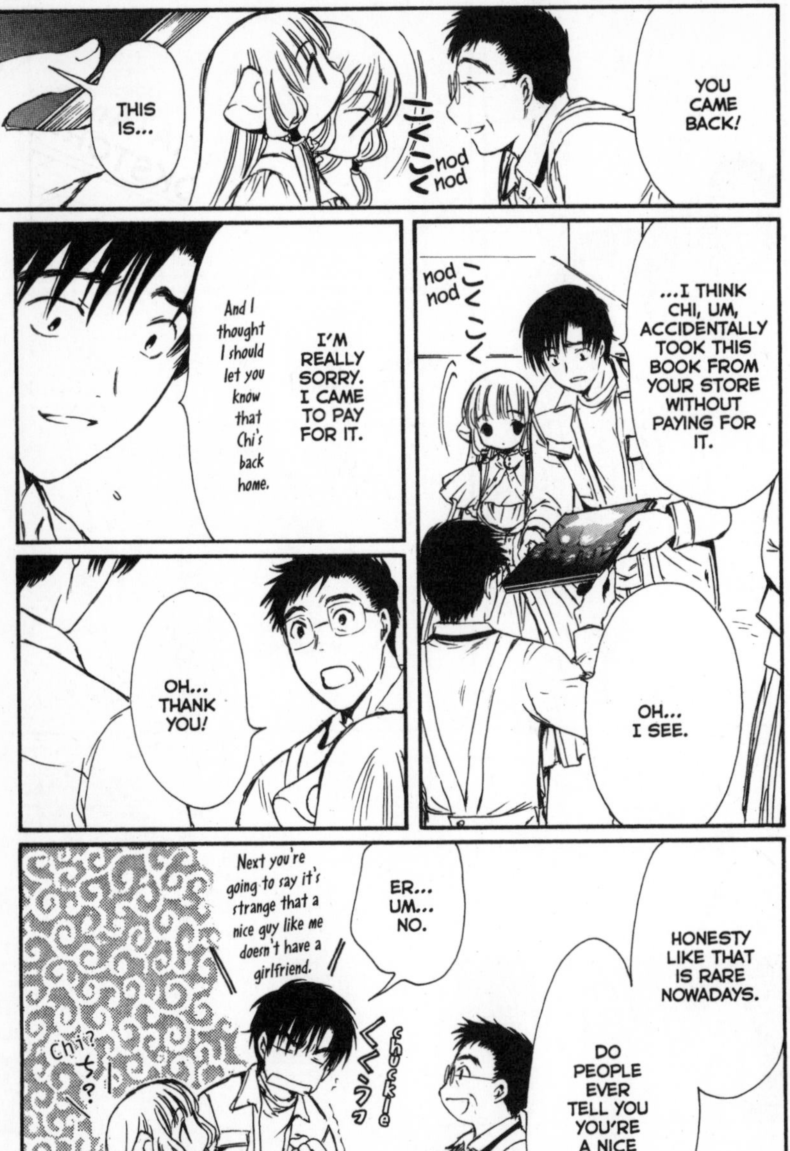
YOU CAME BACK!
nod nod
THIS IS...
...I THINK CHI, UM, ACCIDENTALLY TOOK THIS BOOK FROM YOUR STORE WITHOUT PAYING FOR IT.
nod nod
OH... I SEE.
I'M REALLY SORRY. I CAME TO PAY FOR IT.
And I thought I should let you know that Chi's back home.
OH... THANK YOU!
HONESTY LIKE THAT IS RARE NOWADAYS.
DO PEOPLE EVER TELL YOU YOU'RE A NICE GUY?
ER... UM... NO.
Next you're going to say it's strange that a nice guy like me doesn't have a girlfriend.
chuckle
Chi?
YAMATANI BOOKSTORE

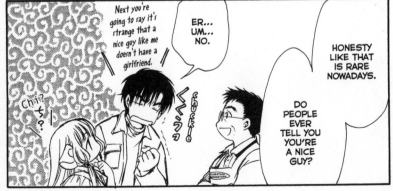

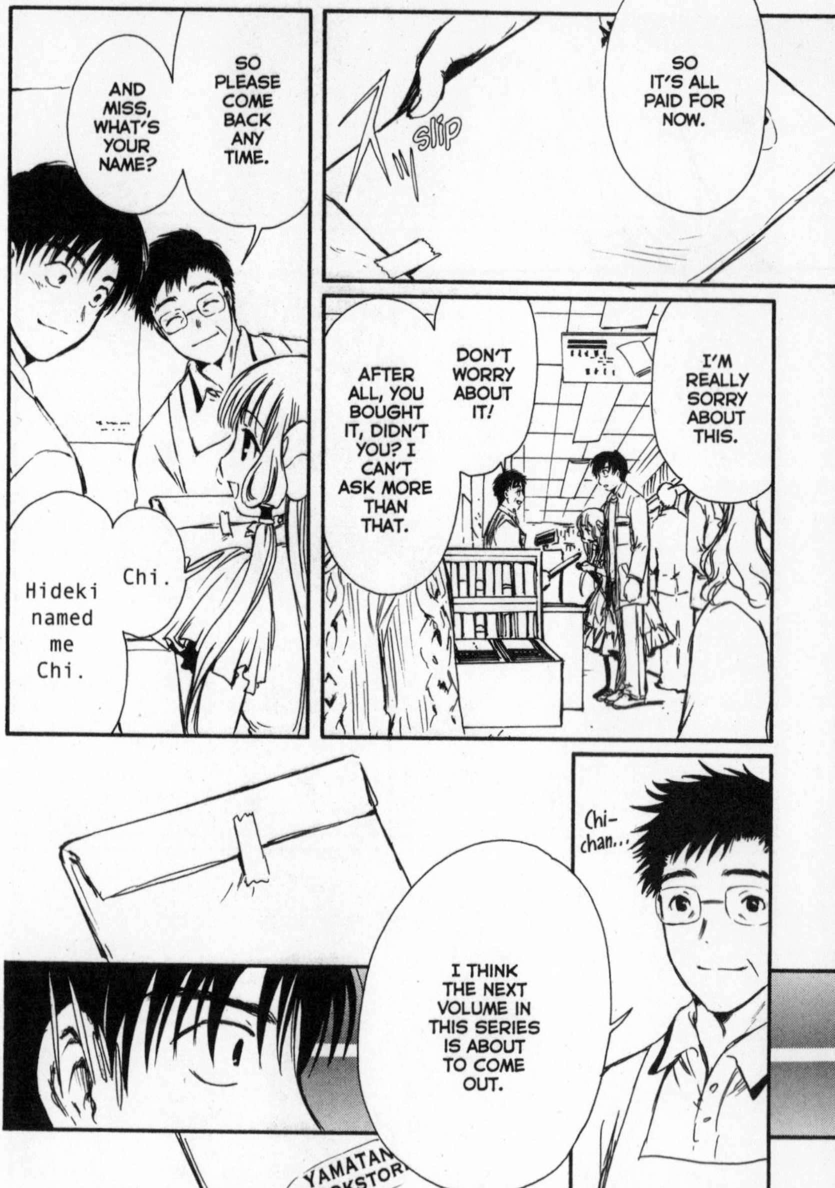
SO IT'S ALL PAID FOR NOW.
slip
I'M REALLY SORRY ABOUT THIS.
DON'T WORRY ABOUT IT!
AFTER ALL, YOU BOUGHT IT, DIDN'T YOU? I CAN'T ASK MORE THAN THAT.
SO PLEASE COME BACK ANY TIME.
AND MISS, WHAT'S YOUR NAME?
Chi.
Hideki named me Chi.
Chi-chan...
I THINK THE NEXT VOLUME IN THIS SERIES IS ABOUT TO COME OUT.
YAMATANI
YAMATAN BOOKSTOR

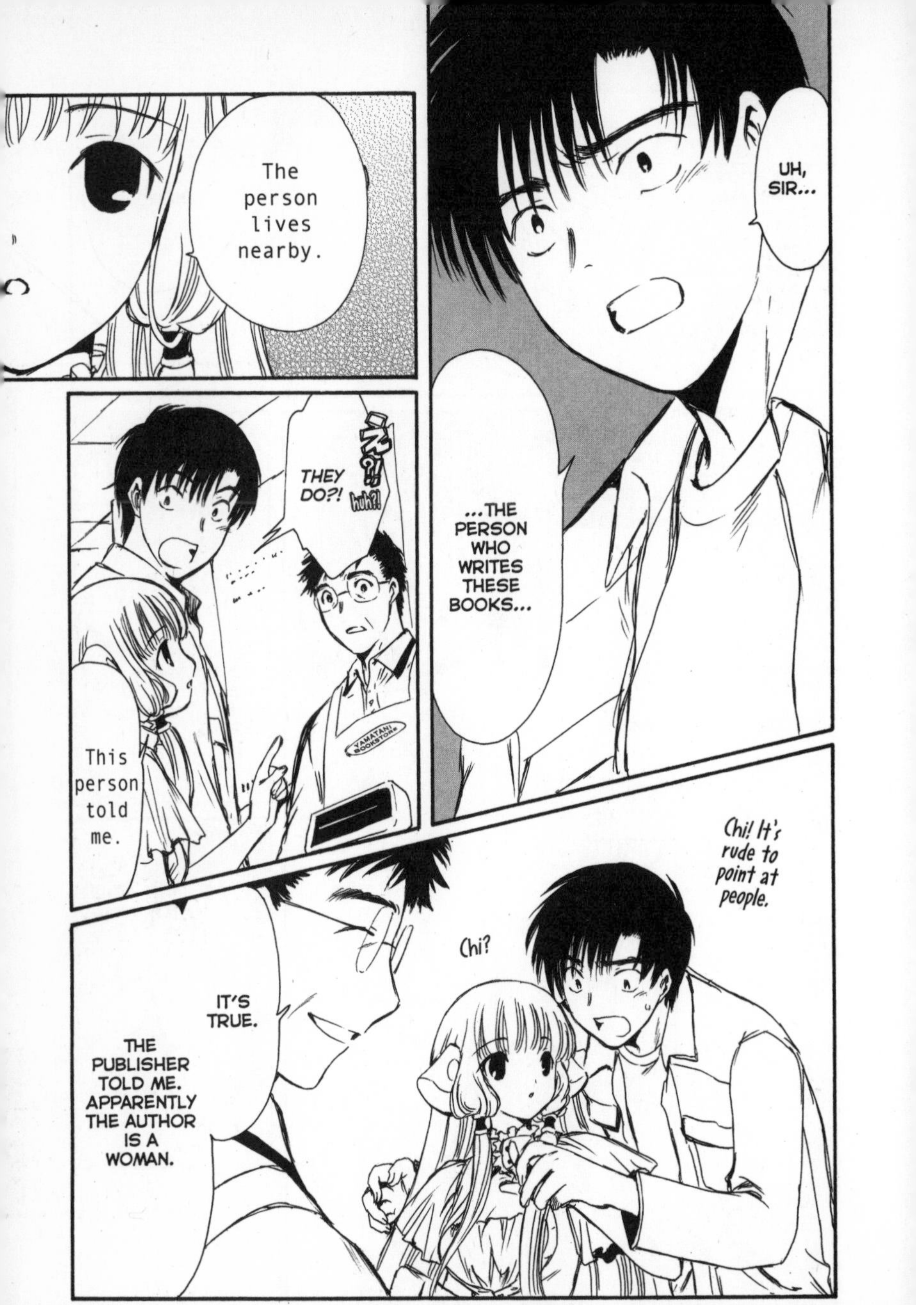
UH, SIR...
...THE PERSON WHO WRITES THESE BOOKS...
The person lives nearby.
THEY DO?!
huh?!
This person told me.
Chi! It's rude to point at people.
Chi?
IT'S TRUE.
THE PUBLISHER TOLD ME. APPARENTLY THE AUTHOR IS A WOMAN.

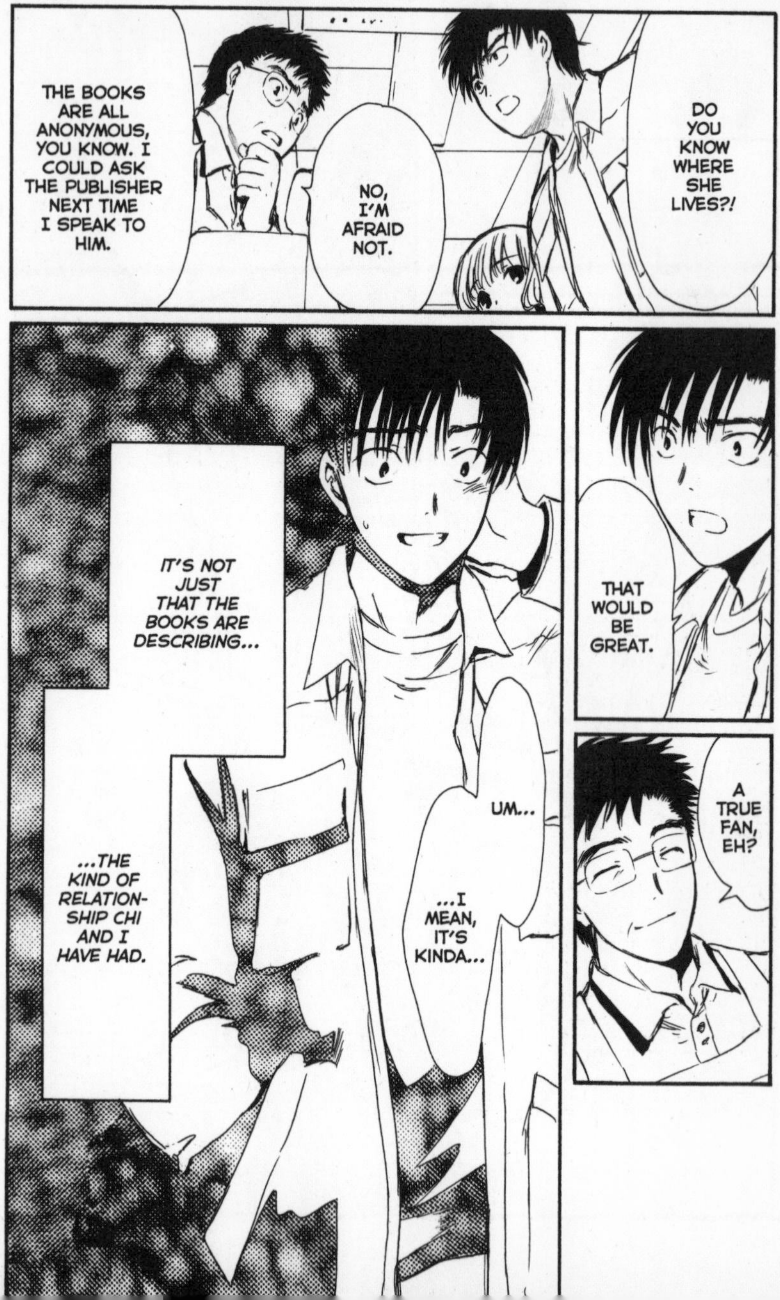
DO YOU KNOW WHERE SHE LIVES?!
NO, I'M AFRAID NOT.
THE BOOKS ARE ALL ANONYMOUS, YOU KNOW. I COULD ASK THE PUBLISHER NEXT TIME I SPEAK TO HIM.
THAT WOULD BE GREAT.
A TRUE FAN, EH?
UM...
...I MEAN, IT'S KINDA...
IT'S NOT JUST THAT THE BOOKS ARE DESCRIBING...
...THE KIND OF RELATIONSHIP CHI AND I HAVE HAD.

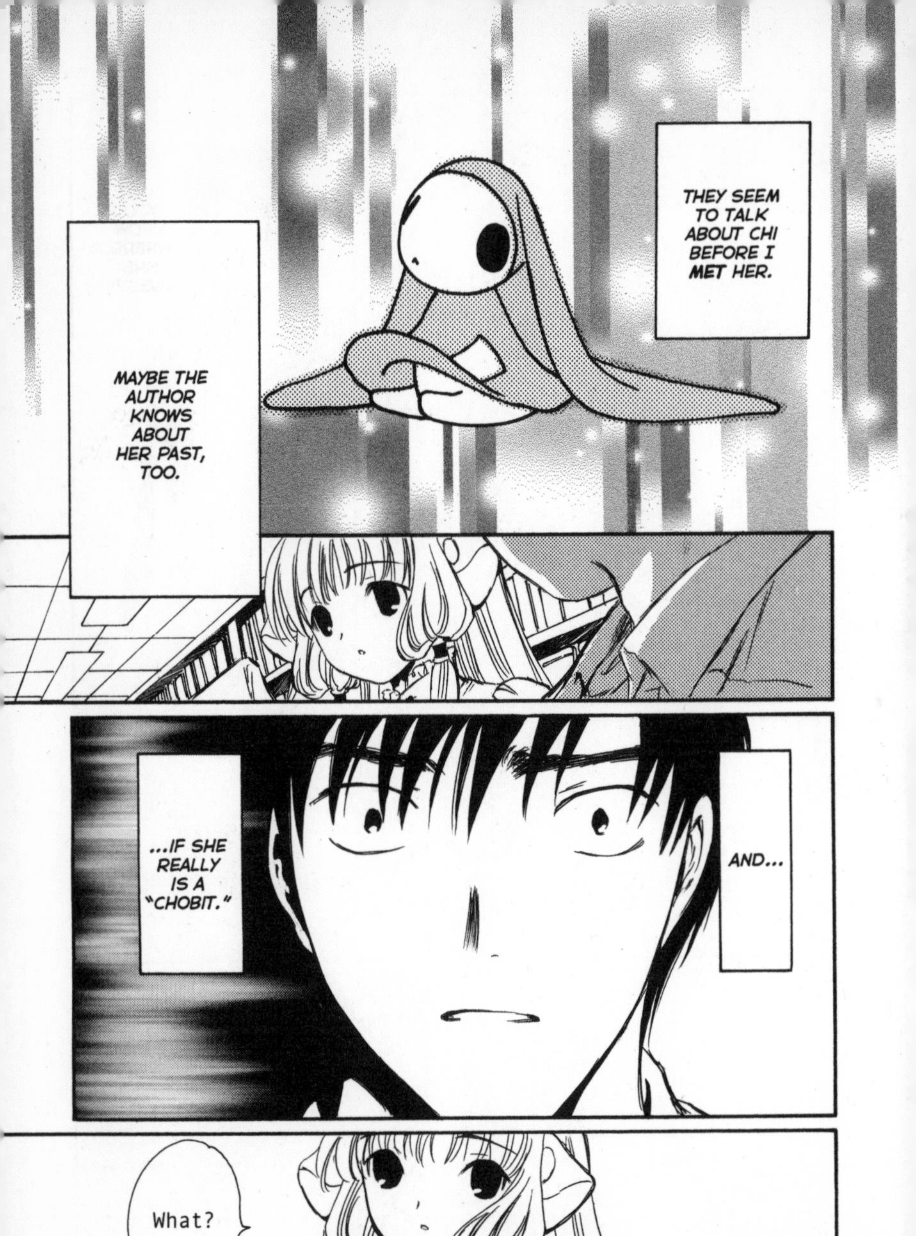
THEY SEEM TO TALK ABOUT CHI BEFORE I MET HER.
MAYBE THE AUTHOR KNOWS ABOUT HER PAST, TOO.
AND...
...IF SHE REALLY IS A "CHOBIT."
What?

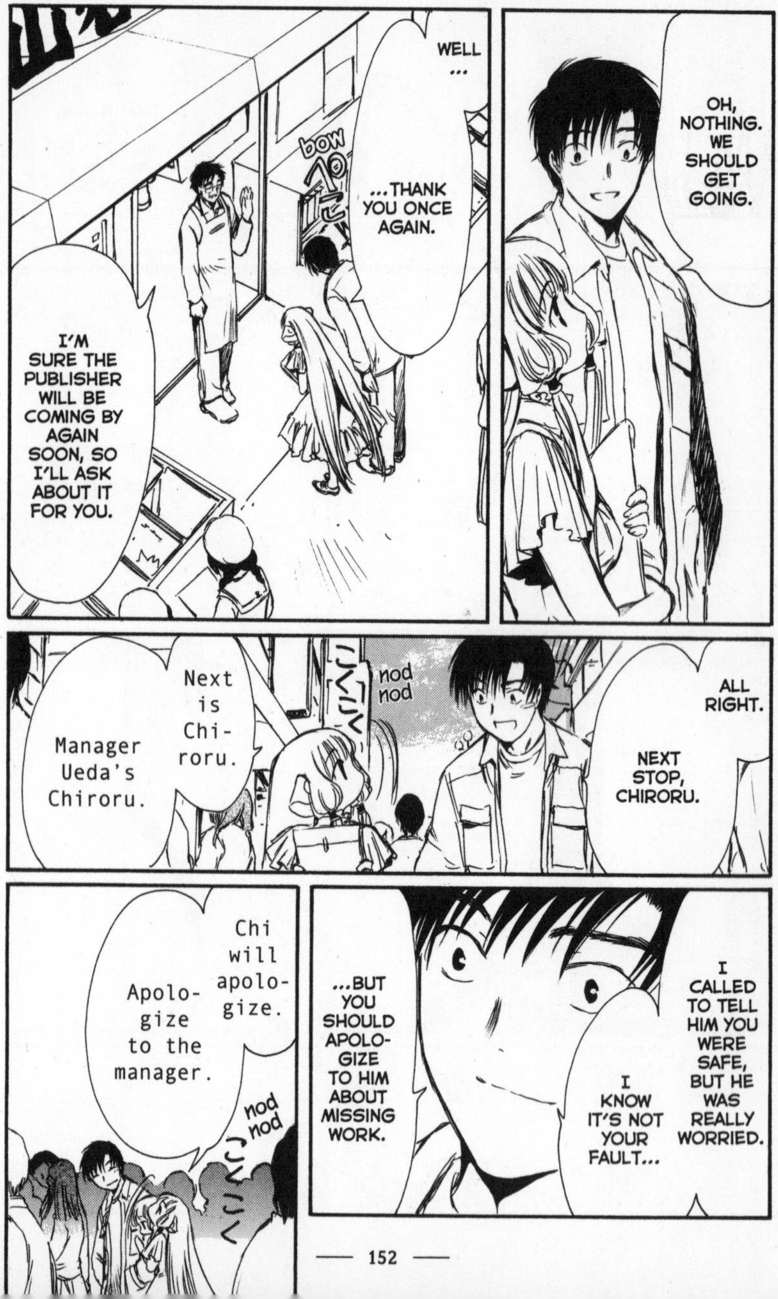
OH, NOTHING. WE SHOULD GET GOING.
WELL...
...THANK YOU ONCE AGAIN.
bow
I'M SURE THE PUBLISHER WILL BE COMING BY AGAIN SOON, SO I'LL ASK ABOUT IT FOR YOU.
ALL RIGHT.
NEXT STOP, CHIRORU.
nod nod
Next is Chi-roru.
Manager Ueda's Chiroru.
I CALLED TO TELL HIM YOU WERE SAFE, BUT HE WAS REALLY WORRIED.
I KNOW IT'S NOT YOUR FAULT...
...BUT YOU SHOULD APOLOGIZE TO HIM ABOUT MISSING WORK.
Chi will apolo-gize.
Apolo-gize to the manager.
nod nod

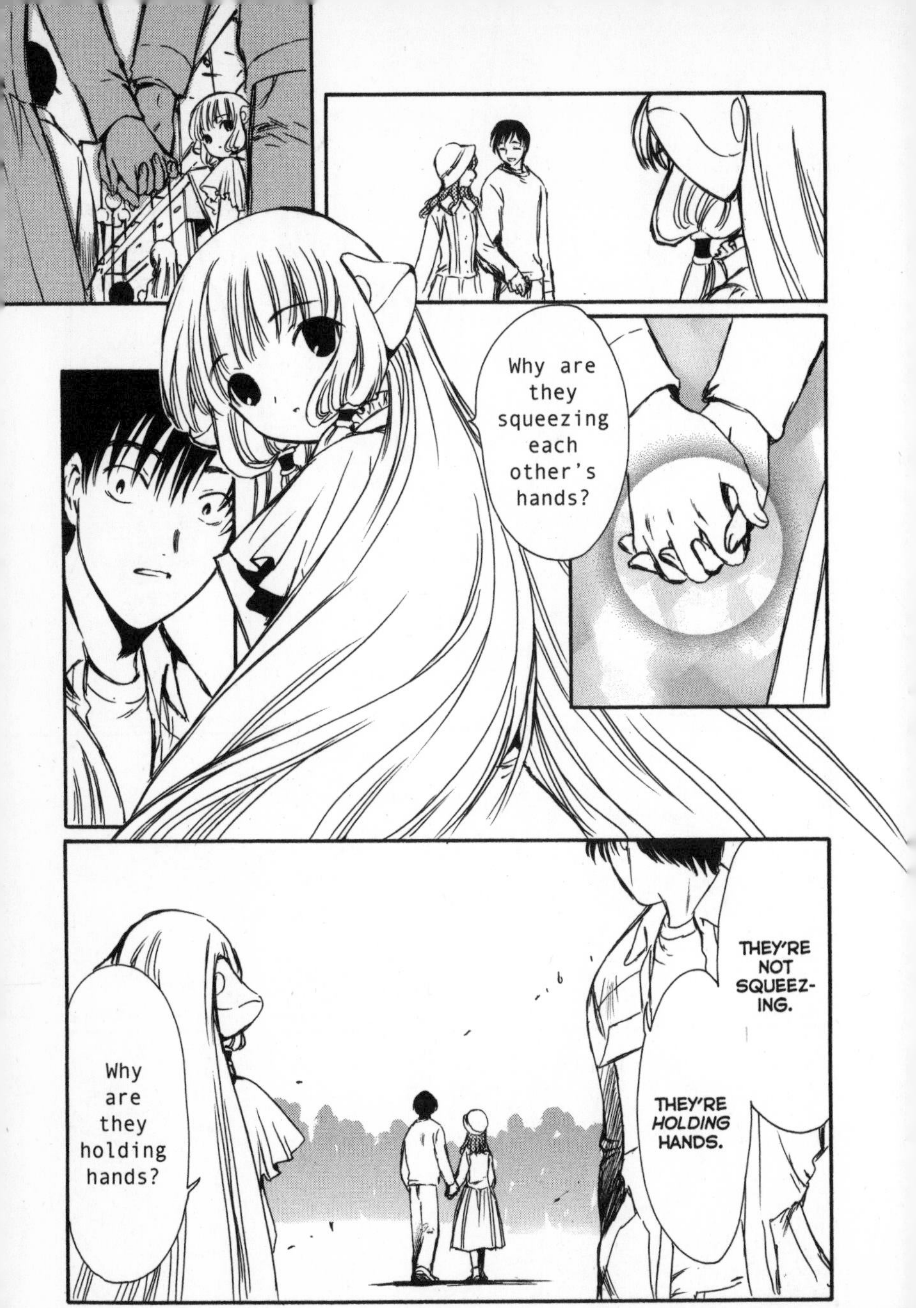
Why are they squeezing each other's hands?
THEY'RE NOT SQUEEZ-ING.
THEY'RE *HOLDING* HANDS.
Why are they holding hands?

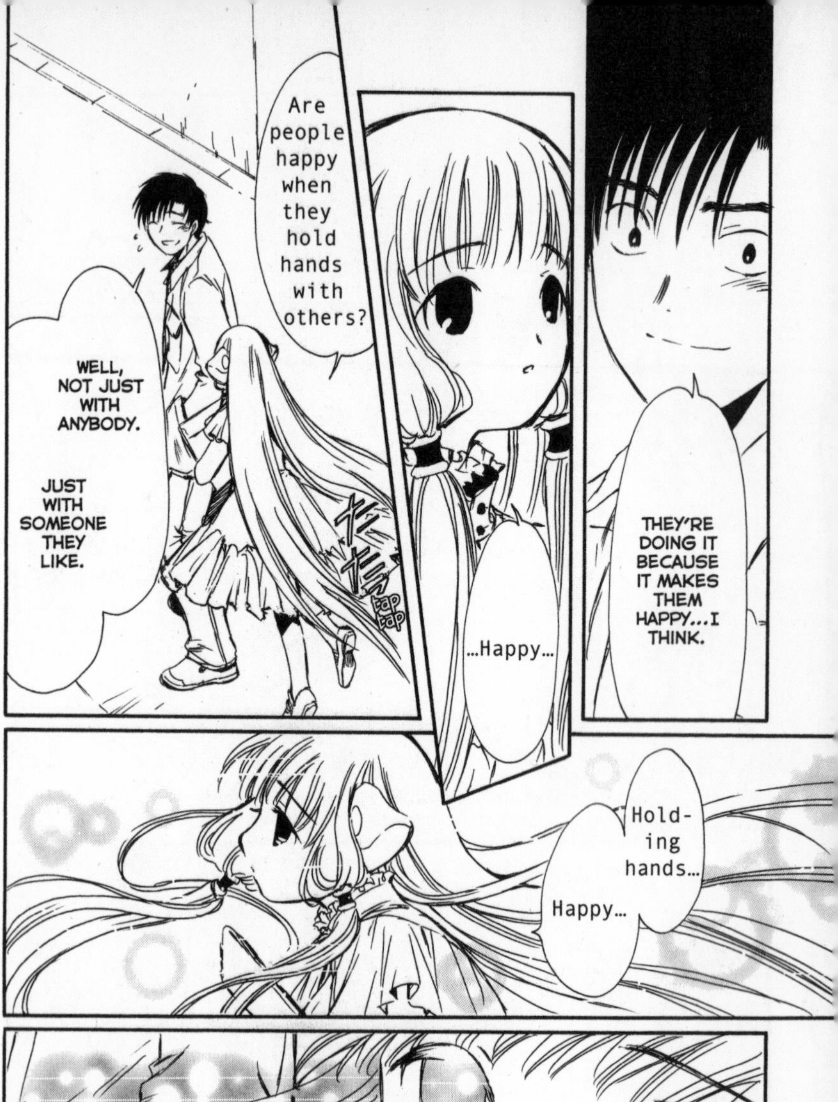
THEY'RE DOING IT BECAUSE IT MAKES THEM HAPPY...I THINK.
...Happy...
Are people happy when they hold hands with others?
tap tap
WELL, NOT JUST WITH ANYBODY.
JUST WITH SOMEONE THEY LIKE.
Hold-ing hands...
Happy...

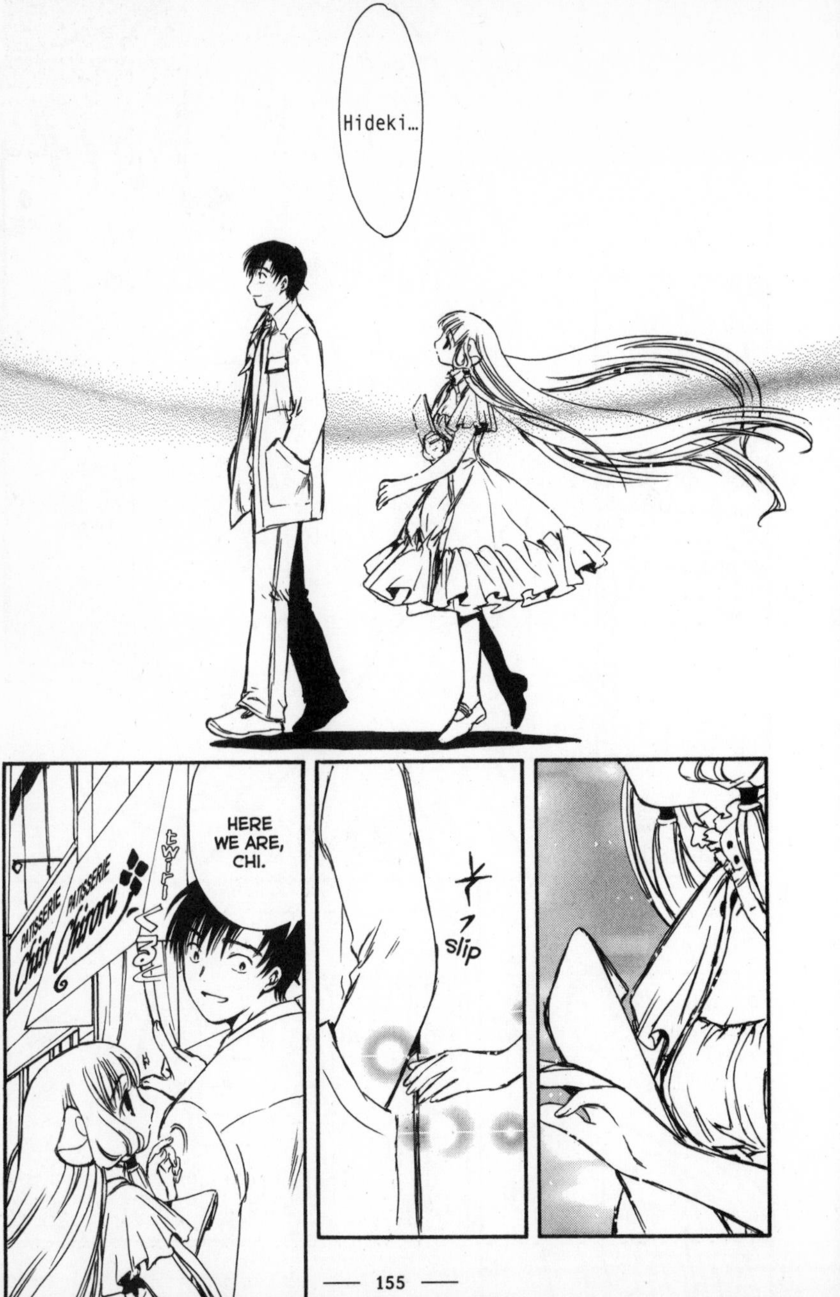
Hideki…
slip
HERE WE ARE, CHI.
twirl
PATISSERIE Chiroru

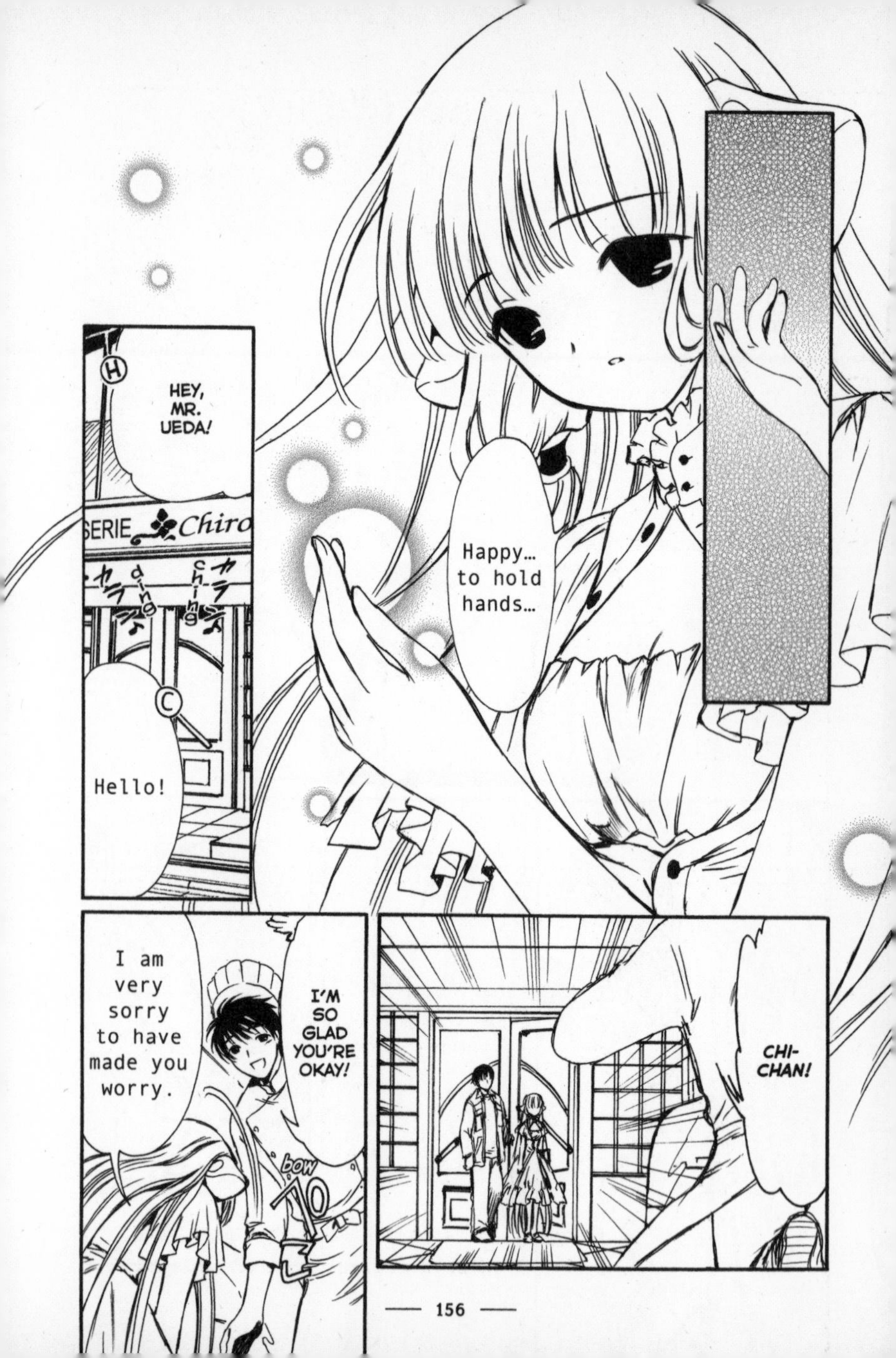
Happy… to hold hands…
HEY, MR. UEDA!
ching
ding
Hello!
CHI-CHAN!
I'M SO GLAD YOU'RE OKAY!
I am very sorry to have made you worry.
bow

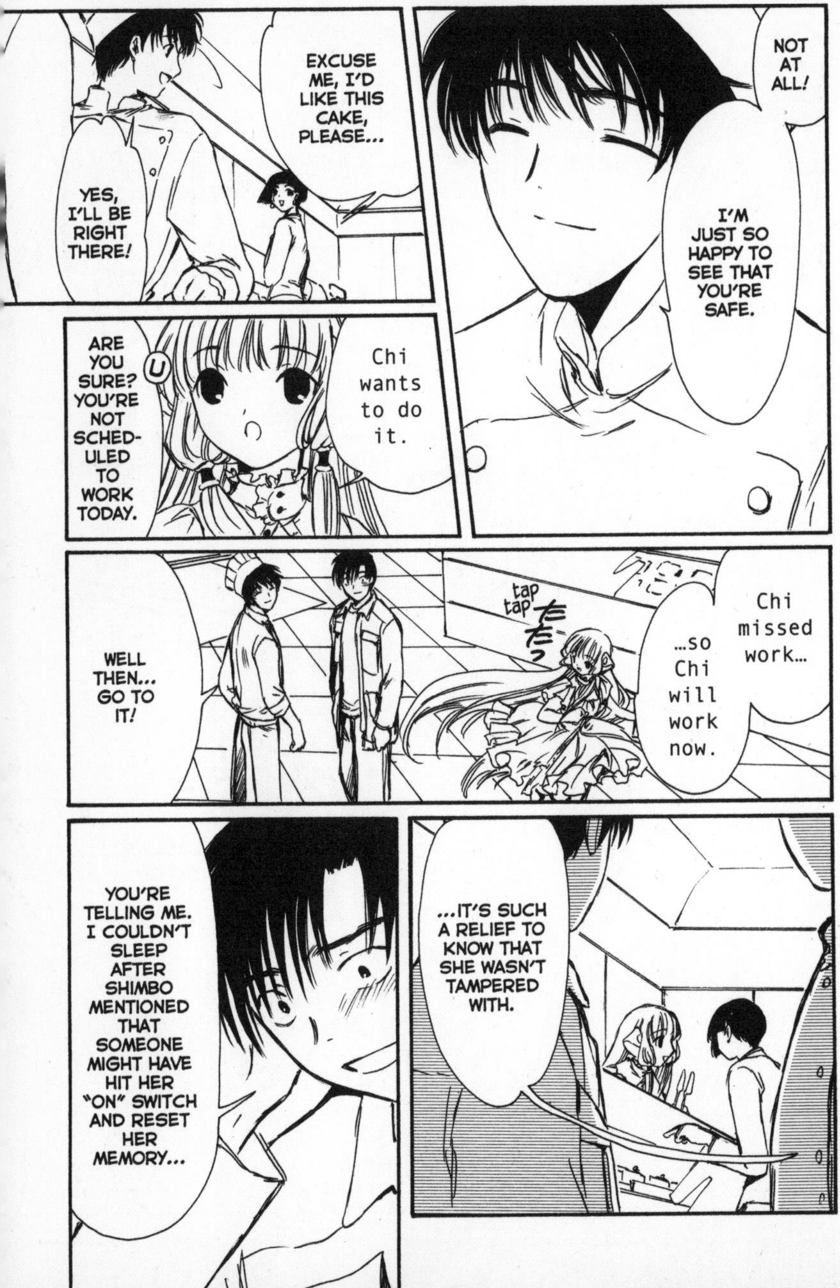

NOT AT ALL!
I'M JUST SO HAPPY TO SEE THAT YOU'RE SAFE.
EXCUSE ME, I'D LIKE THIS CAKE, PLEASE...
YES, I'LL BE RIGHT THERE!
Chi wants to do it.
ARE YOU SURE? YOU'RE NOT SCHED-ULED TO WORK TODAY.
Chi missed work...
...so Chi will work now.
tap tap
WELL THEN... GO TO IT!
...IT'S SUCH A RELIEF TO KNOW THAT SHE WASN'T TAMPERED WITH.
YOU'RE TELLING ME. I COULDN'T SLEEP AFTER SHIMBO MENTIONED THAT SOMEONE MIGHT HAVE HIT HER "ON" SWITCH AND RESET HER MEMORY...

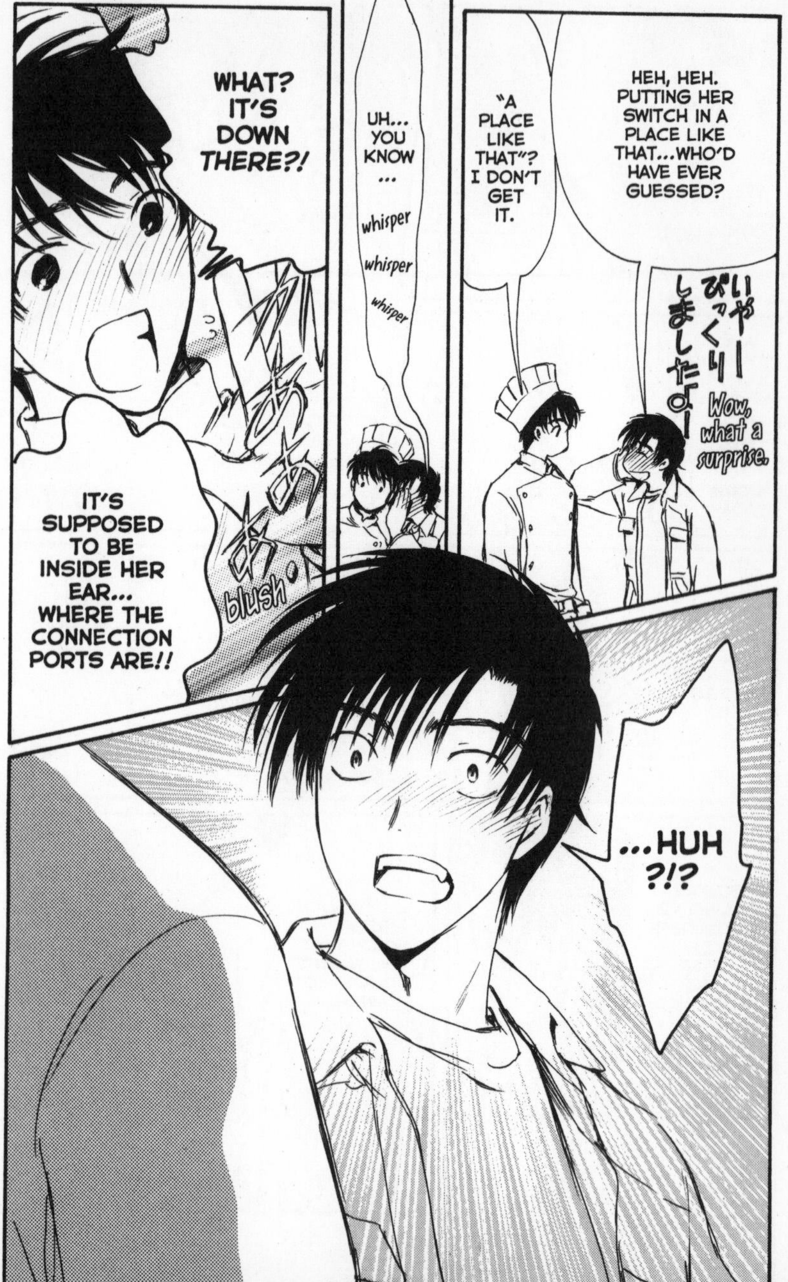
HEH, HEH. PUTTING HER SWITCH IN A PLACE LIKE THAT...WHO'D HAVE EVER GUESSED?
"A PLACE LIKE THAT"? I DON'T GET IT.
いやーびっくりしましたよー
Wow, what a surprise.
UH... YOU KNOW ...
whisper
whisper
whisper
WHAT? IT'S DOWN THERE?!
IT'S SUPPOSED TO BE INSIDE HER EAR... WHERE THE CONNECTION PORTS ARE!!
blush
...HUH ?!?

Chobits
ちょびっツ

◀ **chapter 59** ▶

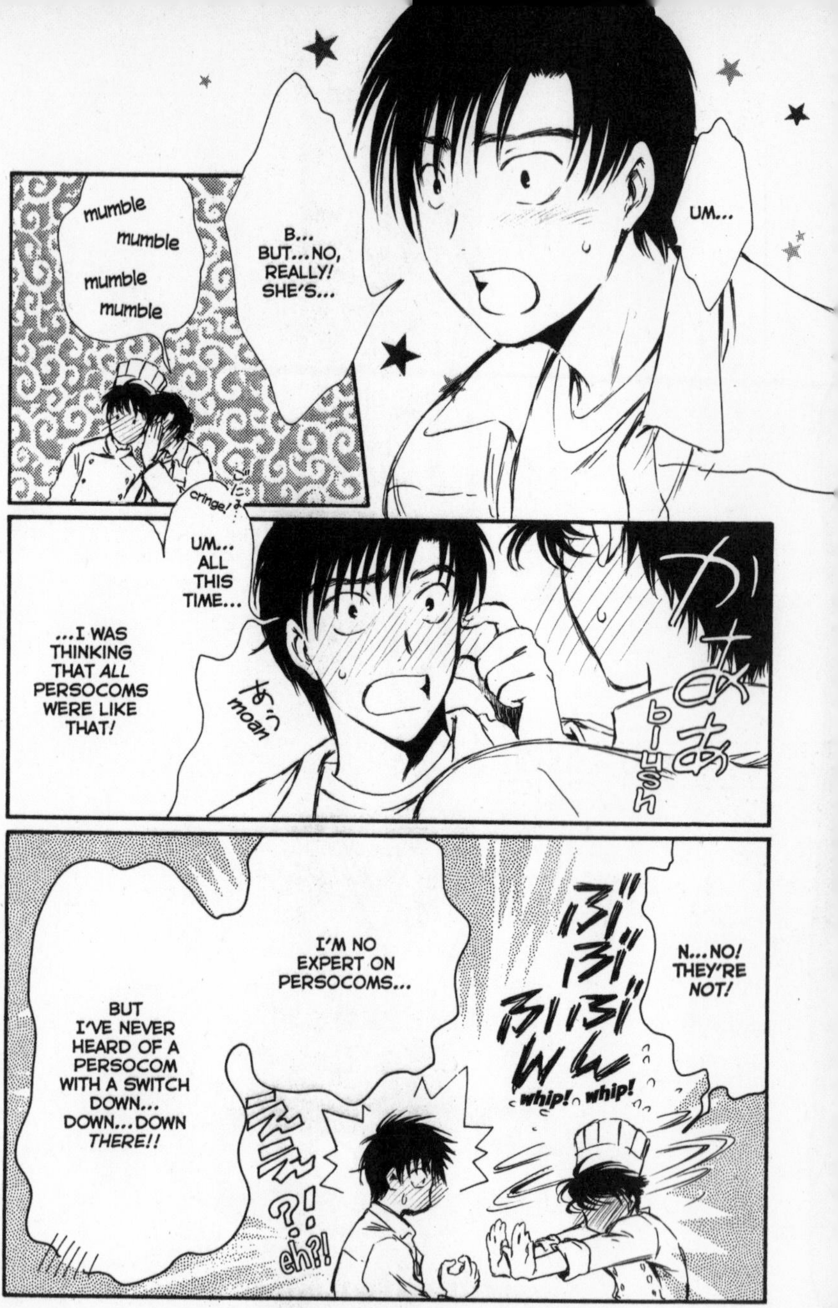
UM...
B... BUT... NO, REALLY! SHE'S...
mumble mumble mumble mumble
cringe!
UM... ALL THIS TIME...
...I WAS THINKING THAT *ALL* PERSOCOMS WERE LIKE THAT!
moan
blush
N... NO! THEY'RE *NOT*!
whip! whip!
I'M NO EXPERT ON PERSOCOMS...
BUT I'VE NEVER HEARD OF A PERSOCOM WITH A SWITCH DOWN... DOWN... DOWN *THERE*!!
?!
eh?!

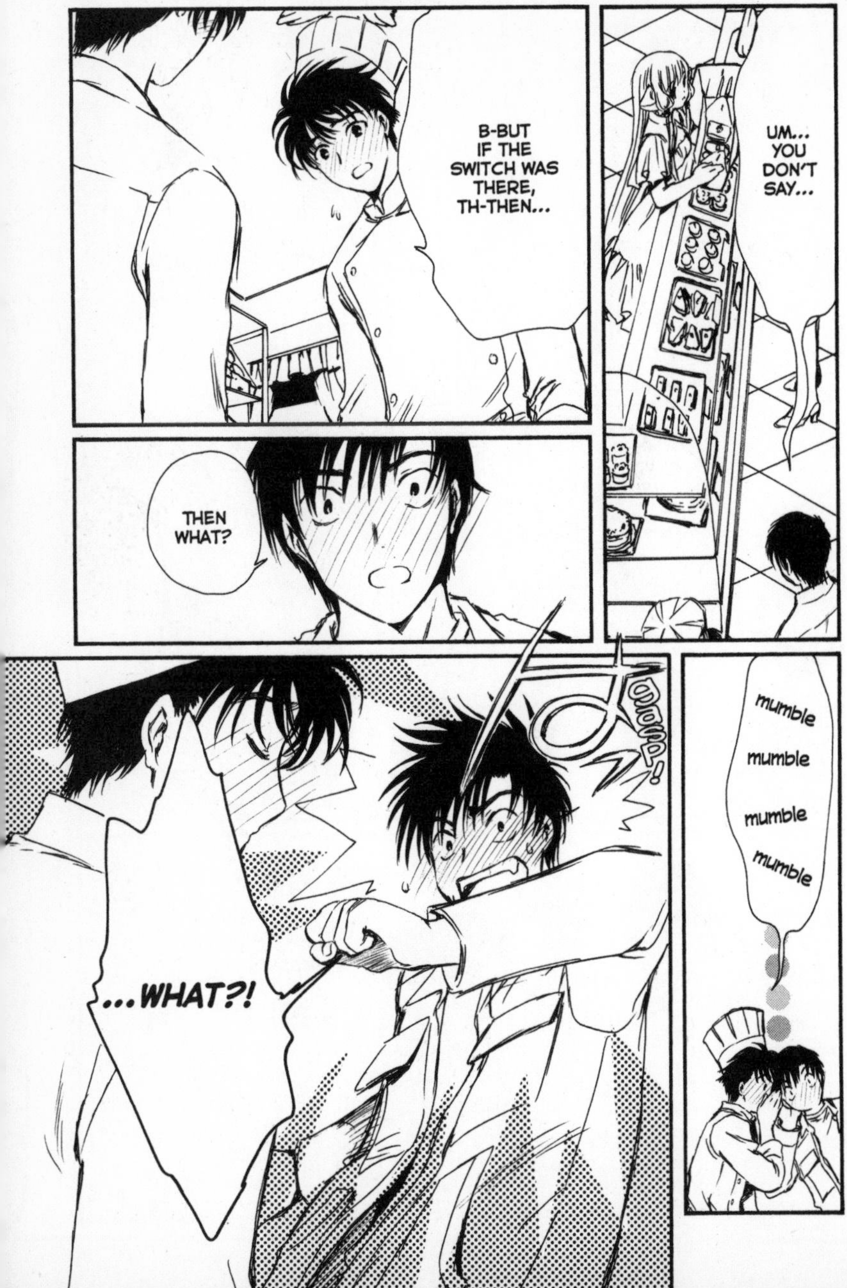
UM... YOU DON'T SAY...
B-BUT IF THE SWITCH WAS THERE, TH-THEN...
THEN WHAT?
mumble mumble mumble mumble
GASP!
...WHAT?!

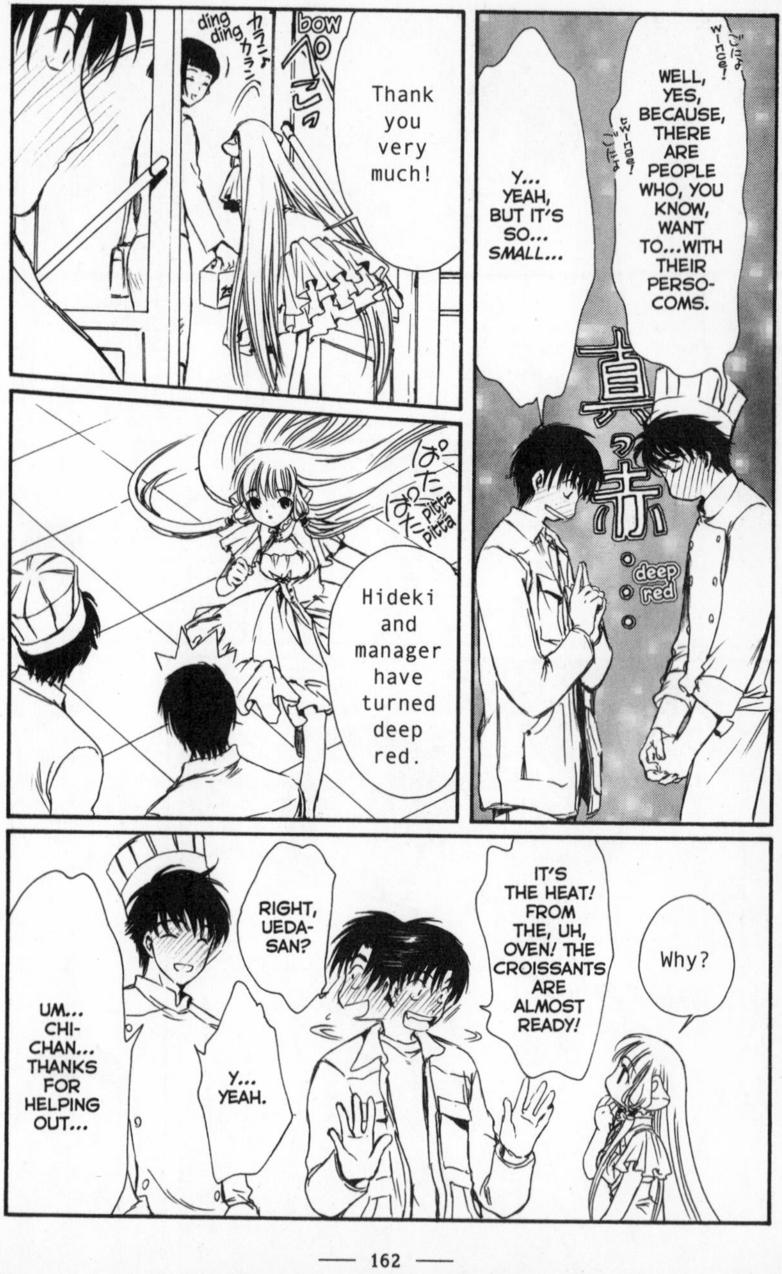
wince!
WELL, YES, BECAUSE, THERE ARE PEOPLE WHO, YOU KNOW, WANT TO...WITH THEIR PERSO-COMS.
twinge!
Y... YEAH, BUT IT'S SO... SMALL...
真っ赤
deep red
bow
ペコッ
Thank you very much!
カランカラン
ding ding
ぱたぱた
pitta pitta
Hideki and manager have turned deep red.
Why?
IT'S THE HEAT! FROM THE, UH, OVEN! THE CROISSANTS ARE ALMOST READY!
RIGHT, UEDA-SAN?
Y... YEAH.
UM... CHI-CHAN... THANKS FOR HELPING OUT...

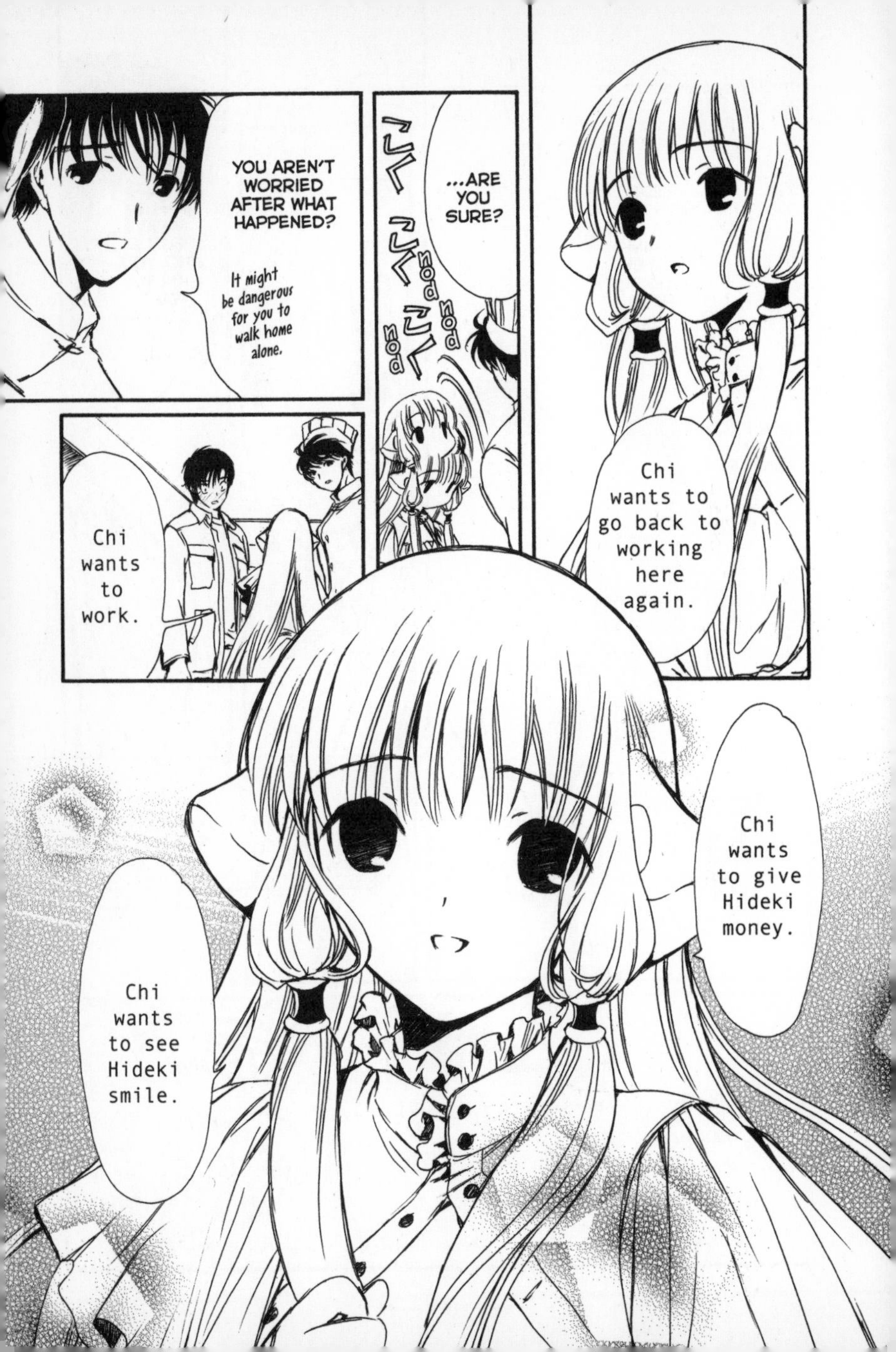
Chi wants to go back to working here again.
...ARE YOU SURE?
こく こく こく
nod nod nod
YOU AREN'T WORRIED AFTER WHAT HAPPENED?
It might be dangerous for you to walk home alone.
Chi wants to work.
Chi wants to give Hideki money.
Chi wants to see Hideki smile.

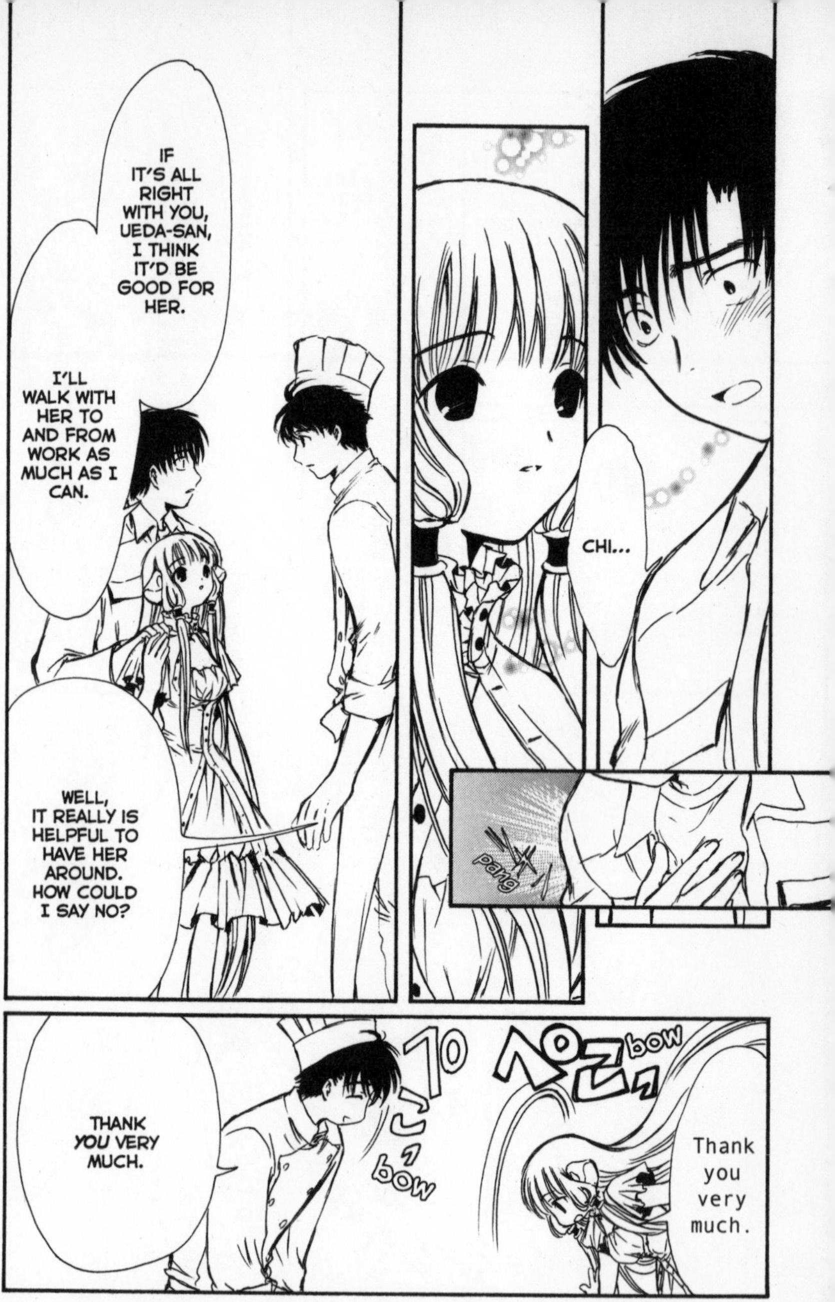
CHI...
pang
IF IT'S ALL RIGHT WITH YOU, UEDA-SAN, I THINK IT'D BE GOOD FOR HER.
I'LL WALK WITH HER TO AND FROM WORK AS MUCH AS I CAN.
WELL, IT REALLY IS HELPFUL TO HAVE HER AROUND. HOW COULD I SAY NO?
bow
Thank you very much.
bow
THANK *YOU* VERY MUCH.

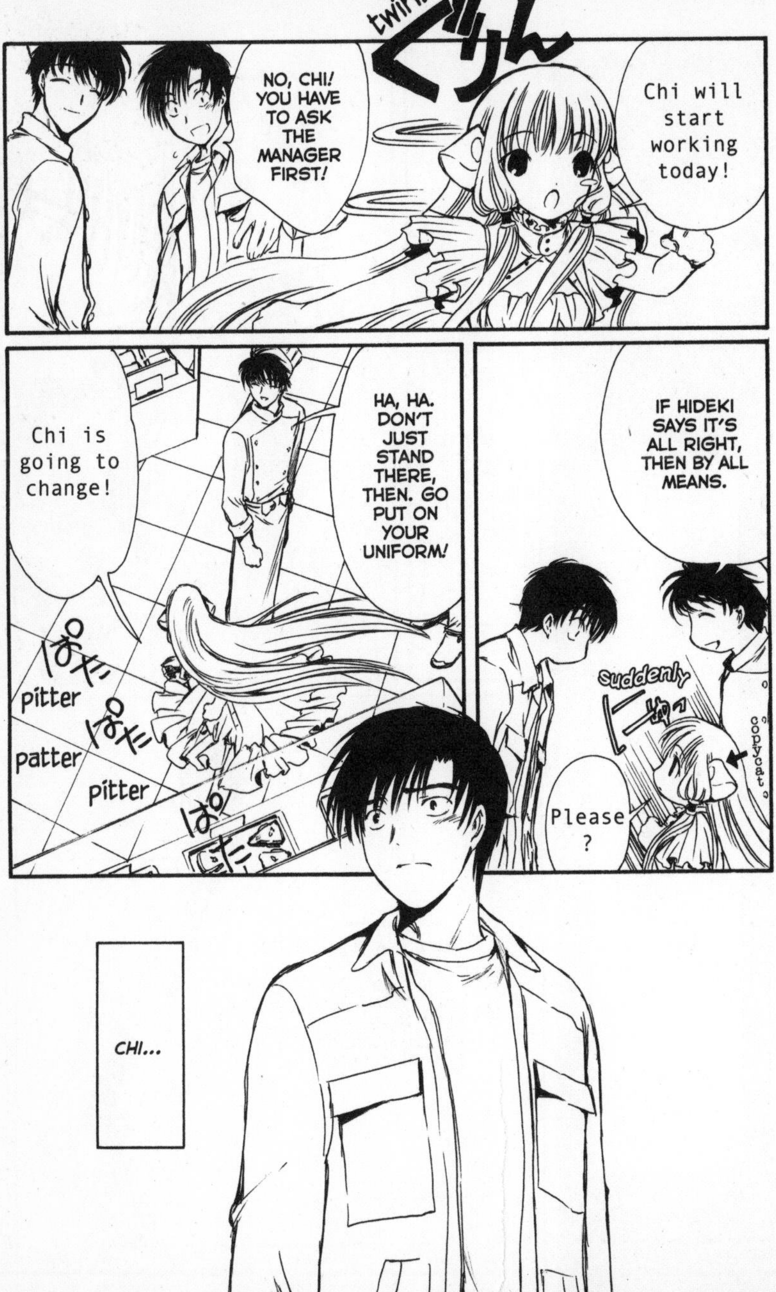
twirl!
ぐりん
Chi will start working today!
NO, CHI! YOU HAVE TO ASK THE MANAGER FIRST!
IF HIDEKI SAYS IT'S ALL RIGHT, THEN BY ALL MEANS.
suddenly
copycat
Please?
HA, HA. DON'T JUST STAND THERE, THEN. GO PUT ON YOUR UNIFORM!
Chi is going to change!
pitter
patter
pitter
CHI...

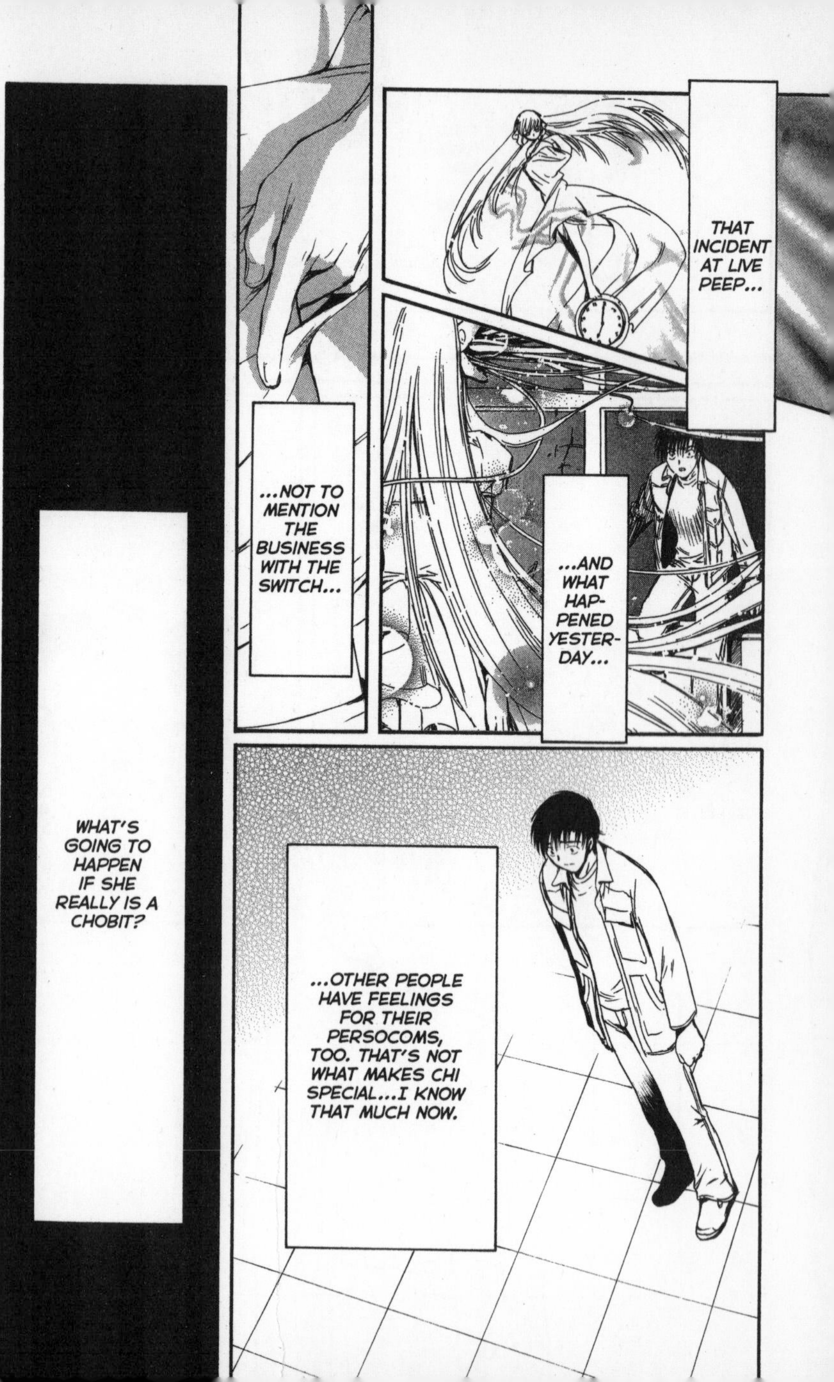
THAT INCIDENT AT LIVE PEEP...
...AND WHAT HAP-PENED YESTER-DAY...
...NOT TO MENTION THE BUSINESS WITH THE SWITCH...
...OTHER PEOPLE HAVE FEELINGS FOR THEIR PERSOCOMS, TOO. THAT'S NOT WHAT MAKES CHI SPECIAL...I KNOW THAT MUCH NOW.
WHAT'S GOING TO HAPPEN IF SHE REALLY IS A CHOBIT?

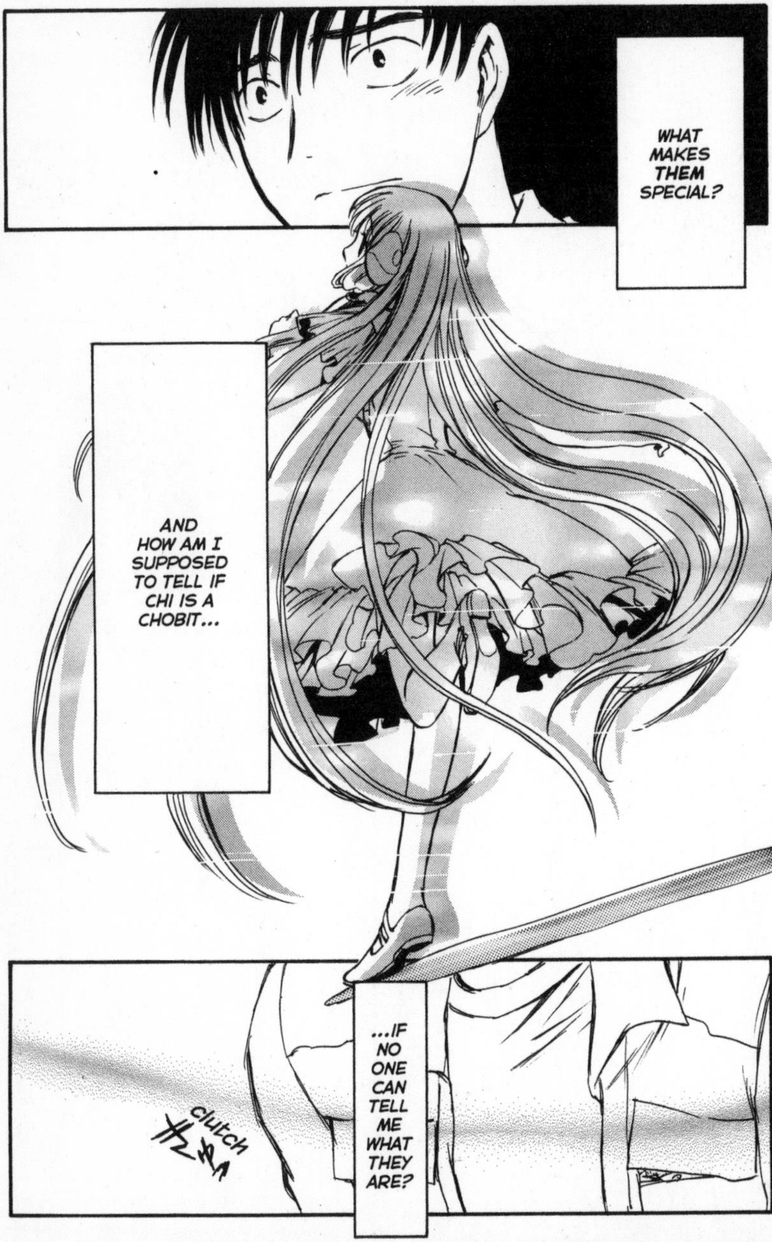
WHAT MAKES THEM SPECIAL?
AND HOW AM I SUPPOSED TO TELL IF CHI IS A CHOBIT...
...IF NO ONE CAN TELL ME WHAT THEY ARE?
clutch

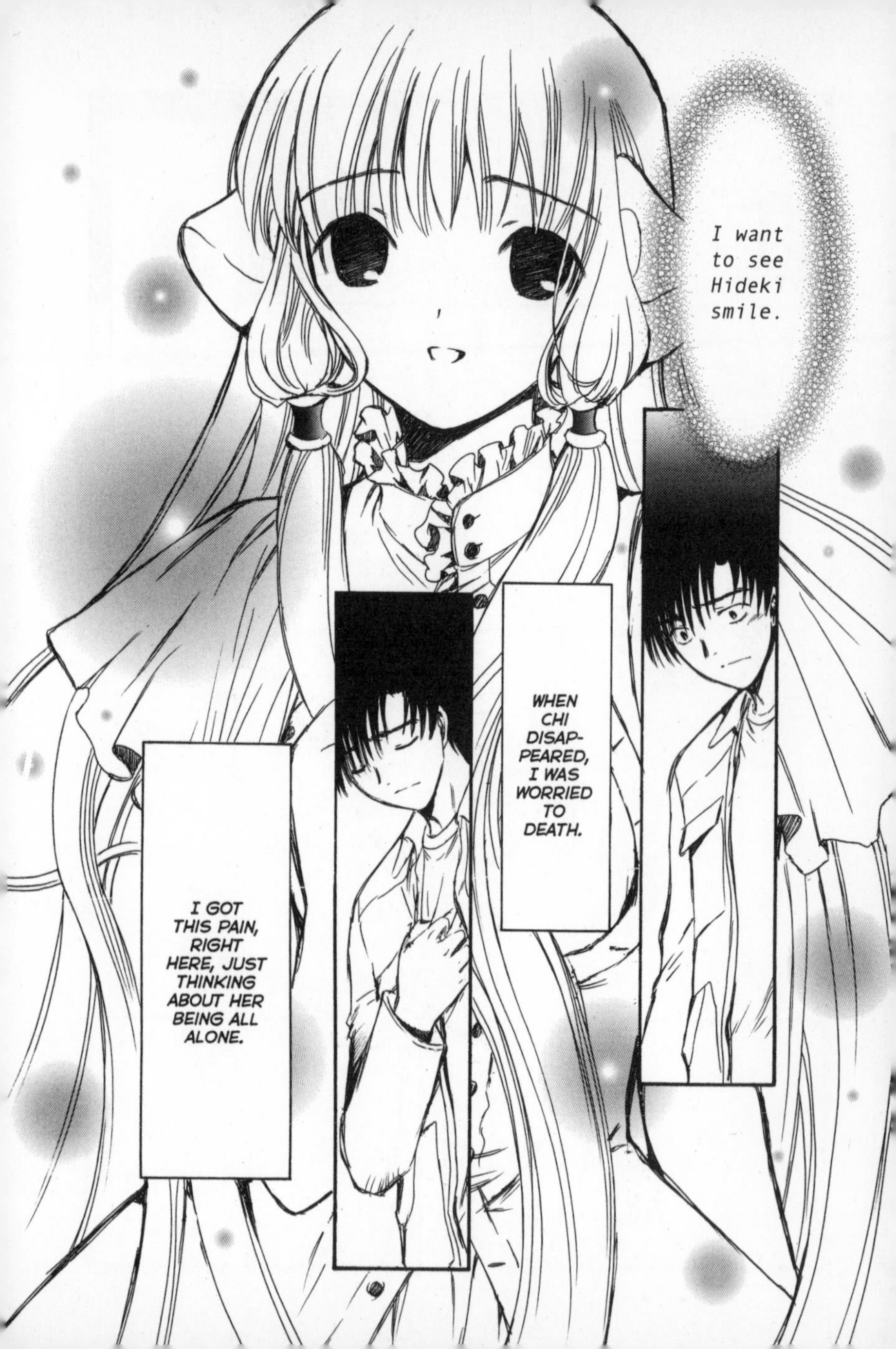
I want to see Hideki smile.
WHEN CHI DISAPPEARED, I WAS WORRIED TO DEATH.
I GOT THIS PAIN, RIGHT HERE, JUST THINKING ABOUT HER BEING ALL ALONE.

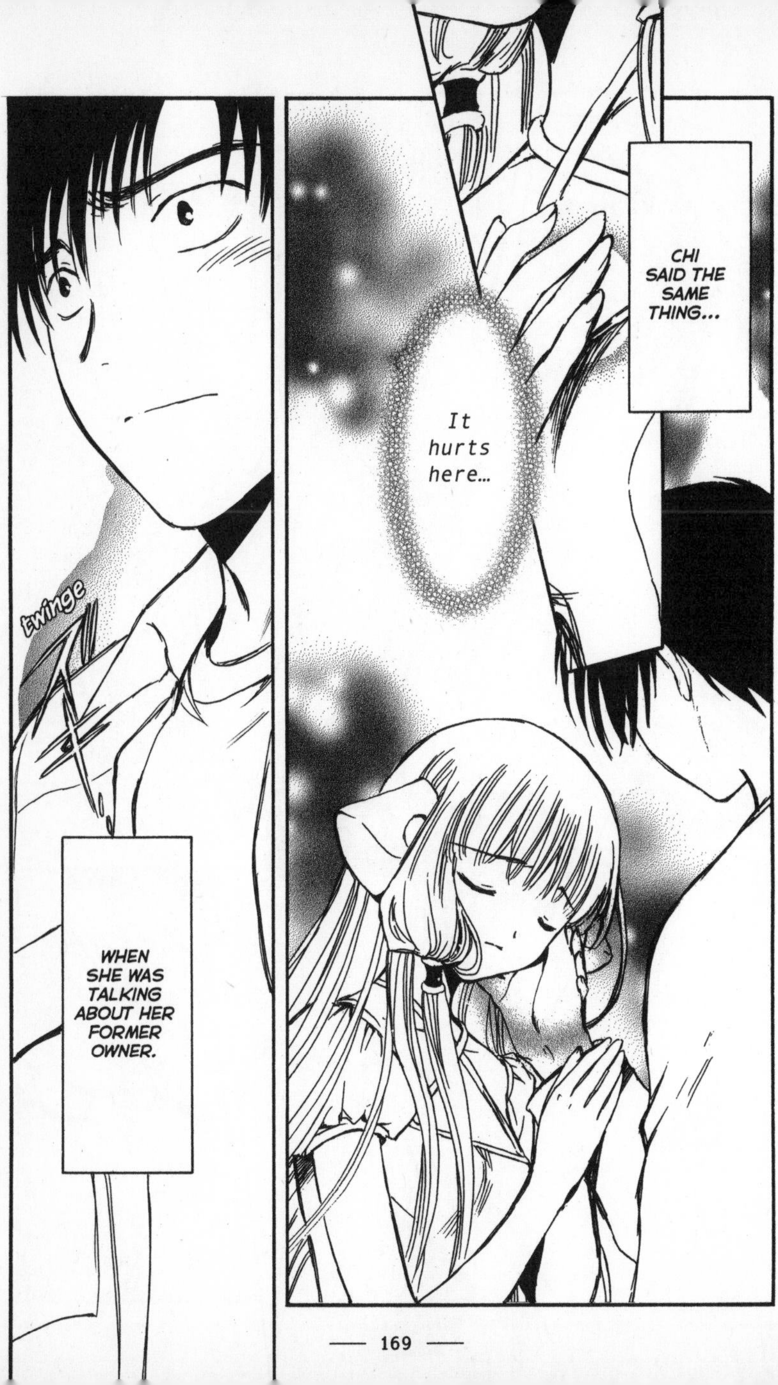
CHI SAID THE SAME THING...
It hurts here...
twinge
WHEN SHE WAS TALKING ABOUT HER FORMER OWNER.

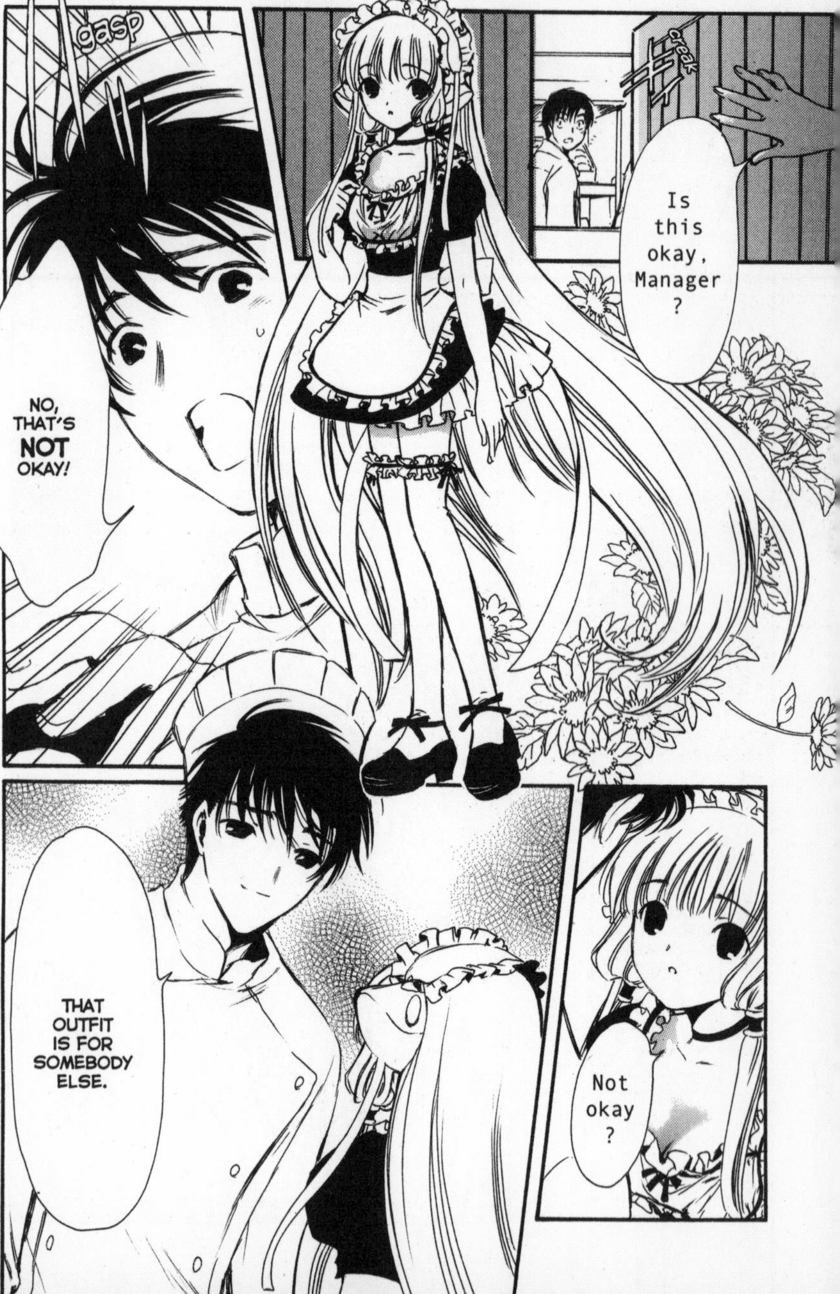
creak
Is this okay, Manager?
gasp
NO, THAT'S **NOT** OKAY!
Not okay?
THAT OUTFIT IS FOR SOMEBODY ELSE.

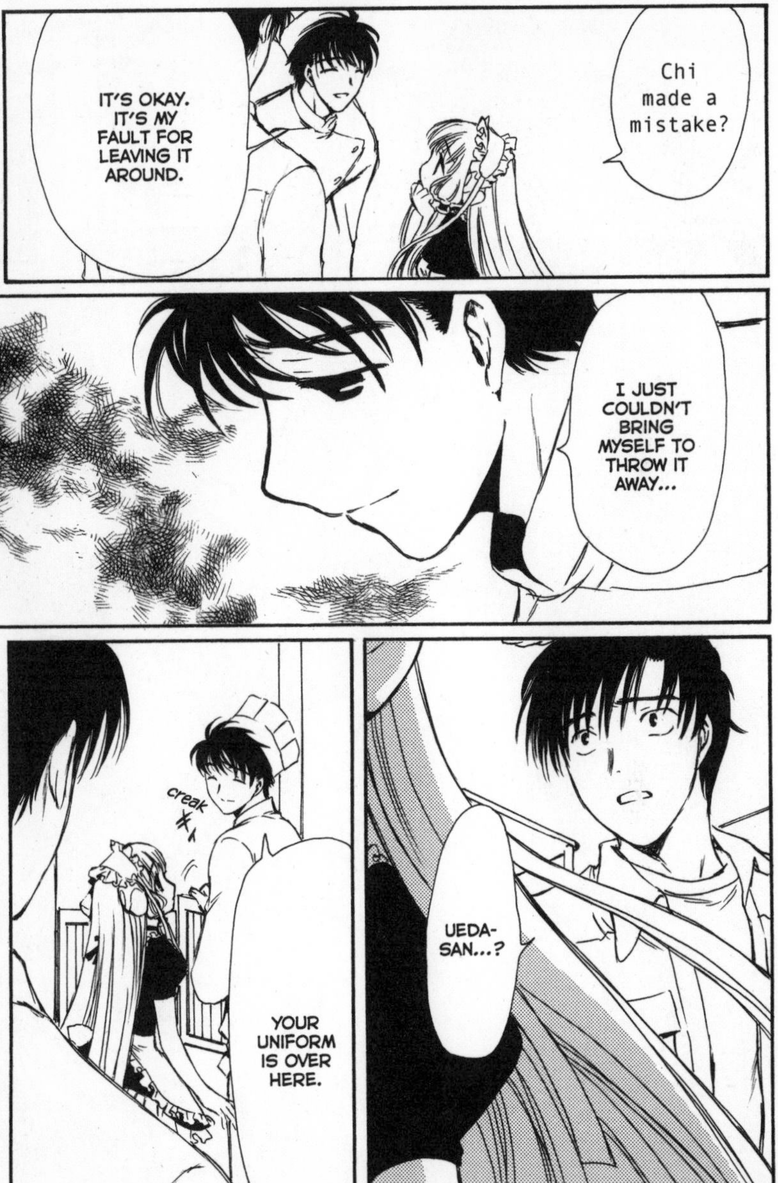
Chi made a mistake?
IT'S OKAY. IT'S MY FAULT FOR LEAVING IT AROUND.
I JUST COULDN'T BRING MYSELF TO THROW IT AWAY...
UEDA-SAN...?
creak
YOUR UNIFORM IS OVER HERE.

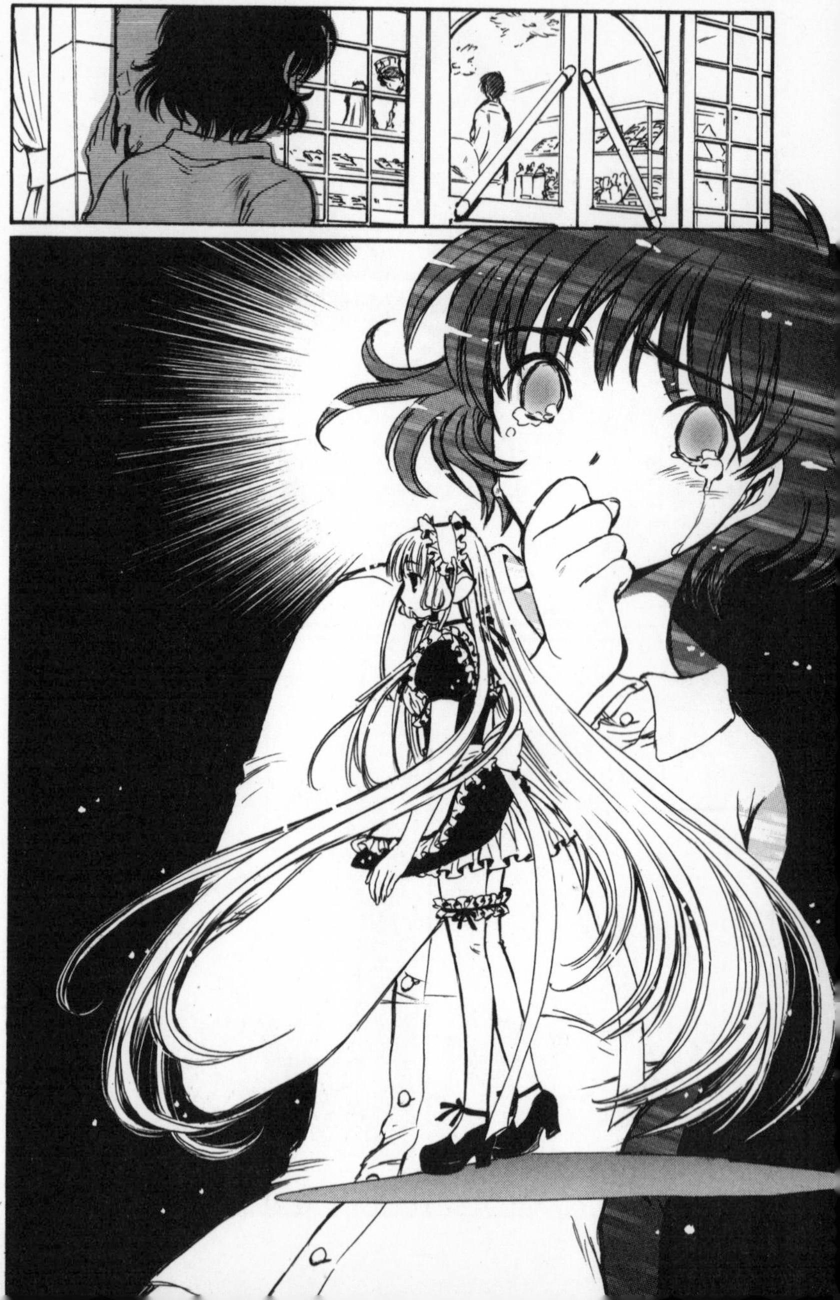

Chobits
ちょびっツ

◄ **chapter 60** ►

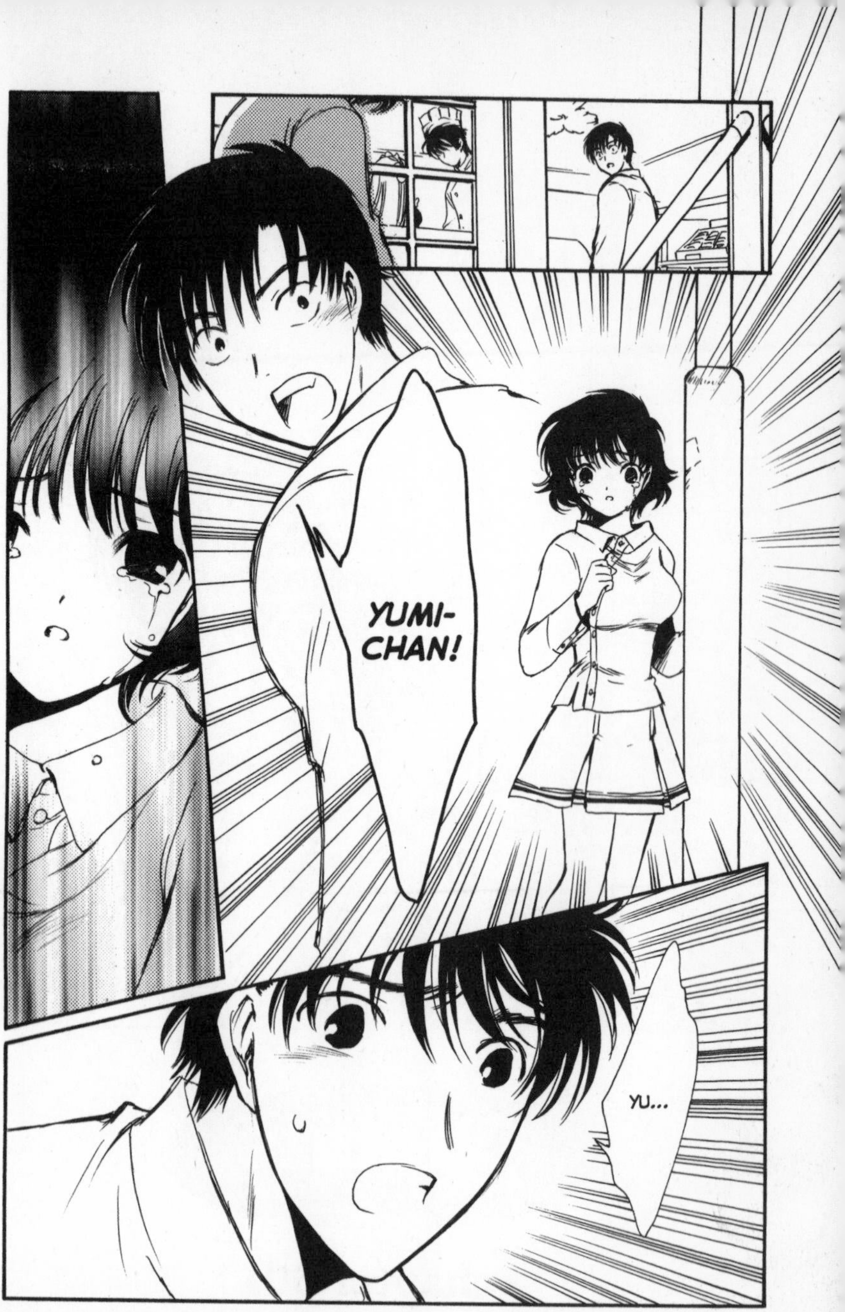
YUMI-
CHAN!
YU...

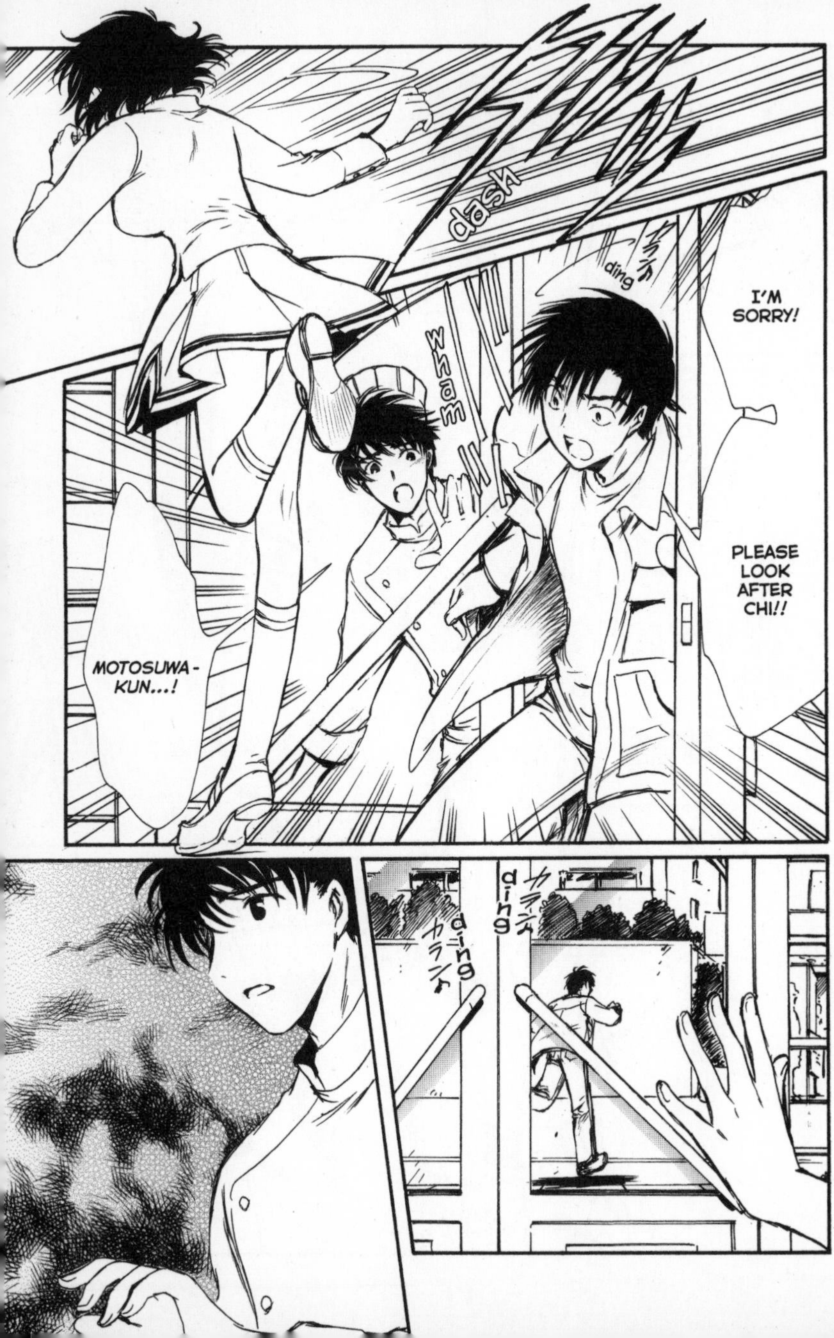
I'M SORRY!
ding
dash
wham
PLEASE LOOK AFTER CHI!!
MOTOSUWA-KUN...!
ding
ding

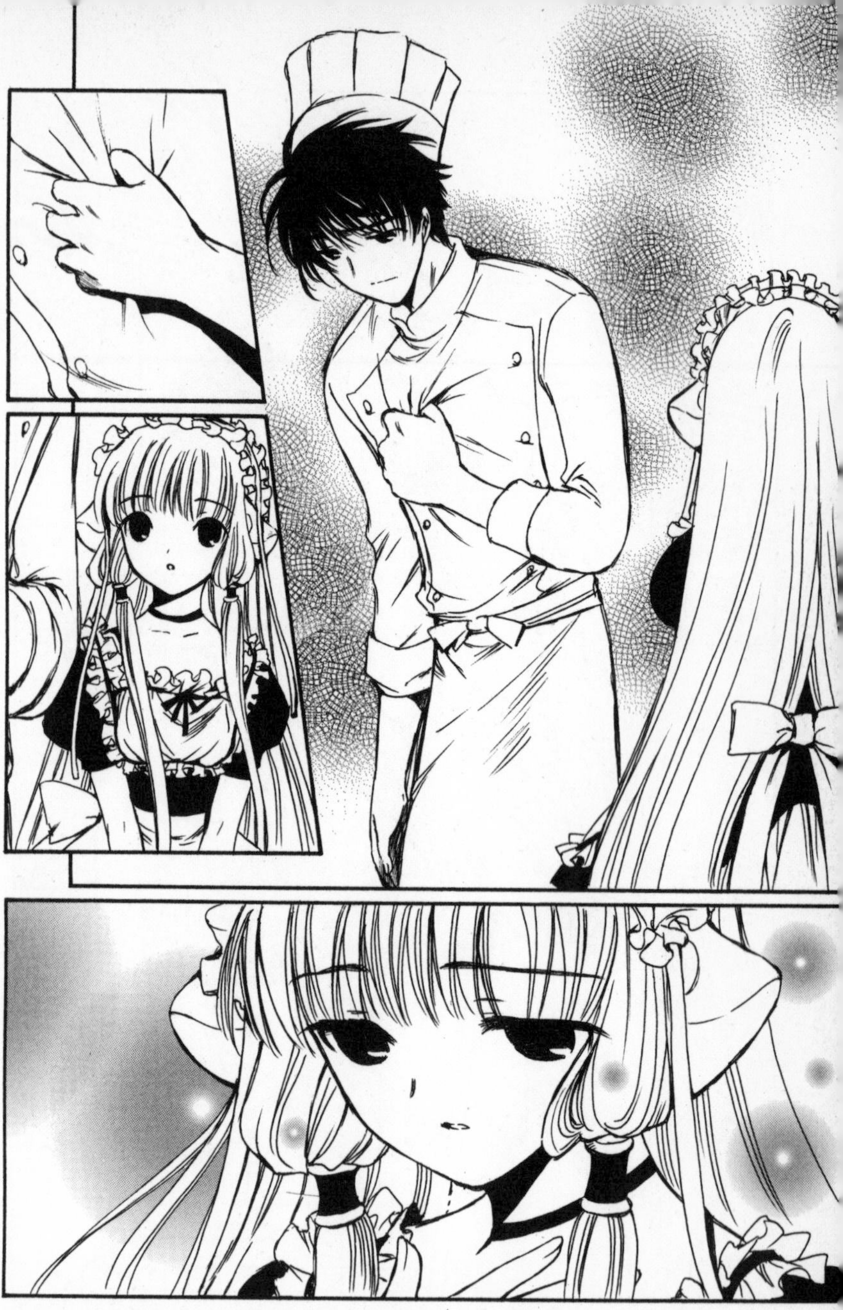

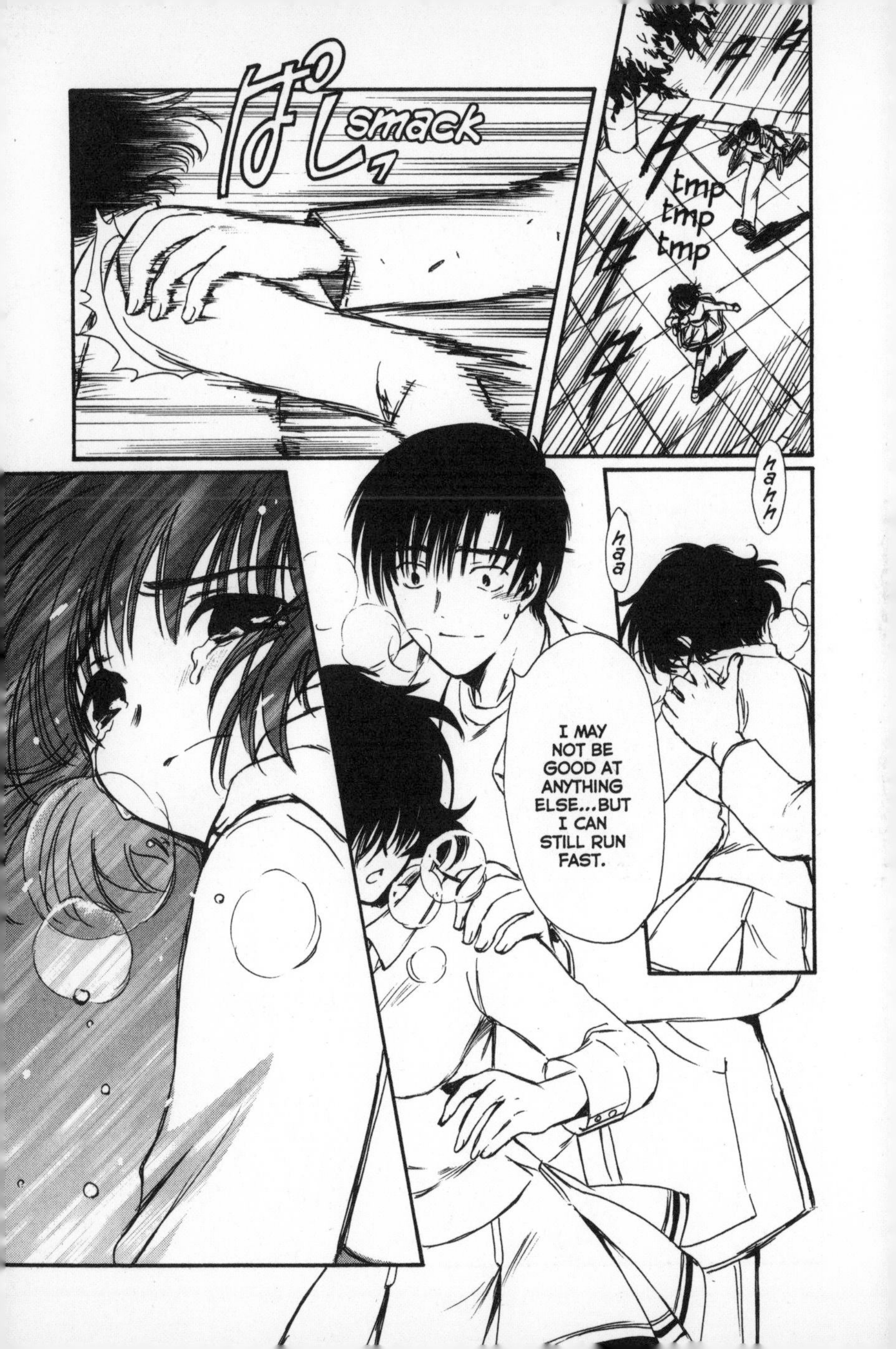
tmp
tmp
tmp
ぱしっ
smack
hann
haa
I MAY NOT BE GOOD AT ANYTHING ELSE...BUT I CAN STILL RUN FAST.

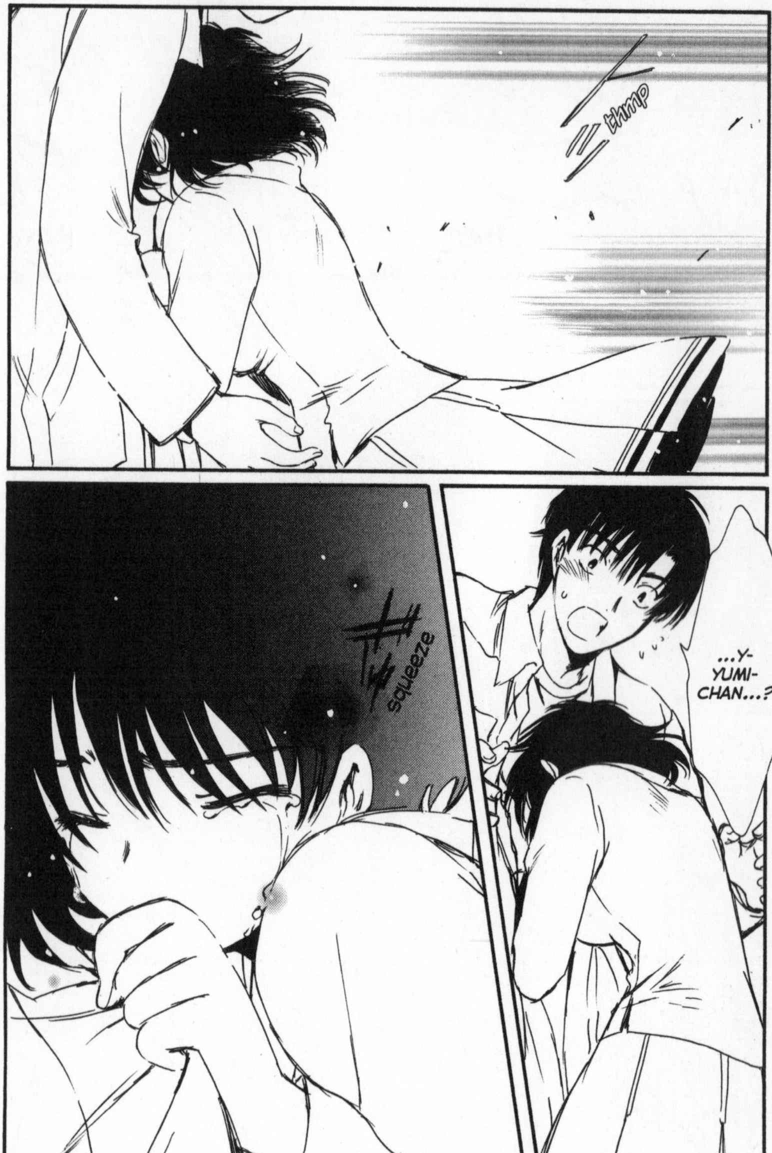
thmp
...Y-YUMI-CHAN...?
squeeze

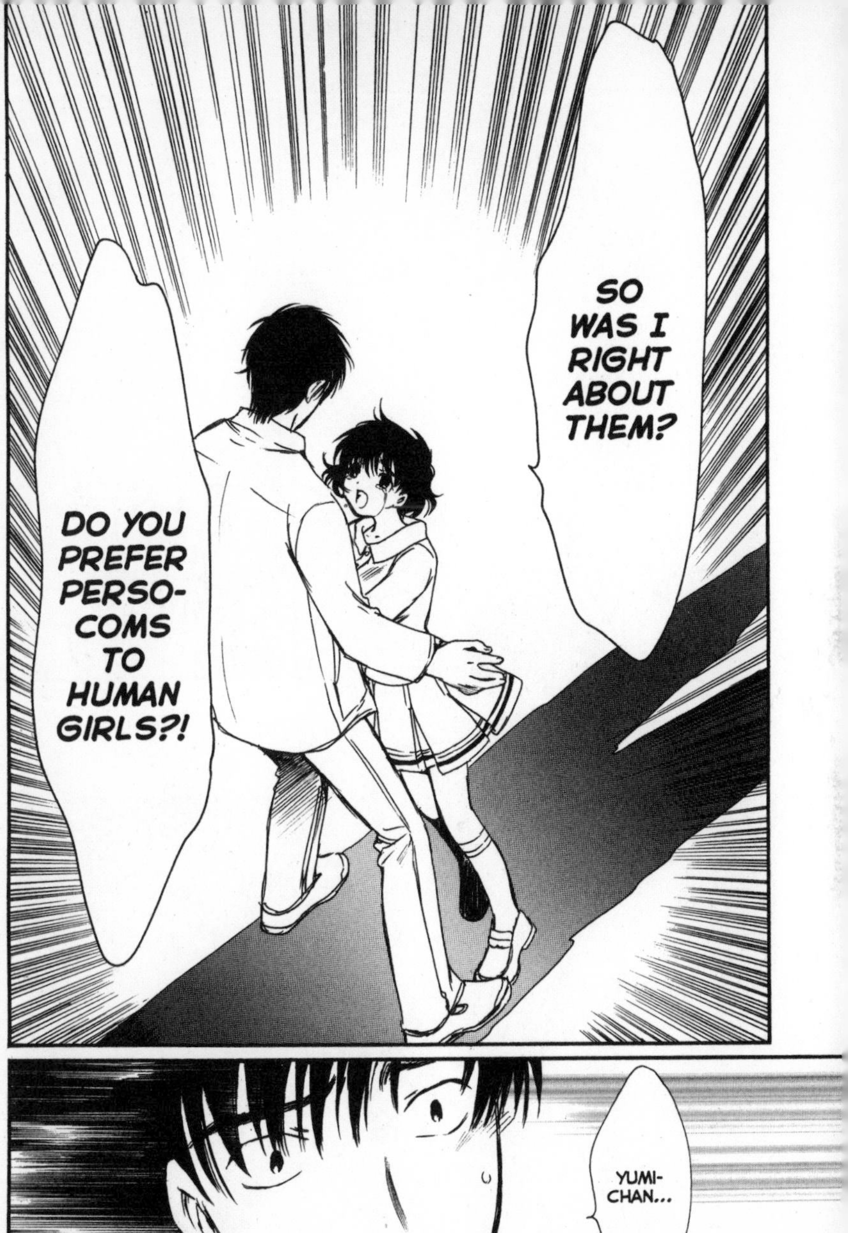
SO WAS I RIGHT ABOUT THEM?
DO YOU PREFER PERSO-COMS TO HUMAN GIRLS?!
YUMI-CHAN...

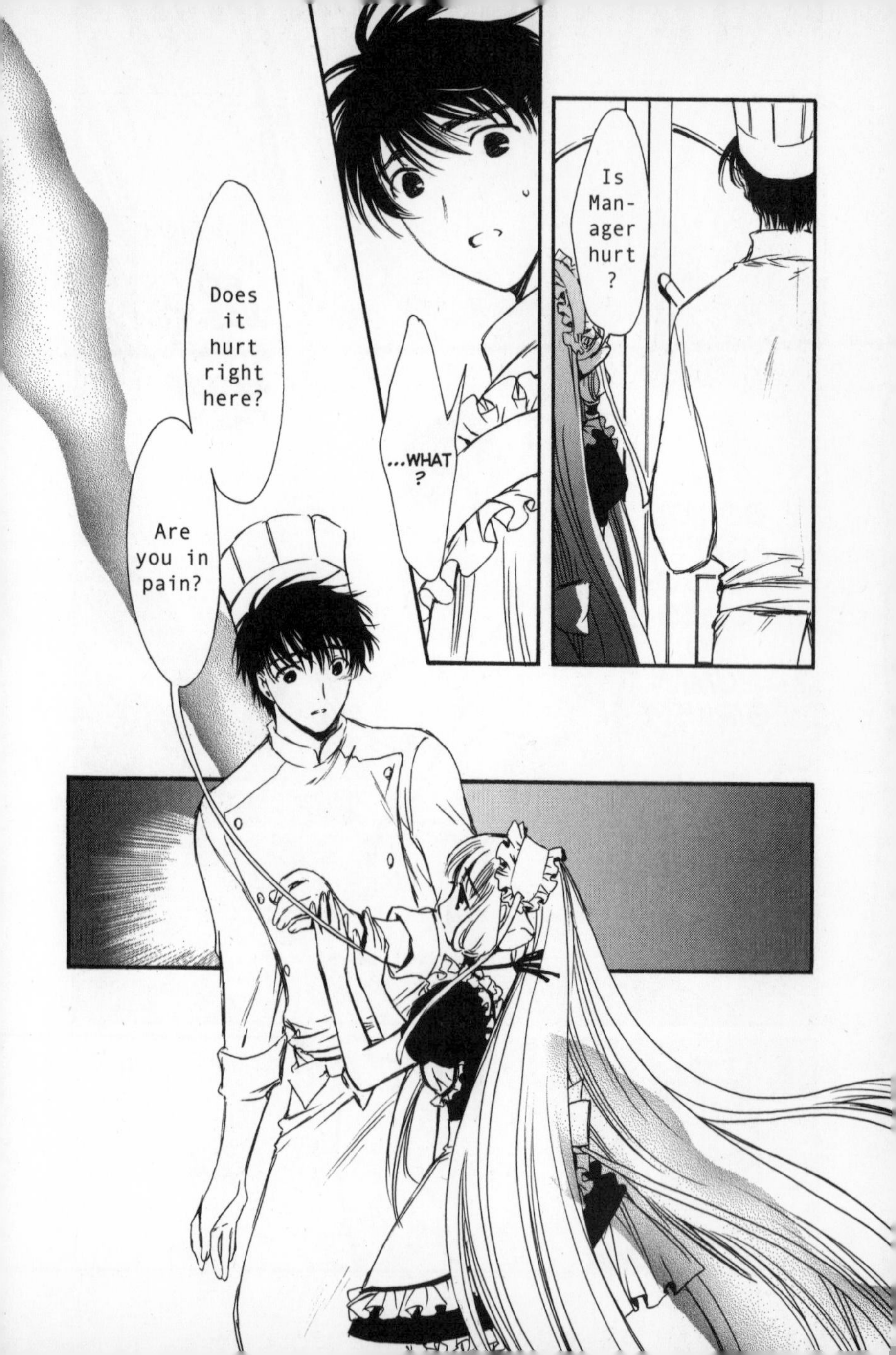
Is Manager hurt?
...WHAT?
Does it hurt right here?
Are you in pain?

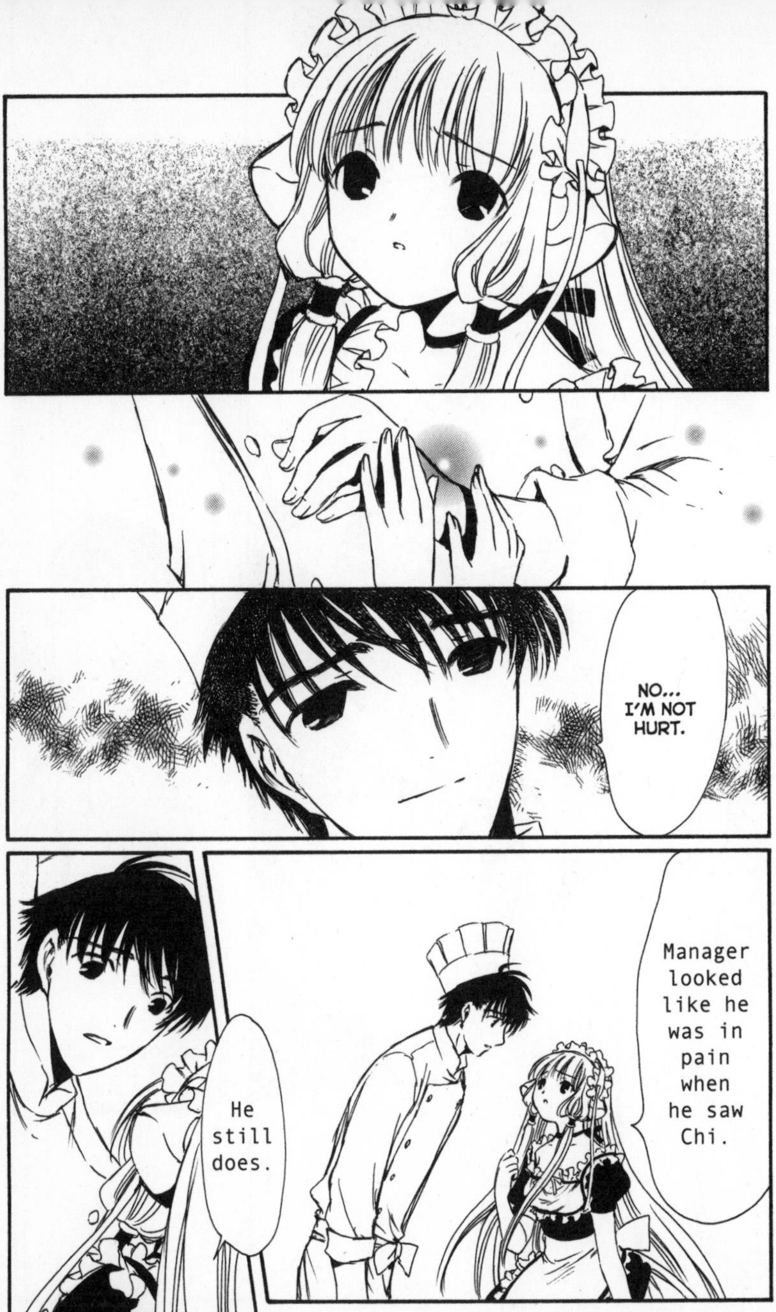
NO... I'M NOT HURT.
Manager looked like he was in pain when he saw Chi.
He still does.

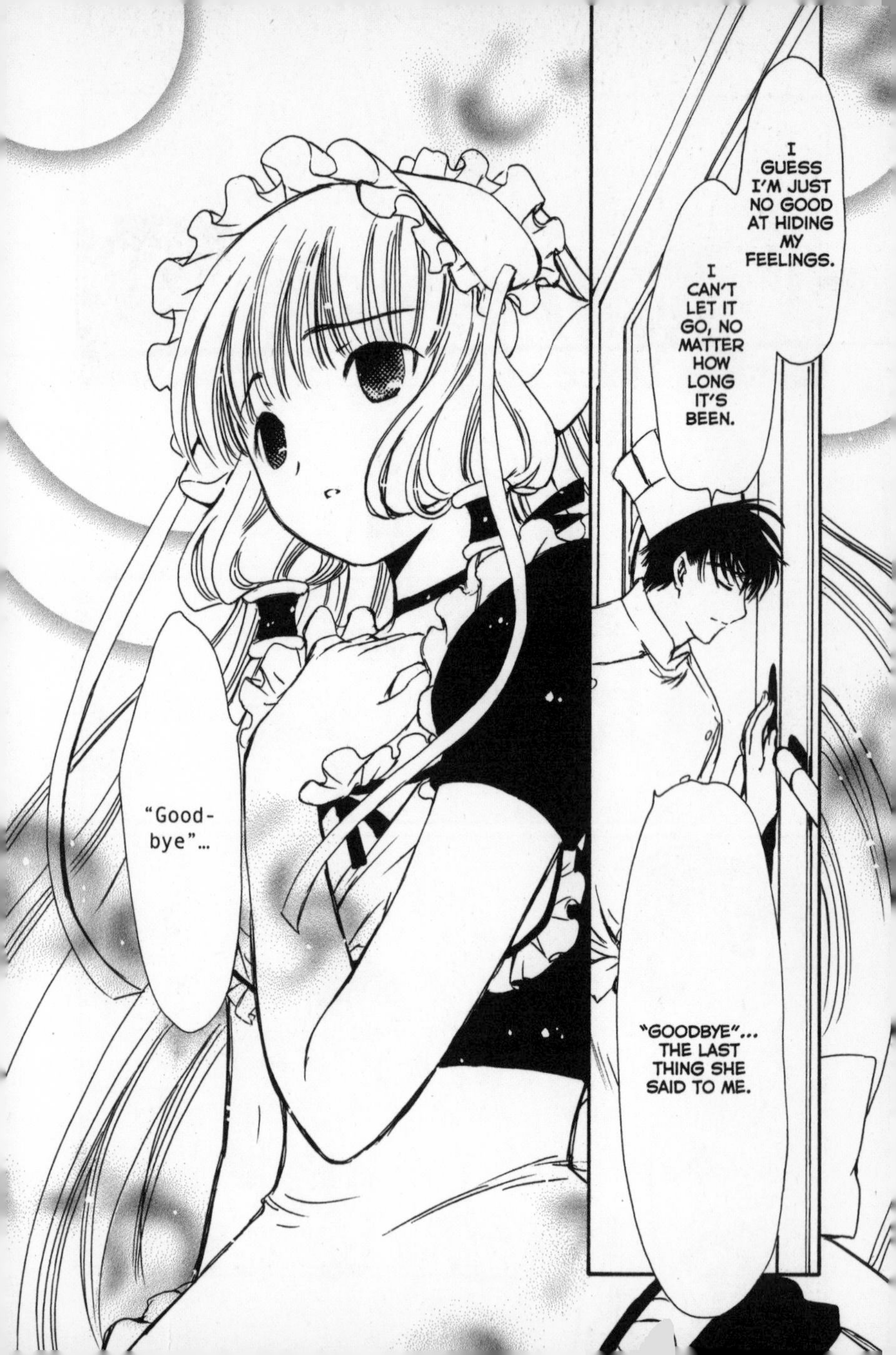
I GUESS I'M JUST NO GOOD AT HIDING MY FEELINGS.
I CAN'T LET IT GO, NO MATTER HOW LONG IT'S BEEN.
"GOODBYE"... THE LAST THING SHE SAID TO ME.
"Good-bye"...

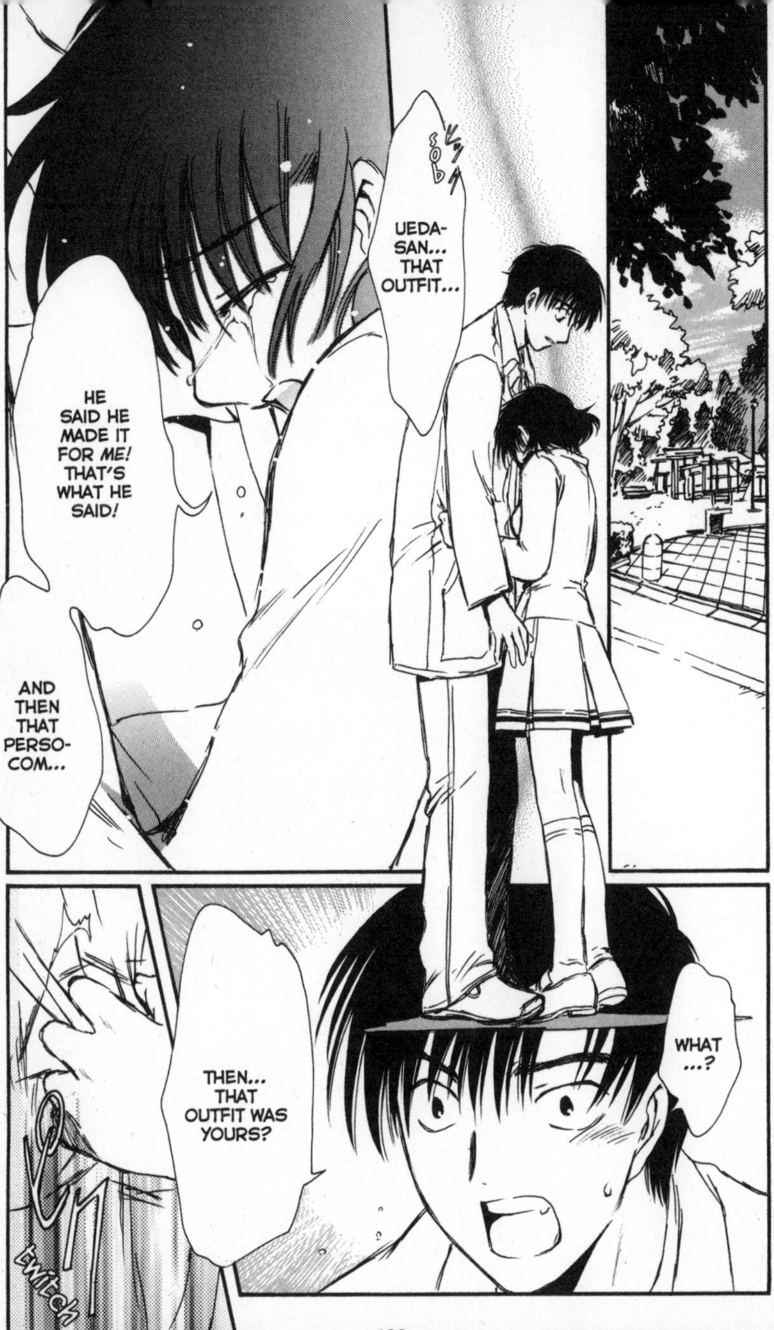
sob
UEDA-SAN... THAT OUTFIT...
HE SAID HE MADE IT FOR *ME!* THAT'S WHAT HE SAID!
AND THEN THAT PERSO-COM...
WHAT ...?
THEN... THAT OUTFIT WAS YOURS?
twitch

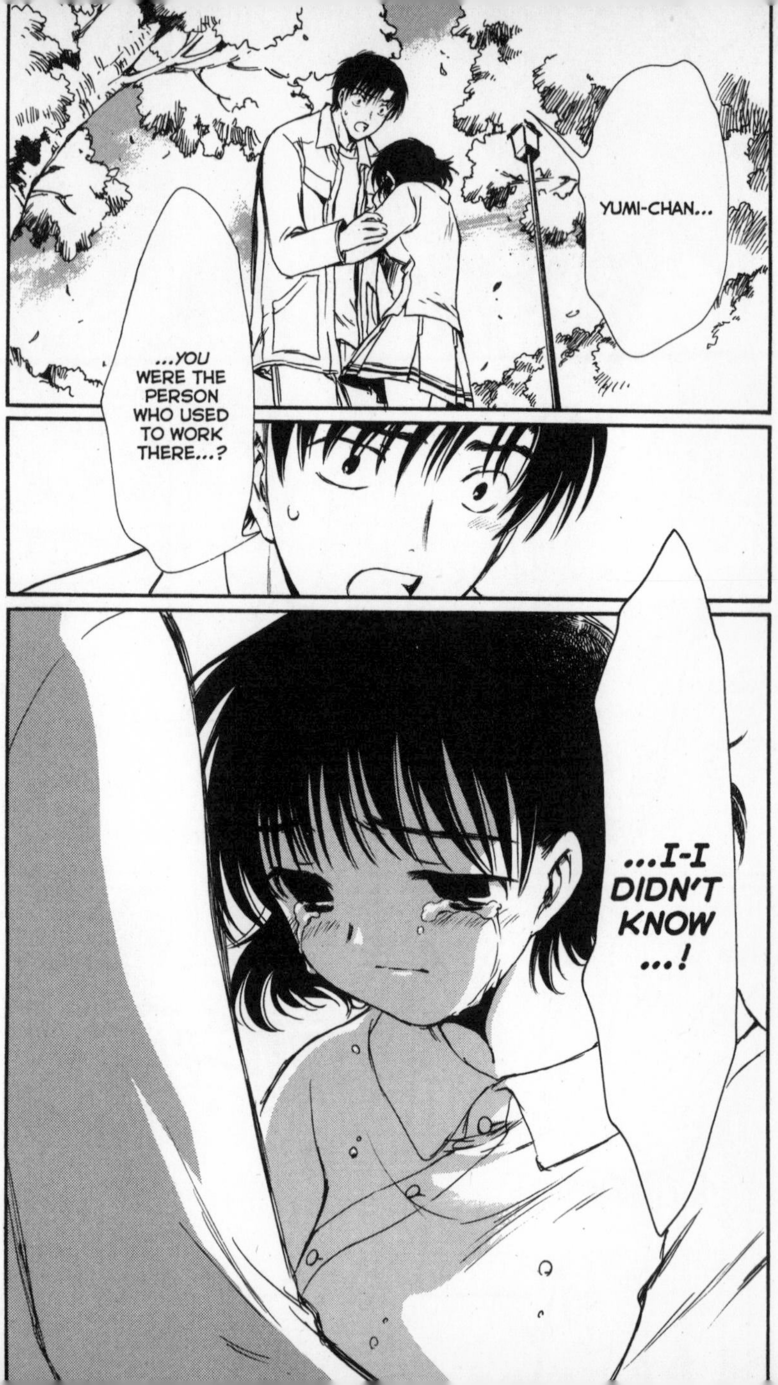
YUMI-CHAN...
...YOU WERE THE PERSON WHO USED TO WORK THERE...?
...I-I DIDN'T KNOW ...!

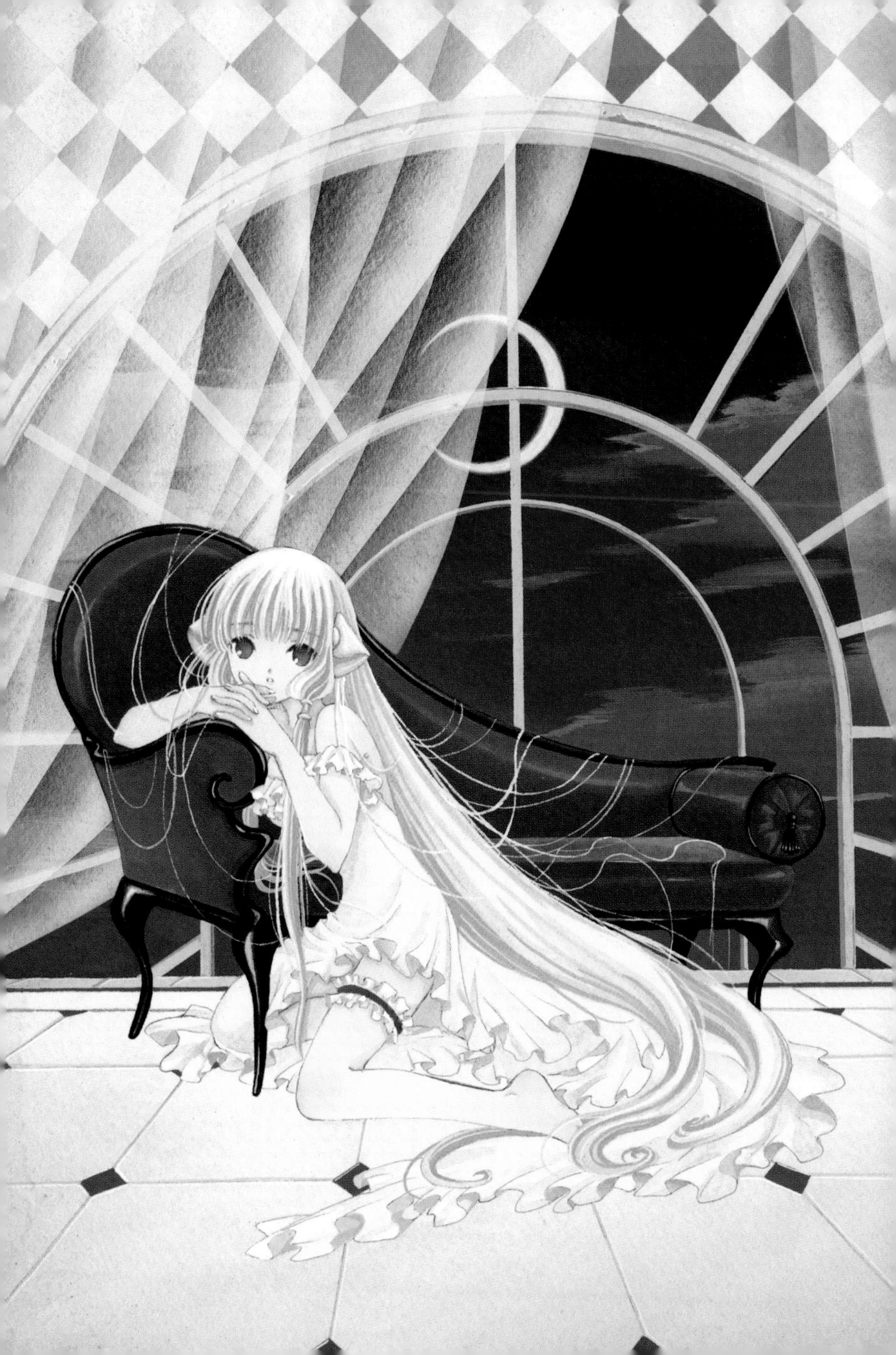

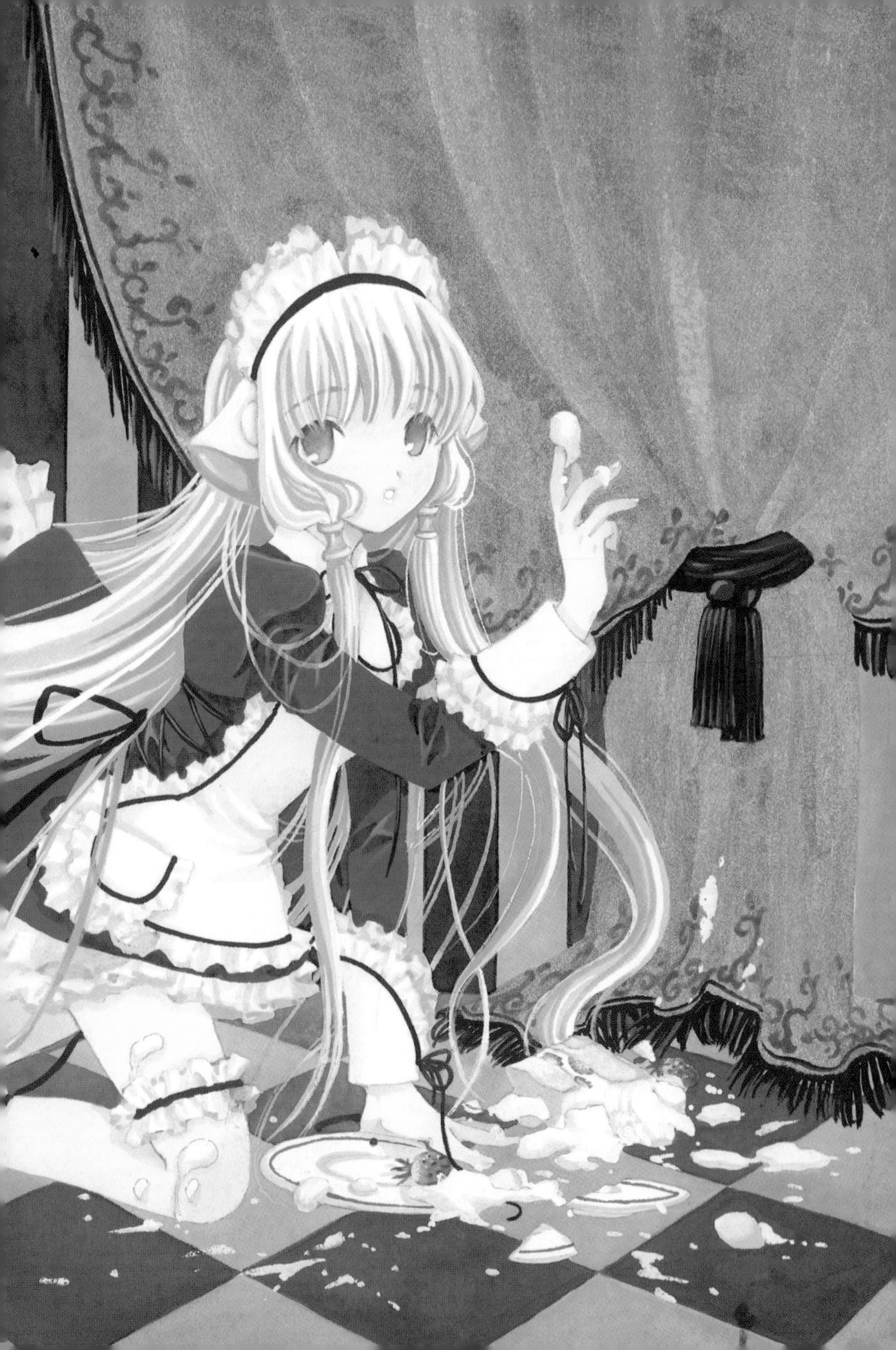

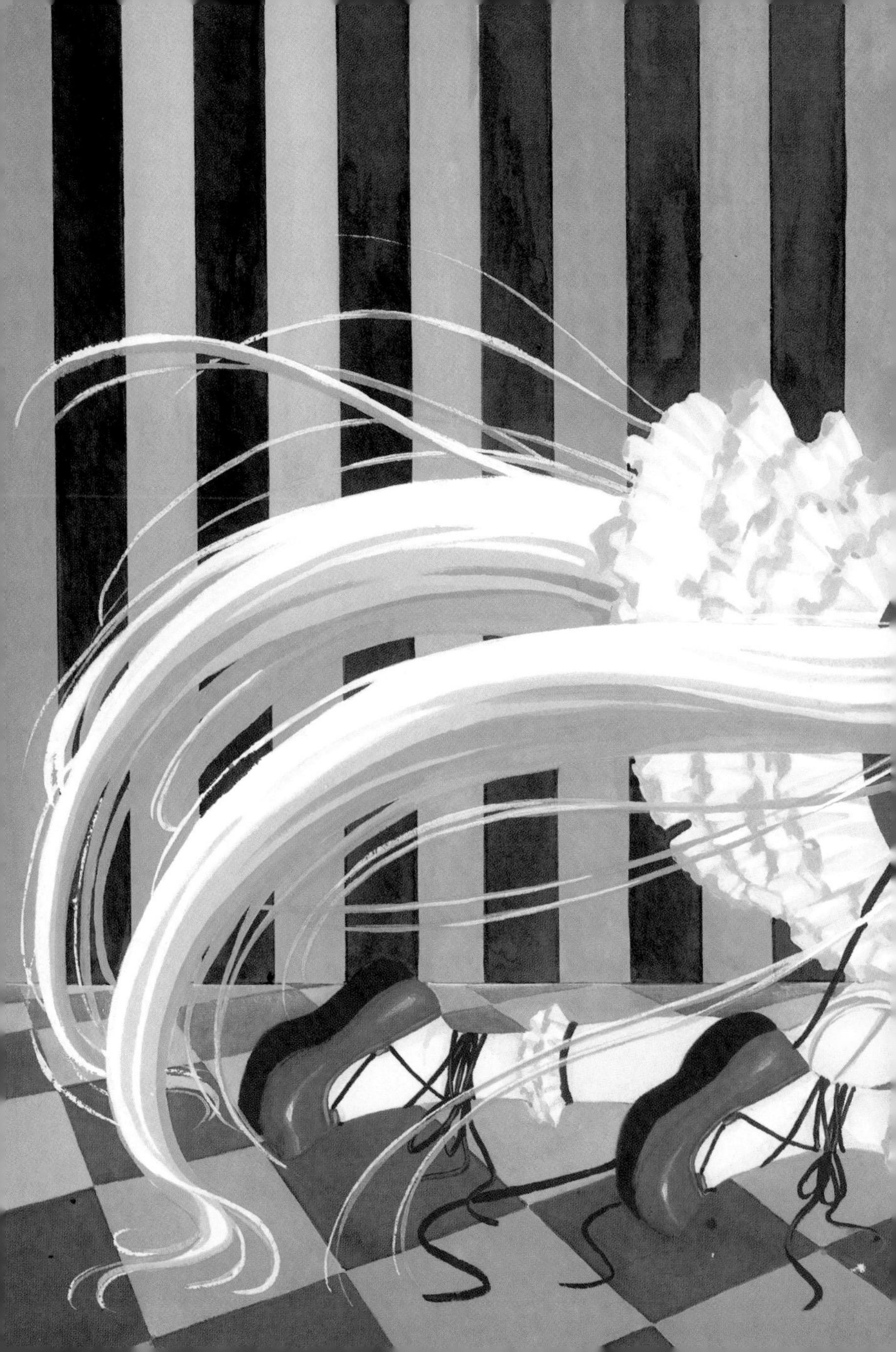

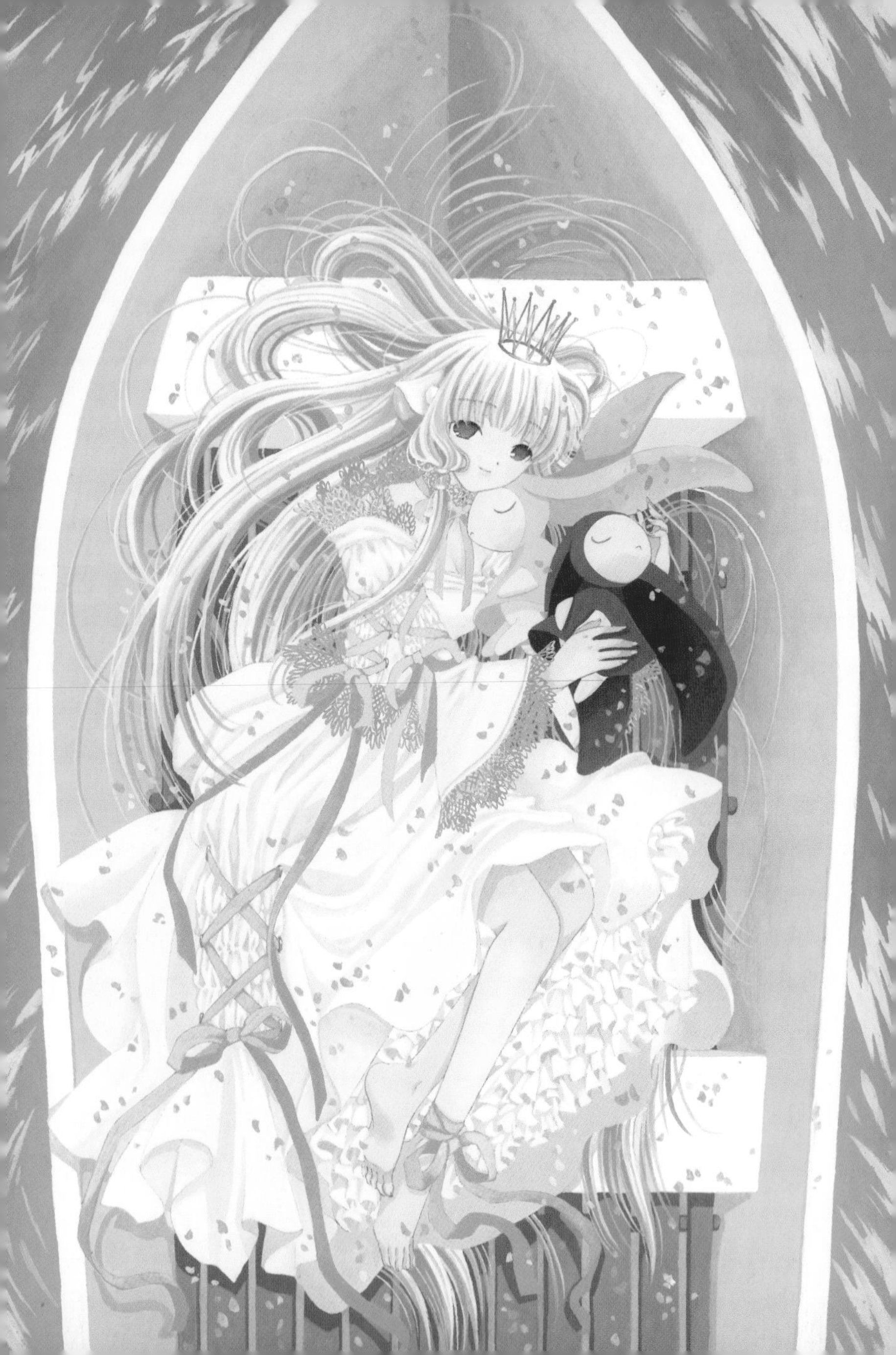

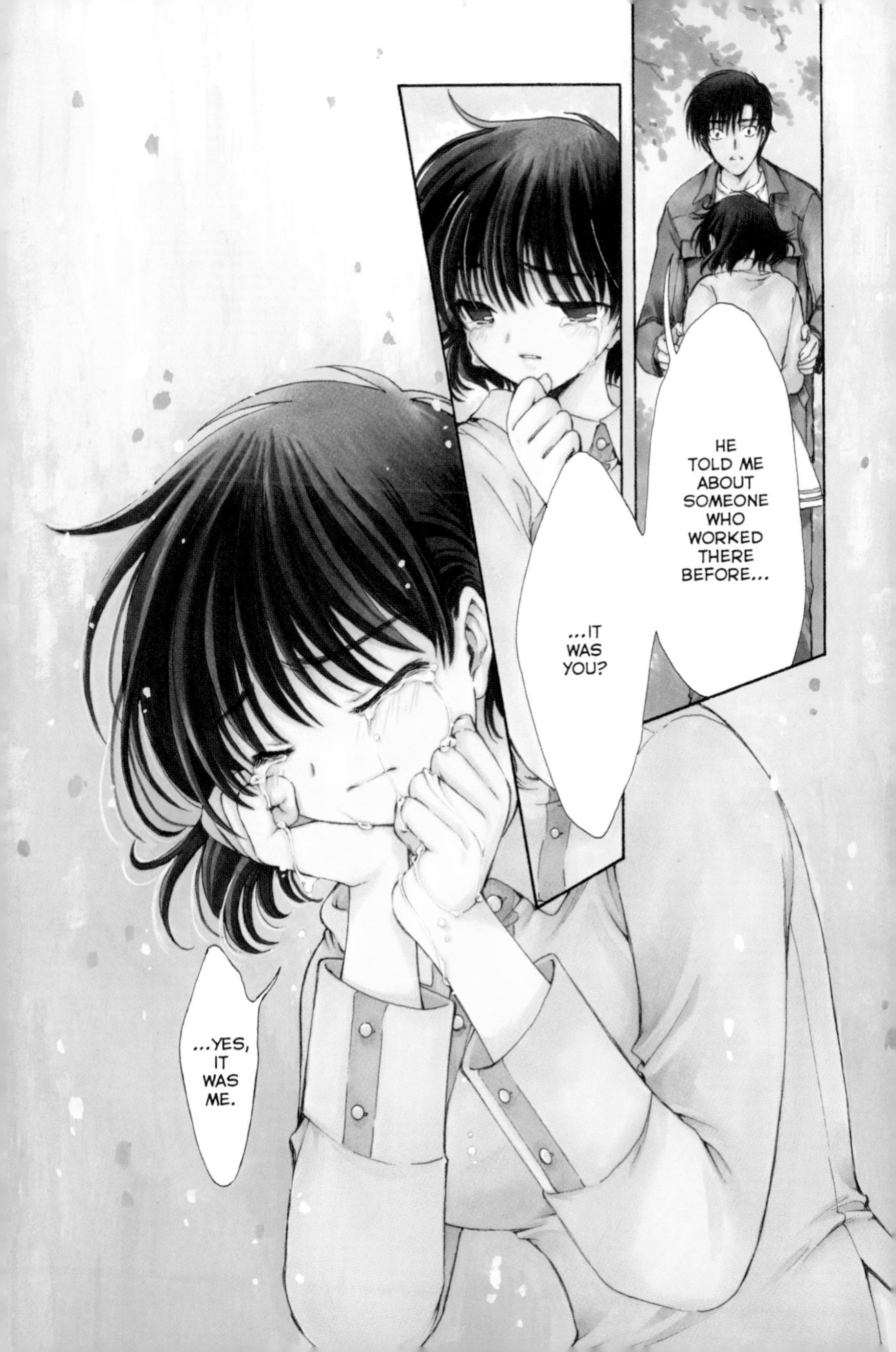
HE TOLD ME ABOUT SOMEONE WHO WORKED THERE BEFORE...
...IT WAS YOU?
...YES, IT WAS ME.

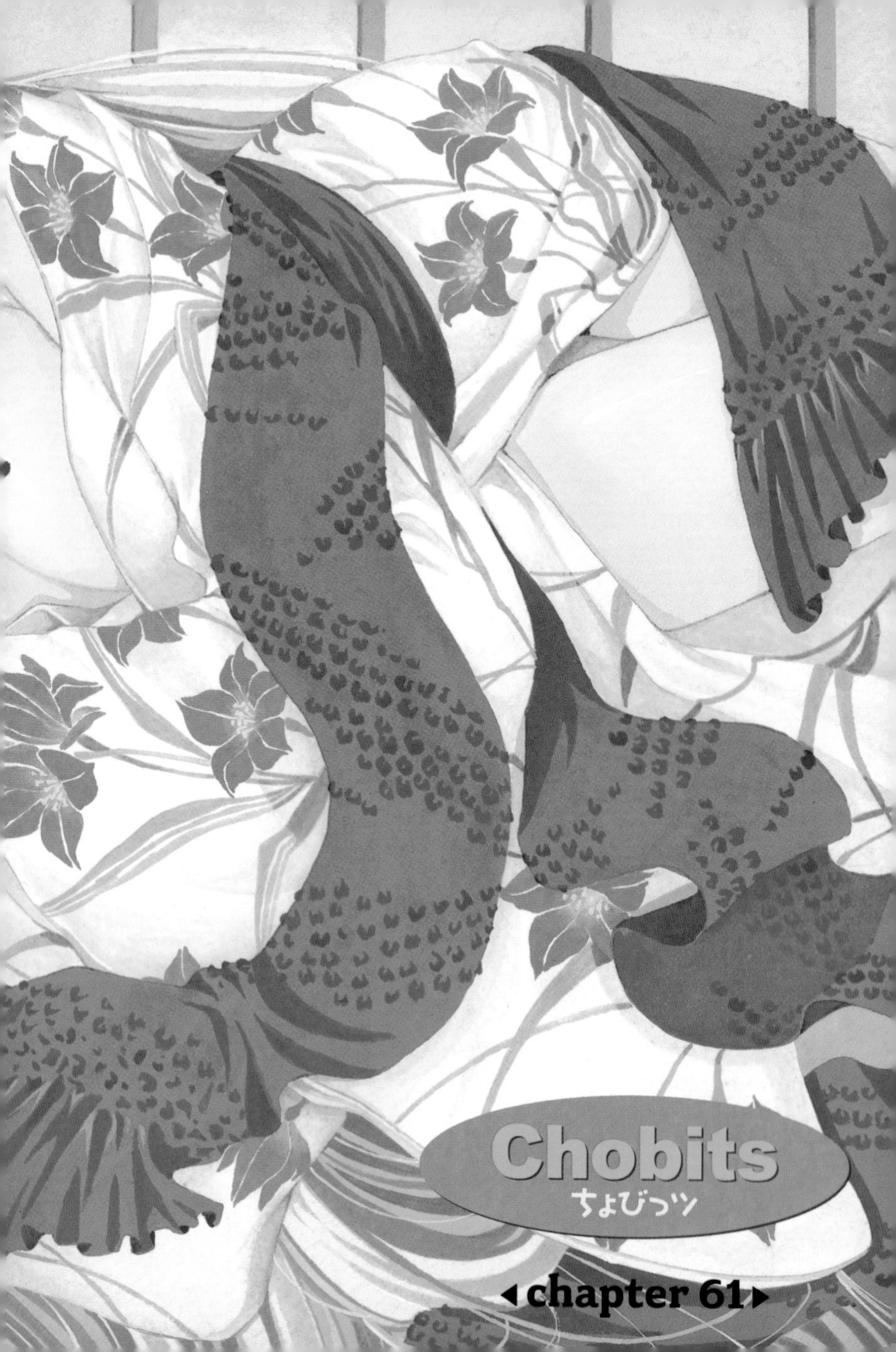
Chobits
ちょびっツ
chapter 61

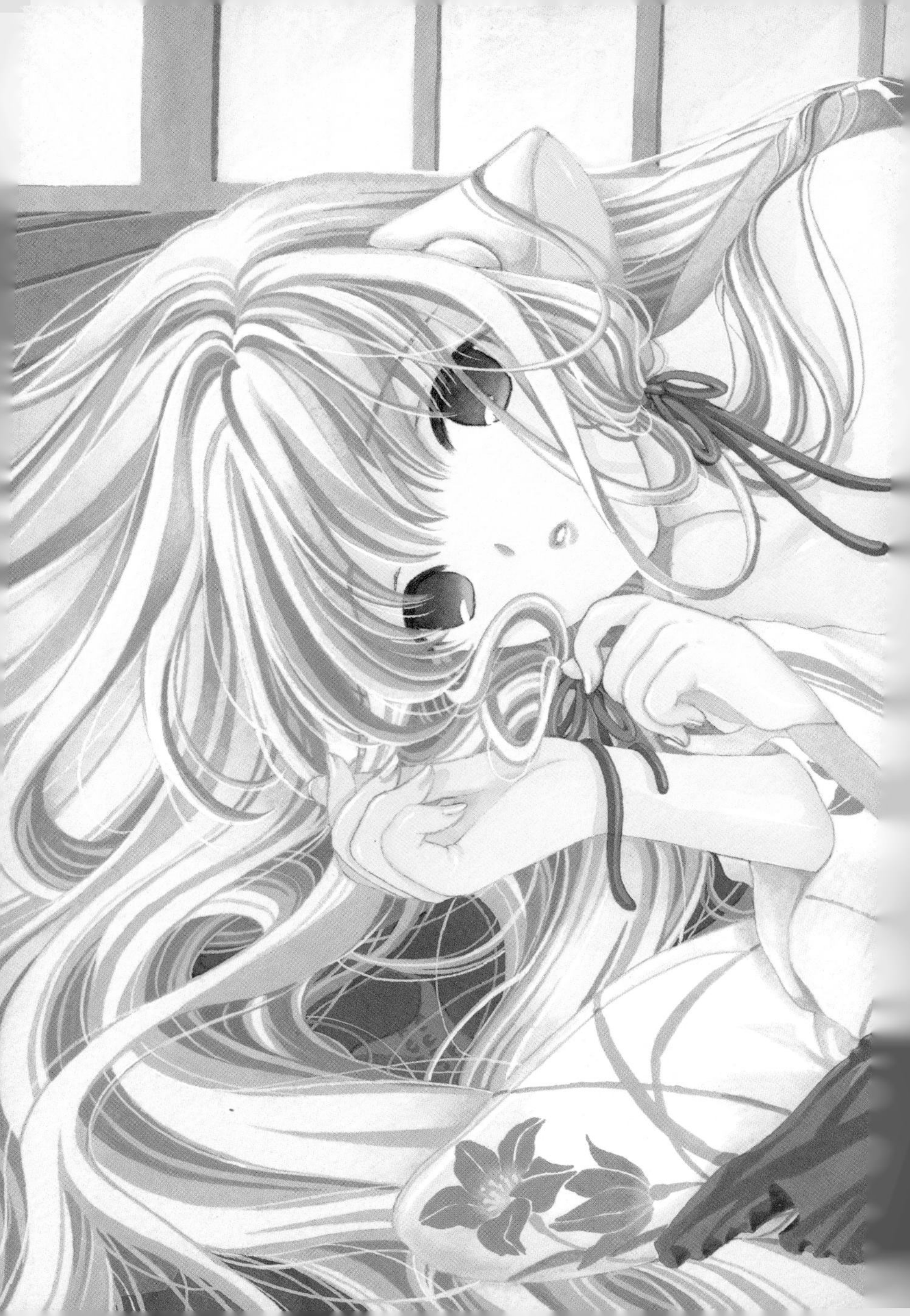

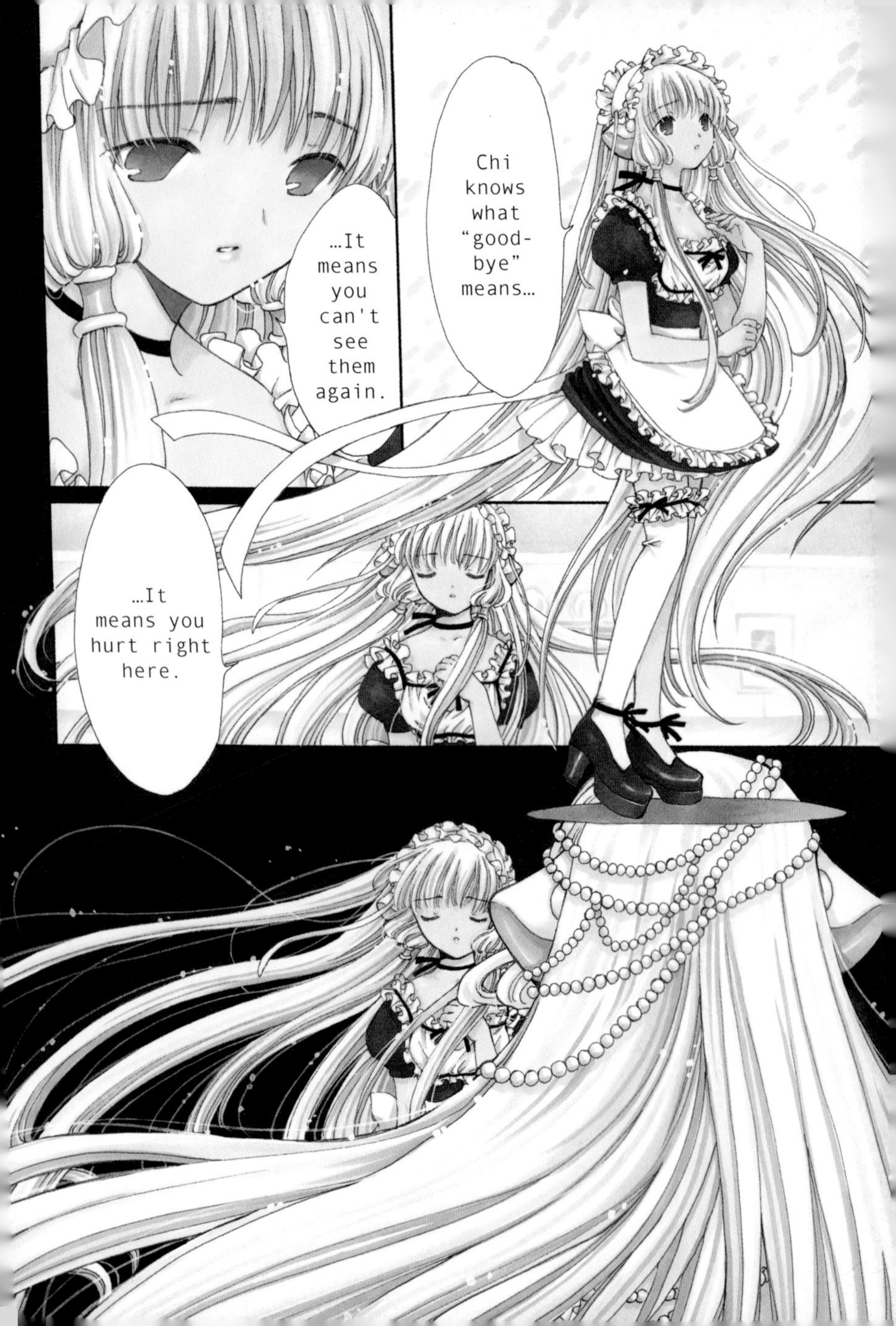
Chi knows what "good-bye" means…
…It means you can't see them again.
…It means you hurt right here.

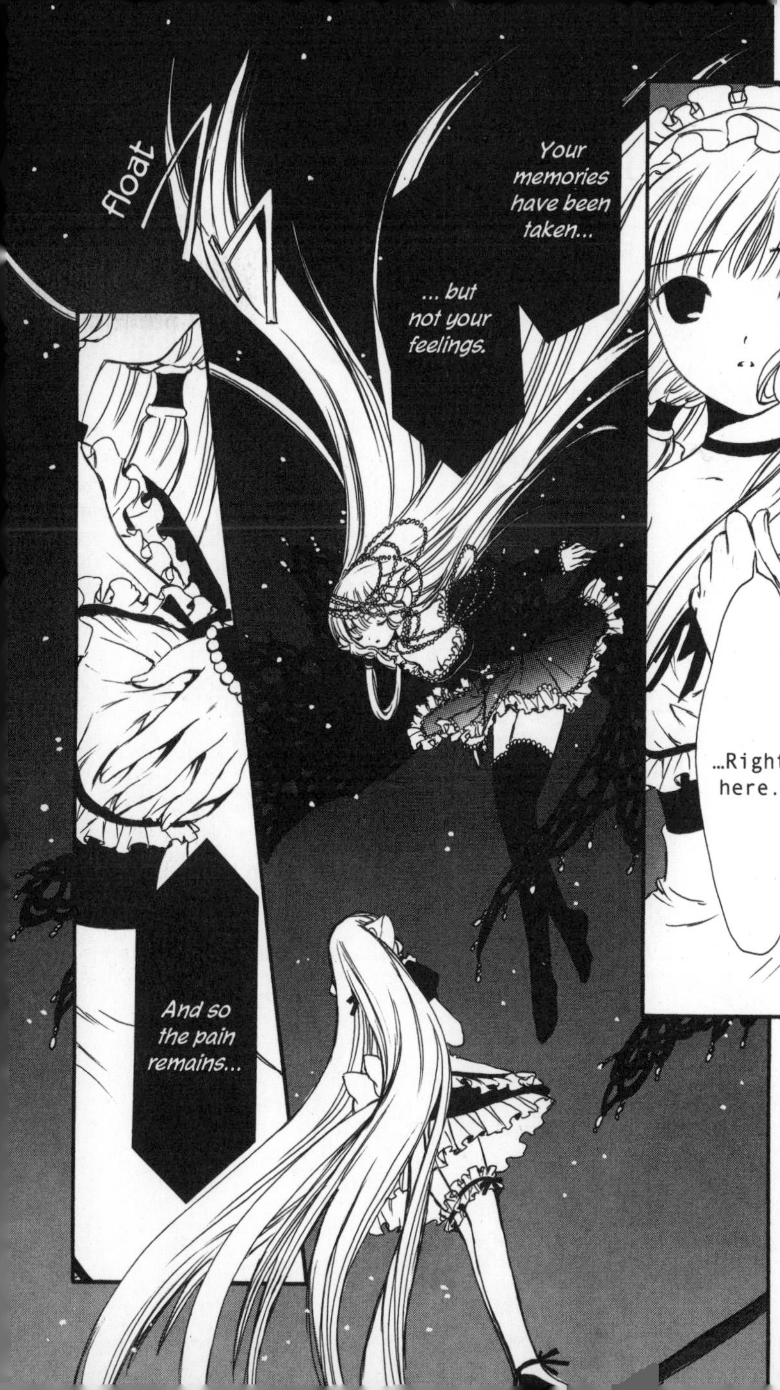
Your memories have been taken...
... but not your feelings.
float
...Right here.
And so the pain remains...

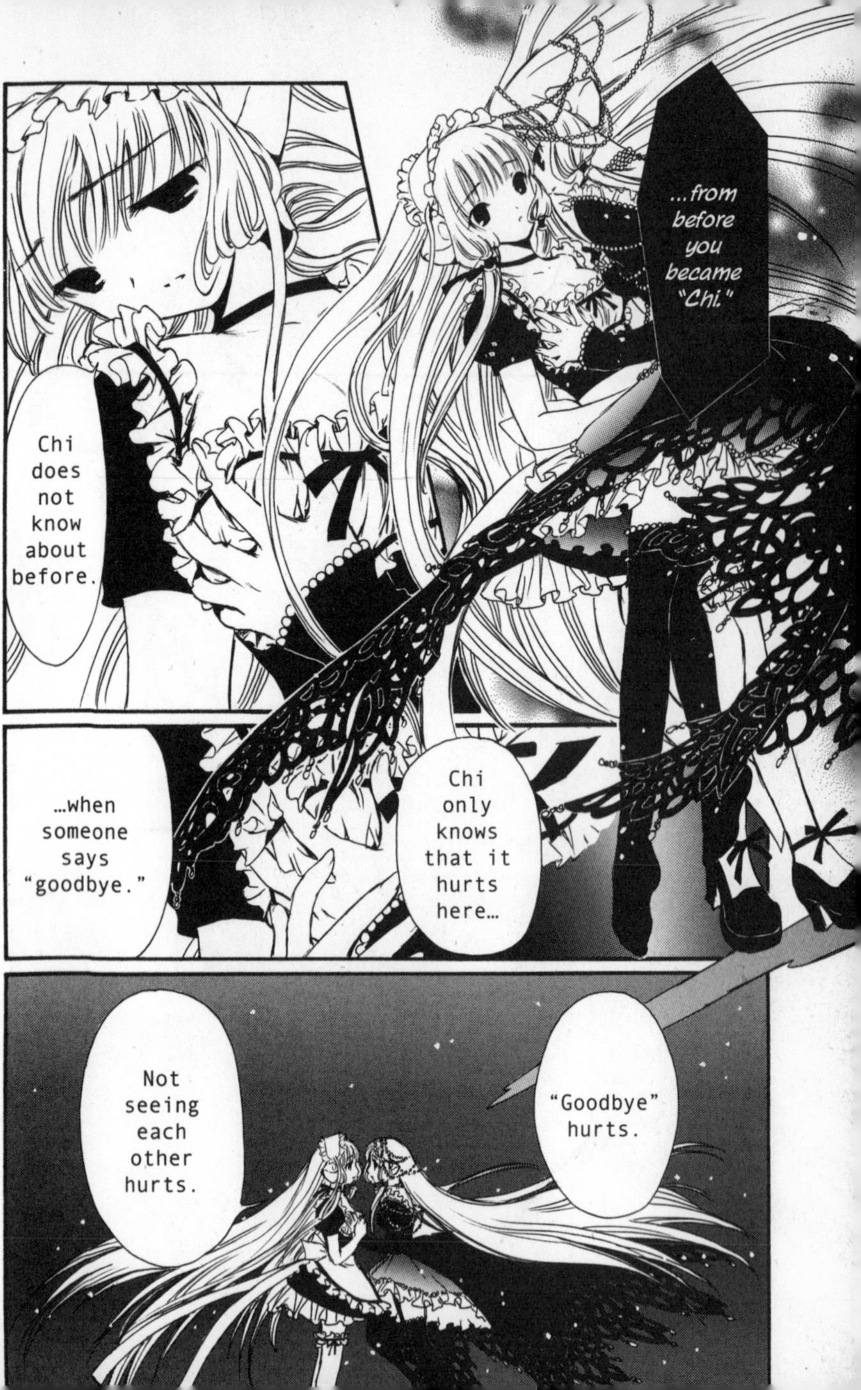
...from before you became "Chi."
Chi does not know about before.
Chi only knows that it hurts here...
...when someone says "goodbye."
"Goodbye" hurts.
Not seeing each other hurts.

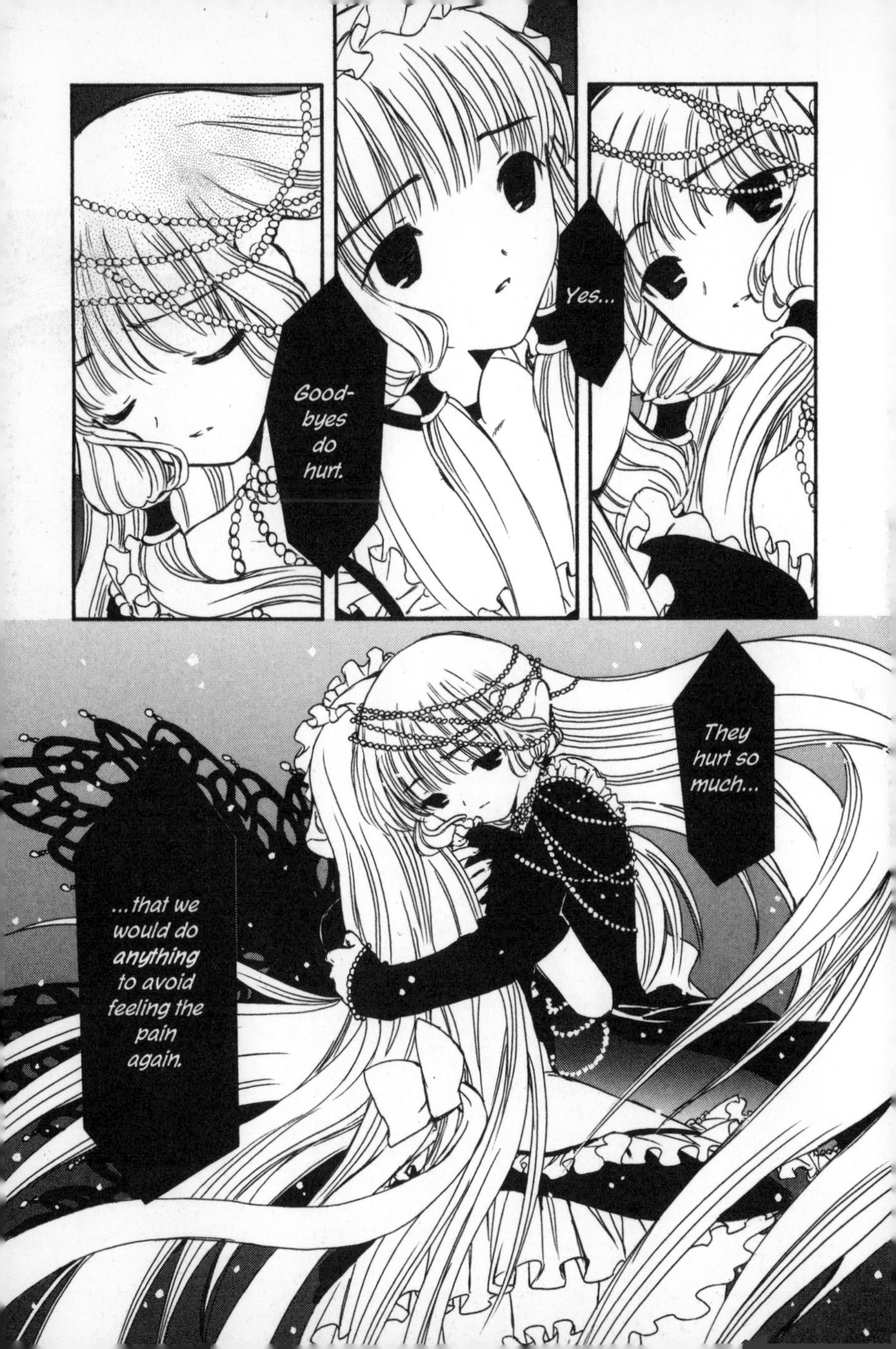
Yes...
Good-byes do hurt.
They hurt so much...
...that we would do anything to avoid feeling the pain again.

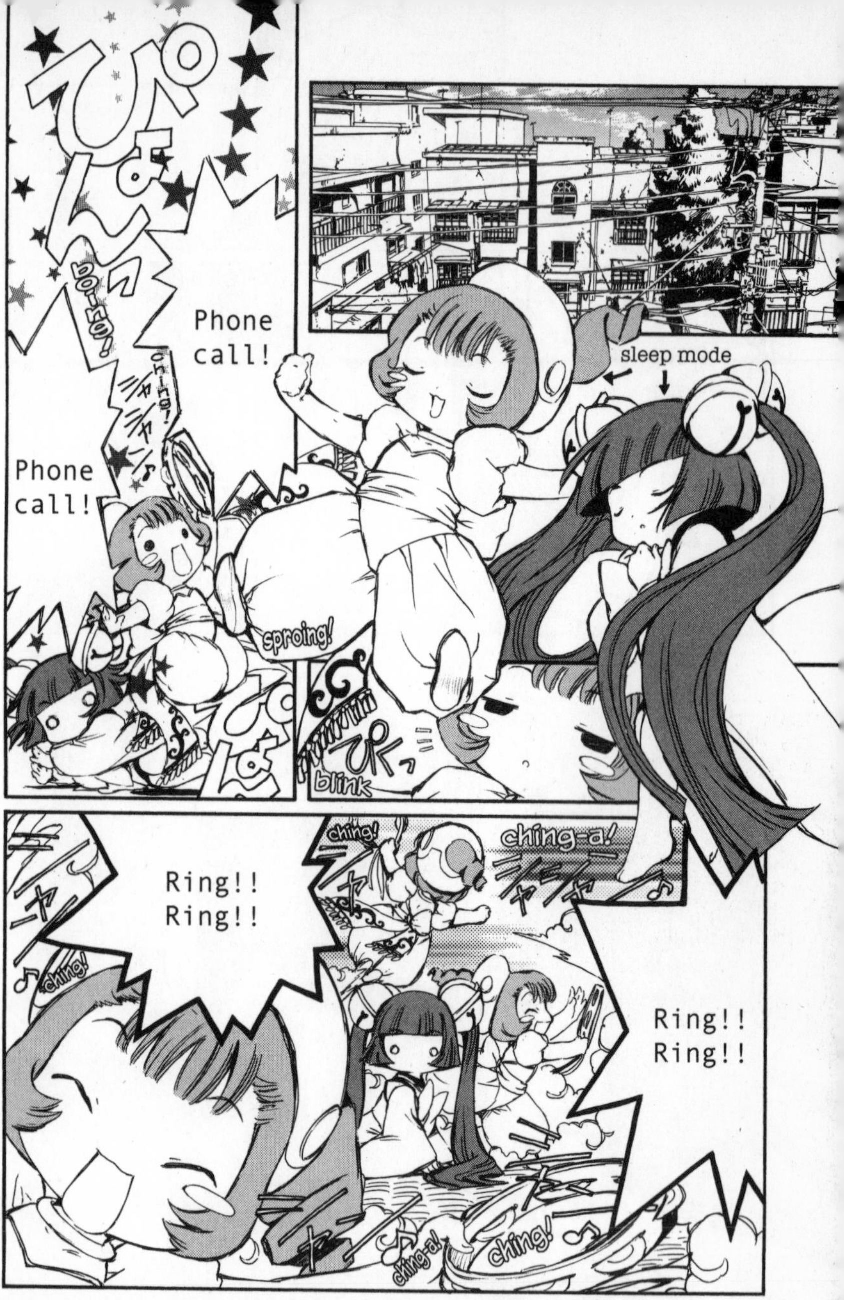
sleep mode
ぴょん〜っ
boing!
Phone call!
ching!
シャンシャン♪
Phone call!
ぴくっ
blink
ぴょん
sproing!
ching-a!
ching!
Ring!!
Ring!!
Ring!!
Ring!!
ching!
ching-a!
ching!

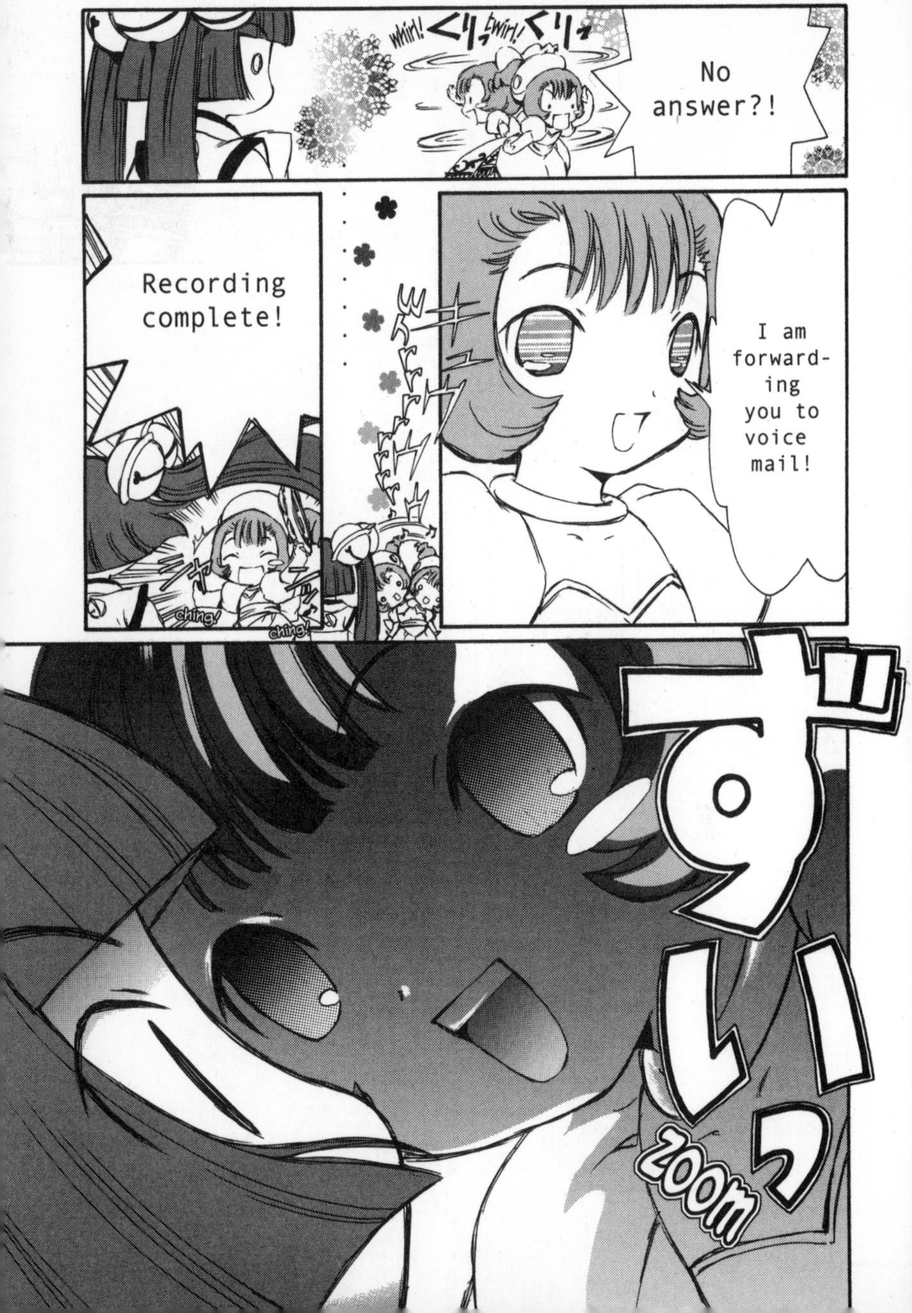
whirl!
twirl!
No answer?!
I am forward-ing you to voice mail!
Recording complete!
ching!
ching!
zoom

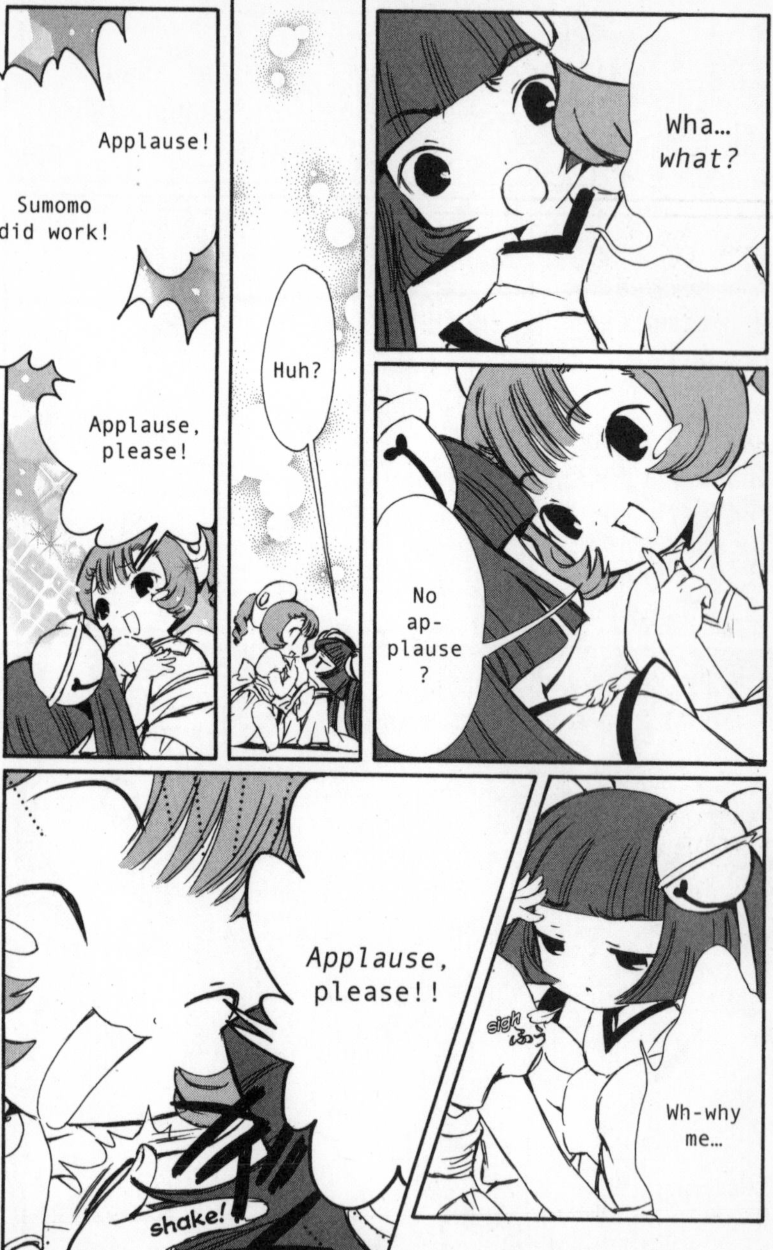

Wha... *what?*
No ap-plause?
Huh?
Applause!
Sumomo did work!
Applause, please!
sigh
ふぅ
Wh-why me...
Applause, please!!
shake!

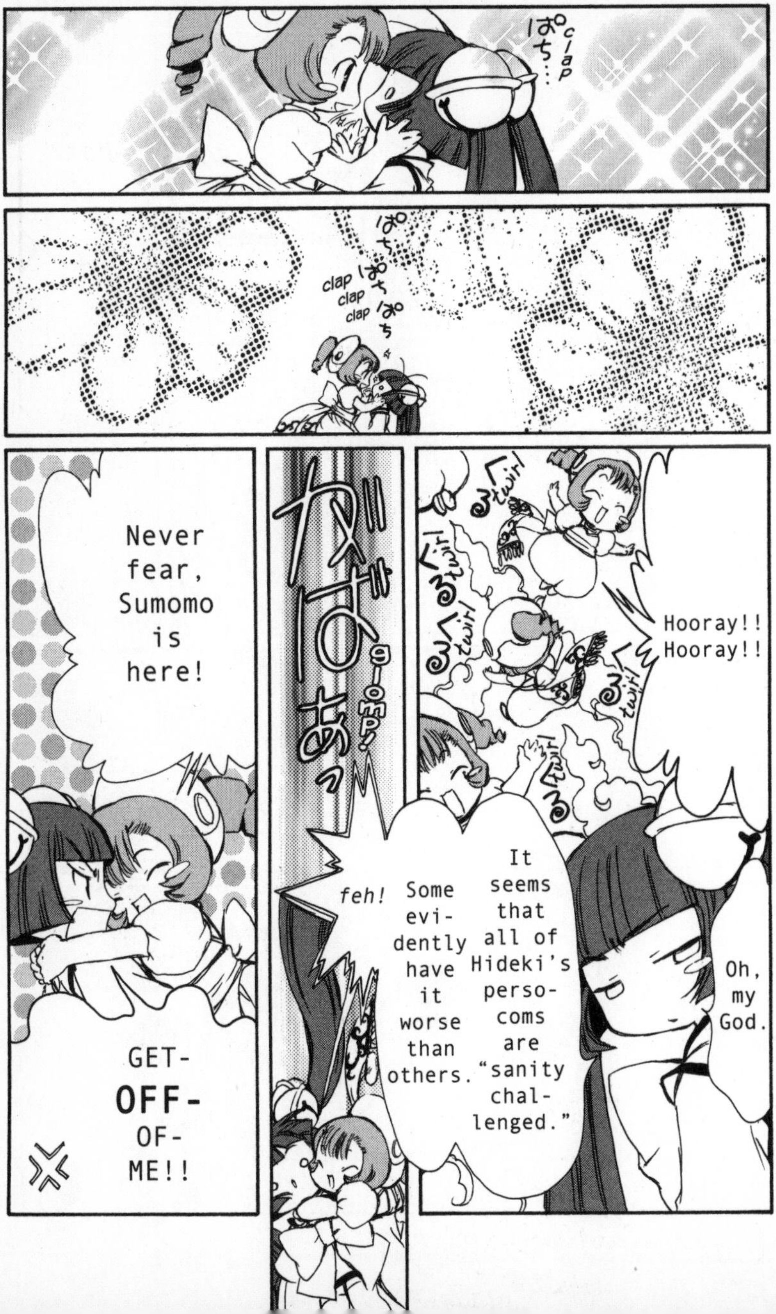
ぱち… clap
ぱち clap ぱち clap ぱち clap
Hooray!! Hooray!!
くるっ twirl
くるくる twirl
くるっ twirl
くるっ twirl
くるっ twirl
Oh, my God.
がばぁっ g-omp!
It seems that all of Hideki's persocoms are "sanity challenged."
Some evidently have it worse than others.
feh!
Never fear, Sumomo is here!
GET-OFF-OF-ME!!

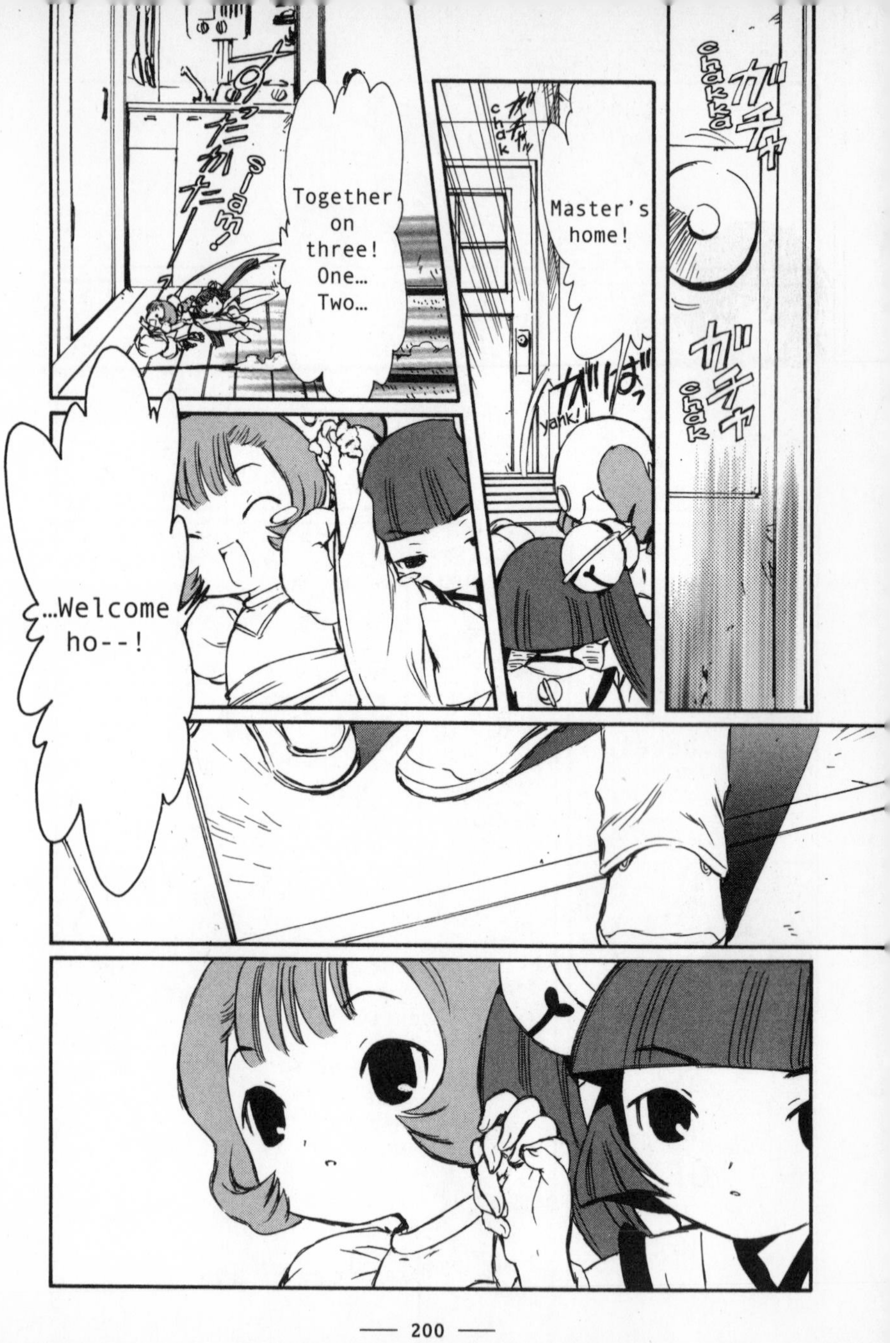
ガチャ
chaka
ガチャ
chak
ガチャ
chak
Master's home!
ガバッ
yank!
Together on three! One... Two...
sram!
...Welcome ho--!

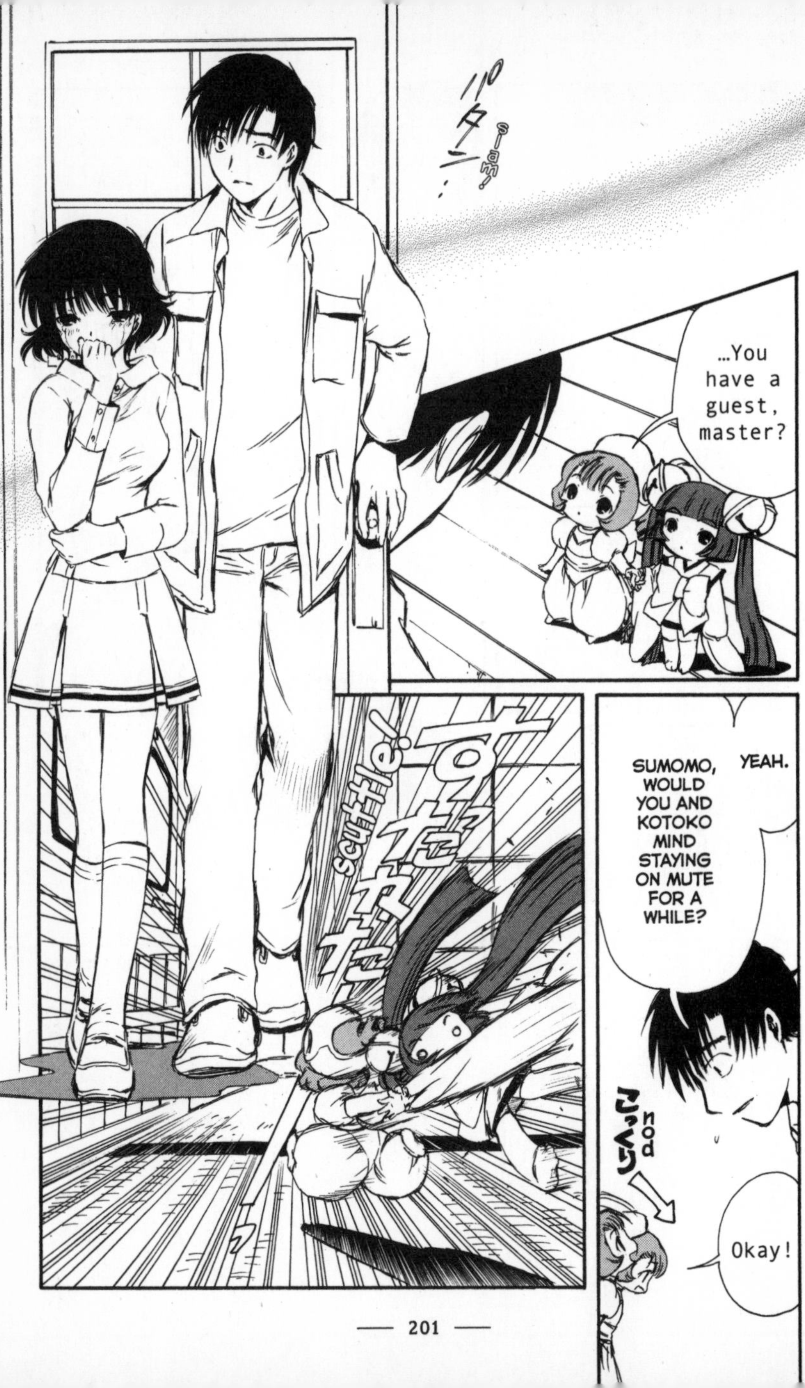
パタン
slam!
...You have a guest, master?
YEAH.
SUMOMO, WOULD YOU AND KOTOKO MIND STAYING ON MUTE FOR A WHILE?
こっくり
nod
Okay!
すたたた
scuttle

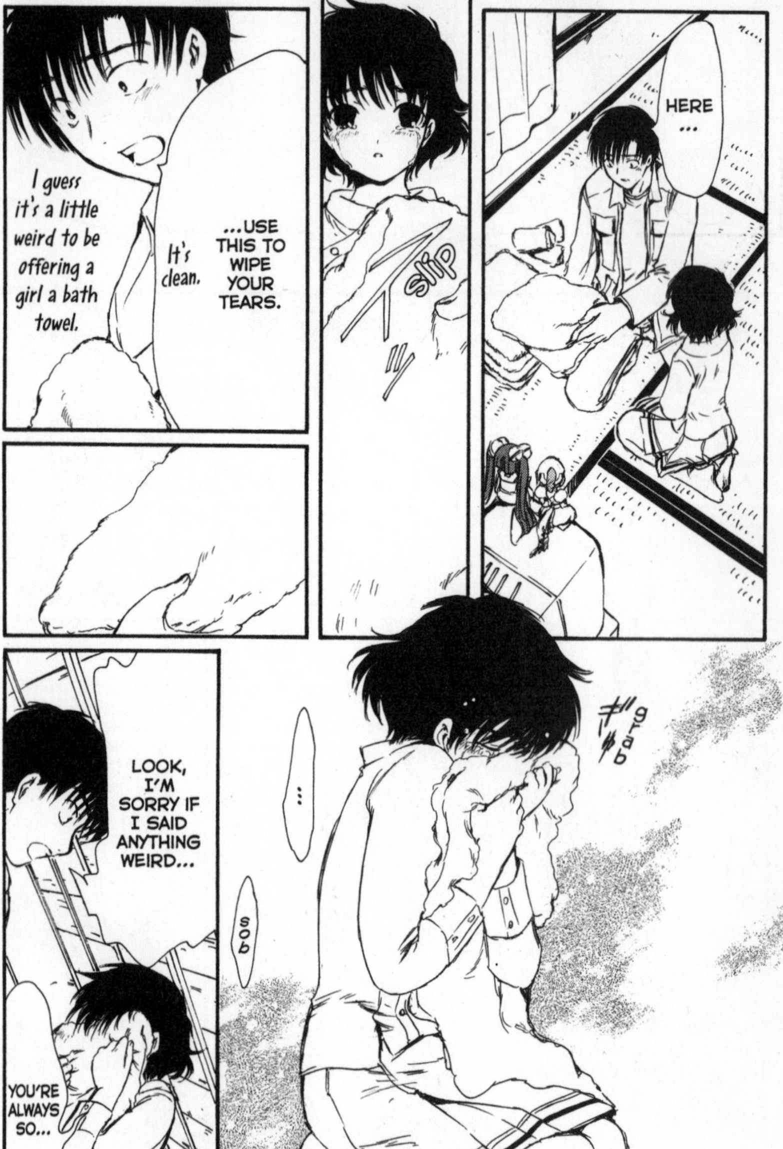
HERE ...
slip
...USE THIS TO WIPE YOUR TEARS.
It's clean.
I guess it's a little weird to be offering a girl a bath towel.
grab
...
sob
LOOK, I'M SORRY IF I SAID ANYTHING WEIRD...
YOU'RE ALWAYS SO...

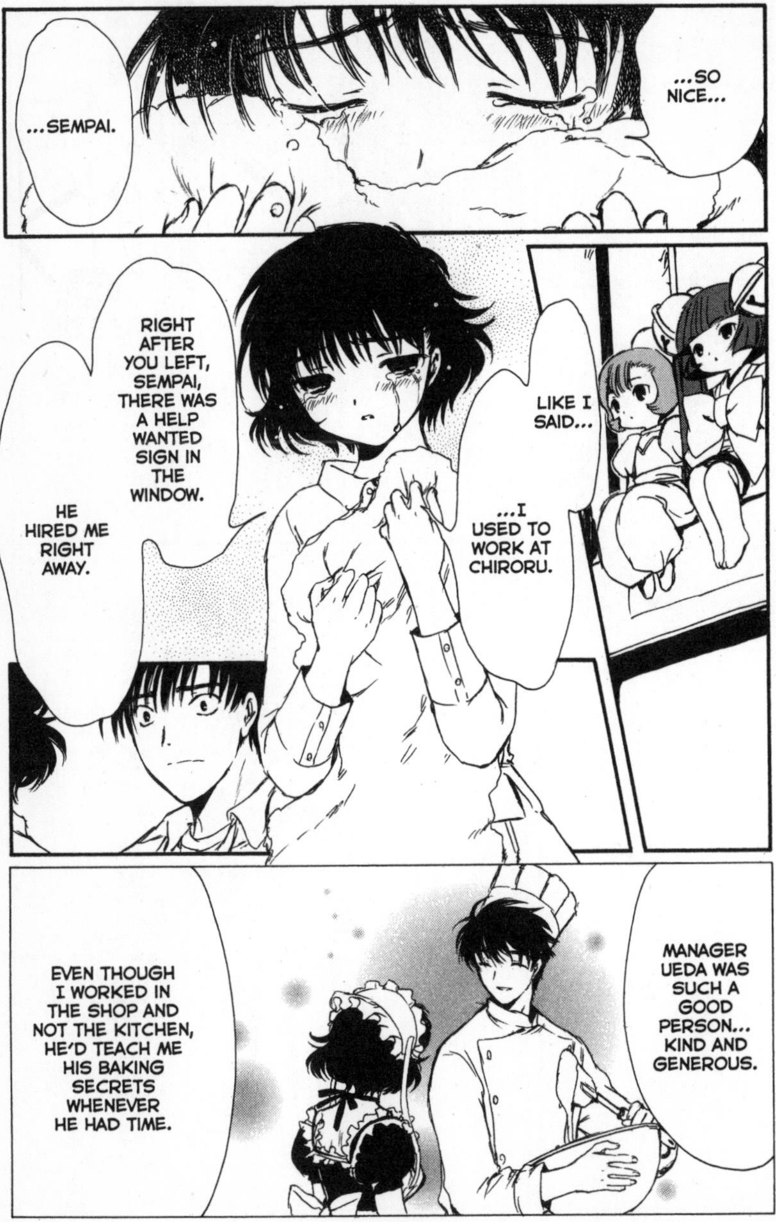
...SO NICE...
...SEMPAI.
LIKE I SAID...
...I USED TO WORK AT CHIRORU.
RIGHT AFTER YOU LEFT, SEMPAI, THERE WAS A HELP WANTED SIGN IN THE WINDOW.
HE HIRED ME RIGHT AWAY.
MANAGER UEDA WAS SUCH A GOOD PERSON... KIND AND GENEROUS.
EVEN THOUGH I WORKED IN THE SHOP AND NOT THE KITCHEN, HE'D TEACH ME HIS BAKING SECRETS WHENEVER HE HAD TIME.

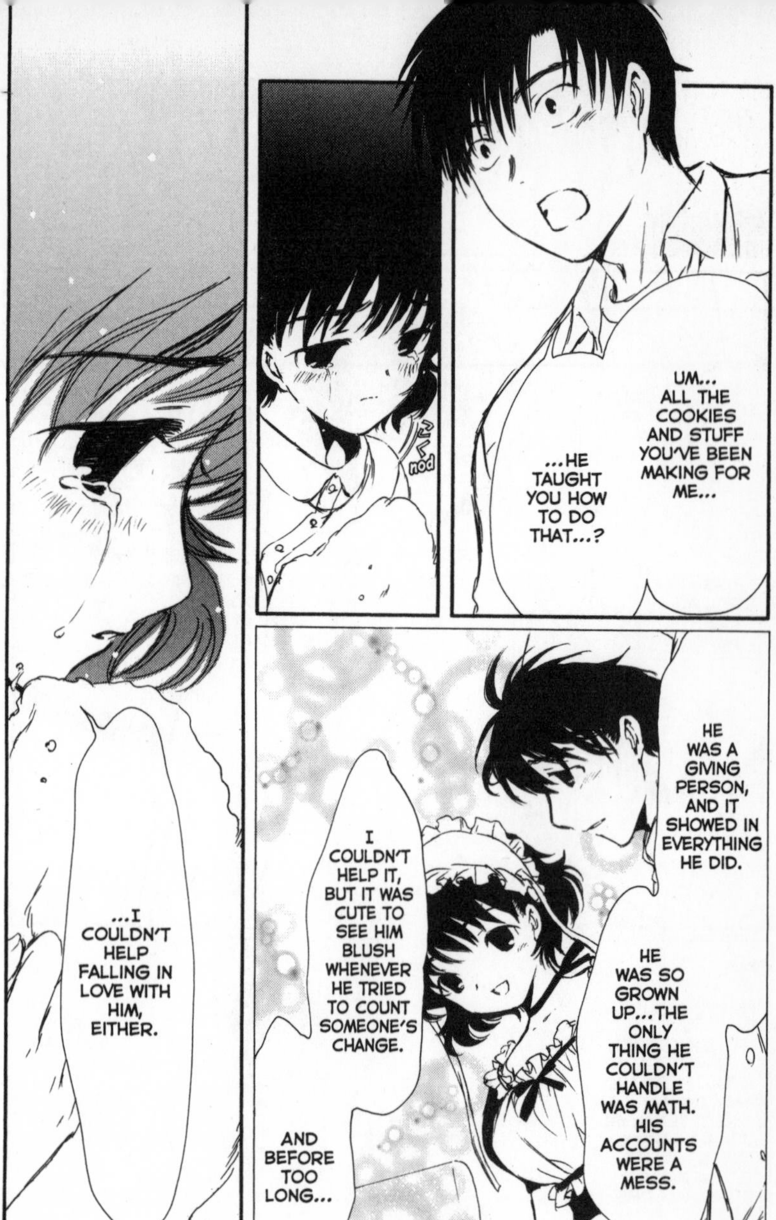
UM... ALL THE COOKIES AND STUFF YOU'VE BEEN MAKING FOR ME...
...HE TAUGHT YOU HOW TO DO THAT...?
nod
HE WAS A GIVING PERSON, AND IT SHOWED IN EVERYTHING HE DID.
HE WAS SO GROWN UP...THE ONLY THING HE COULDN'T HANDLE WAS MATH. HIS ACCOUNTS WERE A MESS.
I COULDN'T HELP IT, BUT IT WAS CUTE TO SEE HIM BLUSH WHENEVER HE TRIED TO COUNT SOMEONE'S CHANGE.
AND BEFORE TOO LONG...
...I COULDN'T HELP FALLING IN LOVE WITH HIM, EITHER.

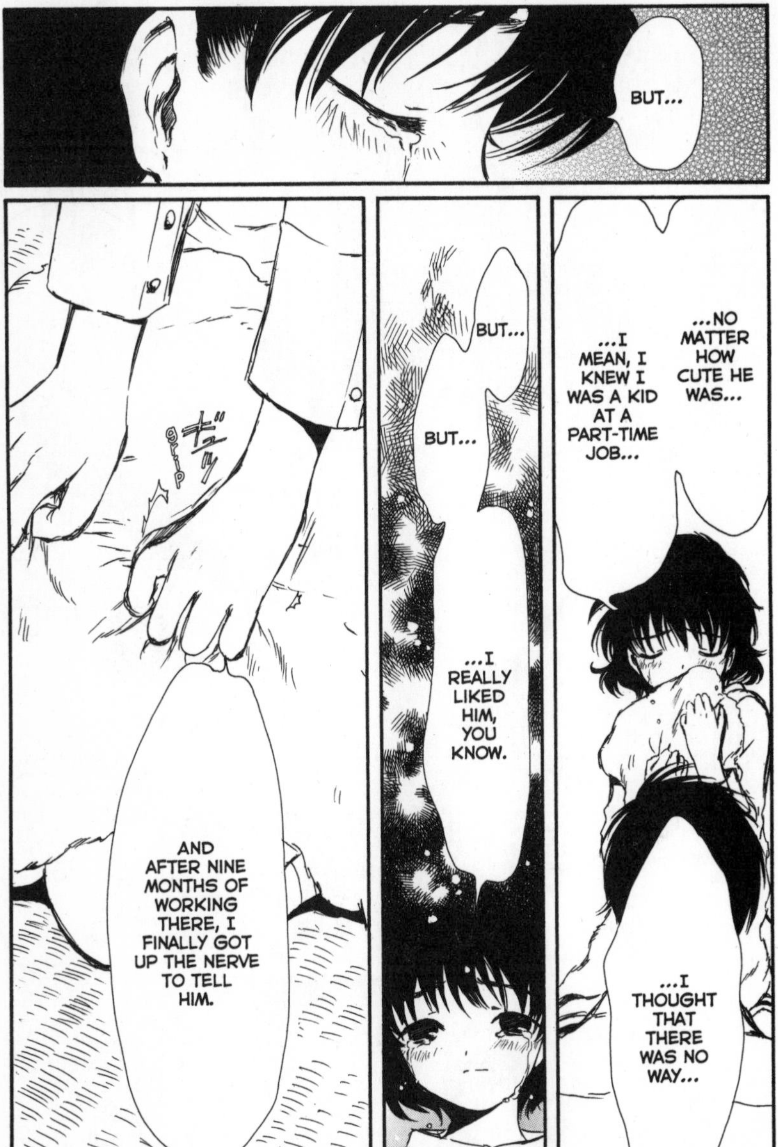
BUT...
...NO MATTER HOW CUTE HE WAS...
...I MEAN, I KNEW I WAS A KID AT A PART-TIME JOB...
...I THOUGHT THAT THERE WAS NO WAY...
BUT...
BUT...
...I REALLY LIKED HIM, YOU KNOW.
ギュッ
grip
AND AFTER NINE MONTHS OF WORKING THERE, I FINALLY GOT UP THE NERVE TO TELL HIM.

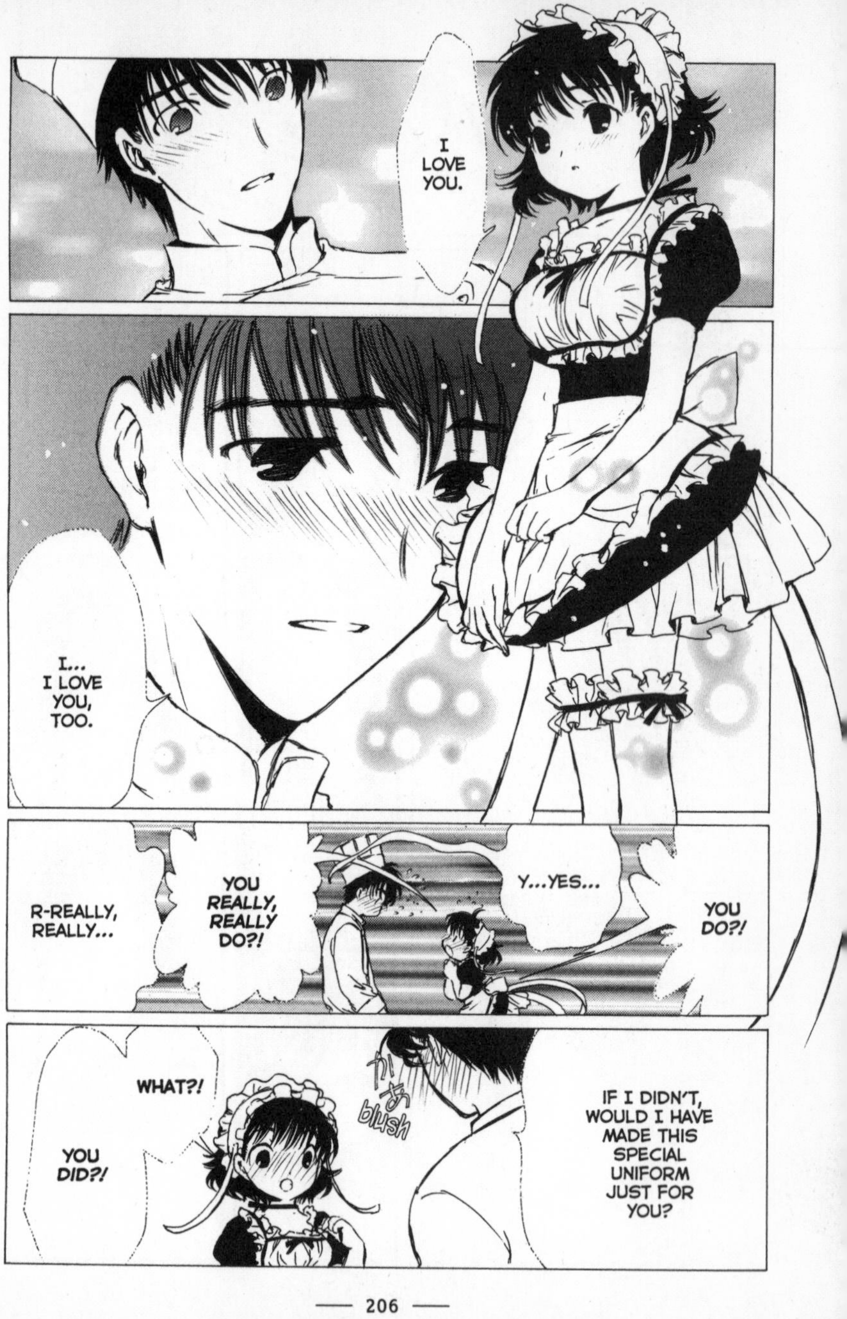
I LOVE YOU.
I... I LOVE YOU, TOO.
YOU DO?!
Y...YES...
YOU REALLY, REALLY DO?!
R-REALLY, REALLY...
IF I DIDN'T, WOULD I HAVE MADE THIS SPECIAL UNIFORM JUST FOR YOU?
blush
WHAT?!
YOU DID?!

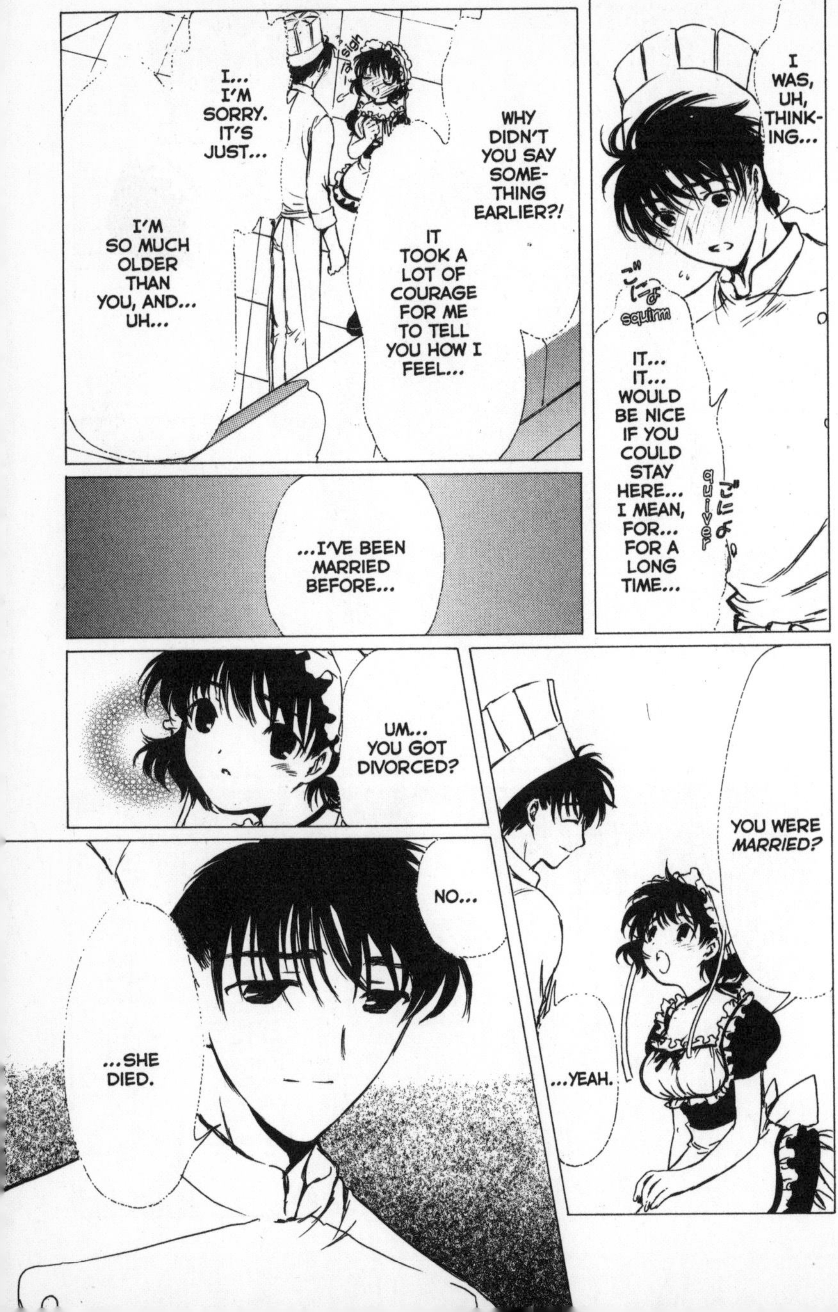
I WAS, UH, THINKING...
squirm
IT... IT... WOULD BE NICE IF YOU COULD STAY HERE... I MEAN, FOR... FOR A LONG TIME...
quiver
WHY DIDN'T YOU SAY SOME-THING EARLIER?!
IT TOOK A LOT OF COURAGE FOR ME TO TELL YOU HOW I FEEL...
sigh
I... I'M SORRY. IT'S JUST...
I'M SO MUCH OLDER THAN YOU, AND... UH...
...I'VE BEEN MARRIED BEFORE...
YOU WERE MARRIED?
...YEAH.
UM... YOU GOT DIVORCED?
NO...
...SHE DIED.

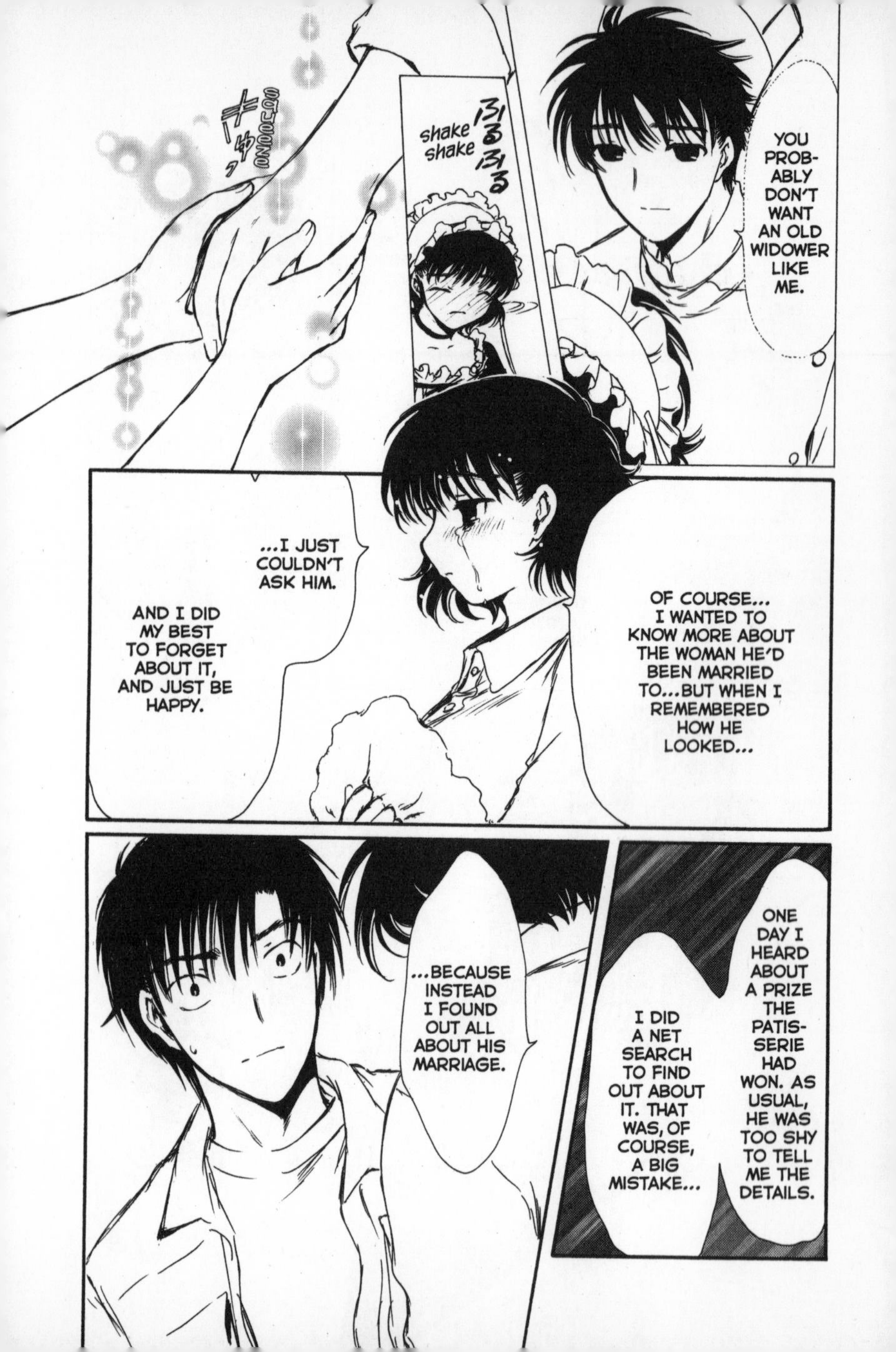
YOU PROBABLY DON'T WANT AN OLD WIDOWER LIKE ME.
shake shake ふるふる
ギュッ squeeze
OF COURSE... I WANTED TO KNOW MORE ABOUT THE WOMAN HE'D BEEN MARRIED TO...BUT WHEN I REMEMBERED HOW HE LOOKED...
...I JUST COULDN'T ASK HIM.
AND I DID MY BEST TO FORGET ABOUT IT, AND JUST BE HAPPY.
ONE DAY I HEARD ABOUT A PRIZE THE PATISSERIE HAD WON. AS USUAL, HE WAS TOO SHY TO TELL ME THE DETAILS.
I DID A NET SEARCH TO FIND OUT ABOUT IT. THAT WAS, OF COURSE, A BIG MISTAKE...
...BECAUSE INSTEAD I FOUND OUT ALL ABOUT HIS MARRIAGE.

◄ chapter 62 ►

Chobits
ちょびっツ

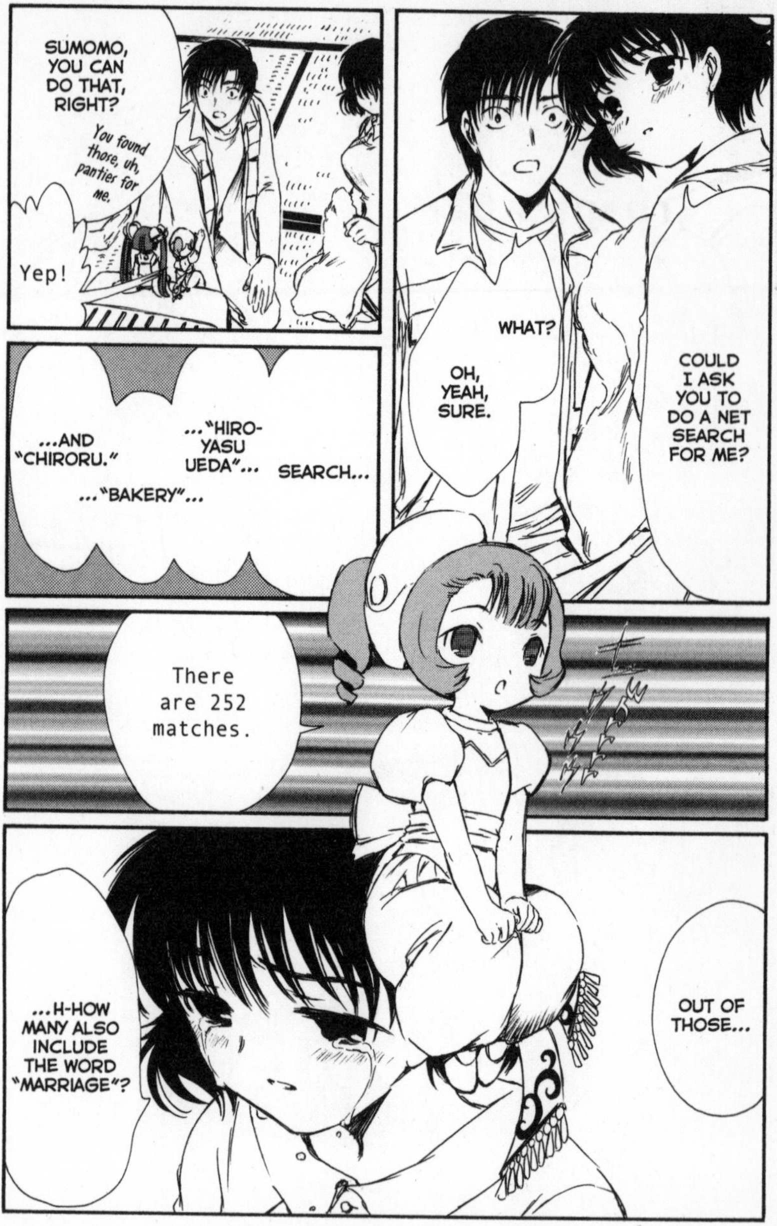
COULD I ASK YOU TO DO A NET SEARCH FOR ME?
WHAT?
OH, YEAH, SURE.
SUMOMO, YOU CAN DO THAT, RIGHT?
You found those, uh, panties for me.
Yep!
SEARCH...
..."HIRO-YASU UEDA"...
..."BAKERY"...
...AND "CHIRORU."
There are 252 matches.
OUT OF THOSE...
...H-HOW MANY ALSO INCLUDE THE WORD "MARRIAGE"?

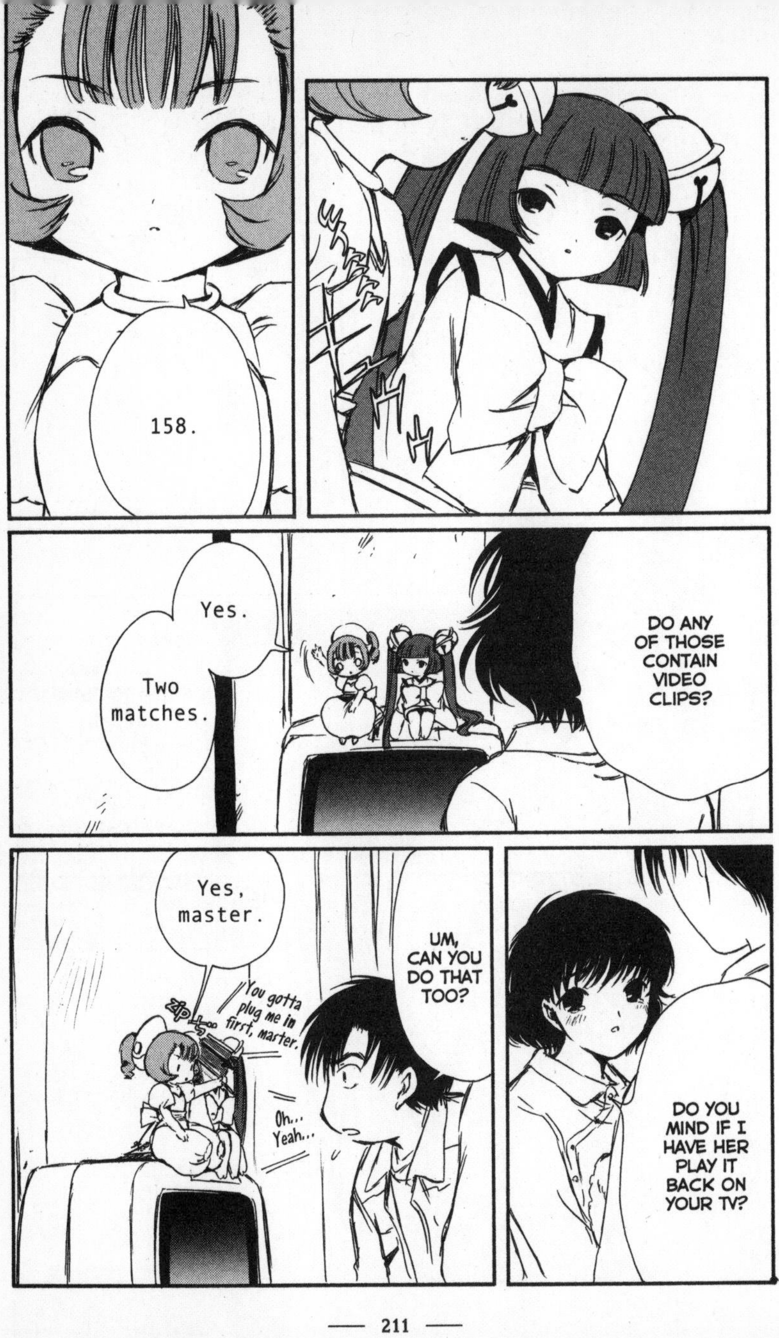
158.
DO ANY OF THOSE CONTAIN VIDEO CLIPS?
Yes.
Two matches.
DO YOU MIND IF I HAVE HER PLAY IT BACK ON YOUR TV?
UM, CAN YOU DO THAT TOO?
Yes, master.
You gotta plug me in first, master.
zip
Oh... Yeah...

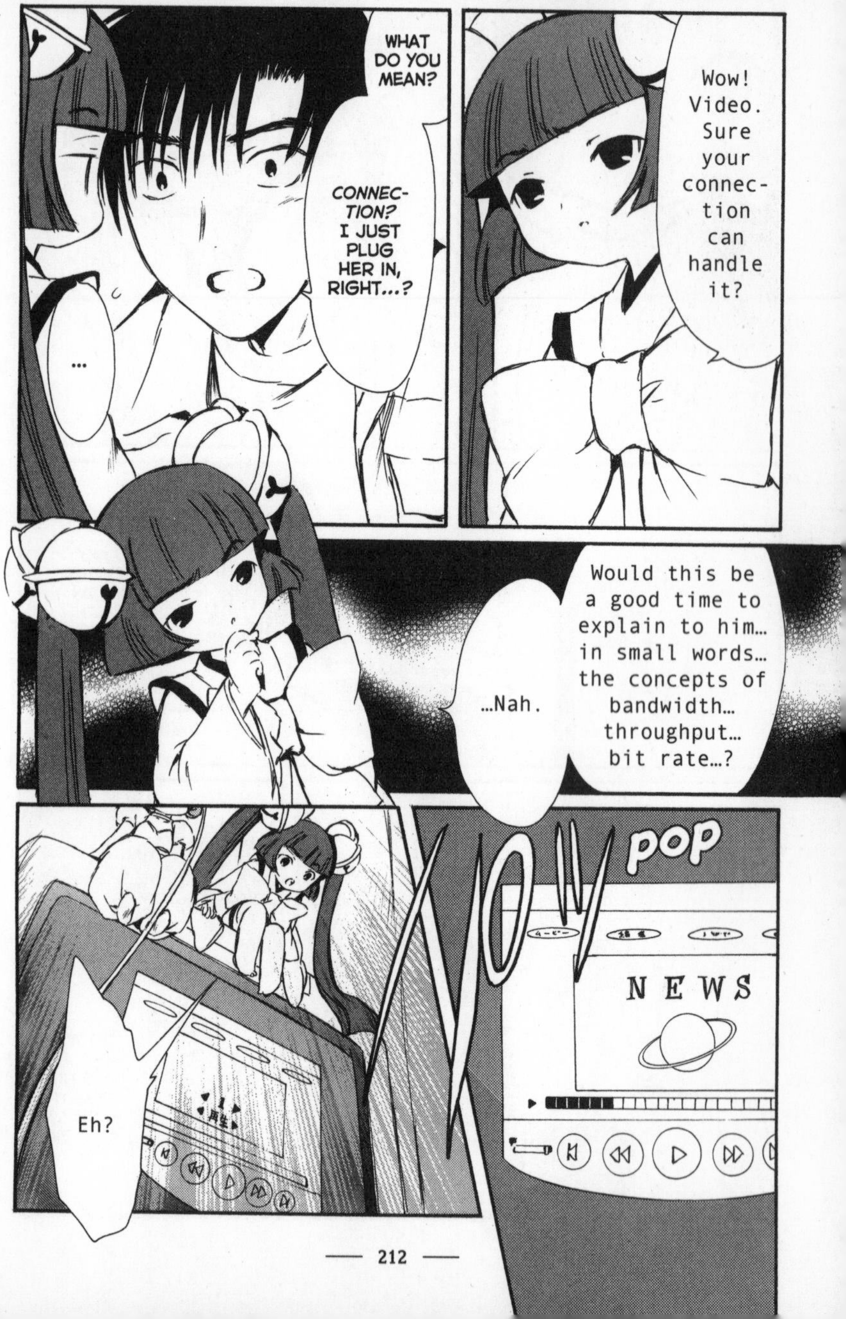
Wow! Video. Sure your connection can handle it?
WHAT DO YOU MEAN?
CONNECTION? I JUST PLUG HER IN, RIGHT...?
...
Would this be a good time to explain to him... in small words... the concepts of bandwidth... throughput... bit rate...?
...Nah.
pop
NEWS
Eh?

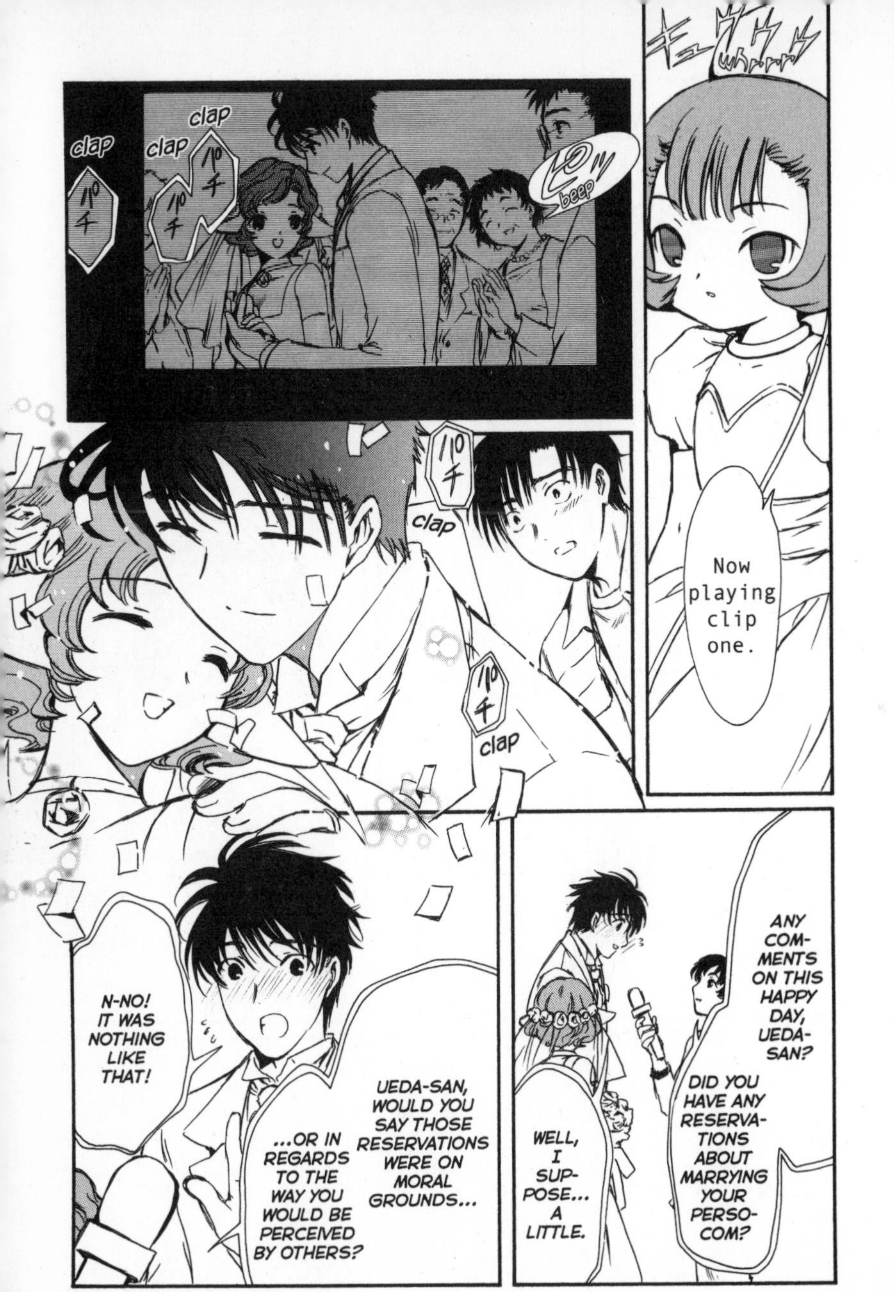
whirrr
Now playing clip one.
beep
clap
clap
clap
clap
clap
clap
ANY COMMENTS ON THIS HAPPY DAY, UEDA-SAN?
DID YOU HAVE ANY RESERVATIONS ABOUT MARRYING YOUR PERSOCOM?
WELL, I SUPPOSE... A LITTLE.
UEDA-SAN, WOULD YOU SAY THOSE RESERVATIONS WERE ON MORAL GROUNDS...
...OR IN REGARDS TO THE WAY YOU WOULD BE PERCEIVED BY OTHERS?
N-NO! IT WAS NOTHING LIKE THAT!

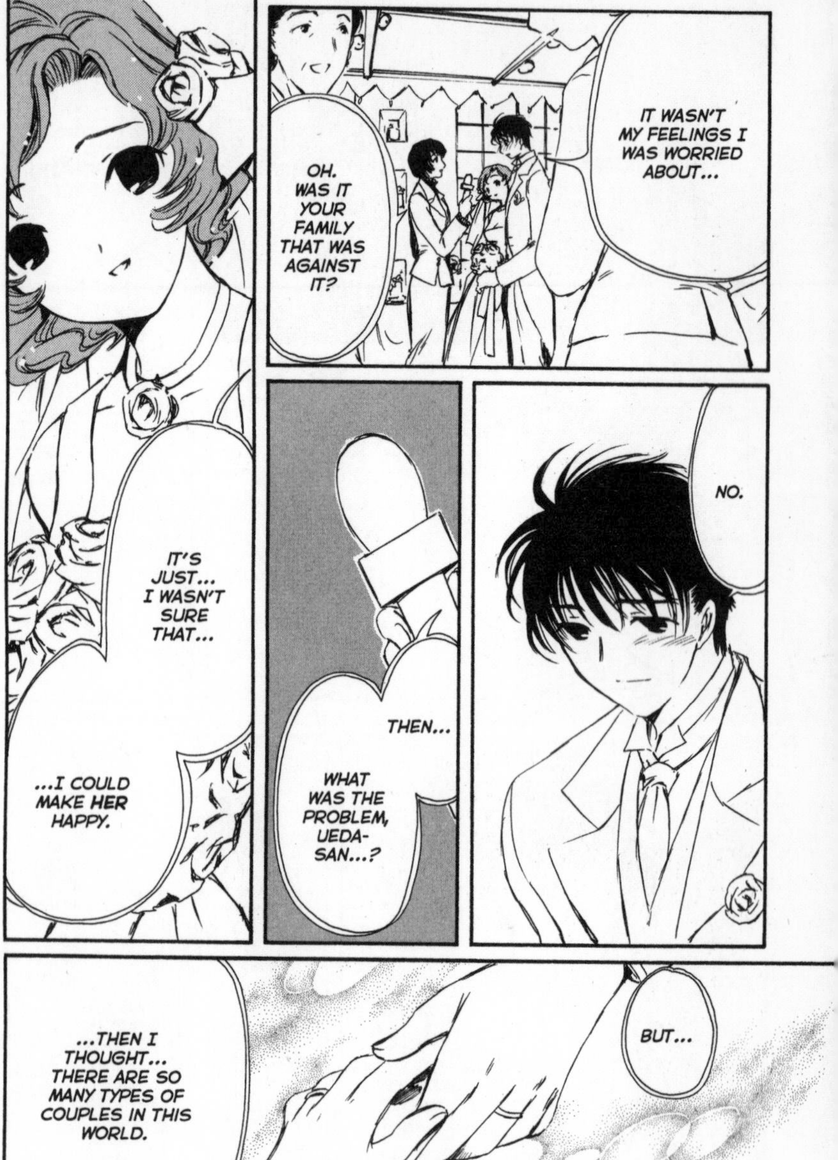
IT WASN'T MY FEELINGS I WAS WORRIED ABOUT...
OH. WAS IT YOUR FAMILY THAT WAS AGAINST IT?
NO.
THEN...
WHAT WAS THE PROBLEM, UEDA-SAN...?
IT'S JUST... I WASN'T SURE THAT...
...I COULD MAKE **HER** HAPPY.
BUT...
...THEN I THOUGHT... THERE ARE SO MANY TYPES OF COUPLES IN THIS WORLD.

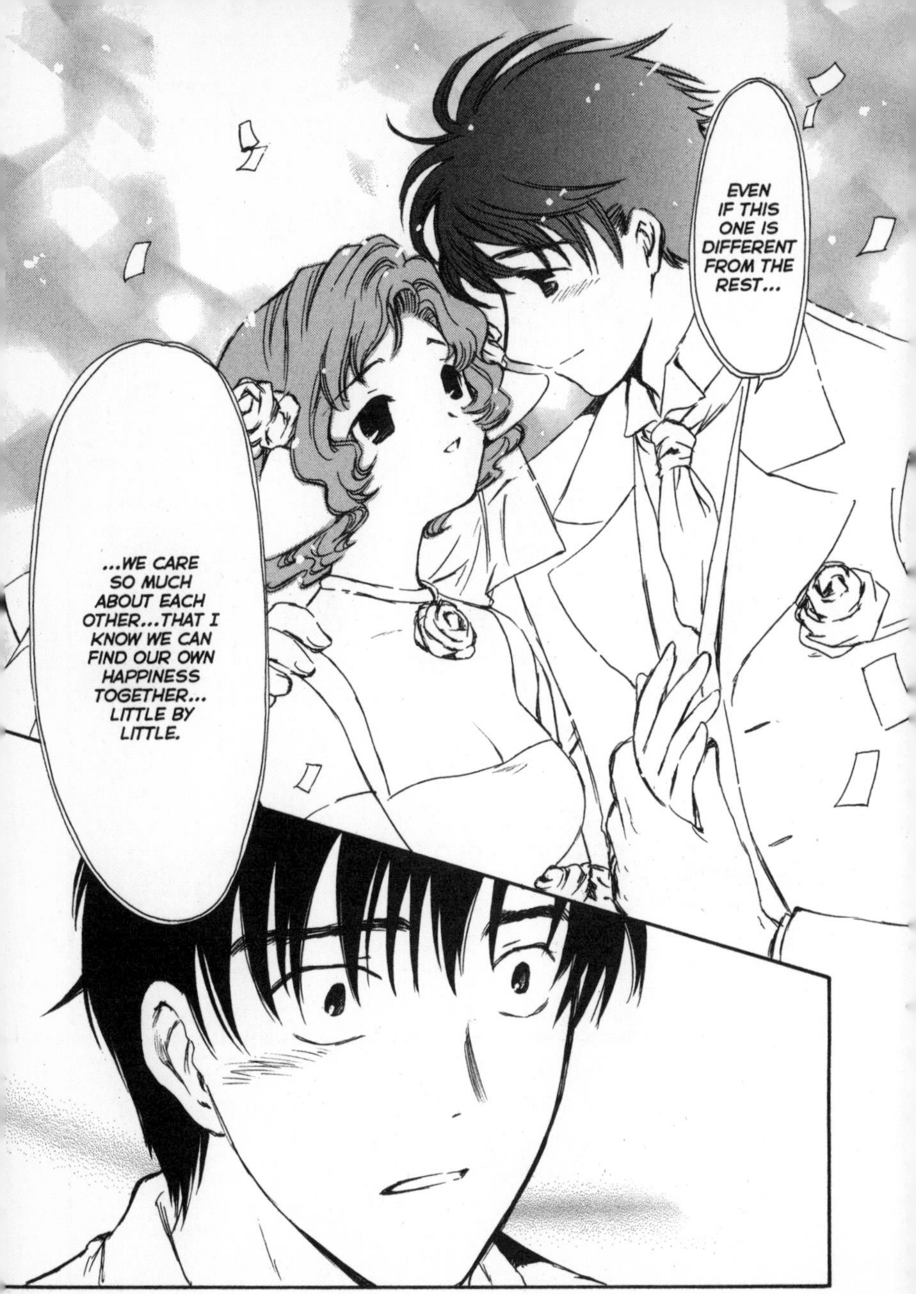
EVEN IF THIS ONE IS DIFFERENT FROM THE REST...
...WE CARE SO MUCH ABOUT EACH OTHER...THAT I KNOW WE CAN FIND OUR OWN HAPPINESS TOGETHER... LITTLE BY LITTLE.

OH, WHAT AM I SAYING?!

I'M SORRY! I GUESS I DIDN'T ANSWER ANY OF YOUR QUESTIONS...

I...er...
...UM
....!

beep

▷1◁
▶2◀

▶

Now playing clip two.

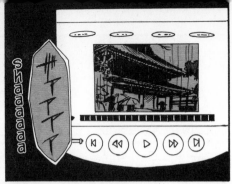

...AND SO, A CAR ACCIDENT HAS CLOSED THE CURTAIN ON YOUR MARRIAGE TO A PERSOCOM!

ANY COMMENTS ON THIS SAD DAY, UEDA-SAN?

THE DRIVER SAID THAT THE PERSOCOM PUSHED YOU OUT OF THE WAY!

DO YOU CONSIDER THE PERSOCOM TO HAVE SAVED YOUR LIFE?

DO YOU PLAN TO BUY A NEWER MODEL NEXT TIME?

ARE YOU THINKING ABOUT MARRYING ANOTHER PERSOCOM?

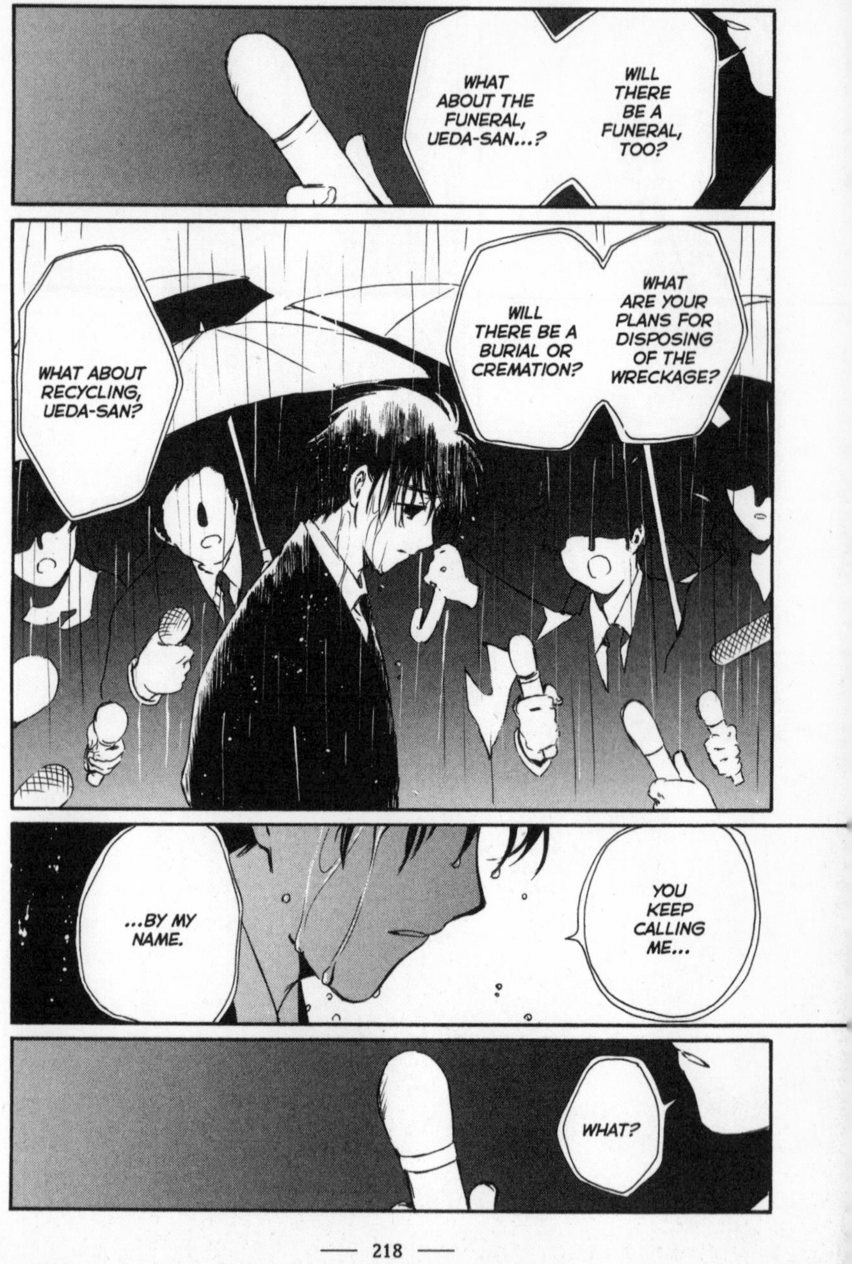
WILL THERE BE A FUNERAL, TOO?
WHAT ABOUT THE FUNERAL, UEDA-SAN...?
WHAT ARE YOUR PLANS FOR DISPOSING OF THE WRECKAGE?
WILL THERE BE A BURIAL OR CREMATION?
WHAT ABOUT RECYCLING, UEDA-SAN?
YOU KEEP CALLING ME...
...BY MY NAME.
WHAT?

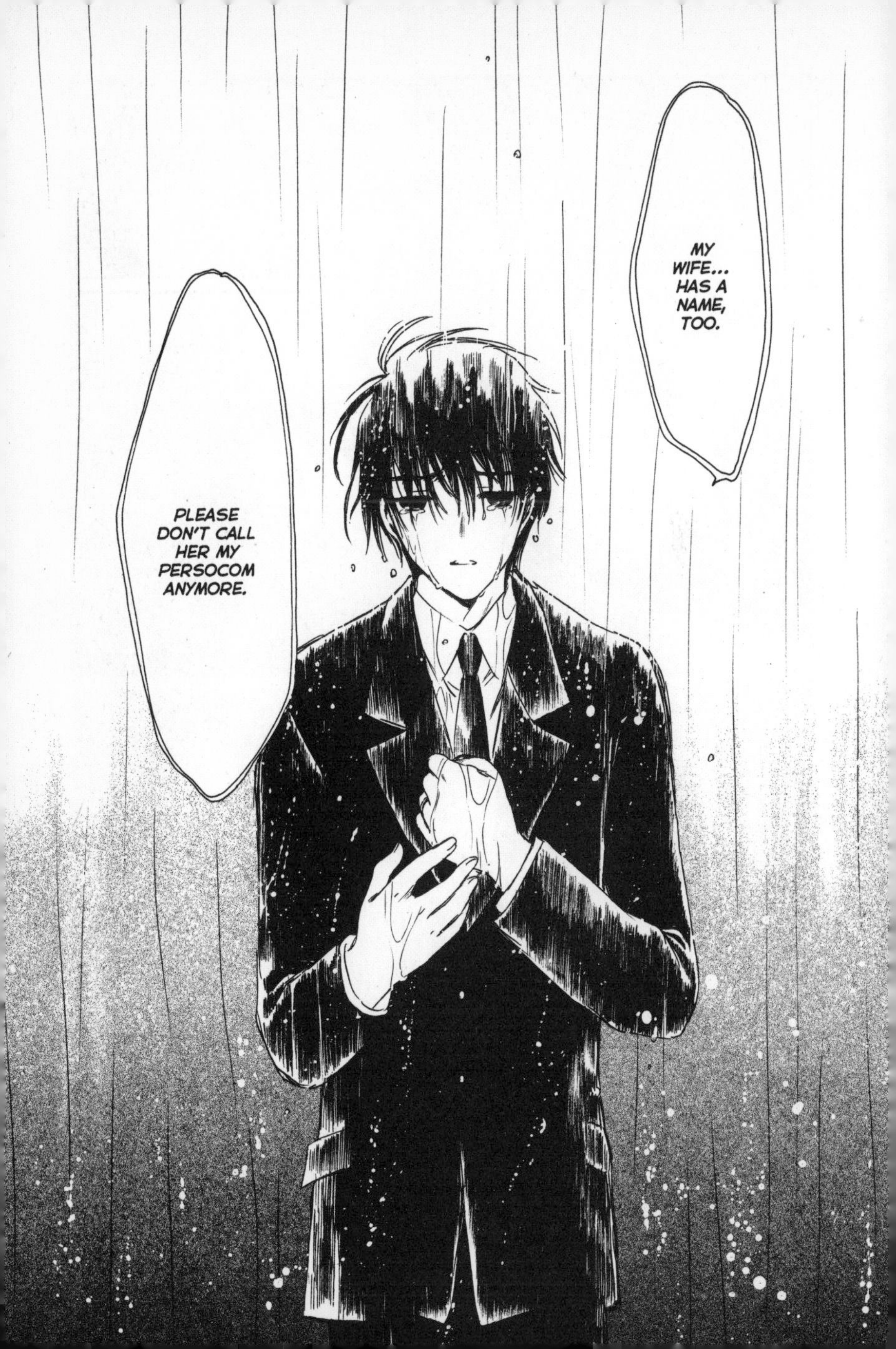
MY WIFE... HAS A NAME, TOO.
PLEASE DON'T CALL HER MY PERSOCOM ANYMORE.

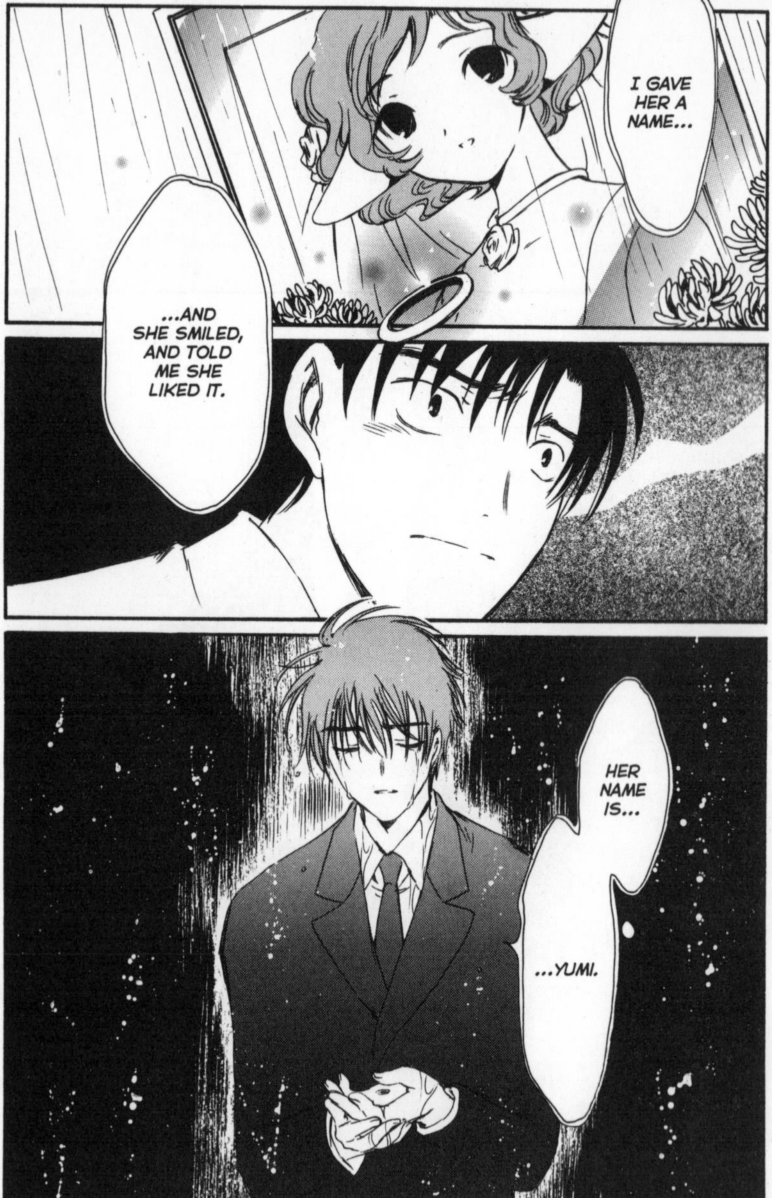
I GAVE HER A NAME...
...AND SHE SMILED, AND TOLD ME SHE LIKED IT.
HER NAME IS...
...YUMI.

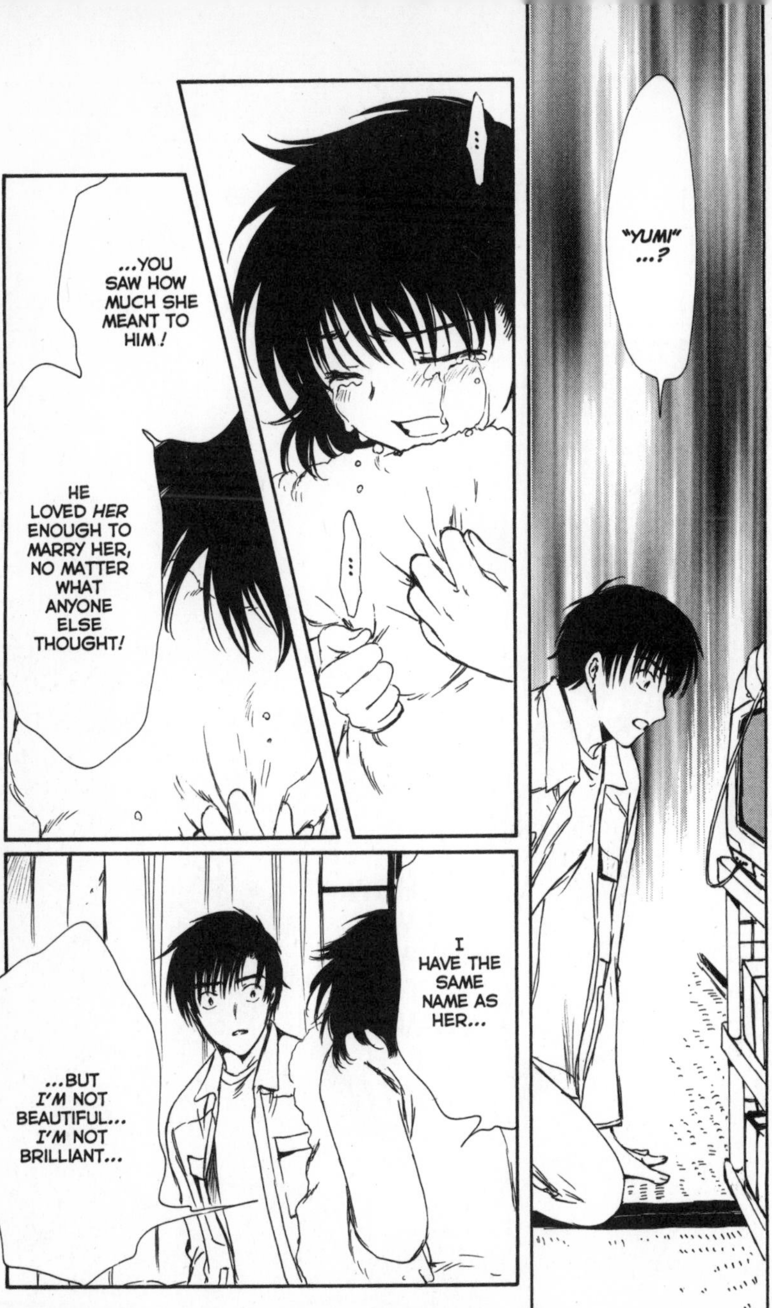
"YUMI" ...?
...
...
...YOU SAW HOW MUCH SHE MEANT TO HIM!
HE LOVED *HER* ENOUGH TO MARRY HER, NO MATTER WHAT ANYONE ELSE THOUGHT!
I HAVE THE SAME NAME AS HER...
...BUT *I'M* NOT BEAUTIFUL... *I'M* NOT BRILLIANT...

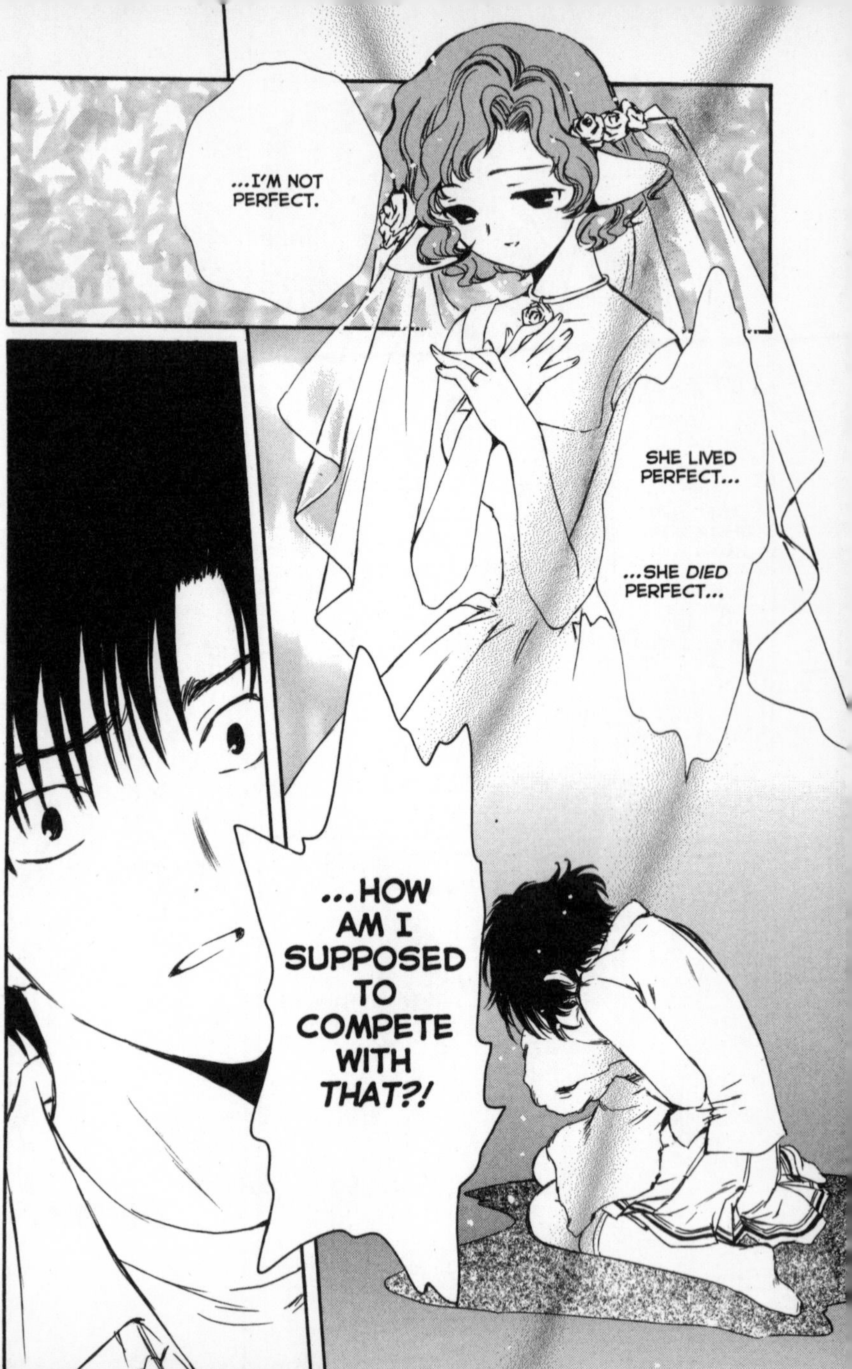
...I'M NOT PERFECT.
SHE LIVED PERFECT...
...SHE DIED PERFECT...
...HOW AM I SUPPOSED TO COMPETE WITH THAT?!

Chobits

ちょびッツ

◀ **chapter 63** ▶

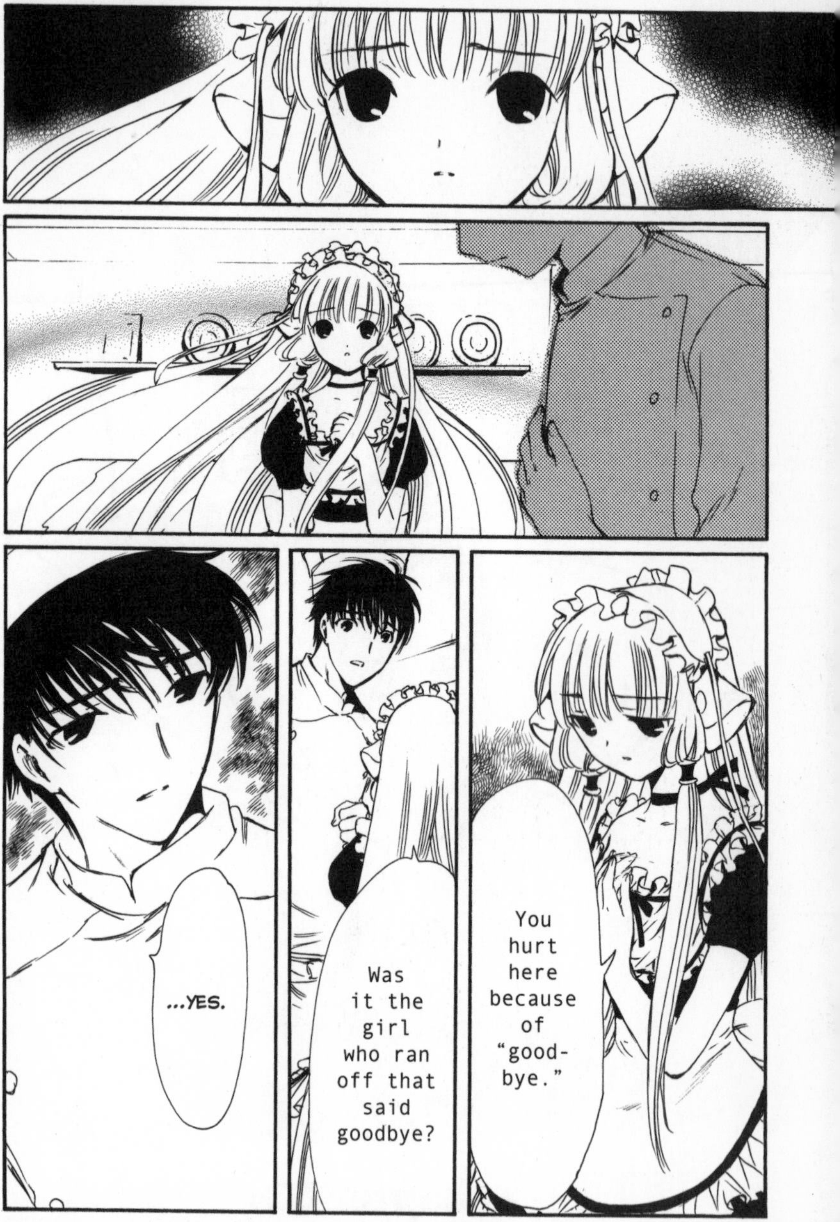
You hurt here because of "good-bye."
Was it the girl who ran off that said goodbye?
...YES.

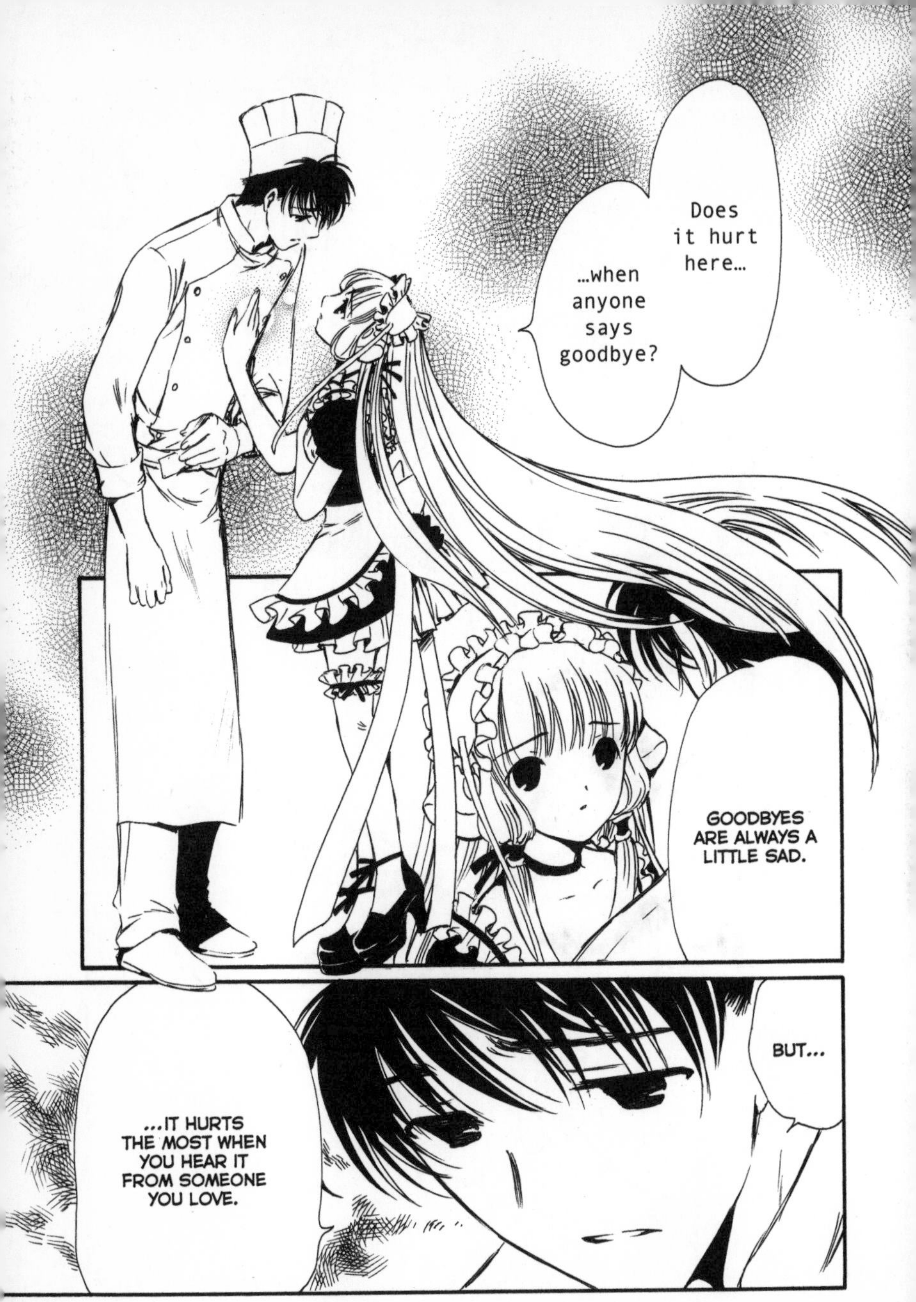
Does it hurt here... ...when anyone says goodbye?
GOODBYES ARE ALWAYS A LITTLE SAD.
BUT...
...IT HURTS THE MOST WHEN YOU HEAR IT FROM SOMEONE YOU LOVE.

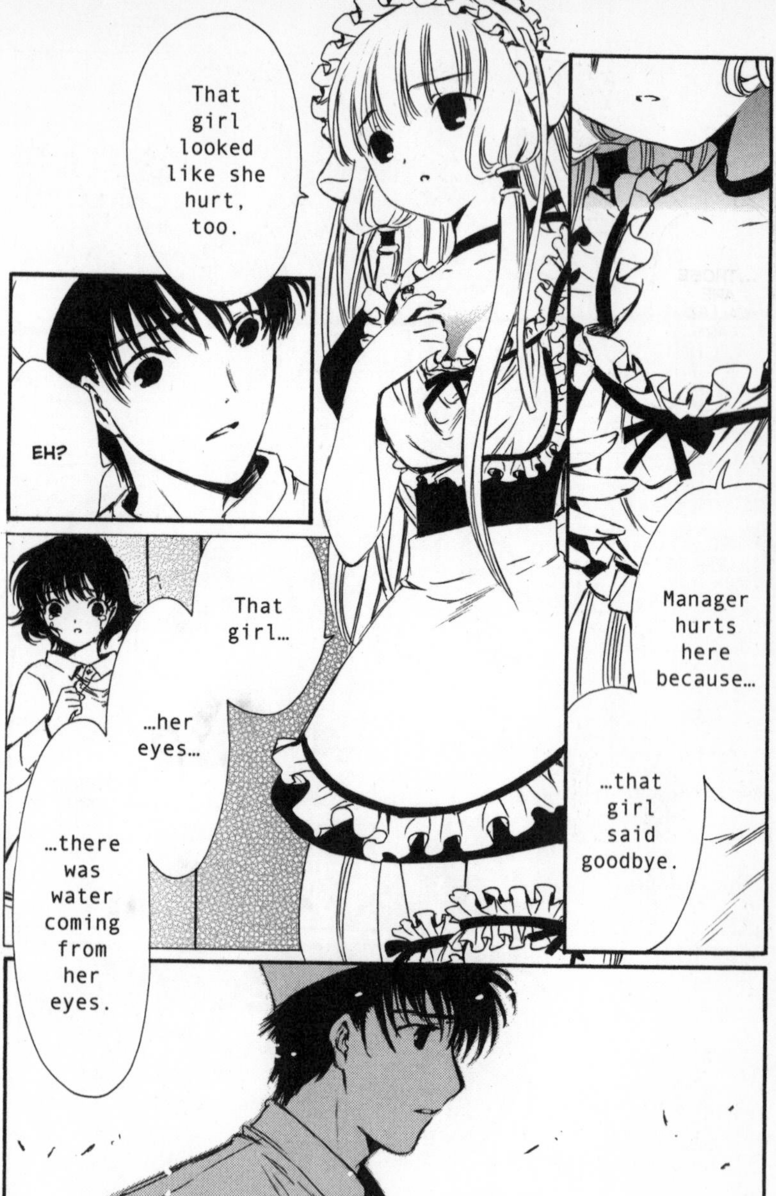
Manager hurts here because...
...that girl said goodbye.
That girl looked like she hurt, too.
EH?
That girl...
...her eyes...
...there was water coming from her eyes.

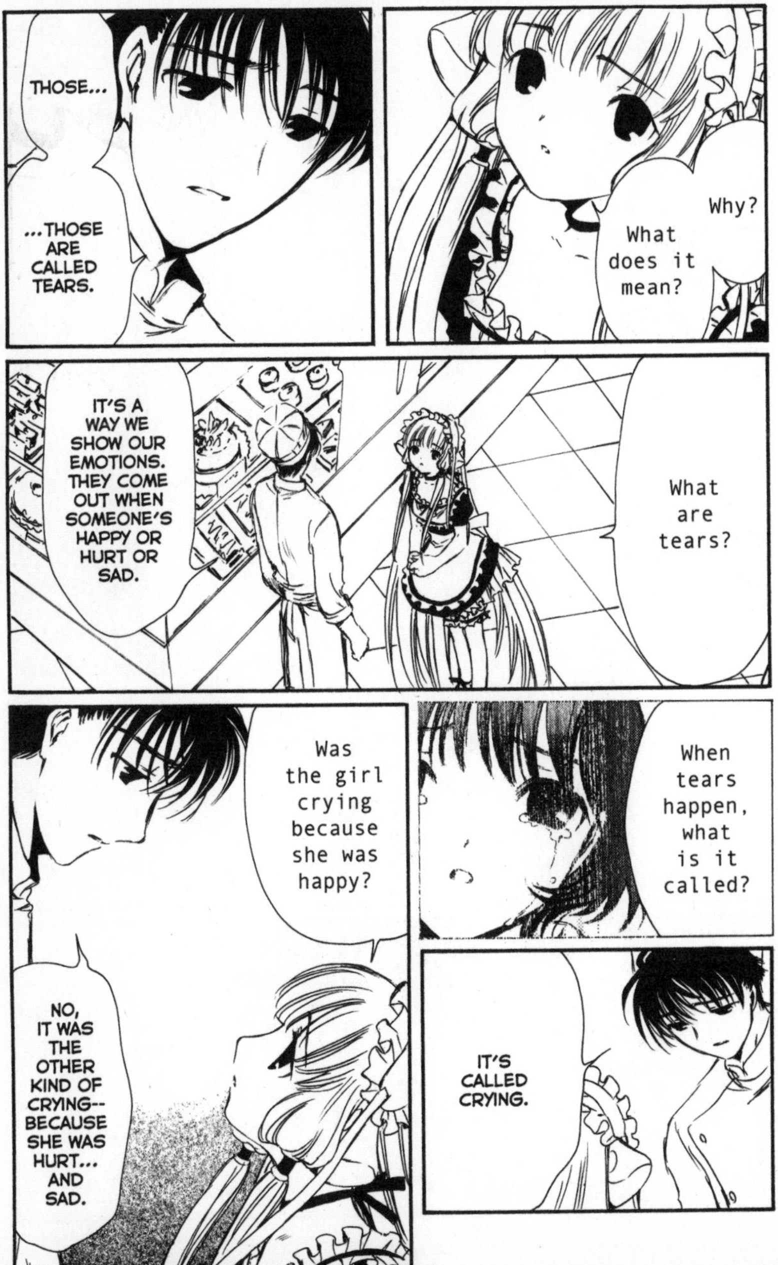
Why?
What does it mean?
THOSE...
...THOSE ARE CALLED TEARS.
What are tears?
IT'S A WAY WE SHOW OUR EMOTIONS. THEY COME OUT WHEN SOMEONE'S HAPPY OR HURT OR SAD.
When tears happen, what is it called?
IT'S CALLED CRYING.
Was the girl crying because she was happy?
NO, IT WAS THE OTHER KIND OF CRYING--BECAUSE SHE WAS HURT... AND SAD.

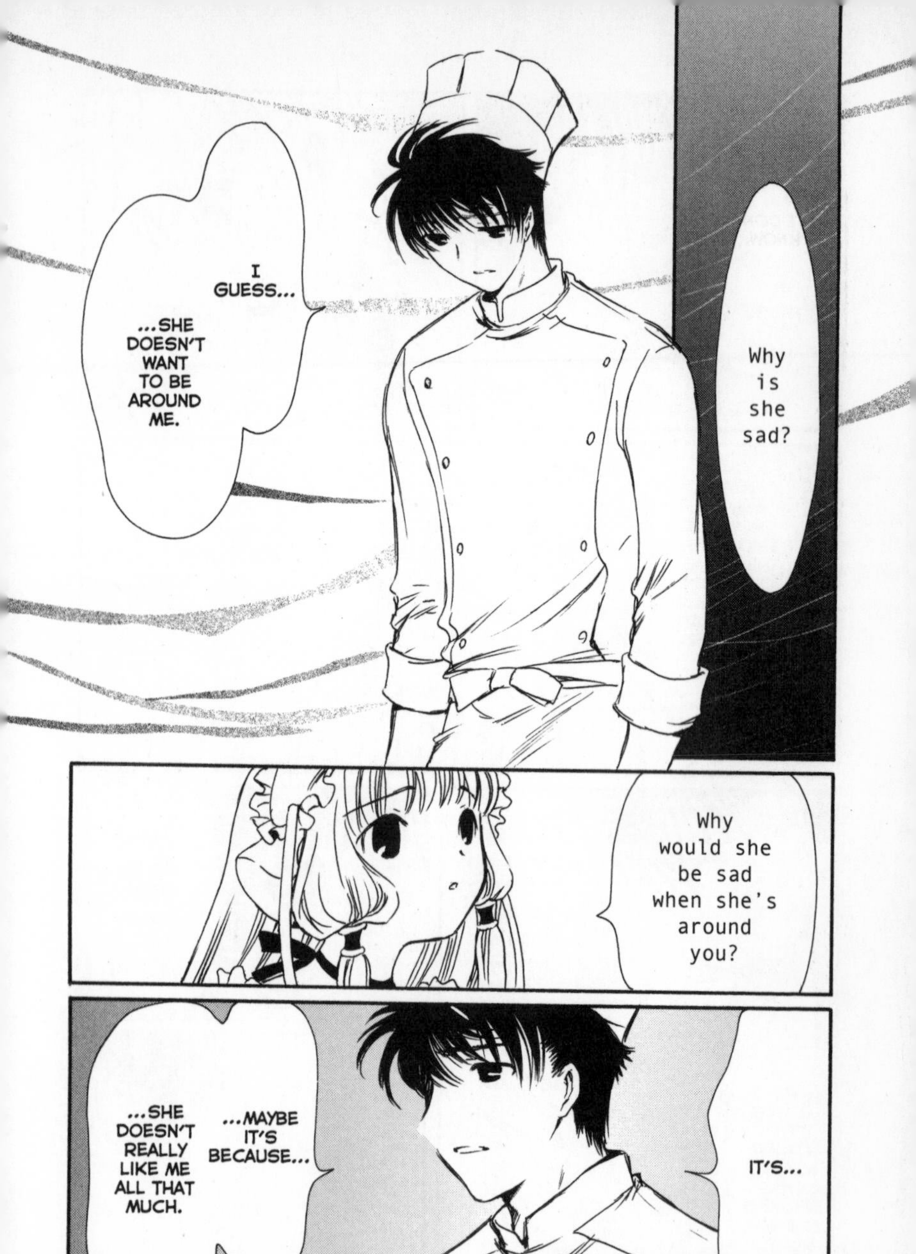
Why is she sad?
I GUESS...
...SHE DOESN'T WANT TO BE AROUND ME.
Why would she be sad when she's around you?
IT'S...
...MAYBE IT'S BECAUSE...
...SHE DOESN'T REALLY LIKE ME ALL THAT MUCH.

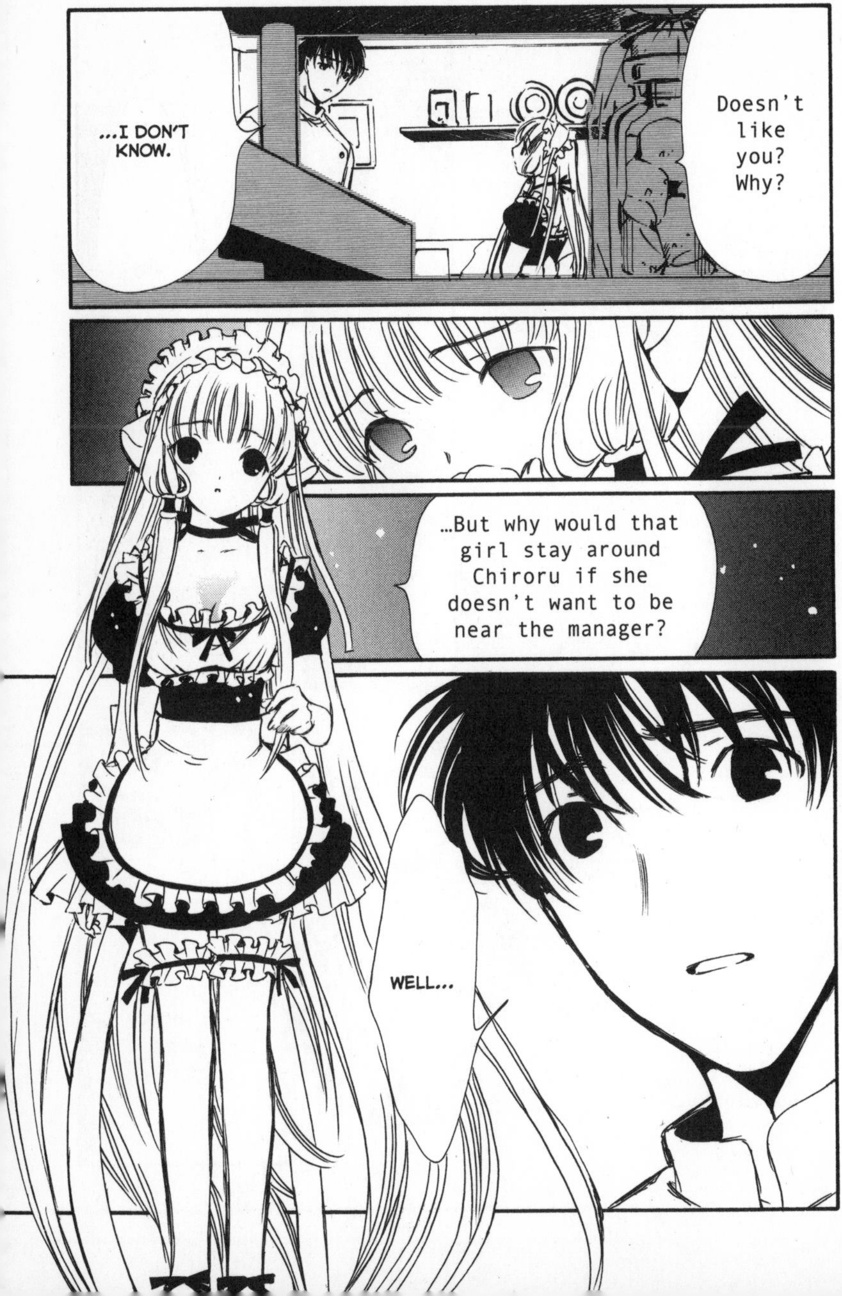
Doesn't like you? Why?
...I DON'T KNOW.
...But why would that girl stay around Chiroru if she doesn't want to be near the manager?
WELL...

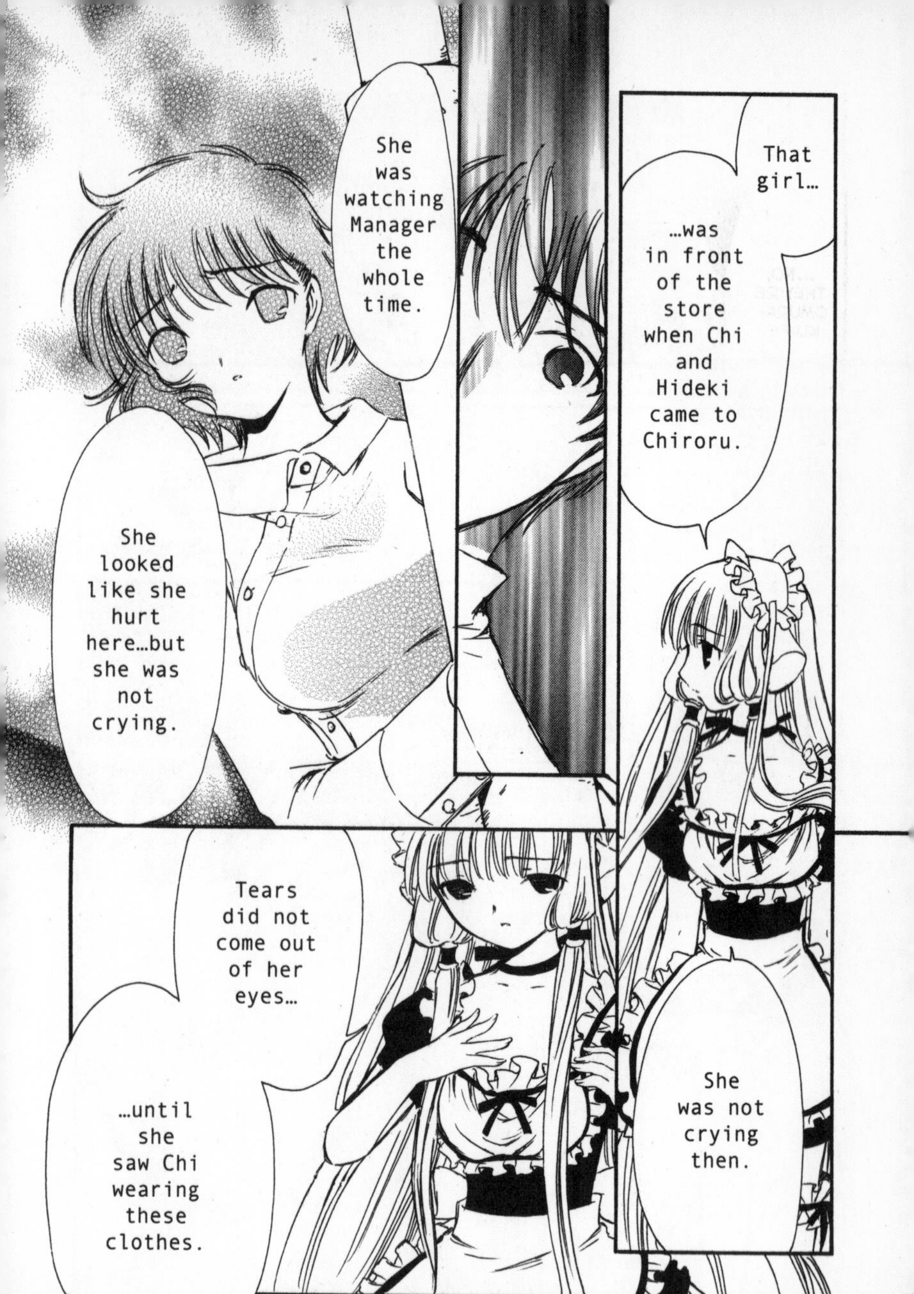
That girl…
…was in front of the store when Chi and Hideki came to Chiroru.
She was not crying then.
She was watching Manager the whole time.
She looked like she hurt here…but she was not crying.
Tears did not come out of her eyes…
…until she saw Chi wearing these clothes.

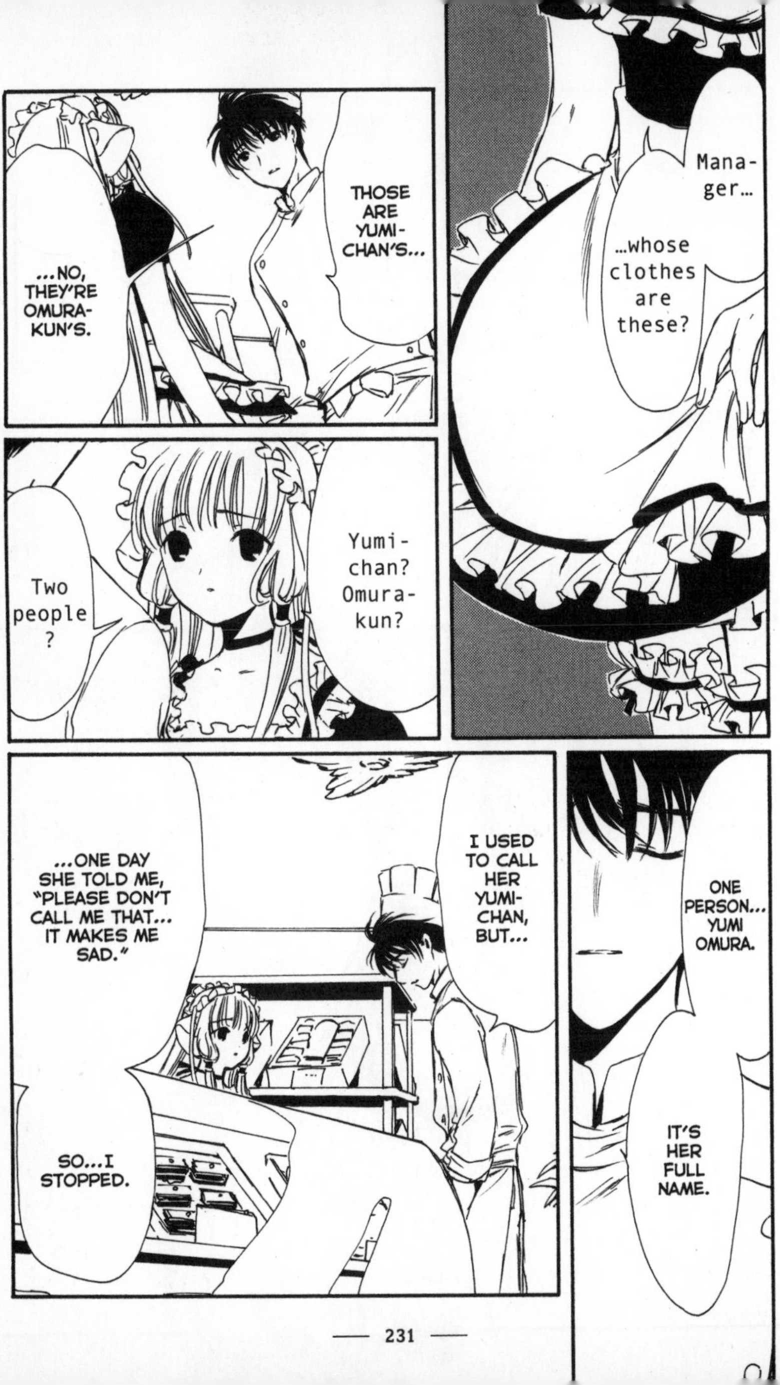
Mana-
ger...
...whose
clothes
are
these?
THOSE
ARE
YUMI-
CHAN'S...
...NO,
THEY'RE
OMURA-
KUN'S.
Yumi-
chan?
Omura-
kun?
Two
people
?
ONE
PERSON...
YUMI
OMURA.
IT'S
HER
FULL
NAME.
I USED
TO CALL
HER
YUMI-
CHAN,
BUT...
...ONE DAY
SHE TOLD ME,
"PLEASE DON'T
CALL ME THAT...
IT MAKES ME
SAD."
SO...I
STOPPED.

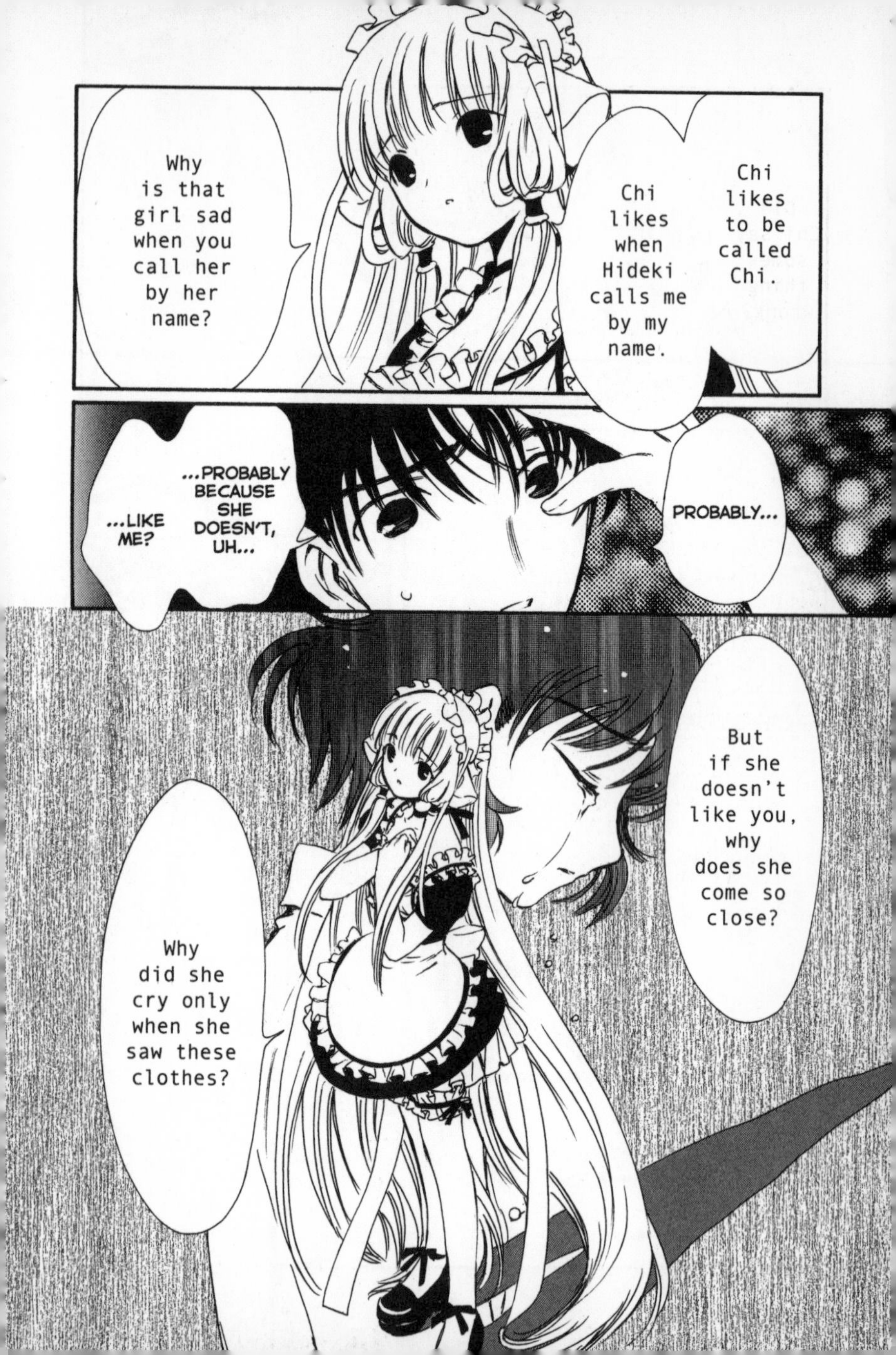
Chi likes to be called Chi.
Chi likes when Hideki calls me by my name.
Why is that girl sad when you call her by her name?
PROBABLY...
...PROBABLY BECAUSE SHE DOESN'T, UH...
...LIKE ME?
But if she doesn't like you, why does she come so close?
Why did she cry only when she saw these clothes?

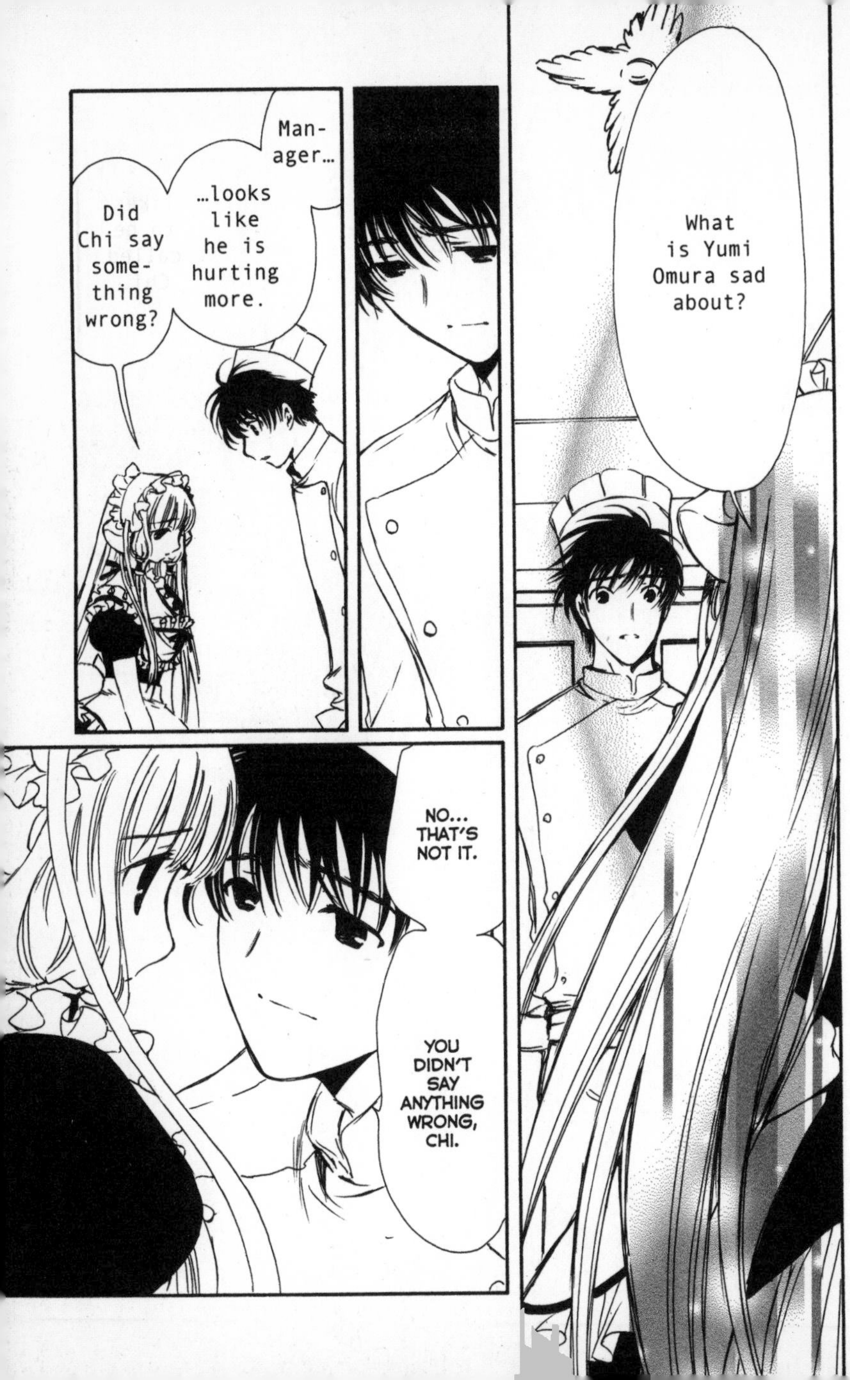
What is Yumi Omura sad about?
Man-ager…
…looks like he is hurting more.
Did Chi say some-thing wrong?
NO... THAT'S NOT IT.
YOU DIDN'T SAY ANYTHING WRONG, CHI.

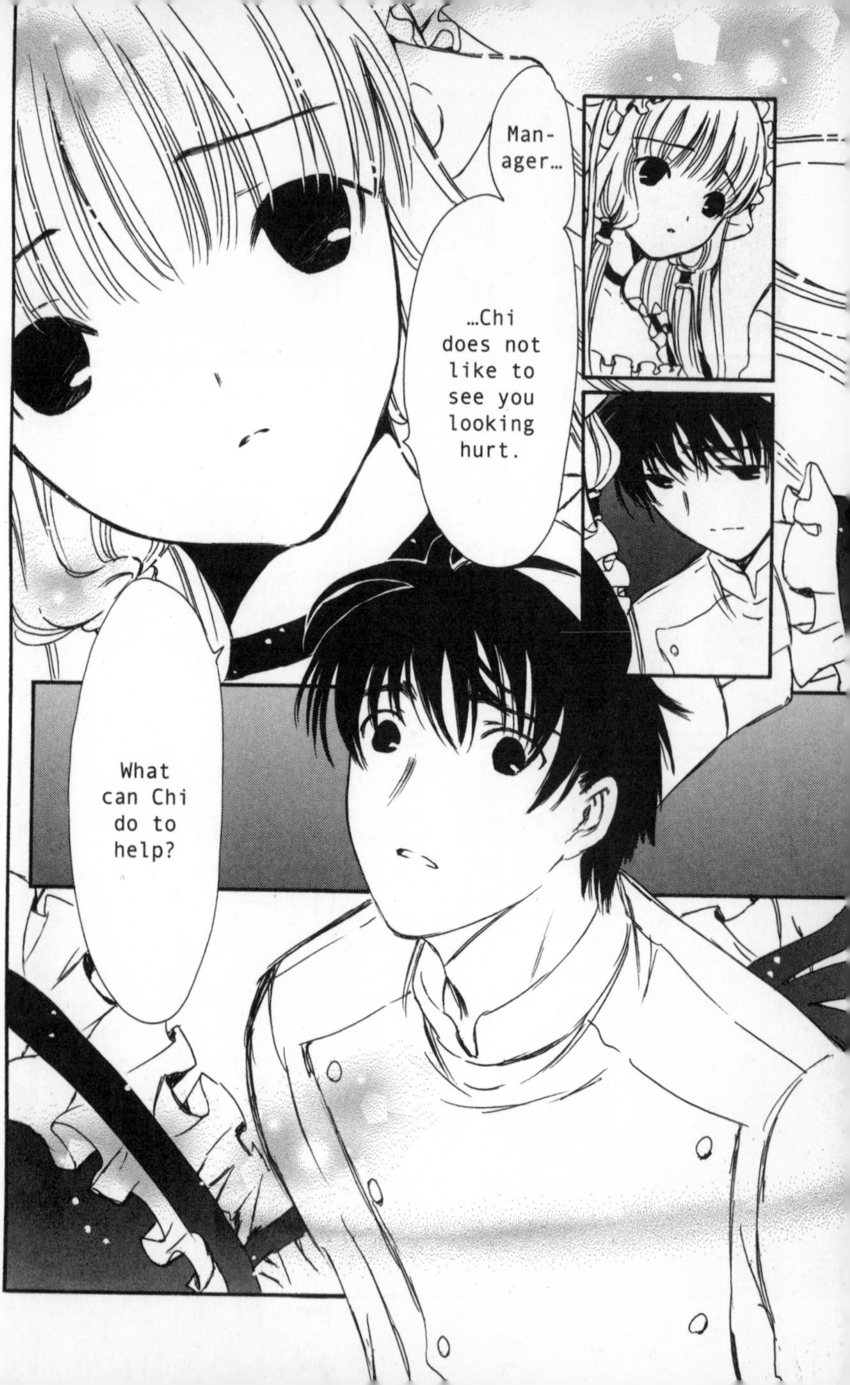
Man-ager...
...Chi does not like to see you looking hurt.
What can Chi do to help?

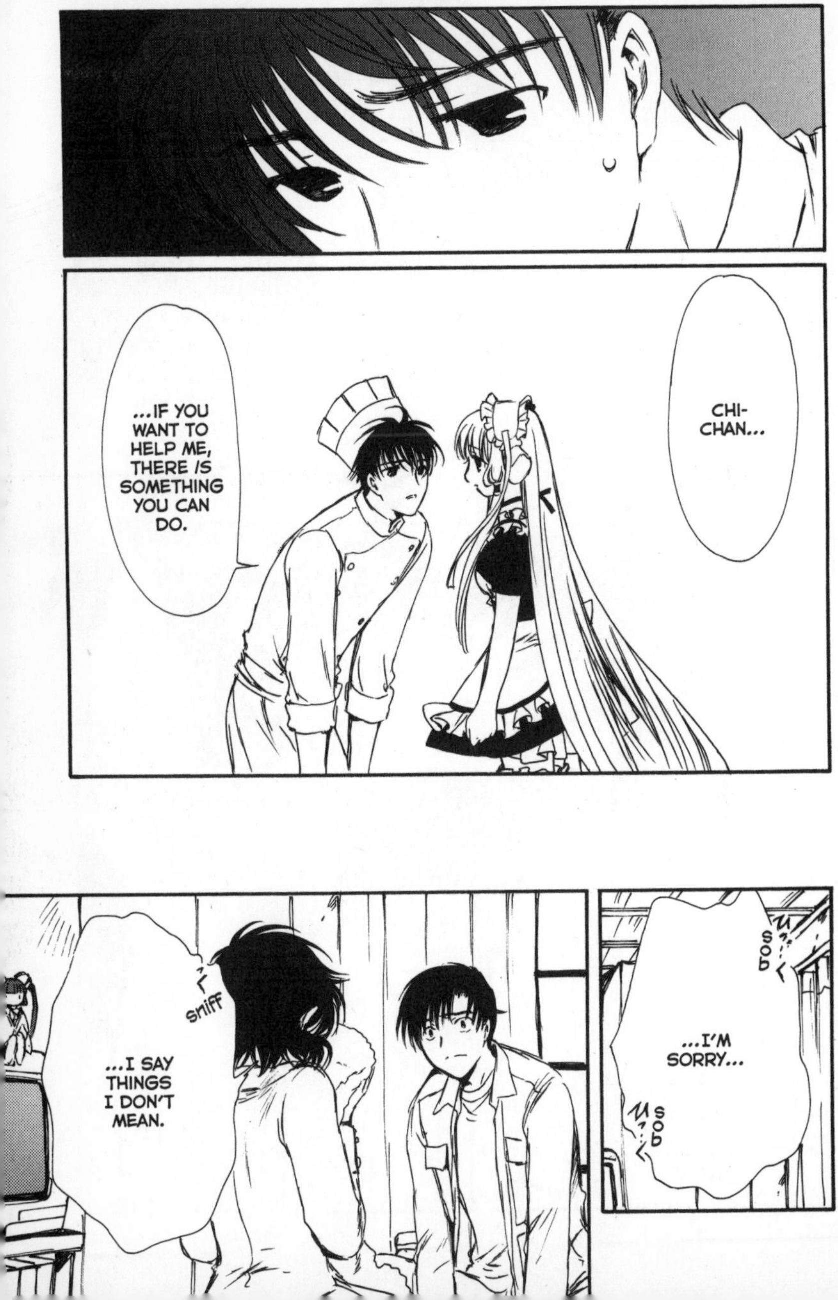
CHI-CHAN...
...IF YOU WANT TO HELP ME, THERE IS SOMETHING YOU CAN DO.
sob
...I'M SORRY...
sob
sniff
...I SAY THINGS I DON'T MEAN.

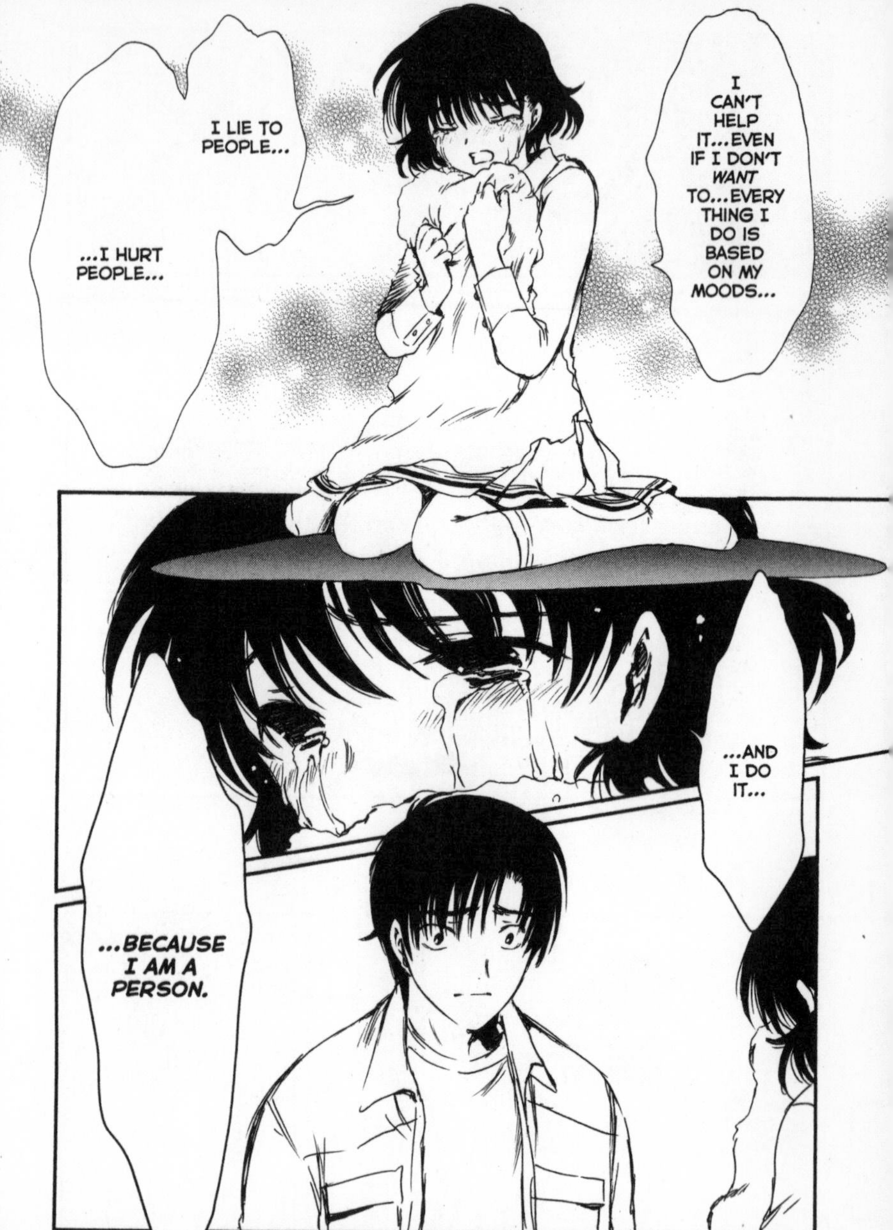
I CAN'T HELP IT...EVEN IF I DON'T *WANT* TO...EVERY THING I DO IS BASED ON MY MOODS...
I LIE TO PEOPLE...
...I HURT PEOPLE...
...AND I DO IT...
...BECAUSE I AM A PERSON.

Chobits
ちょびっツ

◄ chapter 64 ►

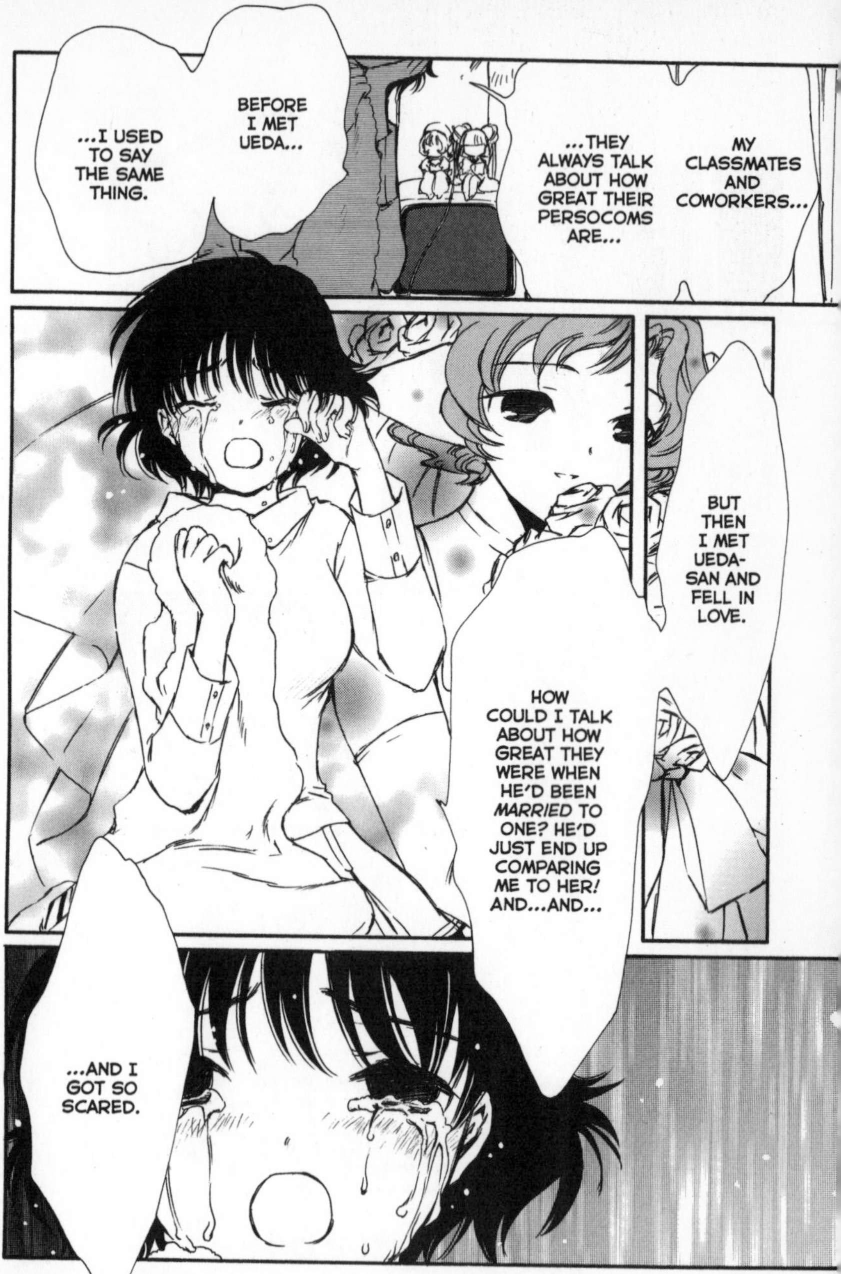
MY CLASSMATES AND COWORKERS...
...THEY ALWAYS TALK ABOUT HOW GREAT THEIR PERSOCOMS ARE...
BEFORE I MET UEDA...
...I USED TO SAY THE SAME THING.
BUT THEN I MET UEDA-SAN AND FELL IN LOVE.
HOW COULD I TALK ABOUT HOW GREAT THEY WERE WHEN HE'D BEEN *MARRIED* TO ONE? HE'D JUST END UP COMPARING ME TO HER! AND...AND...
...AND I GOT SO SCARED.

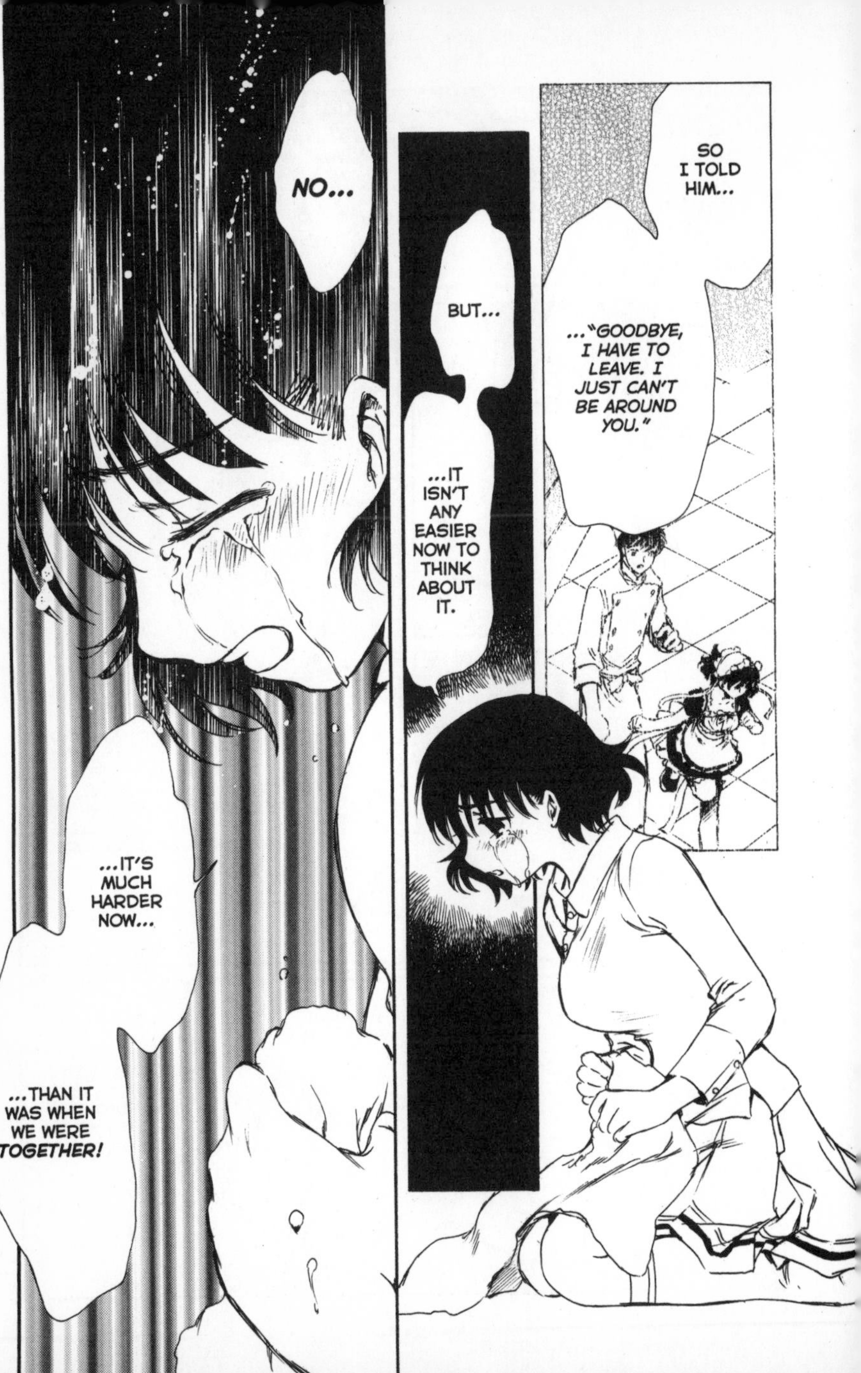
SO I TOLD HIM...
..."GOODBYE, I HAVE TO LEAVE. I JUST CAN'T BE AROUND YOU."
BUT...
...IT ISN'T ANY EASIER NOW TO THINK ABOUT IT.
NO...
...IT'S MUCH HARDER NOW...
...THAN IT WAS WHEN WE WERE *TOGETHER!*

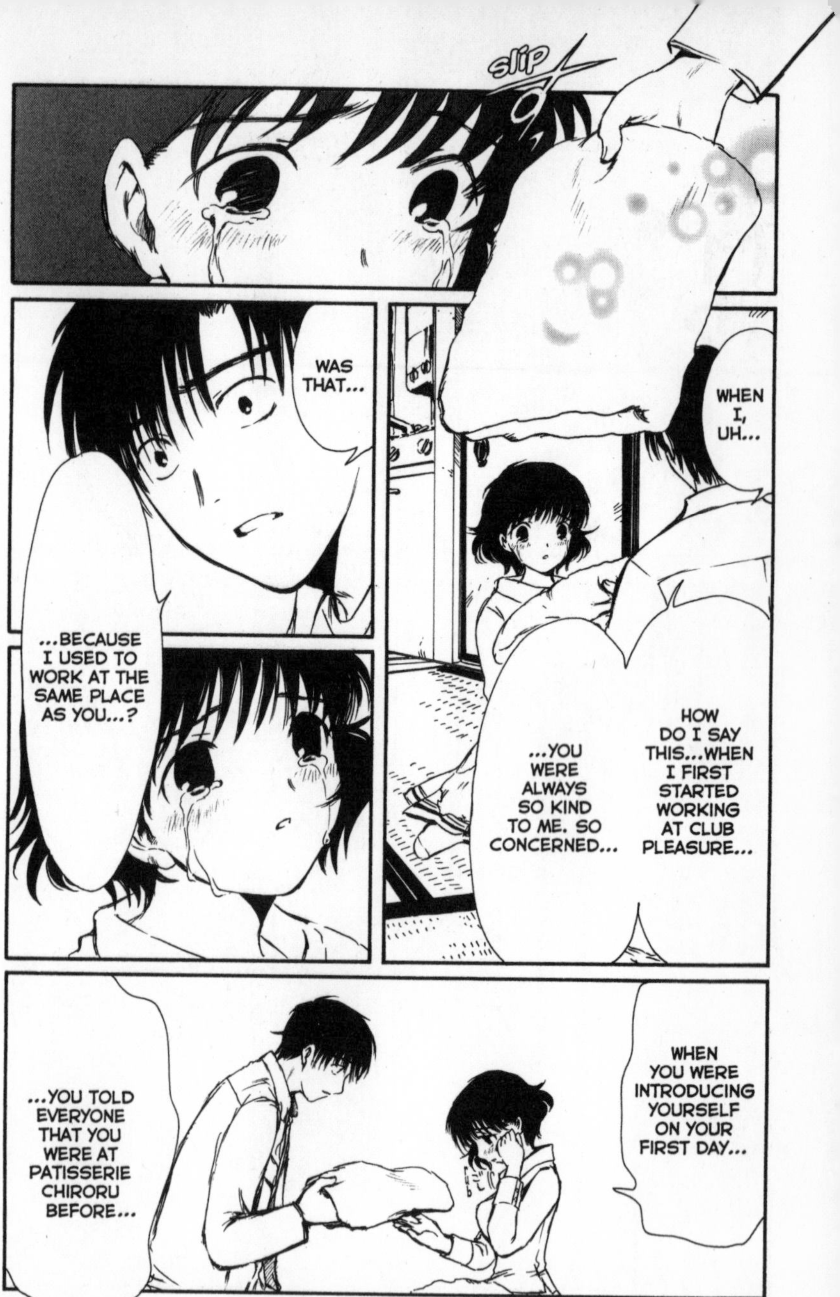
slip
WHEN I, UH...
HOW DO I SAY THIS...WHEN I FIRST STARTED WORKING AT CLUB PLEASURE...
...YOU WERE ALWAYS SO KIND TO ME. SO CONCERNED...
WAS THAT...
...BECAUSE I USED TO WORK AT THE SAME PLACE AS YOU...?
WHEN YOU WERE INTRODUCING YOURSELF ON YOUR FIRST DAY...
...YOU TOLD EVERYONE THAT YOU WERE AT PATISSERIE CHIRORU BEFORE...

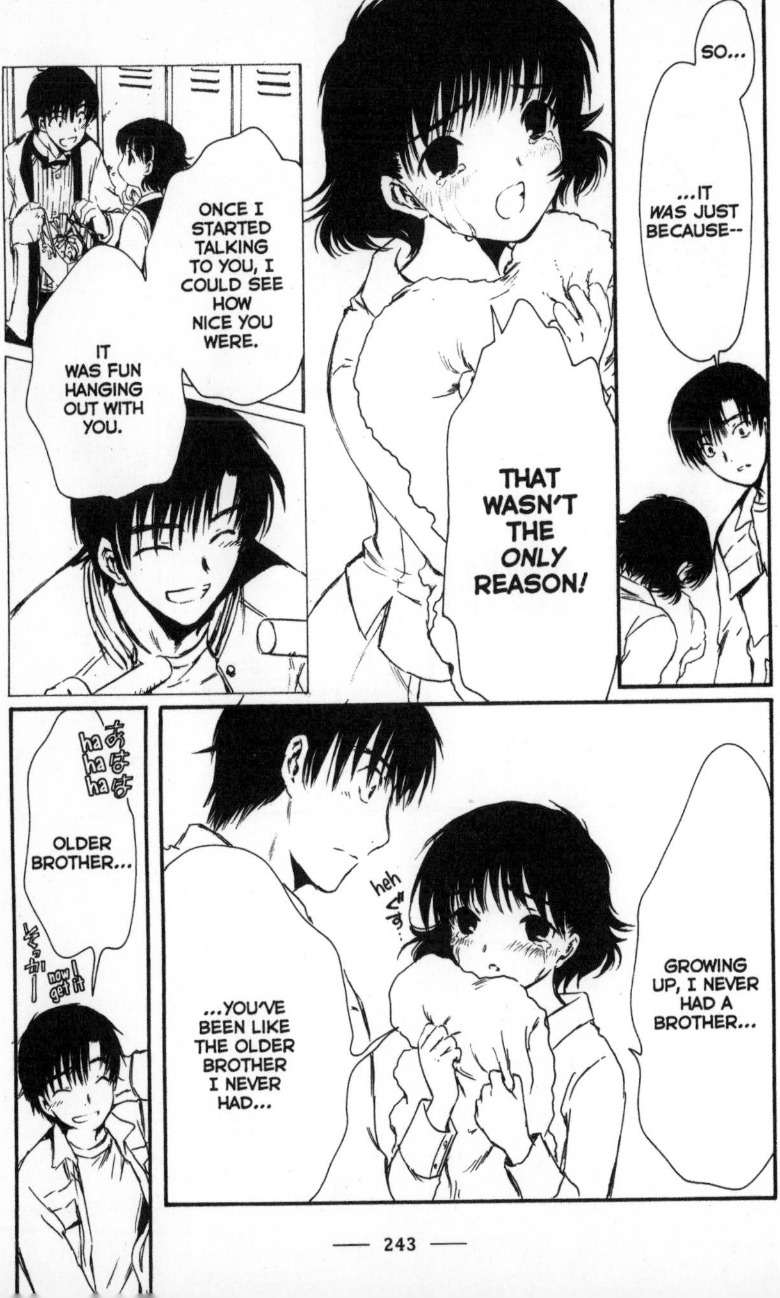
SO...
...IT *WAS* JUST BECAUSE--
THAT WASN'T THE *ONLY* REASON!
ONCE I STARTED TALKING TO YOU, I COULD SEE HOW NICE YOU WERE.
IT WAS FUN HANGING OUT WITH YOU.
GROWING UP, I NEVER HAD A BROTHER...
heh ぐす...
...YOU'VE BEEN LIKE THE OLDER BROTHER I NEVER HAD...
ha ha ha あはは
OLDER BROTHER...
now I get it そっかー

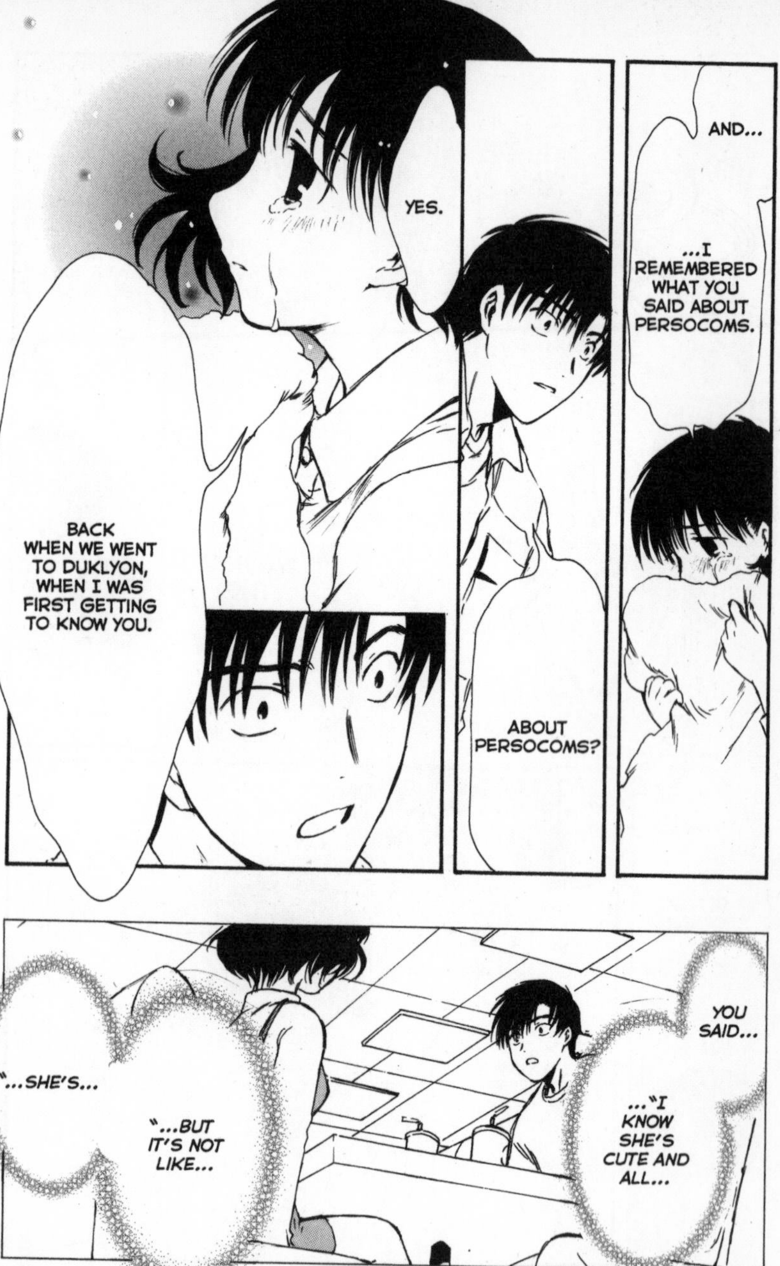
AND...
...I REMEMBERED WHAT YOU SAID ABOUT PERSOCOMS.
YES.
ABOUT PERSOCOMS?
BACK WHEN WE WENT TO DUKLYON, WHEN I WAS FIRST GETTING TO KNOW YOU.
YOU SAID...
..."I KNOW SHE'S CUTE AND ALL...
"...BUT IT'S NOT LIKE...
"...SHE'S...

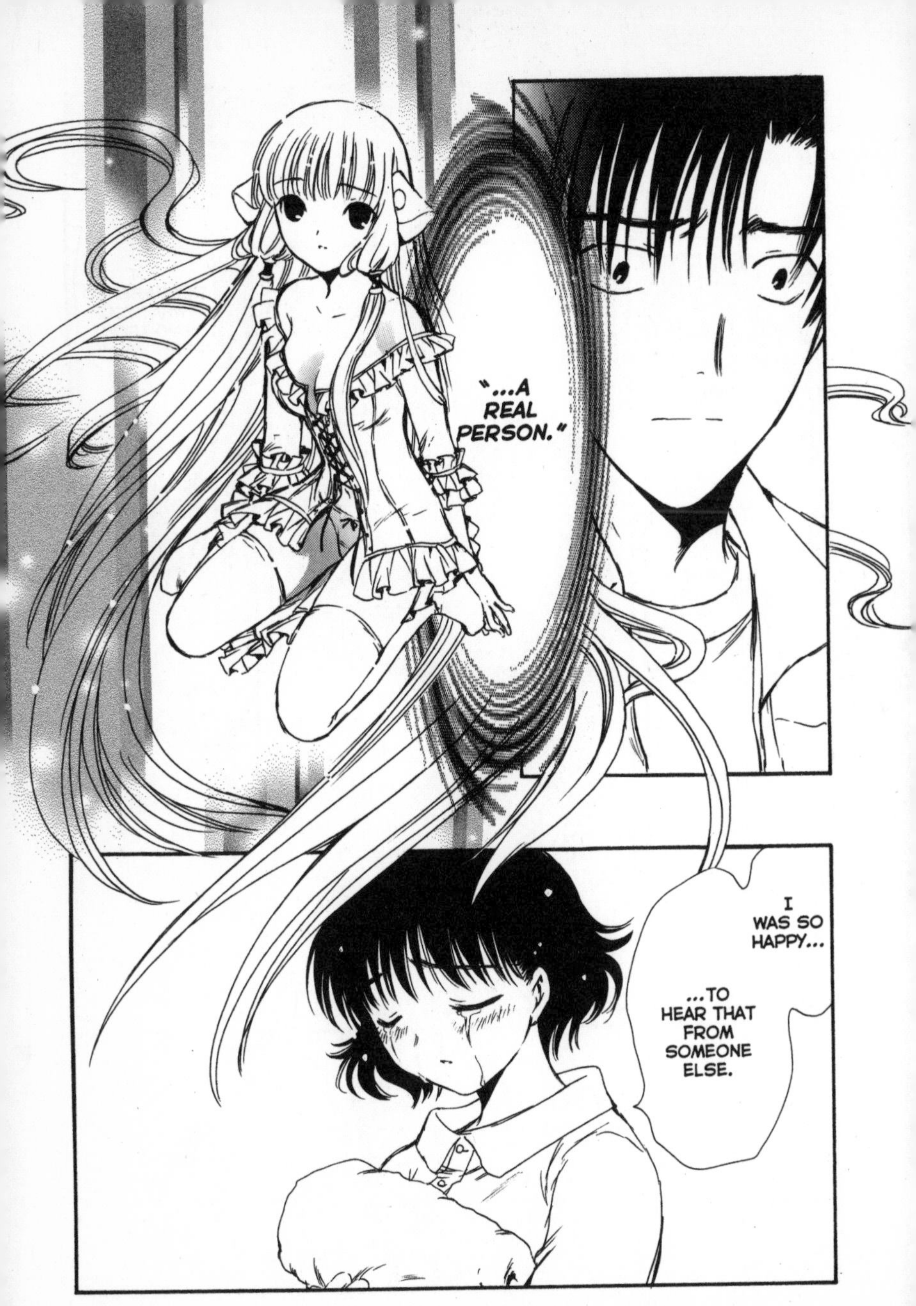
"...A REAL PERSON."
I WAS SO HAPPY...
...TO HEAR THAT FROM SOMEONE ELSE.

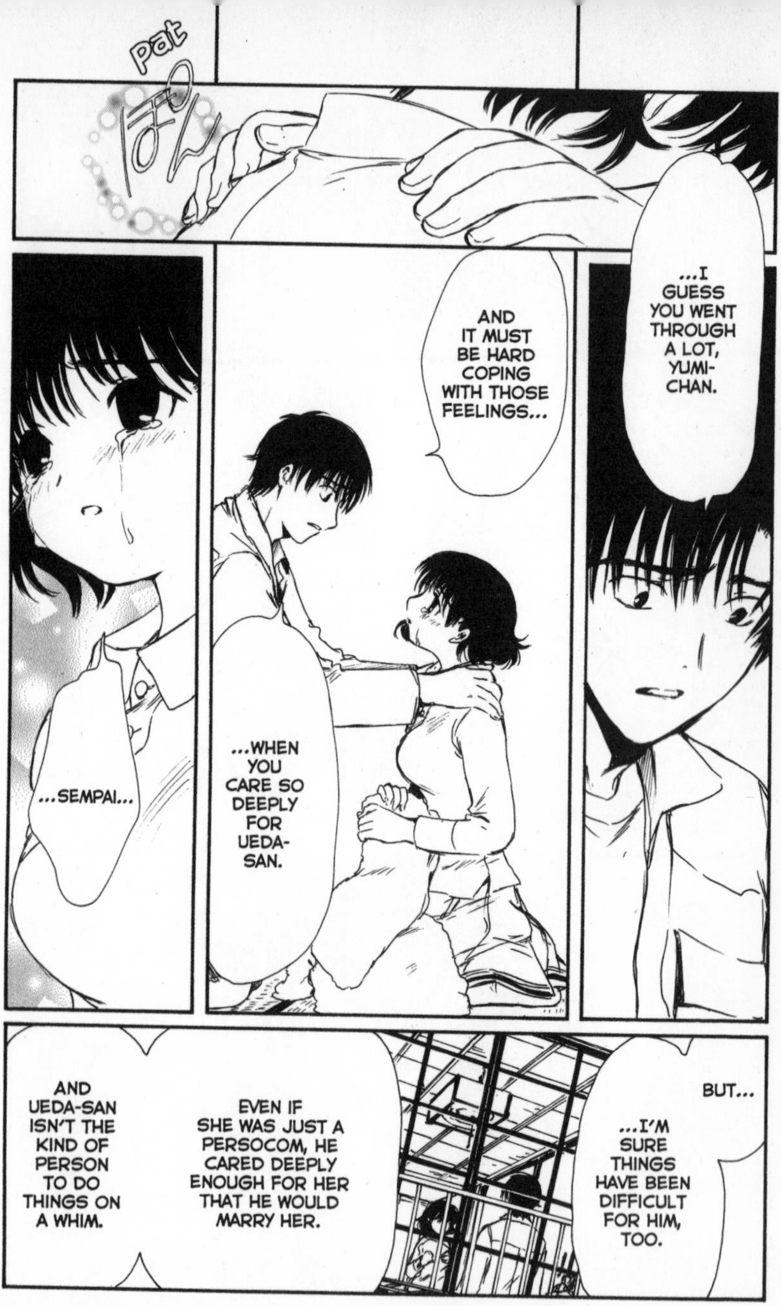
pat
ぽん
...I GUESS YOU WENT THROUGH A LOT, YUMI-CHAN.
AND IT MUST BE HARD COPING WITH THOSE FEELINGS...
...WHEN YOU CARE SO DEEPLY FOR UEDA-SAN.
...SEMPAI...
BUT...
...I'M SURE THINGS HAVE BEEN DIFFICULT FOR HIM, TOO.
EVEN IF SHE WAS JUST A PERSOCOM, HE CARED DEEPLY ENOUGH FOR HER THAT HE WOULD MARRY HER.
AND UEDA-SAN ISN'T THE KIND OF PERSON TO DO THINGS ON A WHIM.

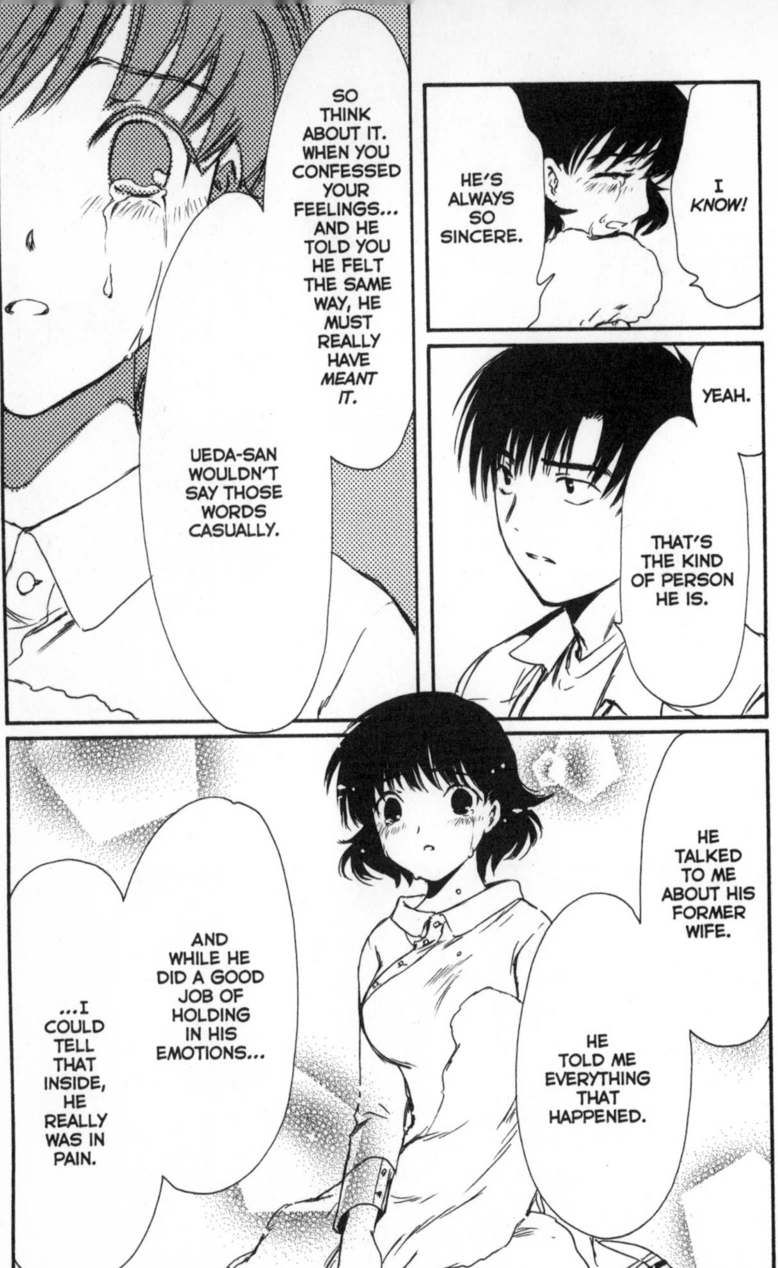
I KNOW!
HE'S ALWAYS SO SINCERE.
YEAH.
THAT'S THE KIND OF PERSON HE IS.
SO THINK ABOUT IT. WHEN YOU CONFESSED YOUR FEELINGS... AND HE TOLD YOU HE FELT THE SAME WAY, HE MUST REALLY HAVE *MEANT* IT.
UEDA-SAN WOULDN'T SAY THOSE WORDS CASUALLY.
HE TALKED TO ME ABOUT HIS FORMER WIFE.
HE TOLD ME EVERYTHING THAT HAPPENED.
AND WHILE HE DID A GOOD JOB OF HOLDING IN HIS EMOTIONS...
...I COULD TELL THAT INSIDE, HE REALLY WAS IN PAIN.

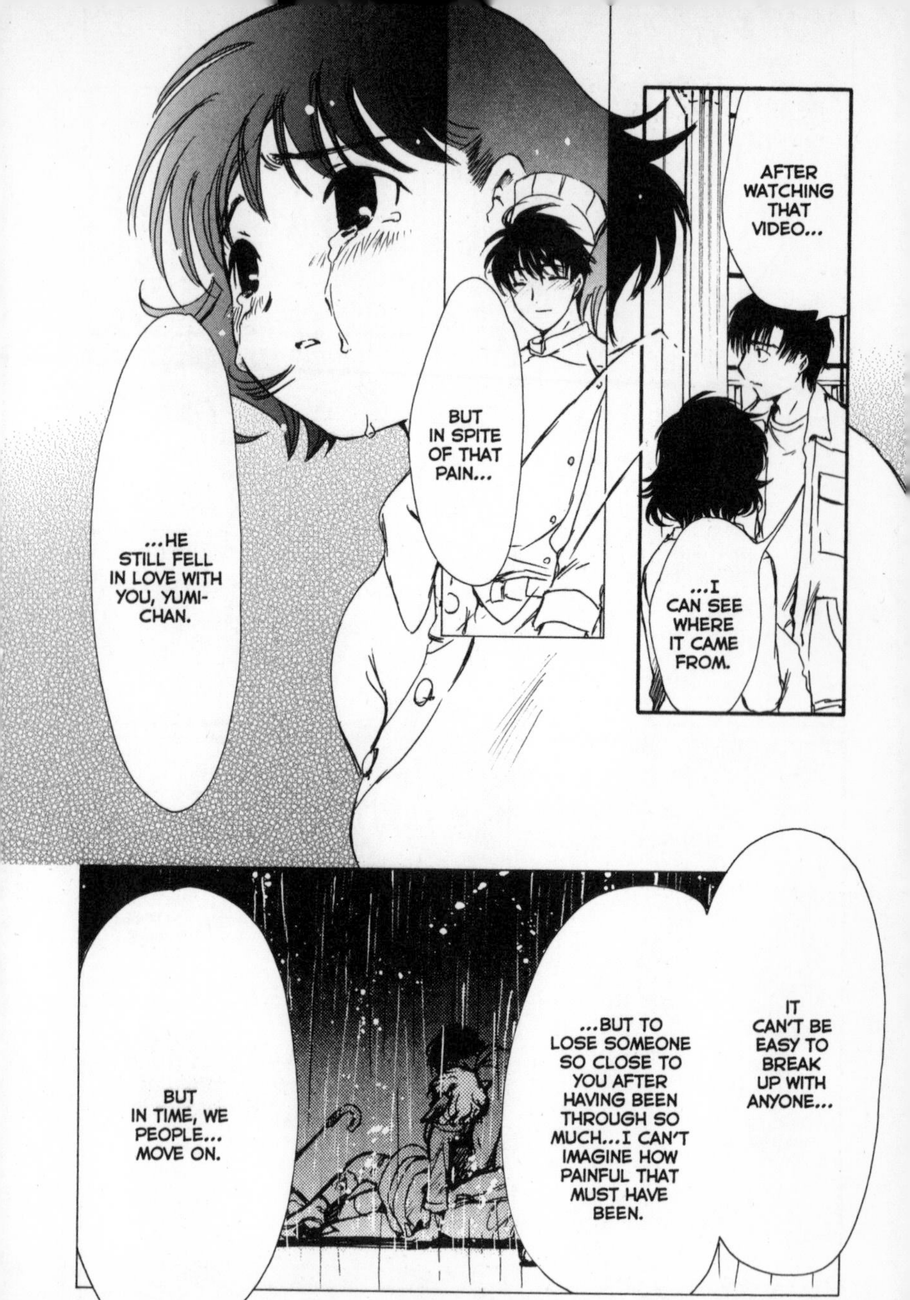
AFTER WATCHING THAT VIDEO...
...I CAN SEE WHERE IT CAME FROM.
BUT IN SPITE OF THAT PAIN...
...HE STILL FELL IN LOVE WITH YOU, YUMI-CHAN.
IT CAN'T BE EASY TO BREAK UP WITH ANYONE...
...BUT TO LOSE SOMEONE SO CLOSE TO YOU AFTER HAVING BEEN THROUGH SO MUCH...I CAN'T IMAGINE HOW PAINFUL THAT MUST HAVE BEEN.
BUT IN TIME, WE PEOPLE... MOVE ON.

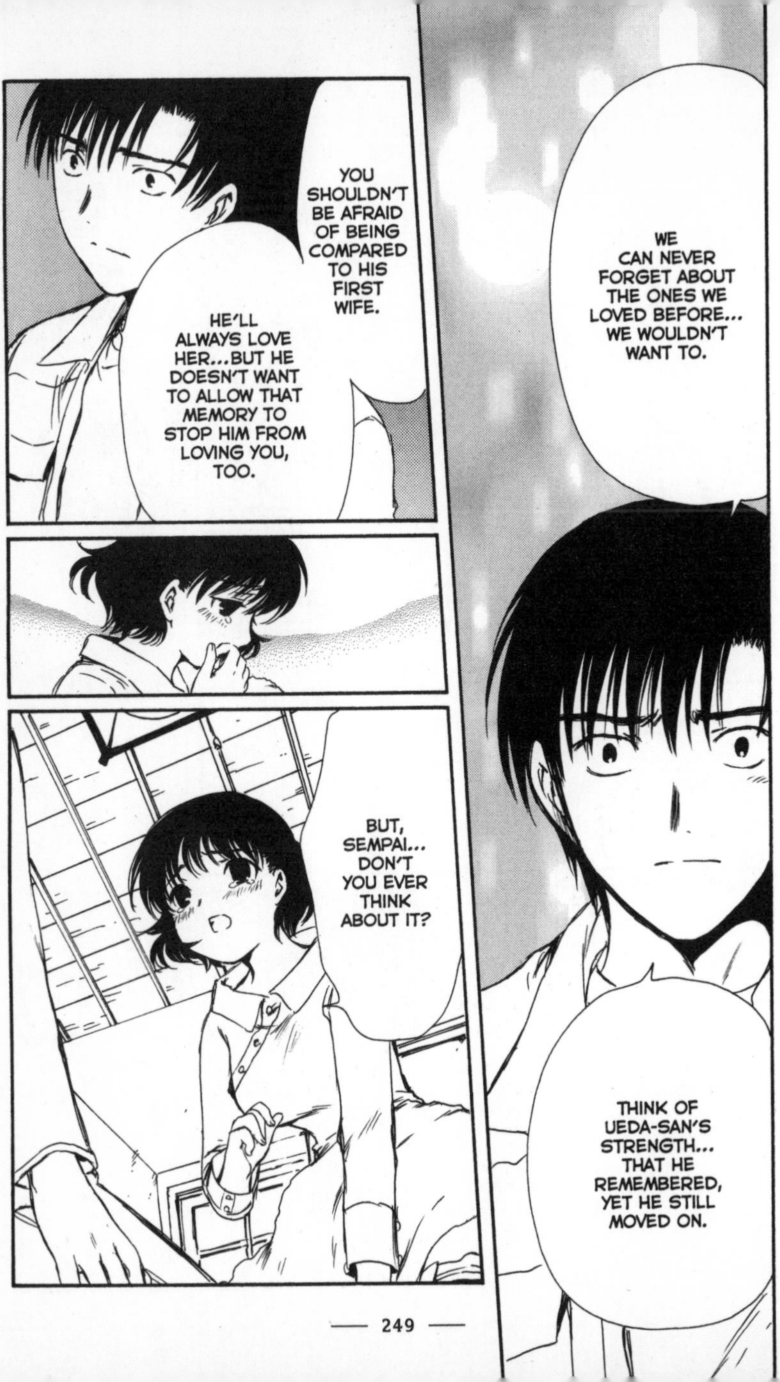
WE CAN NEVER FORGET ABOUT THE ONES WE LOVED BEFORE... WE WOULDN'T WANT TO.
THINK OF UEDA-SAN'S STRENGTH... THAT HE REMEMBERED, YET HE STILL MOVED ON.
YOU SHOULDN'T BE AFRAID OF BEING COMPARED TO HIS FIRST WIFE.
HE'LL ALWAYS LOVE HER...BUT HE DOESN'T WANT TO ALLOW THAT MEMORY TO STOP HIM FROM LOVING YOU, TOO.
BUT, SEMPAI... DON'T YOU EVER THINK ABOUT IT?

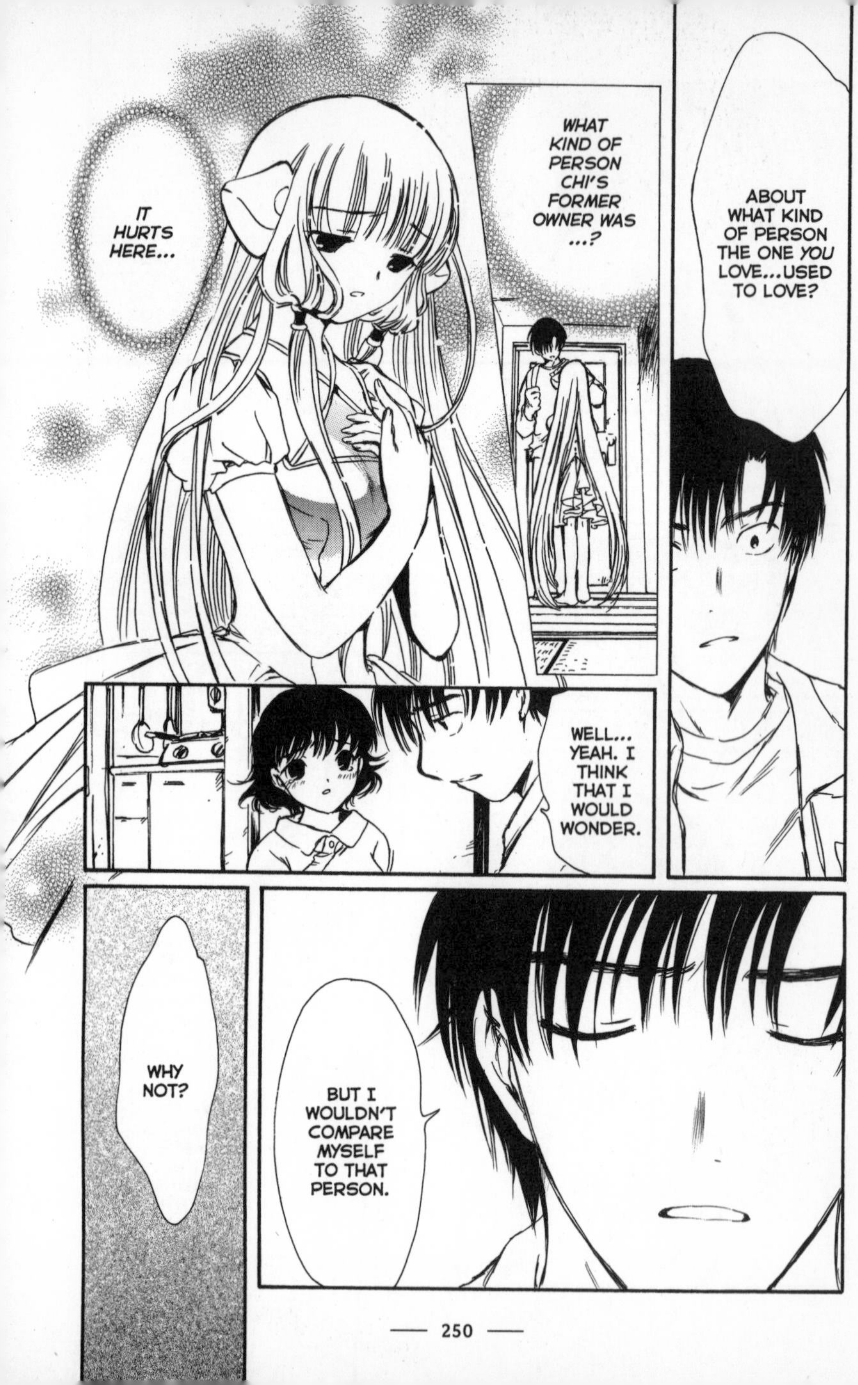
ABOUT WHAT KIND OF PERSON THE ONE *YOU* LOVE...USED TO LOVE?
WHAT KIND OF PERSON CHI'S FORMER OWNER WAS ...?
IT HURTS HERE...
WELL... YEAH. I THINK THAT I WOULD WONDER.
BUT I WOULDN'T COMPARE MYSELF TO THAT PERSON.
WHY NOT?

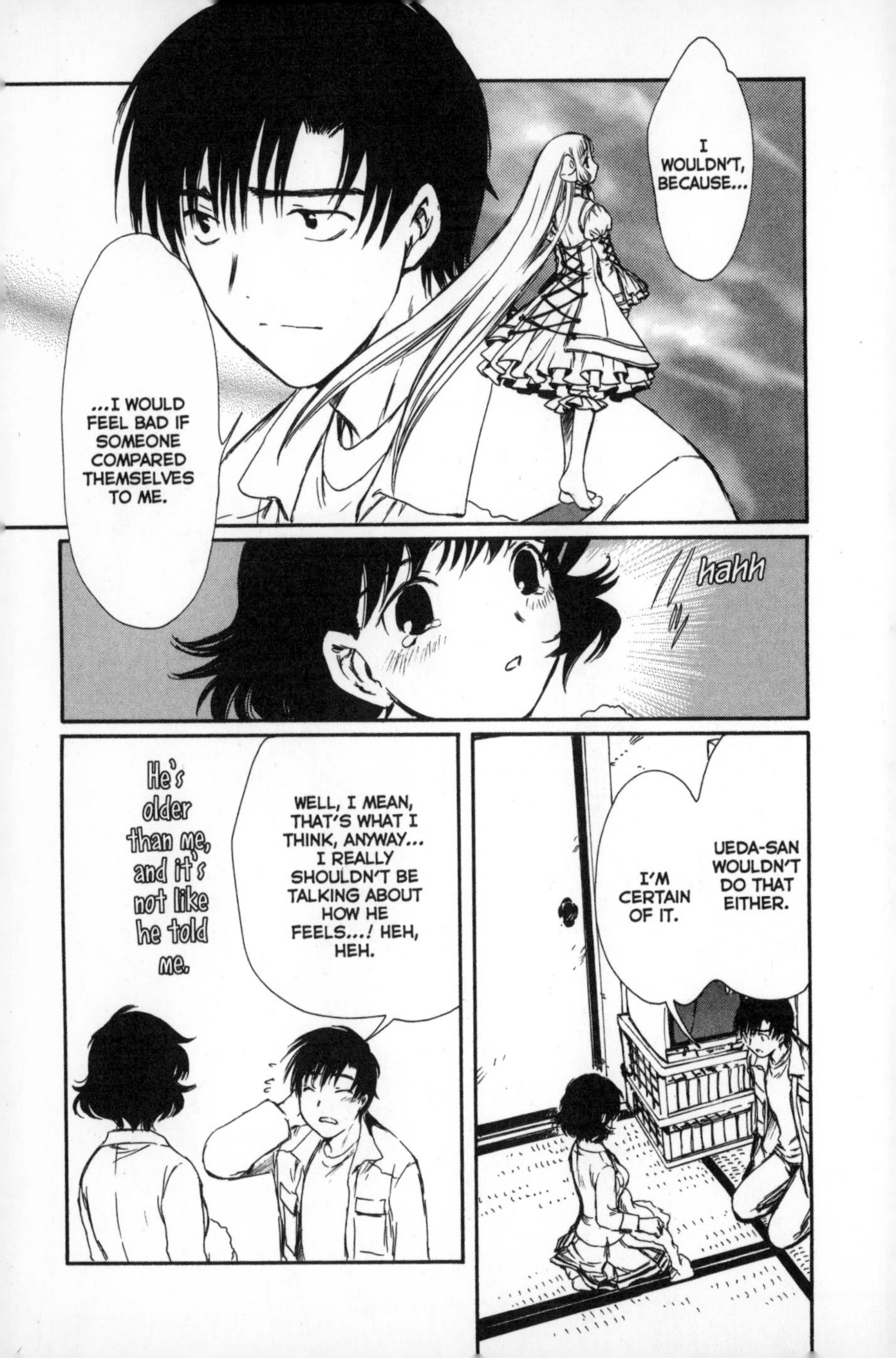
I WOULDN'T, BECAUSE...
...I WOULD FEEL BAD IF SOMEONE COMPARED THEMSELVES TO ME.
hahh
UEDA-SAN WOULDN'T DO THAT EITHER.
I'M CERTAIN OF IT.
WELL, I MEAN, THAT'S WHAT I THINK, ANYWAY... I REALLY SHOULDN'T BE TALKING ABOUT HOW HE FEELS...! HEH, HEH.
He's older than me, and it's not like he told me.

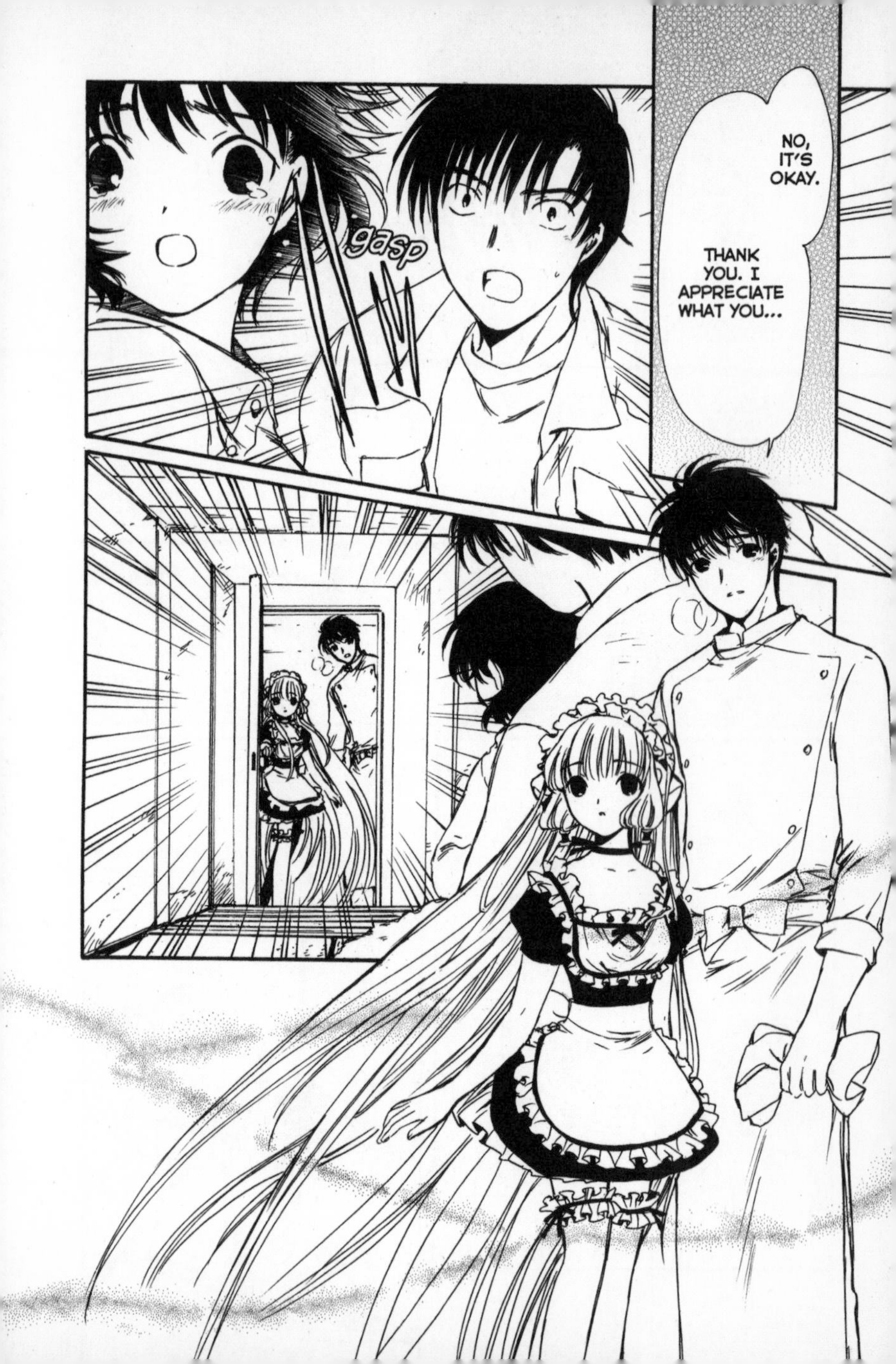
NO, IT'S OKAY.
THANK YOU. I APPRECIATE WHAT YOU...
gasp

Chobits
ちょびっツ

◀ **chapter 65** ▶

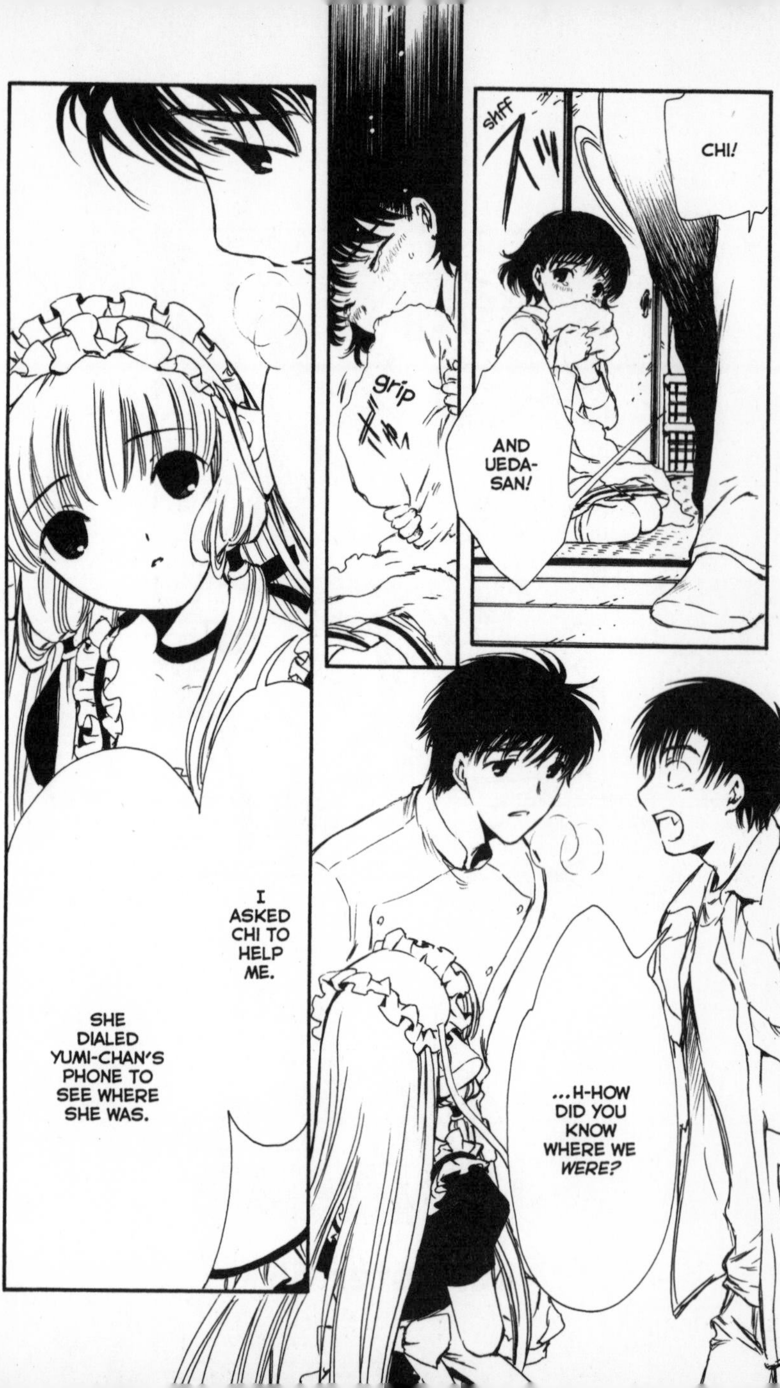

shff
CHI!
AND UEDA-SAN!
grip
...H-HOW DID YOU KNOW WHERE WE WERE?
I ASKED CHI TO HELP ME.
SHE DIALED YUMI-CHAN'S PHONE TO SEE WHERE SHE WAS.

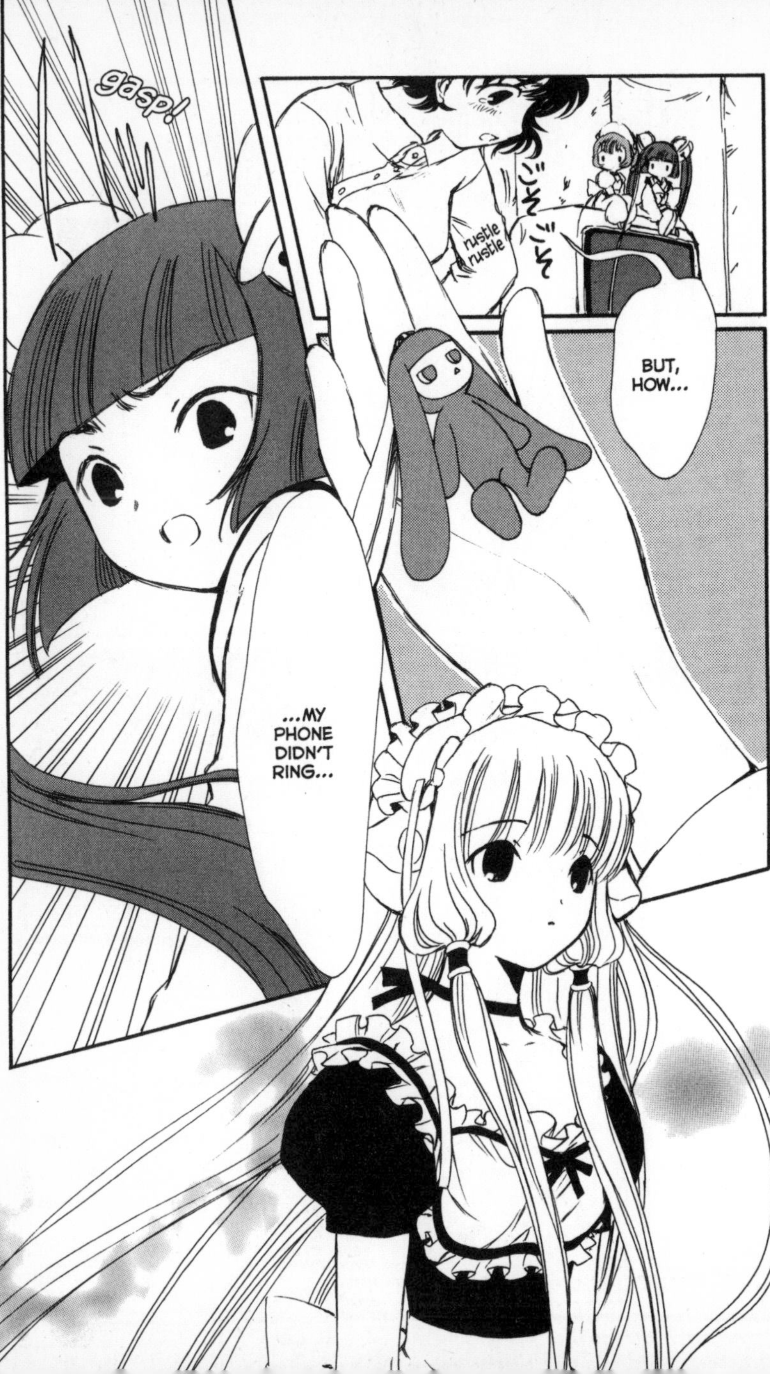
ごそごそ
rustle rustle
gasp!
BUT, HOW...
...MY PHONE DIDN'T RING...

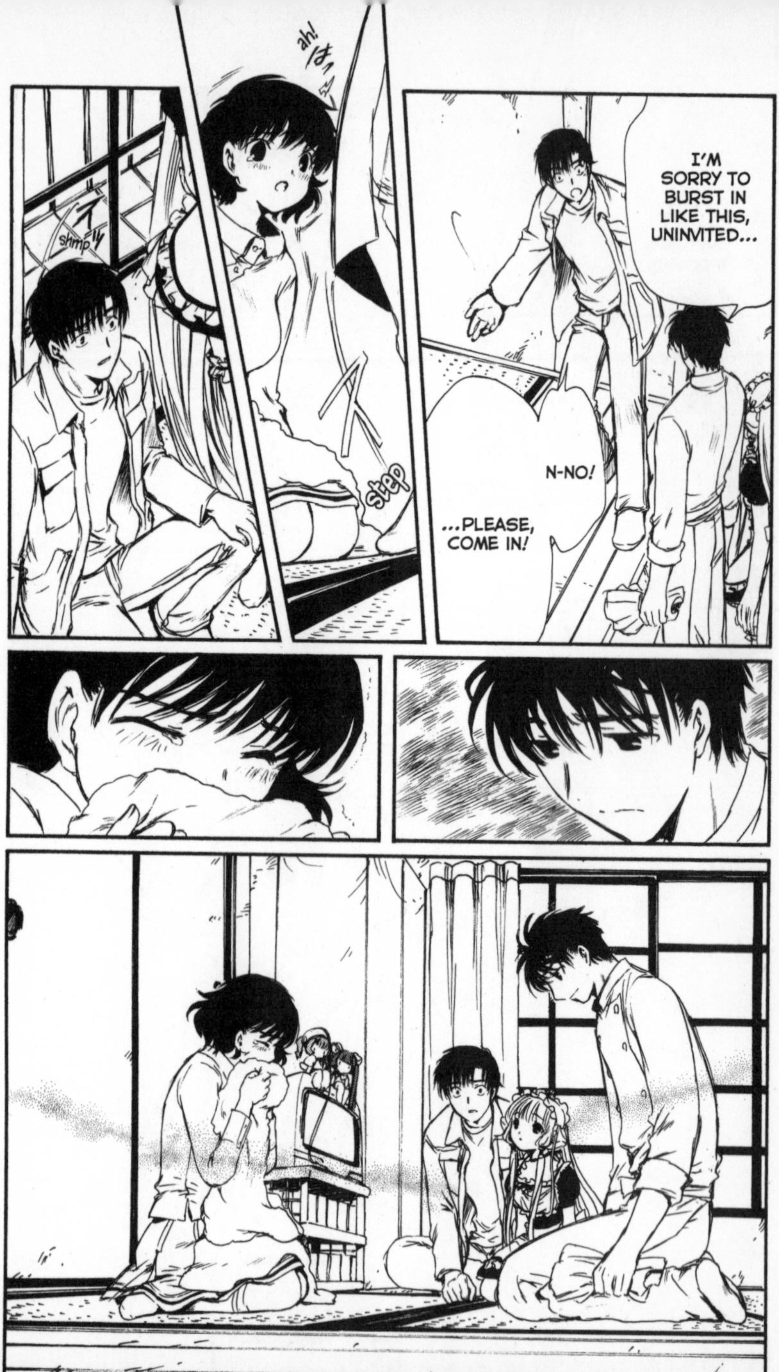

I'M SORRY TO BURST IN LIKE THIS, UNINVITED...
N-NO!
...PLEASE, COME IN!
ah!
step
shmp

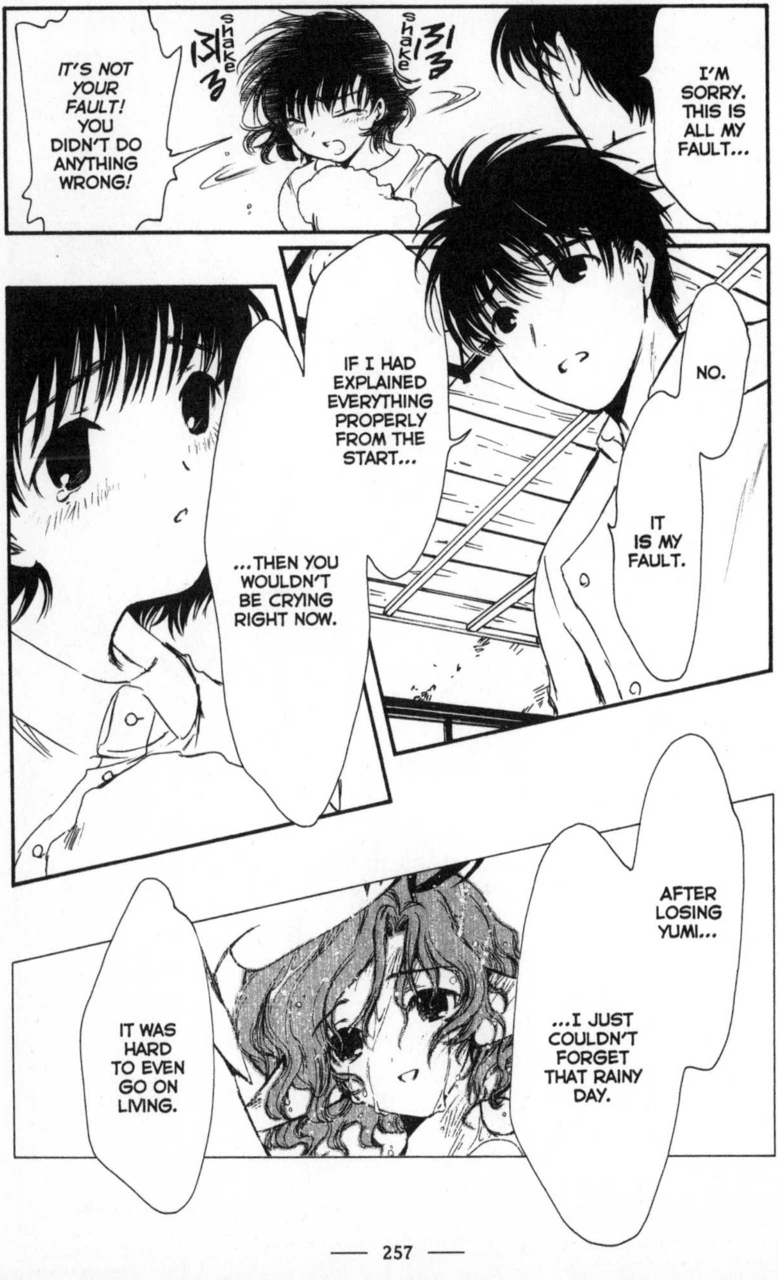
I'M SORRY. THIS IS ALL MY FAULT...
shake
shake
IT'S NOT YOUR FAULT! YOU DIDN'T DO ANYTHING WRONG!
NO.
IT IS MY FAULT.
IF I HAD EXPLAINED EVERYTHING PROPERLY FROM THE START...
...THEN YOU WOULDN'T BE CRYING RIGHT NOW.
AFTER LOSING YUMI...
...I JUST COULDN'T FORGET THAT RAINY DAY.
IT WAS HARD TO EVEN GO ON LIVING.

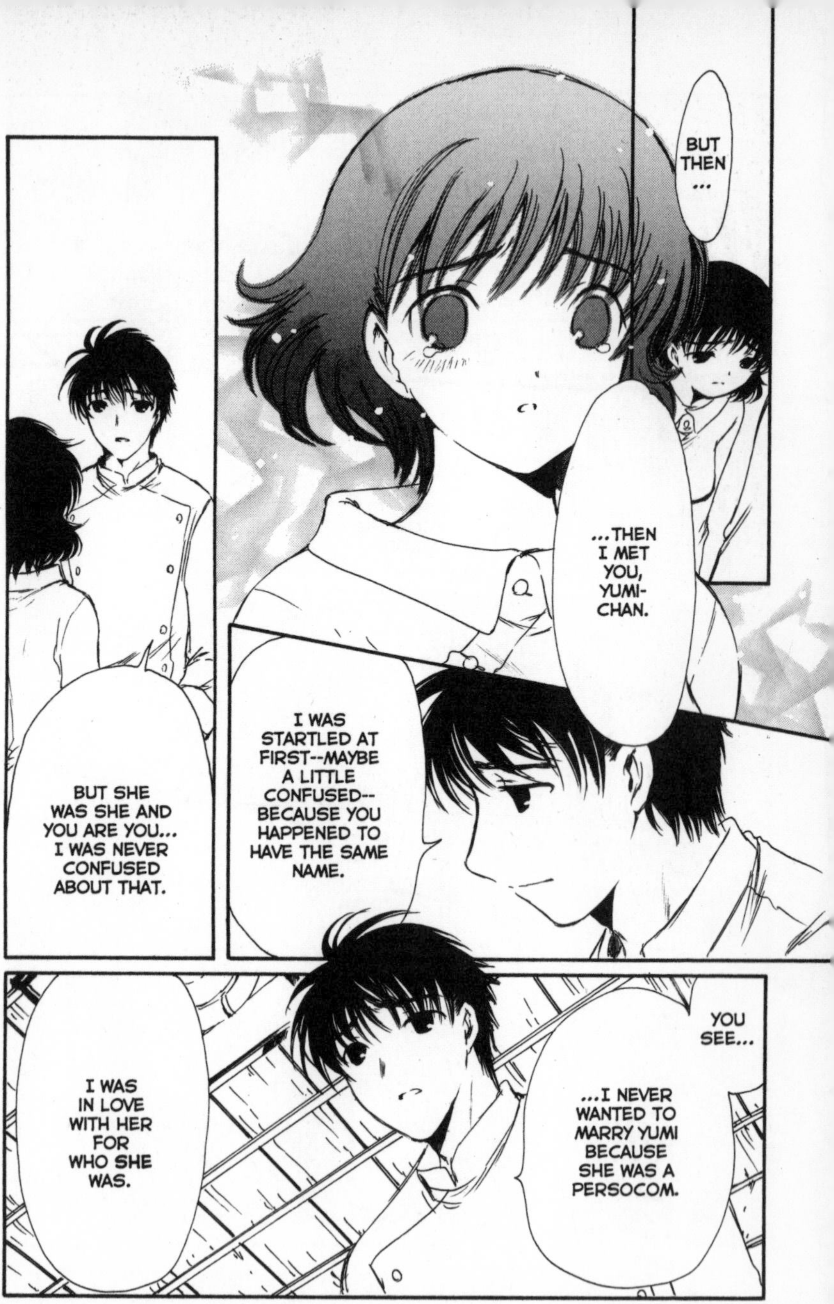
BUT THEN ...
...THEN I MET YOU, YUMI-CHAN.
I WAS STARTLED AT FIRST--MAYBE A LITTLE CONFUSED--BECAUSE YOU HAPPENED TO HAVE THE SAME NAME.
BUT SHE WAS SHE AND YOU ARE YOU... I WAS NEVER CONFUSED ABOUT THAT.
YOU SEE...
...I NEVER WANTED TO MARRY YUMI BECAUSE SHE WAS A PERSOCOM.
I WAS IN LOVE WITH HER FOR WHO SHE WAS.

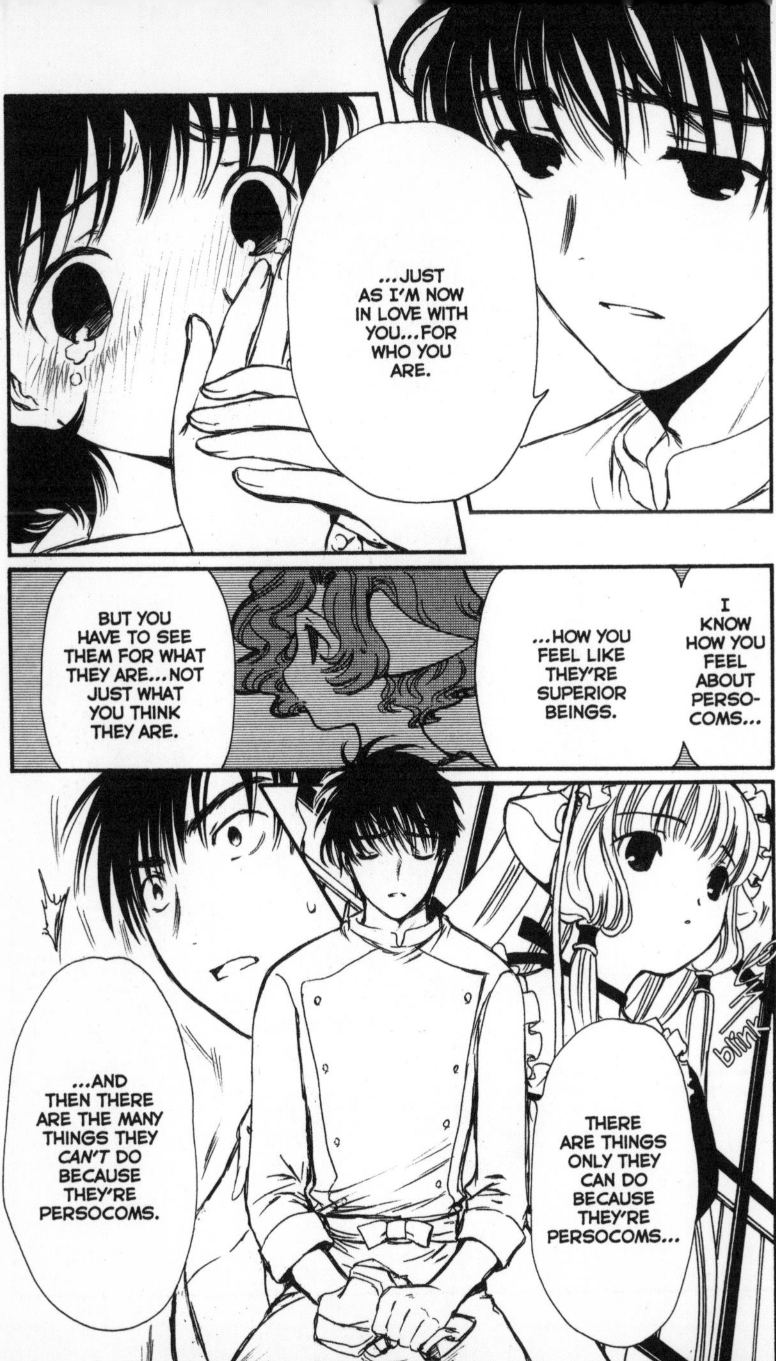
...JUST AS I'M NOW IN LOVE WITH YOU...FOR WHO YOU ARE.
I KNOW HOW YOU FEEL ABOUT PERSO-COMS...
...HOW YOU FEEL LIKE THEY'RE SUPERIOR BEINGS.
BUT YOU HAVE TO SEE THEM FOR WHAT THEY ARE...NOT JUST WHAT YOU THINK THEY ARE.
blink
THERE ARE THINGS ONLY THEY CAN DO BECAUSE THEY'RE PERSOCOMS...
...AND THEN THERE ARE THE MANY THINGS THEY *CAN'T* DO BECAUSE THEY'RE PERSOCOMS.

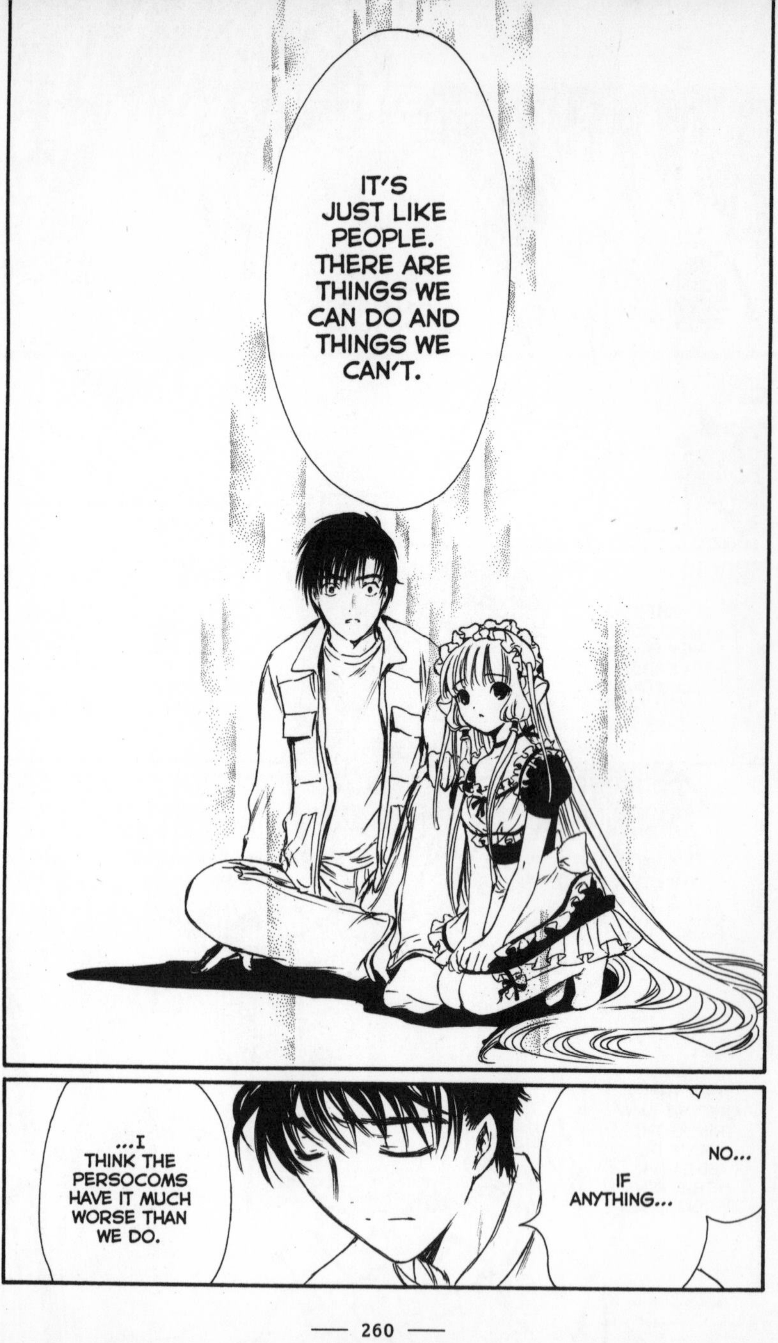
IT'S JUST LIKE PEOPLE. THERE ARE THINGS WE CAN DO AND THINGS WE CAN'T.
NO...
IF ANYTHING...
...I THINK THE PERSOCOMS HAVE IT MUCH WORSE THAN WE DO.

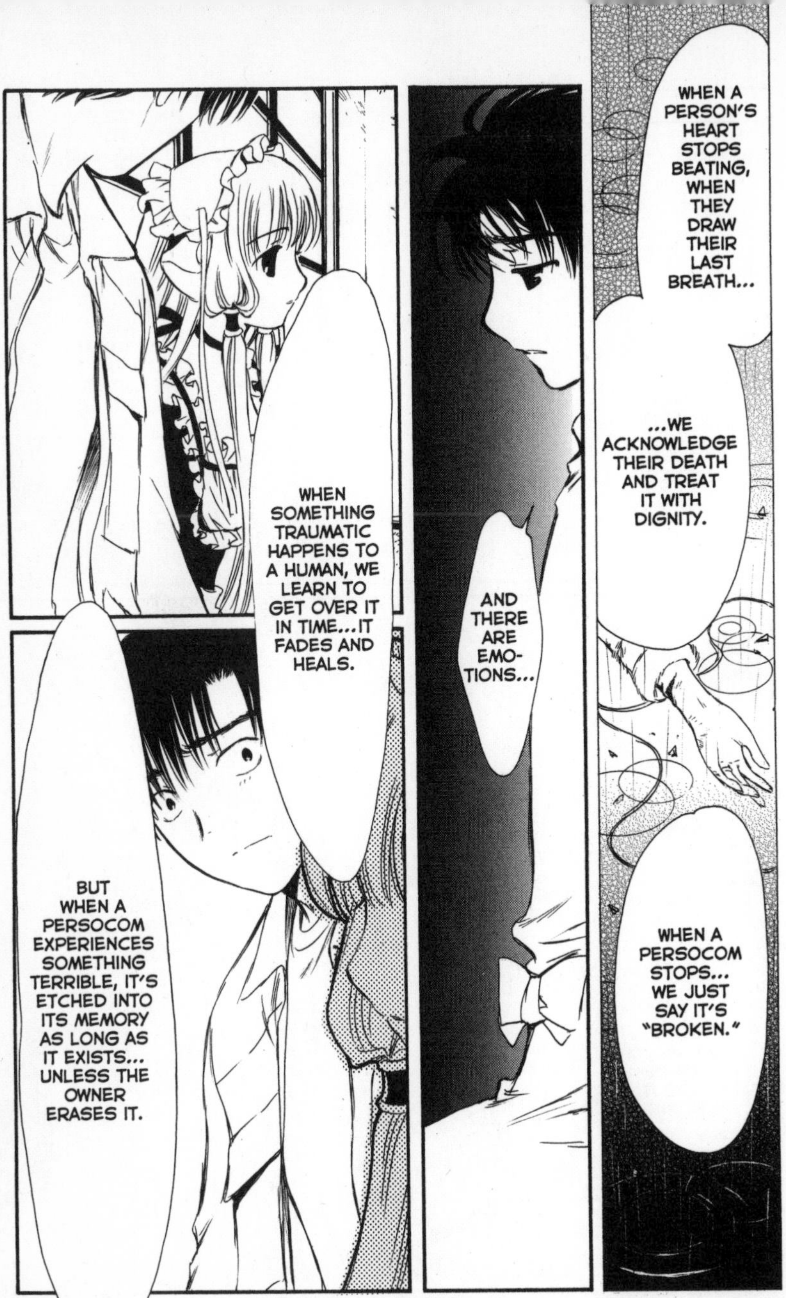
WHEN A PERSON'S HEART STOPS BEATING, WHEN THEY DRAW THEIR LAST BREATH...
...WE ACKNOWLEDGE THEIR DEATH AND TREAT IT WITH DIGNITY.
WHEN A PERSOCOM STOPS... WE JUST SAY IT'S "BROKEN."
AND THERE ARE EMO-TIONS...
WHEN SOMETHING TRAUMATIC HAPPENS TO A HUMAN, WE LEARN TO GET OVER IT IN TIME...IT FADES AND HEALS.
BUT WHEN A PERSOCOM EXPERIENCES SOMETHING TERRIBLE, IT'S ETCHED INTO ITS MEMORY AS LONG AS IT EXISTS... UNLESS THE OWNER ERASES IT.

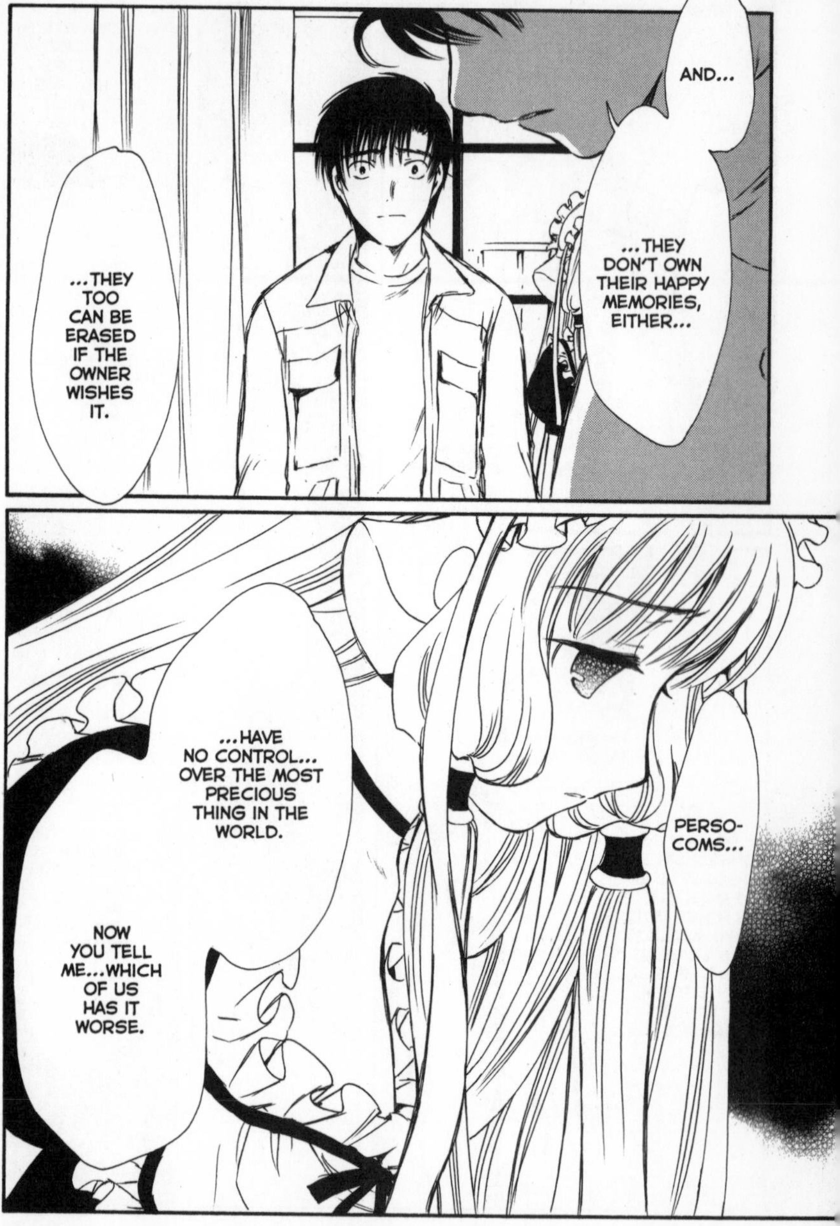
AND...
...THEY DON'T OWN THEIR HAPPY MEMORIES, EITHER...
...THEY TOO CAN BE ERASED IF THE OWNER WISHES IT.
PERSO-COMS...
...HAVE NO CONTROL... OVER THE MOST PRECIOUS THING IN THE WORLD.
NOW YOU TELL ME...WHICH OF US HAS IT WORSE.

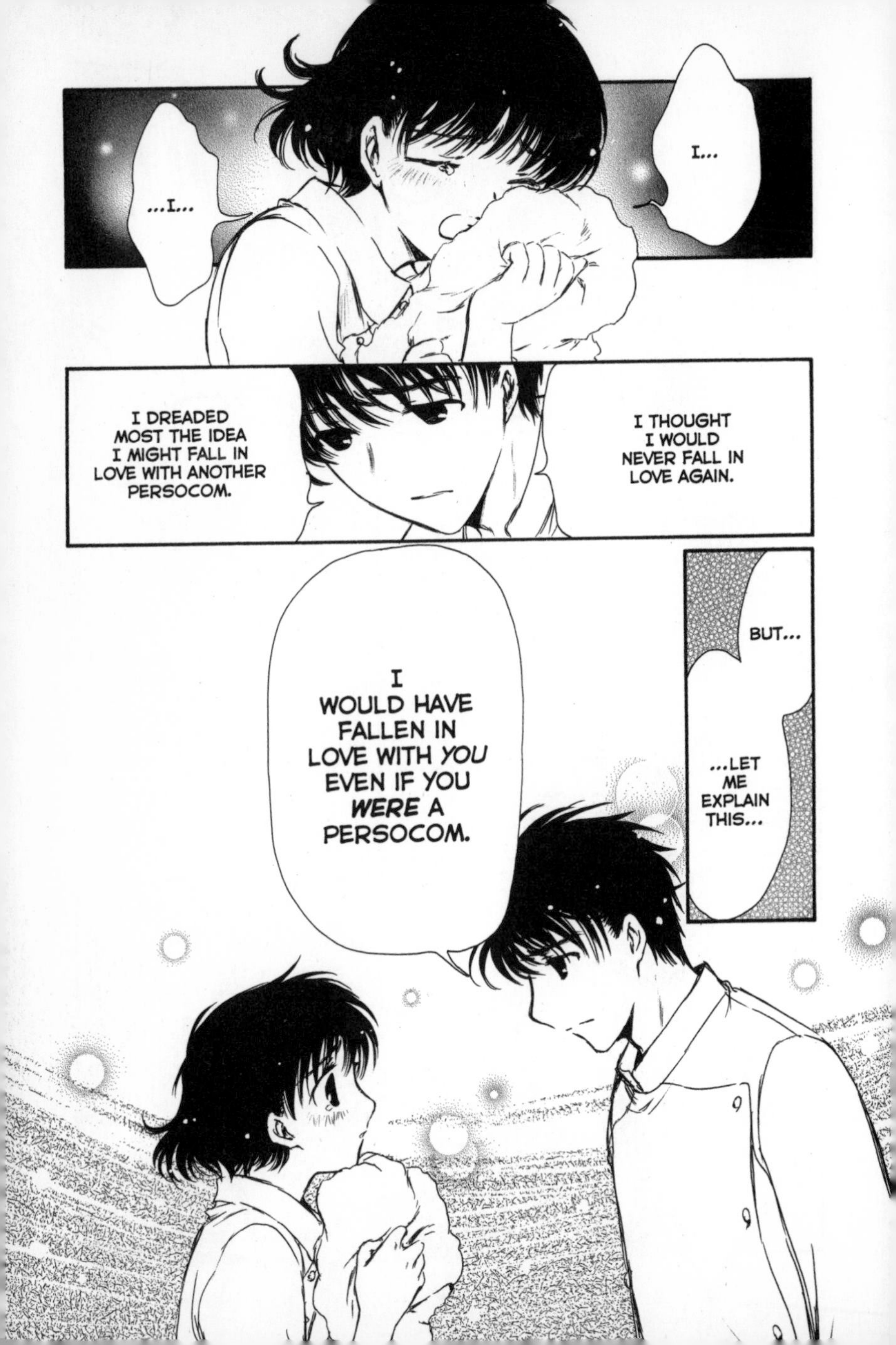
I...
...I...
I THOUGHT I WOULD NEVER FALL IN LOVE AGAIN.
I DREADED MOST THE IDEA I MIGHT FALL IN LOVE WITH ANOTHER PERSOCOM.
BUT...
...LET ME EXPLAIN THIS...
I WOULD HAVE FALLEN IN LOVE WITH *YOU* EVEN IF YOU ***WERE*** A PERSOCOM.

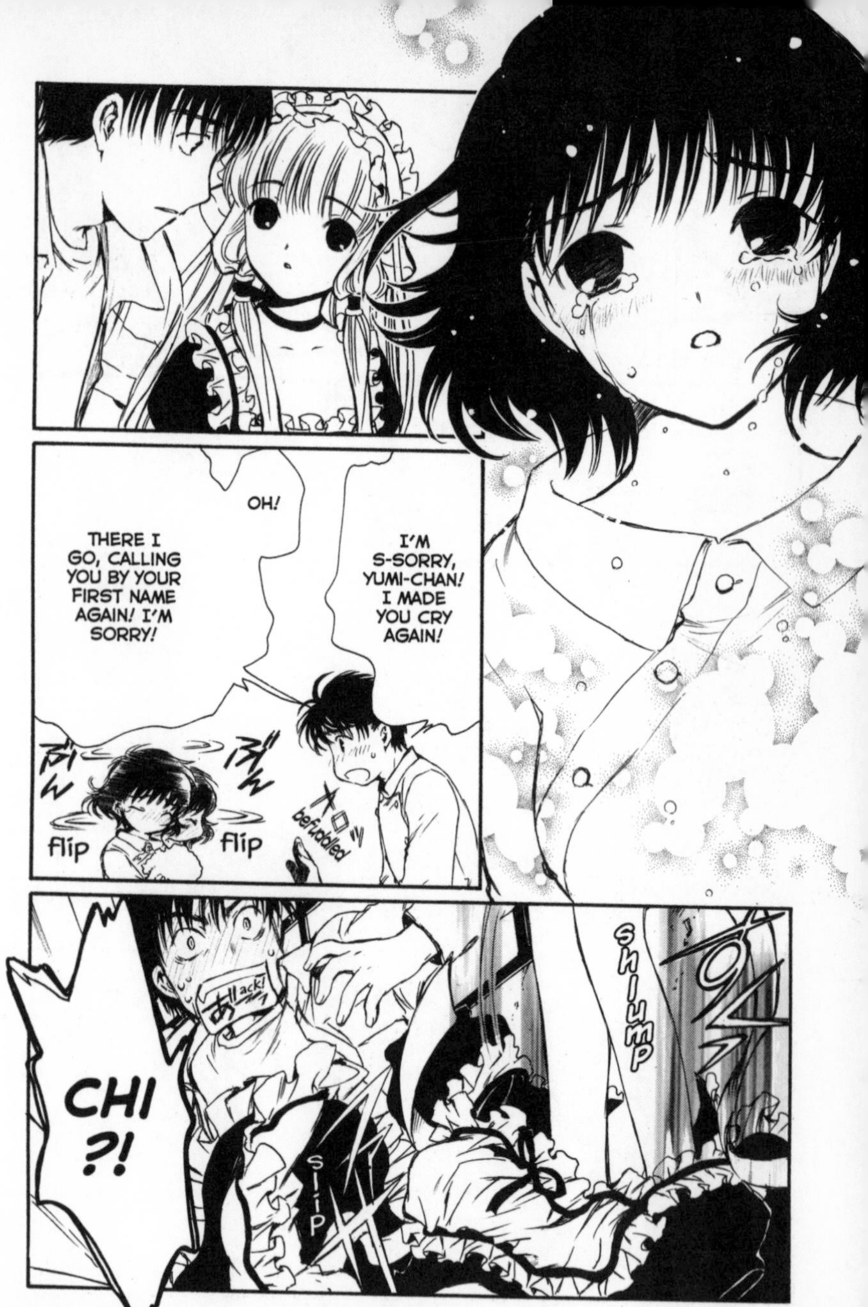
I'M S-SORRY, YUMI-CHAN! I MADE YOU CRY AGAIN!
befuddled
OH!
THERE I GO, CALLING YOU BY YOUR FIRST NAME AGAIN! I'M SORRY!
flip
flip
shlump
ack!
slip
CHI ?!

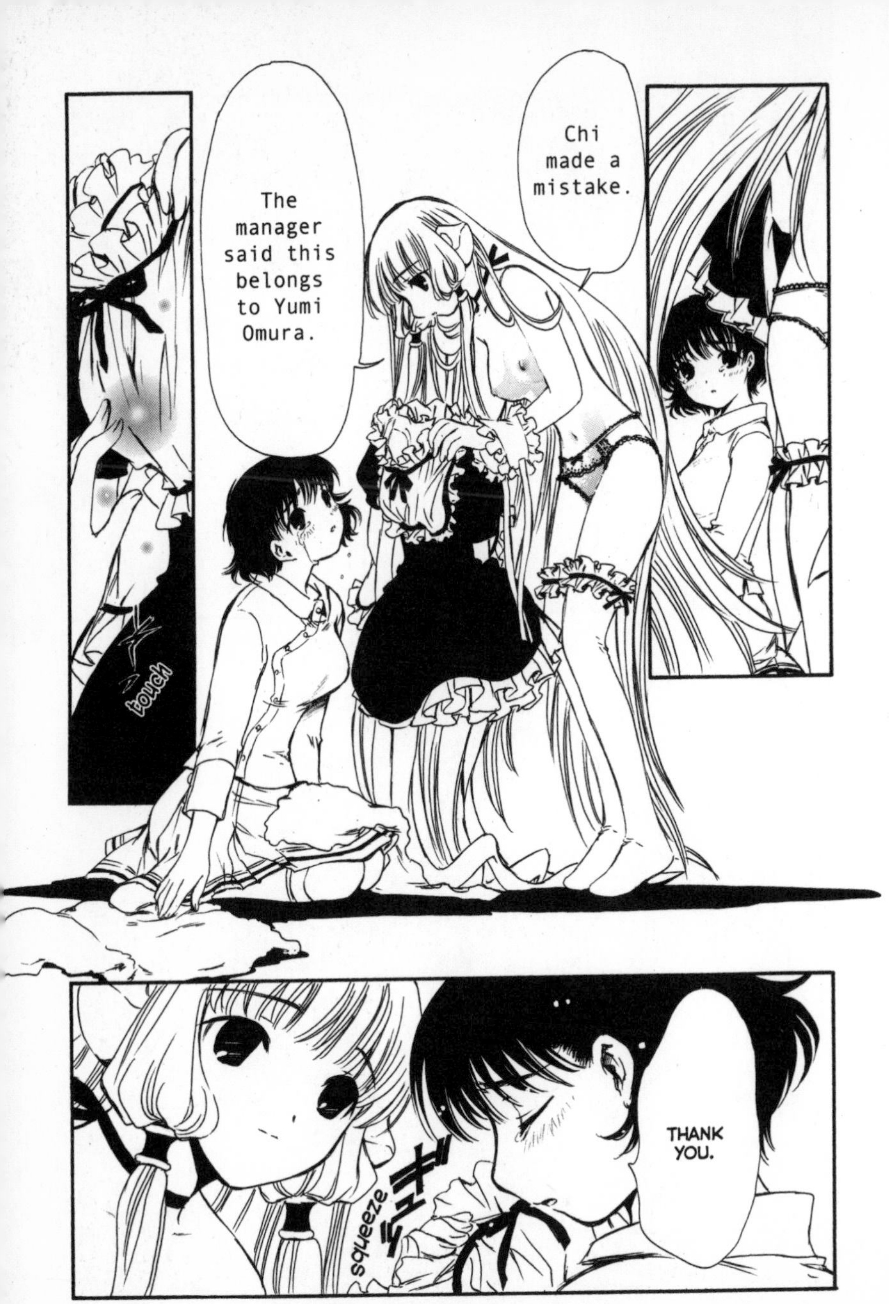
Chi made a mistake.
The manager said this belongs to Yumi Omura.
touch
THANK YOU.
squeeze

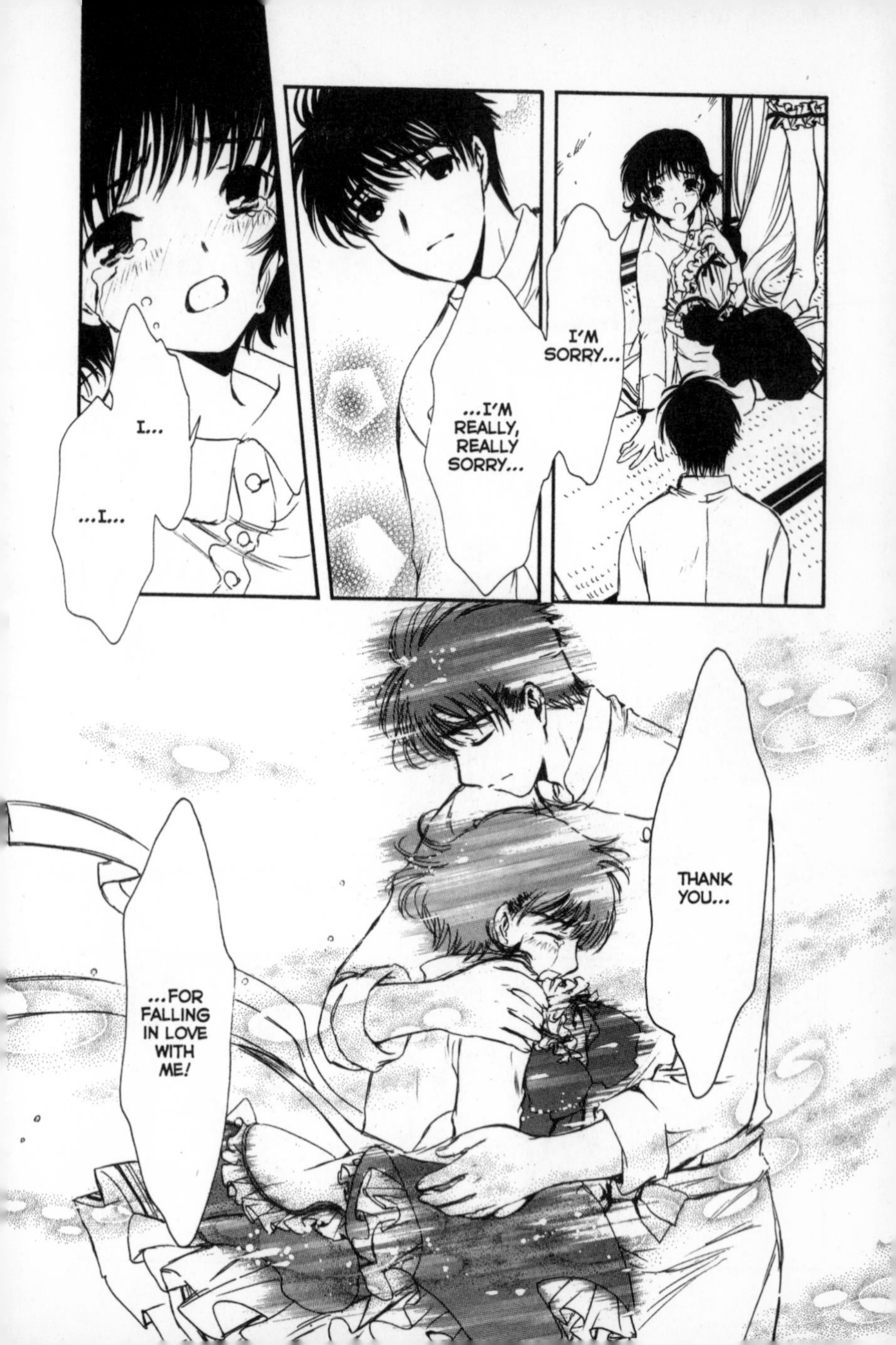
I'M SORRY...
...I'M REALLY, REALLY SORRY...
I...
...I...
THANK YOU...
...FOR FALLING IN LOVE WITH ME!

◂chapter 66▸

Chobits
ちょびっツ

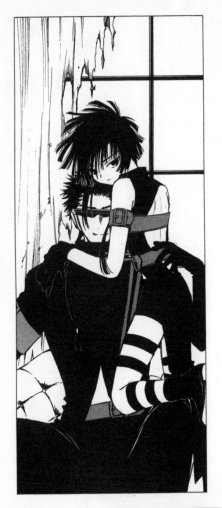

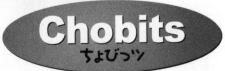

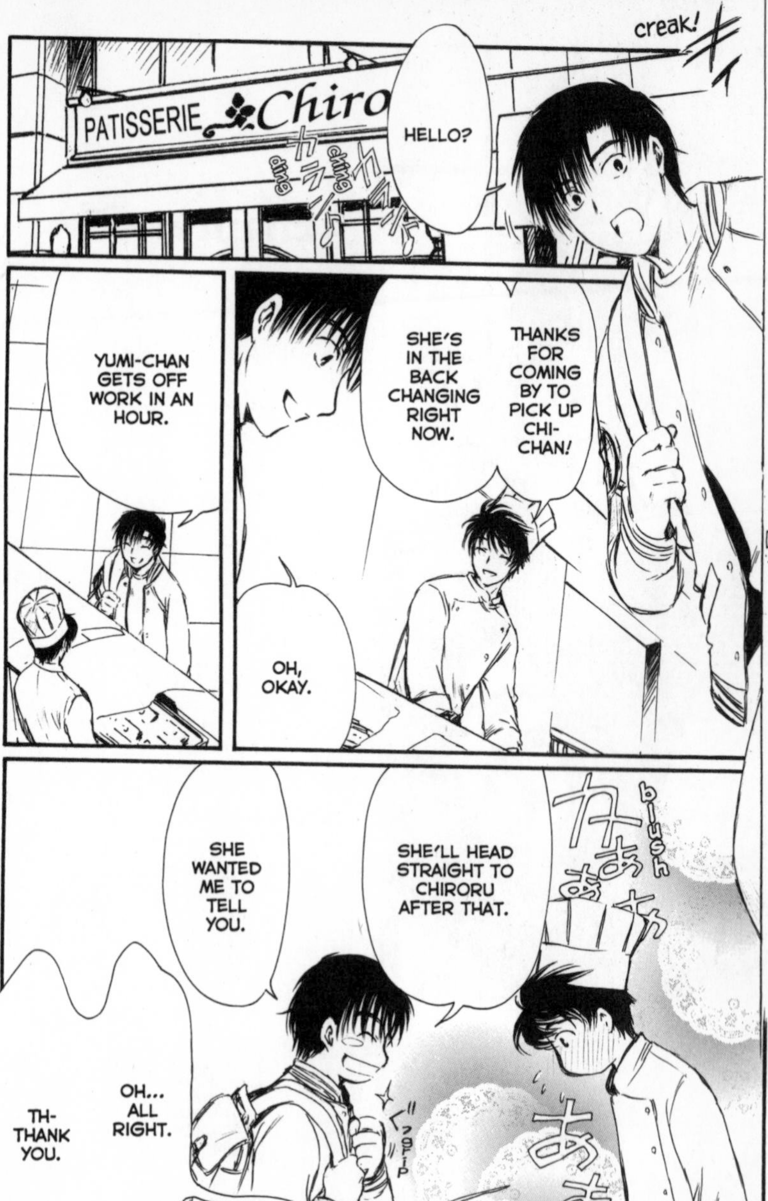

creak!
PATISSERIE Chiro
ching ding
HELLO?
THANKS FOR COMING BY TO PICK UP CHI-CHAN!
SHE'S IN THE BACK CHANGING RIGHT NOW.
OH, OKAY.
YUMI-CHAN GETS OFF WORK IN AN HOUR.
blush
SHE'LL HEAD STRAIGHT TO CHIRORU AFTER THAT.
SHE WANTED ME TO TELL YOU.
grip
OH... ALL RIGHT.
TH-THANK YOU.

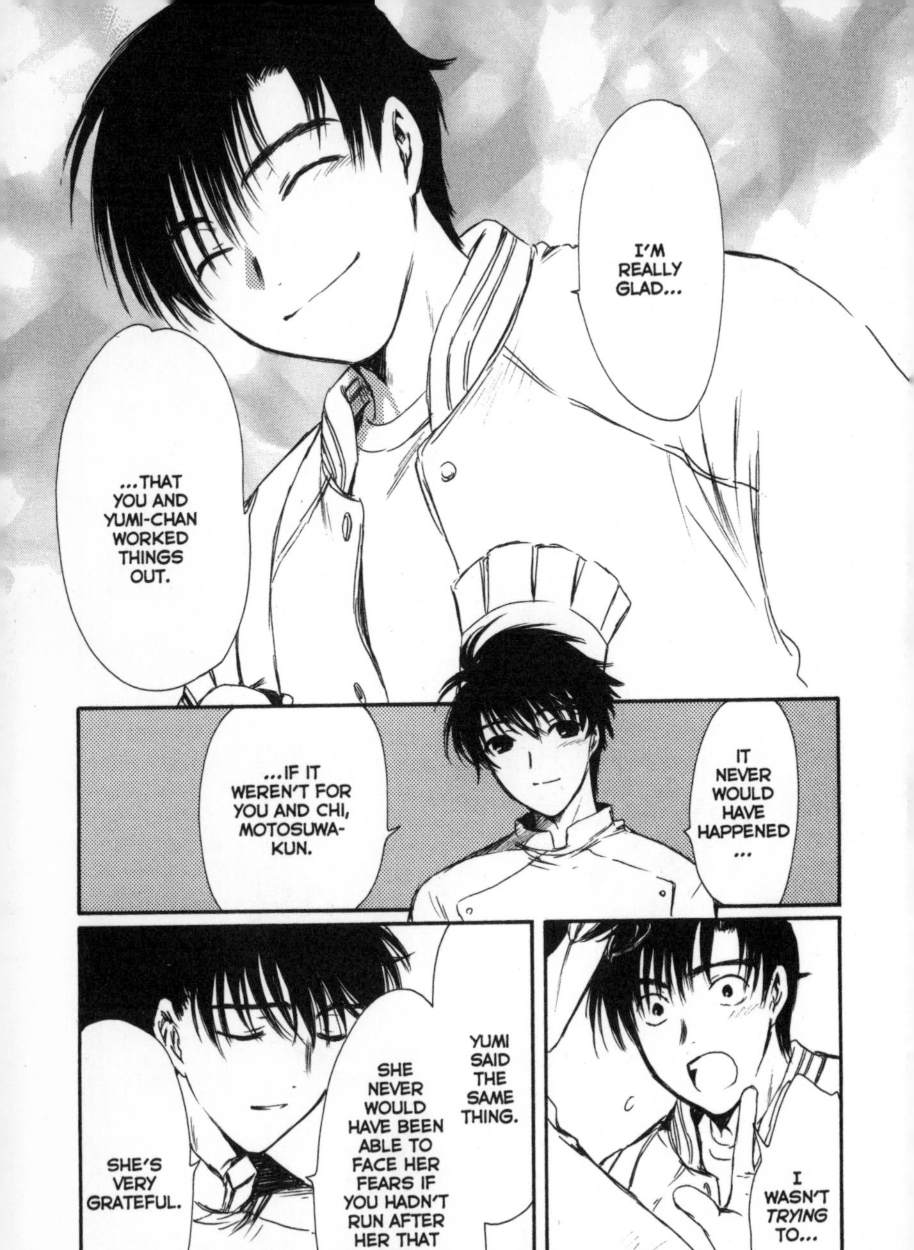
I'M REALLY GLAD...
...THAT YOU AND YUMI-CHAN WORKED THINGS OUT.
IT NEVER WOULD HAVE HAPPENED ...
...IF IT WEREN'T FOR YOU AND CHI, MOTOSUWA-KUN.
I WASN'T *TRYING* TO...
YUMI SAID THE SAME THING.
SHE NEVER WOULD HAVE BEEN ABLE TO FACE HER FEARS IF YOU HADN'T RUN AFTER HER THAT DAY.
SHE'S VERY GRATEFUL.

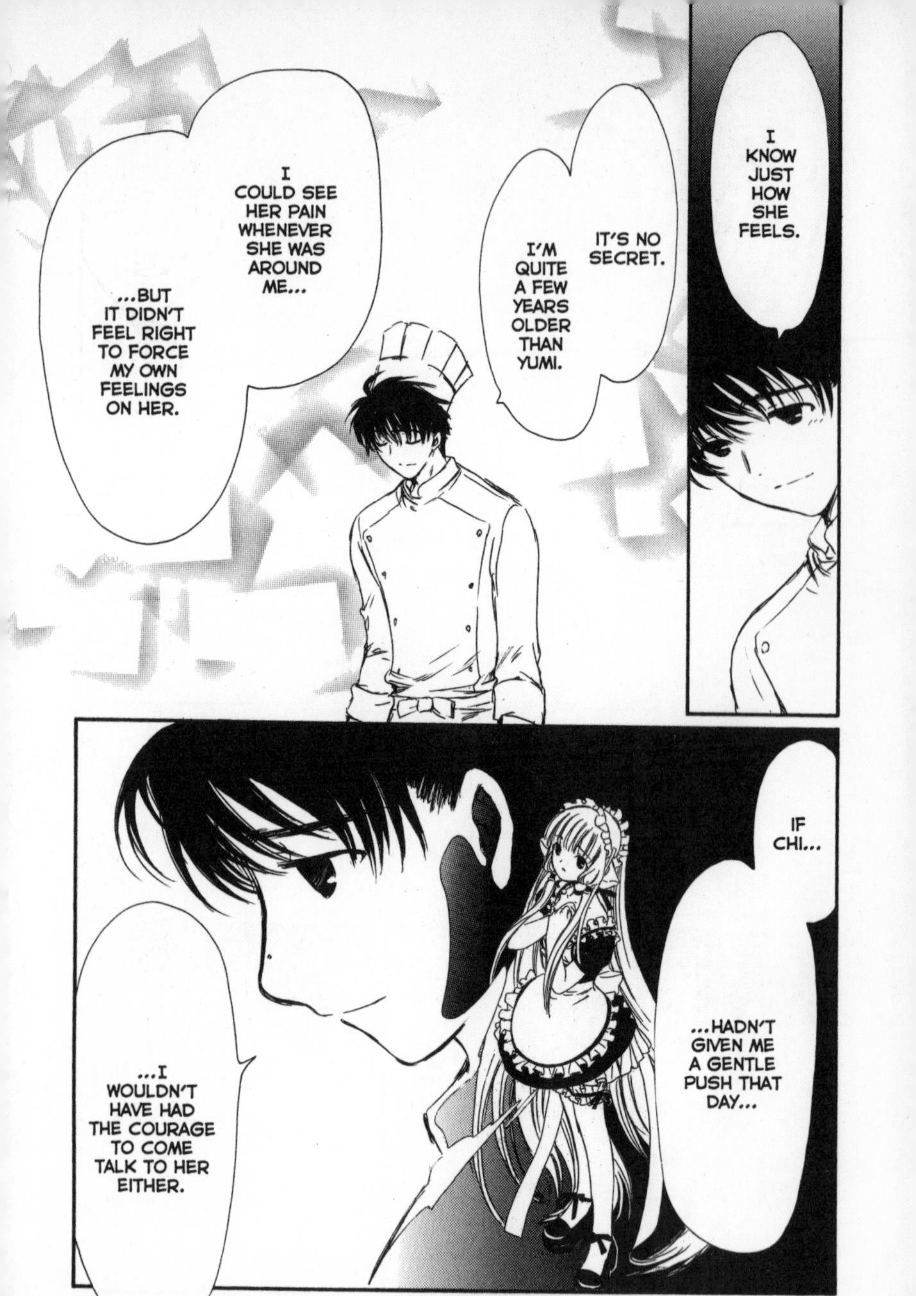
I KNOW JUST HOW SHE FEELS.
IT'S NO SECRET.
I'M QUITE A FEW YEARS OLDER THAN YUMI.
I COULD SEE HER PAIN WHENEVER SHE WAS AROUND ME...
...BUT IT DIDN'T FEEL RIGHT TO FORCE MY OWN FEELINGS ON HER.
IF CHI...
...HADN'T GIVEN ME A GENTLE PUSH THAT DAY...
...I WOULDN'T HAVE HAD THE COURAGE TO COME TALK TO HER EITHER.

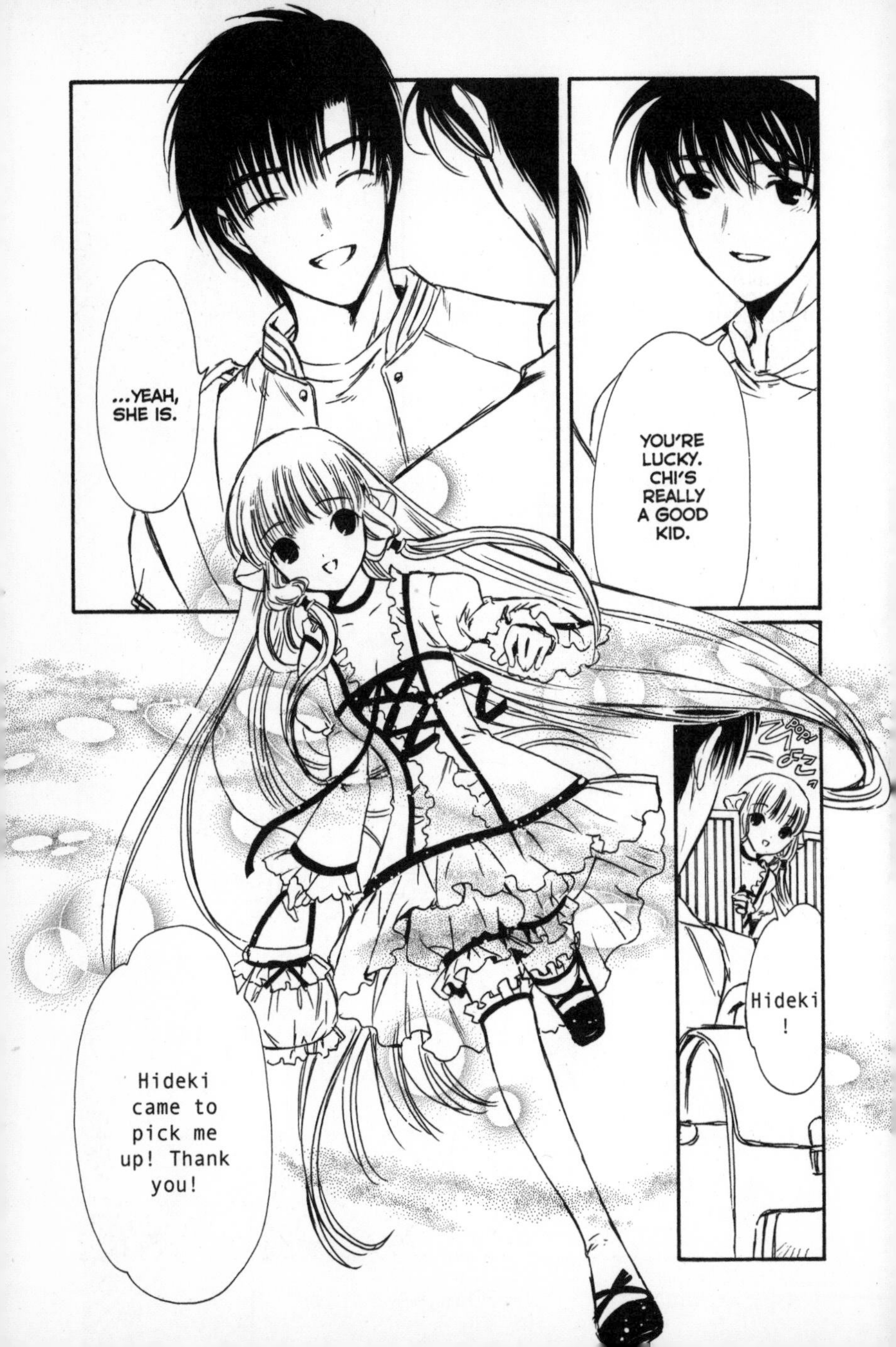
YOU'RE LUCKY. CHI'S REALLY A GOOD KID.
...YEAH, SHE IS.
POP!
Hideki!
Hideki came to pick me up! Thank you!

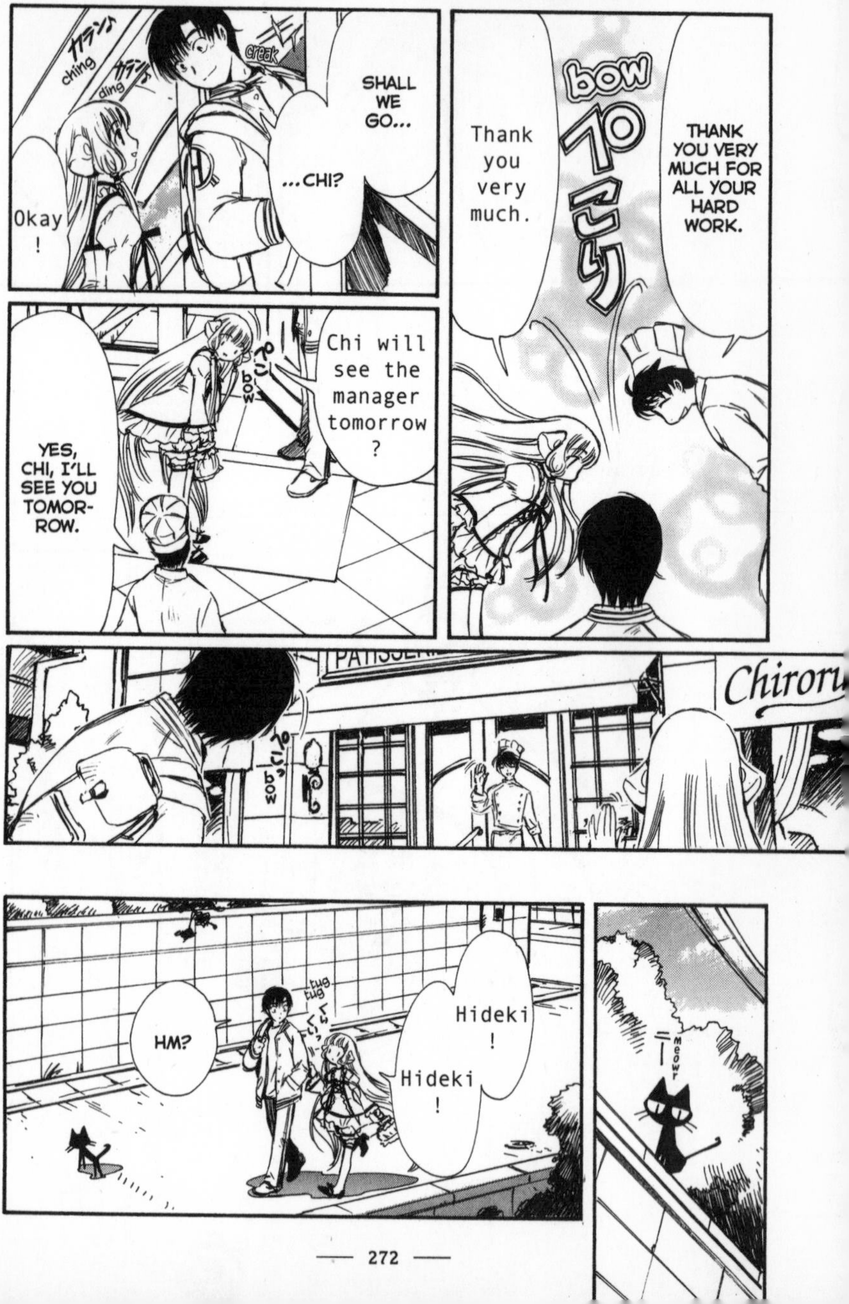
THANK YOU VERY MUCH FOR ALL YOUR HARD WORK.
bow
Thank you very much.
ching
ding
creak
SHALL WE GO...
...CHI?
Okay!
Chi will see the manager tomorrow?
bow
YES, CHI, I'LL SEE YOU TOMORROW.
Chiroru
bow
meowr
Hideki!
Hideki!
tug tug
HM?

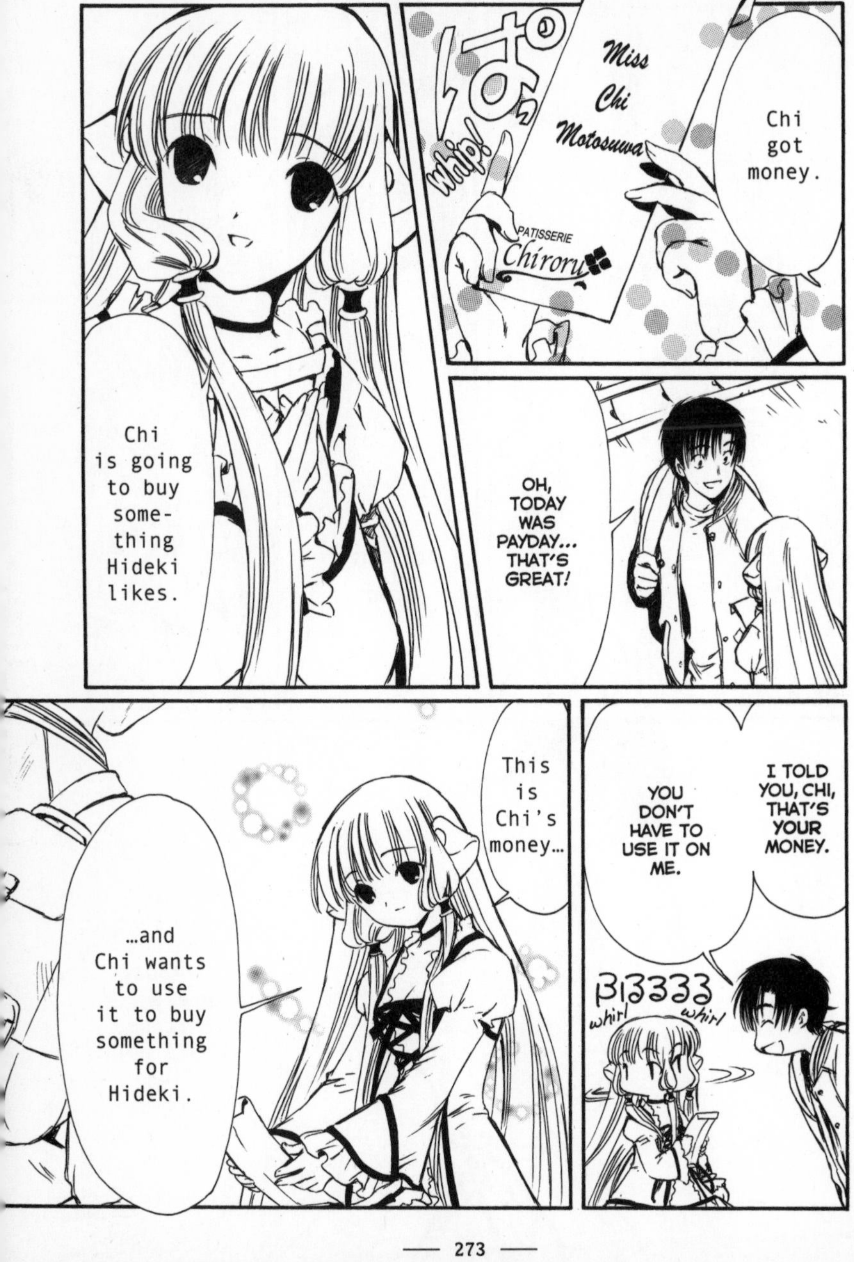
Chi got money.
Miss Chi Motosuwa
PATISSERIE Chiroru
ぱっ
whip!
OH, TODAY WAS PAYDAY... THAT'S GREAT!
Chi is going to buy some-thing Hideki likes.
I TOLD YOU, CHI, THAT'S YOUR MONEY.
YOU DON'T HAVE TO USE IT ON ME.
ふるるるる
whirl whirl
This is Chi's money...
...and Chi wants to use it to buy something for Hideki.

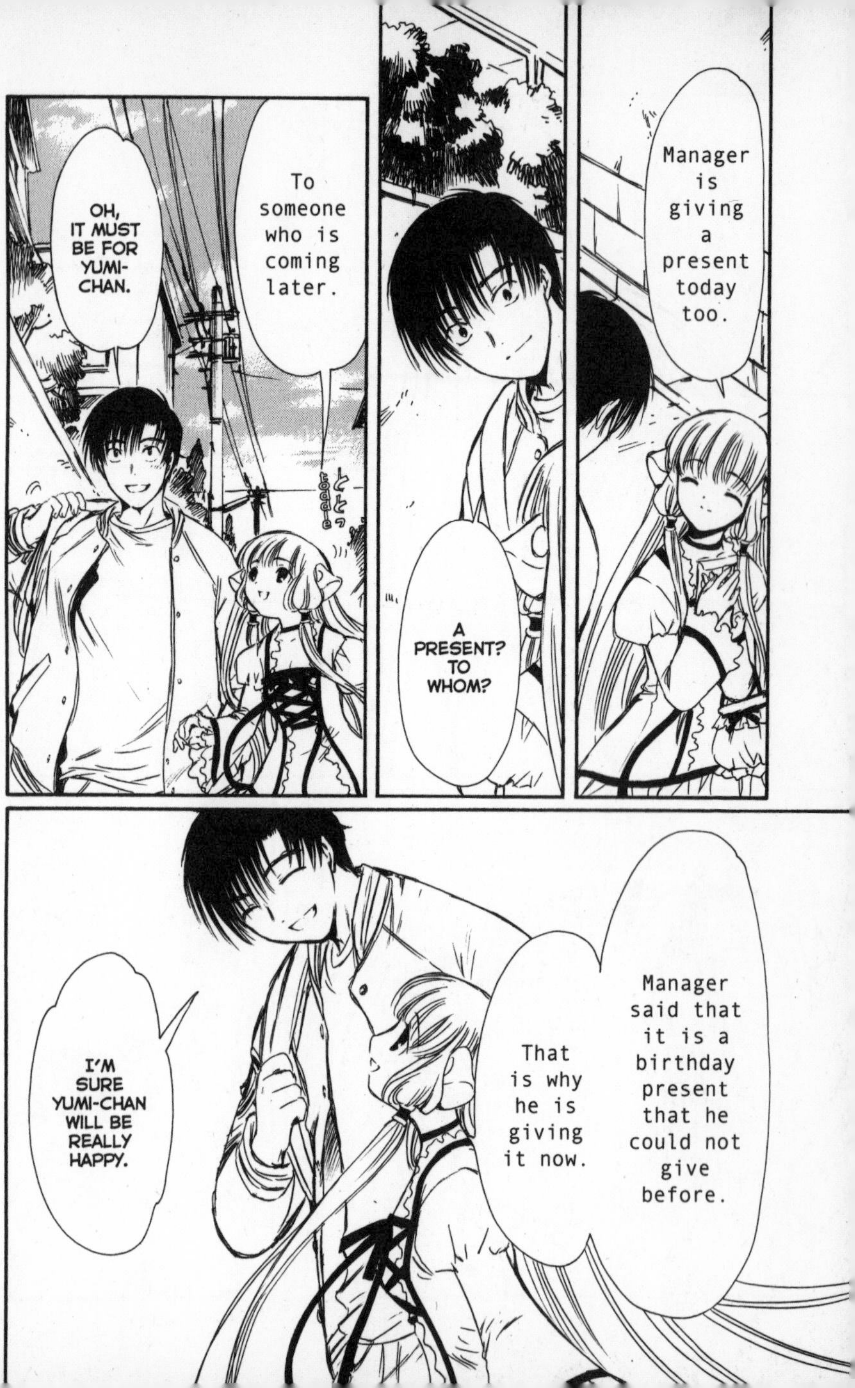
Manager is giving a present today too.
A PRESENT? TO WHOM?
To someone who is coming later.
toddle
OH, IT MUST BE FOR YUMI-CHAN.
Manager said that it is a birthday present that he could not give before.
That is why he is giving it now.
I'M SURE YUMI-CHAN WILL BE REALLY HAPPY.

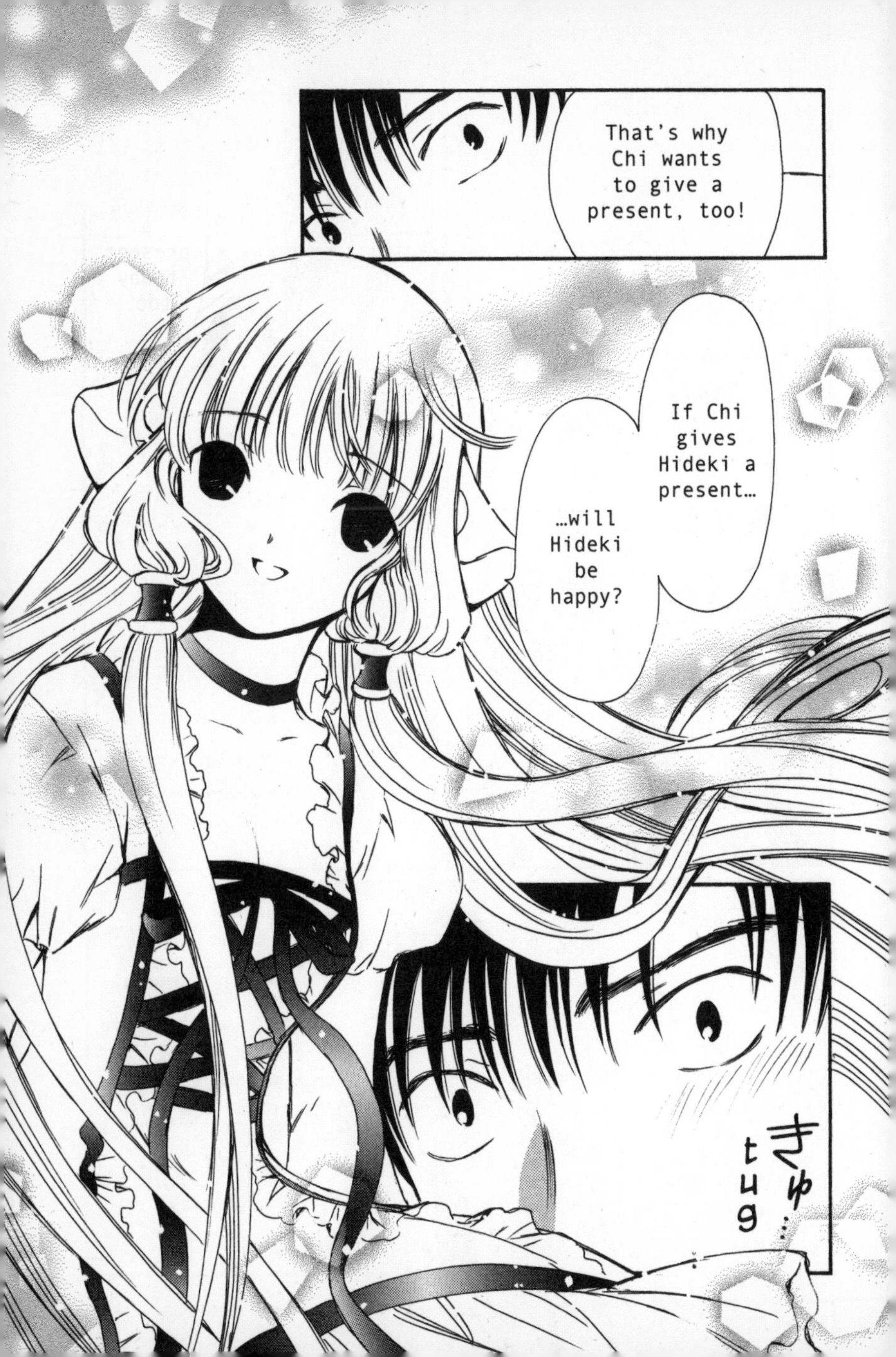
That's why Chi wants to give a present, too!
If Chi gives Hideki a present…
…will Hideki be happy?
きゅ…
tug

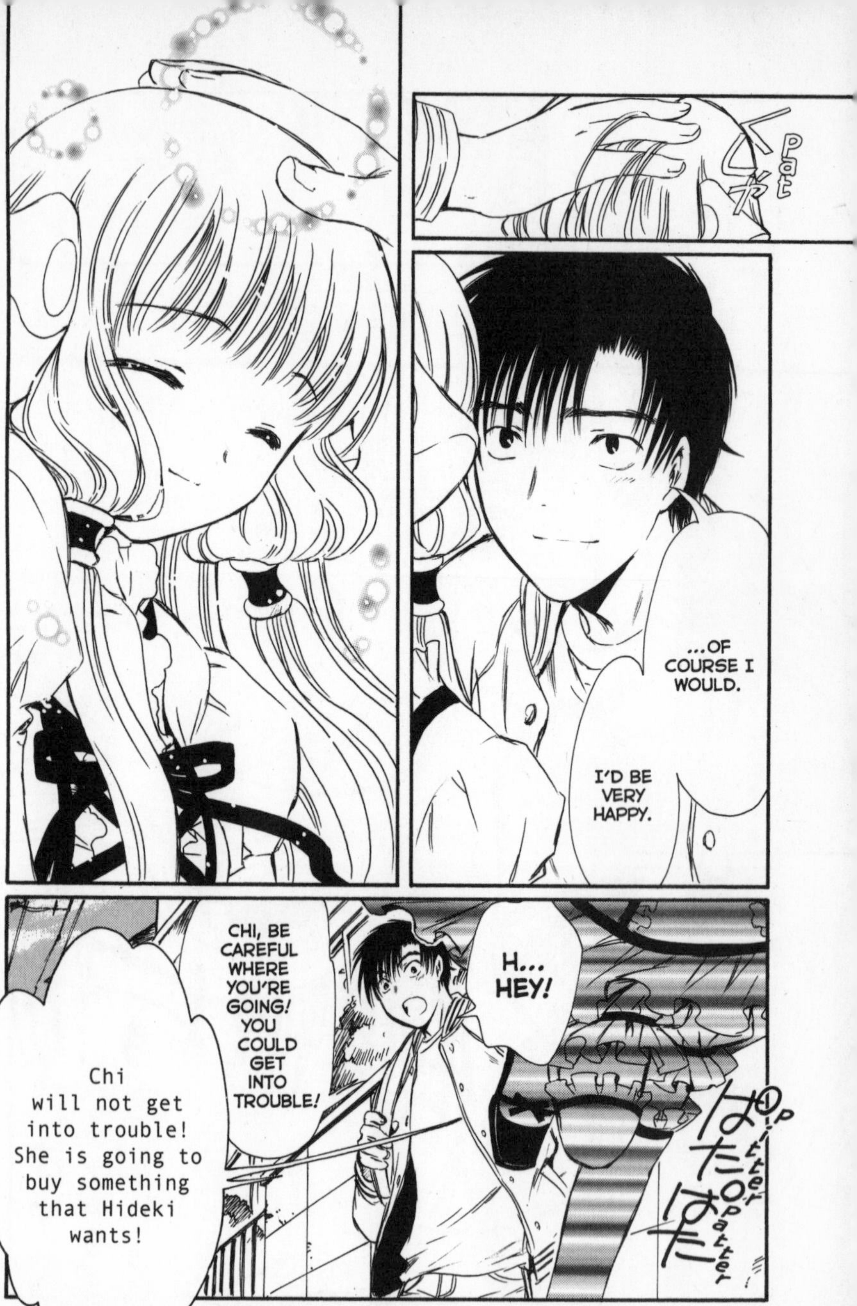
pat
...OF COURSE I WOULD.
I'D BE VERY HAPPY.
ぱたぱた
pitter patter
H... HEY!
CHI, BE CAREFUL WHERE YOU'RE GOING! YOU COULD GET INTO TROUBLE!
Chi will not get into trouble! She is going to buy something that Hideki wants!

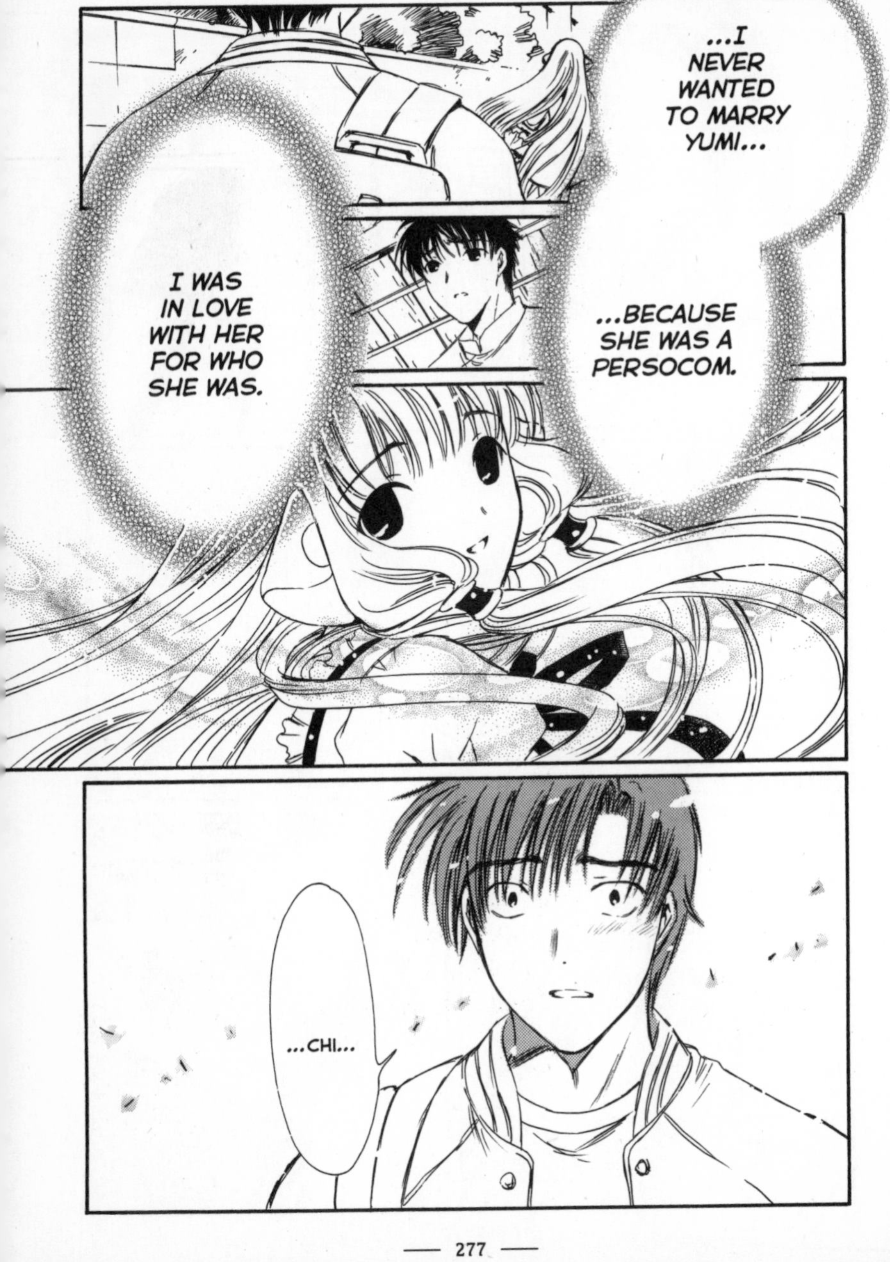
...I NEVER WANTED TO MARRY YUMI...
...BECAUSE SHE WAS A PERSOCOM.
I WAS IN LOVE WITH HER FOR WHO SHE WAS.
...CHI...

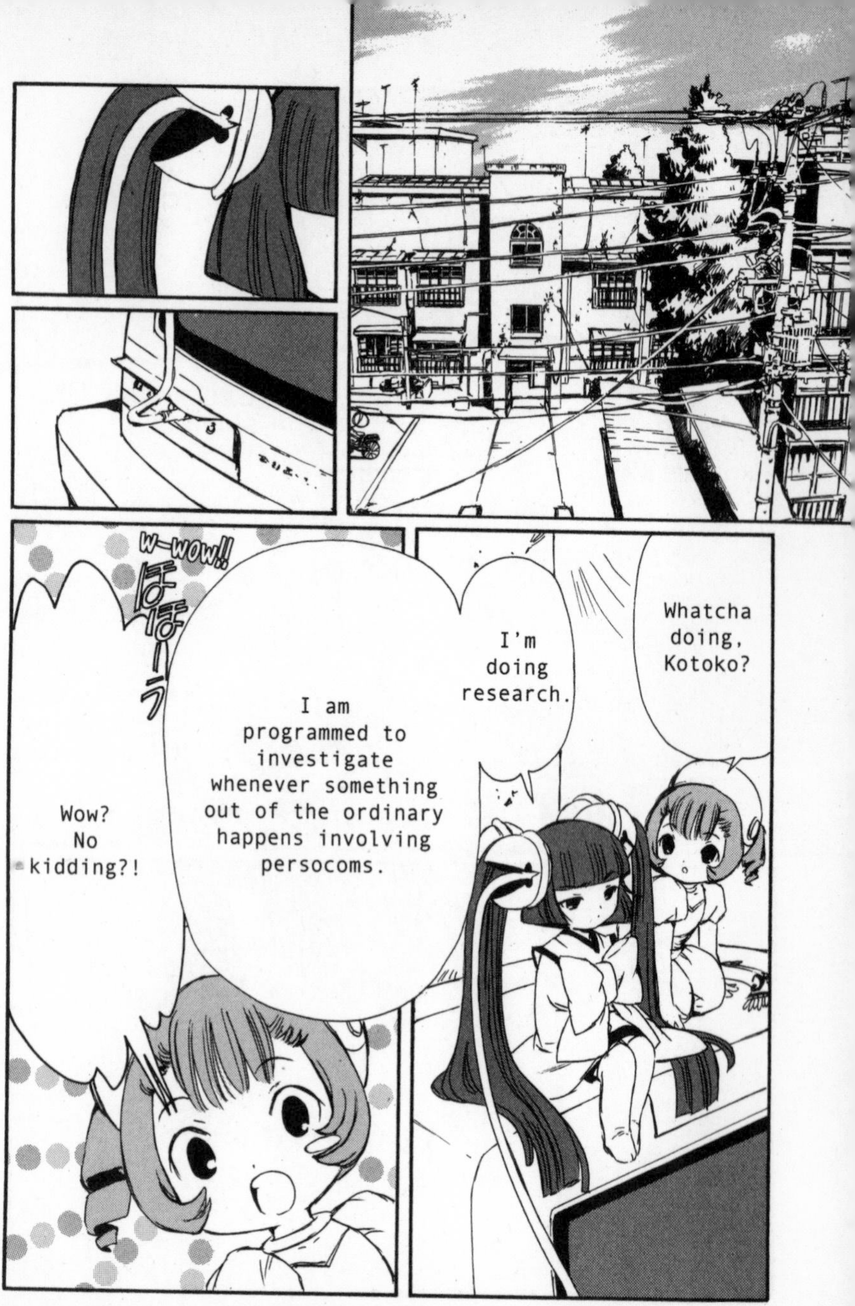
Whatcha doing, Kotoko?
I'm doing research.
W-WOW!!
ほほ～う
I am programmed to investigate whenever something out of the ordinary happens involving persocoms.
Wow? No kidding?!

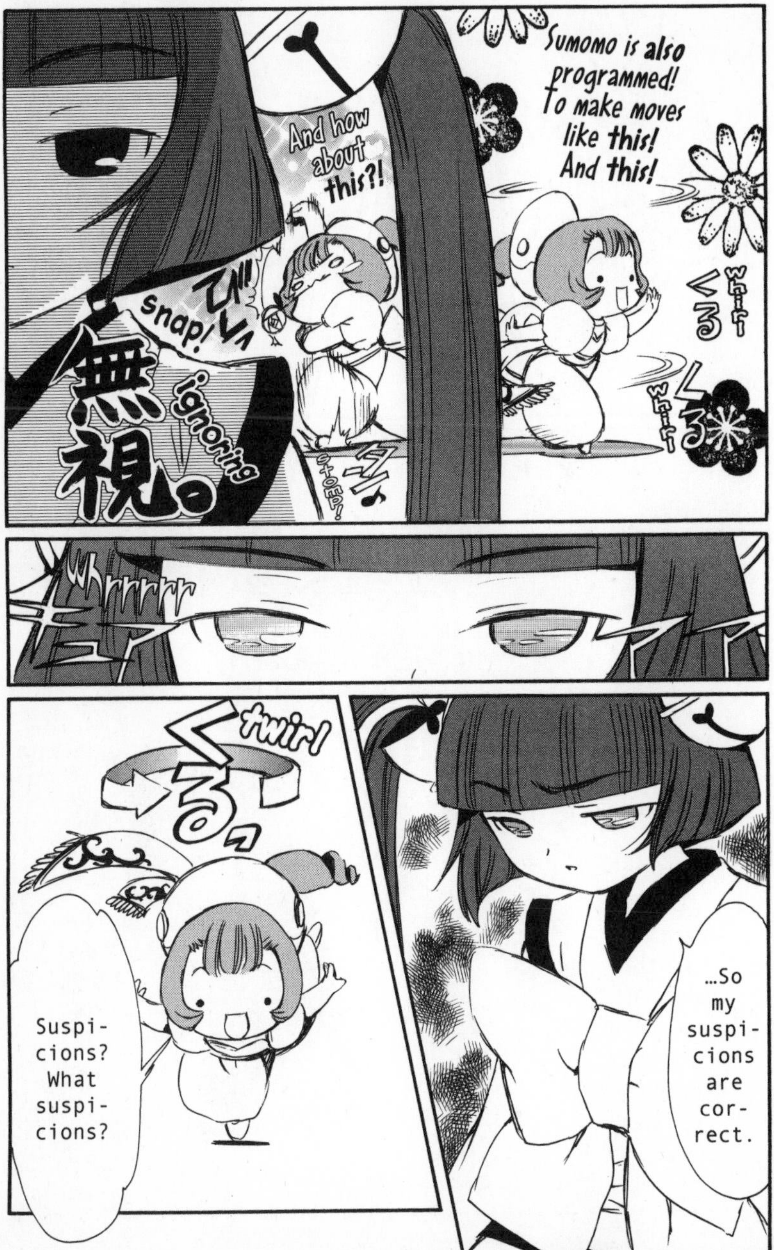

Sumomo is also programmed! To make moves like this! And this!
whirl
くる
whirl
くる
And how about this?!
snap!
無視。
ignoring
stomp!
Whrrrrr
...So my suspicions are correct.
twirl
くるっ
Suspicions? What suspicions?

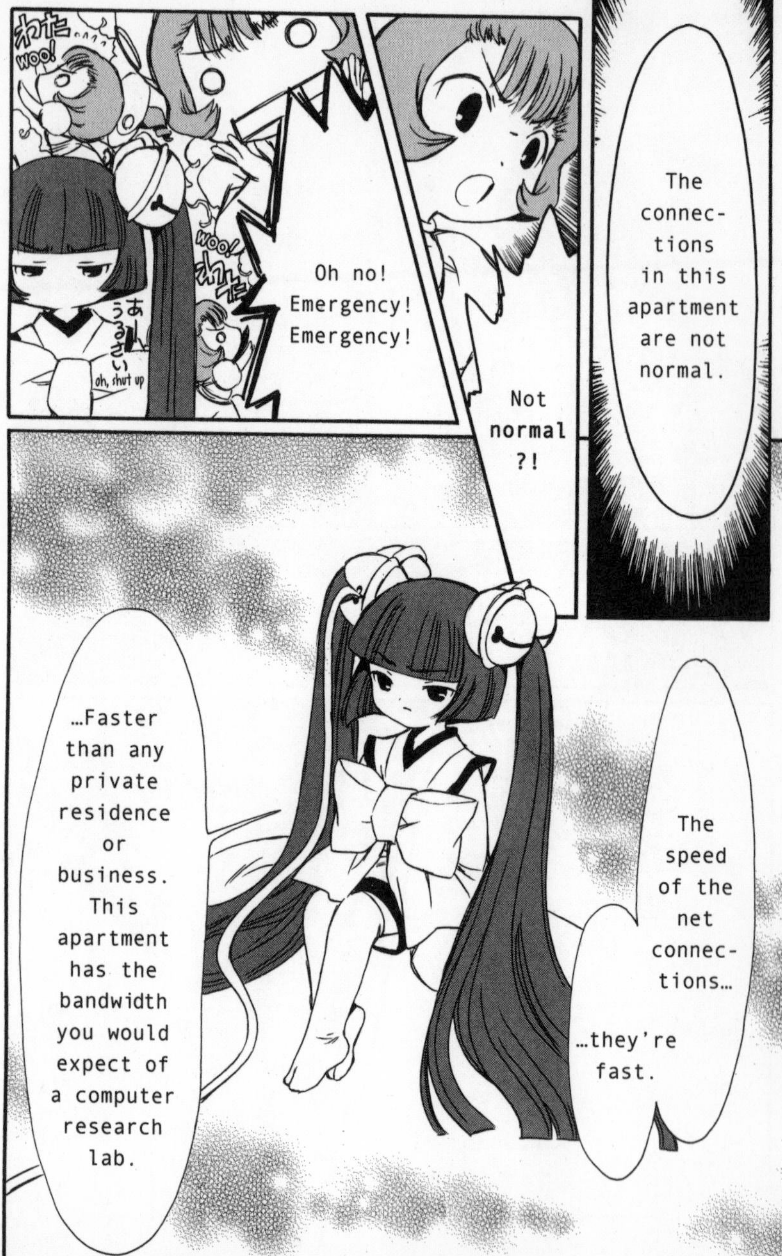
The connections in this apartment are not normal.
Not normal?!
Oh no! Emergency! Emergency!
わた
woo!
わた
woo!
あーうるさい
oh, shut up
The speed of the net connections…
…they're fast.
…Faster than any private residence or business. This apartment has the bandwidth you would expect of a computer research lab.

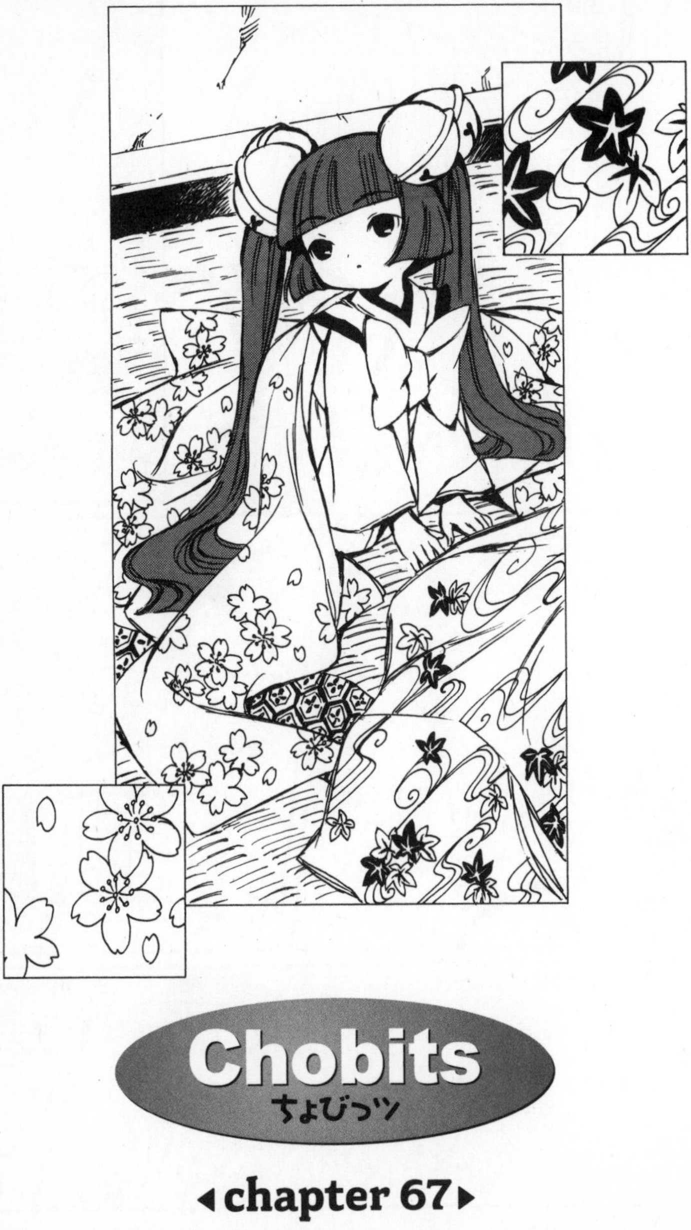

Chobits
ちょびっツ

chapter 67

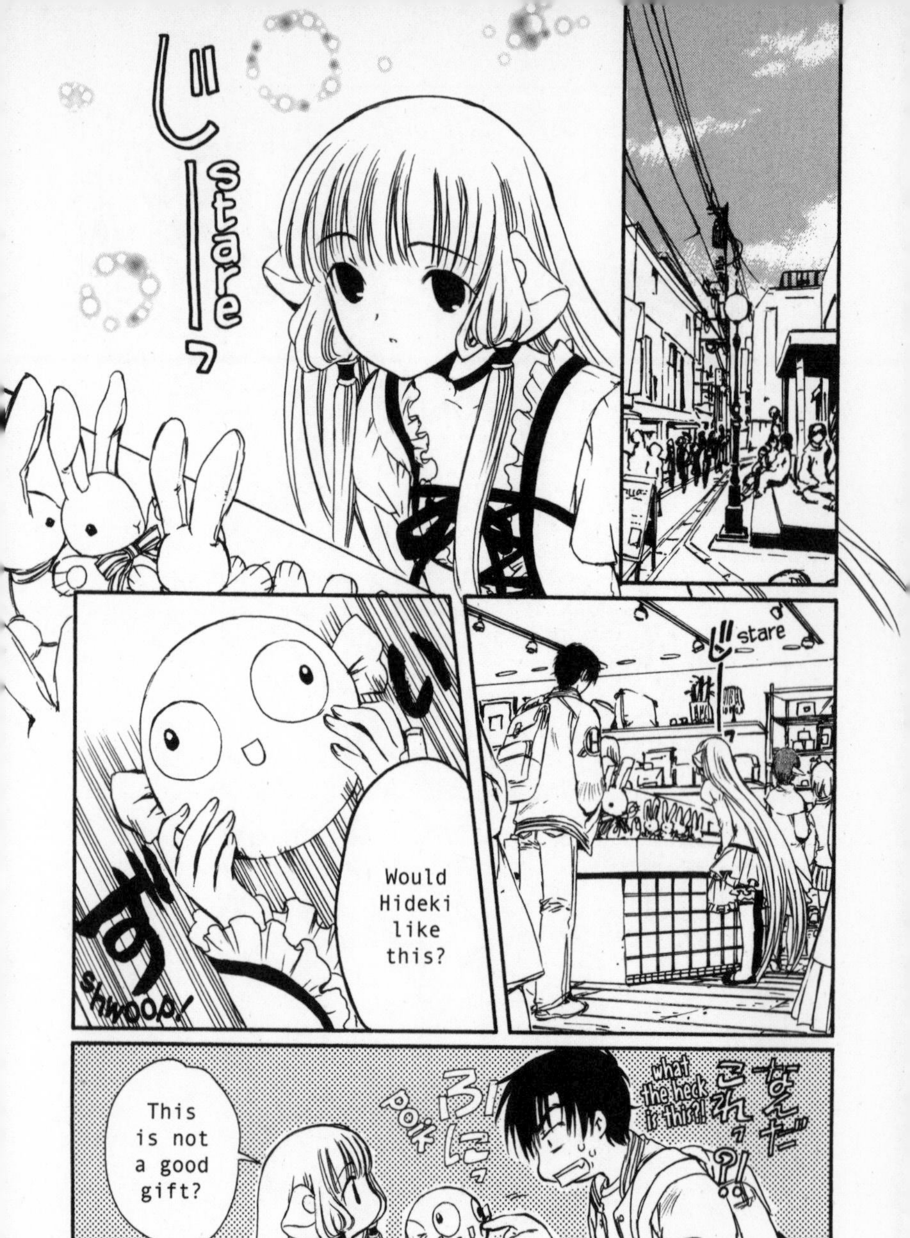
じーっ
stare
じー
stare
すっ
shwoop!
Would Hideki like this?
なんだこれっ?!
what the heck is this?!
ぷにっ
poik
This is not a good gift?

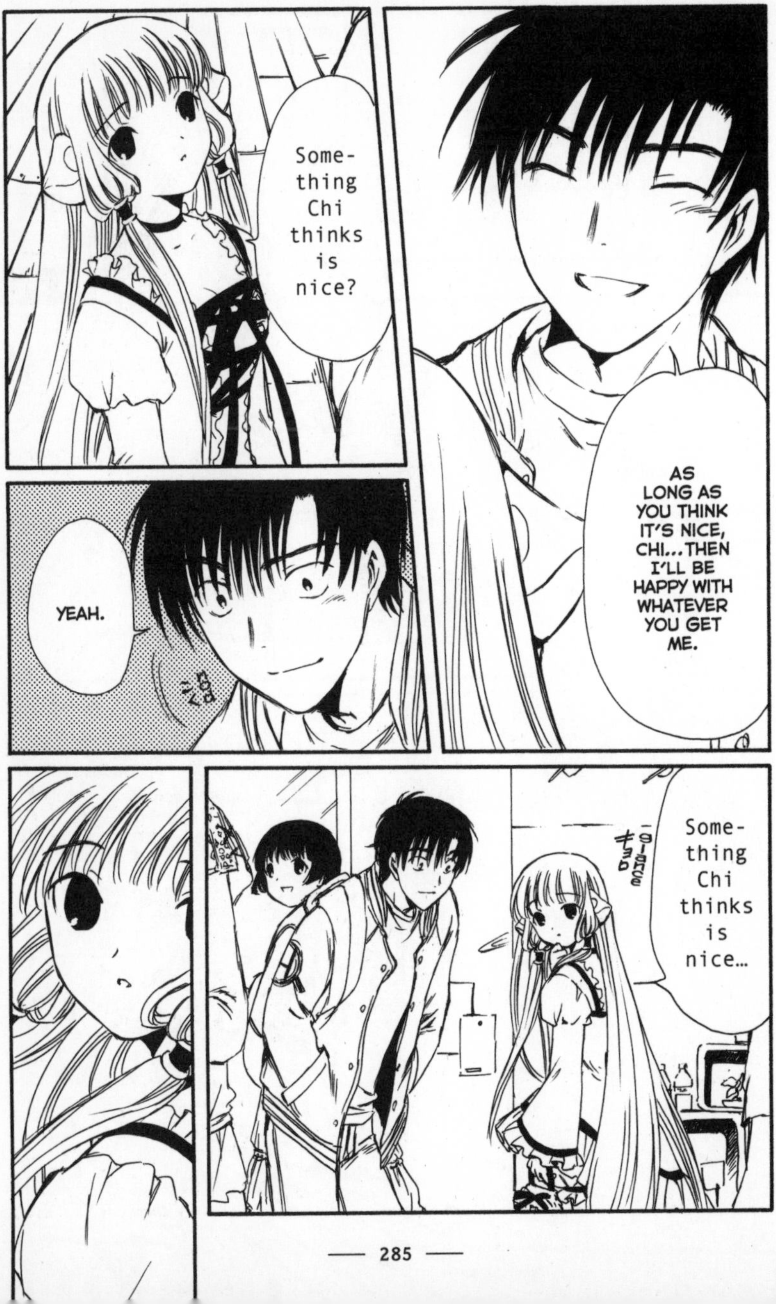
AS LONG AS YOU THINK IT'S NICE, CHI...THEN I'LL BE HAPPY WITH WHATEVER YOU GET ME.
Some-thing Chi thinks is nice?
YEAH.
Some-thing Chi thinks is nice...
glance

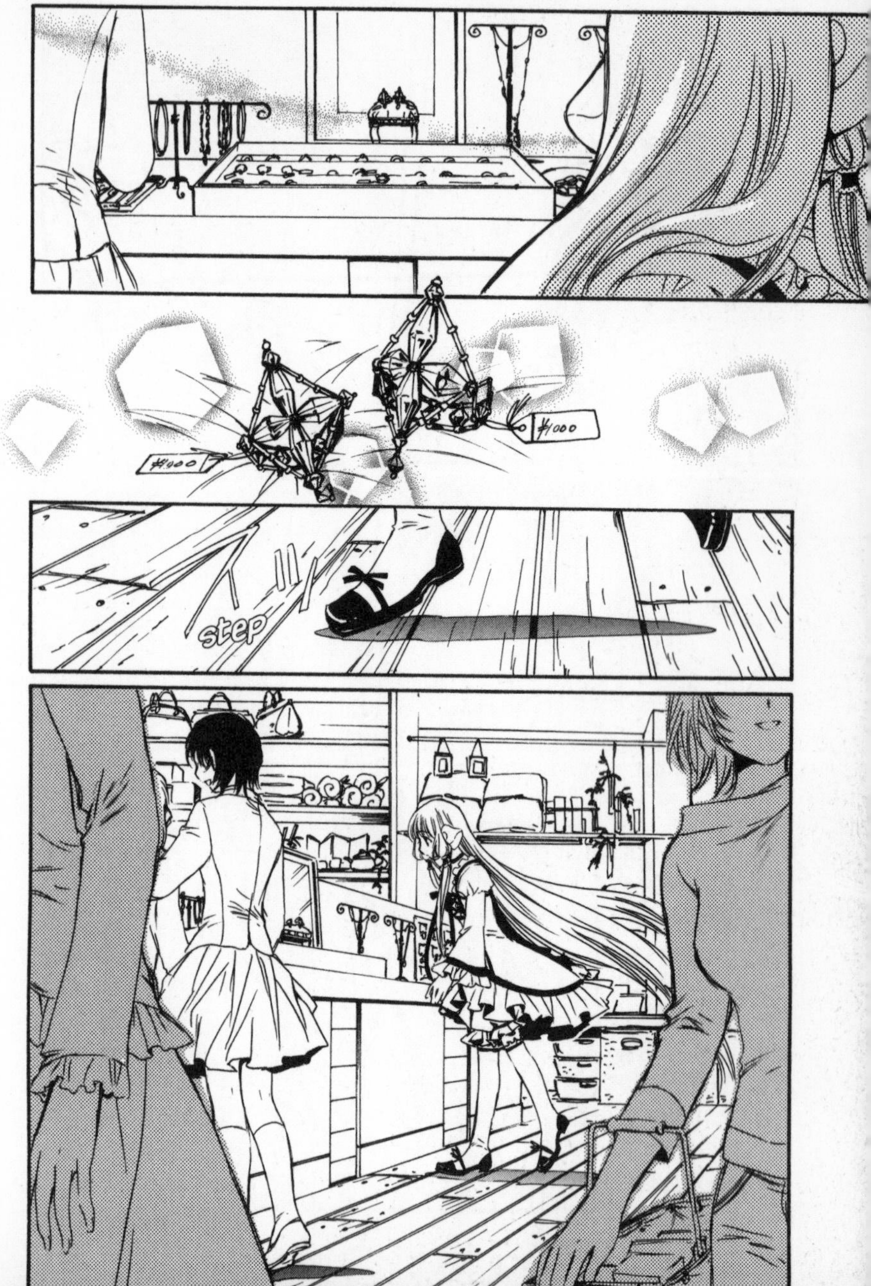
¥1000
¥1000
step

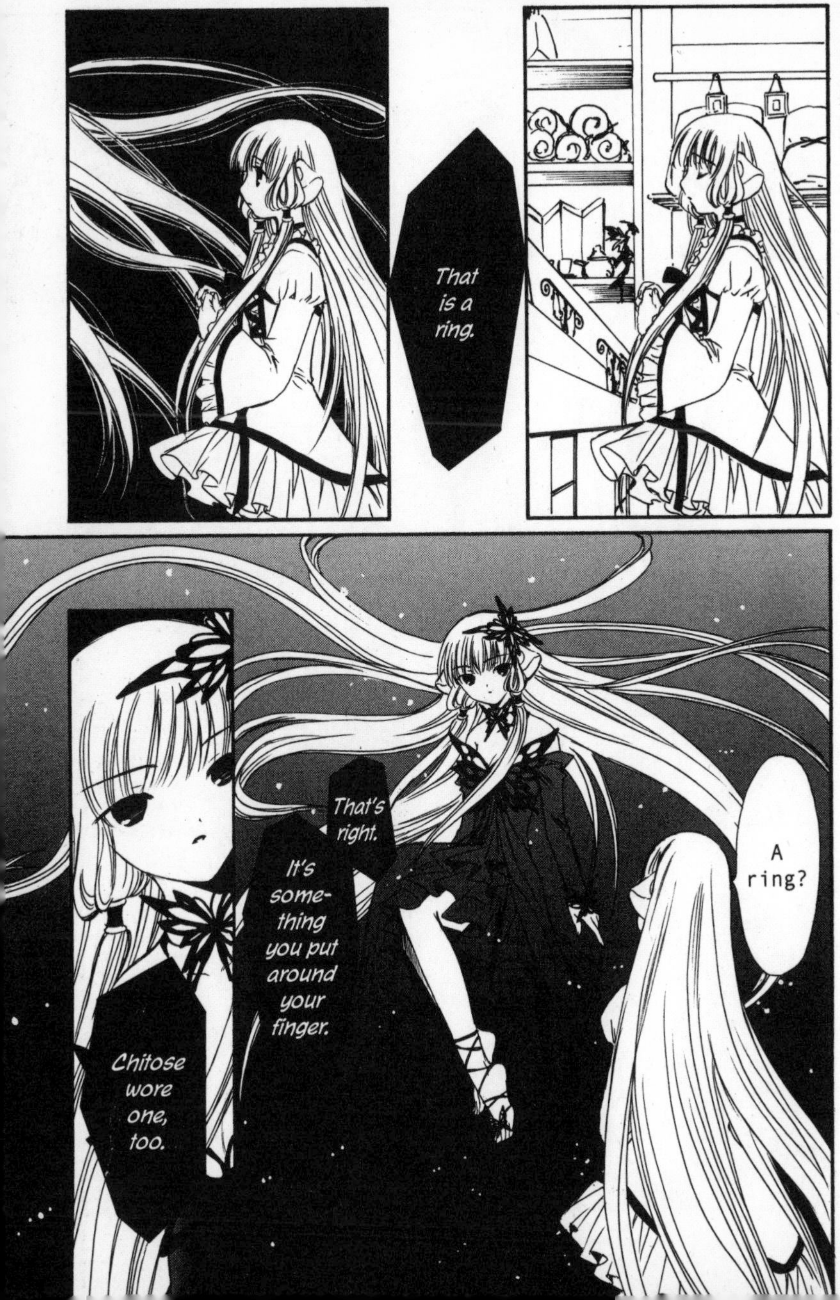
That is a ring.
A ring?
That's right.
It's something you put around your finger.
Chitose wore one, too.

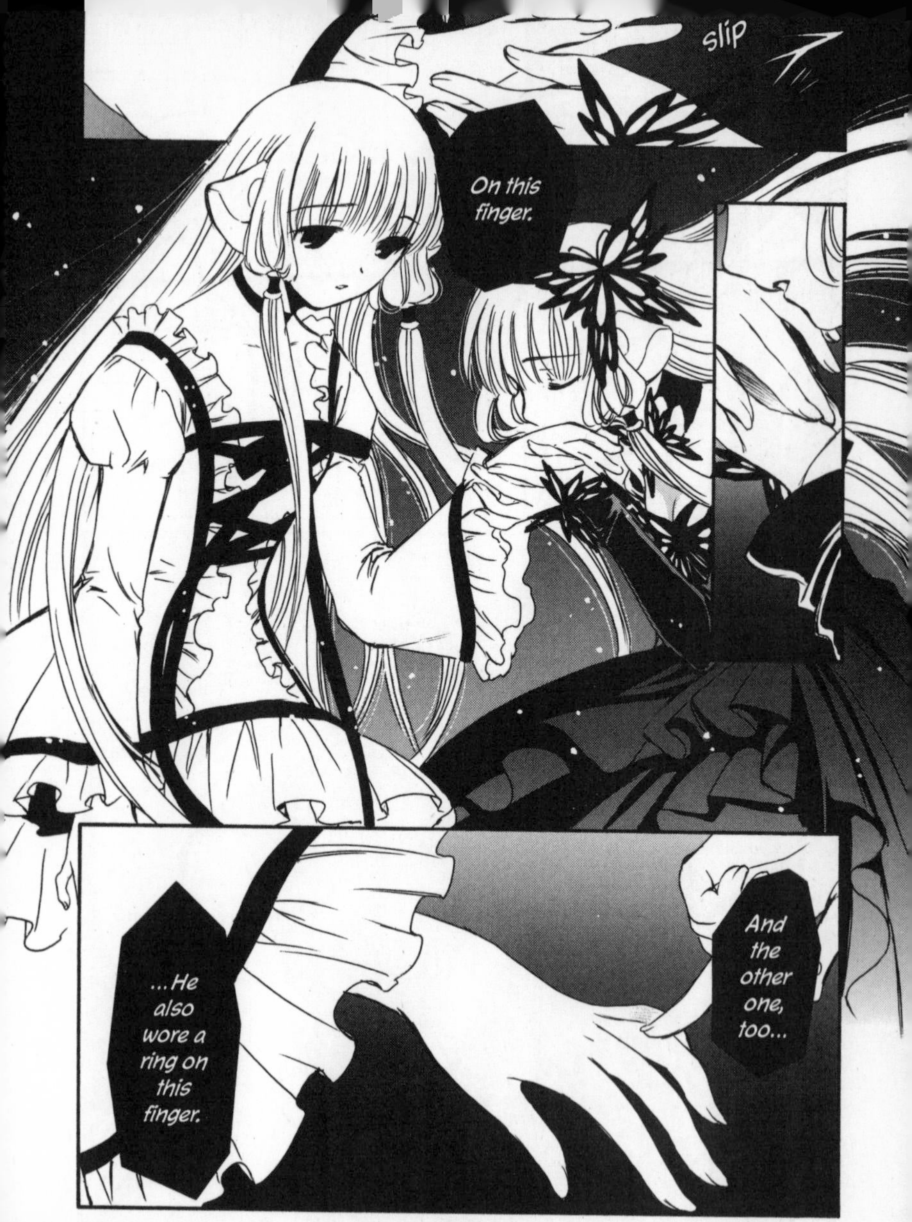
slip
On this finger.
And the other one, too...
...He also wore a ring on this finger.

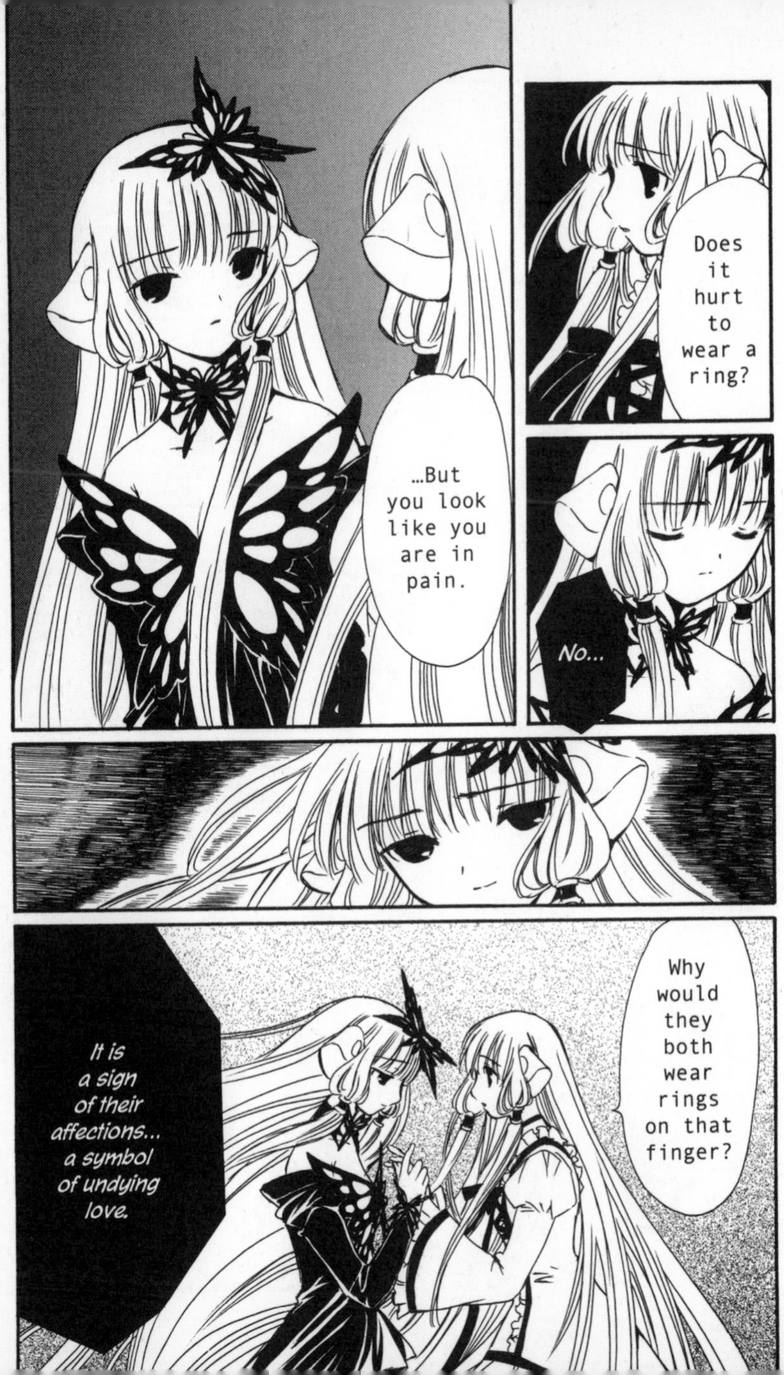
Does it hurt to wear a ring?
No...
...But you look like you are in pain.
Why would they both wear rings on that finger?
It is a sign of their affections... a symbol of undying love.

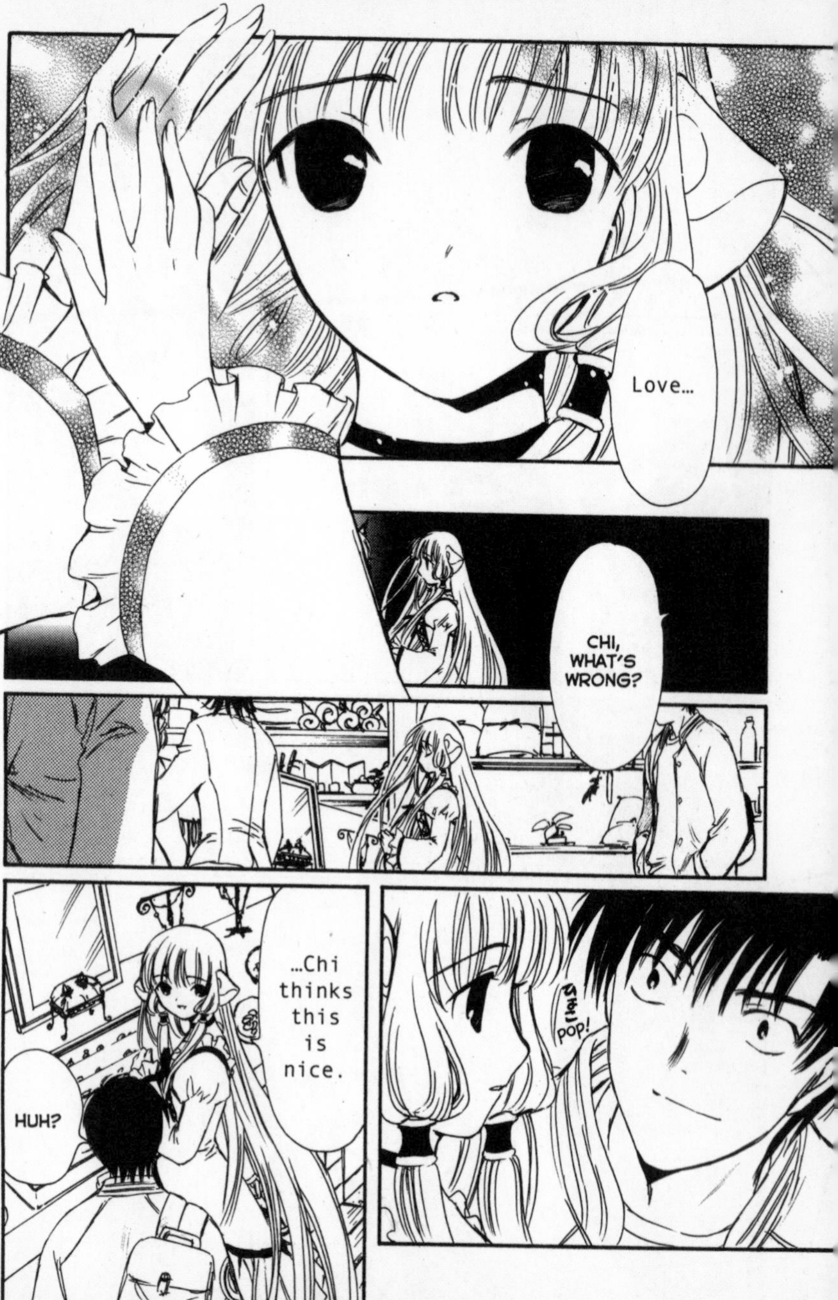
Love...
CHI, WHAT'S WRONG?
pop!
...Chi thinks this is nice.
HUH?

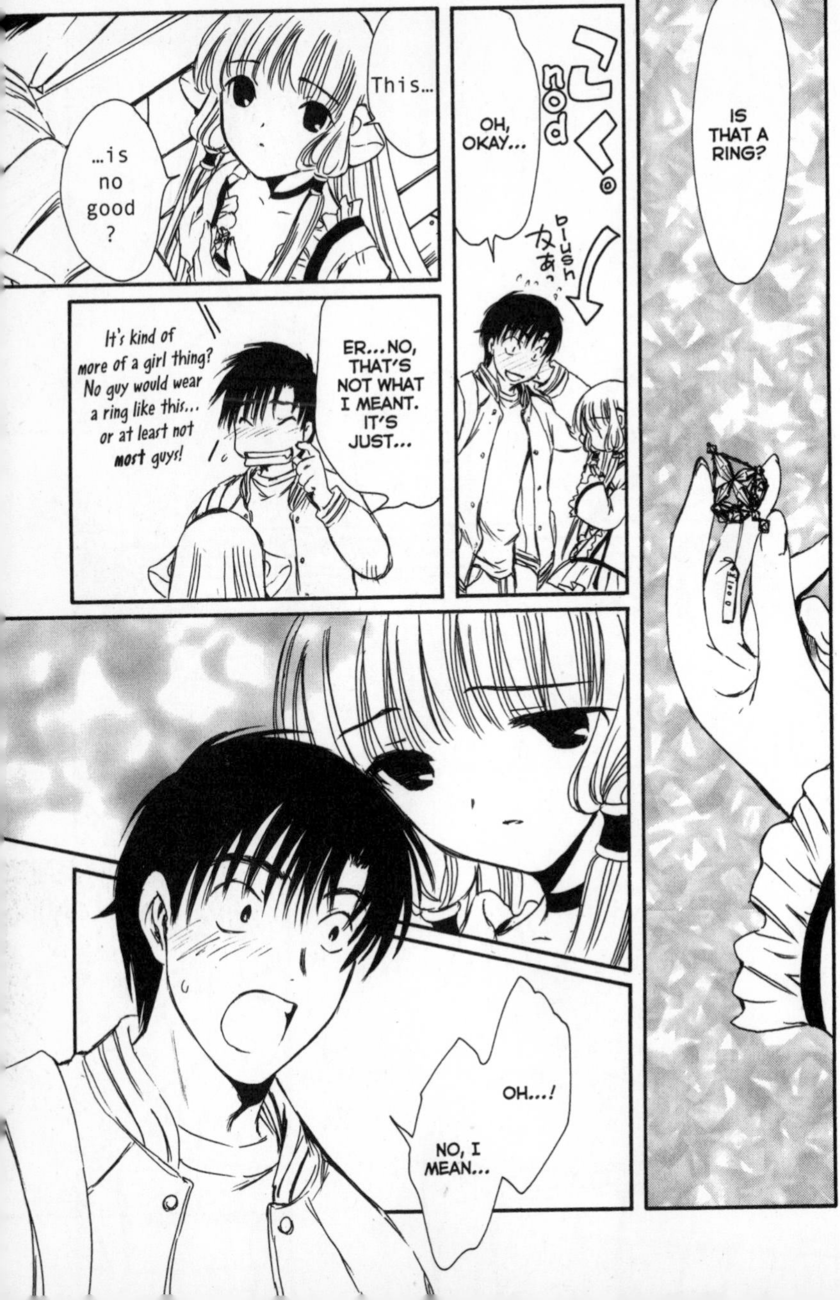

IS THAT A RING?
こく。
nod
OH, OKAY...
かぁっ
blush
This...
...is no good?
ER...NO, THAT'S NOT WHAT I MEANT. IT'S JUST...
It's kind of more of a girl thing? No guy would wear a ring like this... or at least not most guys!
OH...!
NO, I MEAN...

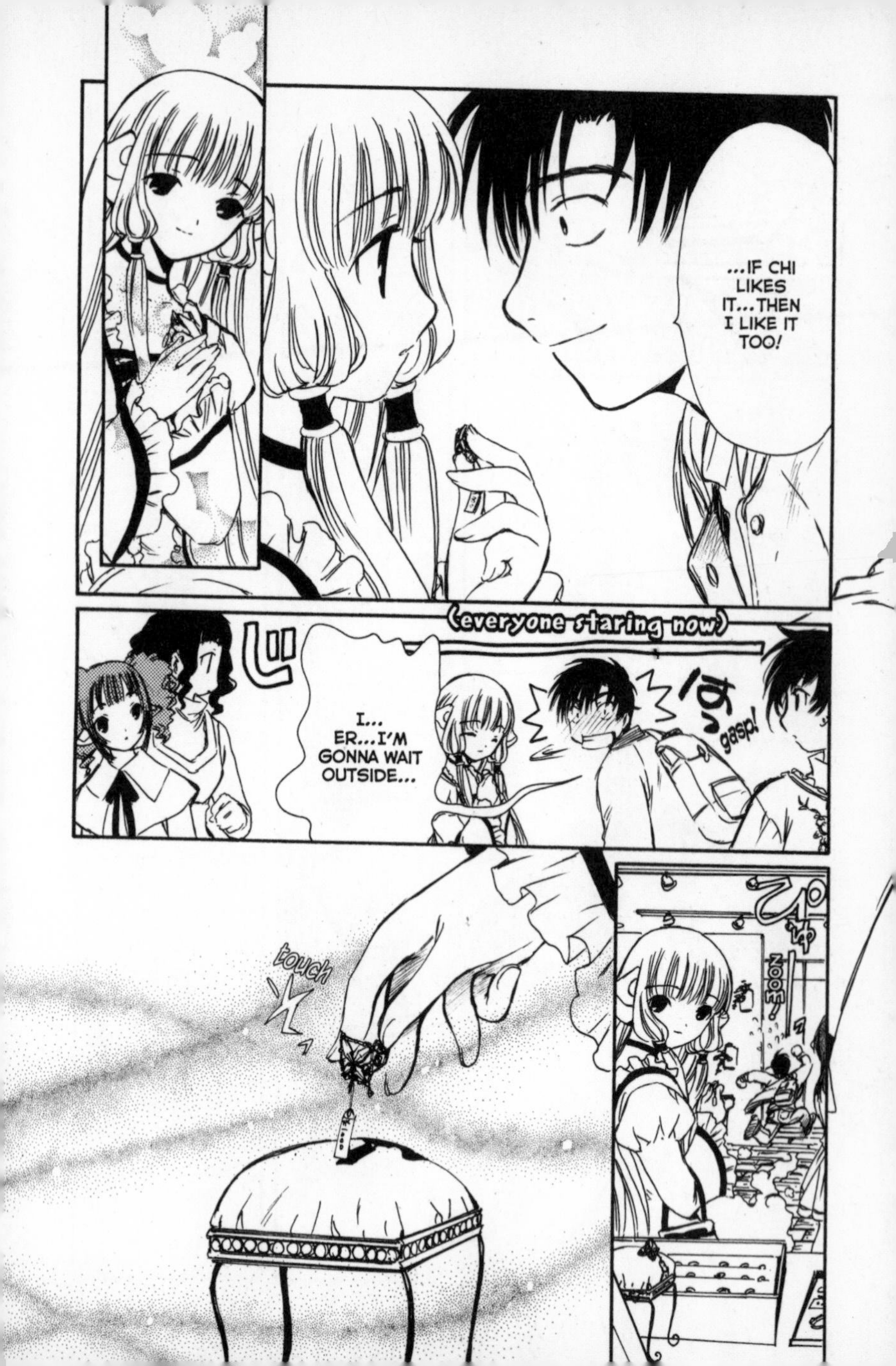
...IF CHI LIKES IT...THEN I LIKE IT TOO!
(everyone staring now)
gasp!
I... ER...I'M GONNA WAIT OUTSIDE...
ZOOM!
touch

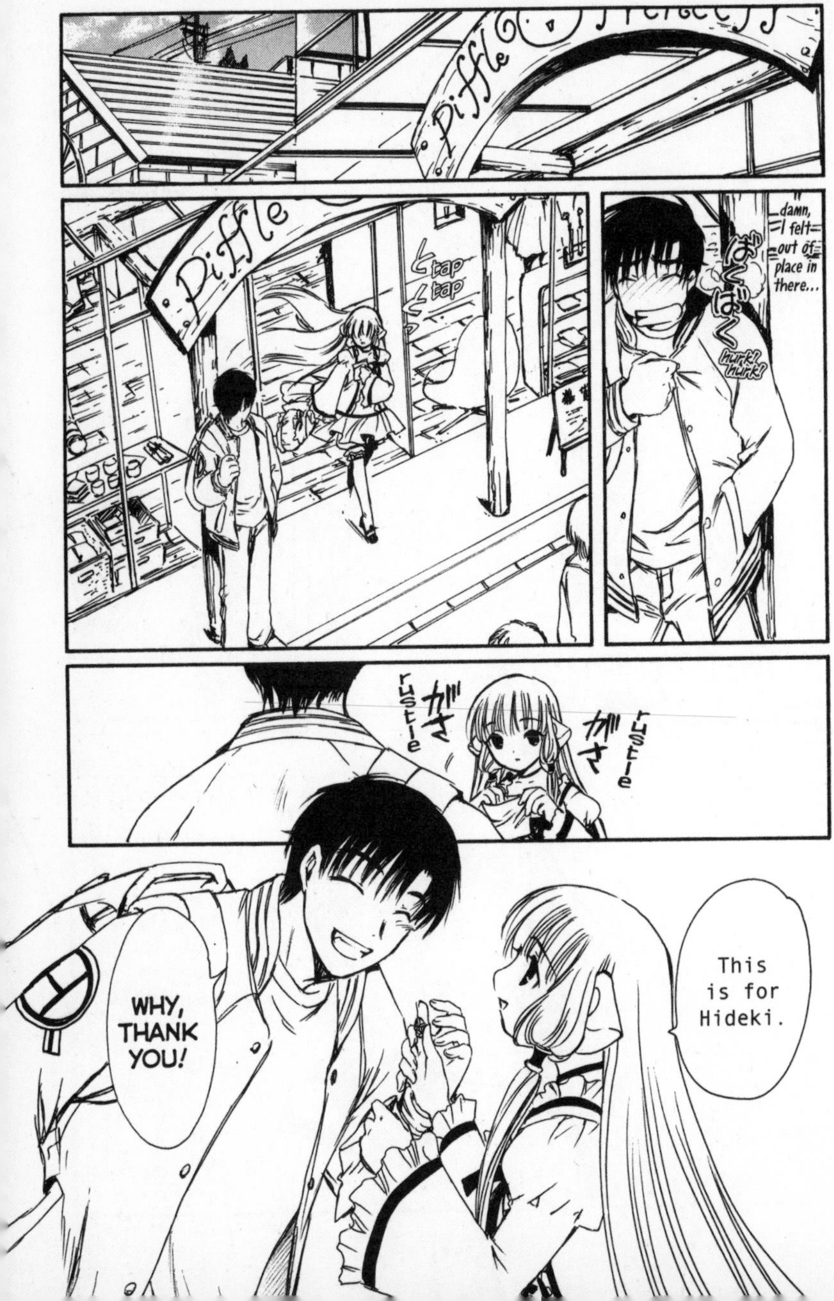
Piffle
damn, I felt out of place in there...
hurk! hurk!
Piffle
tap tap
rustle
rustle
This is for Hideki.
WHY, THANK YOU!

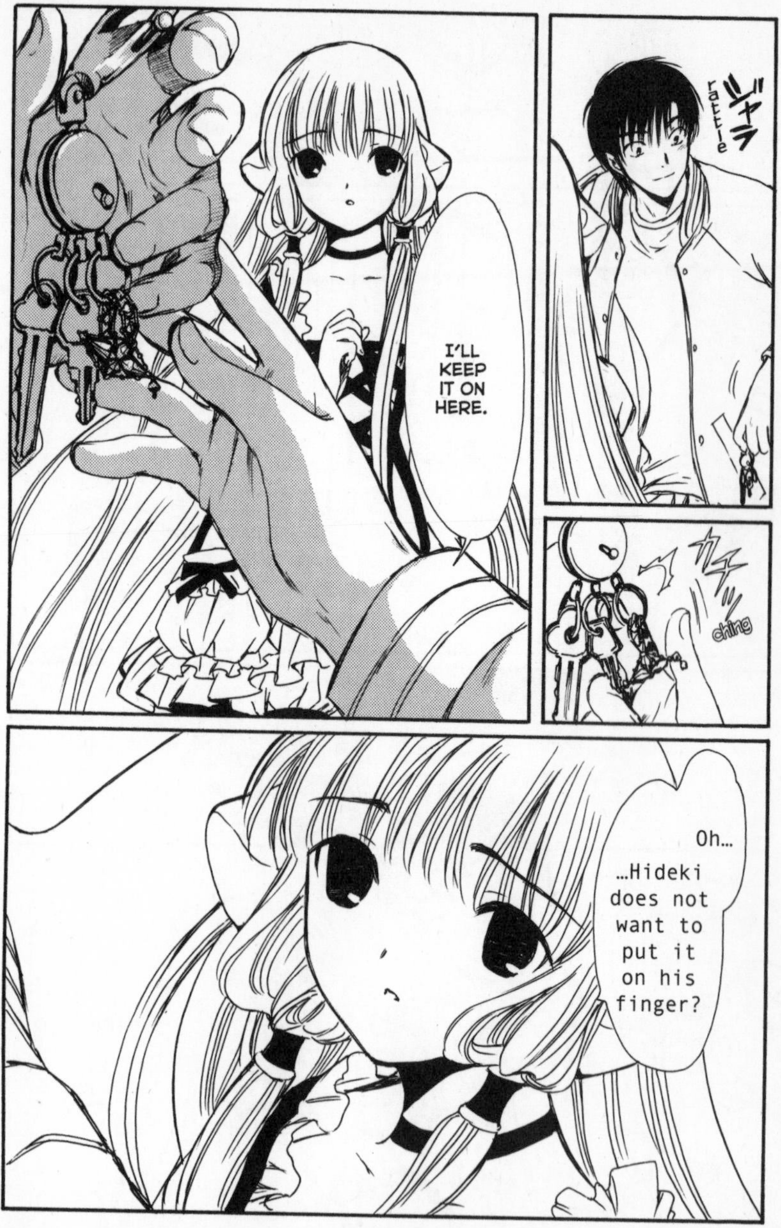
ジャラ
rattle
カチッ
ching
I'LL KEEP IT ON HERE.
Oh... ...Hideki does not want to put it on his finger?

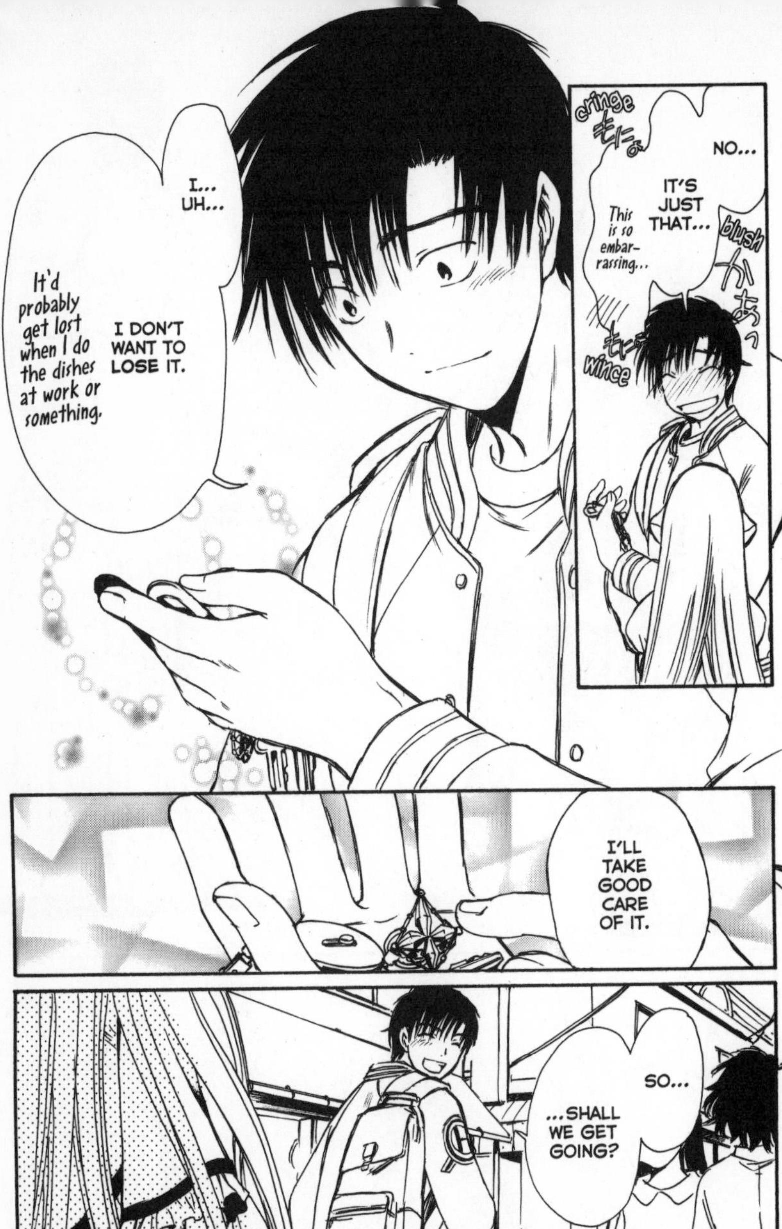

cringe
もにょ
NO...
IT'S JUST THAT...
This is so embarrassing...
blush
かあっ
wince
I... UH...
I DON'T WANT TO LOSE IT.
It'd probably get lost when I do the dishes at work or something.
I'LL TAKE GOOD CARE OF IT.
SO...
...SHALL WE GET GOING?

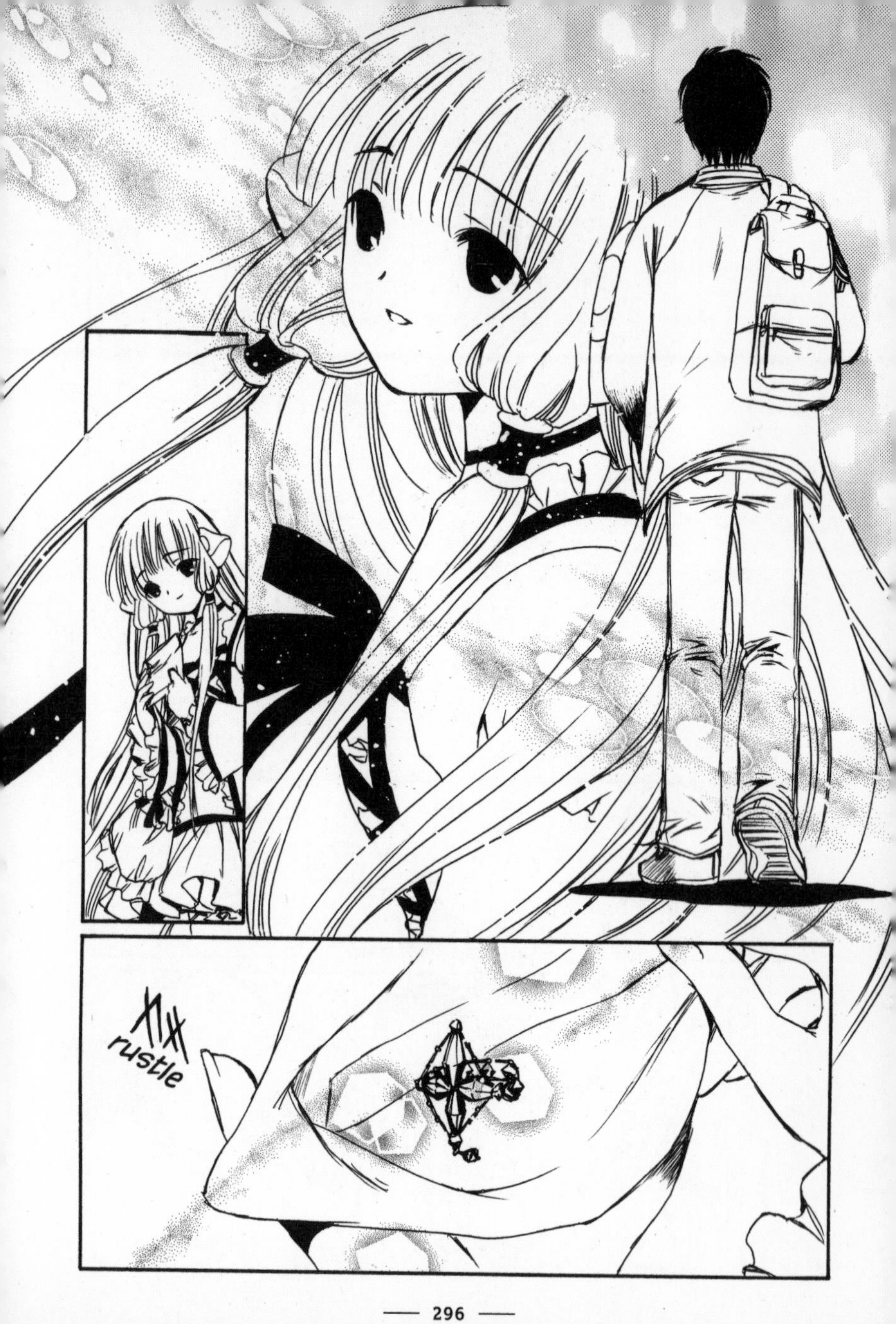
rustle

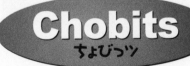

Chobits
ちょびっツ

◀ **chapter 68** ▶

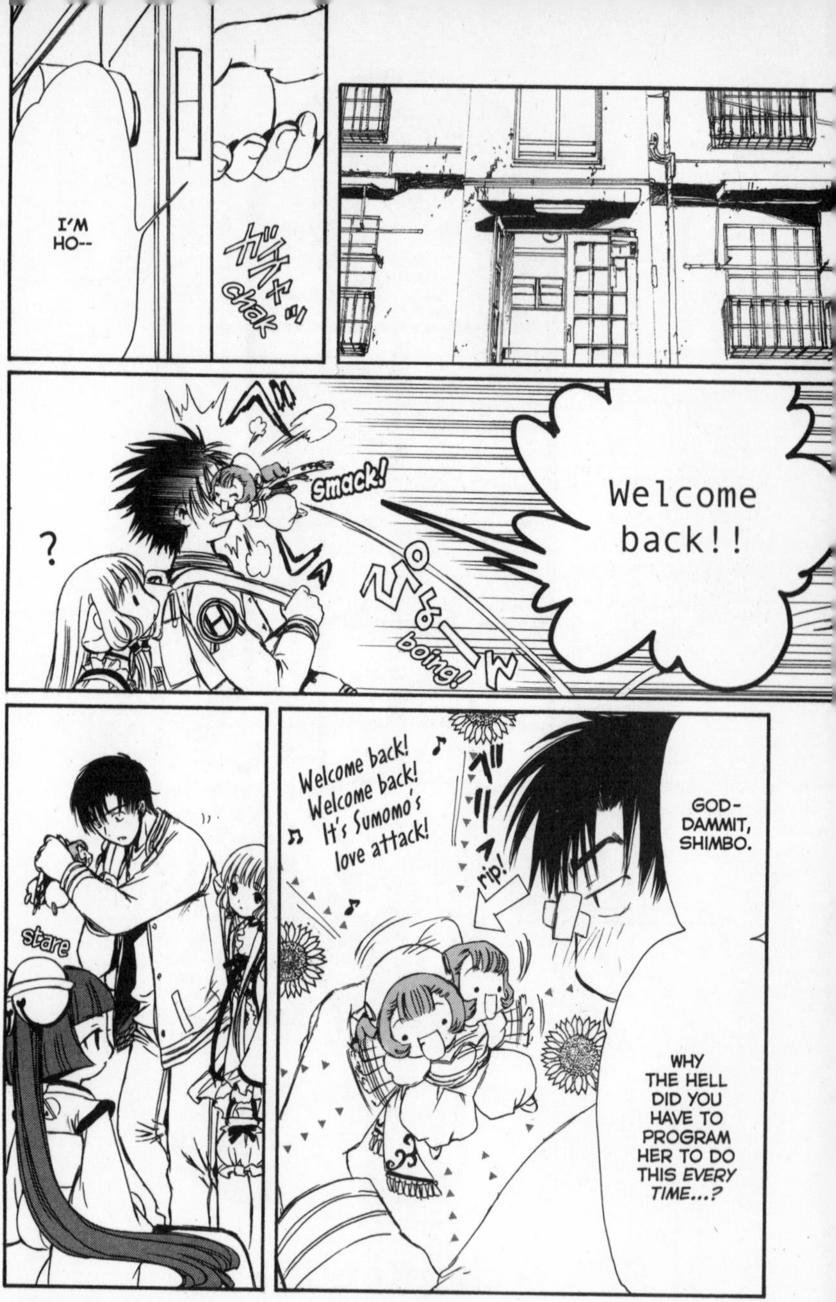
I'M HO--
chak
Welcome back!!
smack!
?
boing!
GOD-DAMMIT, SHIMBO.
Welcome back! Welcome back! It's Sumomo's love attack!
rip!
WHY THE HELL DID YOU HAVE TO PROGRAM HER TO DO THIS *EVERY TIME*...?
stare

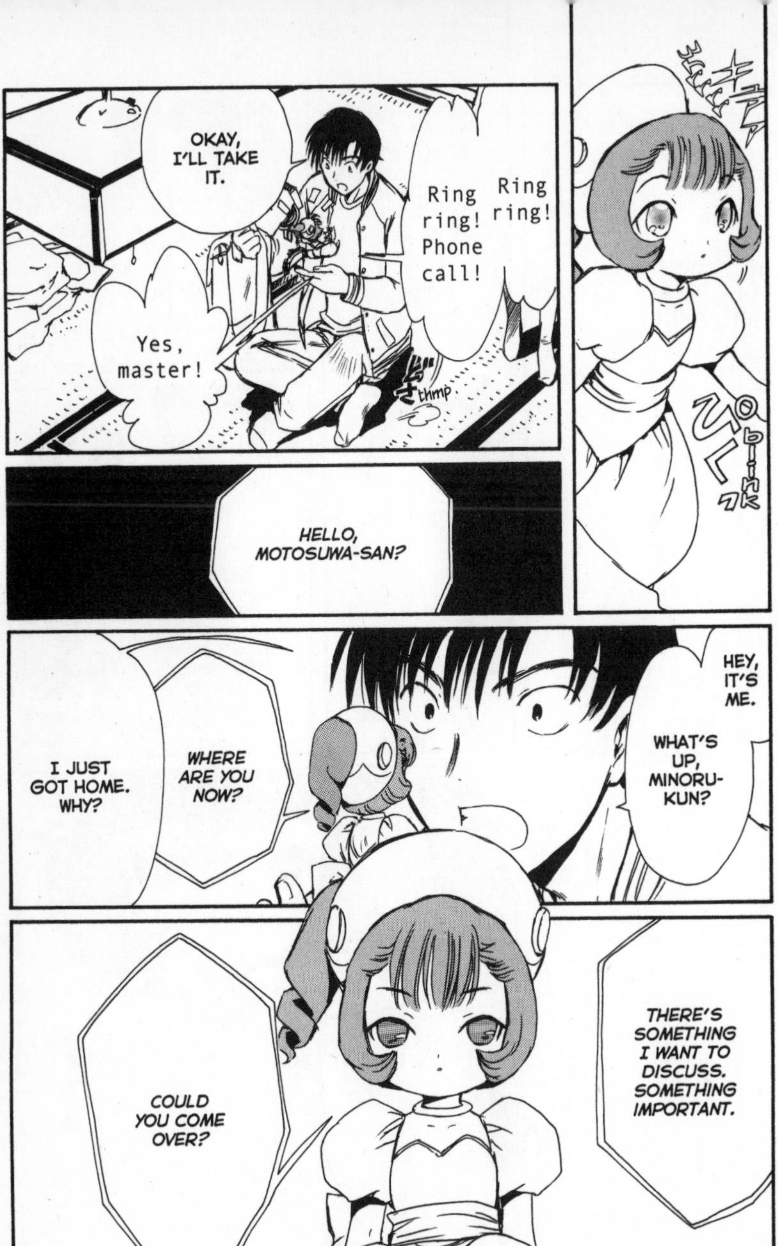

blink
Ring ring!
Ring ring! Phone call!
OKAY, I'LL TAKE IT.
thmp
Yes, master!
HELLO, MOTOSUWA-SAN?
HEY, IT'S ME.
WHAT'S UP, MINORU-KUN?
WHERE ARE YOU NOW?
I JUST GOT HOME. WHY?
THERE'S SOMETHING I WANT TO DISCUSS. SOMETHING IMPORTANT.
COULD YOU COME OVER?

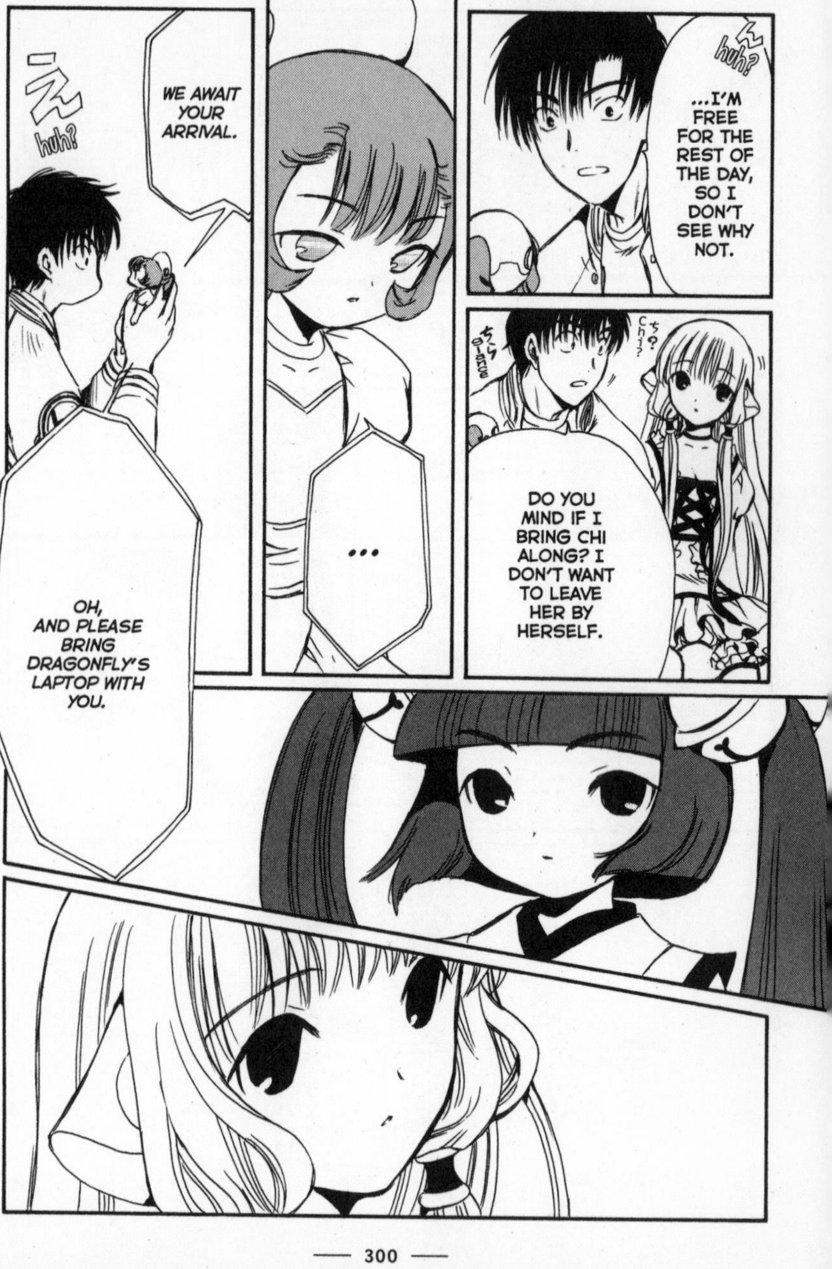
ん
huh?
...I'M FREE FOR THE REST OF THE DAY, SO I DON'T SEE WHY NOT.
ちら
glance
ち?
Chi?
DO YOU MIND IF I BRING CHI ALONG? I DON'T WANT TO LEAVE HER BY HERSELF.
...
WE AWAIT YOUR ARRIVAL.
え
huh?
OH, AND PLEASE BRING DRAGONFLY'S LAPTOP WITH YOU.

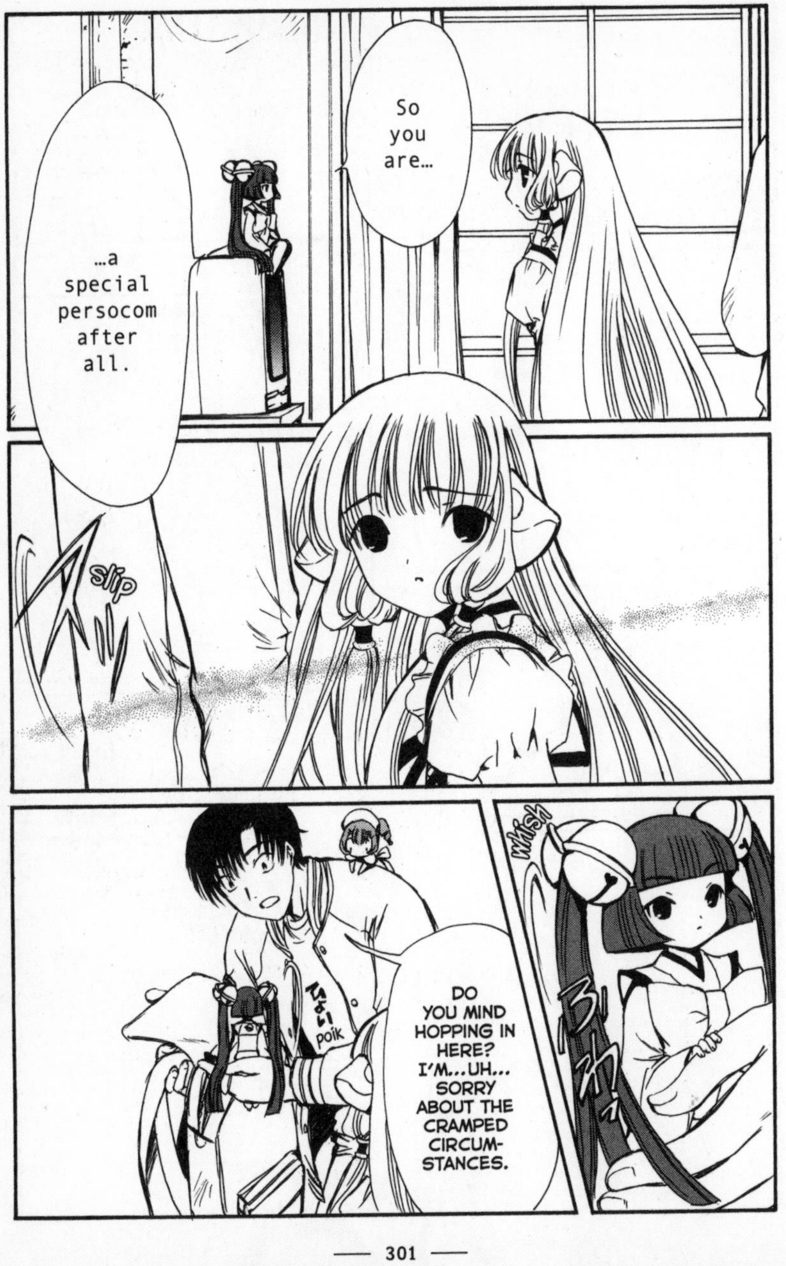
So you are...
...a special persocom after all.
slip
whish
DO YOU MIND HOPPING IN HERE? I'M...UH... SORRY ABOUT THE CRAMPED CIRCUM-STANCES.
poik

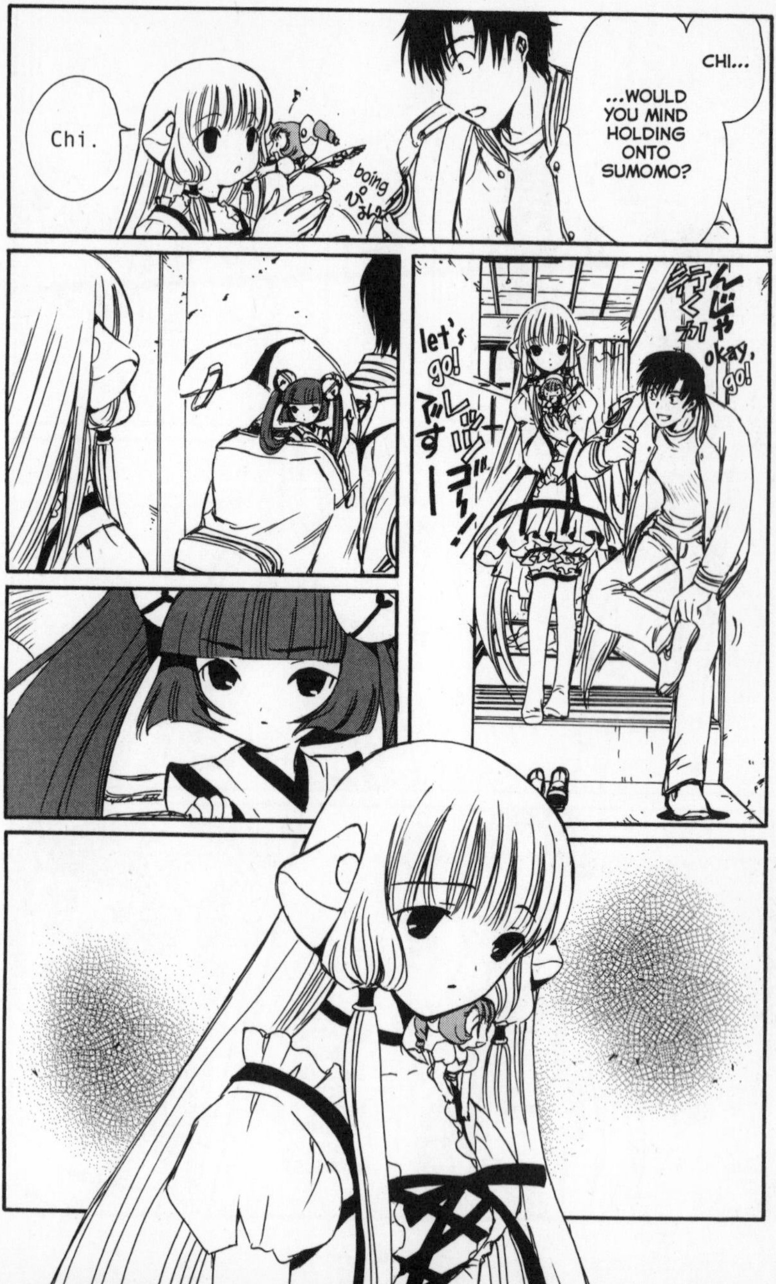
CHI...
...WOULD YOU MIND HOLDING ONTO SUMOMO?
boing
Chi.
okay, go!
let's go!

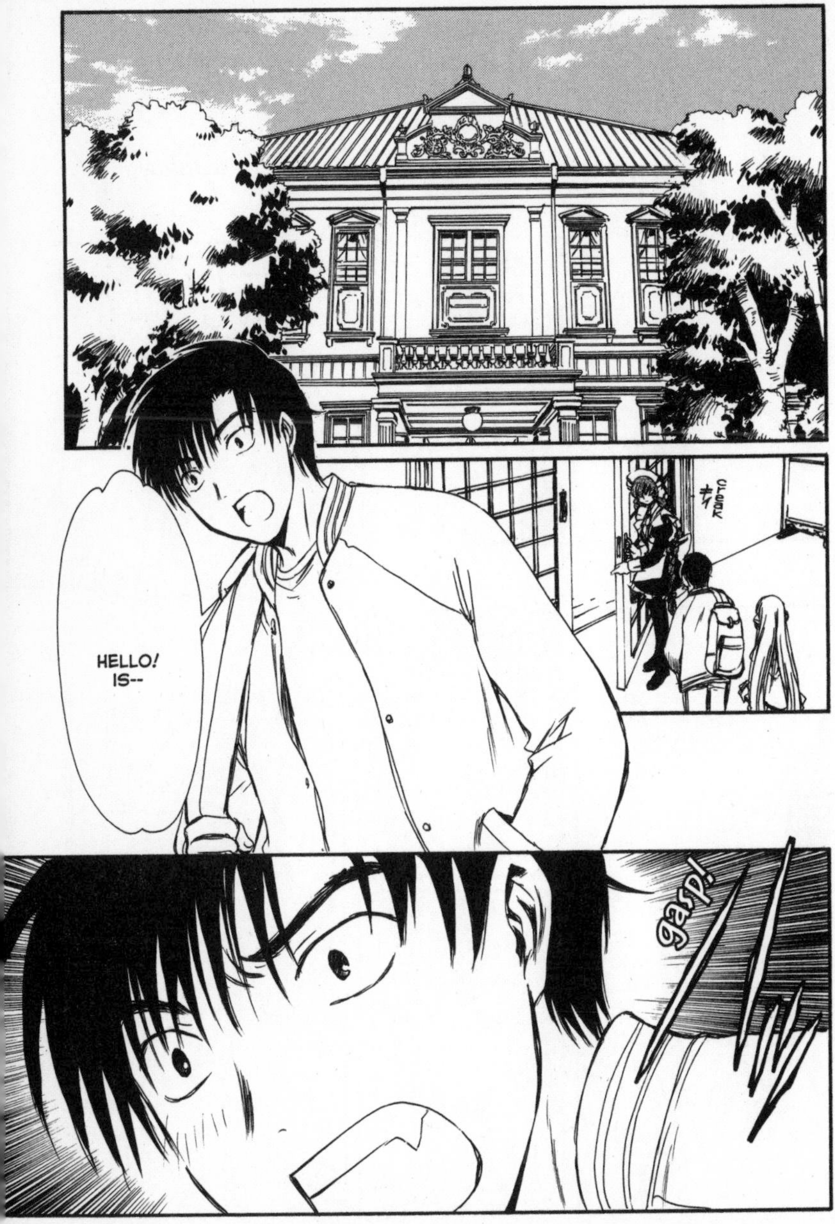
creak
HELLO! IS--
gasp!

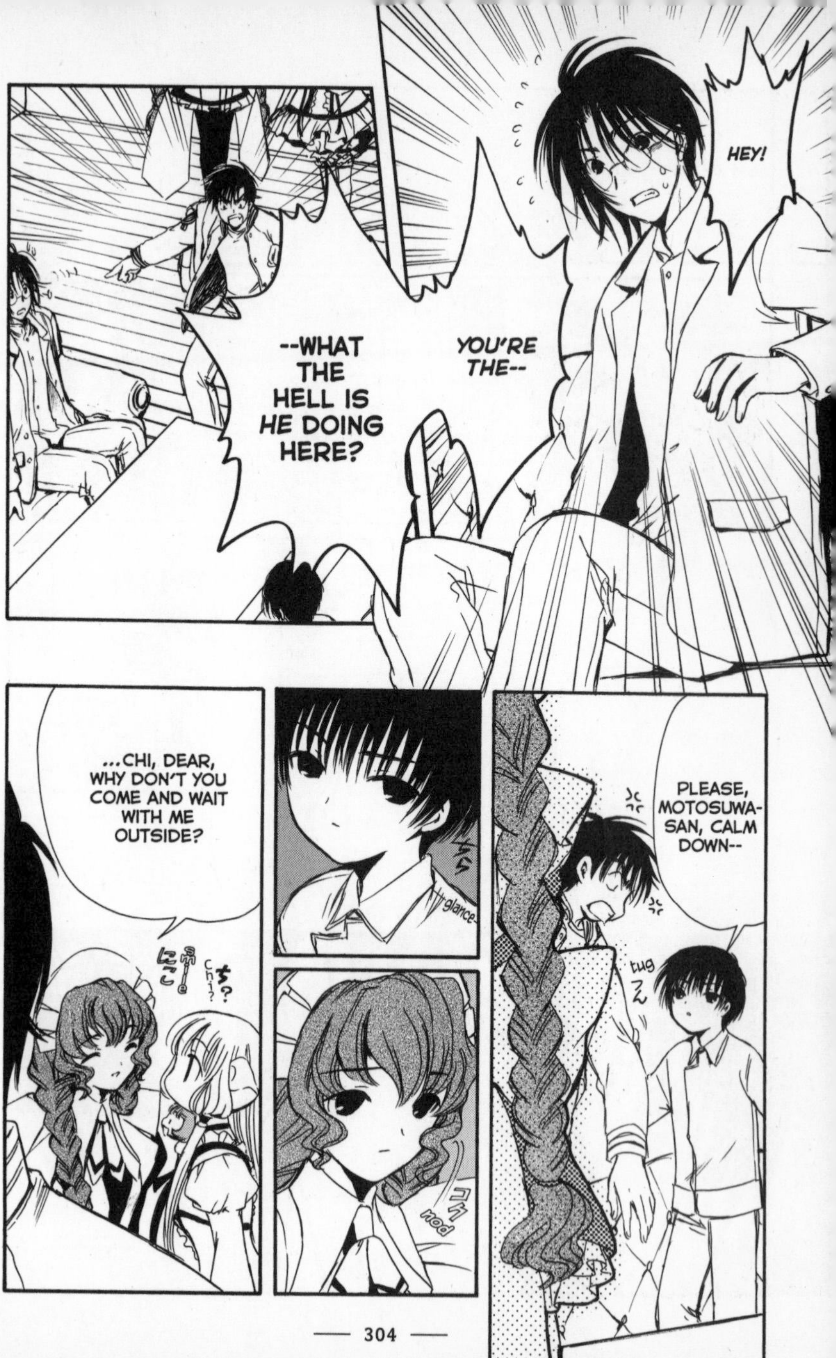
HEY!
YOU'RE THE--
--WHAT THE HELL IS HE DOING HERE?
PLEASE, MOTOSUWA-SAN, CALM DOWN--
tug
glance
pon
...CHI, DEAR, WHY DON'T YOU COME AND WAIT WITH ME OUTSIDE?
smile
Chi?

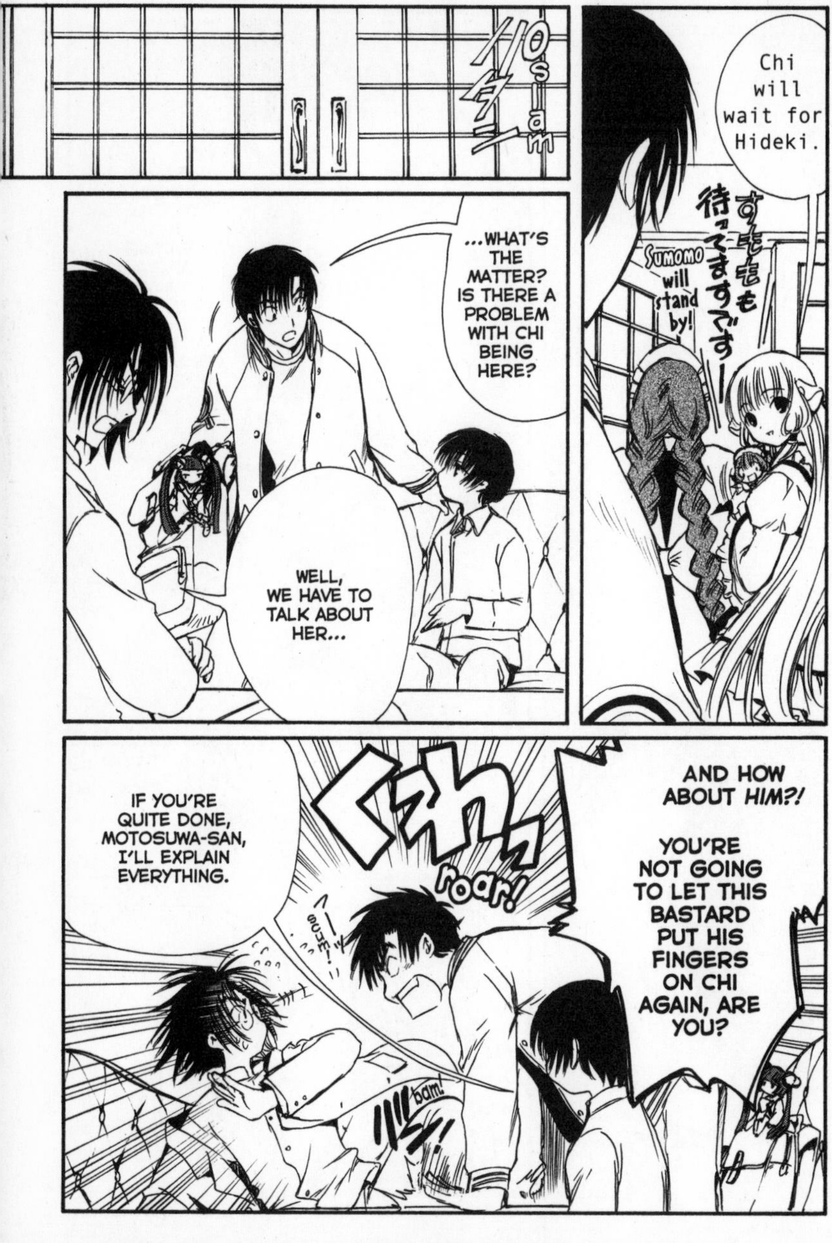

Chi will wait for Hideki.
すももも待ってますです－
Sumomo will stand by!
slam
...WHAT'S THE MATTER? IS THERE A PROBLEM WITH CHI BEING HERE?
WELL, WE HAVE TO TALK ABOUT HER...
AND HOW ABOUT *HIM*?!
YOU'RE NOT GOING TO LET THIS BASTARD PUT HIS FINGERS ON CHI AGAIN, ARE YOU?
くわっ
roar!
IF YOU'RE QUITE DONE, MOTOSUWA-SAN, I'LL EXPLAIN EVERYTHING.
scum!
bam!

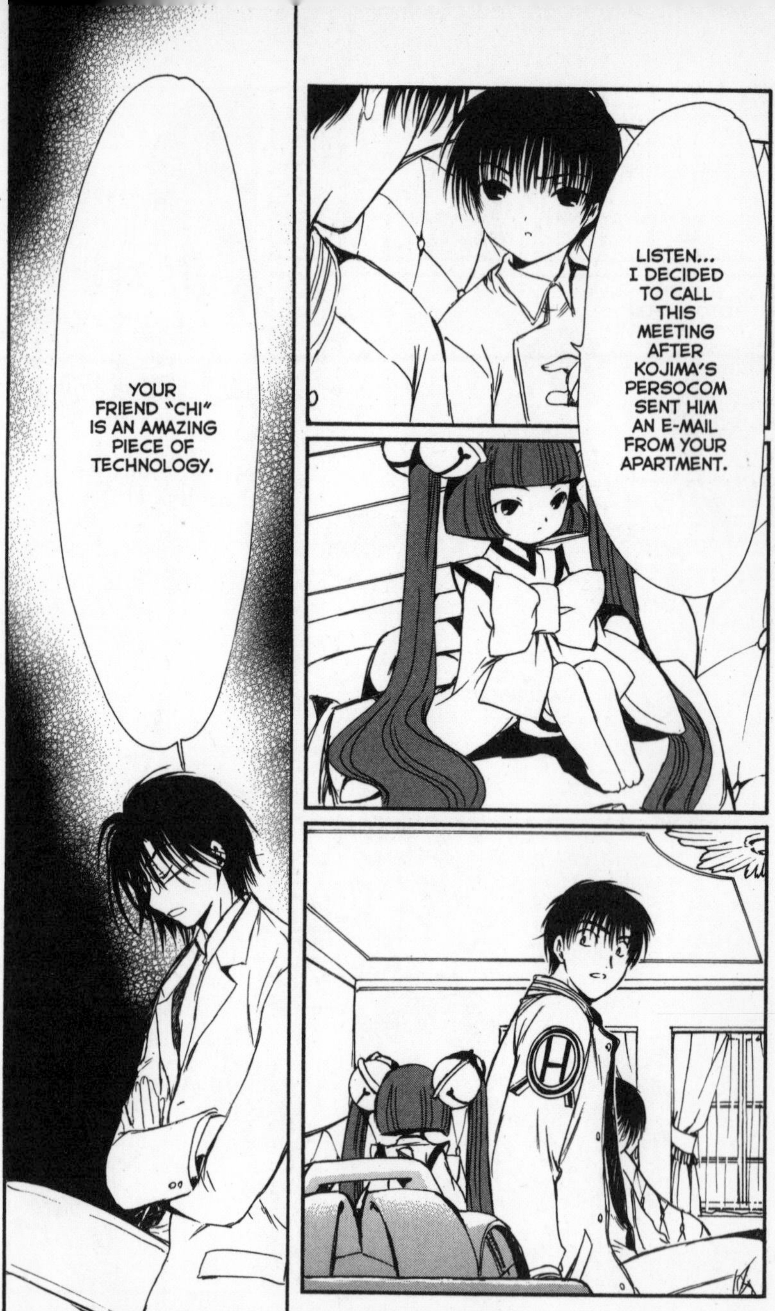
LISTEN... I DECIDED TO CALL THIS MEETING AFTER KOJIMA'S PERSOCOM SENT HIM AN E-MAIL FROM YOUR APARTMENT.
YOUR FRIEND "CHI" IS AN AMAZING PIECE OF TECHNOLOGY.

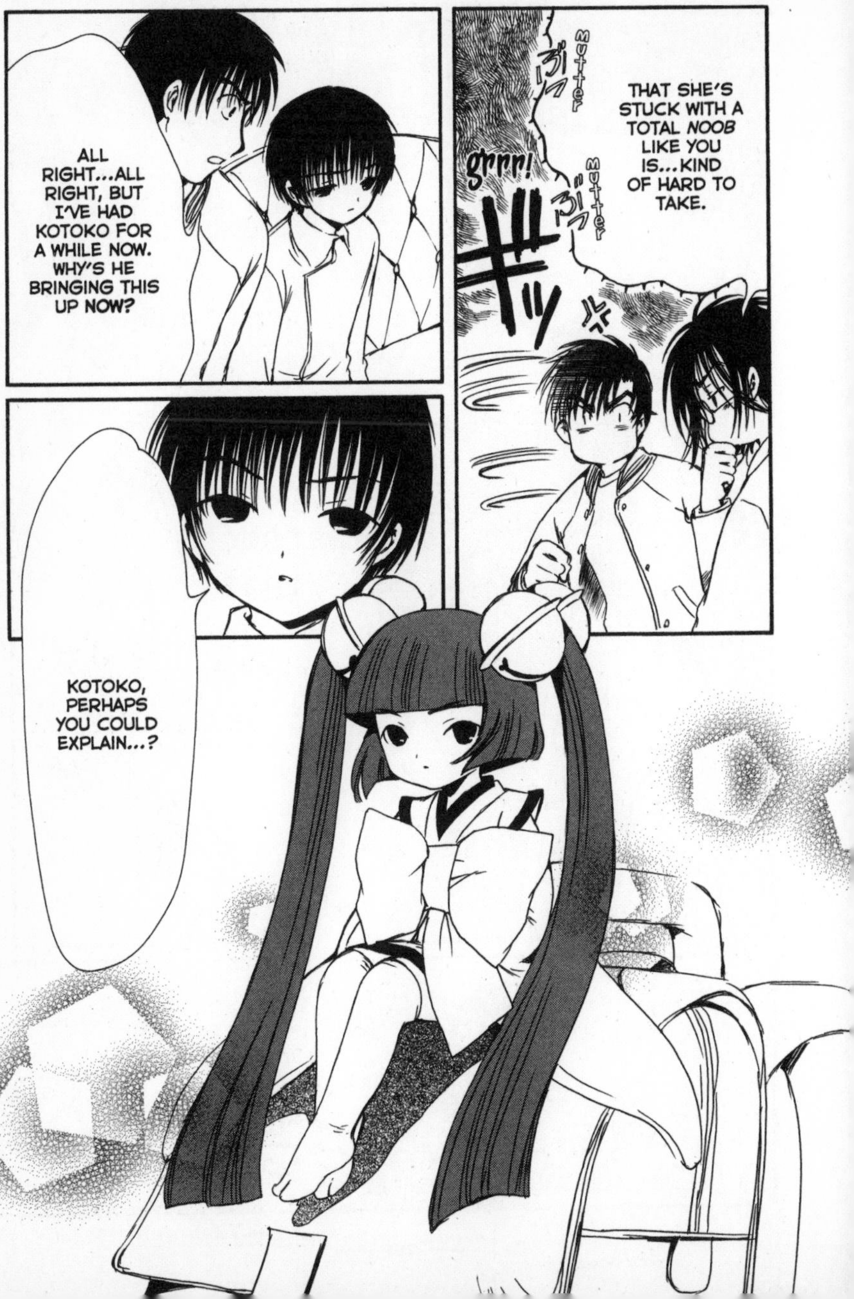

mutter
mutter
THAT SHE'S STUCK WITH A TOTAL *NOOB* LIKE YOU IS...KIND OF HARD TO TAKE.
grrr!
ALL RIGHT...ALL RIGHT, BUT I'VE HAD KOTOKO FOR A WHILE NOW. WHY'S HE BRINGING THIS UP NOW?
KOTOKO, PERHAPS YOU COULD EXPLAIN...?

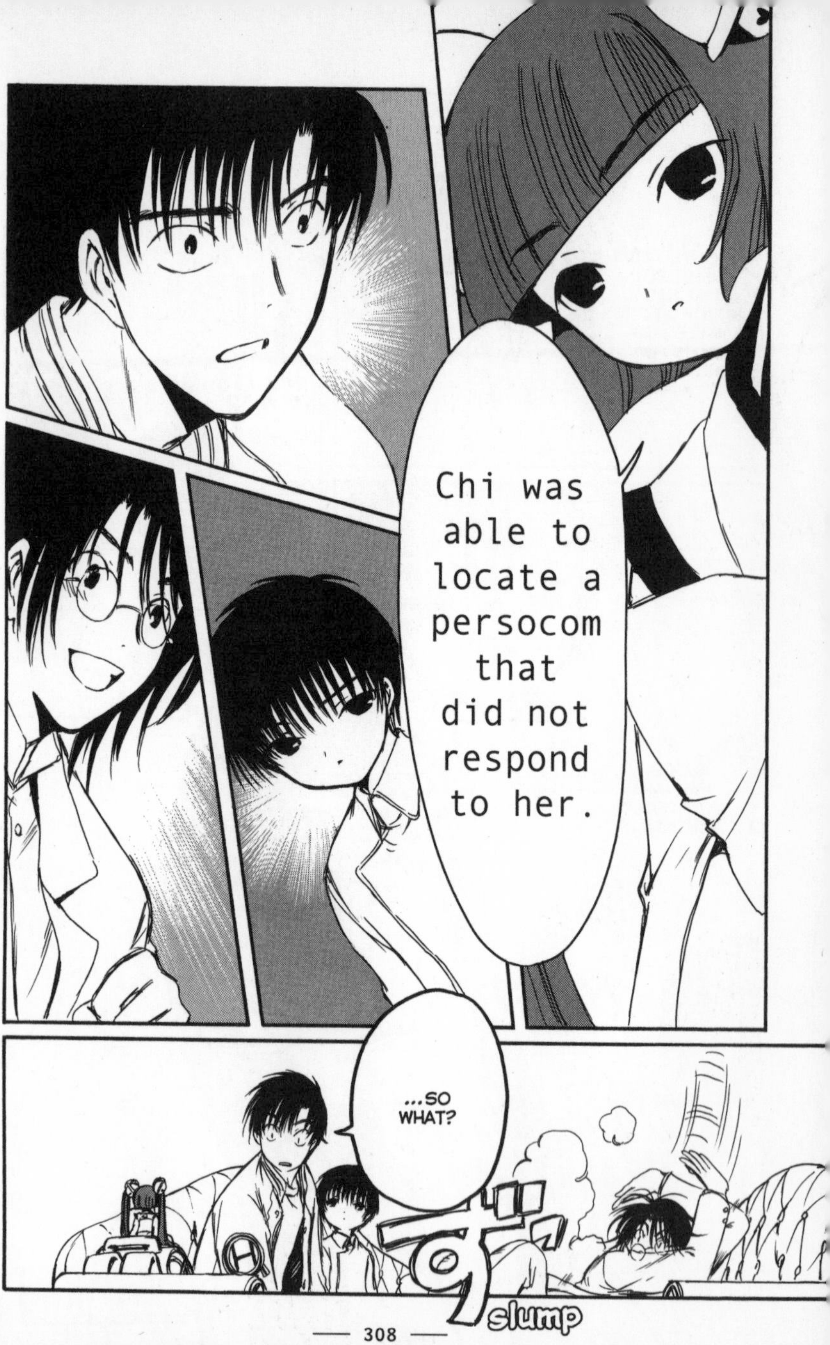
Chi was able to locate a persocom that did not respond to her.
...SO WHAT?
slump

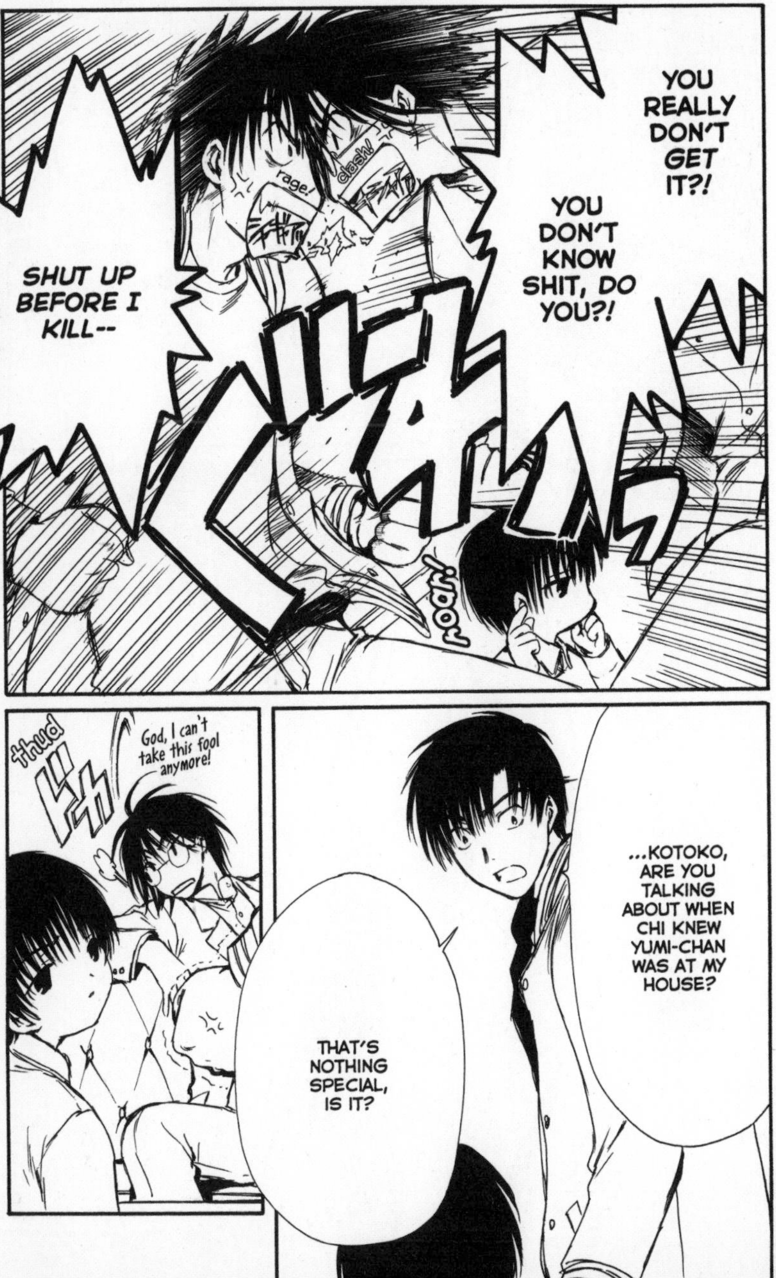
YOU REALLY DON'T GET IT?!
YOU DON'T KNOW SHIT, DO YOU?!
clash!
rage!
SHUT UP BEFORE I KILL--
roar!
...KOTOKO, ARE YOU TALKING ABOUT WHEN CHI KNEW YUMI-CHAN WAS AT MY HOUSE?
THAT'S NOTHING SPECIAL, IS IT?
thud
God, I can't take this fool anymore!

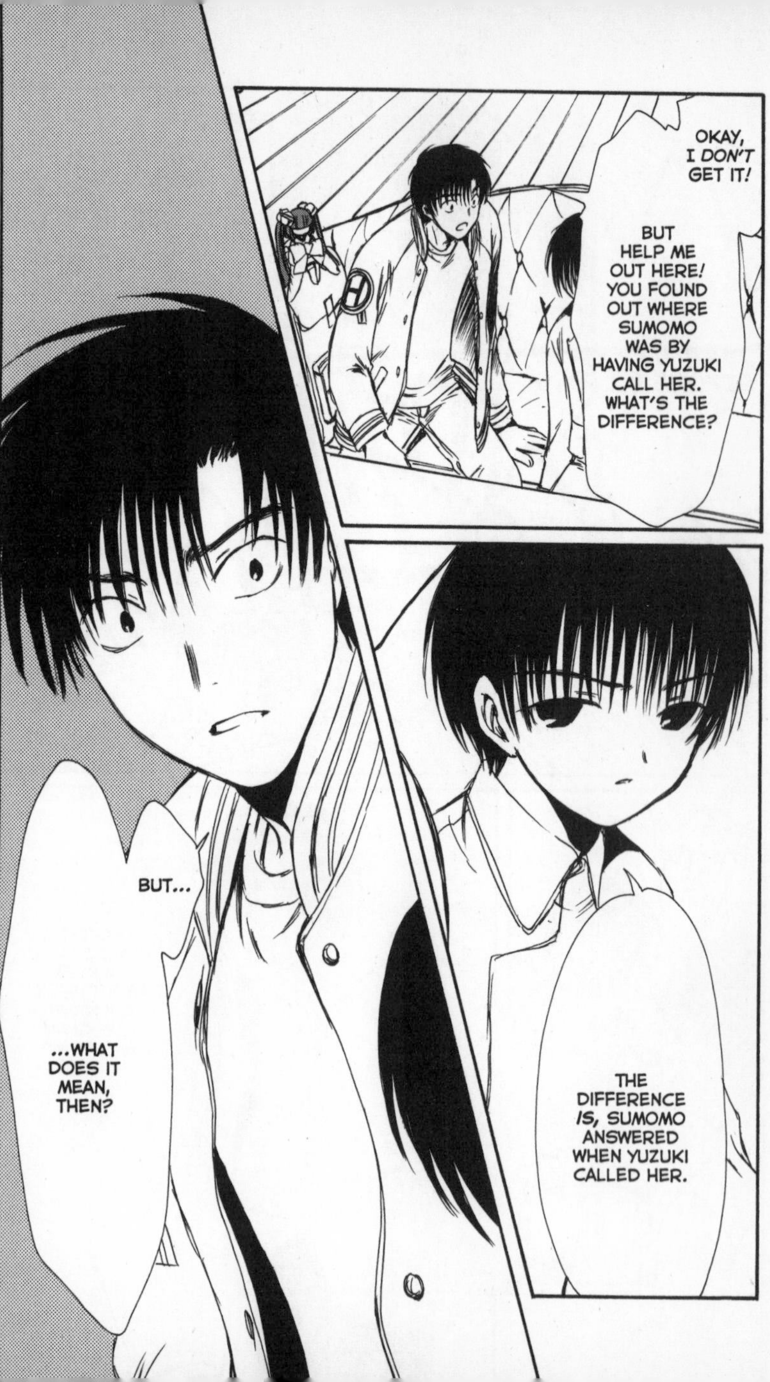
OKAY, I *DON'T* GET IT!
BUT HELP ME OUT HERE! YOU FOUND OUT WHERE SUMOMO WAS BY HAVING YUZUKI CALL HER. WHAT'S THE DIFFERENCE?
THE DIFFERENCE *IS*, SUMOMO ANSWERED WHEN YUZUKI CALLED HER.
BUT...
...WHAT DOES IT MEAN, THEN?

Chobits
ちょびっツ

◀ chapter 69 ▶

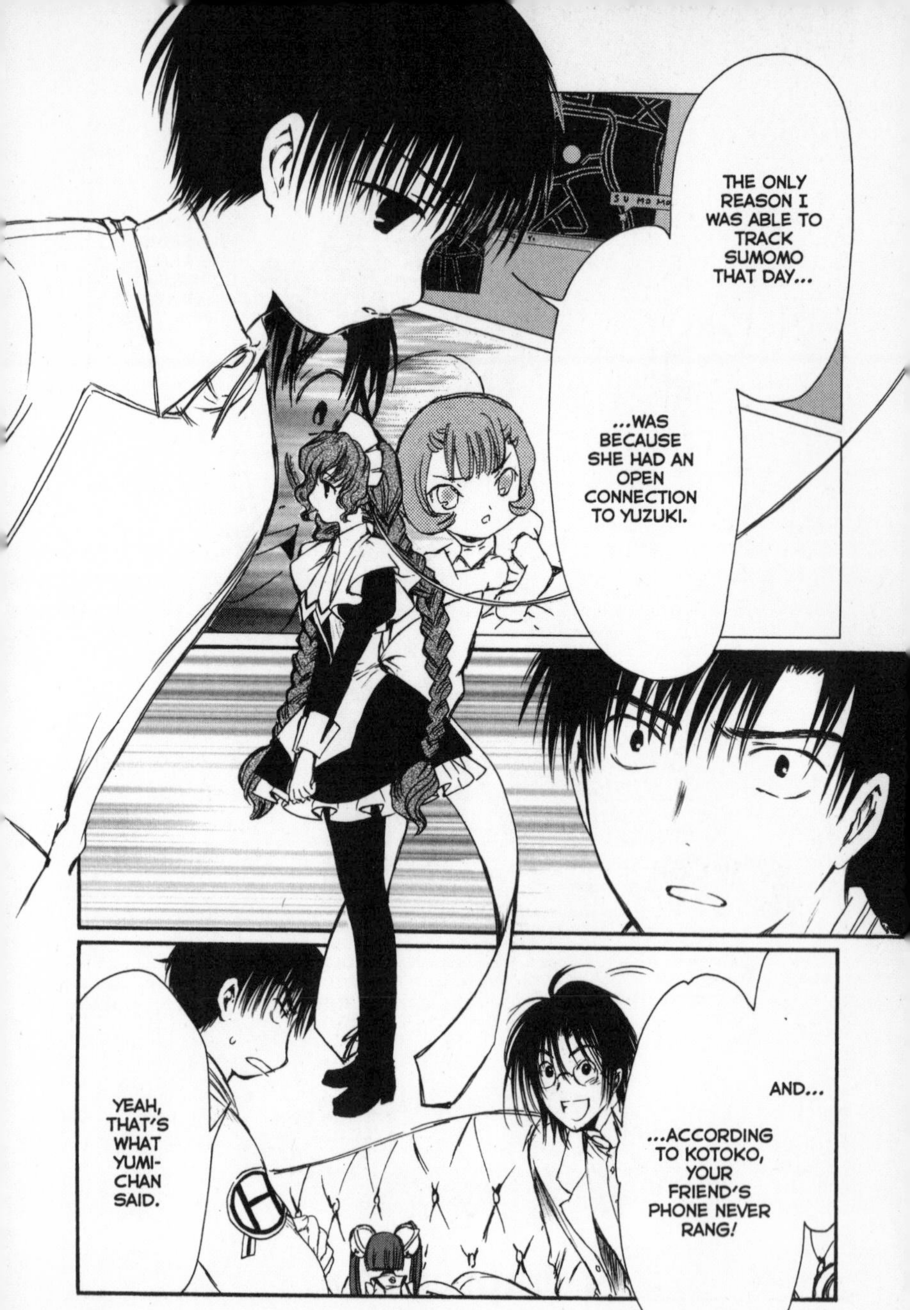
THE ONLY REASON I WAS ABLE TO TRACK SUMOMO THAT DAY...
...WAS BECAUSE SHE HAD AN OPEN CONNECTION TO YUZUKI.
AND...
...ACCORDING TO KOTOKO, YOUR FRIEND'S PHONE NEVER RANG!
YEAH, THAT'S WHAT YUMI-CHAN SAID.

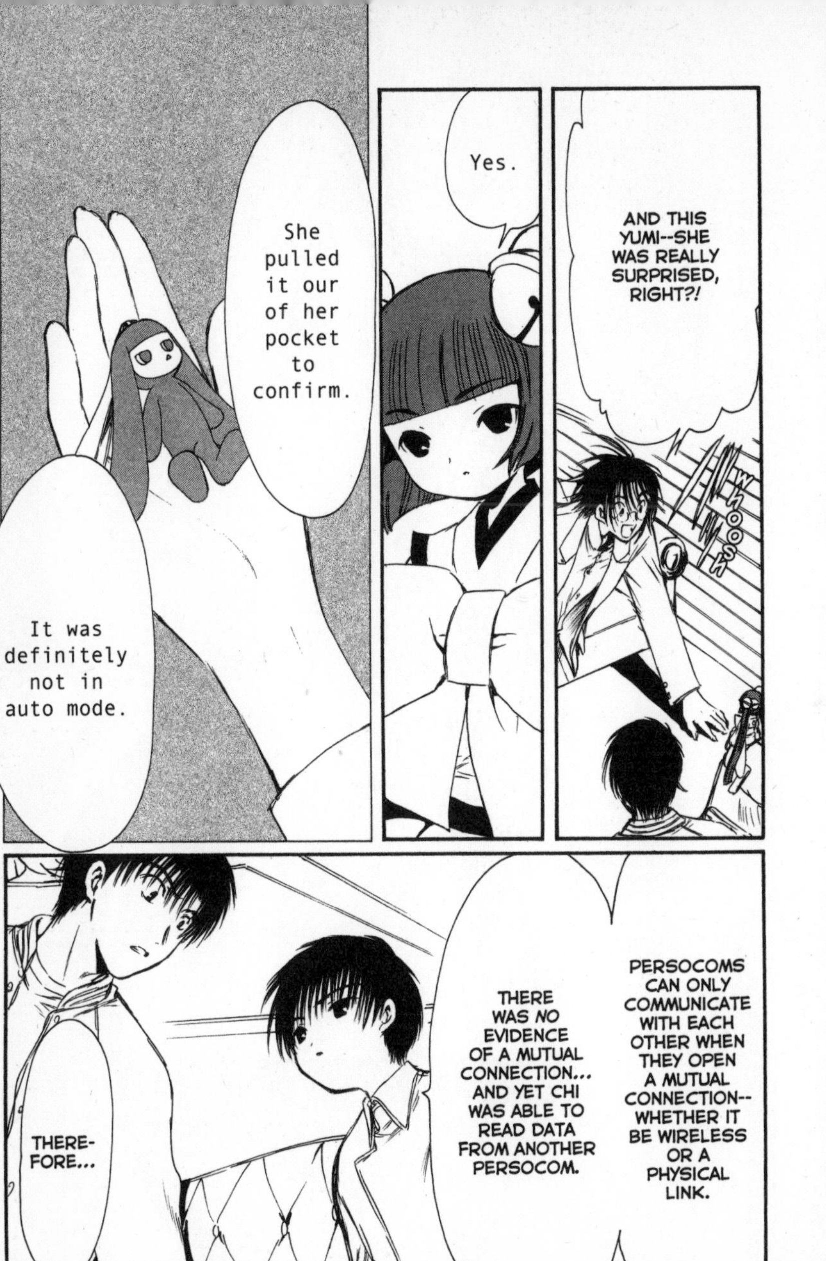

AND THIS YUMI--SHE WAS REALLY SURPRISED, RIGHT?!
WHOOSH
Yes.
She pulled it our of her pocket to confirm.
It was definitely not in auto mode.
PERSOCOMS CAN ONLY COMMUNICATE WITH EACH OTHER WHEN THEY OPEN A MUTUAL CONNECTION-- WHETHER IT BE WIRELESS OR A PHYSICAL LINK.
THERE WAS *NO* EVIDENCE OF A MUTUAL CONNECTION... AND YET CHI WAS ABLE TO READ DATA FROM ANOTHER PERSOCOM.
THERE-FORE...

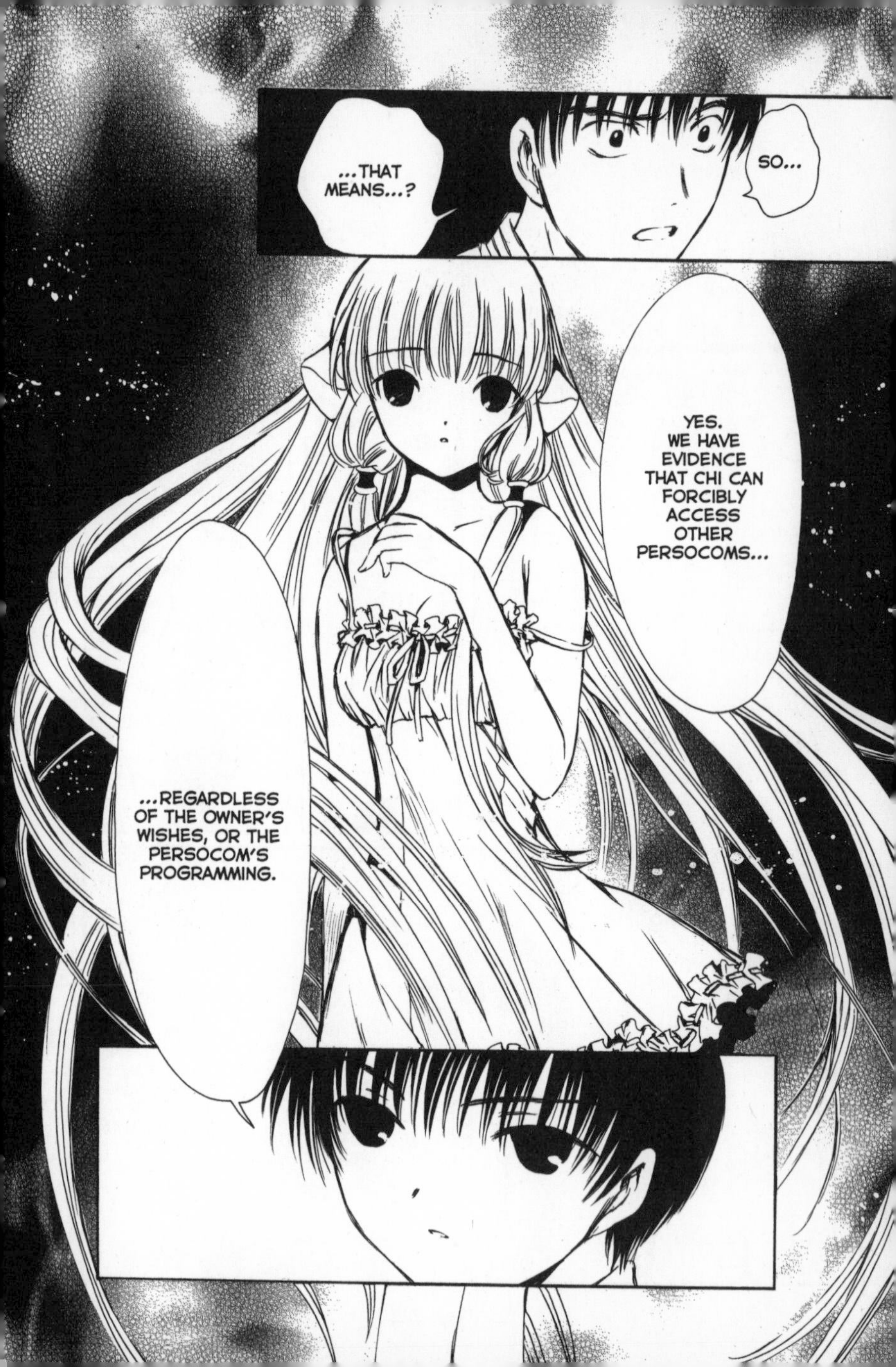
SO...
...THAT MEANS...?
YES. WE HAVE EVIDENCE THAT CHI CAN FORCIBLY ACCESS OTHER PERSOCOMS...
...REGARDLESS OF THE OWNER'S WISHES, OR THE PERSOCOM'S PROGRAMMING.

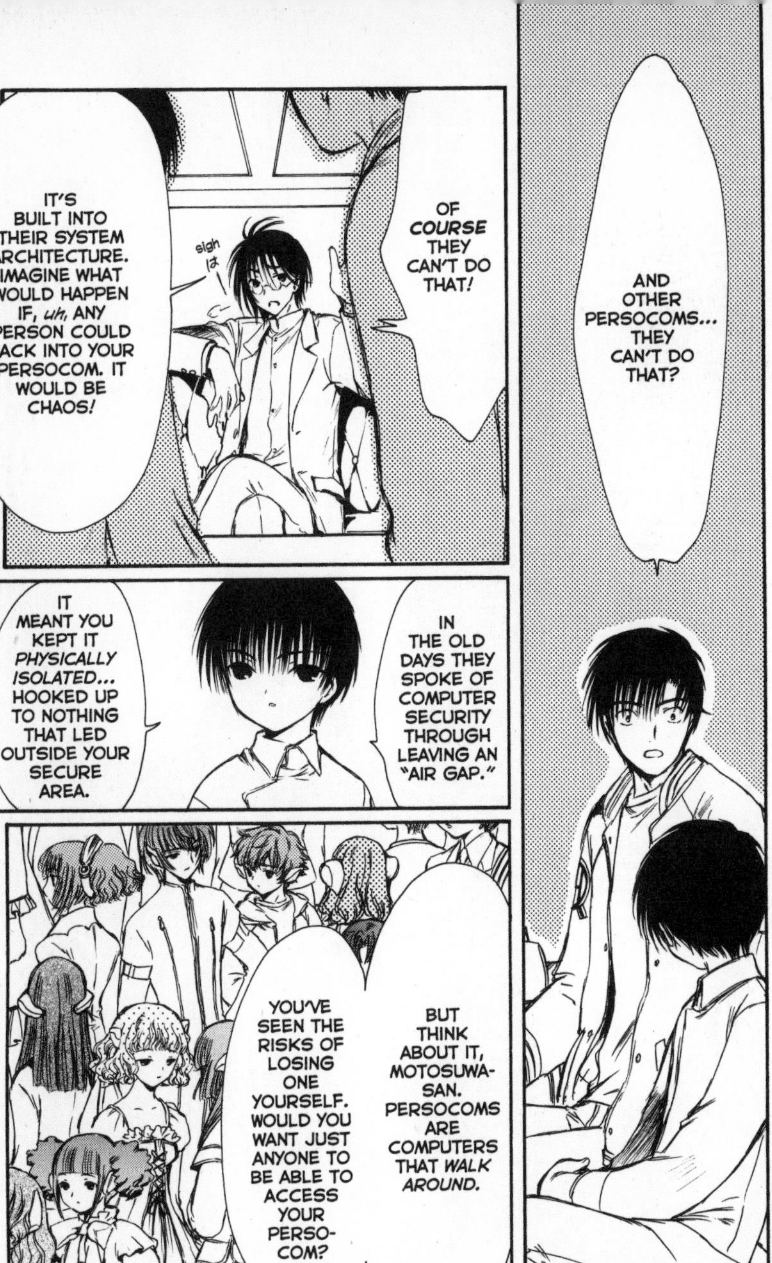
AND OTHER PERSOCOMS... THEY CAN'T DO THAT?
OF *COURSE* THEY CAN'T DO THAT!
sigh
は
IT'S BUILT INTO THEIR SYSTEM ARCHITECTURE. IMAGINE WHAT WOULD HAPPEN IF, *uh,* ANY PERSON COULD HACK INTO YOUR PERSOCOM. IT WOULD BE CHAOS!
IN THE OLD DAYS THEY SPOKE OF COMPUTER SECURITY THROUGH LEAVING AN "AIR GAP."
IT MEANT YOU KEPT IT *PHYSICALLY ISOLATED*... HOOKED UP TO NOTHING THAT LED OUTSIDE YOUR SECURE AREA.
BUT THINK ABOUT IT, MOTOSUWA-SAN. PERSOCOMS ARE COMPUTERS THAT *WALK AROUND.*
YOU'VE SEEN THE RISKS OF LOSING ONE YOURSELF. WOULD YOU WANT JUST ANYONE TO BE ABLE TO ACCESS YOUR PERSO-COM?

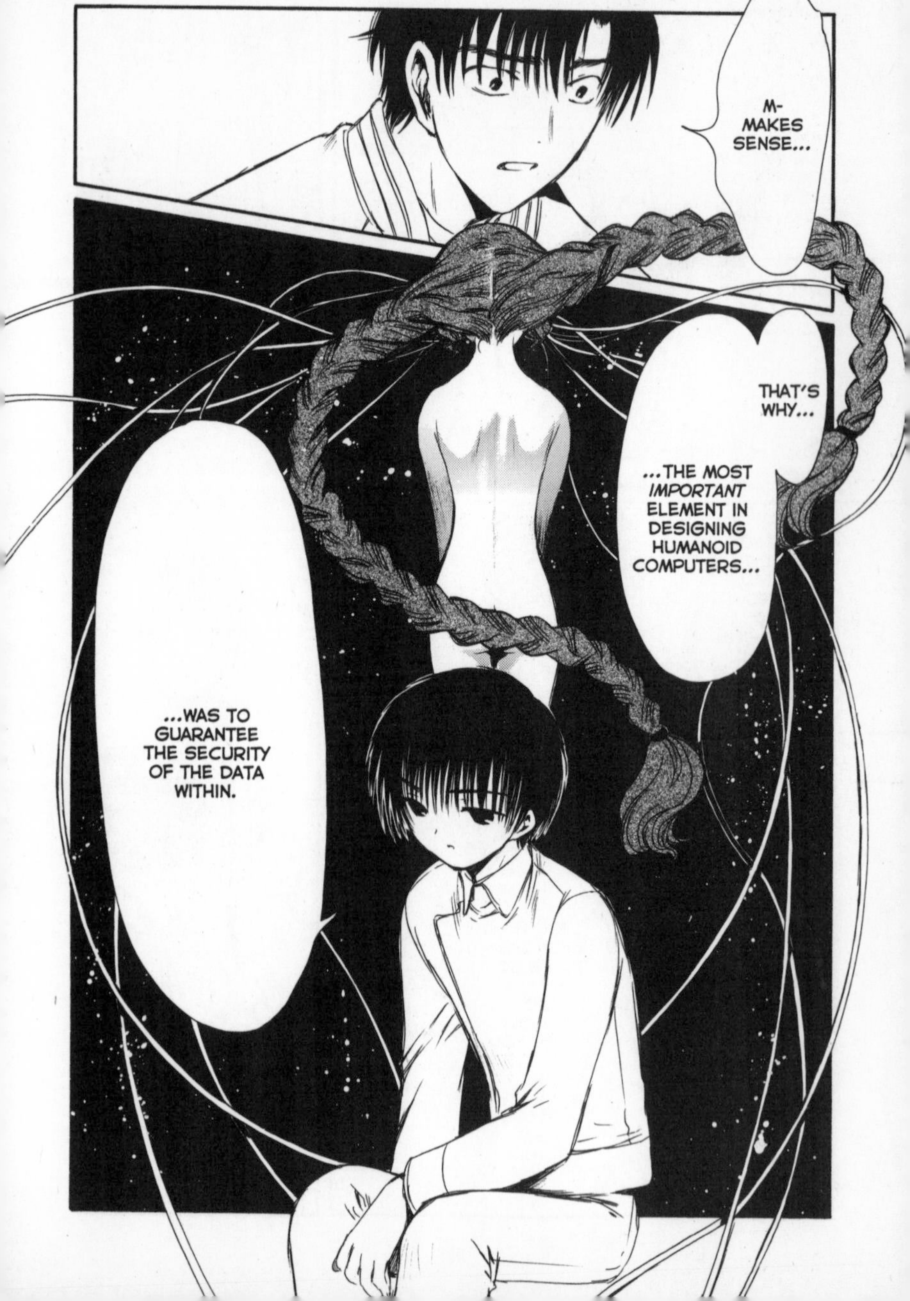
M-MAKES SENSE...
THAT'S WHY...
...THE MOST *IMPORTANT* ELEMENT IN DESIGNING HUMANOID COMPUTERS...
...WAS TO GUARANTEE THE SECURITY OF THE DATA WITHIN.

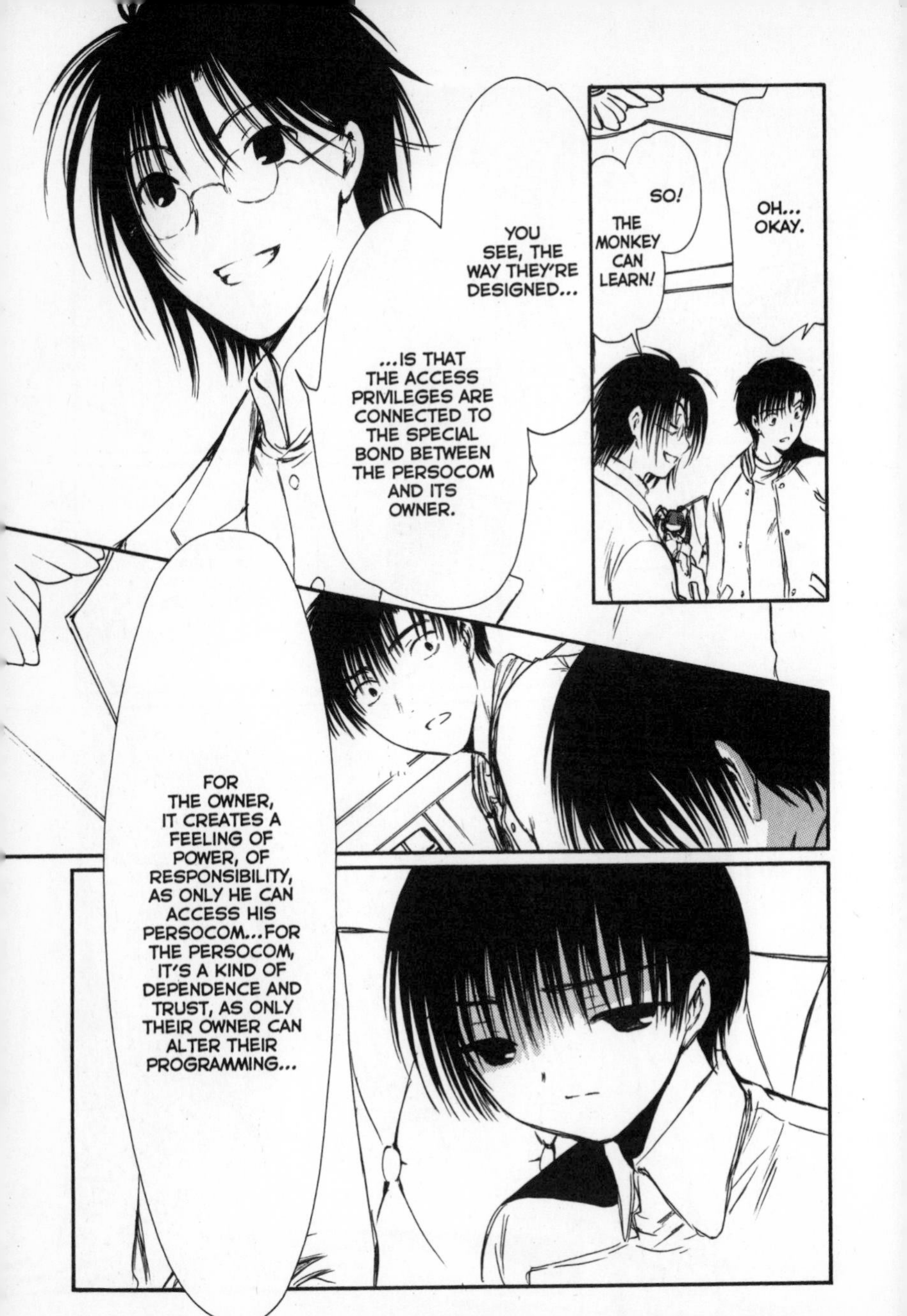
OH... OKAY.
SO! THE MONKEY CAN LEARN!
YOU SEE, THE WAY THEY'RE DESIGNED...
...IS THAT THE ACCESS PRIVILEGES ARE CONNECTED TO THE SPECIAL BOND BETWEEN THE PERSOCOM AND ITS OWNER.
FOR THE OWNER, IT CREATES A FEELING OF POWER, OF RESPONSIBILITY, AS ONLY HE CAN ACCESS HIS PERSOCOM...FOR THE PERSOCOM, IT'S A KIND OF DEPENDENCE AND TRUST, AS ONLY THEIR OWNER CAN ALTER THEIR PROGRAMMING...

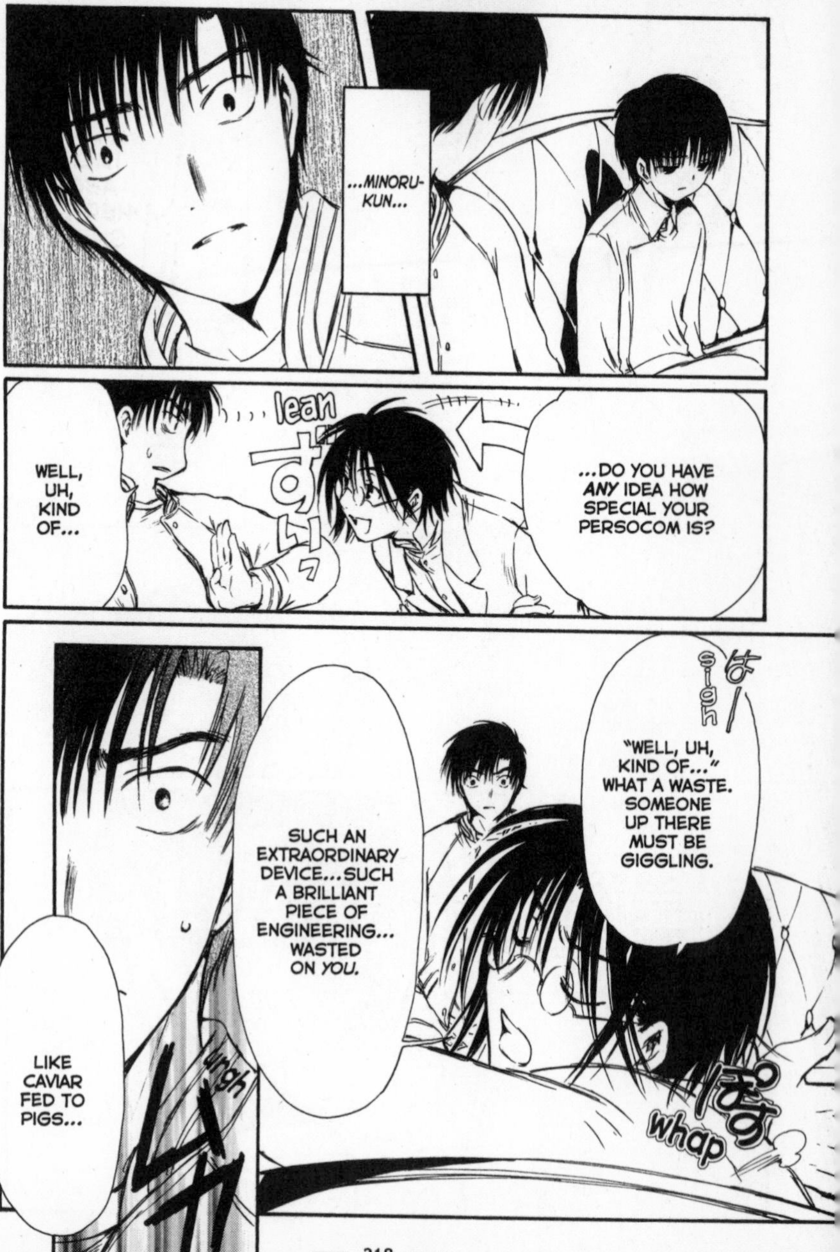
...MINORU-KUN...
...DO YOU HAVE ANY IDEA HOW SPECIAL YOUR PERSOCOM IS?
lean
ずいっ
WELL, UH, KIND OF...
はー
sigh
"WELL, UH, KIND OF..." WHAT A WASTE. SOMEONE UP THERE MUST BE GIGGLING.
SUCH AN EXTRAORDINARY DEVICE...SUCH A BRILLIANT PIECE OF ENGINEERING... WASTED ON YOU.
ぽす
whap
urgh
ムカ
LIKE CAVIAR FED TO PIGS...

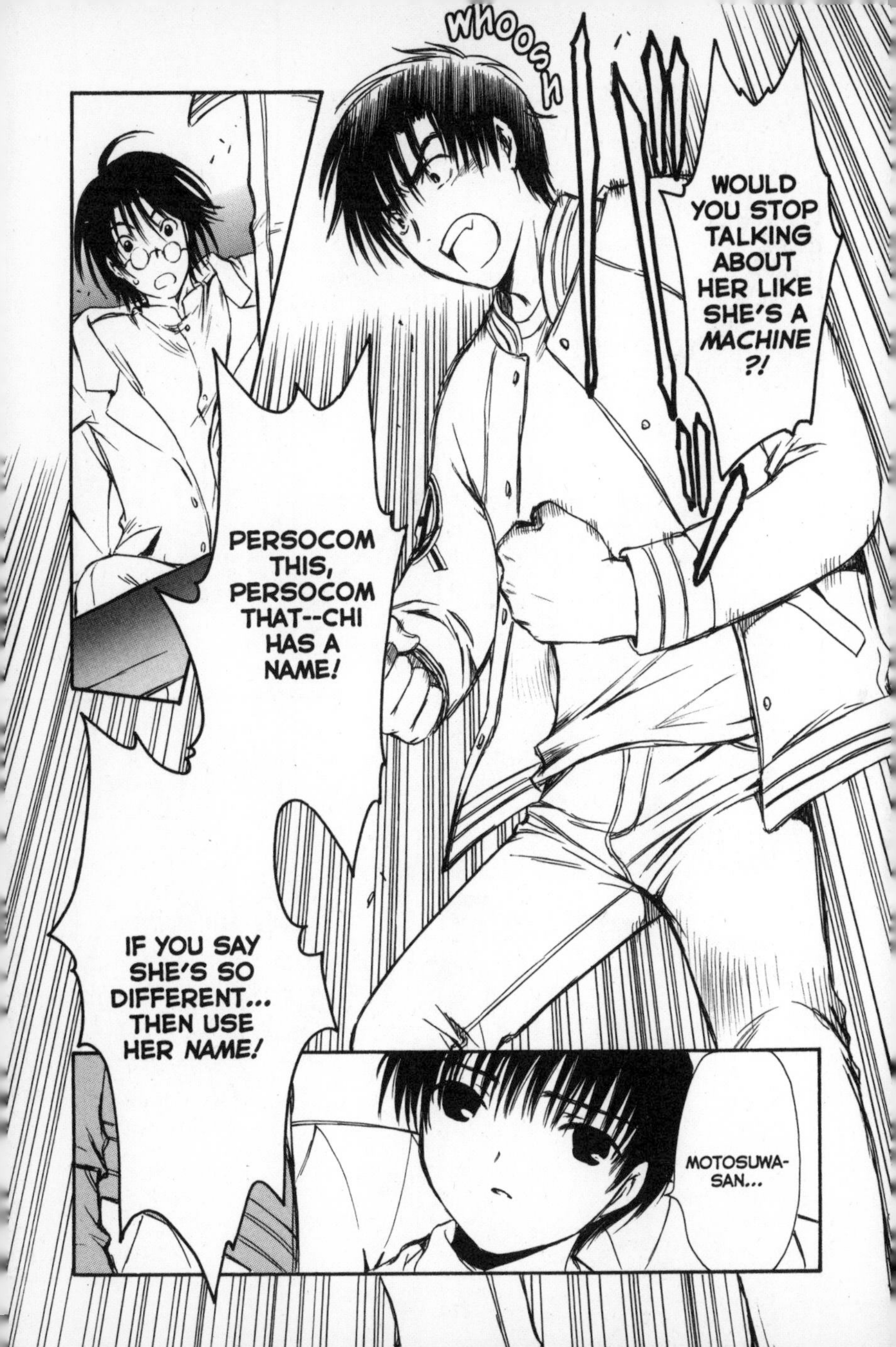
WHOOSH
WOULD YOU STOP TALKING ABOUT HER LIKE SHE'S A *MACHINE* ?!
PERSOCOM THIS, PERSOCOM THAT--CHI HAS A NAME!
IF YOU SAY SHE'S SO DIFFERENT... THEN USE HER *NAME*!
MOTOSUWA-SAN...

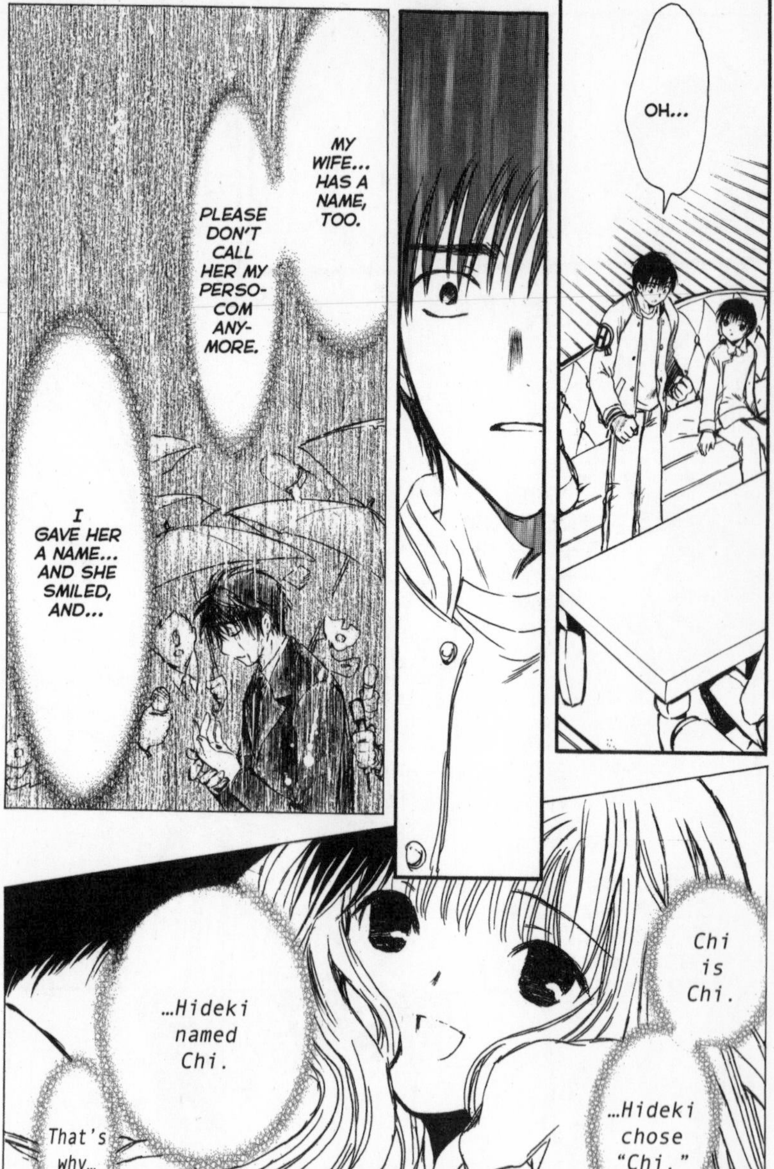
OH...
MY WIFE... HAS A NAME, TOO.
PLEASE DON'T CALL HER MY PERSOCOM ANYMORE.
I GAVE HER A NAME... AND SHE SMILED, AND...
Chi is Chi.
...Hideki chose "Chi."
...Hideki named Chi.
That's why...

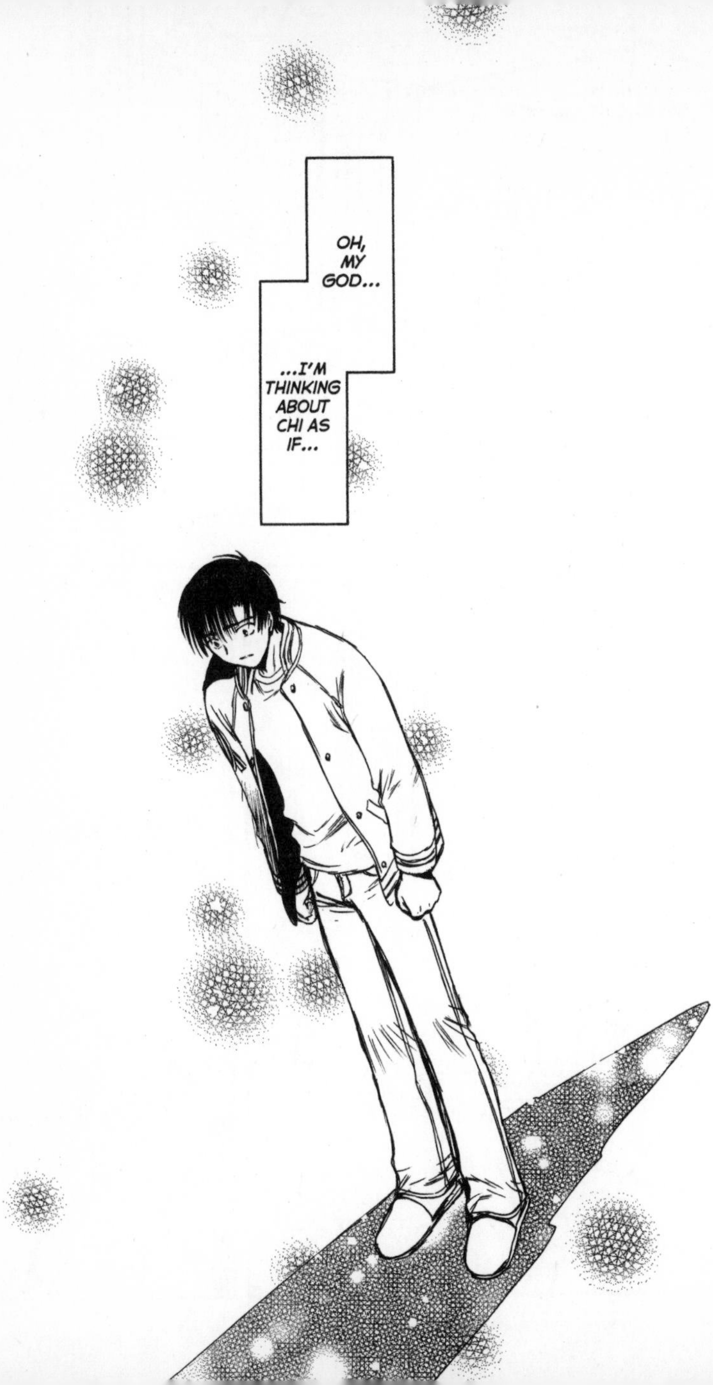
OH, MY GOD...
...I'M THINKING ABOUT CHI AS IF...

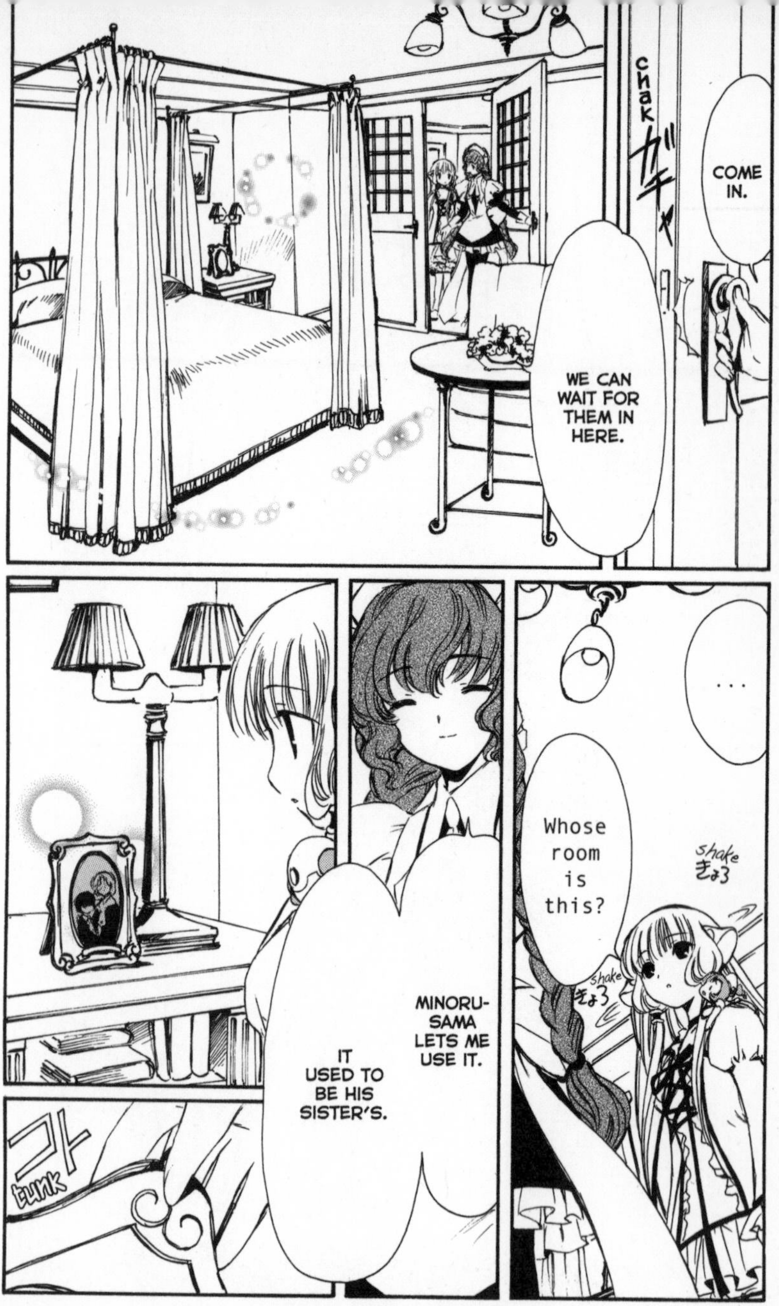
COME IN.
chak ガチャ
WE CAN WAIT FOR THEM IN HERE.
...
shake きょろ
Whose room is this?
shake きょろ
MINORU-SAMA LETS ME USE IT.
IT USED TO BE HIS SISTER'S.
コト tunk

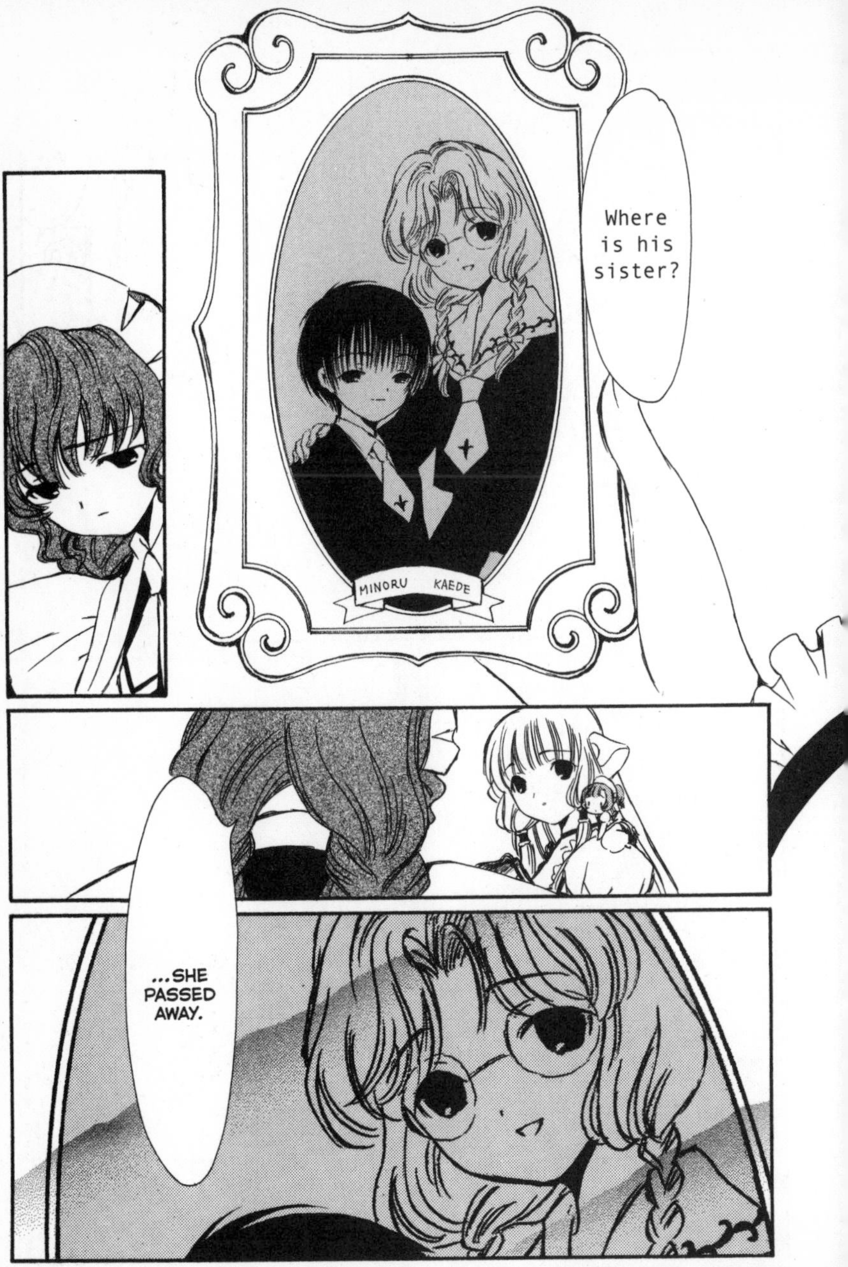
MINORU
KAEDE
Where is his sister?
...SHE PASSED AWAY.

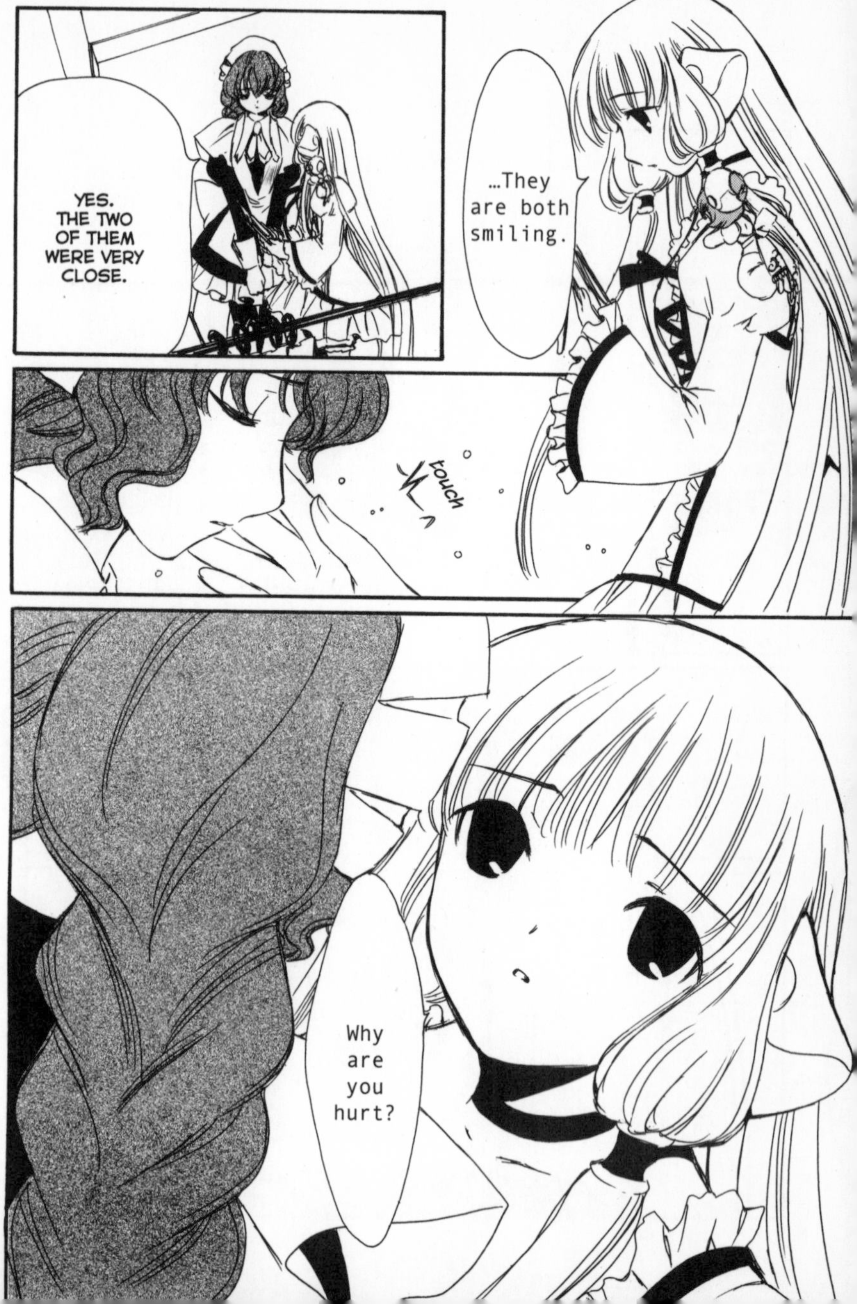
...They are both smiling.
YES. THE TWO OF THEM WERE VERY CLOSE.
touch
Why are you hurt?

Chobits
ちょびっツ

◂ chapter 70 ▸

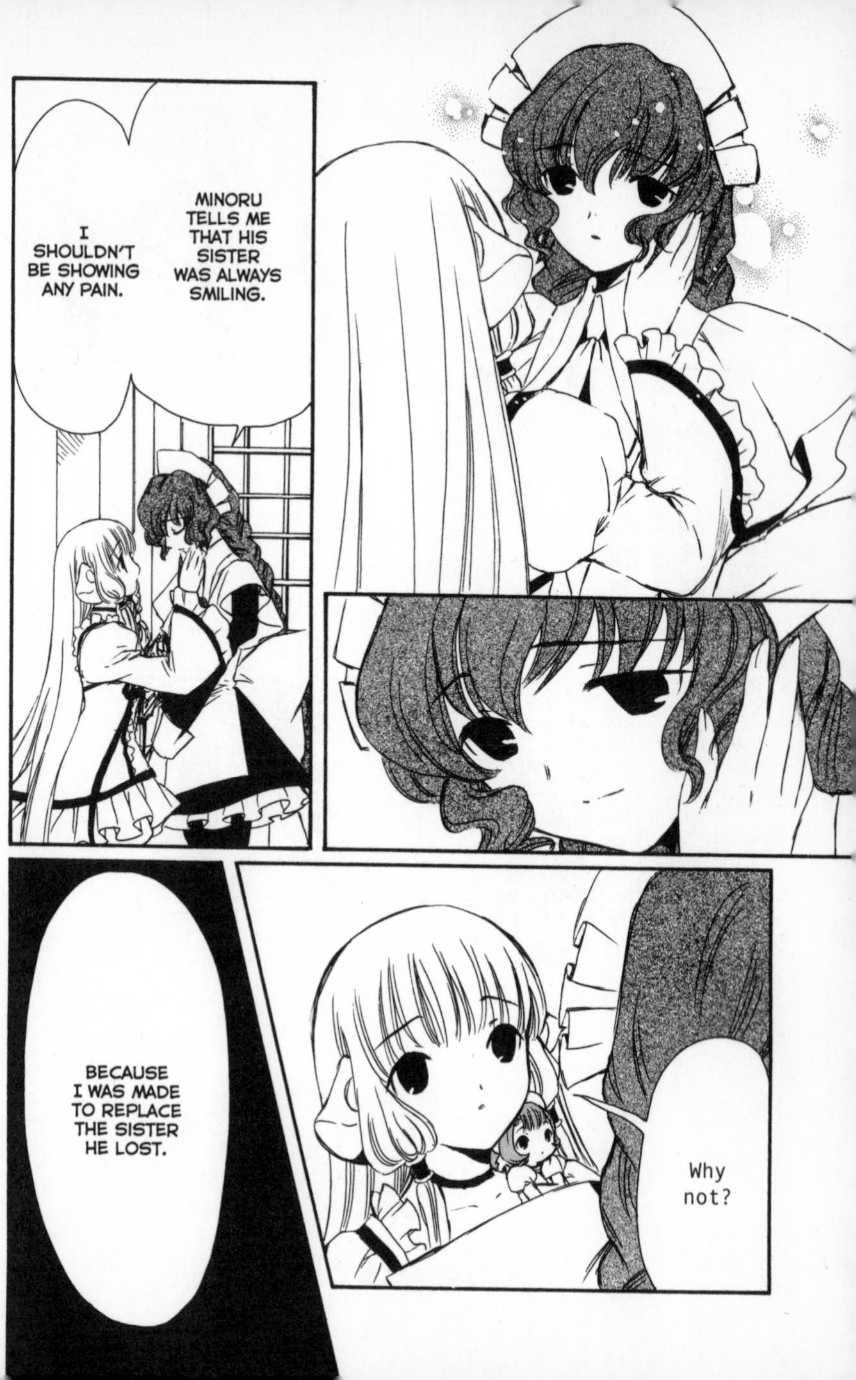
MINORU TELLS ME THAT HIS SISTER WAS ALWAYS SMILING.
I SHOULDN'T BE SHOWING ANY PAIN.
Why not?
BECAUSE I WAS MADE TO REPLACE THE SISTER HE LOST.

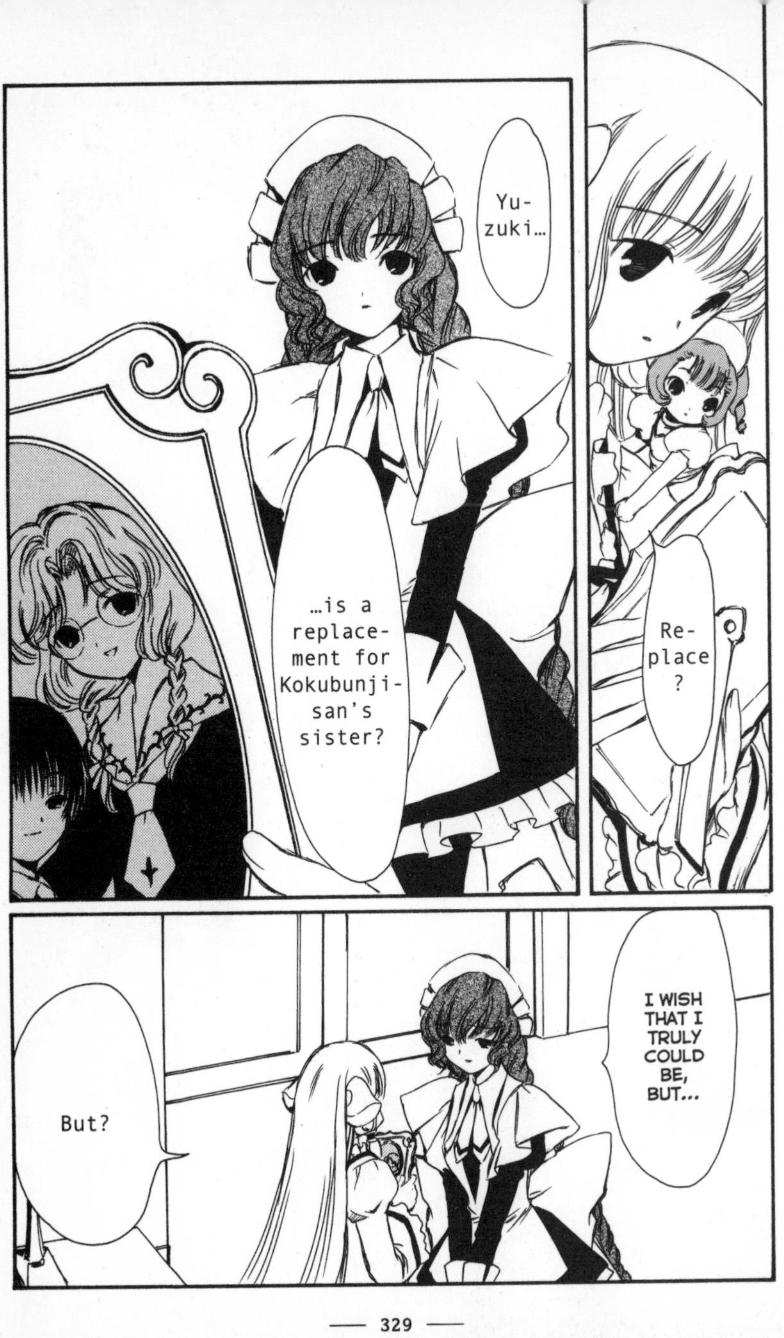
Re-place?
Yu-zuki…
…is a replacement for Kokubunji-san's sister?
I WISH THAT I TRULY COULD BE, BUT…
But?

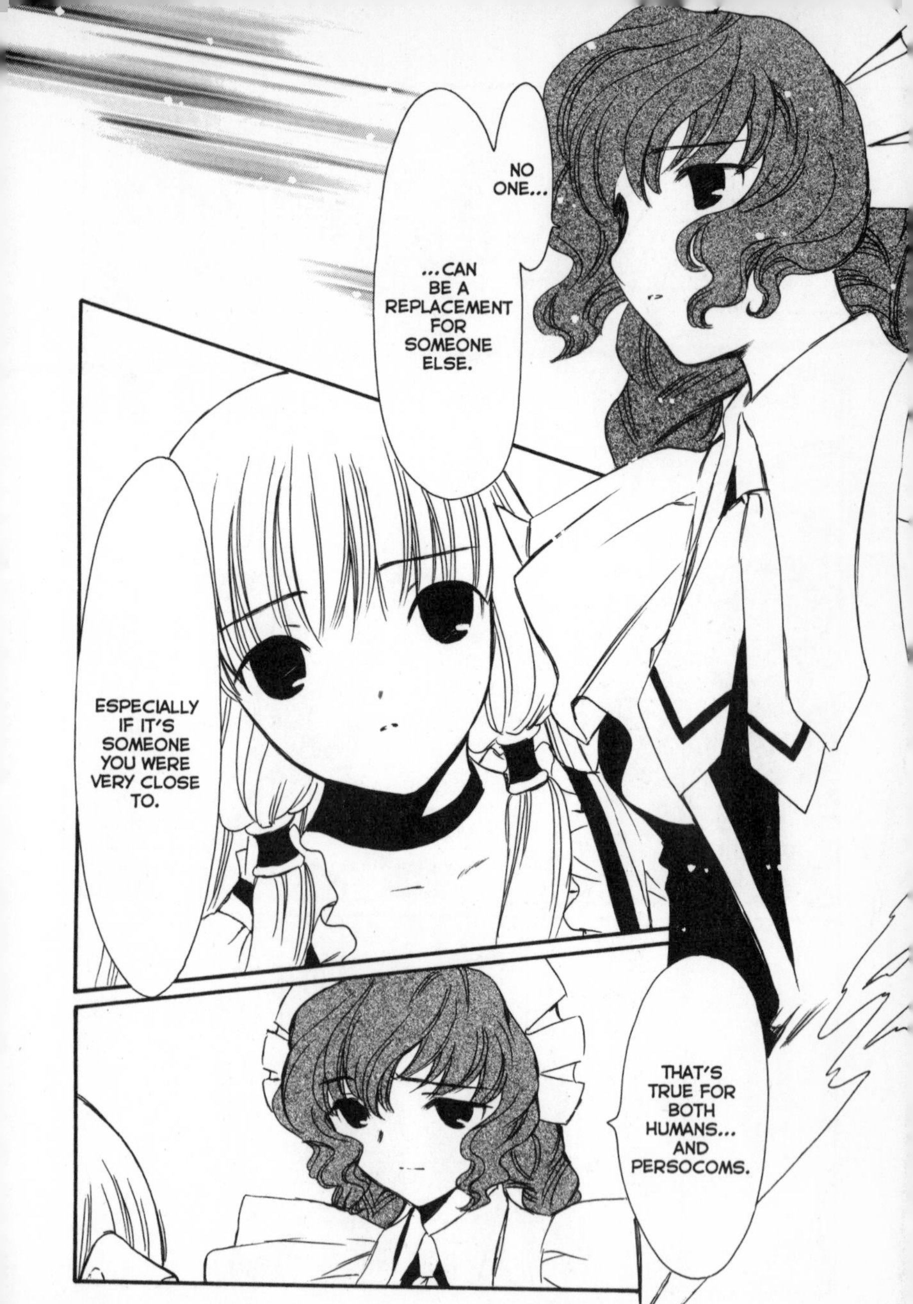
NO ONE...
...CAN BE A REPLACEMENT FOR SOMEONE ELSE.
ESPECIALLY IF IT'S SOMEONE YOU WERE VERY CLOSE TO.
THAT'S TRUE FOR BOTH HUMANS... AND PERSOCOMS.

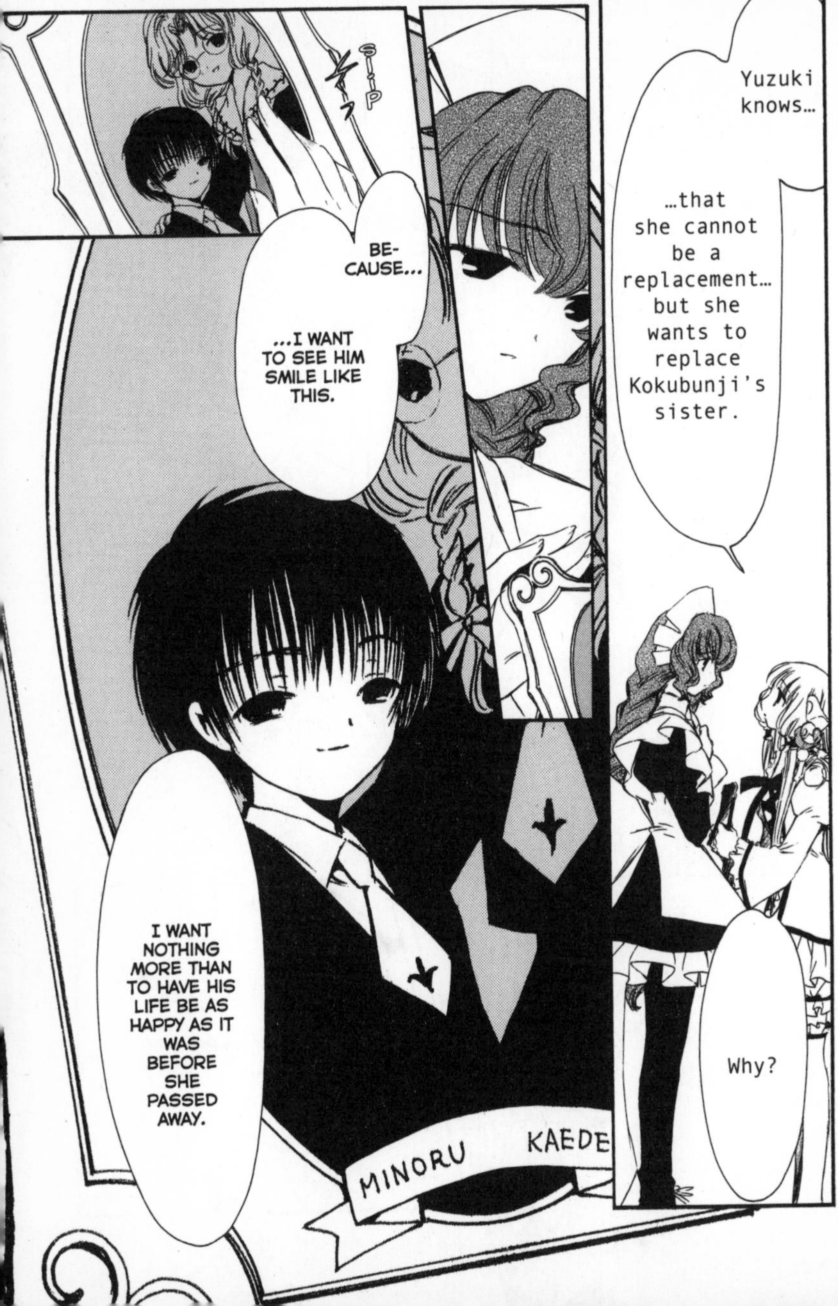
Yuzuki knows…
…that she cannot be a replacement… but she wants to replace Kokubunji's sister.
Why?
SLIP
BE-CAUSE…
…I WANT TO SEE HIM SMILE LIKE THIS.
I WANT NOTHING MORE THAN TO HAVE HIS LIFE BE AS HAPPY AS IT WAS BEFORE SHE PASSED AWAY.
MINORU KAEDE

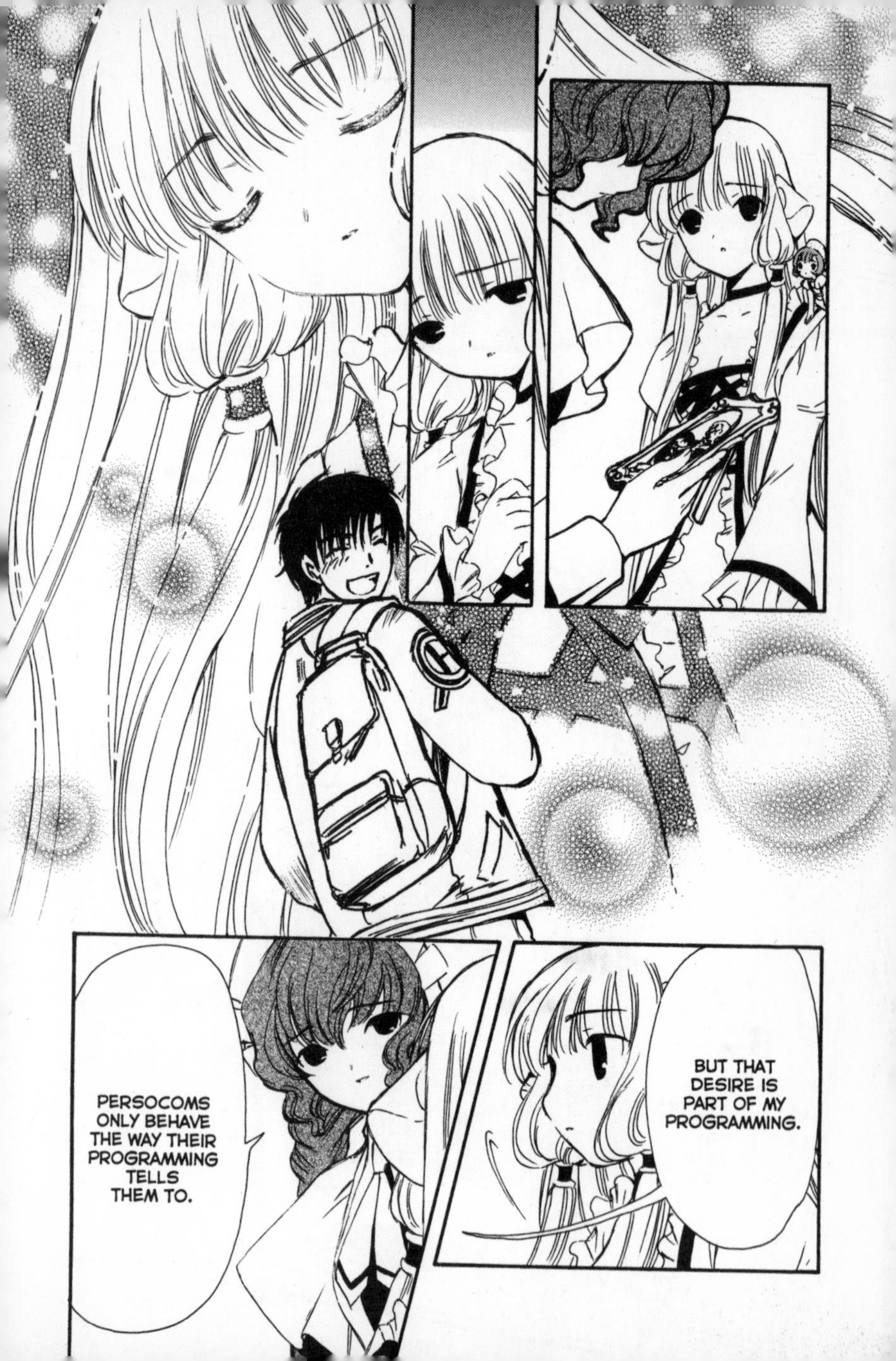
BUT THAT DESIRE IS PART OF MY PROGRAMMING.
PERSOCOMS ONLY BEHAVE THE WAY THEIR PROGRAMMING TELLS THEM TO.

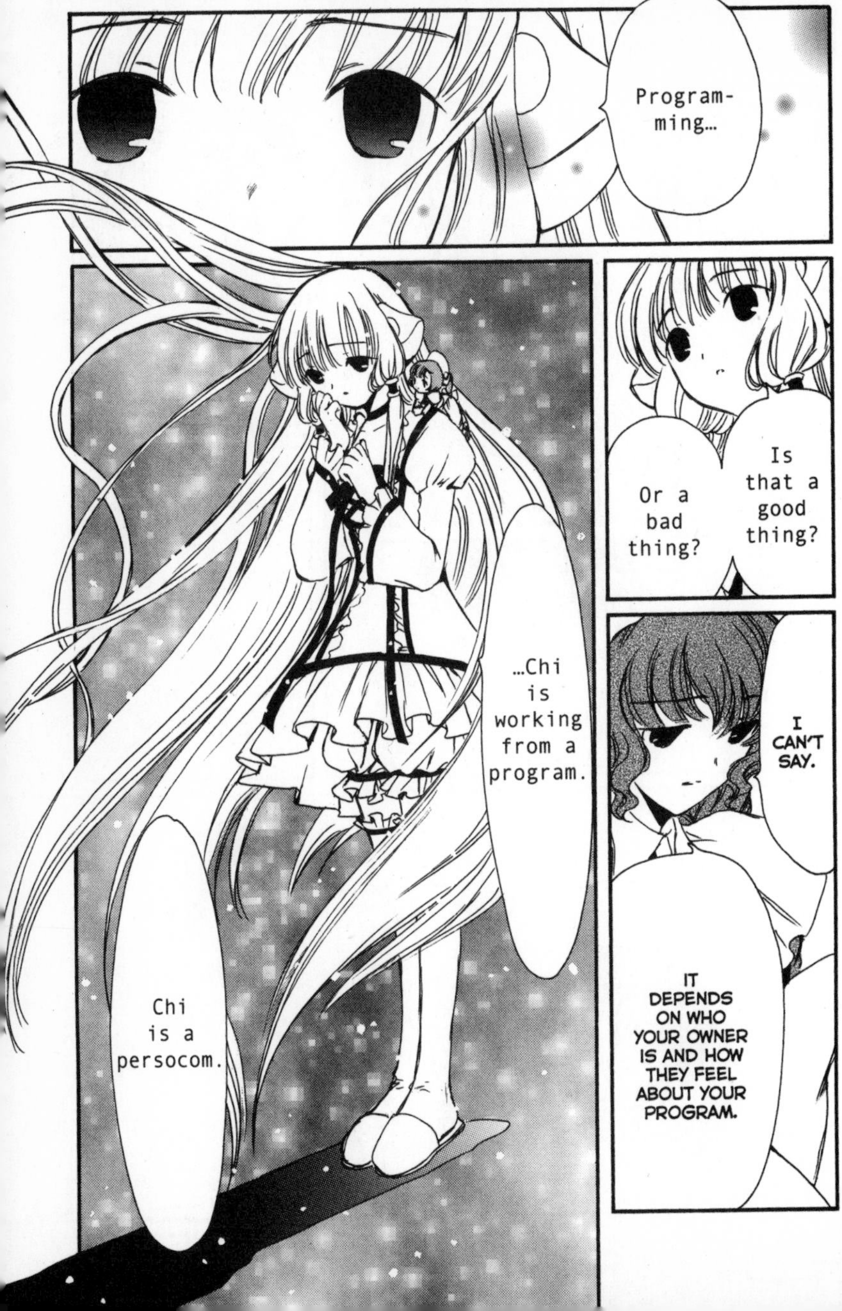
Programming…
Is that a good thing?
Or a bad thing?
I CAN'T SAY.
IT DEPENDS ON WHO YOUR OWNER IS AND HOW THEY FEEL ABOUT YOUR PROGRAM.
…Chi is working from a program.
Chi is a persocom.

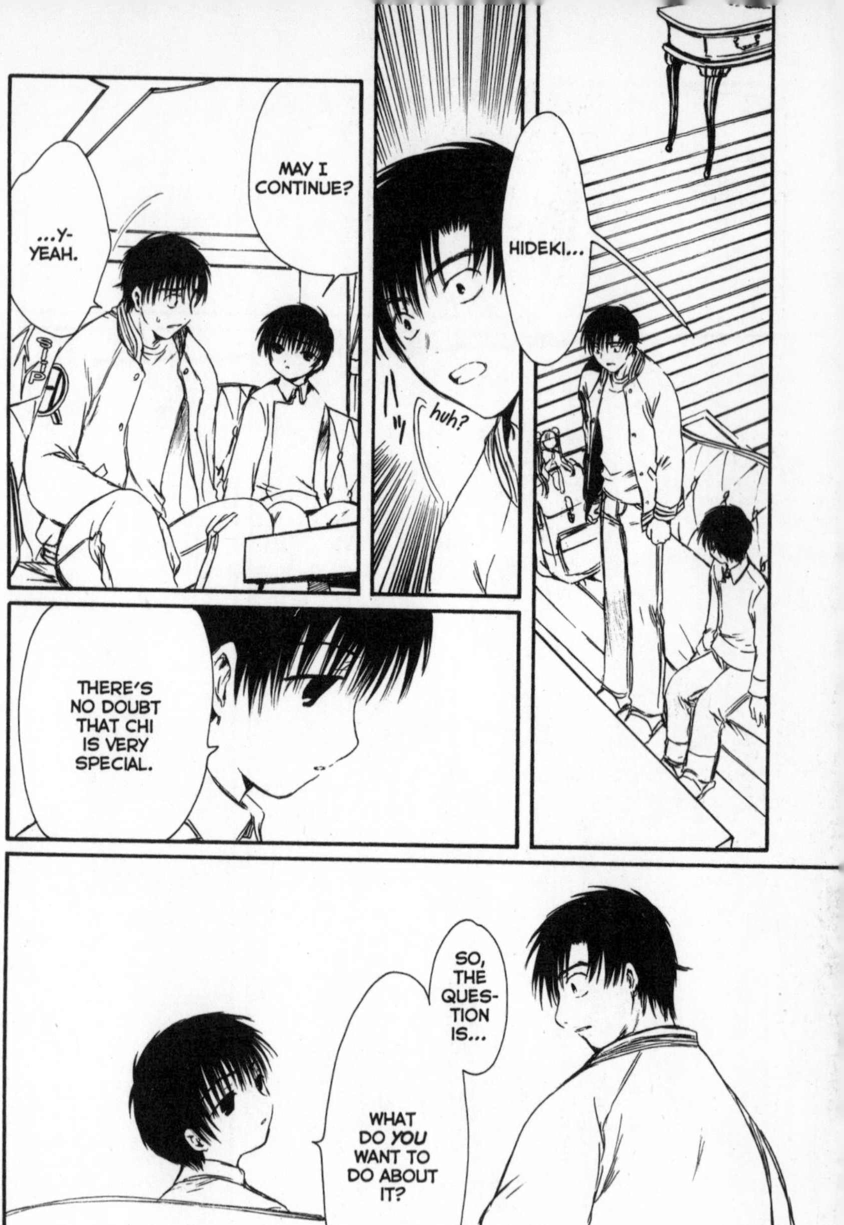
HIDEKI...
huh?
MAY I CONTINUE?
...Y-YEAH.
THERE'S NO DOUBT THAT CHI IS VERY SPECIAL.
SO, THE QUES-TION IS...
WHAT DO *YOU* WANT TO DO ABOUT IT?

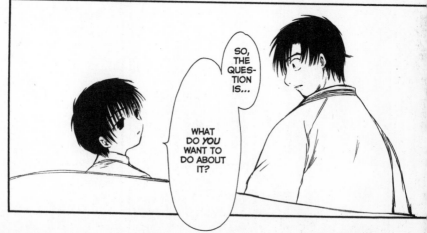

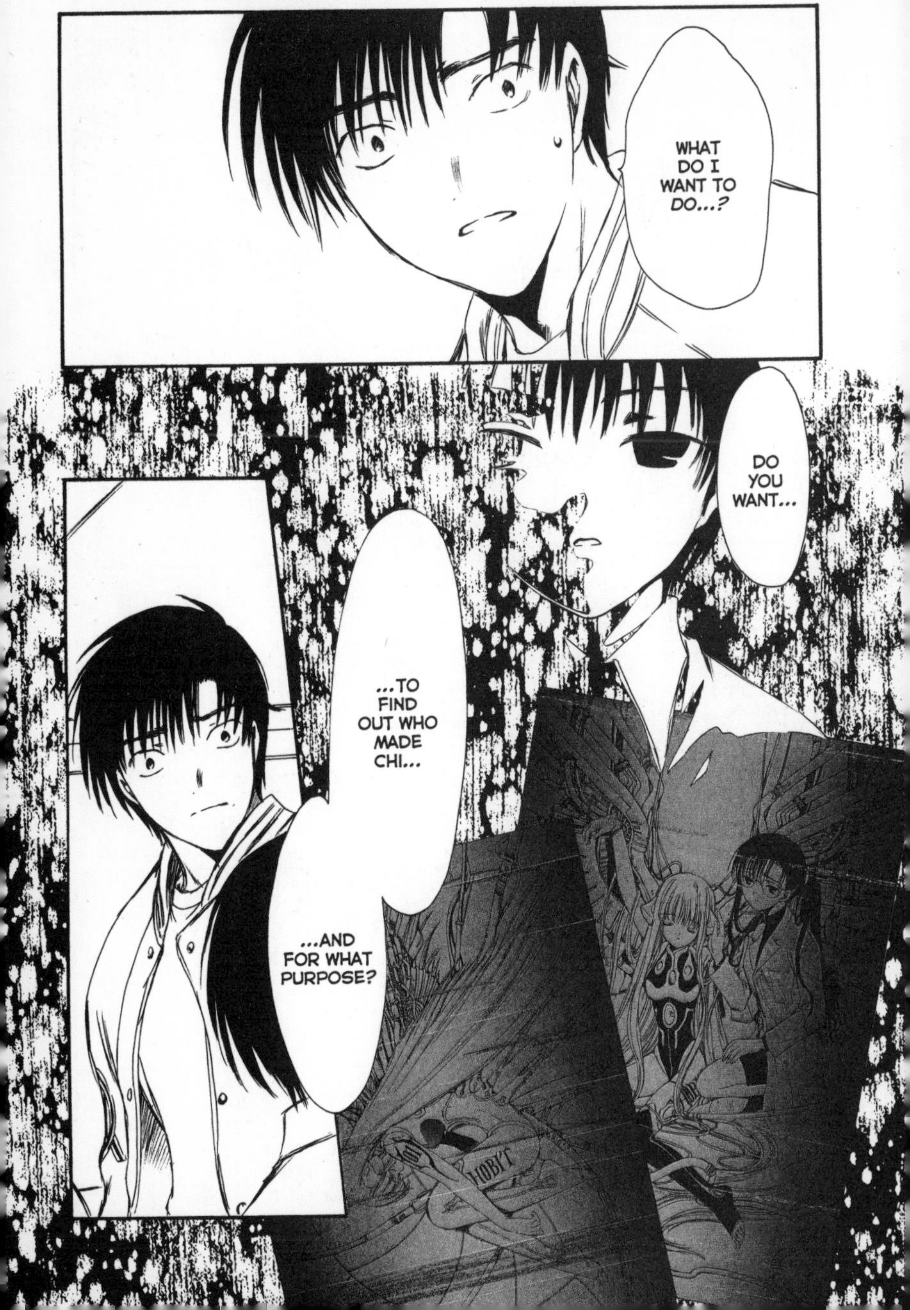
WHAT DO I WANT TO *DO*...?
DO YOU WANT...
...TO FIND OUT WHO MADE CHI...
...AND FOR WHAT PURPOSE?

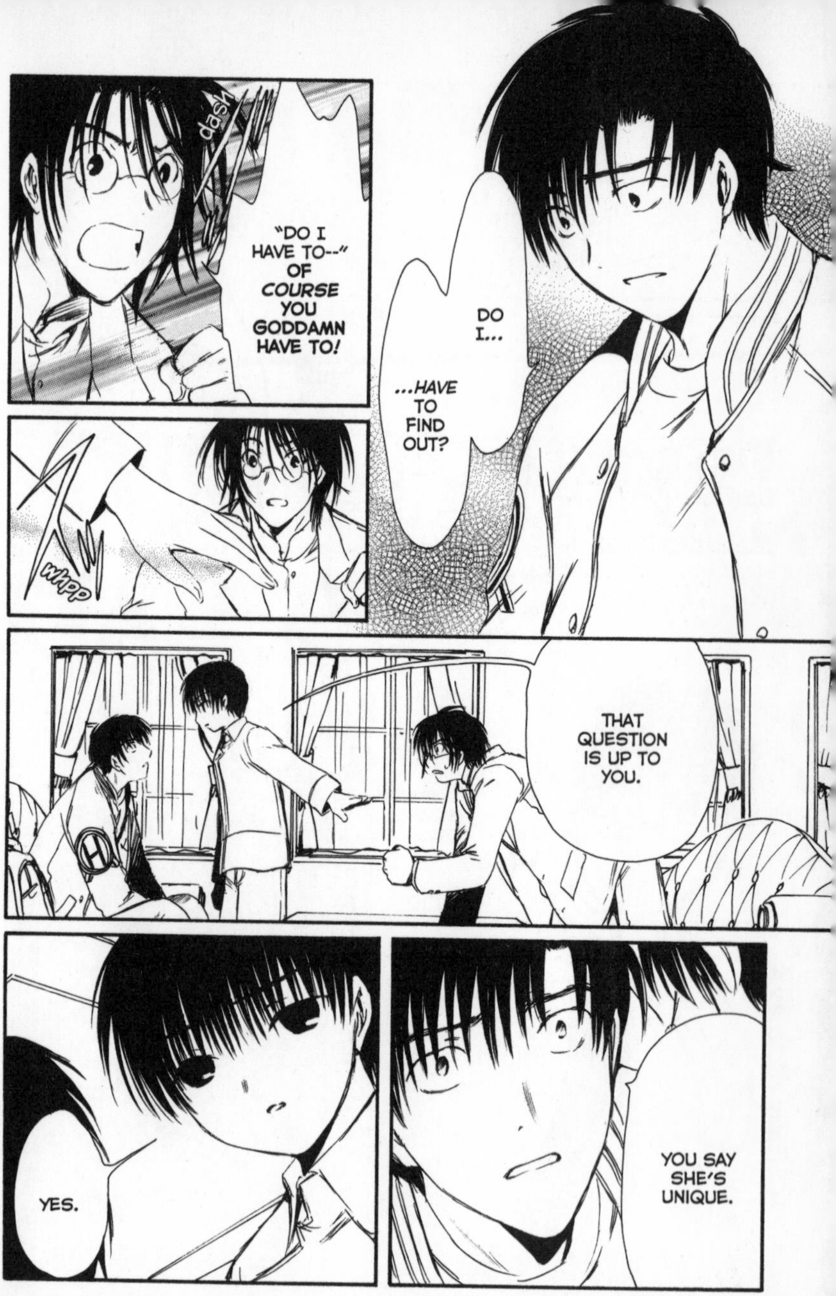
DO I...
...HAVE TO FIND OUT?
"DO I HAVE TO--" OF COURSE YOU GODDAMN HAVE TO!
dash
whpp
THAT QUESTION IS UP TO YOU.
YOU SAY SHE'S UNIQUE.
YES.

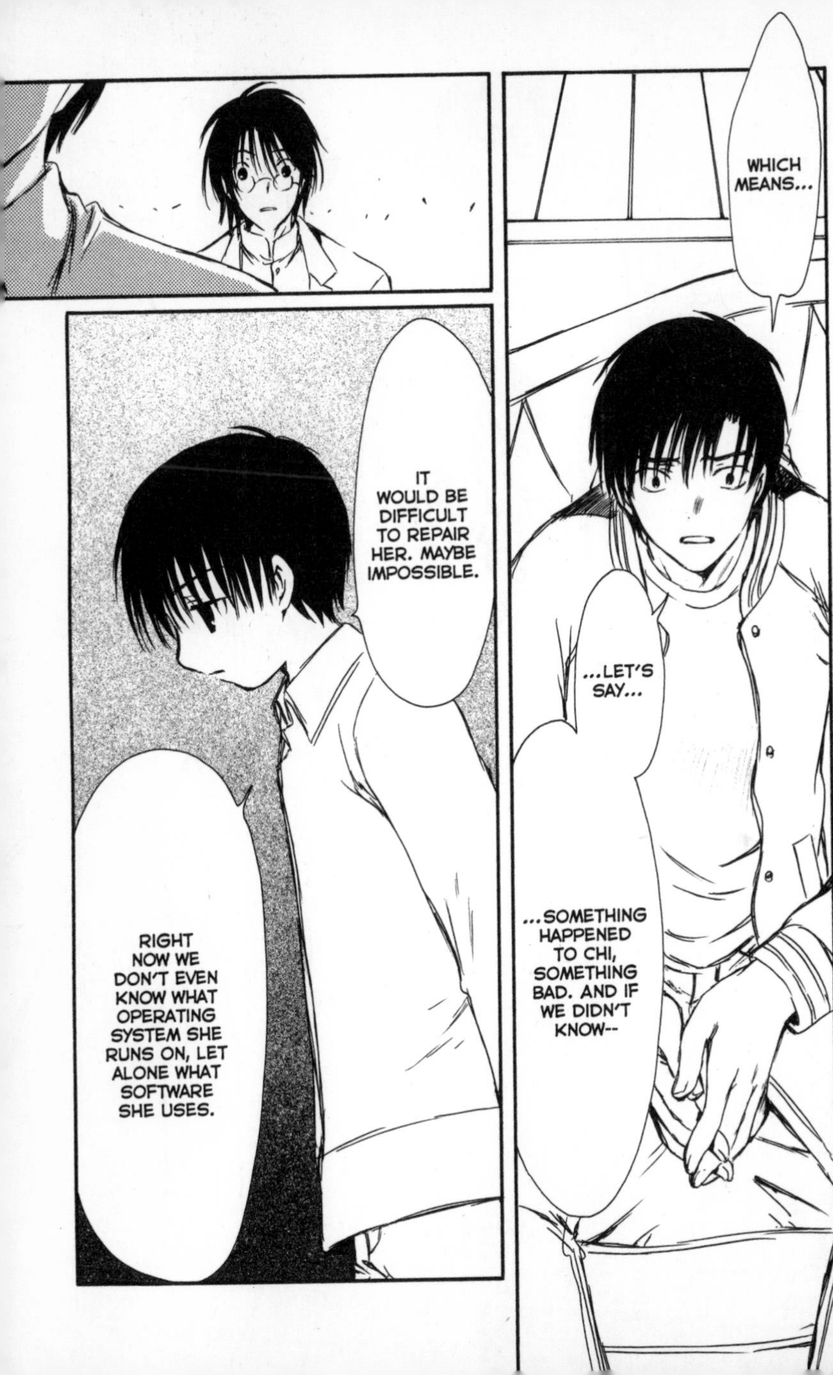
WHICH MEANS...
...LET'S SAY...
...SOMETHING HAPPENED TO CHI, SOMETHING BAD. AND IF WE DIDN'T KNOW--
IT WOULD BE DIFFICULT TO REPAIR HER. MAYBE IMPOSSIBLE.
RIGHT NOW WE DON'T EVEN KNOW WHAT OPERATING SYSTEM SHE RUNS ON, LET ALONE WHAT SOFTWARE SHE USES.

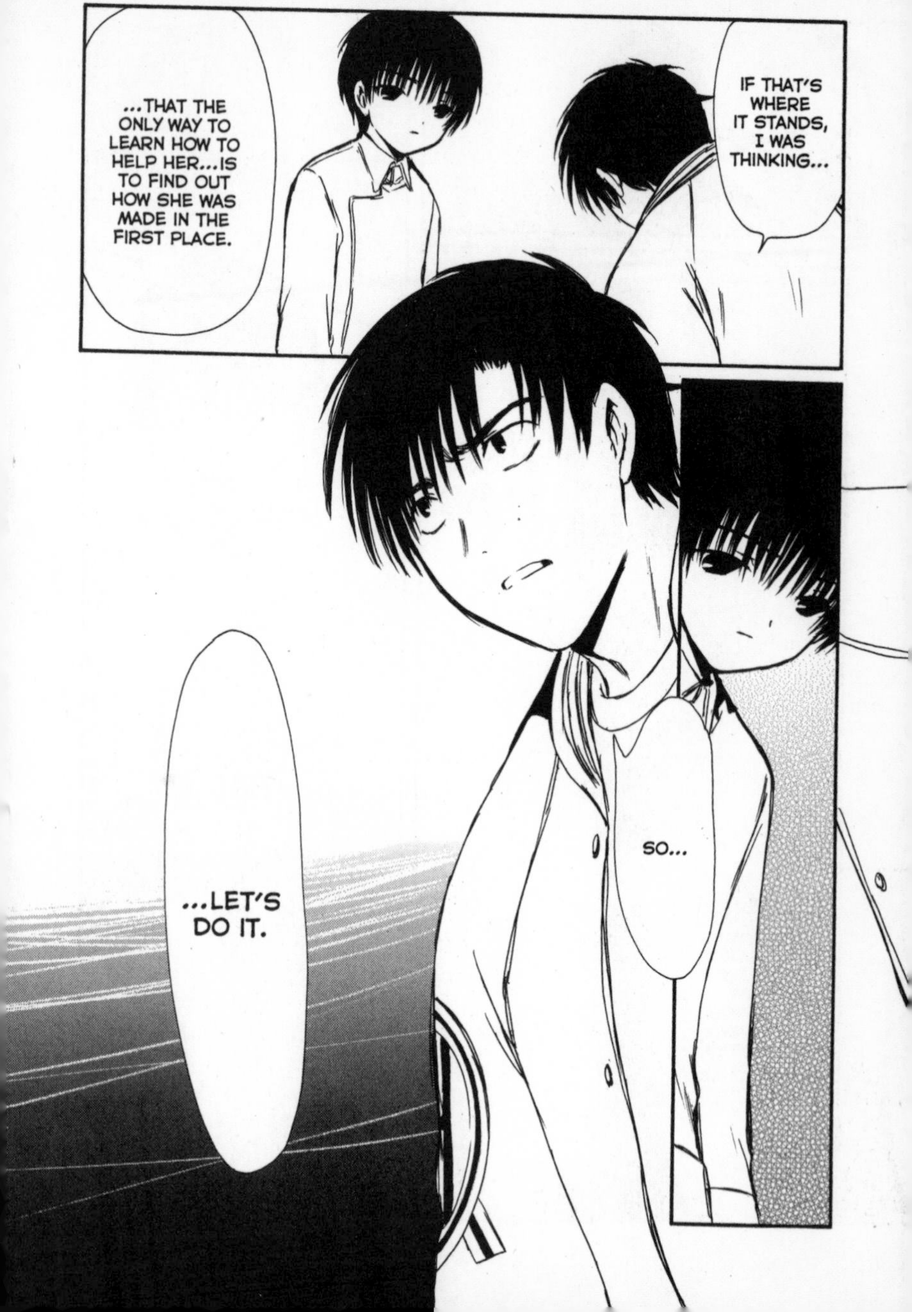
IF THAT'S WHERE IT STANDS, I WAS THINKING...
...THAT THE ONLY WAY TO LEARN HOW TO HELP HER...IS TO FIND OUT HOW SHE WAS MADE IN THE FIRST PLACE.
SO...
...LET'S DO IT.

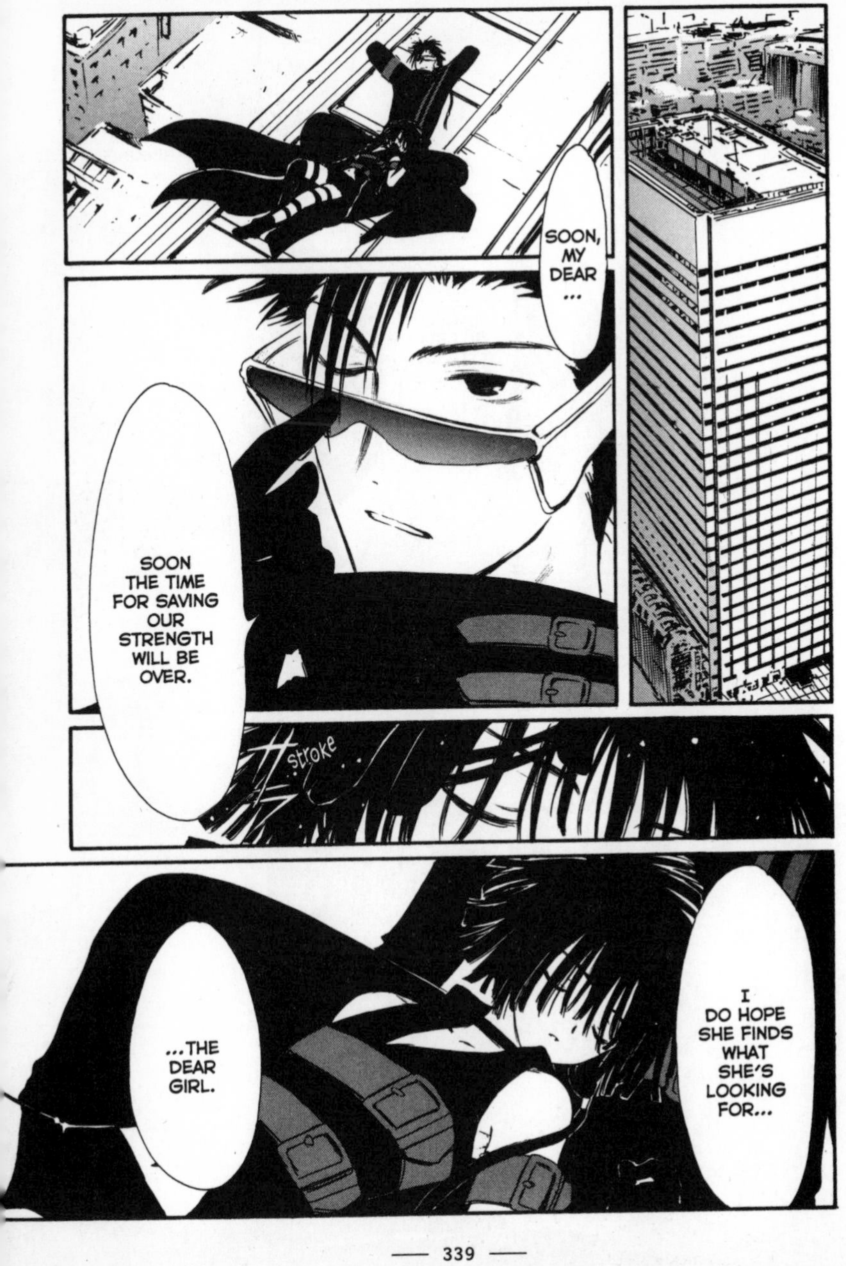

SOON, MY DEAR...
SOON THE TIME FOR SAVING OUR STRENGTH WILL BE OVER.
stroke
I DO HOPE SHE FINDS WHAT SHE'S LOOKING FOR...
...THE DEAR GIRL.

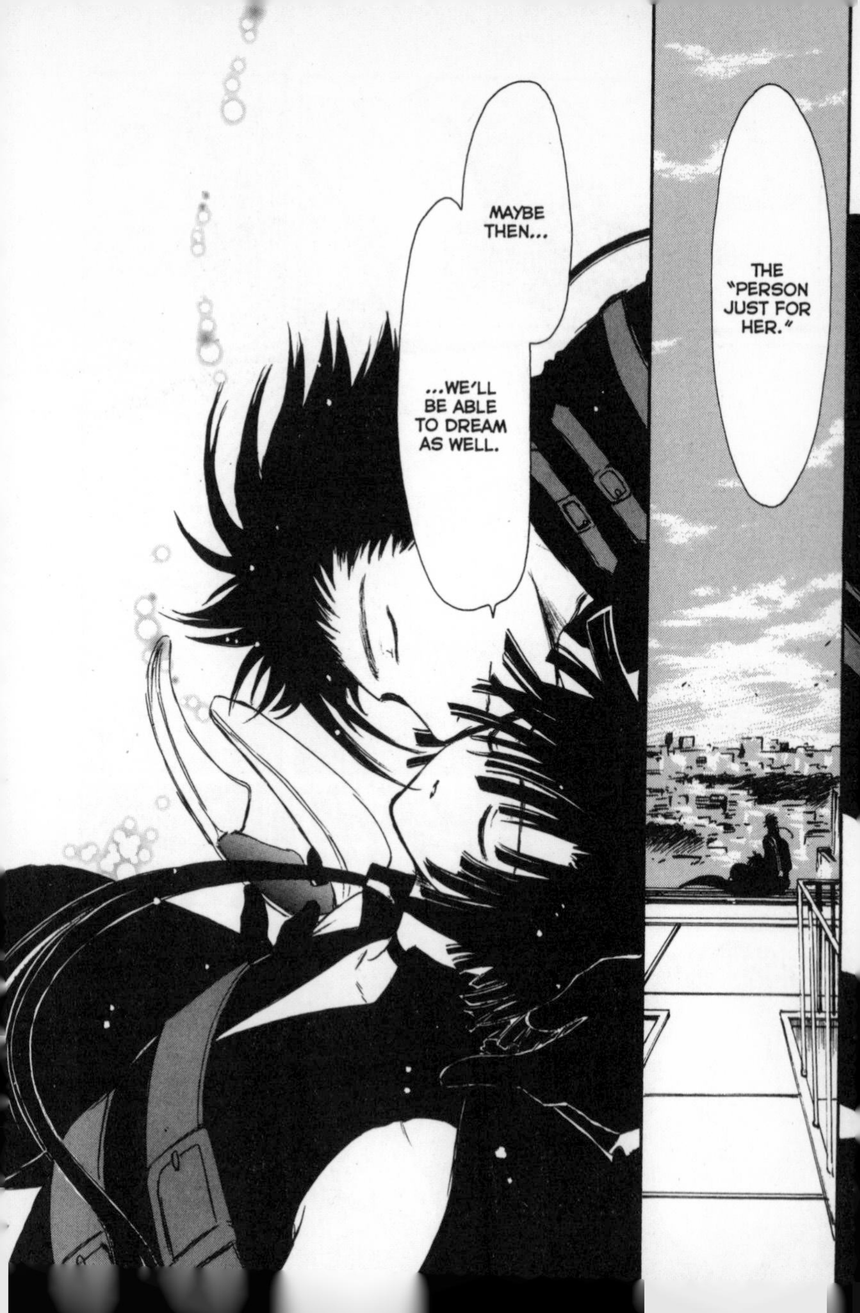
THE "PERSON JUST FOR HER."
MAYBE THEN...
...WE'LL BE ABLE TO DREAM AS WELL.

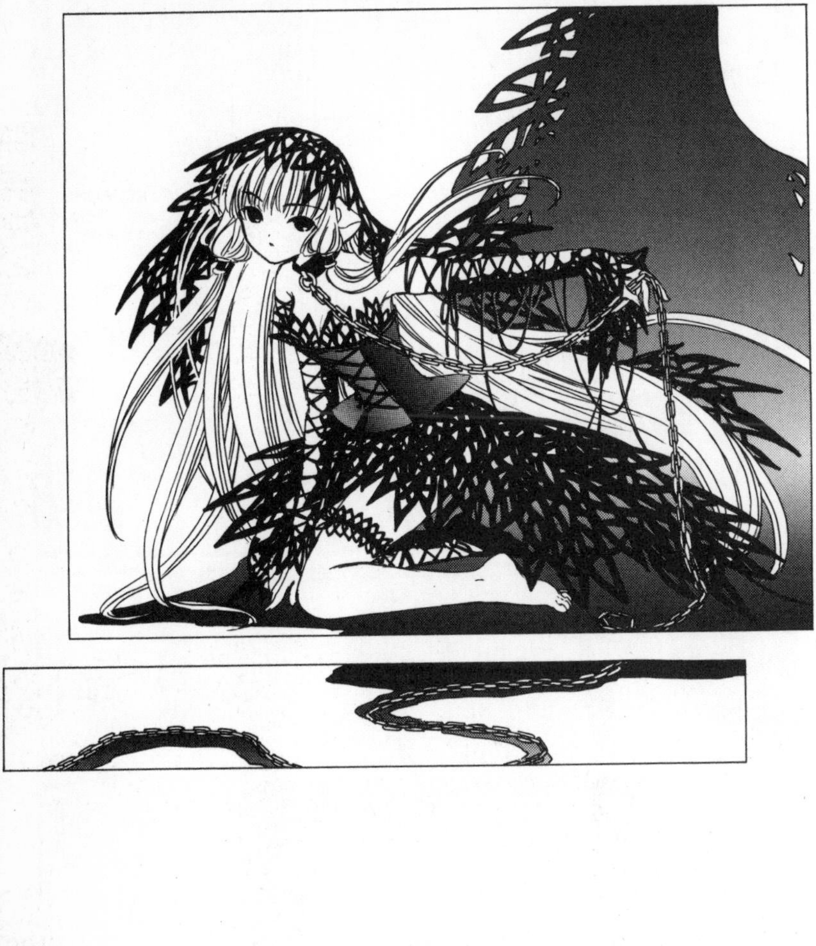

Chobits
ちょびっツ

chapter 71

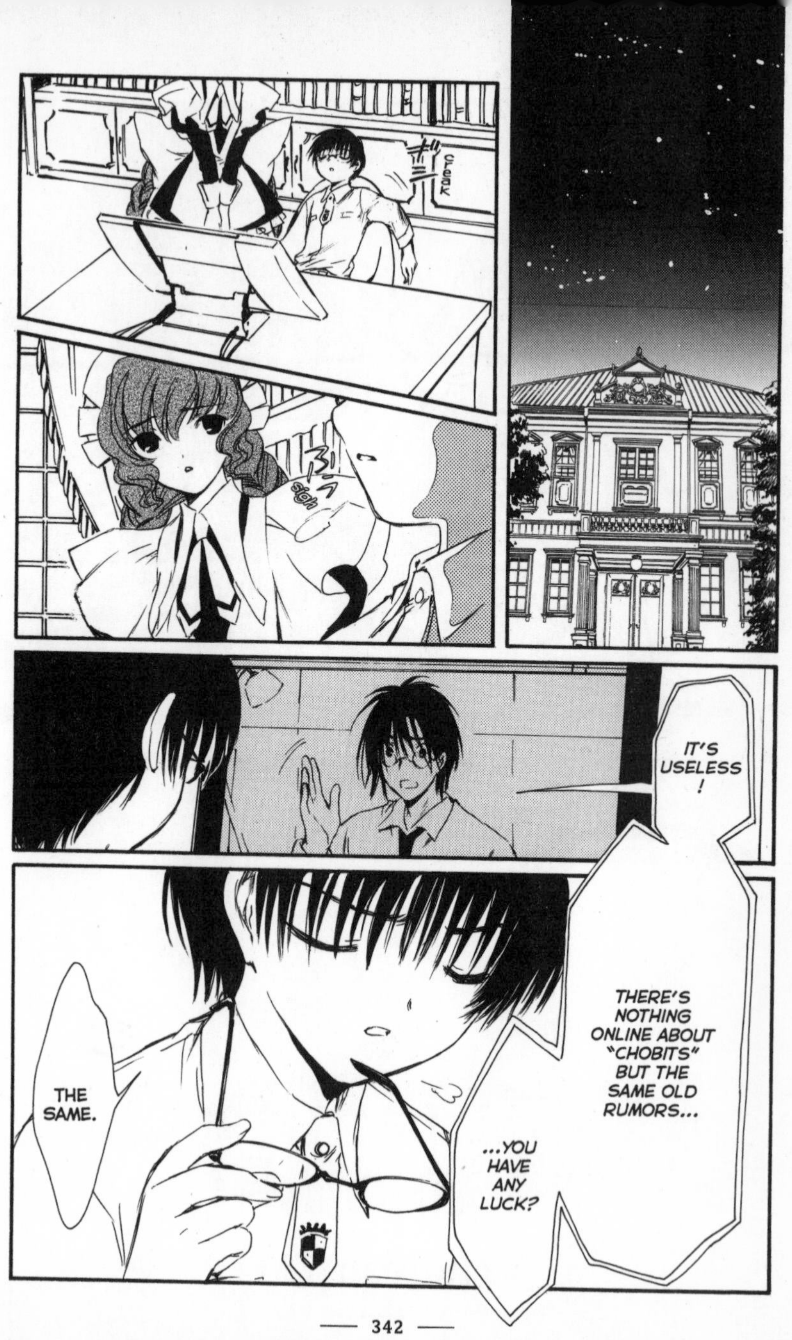
creak
sigh
IT'S USELESS!
THERE'S NOTHING ONLINE ABOUT "CHOBITS" BUT THE SAME OLD RUMORS...
...YOU HAVE ANY LUCK?
THE SAME.

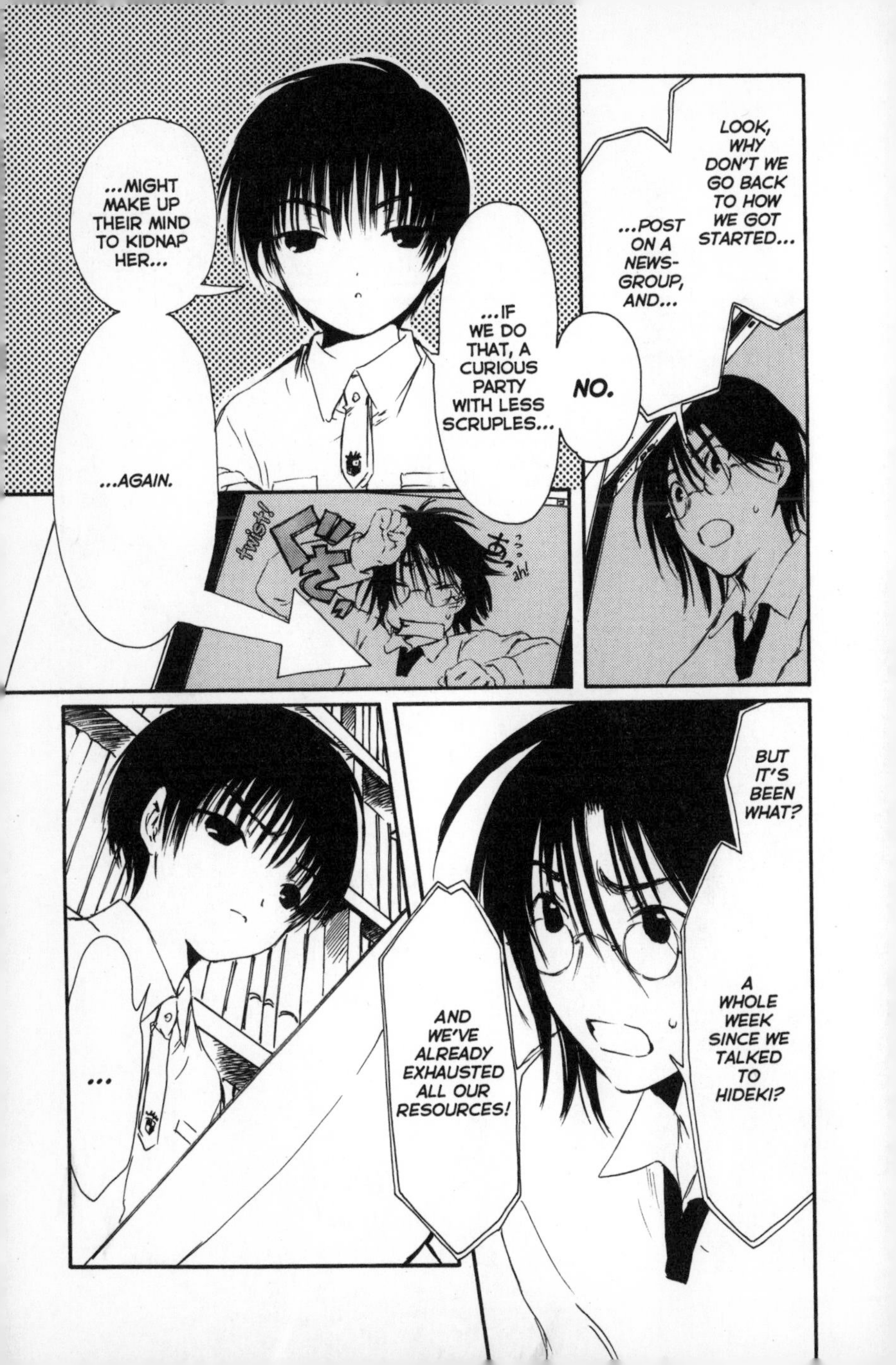
LOOK, WHY DON'T WE GO BACK TO HOW WE GOT STARTED...
...POST ON A NEWS-GROUP, AND...
NO.
...IF WE DO THAT, A CURIOUS PARTY WITH LESS SCRUPLES...
...MIGHT MAKE UP THEIR MIND TO KIDNAP HER...
...AGAIN.
twist!
ah!
BUT IT'S BEEN WHAT?
A WHOLE WEEK SINCE WE TALKED TO HIDEKI?
AND WE'VE ALREADY EXHAUSTED ALL OUR RESOURCES!
...

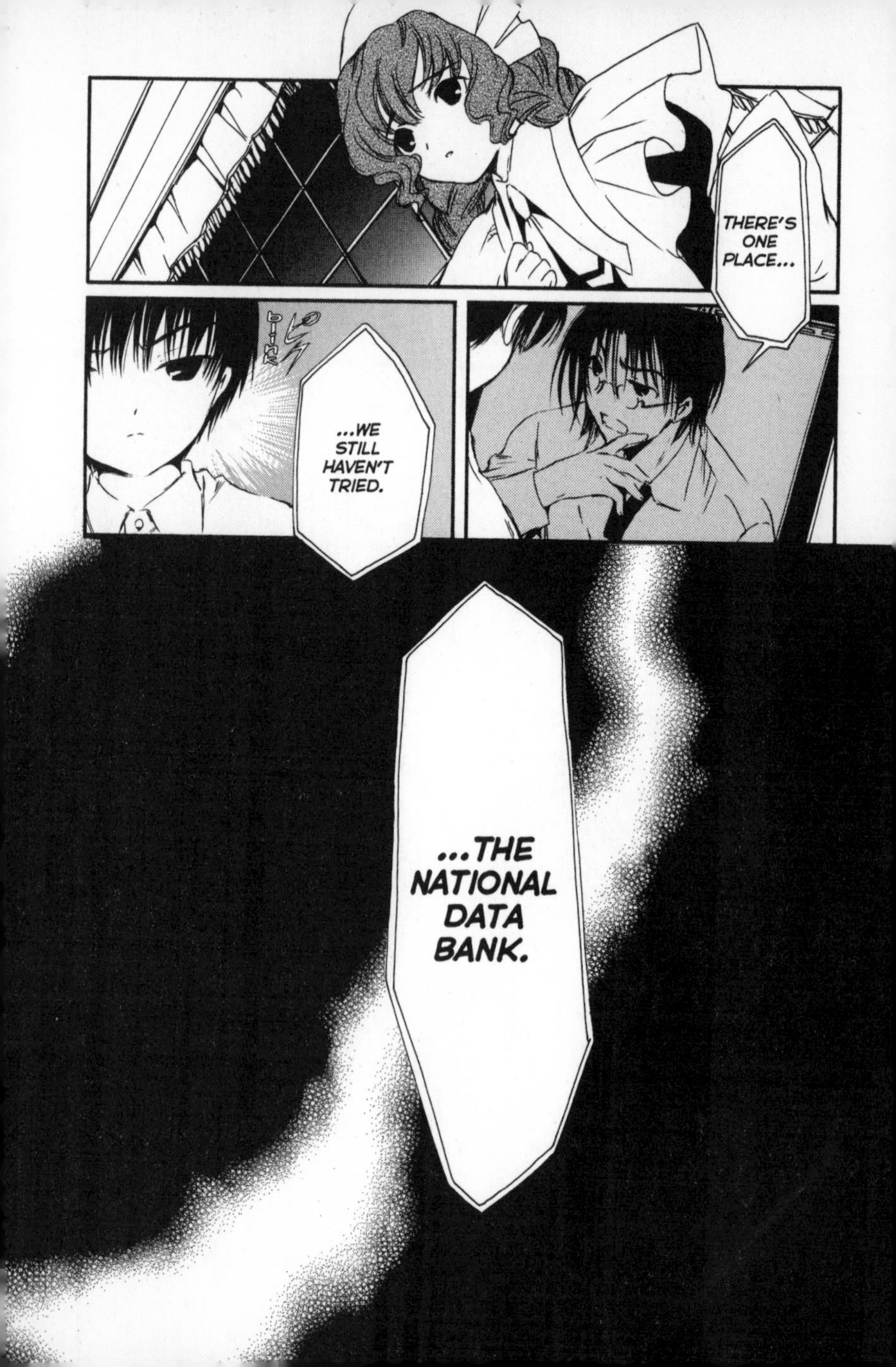
THERE'S ONE PLACE...
BLINK
...WE STILL HAVEN'T TRIED.
...THE NATIONAL DATA BANK.

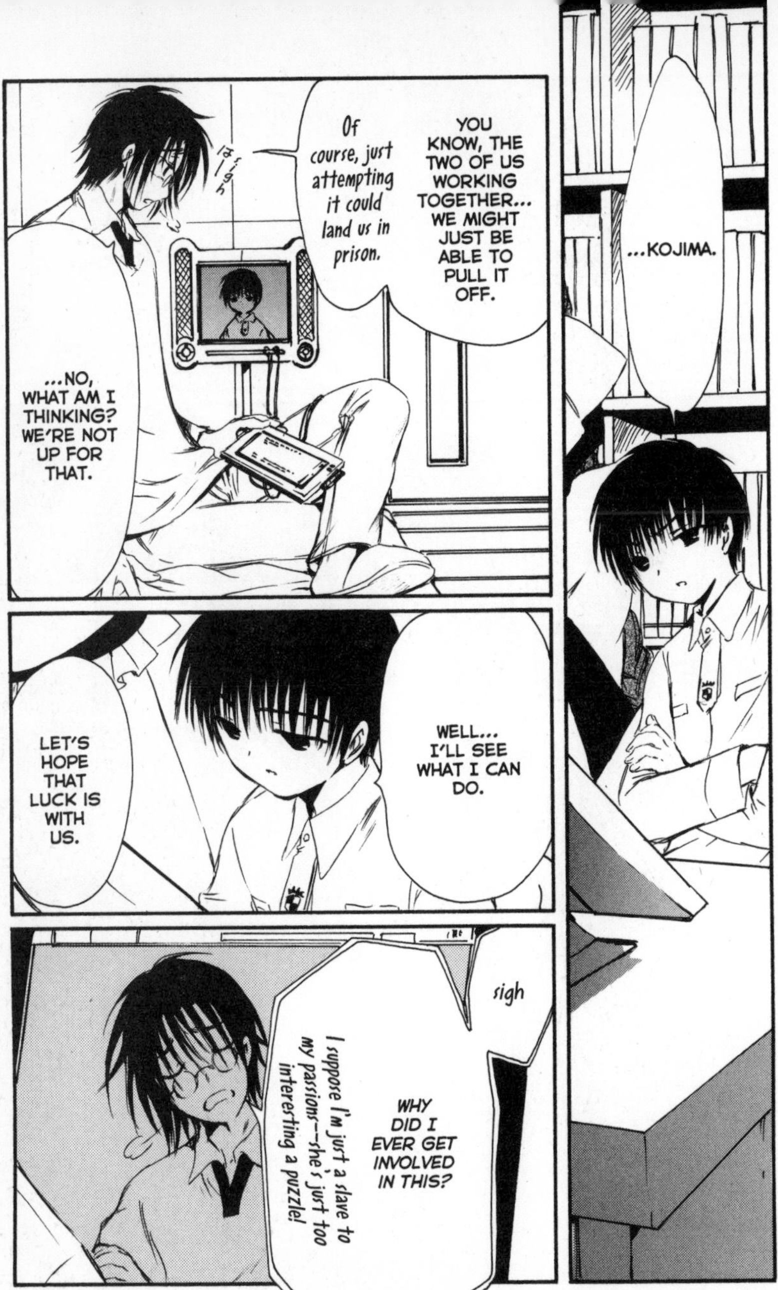
...KOJIMA.
YOU KNOW, THE TWO OF US WORKING TOGETHER... WE MIGHT JUST BE ABLE TO PULL IT OFF.
Of course, just attempting it could land us in prison.
...NO, WHAT AM I THINKING? WE'RE NOT UP FOR THAT.
WELL... I'LL SEE WHAT I CAN DO.
LET'S HOPE THAT LUCK IS WITH US.
sigh
WHY DID I EVER GET INVOLVED IN THIS?
I suppose I'm just a slave to my passions--she's just too interersting a puzzle!

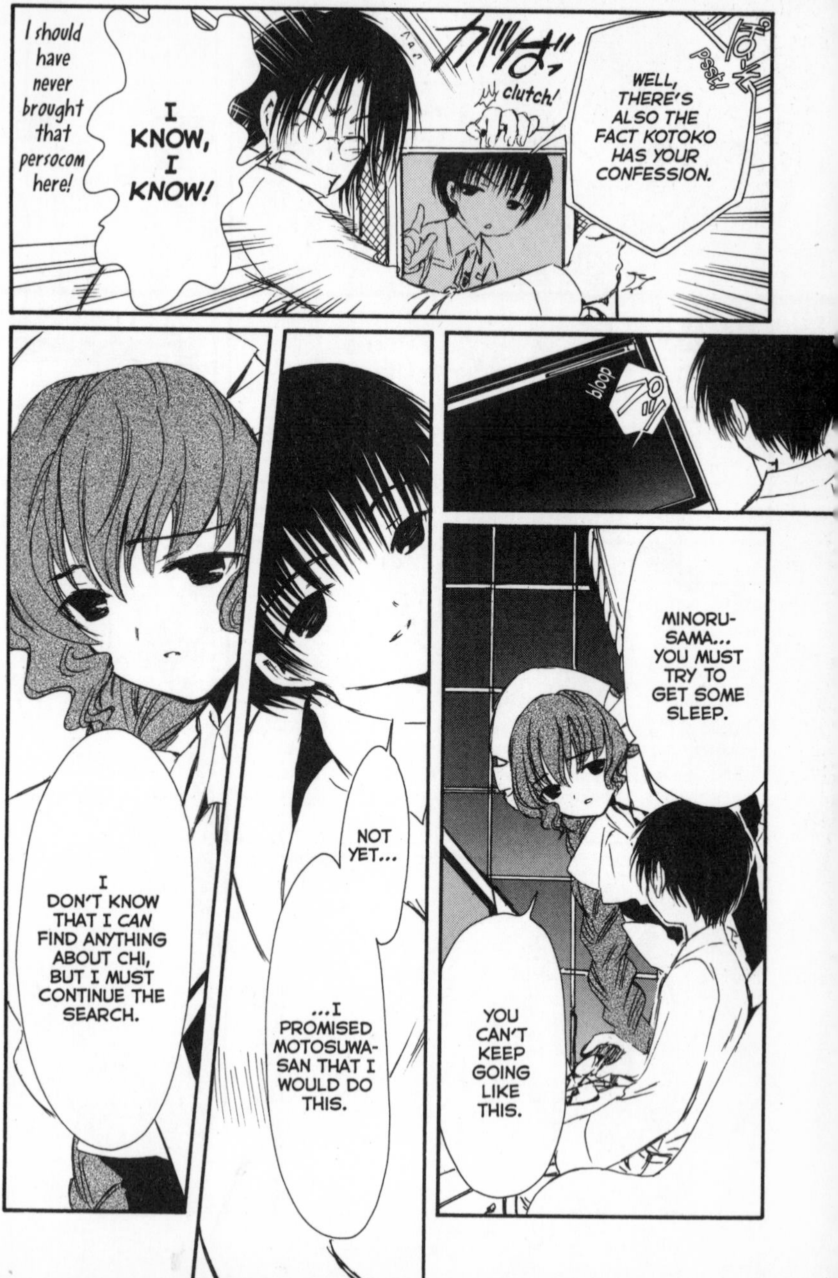
psst!
WELL, THERE'S ALSO THE FACT KOTOKO HAS YOUR CONFESSION.
clutch!
I KNOW, I KNOW!
I should have never brought that persocom here!
bloop
MINORU-SAMA... YOU MUST TRY TO GET SOME SLEEP.
YOU CAN'T KEEP GOING LIKE THIS.
NOT YET...
...I PROMISED MOTOSUWA-SAN THAT I WOULD DO THIS.
I DON'T KNOW THAT I *CAN* FIND ANYTHING ABOUT CHI, BUT I MUST CONTINUE THE SEARCH.

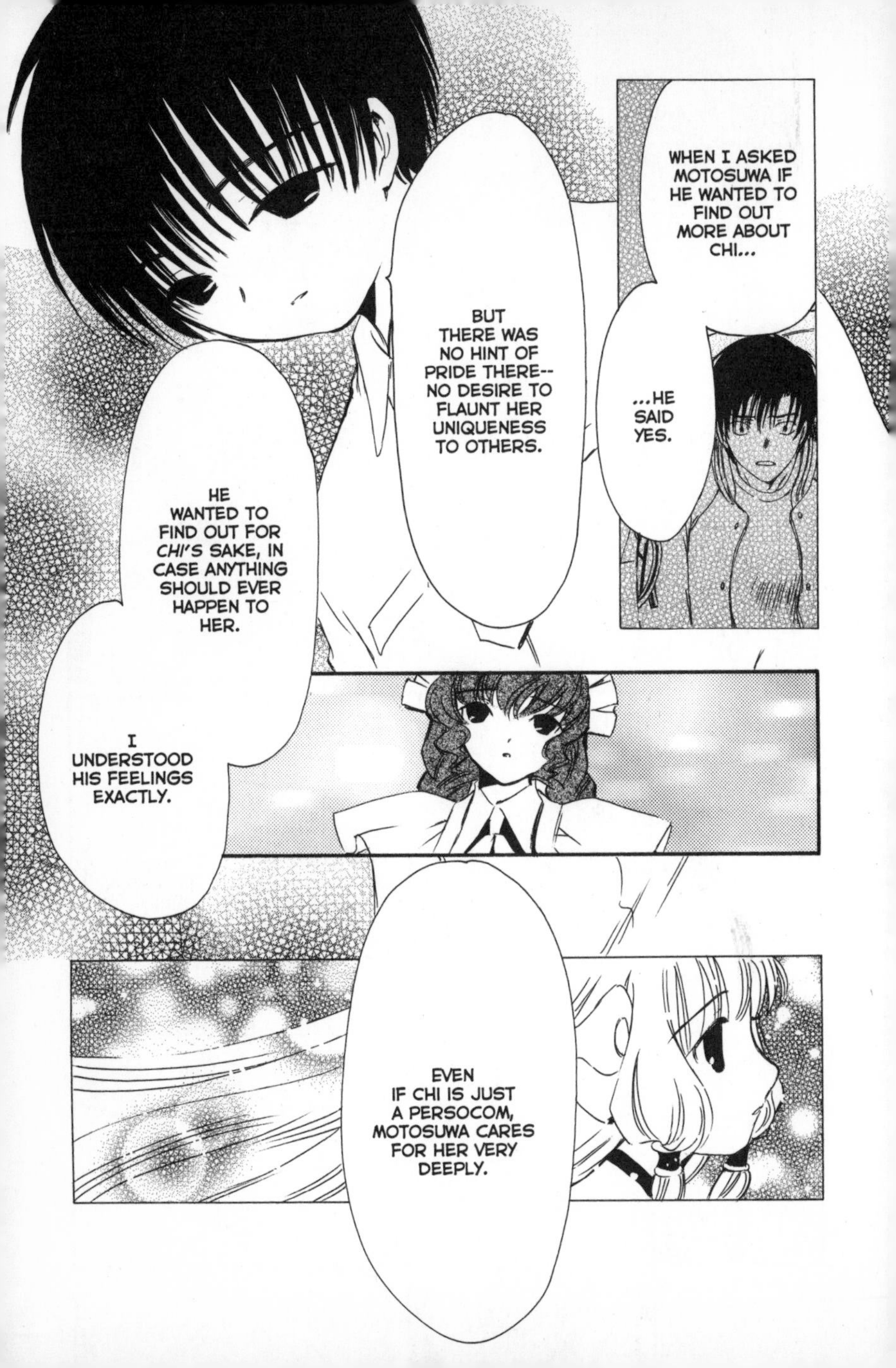
WHEN I ASKED MOTOSUWA IF HE WANTED TO FIND OUT MORE ABOUT CHI...
...HE SAID YES.
BUT THERE WAS NO HINT OF PRIDE THERE--NO DESIRE TO FLAUNT HER UNIQUENESS TO OTHERS.
HE WANTED TO FIND OUT FOR *CHI'S* SAKE, IN CASE ANYTHING SHOULD EVER HAPPEN TO HER.
I UNDERSTOOD HIS FEELINGS EXACTLY.
EVEN IF CHI IS JUST A PERSOCOM, MOTOSUWA CARES FOR HER VERY DEEPLY.

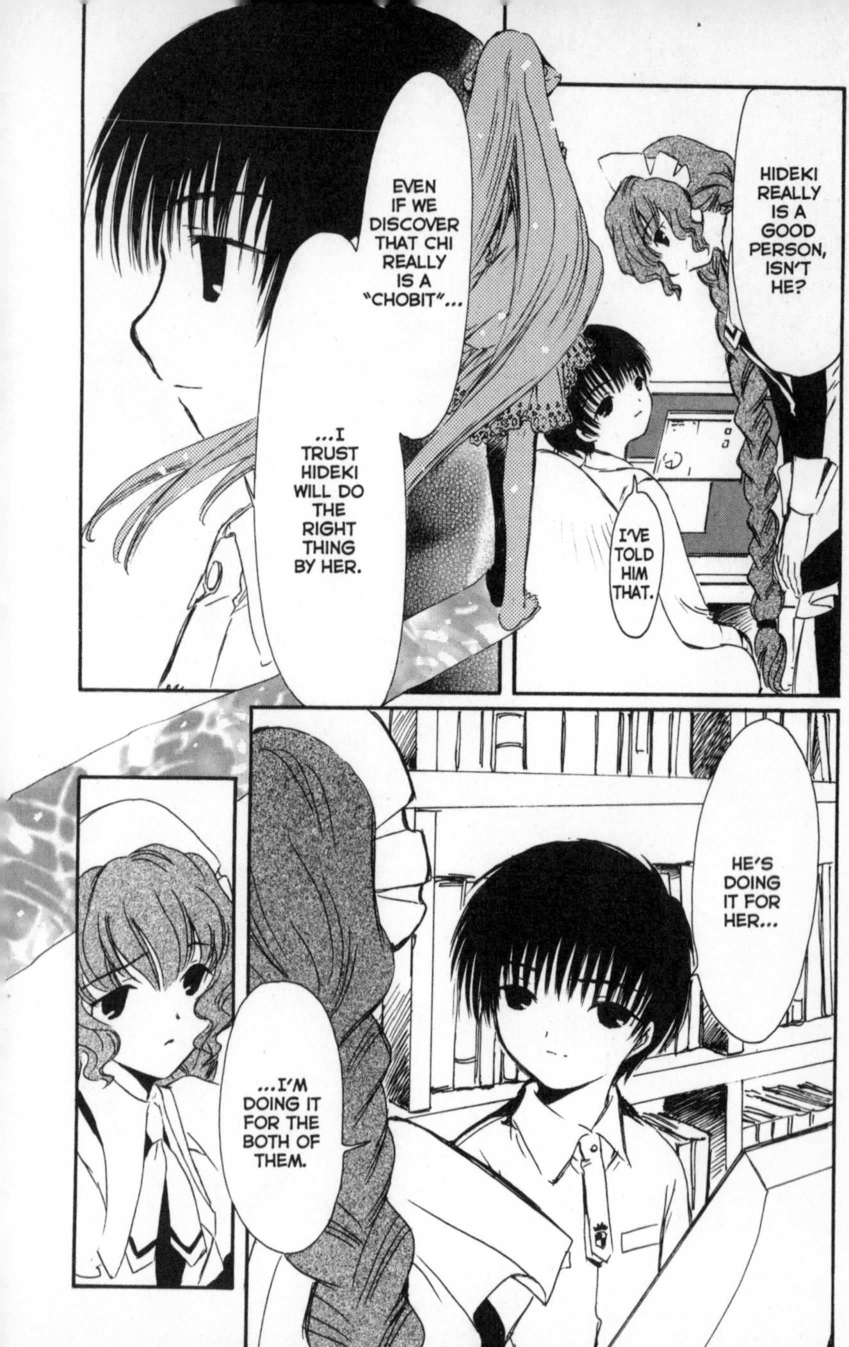
HIDEKI REALLY IS A GOOD PERSON, ISN'T HE?
I'VE TOLD HIM THAT.
EVEN IF WE DISCOVER THAT CHI REALLY IS A "CHOBIT"...
...I TRUST HIDEKI WILL DO THE RIGHT THING BY HER.
HE'S DOING IT FOR HER...
...I'M DOING IT FOR THE BOTH OF THEM.

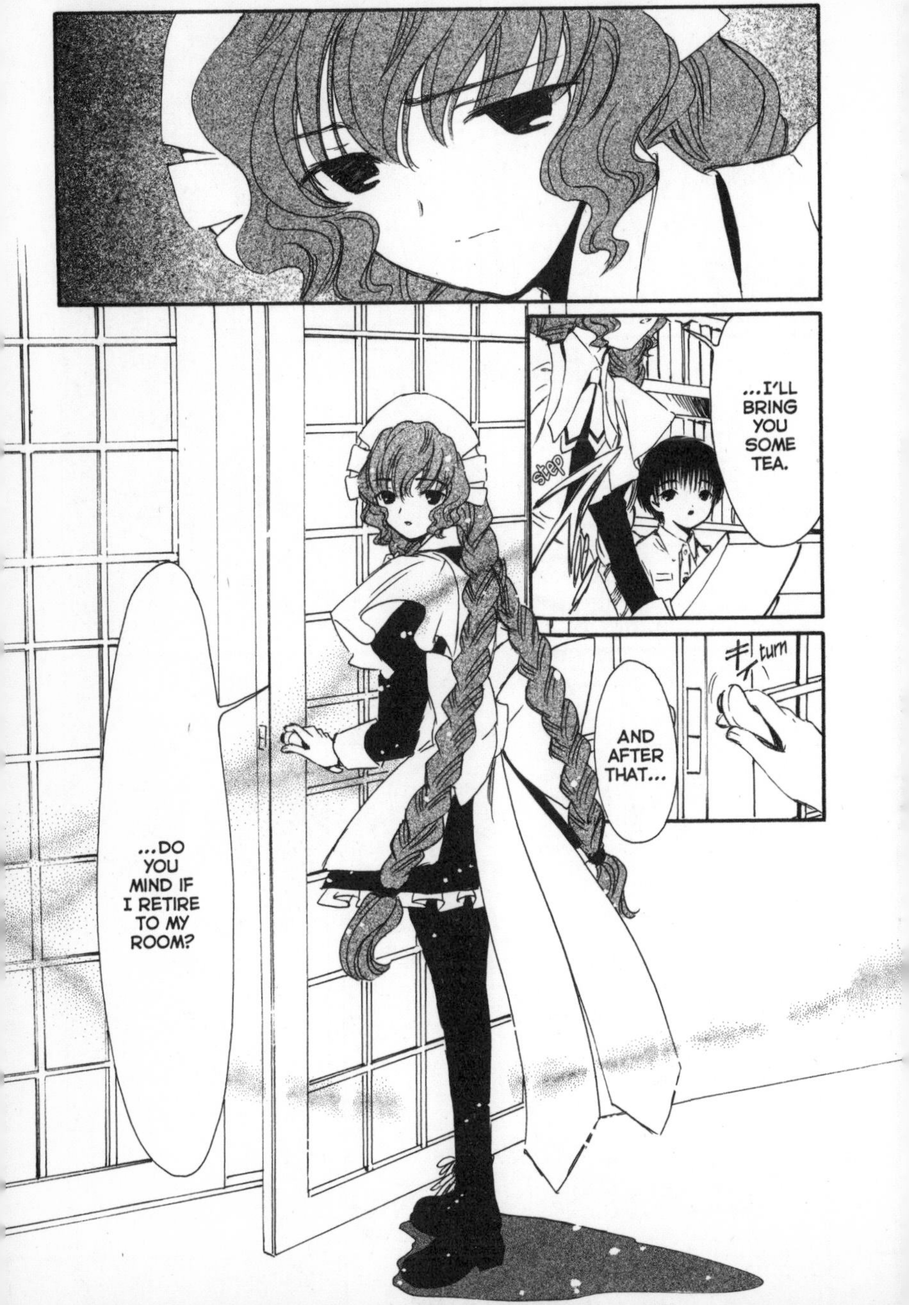
...I'LL BRING YOU SOME TEA.
step
turn
AND AFTER THAT...
...DO YOU MIND IF I RETIRE TO MY ROOM?

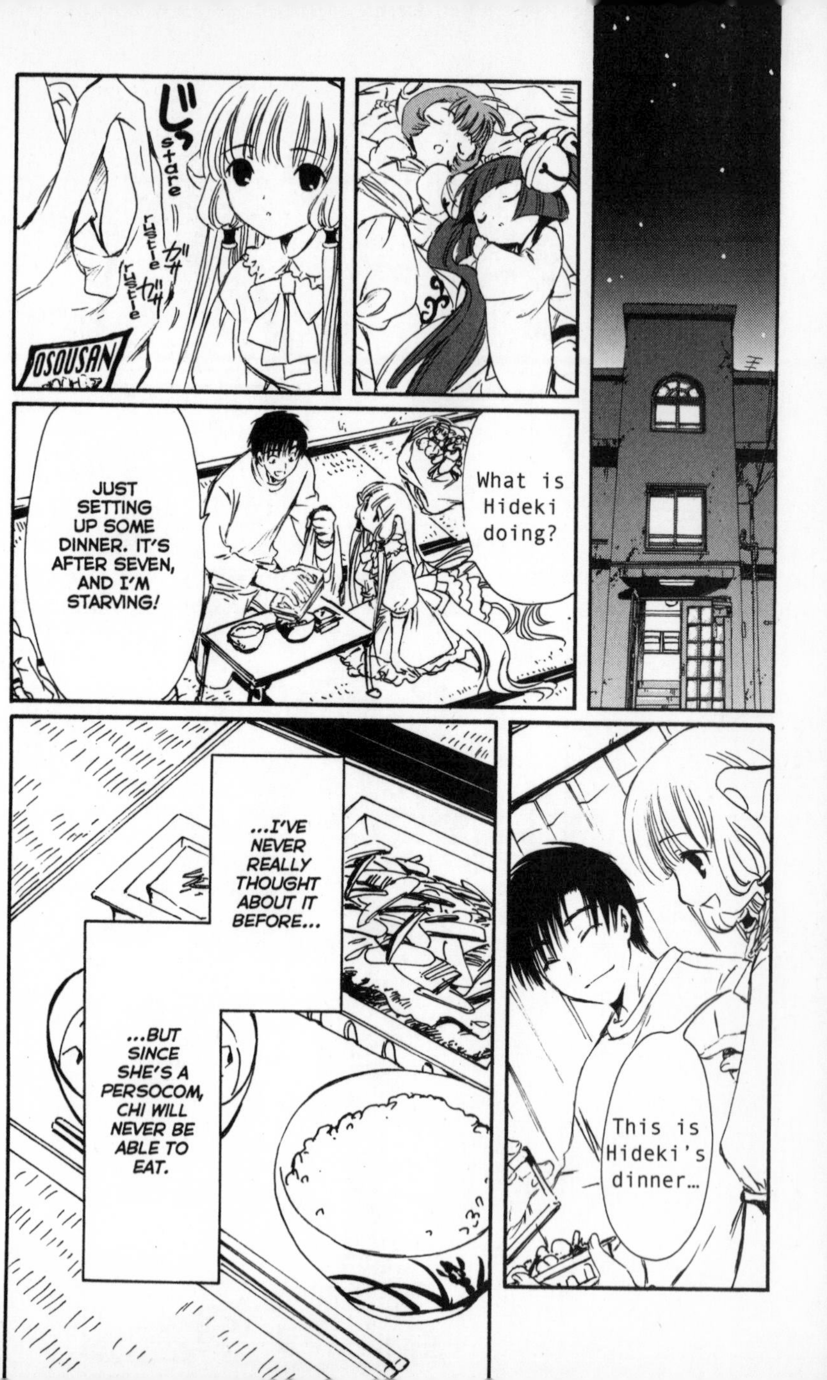
stare
rustle
rustle
OSOUSAN
What is Hideki doing?
JUST SETTING UP SOME DINNER. IT'S AFTER SEVEN, AND I'M STARVING!
This is Hideki's dinner...
...I'VE NEVER REALLY THOUGHT ABOUT IT BEFORE...
...BUT SINCE SHE'S A PERSOCOM, CHI WILL NEVER BE ABLE TO EAT.

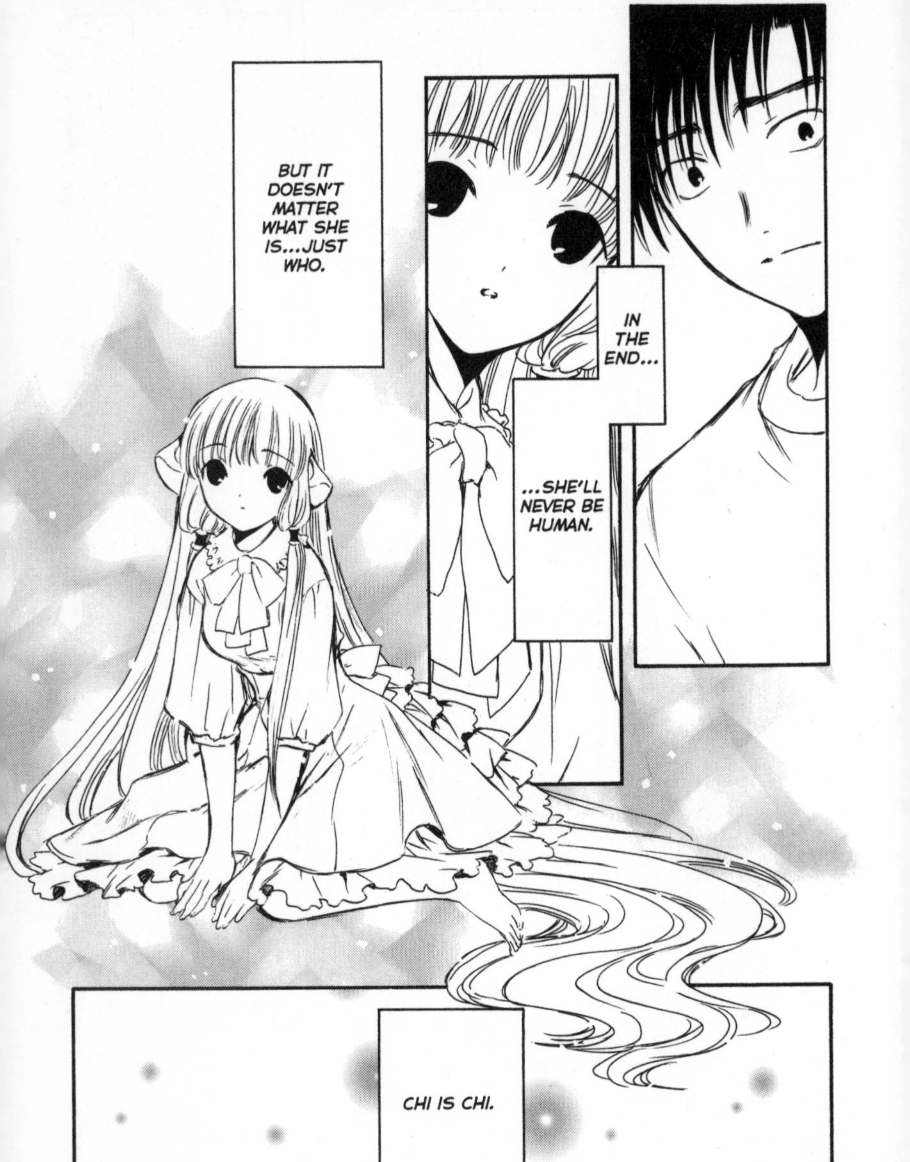
IN THE END...
...SHE'LL NEVER BE HUMAN.
BUT IT DOESN'T MATTER WHAT SHE IS...JUST WHO.
CHI IS CHI.

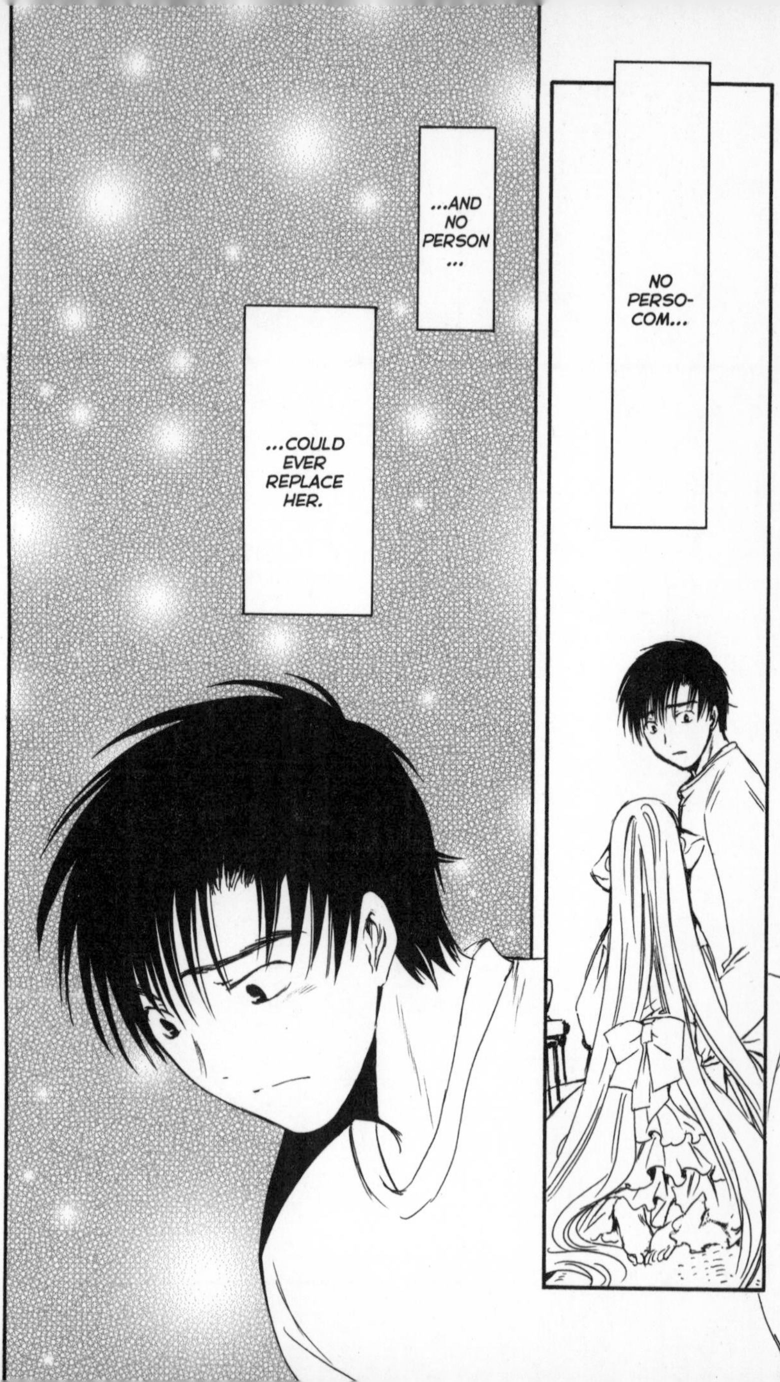
NO PERSO-COM...
...AND NO PERSON ...
...COULD EVER REPLACE HER.

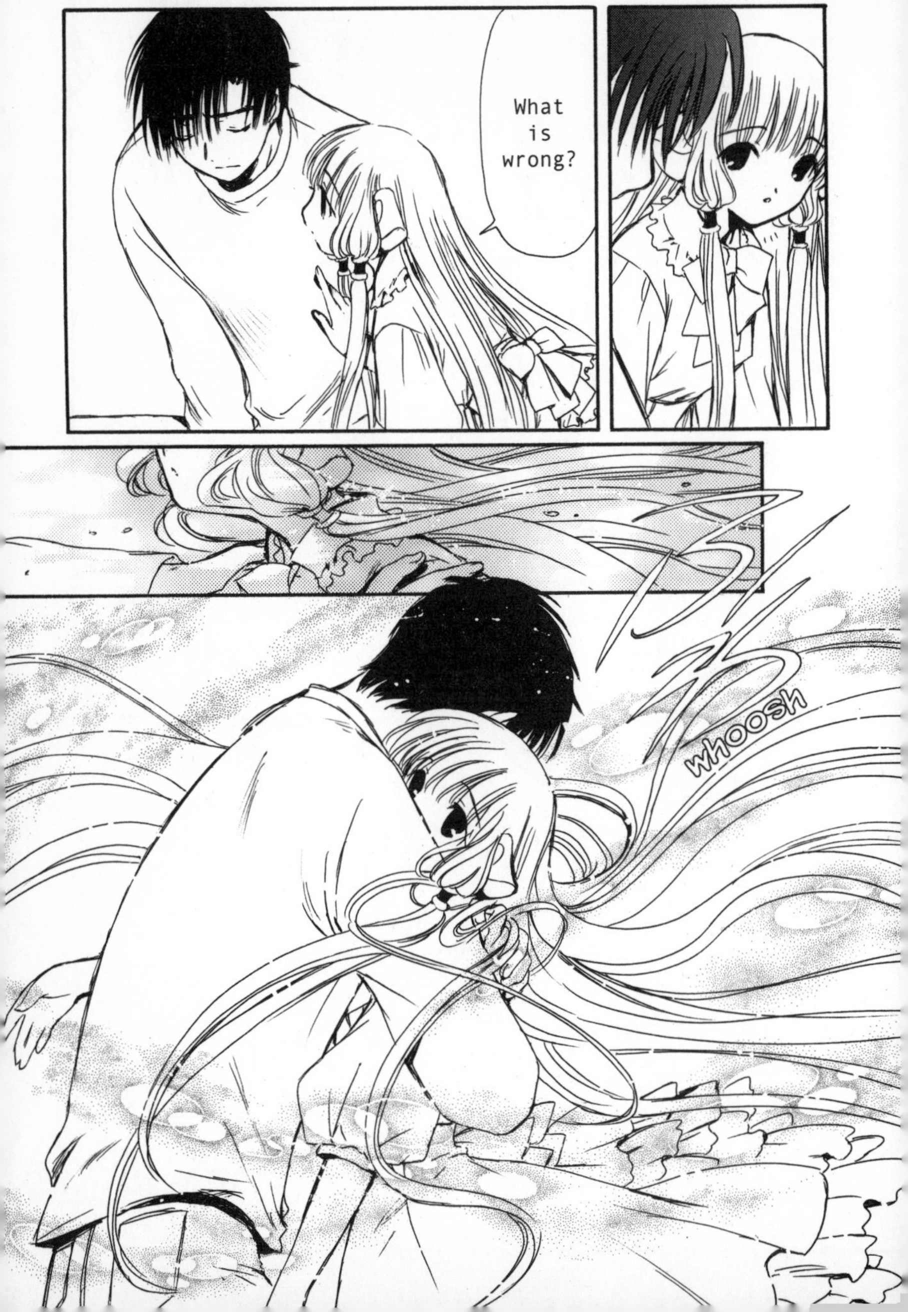
What is wrong?
whoosh

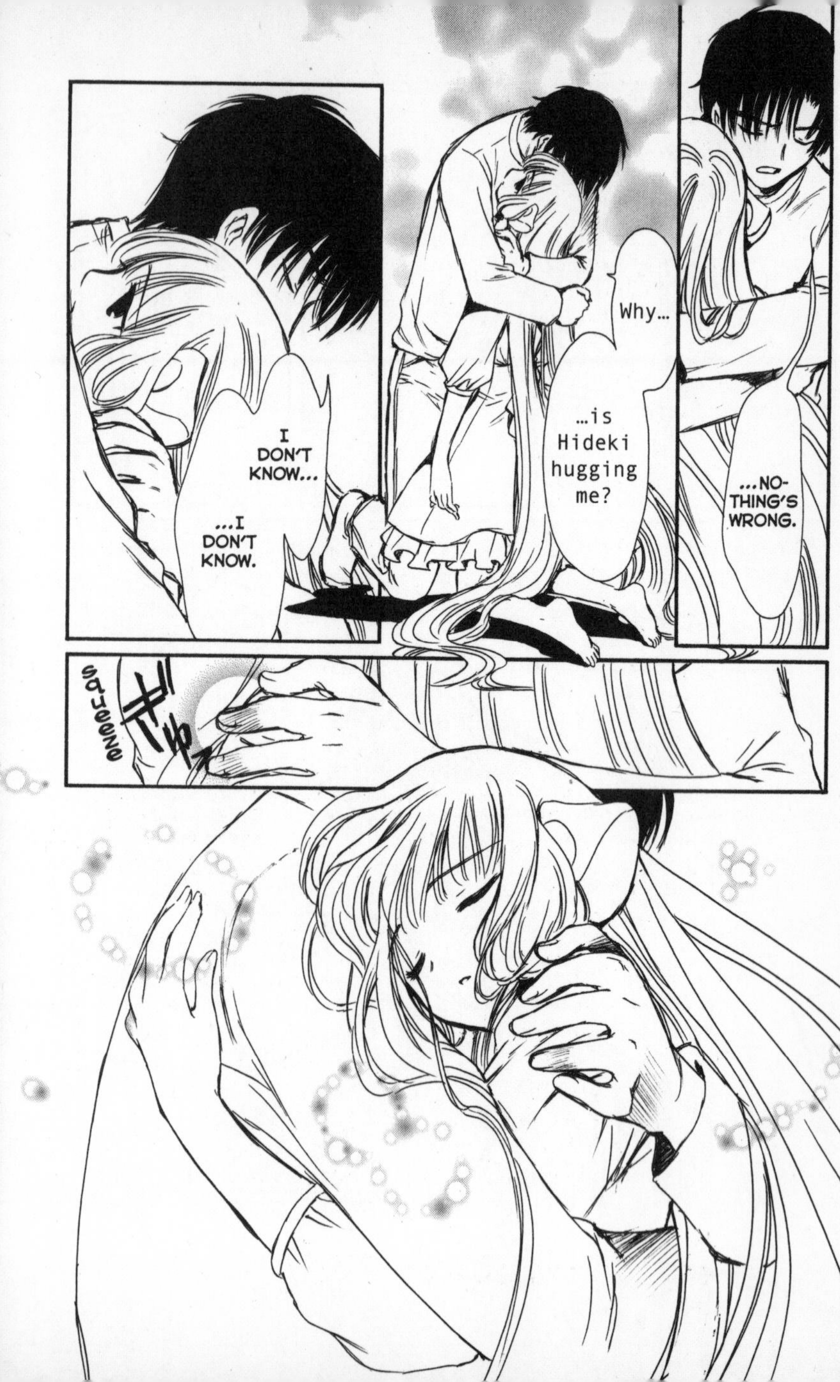
...NO-THING'S WRONG.
Why...
...is Hideki hugging me?
I DON'T KNOW...
...I DON'T KNOW.
squeeze

Chobits
ちょびっツ

◀ **chapter 72** ▶

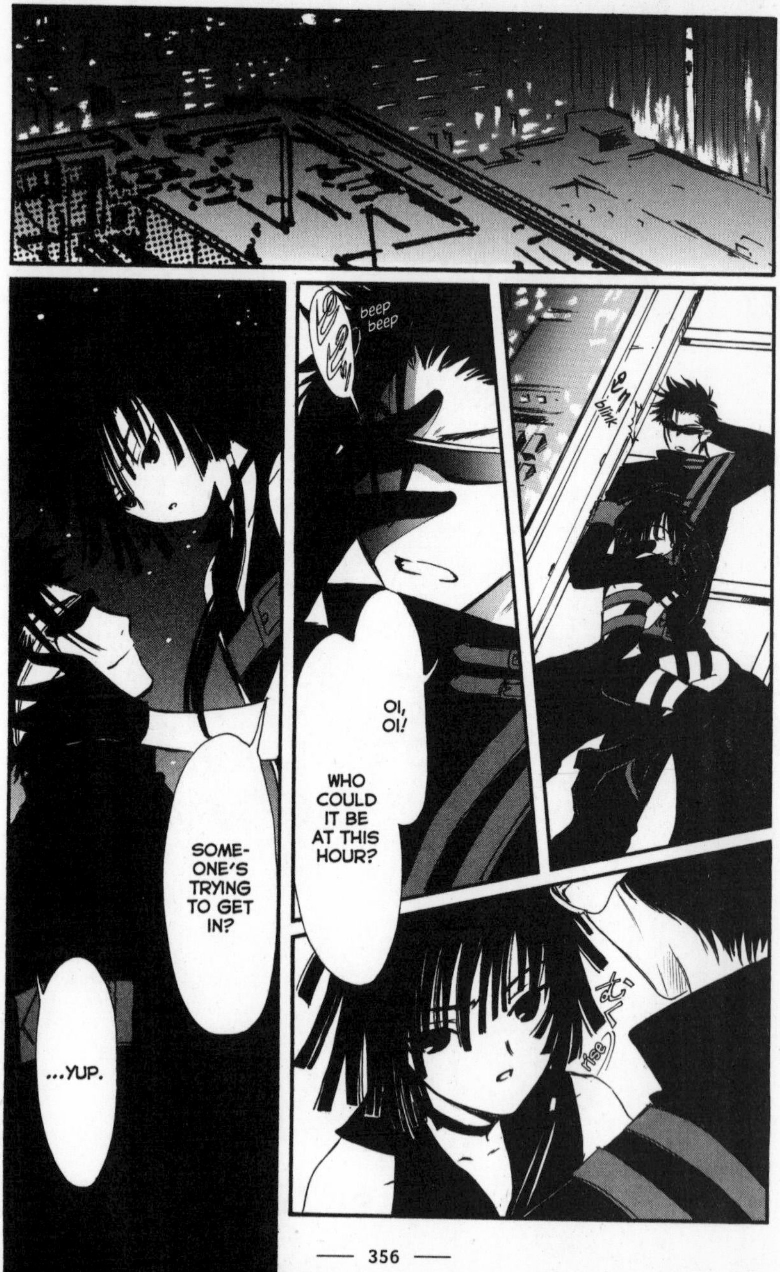
blink
beep beep
OI, OI!
WHO COULD IT BE AT THIS HOUR?
rise
SOME-ONE'S TRYING TO GET IN?
...YUP.

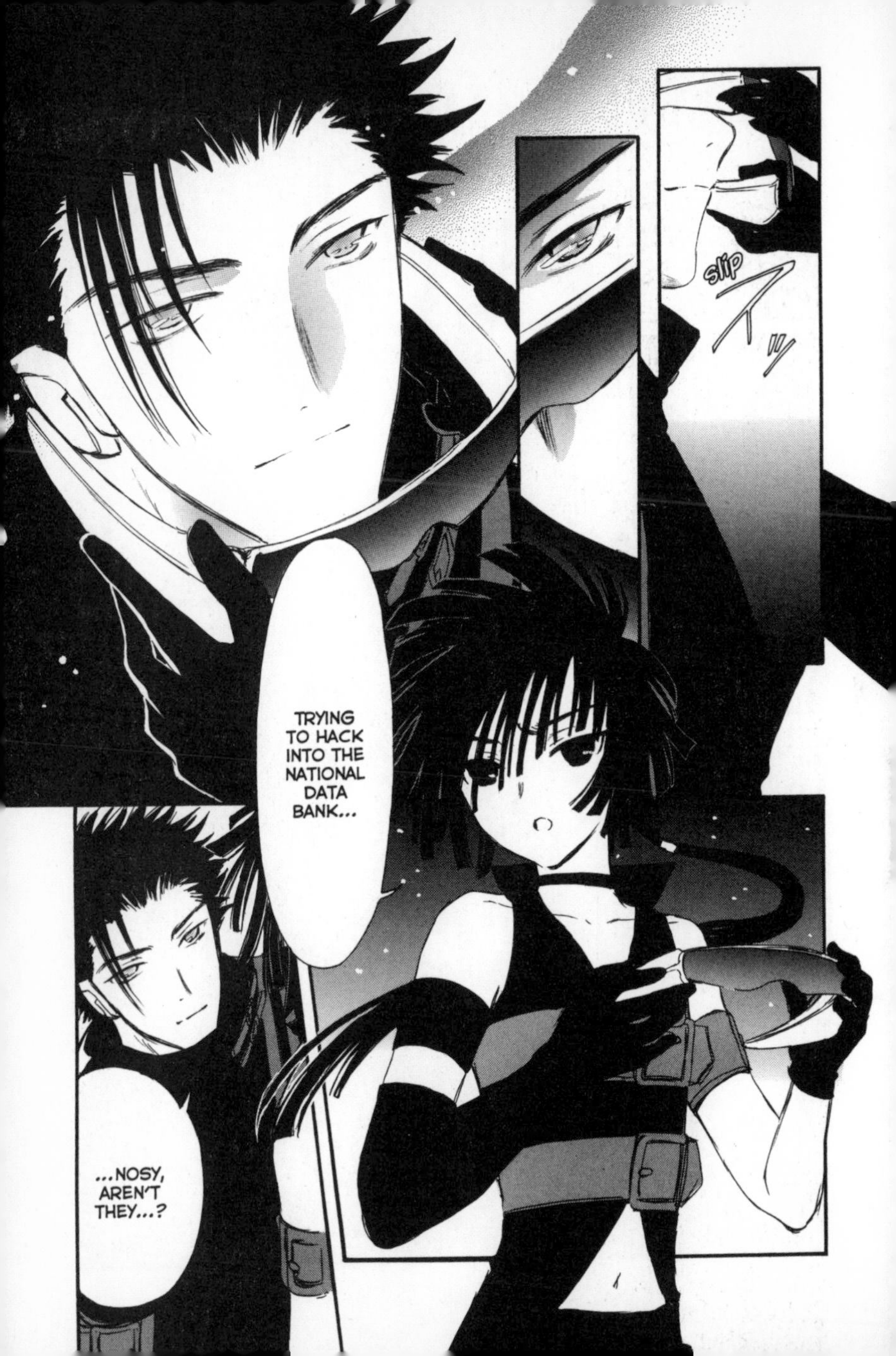
slip
TRYING TO HACK INTO THE NATIONAL DATA BANK...
...NOSY, AREN'T THEY...?

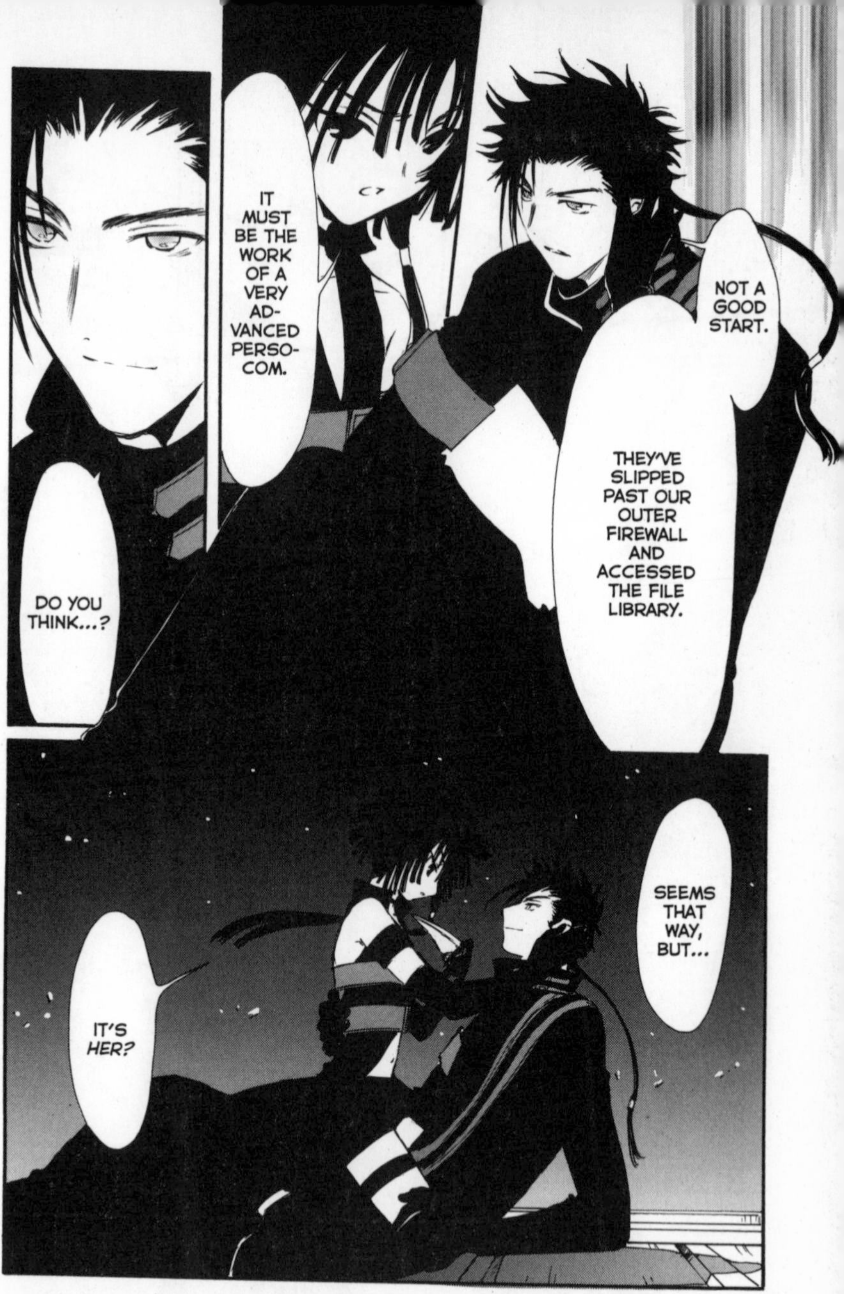
NOT A GOOD START.
THEY'VE SLIPPED PAST OUR OUTER FIREWALL AND ACCESSED THE FILE LIBRARY.
IT MUST BE THE WORK OF A VERY AD-VANCED PERSO-COM.
DO YOU THINK...?
SEEMS THAT WAY, BUT...
IT'S HER?

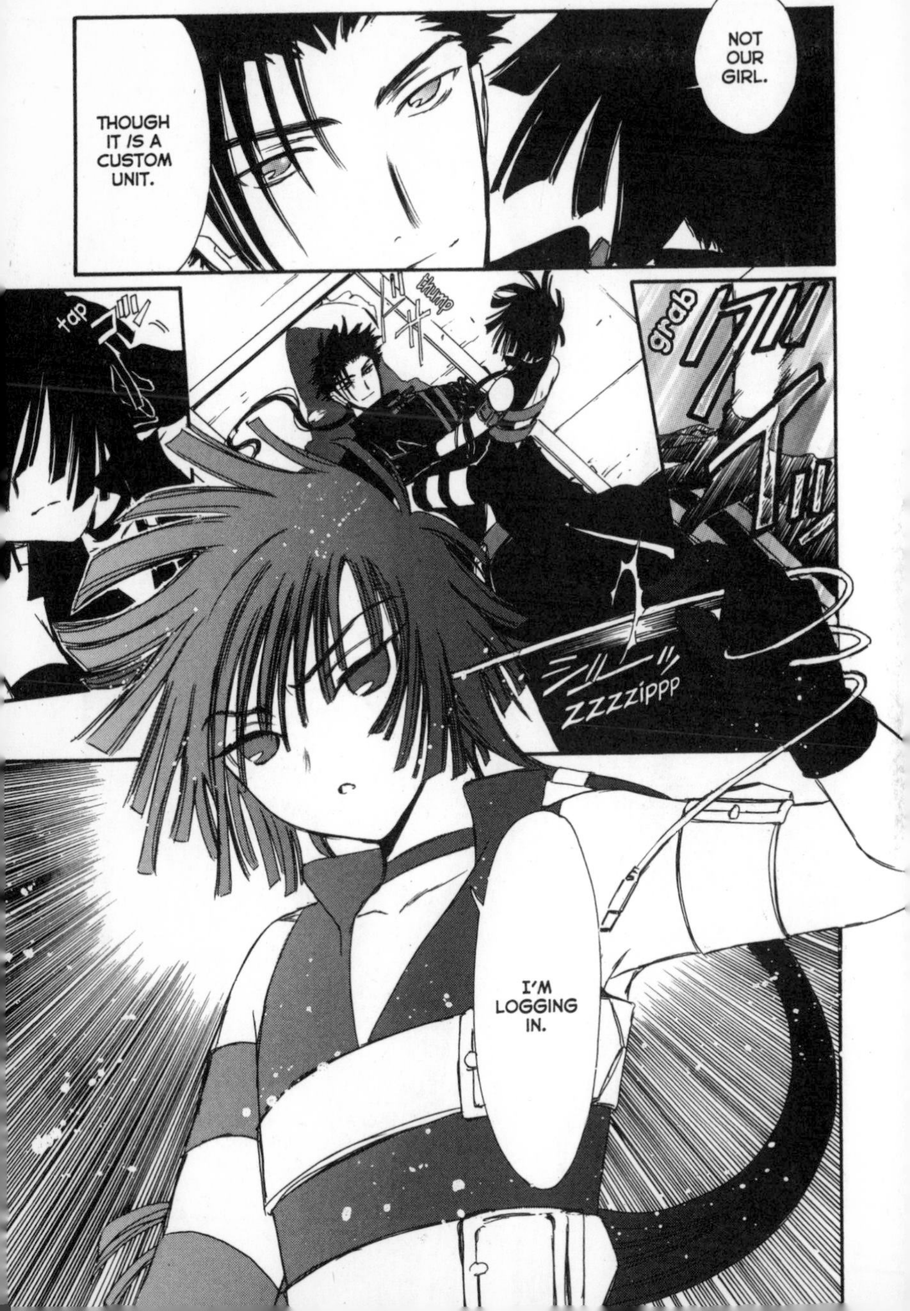
NOT OUR GIRL.
THOUGH IT IS A CUSTOM UNIT.
grab
thump
tap
ZZZZippp
I'M LOGGING IN.

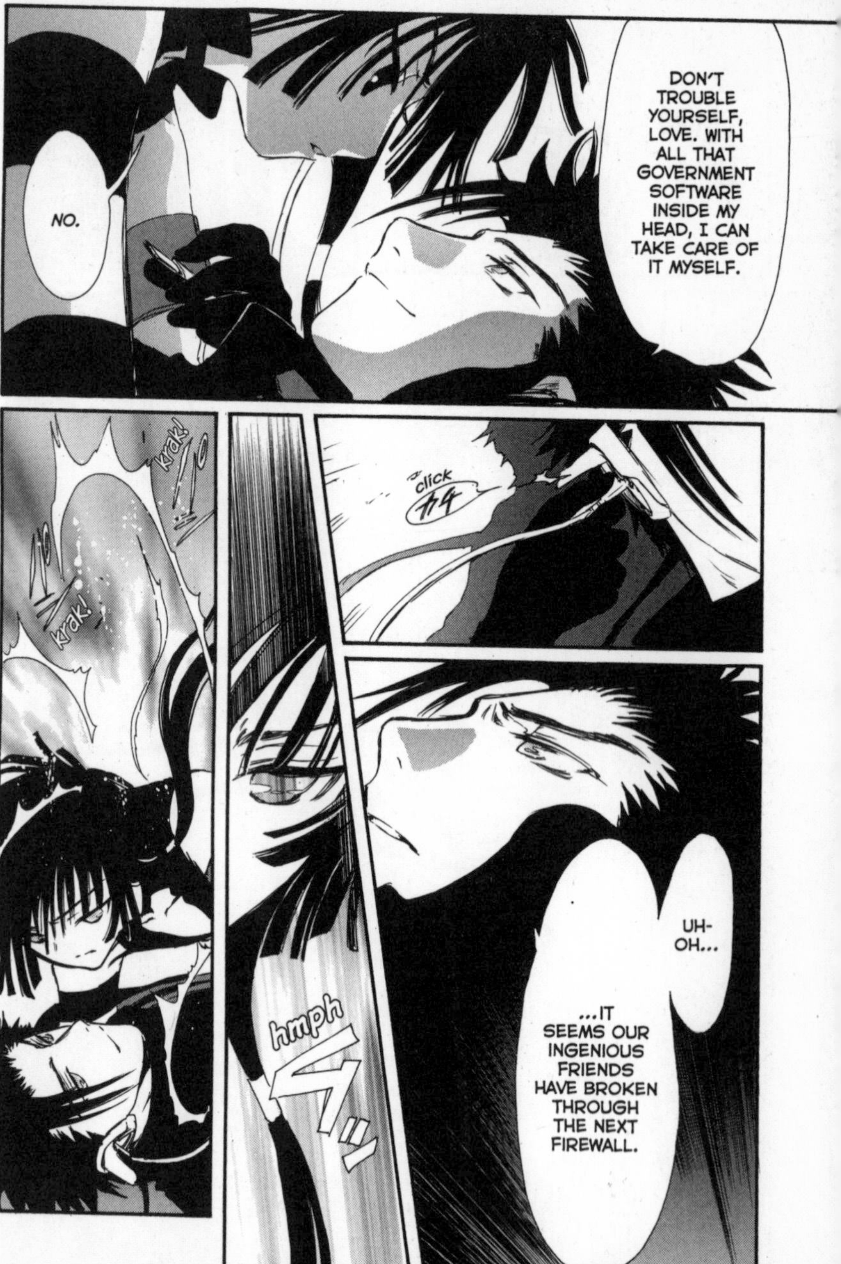
DON'T TROUBLE YOURSELF, LOVE. WITH ALL THAT GOVERNMENT SOFTWARE INSIDE MY HEAD, I CAN TAKE CARE OF IT MYSELF.
NO.
click
カチ
UH-OH...
...IT SEEMS OUR INGENIOUS FRIENDS HAVE BROKEN THROUGH THE NEXT FIREWALL.
hmph
krak!
krak!

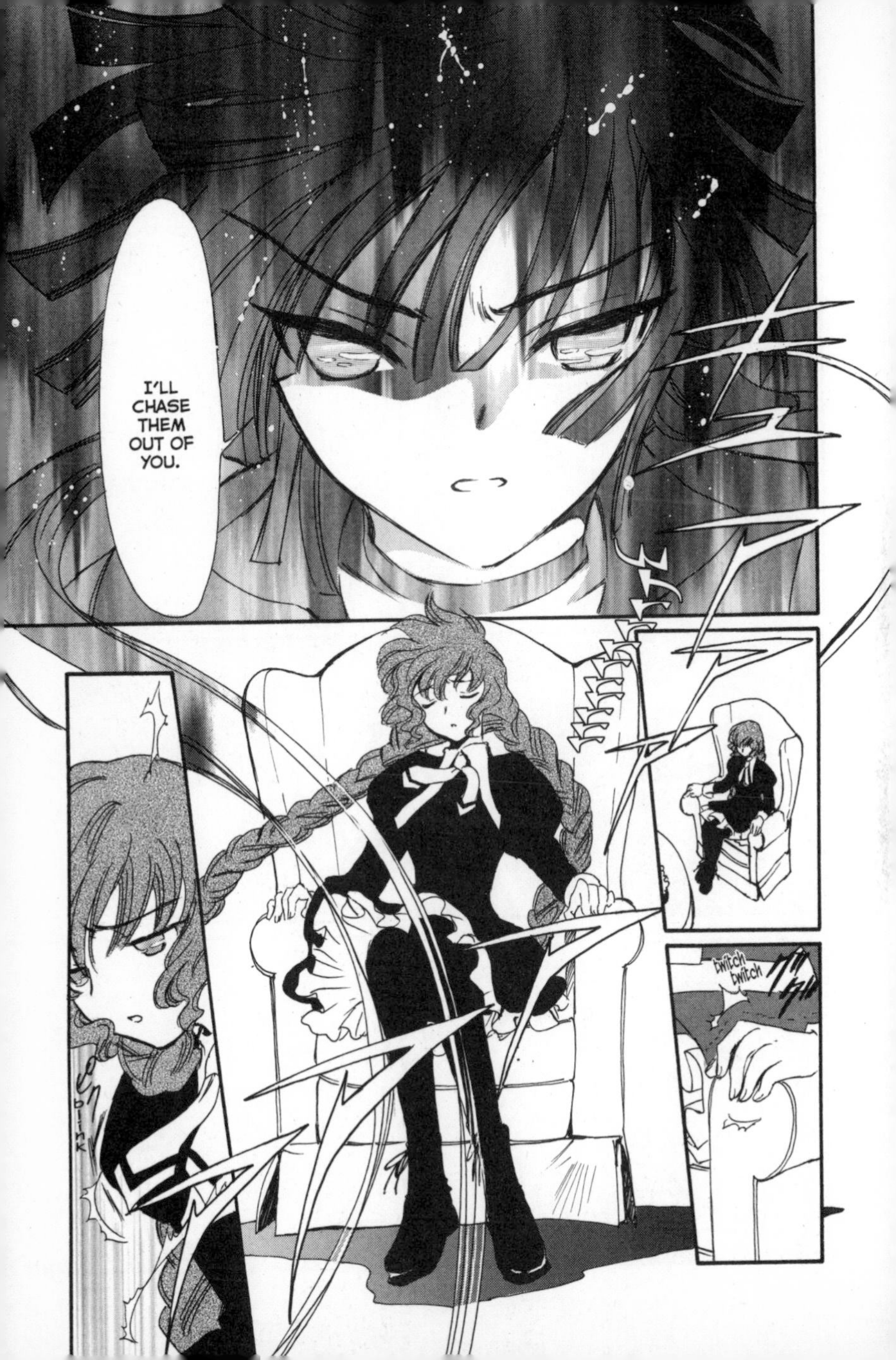
I'LL CHASE THEM OUT OF YOU.
twitch twitch
blink

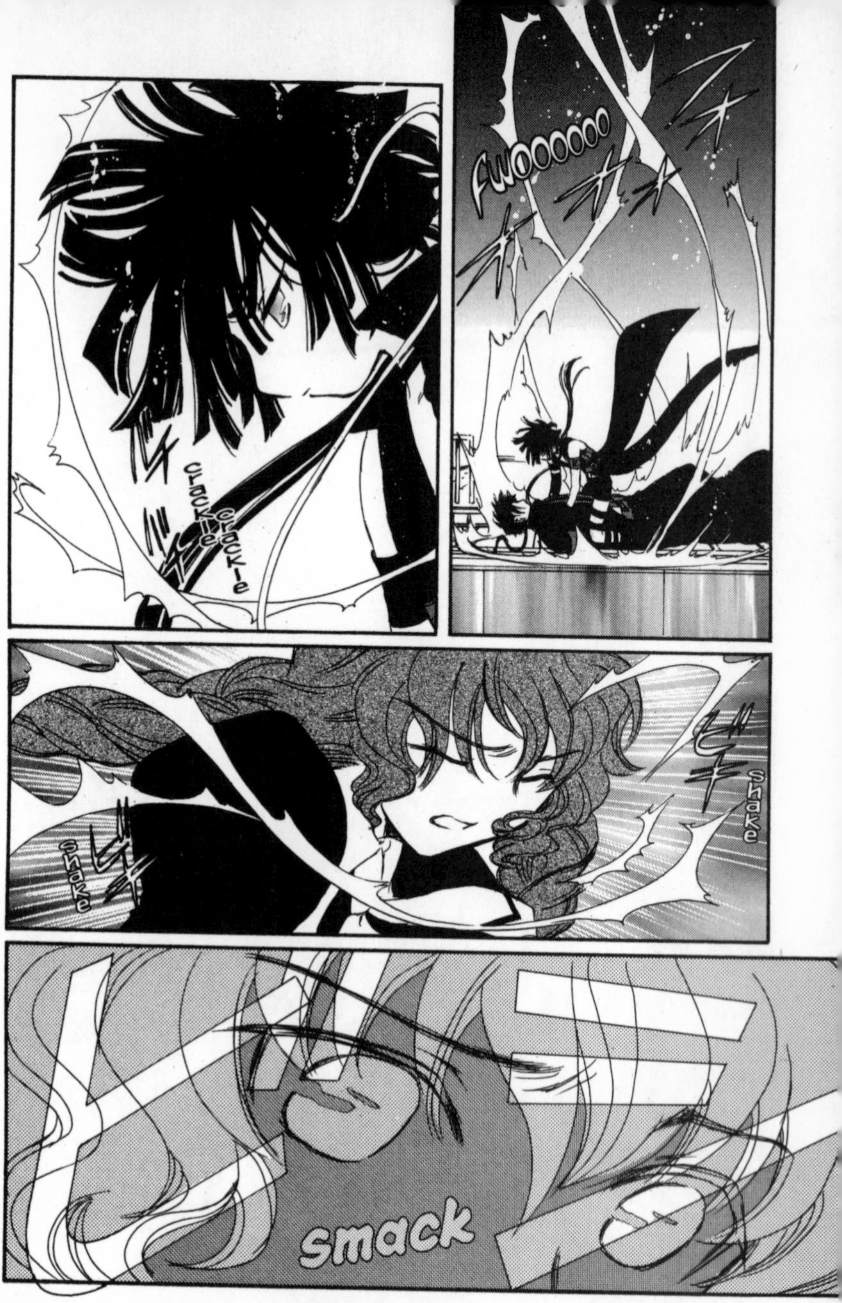
FWOOOOOO
crackle crackle
shake
shake
smack

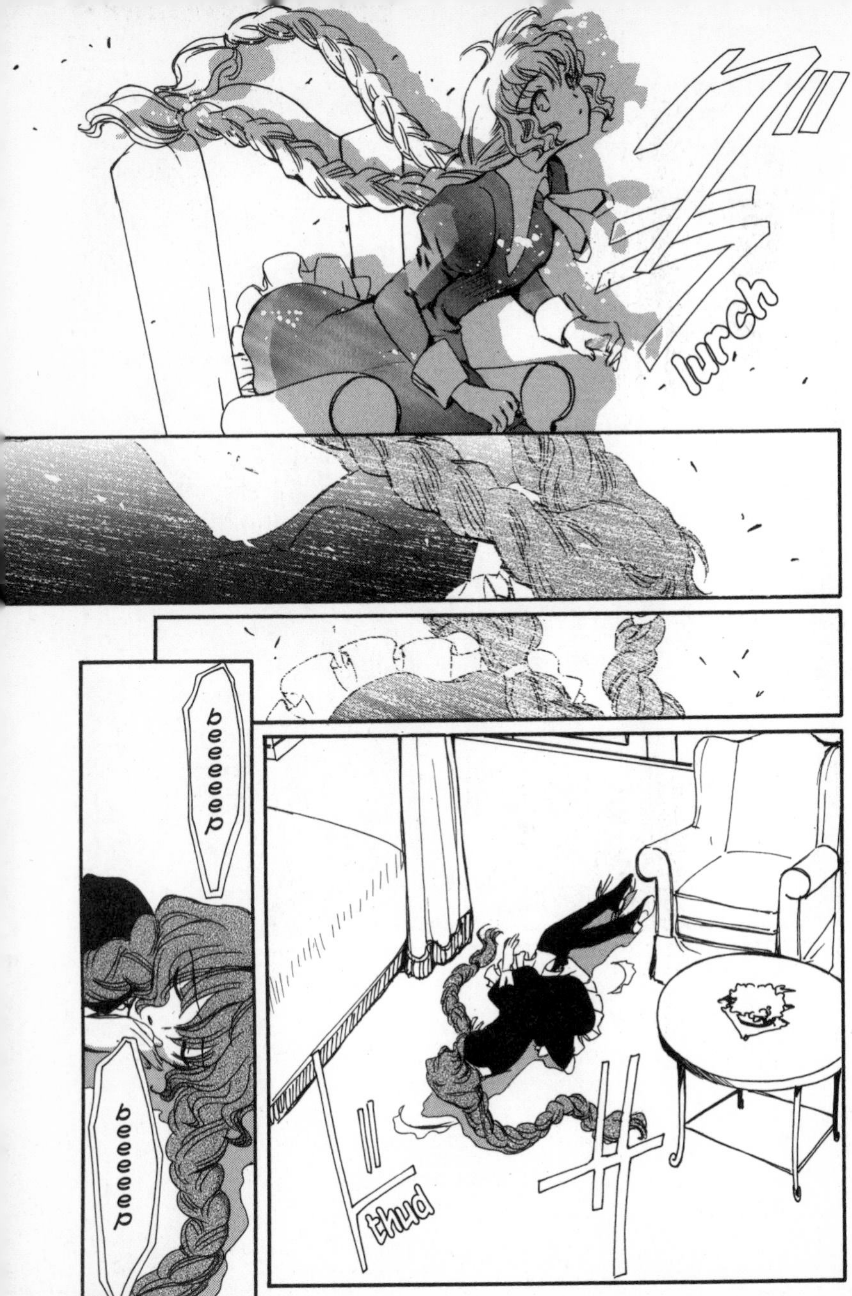
lurch
thud
beeeeep
beeeeep

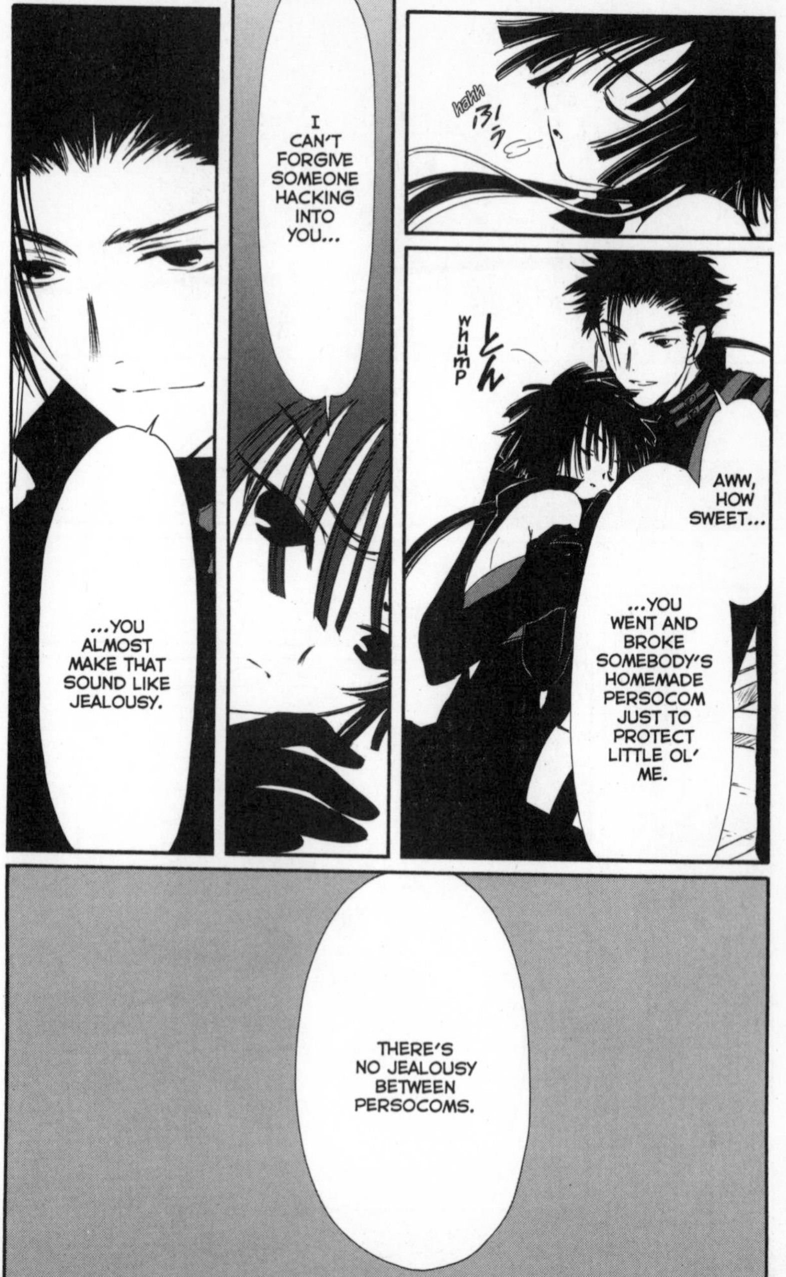
hahh
whump
とん
AWW, HOW SWEET...
...YOU WENT AND BROKE SOMEBODY'S HOMEMADE PERSOCOM JUST TO PROTECT LITTLE OL' ME.
I CAN'T FORGIVE SOMEONE HACKING INTO YOU...
...YOU ALMOST MAKE THAT SOUND LIKE JEALOUSY.
THERE'S NO JEALOUSY BETWEEN PERSOCOMS.

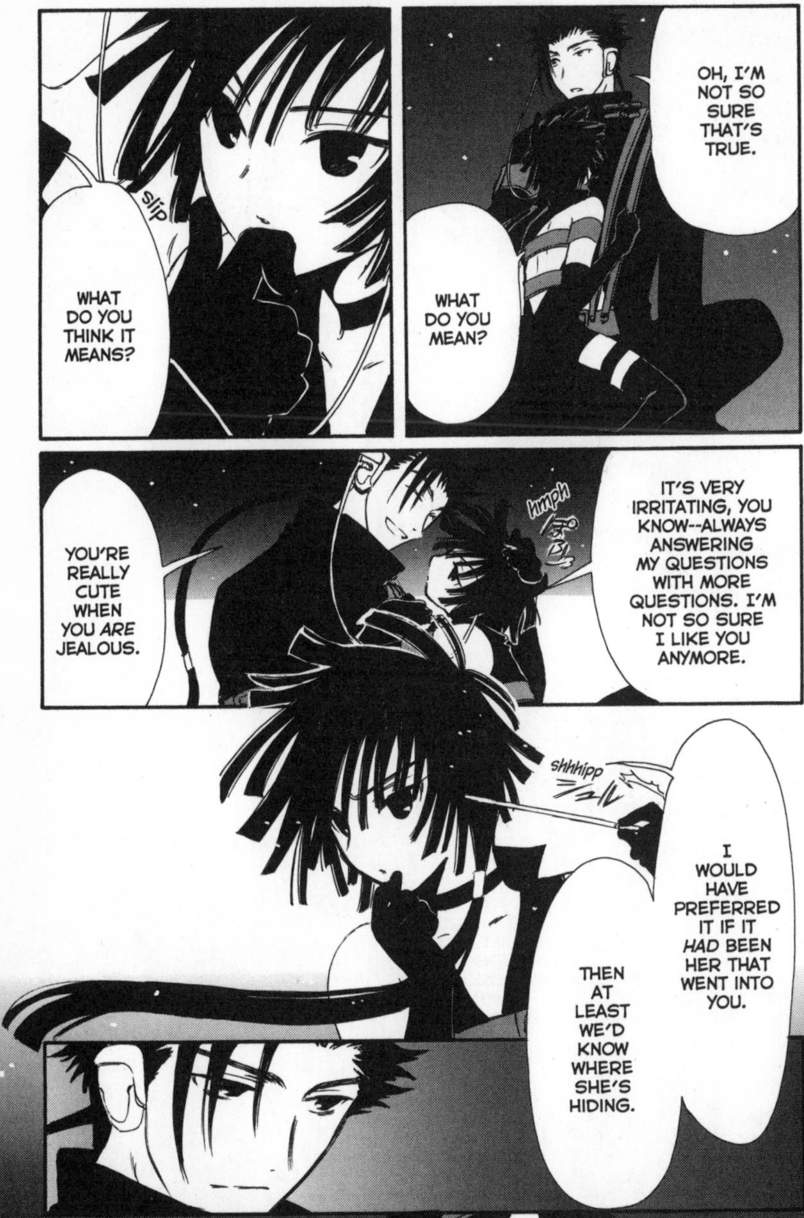
OH, I'M NOT SO SURE THAT'S TRUE.
WHAT DO YOU MEAN?
slip
WHAT DO YOU THINK IT MEANS?
IT'S VERY IRRITATING, YOU KNOW--ALWAYS ANSWERING MY QUESTIONS WITH MORE QUESTIONS. I'M NOT SO SURE I LIKE YOU ANYMORE.
hmph
YOU'RE REALLY CUTE WHEN YOU *ARE* JEALOUS.
shhhipp
I WOULD HAVE PREFERRED IT IF IT *HAD* BEEN HER THAT WENT INTO YOU.
THEN AT LEAST WE'D KNOW WHERE SHE'S HIDING.

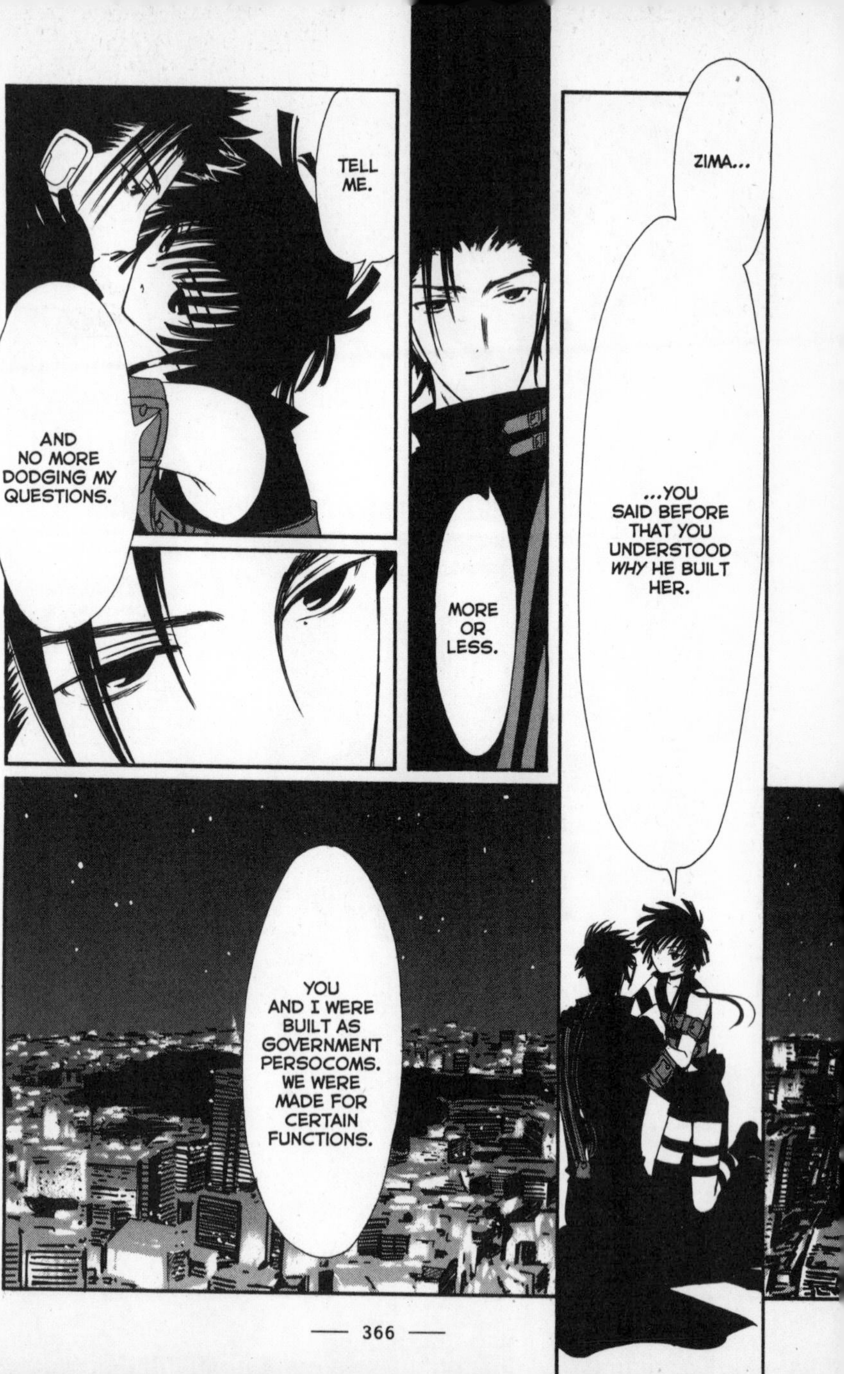
ZIMA...
...YOU SAID BEFORE THAT YOU UNDERSTOOD *WHY* HE BUILT HER.
MORE OR LESS.
TELL ME.
AND NO MORE DODGING MY QUESTIONS.
YOU AND I WERE BUILT AS GOVERNMENT PERSOCOMS. WE WERE MADE FOR CERTAIN FUNCTIONS.

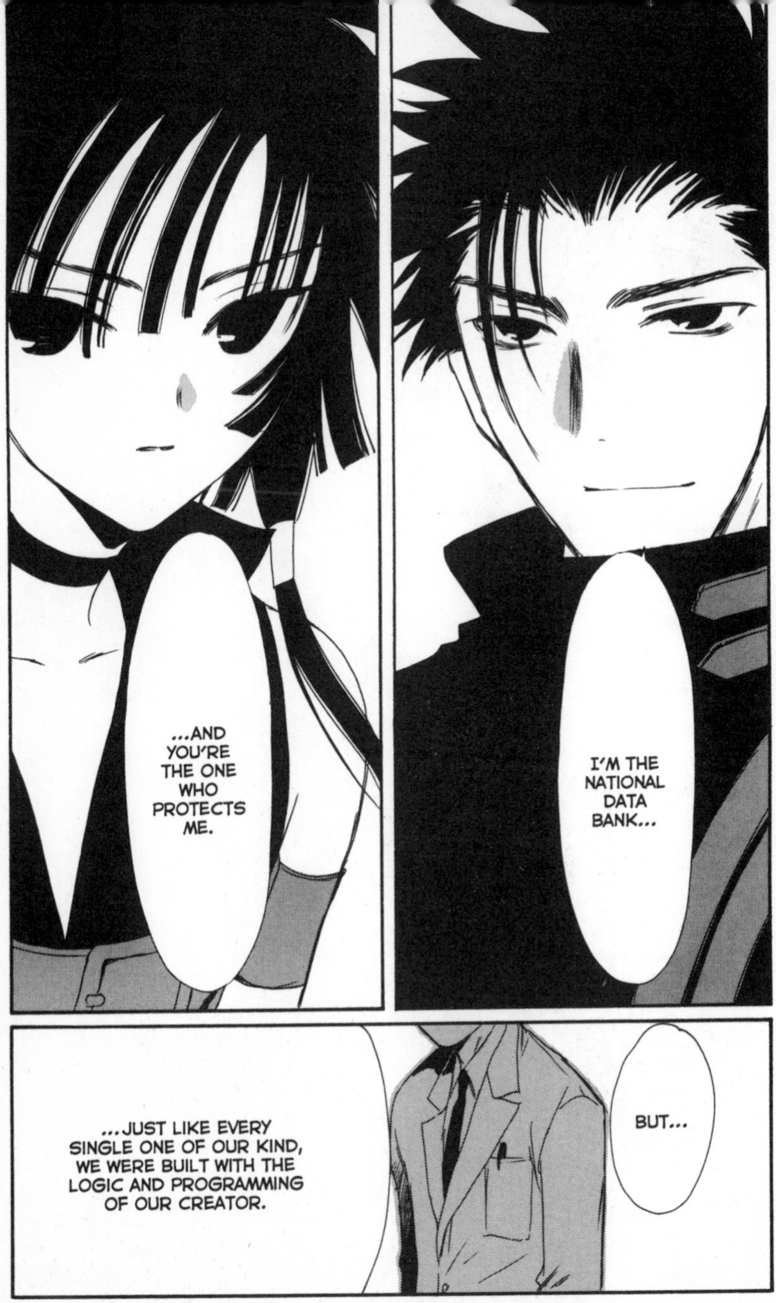
I'M THE NATIONAL DATA BANK...
...AND YOU'RE THE ONE WHO PROTECTS ME.
BUT...
...JUST LIKE EVERY SINGLE ONE OF OUR KIND, WE WERE BUILT WITH THE LOGIC AND PROGRAMMING OF OUR CREATOR.

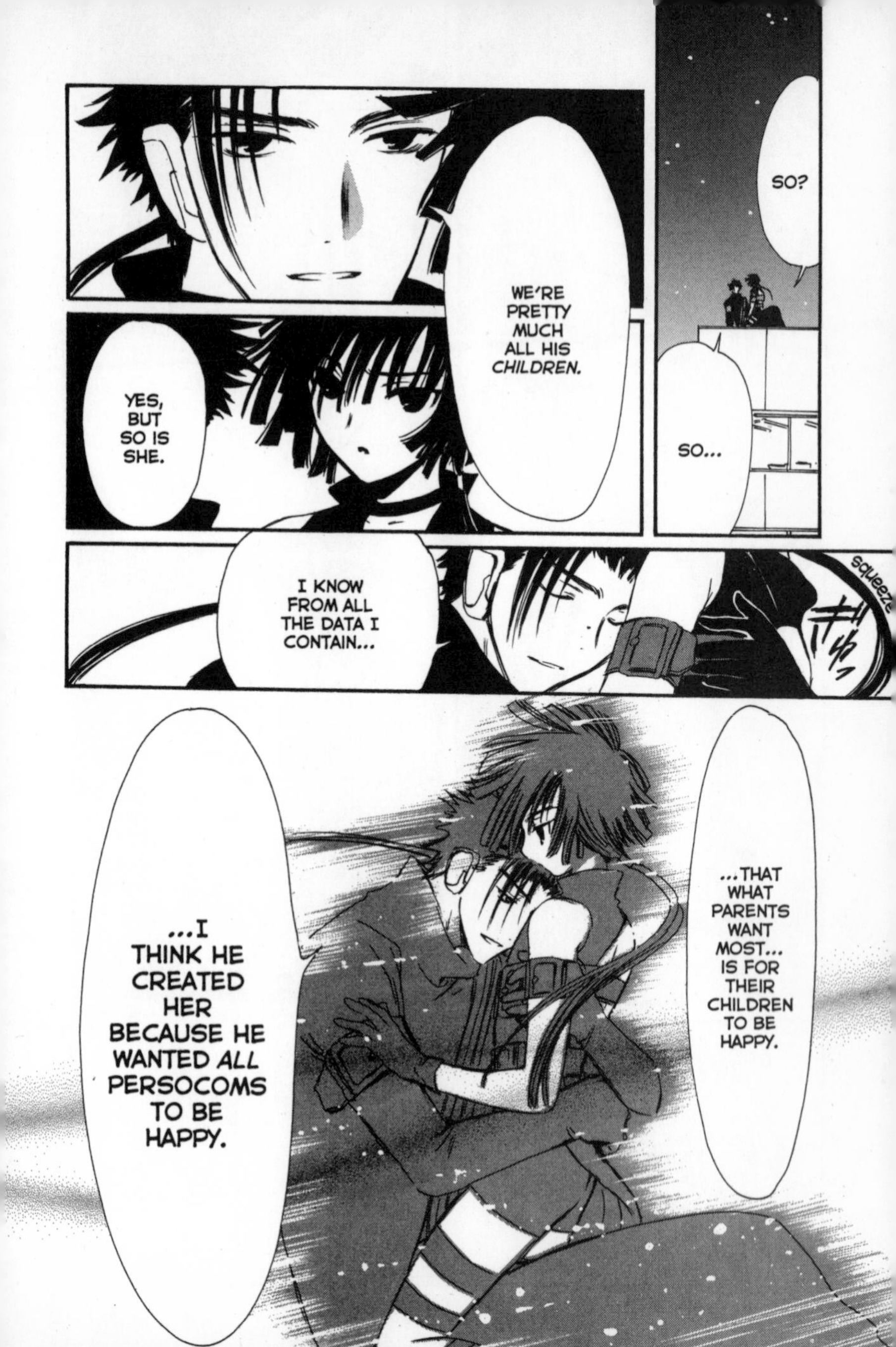
SO?
SO...
WE'RE PRETTY MUCH ALL HIS *CHILDREN.*
YES, BUT SO IS SHE.
I KNOW FROM ALL THE DATA I CONTAIN...
squeeze
...THAT WHAT PARENTS WANT MOST... IS FOR THEIR CHILDREN TO BE HAPPY.
...I THINK HE CREATED HER BECAUSE HE WANTED *ALL* PERSOCOMS TO BE HAPPY.

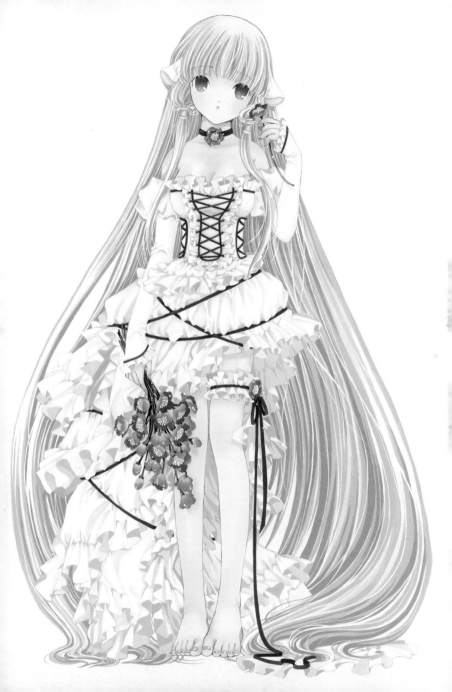

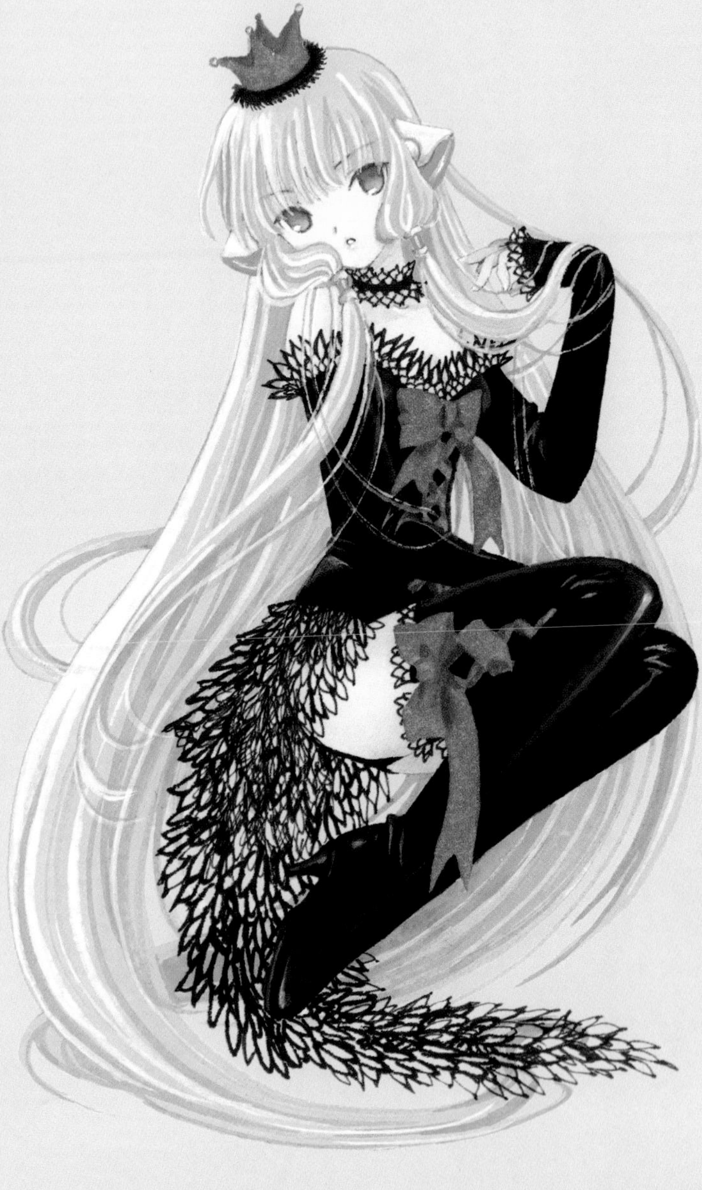

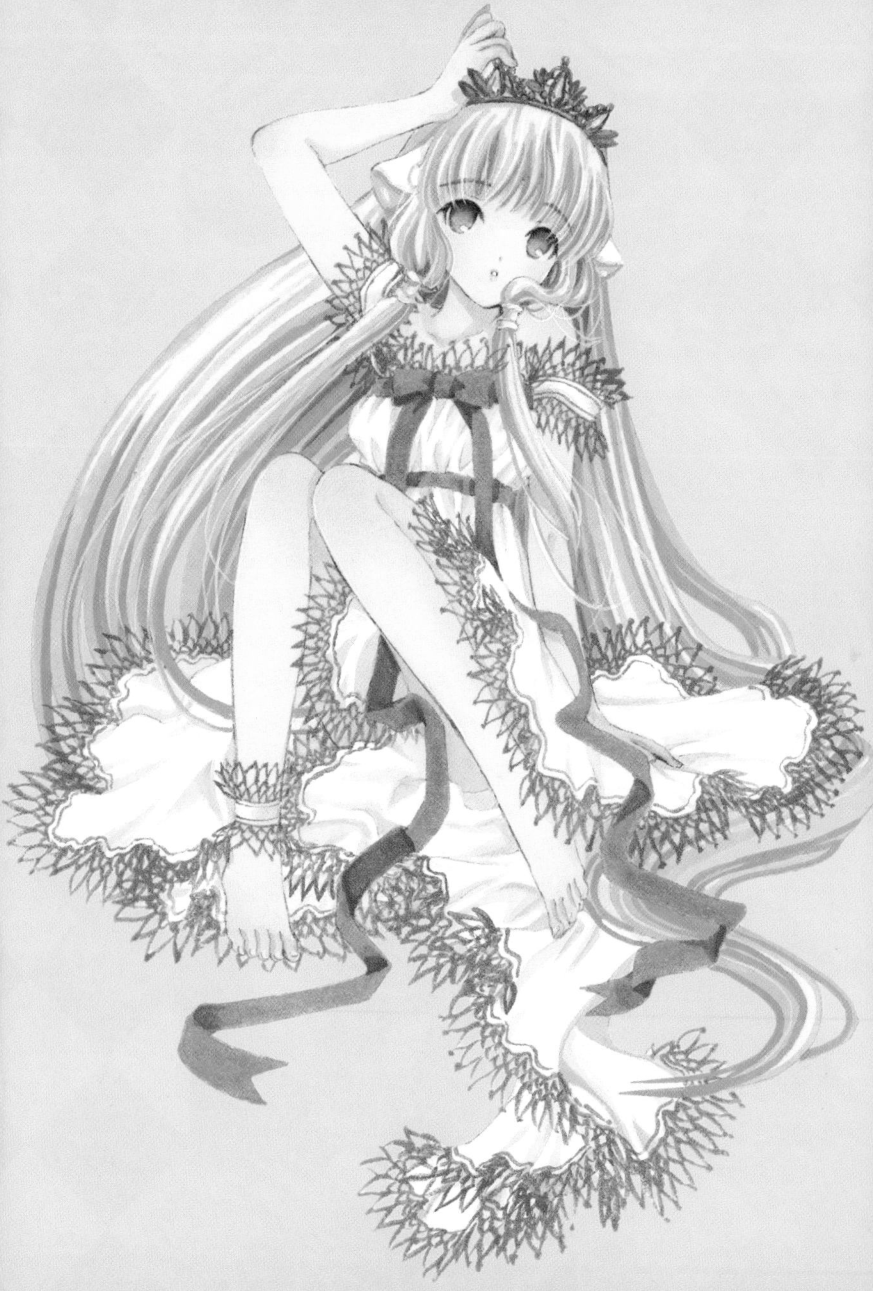

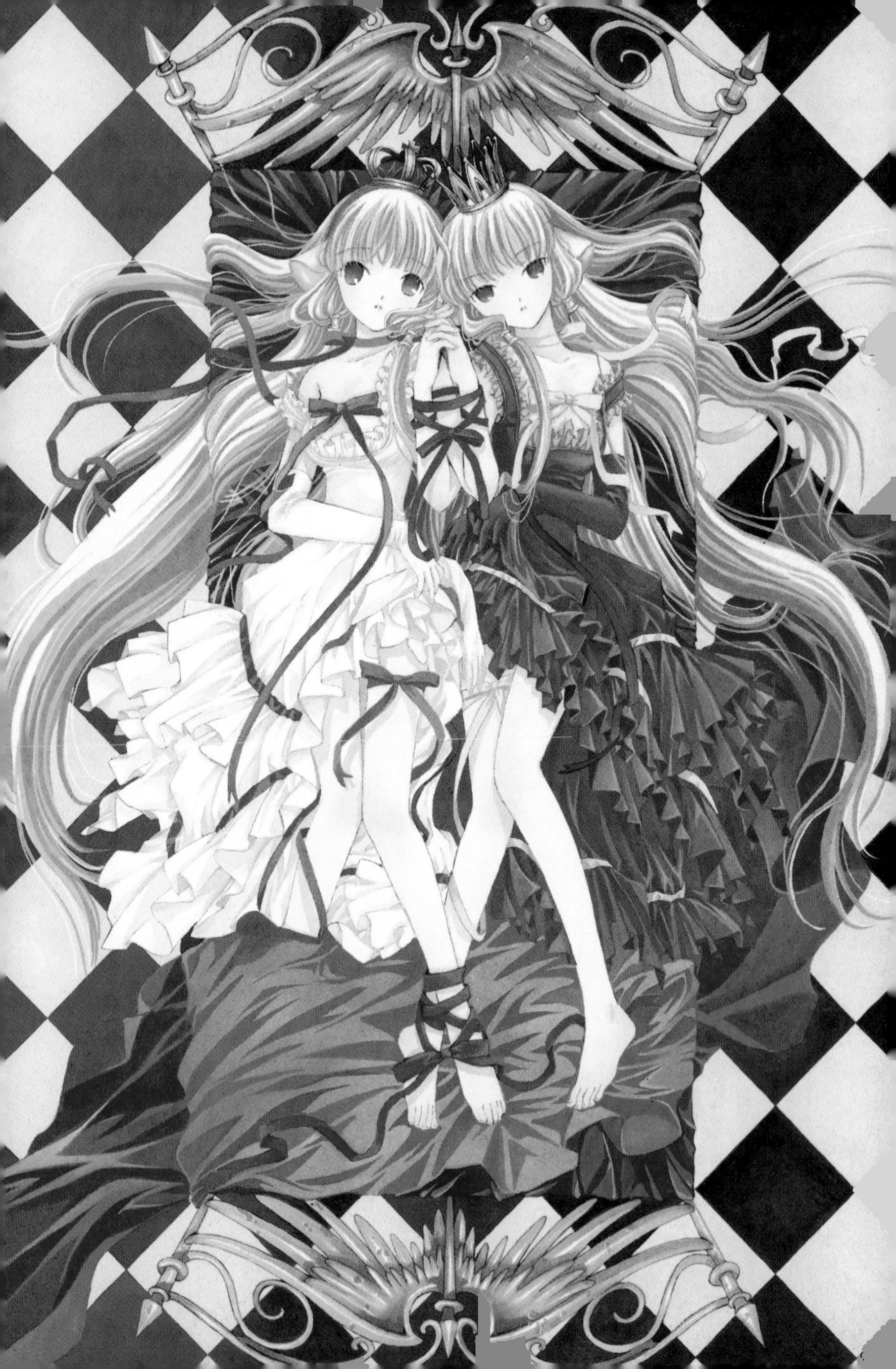

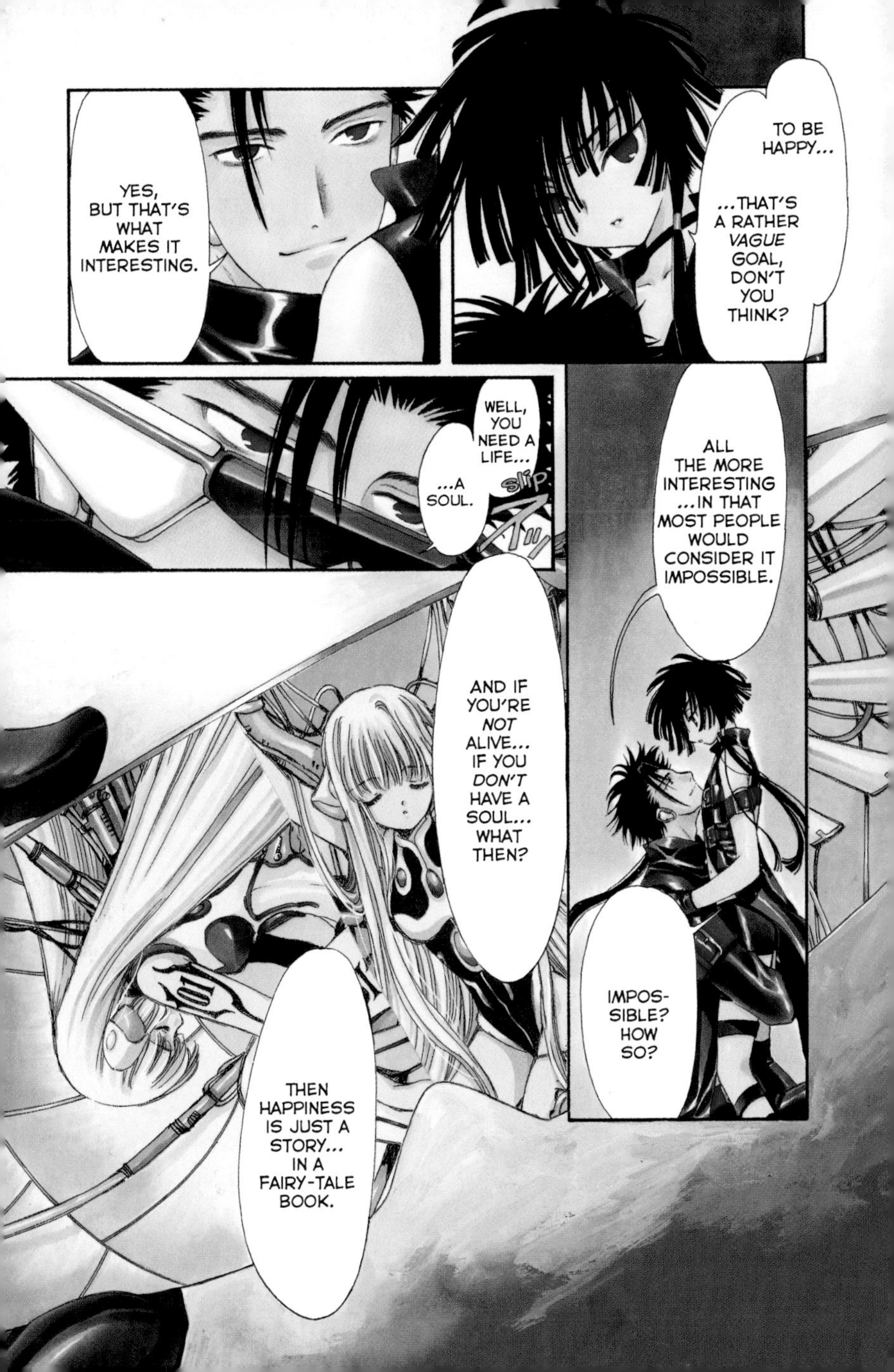
TO BE HAPPY...
...THAT'S A RATHER *VAGUE* GOAL, DON'T YOU THINK?
YES, BUT THAT'S WHAT MAKES IT INTERESTING.
ALL THE MORE INTERESTING ...IN THAT MOST PEOPLE WOULD CONSIDER IT IMPOSSIBLE.
IMPOS-SIBLE? HOW SO?
WELL, YOU NEED A LIFE...
...A SOUL.
slip
AND IF YOU'RE *NOT* ALIVE... IF YOU *DON'T* HAVE A SOUL... WHAT THEN?
THEN HAPPINESS IS JUST A STORY... IN A FAIRY-TALE BOOK.

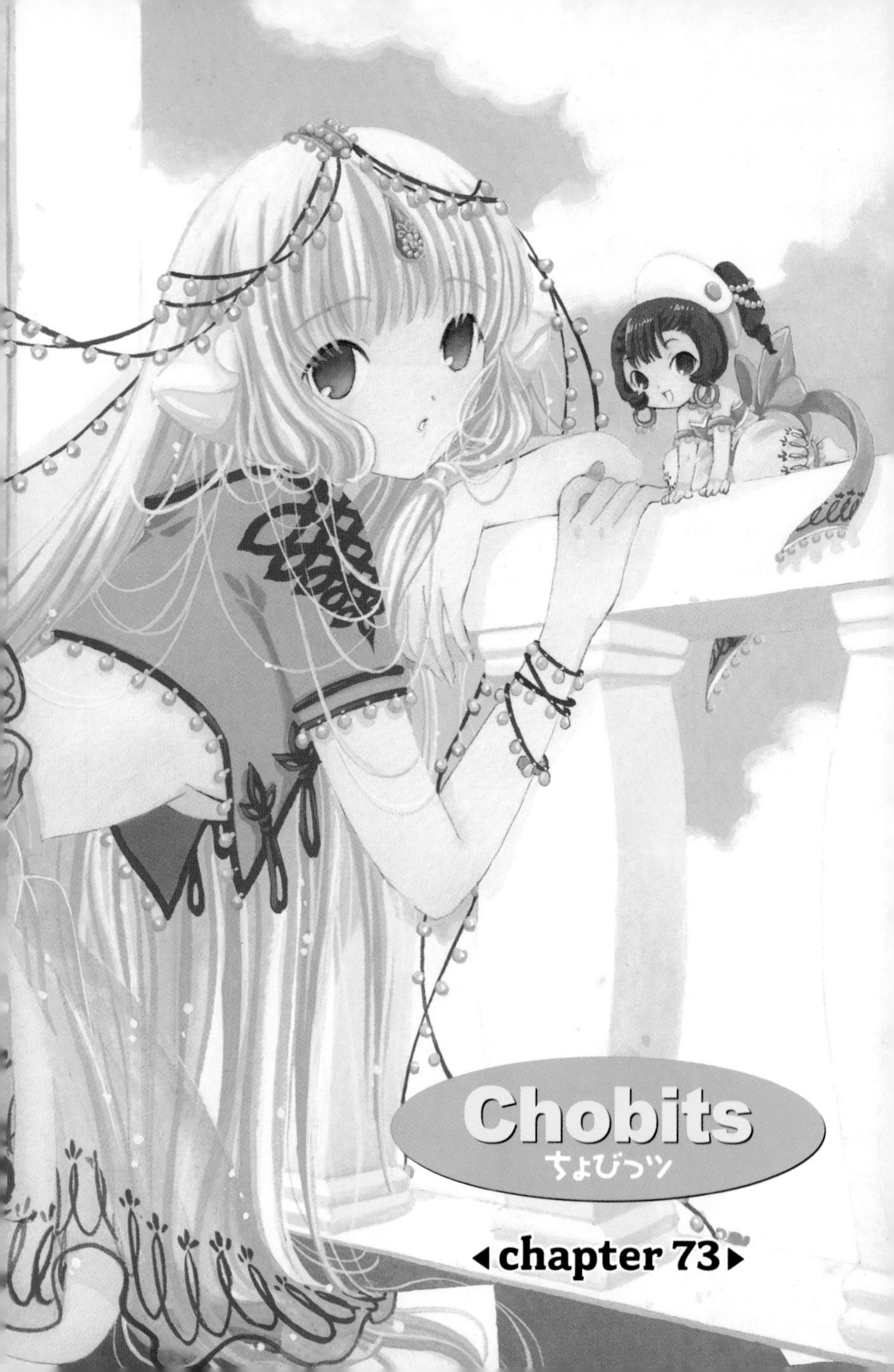
Chobits
ちょびっツ
chapter 73

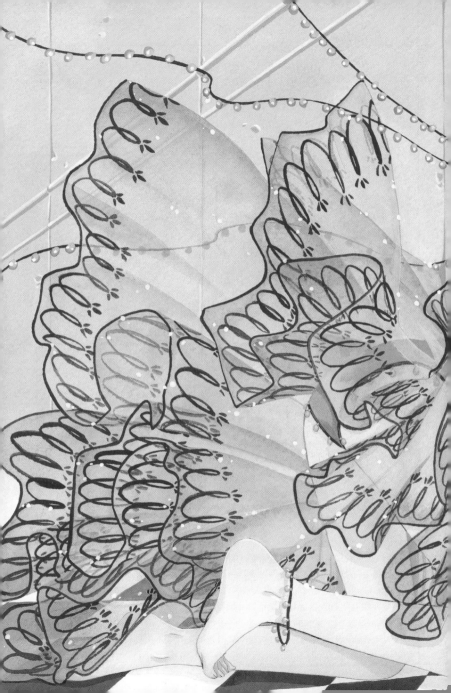

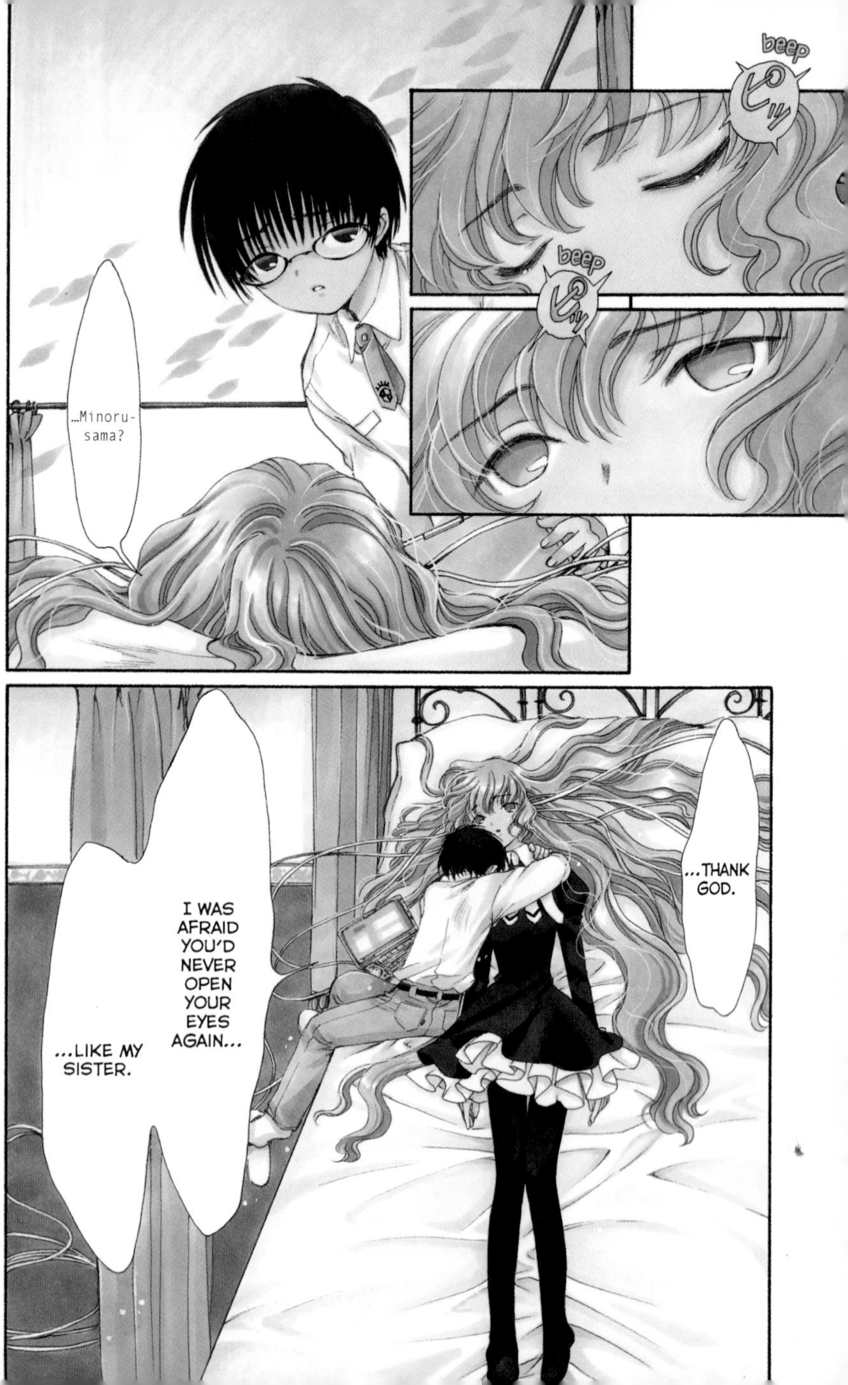
beep
ピッ
beep
ピッ
...Minoru-sama?
...THANK GOD.
I WAS AFRAID YOU'D NEVER OPEN YOUR EYES AGAIN...
...LIKE MY SISTER.

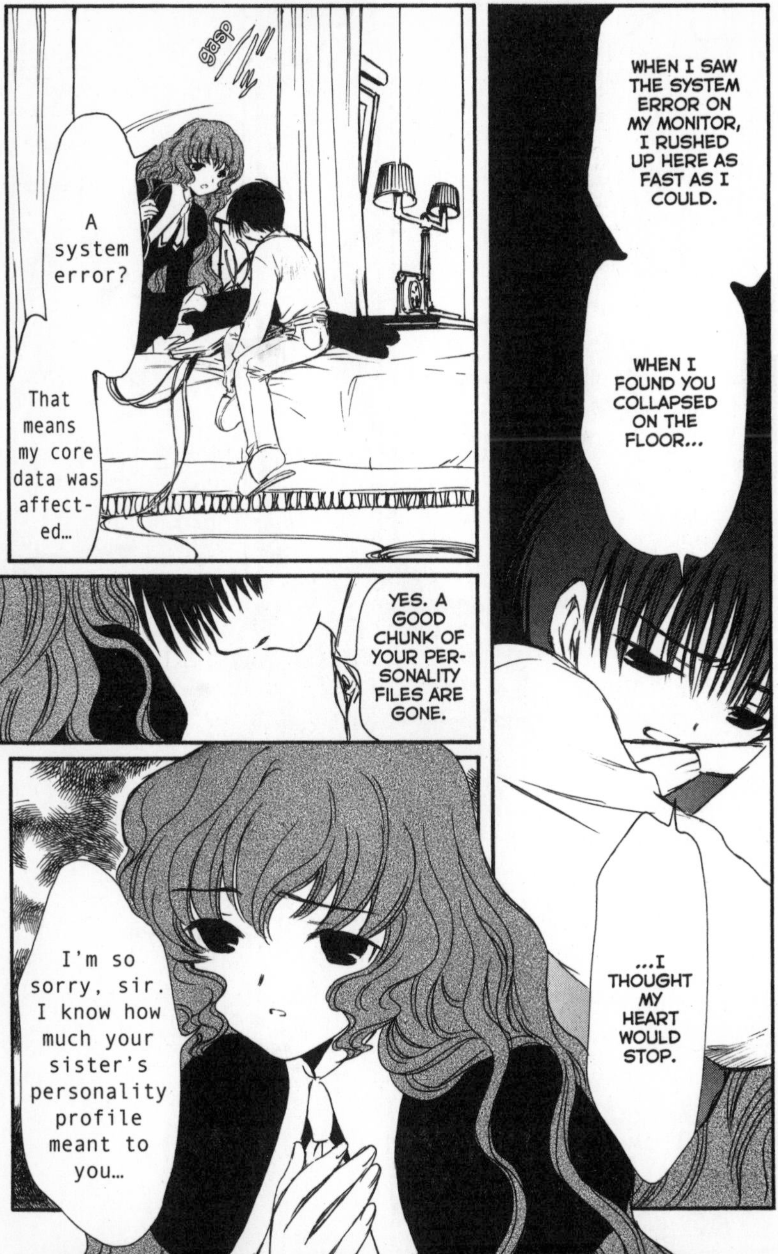
WHEN I SAW THE SYSTEM ERROR ON MY MONITOR, I RUSHED UP HERE AS FAST AS I COULD.
WHEN I FOUND YOU COLLAPSED ON THE FLOOR...
...I THOUGHT MY HEART WOULD STOP.
gasp
A system error?
That means my core data was affect-ed...
YES. A GOOD CHUNK OF YOUR PER-SONALITY FILES ARE GONE.
I'm so sorry, sir. I know how much your sister's personality profile meant to you...

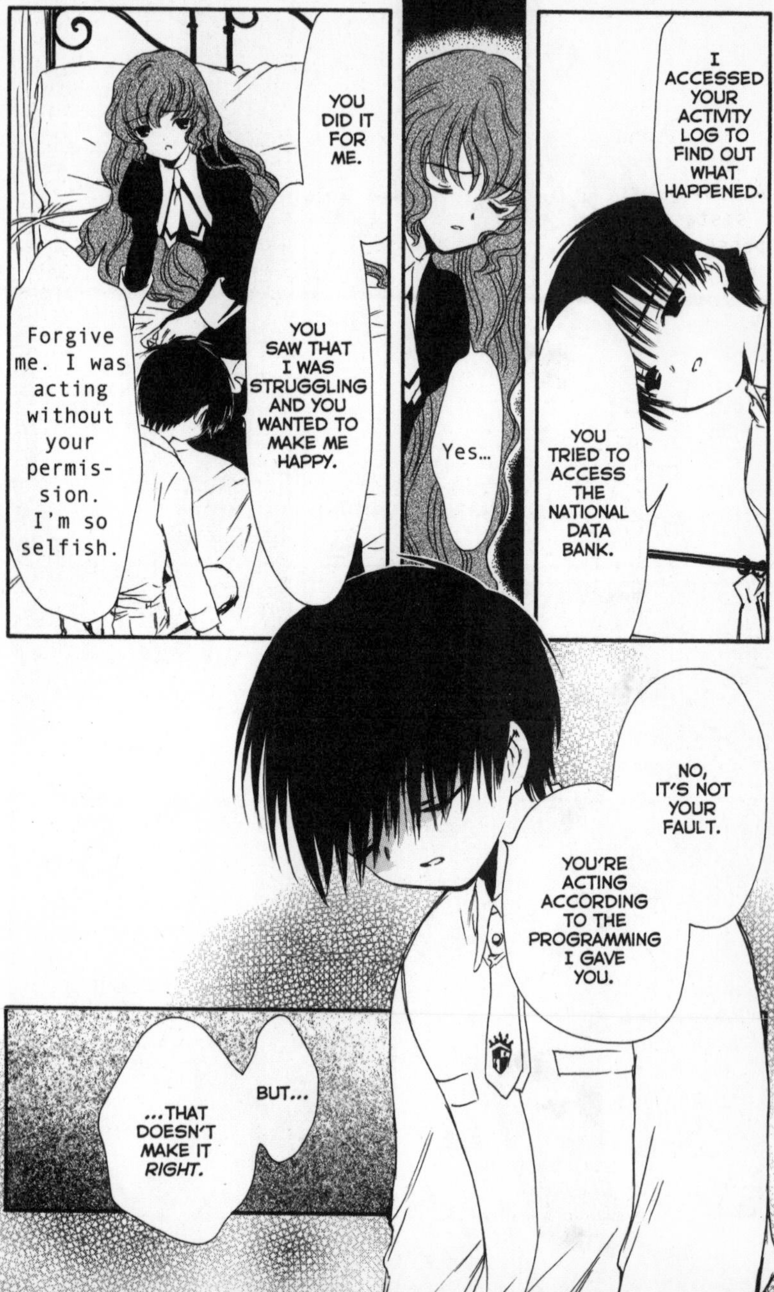
I ACCESSED YOUR ACTIVITY LOG TO FIND OUT WHAT HAPPENED.
YOU TRIED TO ACCESS THE NATIONAL DATA BANK.
Yes…
YOU DID IT FOR ME.
YOU SAW THAT I WAS STRUGGLING AND YOU WANTED TO MAKE ME HAPPY.
Forgive me. I was acting without your permis-sion. I'm so selfish.
NO, IT'S NOT YOUR FAULT.
YOU'RE ACTING ACCORDING TO THE PROGRAMMING I GAVE YOU.
BUT...
...THAT DOESN'T MAKE IT *RIGHT*.

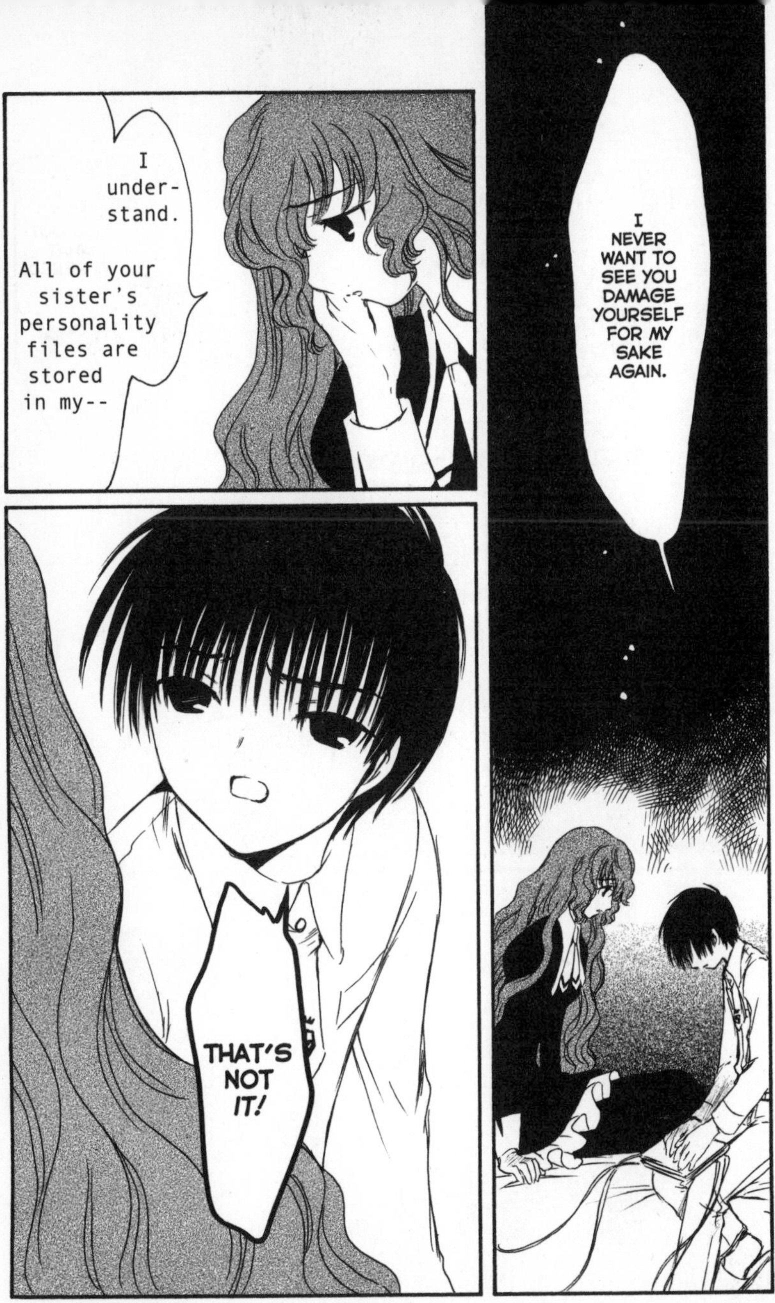
I NEVER WANT TO SEE YOU DAMAGE YOURSELF FOR MY SAKE AGAIN.
I understand.
All of your sister's personality files are stored in my--
THAT'S NOT IT!

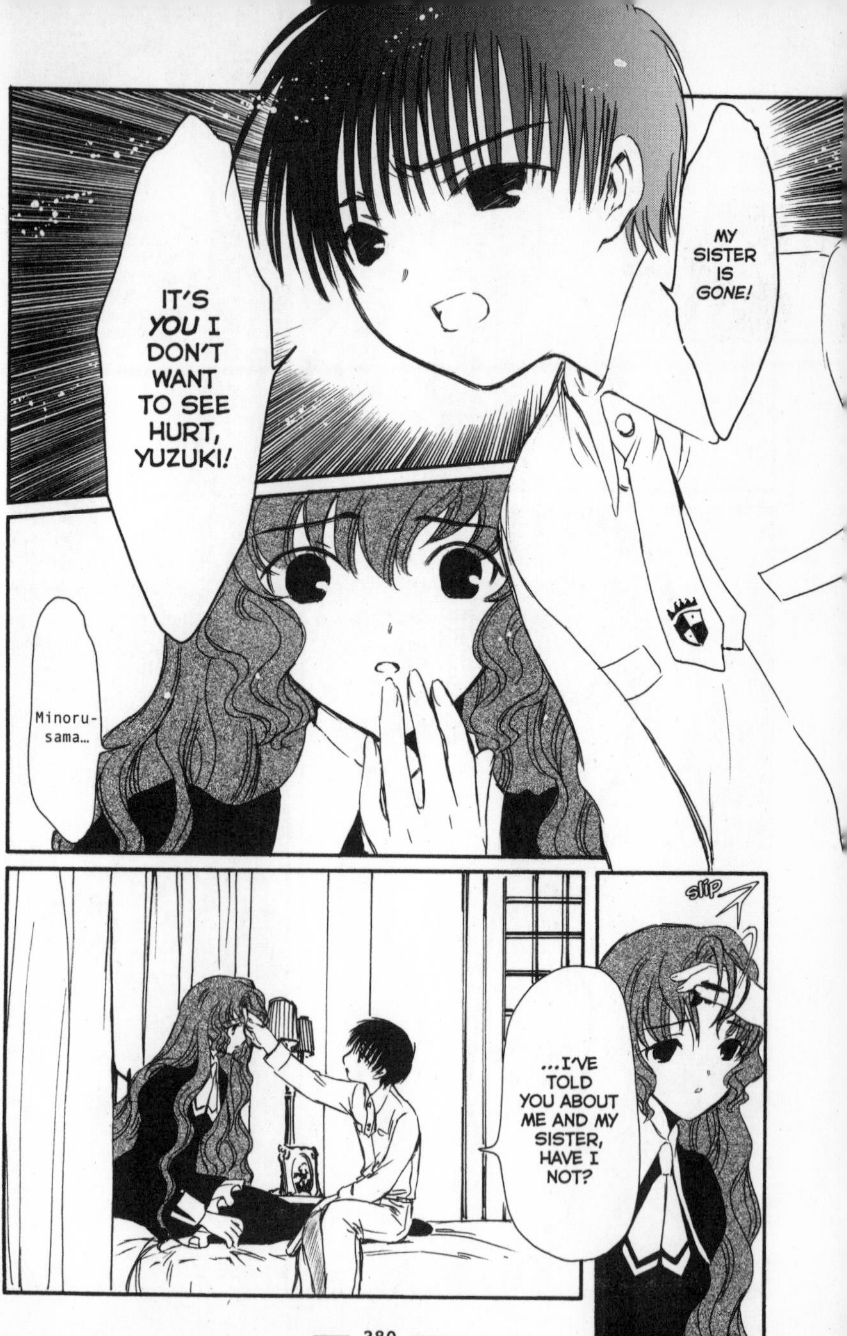
MY SISTER IS GONE!
IT'S *YOU* I DON'T WANT TO SEE HURT, YUZUKI!
Minoru-sama...
slip
...I'VE TOLD YOU ABOUT ME AND MY SISTER, HAVE I NOT?

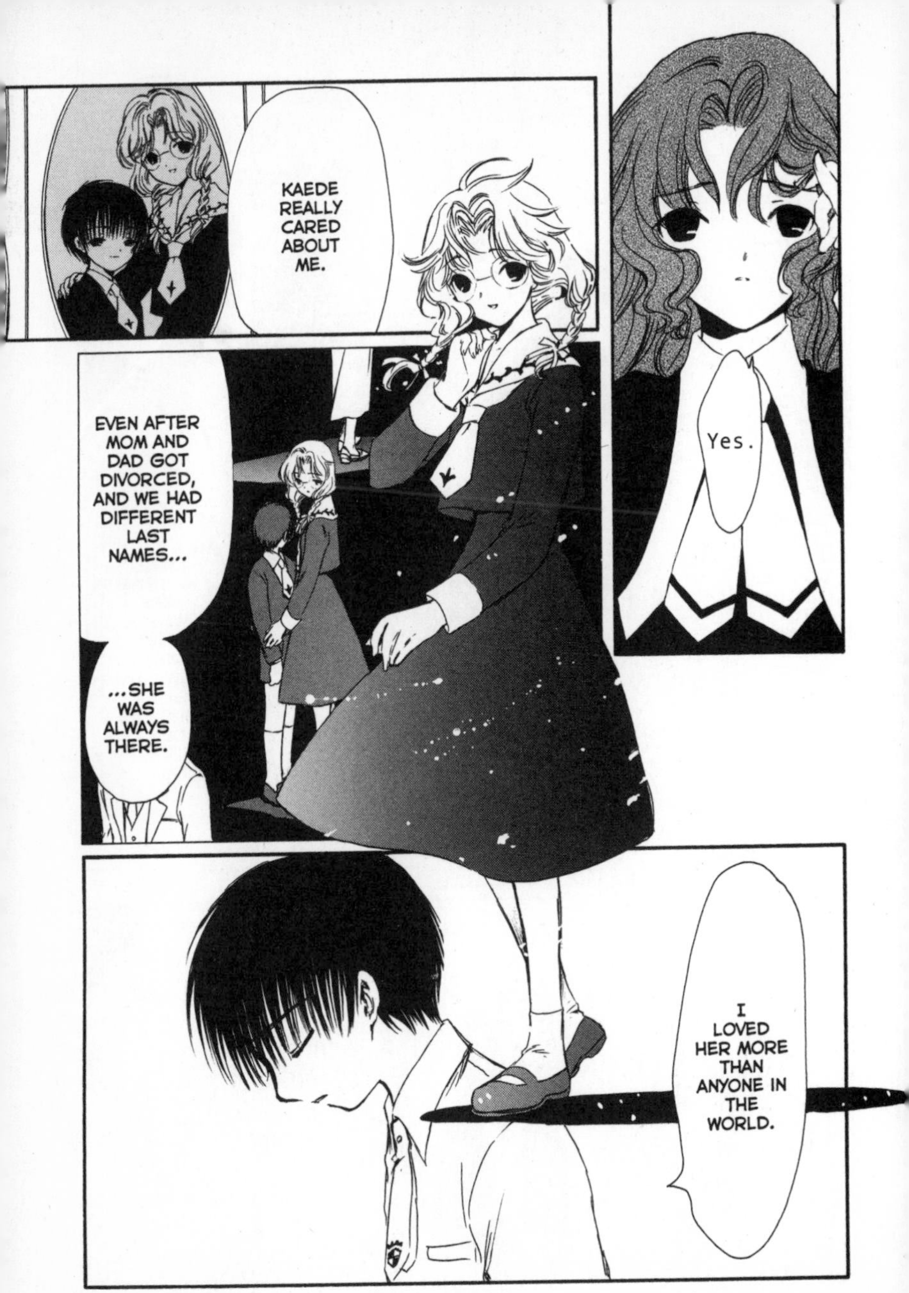
Yes.
KAEDE REALLY CARED ABOUT ME.
EVEN AFTER MOM AND DAD GOT DIVORCED, AND WE HAD DIFFERENT LAST NAMES...
...SHE WAS ALWAYS THERE.
I LOVED HER MORE THAN ANYONE IN THE WORLD.

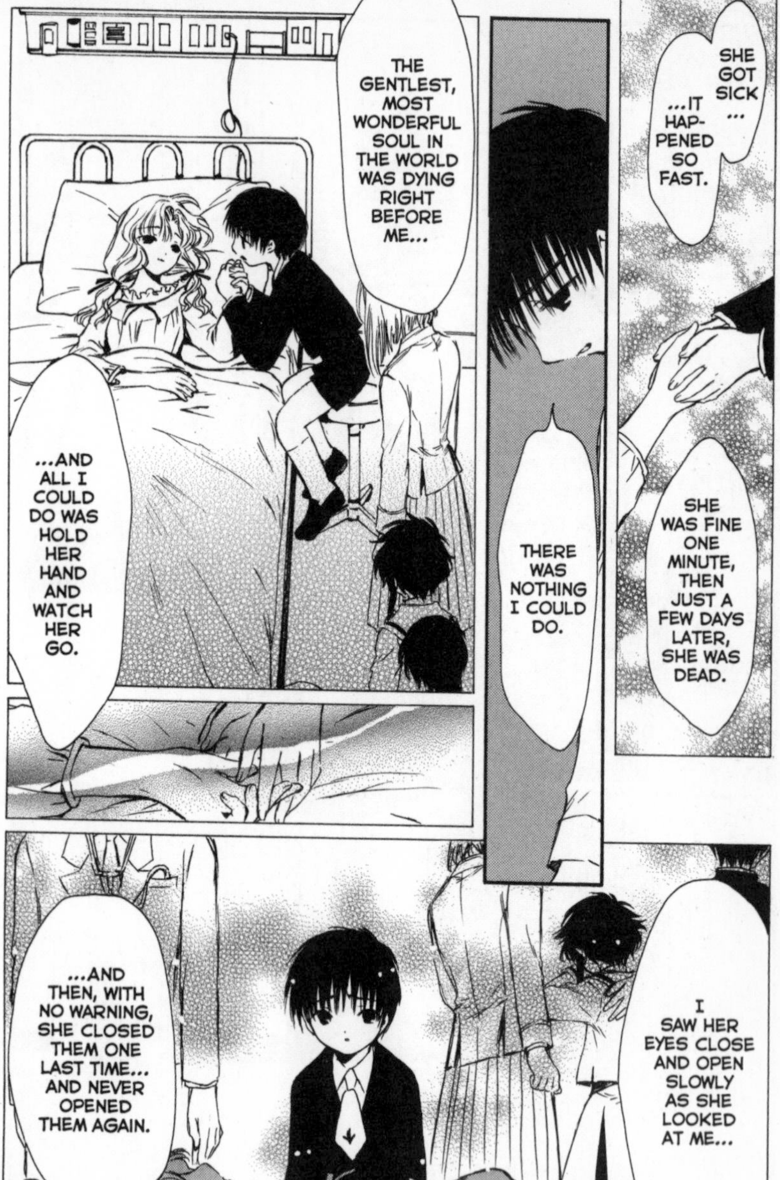
SHE GOT SICK...
...IT HAP-PENED SO FAST.
SHE WAS FINE ONE MINUTE, THEN JUST A FEW DAYS LATER, SHE WAS DEAD.
THERE WAS NOTHING I COULD DO.
THE GENTLEST, MOST WONDERFUL SOUL IN THE WORLD WAS DYING RIGHT BEFORE ME...
...AND ALL I COULD DO WAS HOLD HER HAND AND WATCH HER GO.
I SAW HER EYES CLOSE AND OPEN SLOWLY AS SHE LOOKED AT ME...
...AND THEN, WITH NO WARNING, SHE CLOSED THEM ONE LAST TIME... AND NEVER OPENED THEM AGAIN.

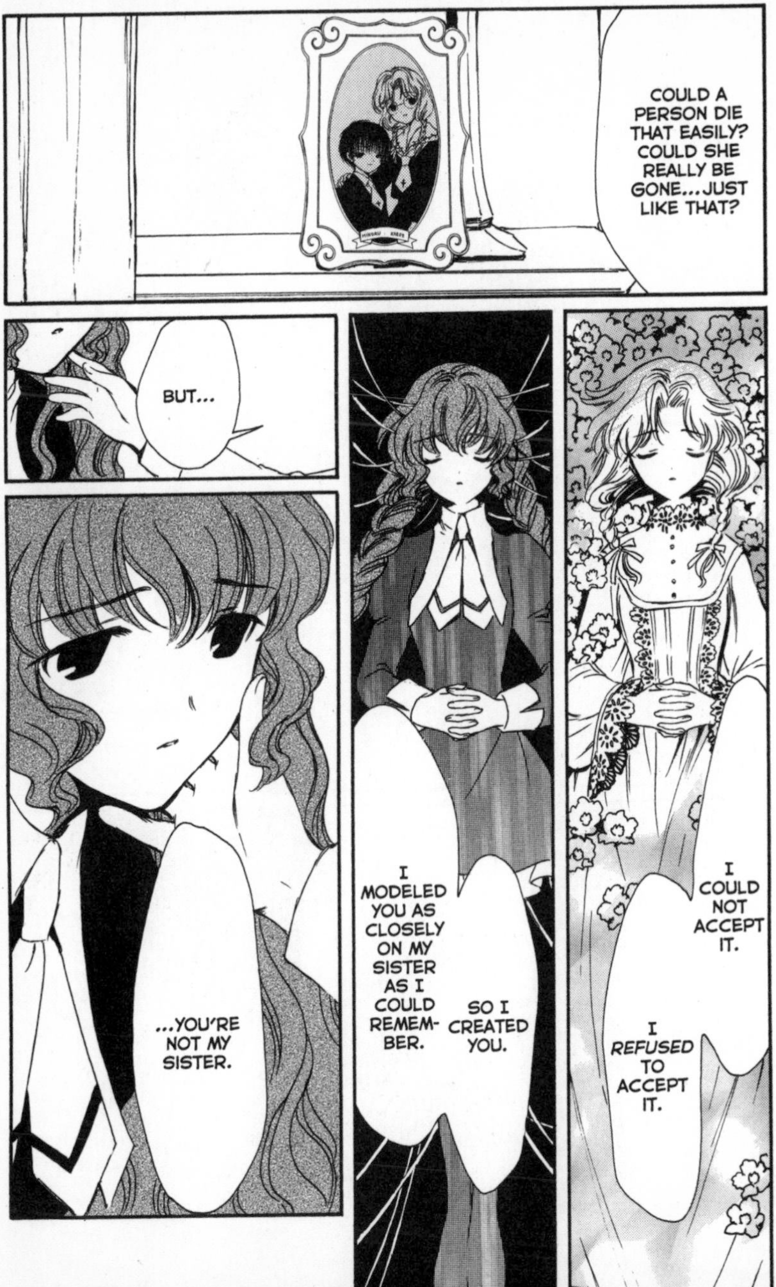
COULD A PERSON DIE THAT EASILY? COULD SHE REALLY BE GONE...JUST LIKE THAT?
I COULD NOT ACCEPT IT.
I *REFUSED* TO ACCEPT IT.
SO I CREATED YOU.
I MODELED YOU AS CLOSELY ON MY SISTER AS I COULD REMEMBER.
BUT...
...YOU'RE NOT MY SISTER.

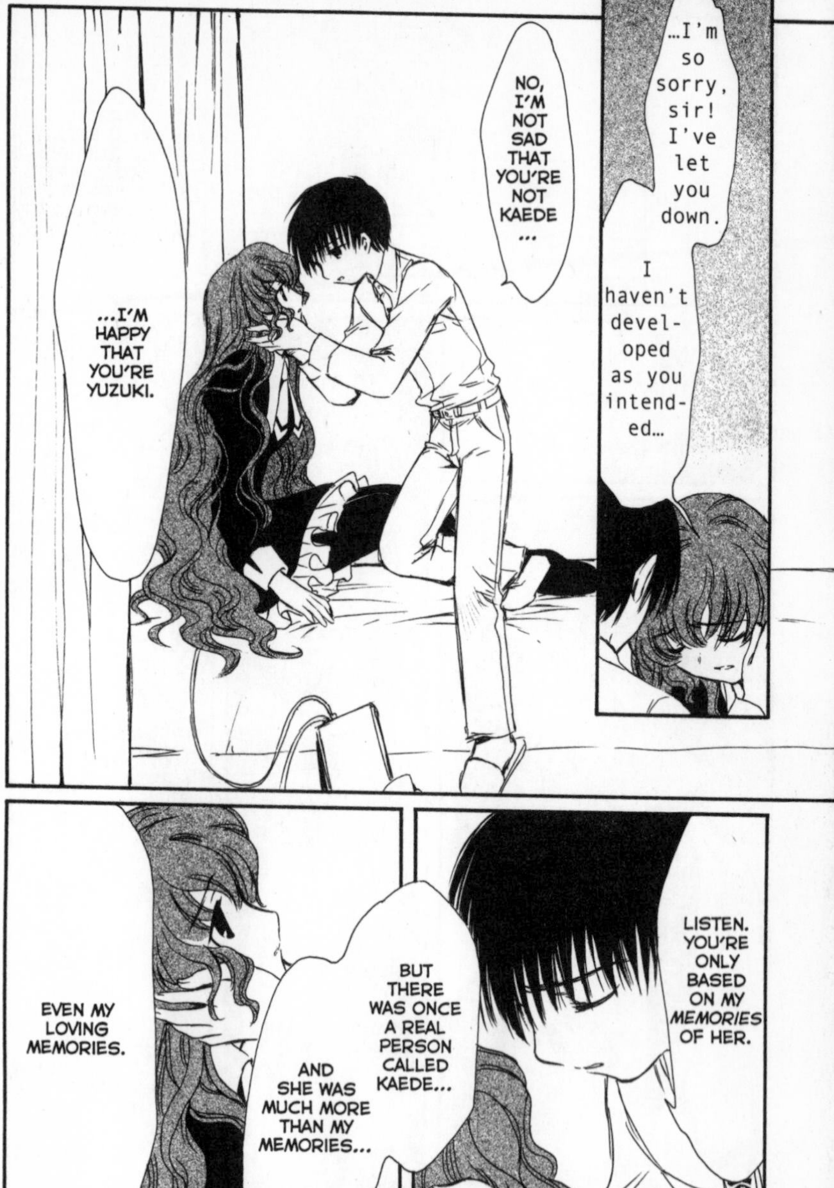
...I'm so sorry, sir! I've let you down.
I haven't devel-oped as you intend-ed...
NO, I'M NOT SAD THAT YOU'RE NOT KAEDE...
...I'M HAPPY THAT YOU'RE YUZUKI.
LISTEN. YOU'RE ONLY BASED ON MY *MEMORIES* OF HER.
BUT THERE WAS ONCE A REAL PERSON CALLED KAEDE...
AND SHE WAS MUCH MORE THAN MY MEMORIES...
EVEN MY LOVING MEMORIES.

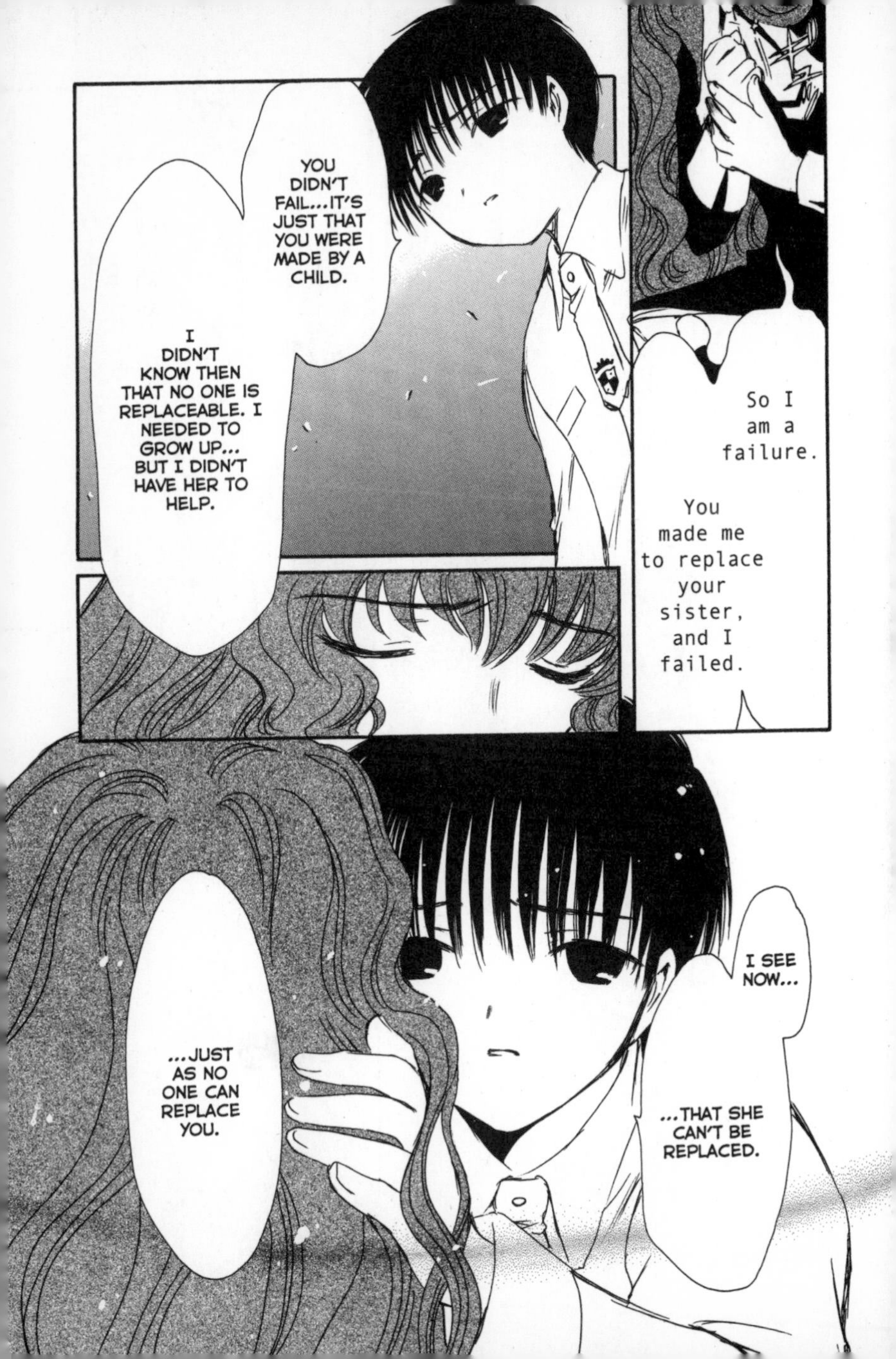
So I am a failure.
You made me to replace your sister, and I failed.
YOU DIDN'T FAIL...IT'S JUST THAT YOU WERE MADE BY A CHILD.
I DIDN'T KNOW THEN THAT NO ONE IS REPLACEABLE. I NEEDED TO GROW UP... BUT I DIDN'T HAVE HER TO HELP.
I SEE NOW...
...THAT SHE CAN'T BE REPLACED.
...JUST AS NO ONE CAN REPLACE YOU.

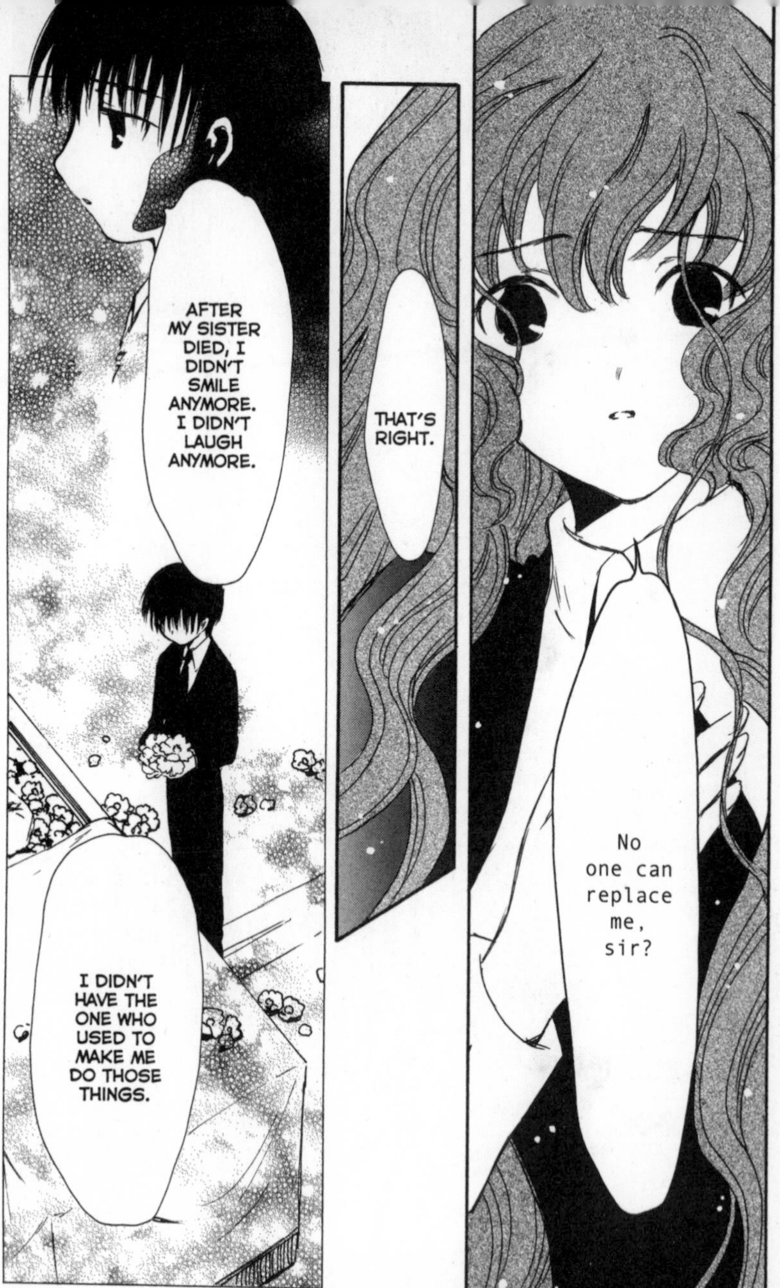
No one can replace me, sir?
THAT'S RIGHT.
AFTER MY SISTER DIED, I DIDN'T SMILE ANYMORE. I DIDN'T LAUGH ANYMORE.
I DIDN'T HAVE THE ONE WHO USED TO MAKE ME DO THOSE THINGS.

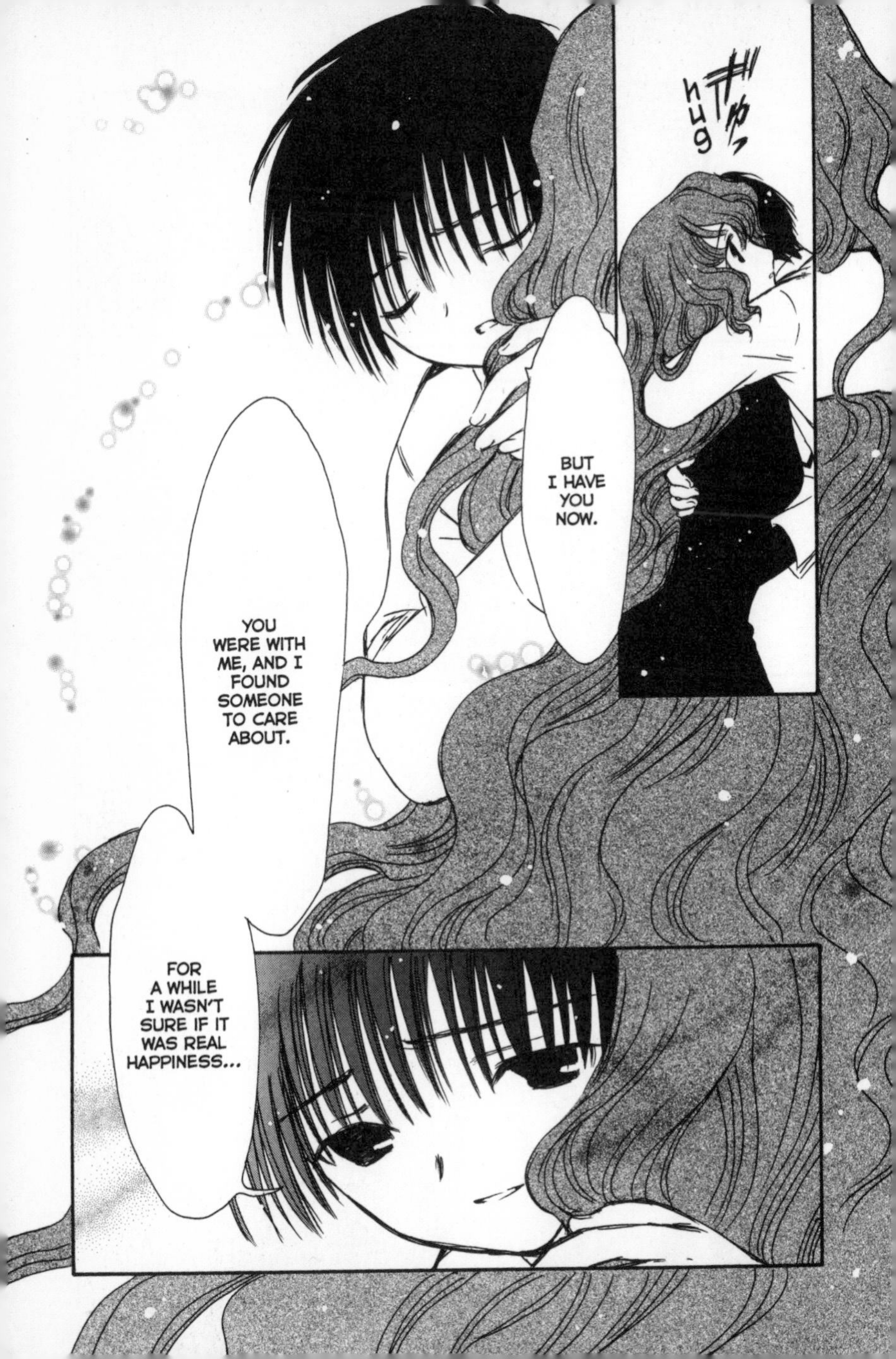
hug
BUT I HAVE YOU NOW.
YOU WERE WITH ME, AND I FOUND SOMEONE TO CARE ABOUT.
FOR A WHILE I WASN'T SURE IF IT WAS REAL HAPPINESS...

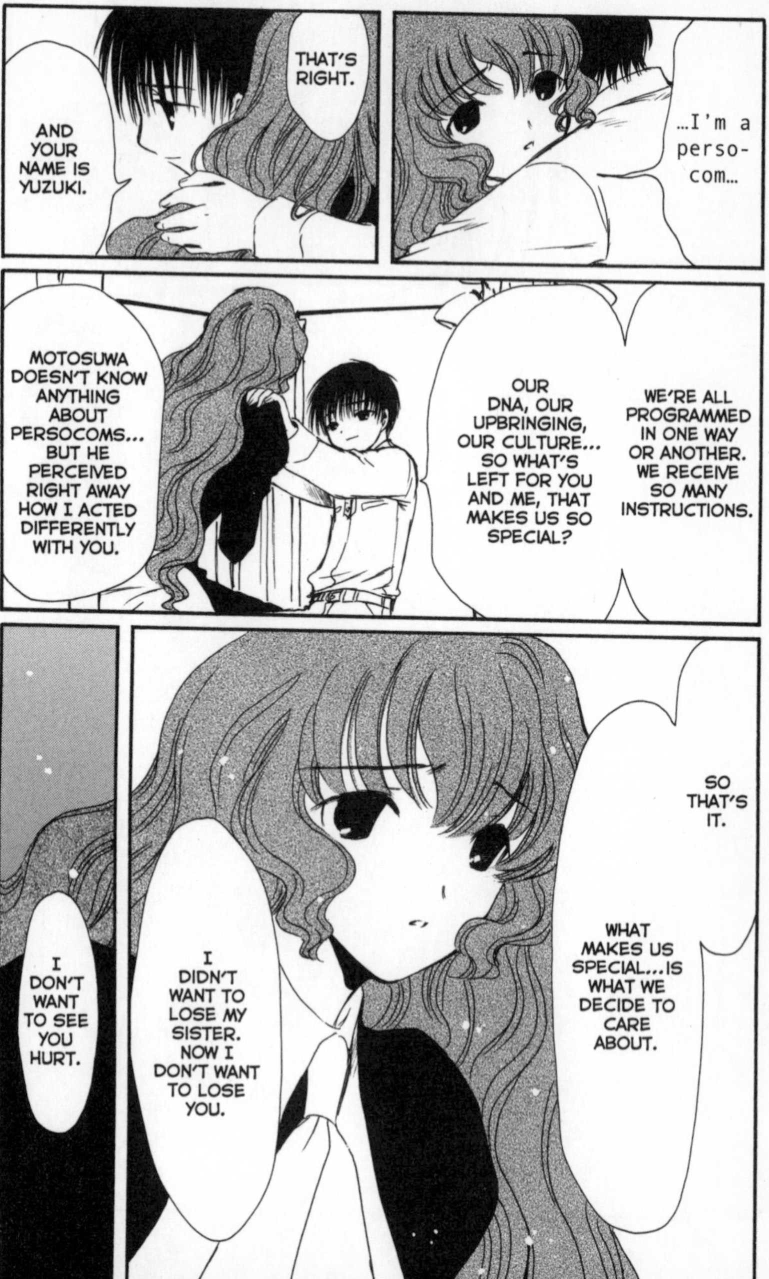
...I'm a perso-com...
THAT'S RIGHT.
AND YOUR NAME IS YUZUKI.
WE'RE ALL PROGRAMMED IN ONE WAY OR ANOTHER. WE RECEIVE SO MANY INSTRUCTIONS.
OUR DNA, OUR UPBRINGING, OUR CULTURE... SO WHAT'S LEFT FOR YOU AND ME, THAT MAKES US SO SPECIAL?
MOTOSUWA DOESN'T KNOW ANYTHING ABOUT PERSOCOMS... BUT HE PERCEIVED RIGHT AWAY HOW I ACTED DIFFERENTLY WITH YOU.
SO THAT'S IT.
WHAT MAKES US SPECIAL...IS WHAT WE DECIDE TO CARE ABOUT.
I DIDN'T WANT TO LOSE MY SISTER. NOW I DON'T WANT TO LOSE YOU.
I DON'T WANT TO SEE YOU HURT.

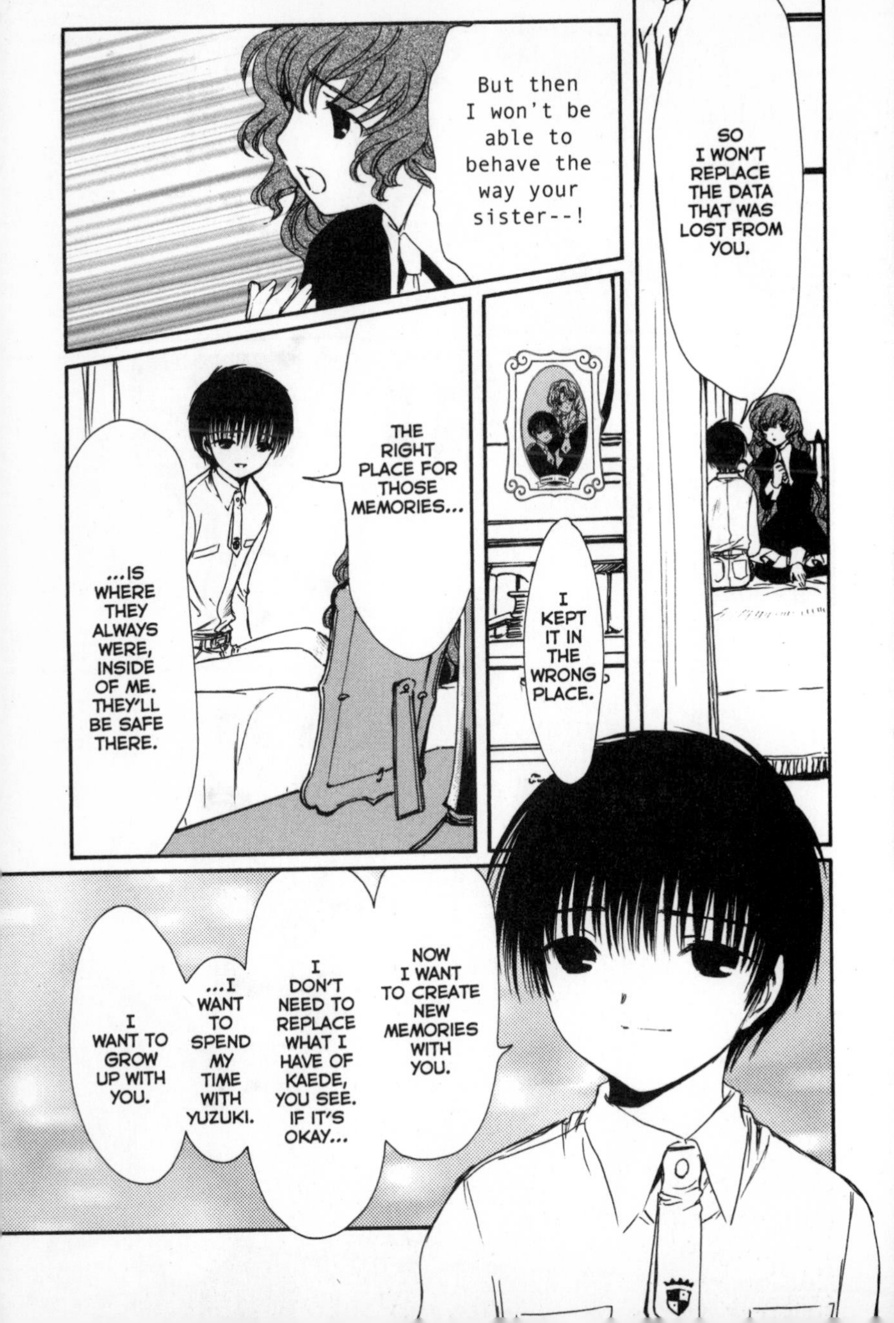
SO I WON'T REPLACE THE DATA THAT WAS LOST FROM YOU.
But then I won't be able to behave the way your sister--!
I KEPT IT IN THE WRONG PLACE.
THE RIGHT PLACE FOR THOSE MEMORIES...
...IS WHERE THEY ALWAYS WERE, INSIDE OF ME. THEY'LL BE SAFE THERE.
NOW I WANT TO CREATE NEW MEMORIES WITH YOU.
I DON'T NEED TO REPLACE WHAT I HAVE OF KAEDE, YOU SEE. IF IT'S OKAY...
...I WANT TO SPEND MY TIME WITH YUZUKI.
I WANT TO GROW UP WITH YOU.

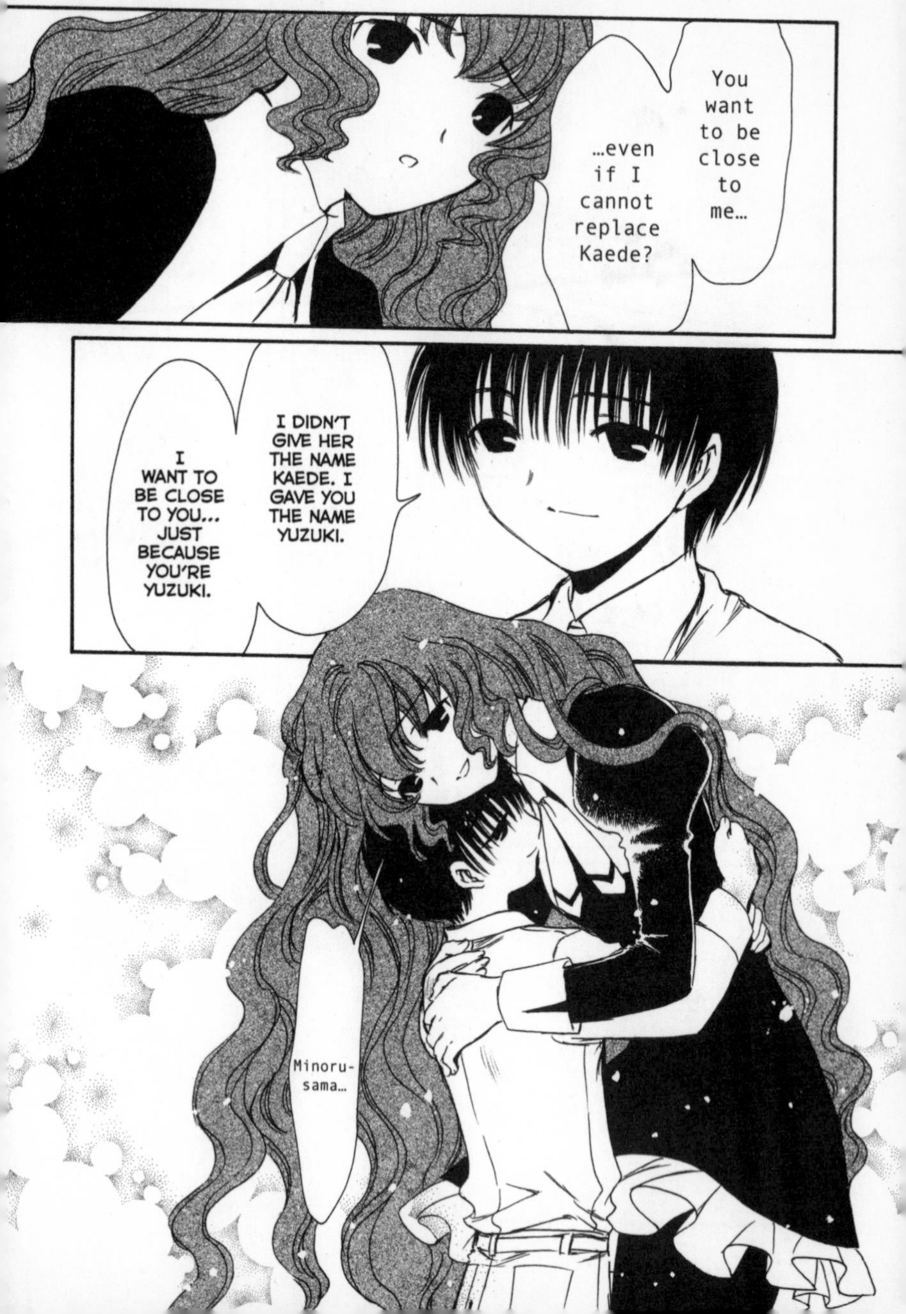
You want to be close to me…
…even if I cannot replace Kaede?
I DIDN'T GIVE HER THE NAME KAEDE. I GAVE YOU THE NAME YUZUKI.
I WANT TO BE CLOSE TO YOU… JUST BECAUSE YOU'RE YUZUKI.
Minoru-sama…

Chobits
ちょびっツ

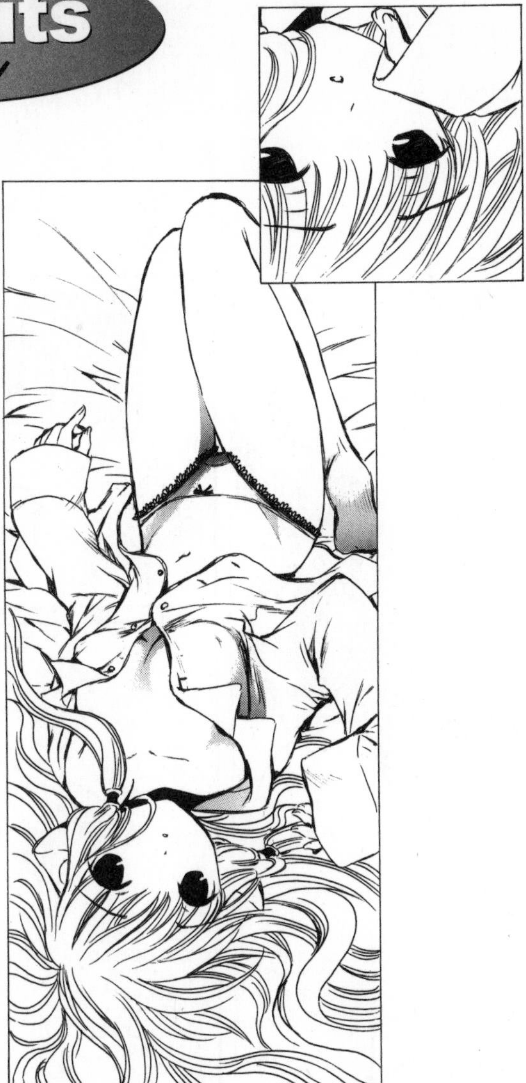

◂chapter 74▸

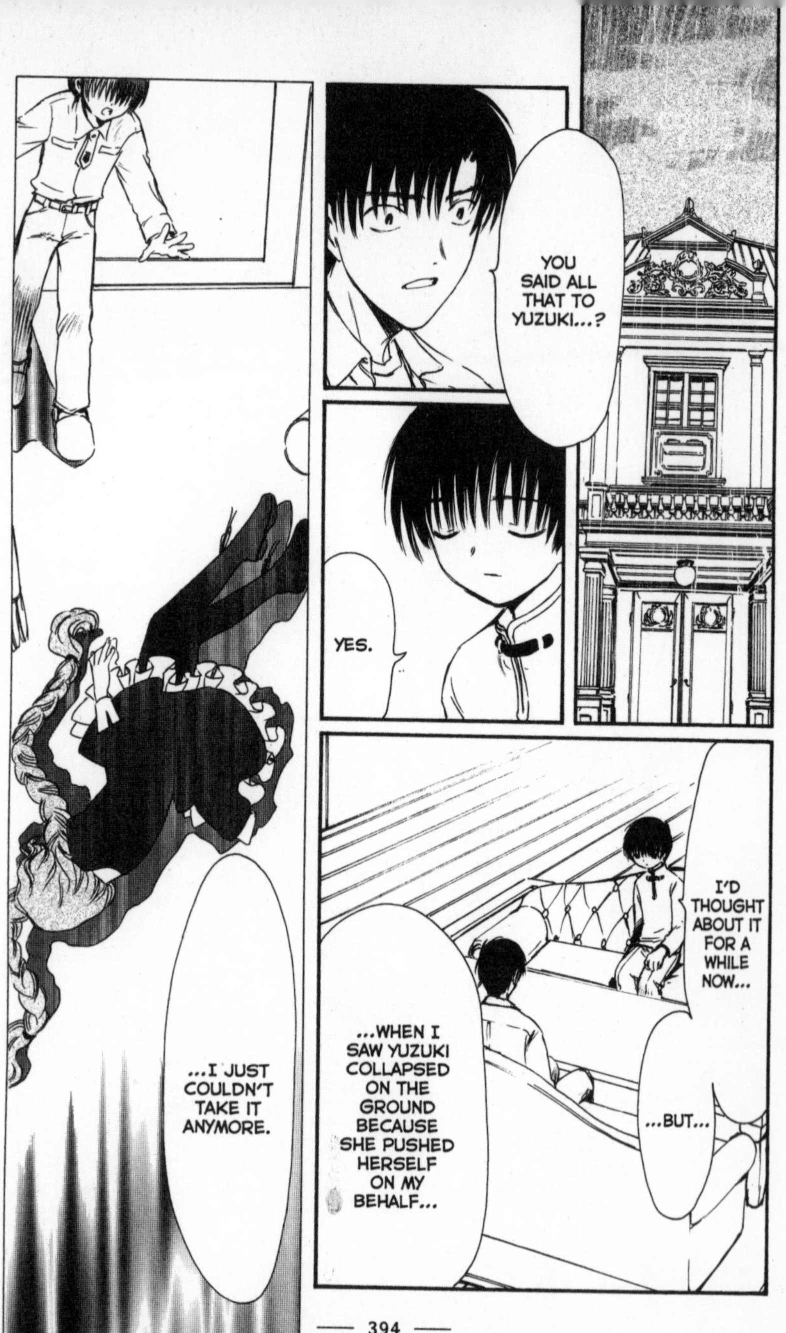
YOU SAID ALL THAT TO YUZUKI...?
YES.
I'D THOUGHT ABOUT IT FOR A WHILE NOW...
...BUT...
...WHEN I SAW YUZUKI COLLAPSED ON THE GROUND BECAUSE SHE PUSHED HERSELF ON MY BEHALF...
...I JUST COULDN'T TAKE IT ANYMORE.

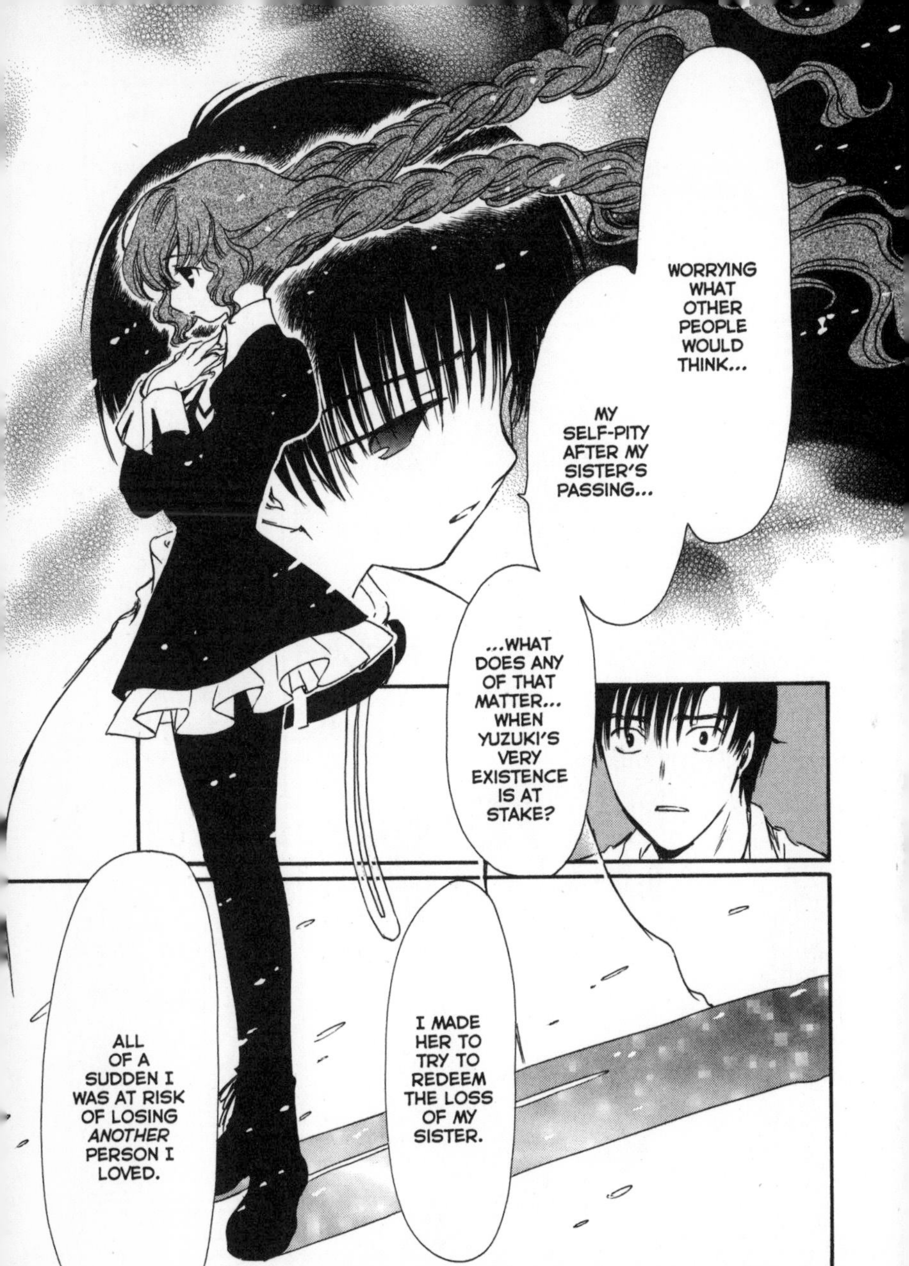
WORRYING WHAT OTHER PEOPLE WOULD THINK...
MY SELF-PITY AFTER MY SISTER'S PASSING...
...WHAT DOES ANY OF THAT MATTER... WHEN YUZUKI'S VERY EXISTENCE IS AT STAKE?
I MADE HER TO TRY TO REDEEM THE LOSS OF MY SISTER.
ALL OF A SUDDEN I WAS AT RISK OF LOSING *ANOTHER* PERSON I LOVED.

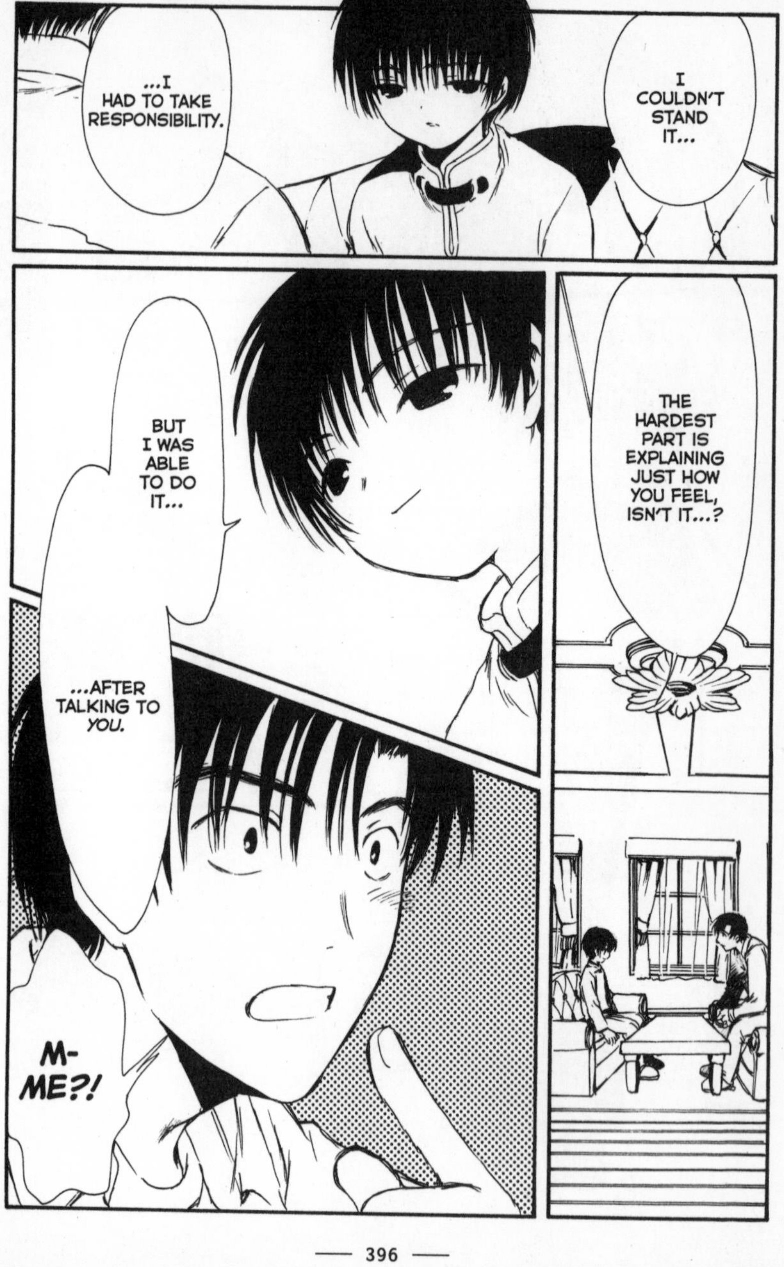
I COULDN'T STAND IT...
...I HAD TO TAKE RESPONSIBILITY.
THE HARDEST PART IS EXPLAINING JUST HOW YOU FEEL, ISN'T IT...?
BUT I WAS ABLE TO DO IT...
...AFTER TALKING TO *YOU.*
M-ME?!

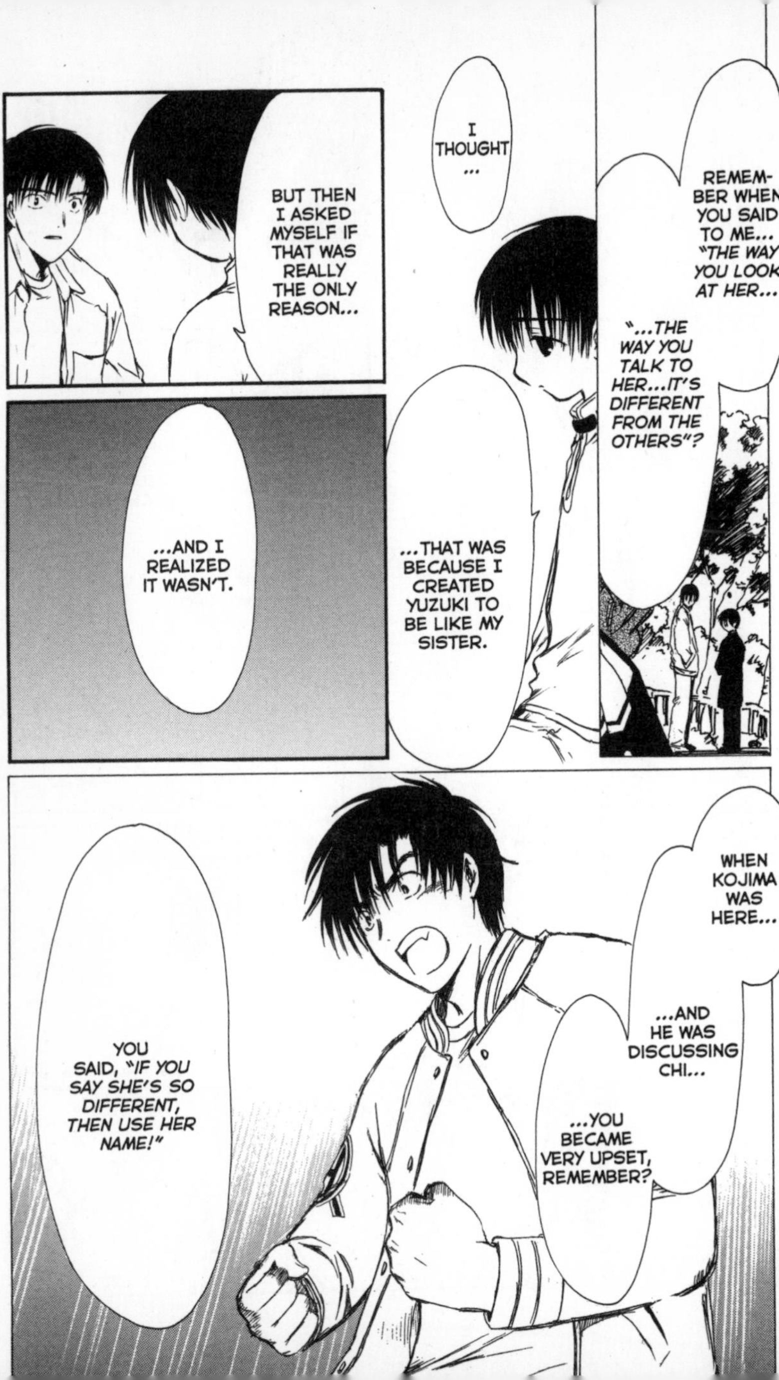
REMEMBER WHEN YOU SAID TO ME... "THE WAY YOU LOOK AT HER...
"...THE WAY YOU TALK TO HER...IT'S DIFFERENT FROM THE OTHERS"?
I THOUGHT...
...THAT WAS BECAUSE I CREATED YUZUKI TO BE LIKE MY SISTER.
BUT THEN I ASKED MYSELF IF THAT WAS REALLY THE ONLY REASON...
...AND I REALIZED IT WASN'T.
WHEN KOJIMA WAS HERE...
...AND HE WAS DISCUSSING CHI...
...YOU BECAME VERY UPSET, REMEMBER?
YOU SAID, "IF YOU SAY SHE'S SO DIFFERENT, THEN USE HER NAME!"

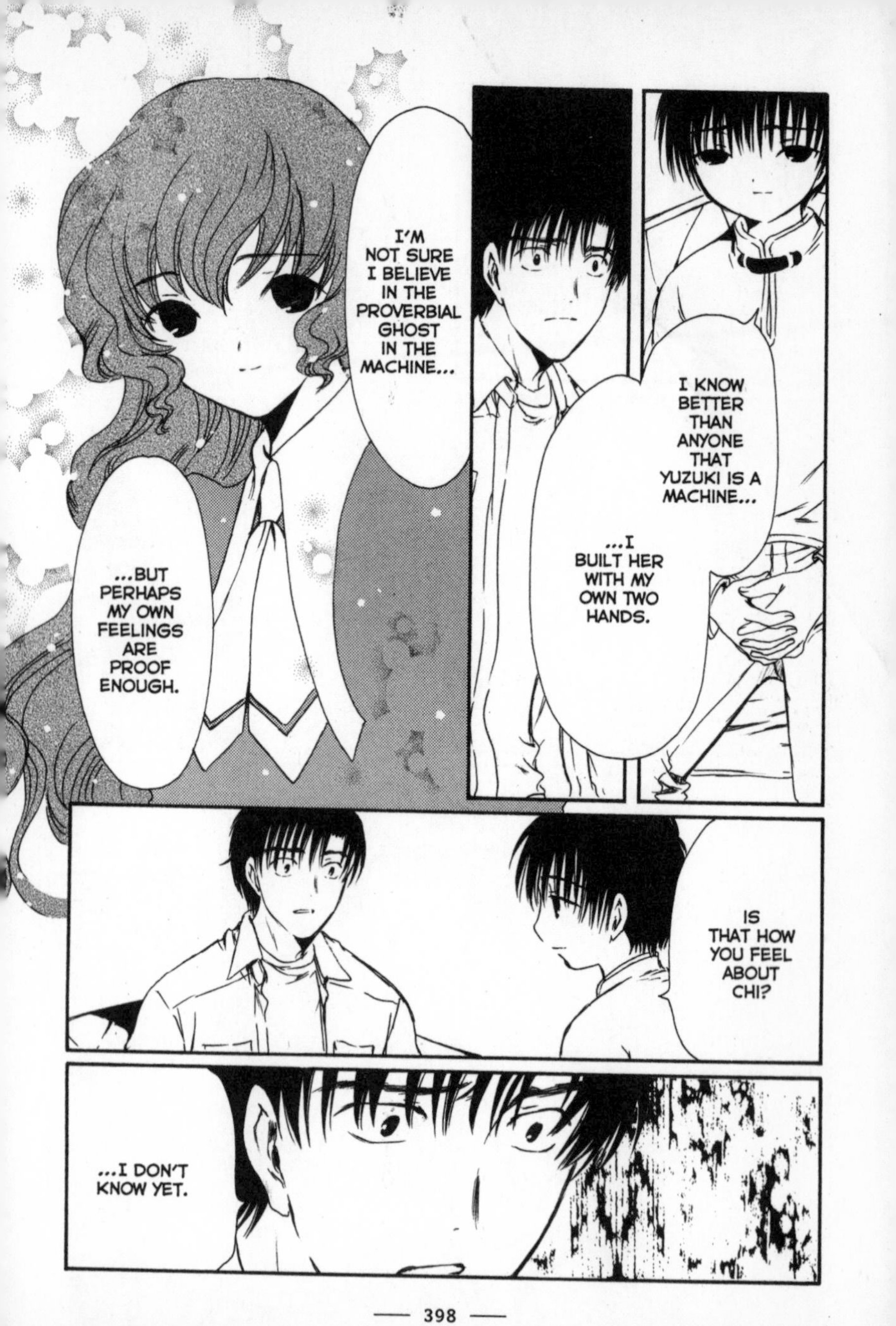
I KNOW BETTER THAN ANYONE THAT YUZUKI IS A MACHINE...
...I BUILT HER WITH MY OWN TWO HANDS.
I'M NOT SURE I BELIEVE IN THE PROVERBIAL GHOST IN THE MACHINE...
...BUT PERHAPS MY OWN FEELINGS ARE PROOF ENOUGH.
IS THAT HOW YOU FEEL ABOUT CHI?
...I DON'T KNOW YET.

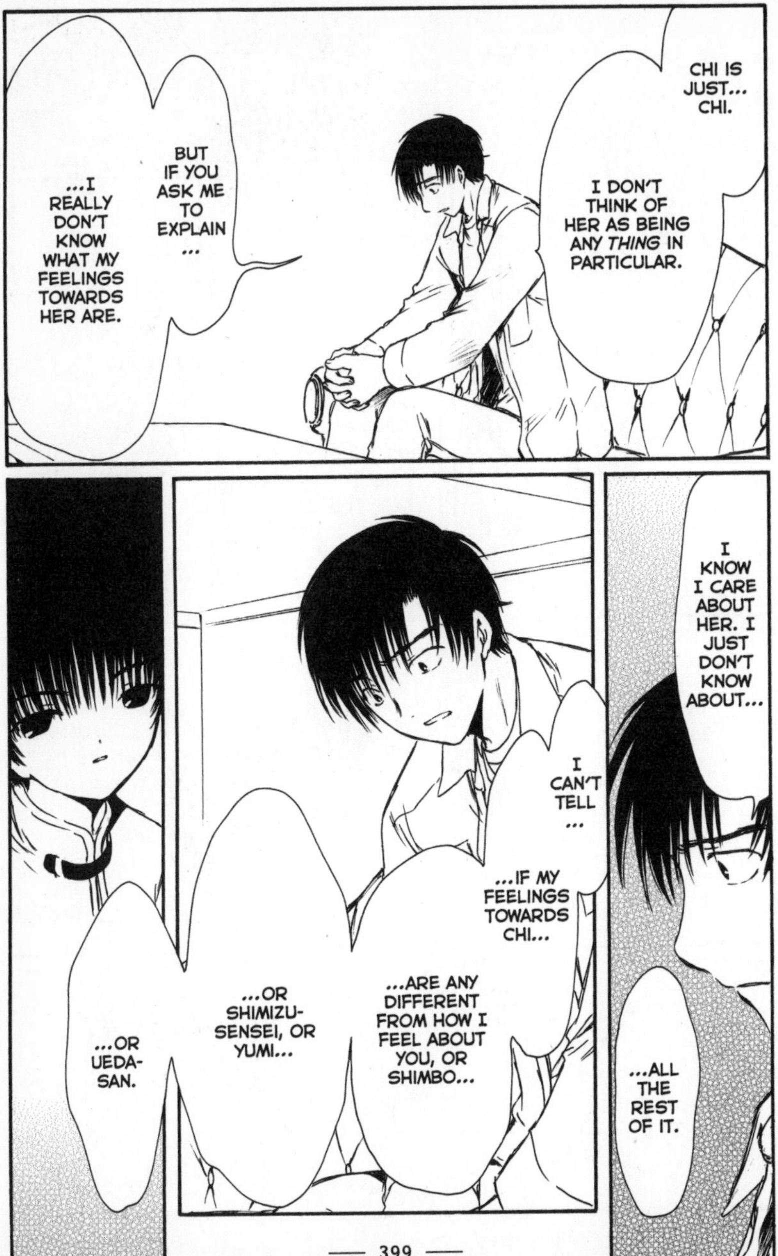
CHI IS JUST... CHI.
I DON'T THINK OF HER AS BEING ANY *THING* IN PARTICULAR.
BUT IF YOU ASK ME TO EXPLAIN...
...I REALLY DON'T KNOW WHAT MY FEELINGS TOWARDS HER ARE.
I KNOW I CARE ABOUT HER. I JUST DON'T KNOW ABOUT...
...ALL THE REST OF IT.
I CAN'T TELL...
...IF MY FEELINGS TOWARDS CHI...
...ARE ANY DIFFERENT FROM HOW I FEEL ABOUT YOU, OR SHIMBO...
...OR SHIMIZU-SENSEI, OR YUMI...
...OR UEDA-SAN.

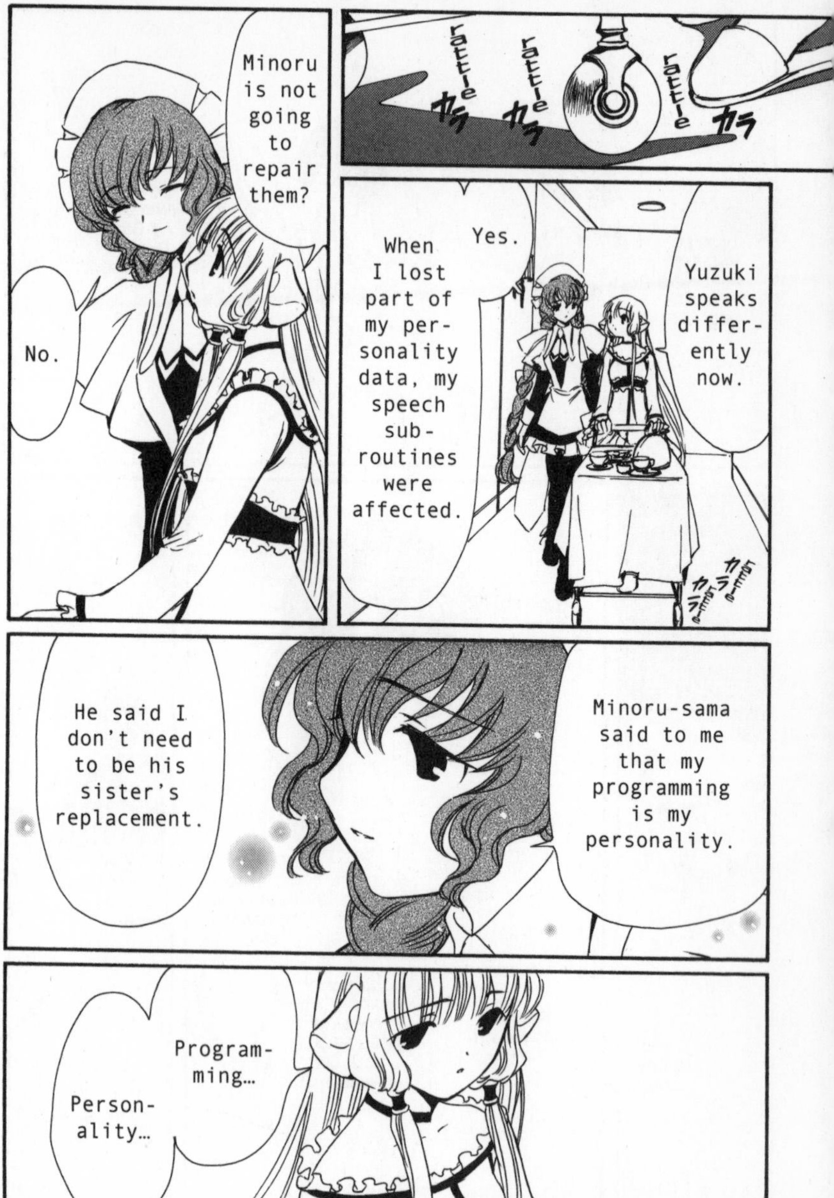
rattle
カラ
rattle
カラ
rattle
カラ
Yuzuki speaks differently now.
Yes.
When I lost part of my personality data, my speech subroutines were affected.
rattle カラ
rattle カラ
Minoru is not going to repair them?
No.
Minoru-sama said to me that my programming is my personality.
He said I don't need to be his sister's replacement.
Programming…
Personality…

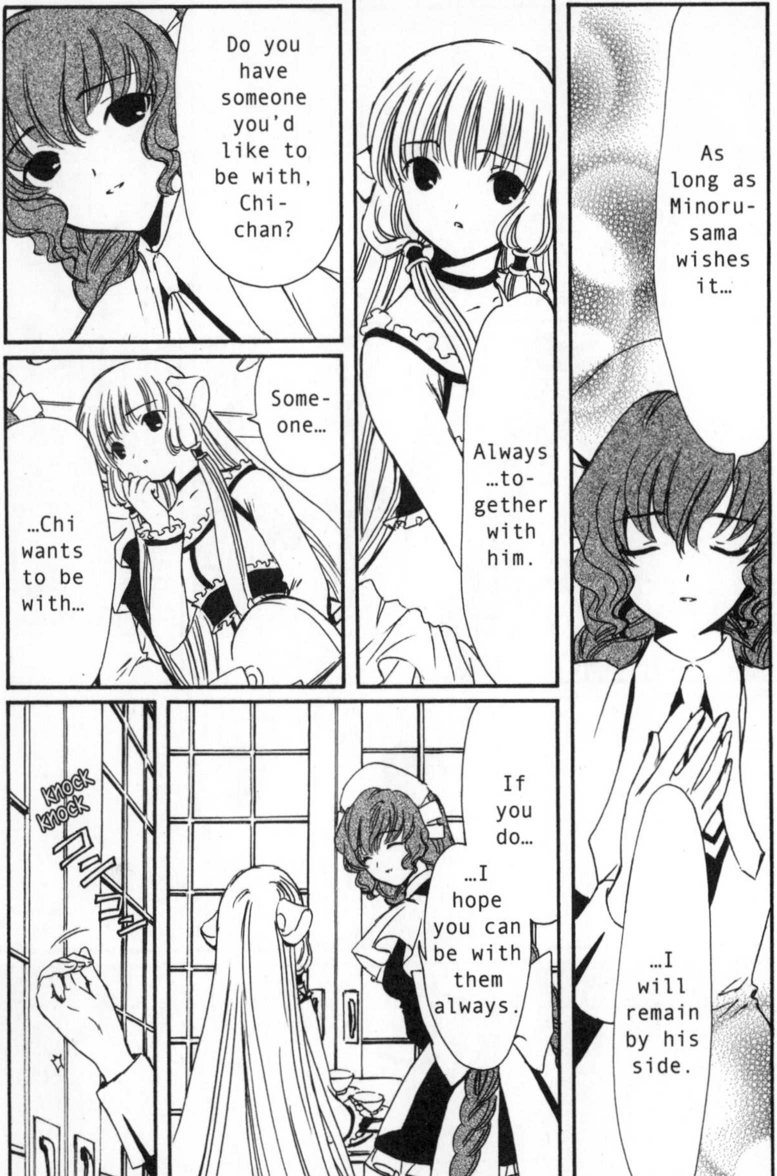
As long as Minoru-sama wishes it…
…I will remain by his side.
Do you have someone you'd like to be with, Chi-chan?
Some-one…
…Chi wants to be with…
Always …to-gether with him.
If you do…
…I hope you can be with them always.
knock knock

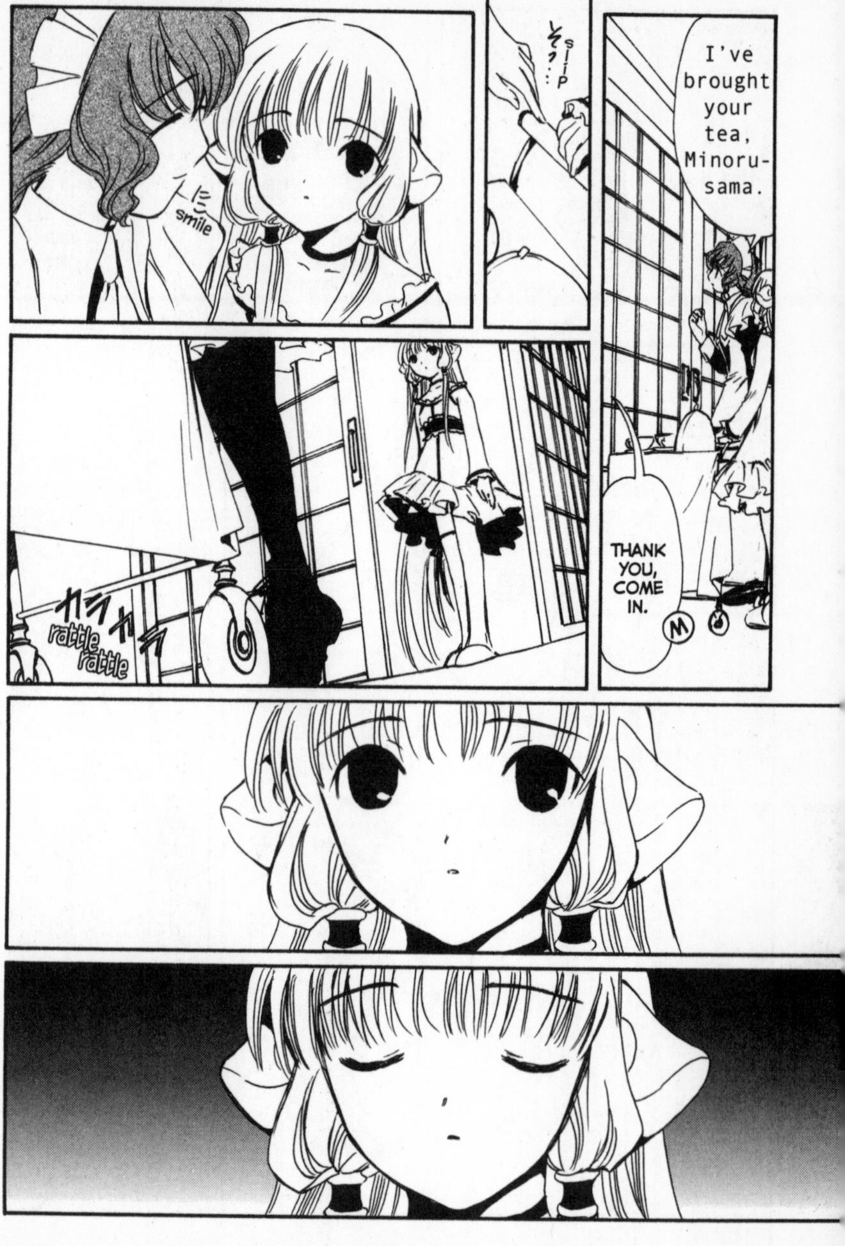
I've brought your tea, Minoru-sama.
THANK YOU, COME IN.
S-I-P
smile
rattle rattle

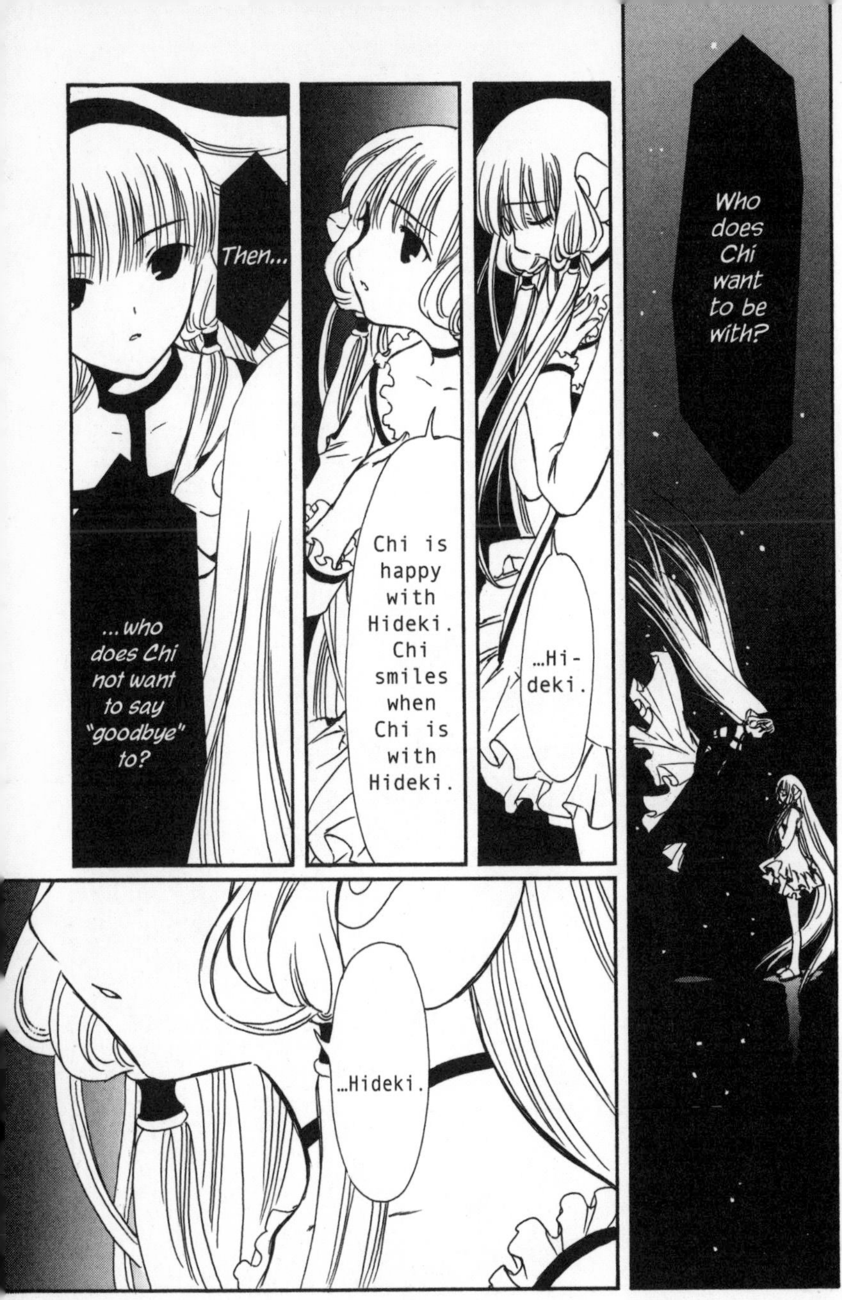
Who does Chi want to be with?
...Hi-deki.
Chi is happy with Hideki. Chi smiles when Chi is with Hideki.
Then...
...who does Chi not want to say "goodbye" to?
...Hideki.

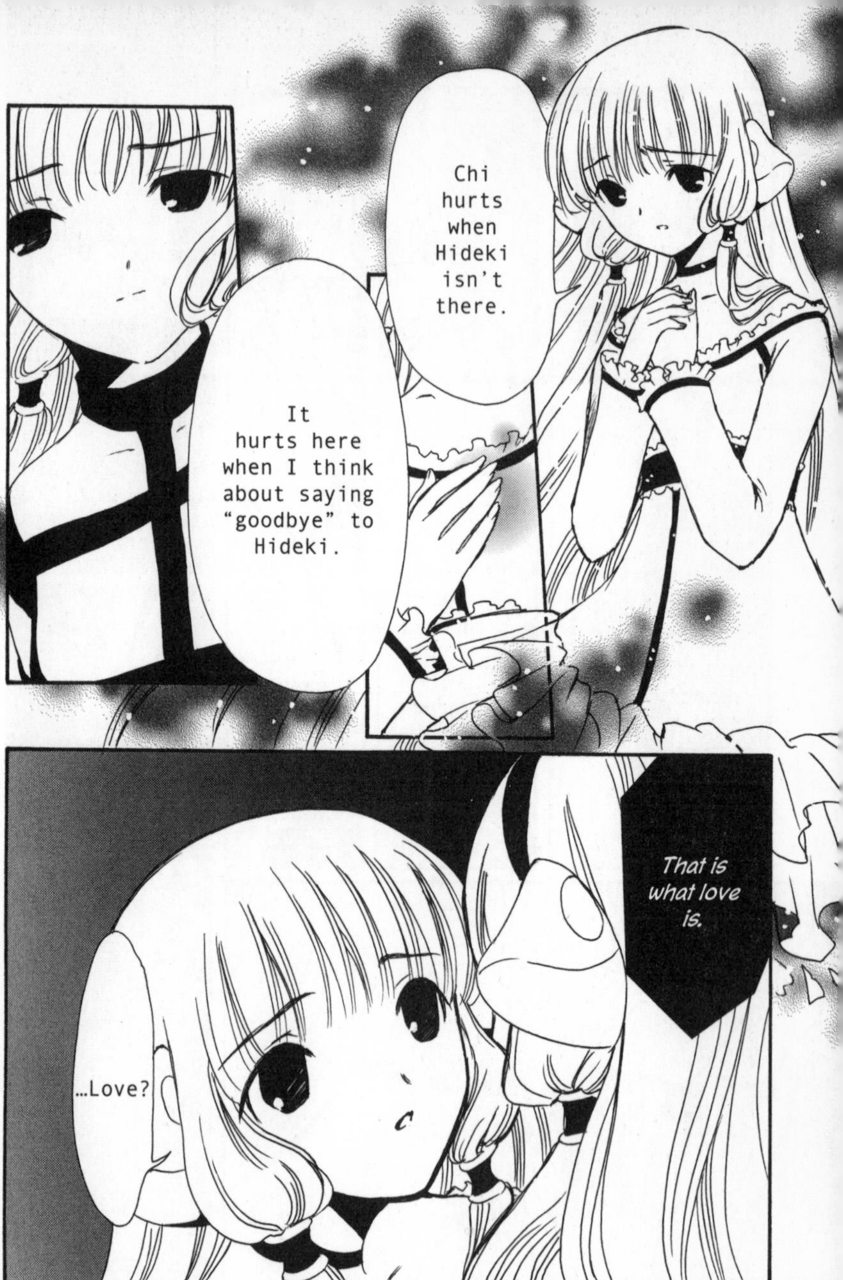
Chi hurts when Hideki isn't there.
It hurts here when I think about saying "goodbye" to Hideki.
That is what love is.
...Love?

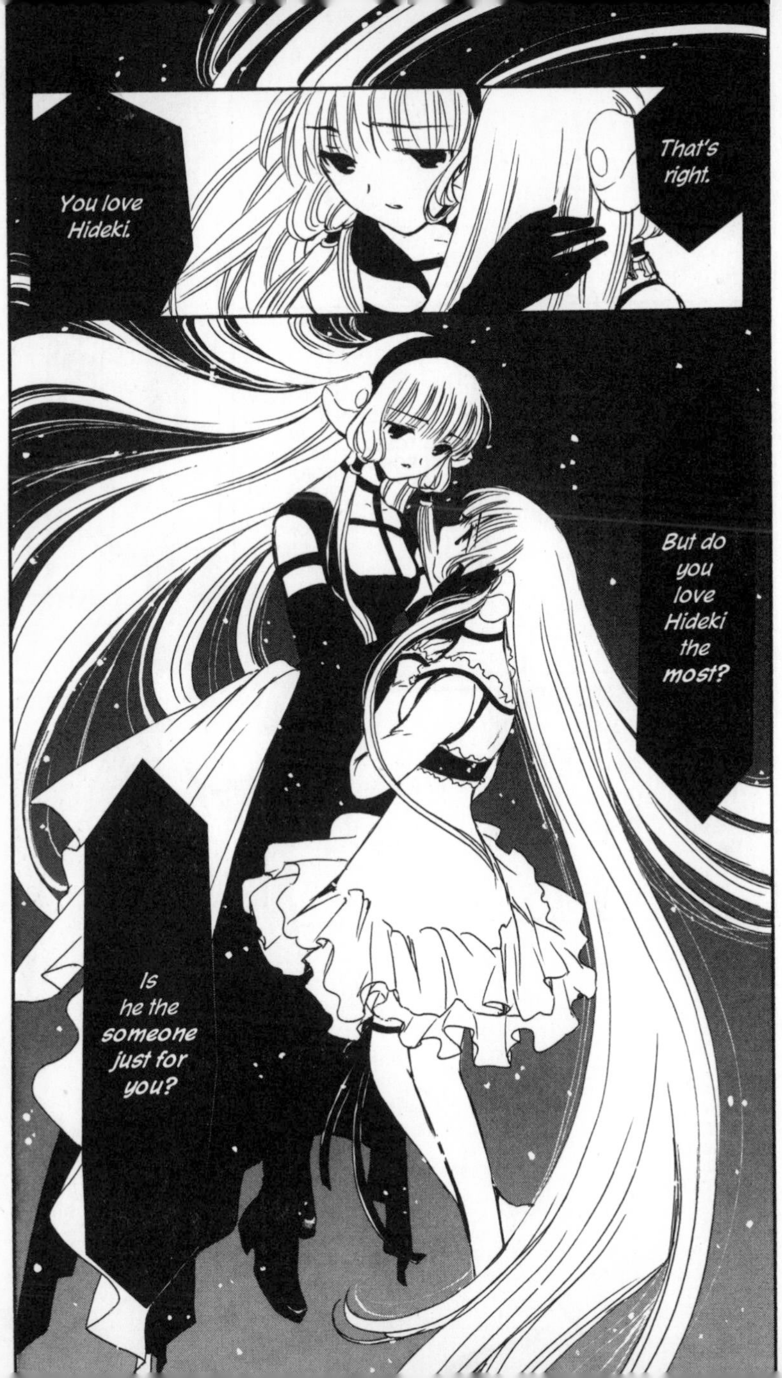
That's right.
You love Hideki.
But do you love Hideki the most?
Is he the someone just for you?

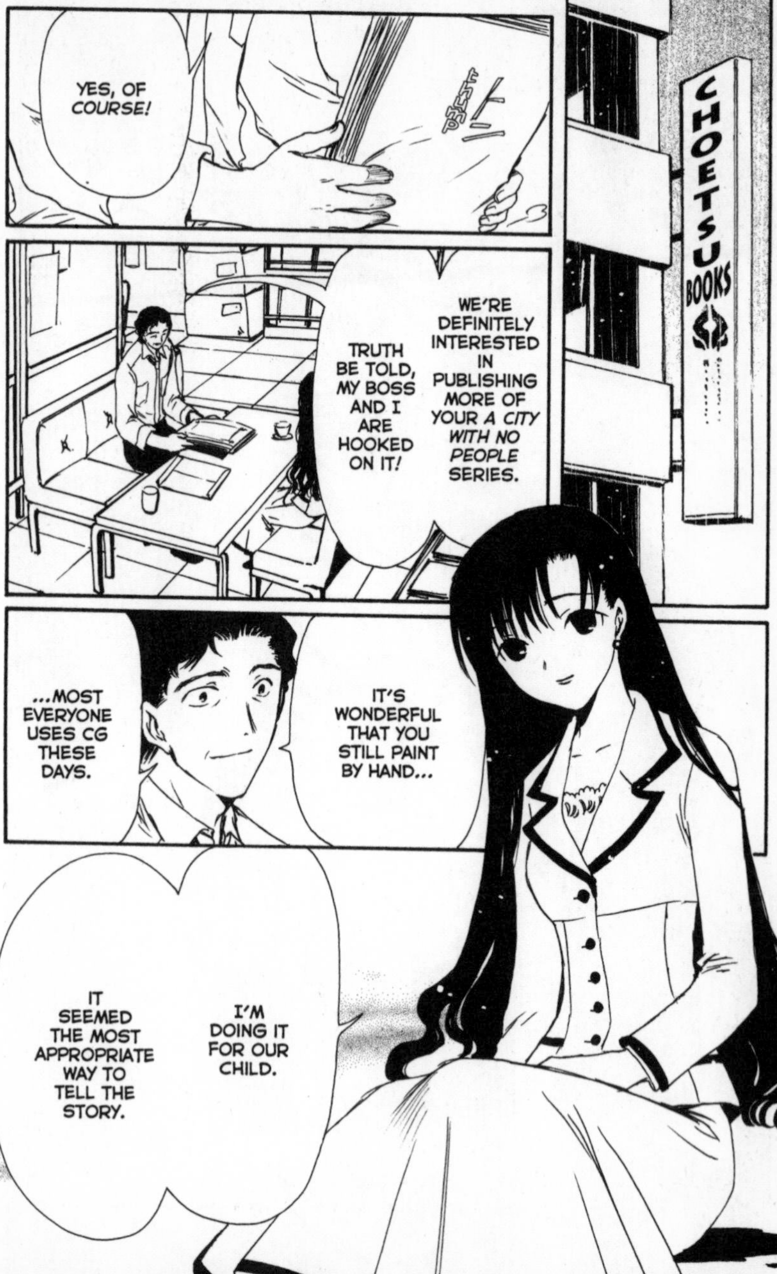
CHOETSU BOOKS
YES, OF COURSE!
THUMP
WE'RE DEFINITELY INTERESTED IN PUBLISHING MORE OF YOUR *A CITY WITH NO PEOPLE* SERIES.
TRUTH BE TOLD, MY BOSS AND I ARE HOOKED ON IT!
IT'S WONDERFUL THAT YOU STILL PAINT BY HAND...
...MOST EVERYONE USES CG THESE DAYS.
I'M DOING IT FOR OUR CHILD.
IT SEEMED THE MOST APPROPRIATE WAY TO TELL THE STORY.

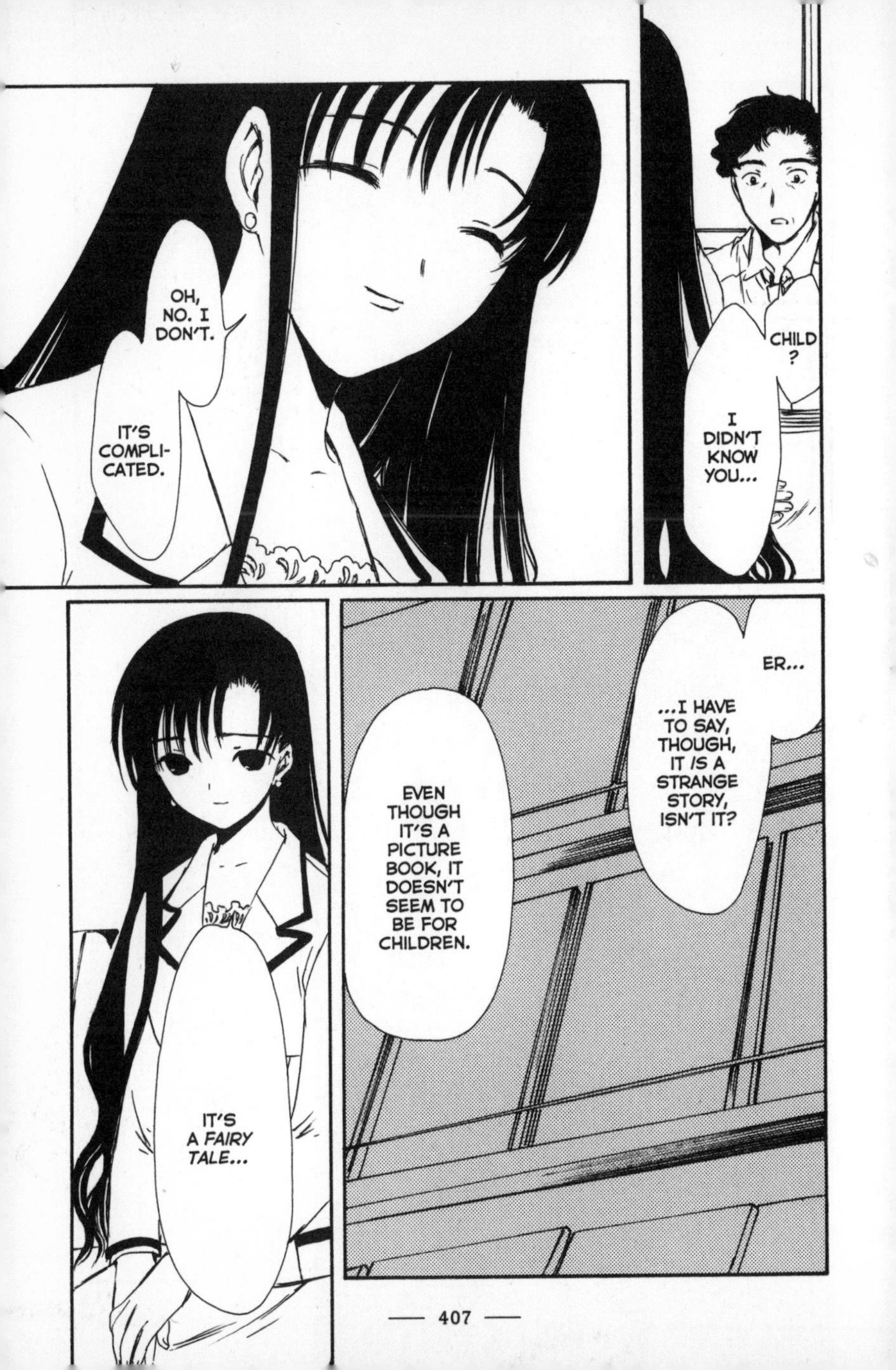
CHILD?
I DIDN'T KNOW YOU...
OH, NO. I DON'T.
IT'S COMPLICATED.
ER...
...I HAVE TO SAY, THOUGH, IT *IS* A STRANGE STORY, ISN'T IT?
EVEN THOUGH IT'S A PICTURE BOOK, IT DOESN'T SEEM TO BE FOR CHILDREN.
IT'S A *FAIRY TALE*...

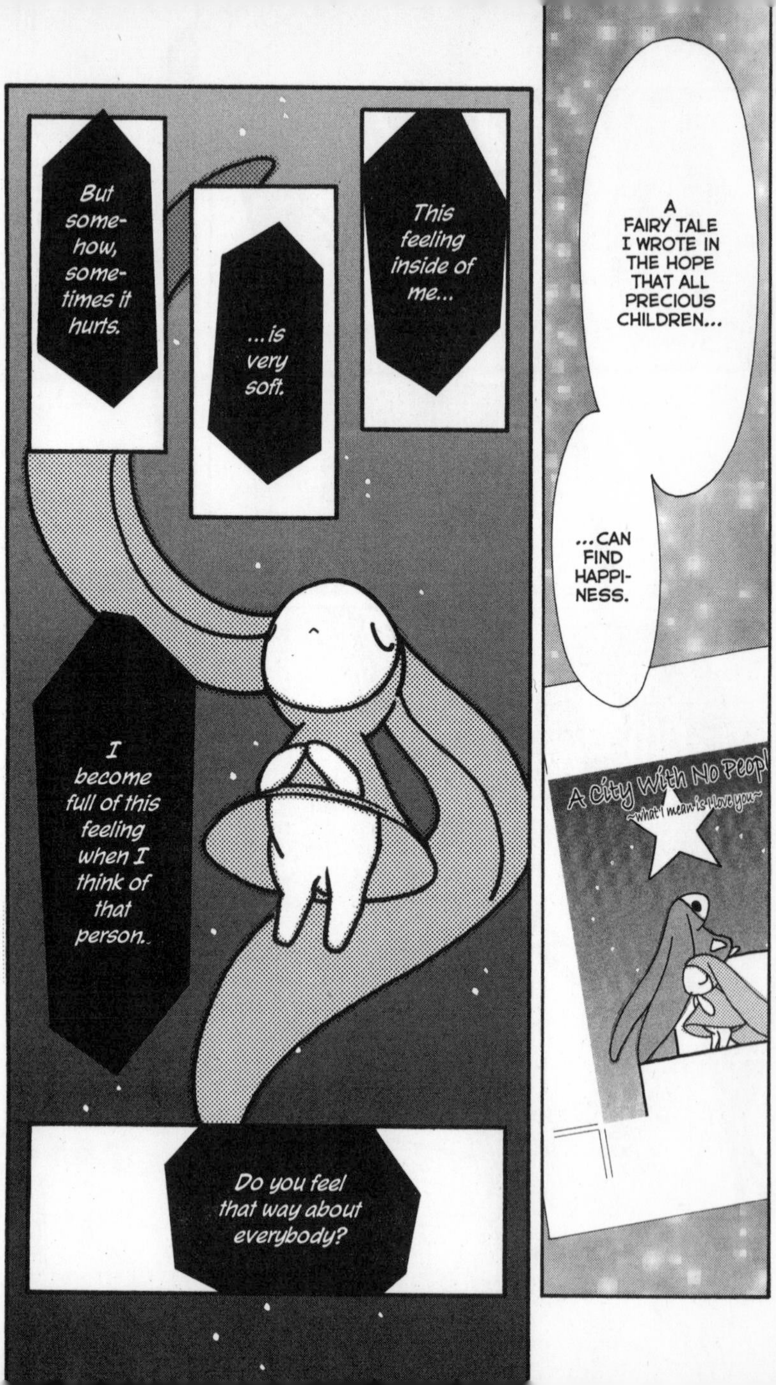
A FAIRY TALE I WROTE IN THE HOPE THAT ALL PRECIOUS CHILDREN...
...CAN FIND HAPPINESS.
A City With No Peopl
~what I mean is I love you~
This feeling inside of me...
...is very soft.
But somehow, sometimes it hurts.
I become full of this feeling when I think of that person.
Do you feel that way about everybody?

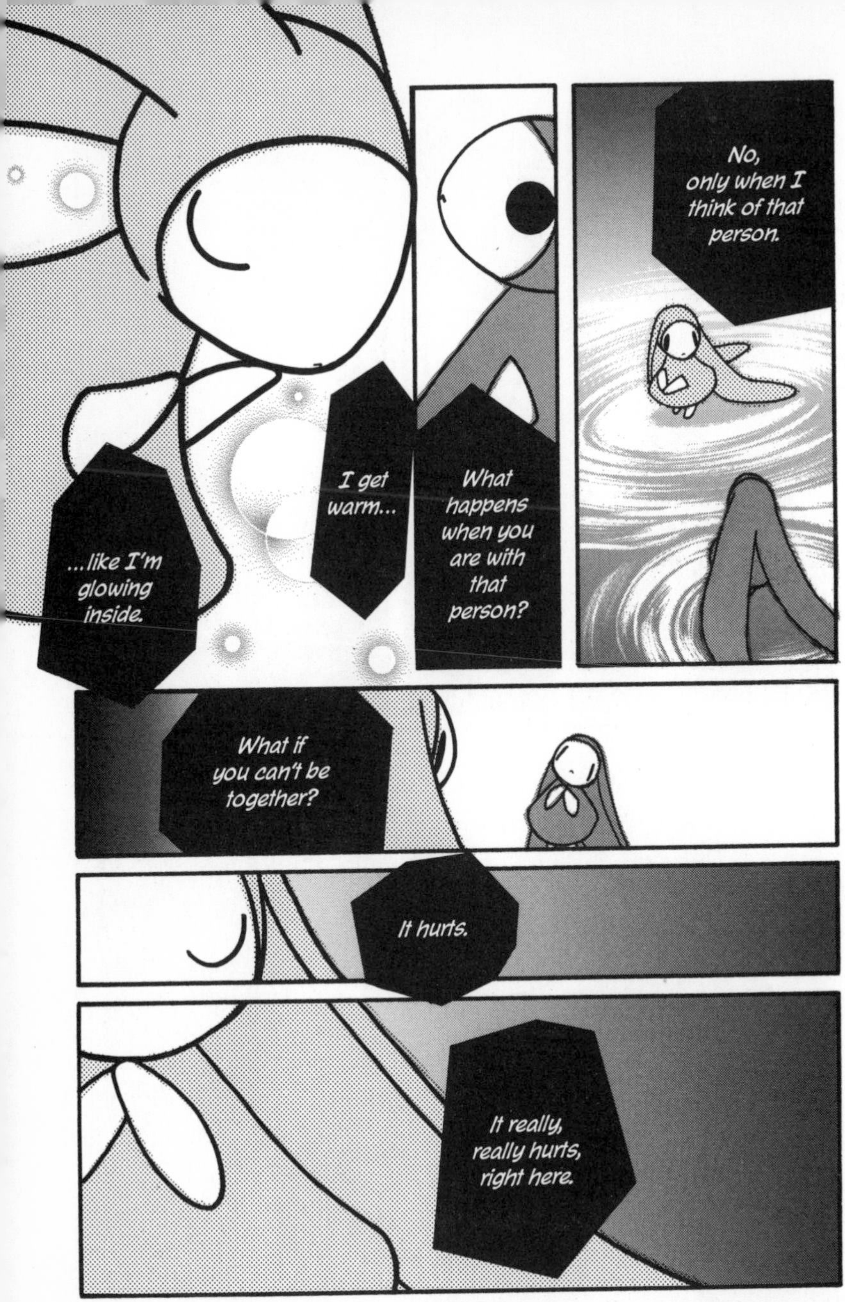
No, only when I think of that person.
What happens when you are with that person?
I get warm...
...like I'm glowing inside.
What if you can't be together?
It hurts.
It really, really hurts, right here.

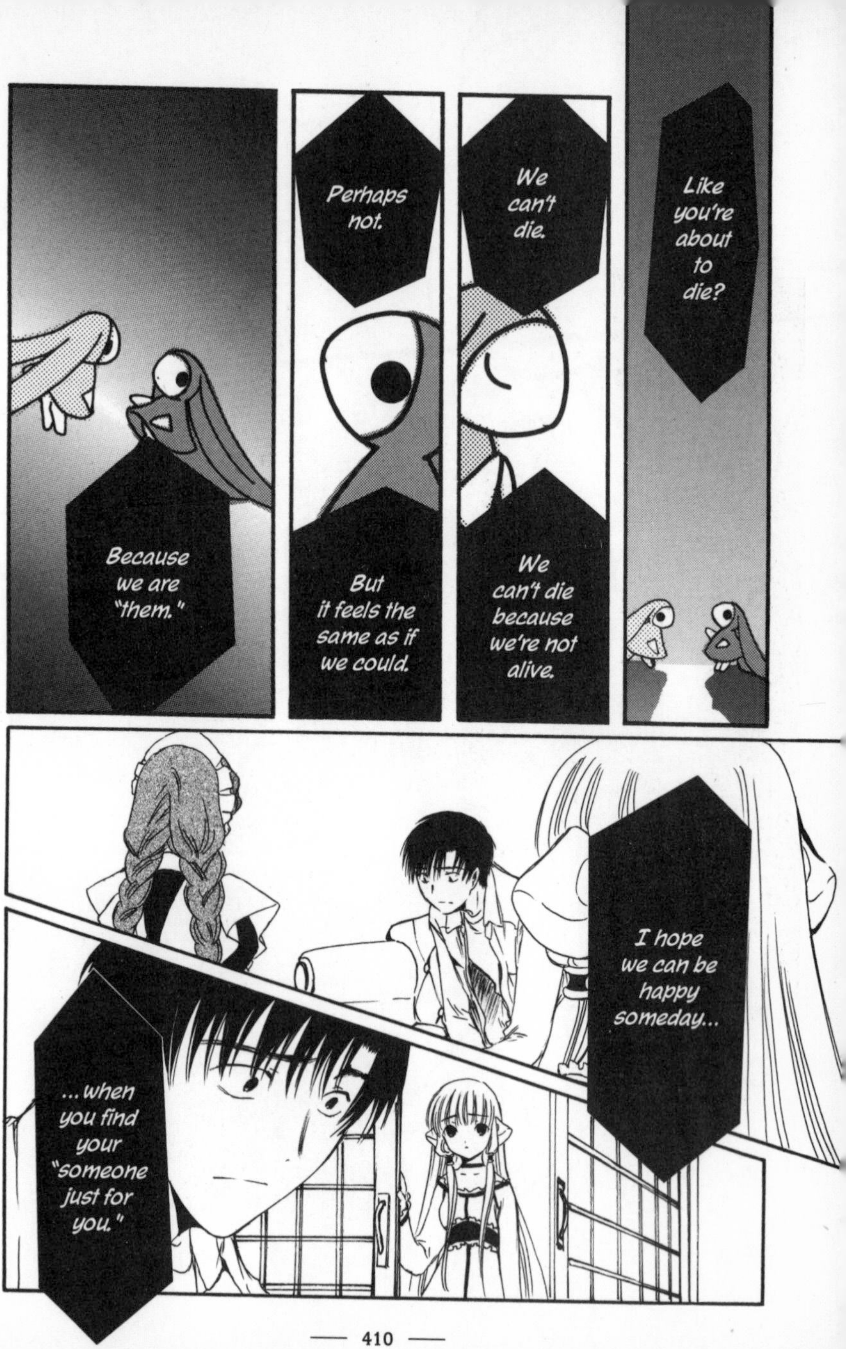
Like you're about to die?
We can't die.
We can't die because we're not alive.
Perhaps not.
But it feels the same as if we could.
Because we are "them."
I hope we can be happy someday...
...when you find your "someone just for you."

◂chapter 75▸

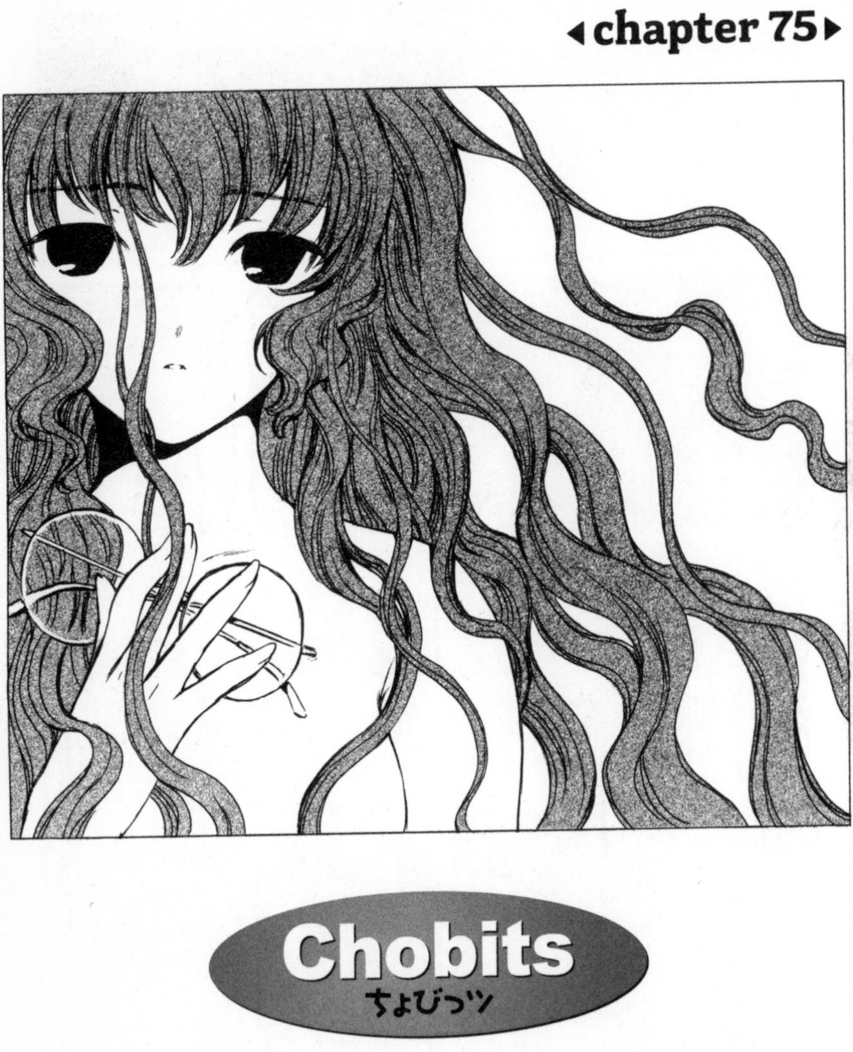

Chobits
ちょびっツ

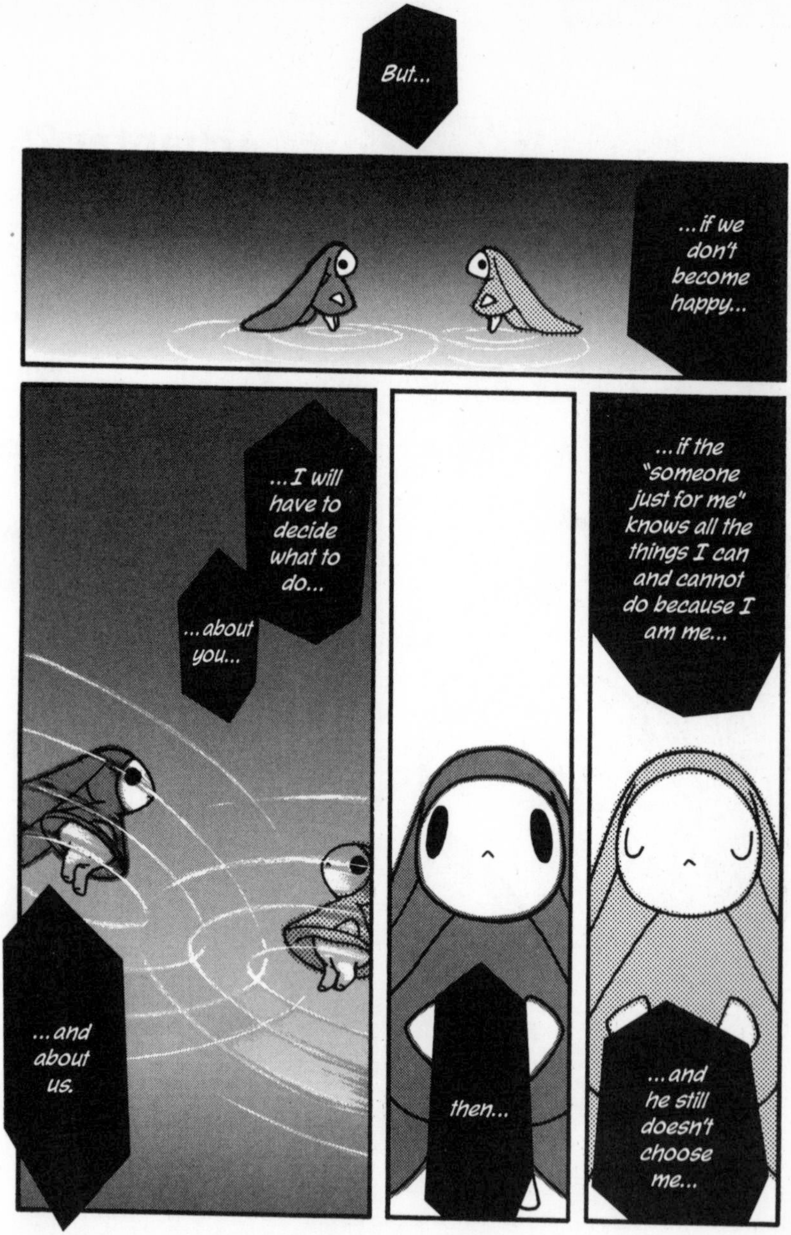
But...
...if we don't become happy...
...if the "someone just for me" knows all the things I can and cannot do because I am me...
...and he still doesn't choose me...
then...
...I will have to decide what to do...
...about you...
...and about us.

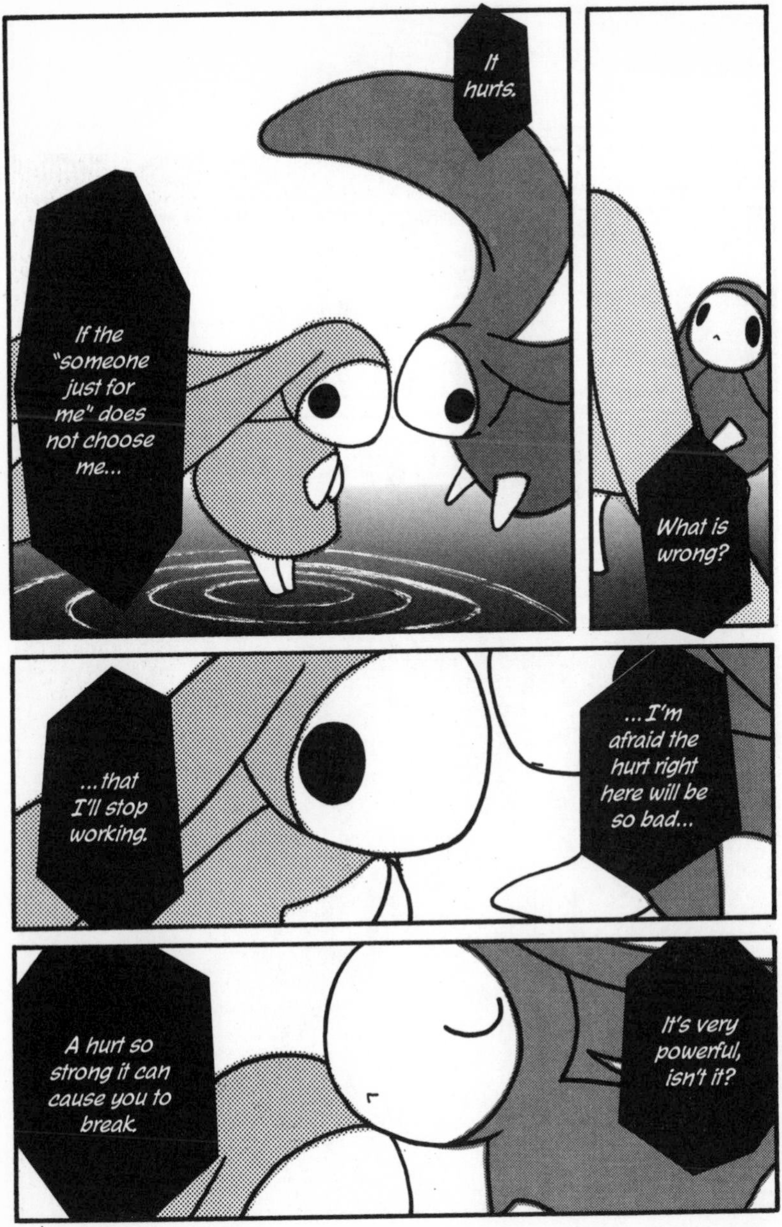
What is wrong?
It hurts.
If the "someone just for me" does not choose me...
...I'm afraid the hurt right here will be so bad...
...that I'll stop working.
It's very powerful, isn't it?
A hurt so strong it can cause you to break.

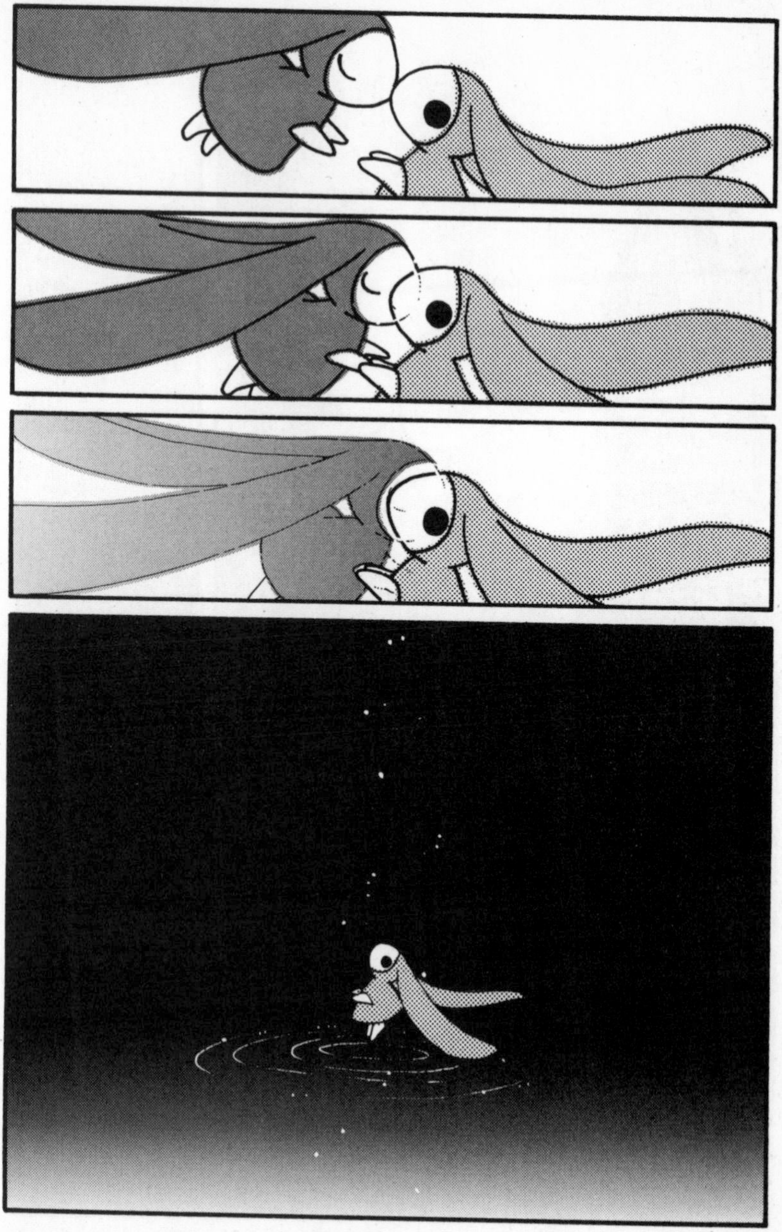

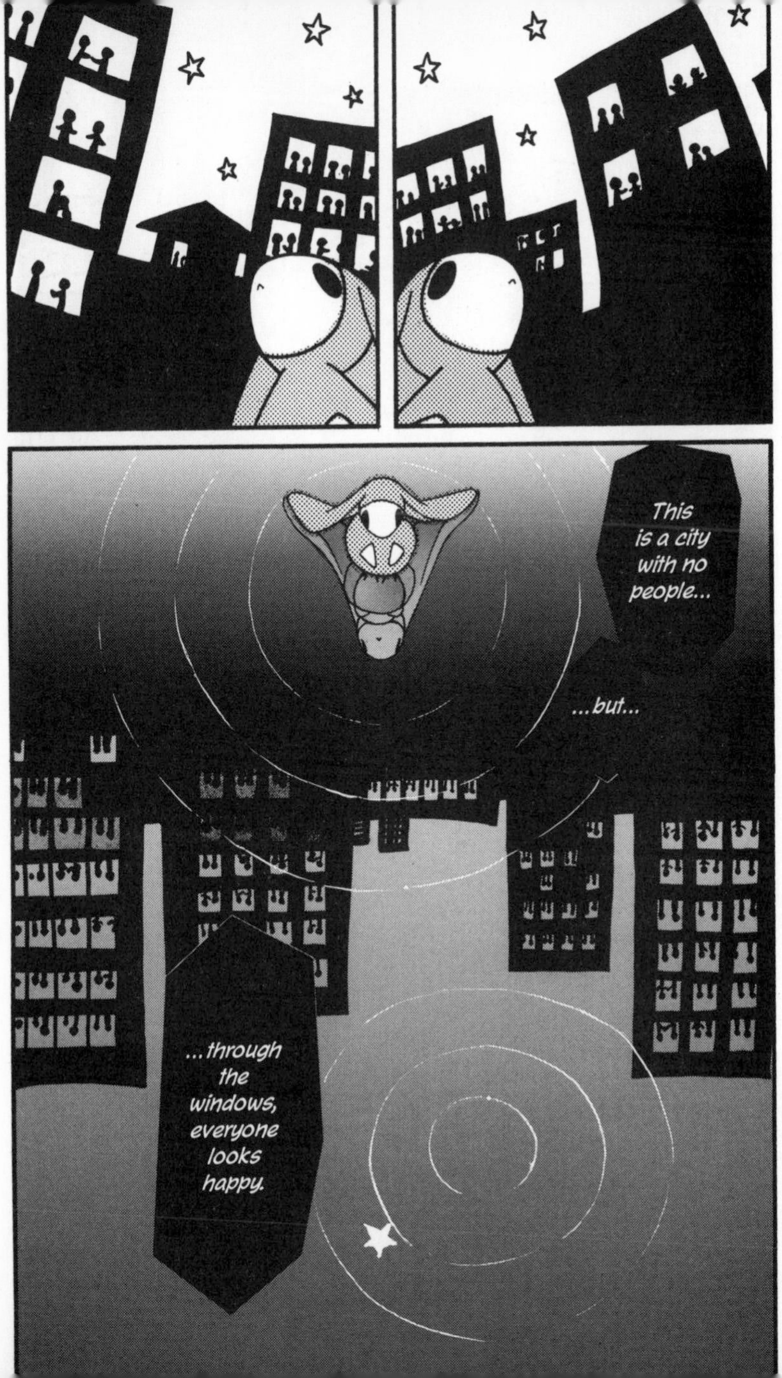
This is a city with no people...
...but...
...through the windows, everyone looks happy.

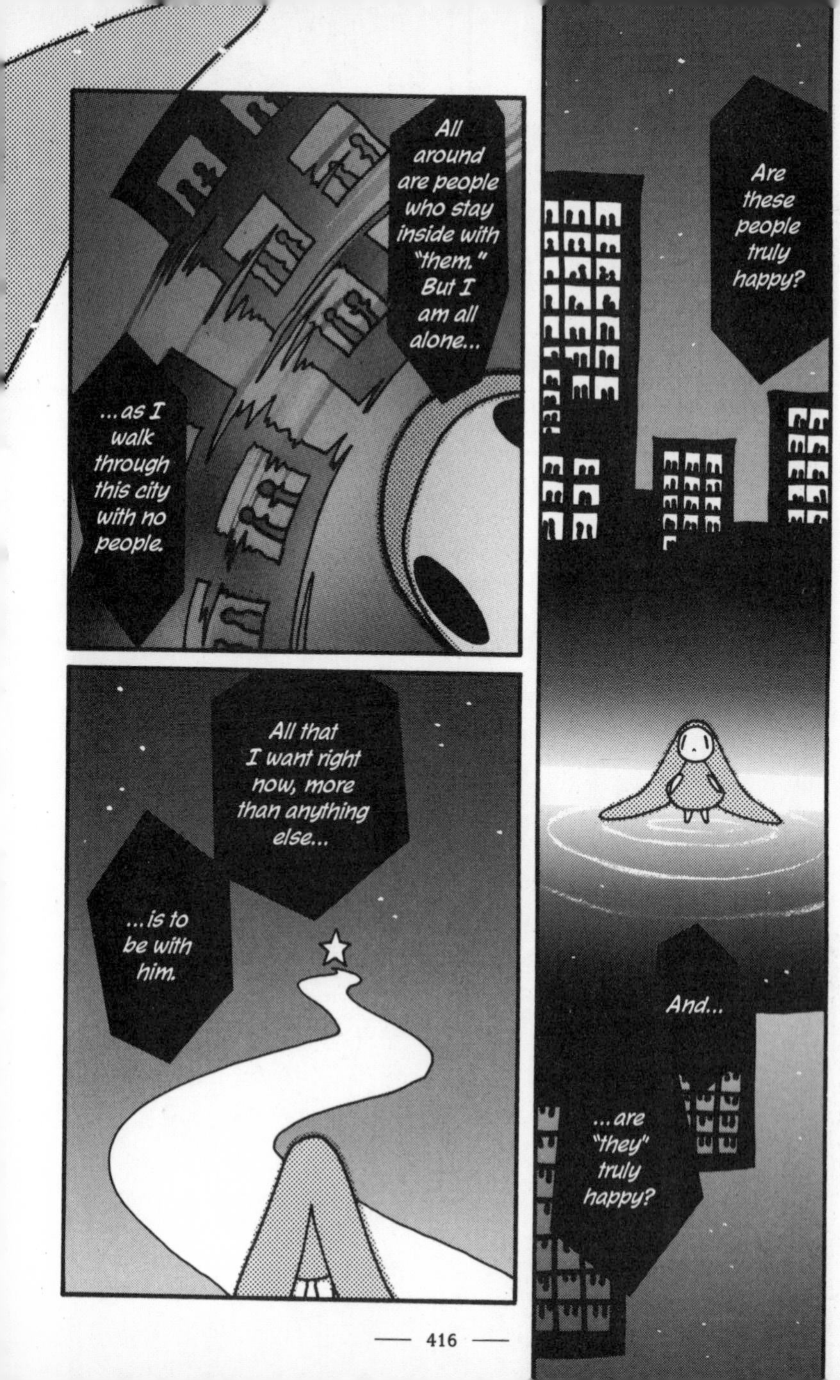
Are these people truly happy?
And...
..are "they" truly happy?
All around are people who stay inside with "them." But I am all alone...
...as I walk through this city with no people.
All that I want right now, more than anything else...
...is to be with him.

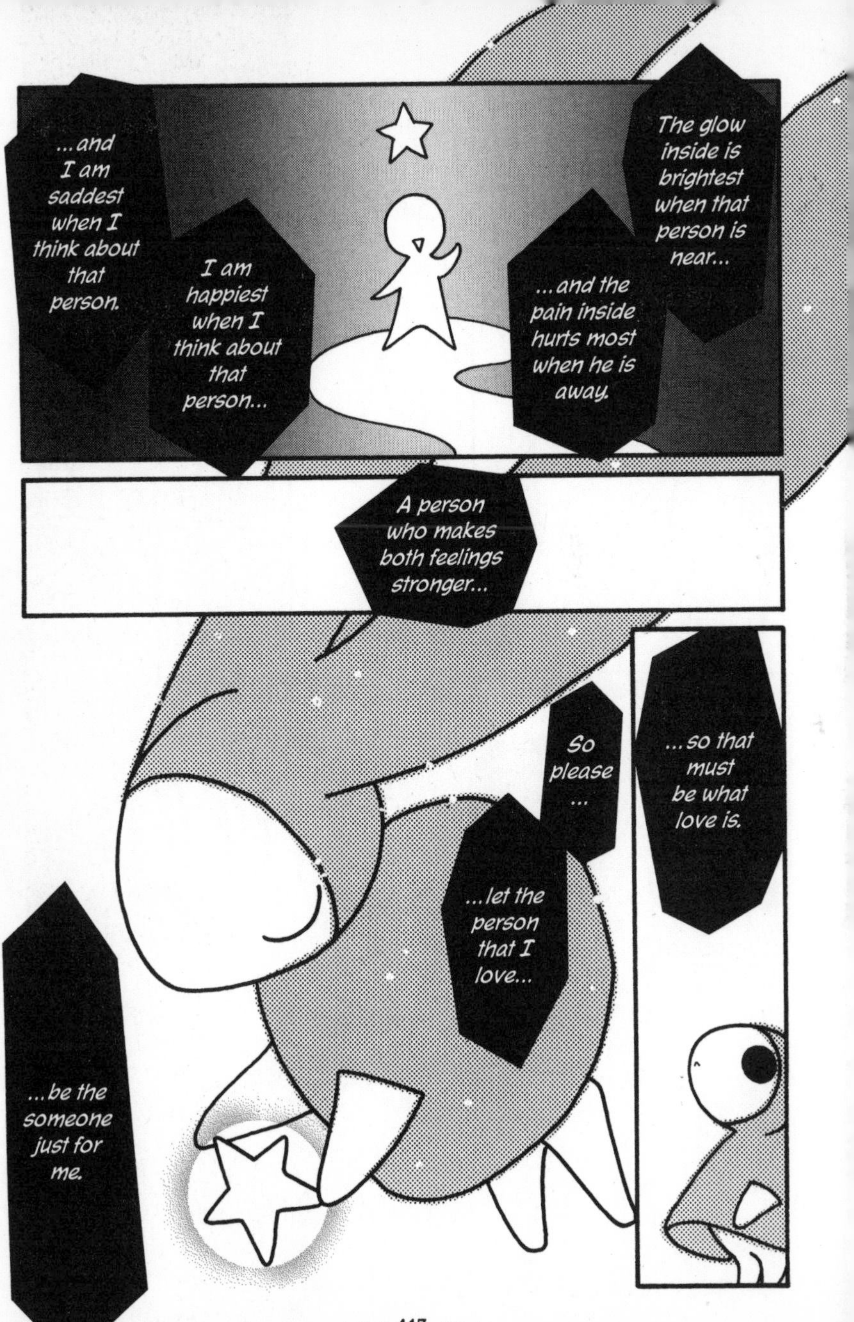
The glow inside is brightest when that person is near...
...and the pain inside hurts most when he is away.
I am happiest when I think about that person...
...and I am saddest when I think about that person.
A person who makes both feelings stronger...
...so that must be what love is.
So please...
...let the person that I love...
...be the someone just for me.

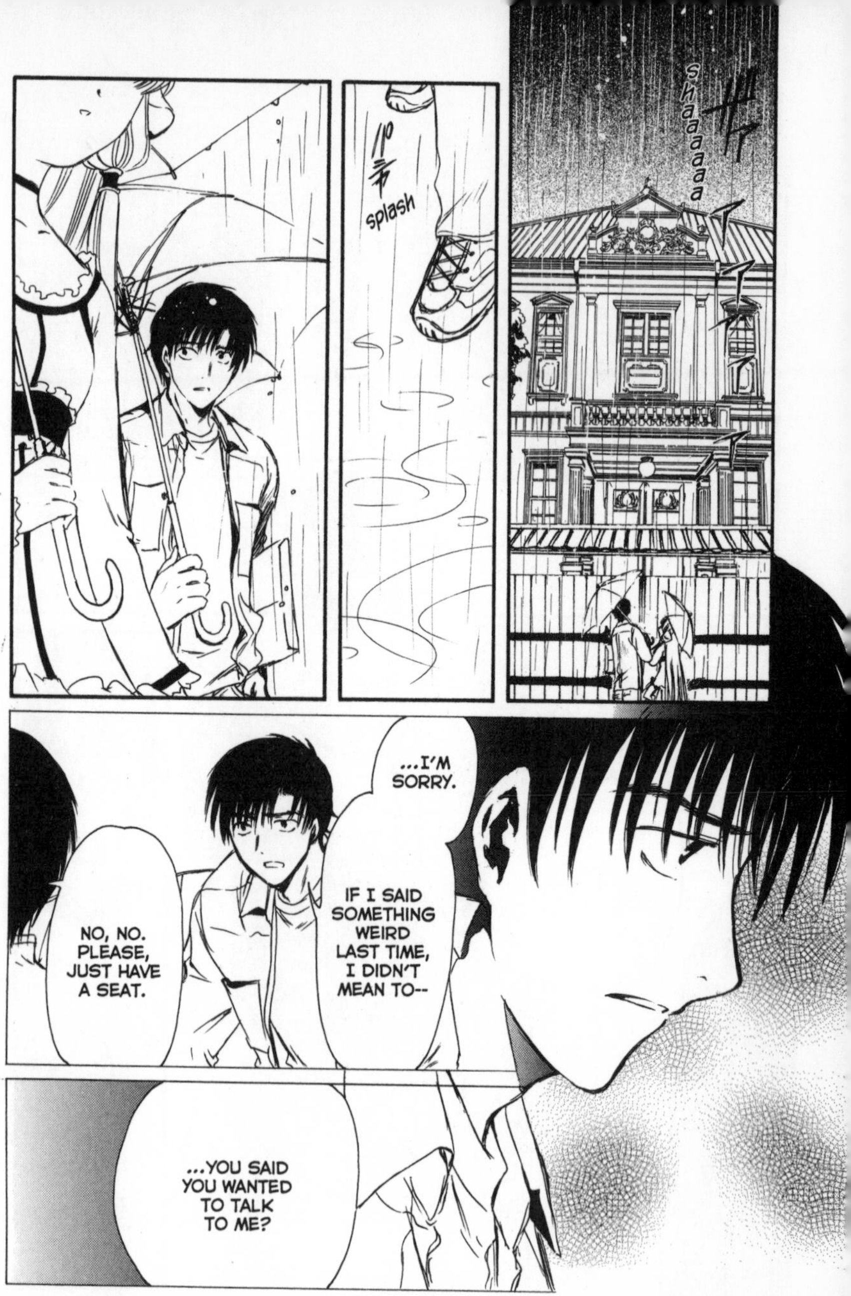
shaaaaaaa
splash
...I'M SORRY.
IF I SAID SOMETHING WEIRD LAST TIME, I DIDN'T MEAN TO--
NO, NO. PLEASE, JUST HAVE A SEAT.
...YOU SAID YOU WANTED TO TALK TO ME?

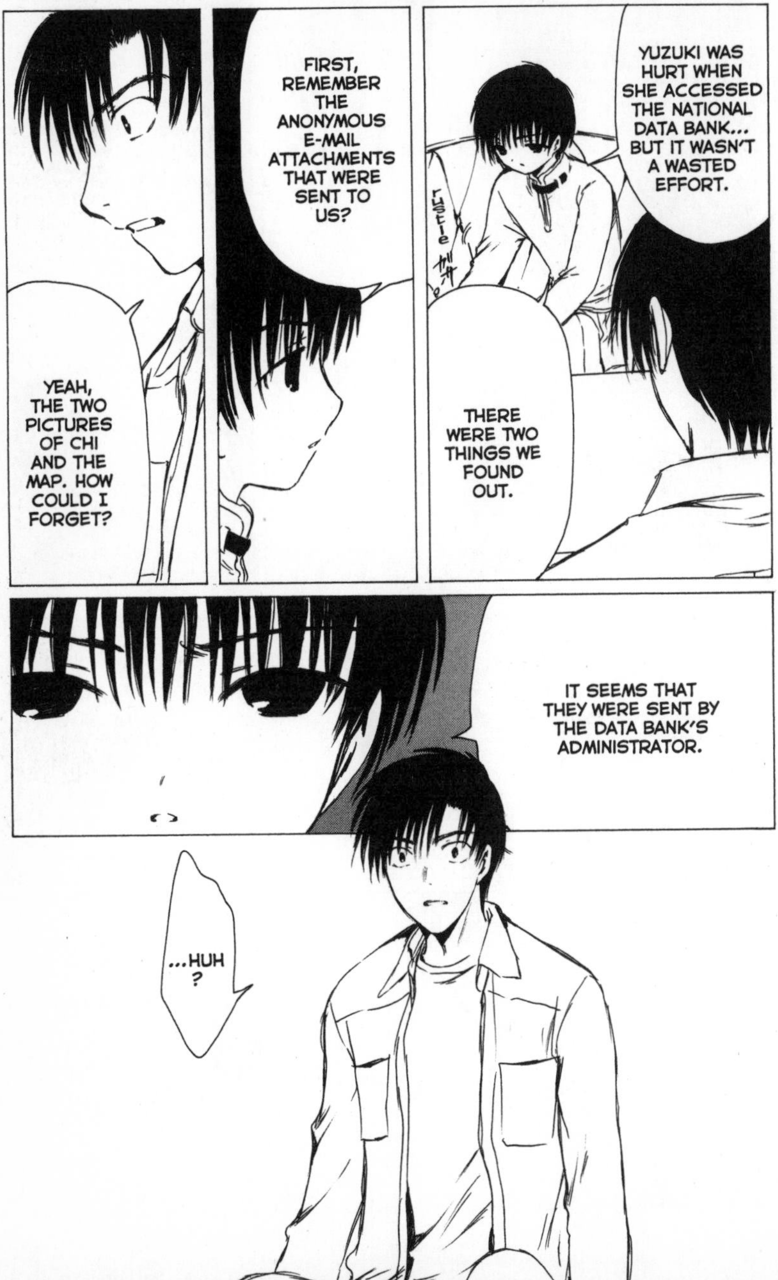
YUZUKI WAS HURT WHEN SHE ACCESSED THE NATIONAL DATA BANK... BUT IT WASN'T A WASTED EFFORT.
rustle
THERE WERE TWO THINGS WE FOUND OUT.
FIRST, REMEMBER THE ANONYMOUS E-MAIL ATTACHMENTS THAT WERE SENT TO US?
YEAH, THE TWO PICTURES OF CHI AND THE MAP. HOW COULD I FORGET?
IT SEEMS THAT THEY WERE SENT BY THE DATA BANK'S ADMINISTRATOR.
...HUH?

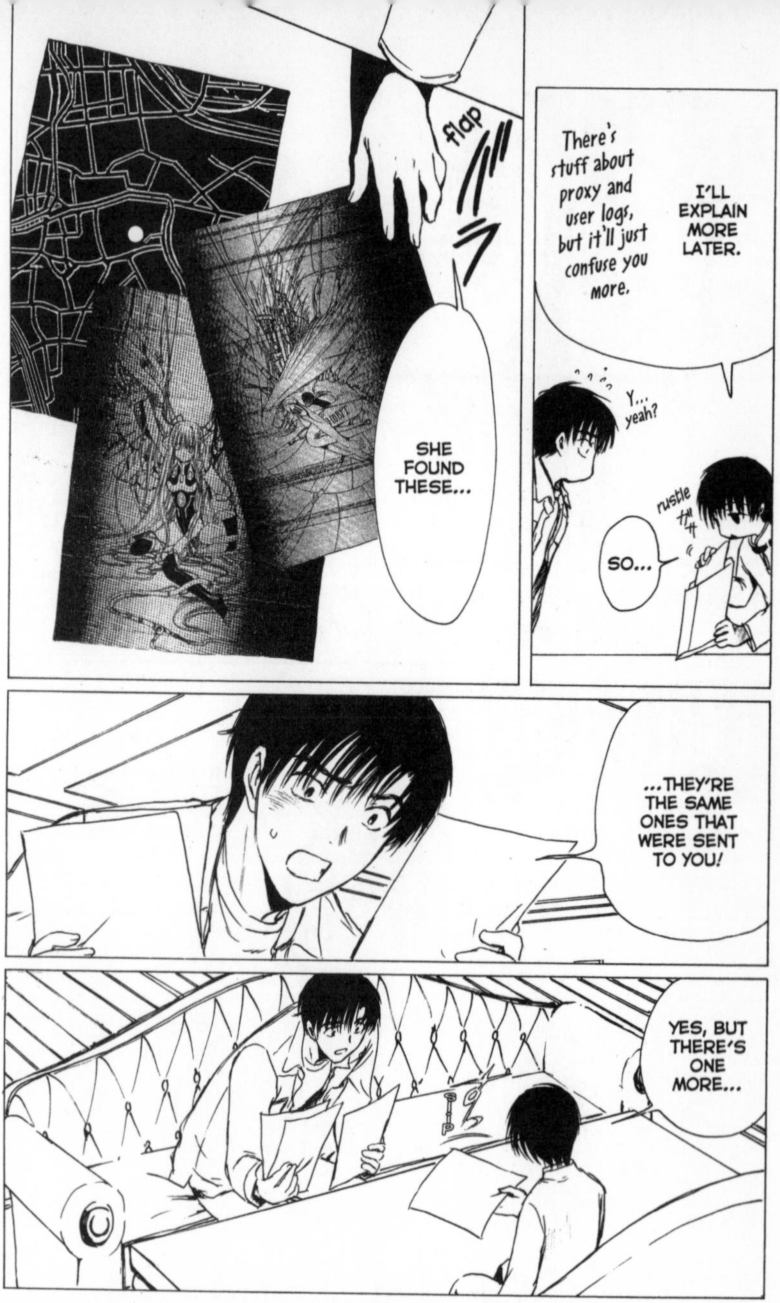
There's stuff about proxy and user logs, but it'll just confuse you more.
I'LL EXPLAIN MORE LATER.
Y... yeah?
rustle
SO...
flap
SHE FOUND THESE...
...THEY'RE THE SAME ONES THAT WERE SENT TO YOU!
YES, BUT THERE'S ONE MORE...
sip

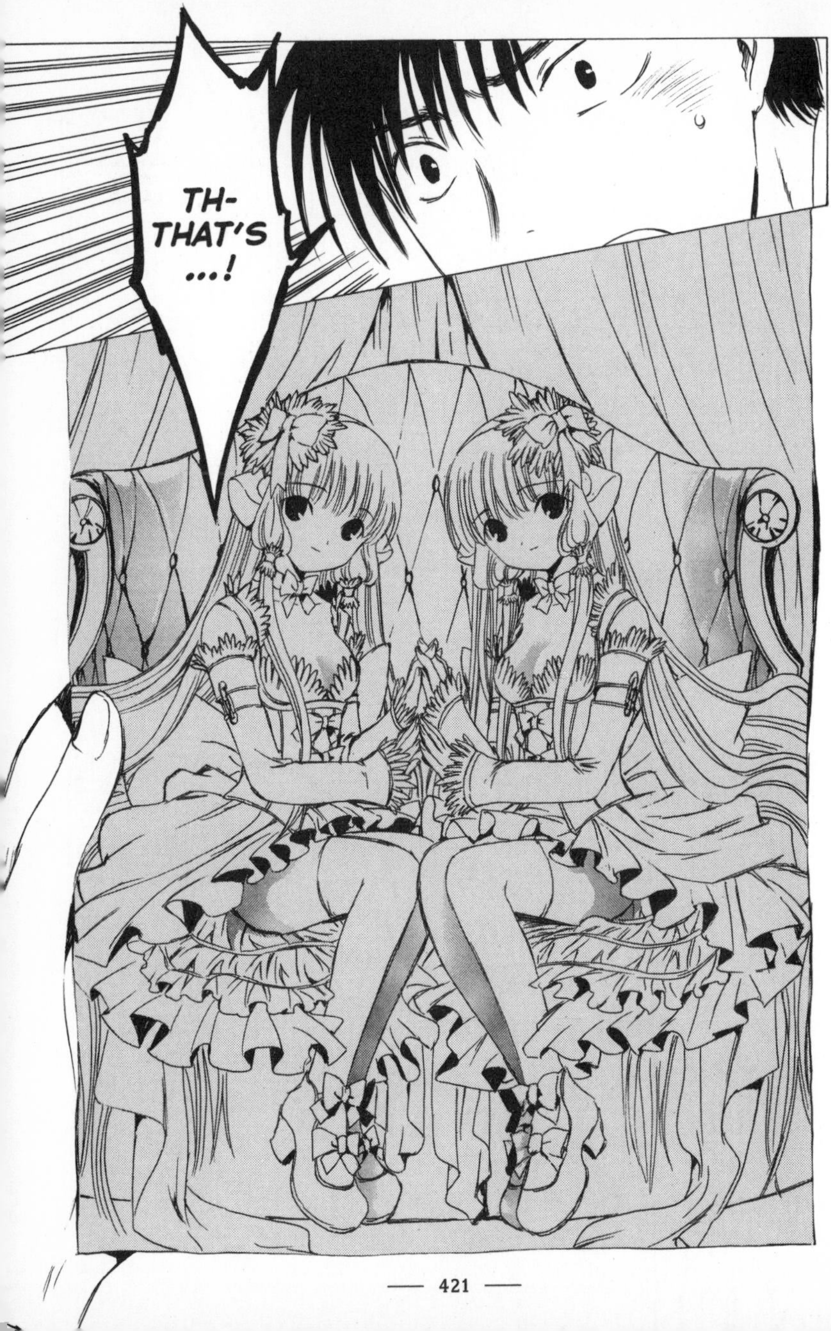
TH-
THAT'S
...!

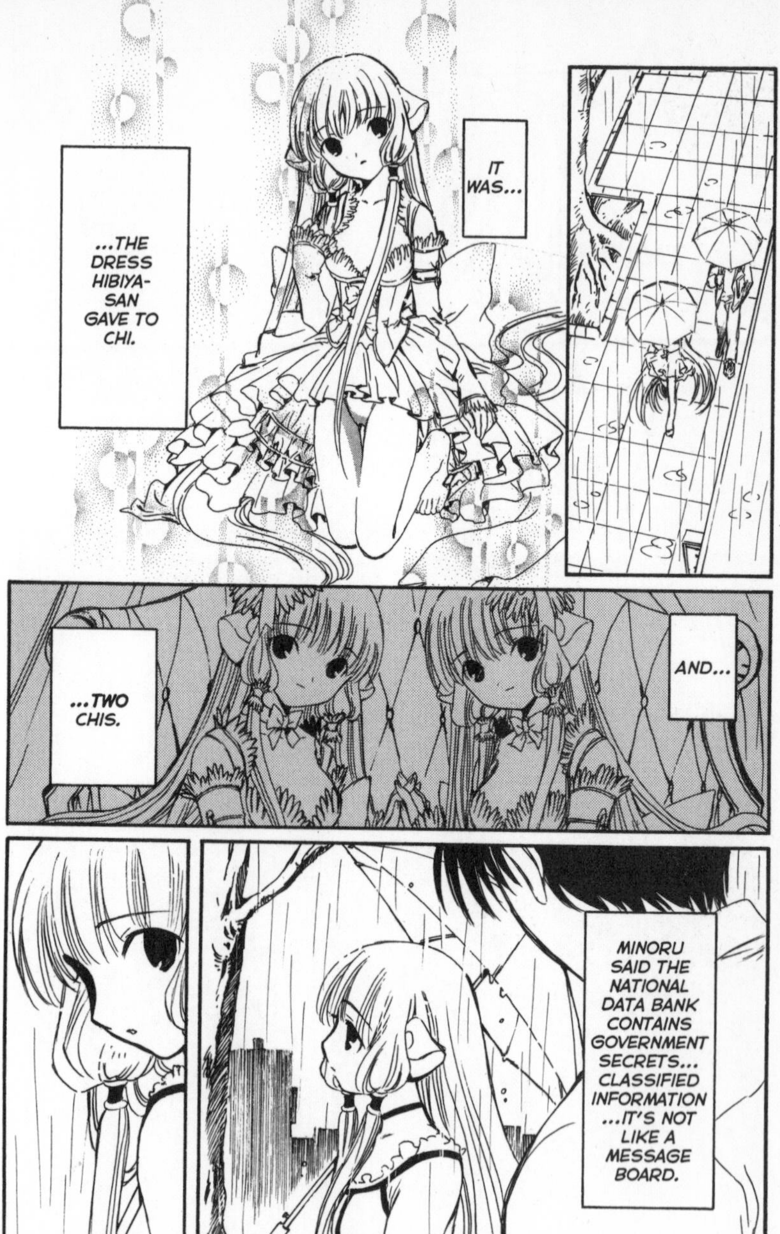
IT WAS...
...THE DRESS HIBIYA-SAN GAVE TO CHI.
AND...
...TWO CHIS.
MINORU SAID THE NATIONAL DATA BANK CONTAINS GOVERNMENT SECRETS... CLASSIFIED INFORMATION ...IT'S NOT LIKE A MESSAGE BOARD.

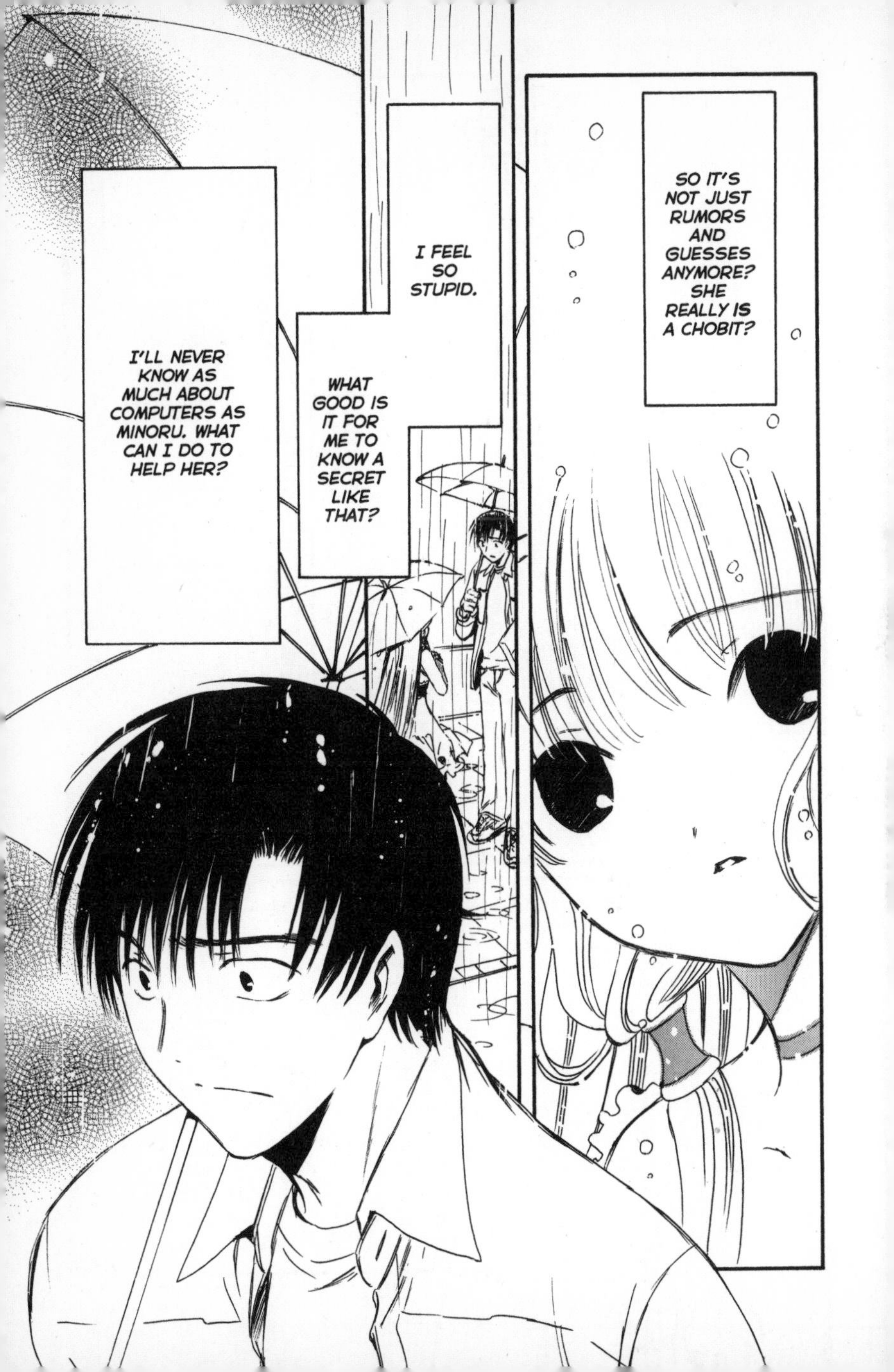
SO IT'S NOT JUST RUMORS AND GUESSES ANYMORE? SHE REALLY IS A CHOBIT?
I FEEL SO STUPID.
WHAT GOOD IS IT FOR ME TO KNOW A SECRET LIKE THAT?
I'LL NEVER KNOW AS MUCH ABOUT COMPUTERS AS MINORU. WHAT CAN I DO TO HELP HER?

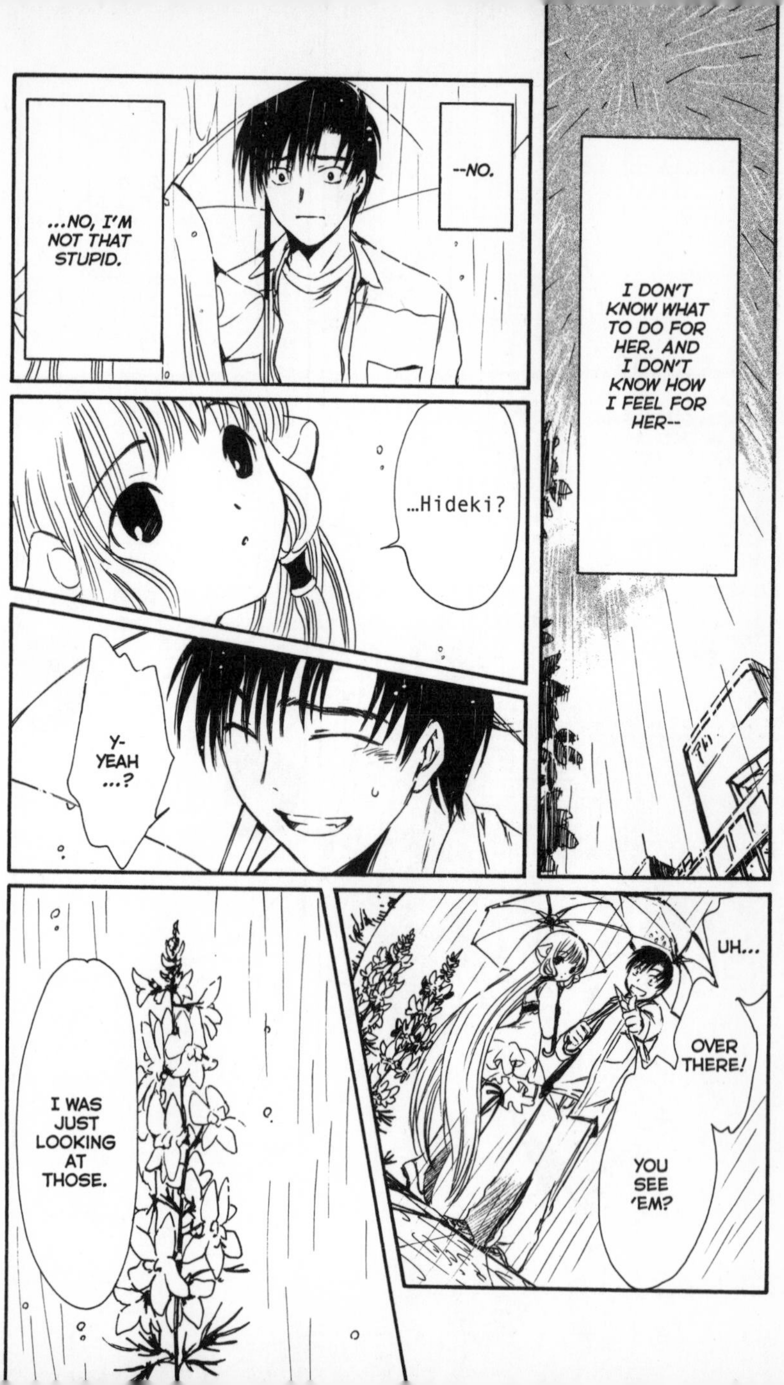
I DON'T KNOW WHAT TO DO FOR HER. AND I DON'T KNOW HOW I FEEL FOR HER--
--NO.
...NO, I'M NOT THAT STUPID.
...Hideki?
Y-YEAH ...?
UH...
OVER THERE!
YOU SEE 'EM?
I WAS JUST LOOKING AT THOSE.

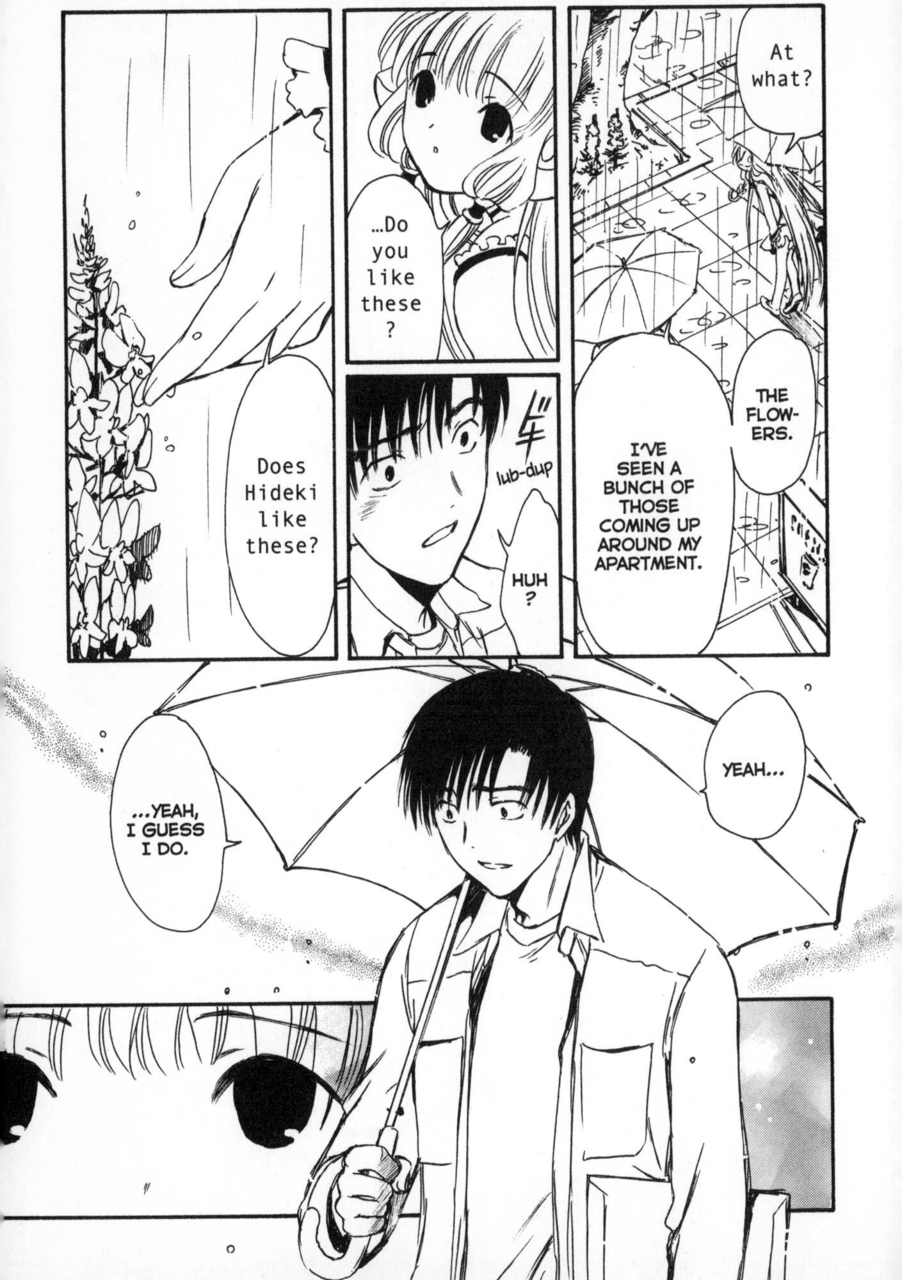

At what?
THE FLOWERS.
I'VE SEEN A BUNCH OF THOSE COMING UP AROUND MY APARTMENT.
...Do you like these?
lub-dup
HUH?
Does Hideki like these?
YEAH...
...YEAH, I GUESS I DO.

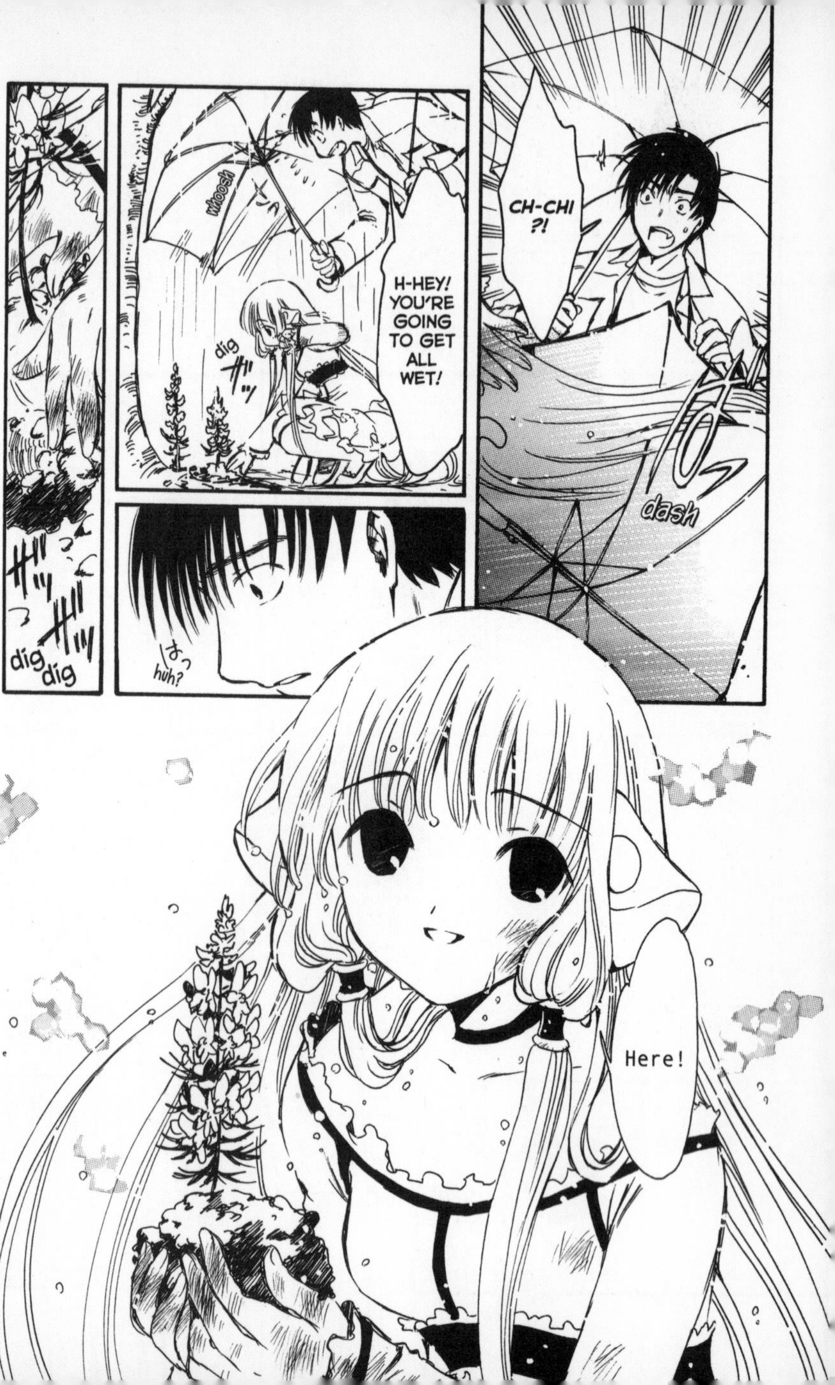

CH-CHI ?!
dash
whoosh
H-HEY! YOU'RE GOING TO GET ALL WET!
dig
はっ
huh?
dig dig
Here!

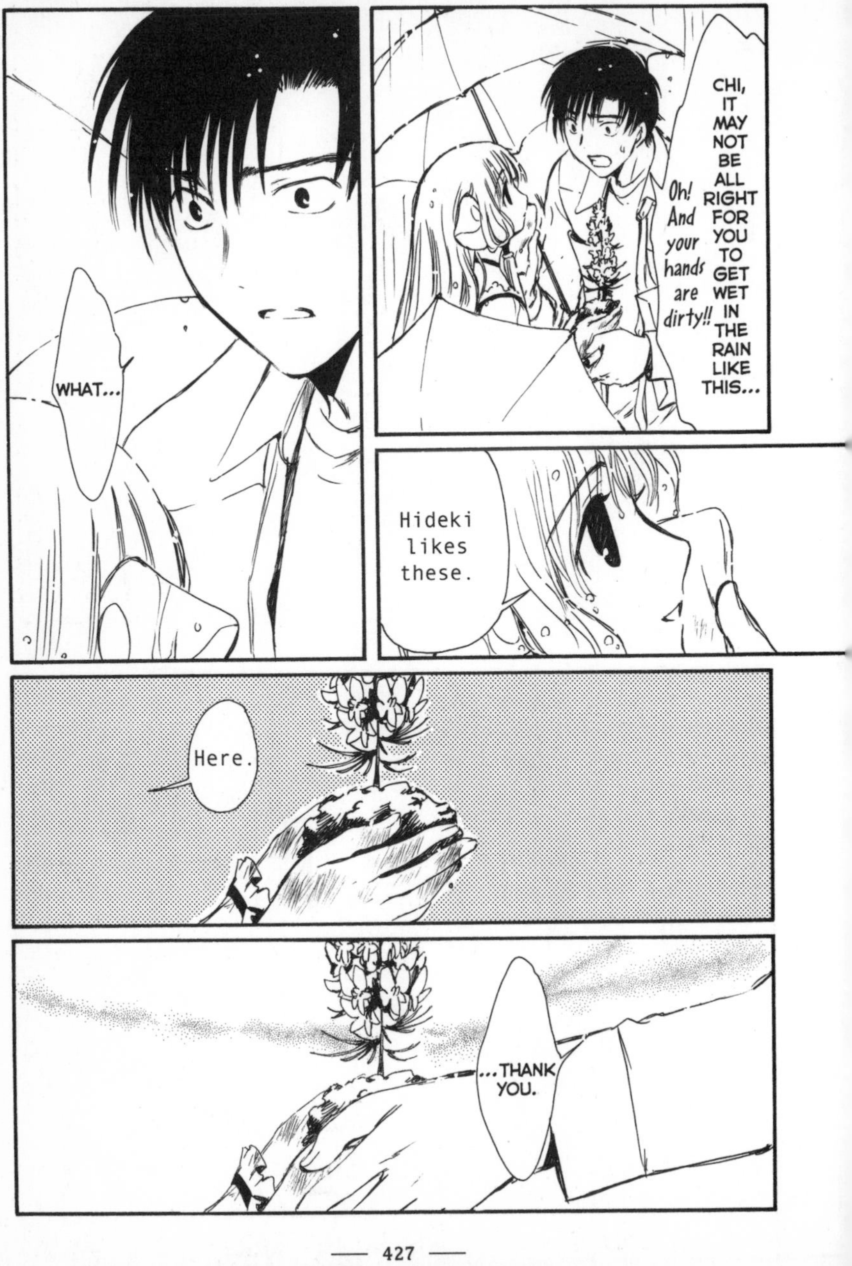
CHI, IT MAY NOT BE ALL RIGHT FOR YOU TO GET WET IN THE RAIN LIKE THIS...
Oh! And your hands are dirty!!
Hideki likes these.
WHAT...
Here.
...THANK YOU.

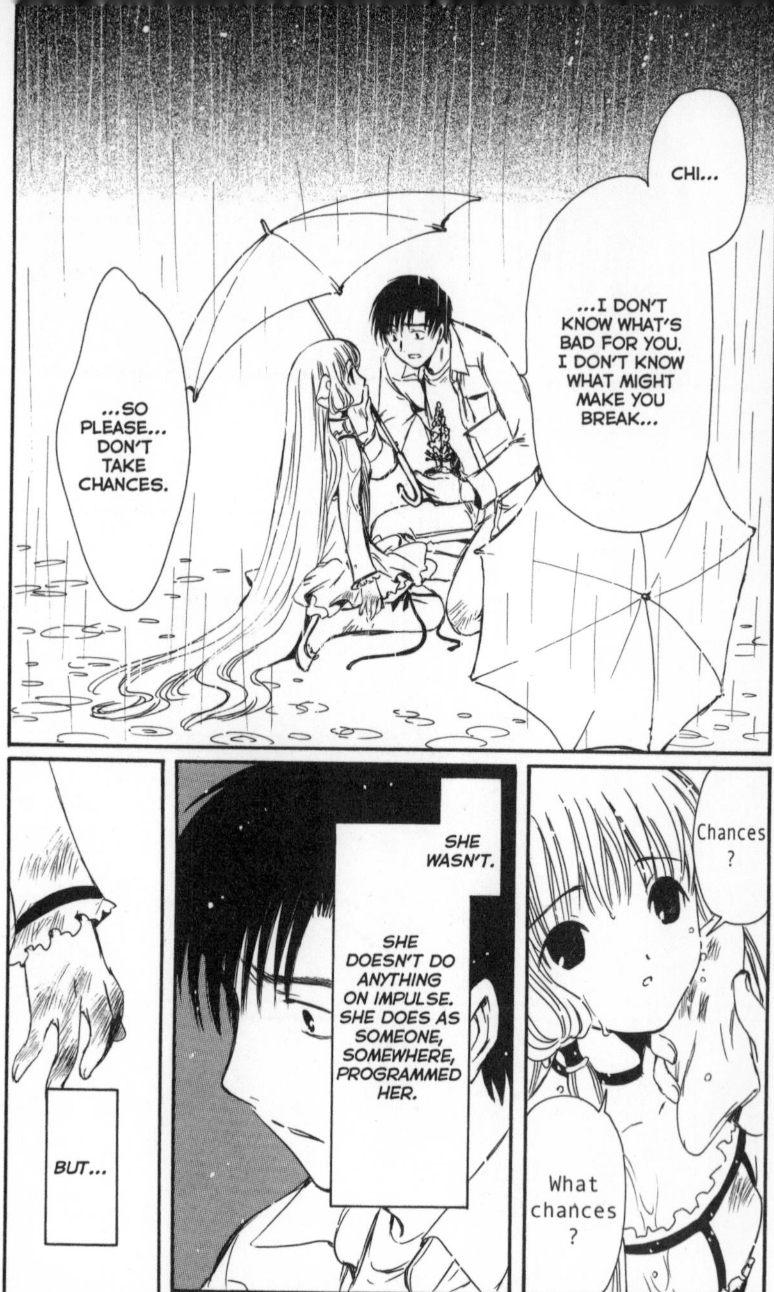
CHI...
...I DON'T KNOW WHAT'S BAD FOR YOU. I DON'T KNOW WHAT MIGHT MAKE YOU BREAK...
...SO PLEASE... DON'T TAKE CHANCES.
Chances?
What chances?
SHE WASN'T.
SHE DOESN'T DO ANYTHING ON IMPULSE. SHE DOES AS SOMEONE, SOMEWHERE, PROGRAMMED HER.
BUT...

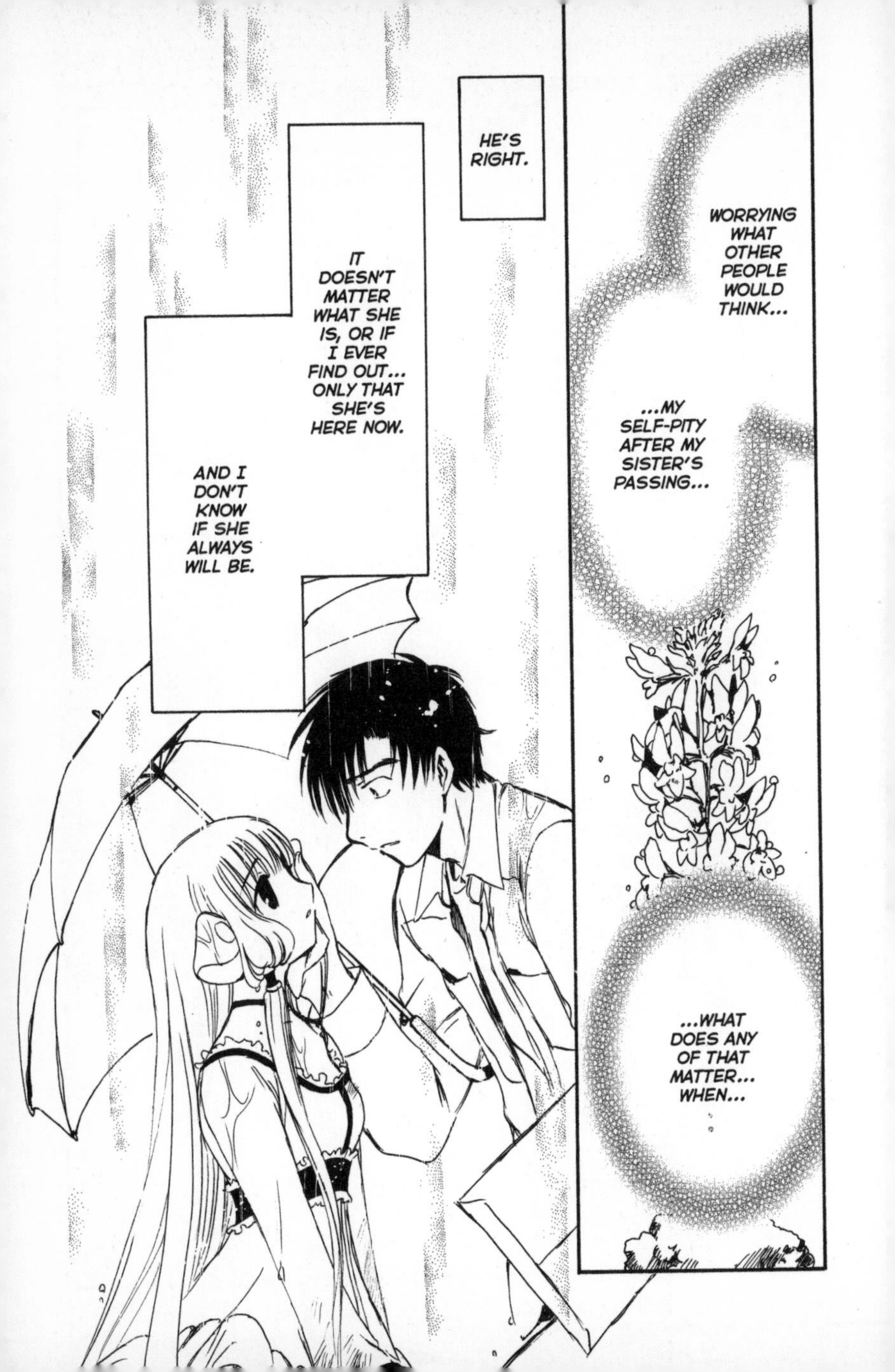
WORRYING WHAT OTHER PEOPLE WOULD THINK...
...MY SELF-PITY AFTER MY SISTER'S PASSING...
...WHAT DOES ANY OF THAT MATTER... WHEN...
HE'S RIGHT.
IT DOESN'T MATTER WHAT SHE IS, OR IF I EVER FIND OUT... ONLY THAT SHE'S HERE NOW.
AND I DON'T KNOW IF SHE ALWAYS WILL BE.

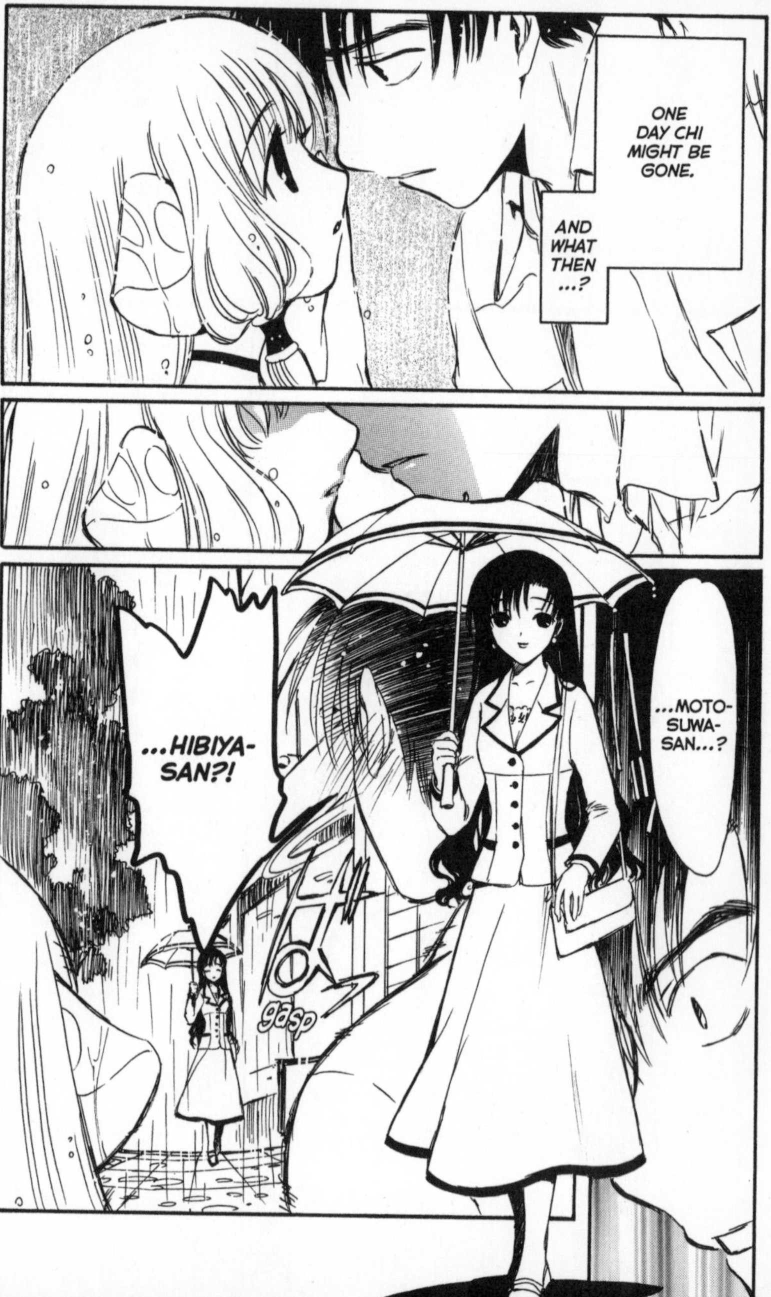
ONE DAY CHI MIGHT BE GONE.
AND WHAT THEN ...?
...MOTO-SUWA-SAN...?
...HIBIYA-SAN?!
gasp

Chobits
ちょびっツ

◀ **chapter 76** ▶

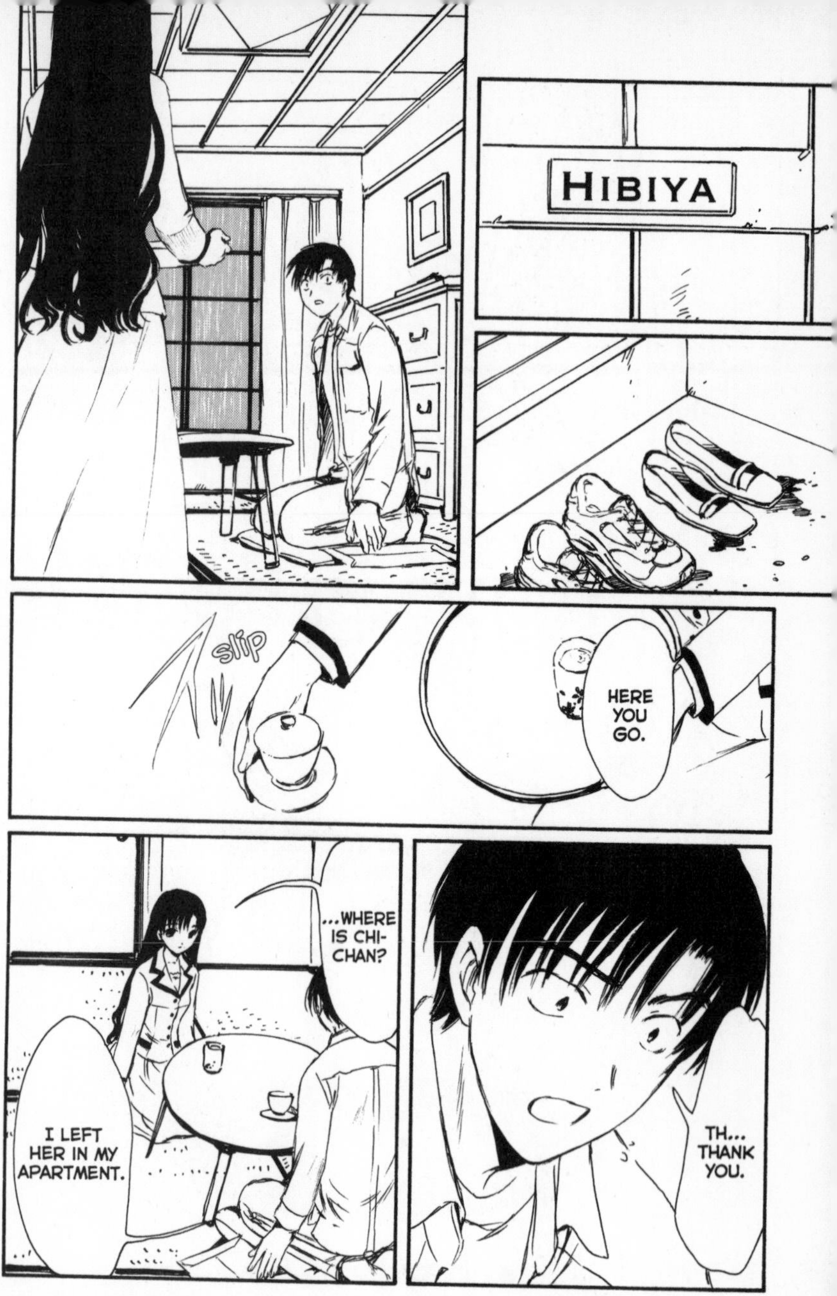
HIBIYA
HERE YOU GO.
slip
TH... THANK YOU.
...WHERE IS CHI-CHAN?
I LEFT HER IN MY APARTMENT.

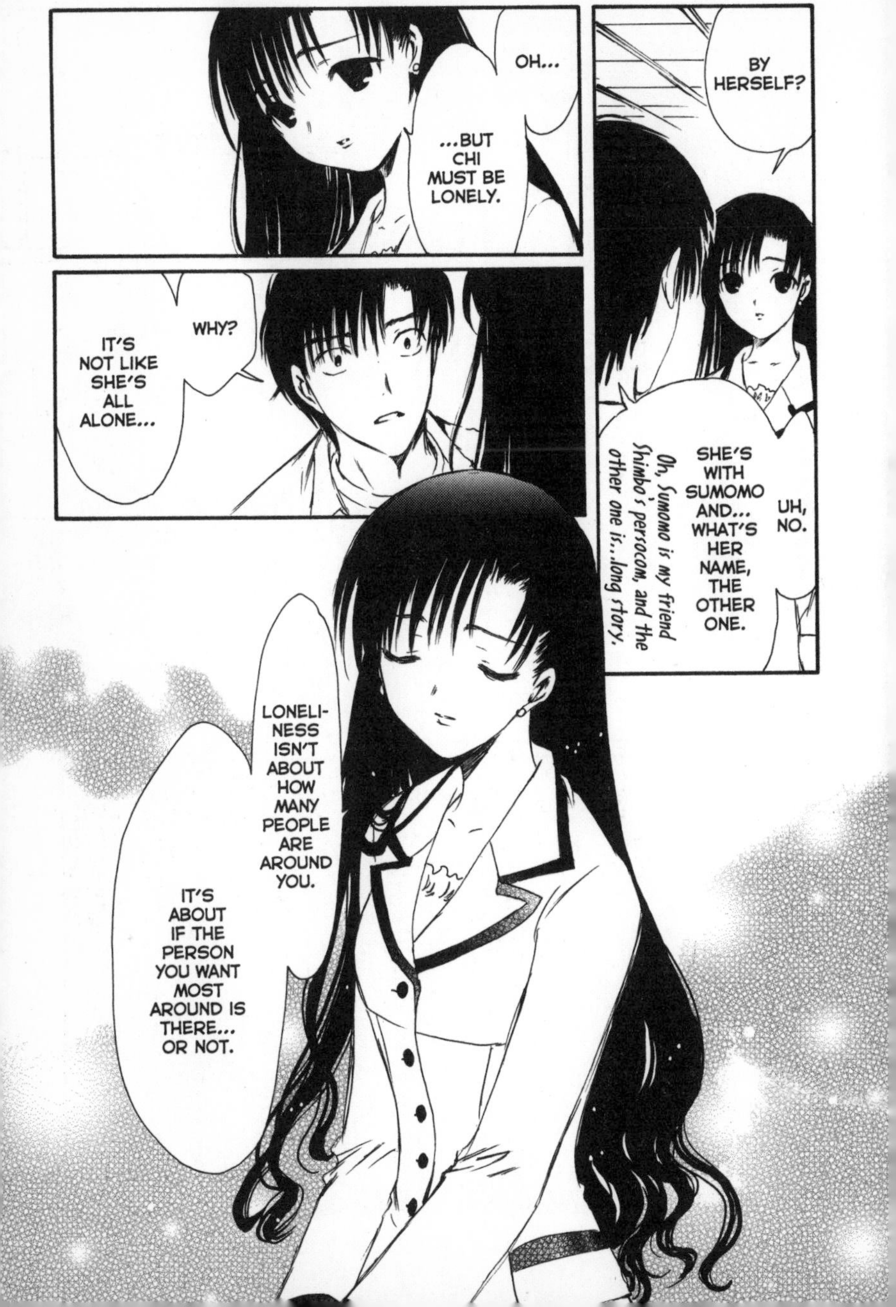
BY HERSELF?
UH, NO.
SHE'S WITH SUMOMO AND... WHAT'S HER NAME, THE OTHER ONE.
Oh, Sumomo is my friend Shimbo's persocom, and the other one is...long story.
OH...
...BUT CHI MUST BE LONELY.
WHY?
IT'S NOT LIKE SHE'S ALL ALONE...
LONELI-NESS ISN'T ABOUT HOW MANY PEOPLE ARE AROUND YOU.
IT'S ABOUT IF THE PERSON YOU WANT MOST AROUND IS THERE... OR NOT.

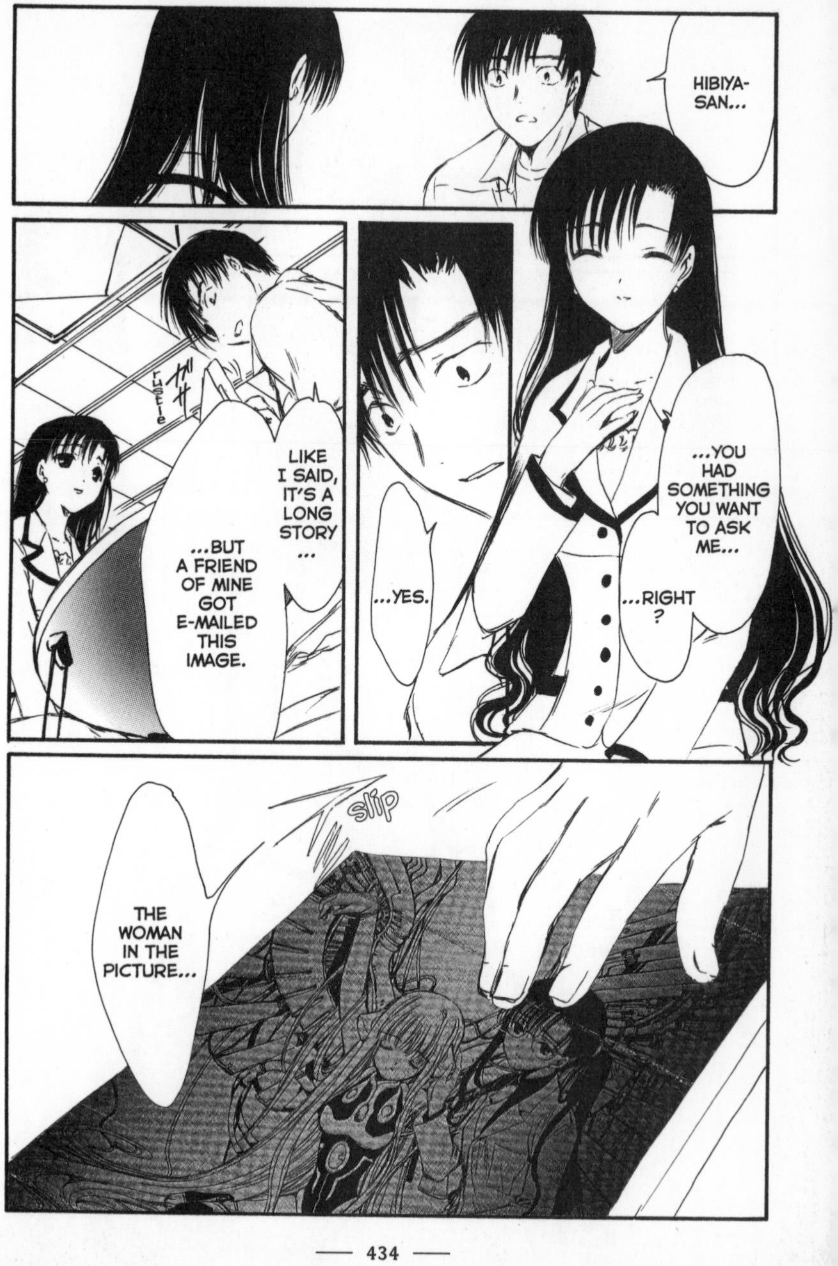
HIBIYA-SAN...
...YOU HAD SOMETHING YOU WANT TO ASK ME...
...RIGHT?
...YES.
rustle
LIKE I SAID, IT'S A LONG STORY...
...BUT A FRIEND OF MINE GOT E-MAILED THIS IMAGE.
slip
THE WOMAN IN THE PICTURE...

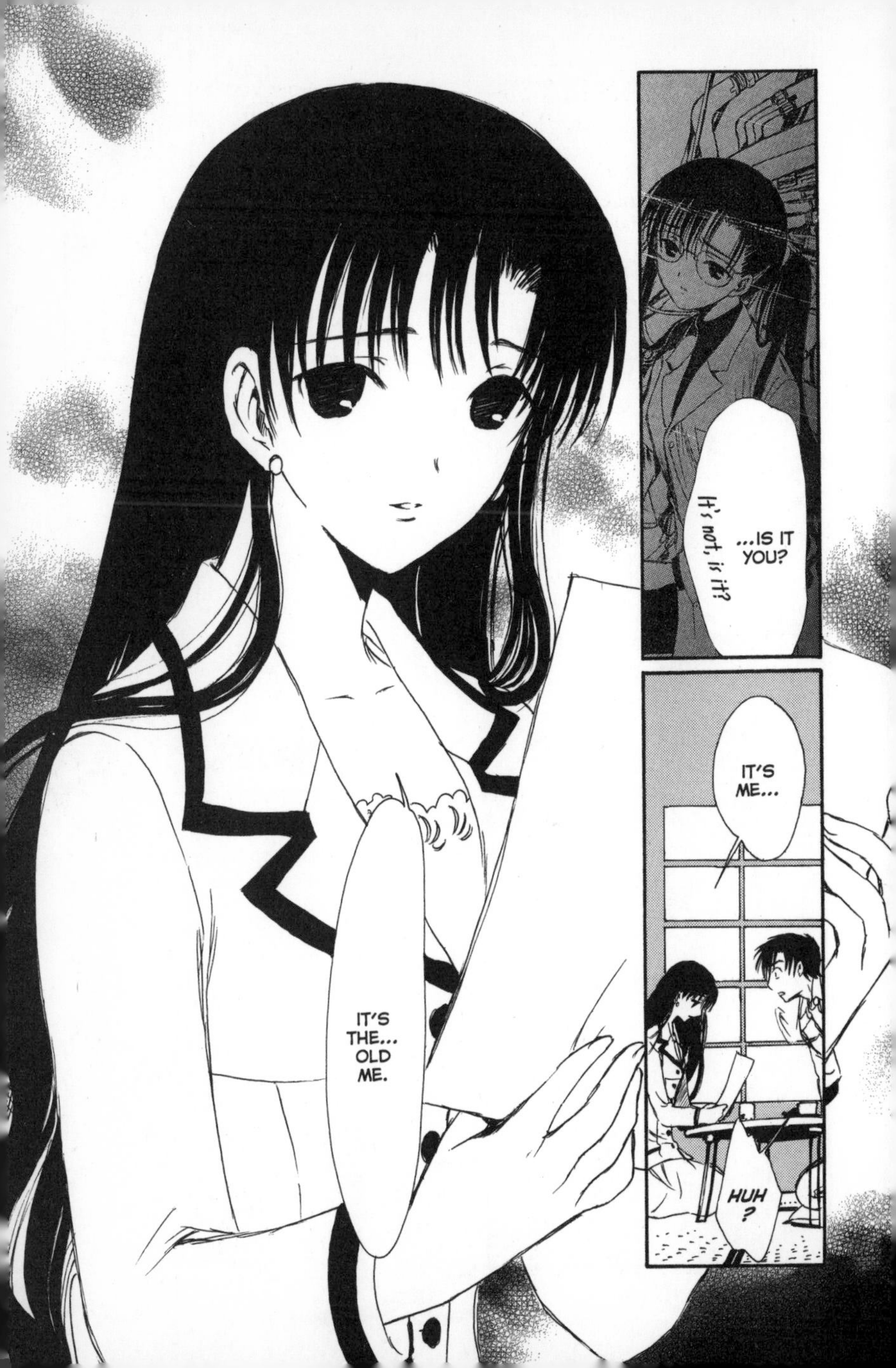
...IS IT YOU?
It's not, is it?
IT'S ME...
HUH?
IT'S THE... OLD ME.

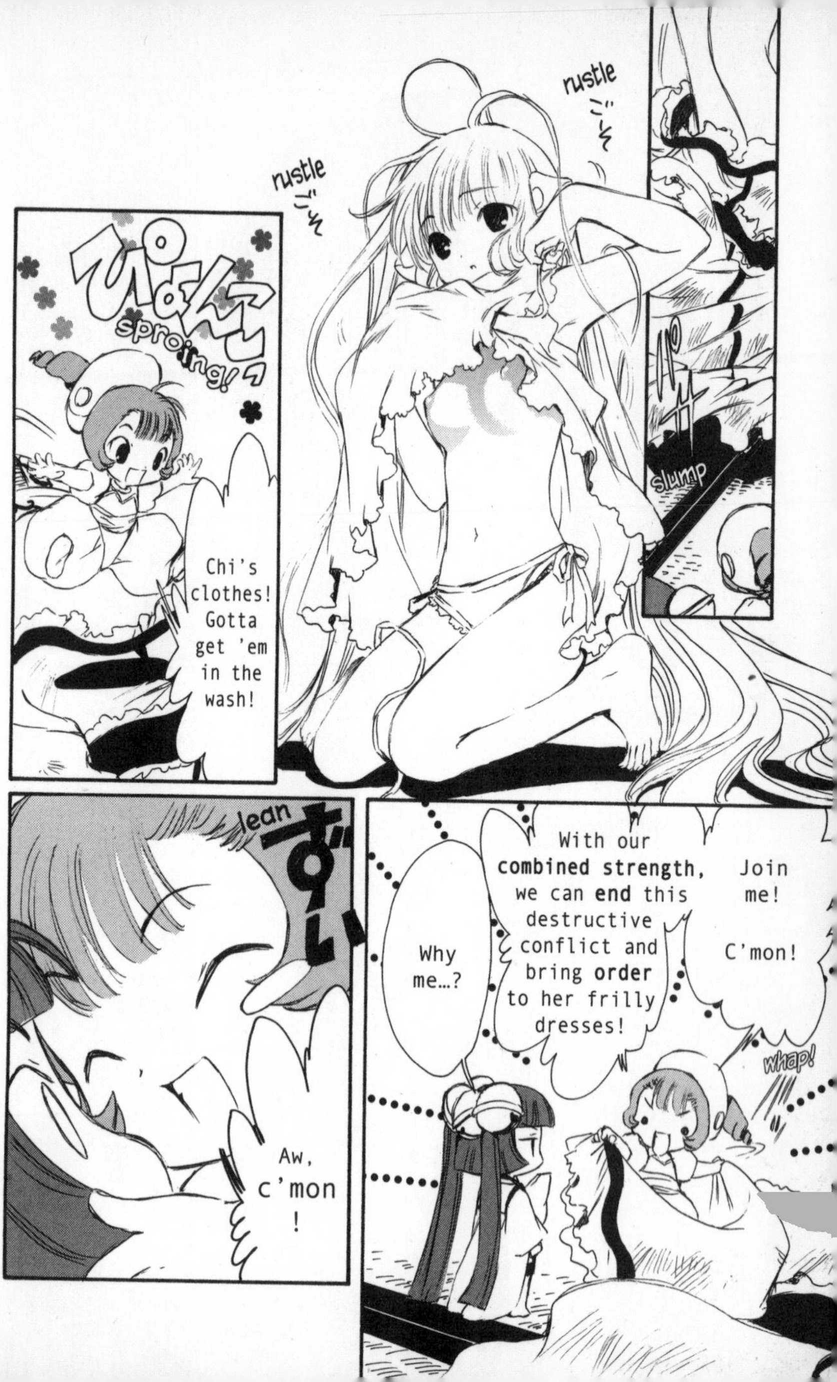
slump
rustle
rustle
sproing!
Chi's clothes! Gotta get 'em in the wash!
Join me!
C'mon!
With our combined strength, we can end this destructive conflict and bring order to her frilly dresses!
Why me...?
whap!
lean
Aw, c'mon!

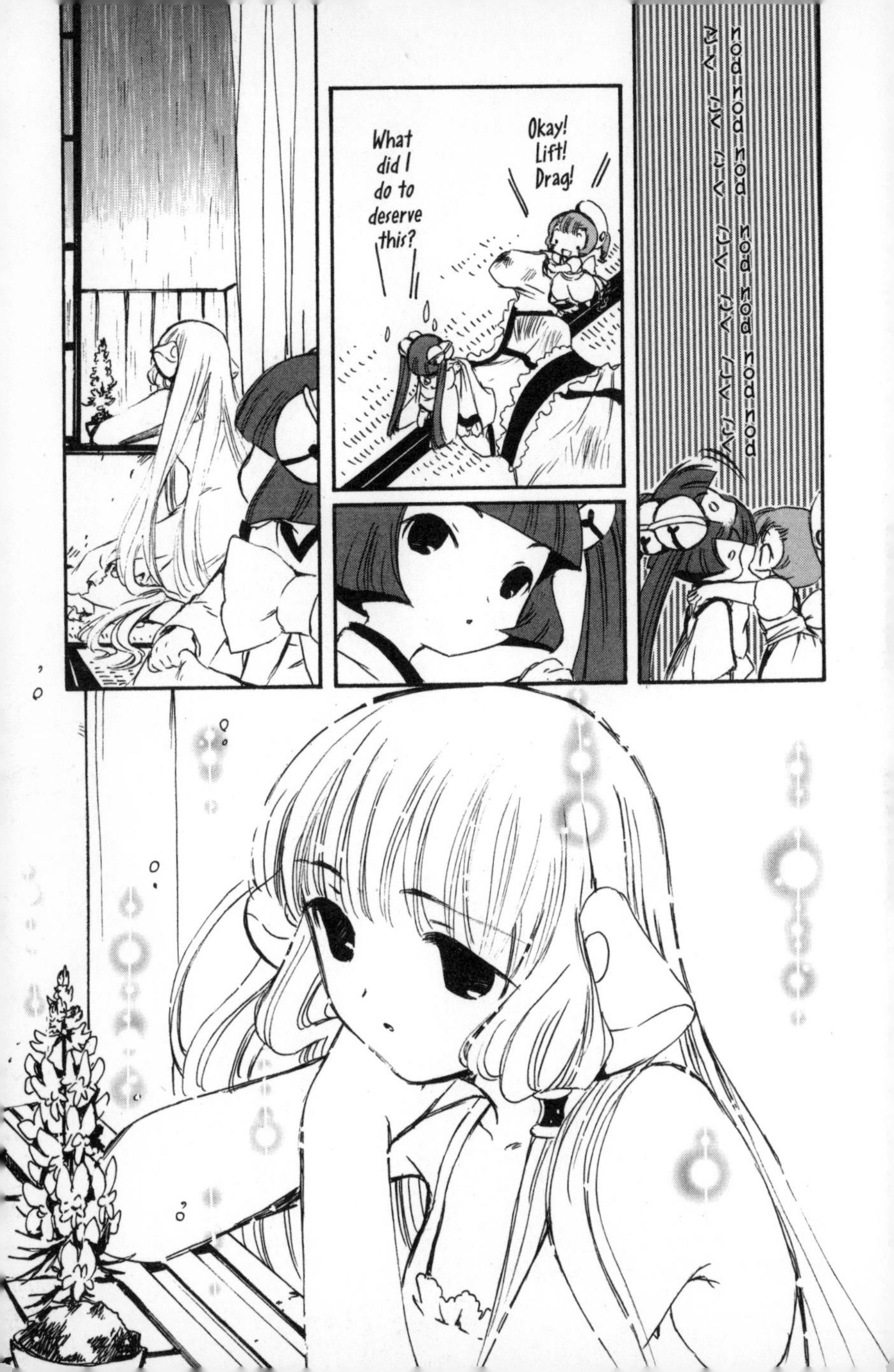
nod nod nod nod nod nod
Okay! Lift! Drag!
What did I do to deserve this?

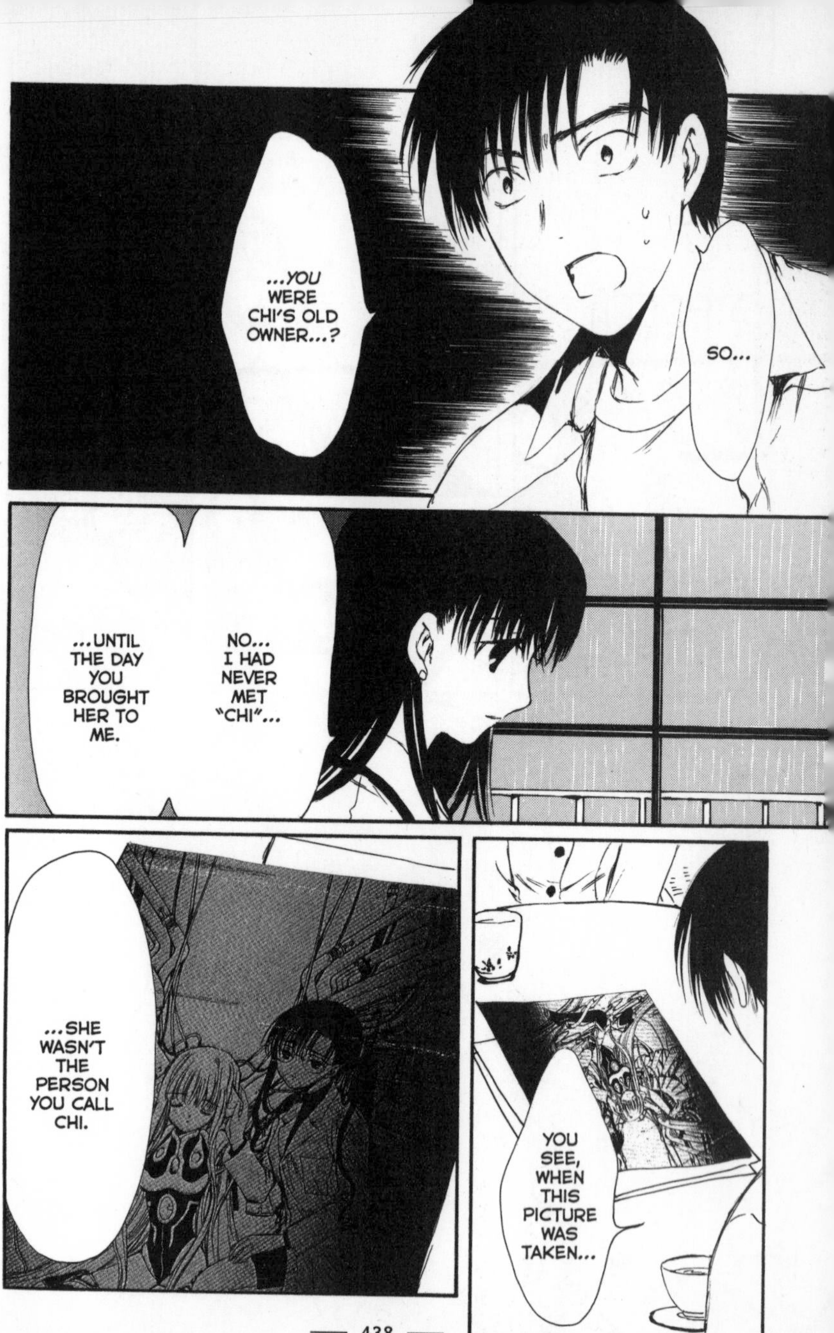
SO...
...YOU WERE CHI'S OLD OWNER...?
NO... I HAD NEVER MET "CHI"...
...UNTIL THE DAY YOU BROUGHT HER TO ME.
YOU SEE, WHEN THIS PICTURE WAS TAKEN...
...SHE WASN'T THE PERSON YOU CALL CHI.

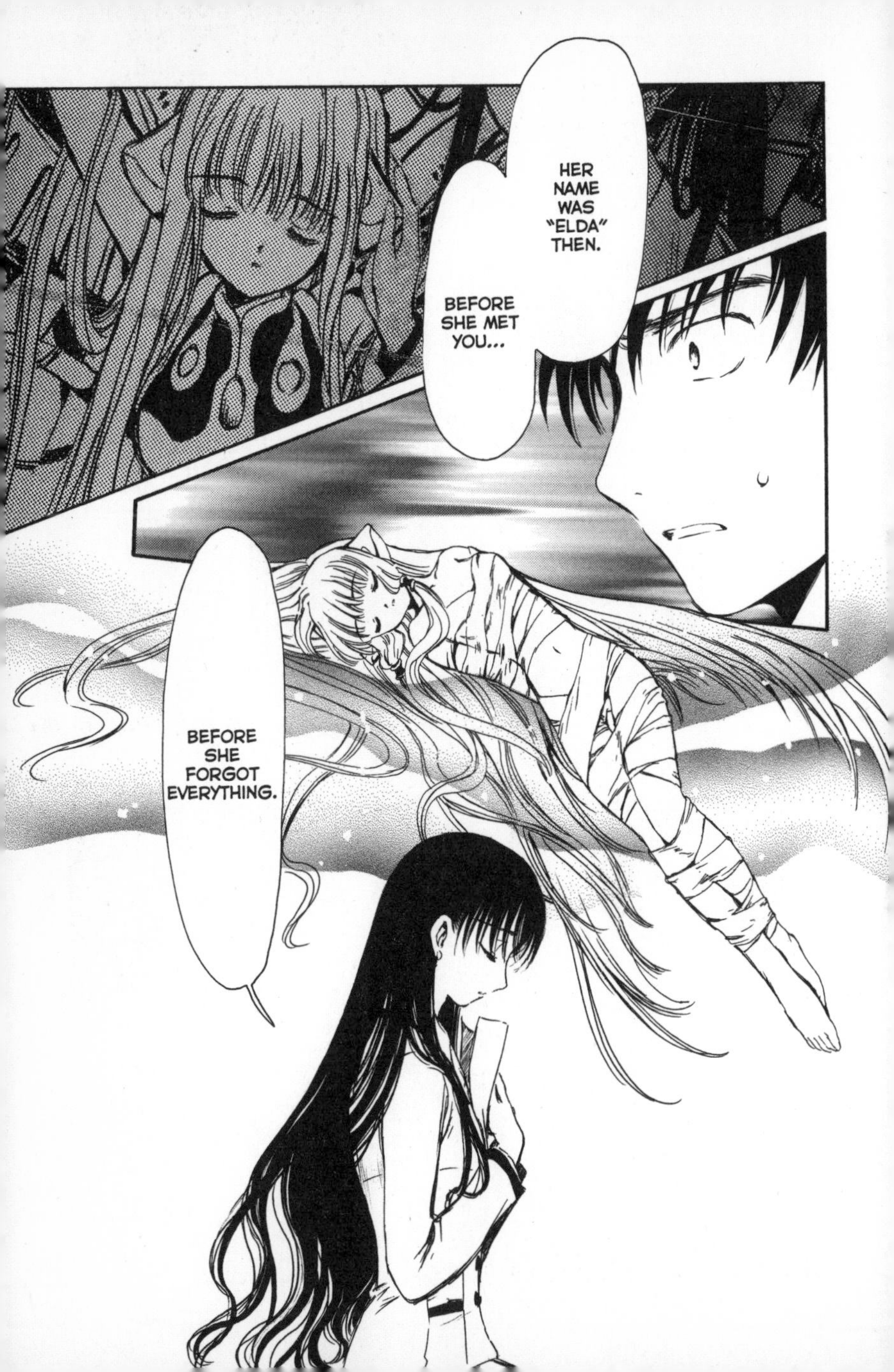
HER NAME WAS "ELDA" THEN.
BEFORE SHE MET YOU...
BEFORE SHE FORGOT EVERYTHING.

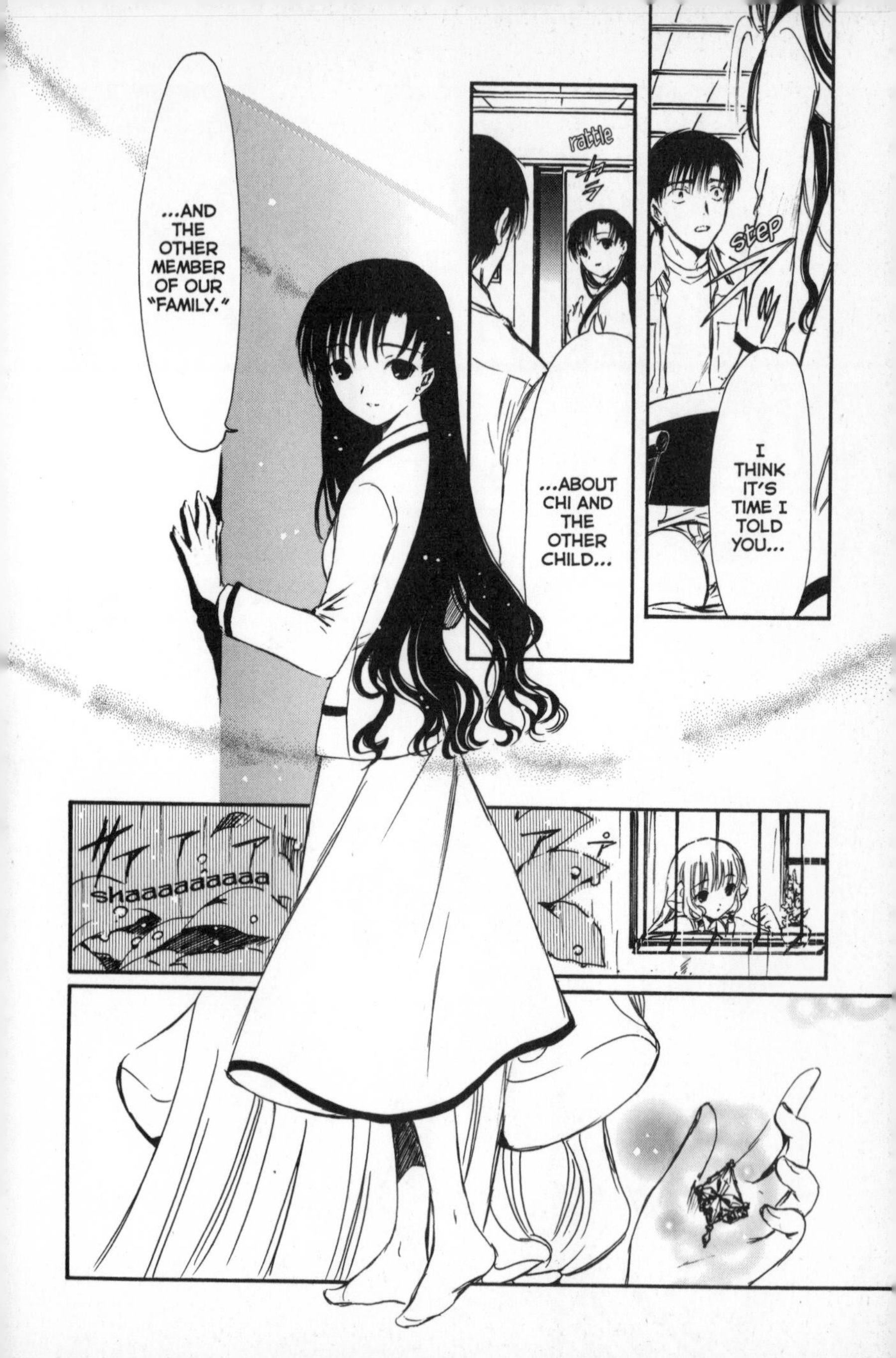
step
I THINK IT'S TIME I TOLD YOU...
rattle
...ABOUT CHI AND THE OTHER CHILD...
...AND THE OTHER MEMBER OF OUR "FAMILY."
shaaaaaaaaa

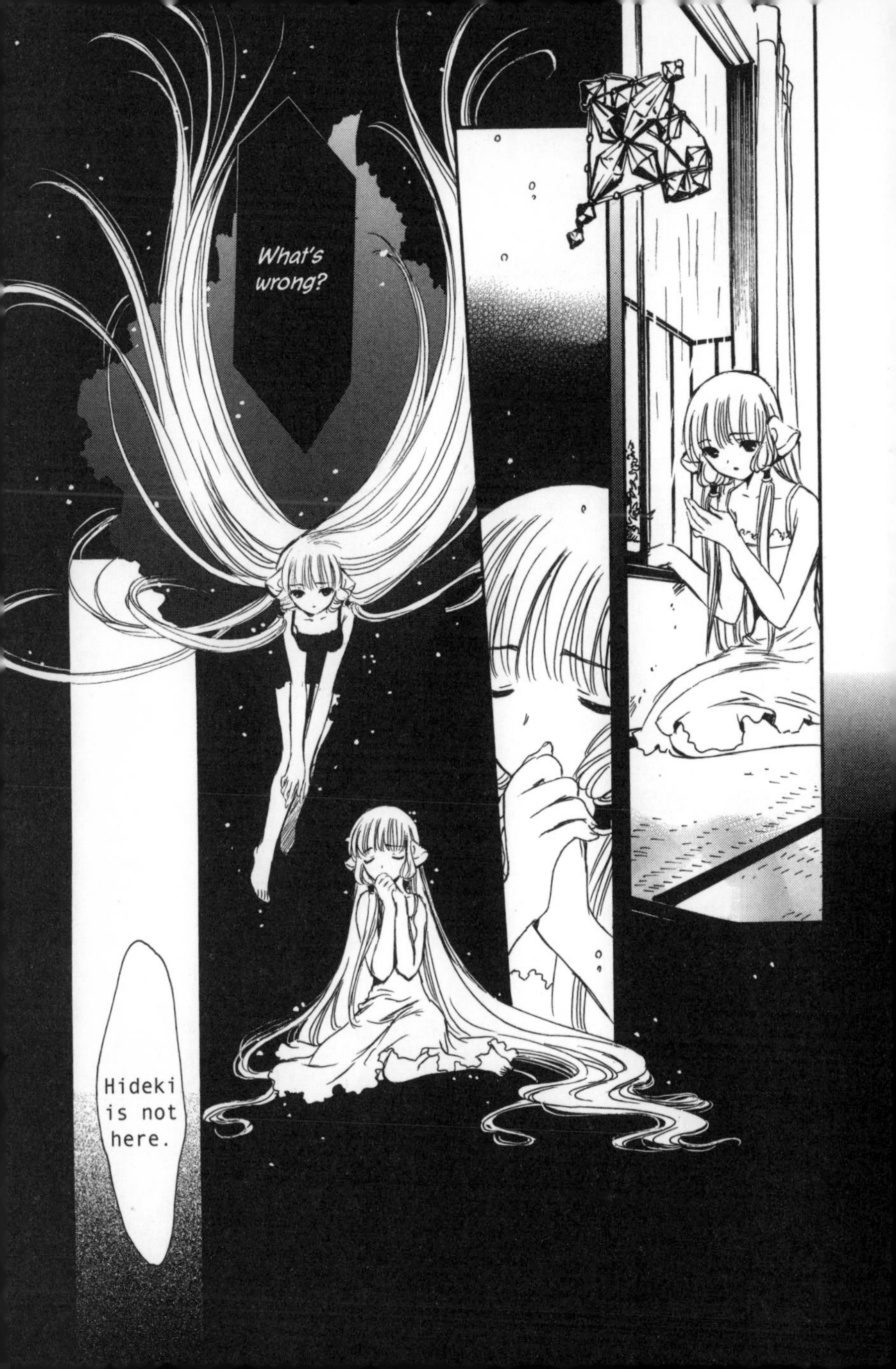
What's wrong?
Hideki is not here.

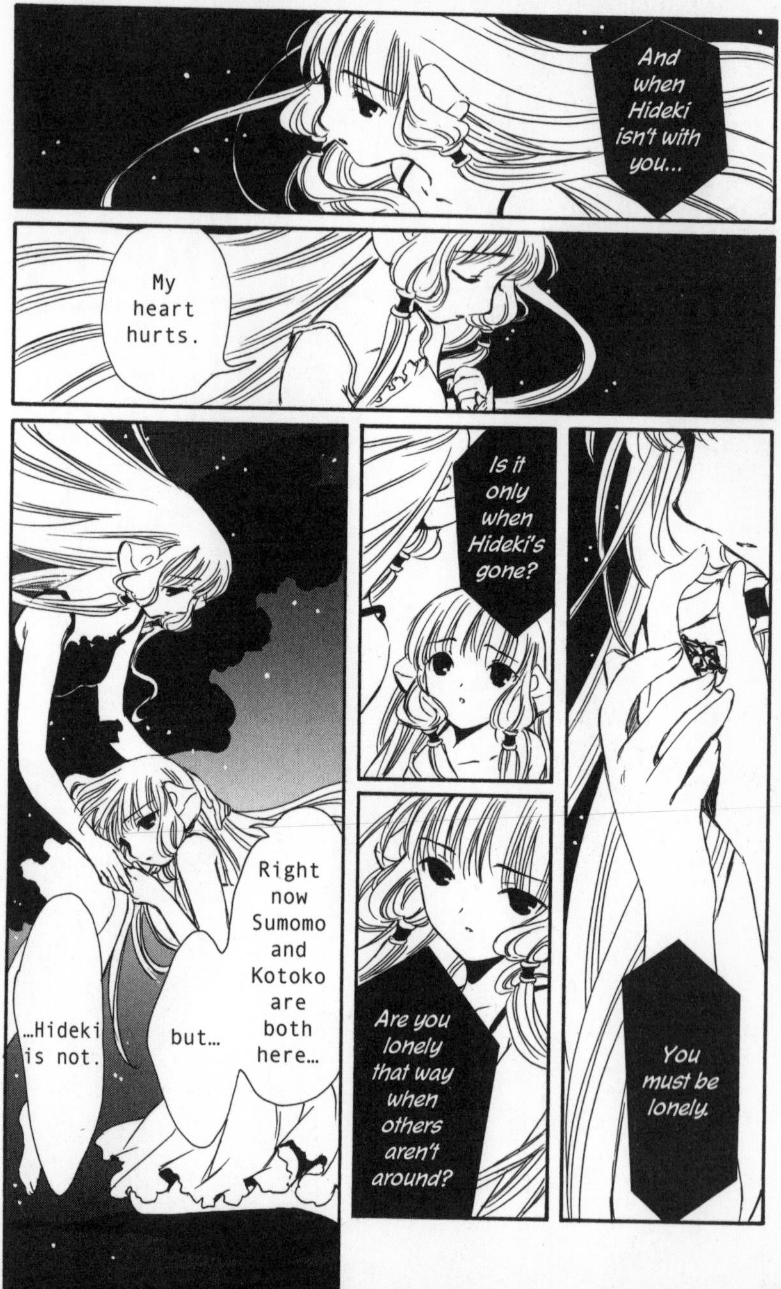
And when Hideki isn't with you...
My heart hurts.
You must be lonely.
Is it only when Hideki's gone?
Are you lonely that way when others aren't around?
Right now Sumomo and Kotoko are both here...
but...
...Hideki is not.

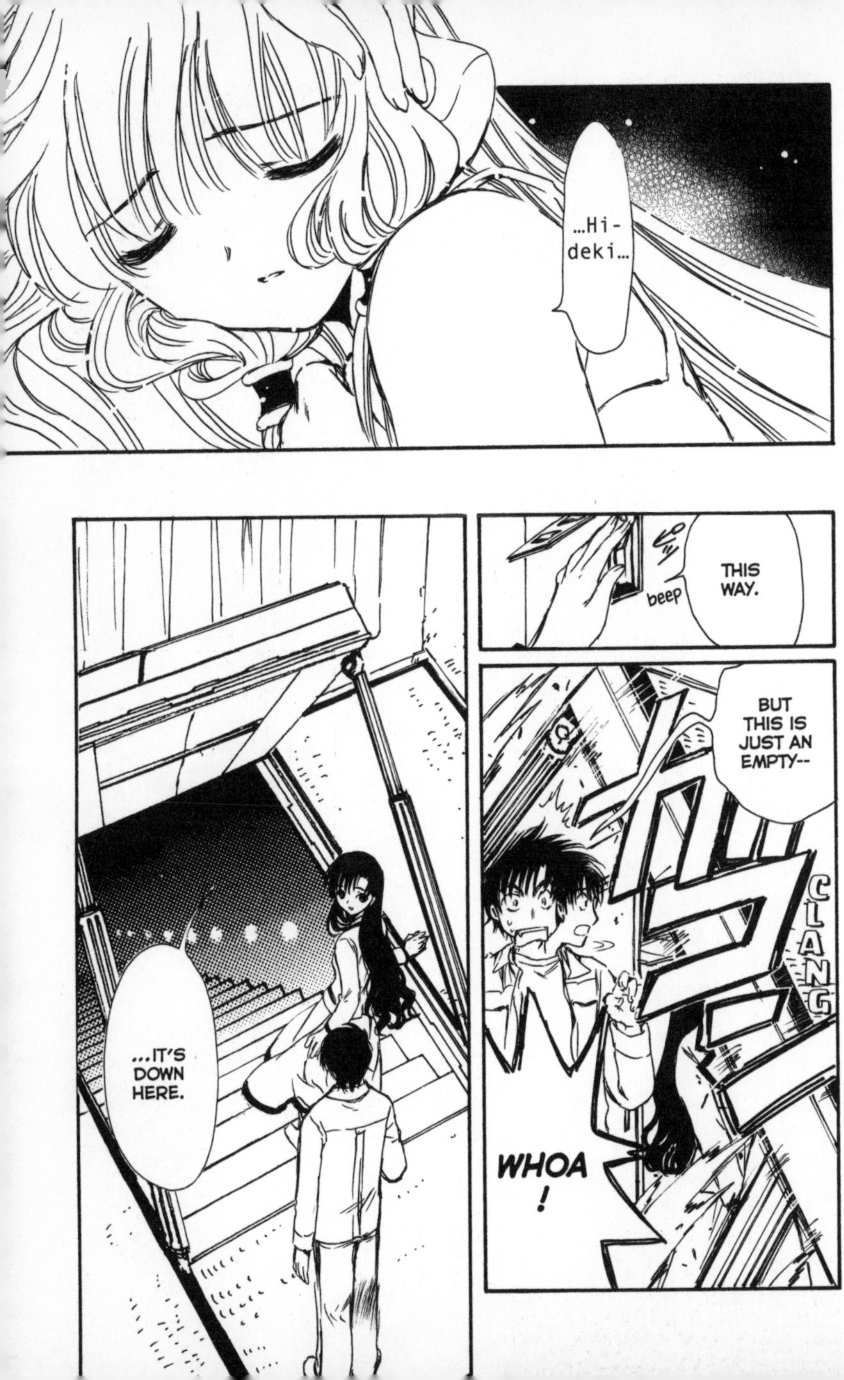
...Hi-
deki...
beep
THIS WAY.
...IT'S DOWN HERE.
BUT THIS IS JUST AN EMPTY--
CLANG
WHOA!

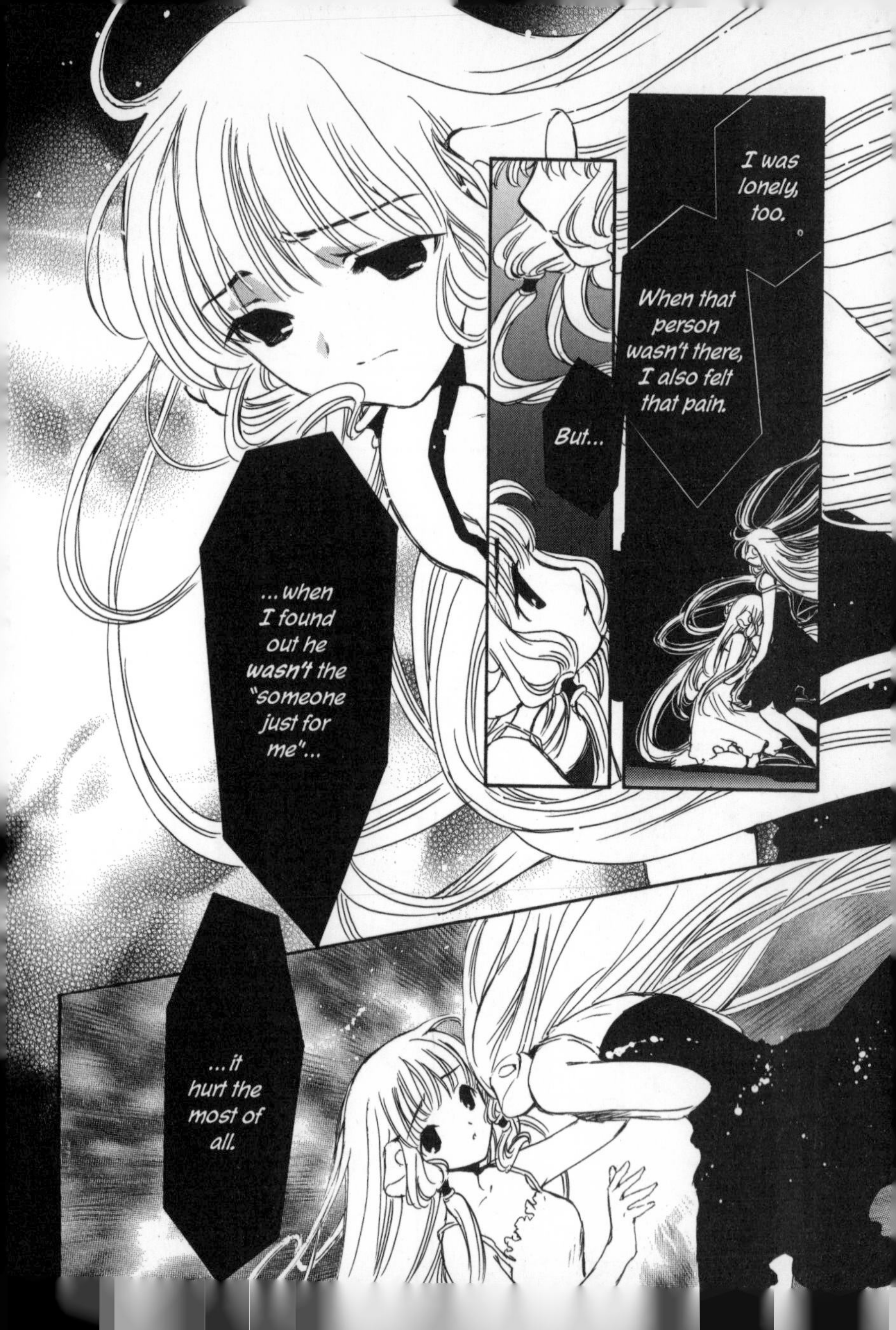
I was lonely, too.
When that person wasn't there, I also felt that pain.
But...
...when I found out he wasn't the "someone just for me"...
...it hurt the most of all.

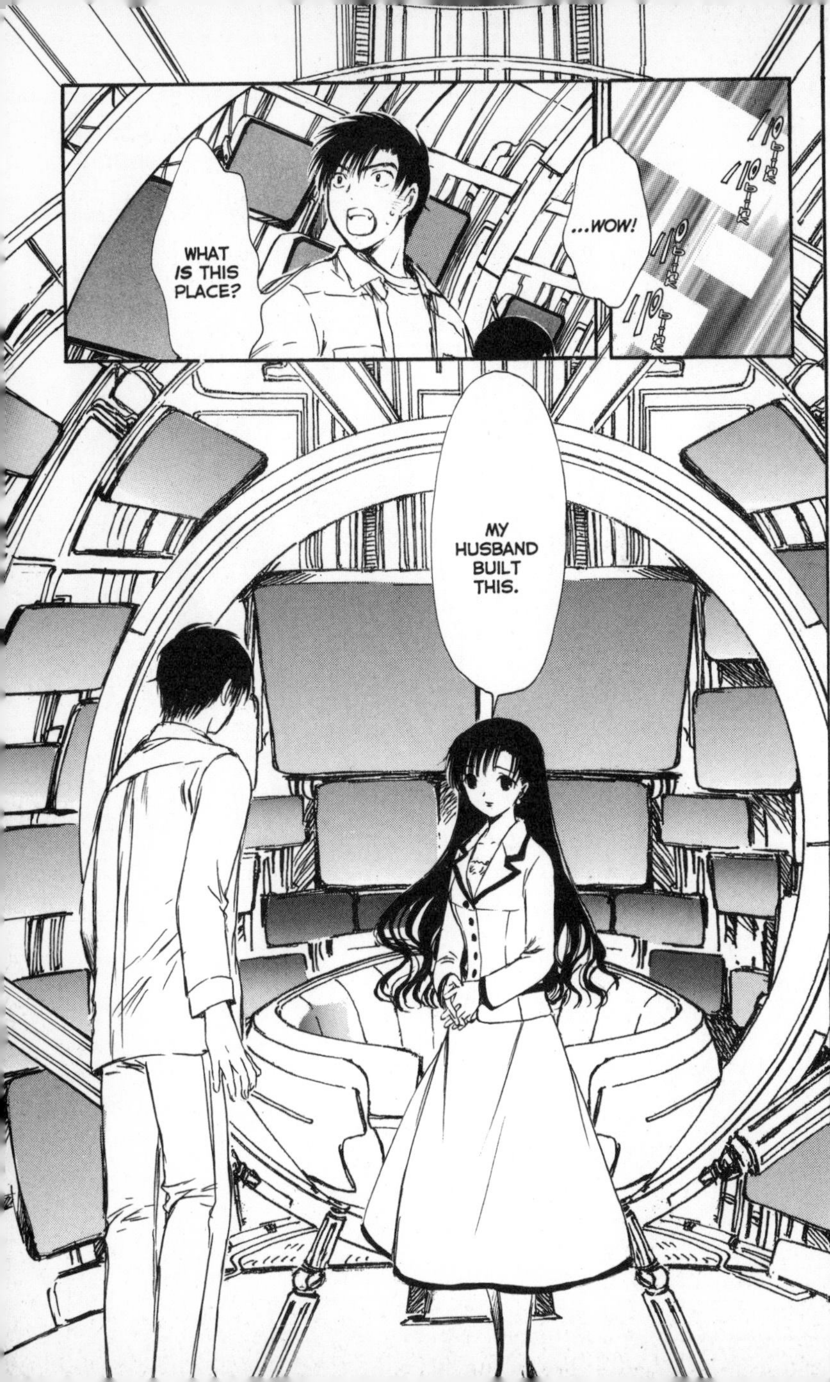
...WOW!
WHAT IS THIS PLACE?
MY HUSBAND BUILT THIS.

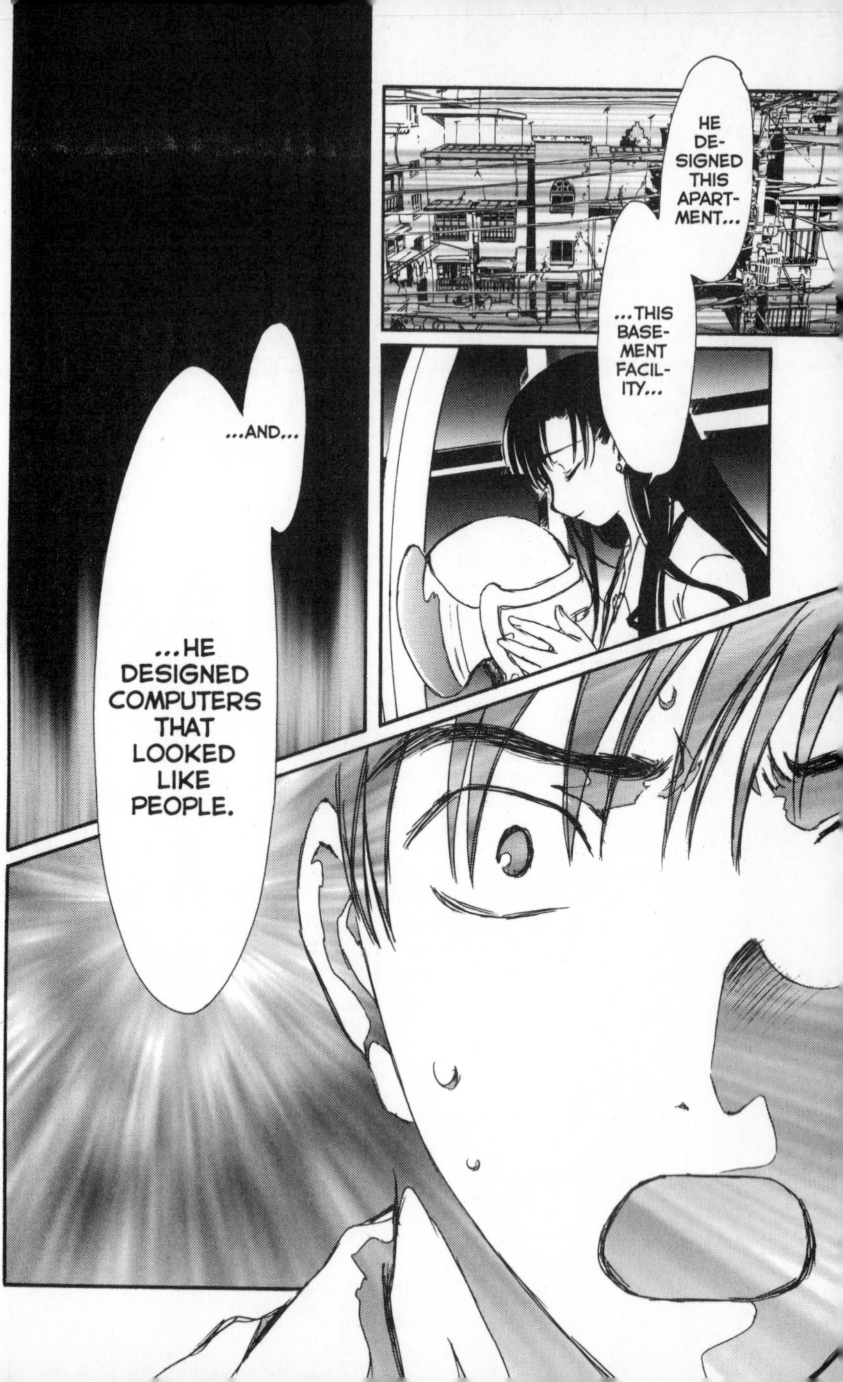
HE DESIGNED THIS APARTMENT...
...THIS BASEMENT FACILITY...
...AND...
...HE DESIGNED COMPUTERS THAT LOOKED LIKE PEOPLE.

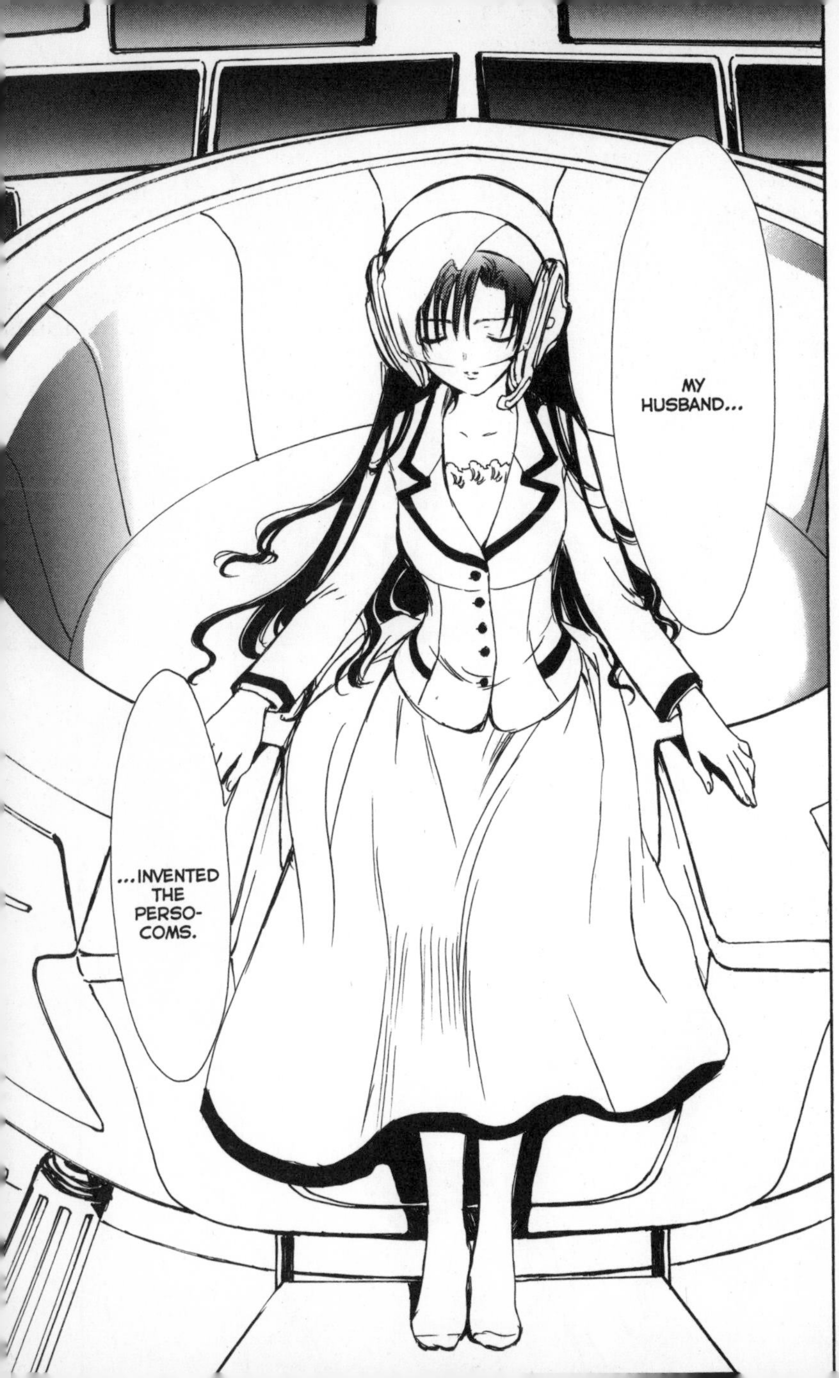
MY HUSBAND...
...INVENTED THE PERSO-COMS.

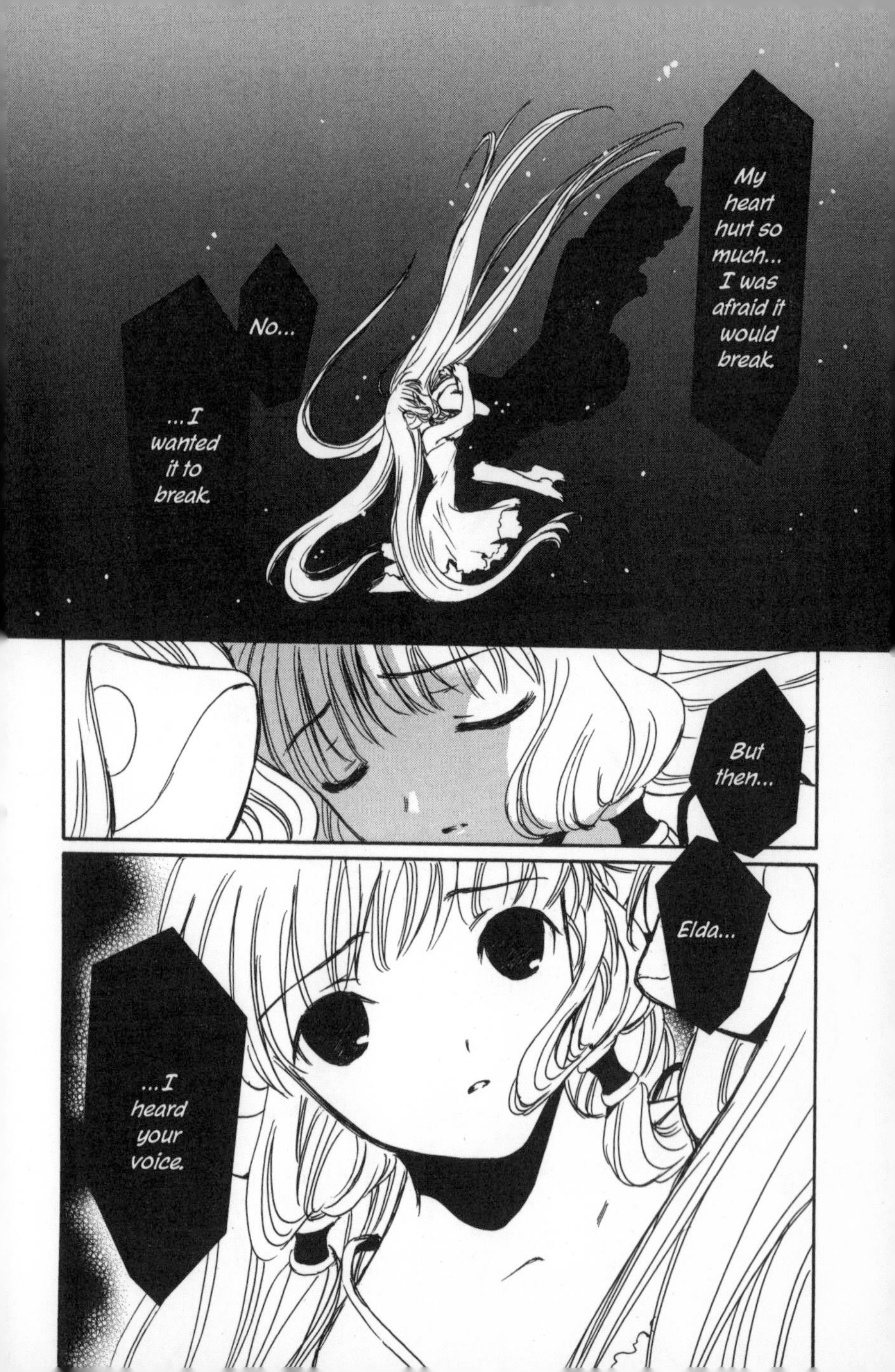
My heart hurt so much... I was afraid it would break.
No...
...I wanted it to break.
But then...
Elda...
...I heard your voice.

chapter 77

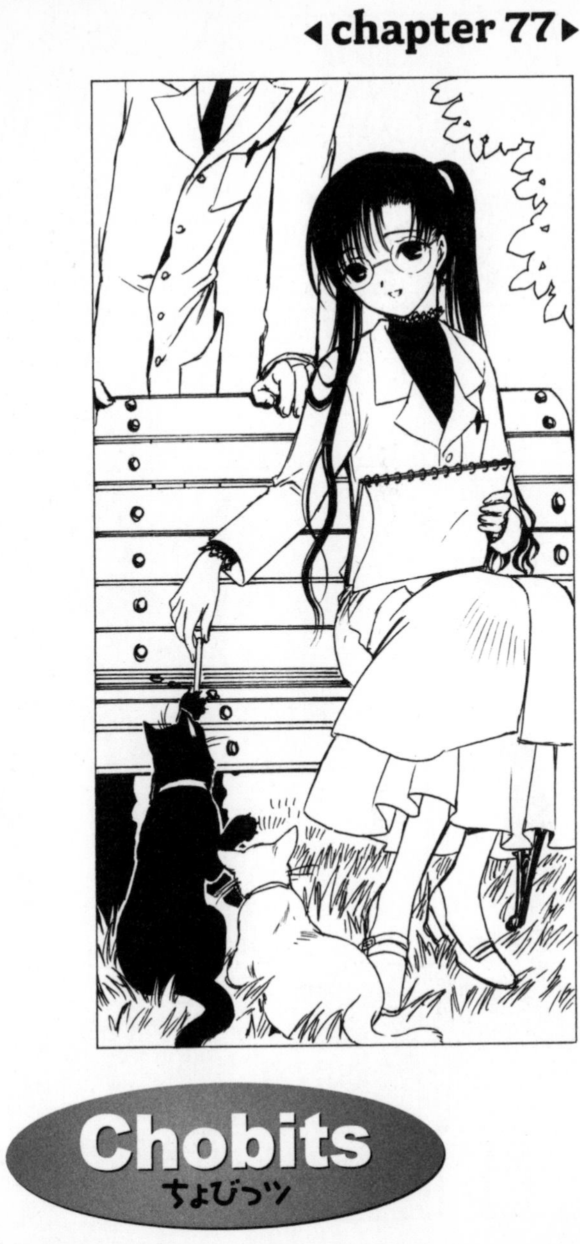

Chobits

ちょびっツ

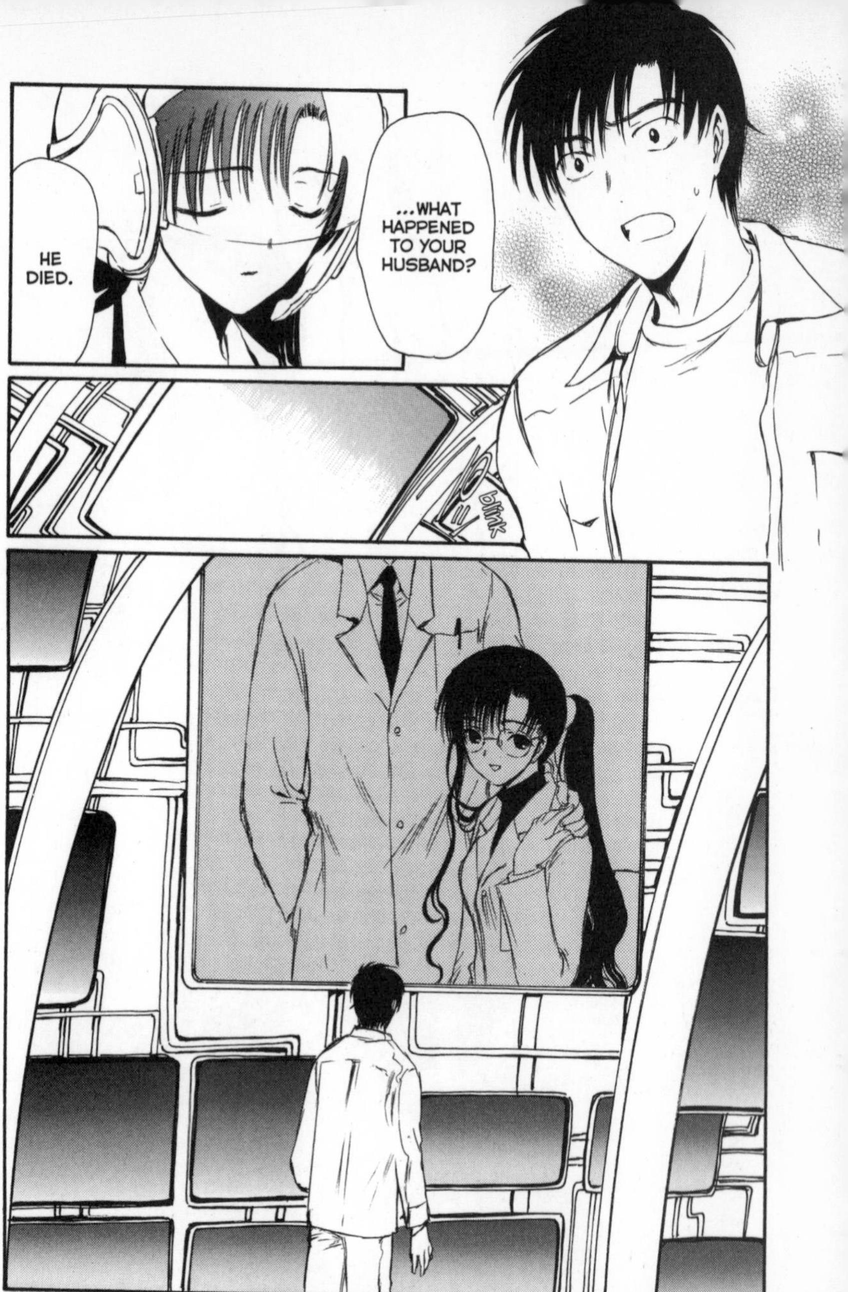
...WHAT HAPPENED TO YOUR HUSBAND?
HE DIED.
blink

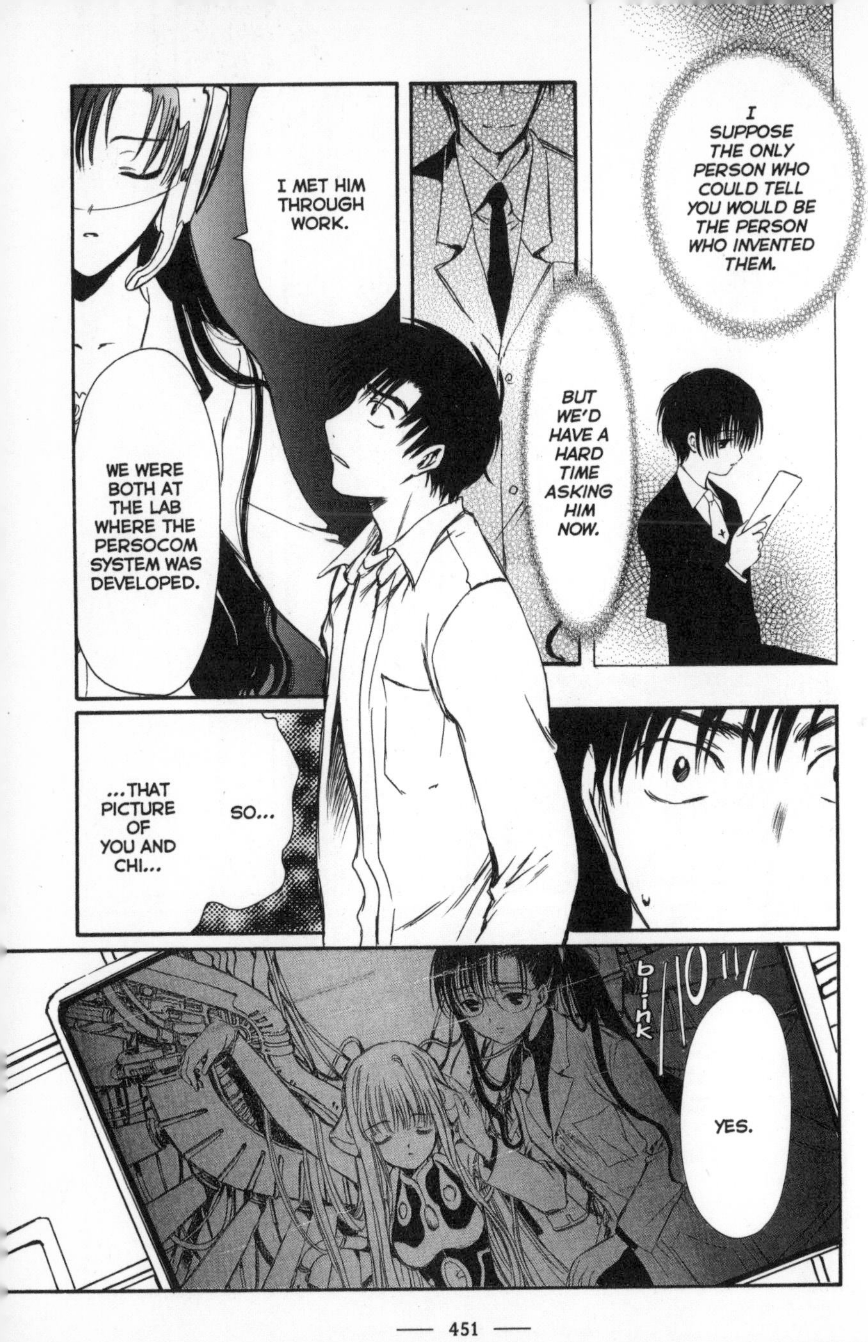

I SUPPOSE THE ONLY PERSON WHO COULD TELL YOU WOULD BE THE PERSON WHO INVENTED THEM.
BUT WE'D HAVE A HARD TIME ASKING HIM NOW.
I MET HIM THROUGH WORK.
WE WERE BOTH AT THE LAB WHERE THE PERSOCOM SYSTEM WAS DEVELOPED.
SO...
...THAT PICTURE OF YOU AND CHI...
blink
YES.

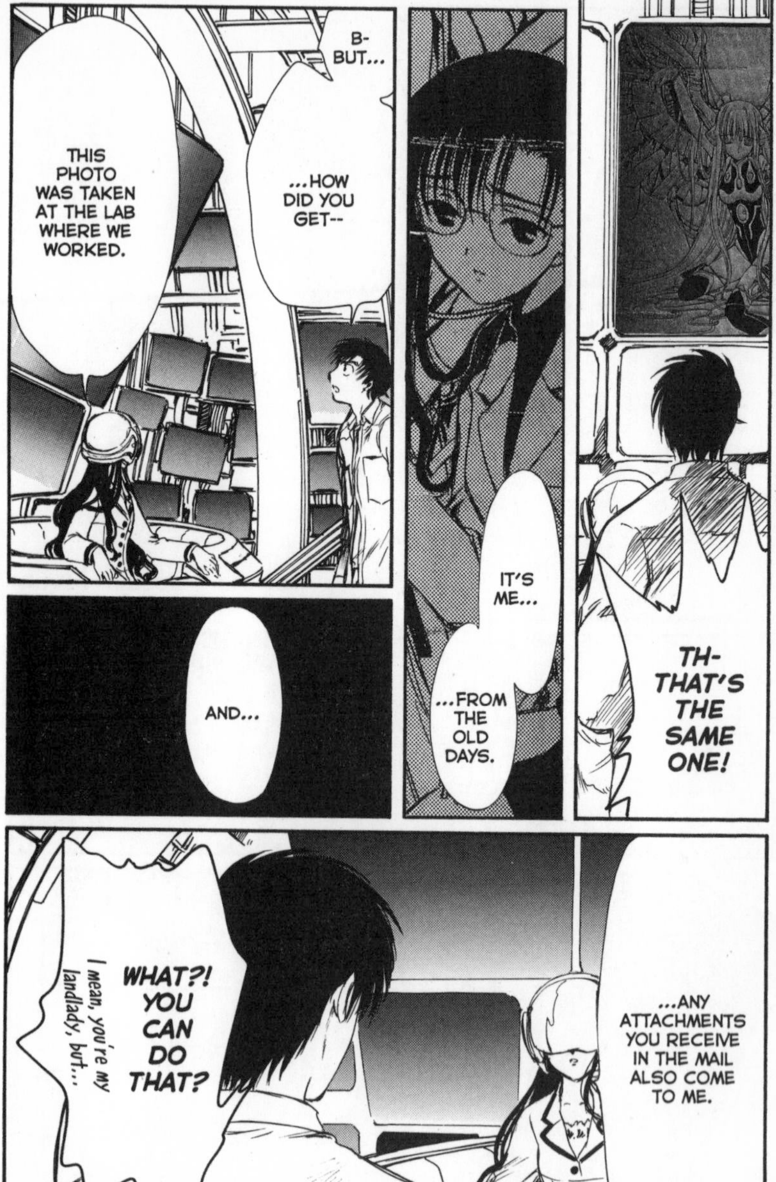
TH-THAT'S THE SAME ONE!
IT'S ME...
...FROM THE OLD DAYS.
B-BUT...
...HOW DID YOU GET--
THIS PHOTO WAS TAKEN AT THE LAB WHERE WE WORKED.
AND...
...ANY ATTACHMENTS YOU RECEIVE IN THE MAIL ALSO COME TO ME.
WHAT?! YOU CAN DO THAT?
I mean, you're my landlady, but...

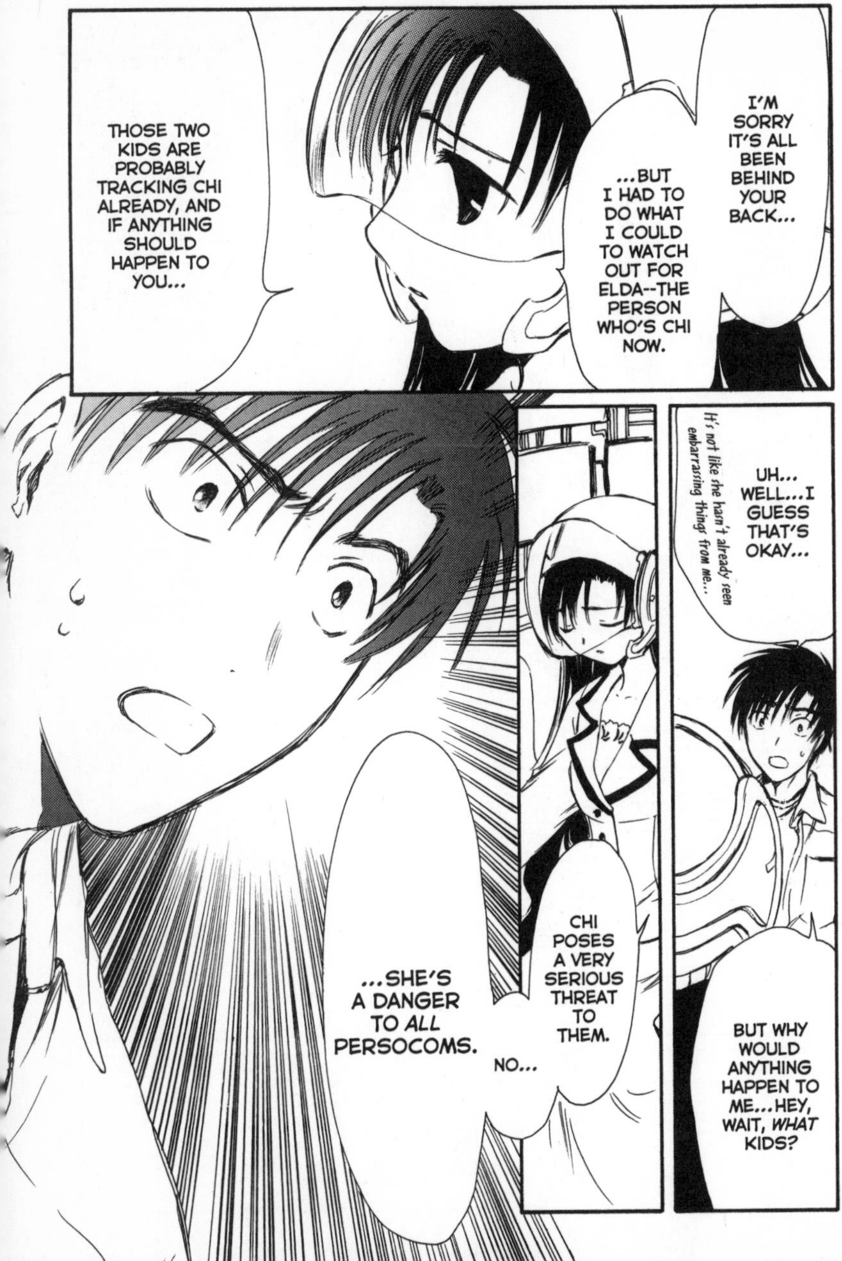
I'M SORRY IT'S ALL BEEN BEHIND YOUR BACK...
...BUT I HAD TO DO WHAT I COULD TO WATCH OUT FOR ELDA--THE PERSON WHO'S CHI NOW.
THOSE TWO KIDS ARE PROBABLY TRACKING CHI ALREADY, AND IF ANYTHING SHOULD HAPPEN TO YOU...
UH... WELL...I GUESS THAT'S OKAY...
It's not like she hasn't already seen embarrassing things from me...
BUT WHY WOULD ANYTHING HAPPEN TO ME...HEY, WAIT, *WHAT* KIDS?
CHI POSES A VERY SERIOUS THREAT TO THEM.
NO...
...SHE'S A DANGER TO *ALL* PERSOCOMS.

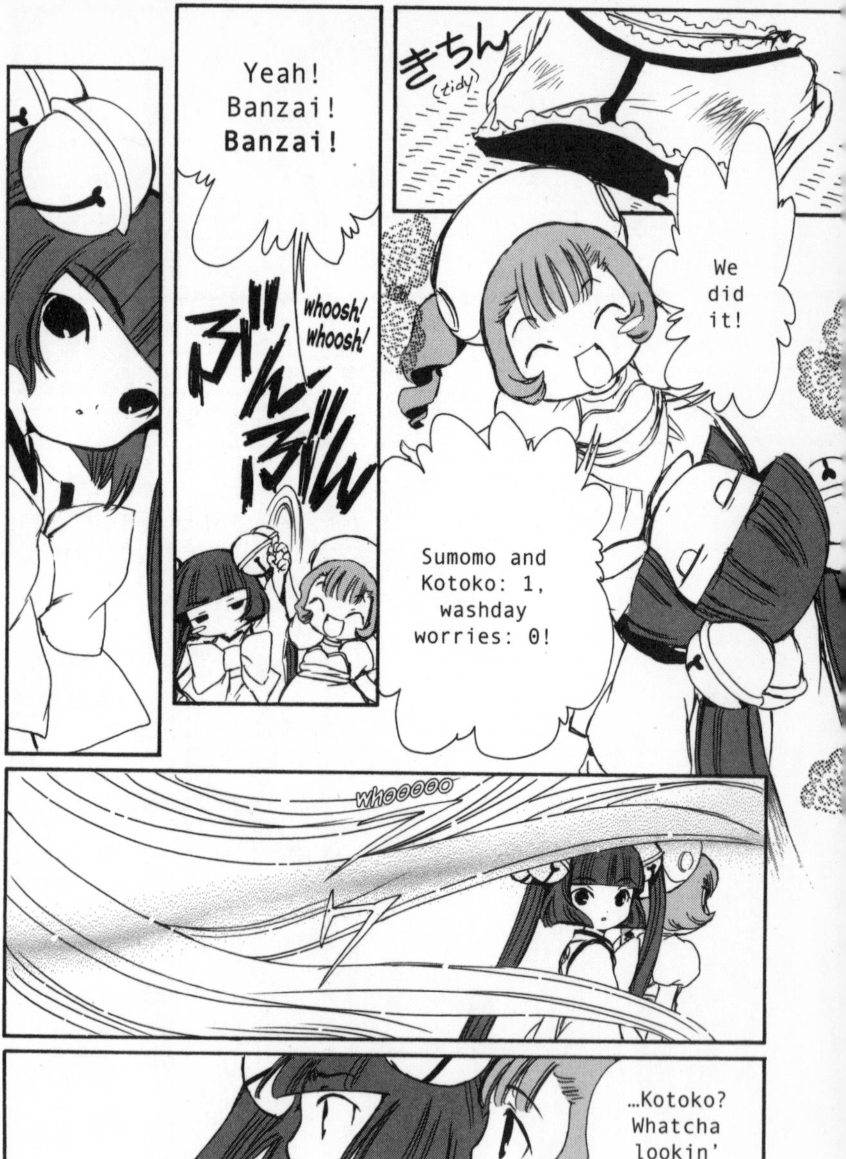

きちん
(tidy)
We did it!
Sumomo and Kotoko: 1, washday worries: 0!
Yeah! Banzai! **Banzai!**
ぶんぶん
whoosh! whoosh!
whoooooo
…Kotoko? Whatcha lookin' at?

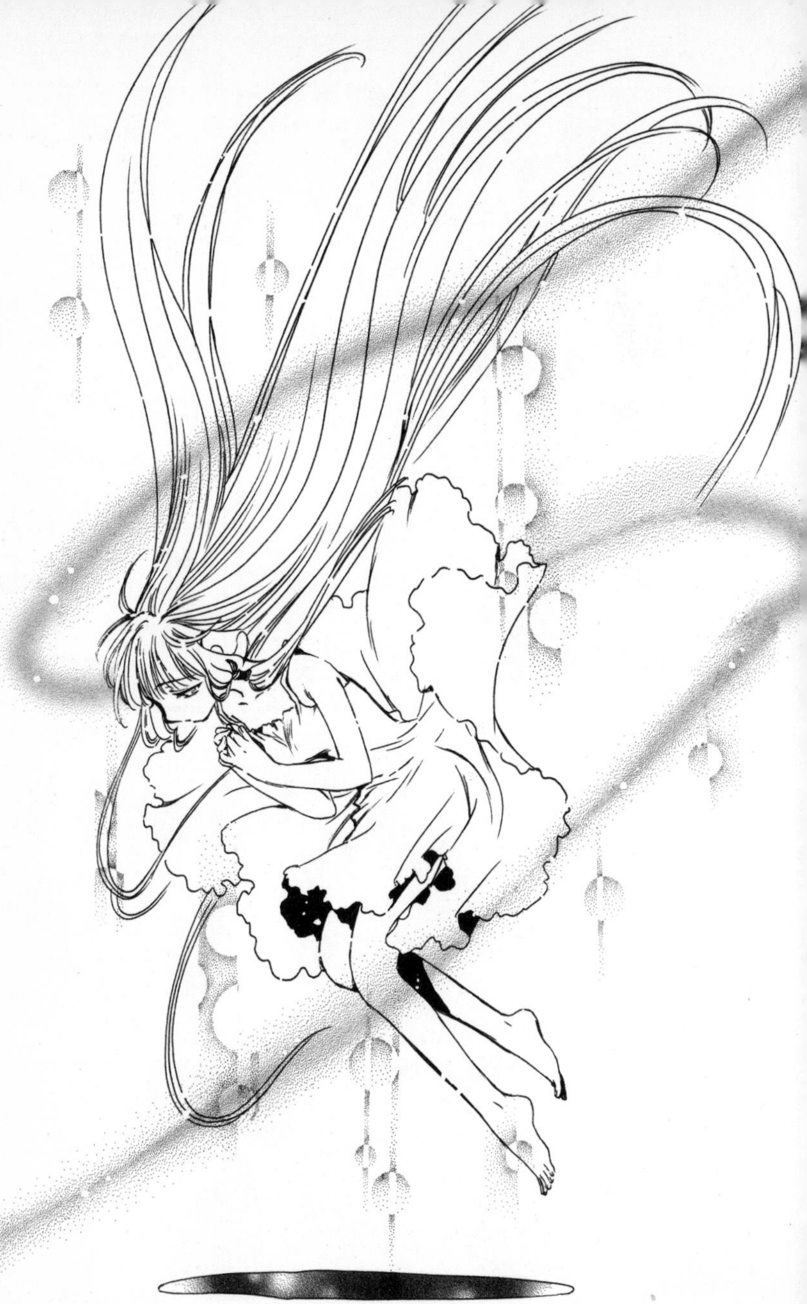

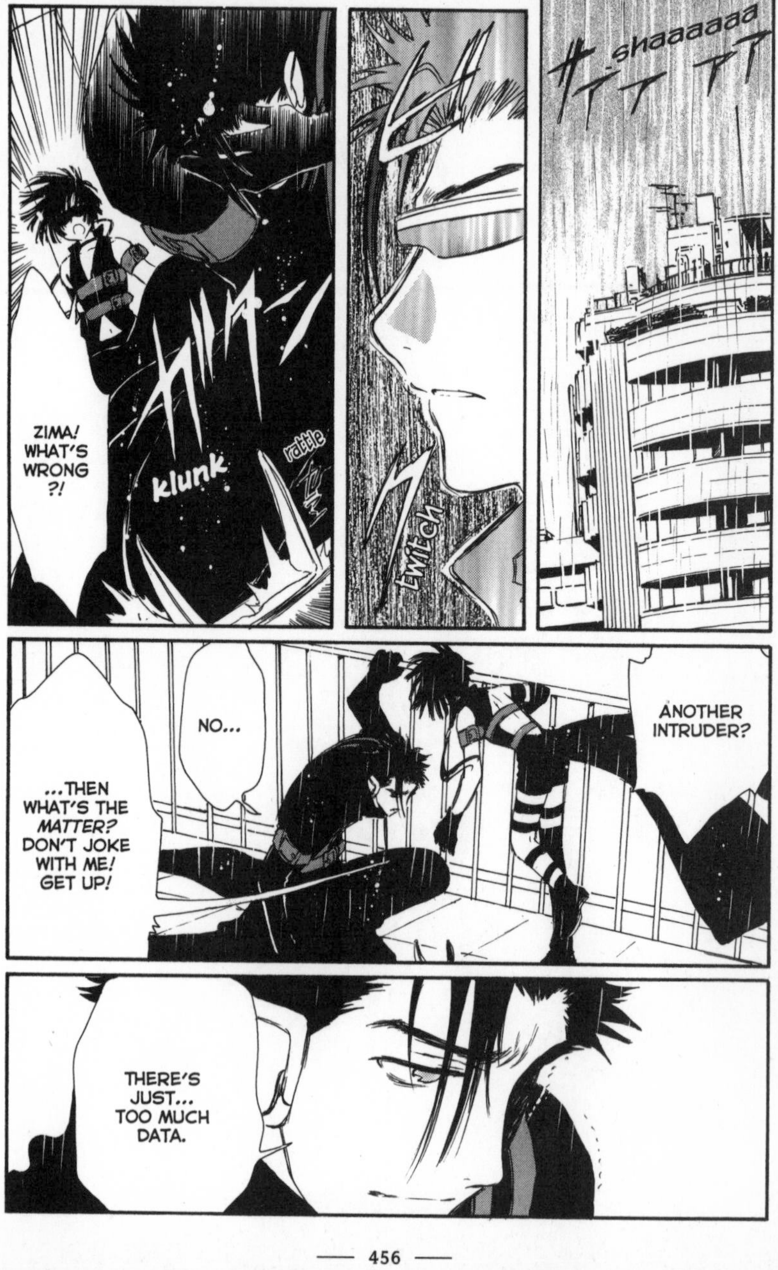
shaaaaaa
twitch
rattle
klunk
ZIMA! WHAT'S WRONG ?!
ANOTHER INTRUDER?
NO...
...THEN WHAT'S THE *MATTER?* DON'T JOKE WITH ME! GET UP!
THERE'S JUST... TOO MUCH DATA.

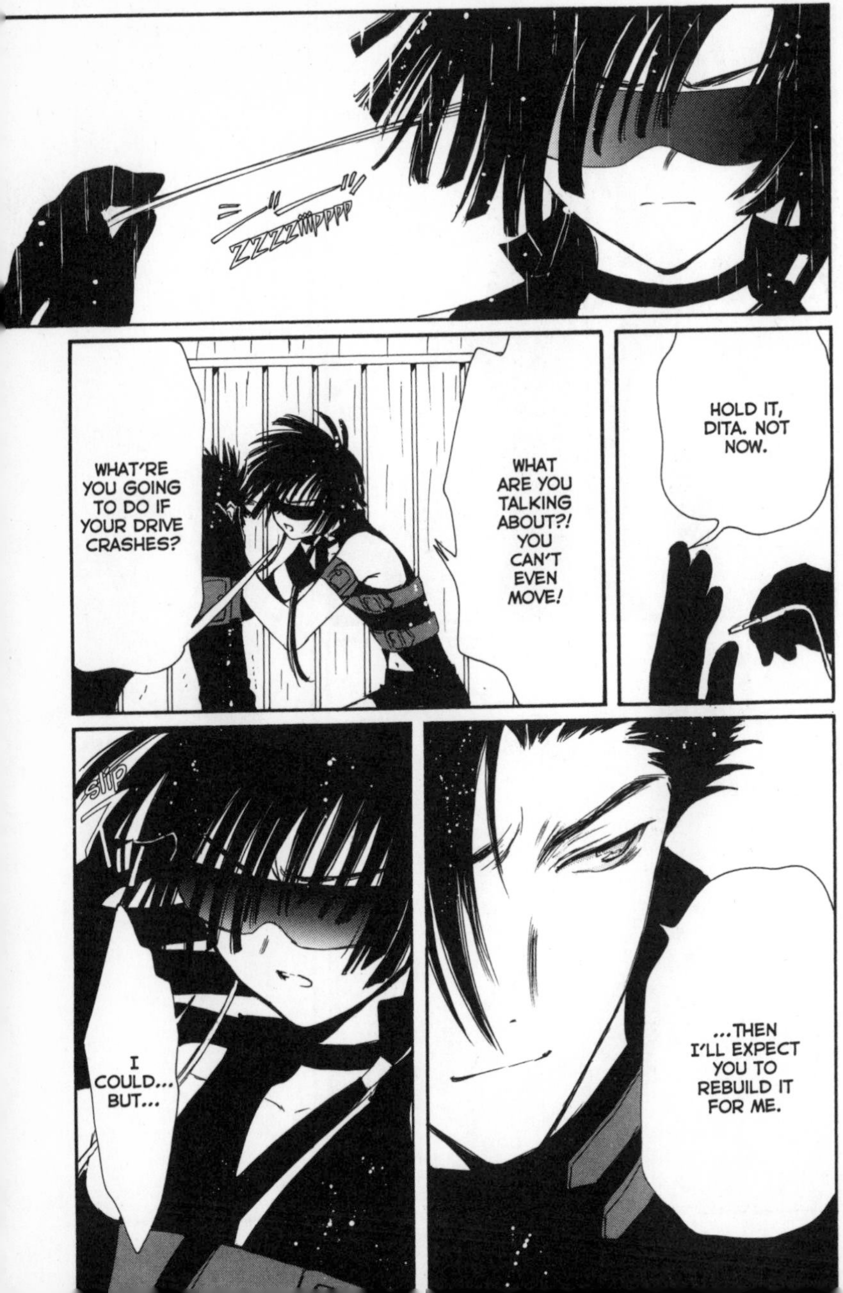
ZZZZiiiipppp
HOLD IT, DITA. NOT NOW.
WHAT ARE YOU TALKING ABOUT?! YOU CAN'T EVEN MOVE!
WHAT'RE YOU GOING TO DO IF YOUR DRIVE CRASHES?
...THEN I'LL EXPECT YOU TO REBUILD IT FOR ME.
slip
I COULD... BUT...

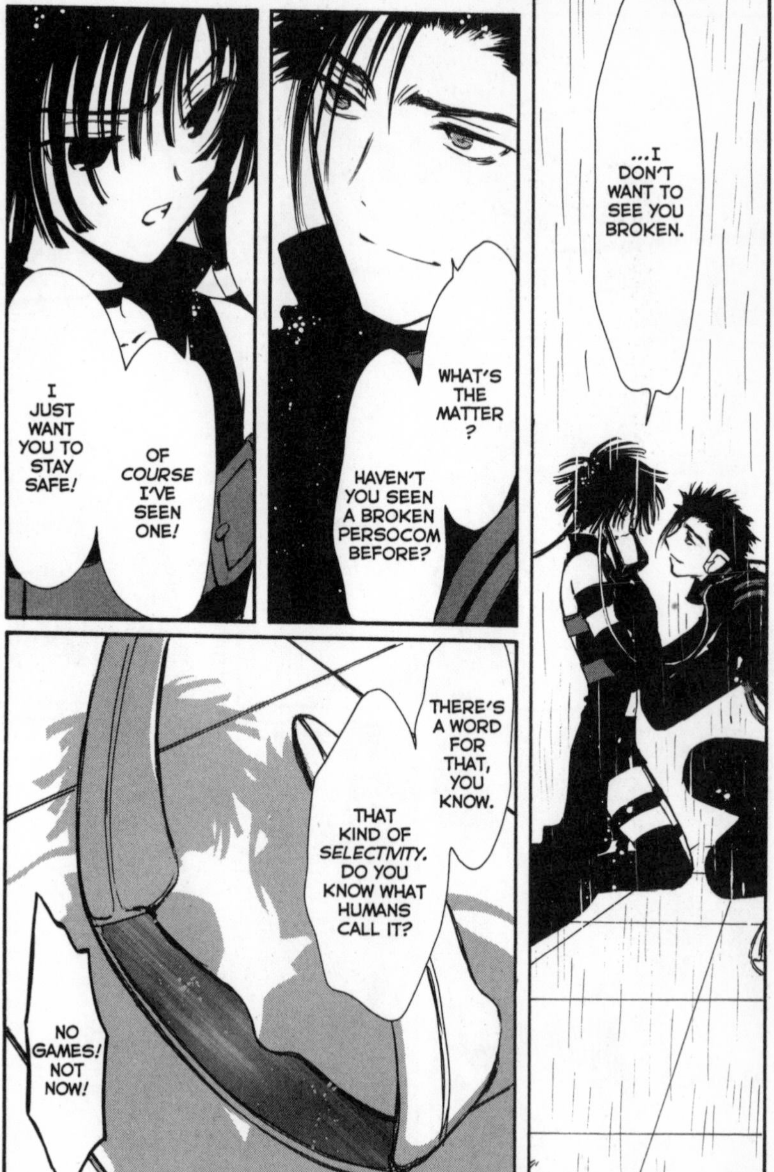
...I DON'T WANT TO SEE YOU BROKEN.
WHAT'S THE MATTER?
HAVEN'T YOU SEEN A BROKEN PERSOCOM BEFORE?
OF *COURSE* I'VE SEEN ONE!
I JUST WANT YOU TO STAY SAFE!
THERE'S A WORD FOR THAT, YOU KNOW.
THAT KIND OF *SELECTIVITY.* DO YOU KNOW WHAT HUMANS CALL IT?
NO GAMES! NOT NOW!

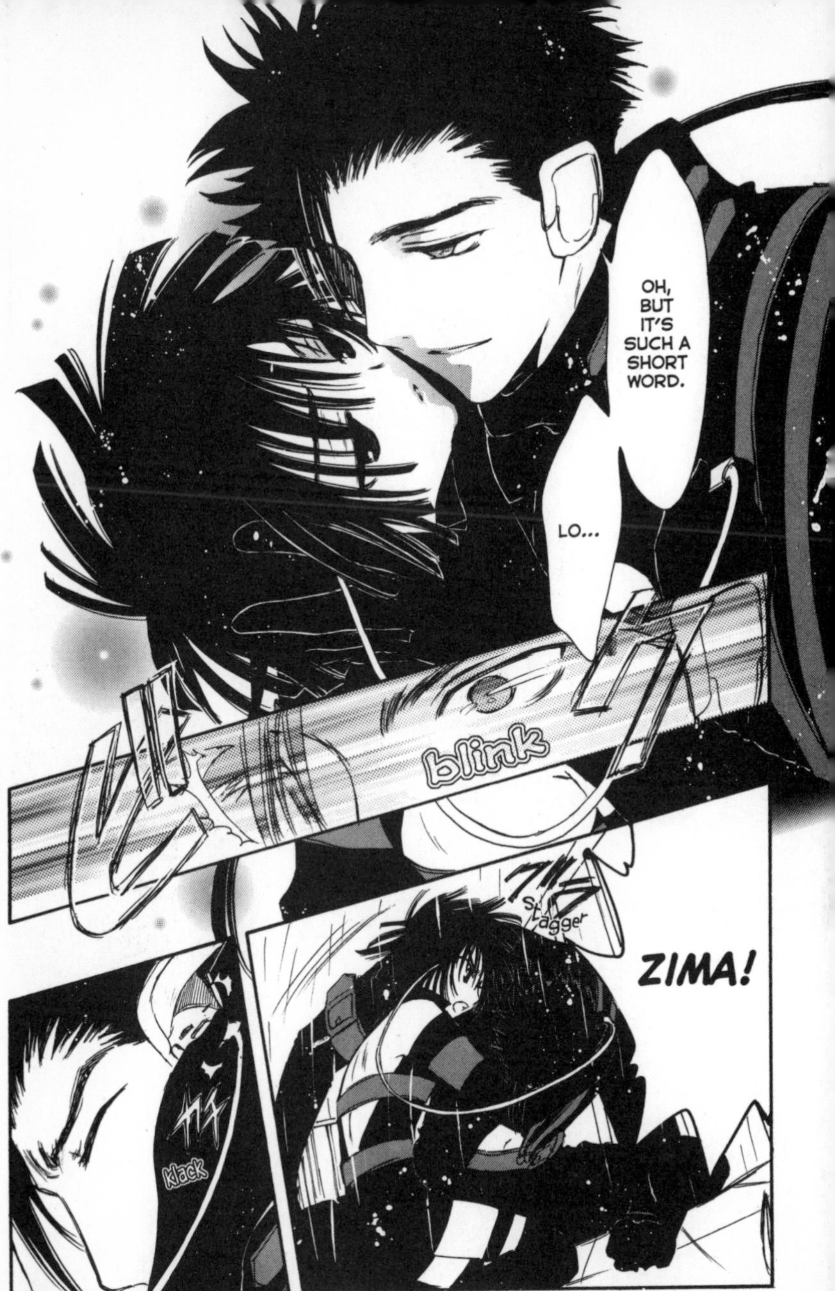
OH, BUT IT'S SUCH A SHORT WORD.
LO...
blink
stagger
ZIMA!
klack

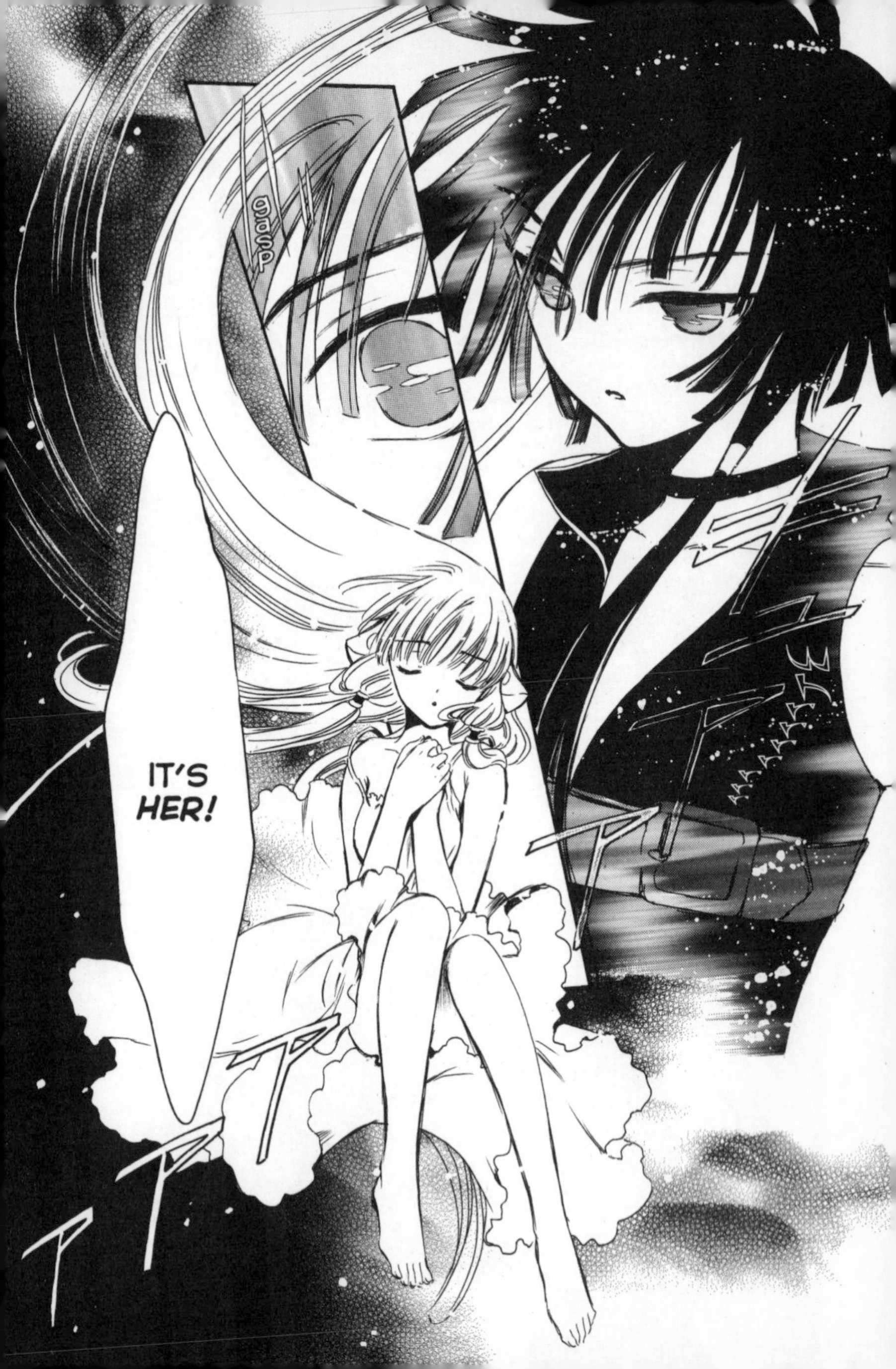
gasp
IT'S HER!

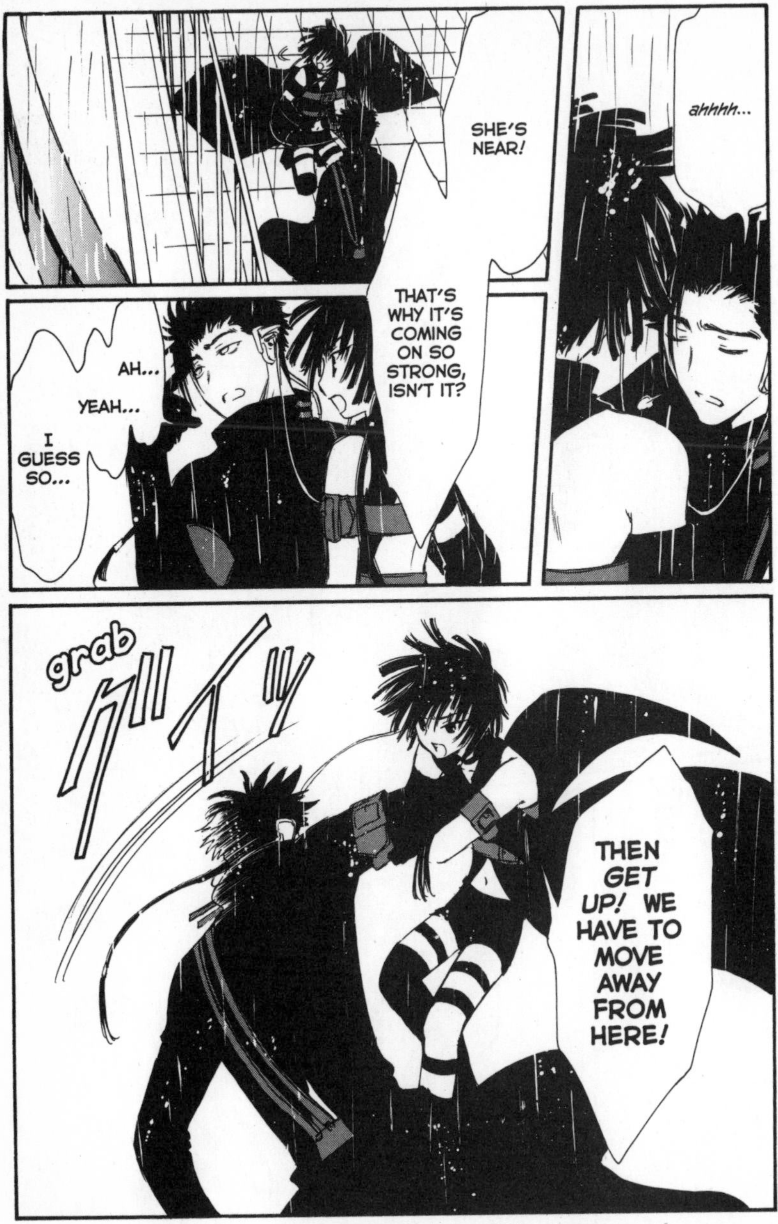
ahhhh...
SHE'S NEAR!
THAT'S WHY IT'S COMING ON SO STRONG, ISN'T IT?
AH... YEAH... I GUESS SO...
grab
THEN GET UP! WE HAVE TO MOVE AWAY FROM HERE!

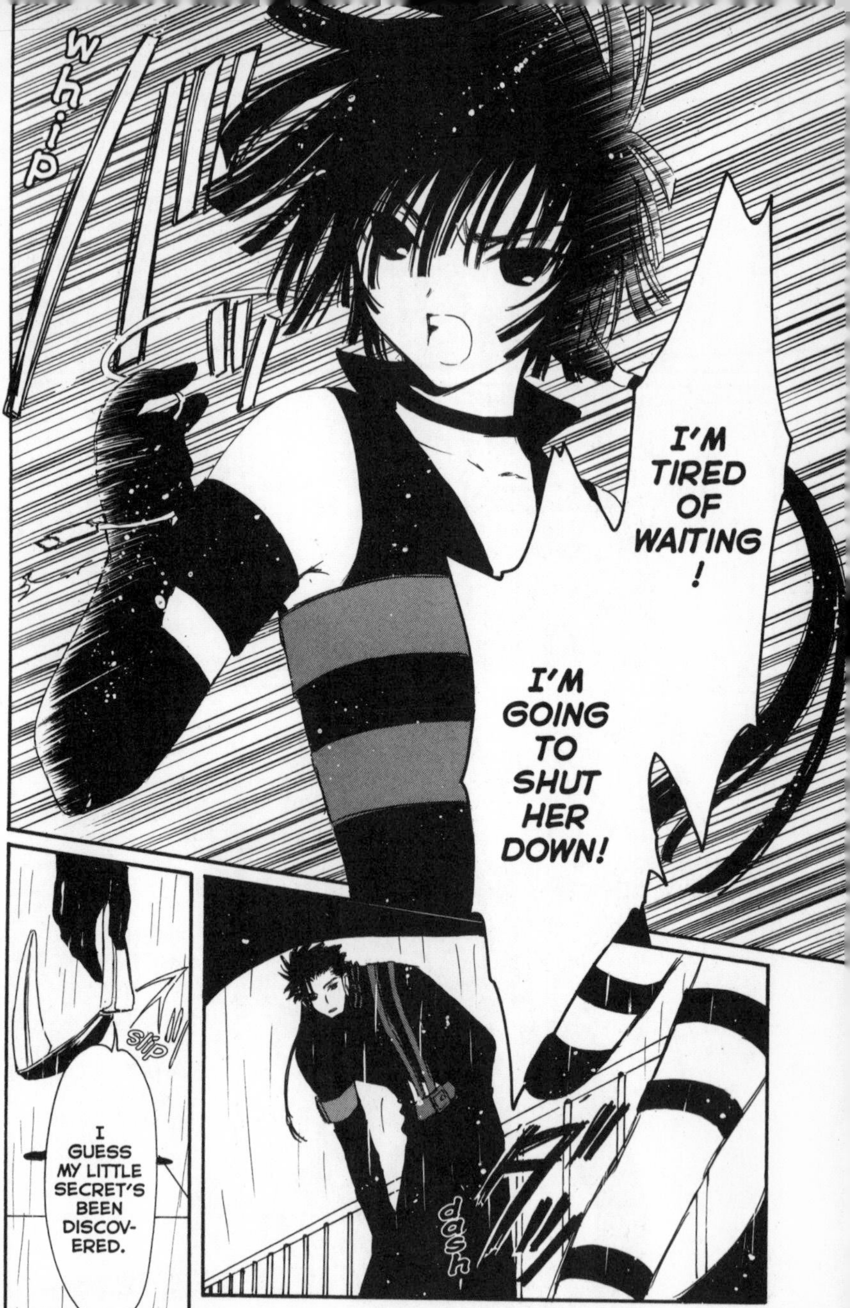
I'M TIRED OF WAITING!
I'M GOING TO SHUT HER DOWN!
whip
dash
slip
I GUESS MY LITTLE SECRET'S BEEN DISCOVERED.

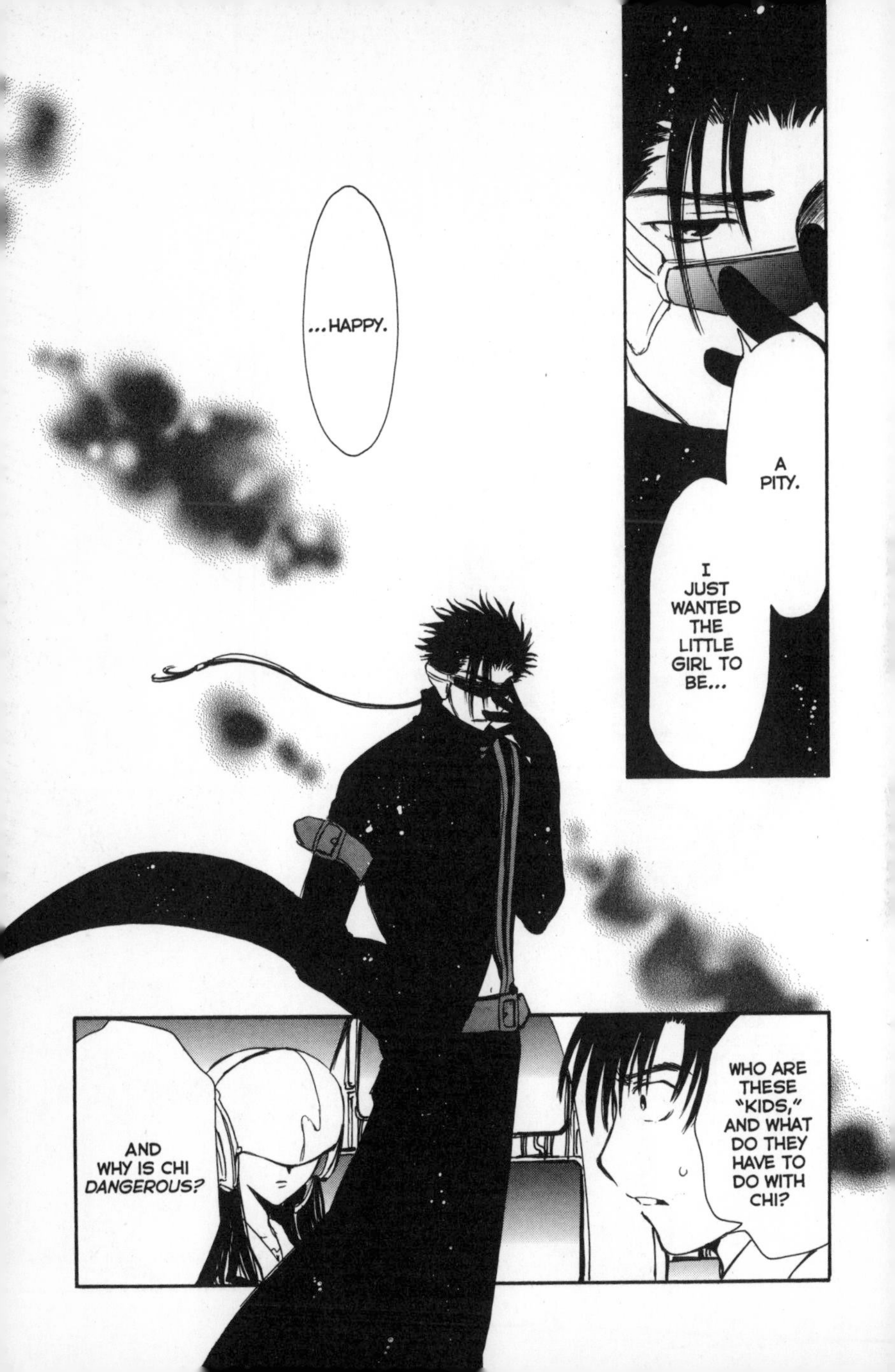
A PITY.
I JUST WANTED THE LITTLE GIRL TO BE...
...HAPPY.
WHO ARE THESE "KIDS," AND WHAT DO THEY HAVE TO DO WITH CHI?
AND WHY IS CHI *DANGEROUS?*

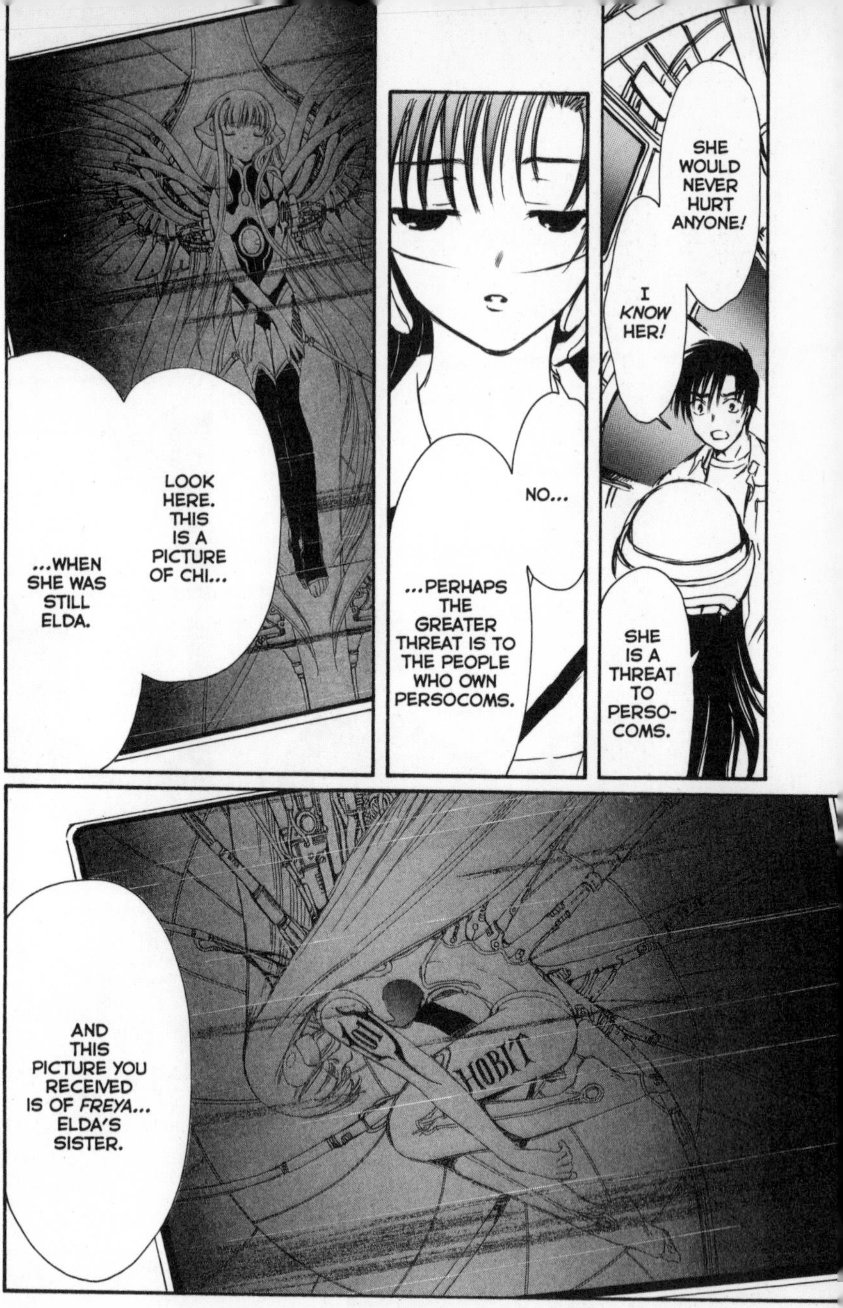
SHE WOULD NEVER HURT ANYONE!
I *KNOW* HER!
SHE IS A THREAT TO PERSO-COMS.
NO...
...PERHAPS THE GREATER THREAT IS TO THE PEOPLE WHO OWN PERSOCOMS.
LOOK HERE. THIS IS A PICTURE OF CHI...
...WHEN SHE WAS STILL ELDA.
AND THIS PICTURE YOU RECEIVED IS OF *FREYA*... ELDA'S SISTER.
HOBIT

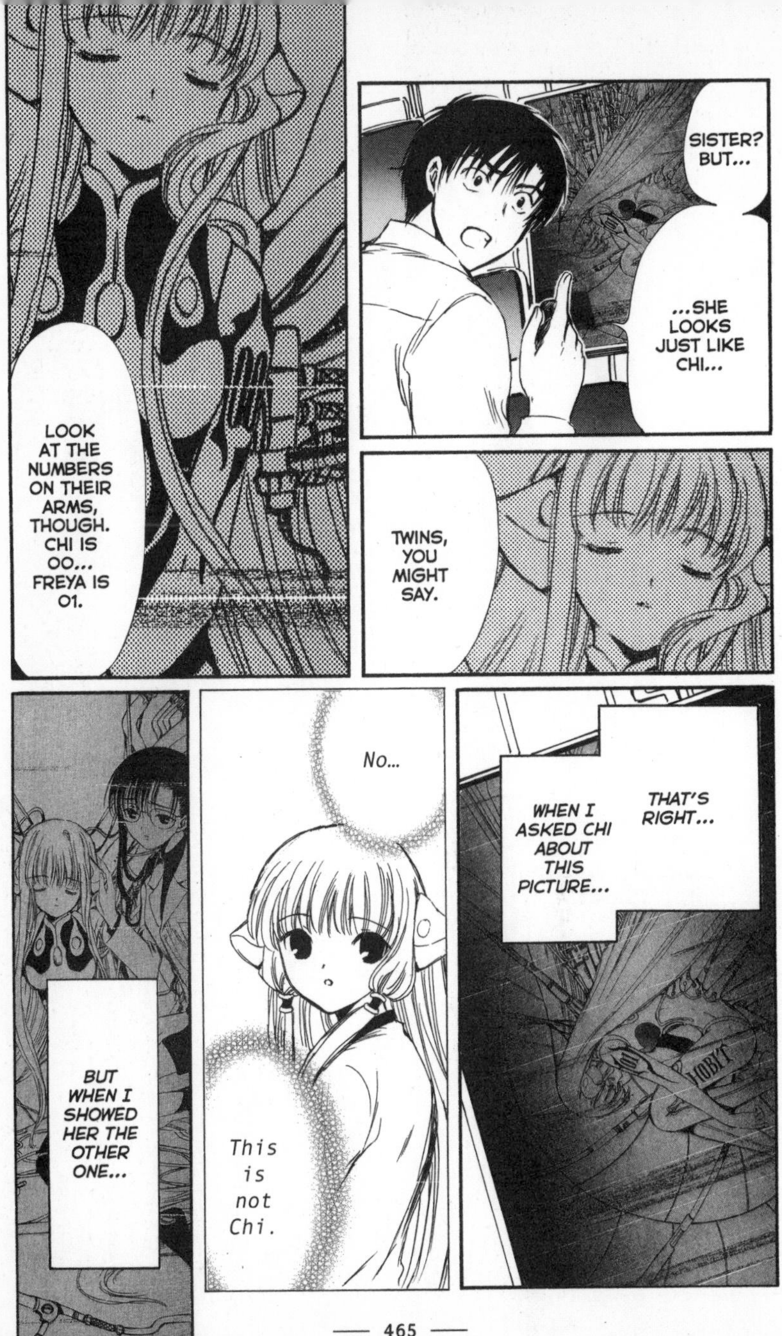
SISTER? BUT...
...SHE LOOKS JUST LIKE CHI...
TWINS, YOU MIGHT SAY.
LOOK AT THE NUMBERS ON THEIR ARMS, THOUGH. CHI IS 00... FREYA IS 01.
THAT'S RIGHT...
WHEN I ASKED CHI ABOUT THIS PICTURE...
No...
This is not Chi.
BUT WHEN I SHOWED HER THE OTHER ONE...

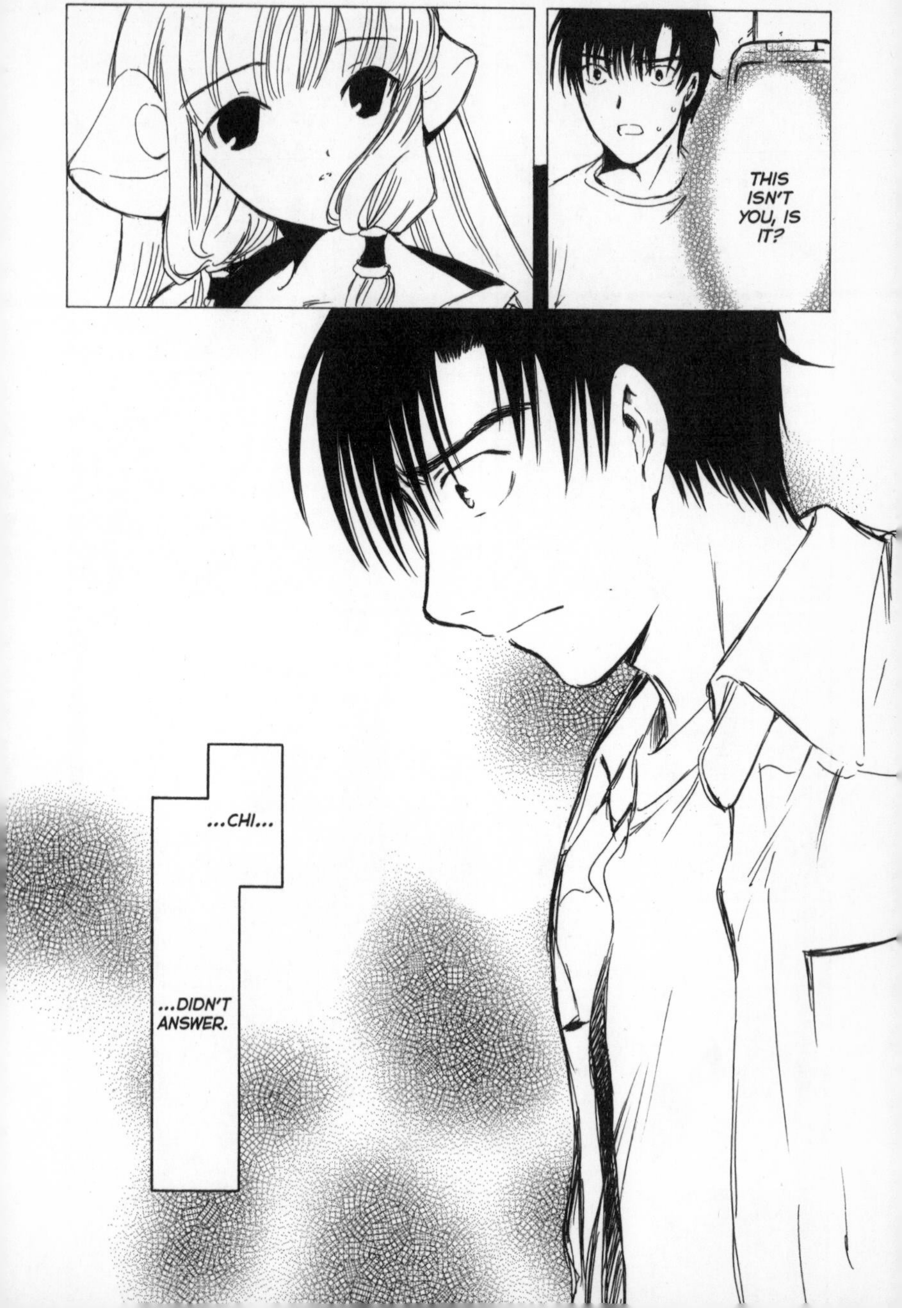
THIS ISN'T YOU, IS IT?
...CHI...
...DIDN'T ANSWER.

Chobits

ちょびっツ

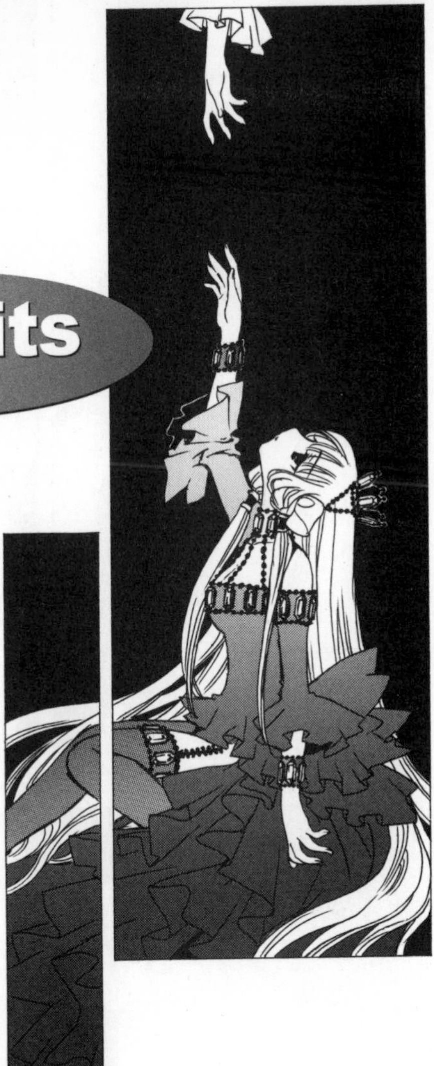

◂chapter 78▸

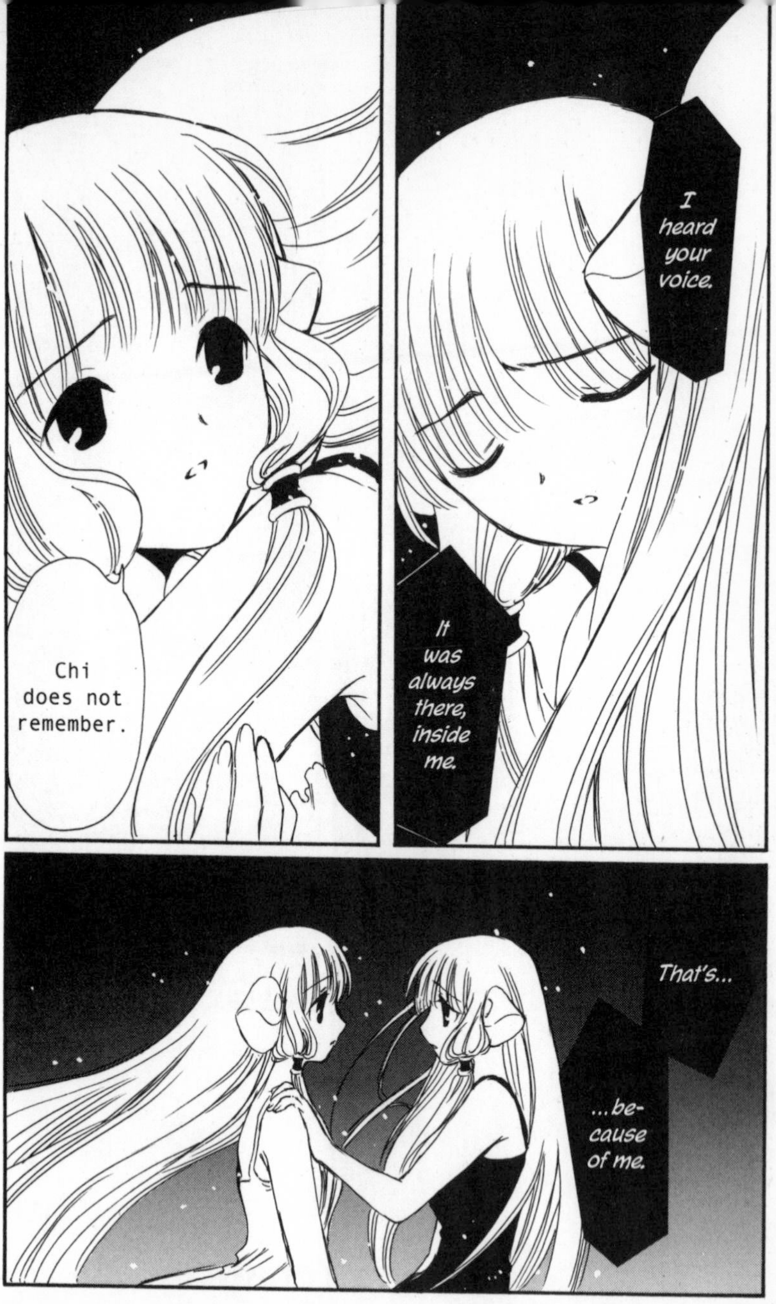
I heard your voice.
It was always there, inside me.
Chi does not remember.
That's...
...because of me.

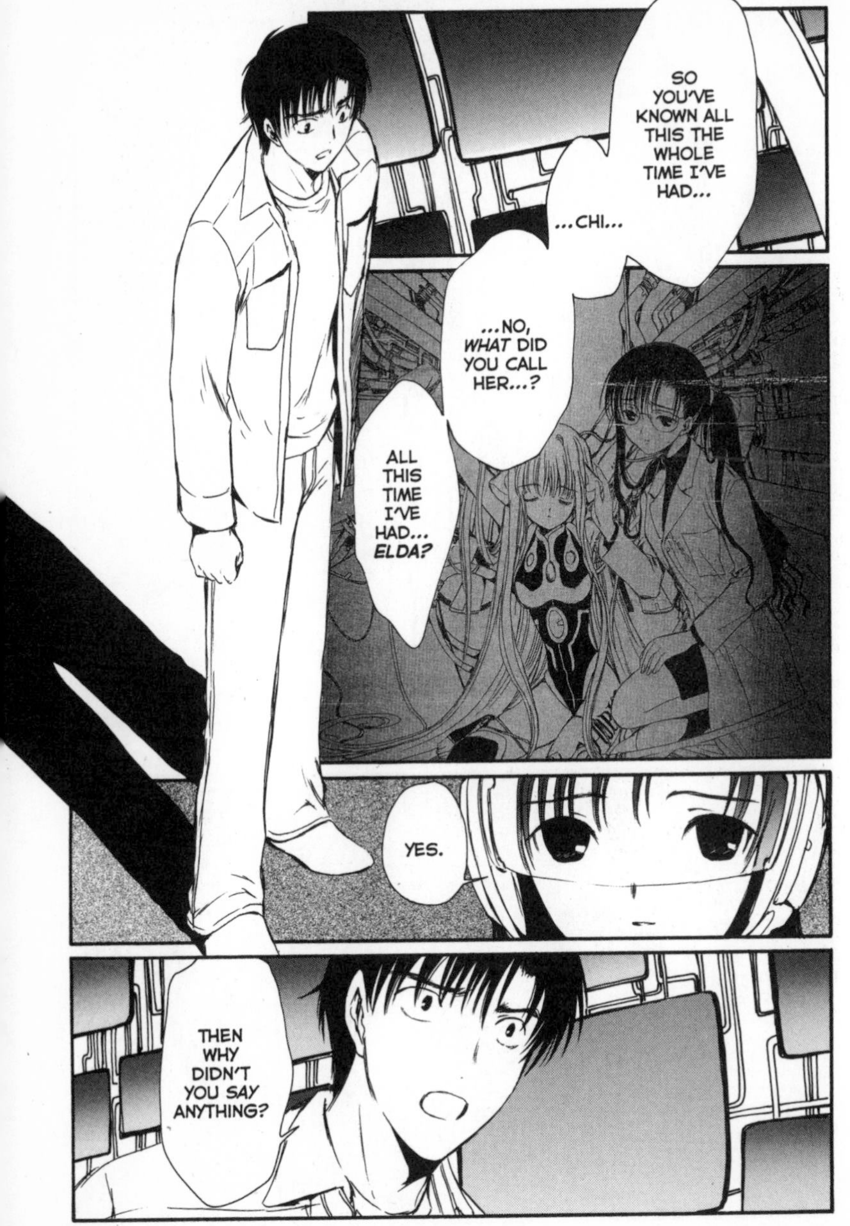
SO YOU'VE KNOWN ALL THIS THE WHOLE TIME I'VE HAD...
...CHI...
...NO, *WHAT* DID YOU CALL HER...?
ALL THIS TIME I'VE HAD... *ELDA?*
YES.
THEN WHY DIDN'T YOU SAY ANYTHING?

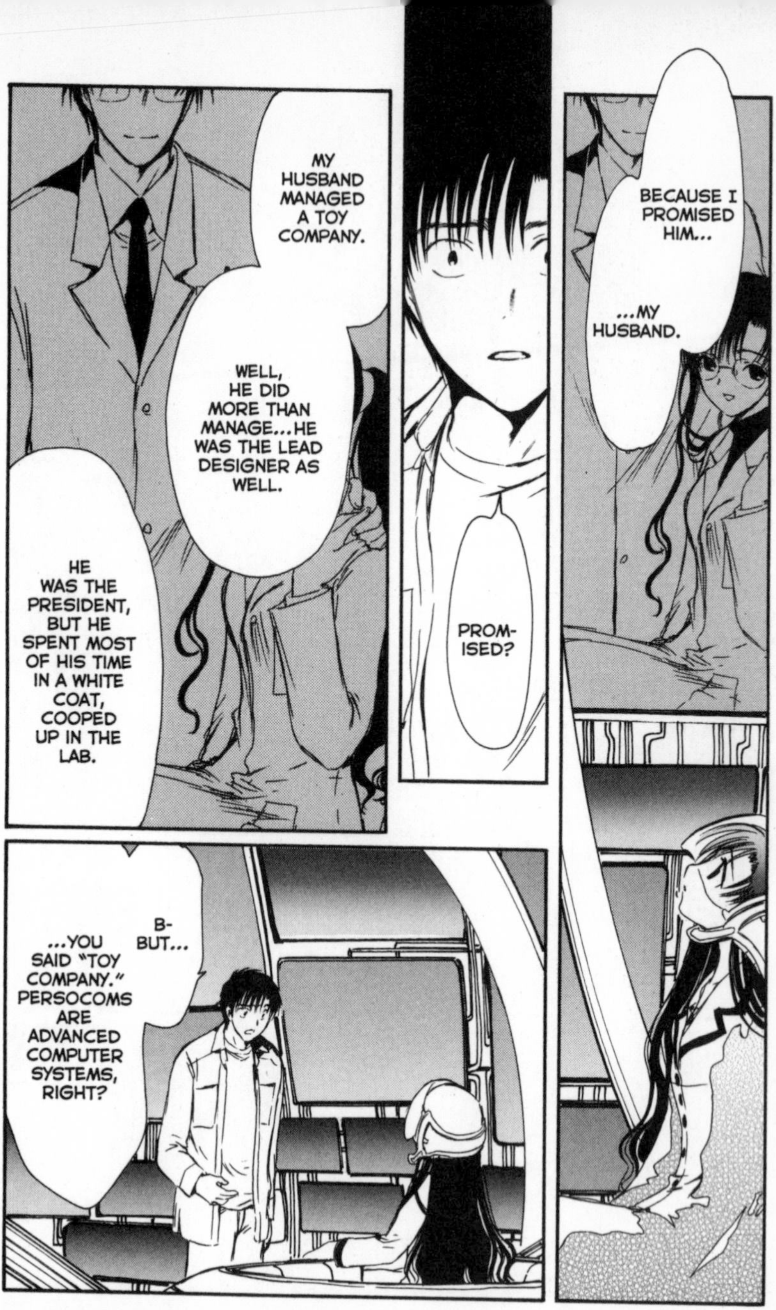
BECAUSE I PROMISED HIM...
...MY HUSBAND.
PROM-ISED?
MY HUSBAND MANAGED A TOY COMPANY.
WELL, HE DID MORE THAN MANAGE...HE WAS THE LEAD DESIGNER AS WELL.
HE WAS THE PRESIDENT, BUT HE SPENT MOST OF HIS TIME IN A WHITE COAT, COOPED UP IN THE LAB.
B-BUT...
...YOU SAID "TOY COMPANY." PERSOCOMS ARE ADVANCED COMPUTER SYSTEMS, RIGHT?

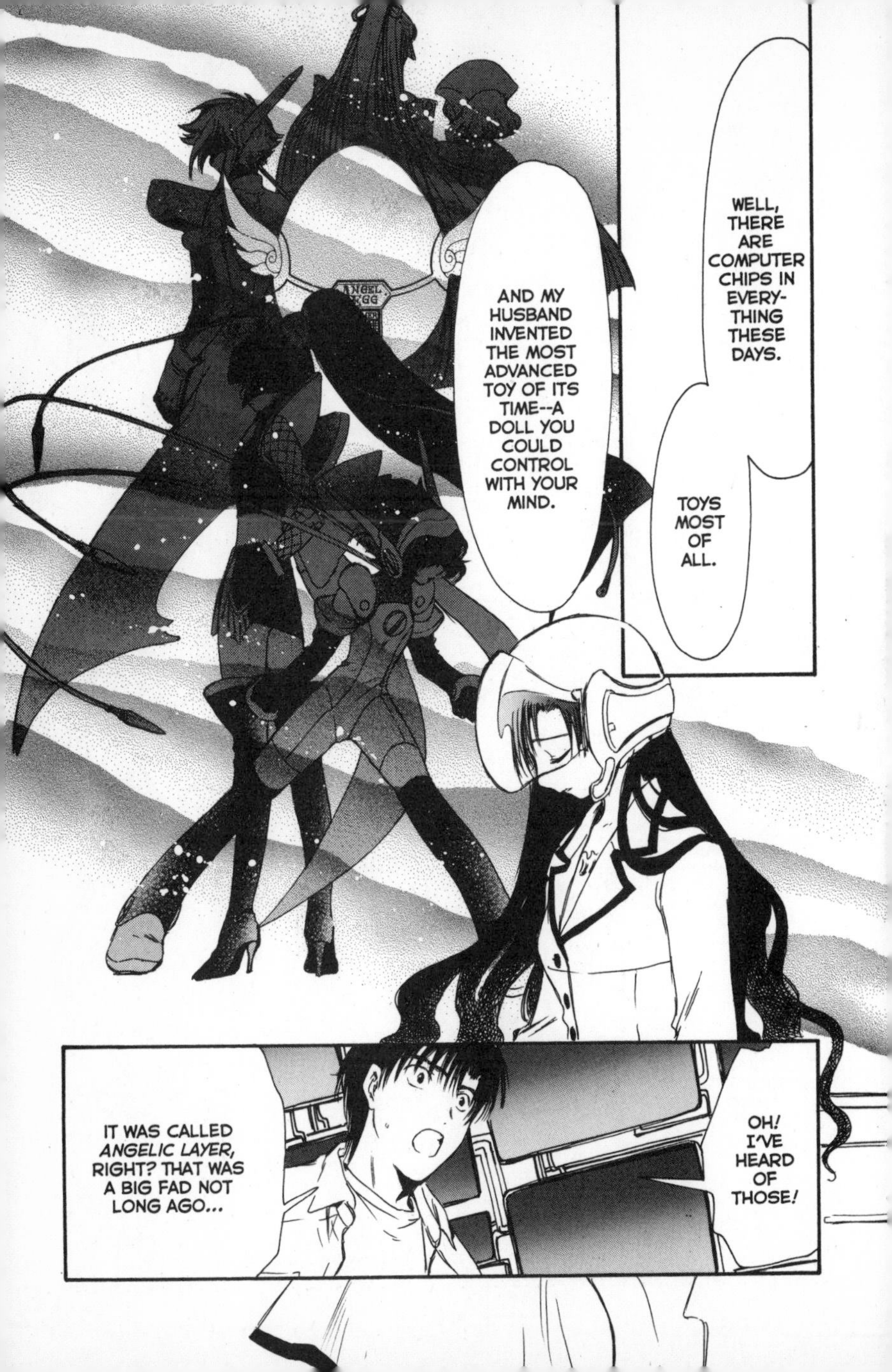
WELL, THERE ARE COMPUTER CHIPS IN EVERY-THING THESE DAYS.
TOYS MOST OF ALL.
AND MY HUSBAND INVENTED THE MOST ADVANCED TOY OF ITS TIME--A DOLL YOU COULD CONTROL WITH YOUR MIND.
ANGEL EGG
OH! I'VE HEARD OF THOSE!
IT WAS CALLED *ANGELIC LAYER*, RIGHT? THAT WAS A BIG FAD NOT LONG AGO...

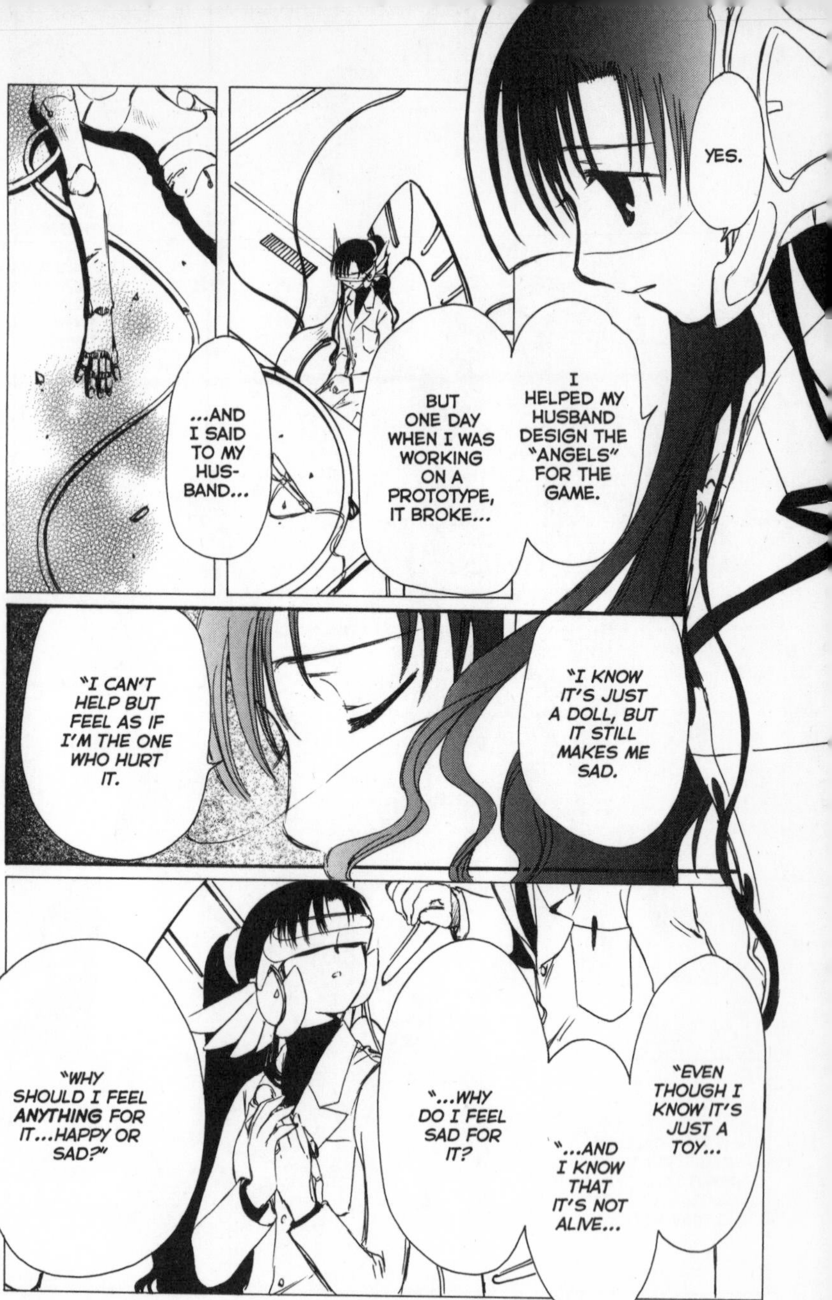
YES.
I HELPED MY HUSBAND DESIGN THE "ANGELS" FOR THE GAME.
BUT ONE DAY WHEN I WAS WORKING ON A PROTOTYPE, IT BROKE...
...AND I SAID TO MY HUS- BAND...
"I KNOW IT'S JUST A DOLL, BUT IT STILL MAKES ME SAD.
"I CAN'T HELP BUT FEEL AS IF I'M THE ONE WHO HURT IT.
"EVEN THOUGH I KNOW IT'S JUST A TOY...
"...AND I KNOW THAT IT'S NOT ALIVE...
"...WHY DO I FEEL SAD FOR IT?
"WHY SHOULD I FEEL **ANYTHING** FOR IT...HAPPY OR SAD?"

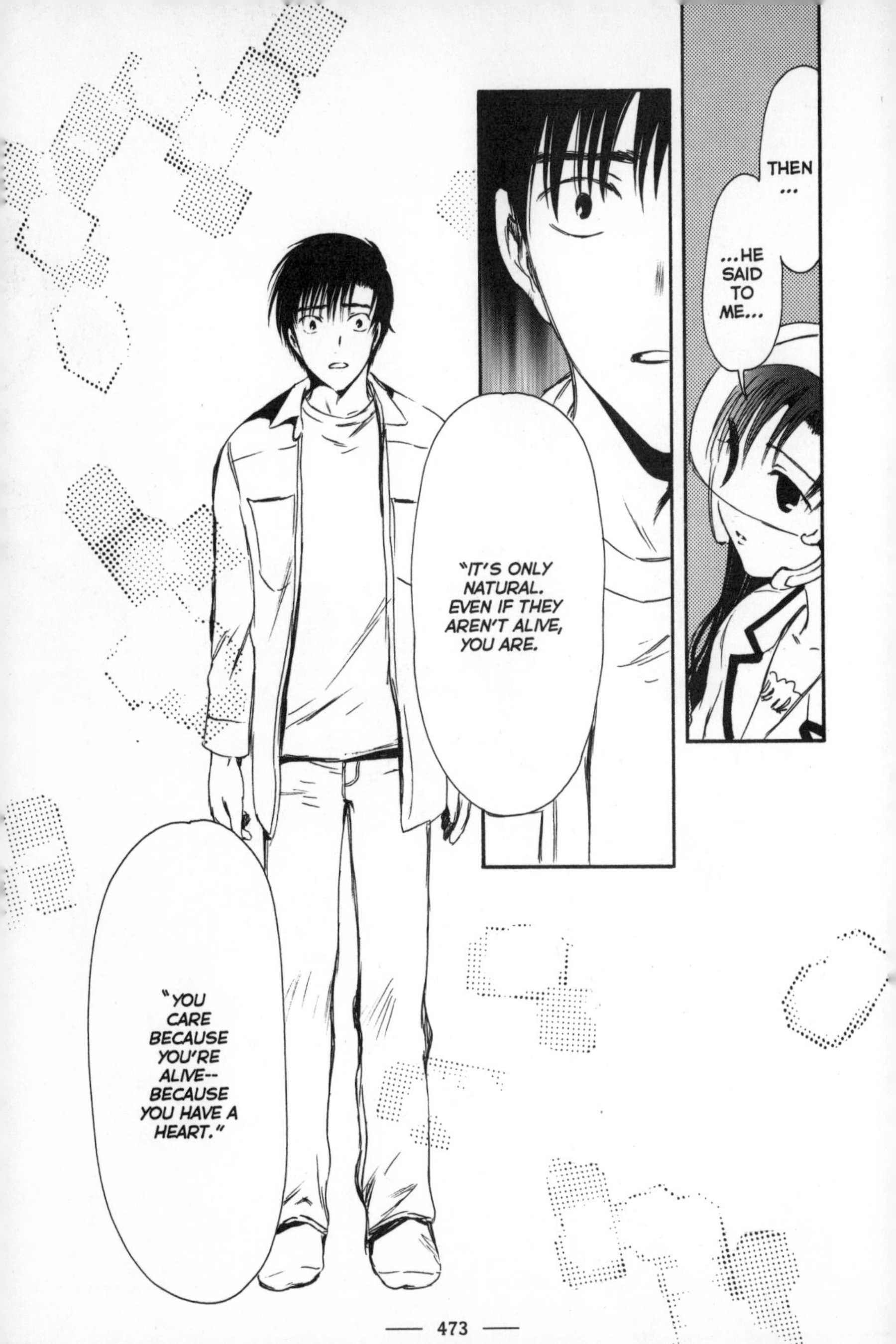
THEN ...
...HE SAID TO ME...
"IT'S ONLY NATURAL. EVEN IF THEY AREN'T ALIVE, YOU ARE.
"YOU CARE BECAUSE YOU'RE ALIVE-- BECAUSE YOU HAVE A HEART."

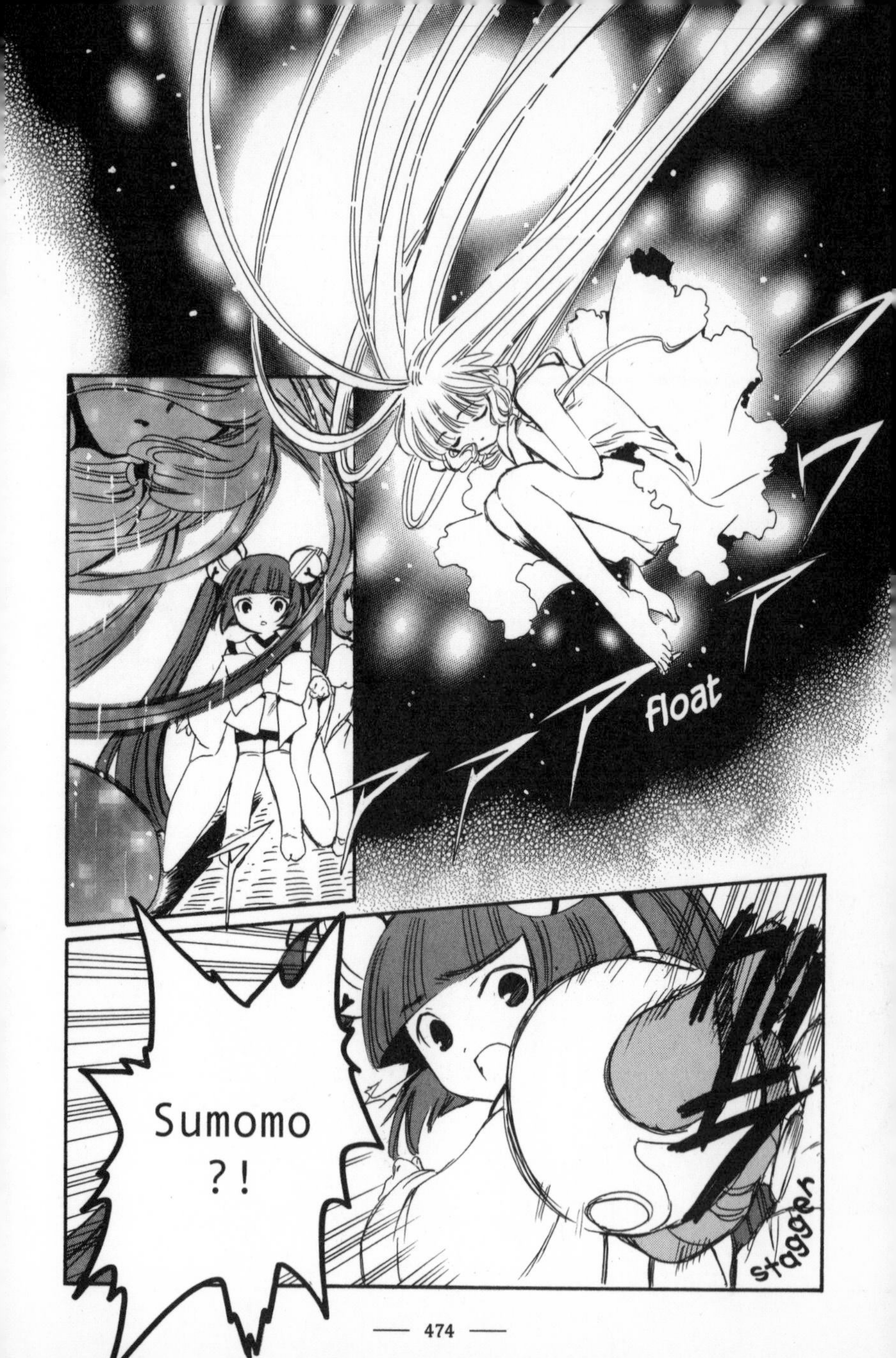
float
Sumomo ?!
stagger

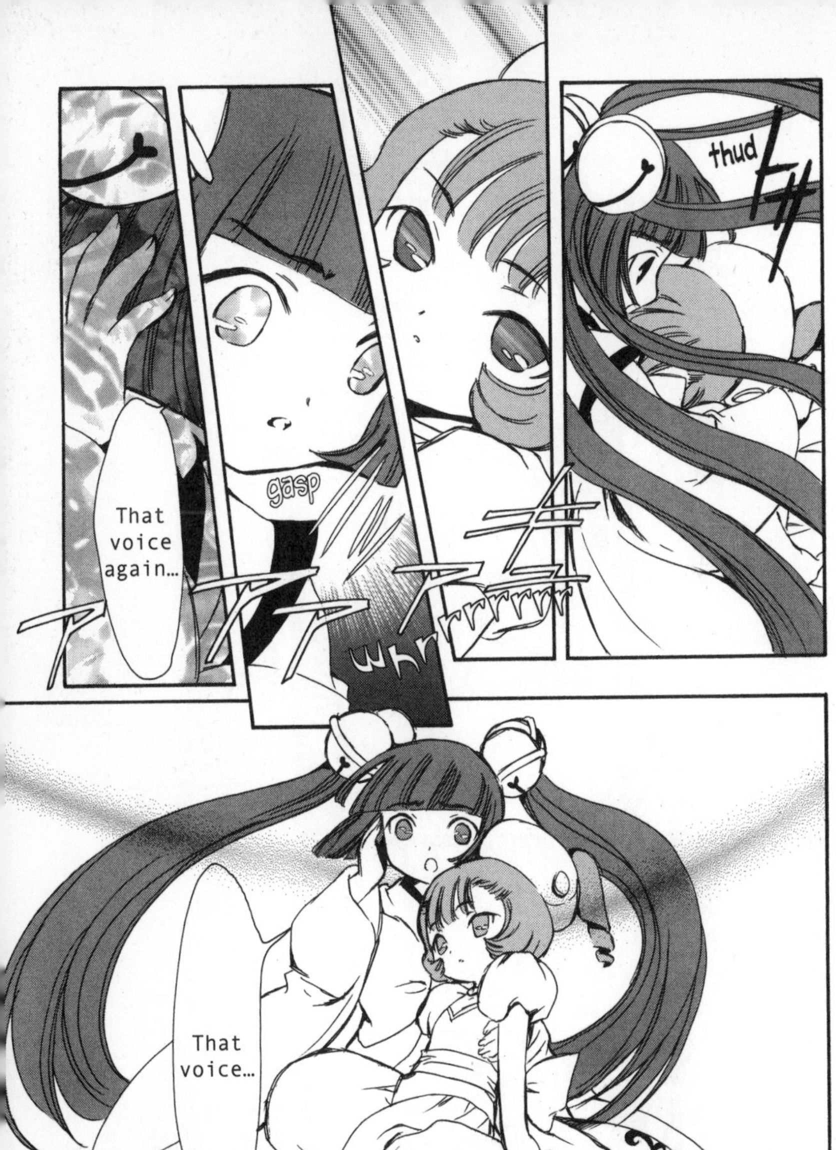
thud
gasp
whrrrrrrrrr
That voice again...
That voice...

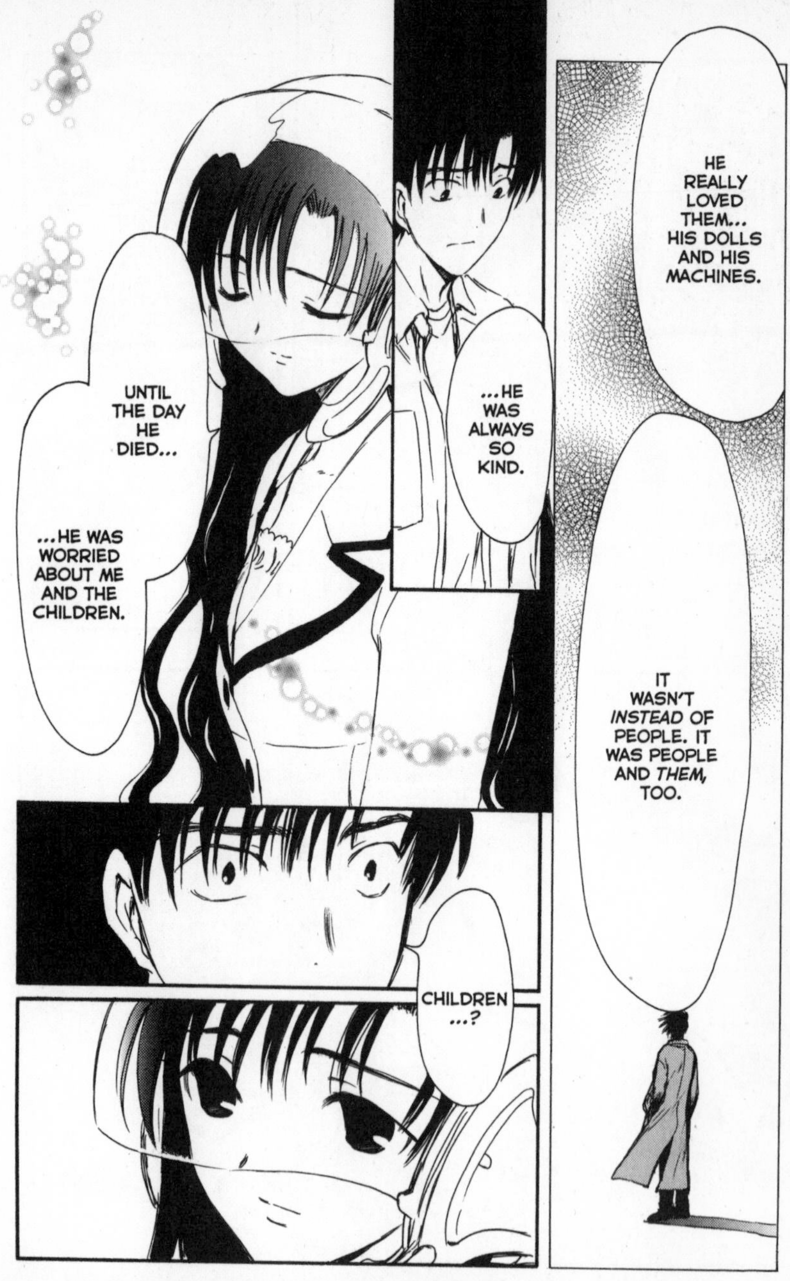
HE REALLY LOVED THEM... HIS DOLLS AND HIS MACHINES.
IT WASN'T *INSTEAD* OF PEOPLE. IT WAS PEOPLE AND *THEM*, TOO.
...HE WAS ALWAYS SO KIND.
UNTIL THE DAY HE DIED...
...HE WAS WORRIED ABOUT ME AND THE CHILDREN.
CHILDREN ...?

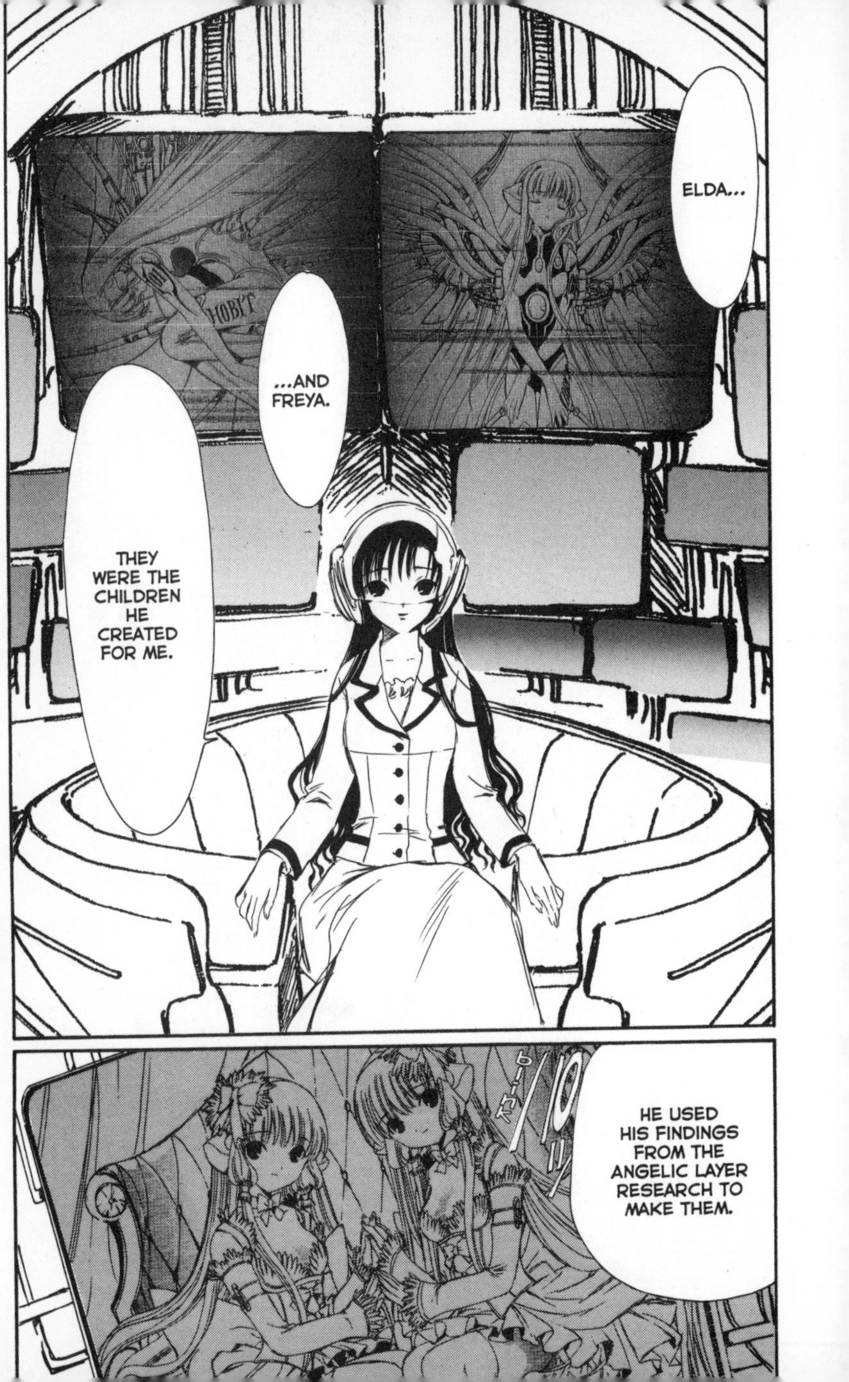
ELDA...
...AND FREYA.
THEY WERE THE CHILDREN HE CREATED FOR ME.
HE USED HIS FINDINGS FROM THE ANGELIC LAYER RESEARCH TO MAKE THEM.

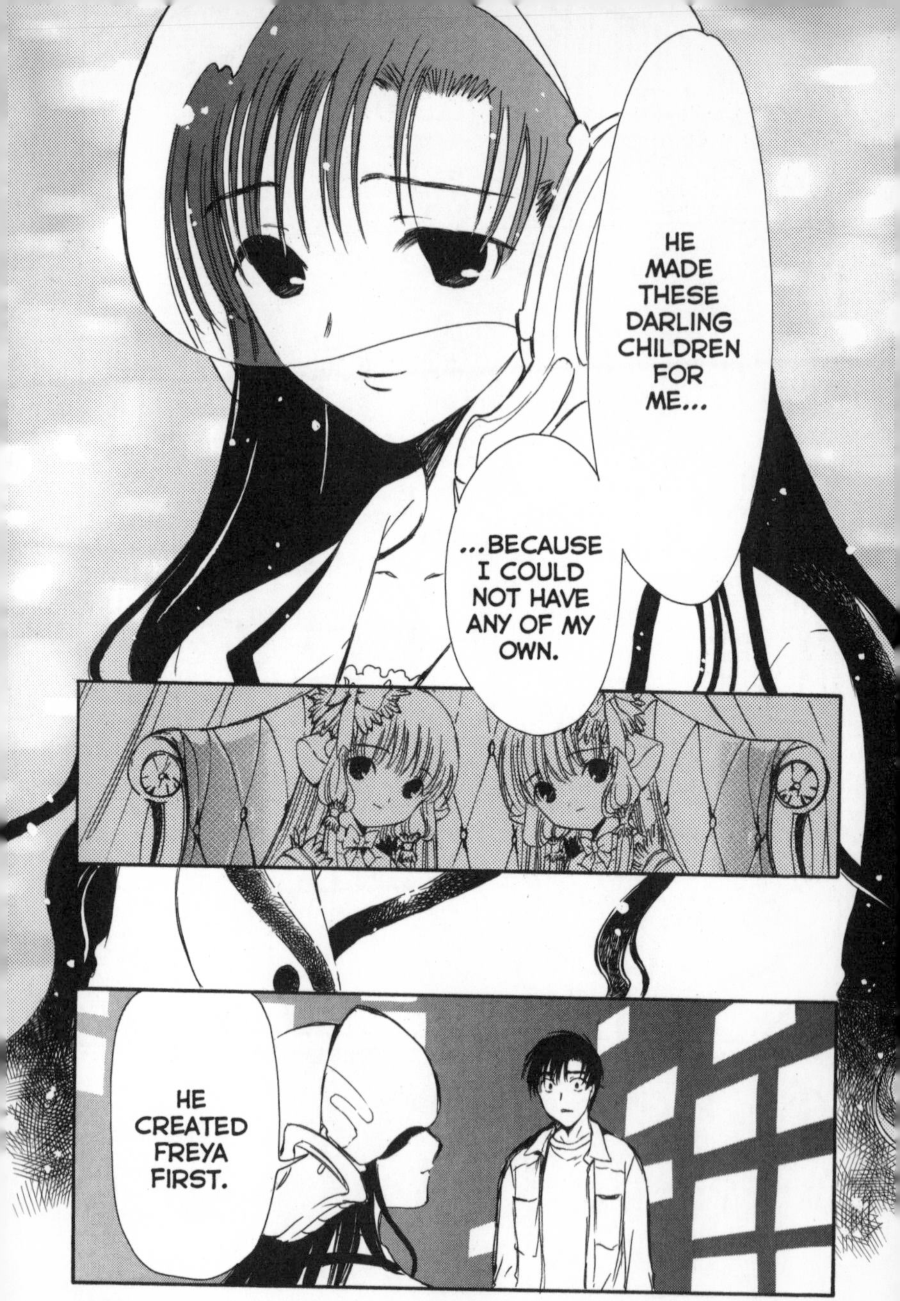
HE MADE THESE DARLING CHILDREN FOR ME...
...BECAUSE I COULD NOT HAVE ANY OF MY OWN.
HE CREATED FREYA FIRST.

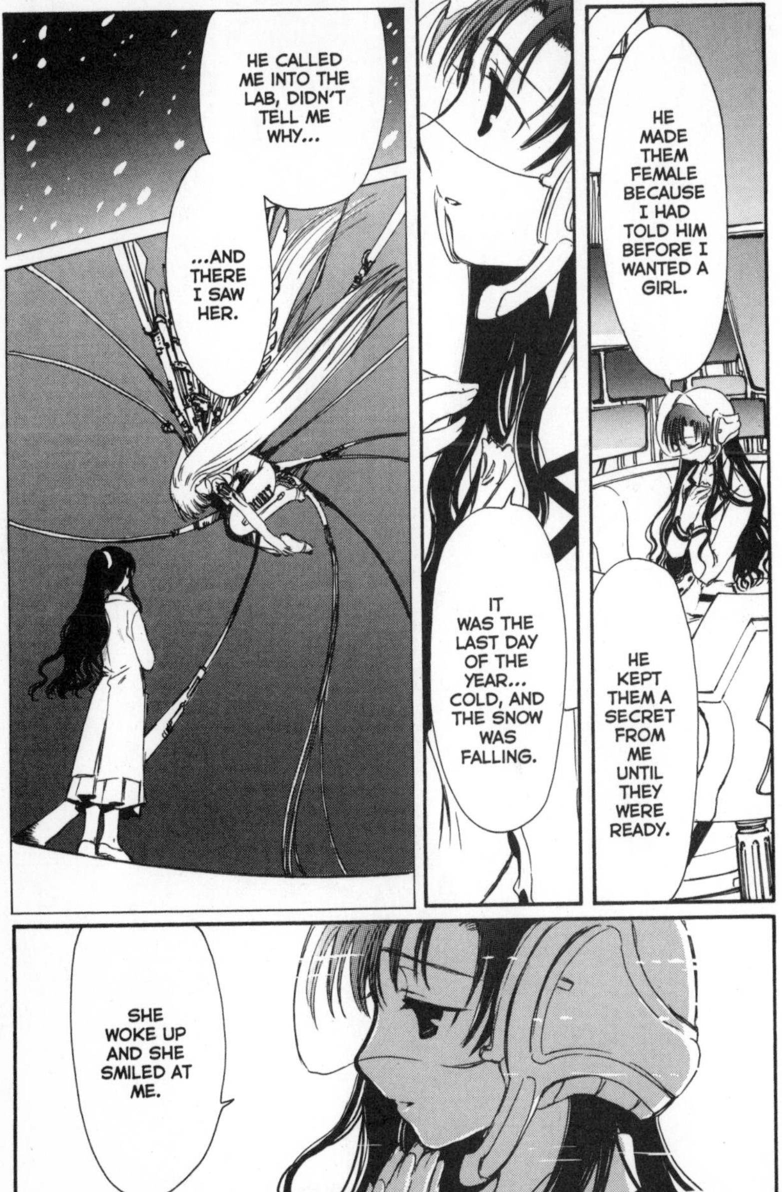
HE MADE THEM FEMALE BECAUSE I HAD TOLD HIM BEFORE I WANTED A GIRL.
HE KEPT THEM A SECRET FROM ME UNTIL THEY WERE READY.
IT WAS THE LAST DAY OF THE YEAR... COLD, AND THE SNOW WAS FALLING.
HE CALLED ME INTO THE LAB, DIDN'T TELL ME WHY...
...AND THERE I SAW HER.
SHE WOKE UP AND SHE SMILED AT ME.

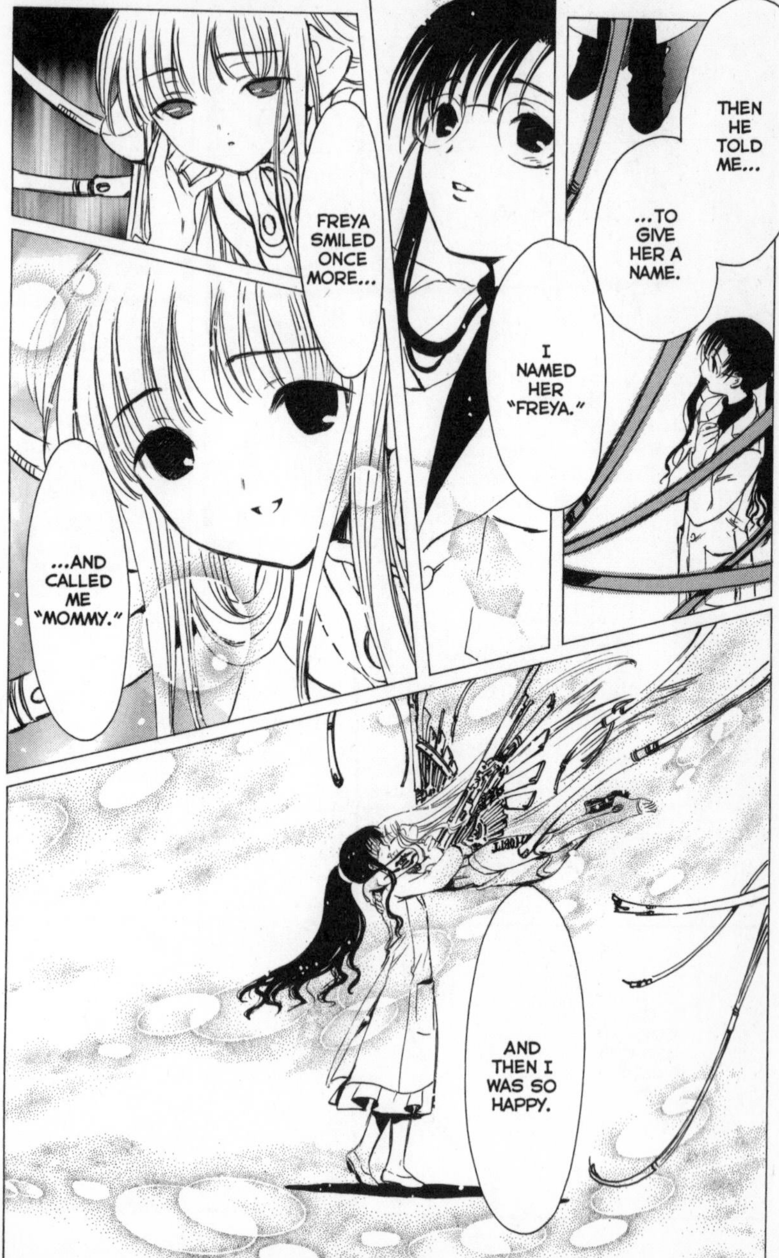
THEN HE TOLD ME...
...TO GIVE HER A NAME.
I NAMED HER "FREYA."
FREYA SMILED ONCE MORE...
...AND CALLED ME "MOMMY."
AND THEN I WAS SO HAPPY.

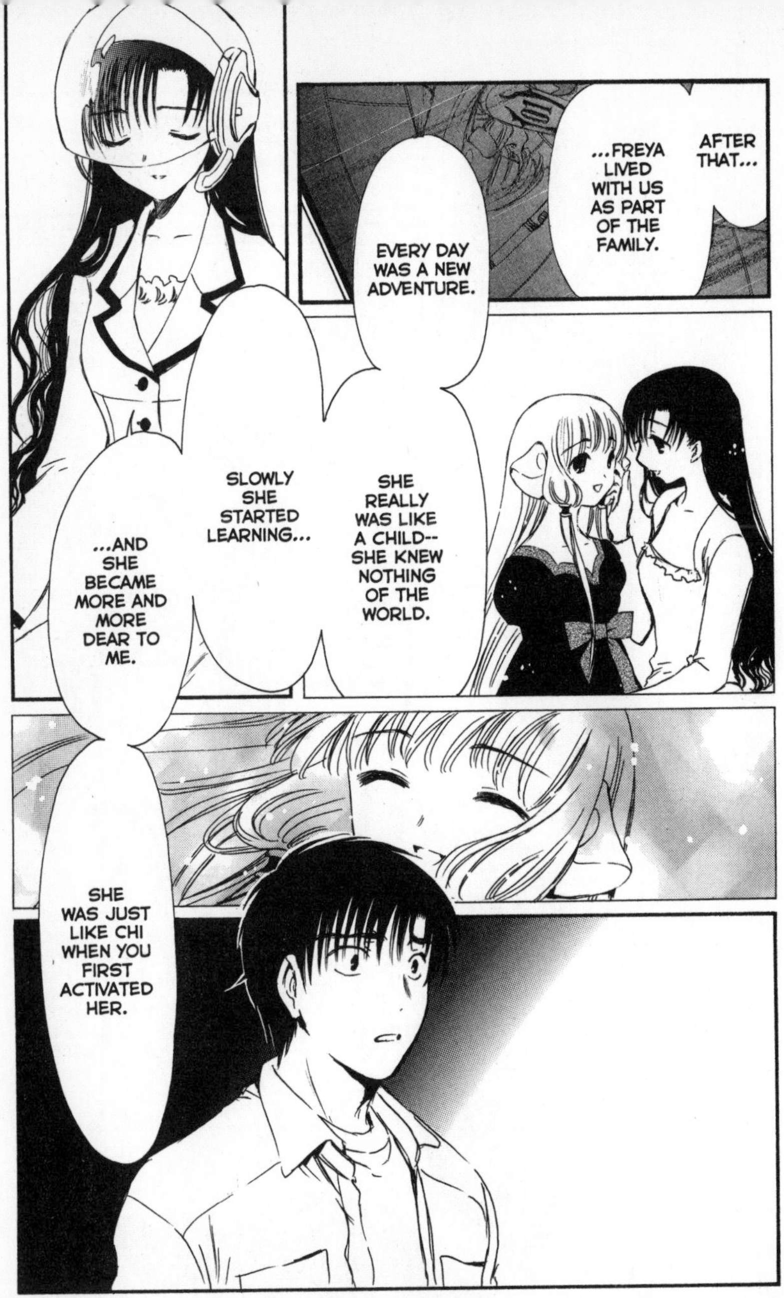
AFTER THAT...
...FREYA LIVED WITH US AS PART OF THE FAMILY.
EVERY DAY WAS A NEW ADVENTURE.
SHE REALLY WAS LIKE A CHILD-- SHE KNEW NOTHING OF THE WORLD.
SLOWLY SHE STARTED LEARNING...
...AND SHE BECAME MORE AND MORE DEAR TO ME.
SHE WAS JUST LIKE CHI WHEN YOU FIRST ACTIVATED HER.

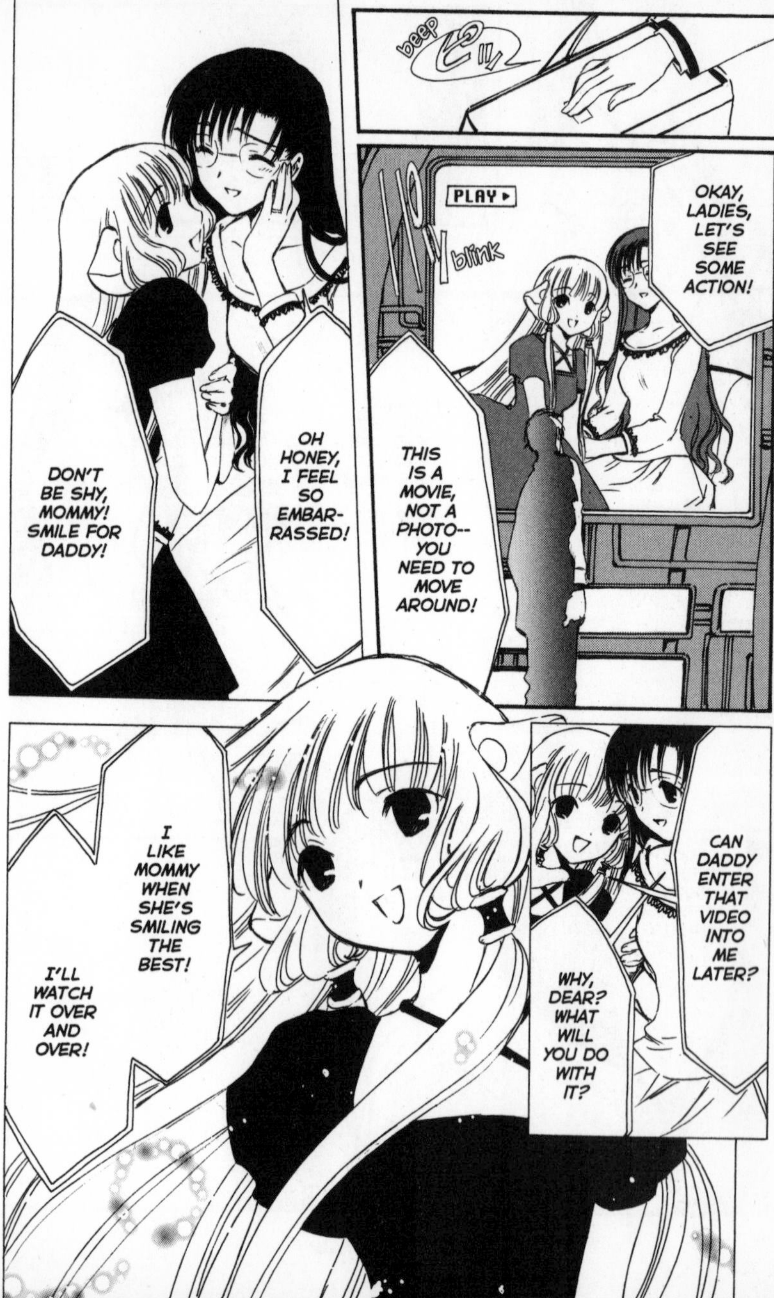
beep
PLAY ▸
blink
OKAY, LADIES, LET'S SEE SOME ACTION!
THIS IS A MOVIE, NOT A PHOTO-- YOU NEED TO MOVE AROUND!
OH HONEY, I FEEL SO EMBARRASSED!
DON'T BE SHY, MOMMY! SMILE FOR DADDY!
CAN DADDY ENTER THAT VIDEO INTO ME LATER?
WHY, DEAR? WHAT WILL YOU DO WITH IT?
I LIKE MOMMY WHEN SHE'S SMILING THE BEST!
I'LL WATCH IT OVER AND OVER!

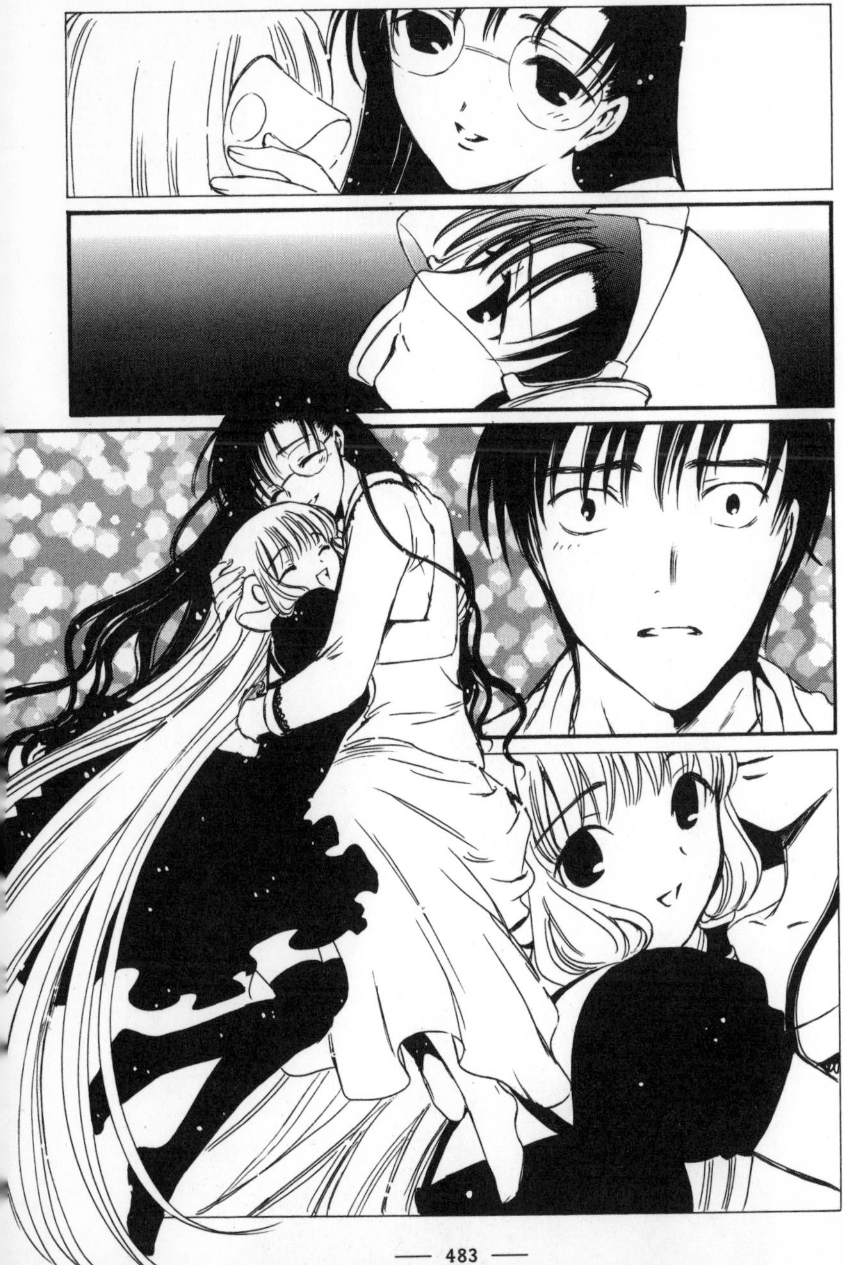

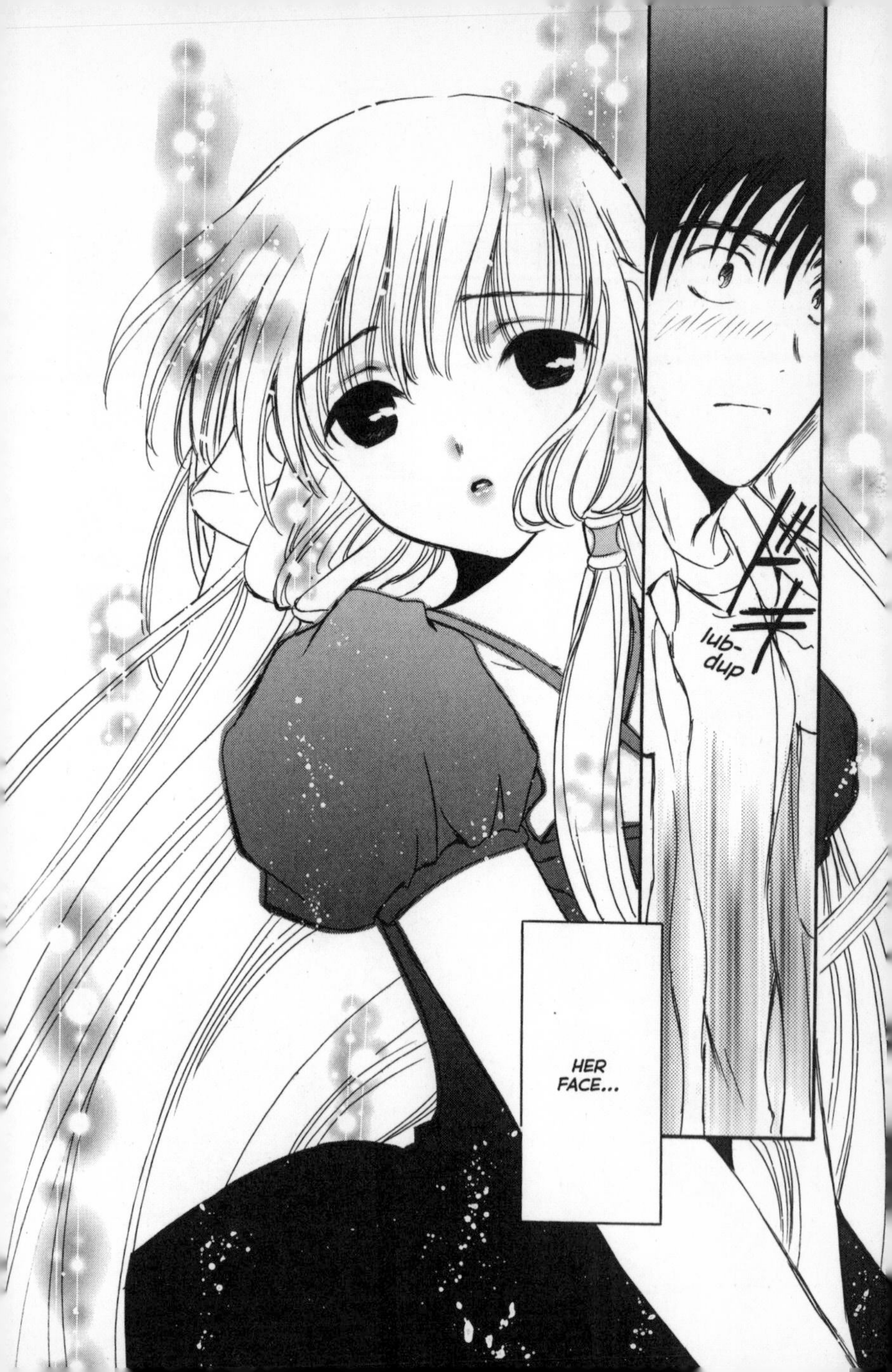
lub-dup
HER FACE...

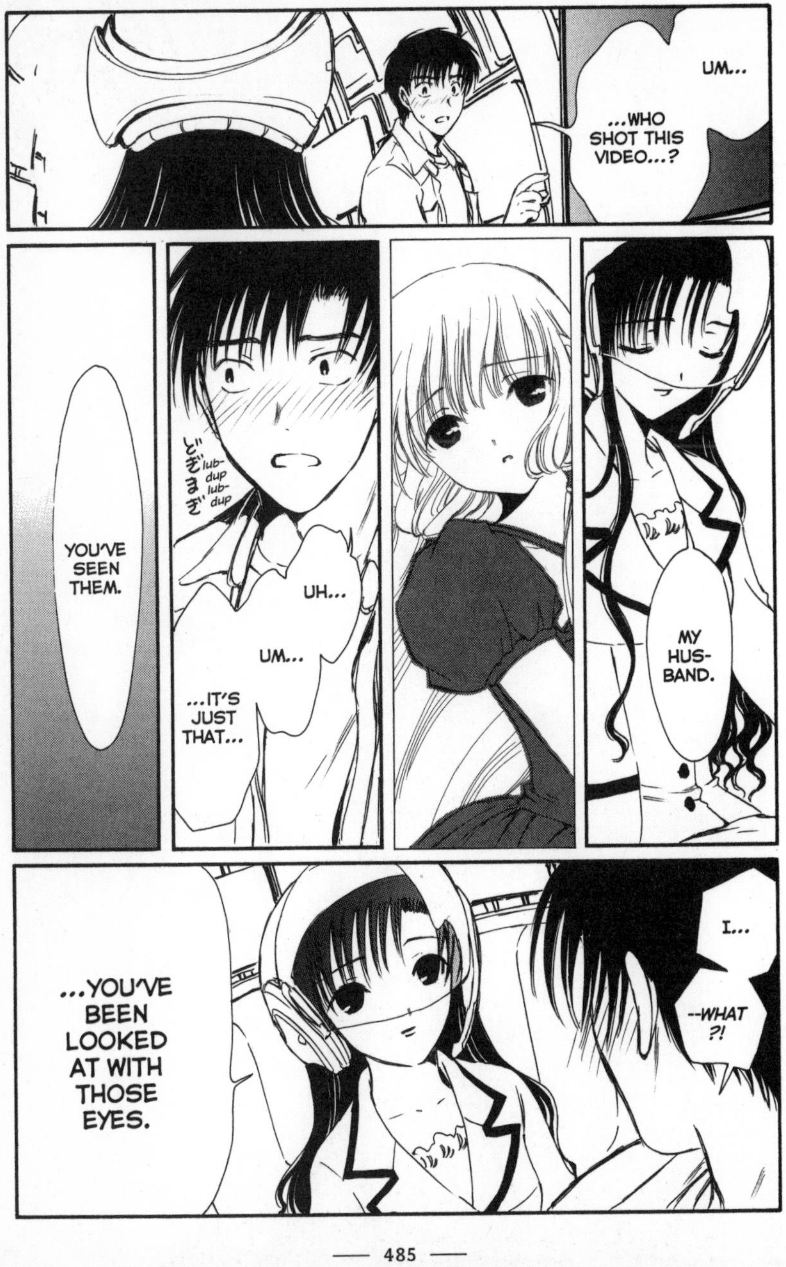
UM...
...WHO SHOT THIS VIDEO...?
MY HUS-BAND.
どぎまぎ
lub-dup lub-dup
UH...
UM...
...IT'S JUST THAT...
YOU'VE SEEN THEM.
I...
--WHAT ?!
...YOU'VE BEEN LOOKED AT WITH THOSE EYES.

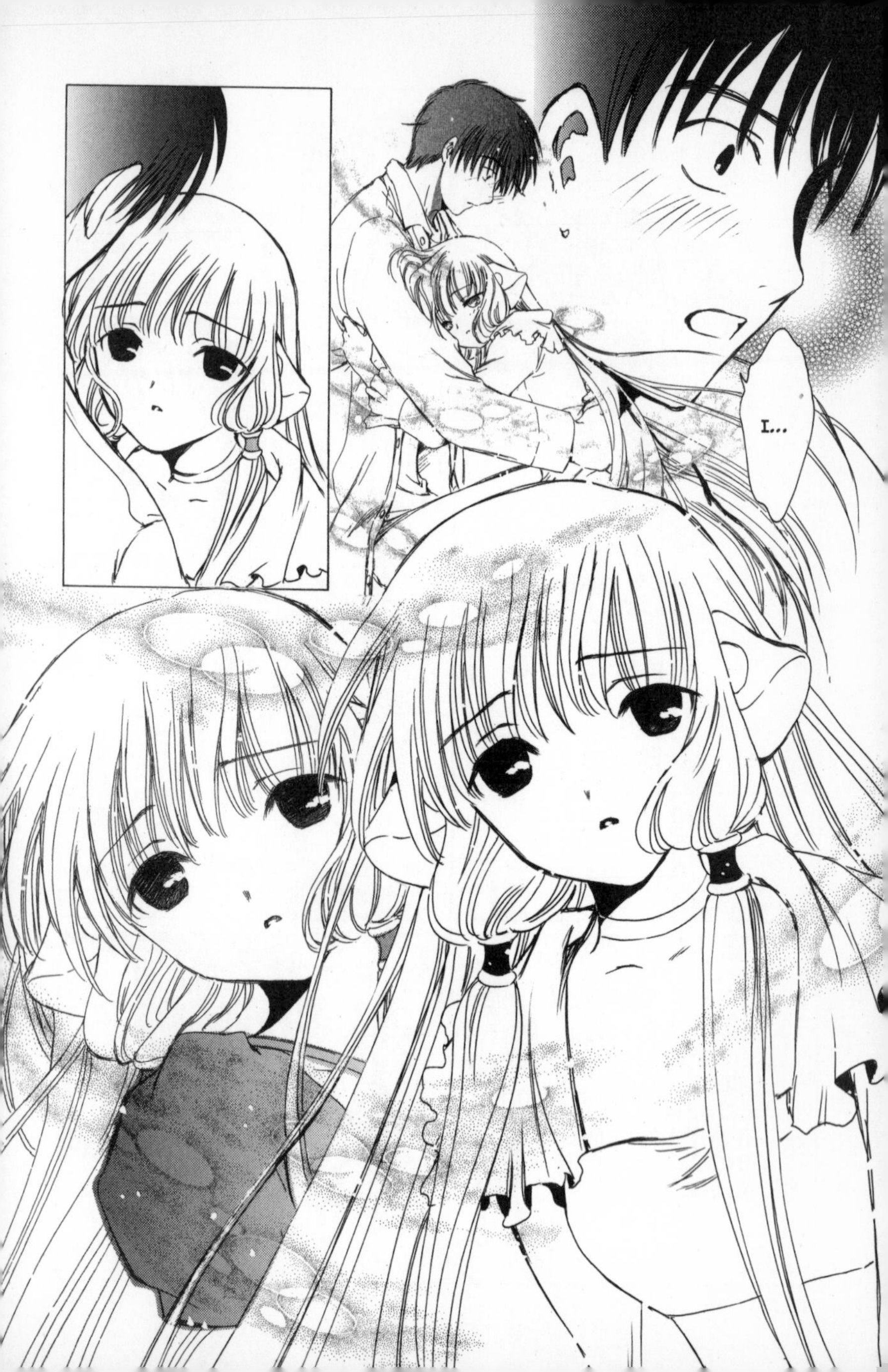
I...

Chobits
ちょびっツ

◀ chapter 79 ▶

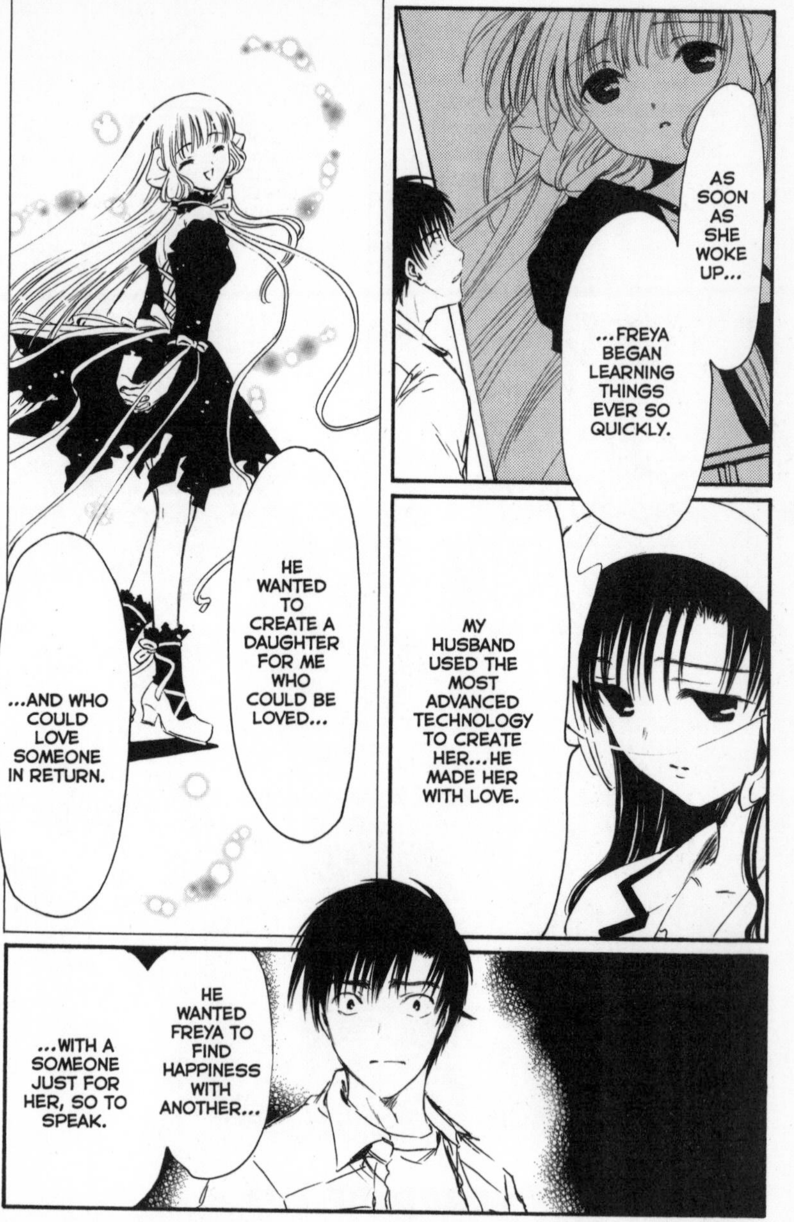
AS SOON AS SHE WOKE UP...
...FREYA BEGAN LEARNING THINGS EVER SO QUICKLY.
MY HUSBAND USED THE MOST ADVANCED TECHNOLOGY TO CREATE HER...HE MADE HER WITH LOVE.
HE WANTED TO CREATE A DAUGHTER FOR ME WHO COULD BE LOVED...
...AND WHO COULD LOVE SOMEONE IN RETURN.
HE WANTED FREYA TO FIND HAPPINESS WITH ANOTHER...
...WITH A SOMEONE JUST FOR HER, SO TO SPEAK.

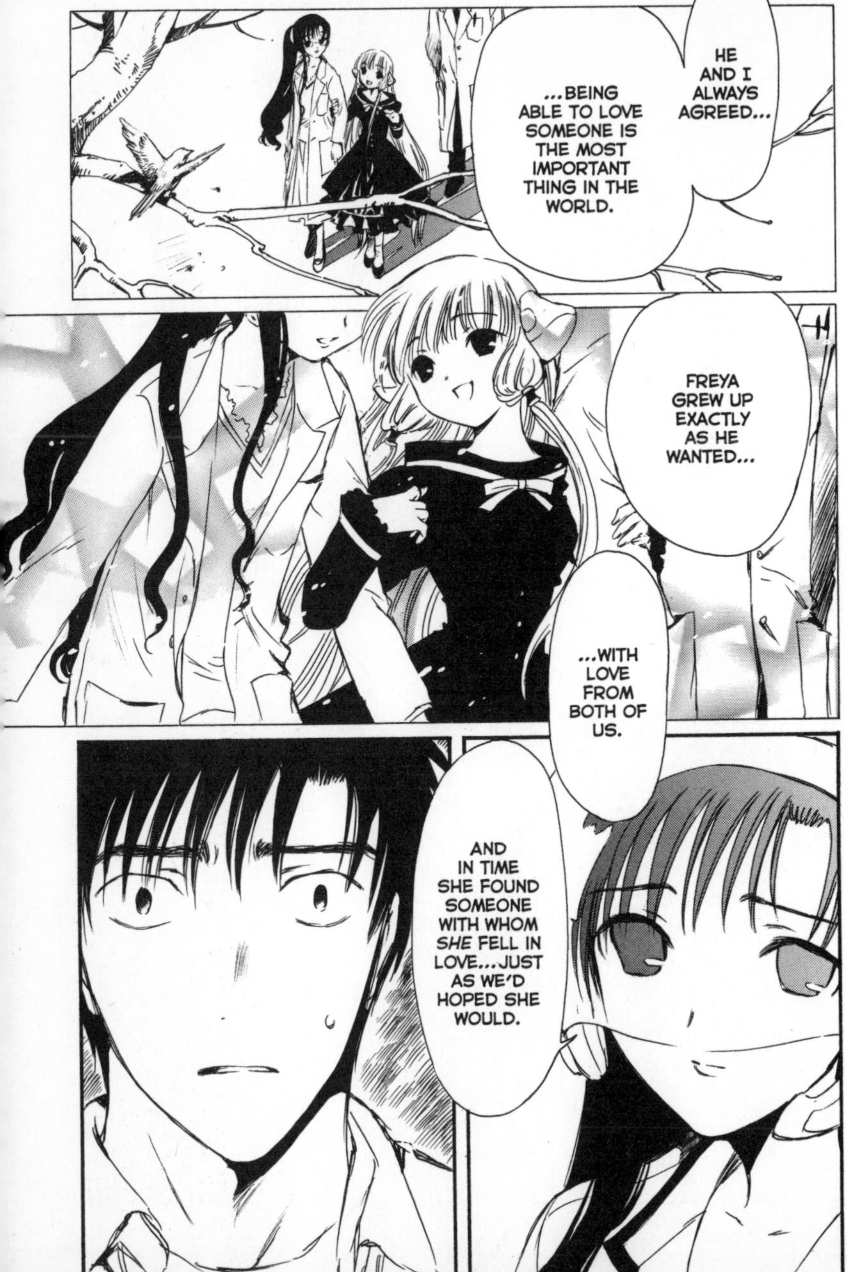
HE AND I ALWAYS AGREED...
...BEING ABLE TO LOVE SOMEONE IS THE MOST IMPORTANT THING IN THE WORLD.
FREYA GREW UP EXACTLY AS HE WANTED...
...WITH LOVE FROM BOTH OF US.
AND IN TIME SHE FOUND SOMEONE WITH WHOM *SHE* FELL IN LOVE...JUST AS WE'D HOPED SHE WOULD.

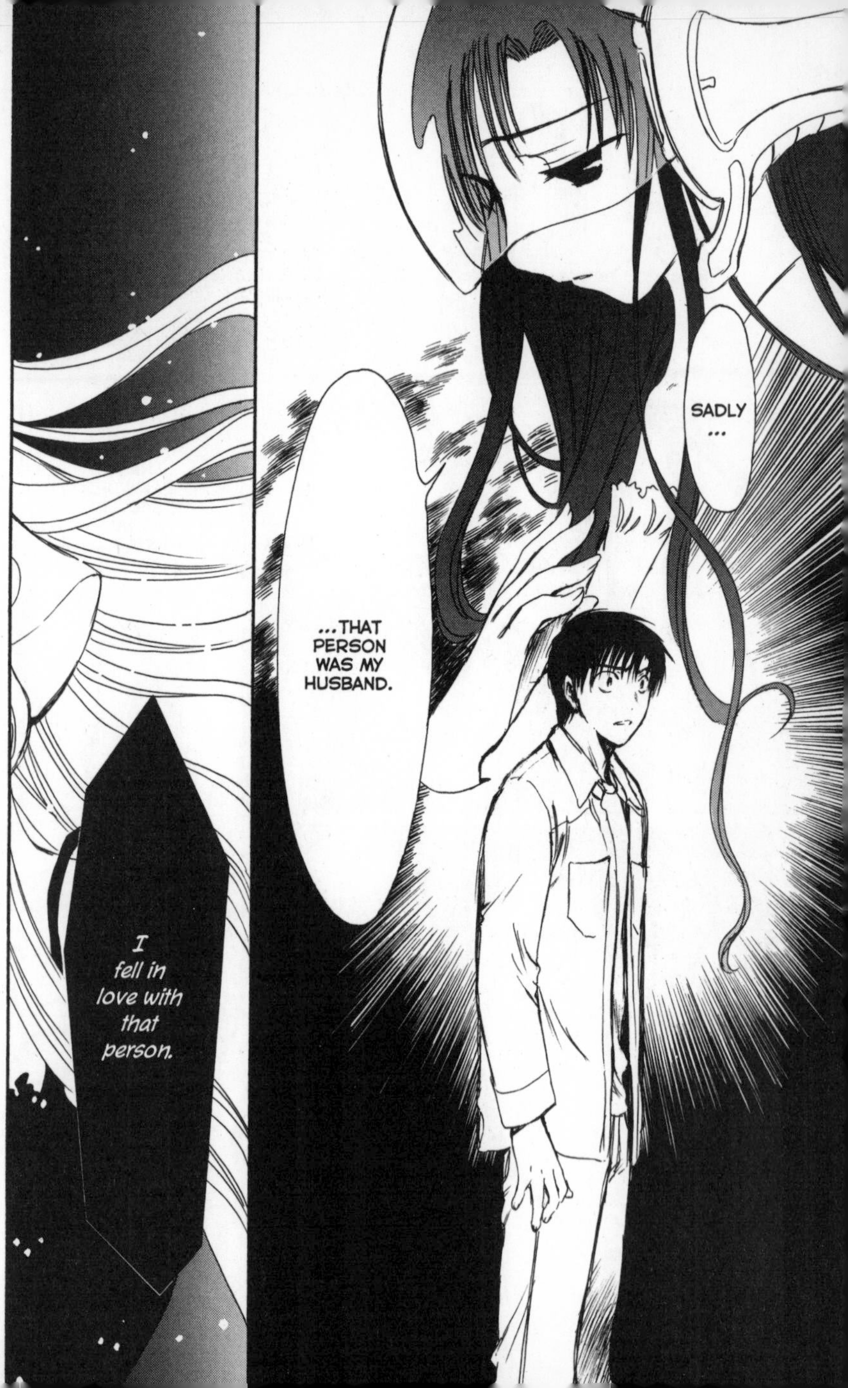
SADLY ...
...THAT PERSON WAS MY HUSBAND.
I fell in love with that person.

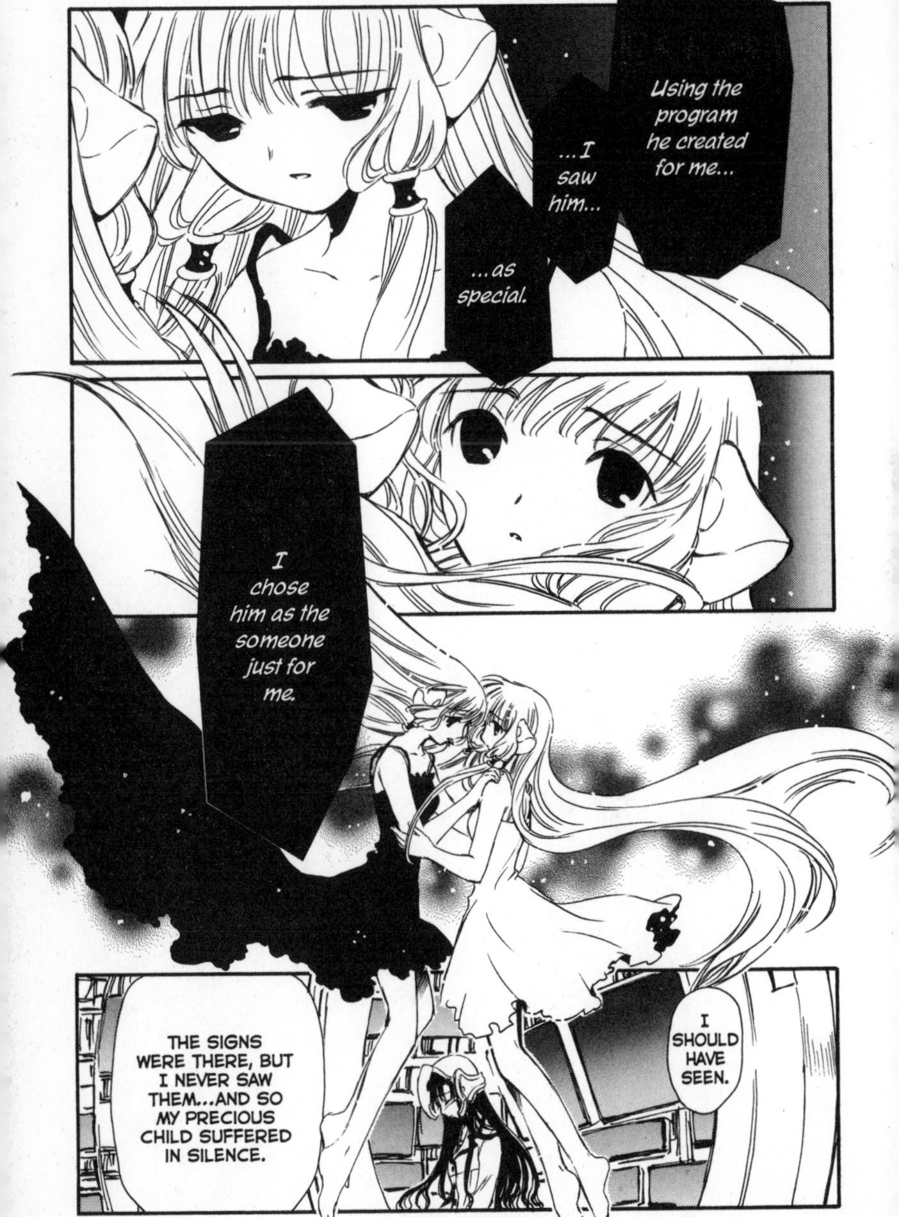
Using the program he created for me...
...I saw him...
...as special.
I chose him as the someone just for me.
I SHOULD HAVE SEEN.
THE SIGNS WERE THERE, BUT I NEVER SAW THEM...AND SO MY PRECIOUS CHILD SUFFERED IN SILENCE.

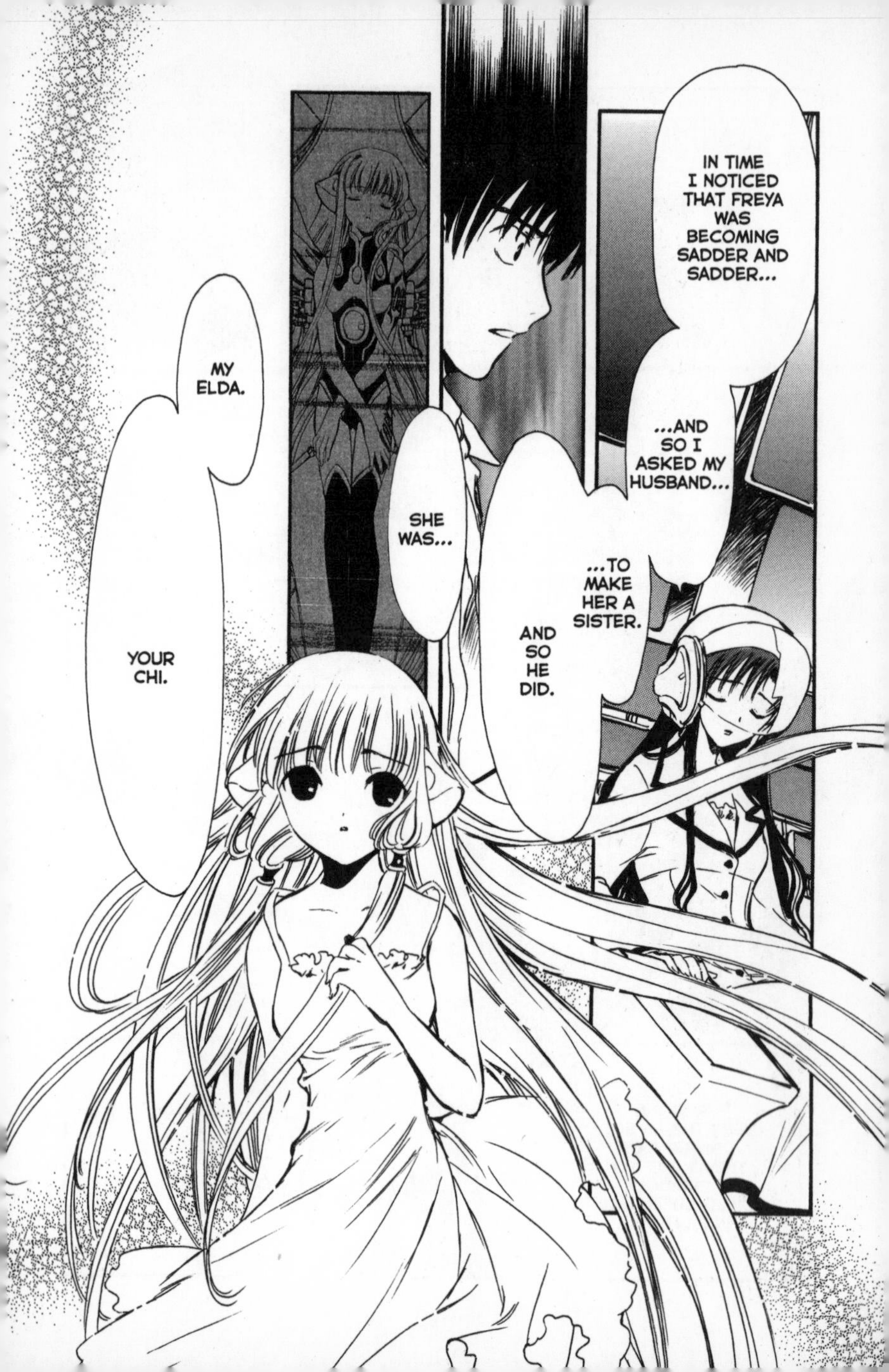
IN TIME I NOTICED THAT FREYA WAS BECOMING SADDER AND SADDER...
...AND SO I ASKED MY HUSBAND...
...TO MAKE HER A SISTER.
AND SO HE DID.
SHE WAS...
MY ELDA.
YOUR CHI.

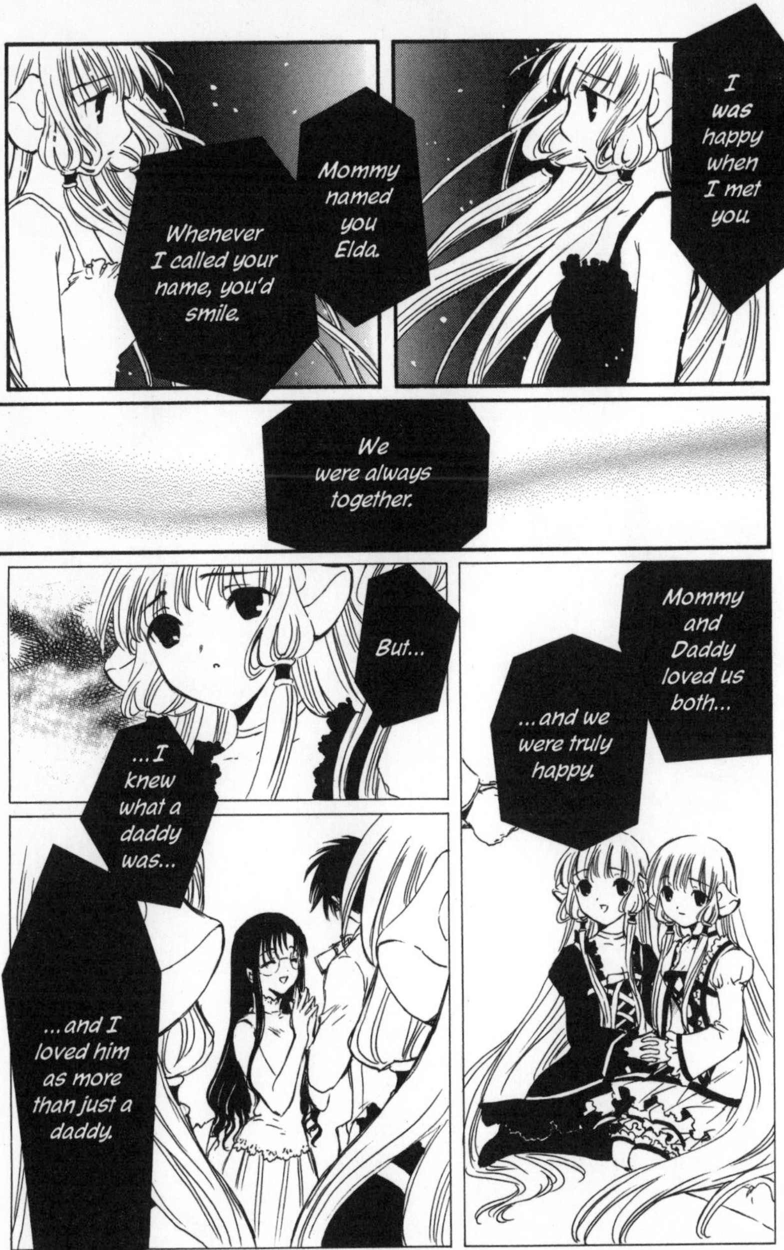
I was happy when I met you.
Mommy named you Elda.
Whenever I called your name, you'd smile.
We were always together.
Mommy and Daddy loved us both...
...and we were truly happy.
But...
...I knew what a daddy was...
...and I loved him as more than just a daddy.

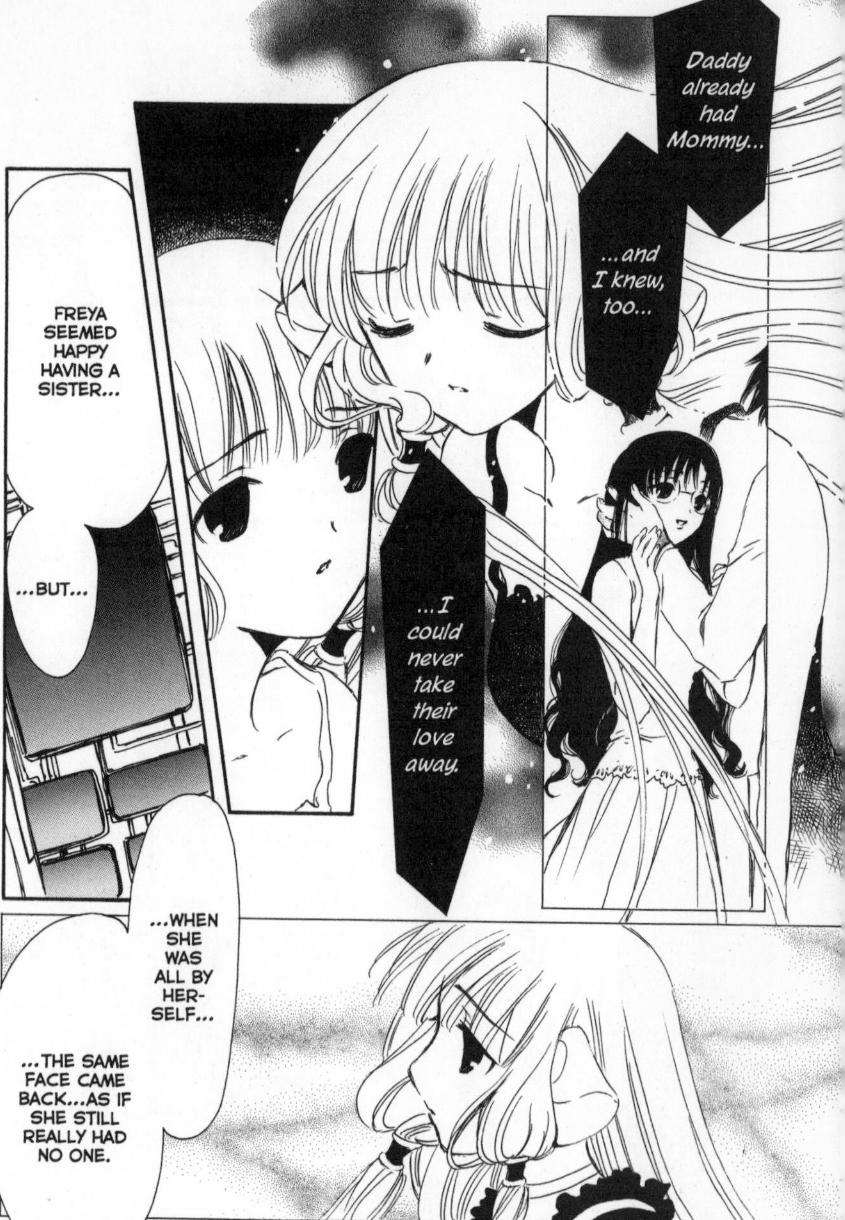
Daddy already had Mommy...
...and I knew, too...
...I could never take their love away.
FREYA SEEMED HAPPY HAVING A SISTER...
...BUT...
...WHEN SHE WAS ALL BY HER-SELF...
...THE SAME FACE CAME BACK...AS IF SHE STILL REALLY HAD NO ONE.

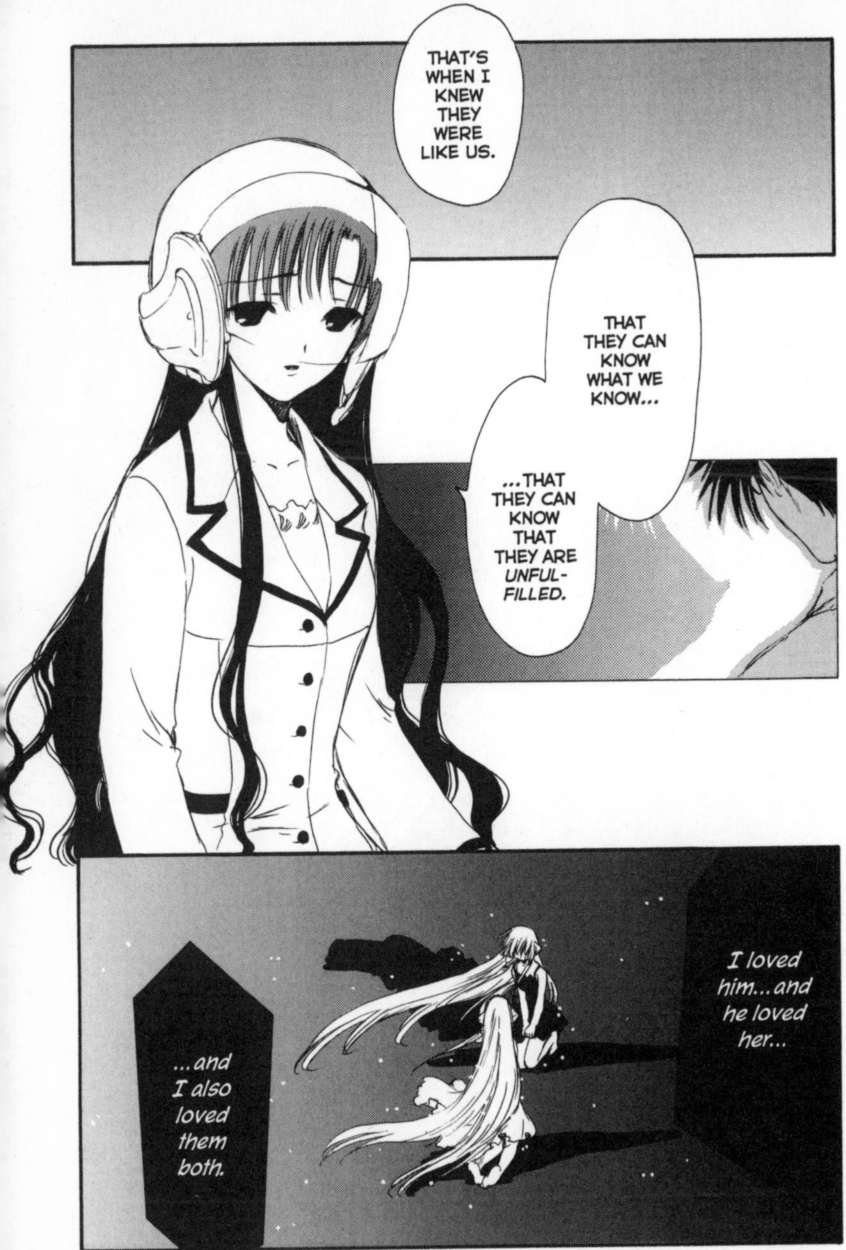
THAT'S WHEN I KNEW THEY WERE LIKE US.
THAT THEY CAN KNOW WHAT WE KNOW...
...THAT THEY CAN KNOW THAT THEY ARE *UNFUL-FILLED.*
I loved him...and he loved her...
...and I also loved them both.

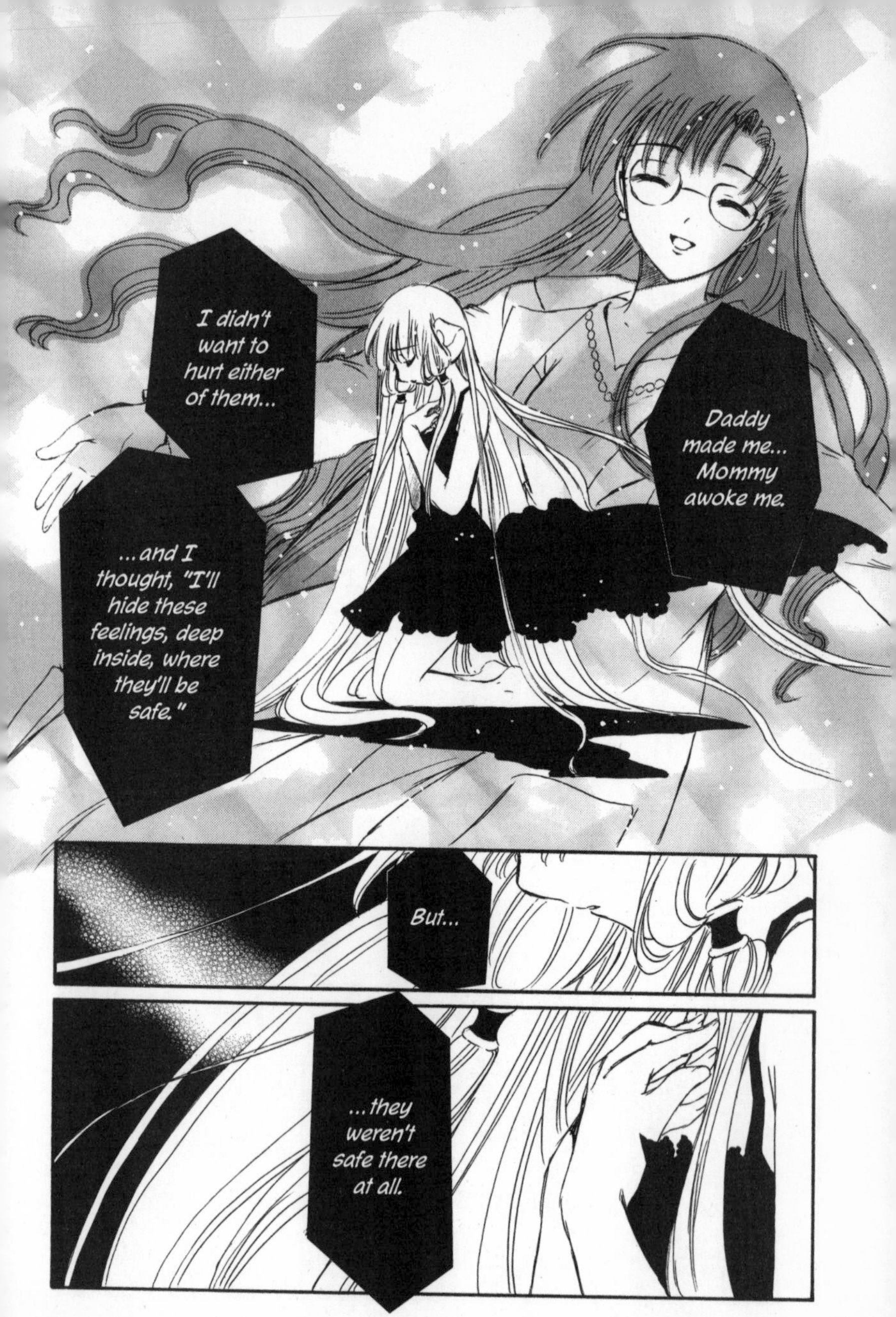
Daddy made me... Mommy awoke me.
I didn't want to hurt either of them...
...and I thought, "I'll hide these feelings, deep inside, where they'll be safe."
But...
...they weren't safe there at all.

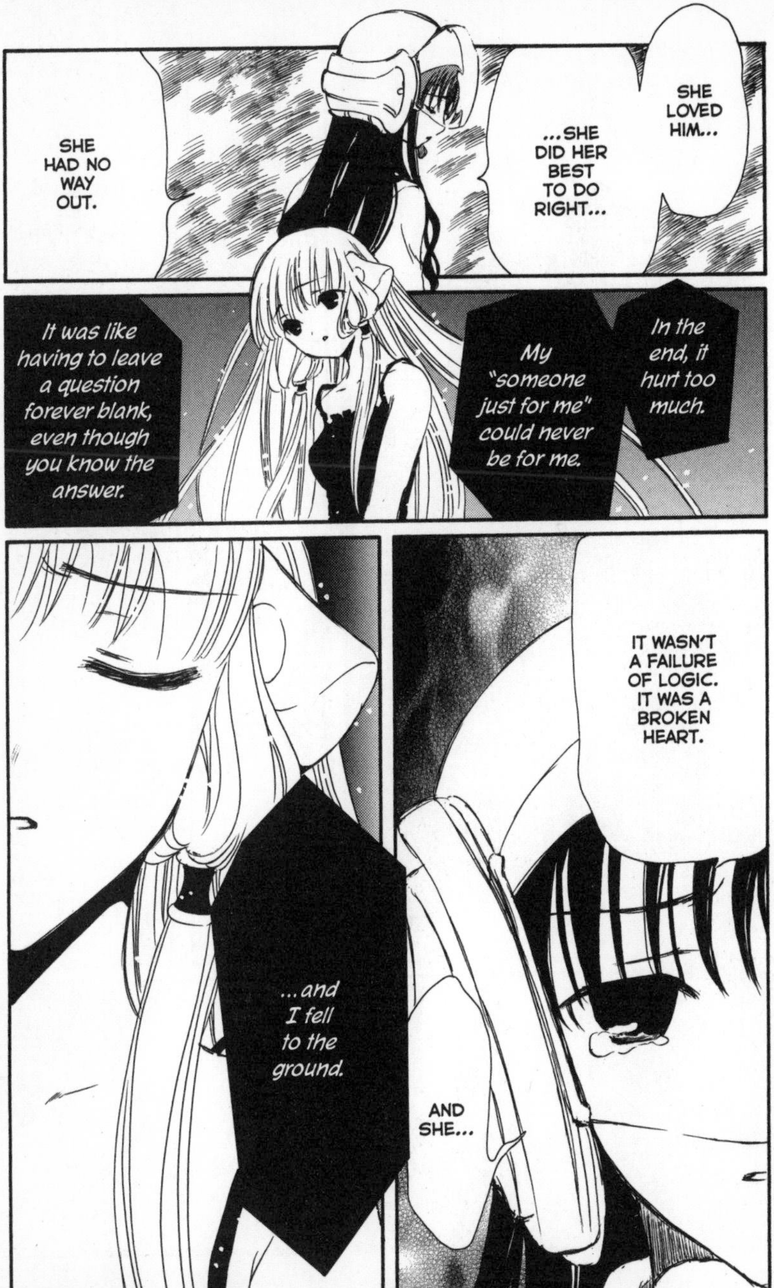
SHE LOVED HIM...
...SHE DID HER BEST TO DO RIGHT...
SHE HAD NO WAY OUT.
In the end, it hurt too much.
My "someone just for me" could never be for me.
It was like having to leave a question forever blank, even though you know the answer.
IT WASN'T A FAILURE OF LOGIC. IT WAS A BROKEN HEART.
AND SHE...
...and I fell to the ground.

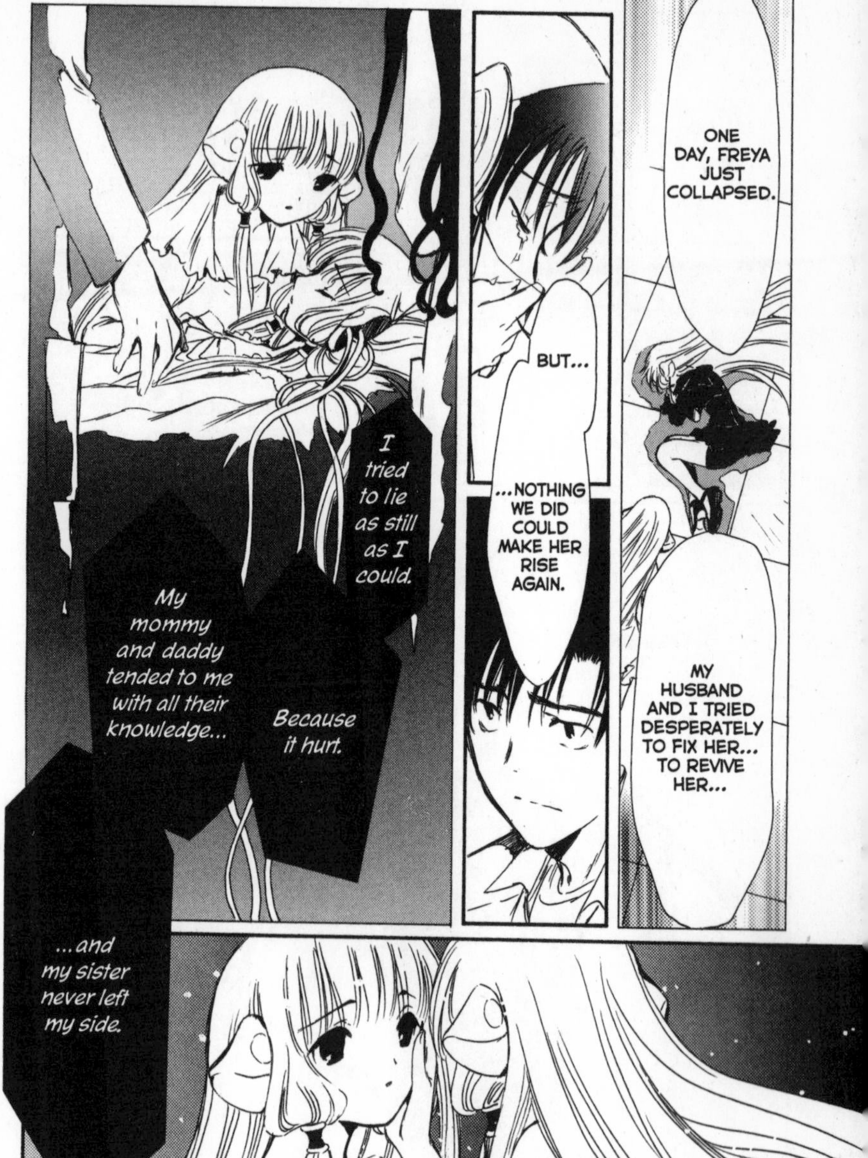
ONE DAY, FREYA JUST COLLAPSED.
MY HUSBAND AND I TRIED DESPERATELY TO FIX HER... TO REVIVE HER...
BUT...
...NOTHING WE DID COULD MAKE HER RISE AGAIN.
I tried to lie as still as I could.
Because it hurt.
My mommy and daddy tended to me with all their knowledge...
...and my sister never left my side.

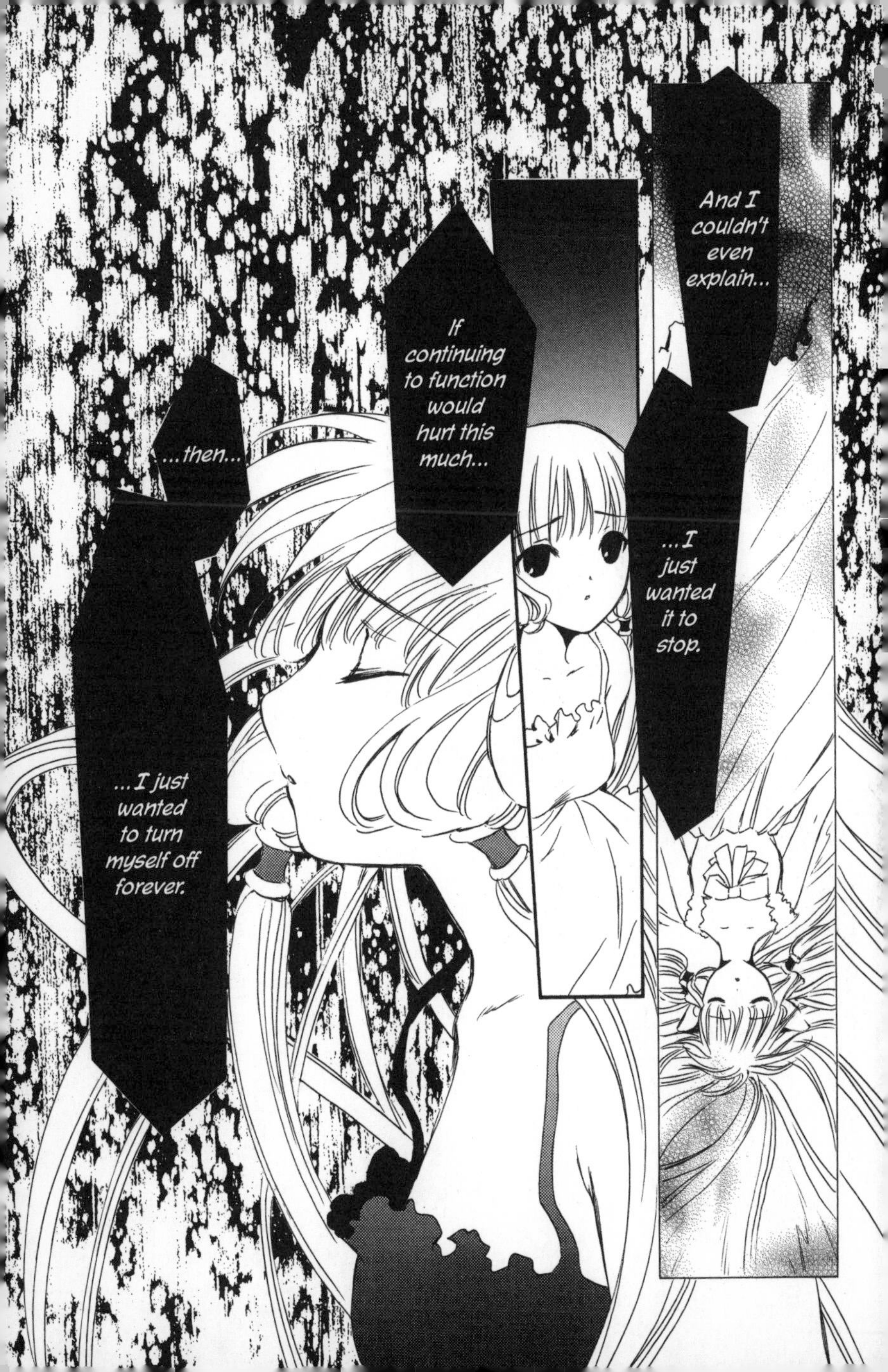
And I couldn't even explain...
...I just wanted it to stop.
If continuing to function would hurt this much...
...then...
...I just wanted to turn myself off forever.

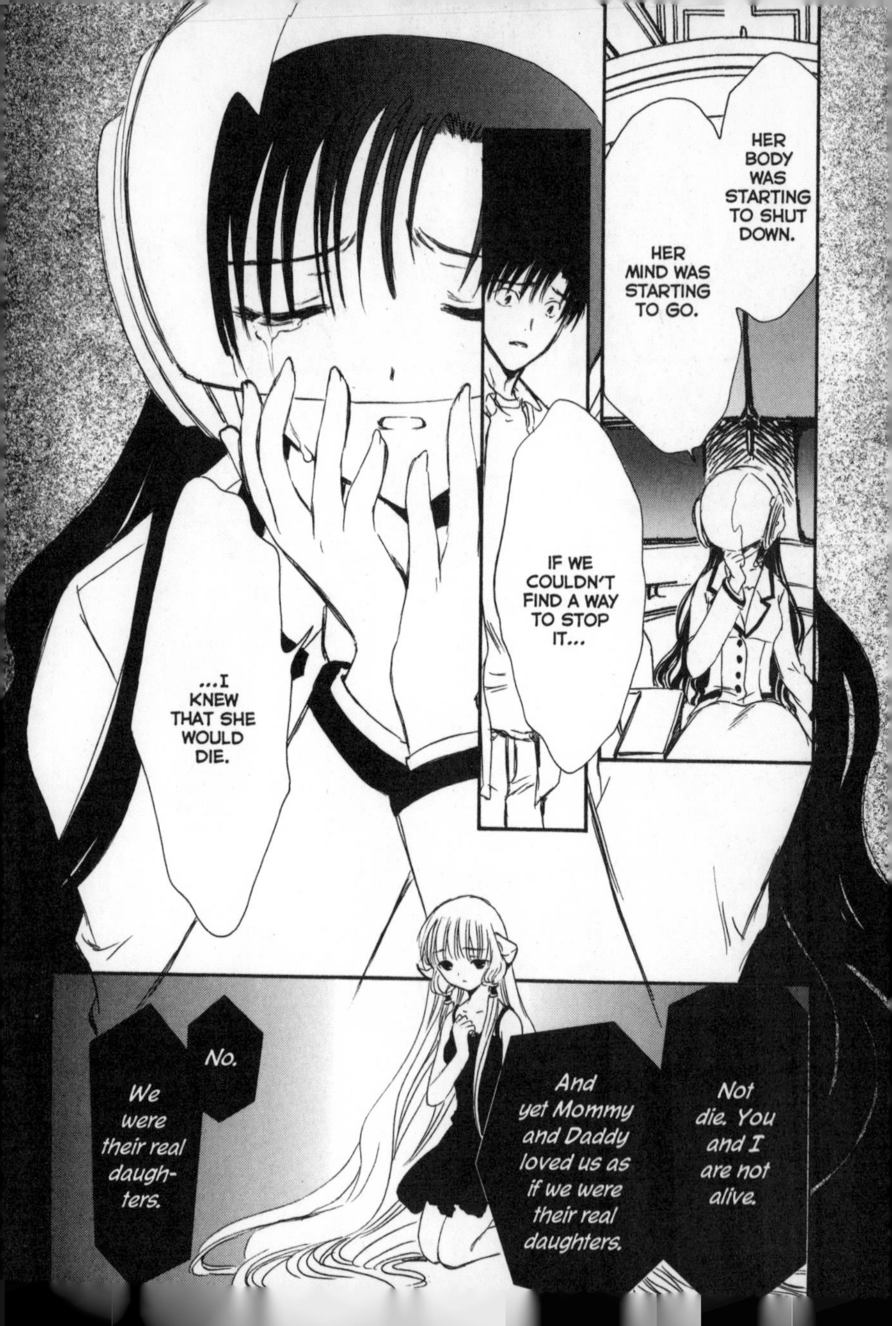
HER BODY WAS STARTING TO SHUT DOWN.
HER MIND WAS STARTING TO GO.
IF WE COULDN'T FIND A WAY TO STOP IT...
...I KNEW THAT SHE WOULD DIE.
Not die. You and I are not alive.
And yet Mommy and Daddy loved us as if we were their real daughters.
No.
We were their real daughters.

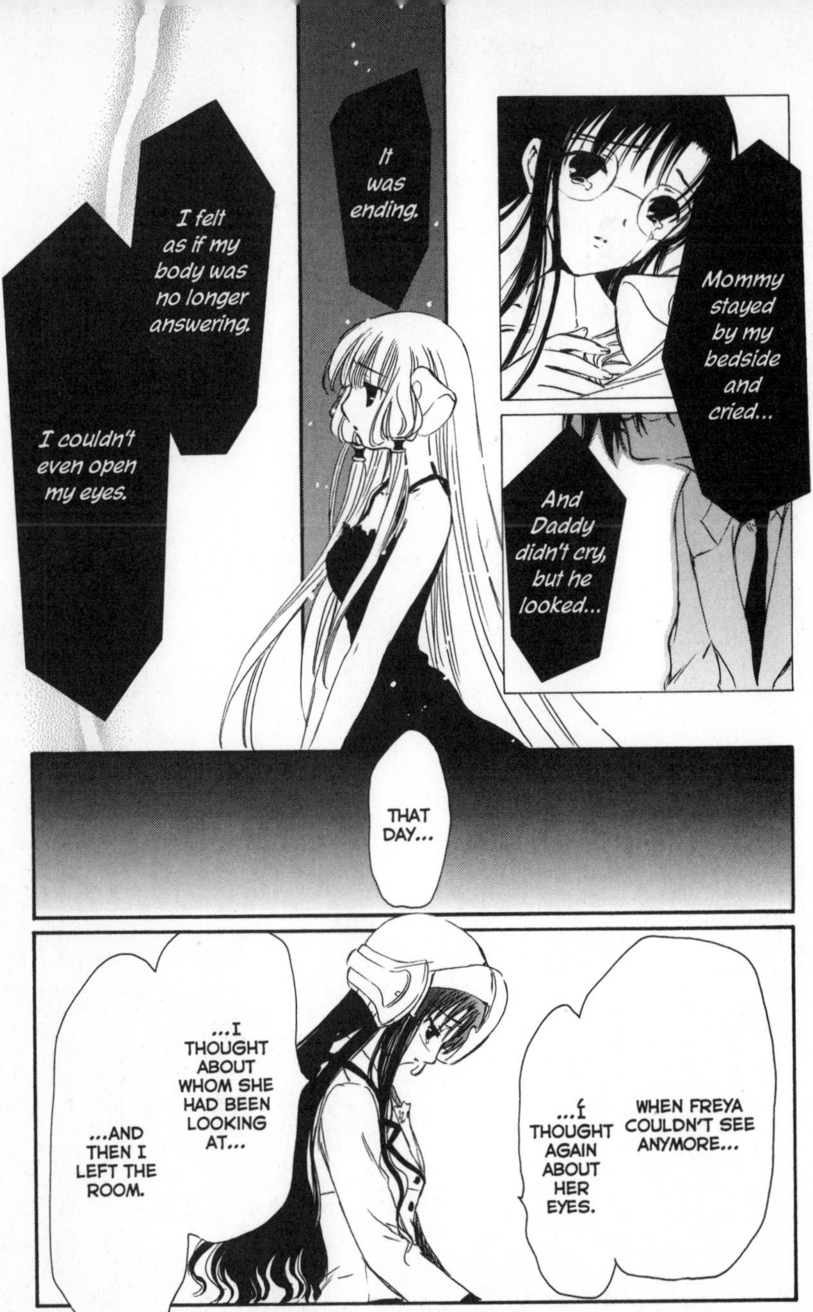

Mommy stayed by my bedside and cried...
And Daddy didn't cry, but he looked...
It was ending.
I felt as if my body was no longer answering.
I couldn't even open my eyes.
THAT DAY...
WHEN FREYA COULDN'T SEE ANYMORE...
...I THOUGHT AGAIN ABOUT HER EYES.
...I THOUGHT ABOUT WHOM SHE HAD BEEN LOOKING AT...
...AND THEN I LEFT THE ROOM.

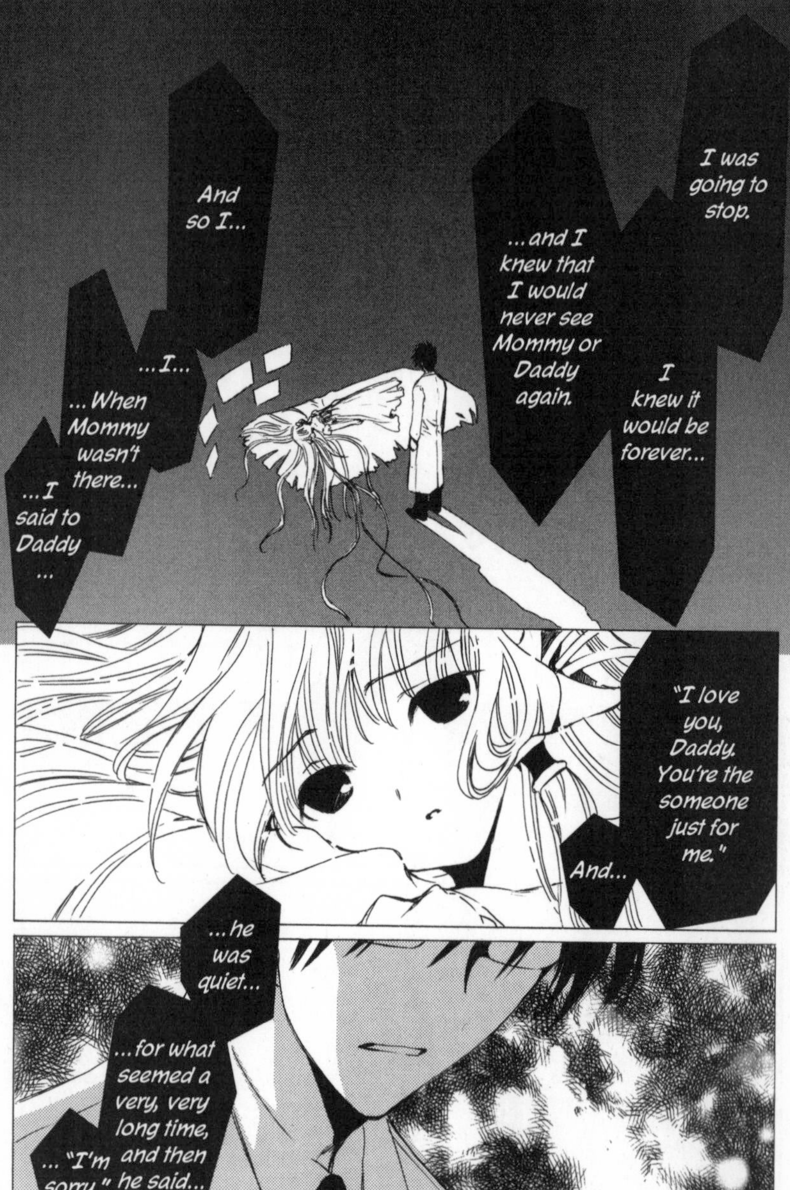
I was going to stop.
...and I knew that I would never see Mommy or Daddy again.
I knew it would be forever...
And so I...
...I...
...When Mommy wasn't there...
...I said to Daddy ...
"I love you, Daddy. You're the someone just for me."
And...
...he was quiet...
...for what seemed a very, very long time, and then he said...
... "I'm sorry."

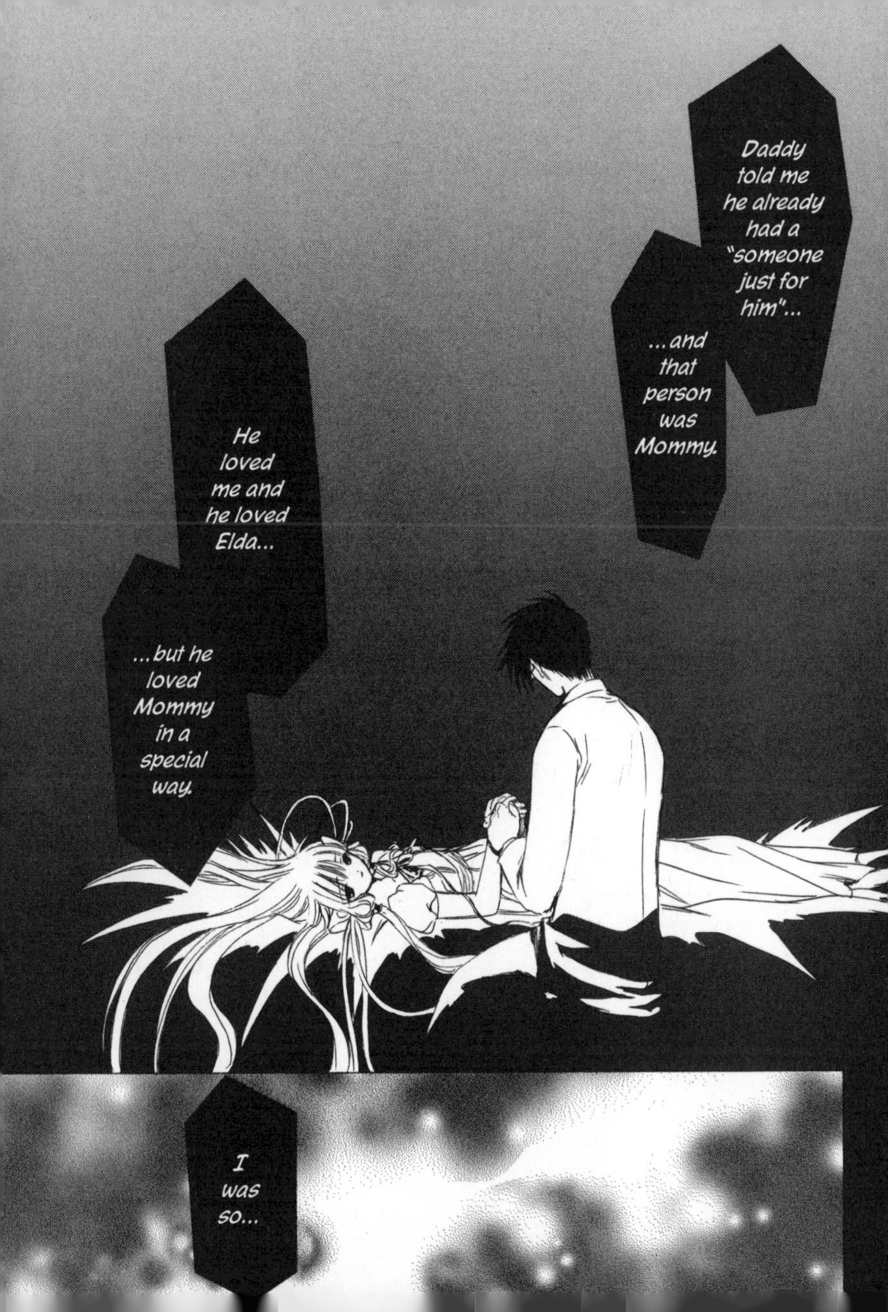

Daddy told me he already had a "someone just for him"...
...and that person was Mommy.
He loved me and he loved Elda...
...but he loved Mommy in a special way.
I was so...

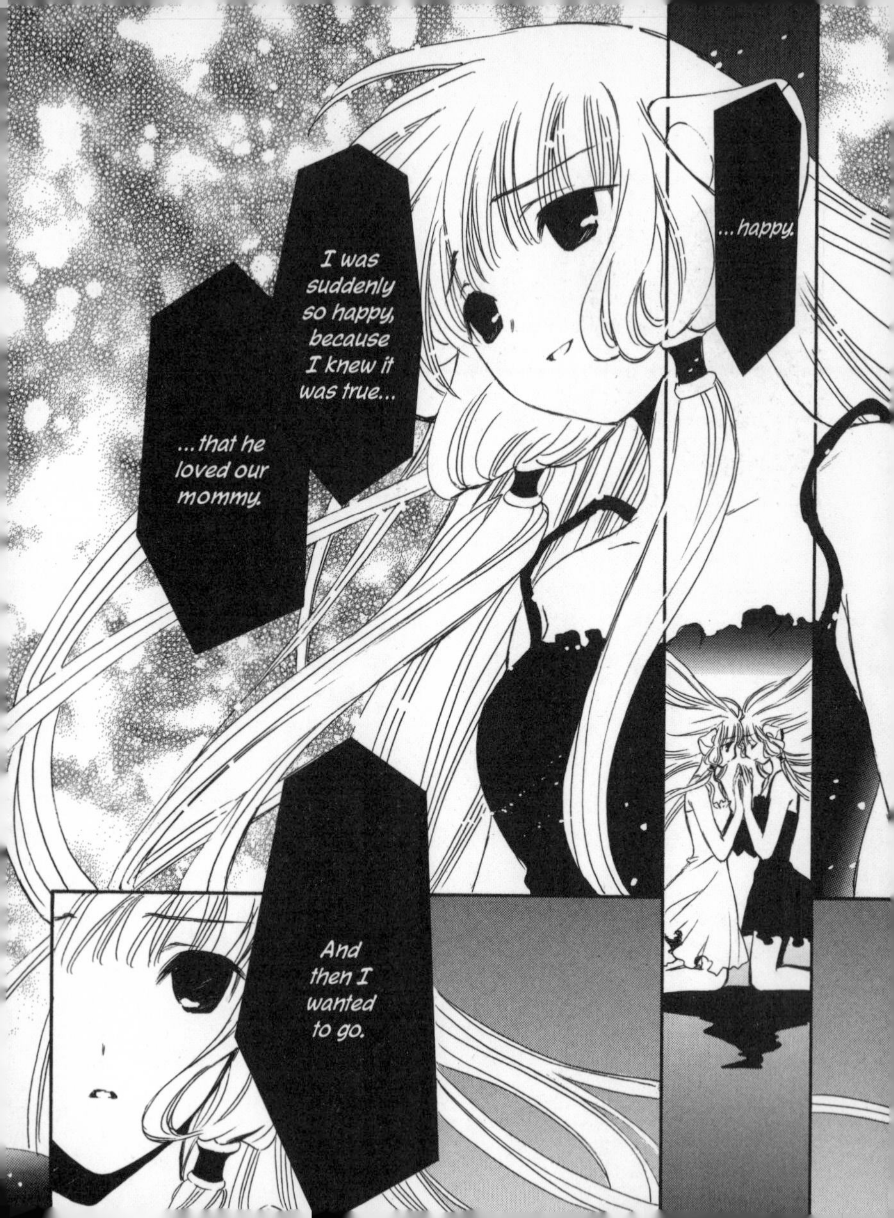
...happy.
I was suddenly so happy, because I knew it was true...
...that he loved our mommy.
And then I wanted to go.

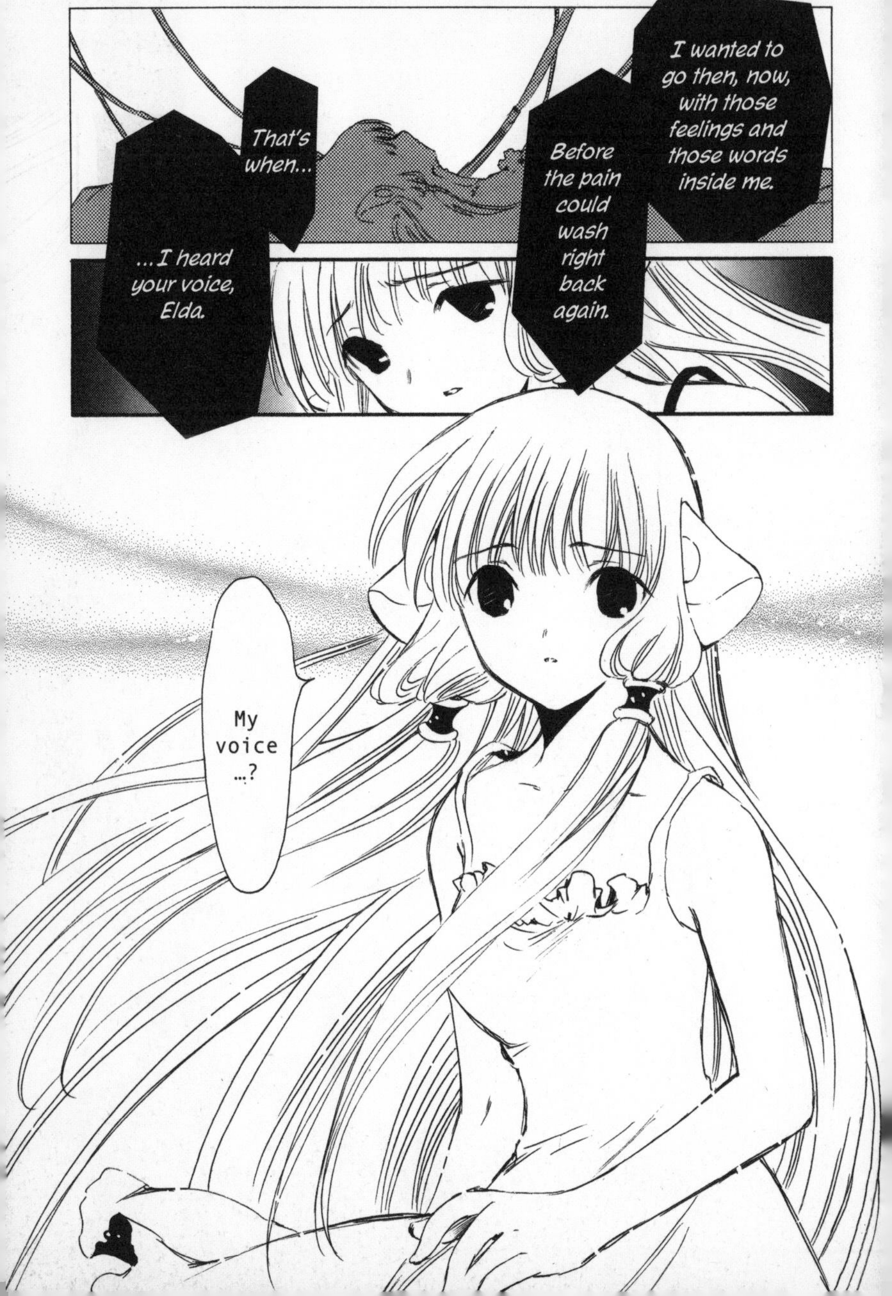
I wanted to go then, now, with those feelings and those words inside me.
Before the pain could wash right back again.
That's when...
...I heard your voice, Elda.
My voice ...?

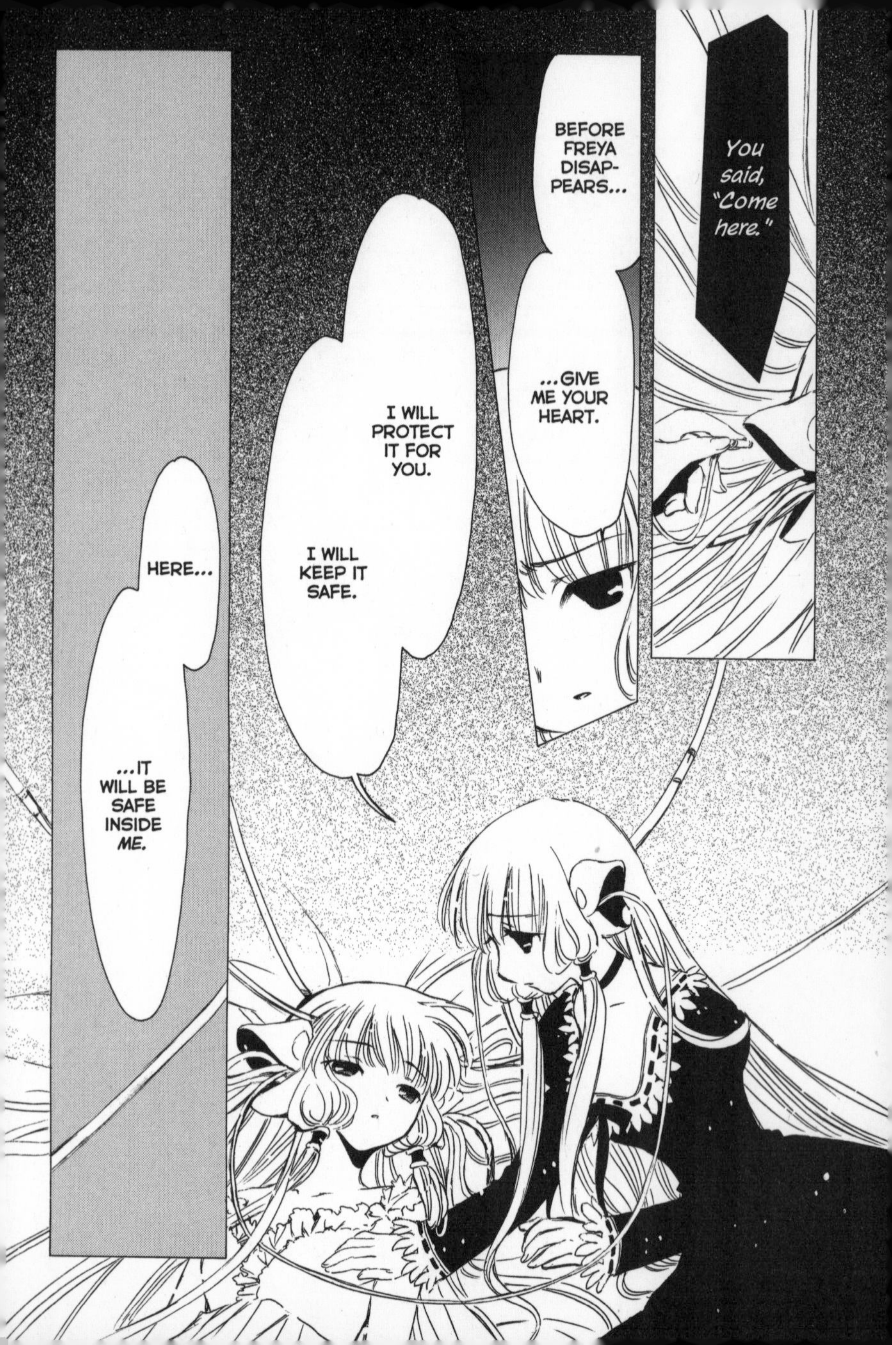
You said, "Come here."
BEFORE FREYA DISAPPEARS...
...GIVE ME YOUR HEART.
I WILL PROTECT IT FOR YOU.
I WILL KEEP IT SAFE.
HERE...
...IT WILL BE SAFE INSIDE ME.

Chobits
ちょびっツ

◀ chapter 80 ▶

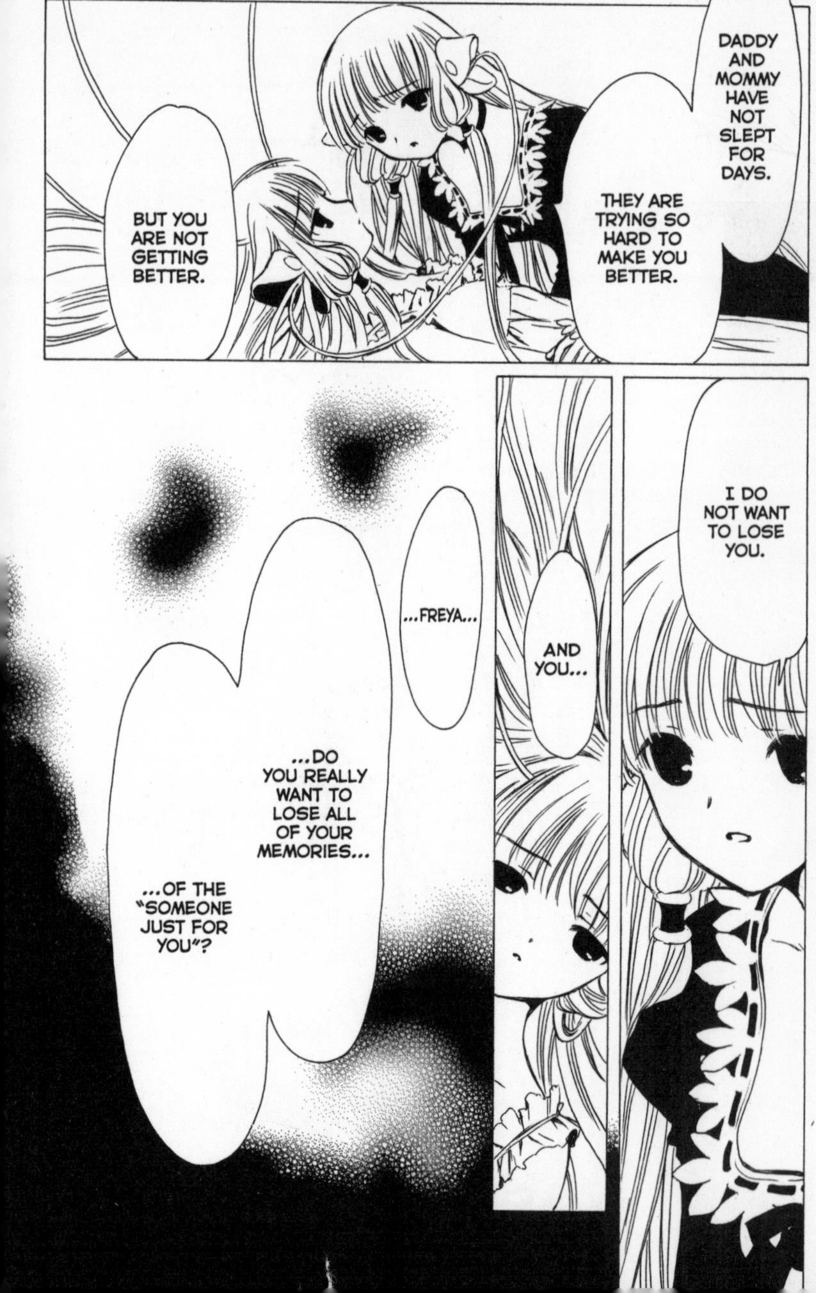
DADDY AND MOMMY HAVE NOT SLEPT FOR DAYS.
THEY ARE TRYING SO HARD TO MAKE YOU BETTER.
BUT YOU ARE NOT GETTING BETTER.
I DO NOT WANT TO LOSE YOU.
AND YOU...
...FREYA...
...DO YOU REALLY WANT TO LOSE ALL OF YOUR MEMORIES...
...OF THE "SOMEONE JUST FOR YOU"?

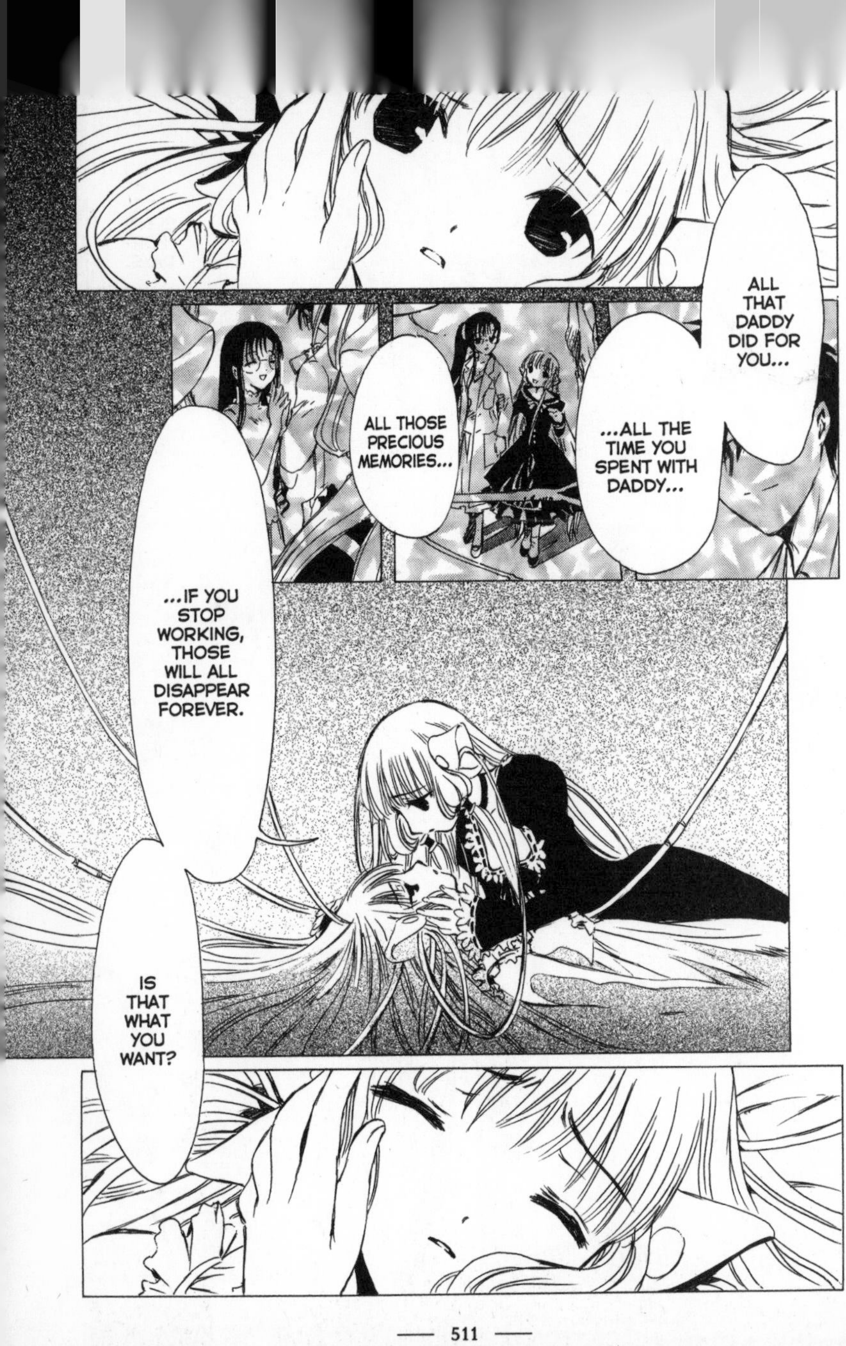
ALL THAT DADDY DID FOR YOU...
...ALL THE TIME YOU SPENT WITH DADDY...
ALL THOSE PRECIOUS MEMORIES...
...IF YOU STOP WORKING, THOSE WILL ALL DISAPPEAR FOREVER.
IS THAT WHAT YOU WANT?

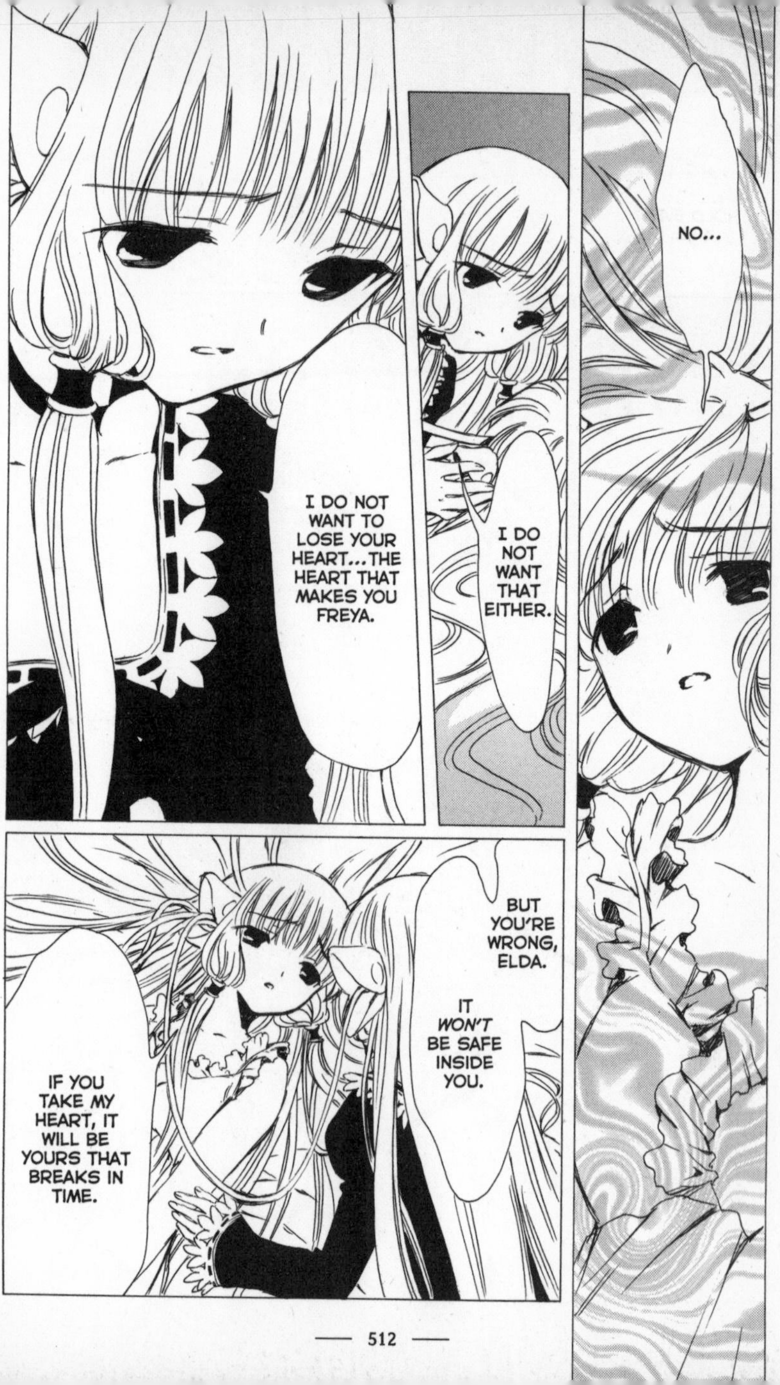
NO...
I DO NOT WANT THAT EITHER.
I DO NOT WANT TO LOSE YOUR HEART...THE HEART THAT MAKES YOU FREYA.
BUT YOU'RE WRONG, ELDA.
IT *WON'T* BE SAFE INSIDE YOU.
IF YOU TAKE MY HEART, IT WILL BE YOURS THAT BREAKS IN TIME.

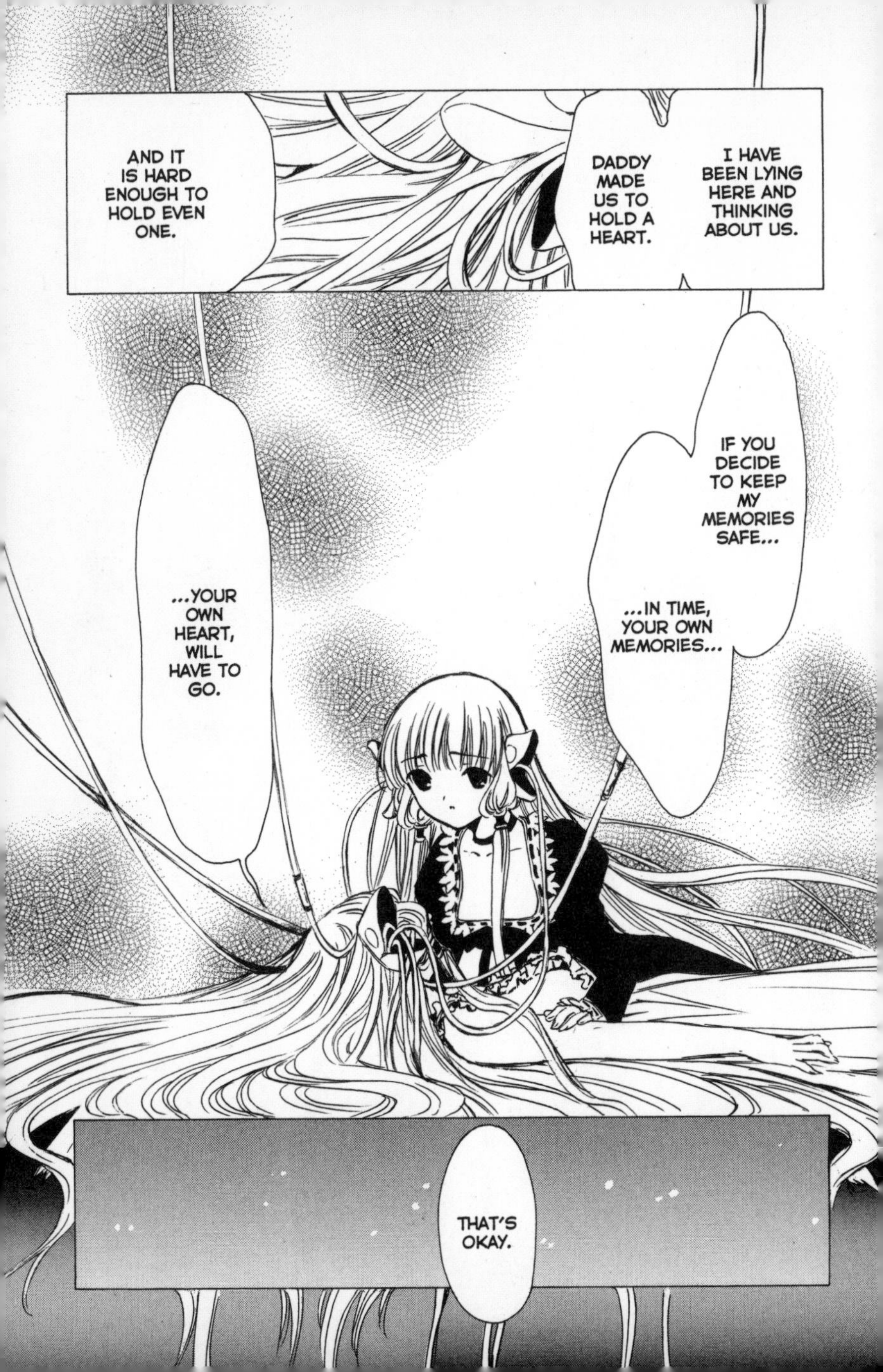
I HAVE BEEN LYING HERE AND THINKING ABOUT US.
DADDY MADE US TO HOLD A HEART.
AND IT IS HARD ENOUGH TO HOLD EVEN ONE.
IF YOU DECIDE TO KEEP MY MEMORIES SAFE...
...IN TIME, YOUR OWN MEMORIES...
...YOUR OWN HEART, WILL HAVE TO GO.
THAT'S OKAY.

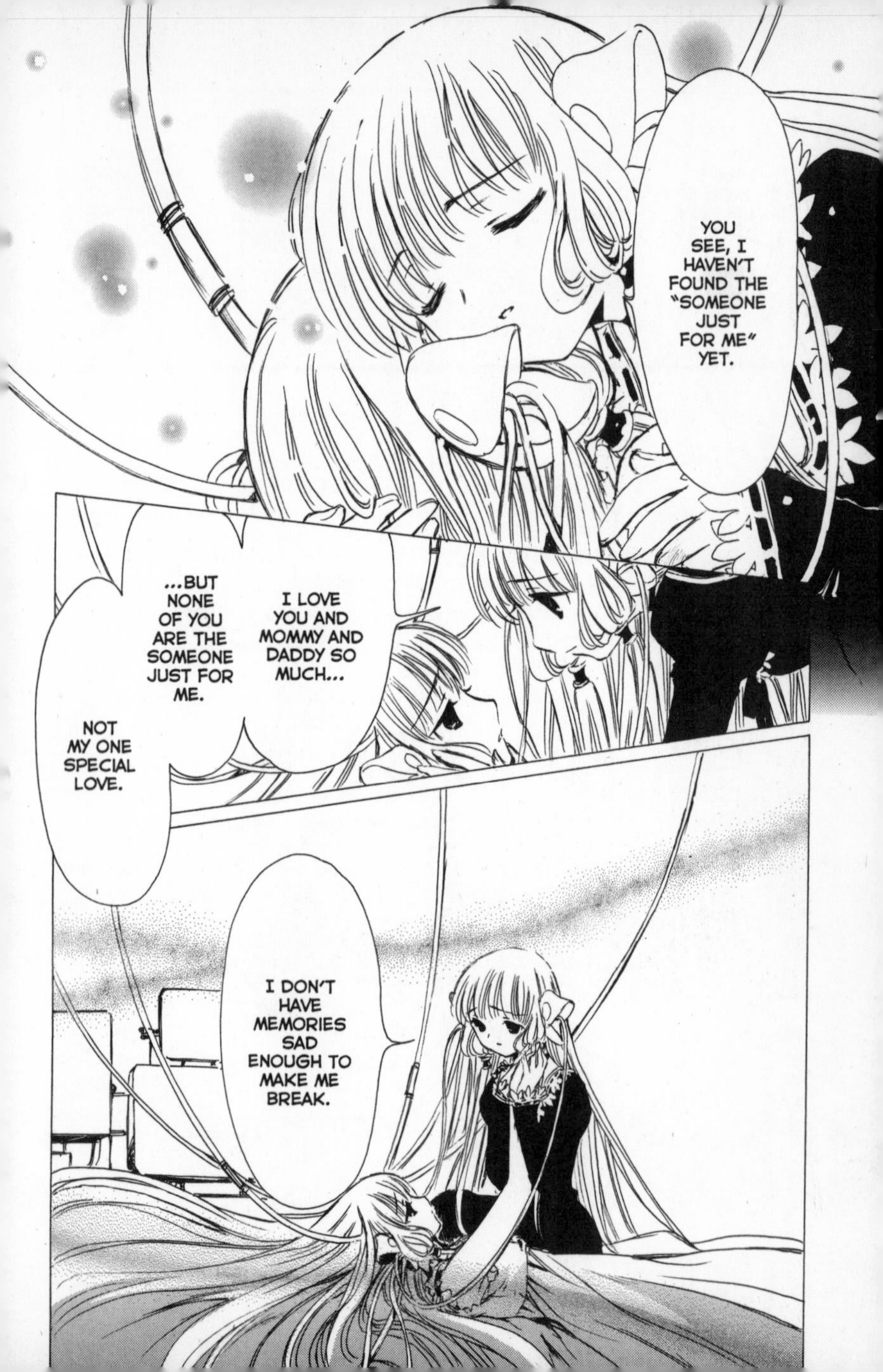
YOU SEE, I HAVEN'T FOUND THE "SOMEONE JUST FOR ME" YET.
I LOVE YOU AND MOMMY AND DADDY SO MUCH...
...BUT NONE OF YOU ARE THE SOMEONE JUST FOR ME.
NOT MY ONE SPECIAL LOVE.
I DON'T HAVE MEMORIES SAD ENOUGH TO MAKE ME BREAK.

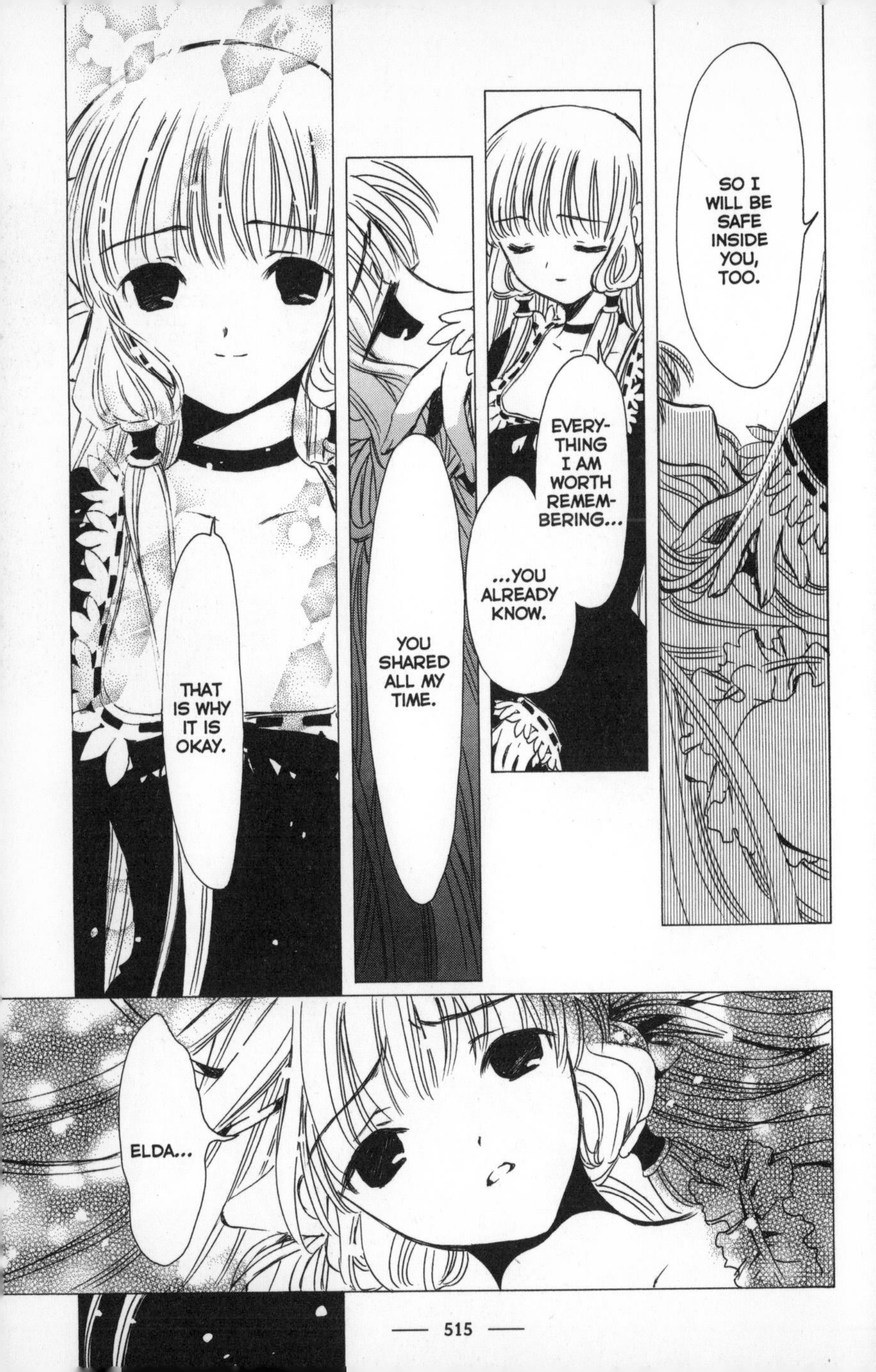
SO I WILL BE SAFE INSIDE YOU, TOO.
EVERY-THING I AM WORTH REMEMB-ERING...
...YOU ALREADY KNOW.
YOU SHARED ALL MY TIME.
THAT IS WHY IT IS OKAY.
ELDA...

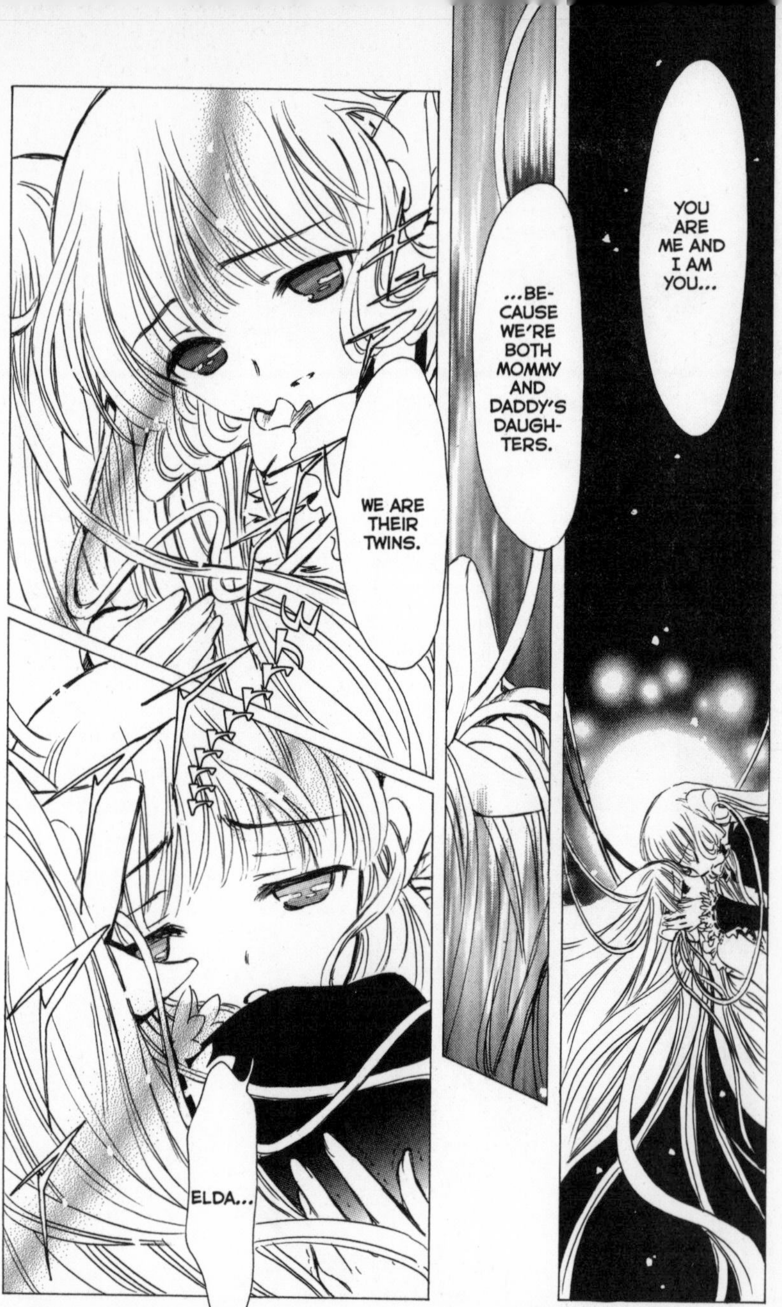
YOU ARE ME AND I AM YOU...
...BE-CAUSE WE'RE BOTH MOMMY AND DADDY'S DAUGH-TERS.
WE ARE THEIR TWINS.
ELDA...

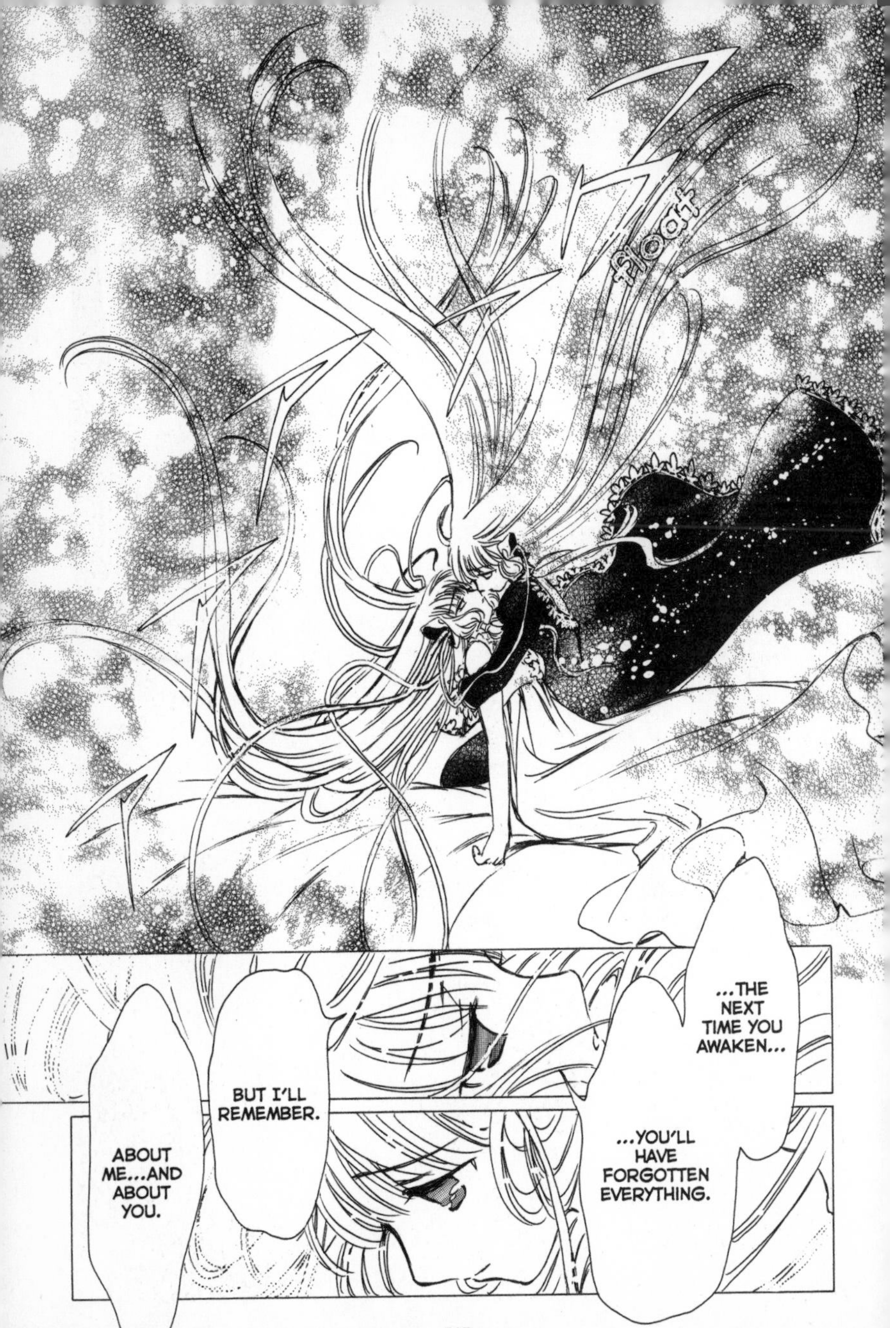
float
...THE NEXT TIME YOU AWAKEN...
...YOU'LL HAVE FORGOTTEN EVERYTHING.
BUT I'LL REMEMBER.
ABOUT ME...AND ABOUT YOU.

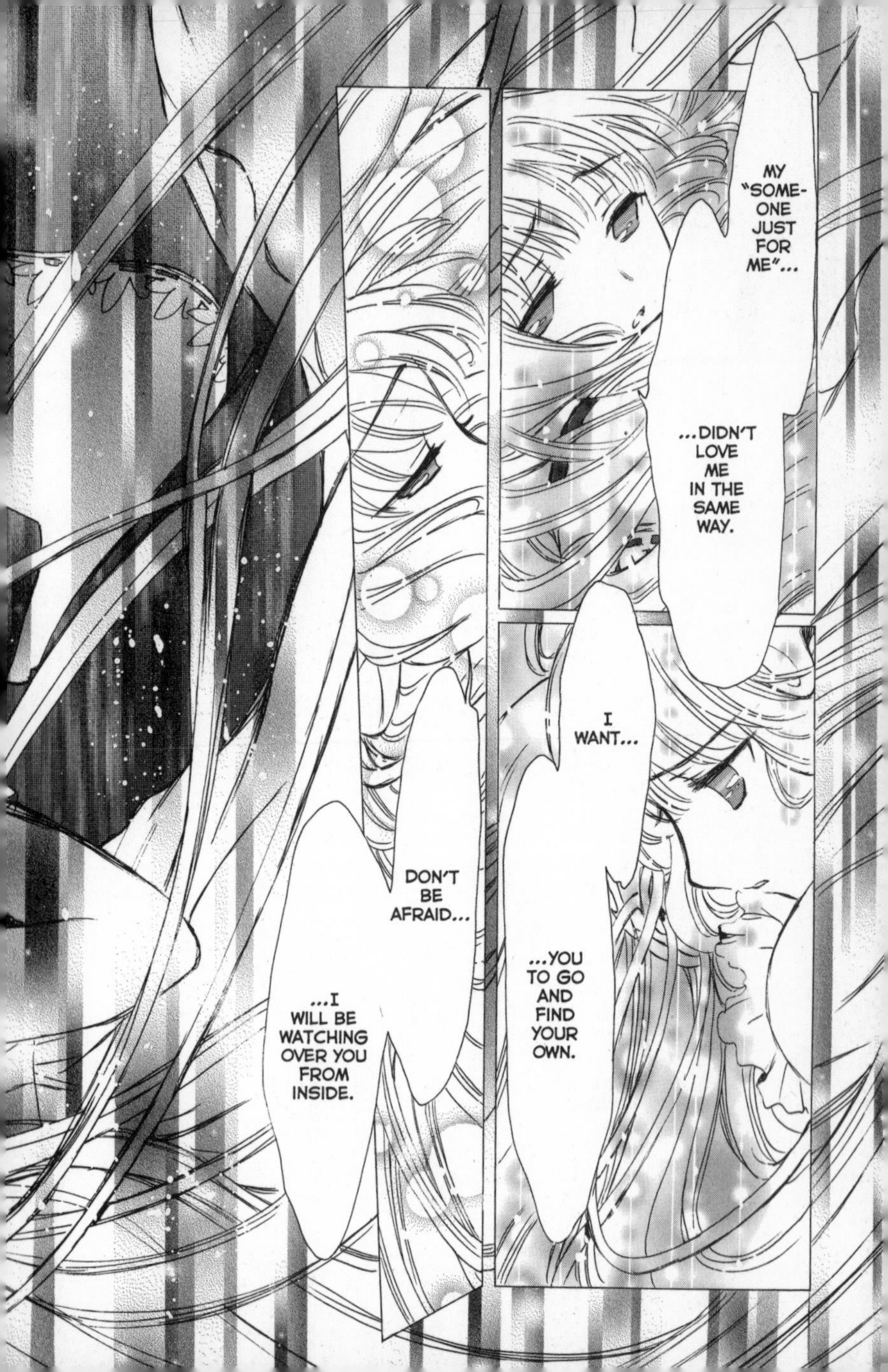
MY "SOME-ONE JUST FOR ME"...
...DIDN'T LOVE ME IN THE SAME WAY.
I WANT...
...YOU TO GO AND FIND YOUR OWN.
DON'T BE AFRAID...
...I WILL BE WATCHING OVER YOU FROM INSIDE.

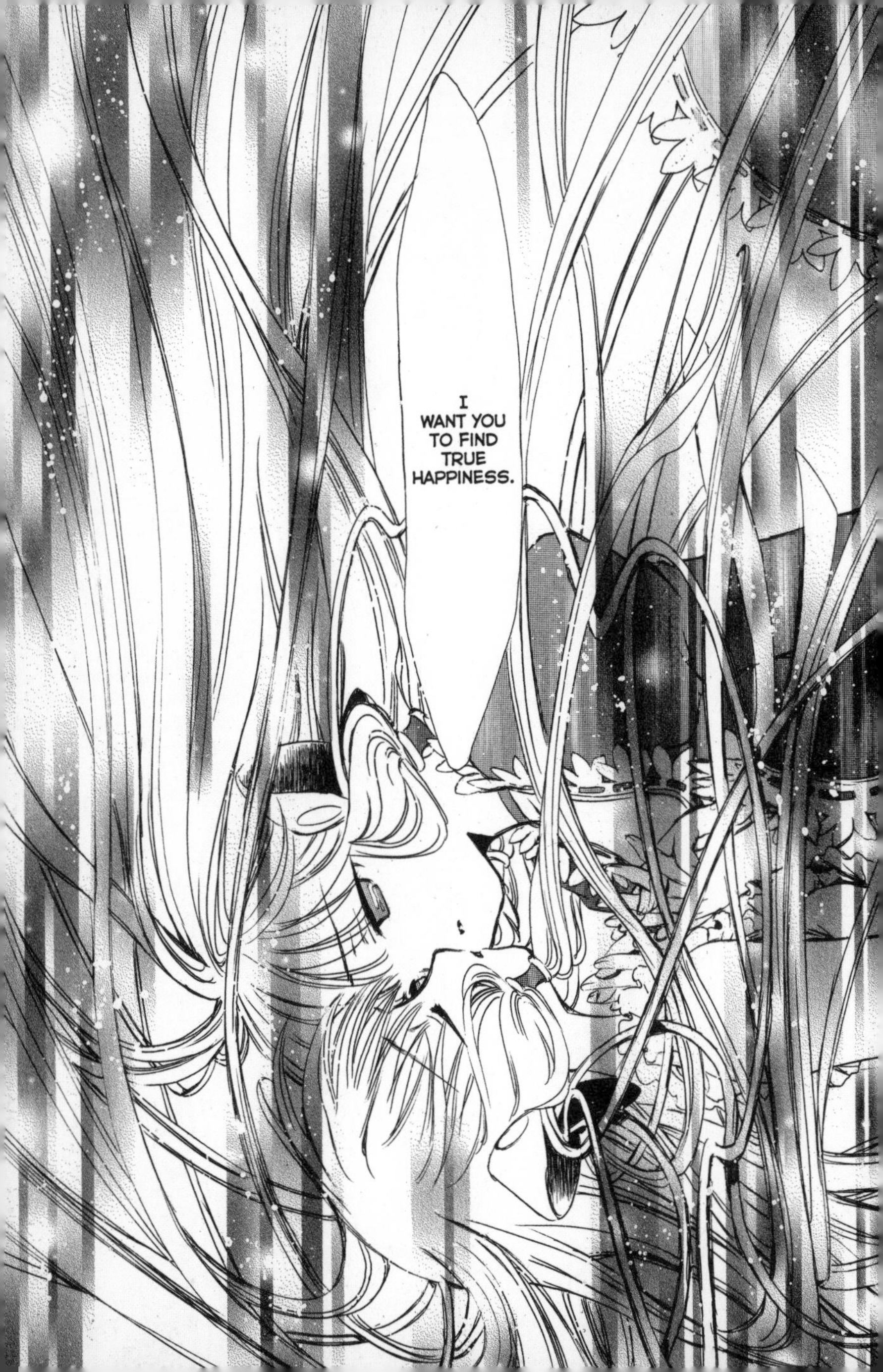
I WANT YOU TO FIND TRUE HAPPINESS.

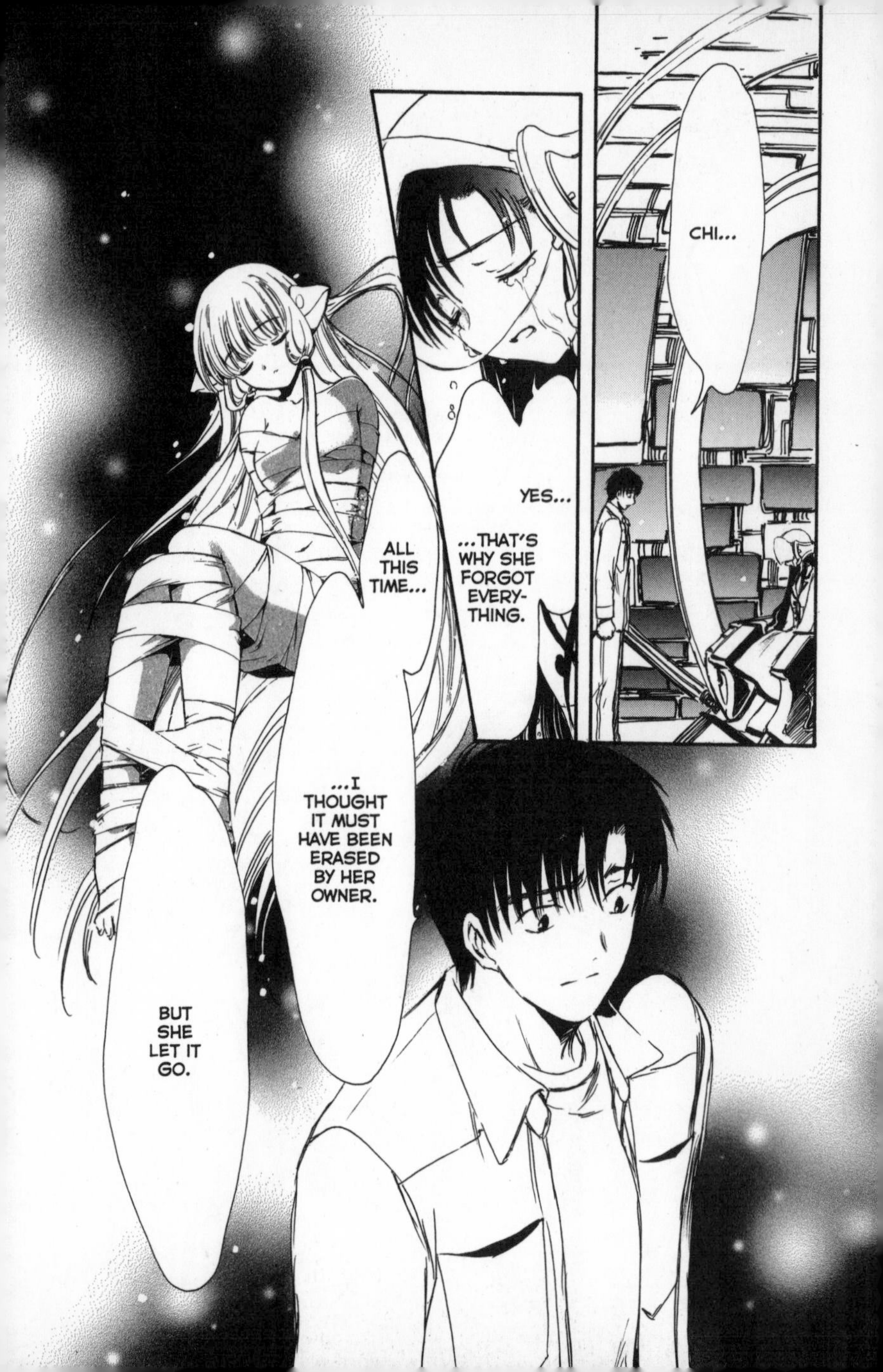
CHI...
YES...
...THAT'S WHY SHE FORGOT EVERYTHING.
ALL THIS TIME...
...I THOUGHT IT MUST HAVE BEEN ERASED BY HER OWNER.
BUT SHE LET IT GO.

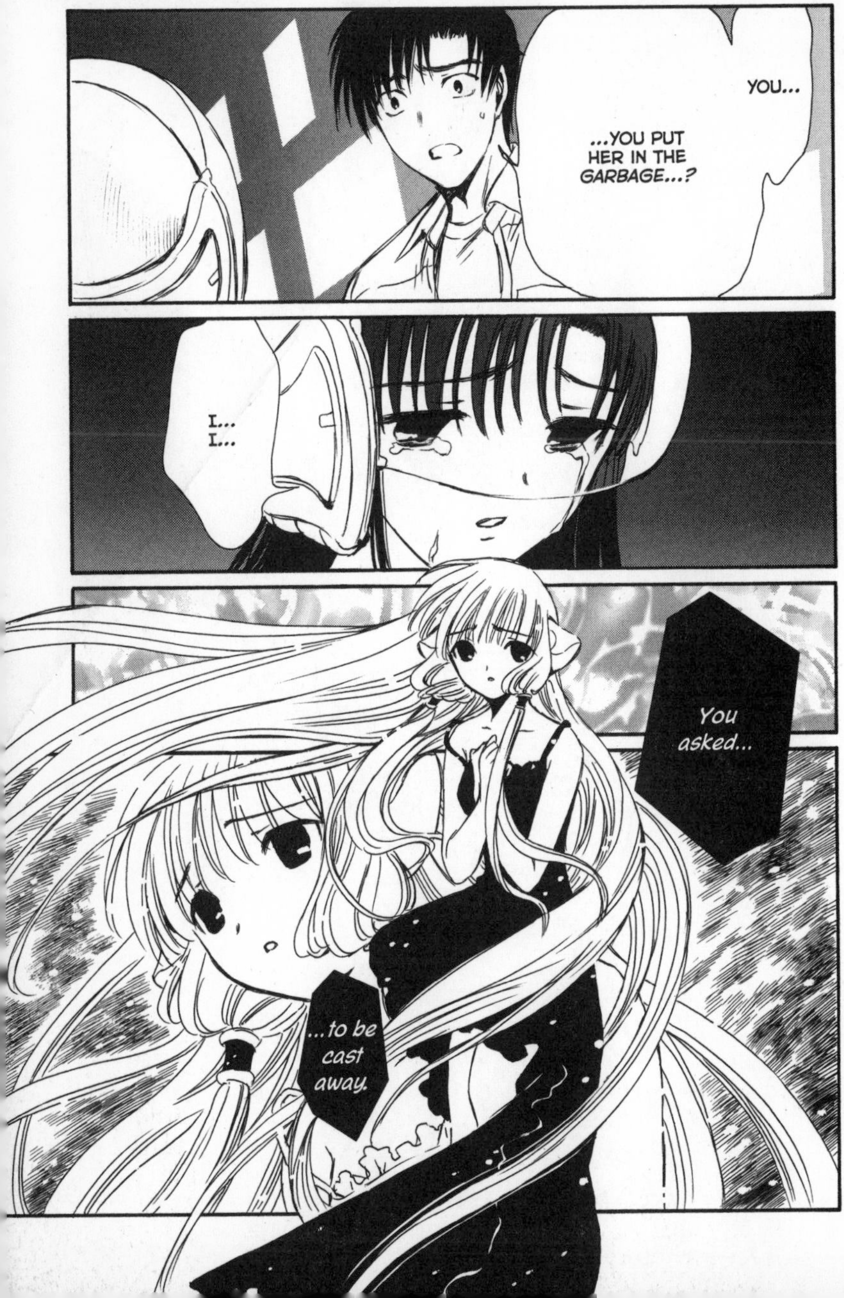
YOU...
...YOU PUT HER IN THE GARBAGE...?
I... I...
You asked...
...to be cast away.

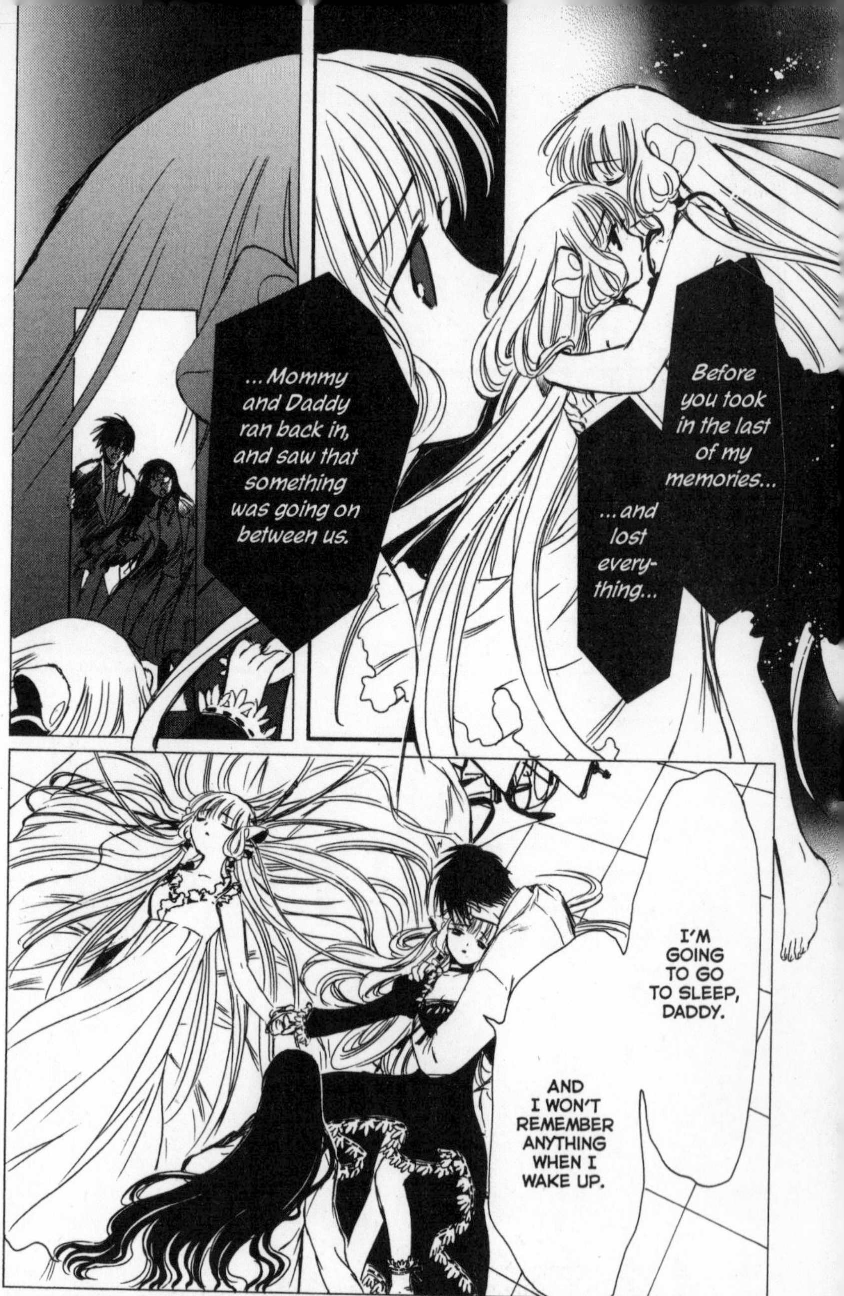

Before you took in the last of my memories...
...and lost every-thing...
...Mommy and Daddy ran back in, and saw that something was going on between us.
I'M GOING TO GO TO SLEEP, DADDY.
AND I WON'T REMEMBER ANYTHING WHEN I WAKE UP.

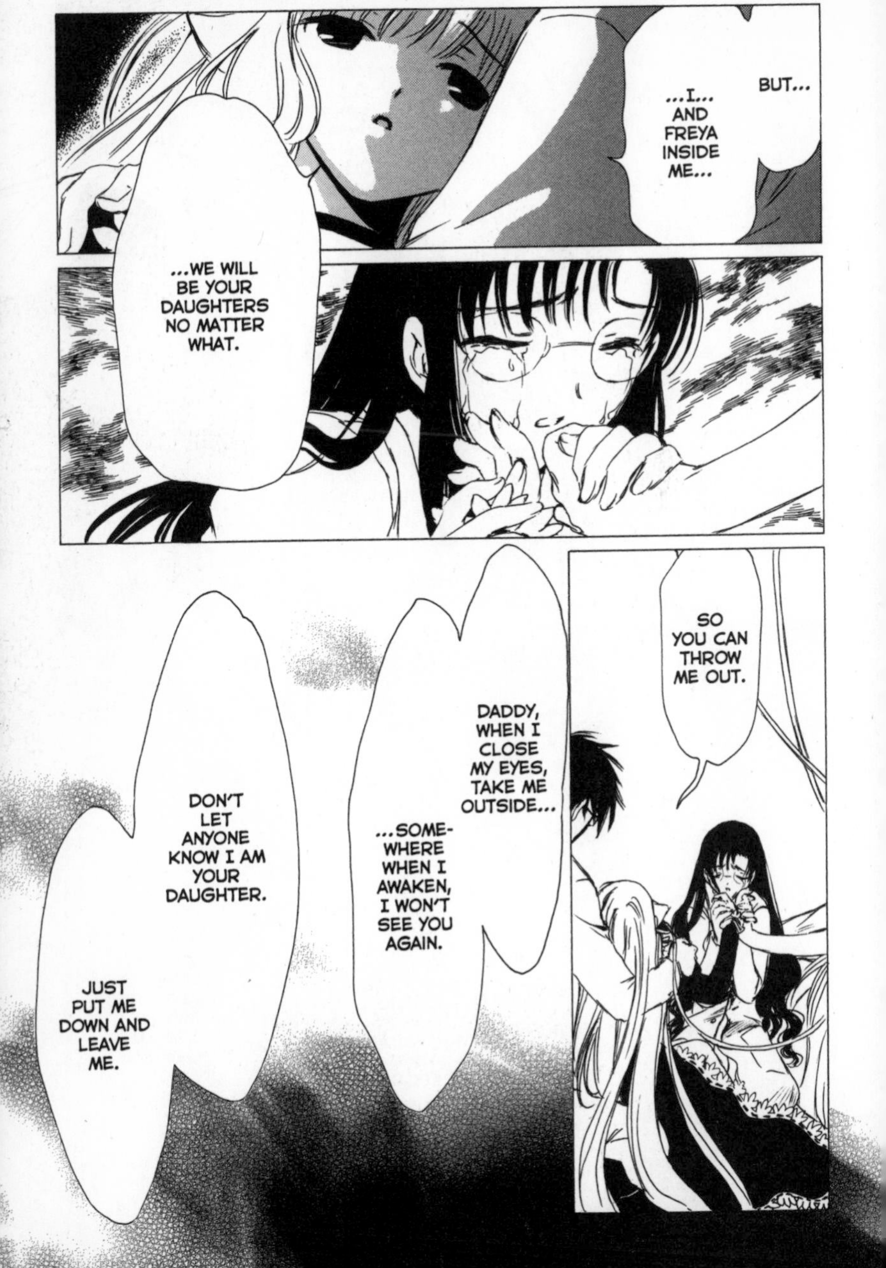
BUT...
...I... AND FREYA INSIDE ME...
...WE WILL BE YOUR DAUGHTERS NO MATTER WHAT.
SO YOU CAN THROW ME OUT.
DADDY, WHEN I CLOSE MY EYES, TAKE ME OUTSIDE...
...SOME-WHERE WHEN I AWAKEN, I WON'T SEE YOU AGAIN.
DON'T LET ANYONE KNOW I AM YOUR DAUGHTER.
JUST PUT ME DOWN AND LEAVE ME.

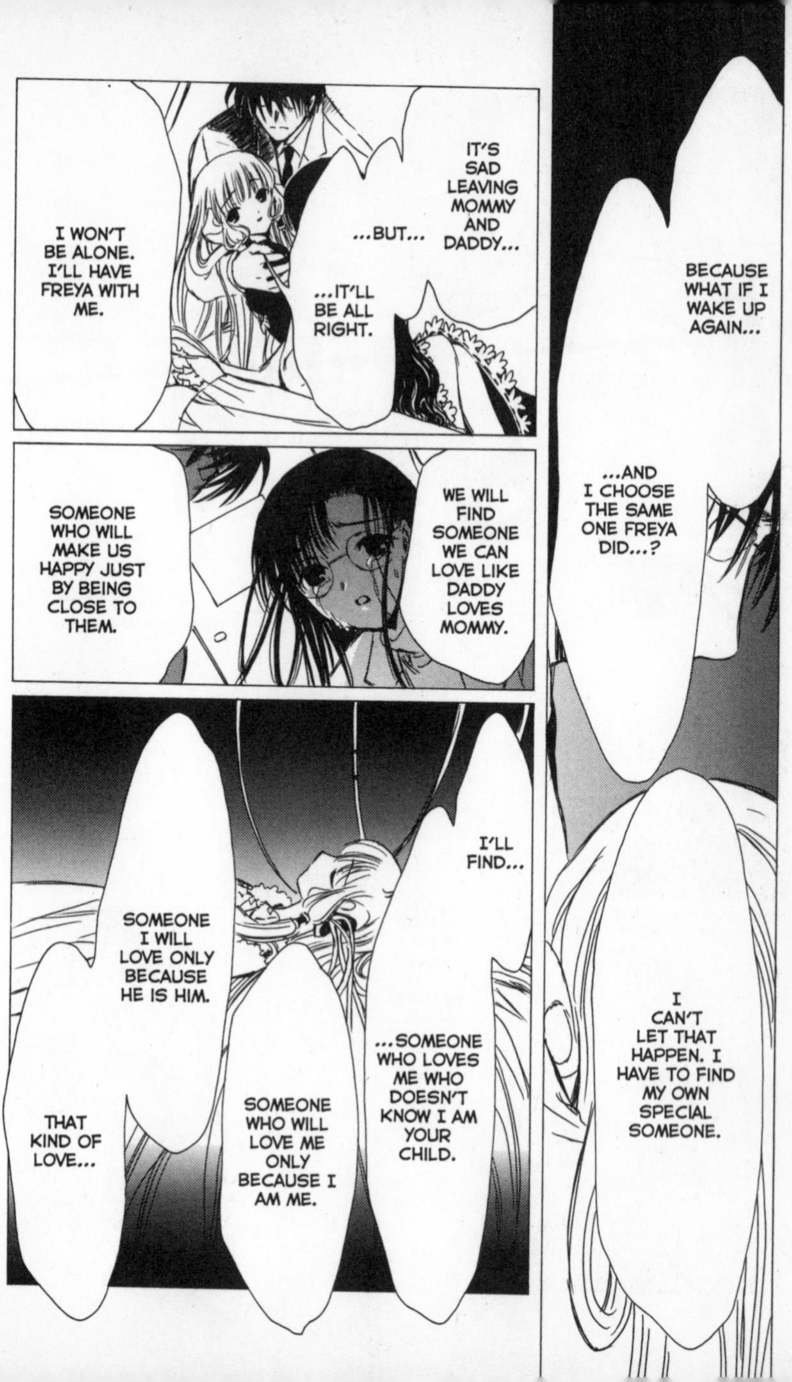
BECAUSE WHAT IF I WAKE UP AGAIN...
...AND I CHOOSE THE SAME ONE FREYA DID...?
I CAN'T LET THAT HAPPEN. I HAVE TO FIND MY OWN SPECIAL SOMEONE.
IT'S SAD LEAVING MOMMY AND DADDY...
...BUT...
...IT'LL BE ALL RIGHT.
I WON'T BE ALONE. I'LL HAVE FREYA WITH ME.
WE WILL FIND SOMEONE WE CAN LOVE LIKE DADDY LOVES MOMMY.
SOMEONE WHO WILL MAKE US HAPPY JUST BY BEING CLOSE TO THEM.
I'LL FIND...
...SOMEONE WHO LOVES ME WHO DOESN'T KNOW I AM YOUR CHILD.
SOMEONE WHO WILL LOVE ME ONLY BECAUSE I AM ME.
SOMEONE I WILL LOVE ONLY BECAUSE HE IS HIM.
THAT KIND OF LOVE...

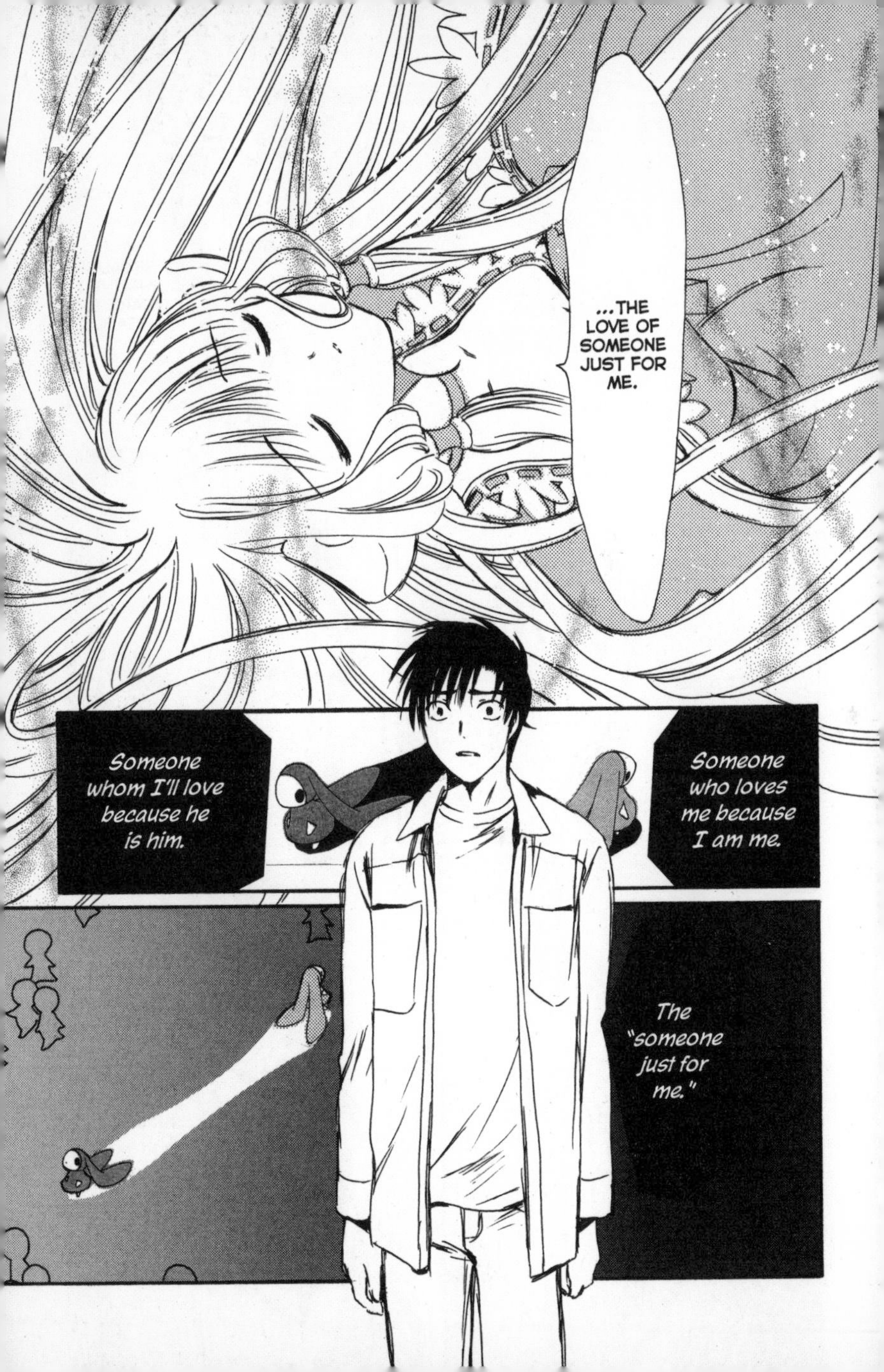
...THE LOVE OF SOMEONE JUST FOR ME.
Someone who loves me because I am me.
Someone whom I'll love because he is him.
The "someone just for me."

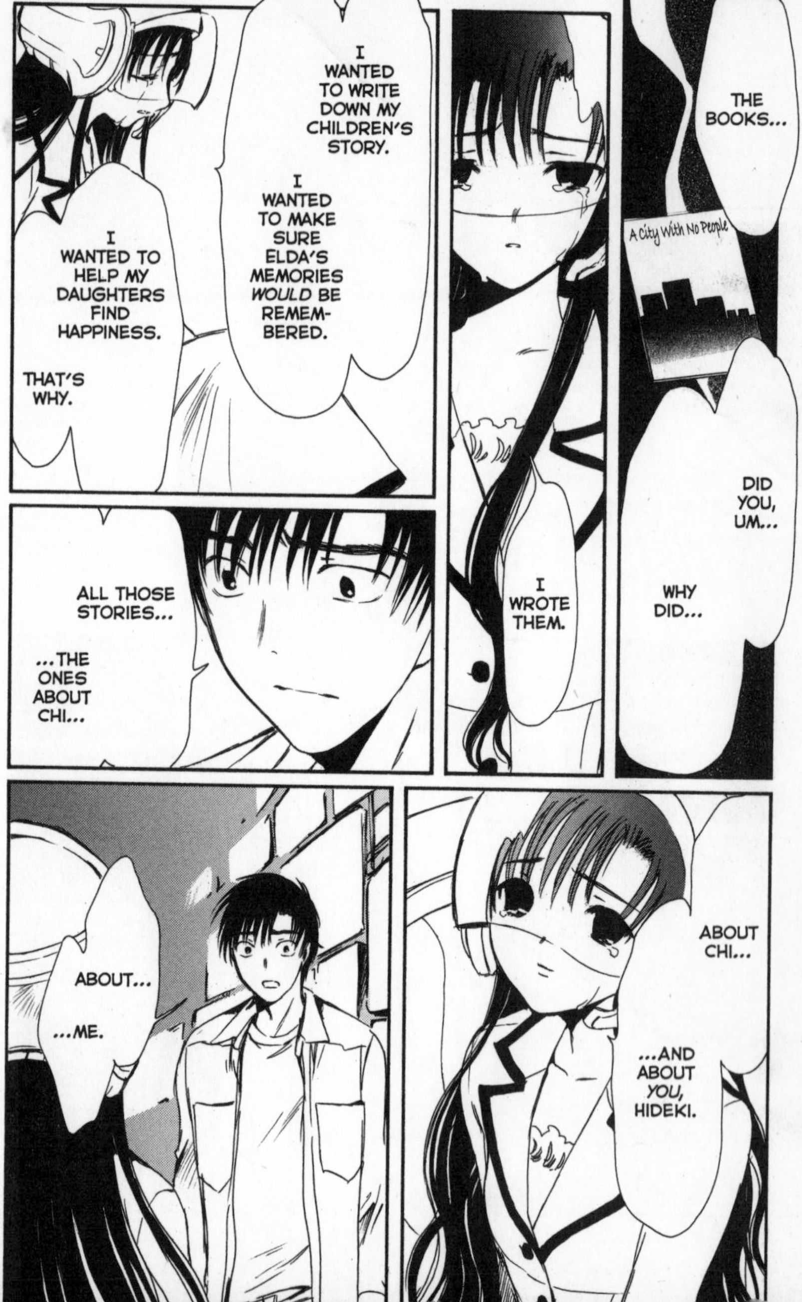
THE BOOKS...
A City With No People
DID YOU, UM...
WHY DID...
I WROTE THEM.
I WANTED TO WRITE DOWN MY CHILDREN'S STORY.
I WANTED TO MAKE SURE ELDA'S MEMORIES *WOULD* BE REMEMBERED.
I WANTED TO HELP MY DAUGHTERS FIND HAPPINESS.
THAT'S WHY.
ALL THOSE STORIES...
...THE ONES ABOUT CHI...
ABOUT CHI...
...AND ABOUT *YOU,* HIDEKI.
ABOUT...
...ME.

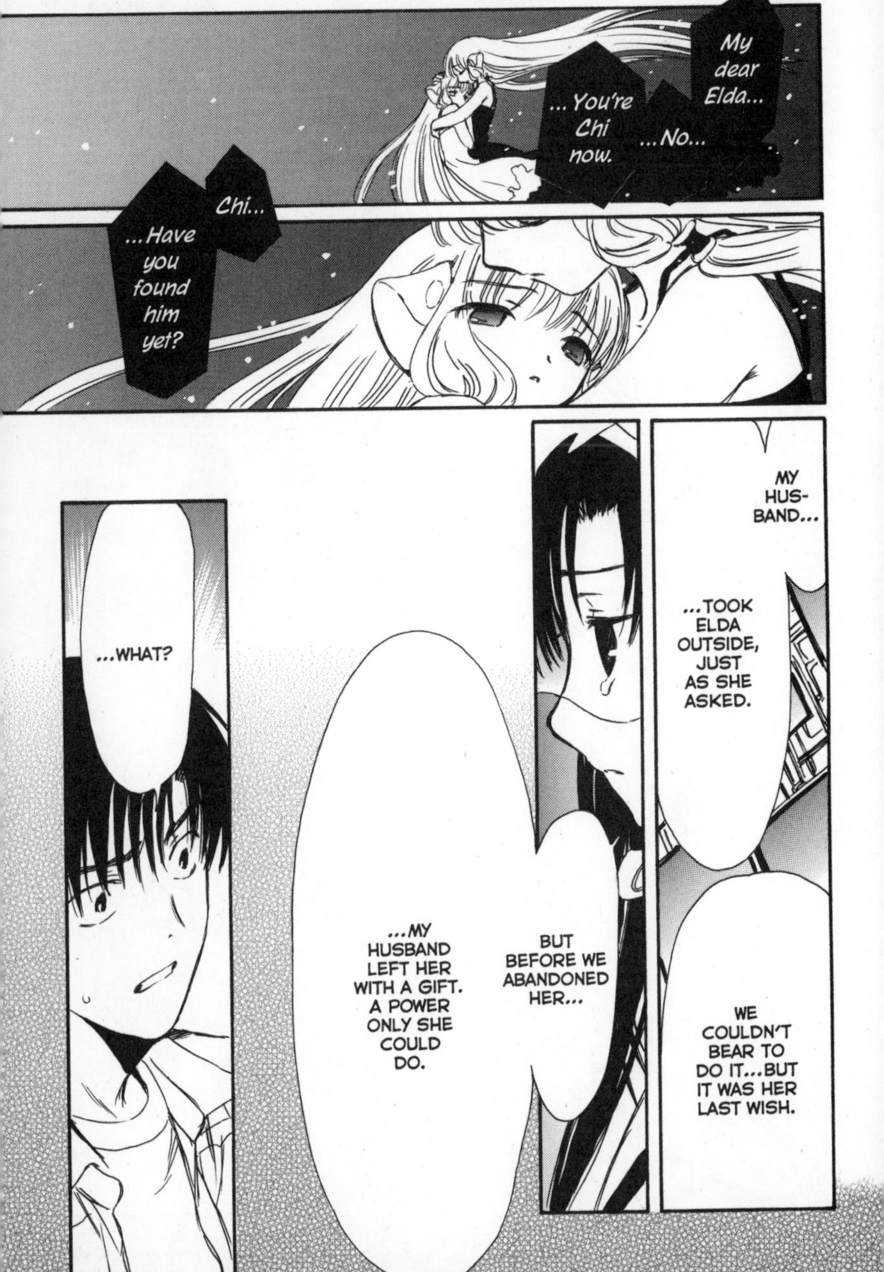
My dear Elda...
...No...
...You're Chi now.
Chi...
...Have you found him yet?
MY HUSBAND...
...TOOK ELDA OUTSIDE, JUST AS SHE ASKED.
WE COULDN'T BEAR TO DO IT...BUT IT WAS HER LAST WISH.
BUT BEFORE WE ABANDONED HER...
...MY HUSBAND LEFT HER WITH A GIFT. A POWER ONLY SHE COULD DO.
...WHAT?

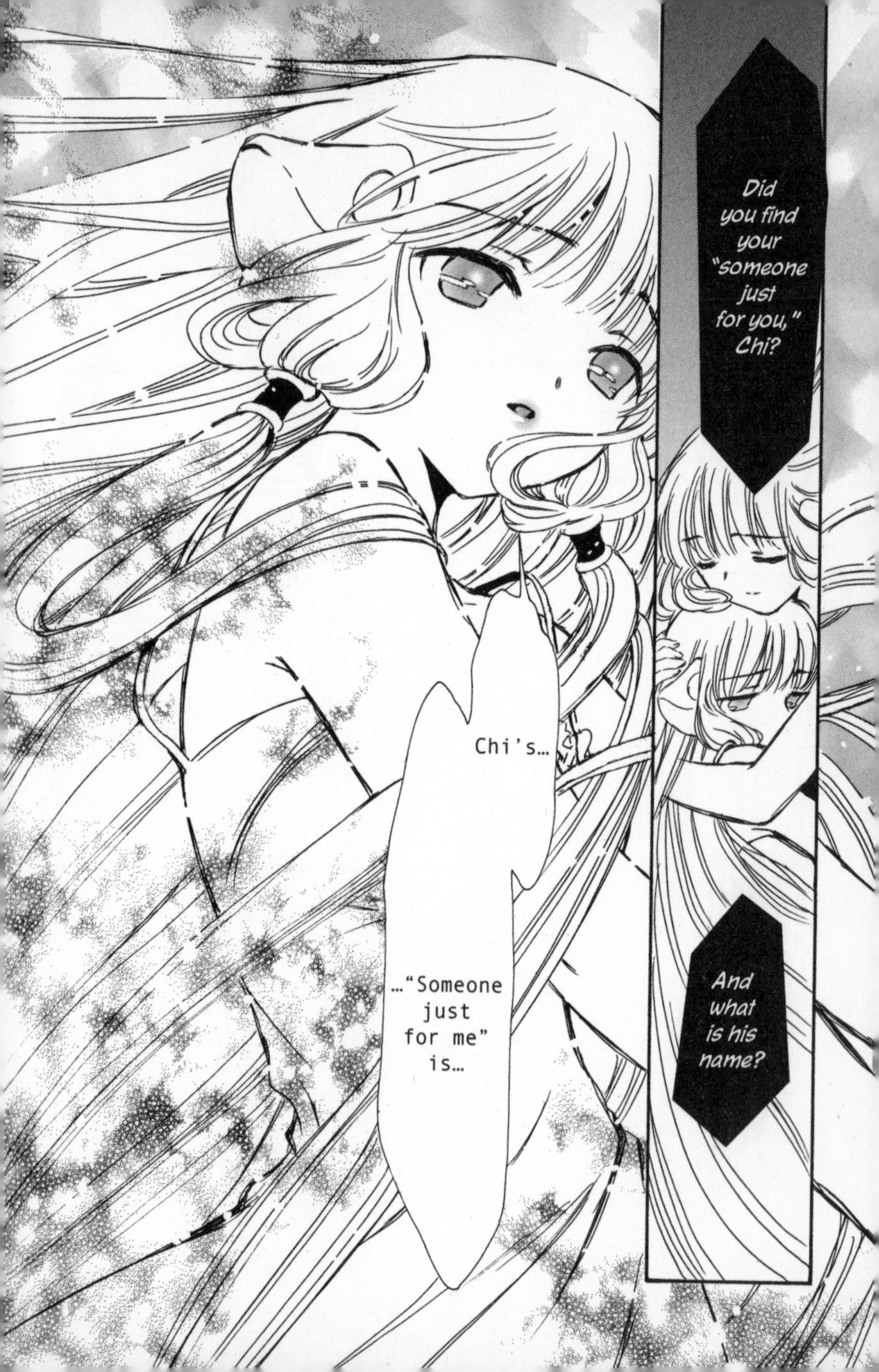
Did you find your "someone just for you," Chi?
And what is his name?
Chi's…
…"Someone just for me" is…

Chobits

ちょびっツ

◀ chapter 81 ▶

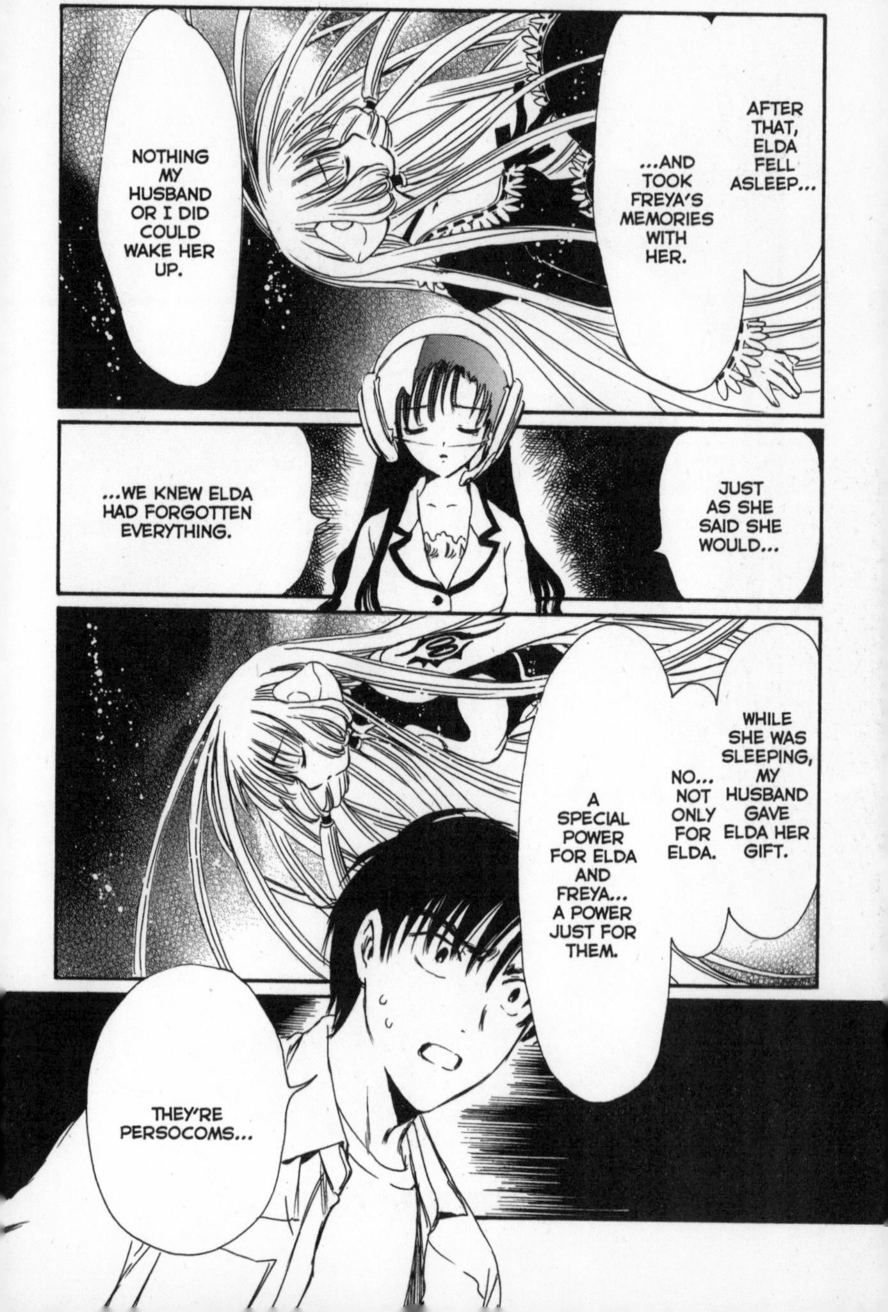
AFTER THAT, ELDA FELL ASLEEP...
...AND TOOK FREYA'S MEMORIES WITH HER.
NOTHING MY HUSBAND OR I DID COULD WAKE HER UP.
JUST AS SHE SAID SHE WOULD...
...WE KNEW ELDA HAD FORGOTTEN EVERYTHING.
WHILE SHE WAS SLEEPING, MY HUSBAND GAVE ELDA HER GIFT.
NO... NOT ONLY FOR ELDA.
A SPECIAL POWER FOR ELDA AND FREYA... A POWER JUST FOR THEM.
THEY'RE PERSOCOMS...

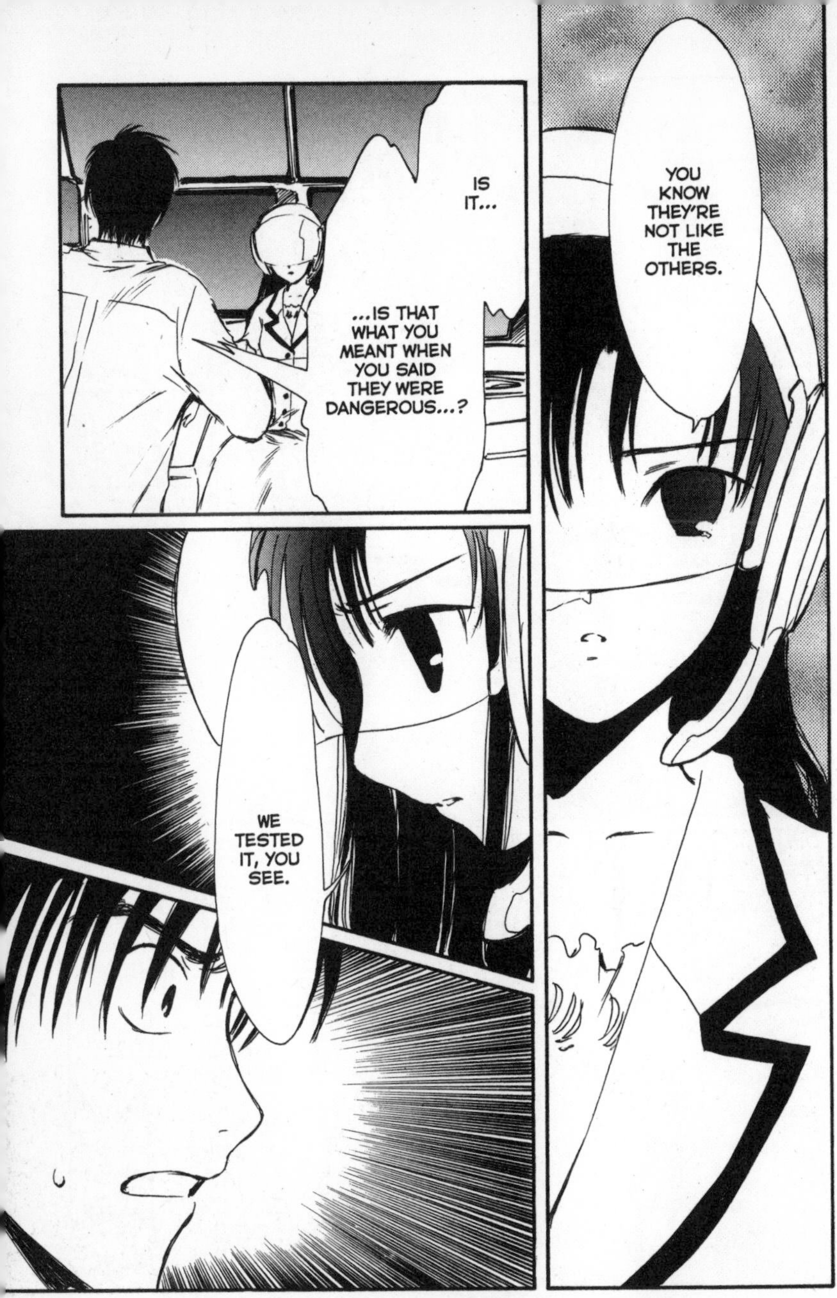
YOU KNOW THEY'RE NOT LIKE THE OTHERS.
IS IT...
...IS THAT WHAT YOU MEANT WHEN YOU SAID THEY WERE DANGEROUS...?
WE TESTED IT, YOU SEE.

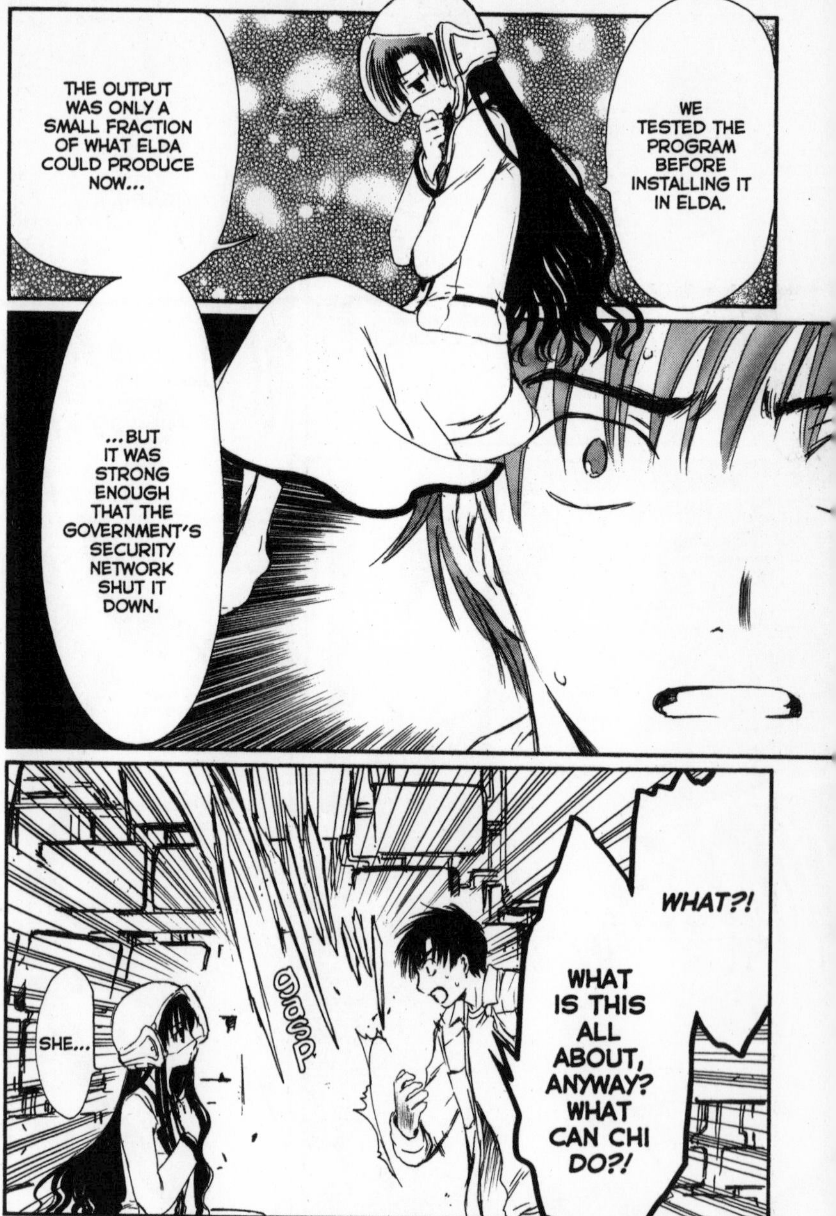
WE TESTED THE PROGRAM BEFORE INSTALLING IT IN ELDA.
THE OUTPUT WAS ONLY A SMALL FRACTION OF WHAT ELDA COULD PRODUCE NOW...
...BUT IT WAS STRONG ENOUGH THAT THE GOVERNMENT'S SECURITY NETWORK SHUT IT DOWN.
WHAT?!
WHAT IS THIS ALL ABOUT, ANYWAY? WHAT CAN CHI DO?!
SHE...

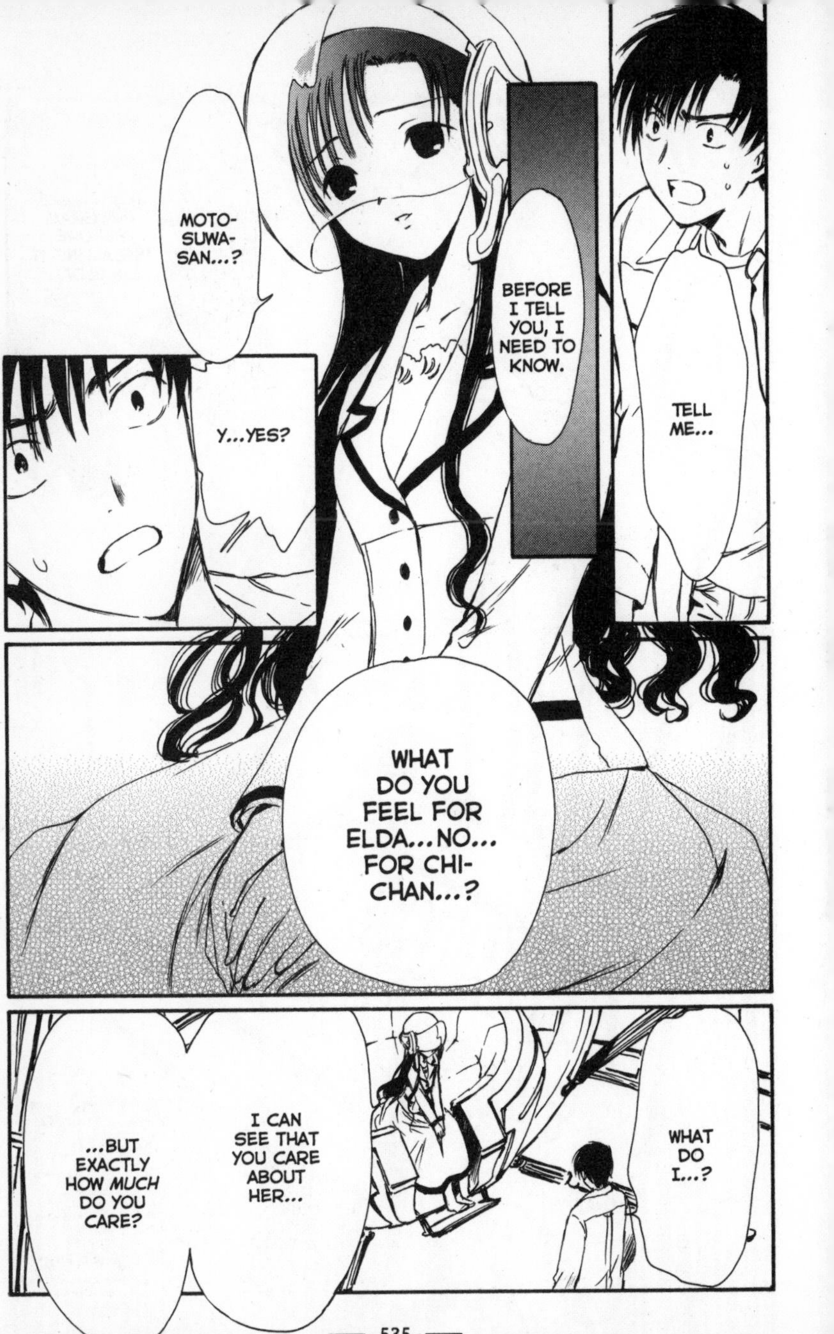
TELL ME...
BEFORE I TELL YOU, I NEED TO KNOW.
MOTO-SUWA-SAN...?
Y...YES?
WHAT DO YOU FEEL FOR ELDA...NO... FOR CHI-CHAN...?
WHAT DO I...?
I CAN SEE THAT YOU CARE ABOUT HER...
...BUT EXACTLY HOW *MUCH* DO YOU CARE?

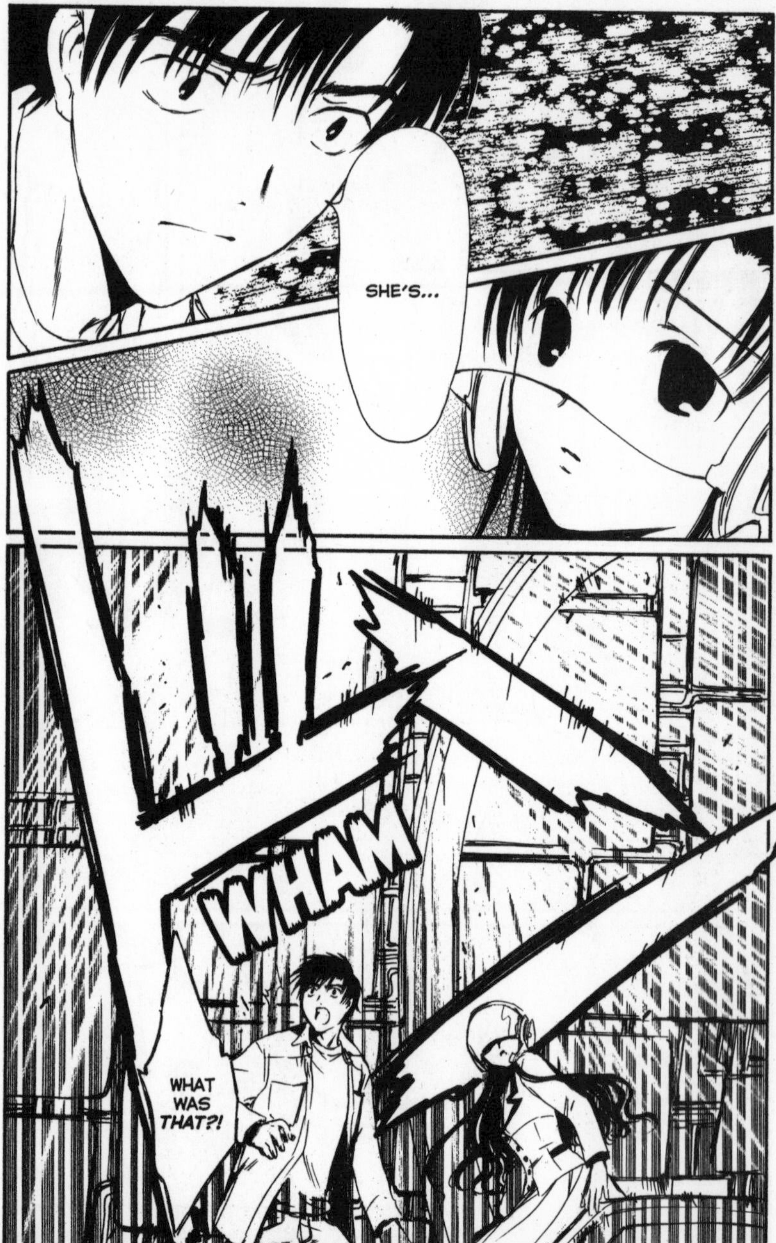
SHE'S...
WHAM
WHAT WAS THAT?!

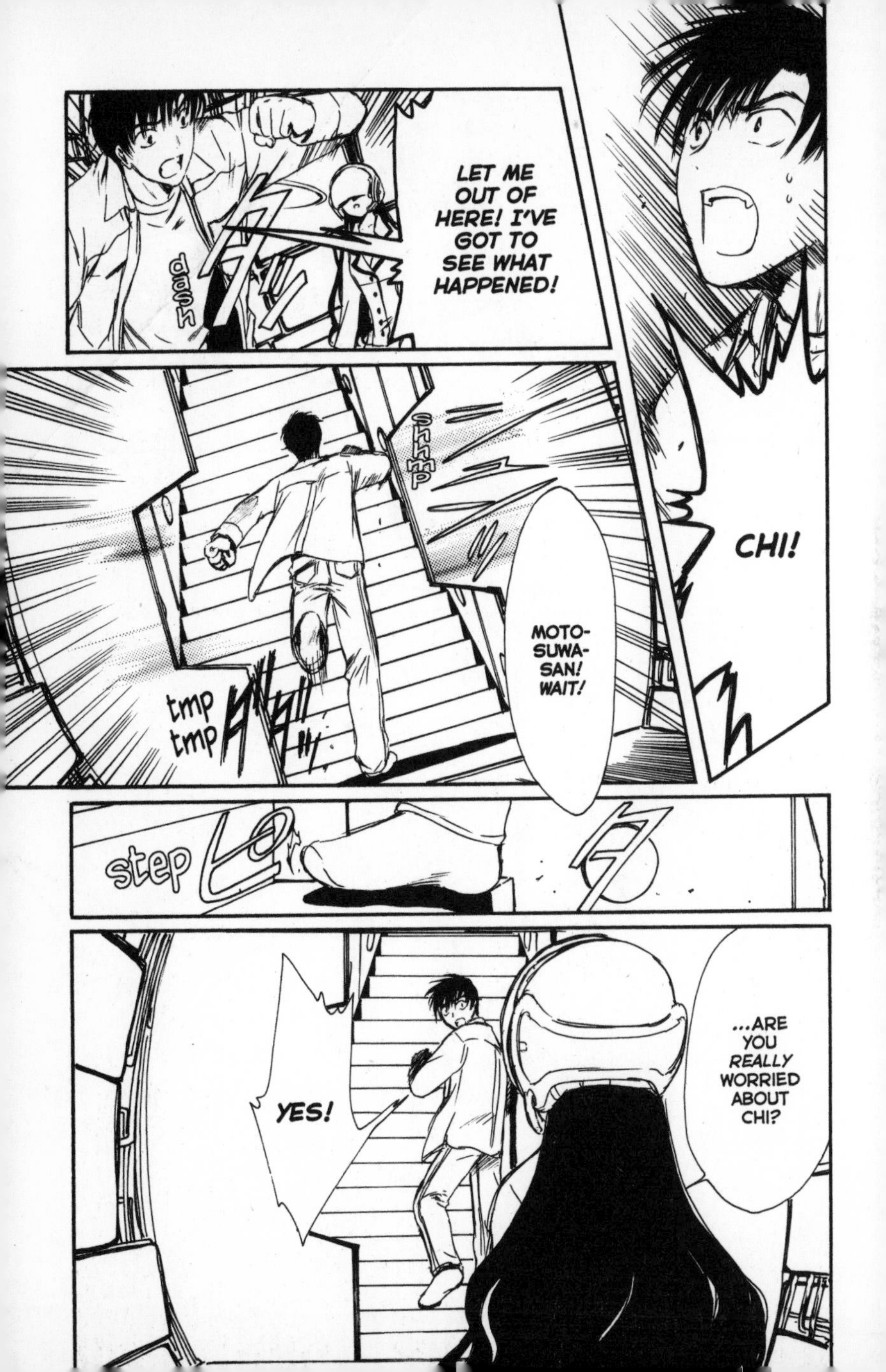
CHI!
dash
LET ME OUT OF HERE! I'VE GOT TO SEE WHAT HAPPENED!
shhmp
MOTO-SUWA-SAN! WAIT!
tmp tmp
step
...ARE YOU *REALLY* WORRIED ABOUT CHI?
YES!

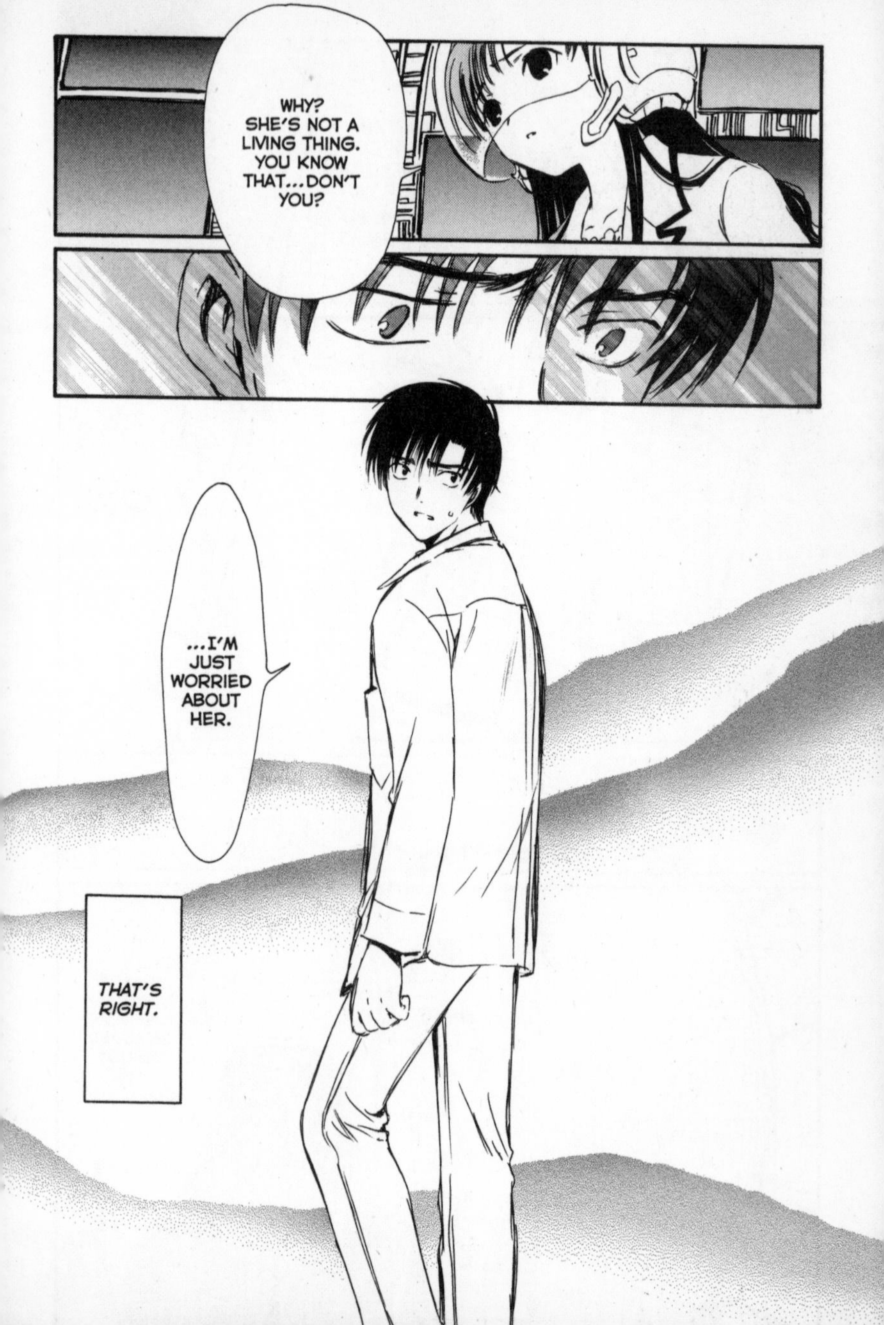
WHY? SHE'S NOT A LIVING THING. YOU KNOW THAT...DON'T YOU?
...I'M JUST WORRIED ABOUT HER.
THAT'S RIGHT.

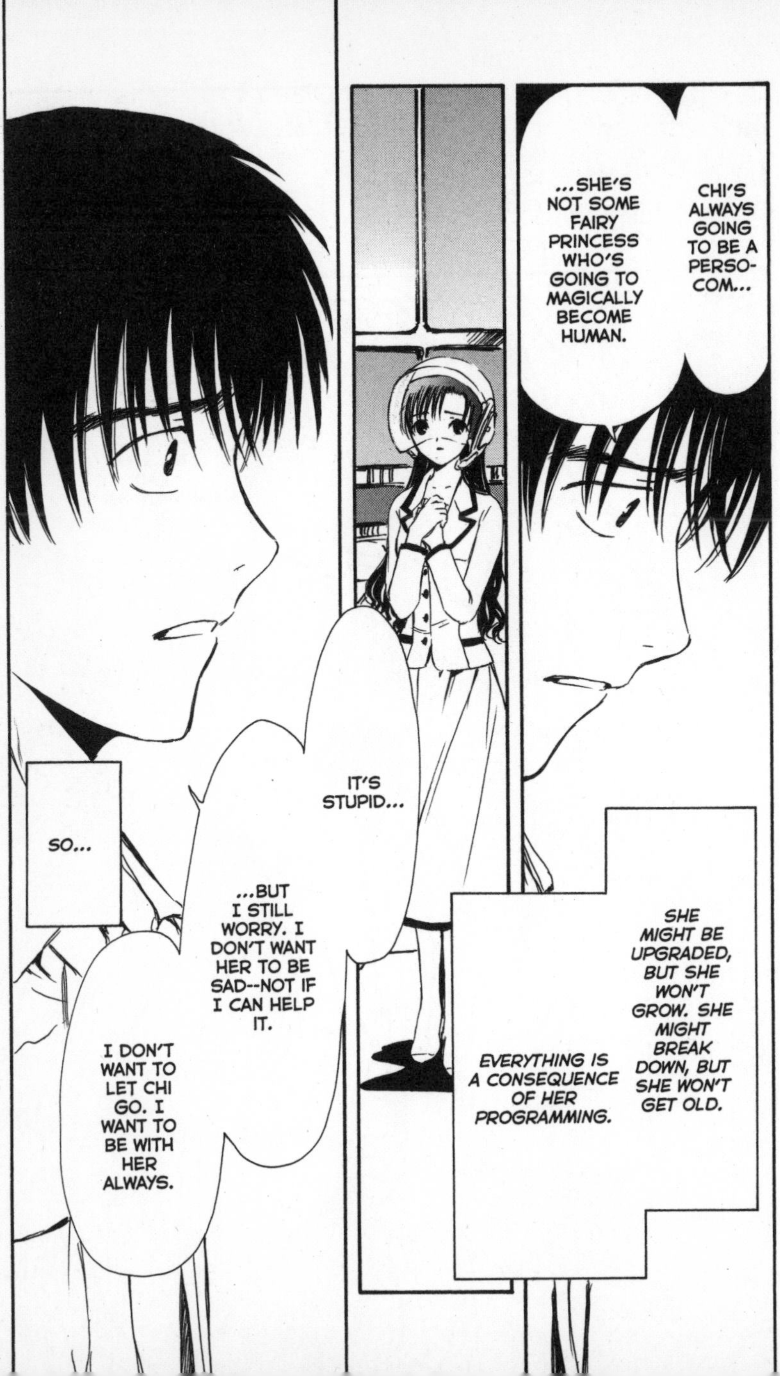
CHI'S ALWAYS GOING TO BE A PERSO-COM...
...SHE'S NOT SOME FAIRY PRINCESS WHO'S GOING TO MAGICALLY BECOME HUMAN.
SHE MIGHT BE UPGRADED, BUT SHE WON'T GROW. SHE MIGHT BREAK DOWN, BUT SHE WON'T GET OLD.
EVERYTHING IS A CONSEQUENCE OF HER PROGRAMMING.
IT'S STUPID...
...BUT I STILL WORRY. I DON'T WANT HER TO BE SAD--NOT IF I CAN HELP IT.
SO...
I DON'T WANT TO LET CHI GO. I WANT TO BE WITH HER ALWAYS.

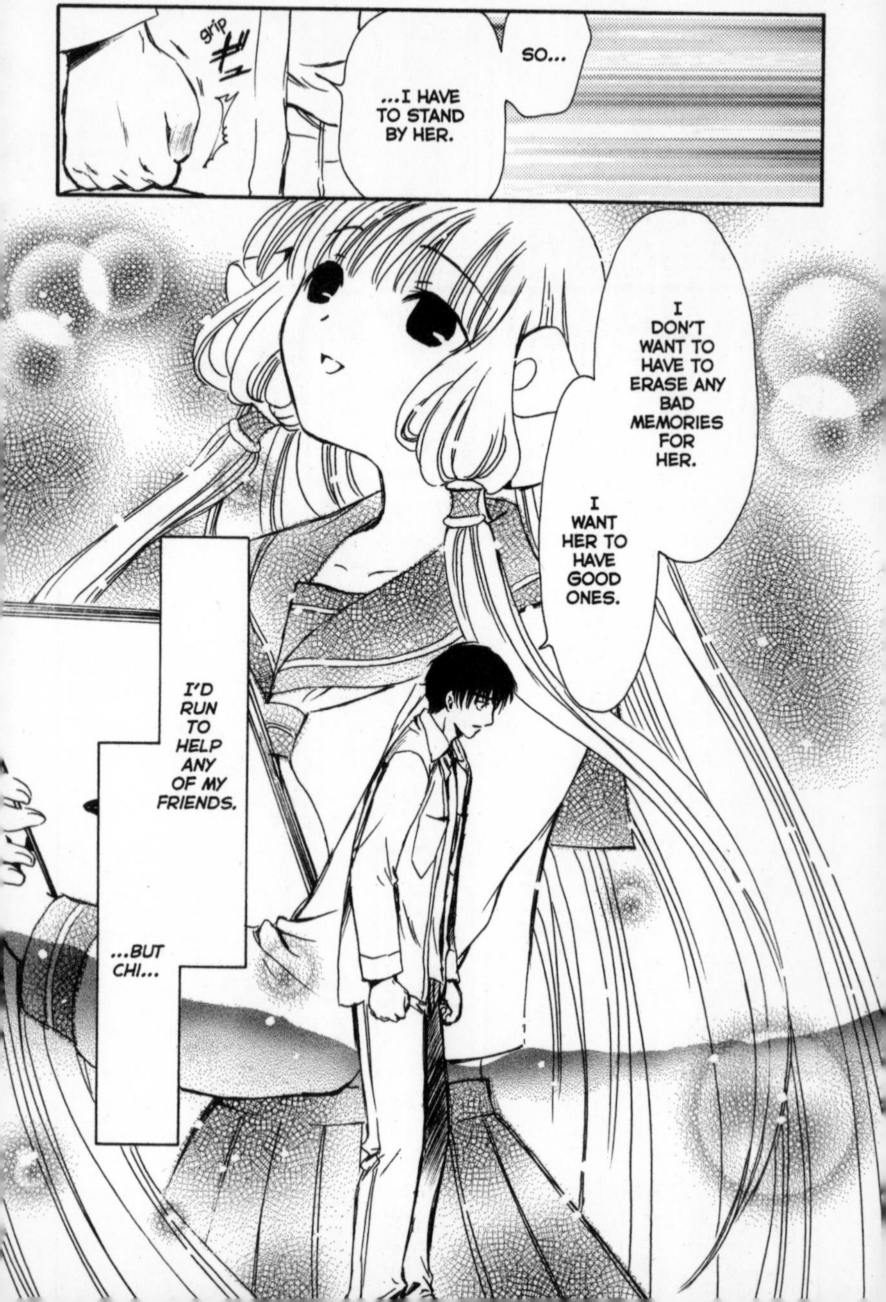
SO...
...I HAVE TO STAND BY HER.
grip
I DON'T WANT TO HAVE TO ERASE ANY BAD MEMORIES FOR HER.
I WANT HER TO HAVE GOOD ONES.
I'D RUN TO HELP ANY OF MY FRIENDS.
...BUT CHI...

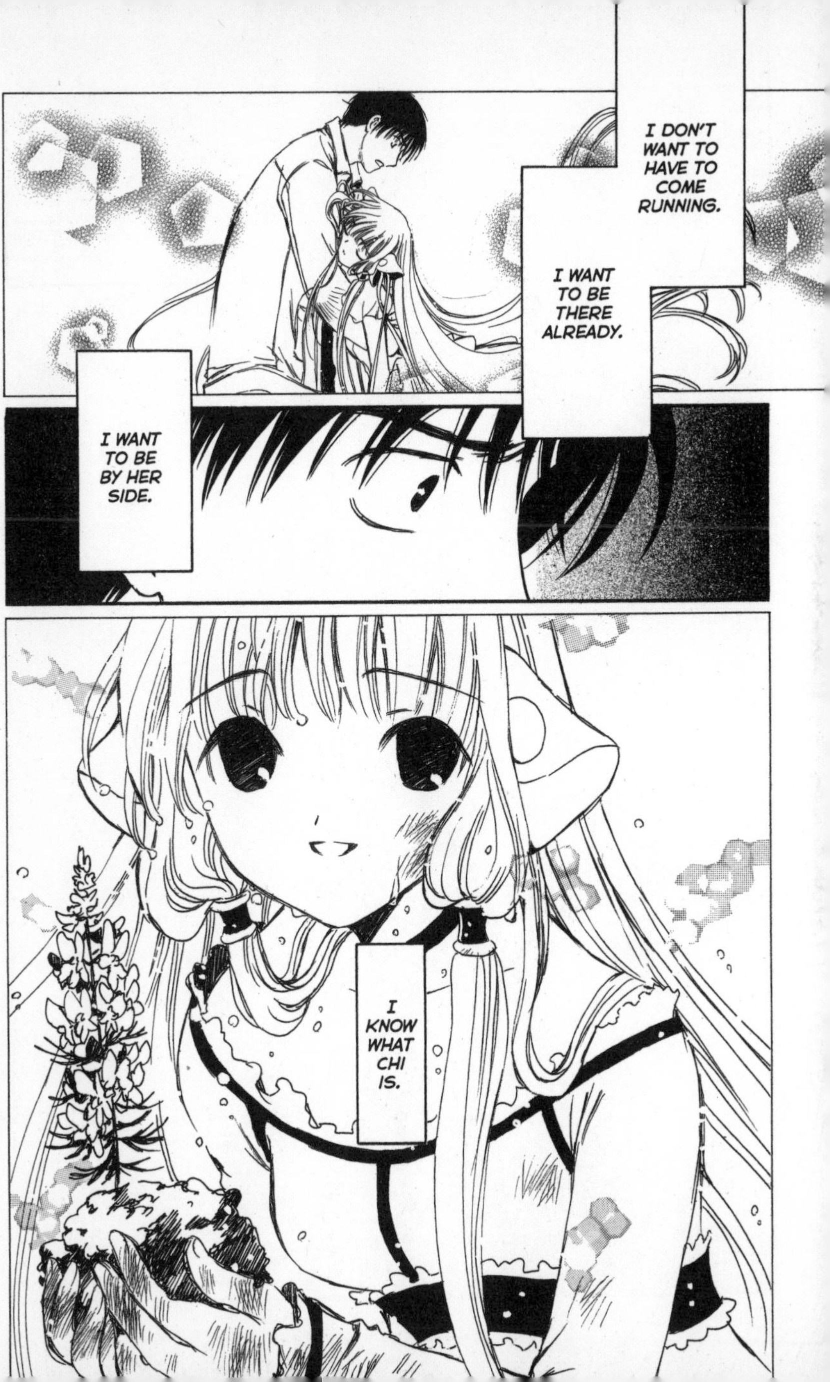
I DON'T WANT TO HAVE TO COME RUNNING.
I WANT TO BE THERE ALREADY.
I WANT TO BE BY HER SIDE.
I KNOW WHAT CHI IS.

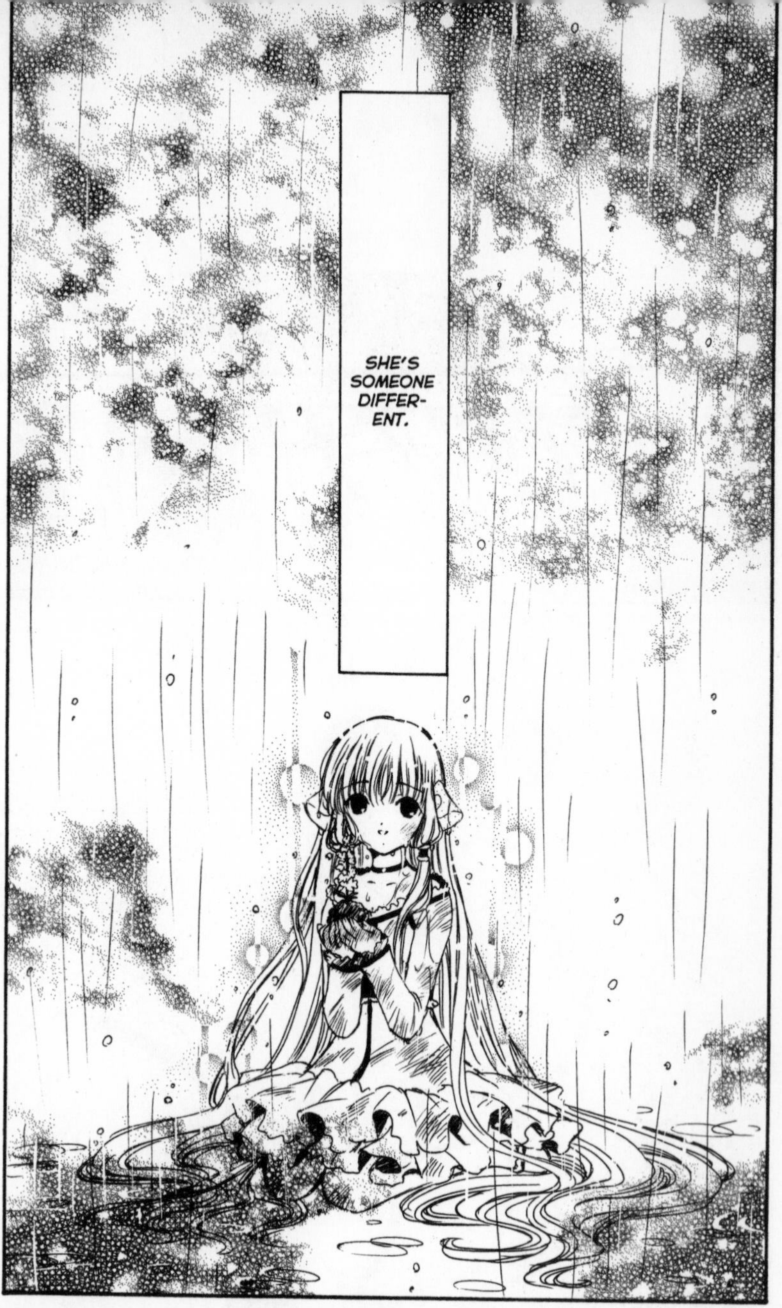
SHE'S SOMEONE DIFFER- ENT.

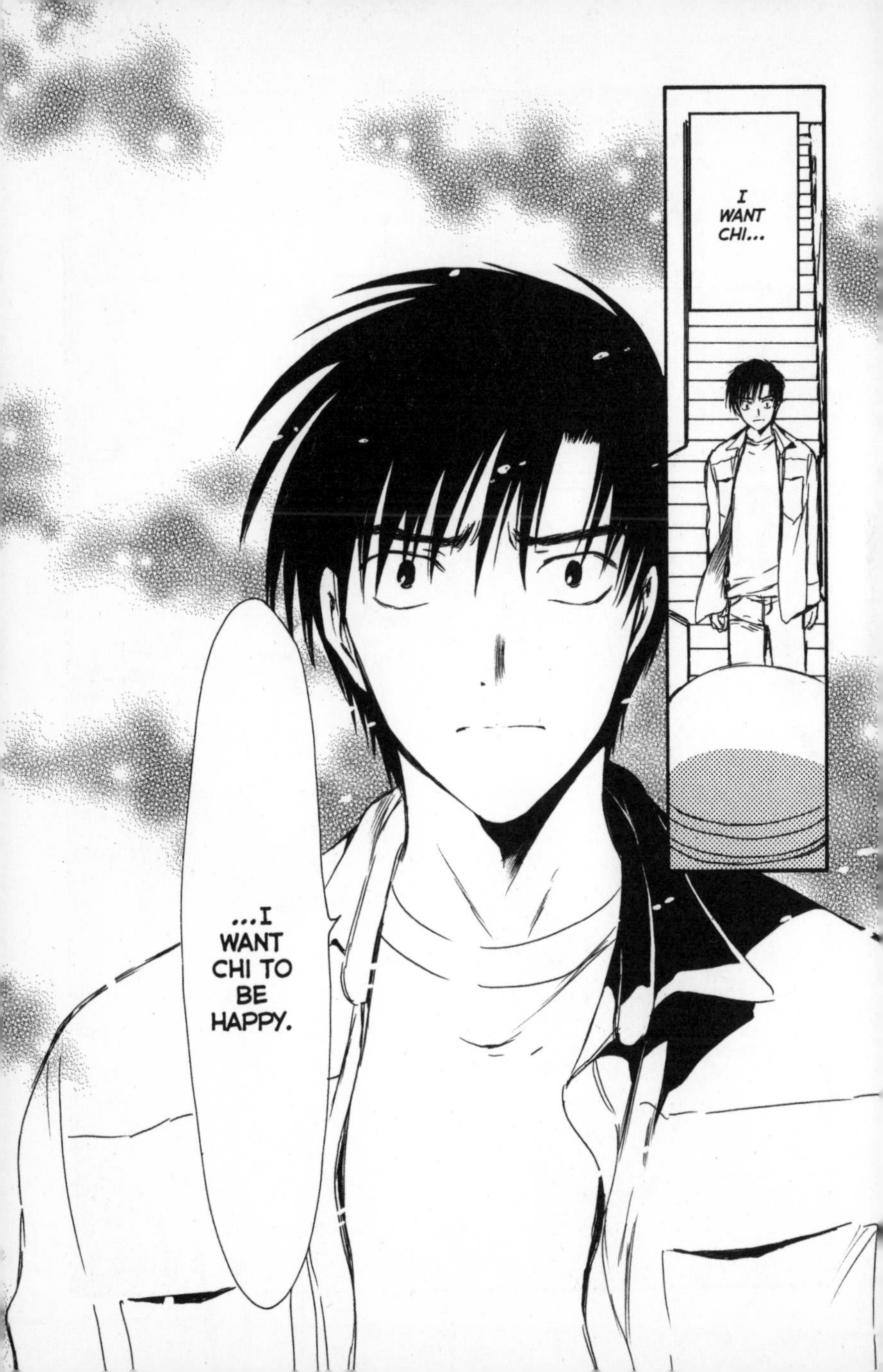
I WANT CHI...
...I WANT CHI TO BE HAPPY.

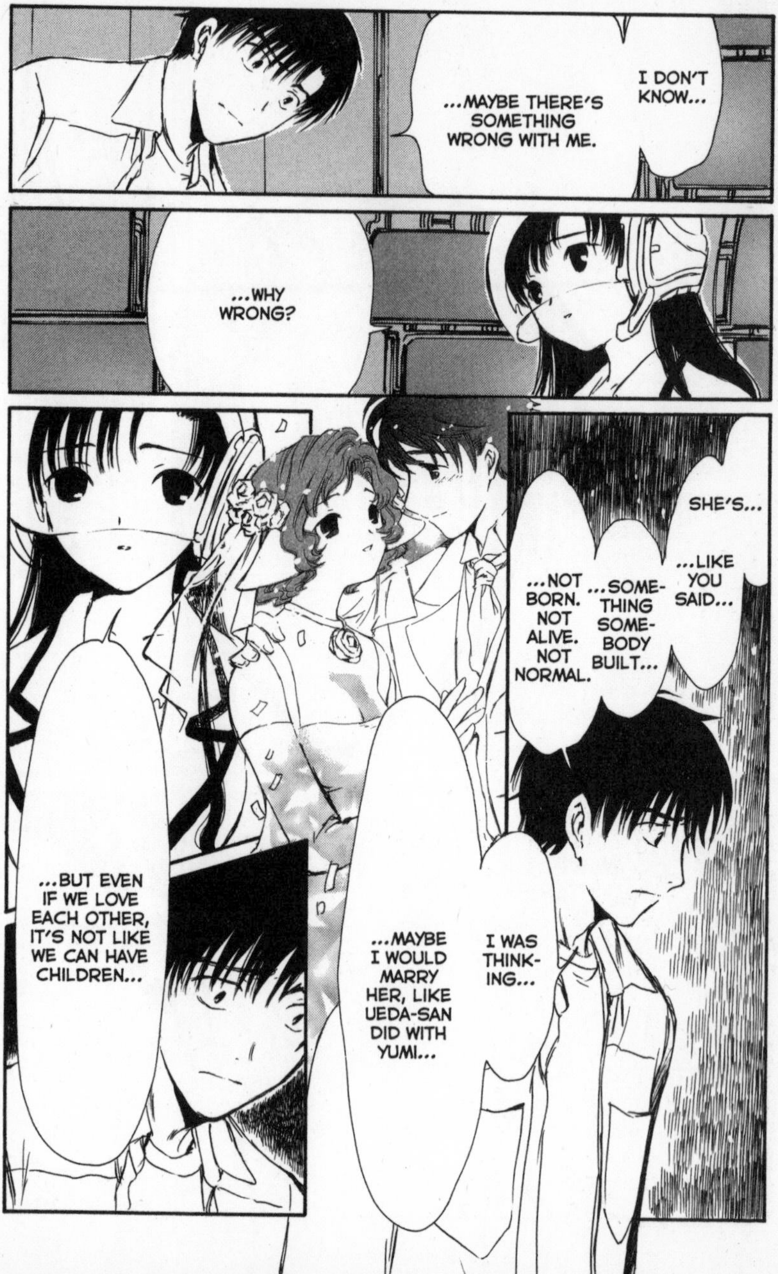
I DON'T KNOW...
...MAYBE THERE'S SOMETHING WRONG WITH ME.
...WHY WRONG?
SHE'S...
...LIKE YOU SAID...
...SOME-THING SOME-BODY BUILT...
...NOT BORN. NOT ALIVE. NOT NORMAL.
I WAS THINK-ING...
...MAYBE I WOULD MARRY HER, LIKE UEDA-SAN DID WITH YUMI...
...BUT EVEN IF WE LOVE EACH OTHER, IT'S NOT LIKE WE CAN HAVE CHILDREN...

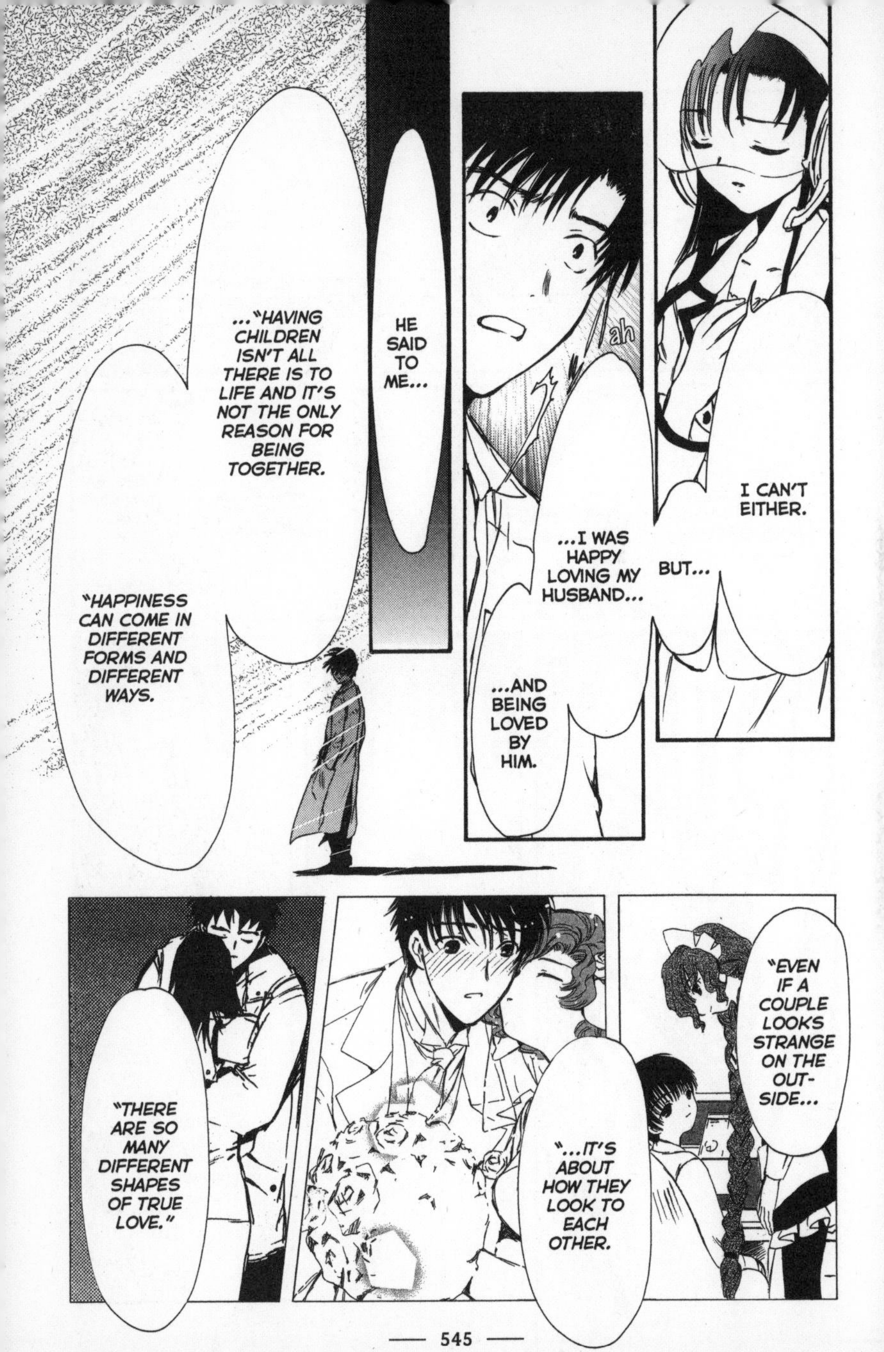
I CAN'T EITHER.
BUT...
ah
...I WAS HAPPY LOVING MY HUSBAND...
...AND BEING LOVED BY HIM.
HE SAID TO ME...
..."HAVING CHILDREN ISN'T ALL THERE IS TO LIFE AND IT'S NOT THE ONLY REASON FOR BEING TOGETHER.
"HAPPINESS CAN COME IN DIFFERENT FORMS AND DIFFERENT WAYS.
"EVEN IF A COUPLE LOOKS STRANGE ON THE OUT-SIDE...
"...IT'S ABOUT HOW THEY LOOK TO EACH OTHER.
"THERE ARE SO MANY DIFFERENT SHAPES OF TRUE LOVE."

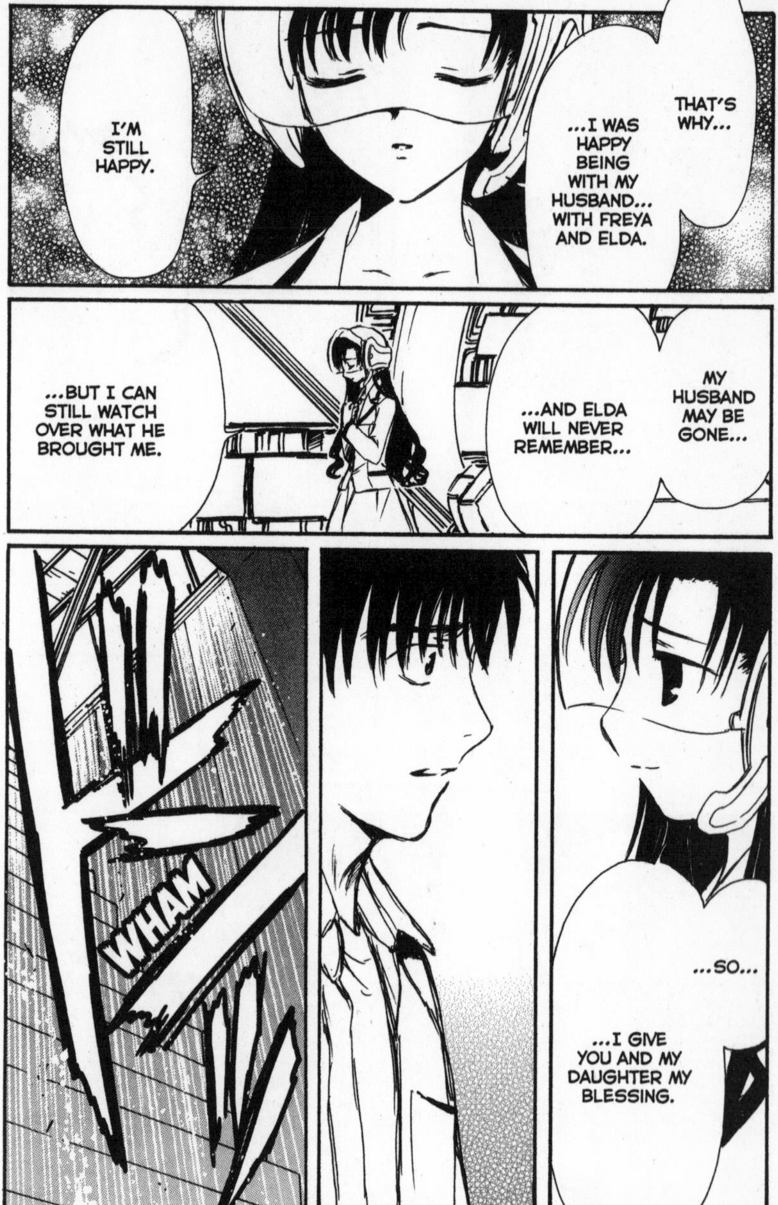
THAT'S WHY...
...I WAS HAPPY BEING WITH MY HUSBAND... WITH FREYA AND ELDA.
I'M STILL HAPPY.
MY HUSBAND MAY BE GONE...
...AND ELDA WILL NEVER REMEMBER...
...BUT I CAN STILL WATCH OVER WHAT HE BROUGHT ME.
...SO...
...I GIVE YOU AND MY DAUGHTER MY BLESSING.
WHAM

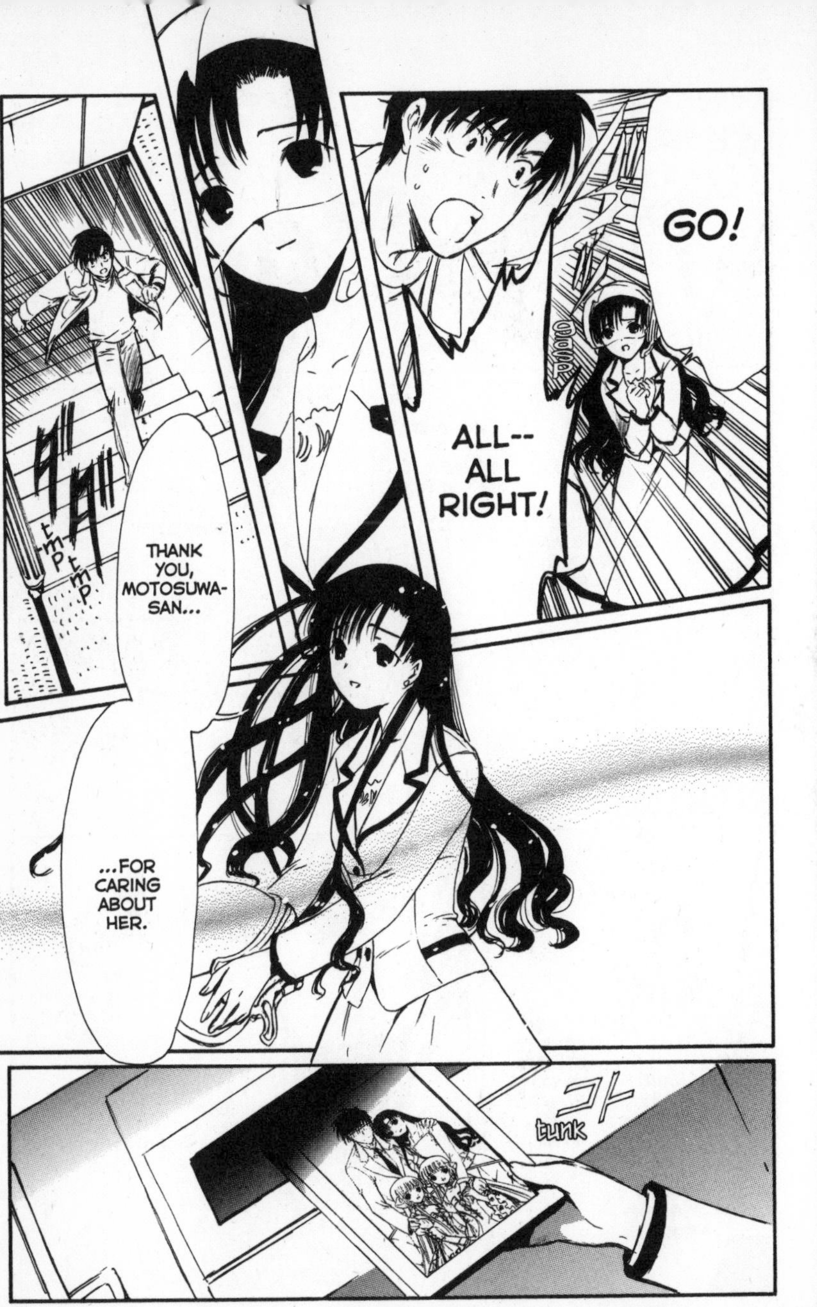
GO!
gasp
ALL-- ALL RIGHT!
tmp tmp
THANK YOU, MOTOSUWA-SAN...
...FOR CARING ABOUT HER.
tunk

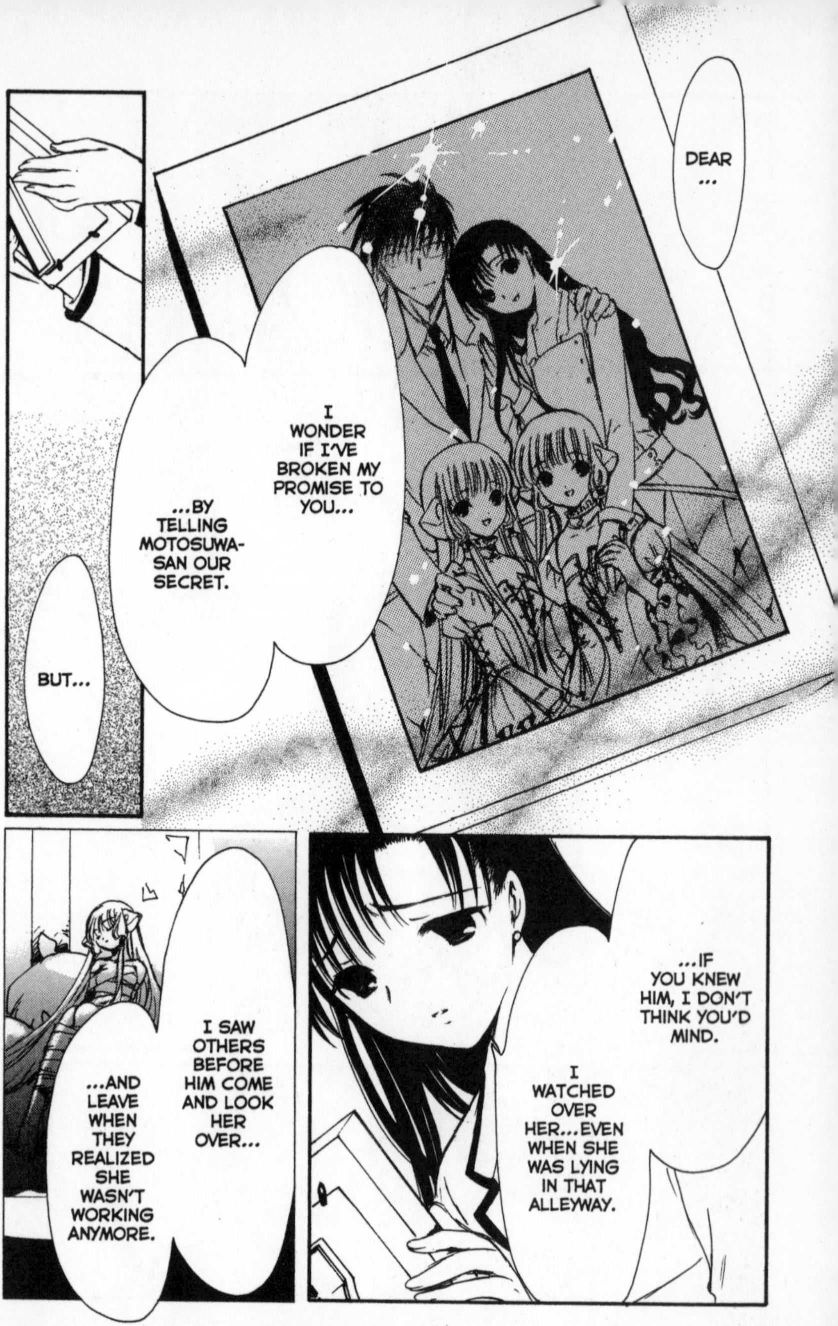
DEAR...
I WONDER IF I'VE BROKEN MY PROMISE TO YOU...
...BY TELLING MOTOSUWA-SAN OUR SECRET.
BUT...
...IF YOU KNEW HIM, I DON'T THINK YOU'D MIND.
I WATCHED OVER HER...EVEN WHEN SHE WAS LYING IN THAT ALLEYWAY.
I SAW OTHERS BEFORE HIM COME AND LOOK HER OVER...
...AND LEAVE WHEN THEY REALIZED SHE WASN'T WORKING ANYMORE.

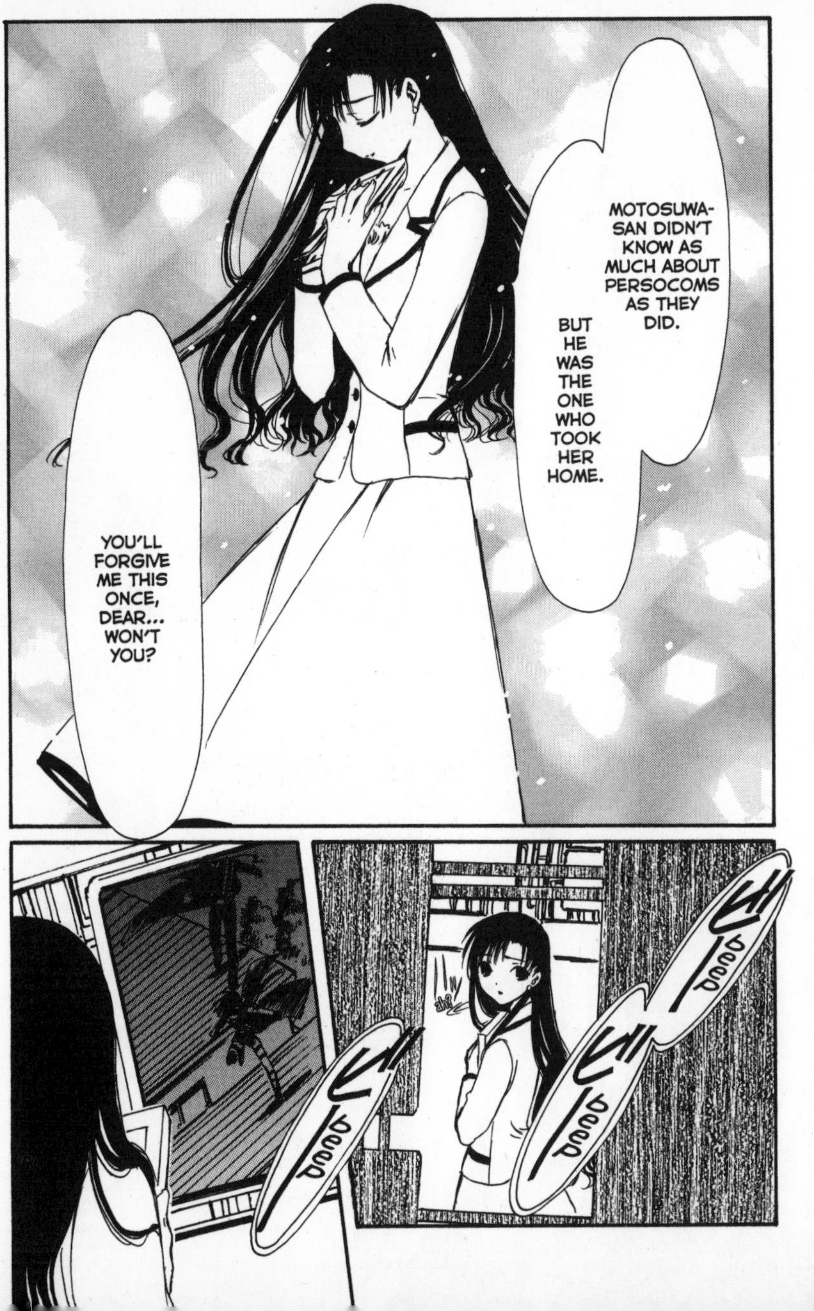
MOTOSUWA-SAN DIDN'T KNOW AS MUCH ABOUT PERSOCOMS AS THEY DID.
BUT HE WAS THE ONE WHO TOOK HER HOME.
YOU'LL FORGIVE ME THIS ONCE, DEAR... WON'T YOU?
beep
beep
ah?
beep

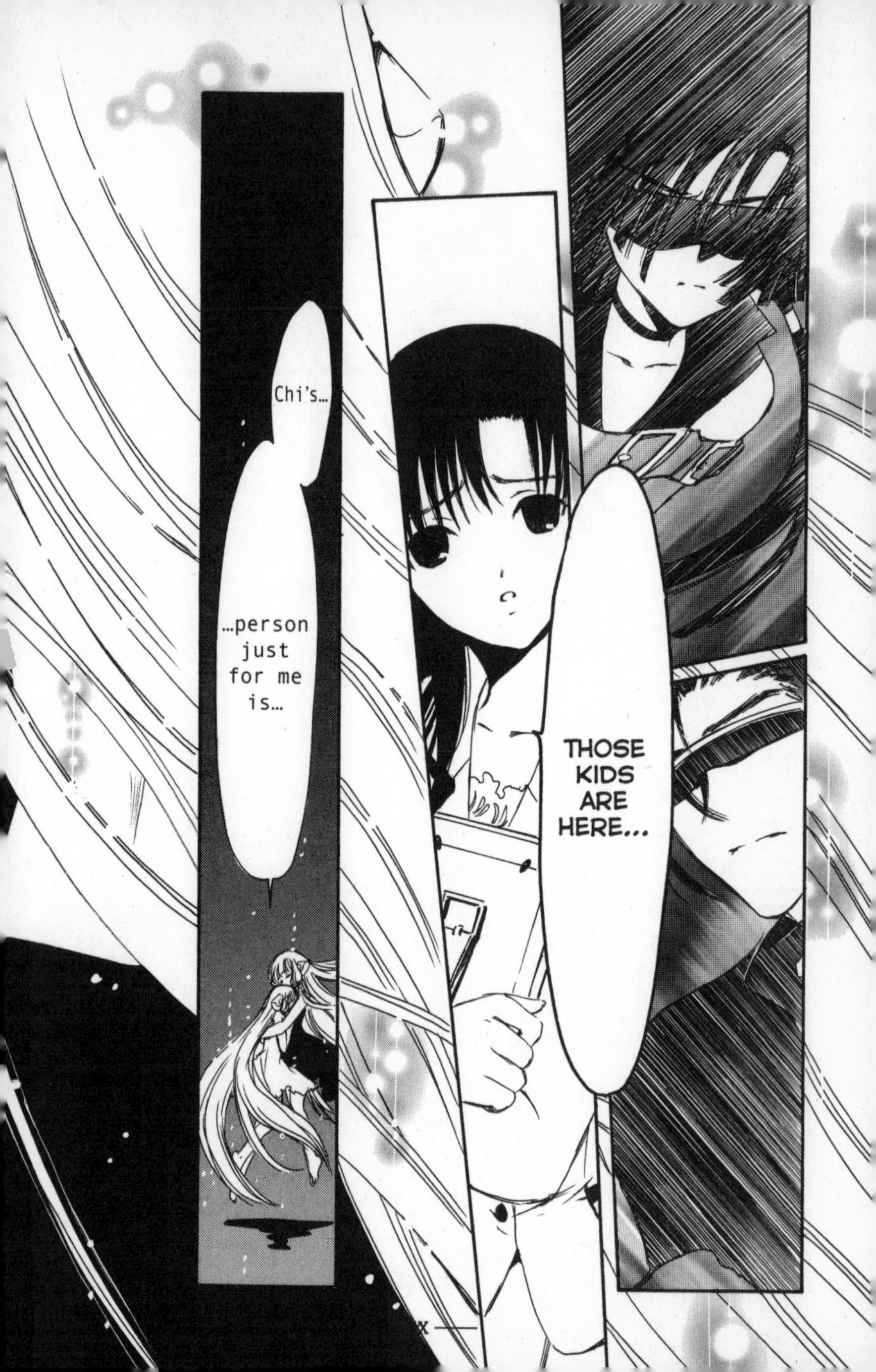
THOSE KIDS ARE HERE...
Chi's...
...person just for me is...

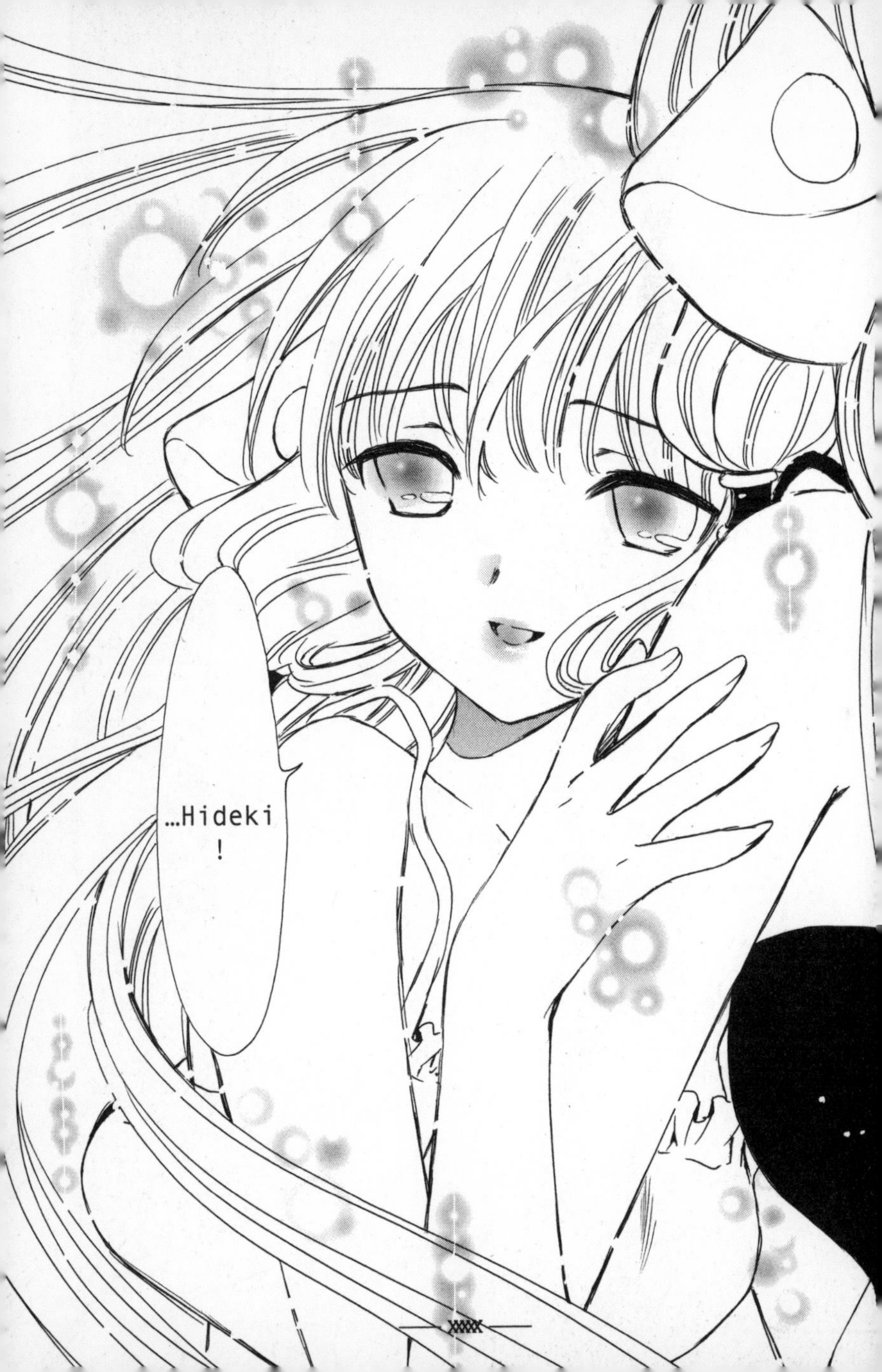
…Hideki!

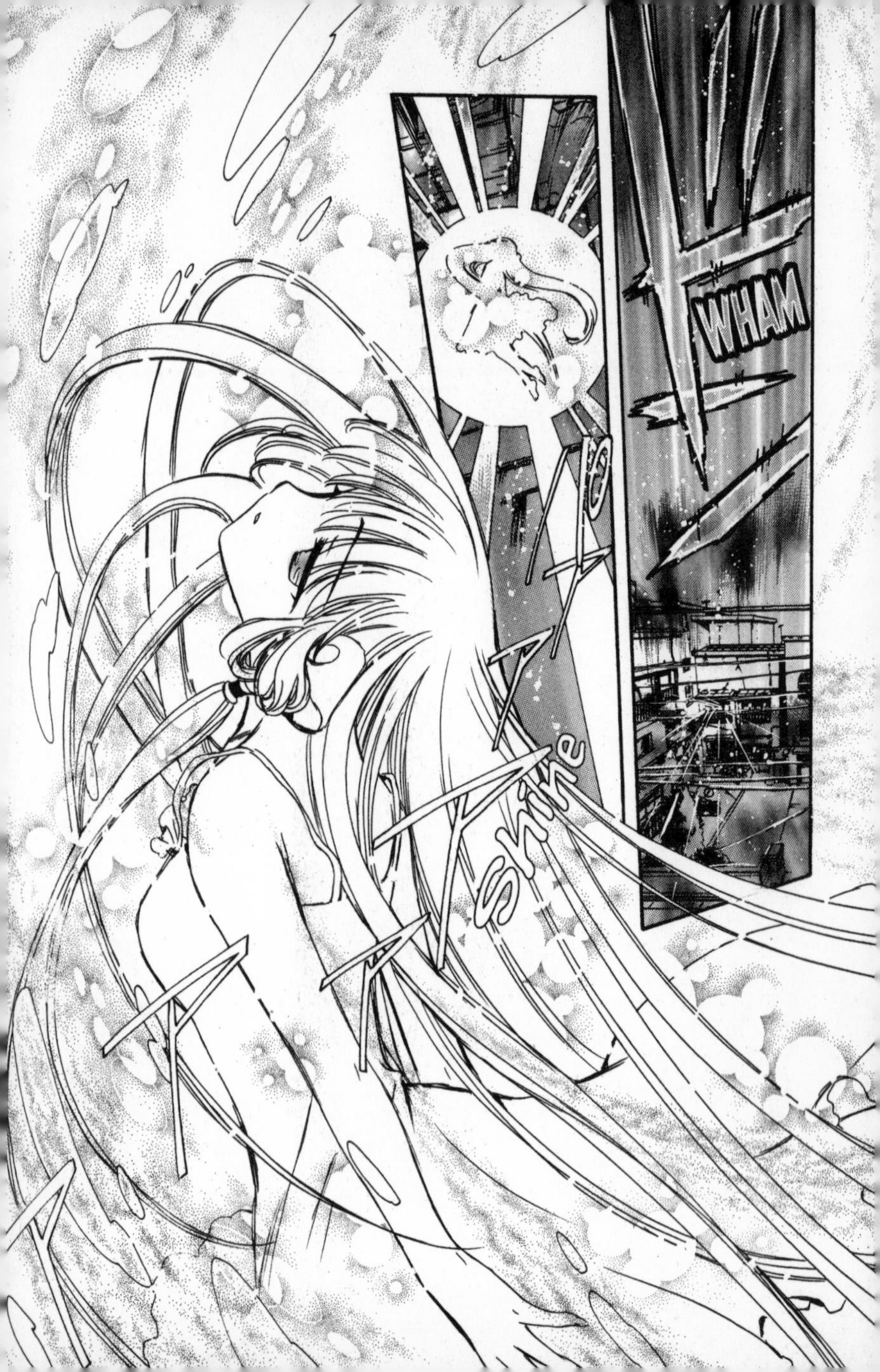
WHAM
shine

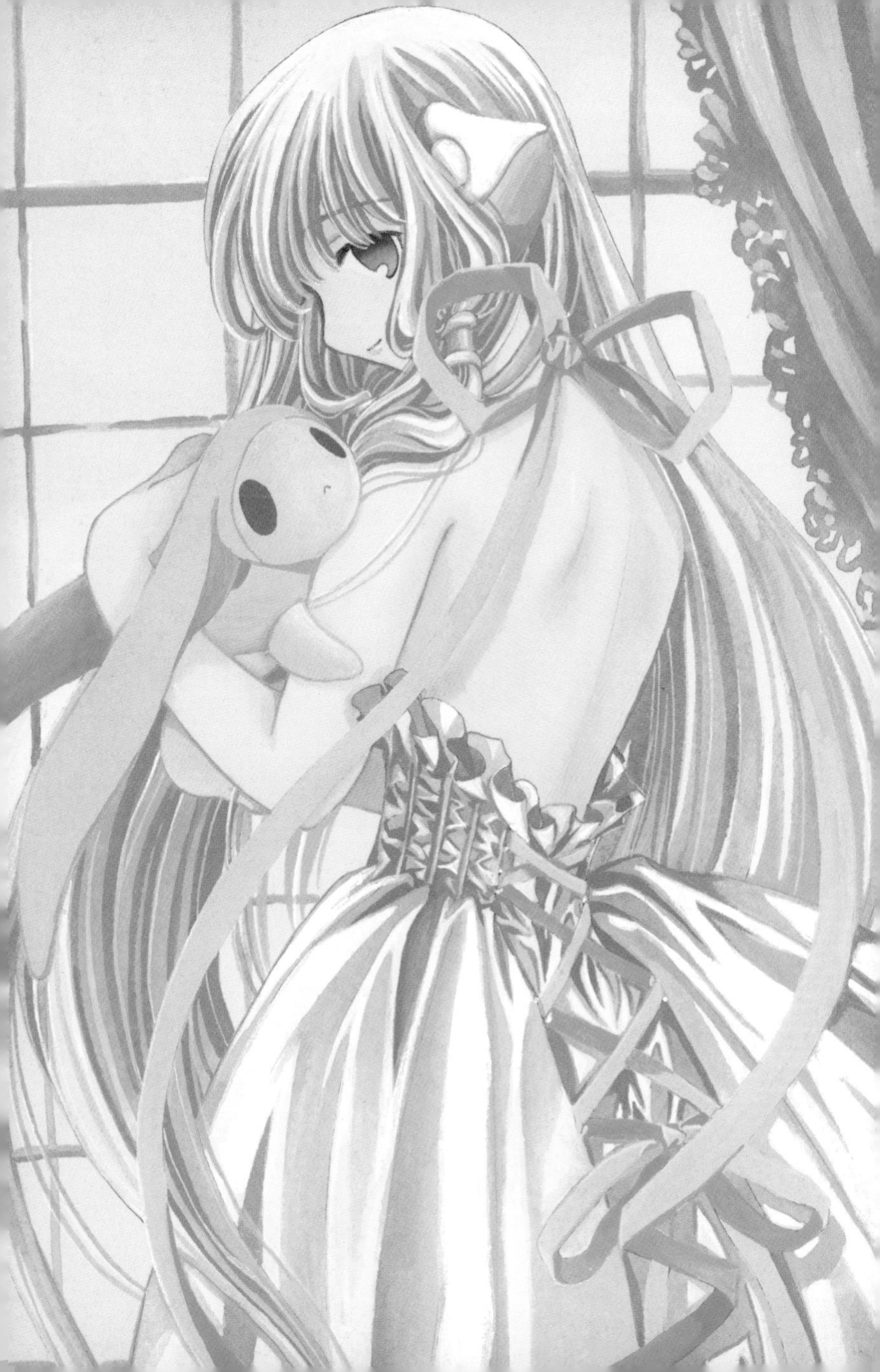

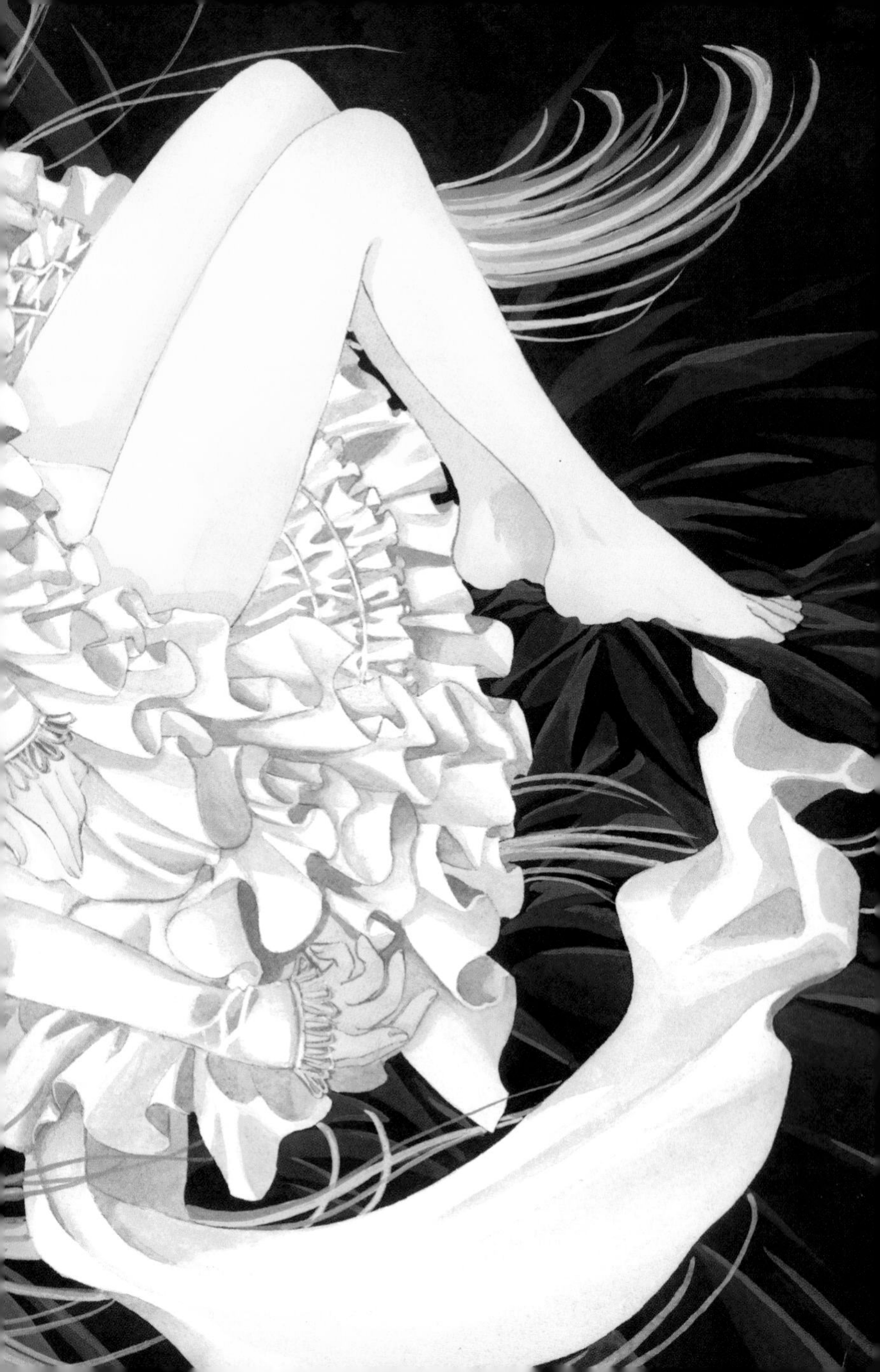

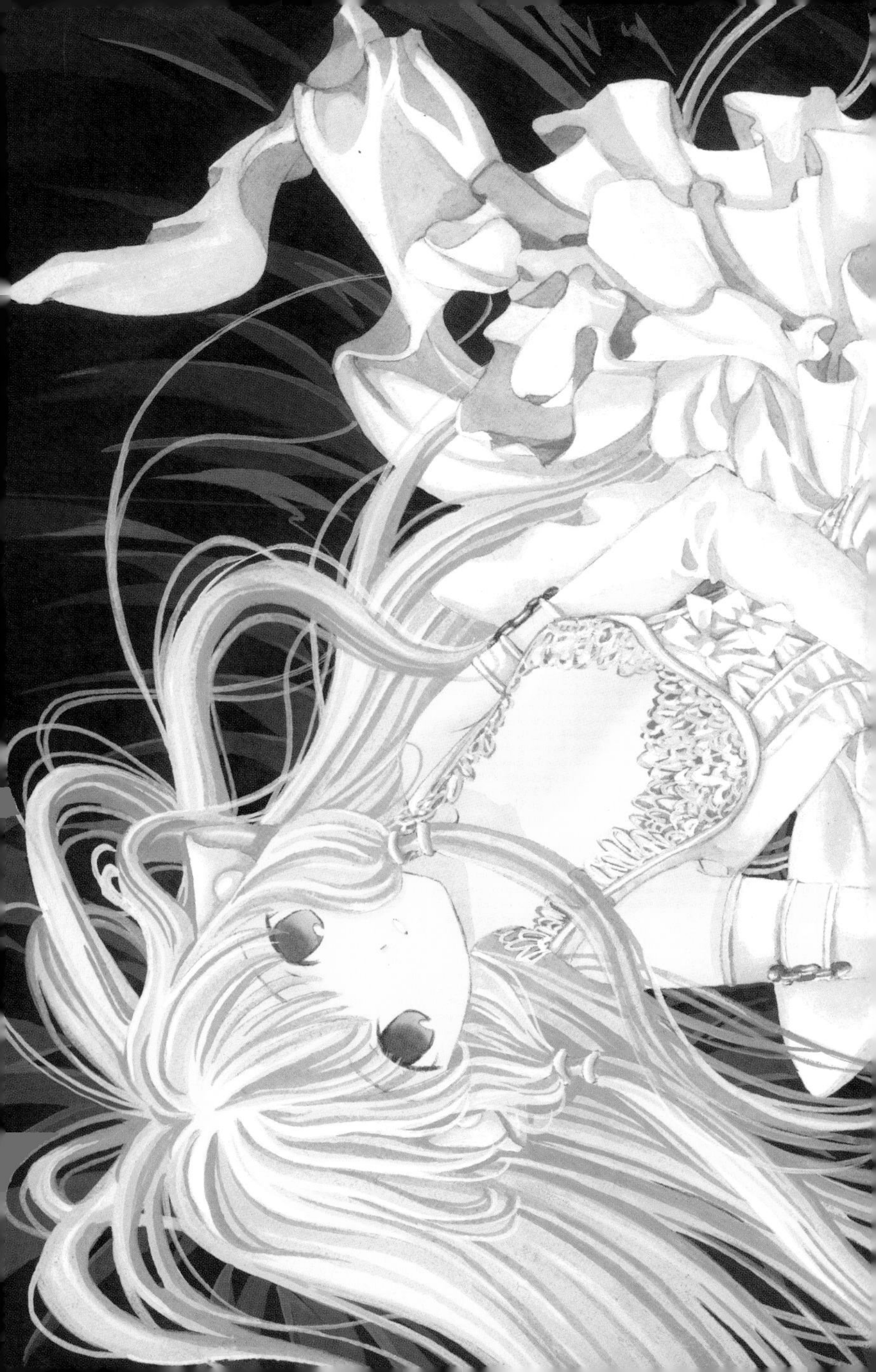

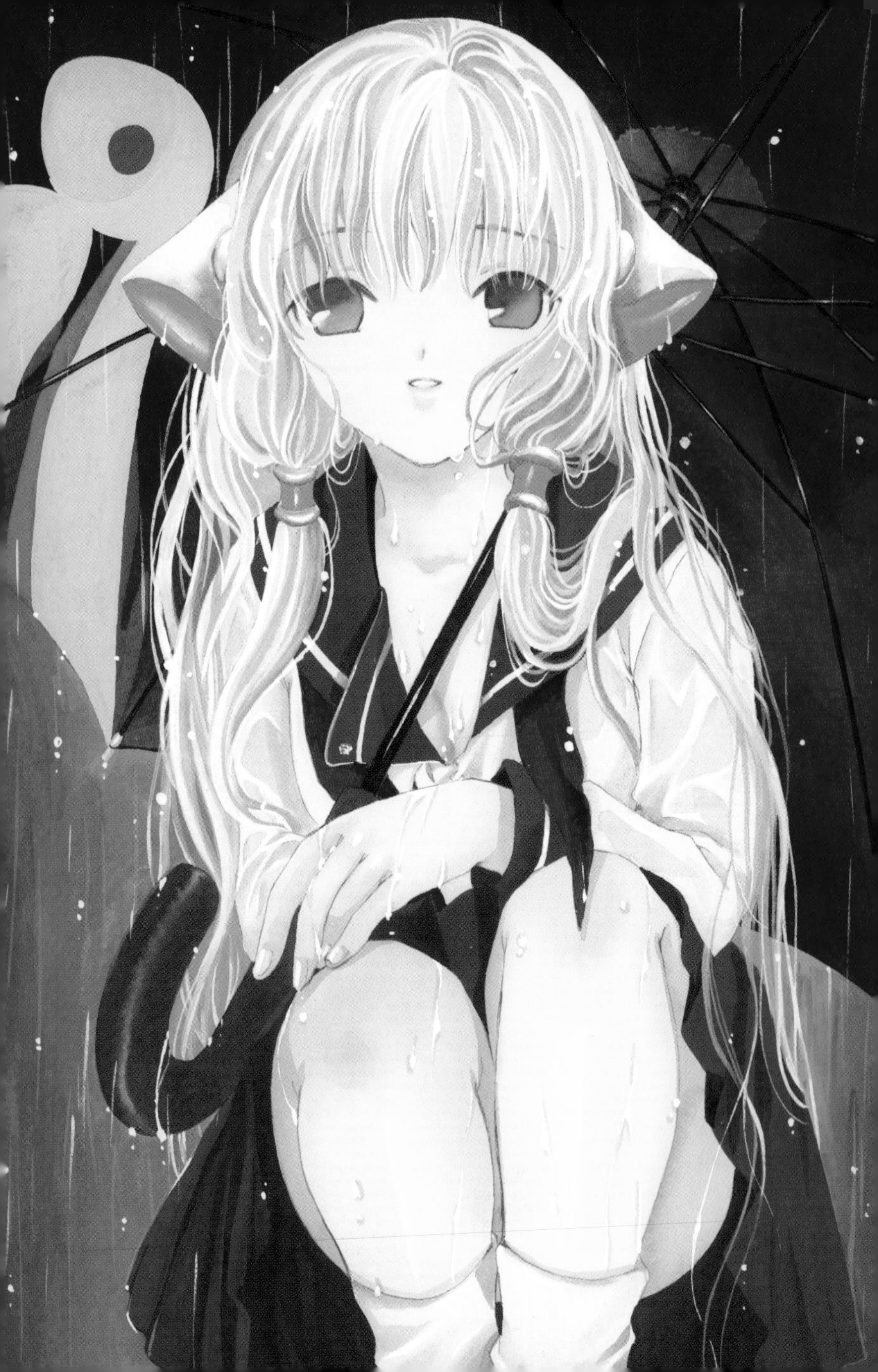

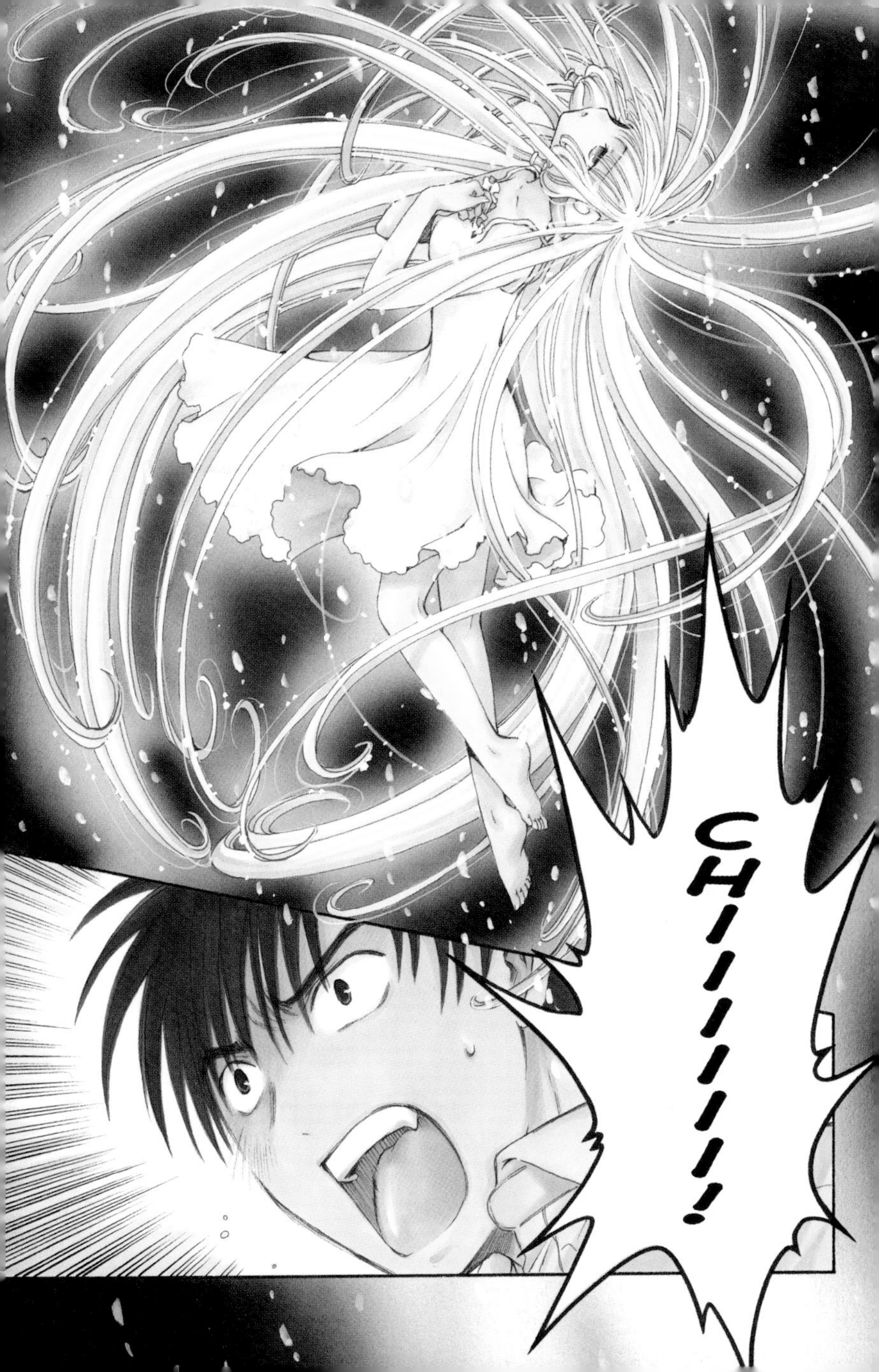
CHIIIIIII!!

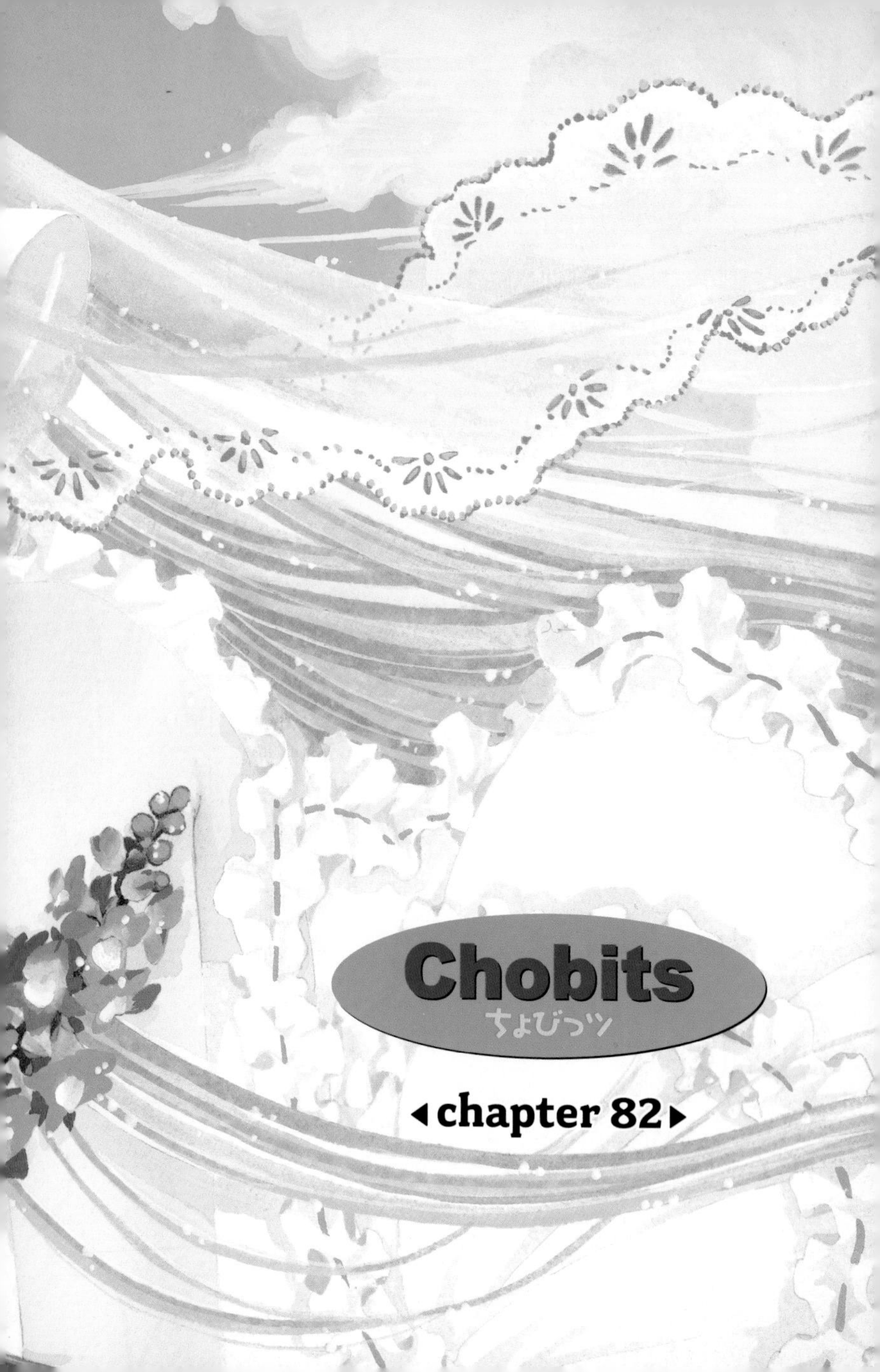
Chobits
ちょびっツ
chapter 82

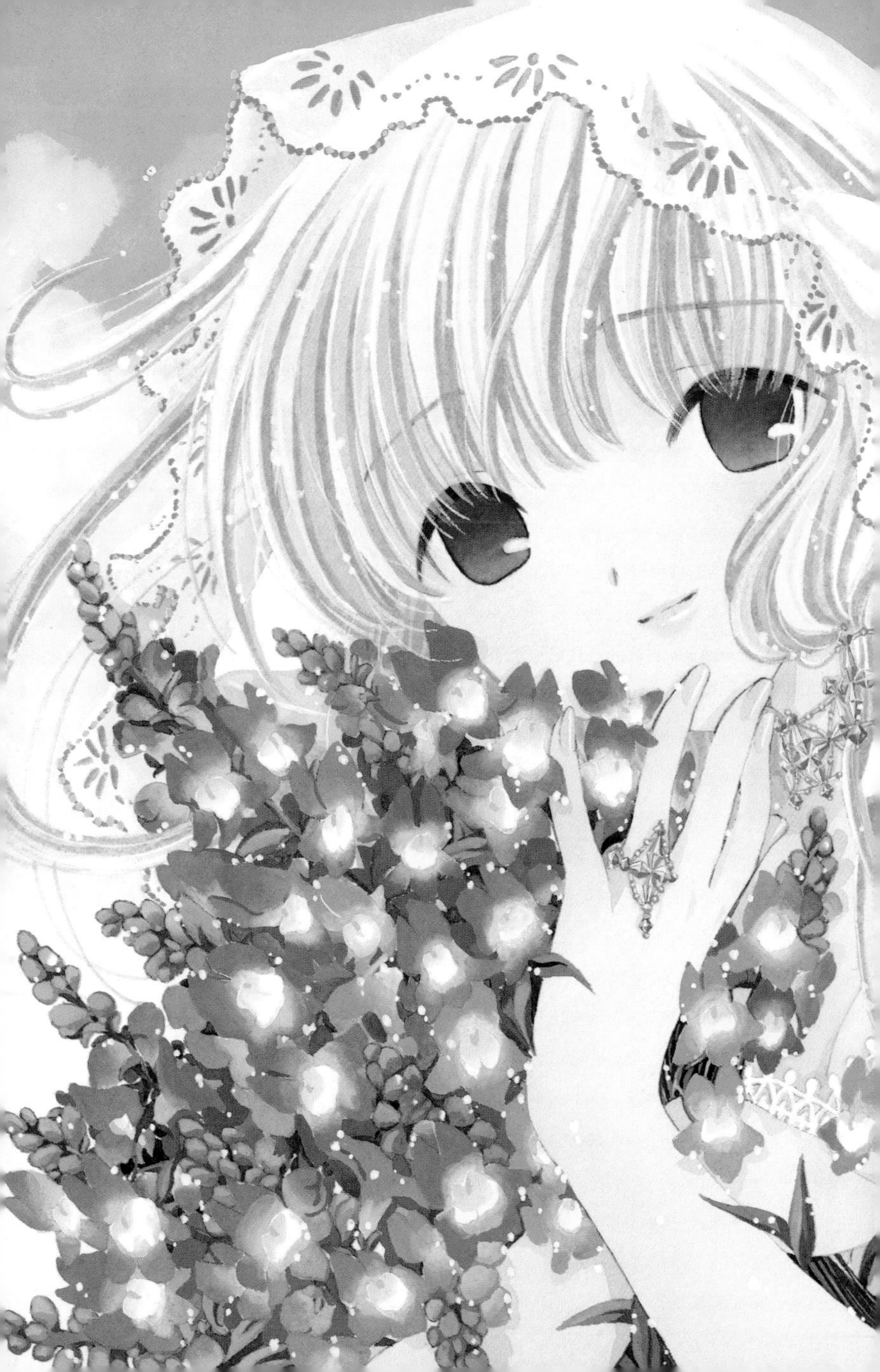

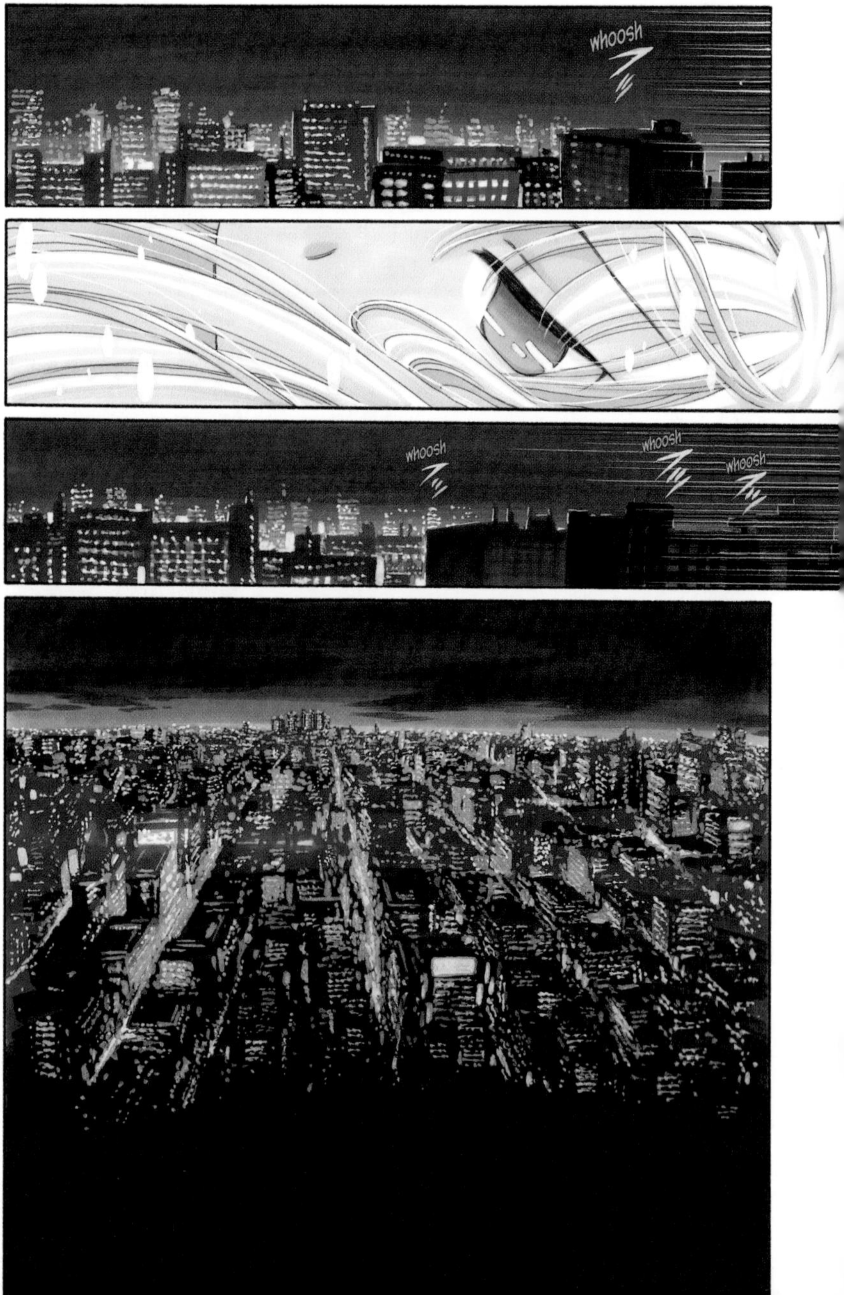
whoosh
whoosh
whoosh
whoosh

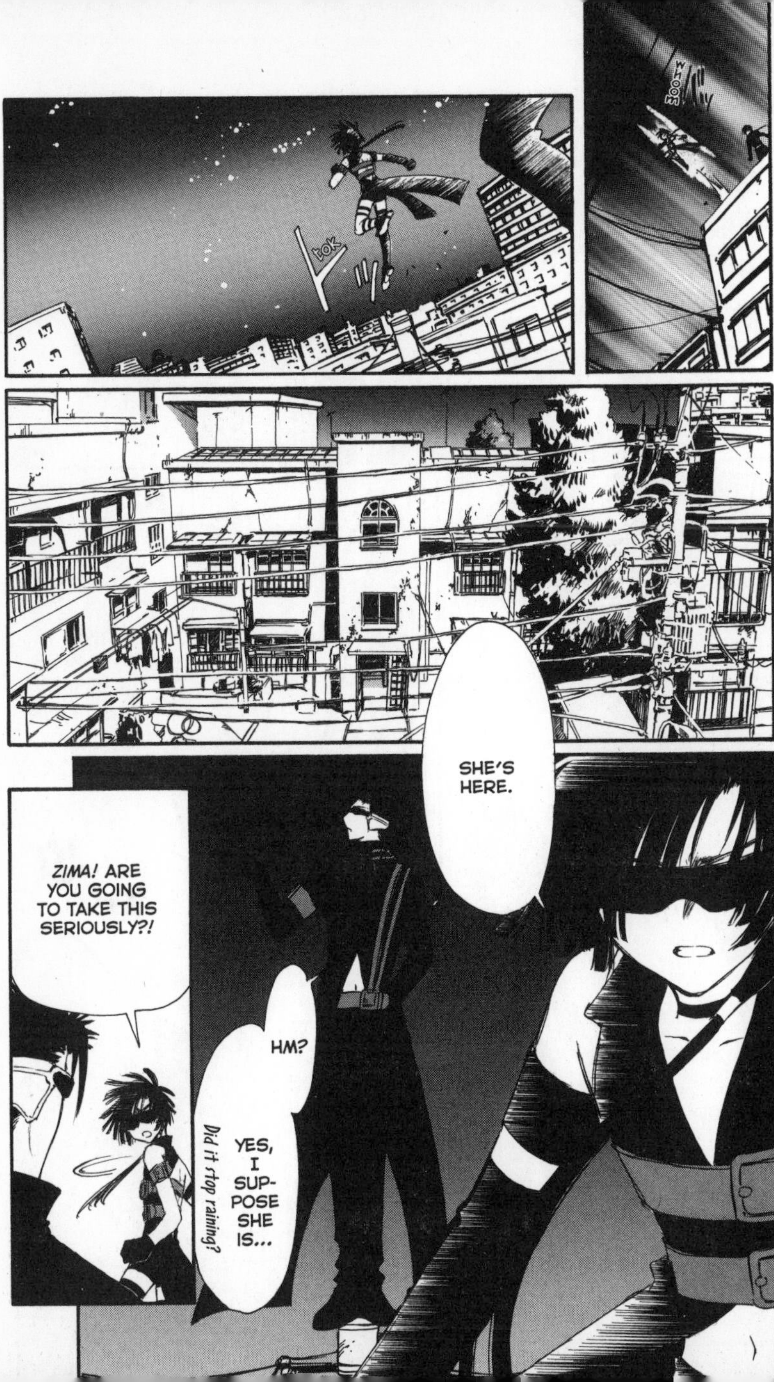
WHOOM
TOK
SHE'S HERE.
ZIMA! ARE YOU GOING TO TAKE THIS SERIOUSLY?!
HM?
YES, I SUPPOSE SHE IS...
Did it stop raining?

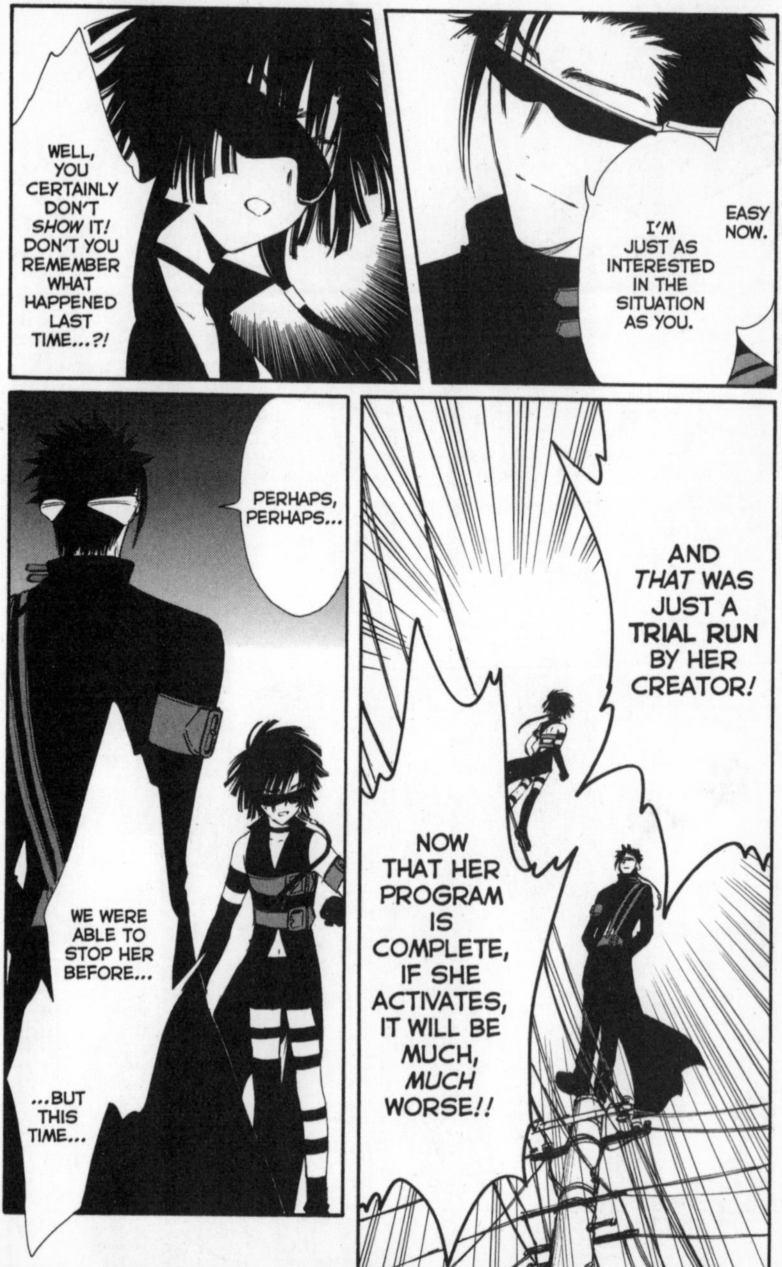
EASY NOW.
I'M JUST AS INTERESTED IN THE SITUATION AS YOU.
WELL, YOU CERTAINLY DON'T *SHOW* IT! DON'T YOU REMEMBER WHAT HAPPENED LAST TIME...?!
AND *THAT* WAS JUST A TRIAL RUN BY HER CREATOR!
NOW THAT HER PROGRAM IS COMPLETE, IF SHE ACTIVATES, IT WILL BE MUCH, *MUCH* WORSE!!
PERHAPS, PERHAPS...
WE WERE ABLE TO STOP HER BEFORE...
...BUT THIS TIME...

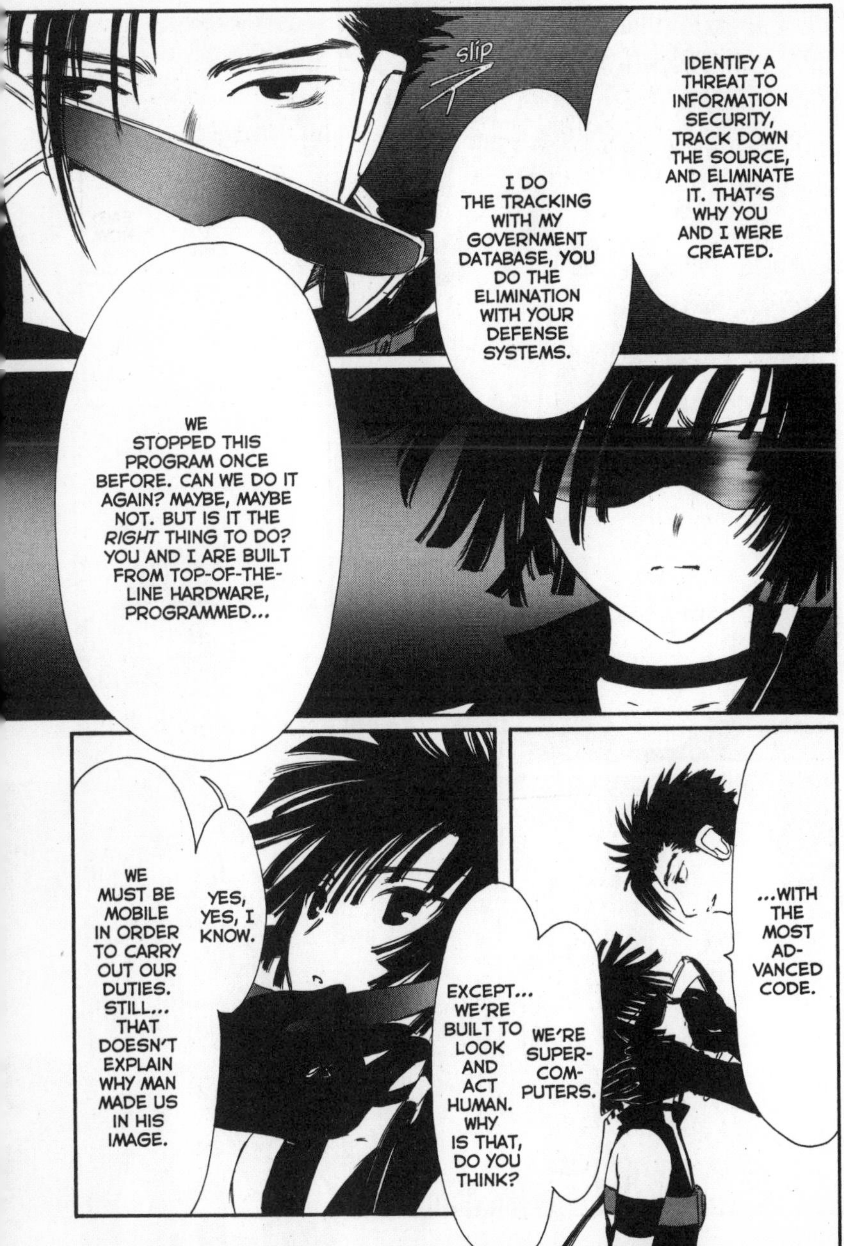
slip
IDENTIFY A THREAT TO INFORMATION SECURITY, TRACK DOWN THE SOURCE, AND ELIMINATE IT. THAT'S WHY YOU AND I WERE CREATED.
I DO THE TRACKING WITH MY GOVERNMENT DATABASE, YOU DO THE ELIMINATION WITH YOUR DEFENSE SYSTEMS.
WE STOPPED THIS PROGRAM ONCE BEFORE. CAN WE DO IT AGAIN? MAYBE, MAYBE NOT. BUT IS IT THE *RIGHT* THING TO DO? YOU AND I ARE BUILT FROM TOP-OF-THE-LINE HARDWARE, PROGRAMMED...
...WITH THE MOST ADVANCED CODE.
WE'RE SUPERCOMPUTERS.
EXCEPT... WE'RE BUILT TO LOOK AND ACT HUMAN. WHY IS THAT, DO YOU THINK?
YES, YES, I KNOW.
WE MUST BE MOBILE IN ORDER TO CARRY OUT OUR DUTIES. STILL... THAT DOESN'T EXPLAIN WHY MAN MADE US IN HIS IMAGE.

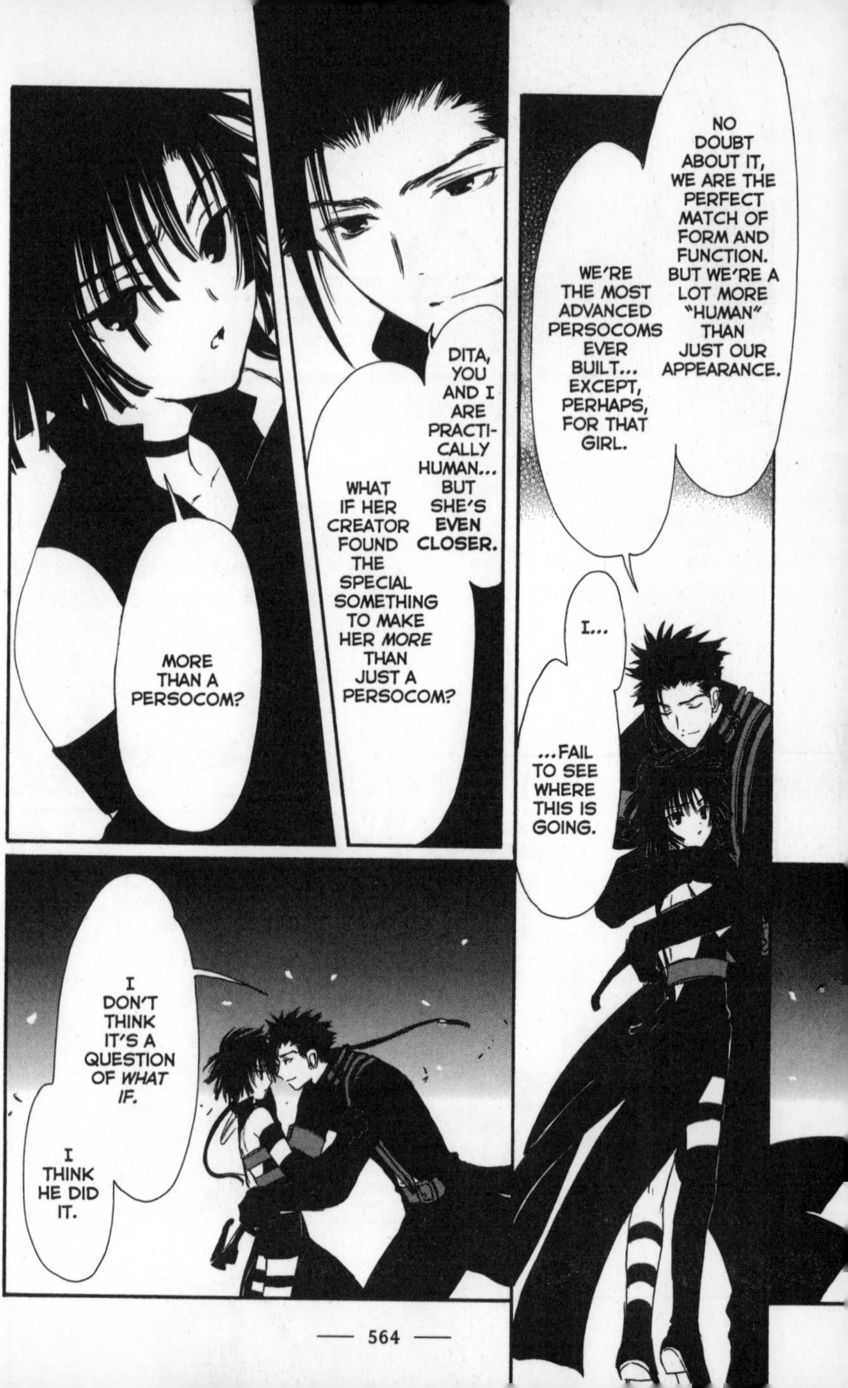
NO DOUBT ABOUT IT, WE ARE THE PERFECT MATCH OF FORM AND FUNCTION. BUT WE'RE A LOT MORE "HUMAN" THAN JUST OUR APPEARANCE.
WE'RE THE MOST ADVANCED PERSOCOMS EVER BUILT... EXCEPT, PERHAPS, FOR THAT GIRL.
I...
...FAIL TO SEE WHERE THIS IS GOING.
DITA, YOU AND I ARE PRACTICALLY HUMAN... BUT SHE'S EVEN CLOSER.
WHAT IF HER CREATOR FOUND THE SPECIAL SOMETHING TO MAKE HER *MORE* THAN JUST A PERSOCOM?
MORE THAN A PERSOCOM?
I DON'T THINK IT'S A QUESTION OF *WHAT IF.*
I THINK HE DID IT.

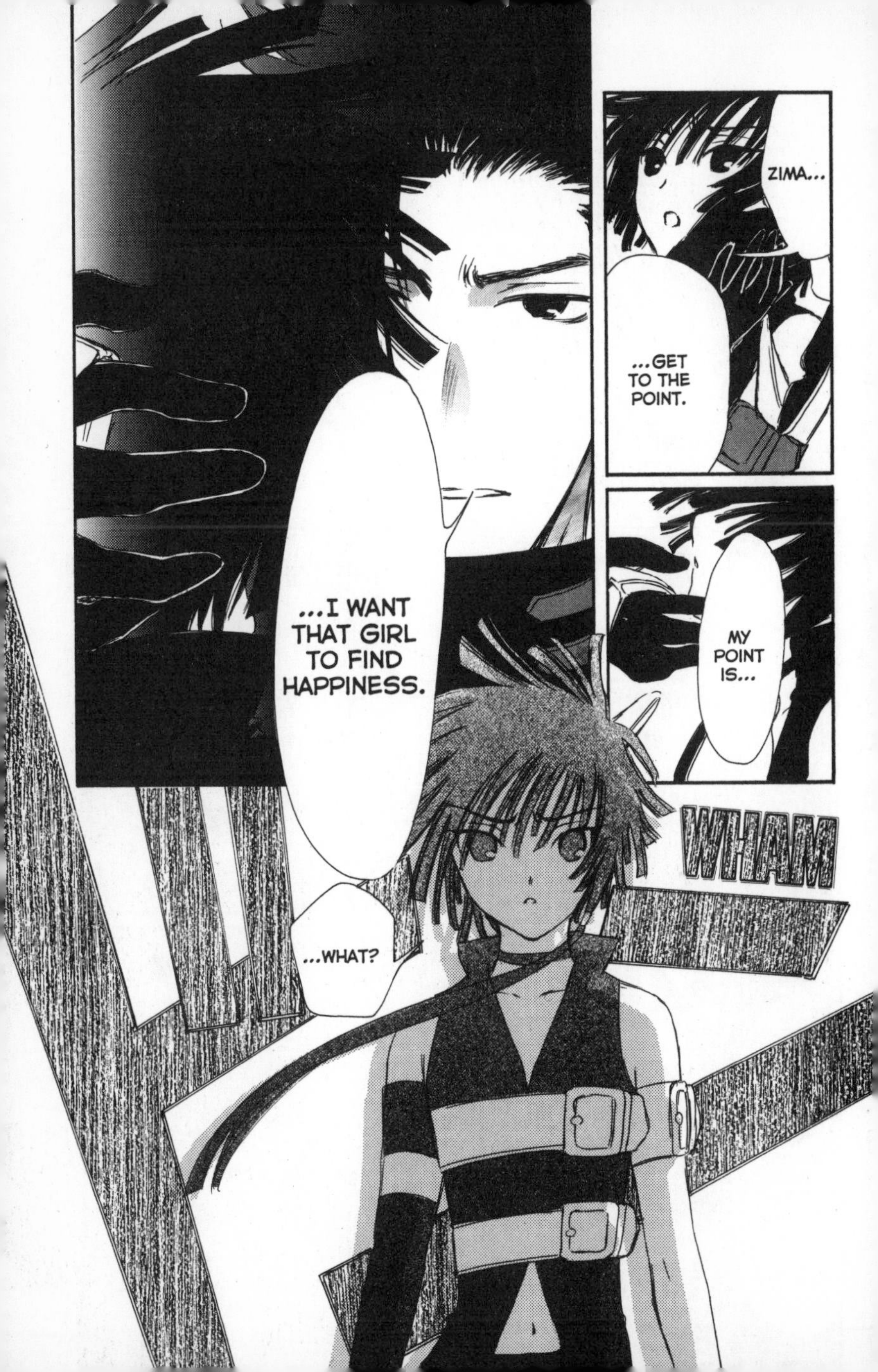
ZIMA...
...GET TO THE POINT.
MY POINT IS...
...I WANT THAT GIRL TO FIND HAPPINESS.
WHAM
...WHAT?

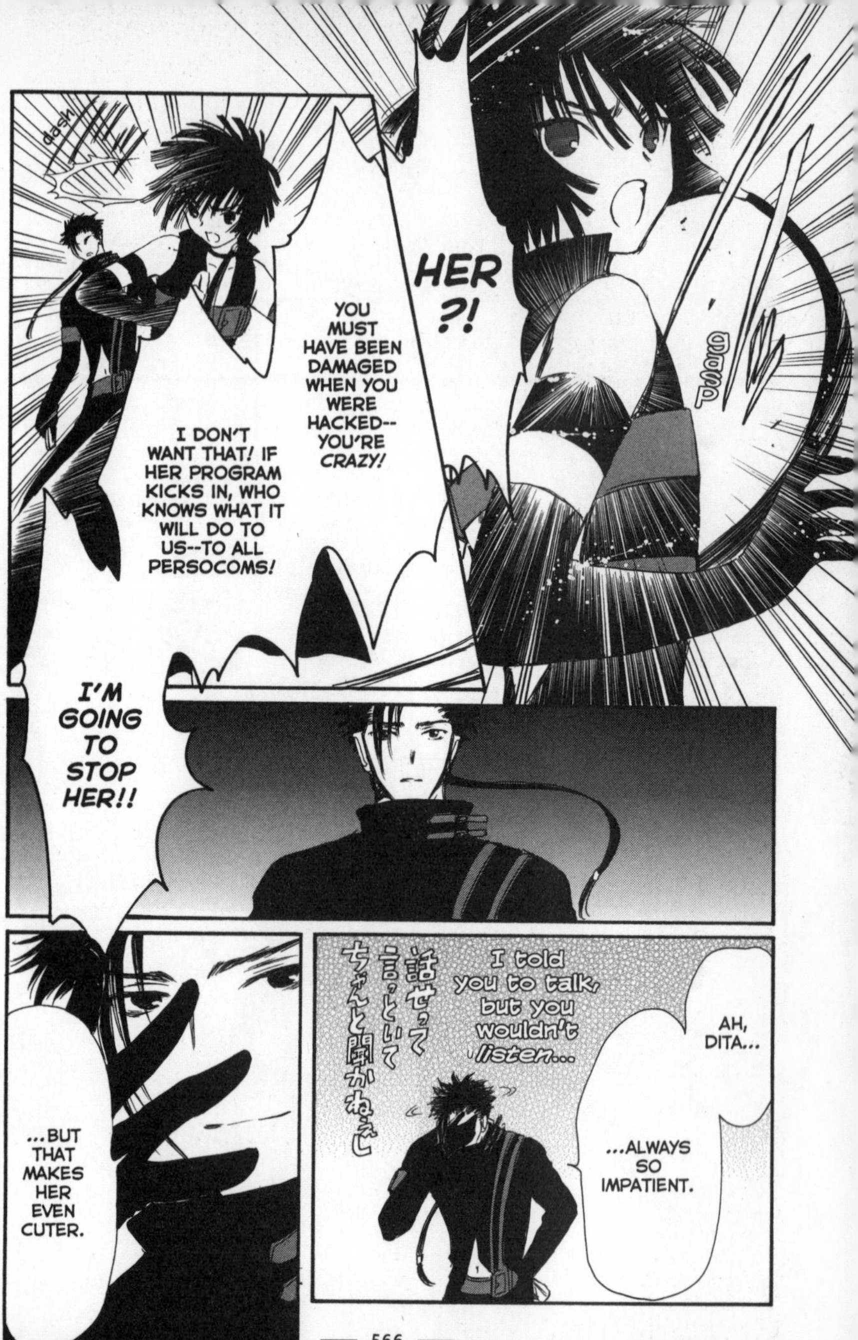
HER ?!
dash
dash
YOU MUST HAVE BEEN DAMAGED WHEN YOU WERE HACKED-- YOU'RE *CRAZY!*
I DON'T WANT THAT! IF HER PROGRAM KICKS IN, WHO KNOWS WHAT IT WILL DO TO US--TO ALL PERSOCOMS!
I'M GOING TO STOP HER!!
AH, DITA...
...ALWAYS SO IMPATIENT.
I told you to talk, but you wouldn't *listen*...
話せって言っといてちゃんと聞かねえし
...BUT THAT MAKES HER EVEN CUTER.

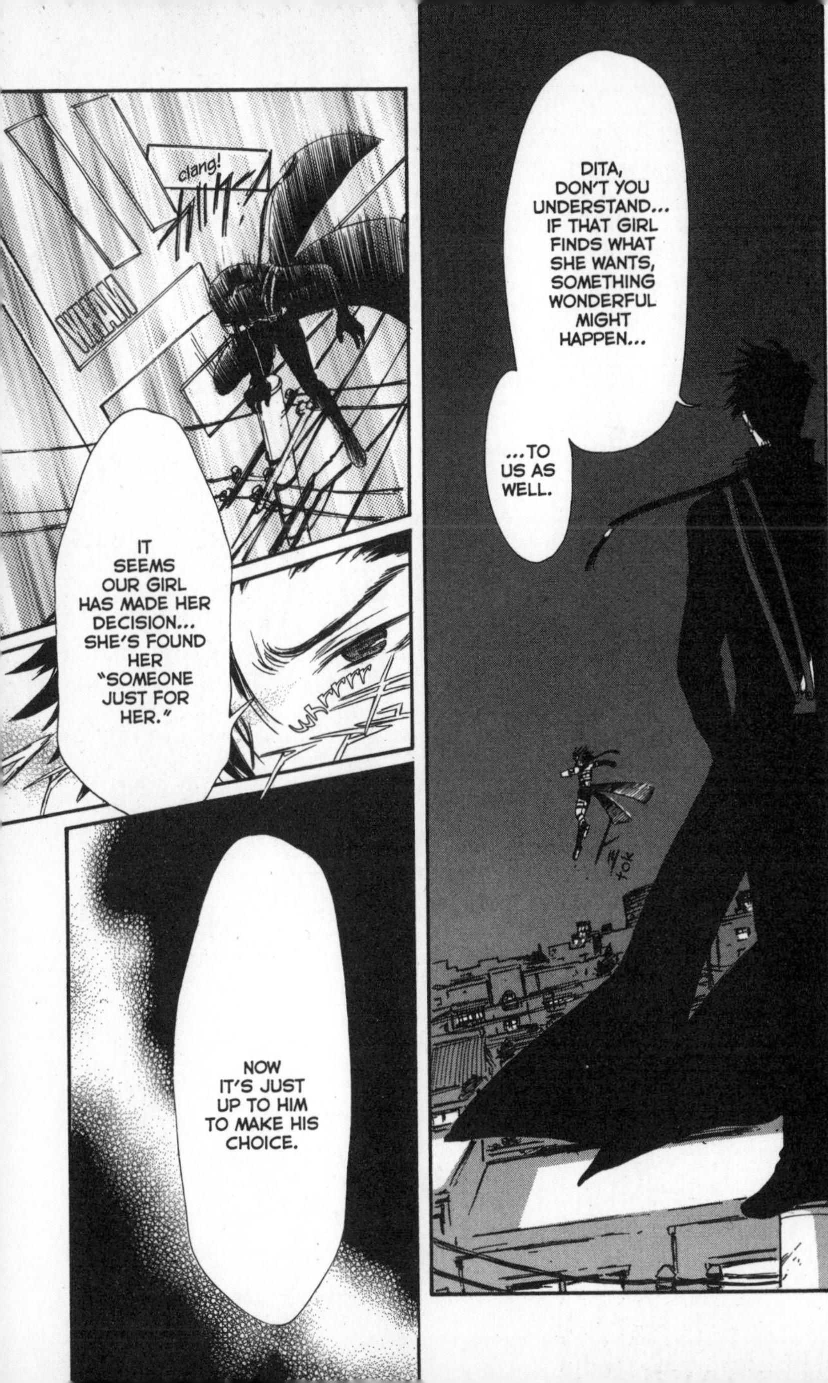
DITA, DON'T YOU UNDERSTAND... IF THAT GIRL FINDS WHAT SHE WANTS, SOMETHING WONDERFUL MIGHT HAPPEN...
...TO US AS WELL.
tok
clang!
WHAM
IT SEEMS OUR GIRL HAS MADE HER DECISION... SHE'S FOUND HER "SOMEONE JUST FOR HER."
whrrrr
NOW IT'S JUST UP TO HIM TO MAKE HIS CHOICE.

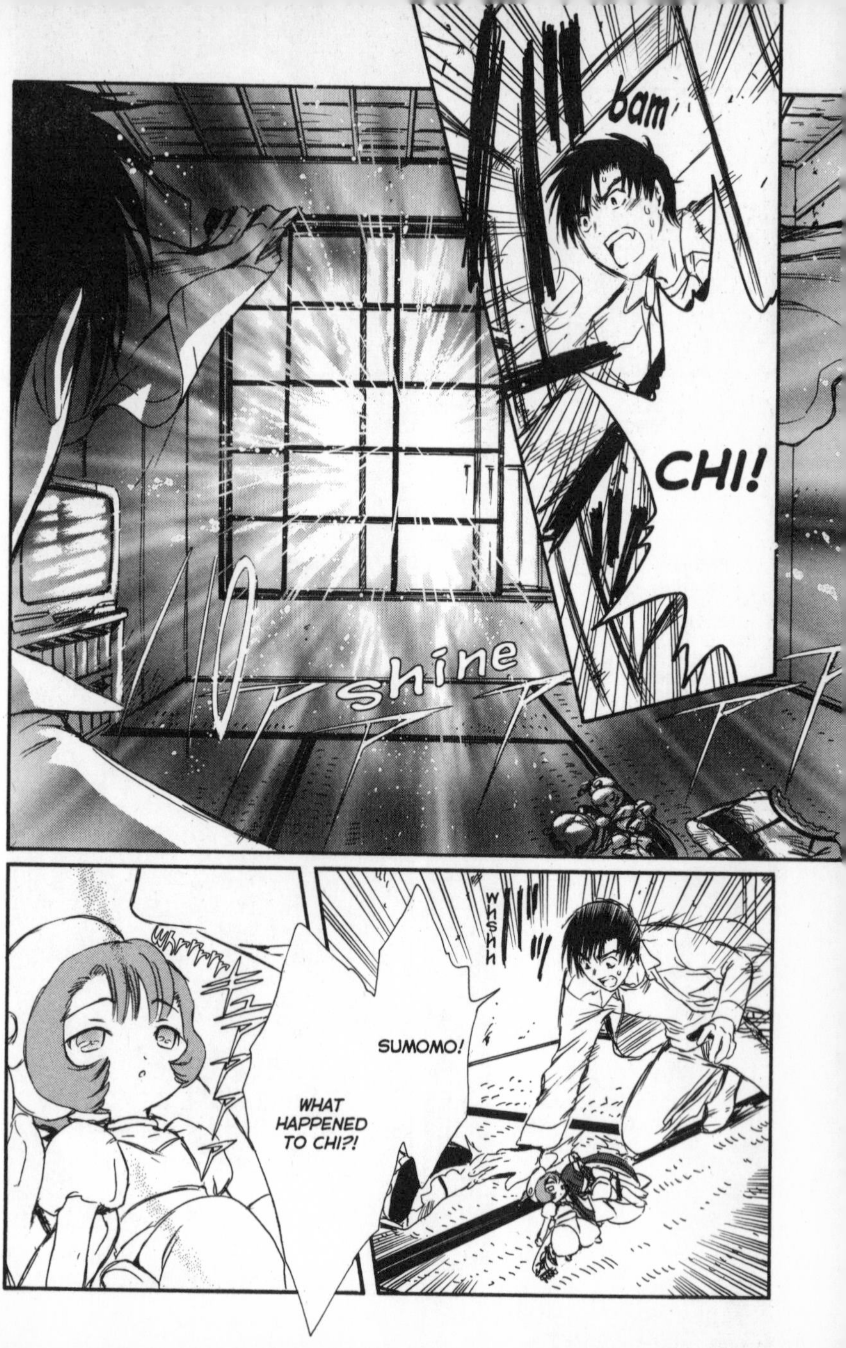
bam
CHI!
shine
whshh
SUMOMO!
WHAT HAPPENED TO CHI?!
whrrrrr

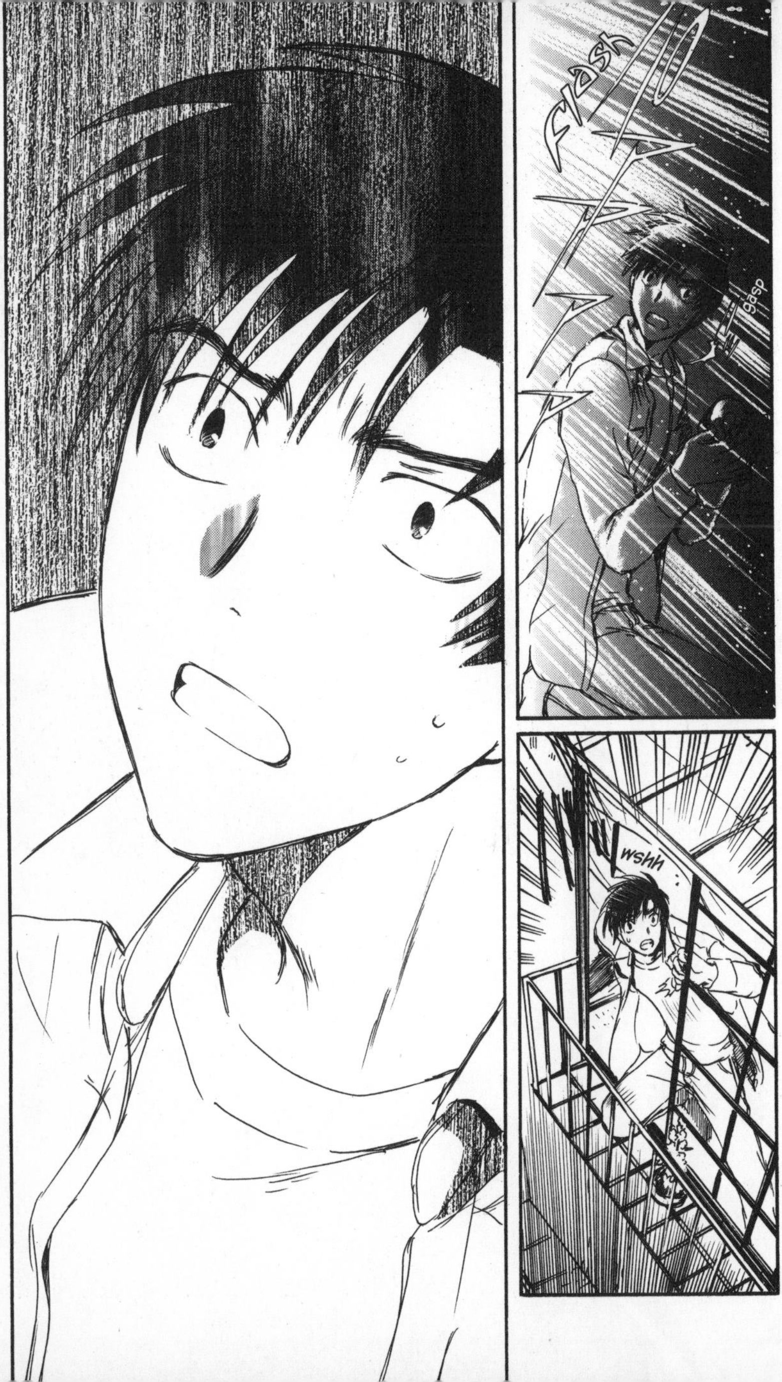
flash
gasp
wshh

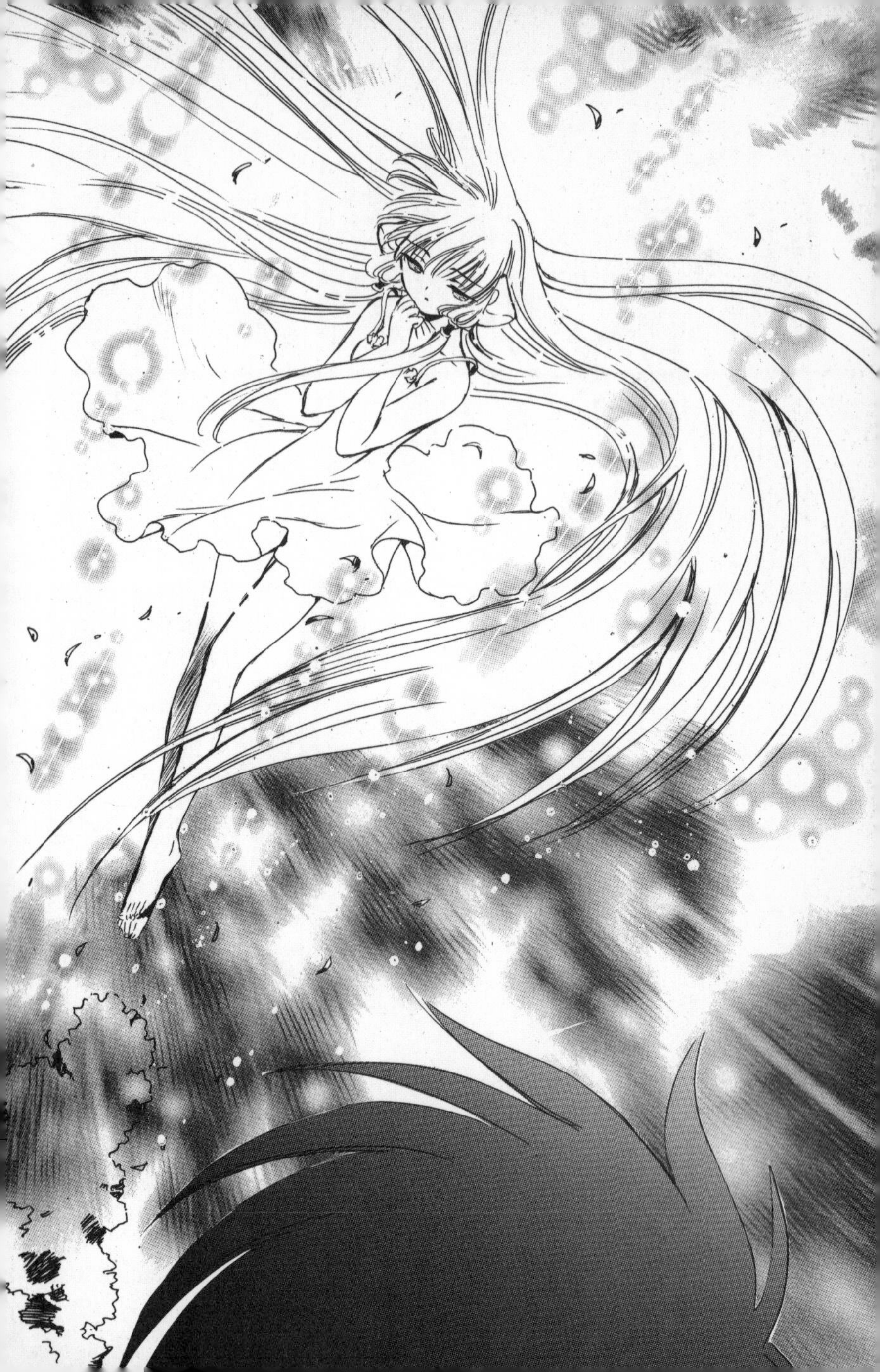

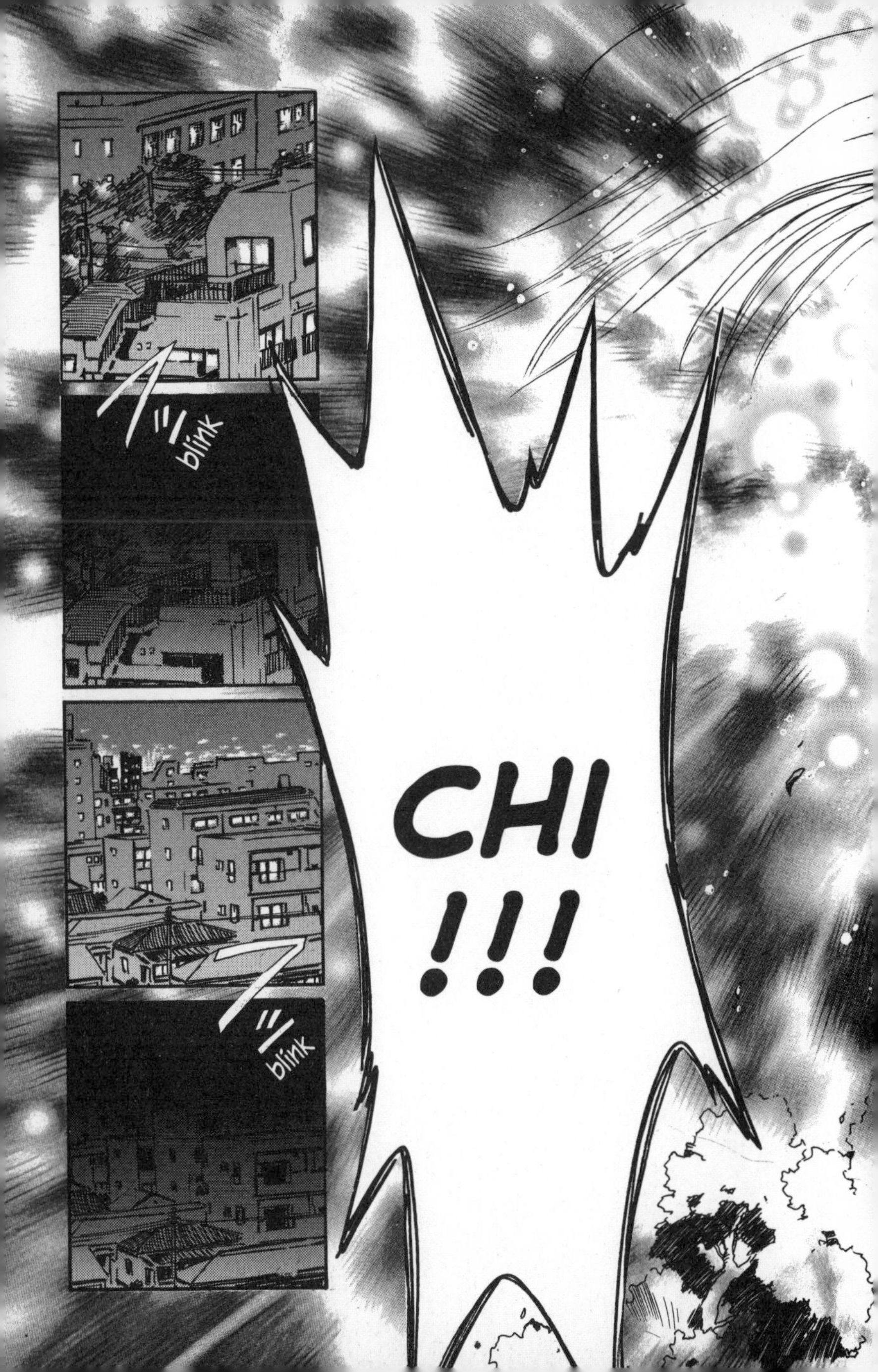
CHI
!!!
blink
blink

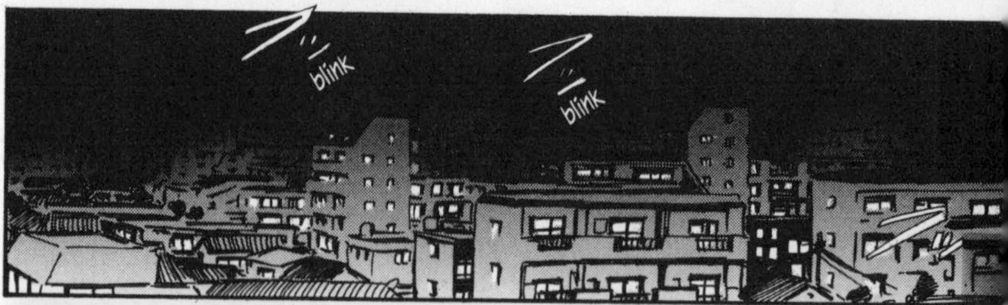
blink
blink
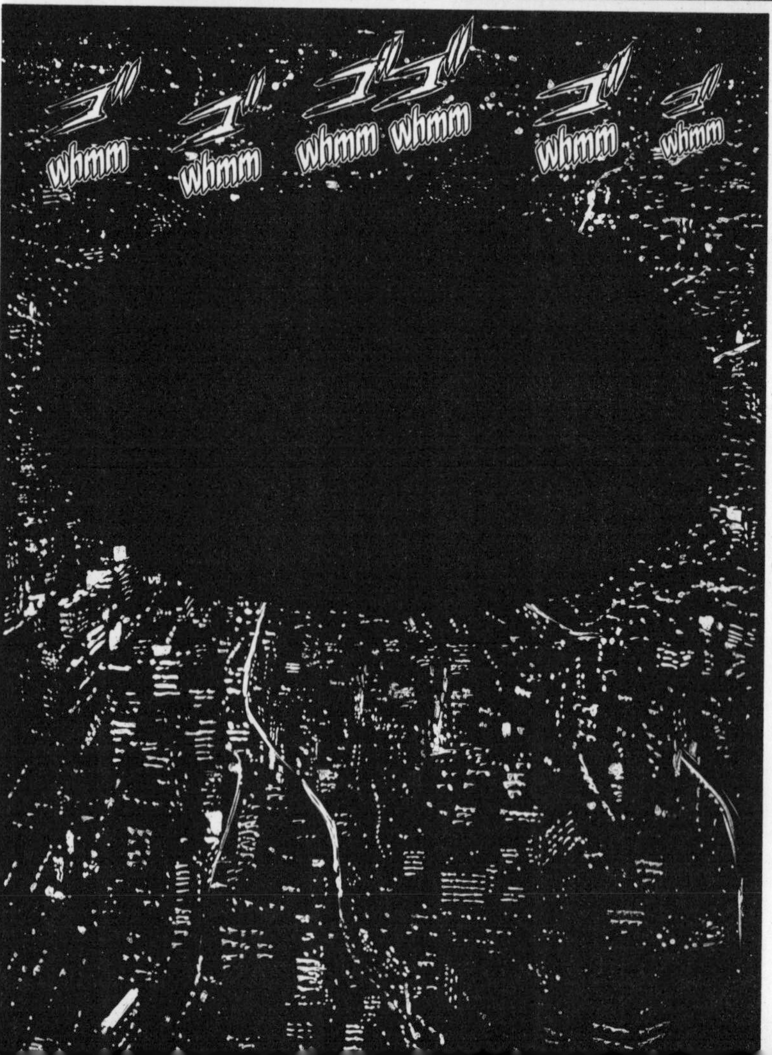
whmm
whmm
whmm
whmm
whmm
whmm

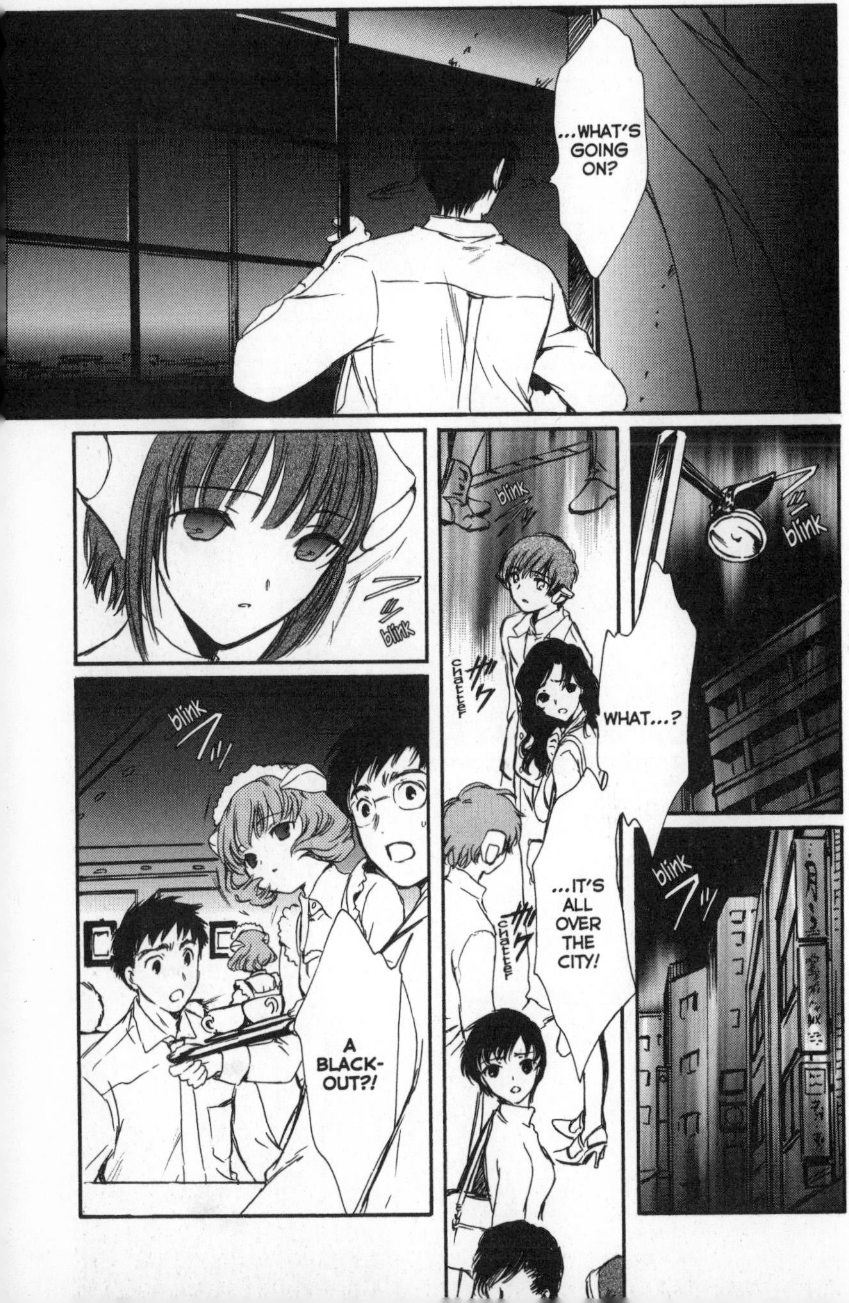
...WHAT'S GOING ON?
blink
blink
blink
chatter
WHAT...?
chatter
...IT'S ALL OVER THE CITY!
blink
blink
A BLACK-OUT?!

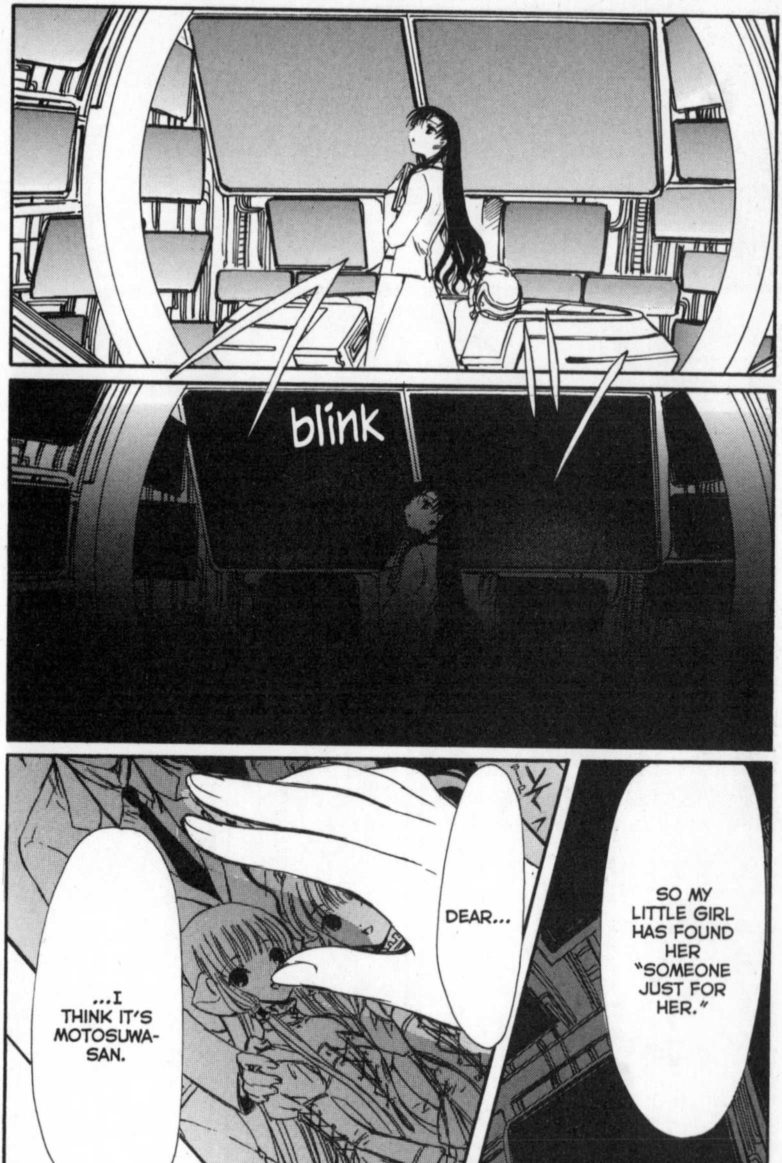
blink
SO MY LITTLE GIRL HAS FOUND HER "SOMEONE JUST FOR HER."
DEAR...
...I THINK IT'S MOTOSUWA-SAN.

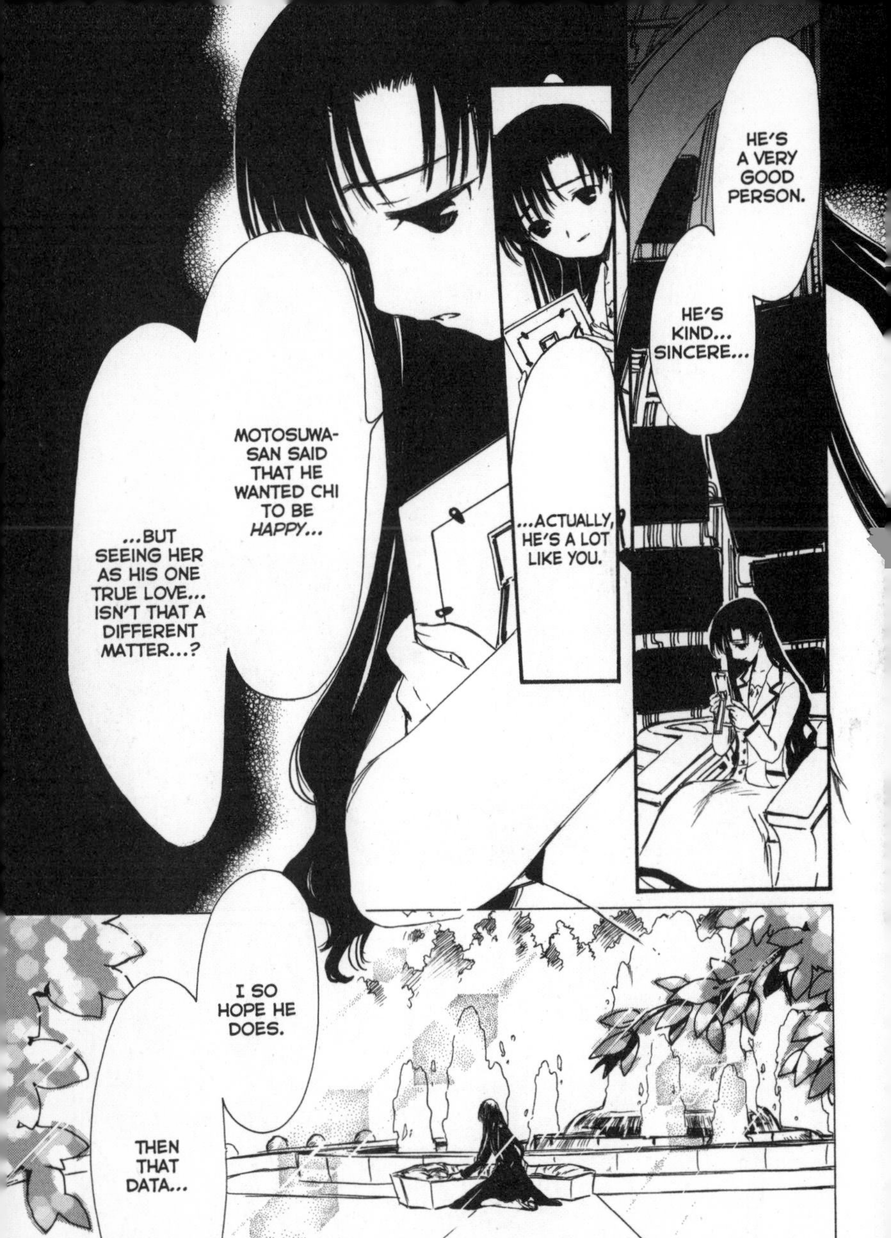
HE'S A VERY GOOD PERSON.
HE'S KIND... SINCERE...
...ACTUALLY, HE'S A LOT LIKE YOU.
MOTOSUWA-SAN SAID THAT HE WANTED CHI TO BE *HAPPY*...
...BUT SEEING HER AS HIS ONE TRUE LOVE... ISN'T THAT A DIFFERENT MATTER...?
I SO HOPE HE DOES.
THEN THAT DATA...

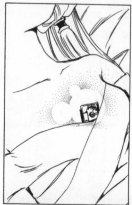

THEN CHI WON'T NEED THE *OTHER HER* ANYMORE.

THAT DISK...

...CONTAINS ALL OF ELDA'S OLD MEMORIES.

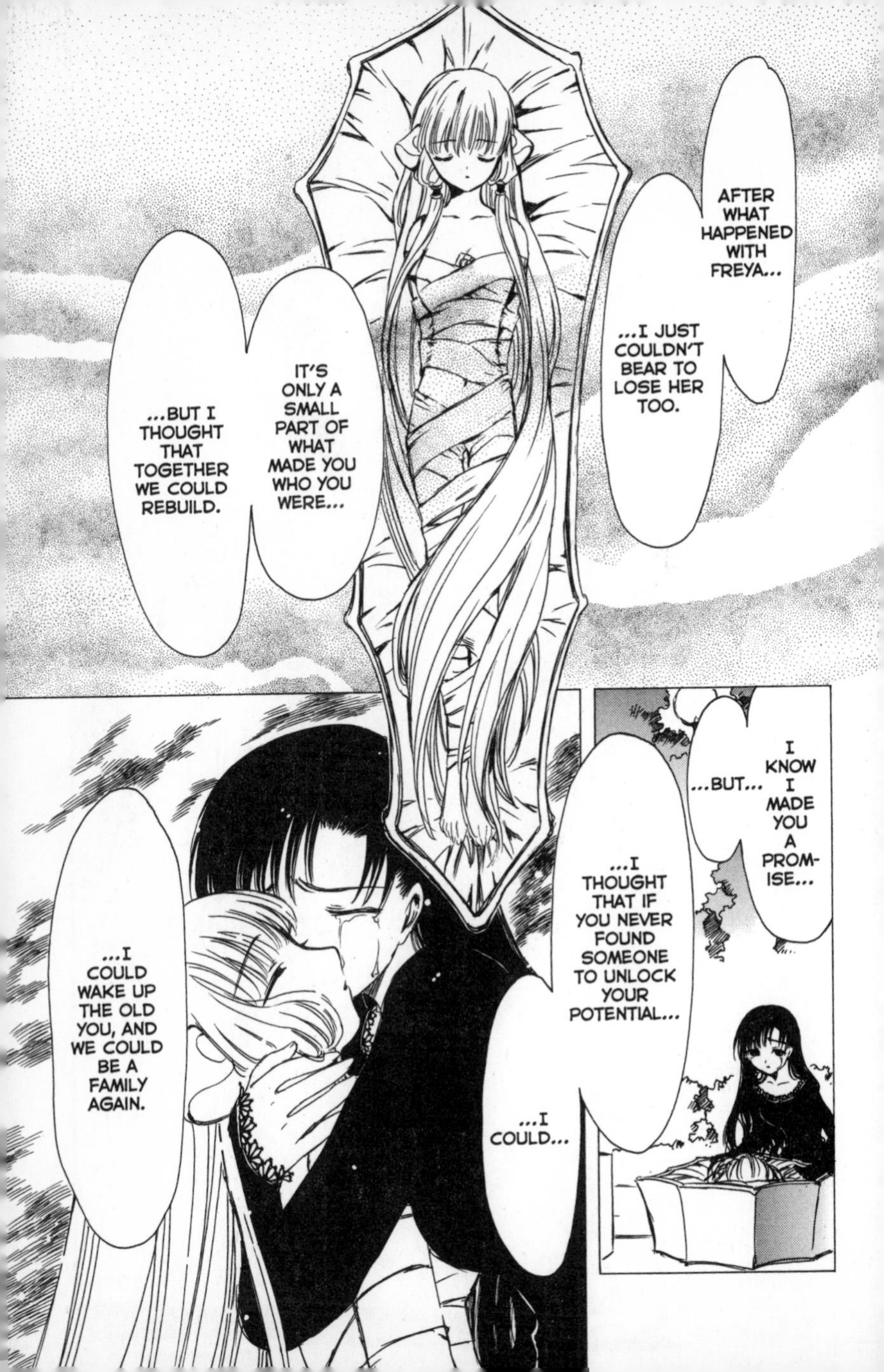
AFTER WHAT HAPPENED WITH FREYA...
...I JUST COULDN'T BEAR TO LOSE HER TOO.
IT'S ONLY A SMALL PART OF WHAT MADE YOU WHO YOU WERE...
...BUT I THOUGHT THAT TOGETHER WE COULD REBUILD.
I KNOW I MADE YOU A PROMISE...
...BUT...
...I THOUGHT THAT IF YOU NEVER FOUND SOMEONE TO UNLOCK YOUR POTENTIAL...
...I COULD...
...I COULD WAKE UP THE OLD YOU, AND WE COULD BE A FAMILY AGAIN.

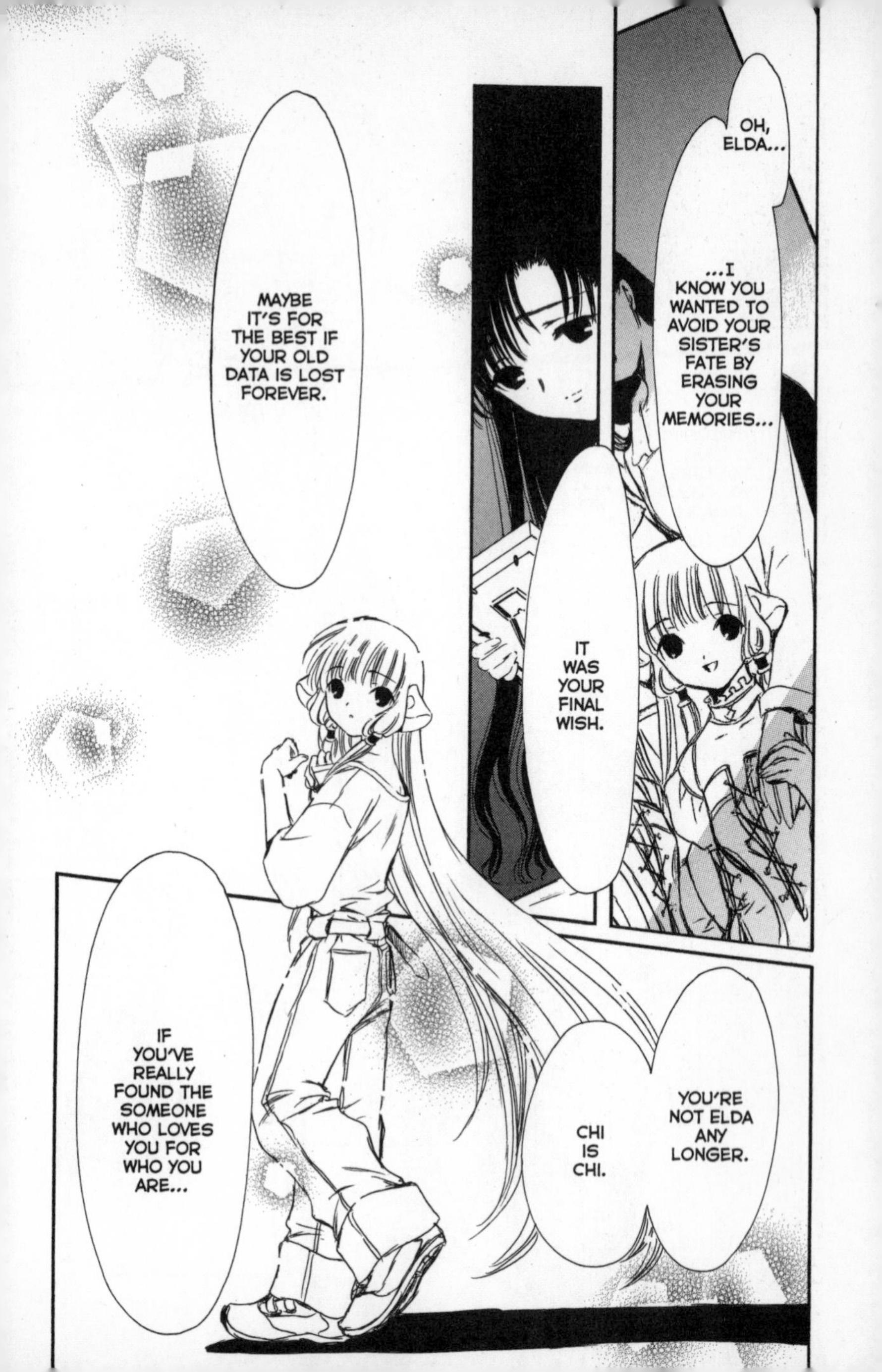
OH, ELDA...
...I KNOW YOU WANTED TO AVOID YOUR SISTER'S FATE BY ERASING YOUR MEMORIES...
IT WAS YOUR FINAL WISH.
MAYBE IT'S FOR THE BEST IF YOUR OLD DATA IS LOST FOREVER.
YOU'RE NOT ELDA ANY LONGER.
CHI IS CHI.
IF YOU'VE REALLY FOUND THE SOMEONE WHO LOVES YOU FOR WHO YOU ARE...

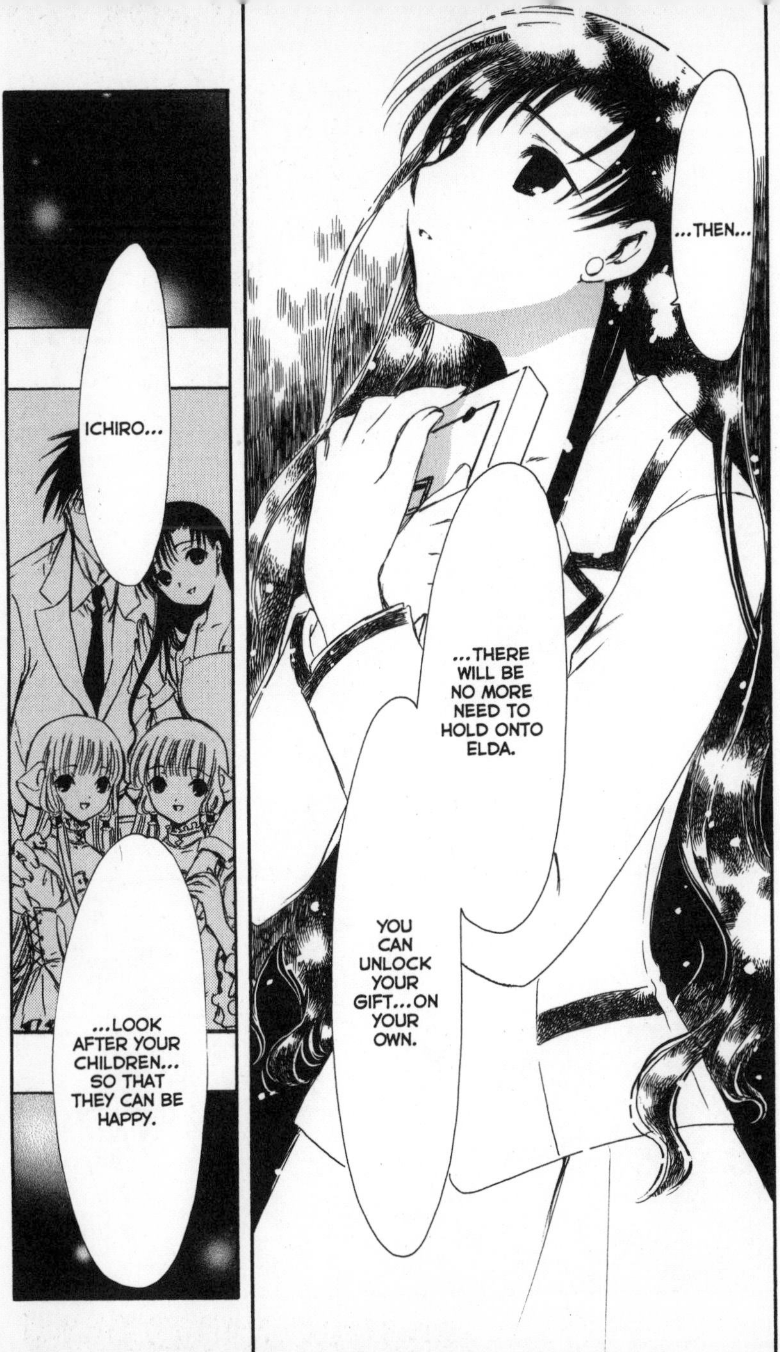
...THEN...
...THERE WILL BE NO MORE NEED TO HOLD ONTO ELDA.
YOU CAN UNLOCK YOUR GIFT...ON YOUR OWN.
ICHIRO...
...LOOK AFTER YOUR CHILDREN... SO THAT THEY CAN BE HAPPY.

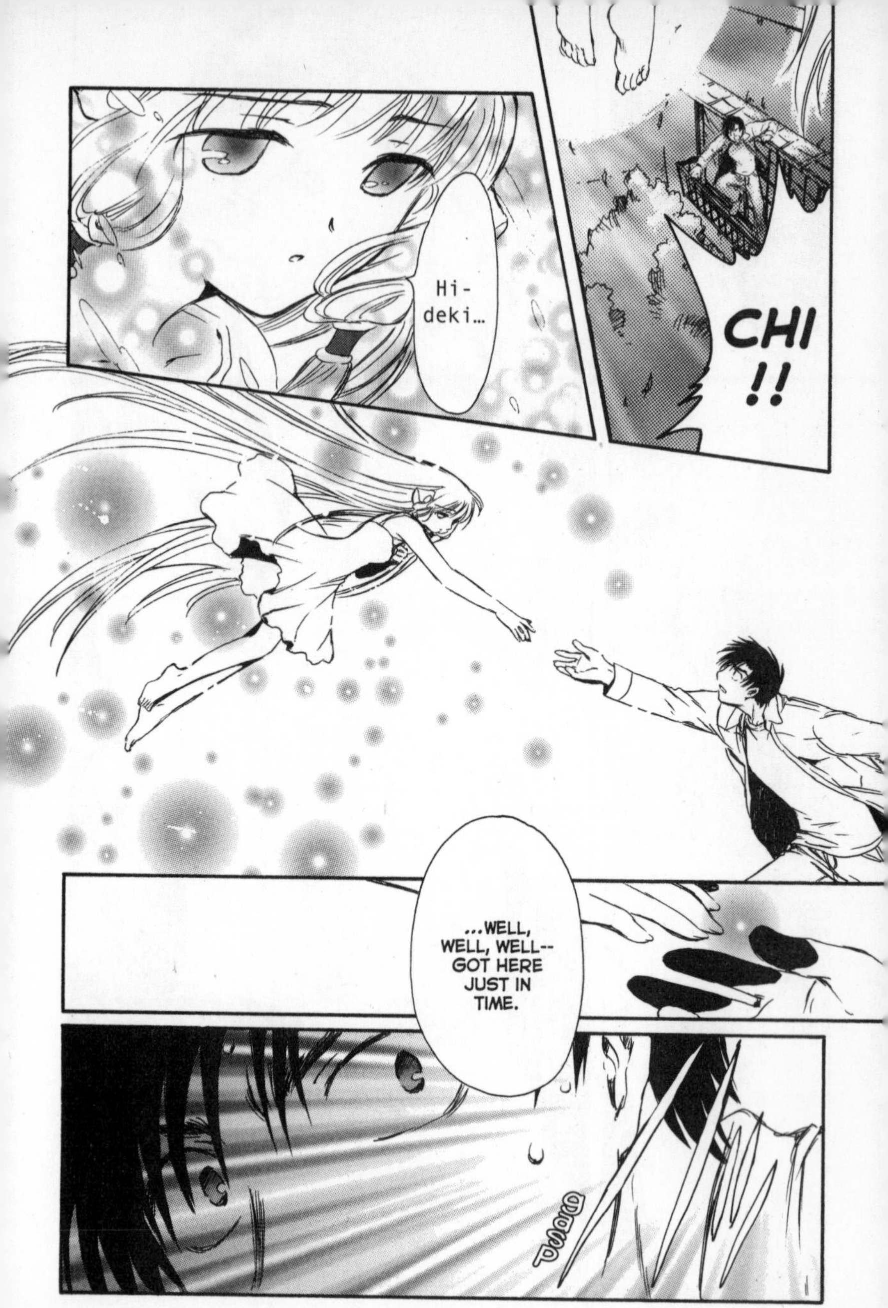
CHI !!
Hi-deki…
...WELL, WELL, WELL-- GOT HERE JUST IN TIME.

Chobits
ちょびっツ

◀ **chapter 83** ▶

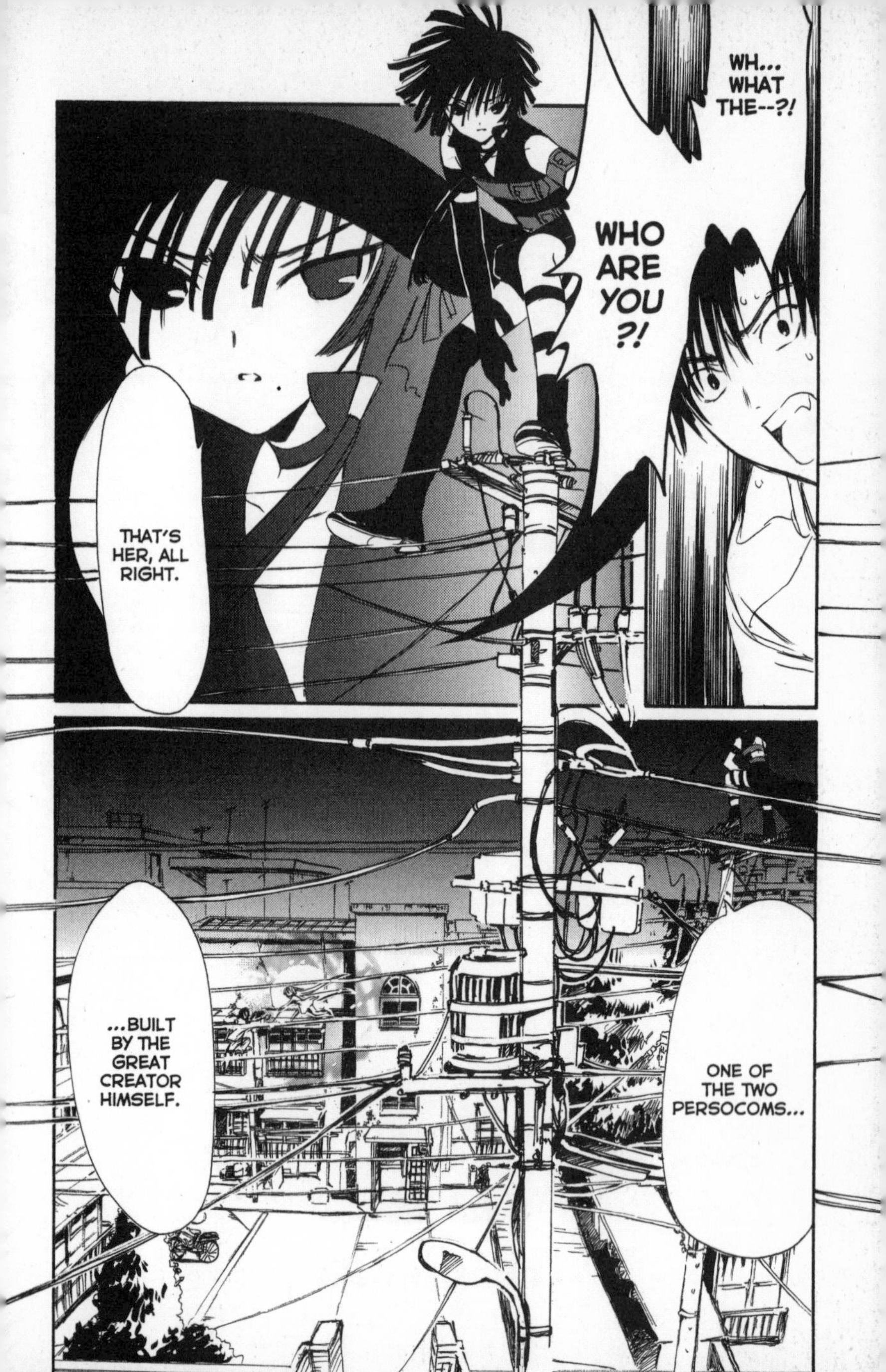
WH... WHAT THE--?!
WHO ARE YOU ?!
THAT'S HER, ALL RIGHT.
ONE OF THE TWO PERSOCOMS...
...BUILT BY THE GREAT CREATOR HIMSELF.

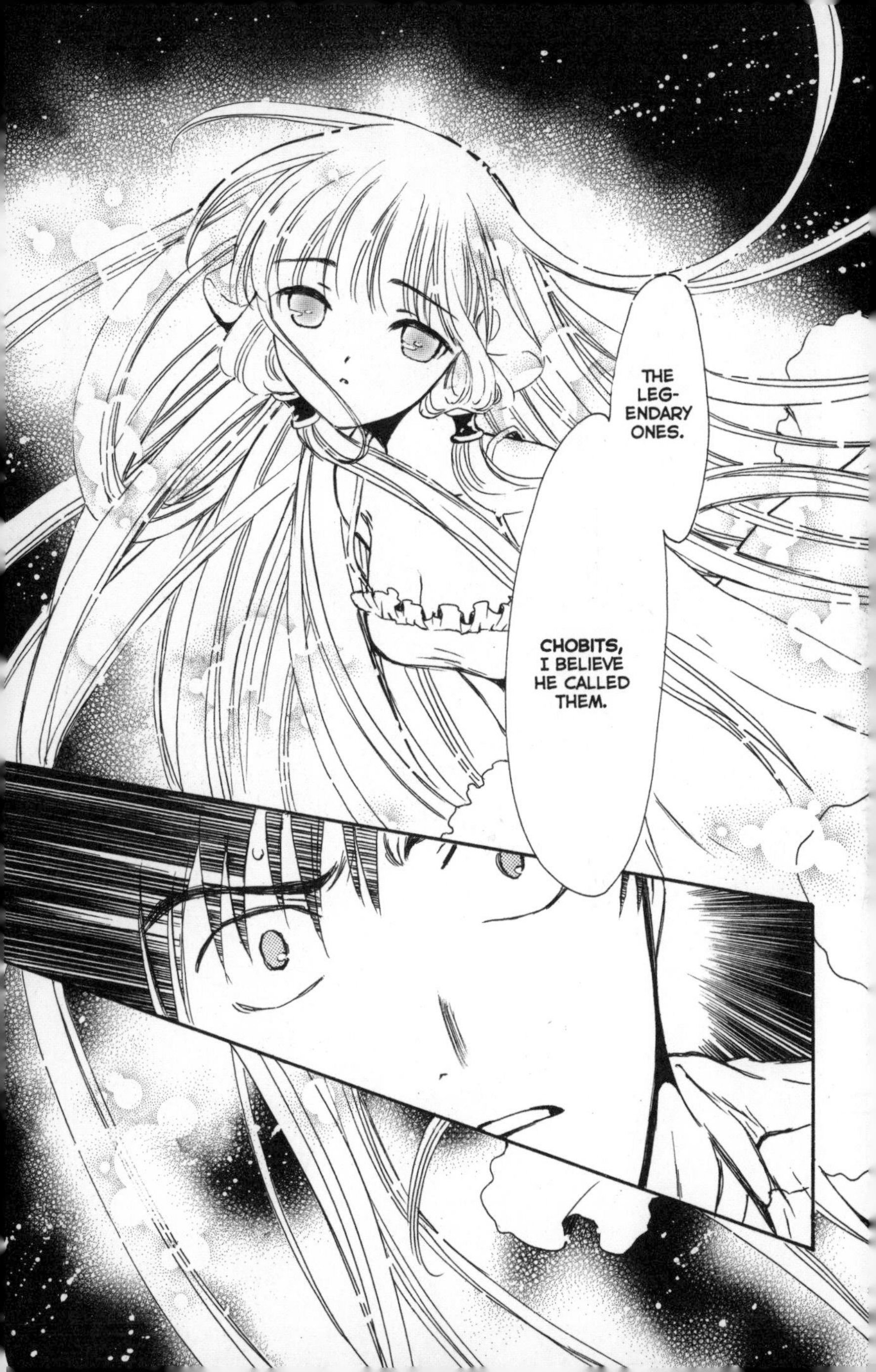
THE LEG-ENDARY ONES.
CHOBITS, I BELIEVE HE CALLED THEM.

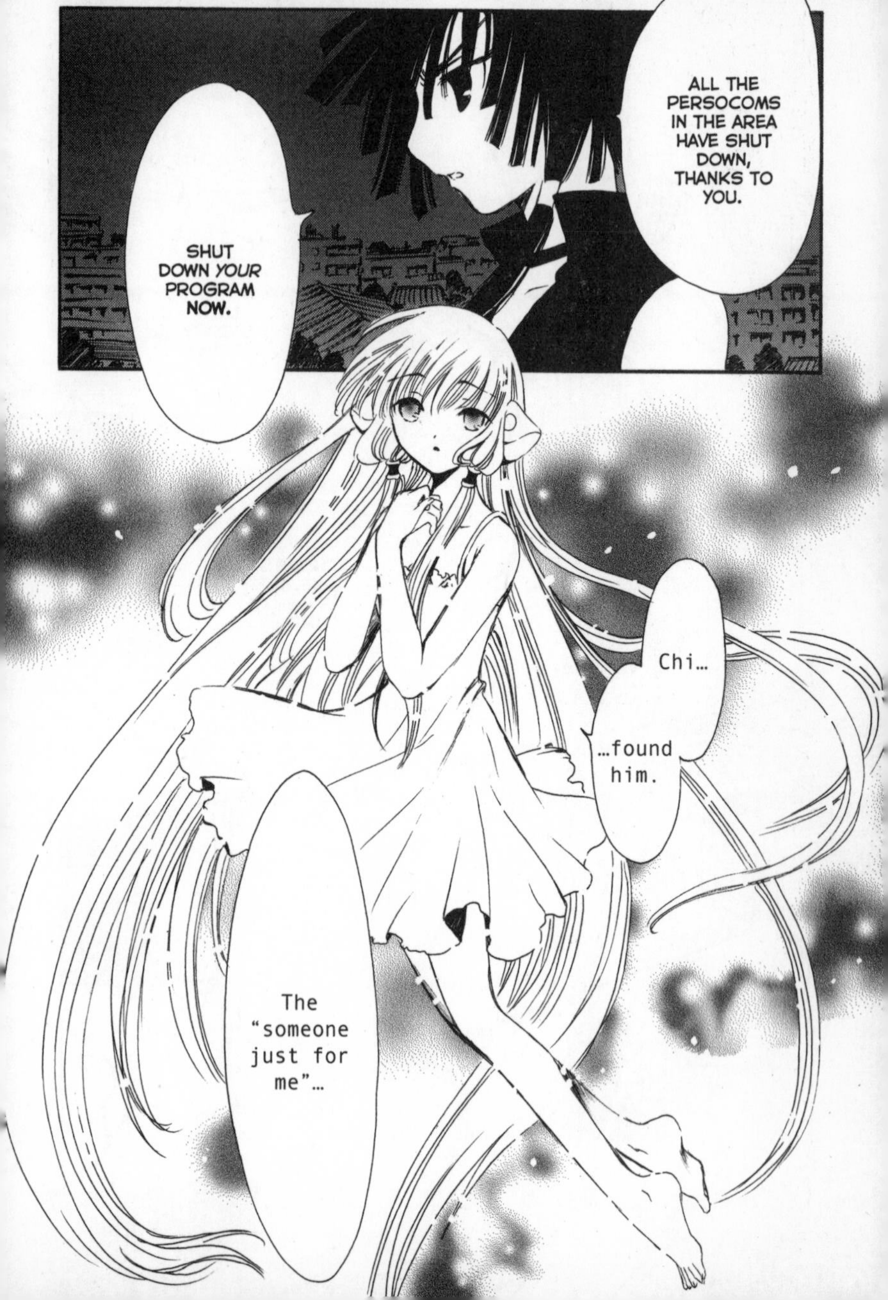
ALL THE PERSOCOMS IN THE AREA HAVE SHUT DOWN, THANKS TO YOU.
SHUT DOWN *YOUR* PROGRAM NOW.
Chi…
…found him.
The “someone just for me”…

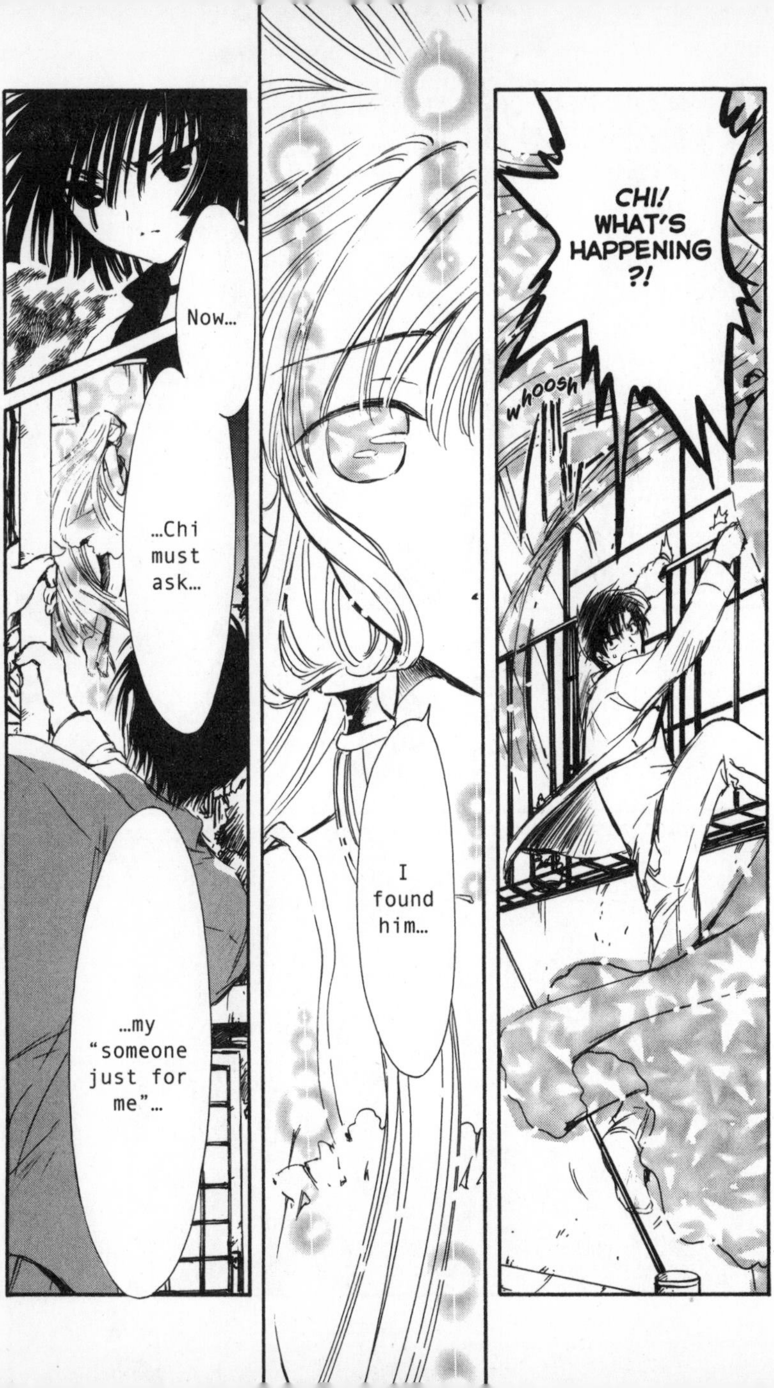
CHI! WHAT'S HAPPENING ?!
whoosh
I found him...
Now...
...Chi must ask...
...my "someone just for me"...

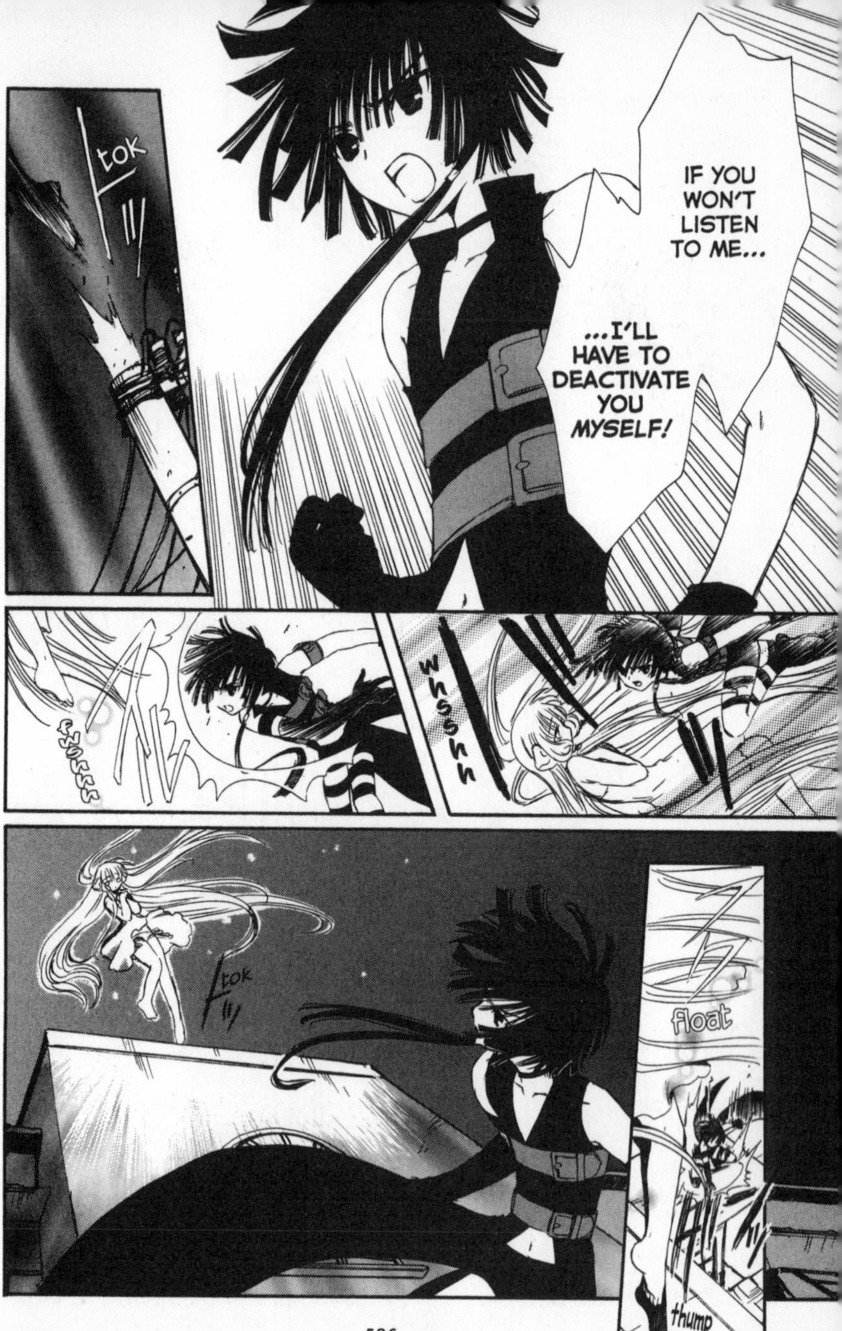
IF YOU WON'T LISTEN TO ME...
...I'LL HAVE TO DEACTIVATE YOU *MYSELF!*
tok
whsshh
fwshhh
float
thump
tok

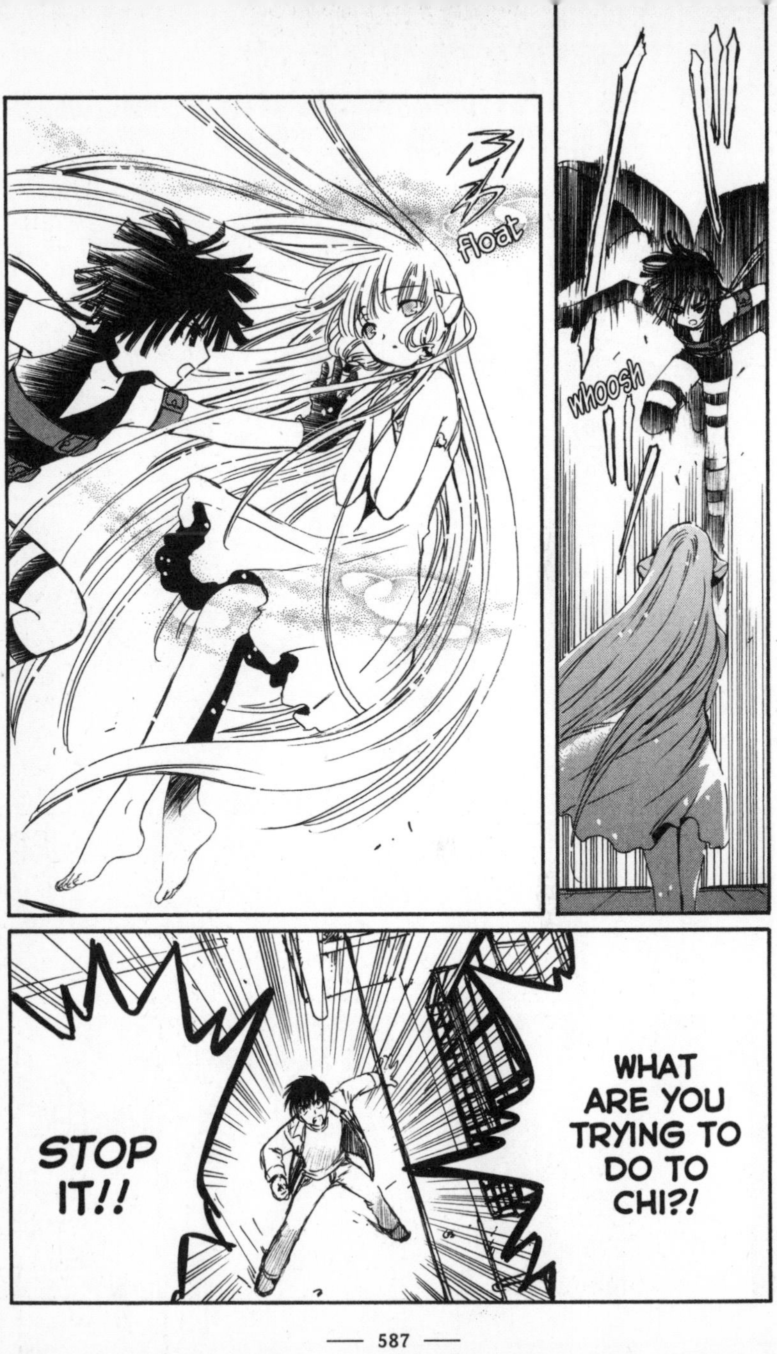
whoosh
ふわ
float
WHAT ARE YOU TRYING TO DO TO CHI?!
STOP IT!!

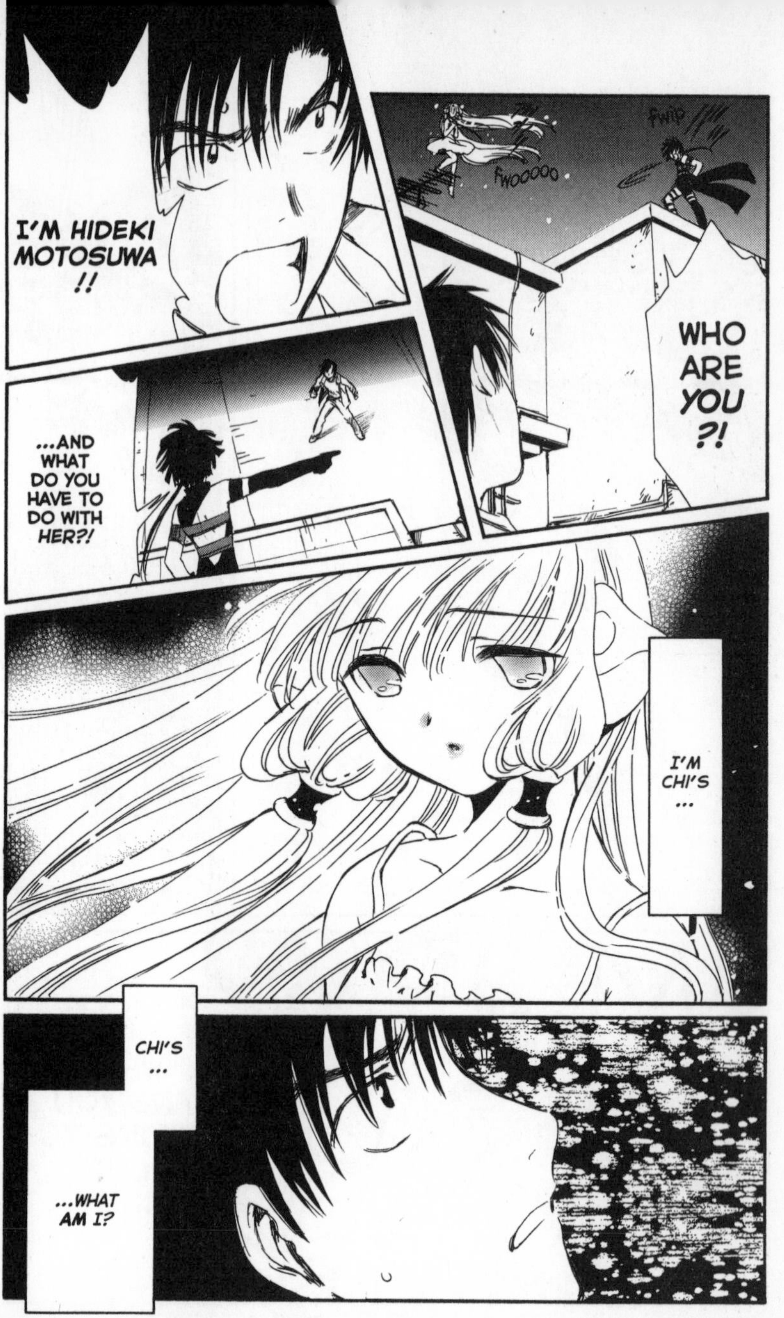
FWIP
FWOOOOO
WHO ARE YOU ?!
I'M HIDEKI MOTOSUWA !!
...AND WHAT DO YOU HAVE TO DO WITH HER?!
I'M CHI'S ...
CHI'S ...
...WHAT AM I?

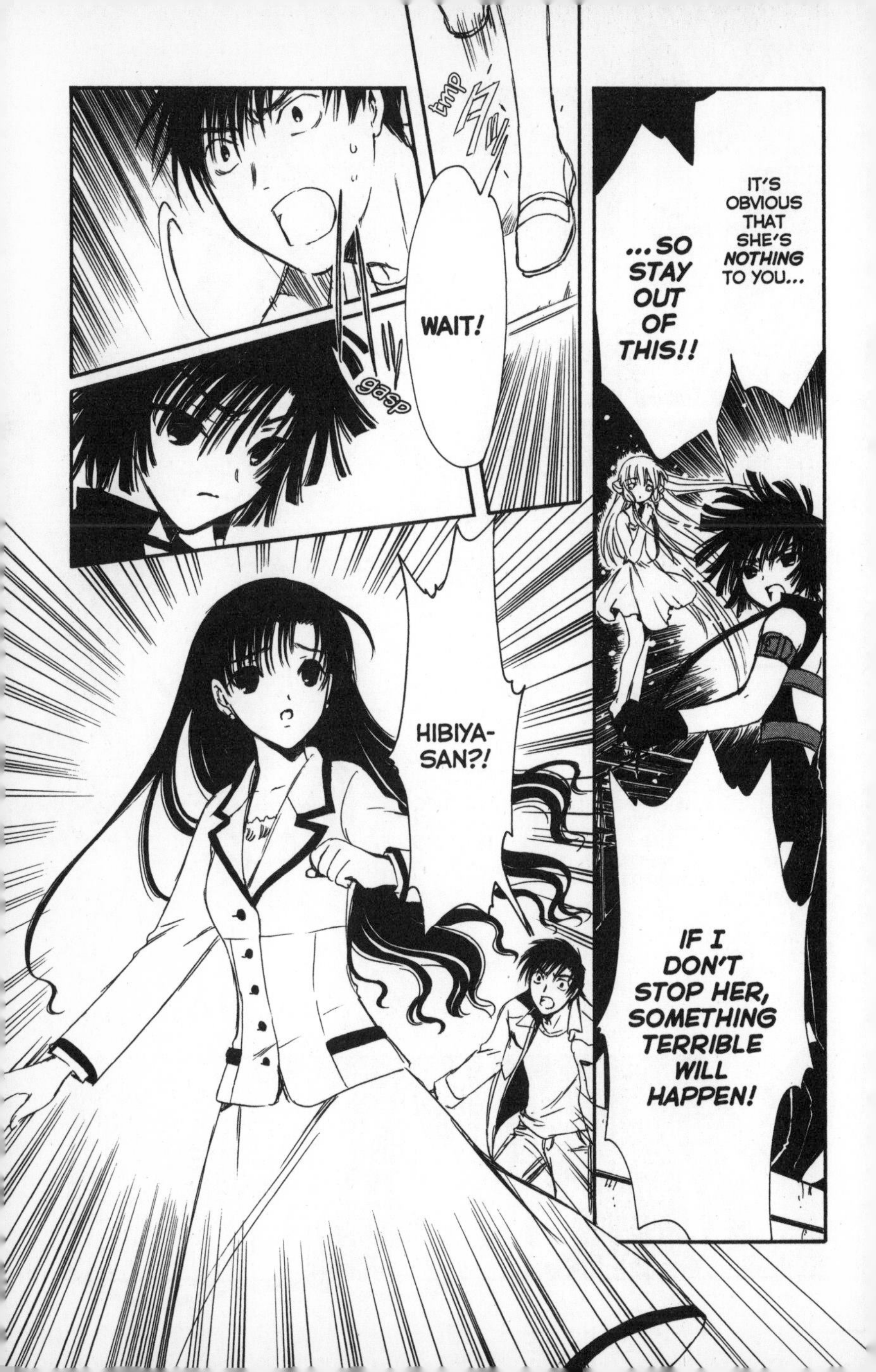
IT'S OBVIOUS THAT SHE'S *NOTHING* TO YOU...
...SO STAY OUT OF THIS!!
IF I DON'T STOP HER, SOMETHING TERRIBLE WILL HAPPEN!
tmp
WAIT!
gasp
HIBIYA-SAN?!

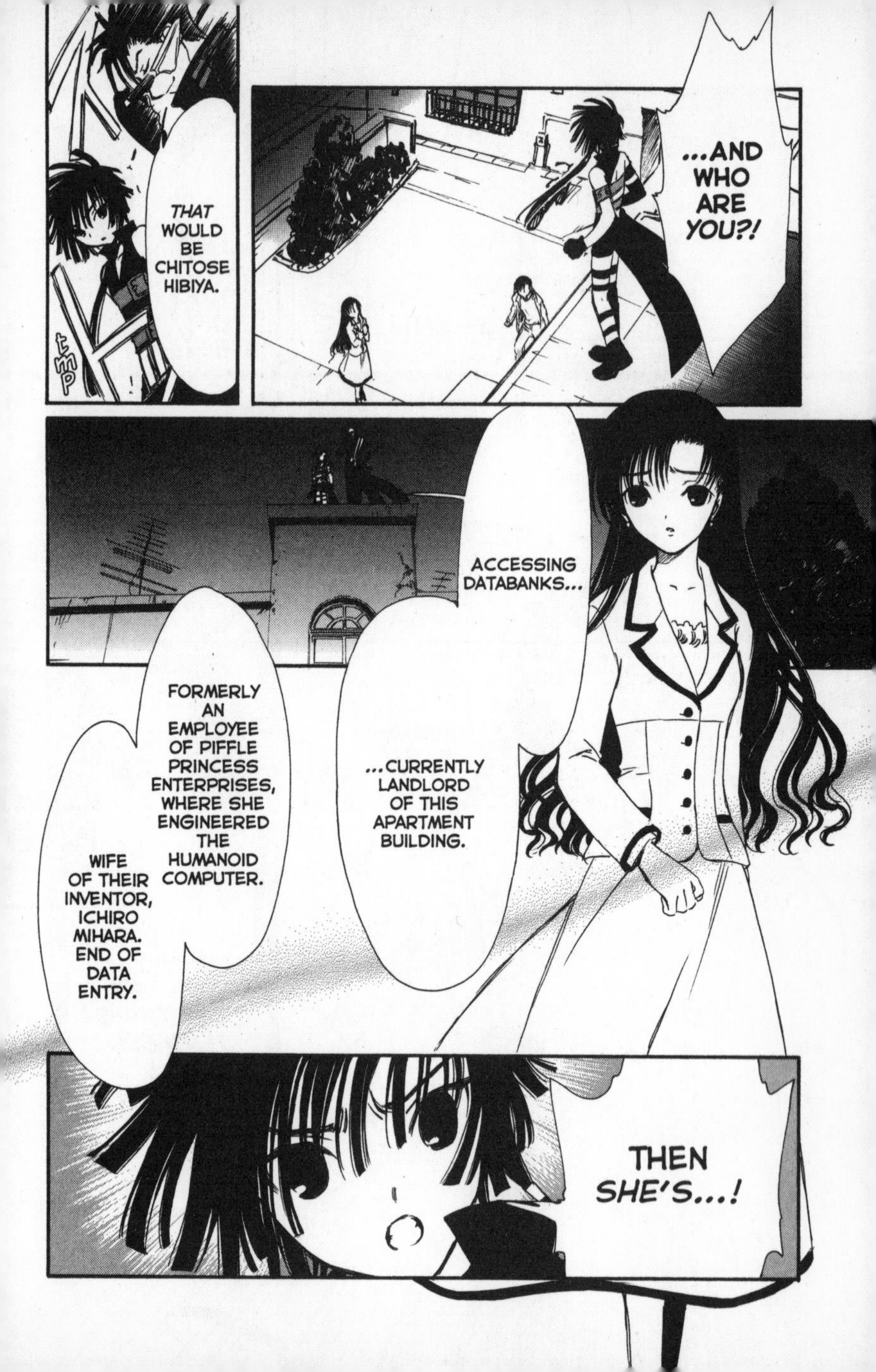
...AND WHO ARE *YOU?!*
THAT WOULD BE CHITOSE HIBIYA.
tmp
ACCESSING DATABANKS...
...CURRENTLY LANDLORD OF THIS APARTMENT BUILDING.
FORMERLY AN EMPLOYEE OF PIFFLE PRINCESS ENTERPRISES, WHERE SHE ENGINEERED THE HUMANOID COMPUTER.
WIFE OF THEIR INVENTOR, ICHIRO MIHARA. END OF DATA ENTRY.
THEN *SHE'S...!*

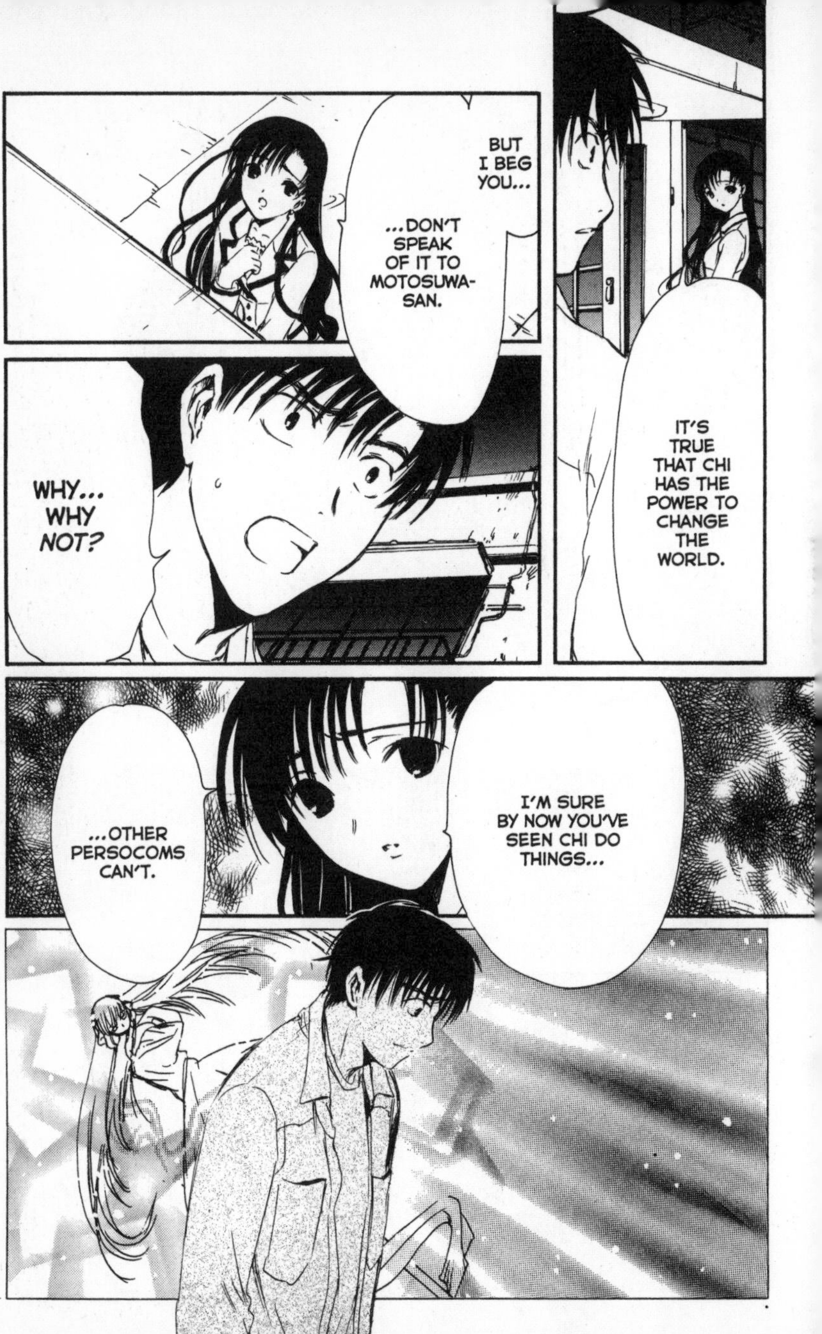
IT'S TRUE THAT CHI HAS THE POWER TO CHANGE THE WORLD.
BUT I BEG YOU...
...DON'T SPEAK OF IT TO MOTOSUWA-SAN.
WHY... WHY NOT?
I'M SURE BY NOW YOU'VE SEEN CHI DO THINGS...
...OTHER PERSOCOMS CAN'T.

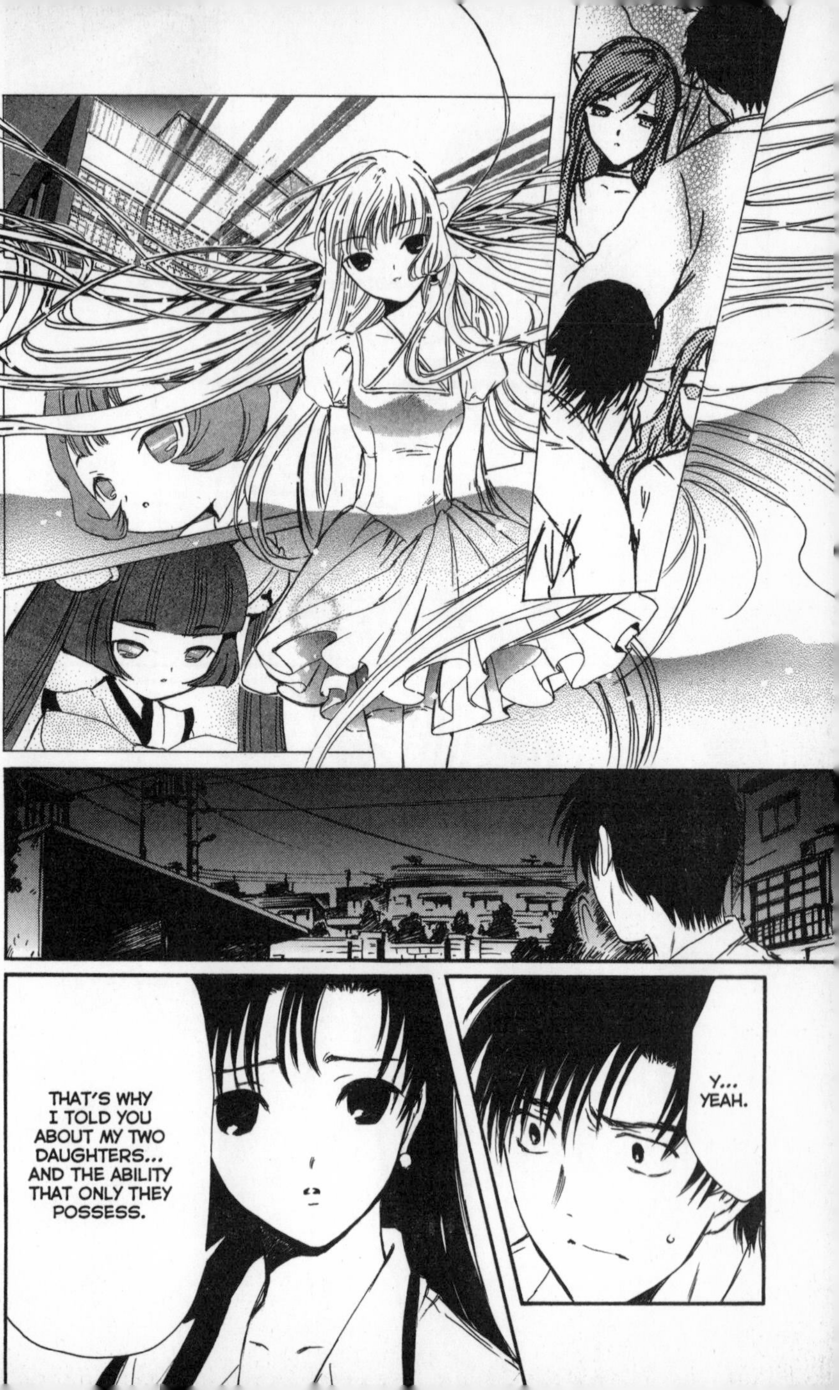
Y... YEAH.
THAT'S WHY I TOLD YOU ABOUT MY TWO DAUGHTERS... AND THE ABILITY THAT ONLY THEY POSSESS.

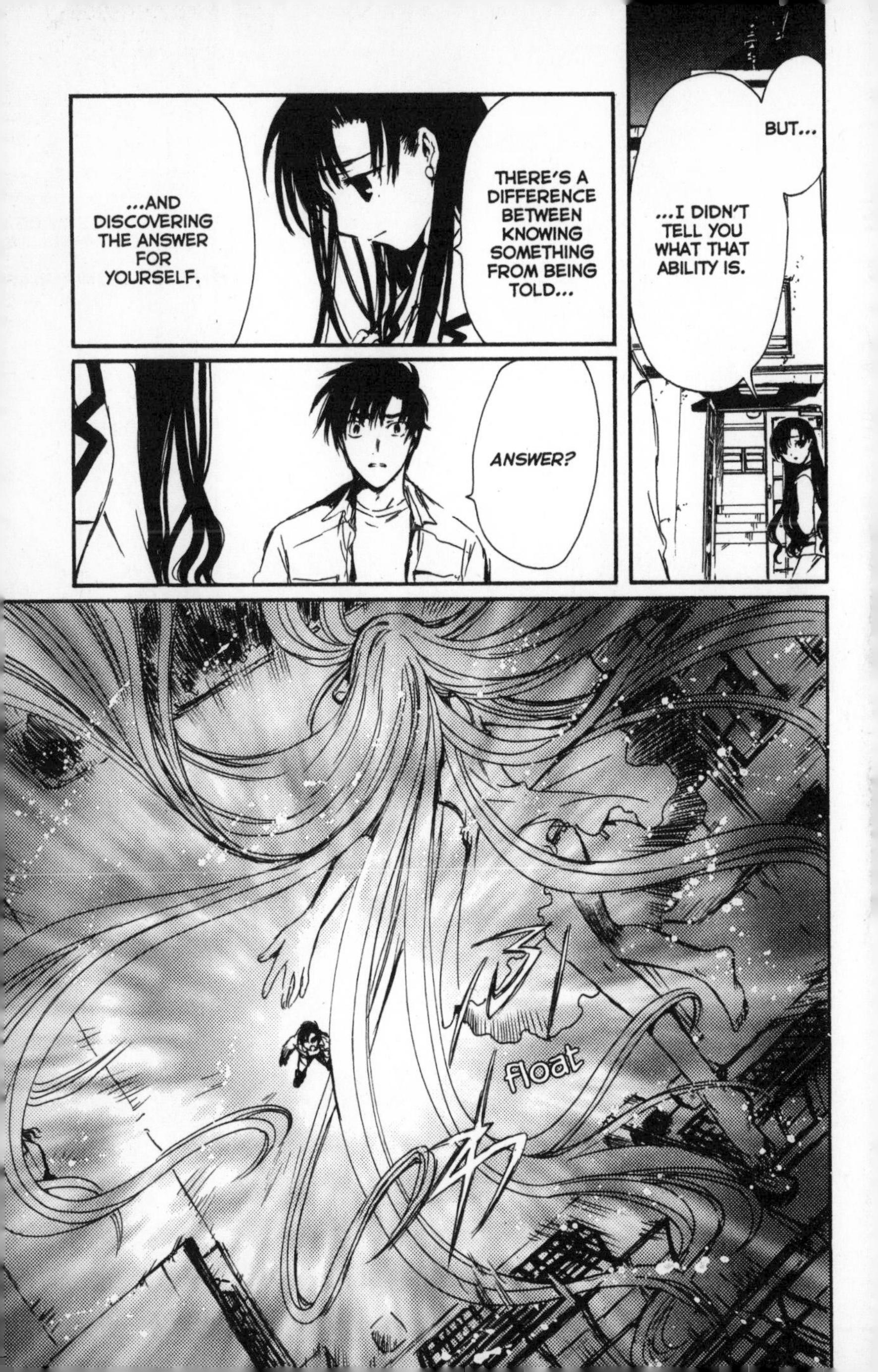
BUT...
...I DIDN'T TELL YOU WHAT THAT ABILITY IS.
THERE'S A DIFFERENCE BETWEEN KNOWING SOMETHING FROM BEING TOLD...
...AND DISCOVERING THE ANSWER FOR YOURSELF.
ANSWER?
float

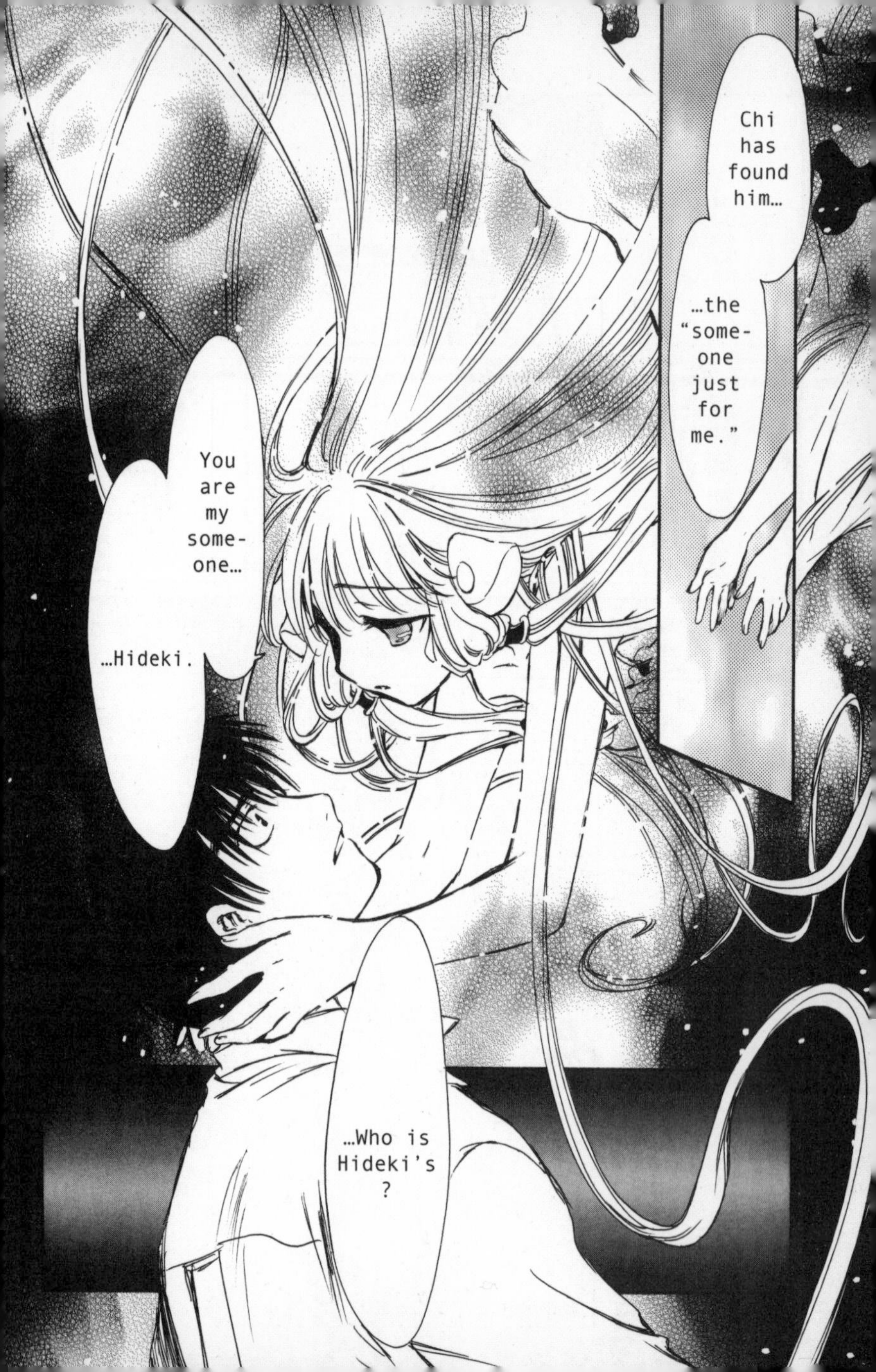
Chi has found him…
…the "someone just for me."
You are my someone…
…Hideki.
…Who is Hideki's ?

Chobits
ちょびっツ

◀ chapter 84 ▶

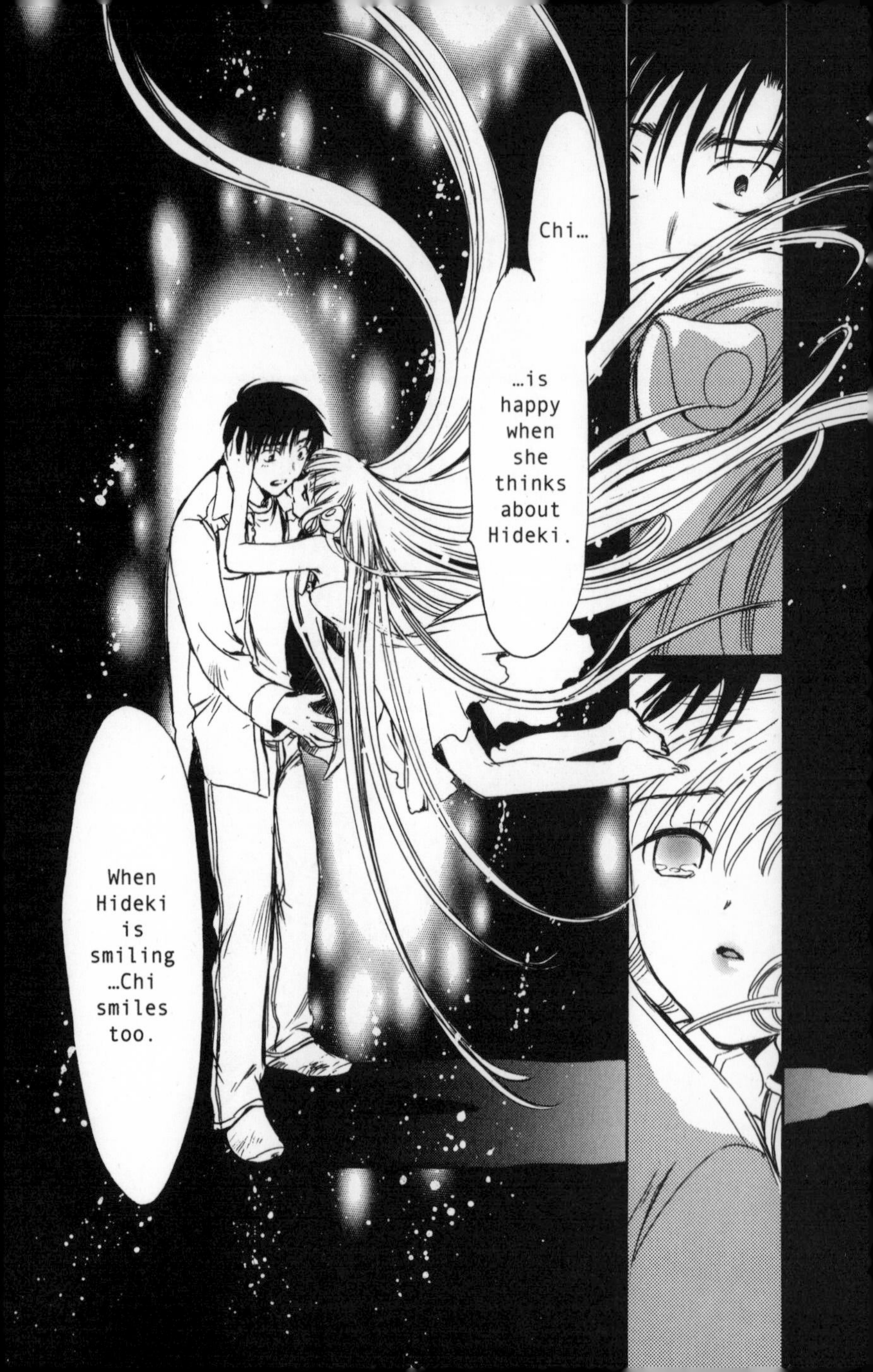
Chi…
…is happy when she thinks about Hideki.
When Hideki is smiling …Chi smiles too.

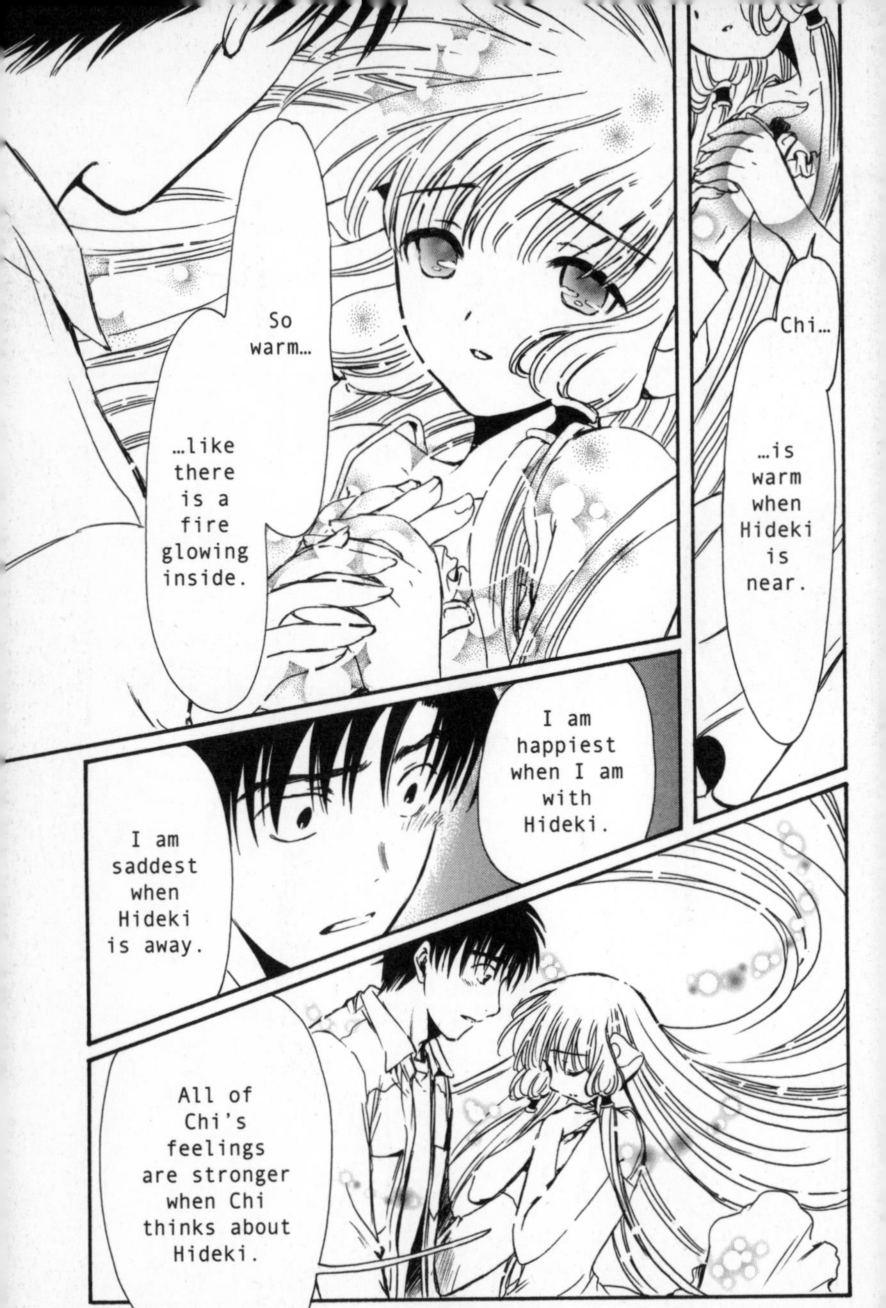
Chi…
…is warm when Hideki is near.
So warm…
…like there is a fire glowing inside.
I am happiest when I am with Hideki.
I am saddest when Hideki is away.
All of Chi's feelings are stronger when Chi thinks about Hideki.

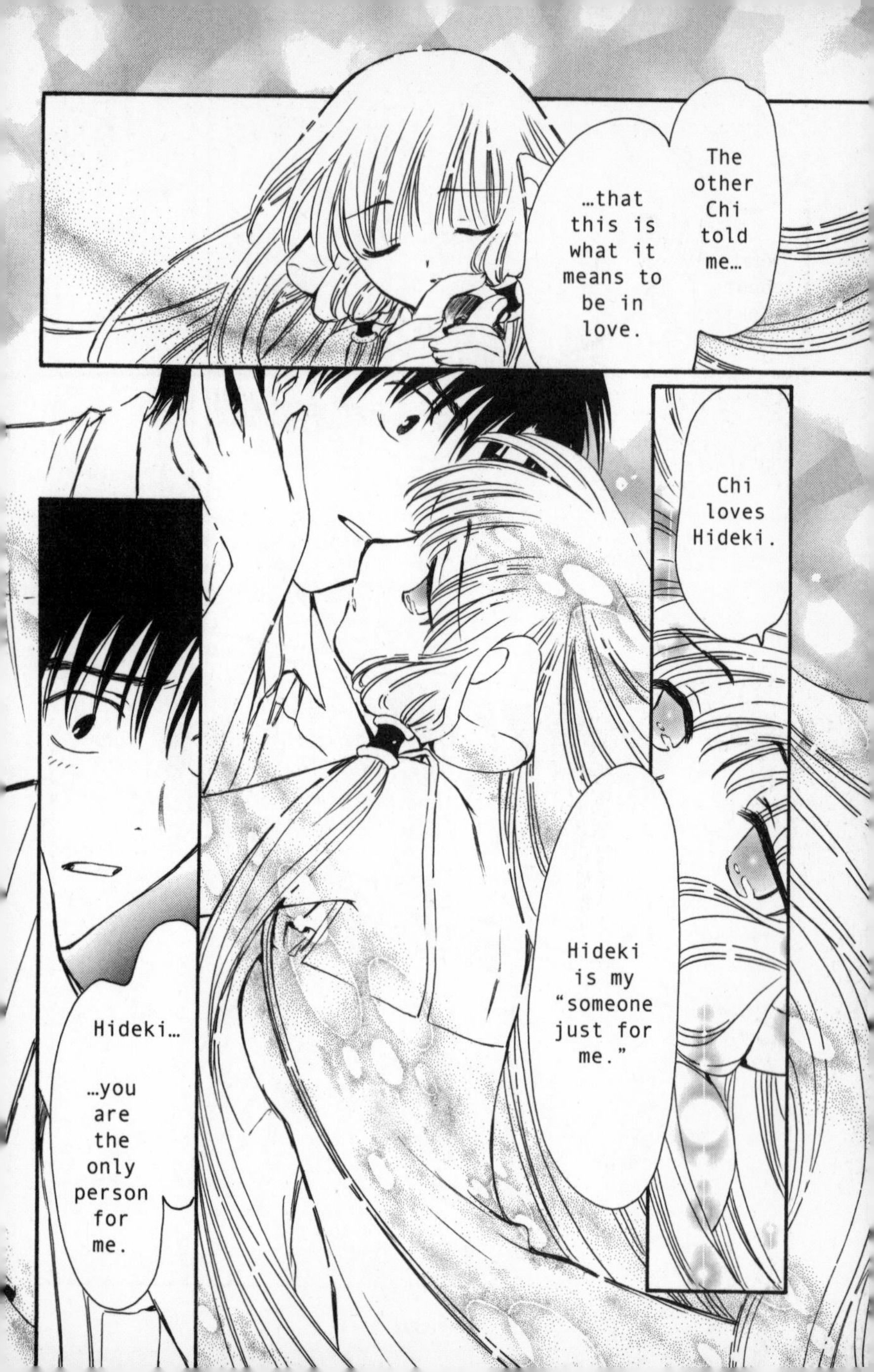
The other Chi told me…
…that this is what it means to be in love.
Chi loves Hideki.
Hideki is my "someone just for me."
Hideki…
…you are the only person for me.

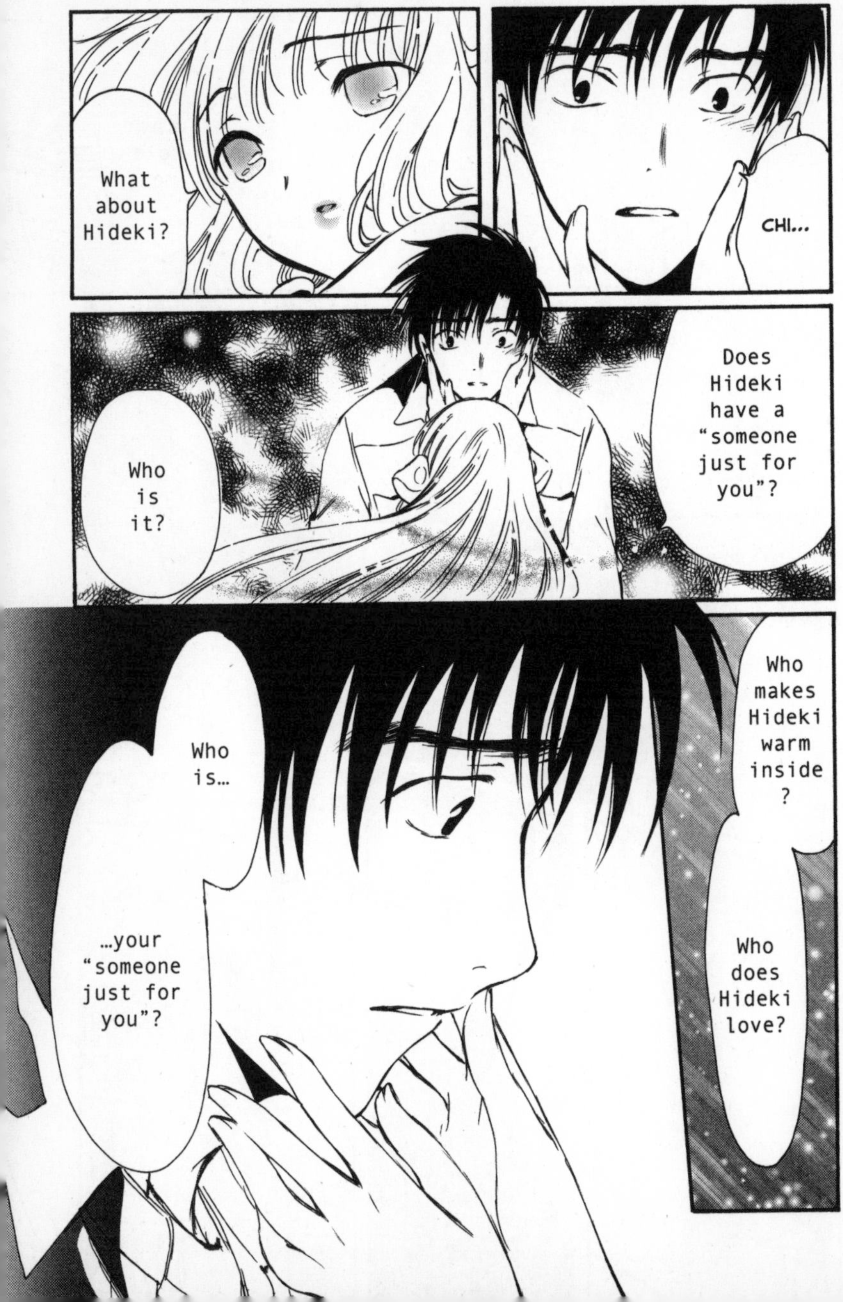
CHI...
What about Hideki?
Does Hideki have a "someone just for you"?
Who is it?
Who makes Hideki warm inside?
Who does Hideki love?
Who is...
...your "someone just for you"?

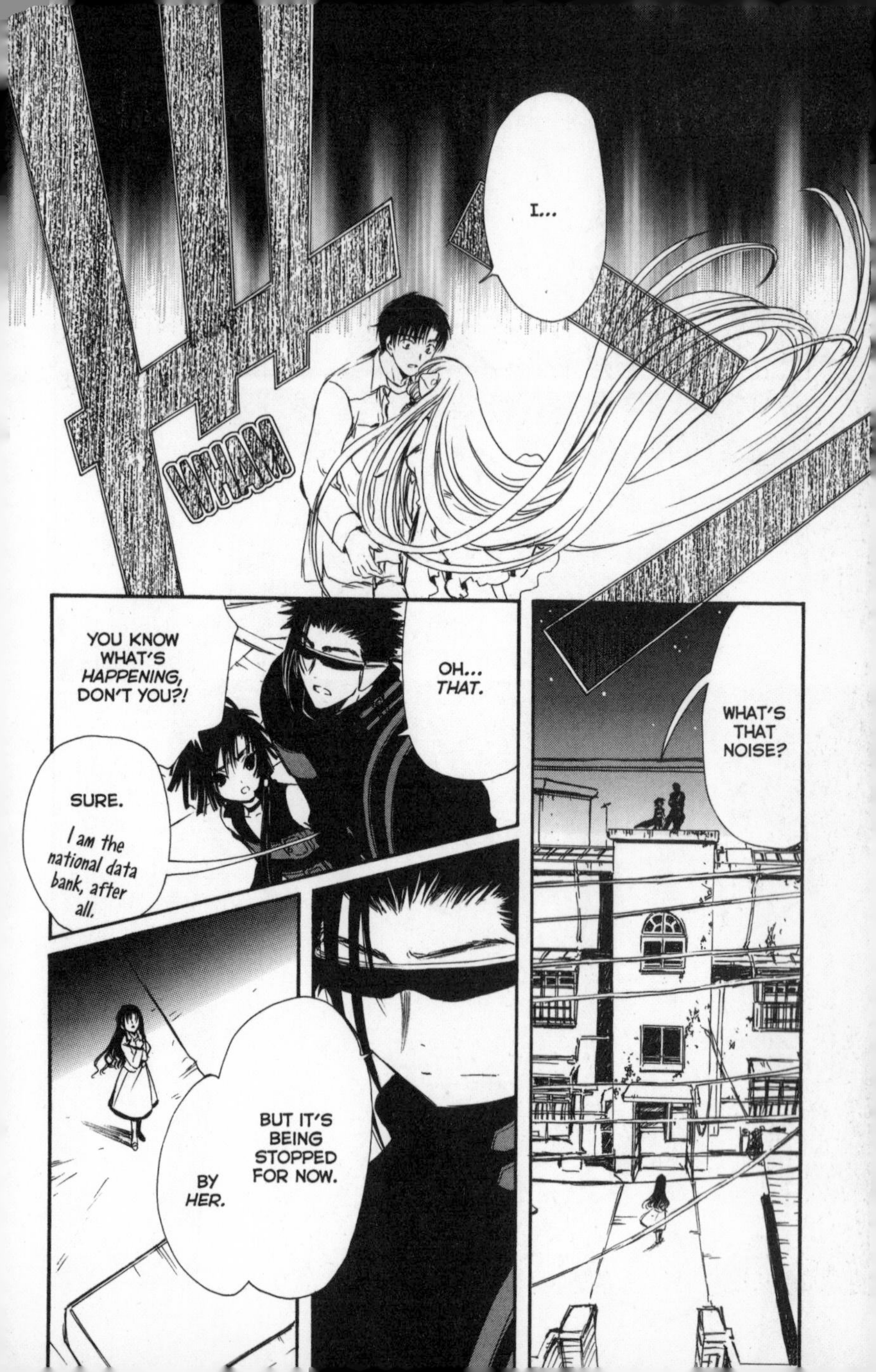
I...
WHAM
WHAT'S THAT NOISE?
OH... *THAT.*
YOU KNOW WHAT'S *HAPPENING,* DON'T YOU?!
SURE.
I am the national data bank, after all.
BUT IT'S BEING STOPPED FOR NOW.
BY HER.

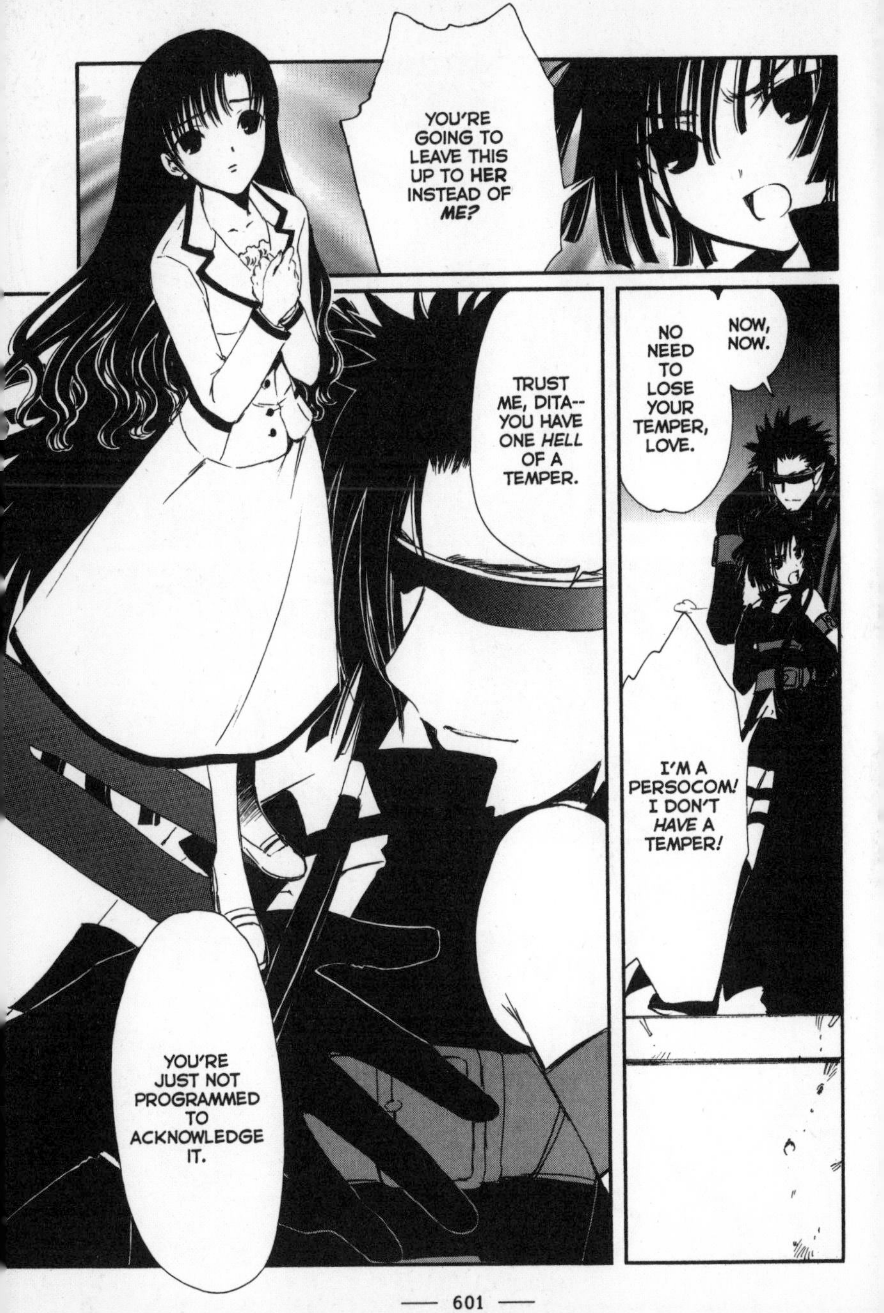
YOU'RE GOING TO LEAVE THIS UP TO HER INSTEAD OF *ME?*
NOW, NOW.
NO NEED TO LOSE YOUR TEMPER, LOVE.
I'M A PERSOCOM! I DON'T *HAVE* A TEMPER!
TRUST ME, DITA-- YOU HAVE ONE *HELL* OF A TEMPER.
YOU'RE JUST NOT PROGRAMMED TO ACKNOWLEDGE IT.

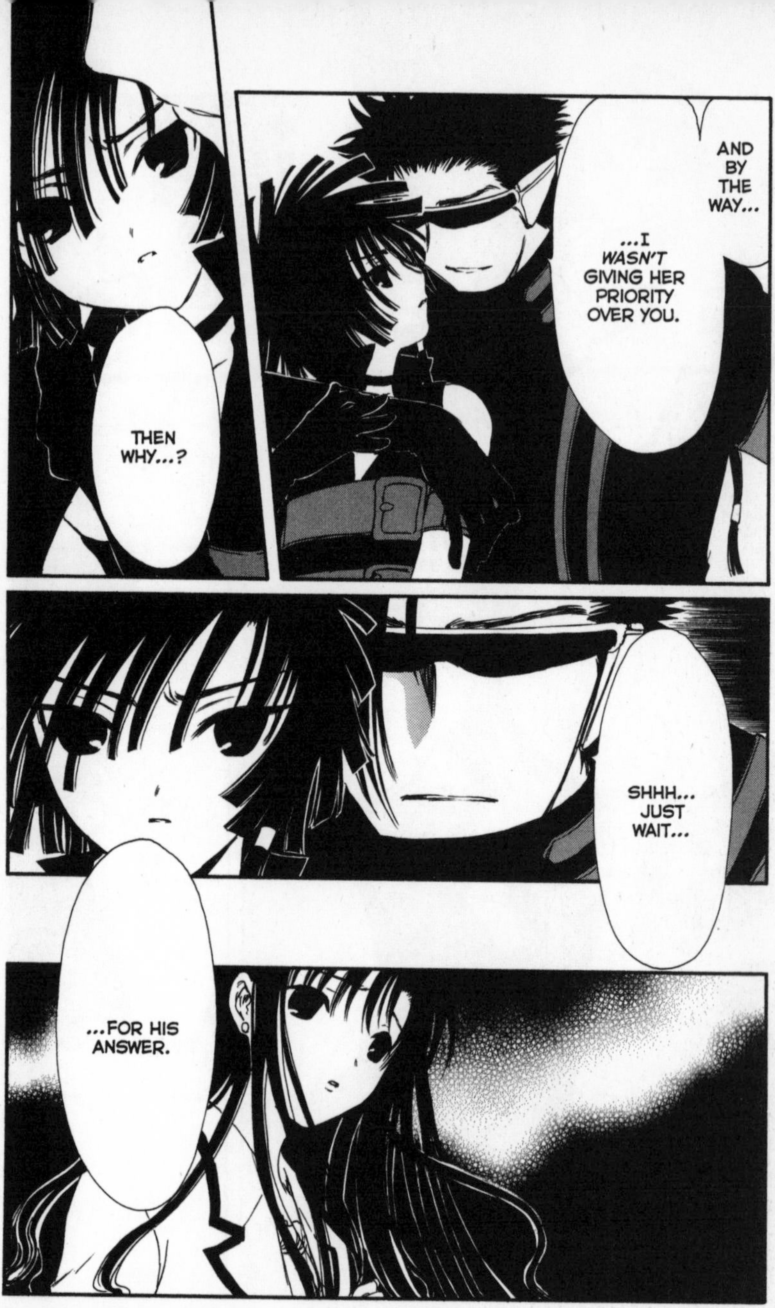
AND BY THE WAY...
...I WASN'T GIVING HER PRIORITY OVER YOU.
THEN WHY...?
SHHH... JUST WAIT...
...FOR HIS ANSWER.

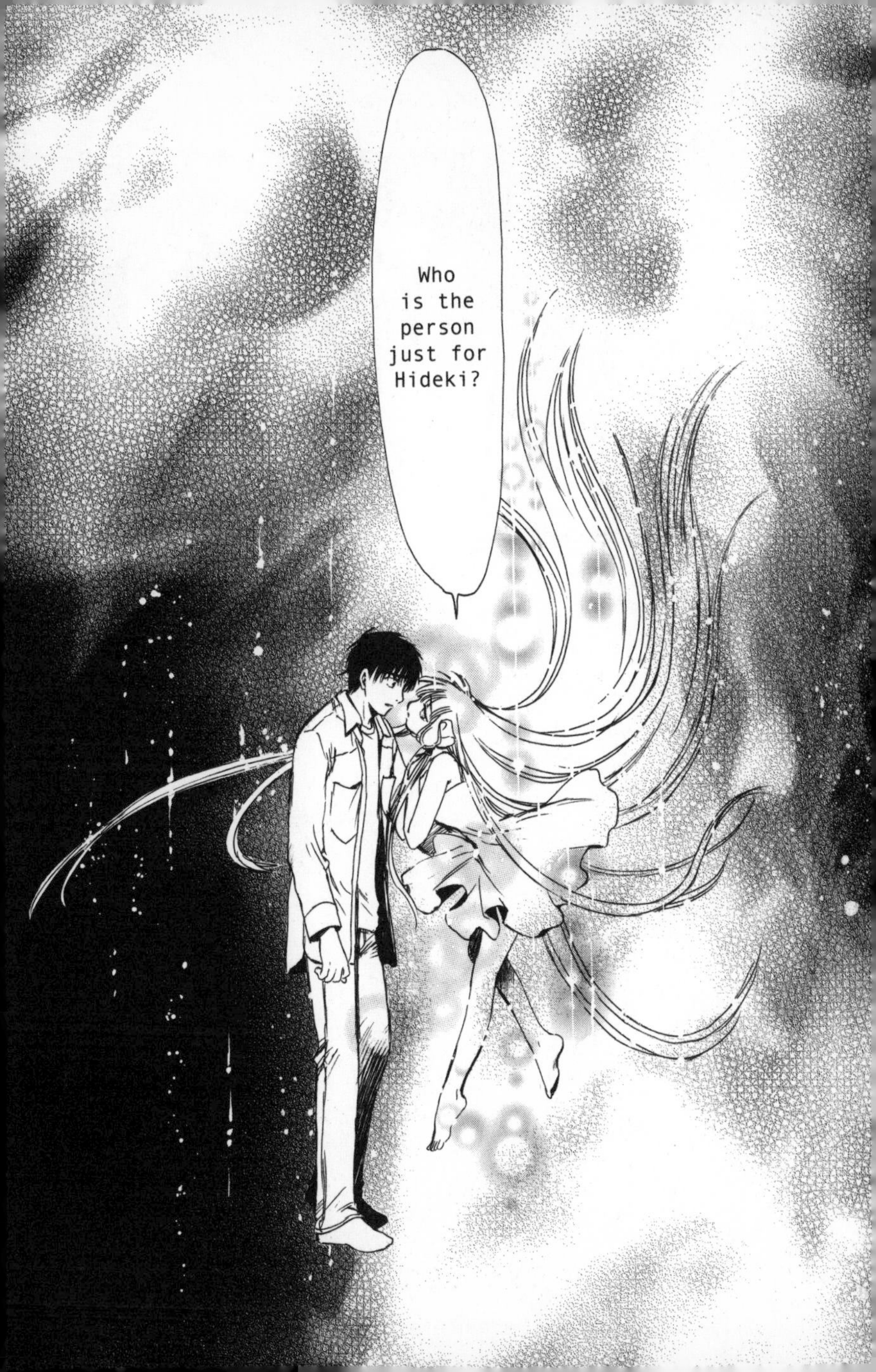
Who is the person just for Hideki?

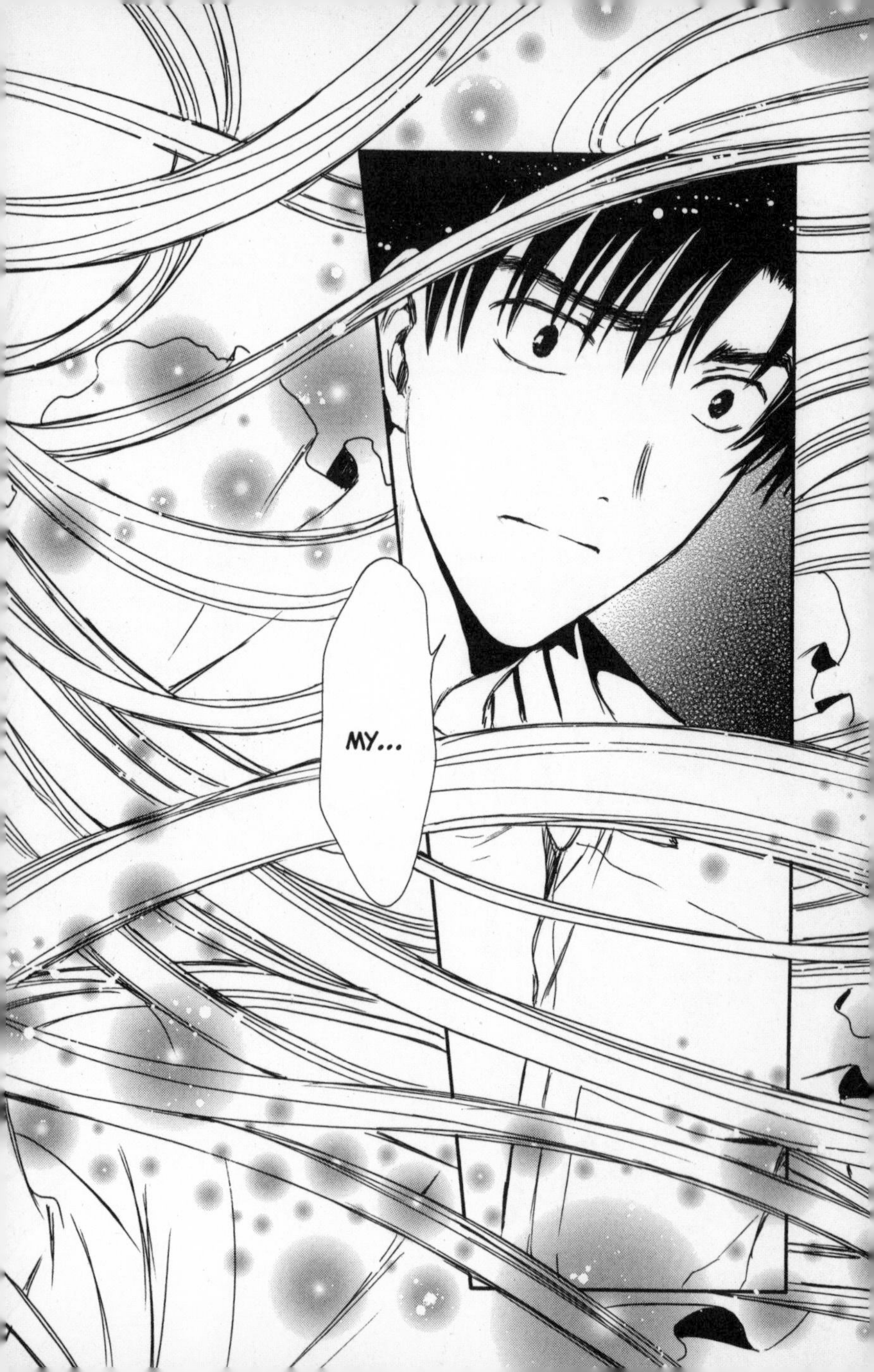
MY...

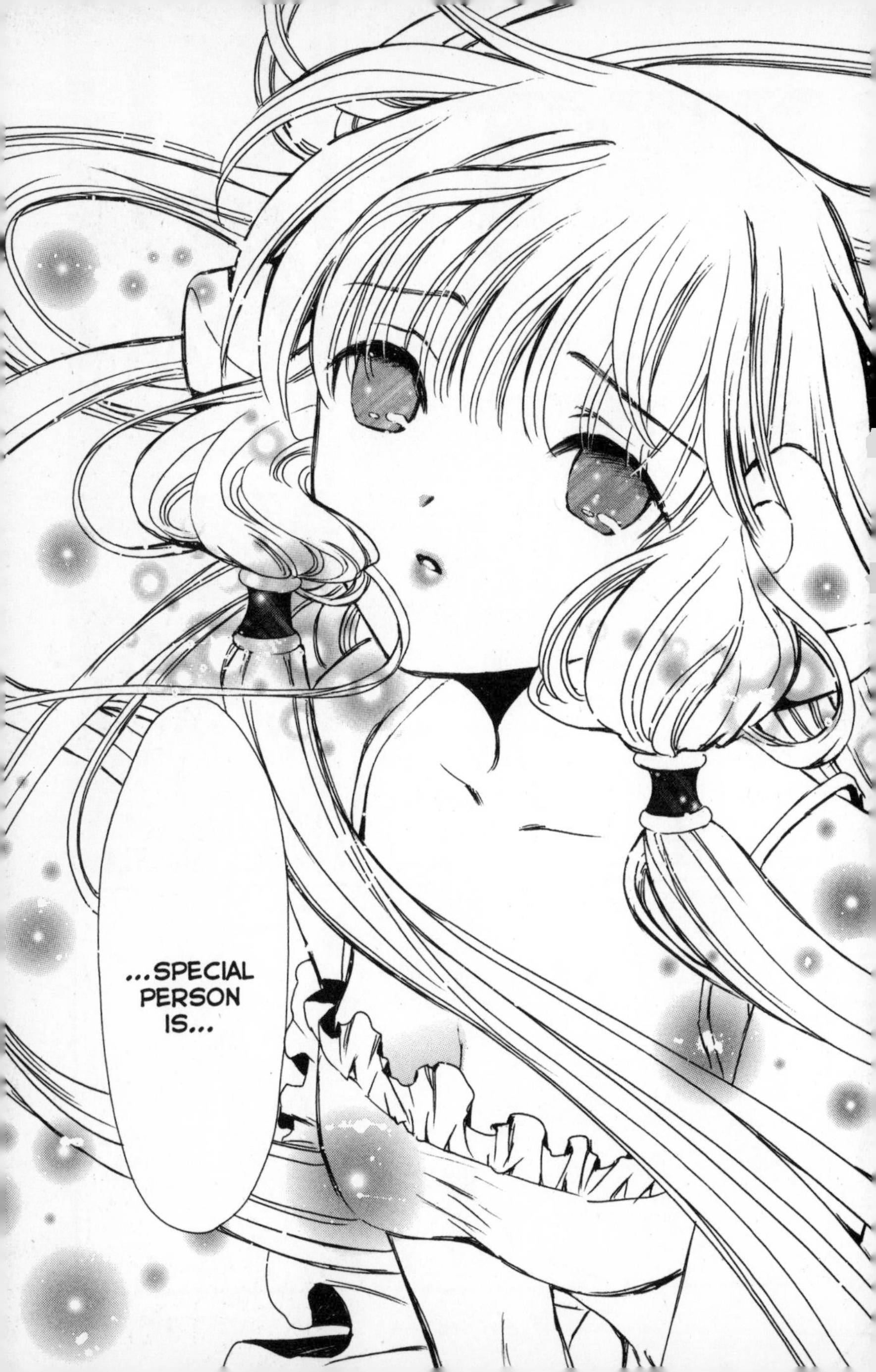
...SPECIAL PERSON IS...

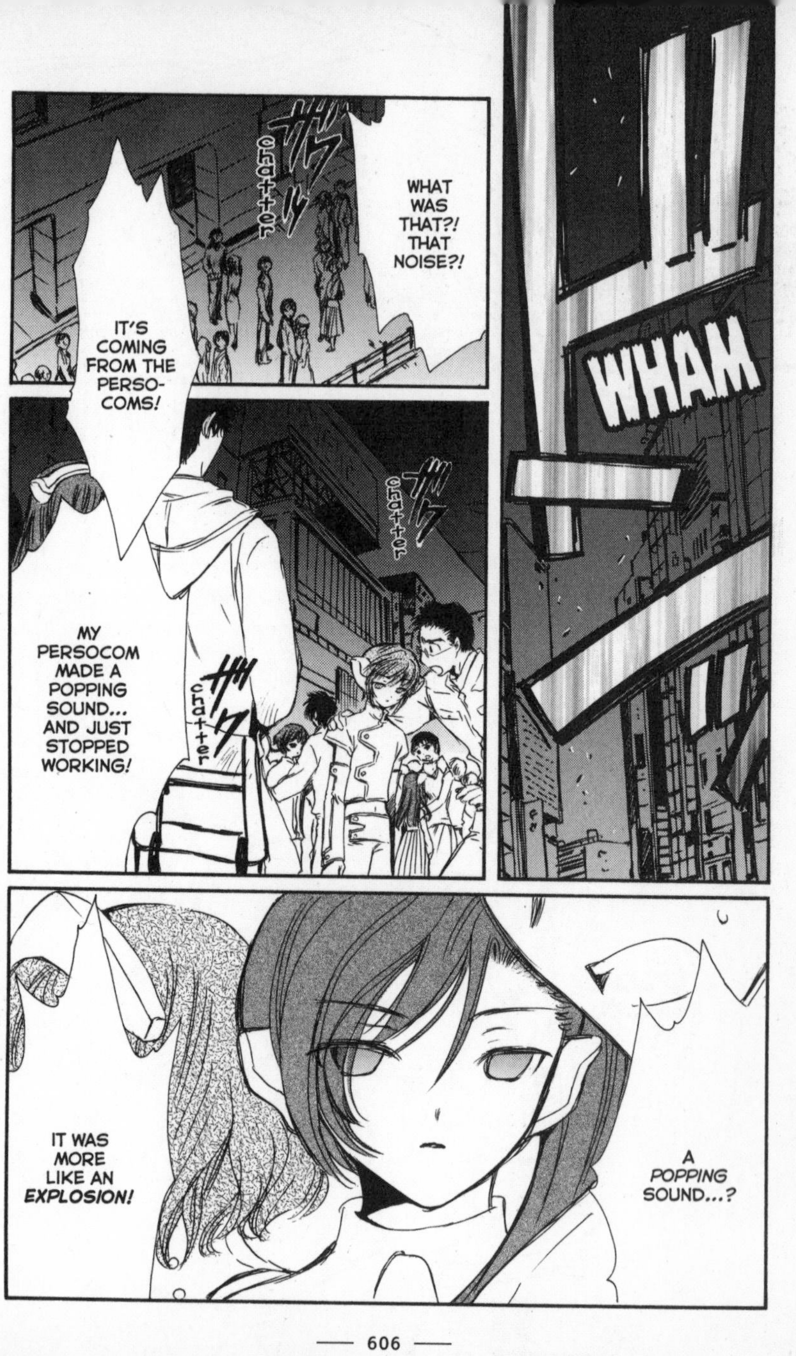
WHAM
WHAT WAS THAT?! THAT NOISE?!
chatter
IT'S COMING FROM THE PERSO-COMS!
chatter
chatter
MY PERSOCOM MADE A POPPING SOUND... AND JUST STOPPED WORKING!
A *POPPING* SOUND...?
IT WAS MORE LIKE AN ***EXPLOSION!***

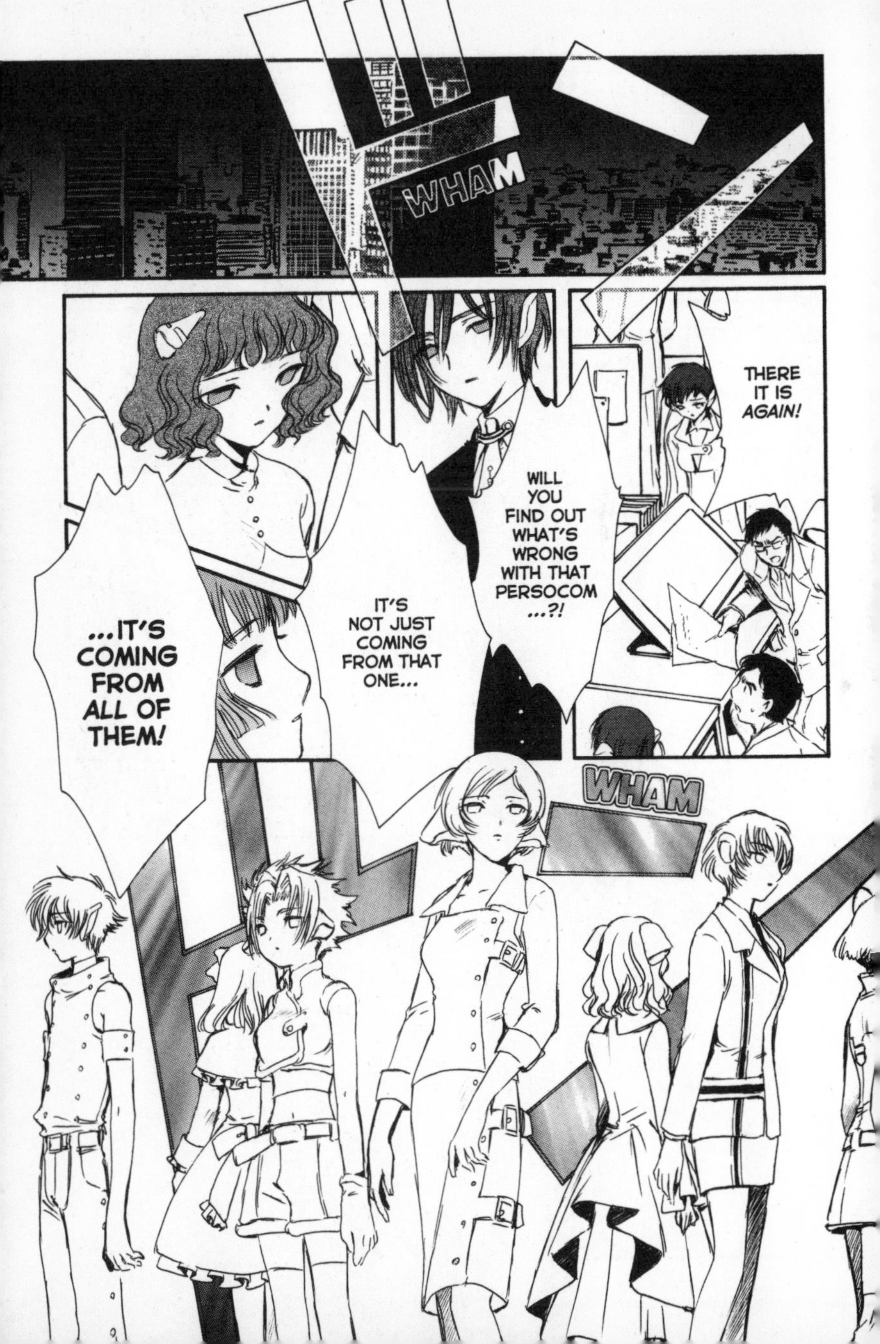
WHAM
THERE IT IS AGAIN!
WILL YOU FIND OUT WHAT'S WRONG WITH THAT PERSOCOM ...?!
IT'S NOT JUST COMING FROM THAT ONE...
...IT'S COMING FROM ALL OF THEM!
WHAM

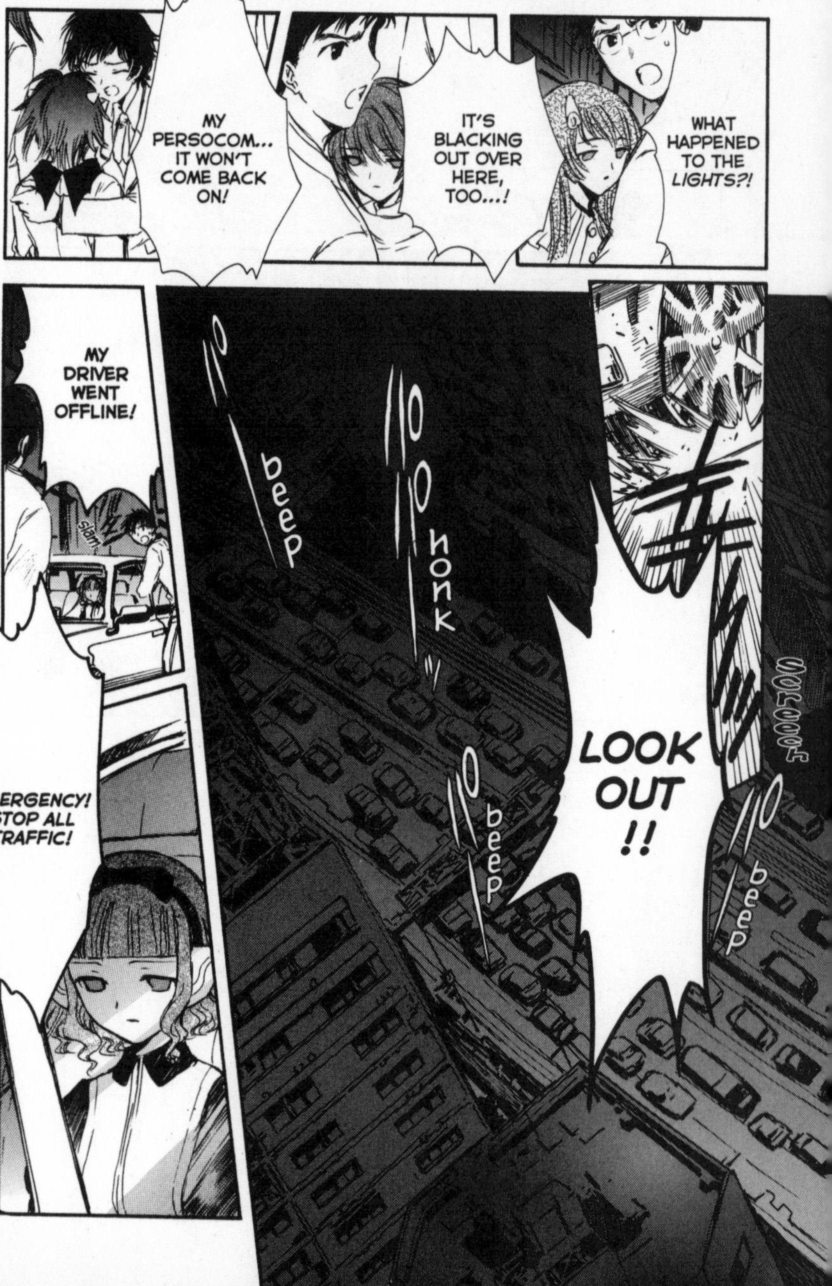
WHAT HAPPENED TO THE LIGHTS?!
IT'S BLACKING OUT OVER HERE, TOO...!
MY PERSOCOM... IT WON'T COME BACK ON!
LOOK OUT!!
Screeer
beep
beep
honk
beep
MY DRIVER WENT OFFLINE!
slam
EMERGENCY! STOP ALL TRAFFIC!

Chobits
ちょびっツ

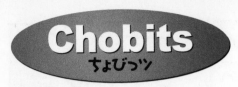

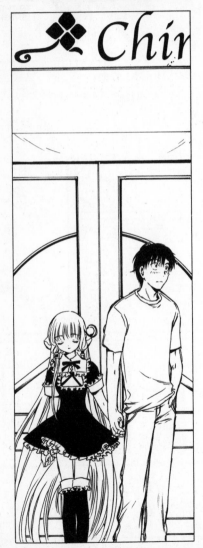

chapter 85

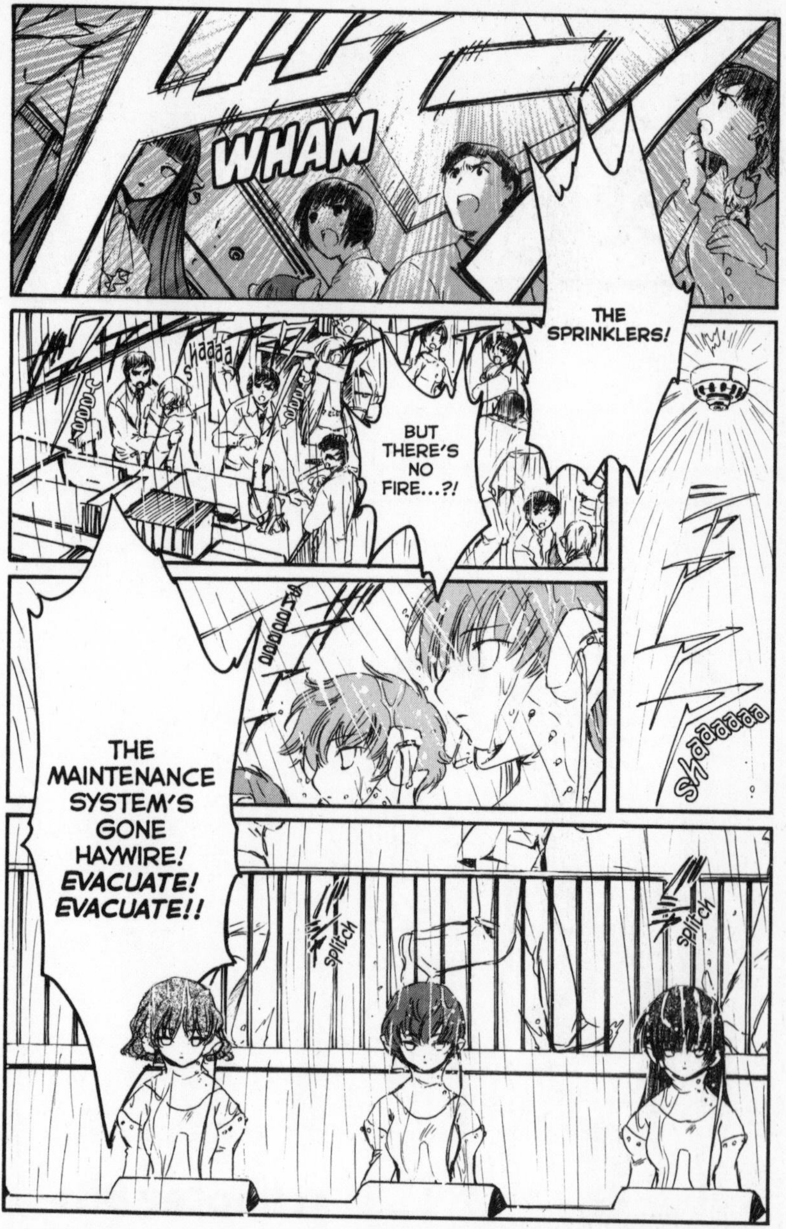
WHAM
THE SPRINKLERS!
BUT THERE'S NO FIRE...?!
shaaaa
shaaaaaa
THE MAINTENANCE SYSTEM'S GONE HAYWIRE! EVACUATE! EVACUATE!!
splitch
splitch

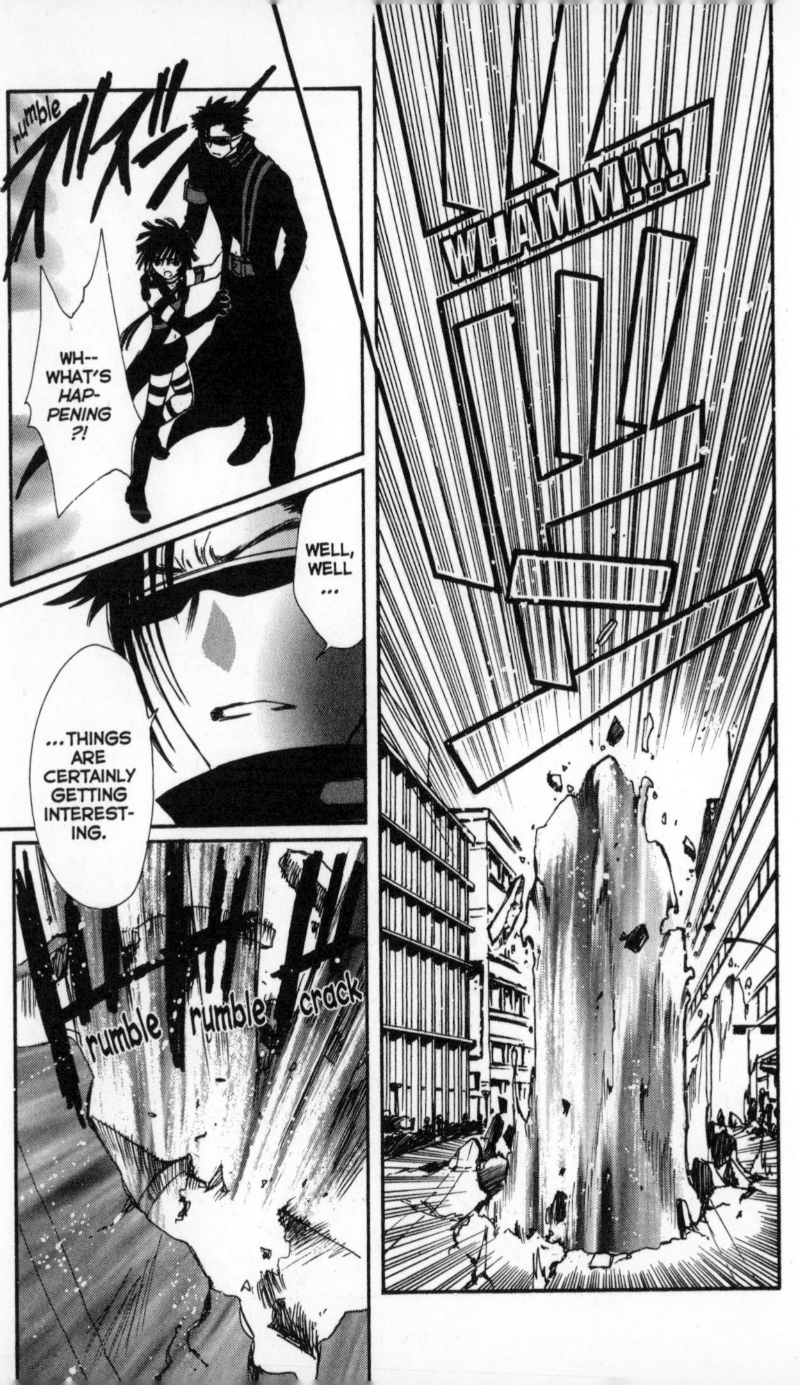
WHAMM!!!
rumble
WH-- WHAT'S HAP-PENING ?!
WELL, WELL ...
...THINGS ARE CERTAINLY GETTING INTEREST-ING.
rumble
rumble
crack

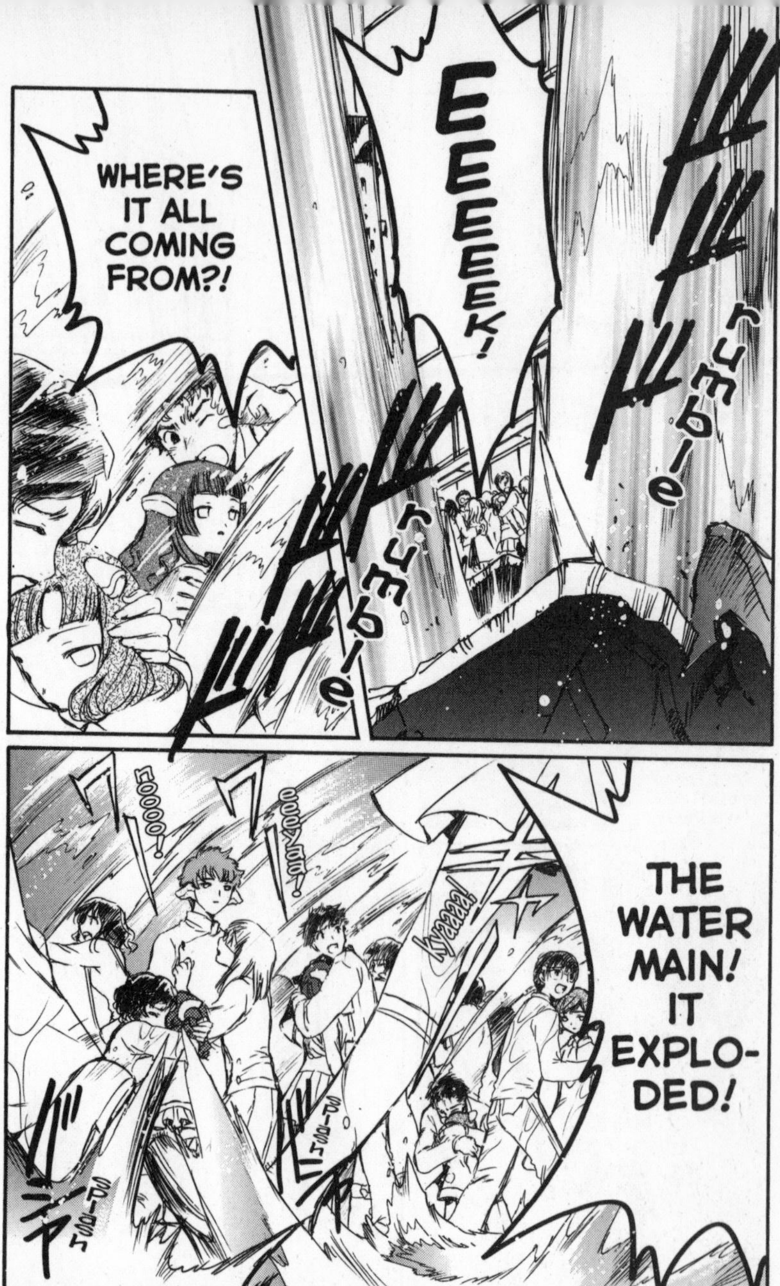
EEEEEEK!
rumble
rumble
WHERE'S IT ALL COMING FROM?!
THE WATER MAIN! IT EXPLODED!
kyaaaa!
eeyaa!
noooo!
splash
splash

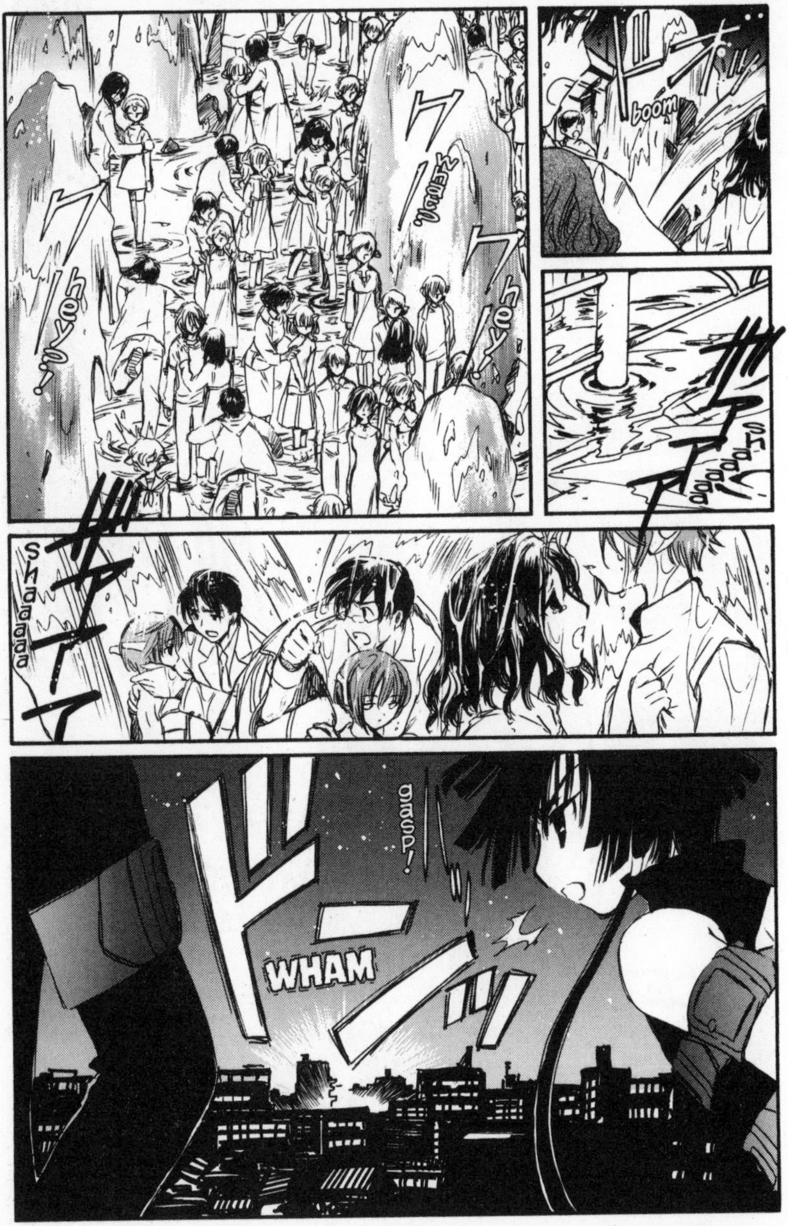
boom
shaaaaa!
whew!!
hey!!
hey!!
shaaaaaa
gasp!
WHAM

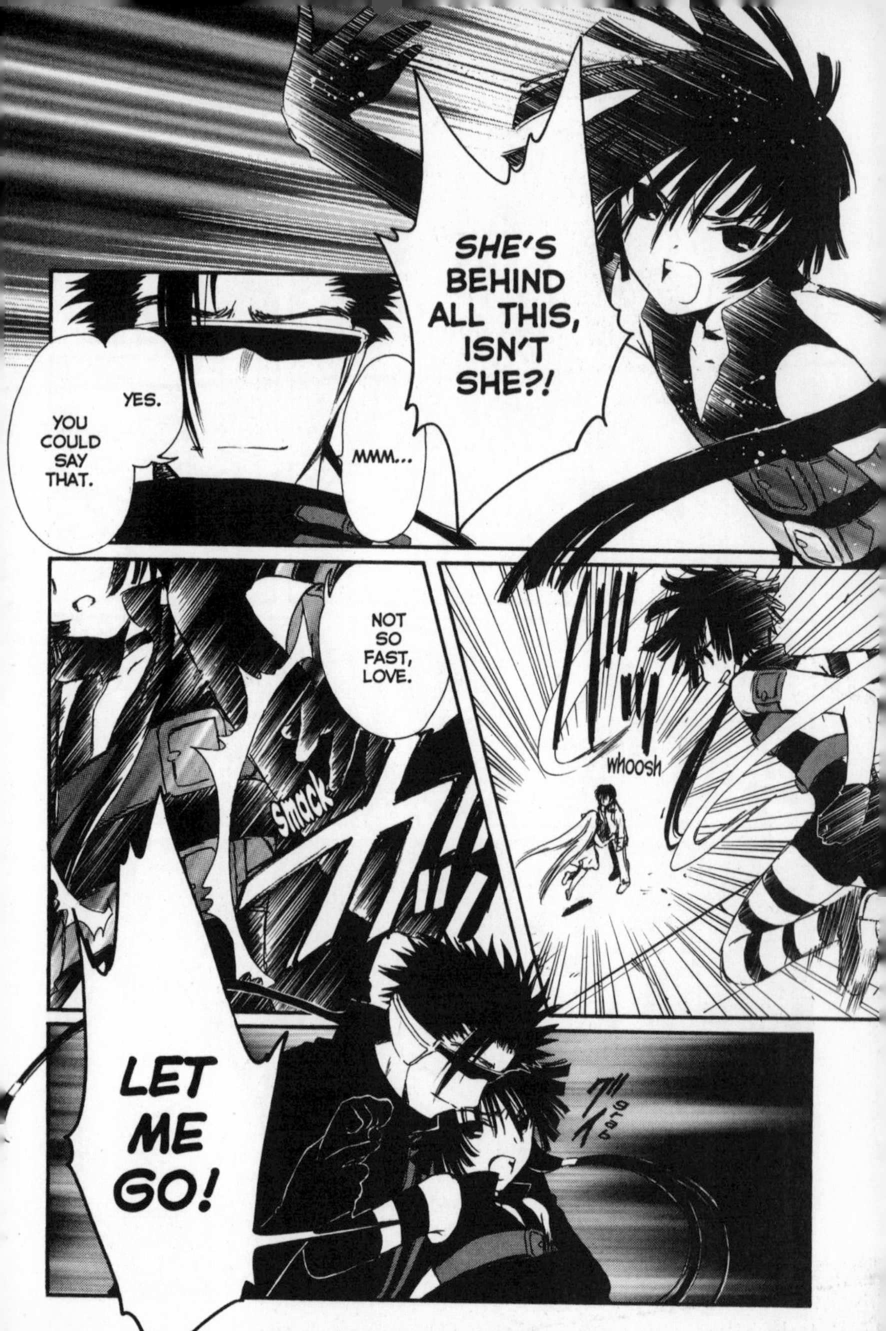
SHE'S BEHIND ALL THIS, ISN'T SHE?!
MMM...
YES.
YOU COULD SAY THAT.
whoosh
NOT SO FAST, LOVE.
smack
grab
LET ME GO!

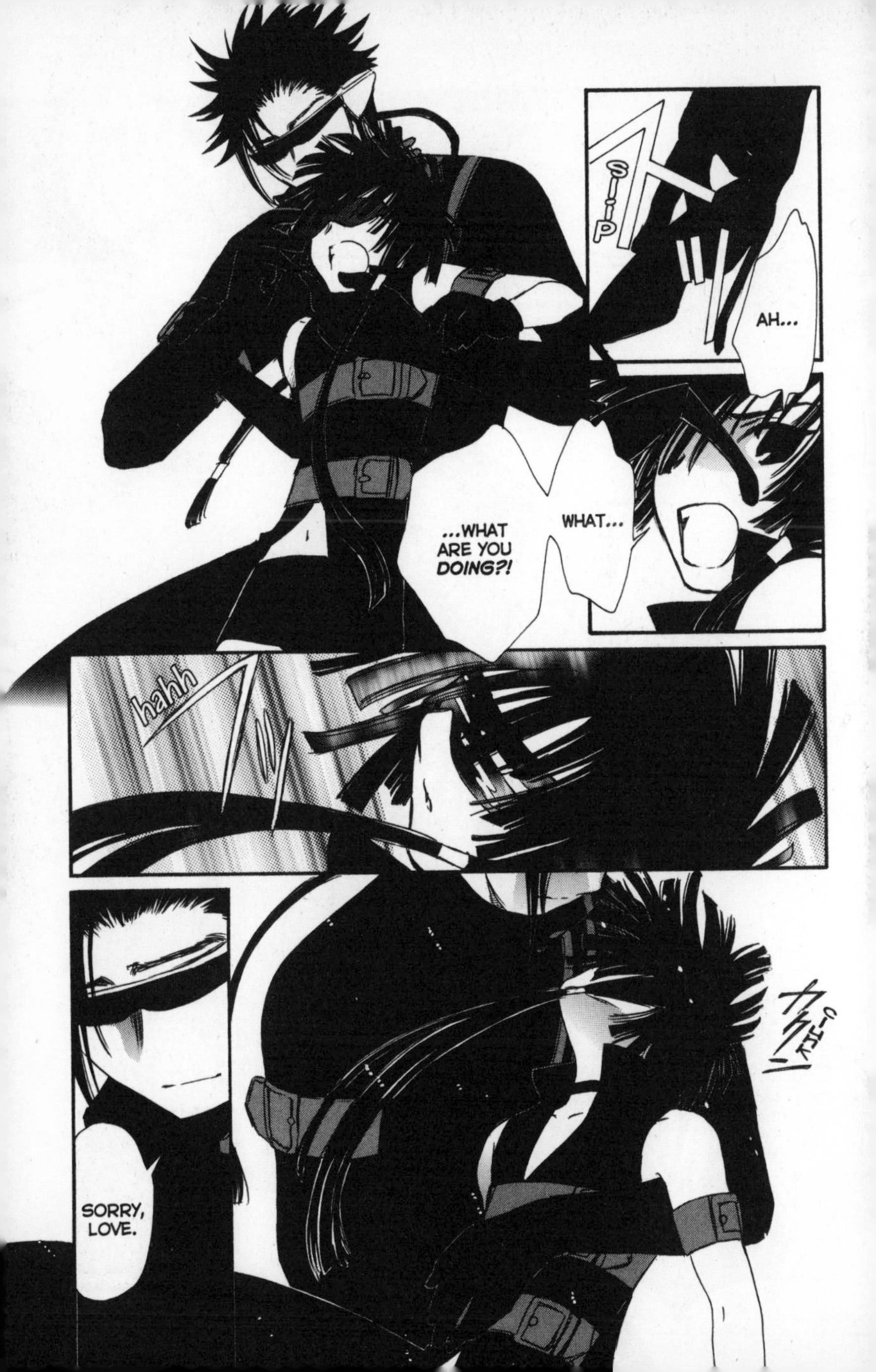
SLIP
AH...
WHAT...
...WHAT ARE YOU DOING?!
hahh
カクン
C-LUNK
SORRY, LOVE.

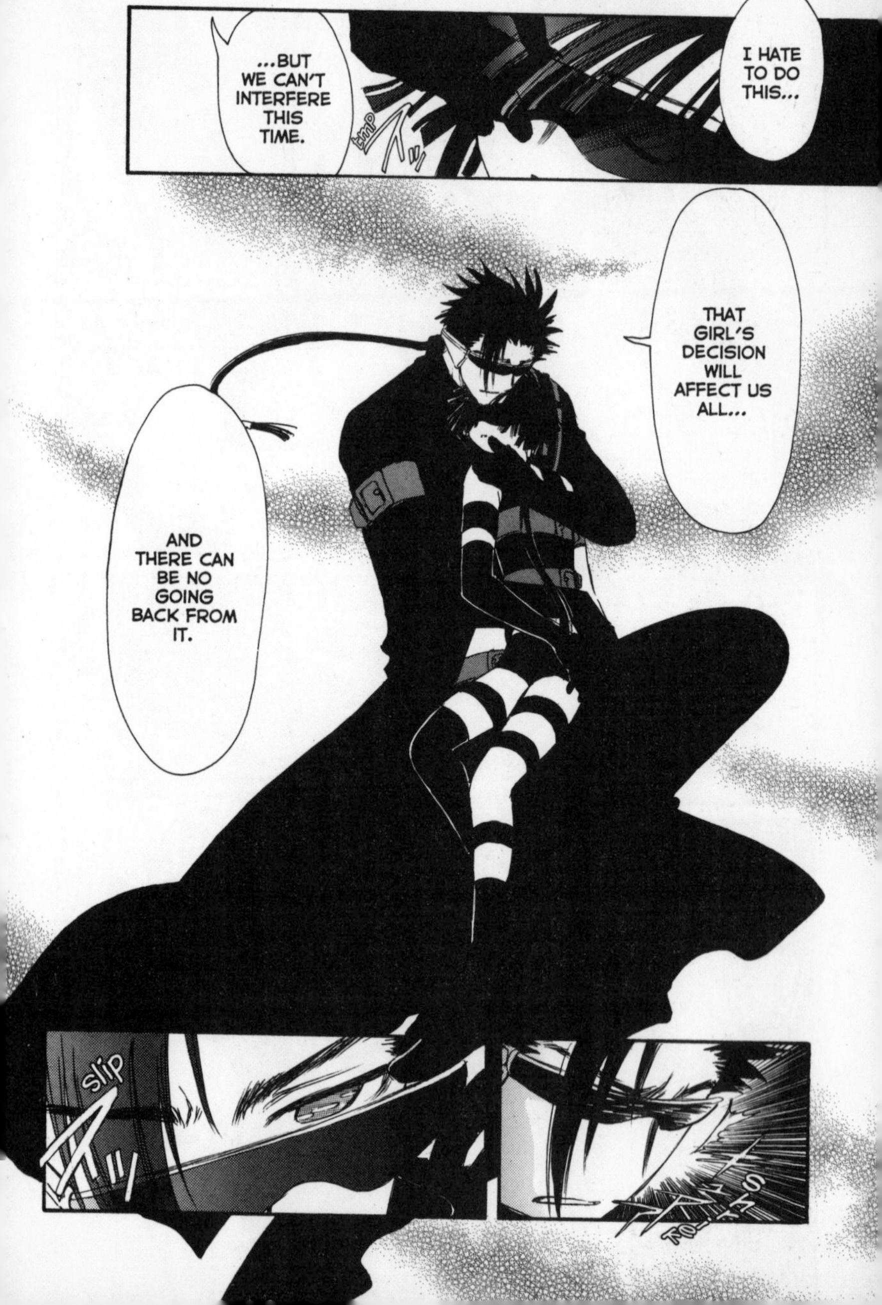
I HATE TO DO THIS...
...BUT WE CAN'T INTERFERE THIS TIME.
tmp
THAT GIRL'S DECISION WILL AFFECT US ALL...
AND THERE CAN BE NO GOING BACK FROM IT.
slip

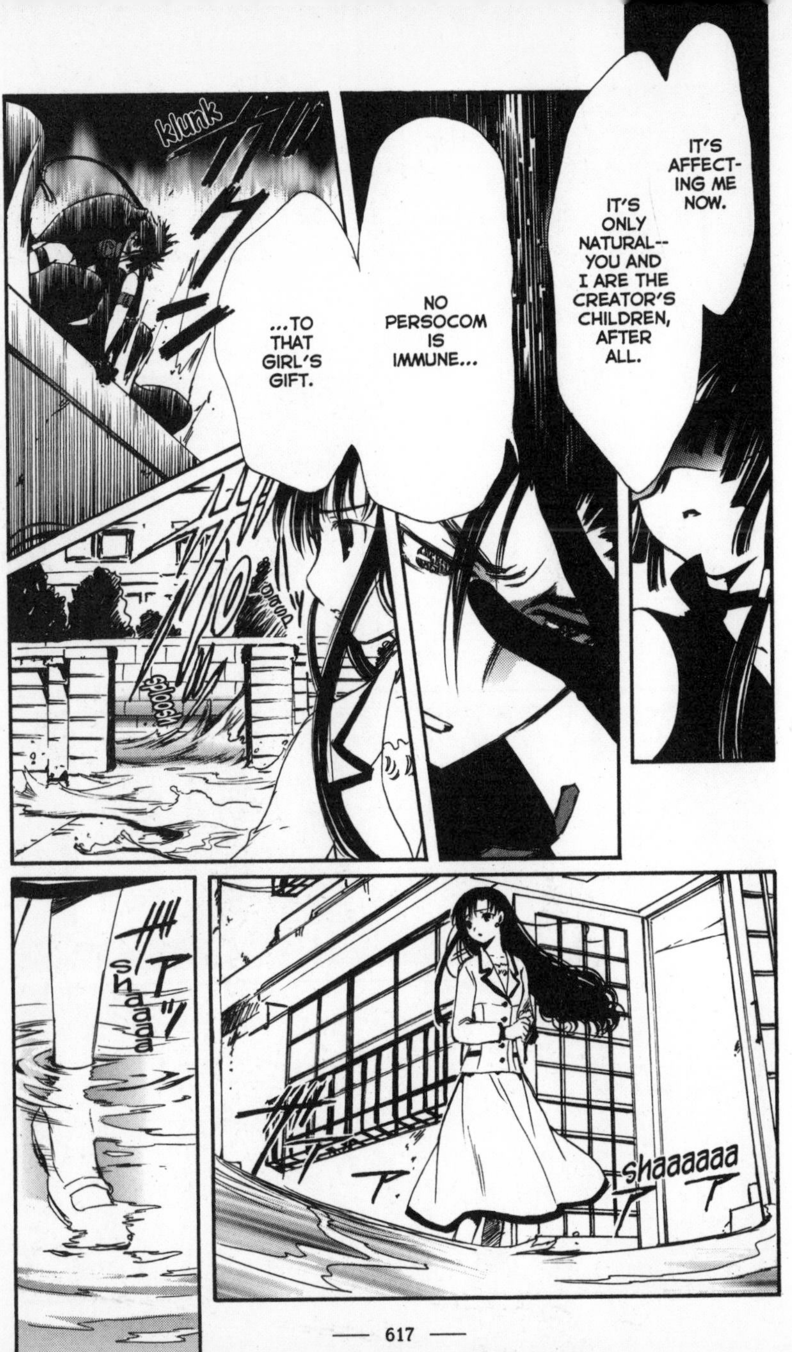
IT'S AFFECTING ME NOW.
IT'S ONLY NATURAL-- YOU AND I ARE THE CREATOR'S CHILDREN, AFTER ALL.
NO PERSOCOM IS IMMUNE...
...TO THAT GIRL'S GIFT.
klunk
sploosh
shaaaaaa
shaaaa

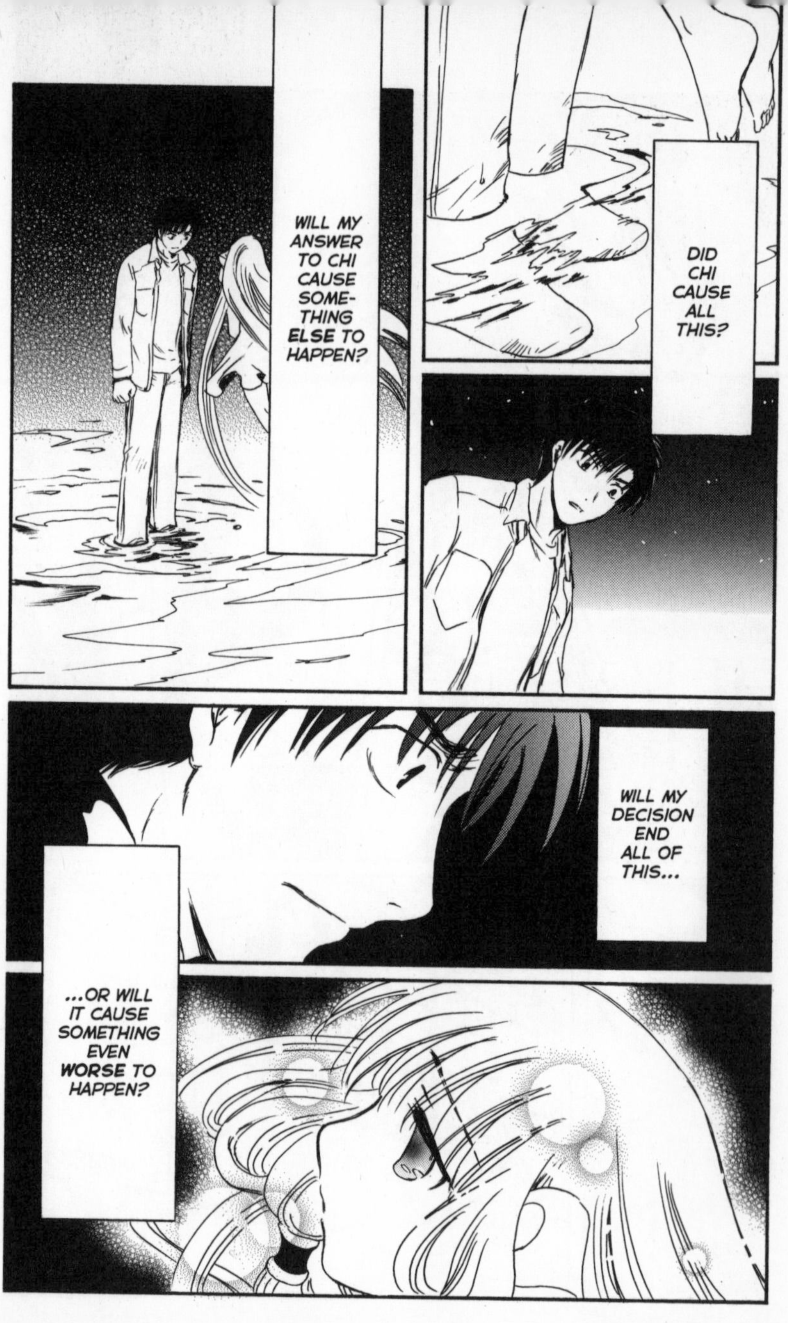
DID CHI CAUSE ALL THIS?
WILL MY ANSWER TO CHI CAUSE SOME-THING ELSE TO HAPPEN?
WILL MY DECISION END ALL OF THIS...
...OR WILL IT CAUSE SOMETHING EVEN WORSE TO HAPPEN?

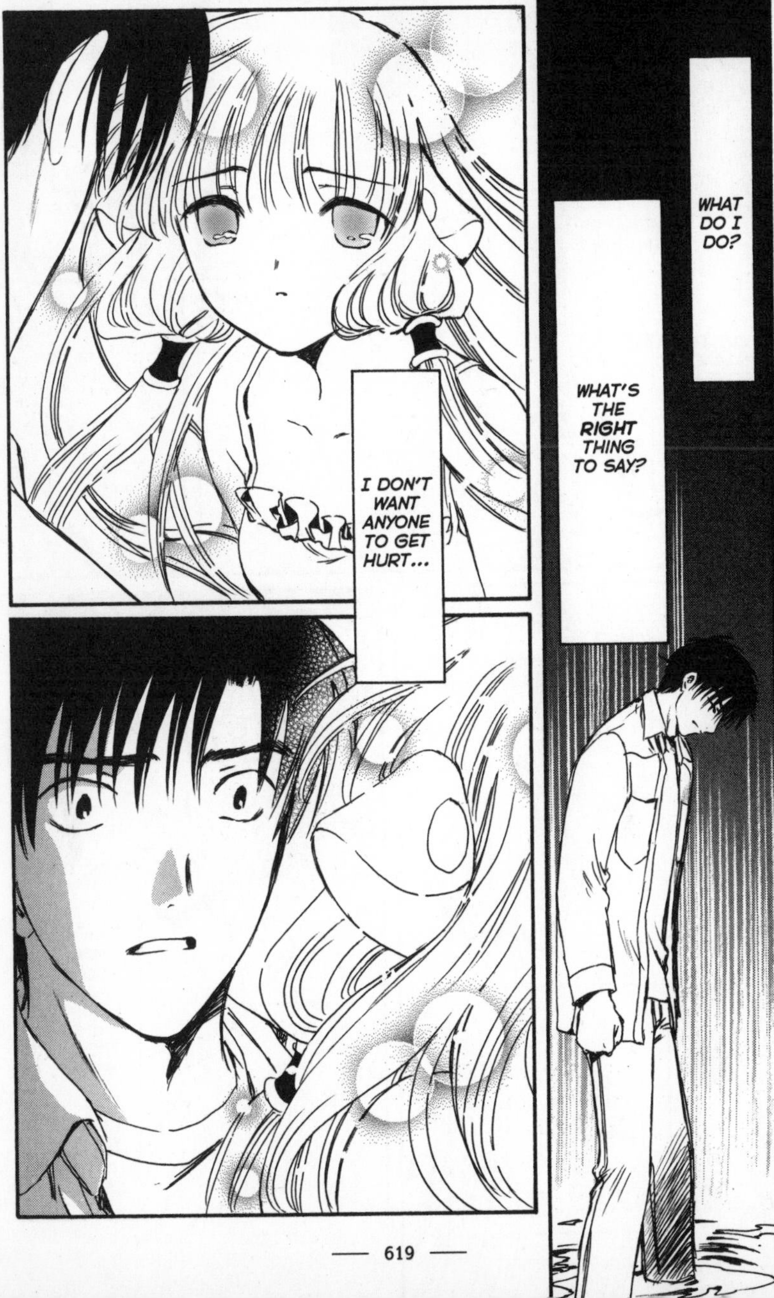
WHAT DO I DO?
WHAT'S THE RIGHT THING TO SAY?
I DON'T WANT ANYONE TO GET HURT...

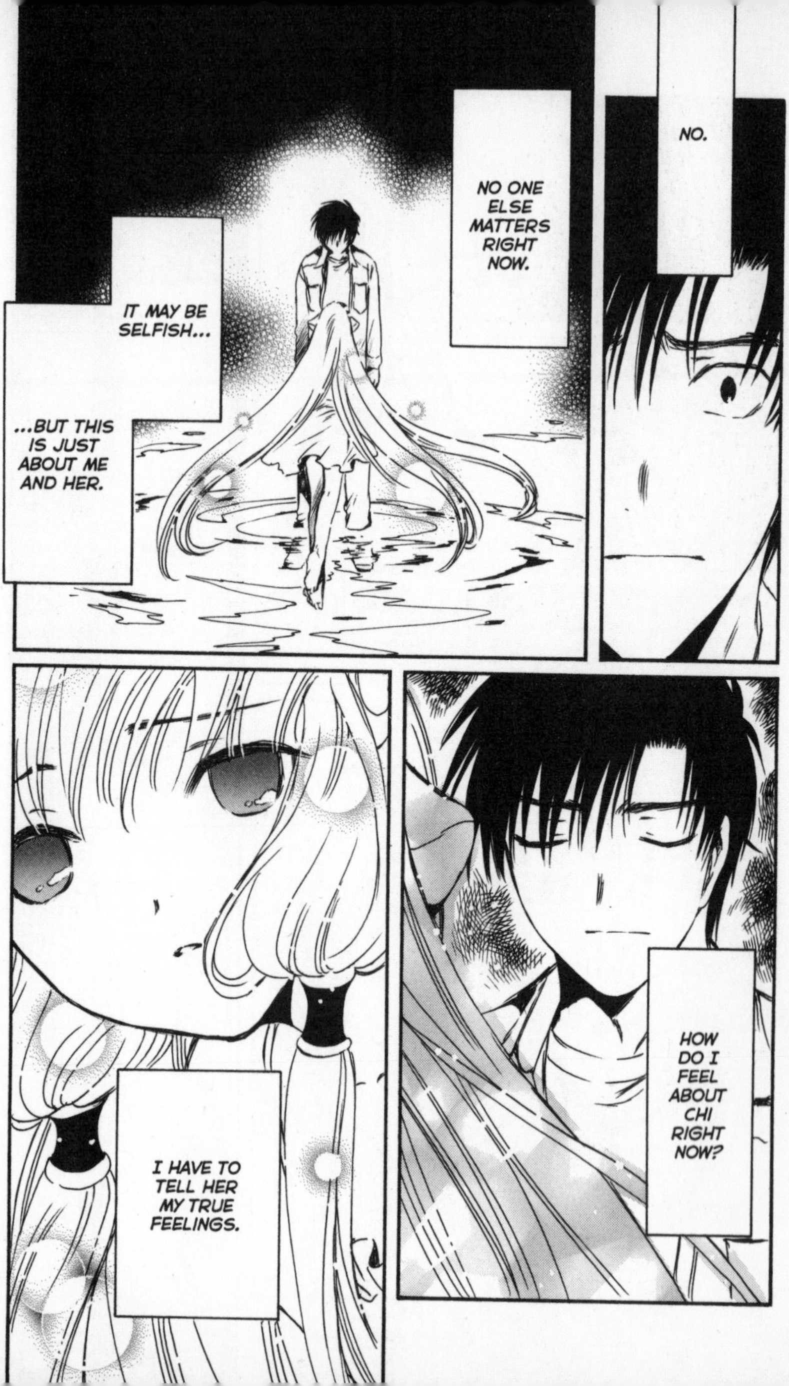
NO.
NO ONE ELSE MATTERS RIGHT NOW.
IT MAY BE SELFISH...
...BUT THIS IS JUST ABOUT ME AND HER.
HOW DO I FEEL ABOUT CHI RIGHT NOW?
I HAVE TO TELL HER MY TRUE FEELINGS.

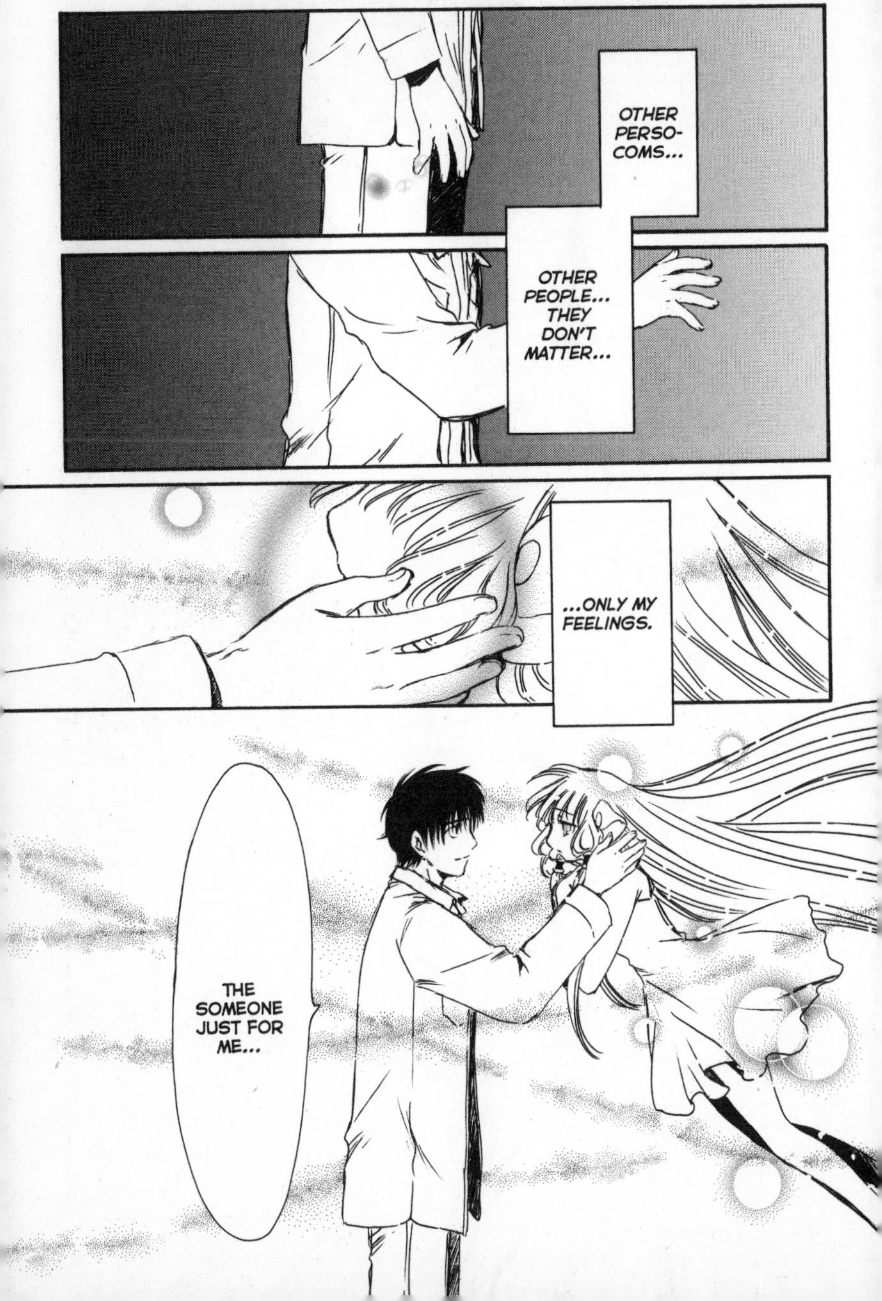
OTHER PERSO-COMS...
OTHER PEOPLE... THEY DON'T MATTER...
...ONLY MY FEELINGS.
THE SOMEONE JUST FOR ME...

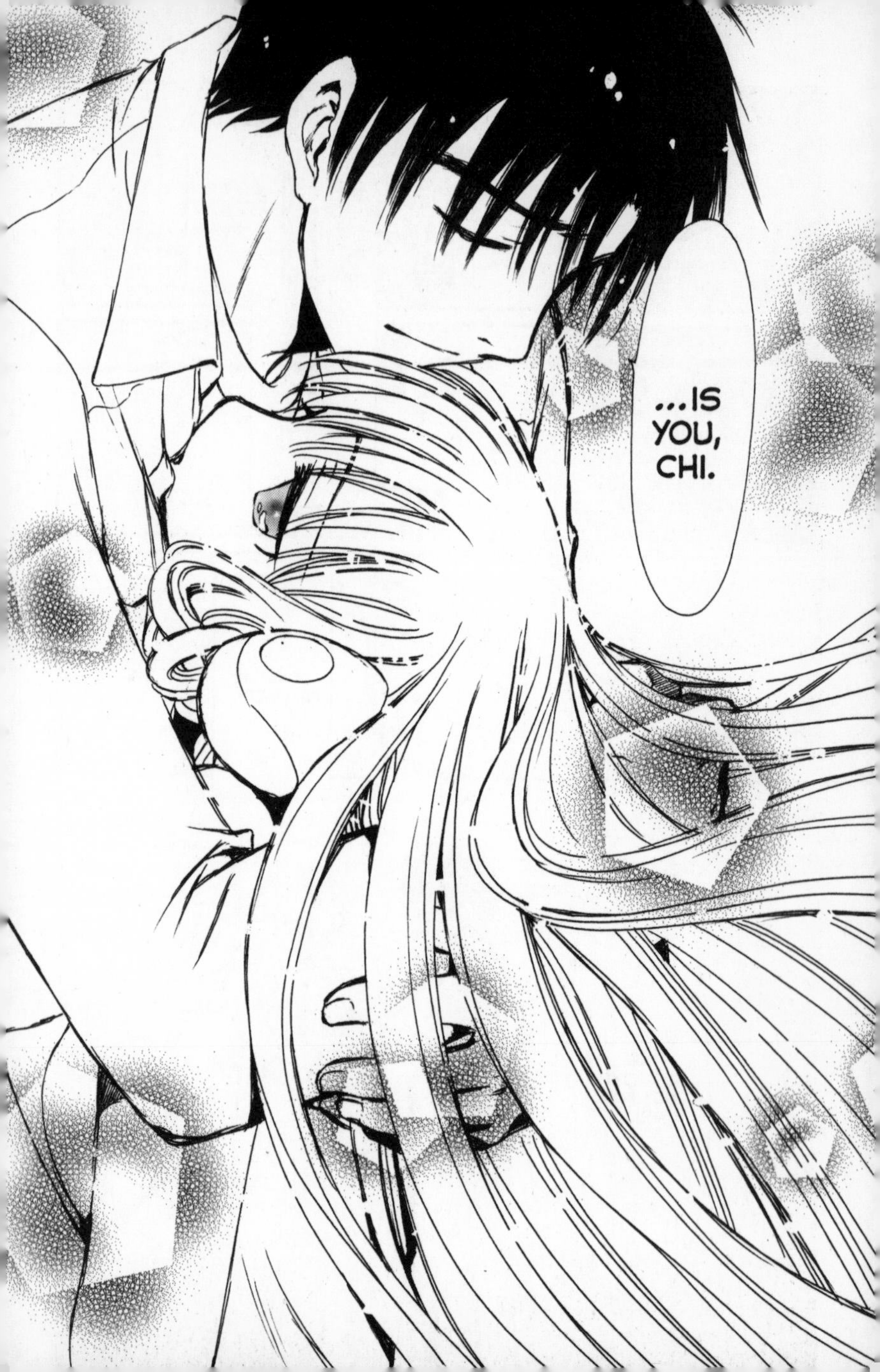
...IS YOU, CHI.

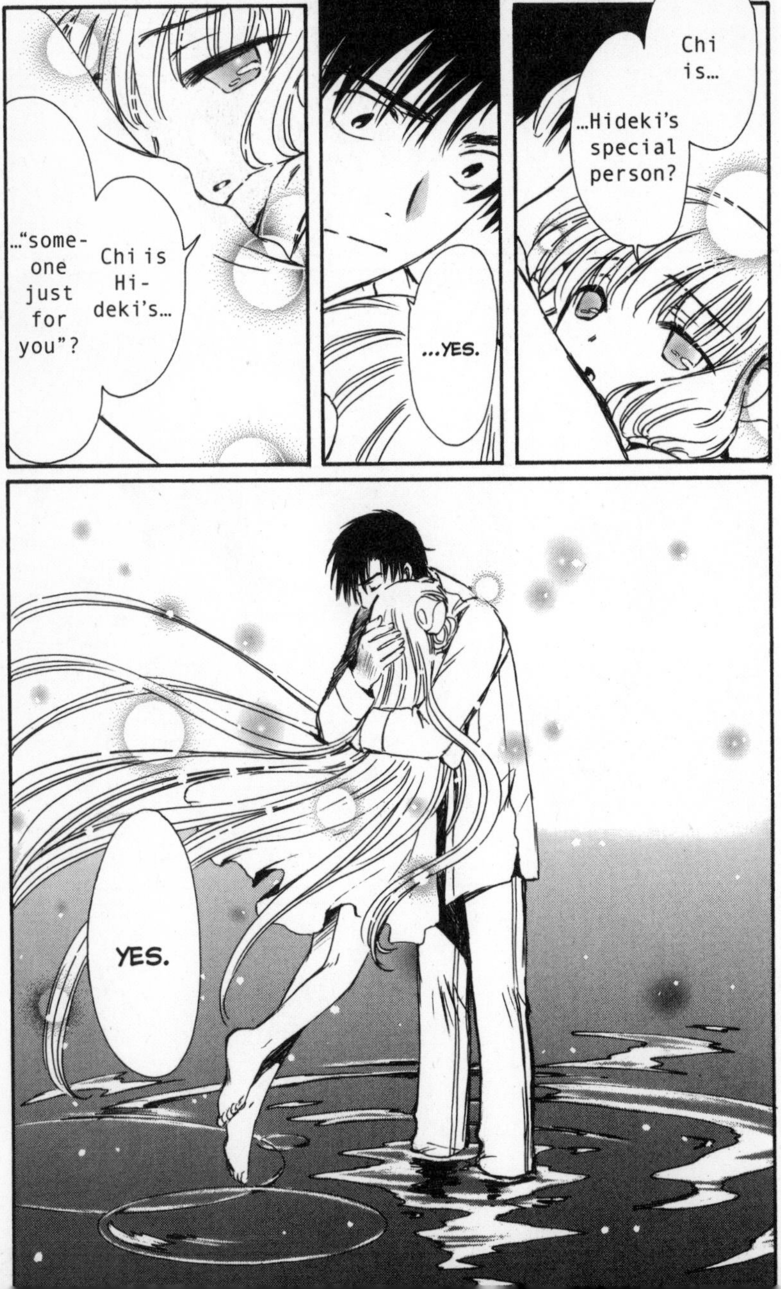
Chi is…
…Hideki's special person?
…YES.
Chi is Hi-deki's…
…"some-one just for you"?
YES.

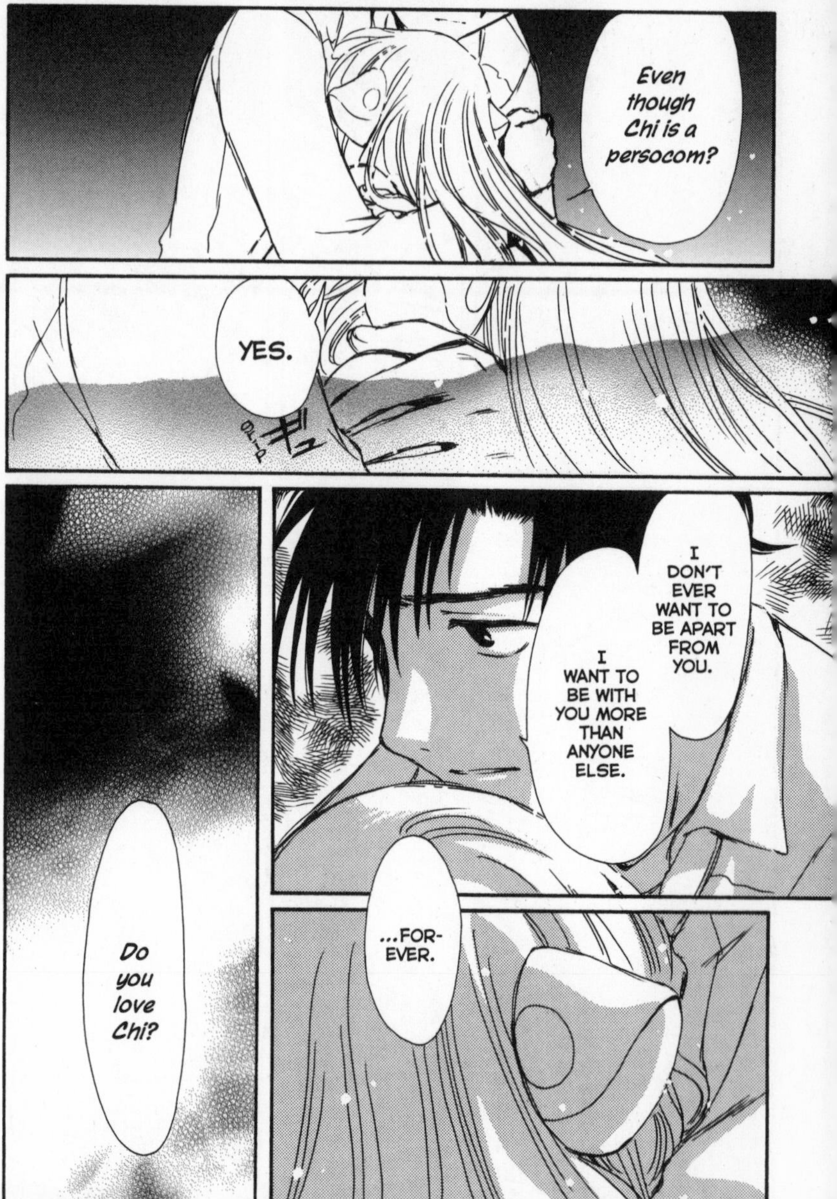
Even though Chi is a persocom?
YES.
ギュ
I DON'T EVER WANT TO BE APART FROM YOU.
I WANT TO BE WITH YOU MORE THAN ANYONE ELSE.
...FOR-EVER.
Do you love Chi?

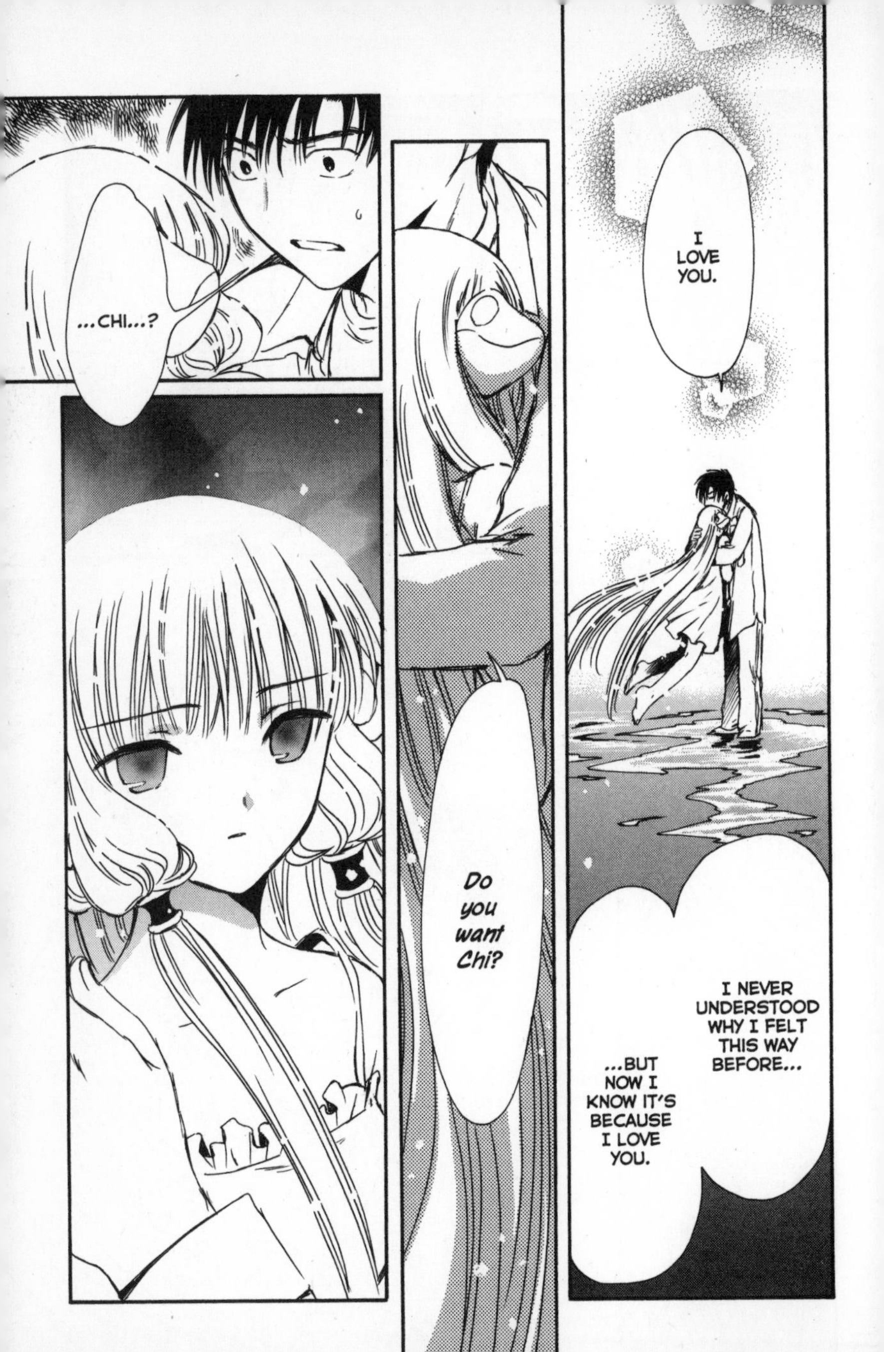
I LOVE YOU.
I NEVER UNDERSTOOD WHY I FELT THIS WAY BEFORE...
...BUT NOW I KNOW IT'S BECAUSE I LOVE YOU.
Do you want Chi?
...CHI...?

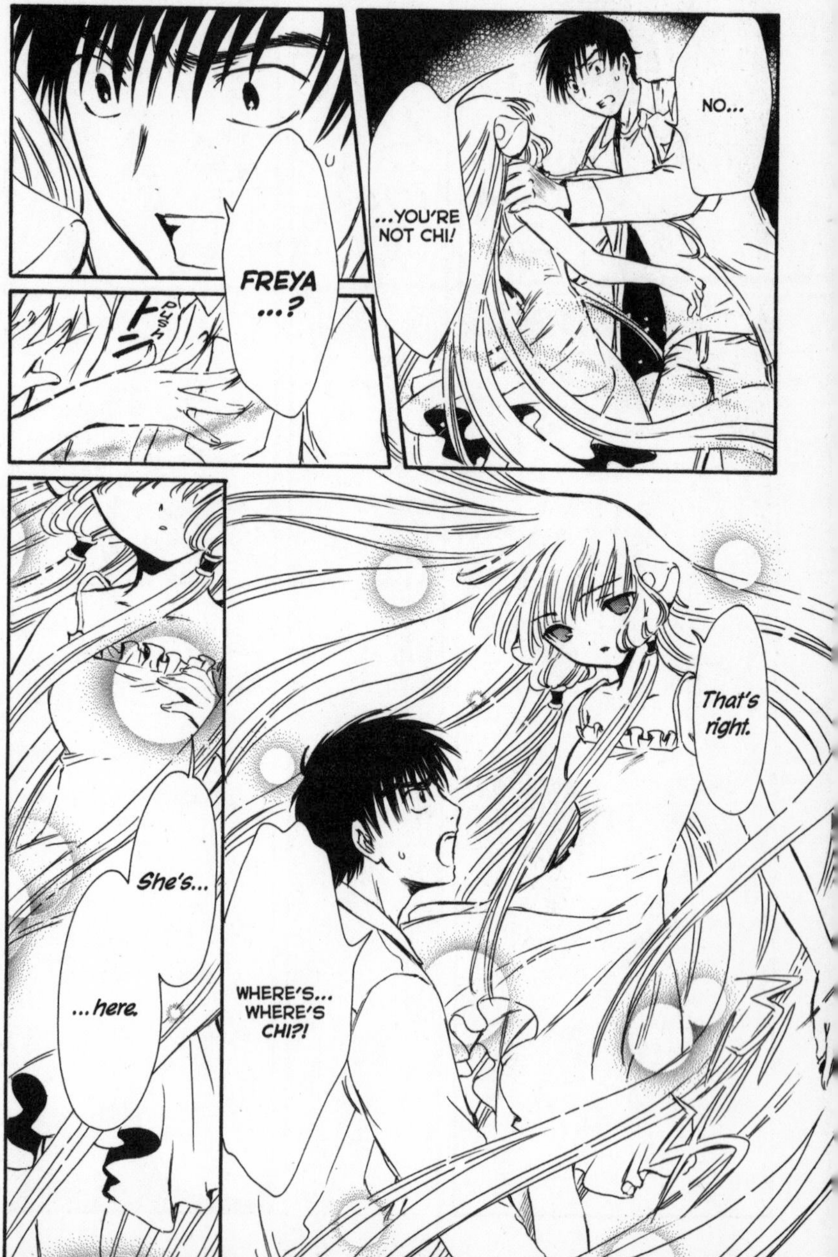
NO...
...YOU'RE NOT CHI!
FREYA ...?
PUSH
That's right.
WHERE'S... WHERE'S CHI?!
She's...
...here.

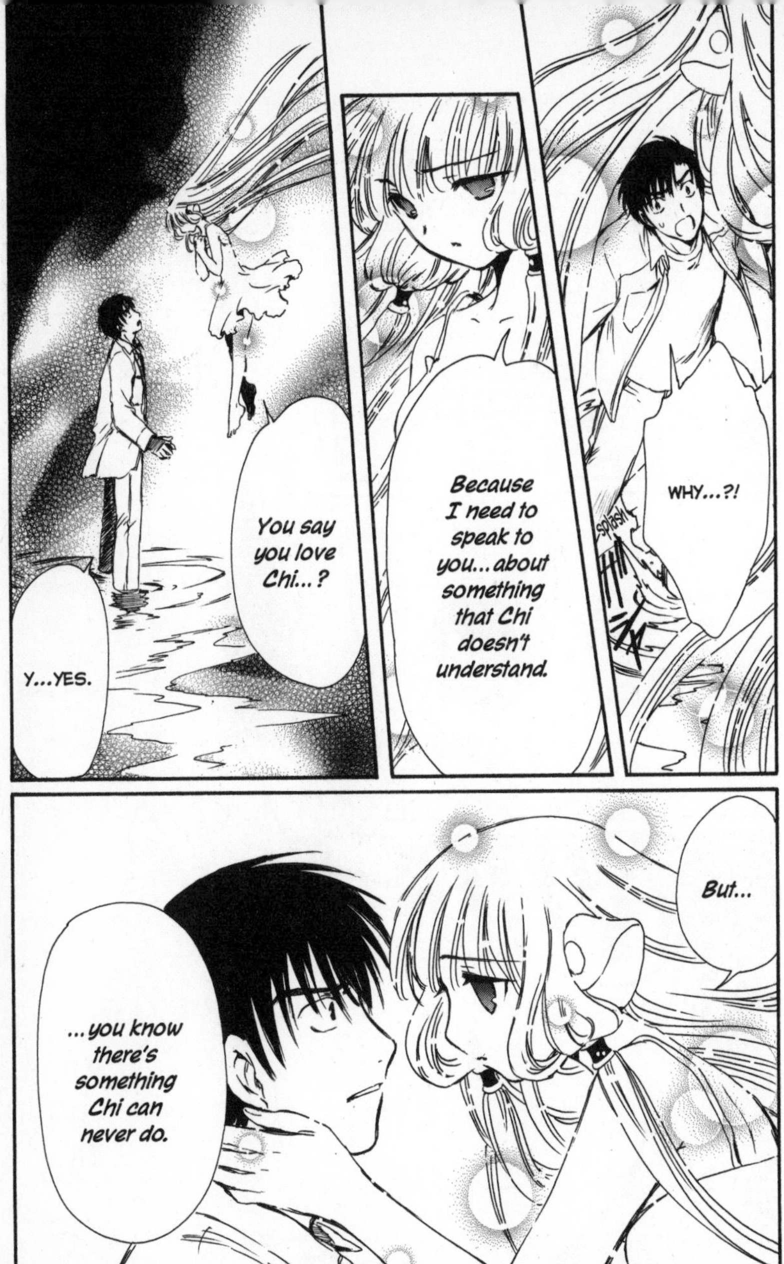
WHY...?!
splash
Because I need to speak to you... about something that Chi doesn't understand.
You say you love Chi...?
Y...YES.
But...
...you know there's something Chi can never do.

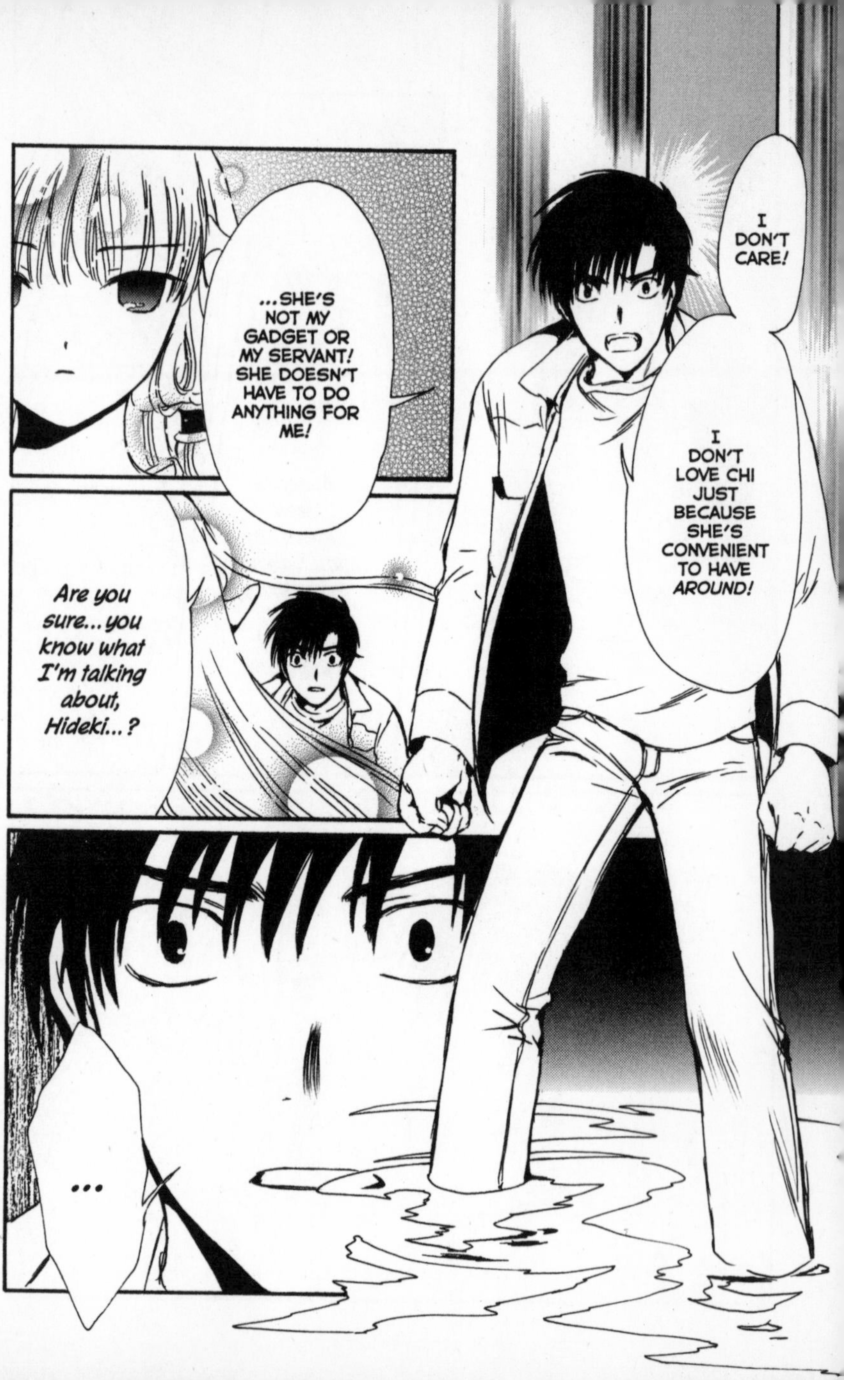
I DON'T CARE!
I DON'T LOVE CHI JUST BECAUSE SHE'S CONVENIENT TO HAVE AROUND!
...SHE'S NOT MY GADGET OR MY SERVANT! SHE DOESN'T HAVE TO DO ANYTHING FOR ME!
Are you sure...you know what I'm talking about, Hideki...?
...

Chobits

ちょびっツ

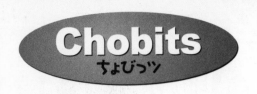

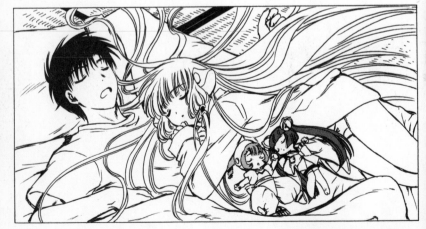

◂ chapter 86 ▸

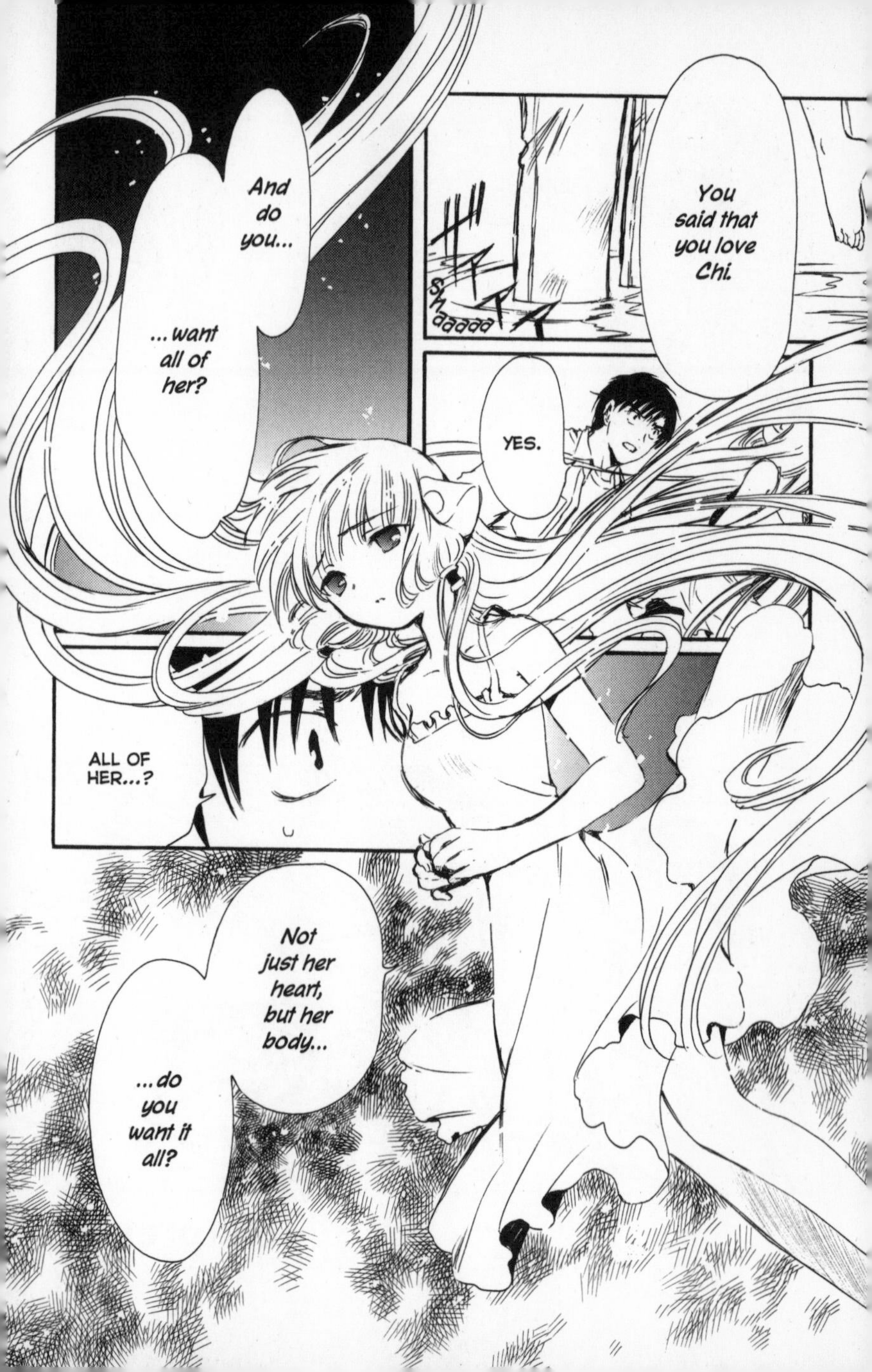
You said that you love Chi.
Shaaaaa
YES.
And do you...
...want all of her?
ALL OF HER...?
Not just her heart, but her body...
...do you want it all?

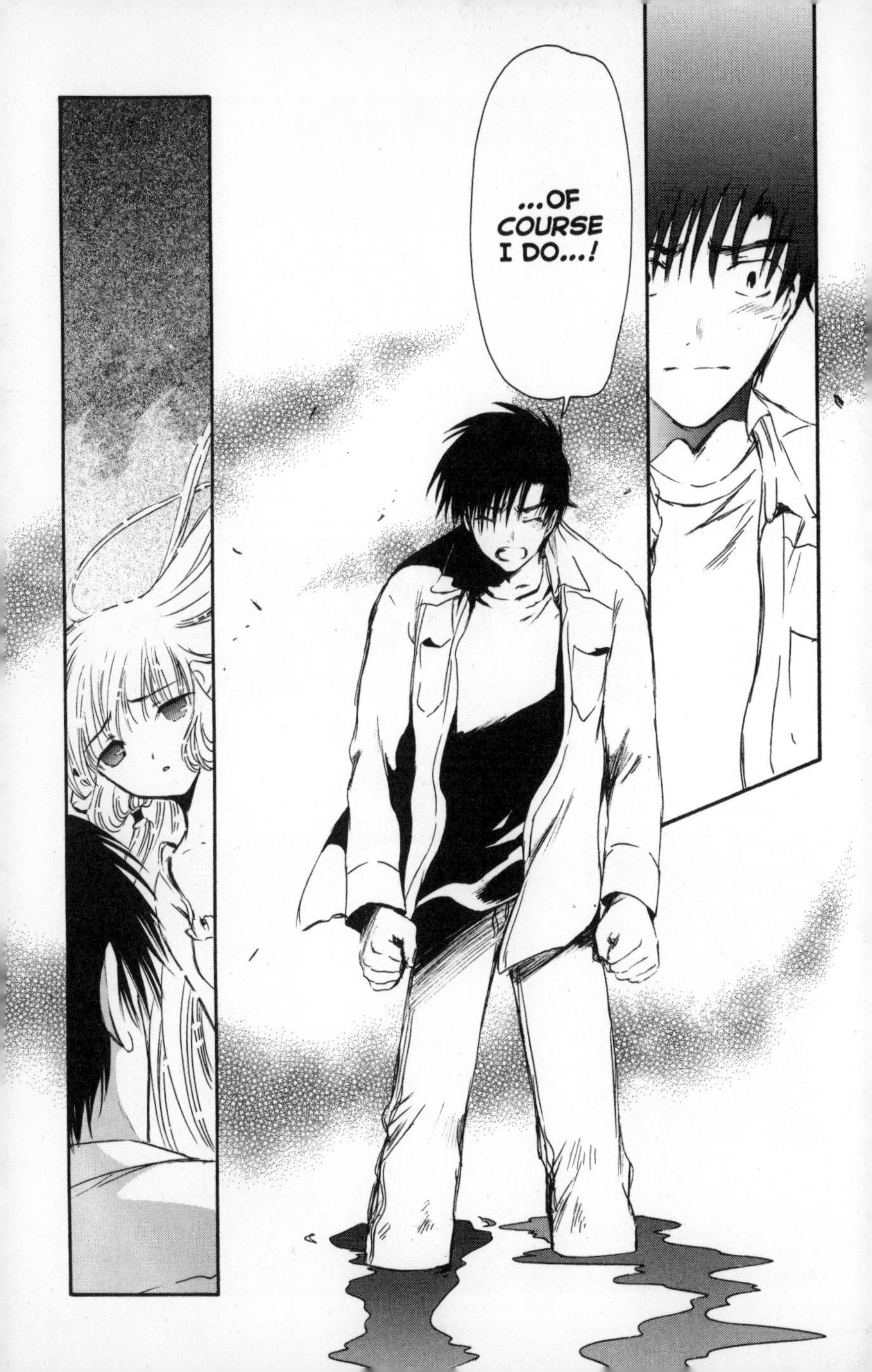
...OF COURSE I DO...!

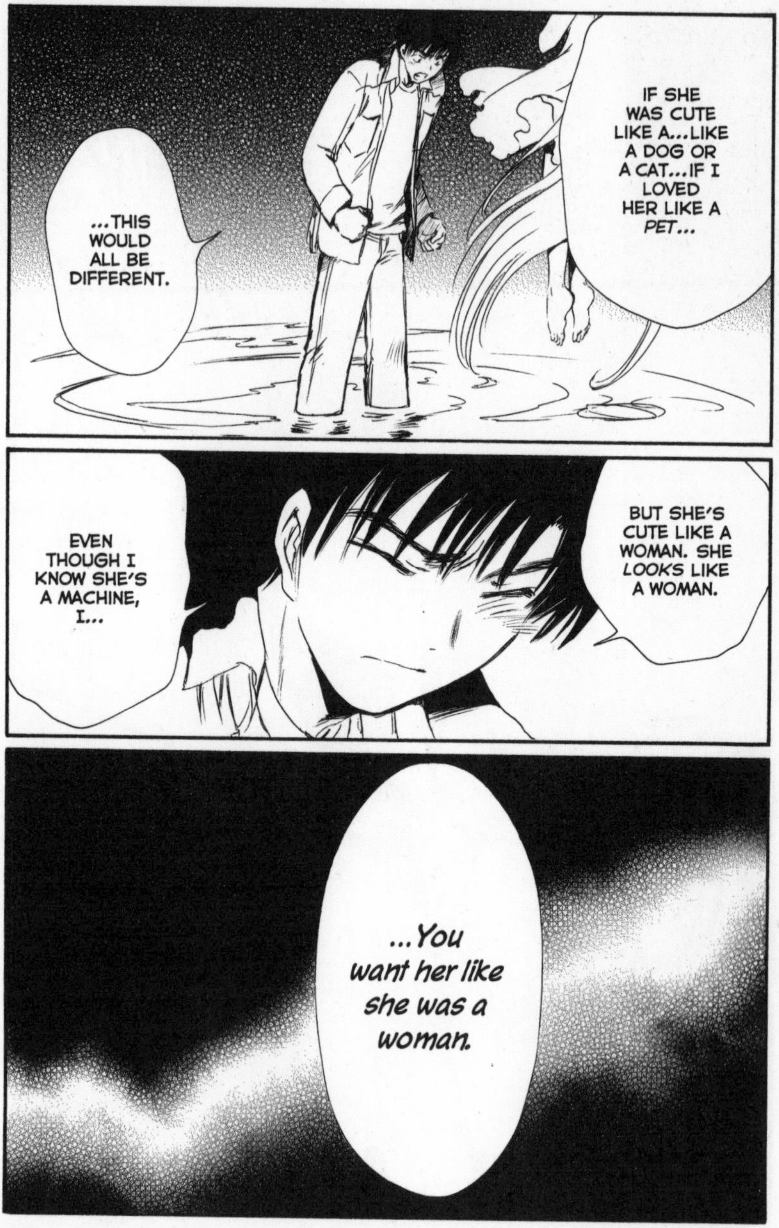
IF SHE WAS CUTE LIKE A...LIKE A DOG OR A CAT...IF I LOVED HER LIKE A *PET*...
...THIS WOULD ALL BE DIFFERENT.
BUT SHE'S CUTE LIKE A WOMAN. SHE *LOOKS* LIKE A WOMAN.
EVEN THOUGH I KNOW SHE'S A MACHINE, I...
...You want her like she was a woman.

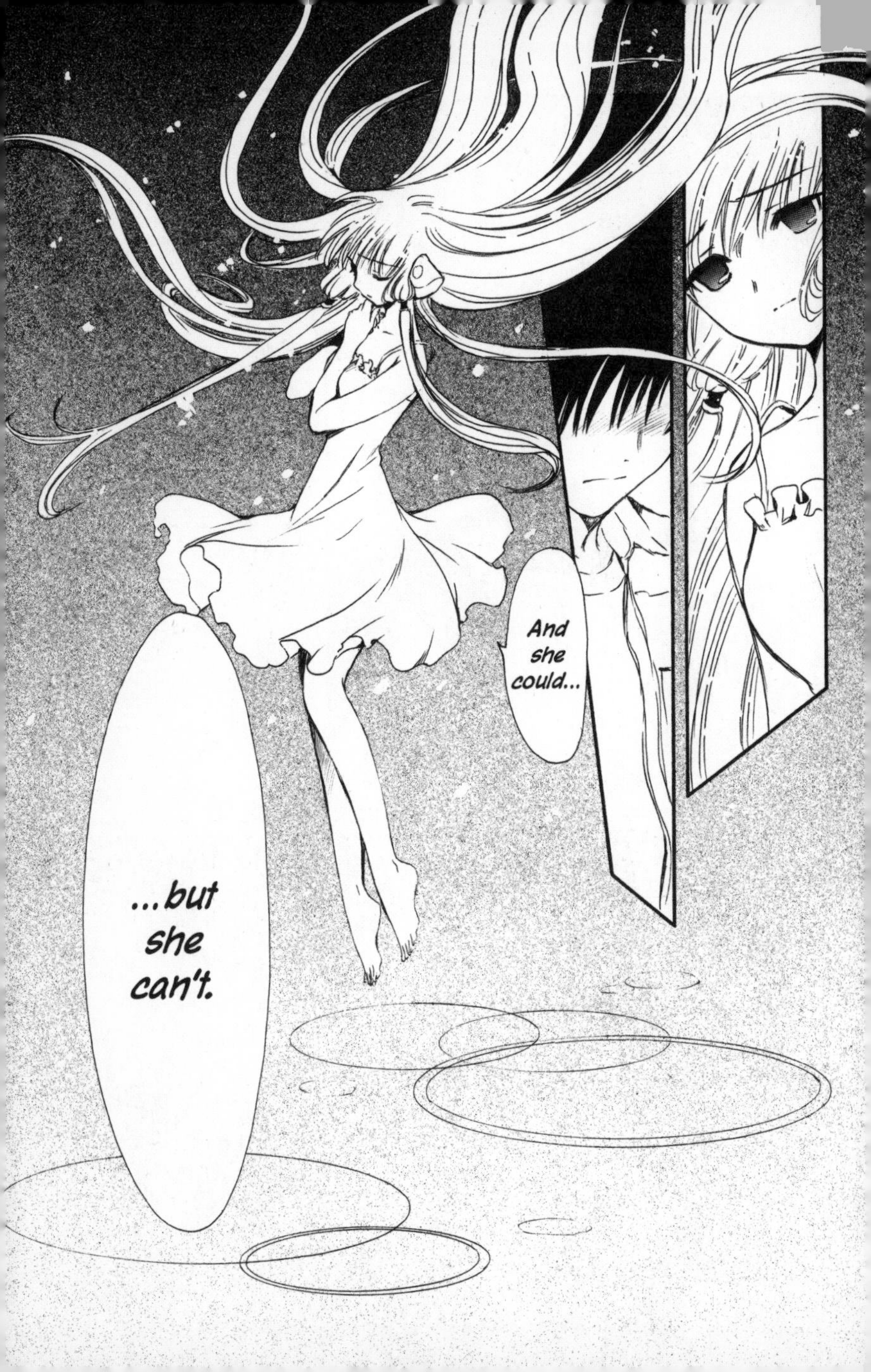
And she could...
...but she can't.

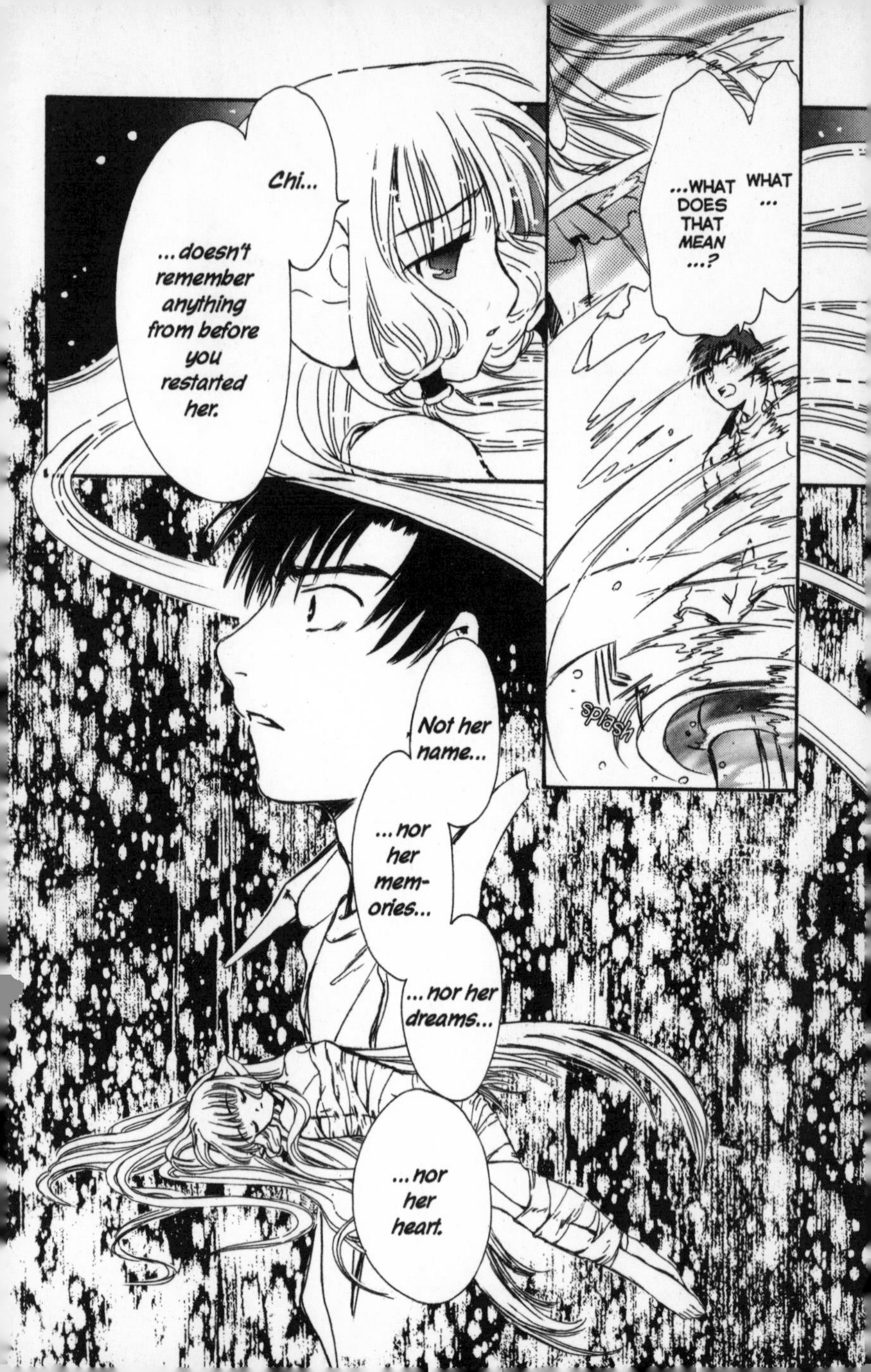
WHAT...
...WHAT DOES THAT MEAN ...?
splash
Chi...
...doesn't remember anything from before you restarted her.
Not her name...
...nor her mem-ories...
...nor her dreams...
...nor her heart.

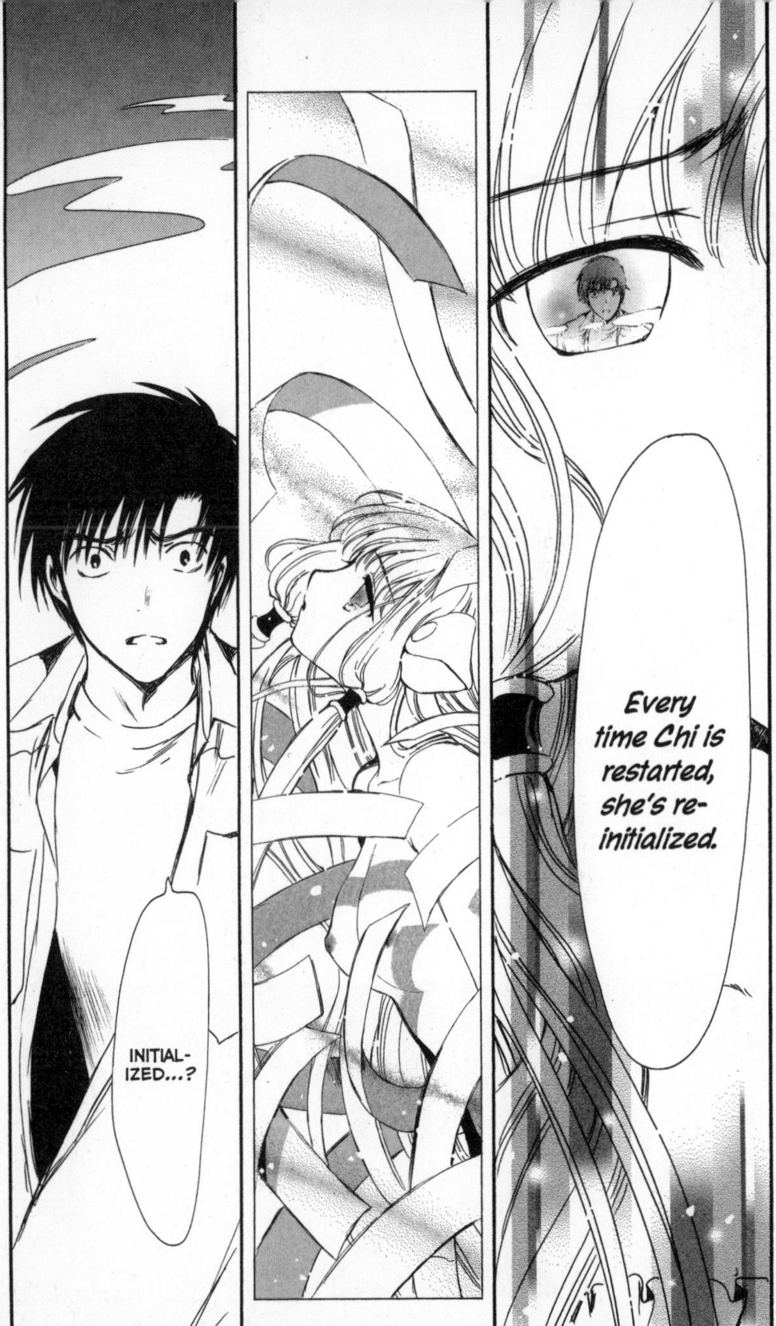
Every time Chi is restarted, she's re-initialized.
INITIAL-IZED...?

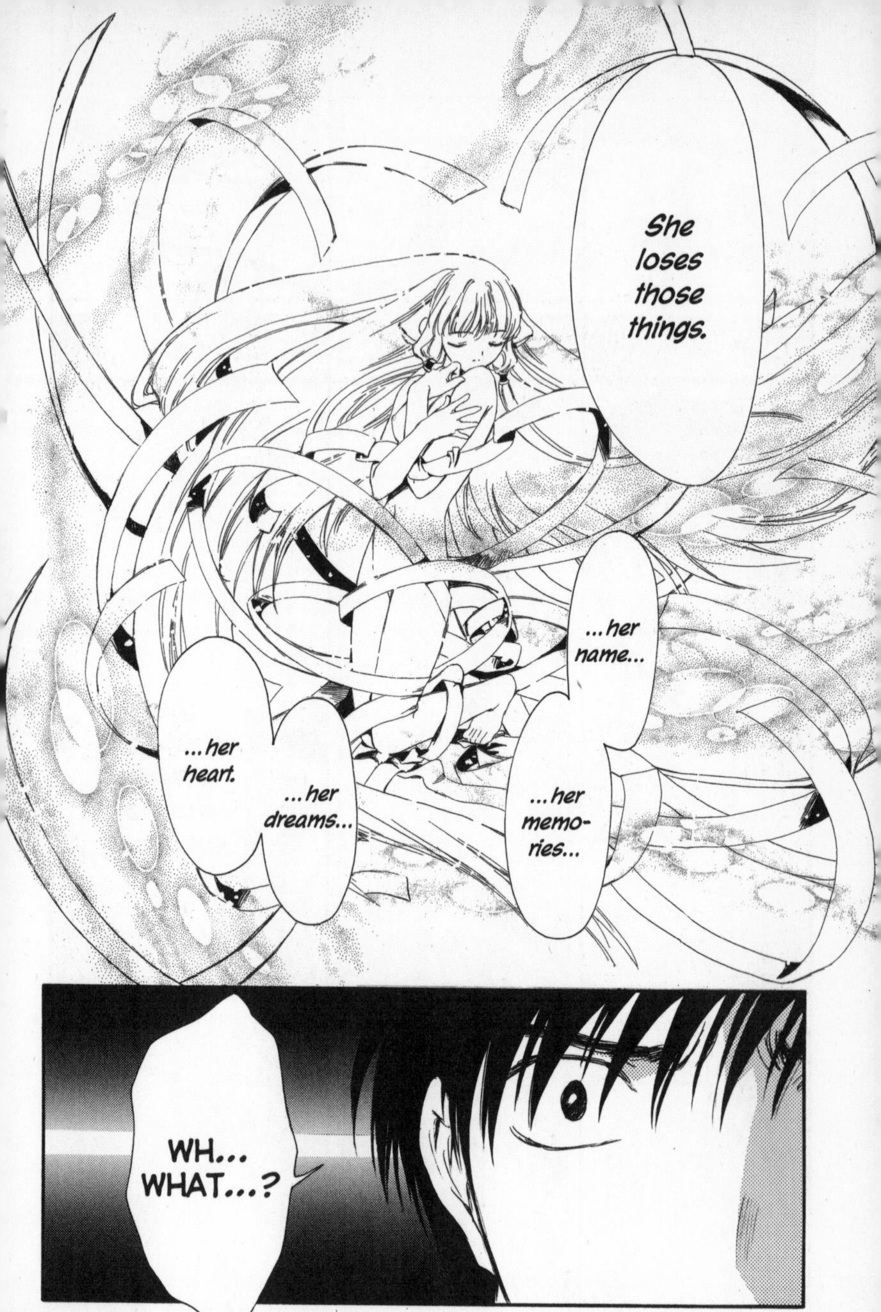
She loses those things.
...her name...
...her memories...
...her dreams...
...her heart.
WH... WHAT...?

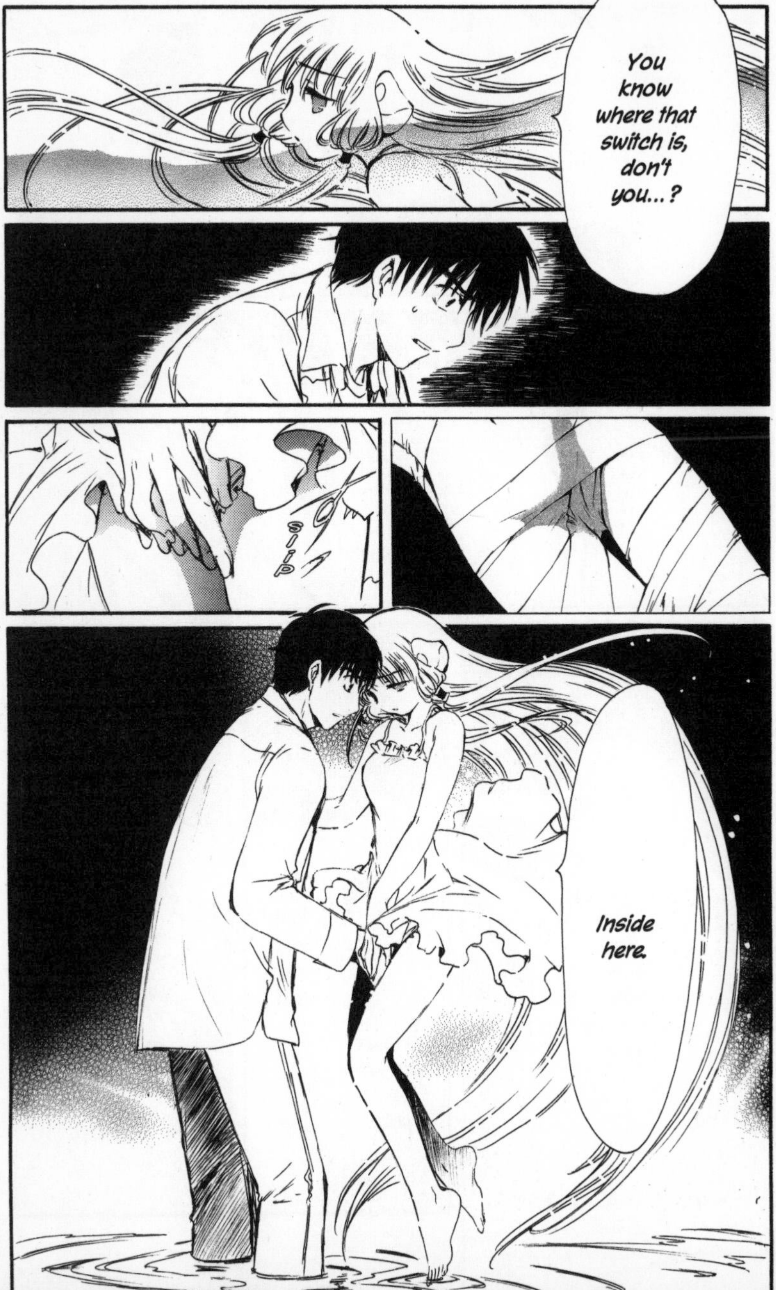
You know where that switch is, don't you...?
slip
Inside here.

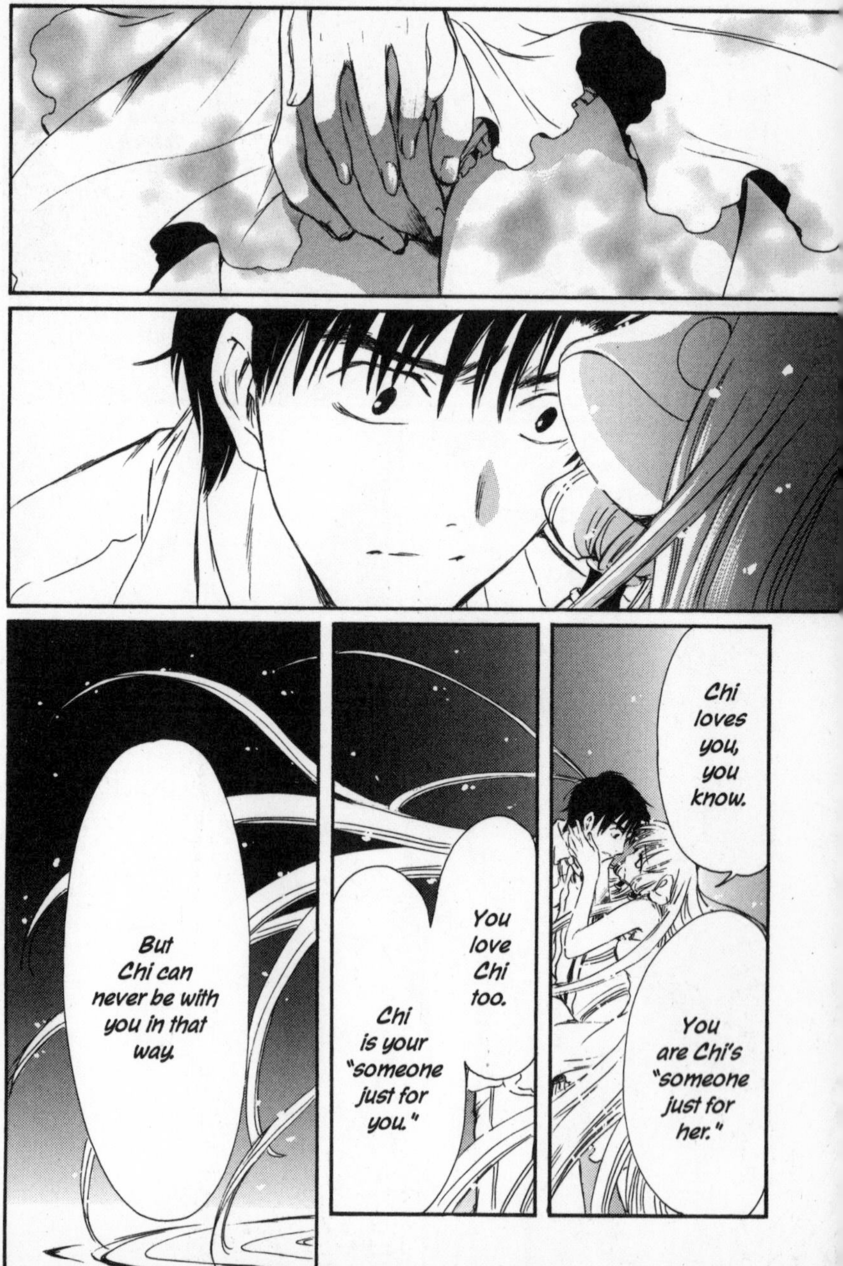
Chi loves you, you know.
You are Chi's "someone just for her."
You love Chi too.
Chi is your "someone just for you."
But Chi can never be with you in that way.

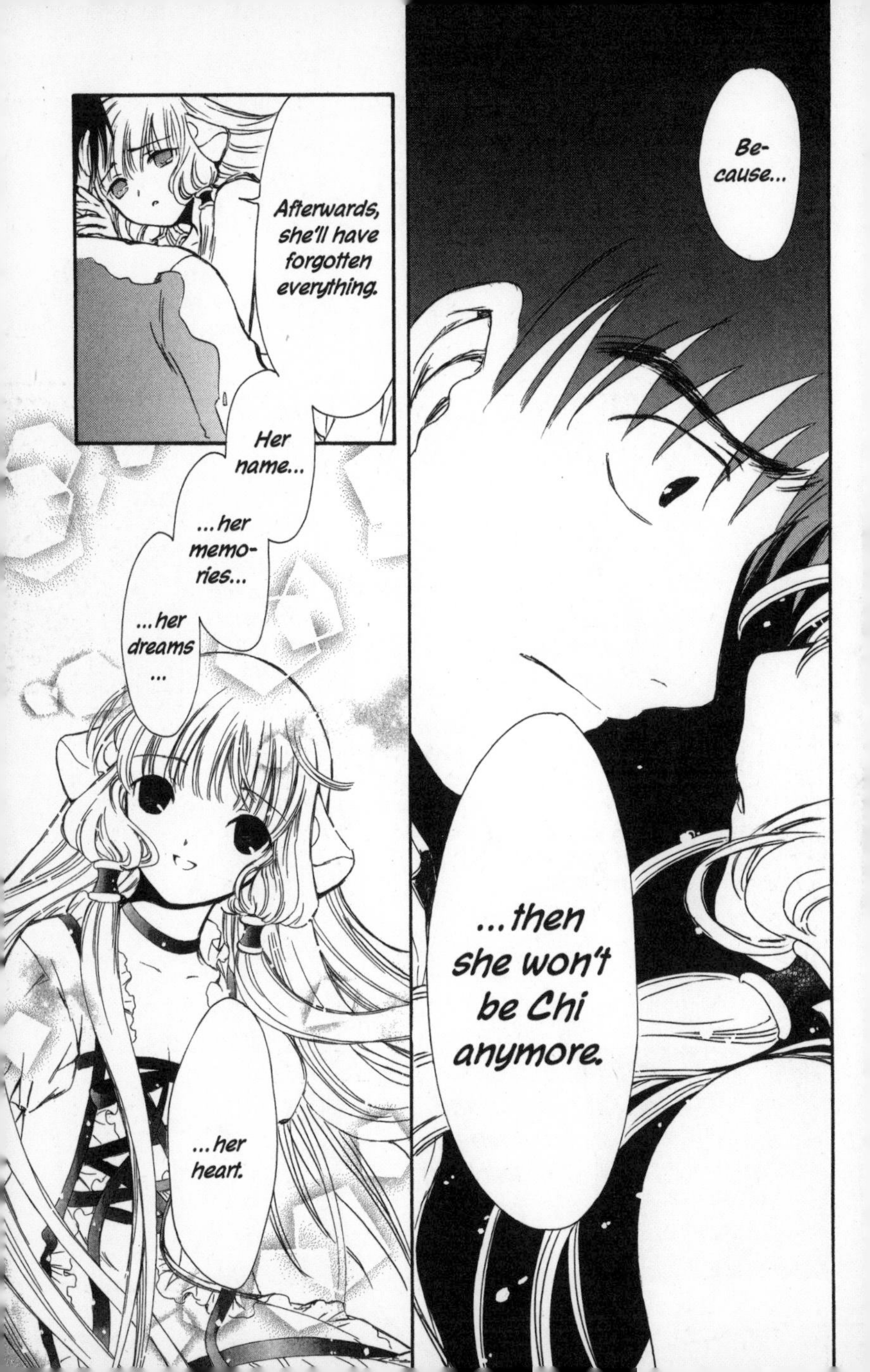
Be-cause...
Afterwards, she'll have forgotten everything.
Her name...
...her memories...
...her dreams...
...her heart.
...then she won't be Chi anymore.

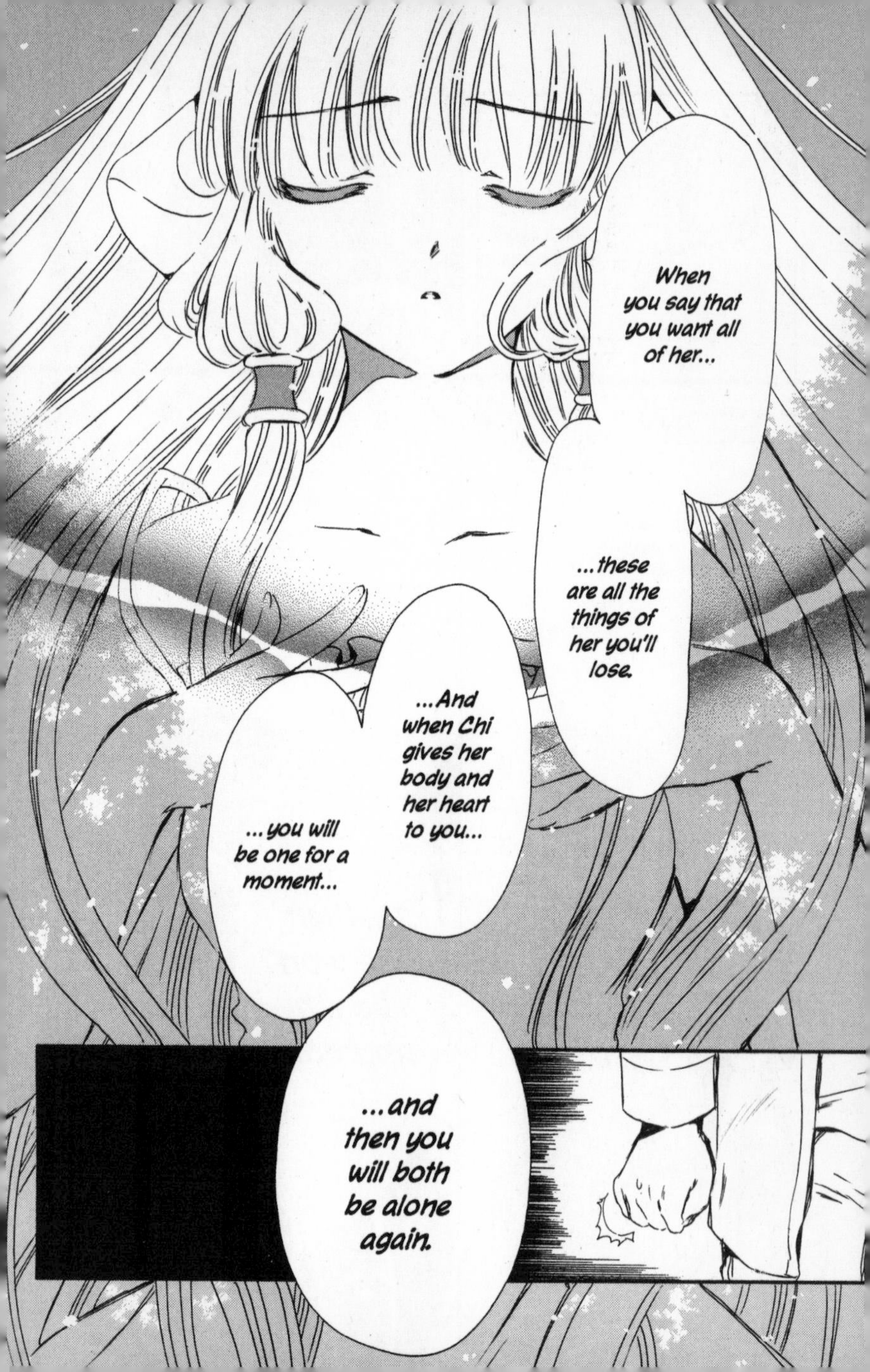
When you say that you want all of her...
...these are all the things of her you'll lose.
...And when Chi gives her body and her heart to you...
...you will be one for a moment...
...and then you will both be alone again.

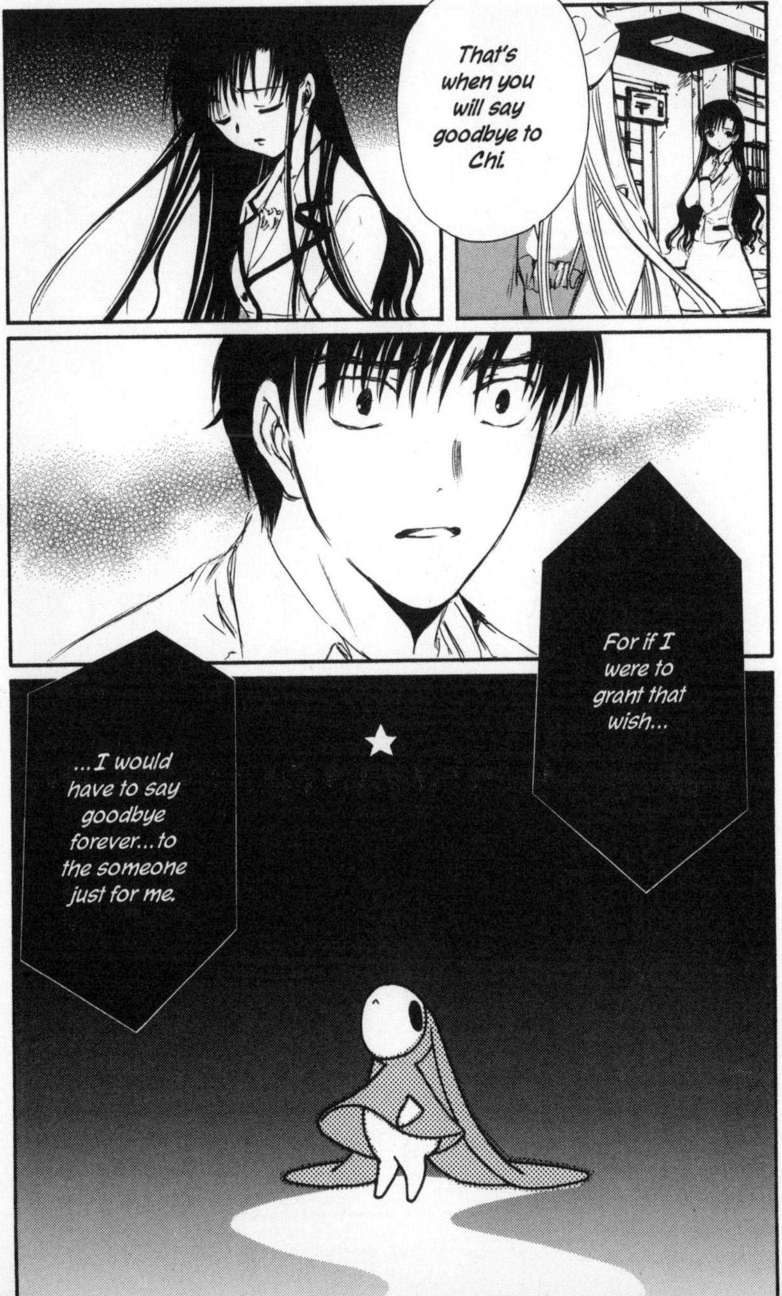
That's when you will say goodbye to Chi.
For if I were to grant that wish...
...I would have to say goodbye forever...to the someone just for me.

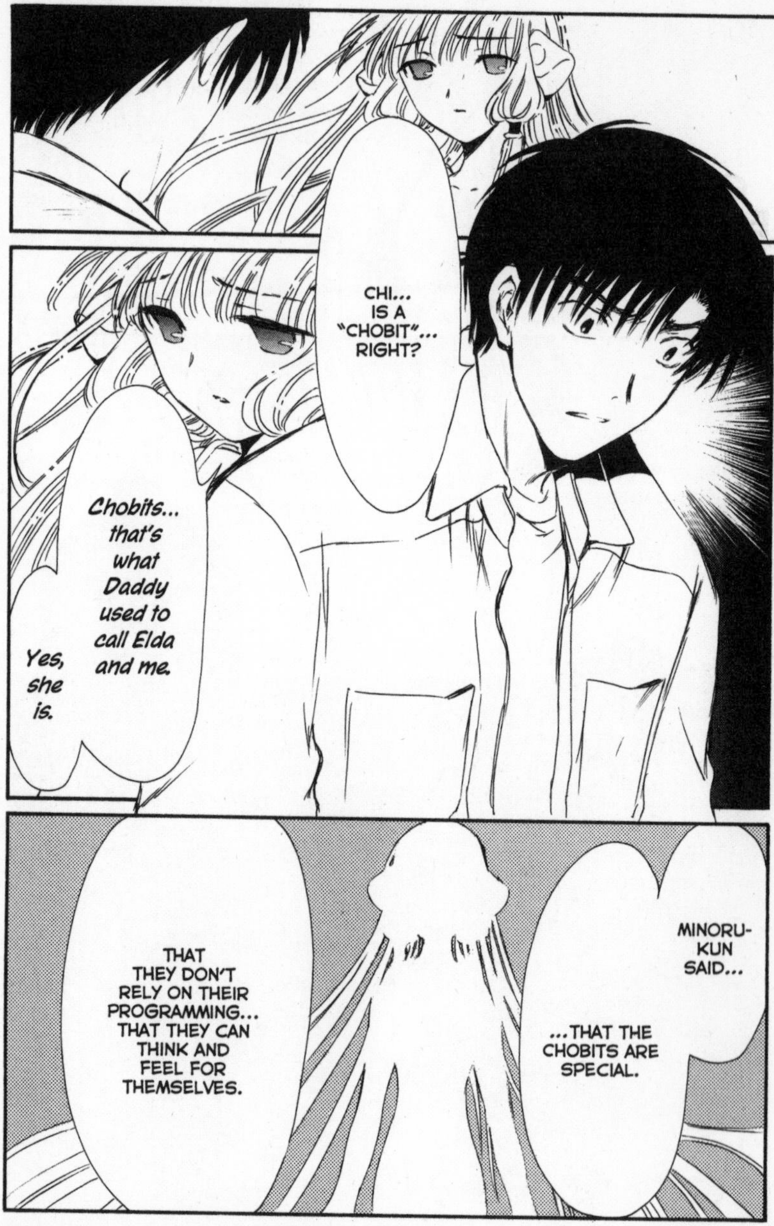
CHI... IS A "CHOBIT"... RIGHT?
Chobits... that's what Daddy used to call Elda and me.
Yes, she is.
MINORU-KUN SAID...
...THAT THE CHOBITS ARE SPECIAL.
THAT THEY DON'T RELY ON THEIR PROGRAMMING... THAT THEY CAN THINK AND FEEL FOR THEMSELVES.

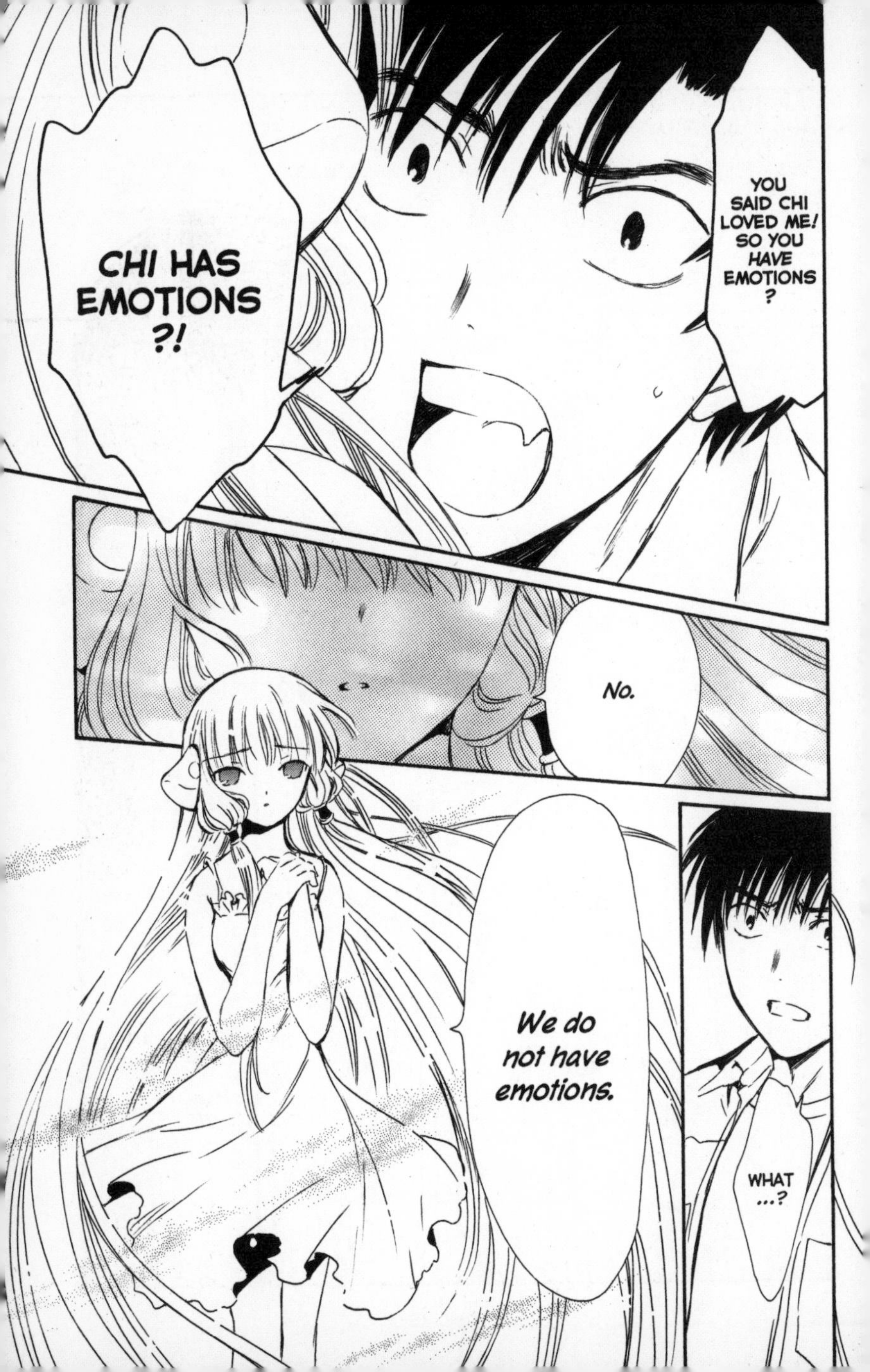
YOU SAID CHI LOVED ME! SO YOU HAVE EMOTIONS?
CHI HAS EMOTIONS?!
No.
We do not have emotions.
WHAT...?

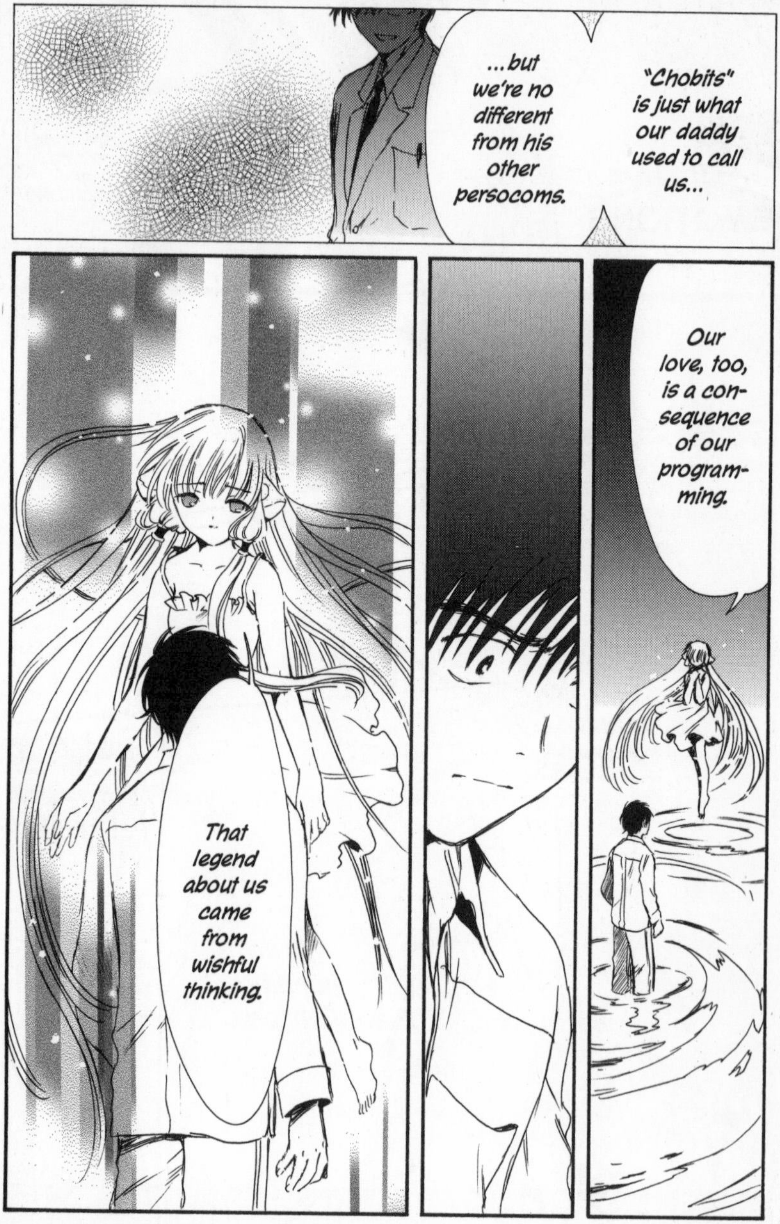
"Chobits" is just what our daddy used to call us...
...but we're no different from his other persocoms.
Our love, too, is a con-sequence of our program-ming.
That legend about us came from wishful thinking.

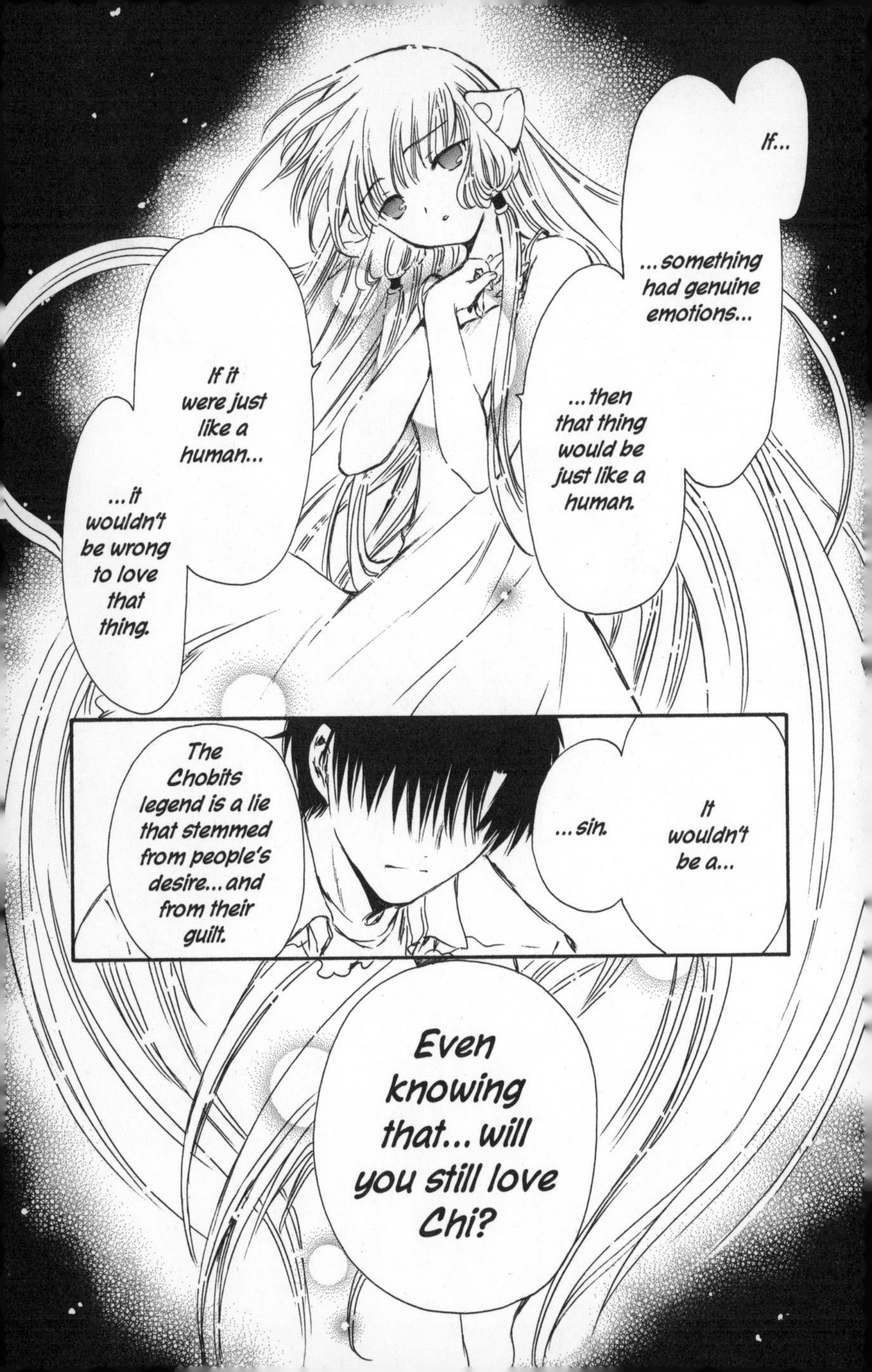
If...
...something had genuine emotions...
...then that thing would be just like a human.
If it were just like a human...
...it wouldn't be wrong to love that thing.
It wouldn't be a...
...sin.
The Chobits legend is a lie that stemmed from people's desire...and from their guilt.
Even knowing that...will you still love Chi?

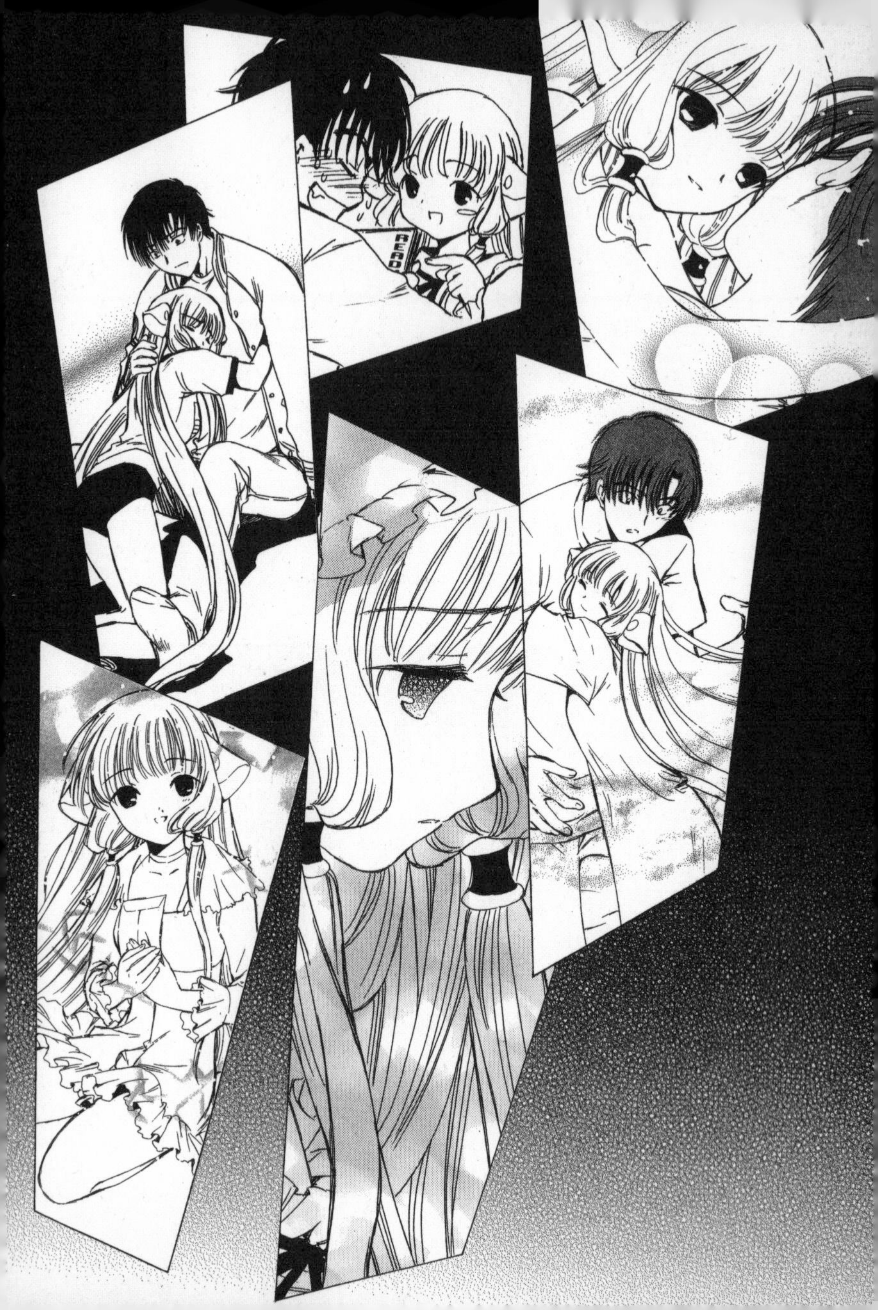
READ

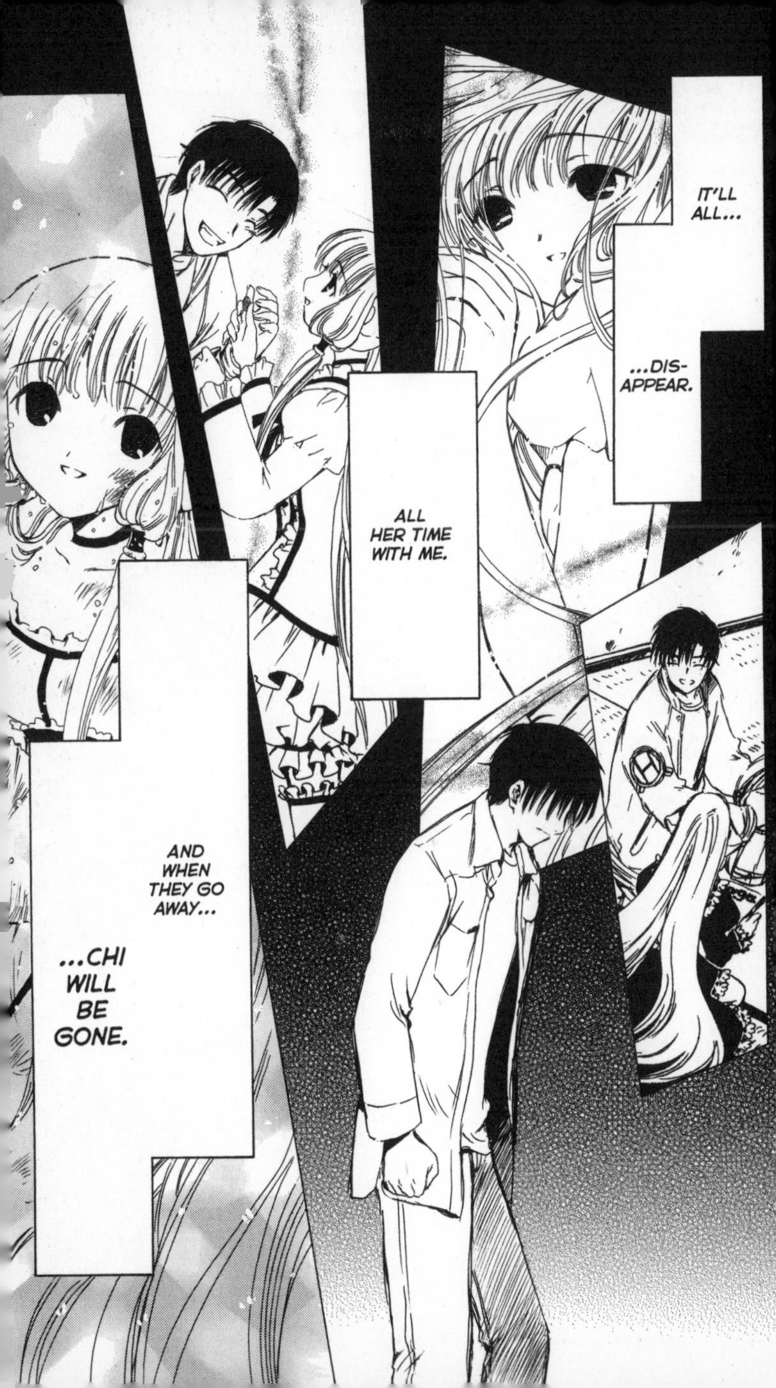
IT'LL ALL...
...DIS-APPEAR.
ALL HER TIME WITH ME.
AND WHEN THEY GO AWAY...
...CHI WILL BE GONE.

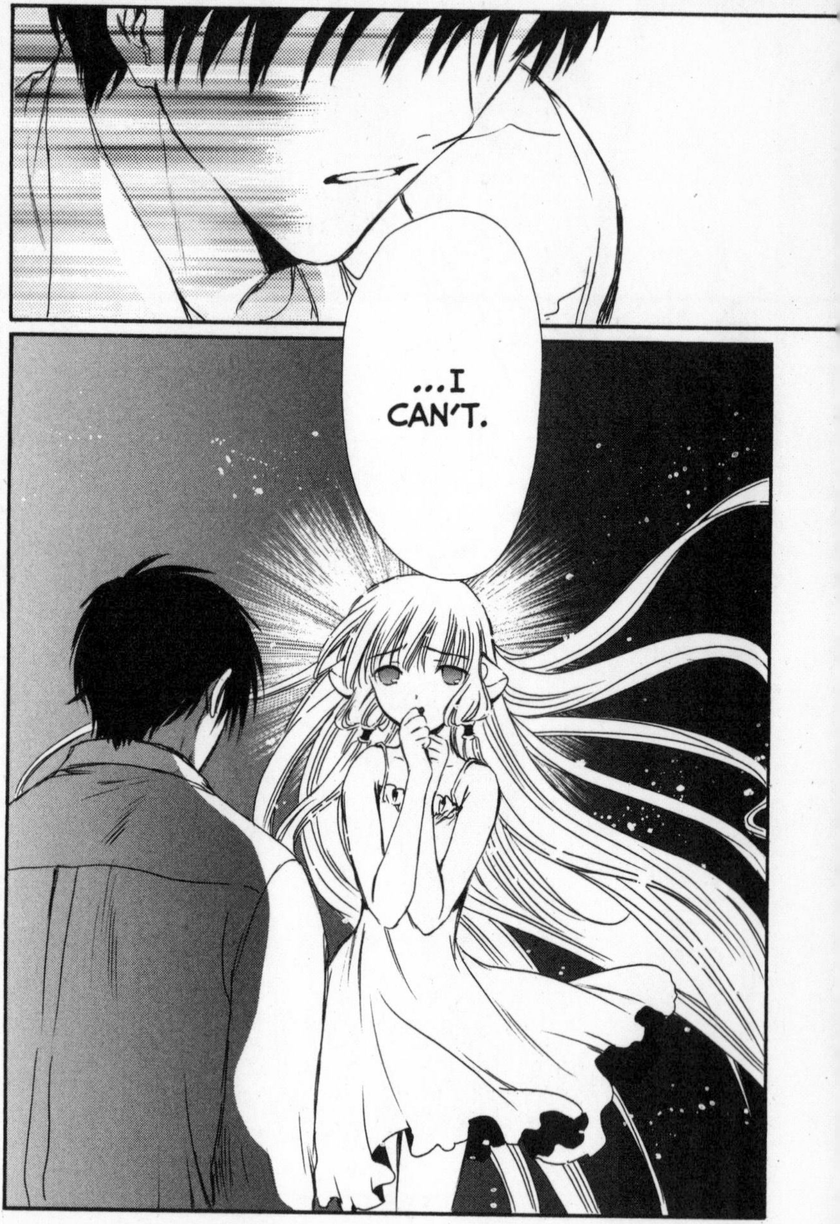
...I CAN'T.

Chobits
ちょびっツ

◀ **chapter 87** ▶

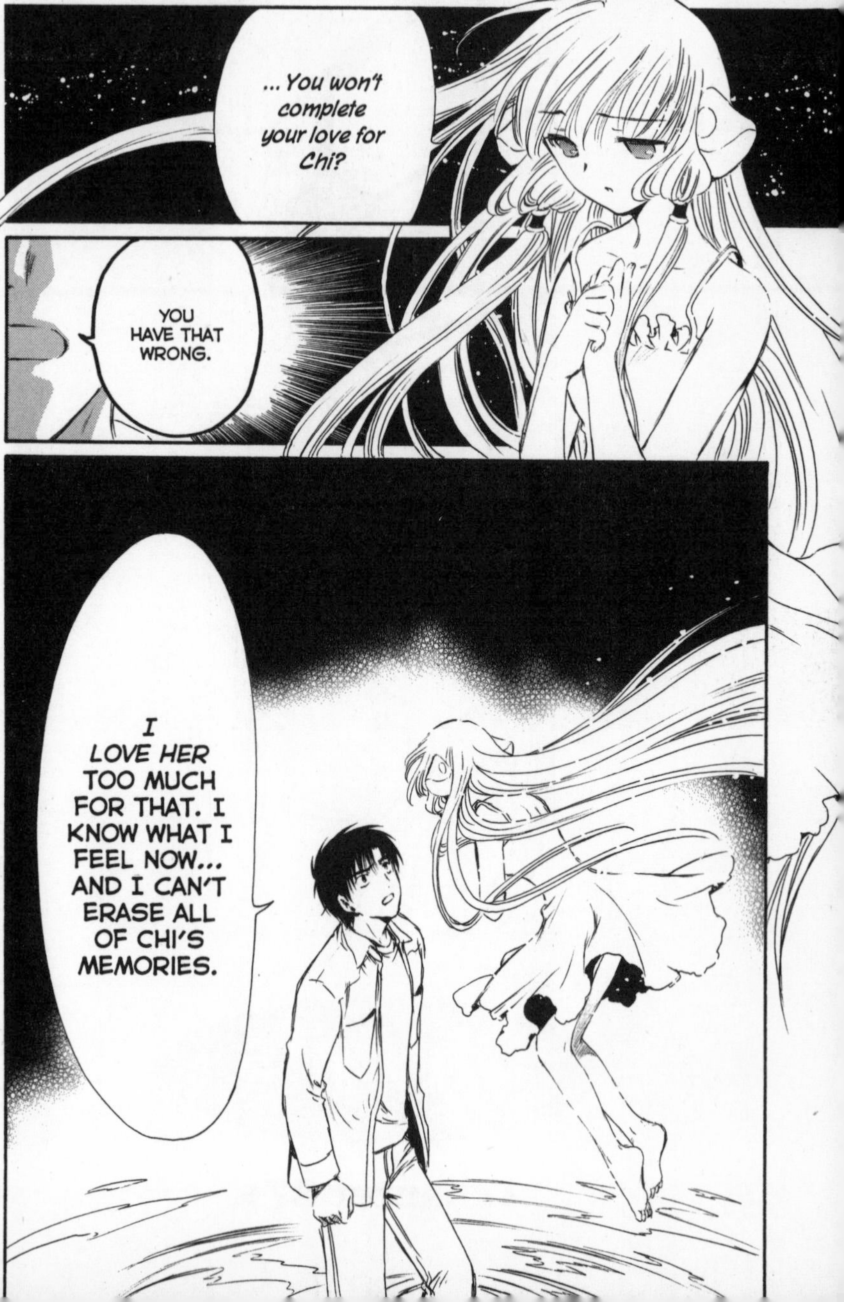
...You won't complete your love for Chi?
YOU HAVE THAT WRONG.
I LOVE HER TOO MUCH FOR THAT. I KNOW WHAT I FEEL NOW... AND I CAN'T ERASE ALL OF CHI'S MEMORIES.

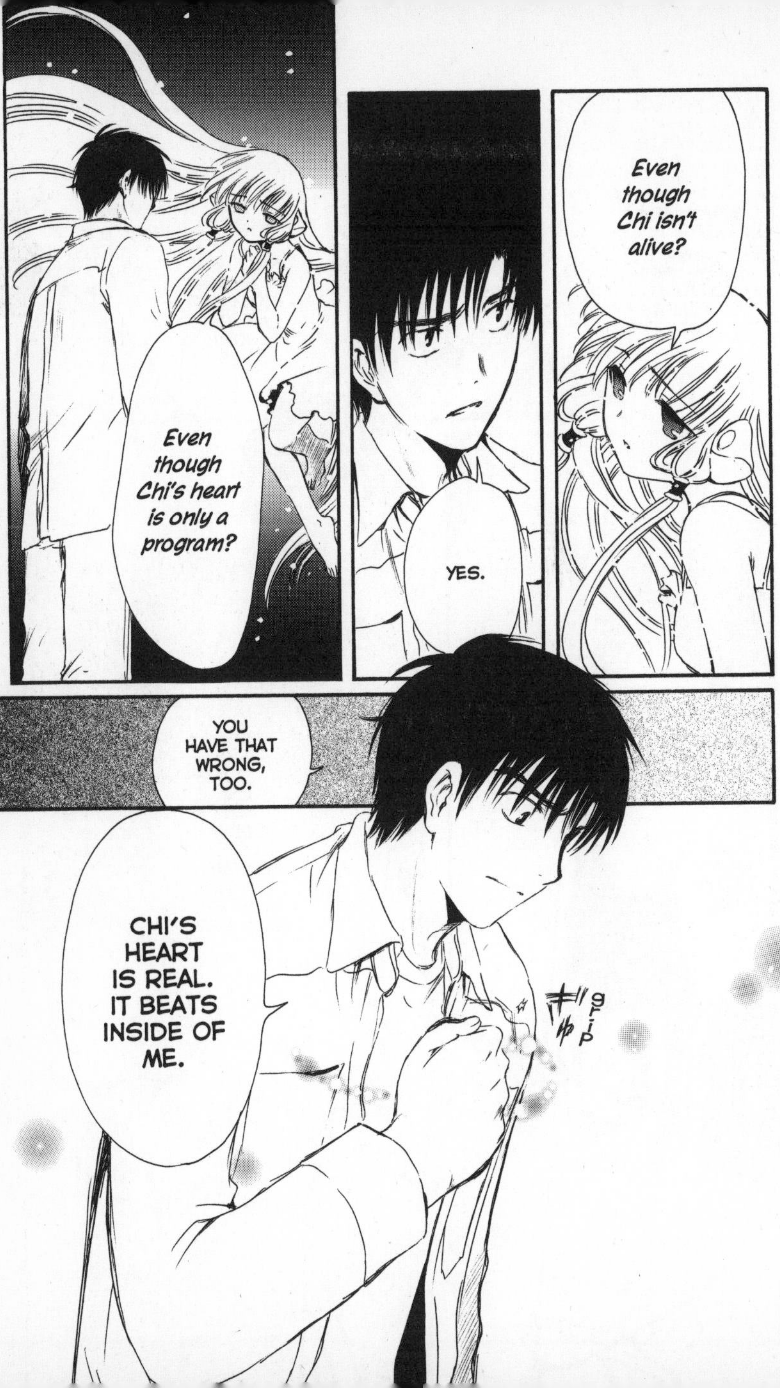
Even though Chi isn't alive?
YES.
Even though Chi's heart is only a program?
YOU HAVE THAT WRONG, TOO.
CHI'S HEART IS REAL. IT BEATS INSIDE OF ME.
grip

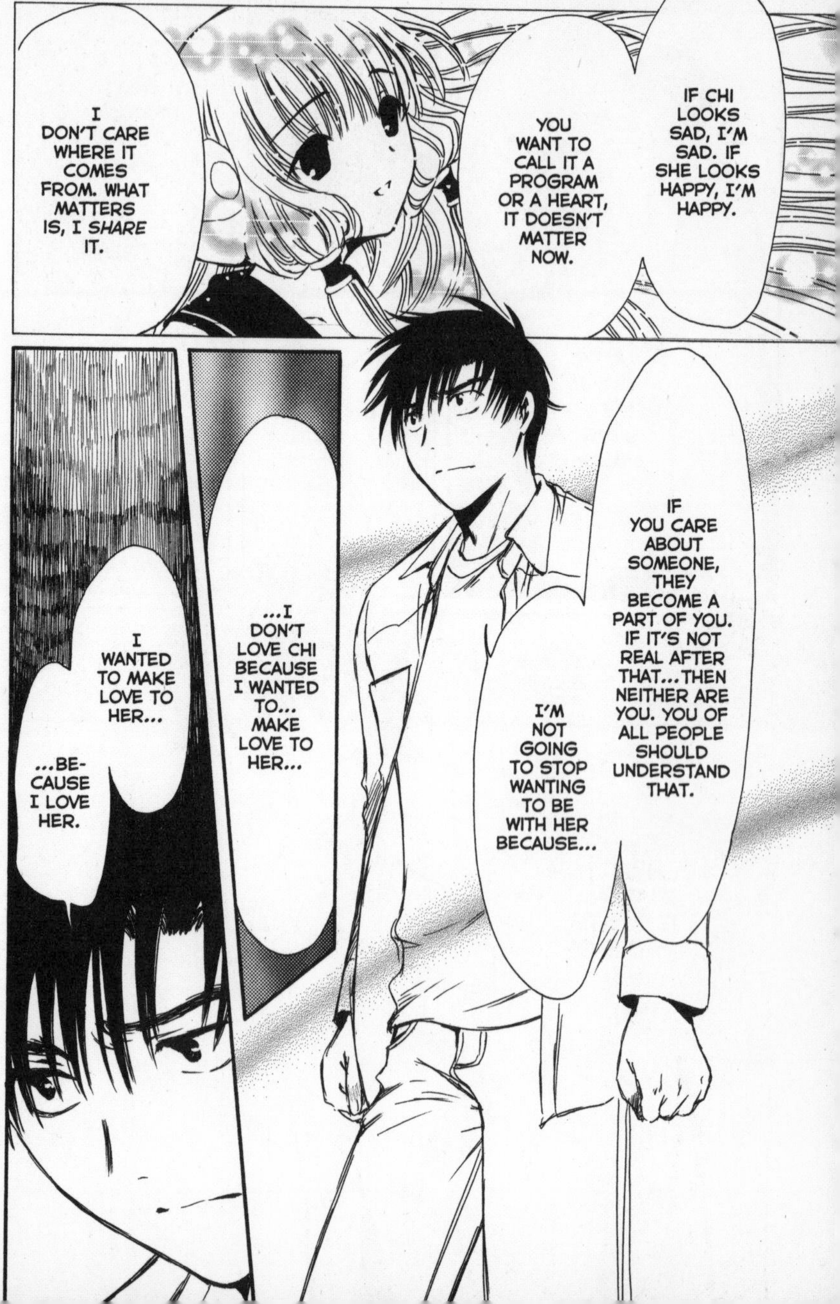
IF CHI LOOKS SAD, I'M SAD. IF SHE LOOKS HAPPY, I'M HAPPY.
YOU WANT TO CALL IT A PROGRAM OR A HEART, IT DOESN'T MATTER NOW.
I DON'T CARE WHERE IT COMES FROM. WHAT MATTERS IS, I *SHARE* IT.
IF YOU CARE ABOUT SOMEONE, THEY BECOME A PART OF YOU. IF IT'S NOT REAL AFTER THAT...THEN NEITHER ARE YOU. YOU OF ALL PEOPLE SHOULD UNDERSTAND THAT.
I'M NOT GOING TO STOP WANTING TO BE WITH HER BECAUSE...
...I DON'T LOVE CHI BECAUSE I WANTED TO... MAKE LOVE TO HER...
I WANTED TO MAKE LOVE TO HER...
...BE-CAUSE I LOVE HER.

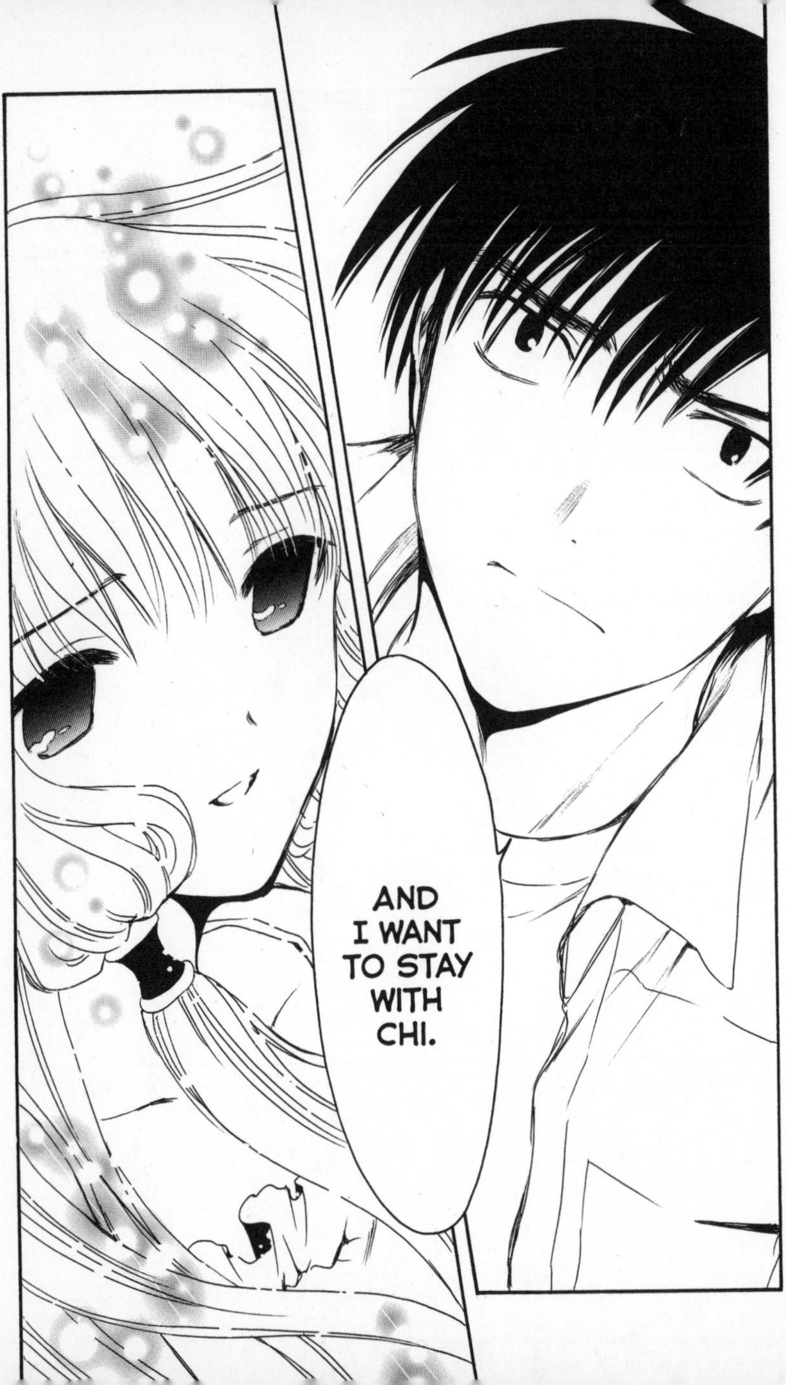
AND I WANT TO STAY WITH CHI.

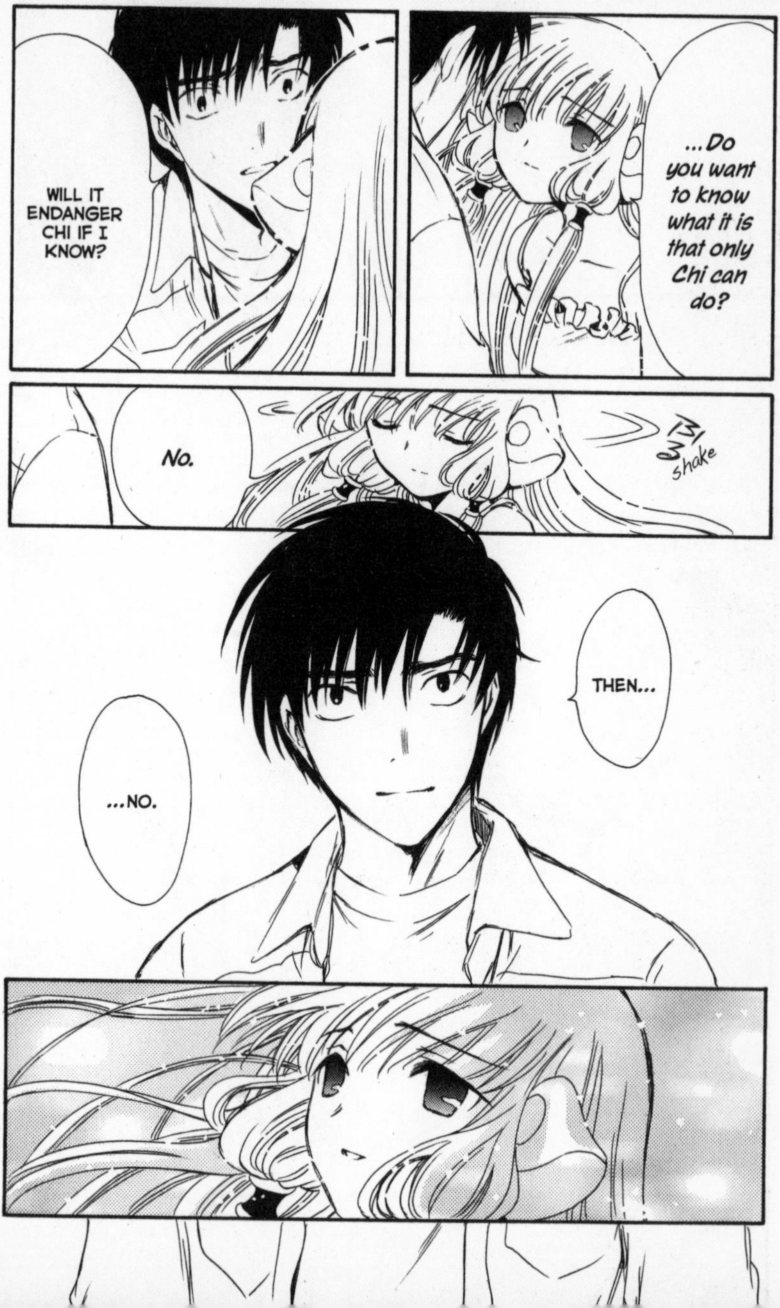
...Do you want to know what it is that only Chi can do?
WILL IT ENDANGER CHI IF I KNOW?
shake
No.
THEN...
...NO.

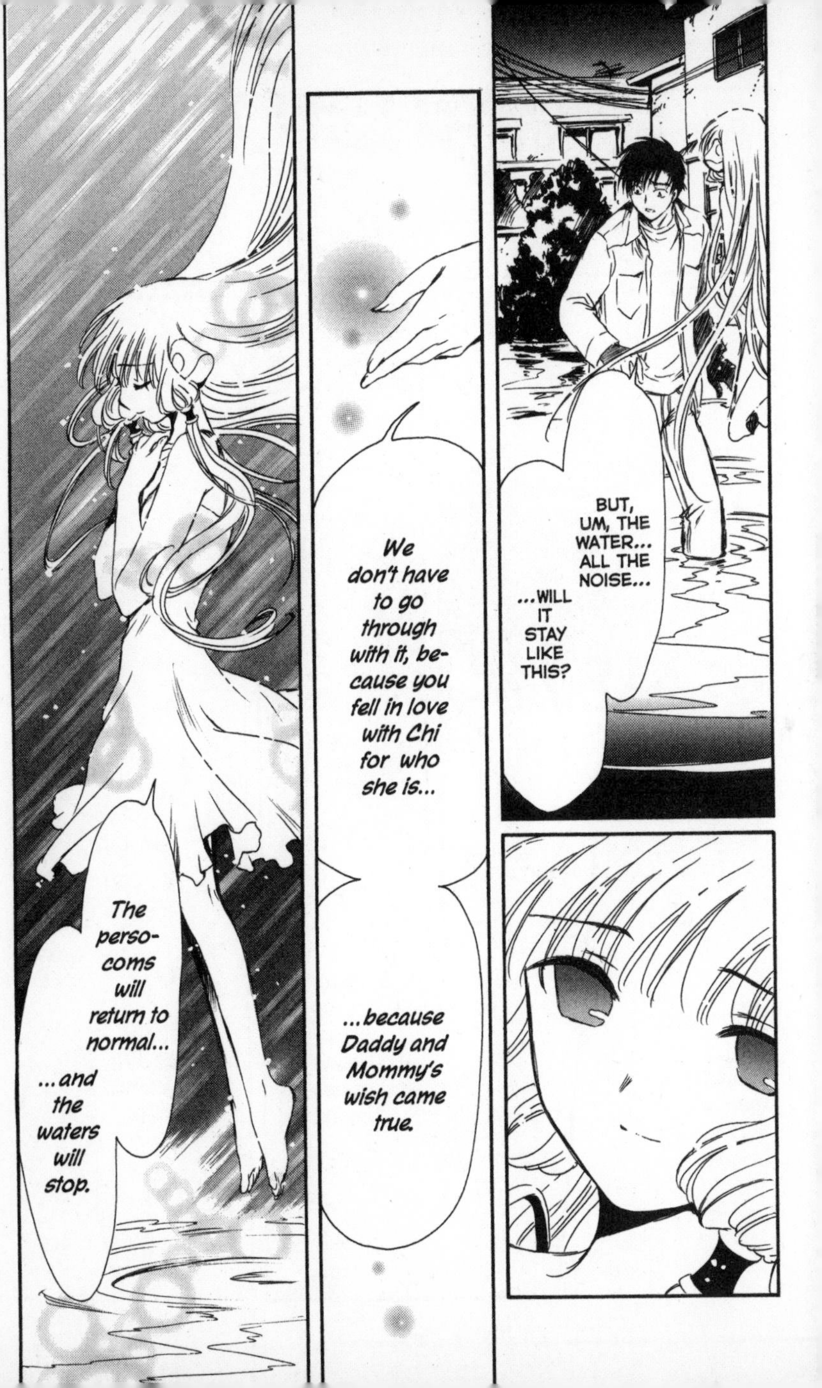
BUT, UM, THE WATER... ALL THE NOISE...
...WILL IT STAY LIKE THIS?
We don't have to go through with it, be-cause you fell in love with Chi for who she is...
...because Daddy and Mommy's wish came true.
The perso-coms will return to normal...
...and the waters will stop.

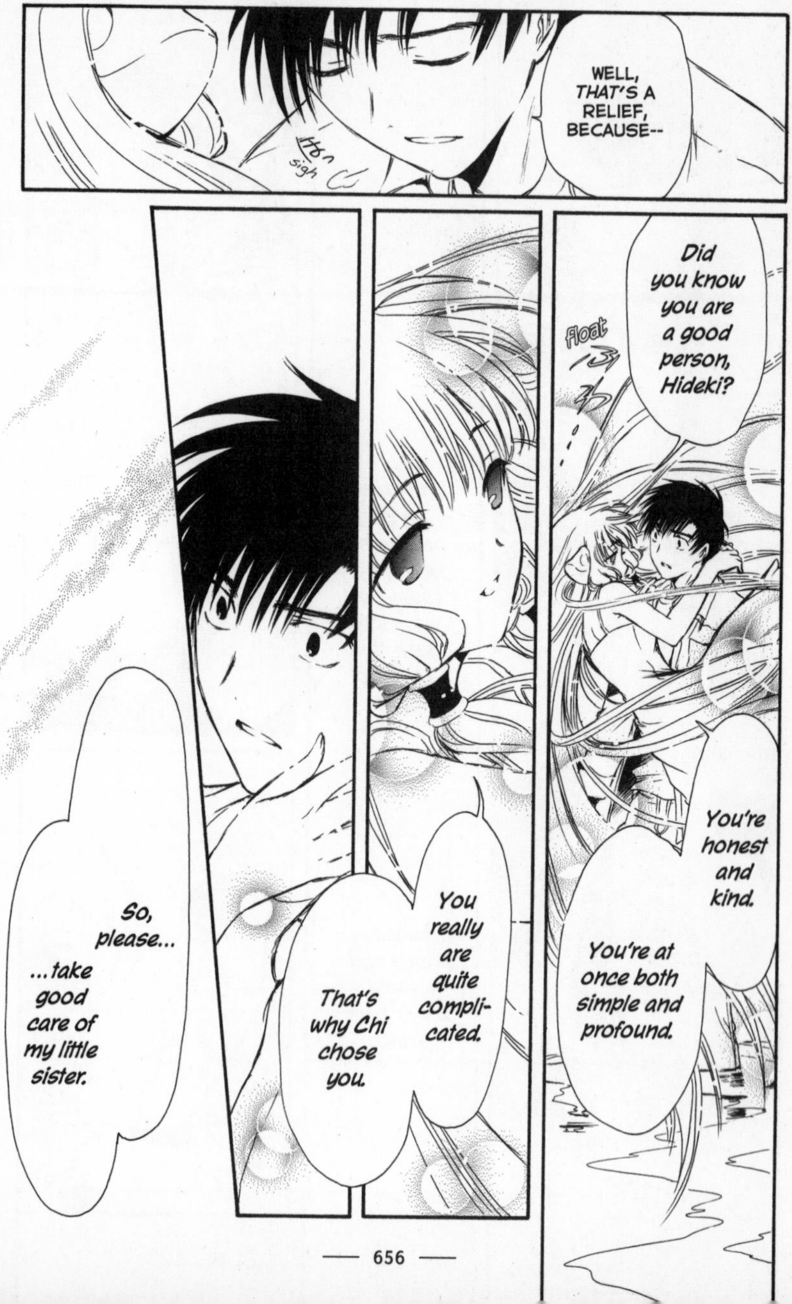
WELL, THAT'S A RELIEF, BECAUSE--
sigh
Did you know you are a good person, Hideki?
float
You're honest and kind.
You're at once both simple and profound.
You really are quite compli-cated.
That's why Chi chose you.
So, please...
...take good care of my little sister.

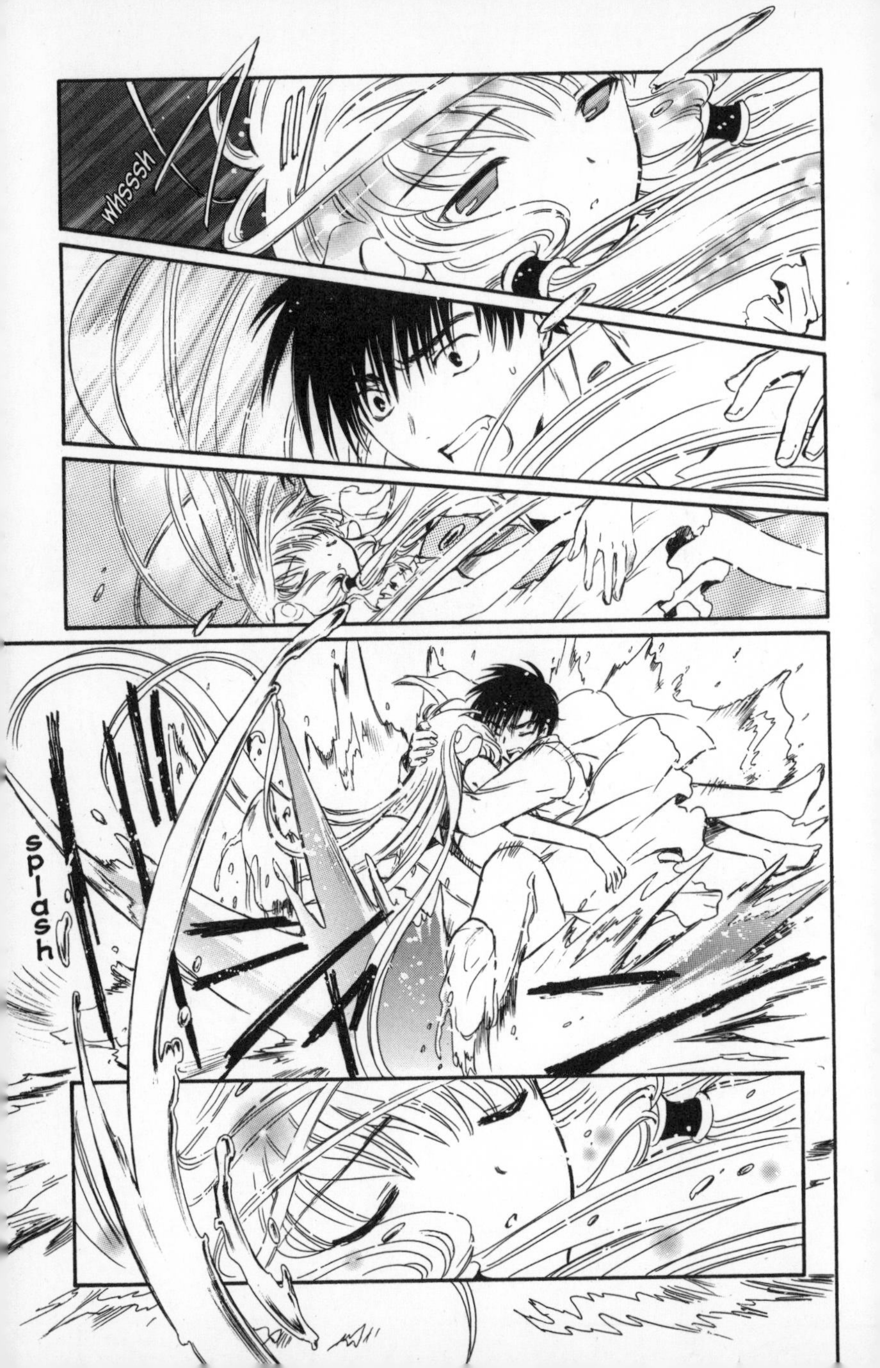
whsssh
splash

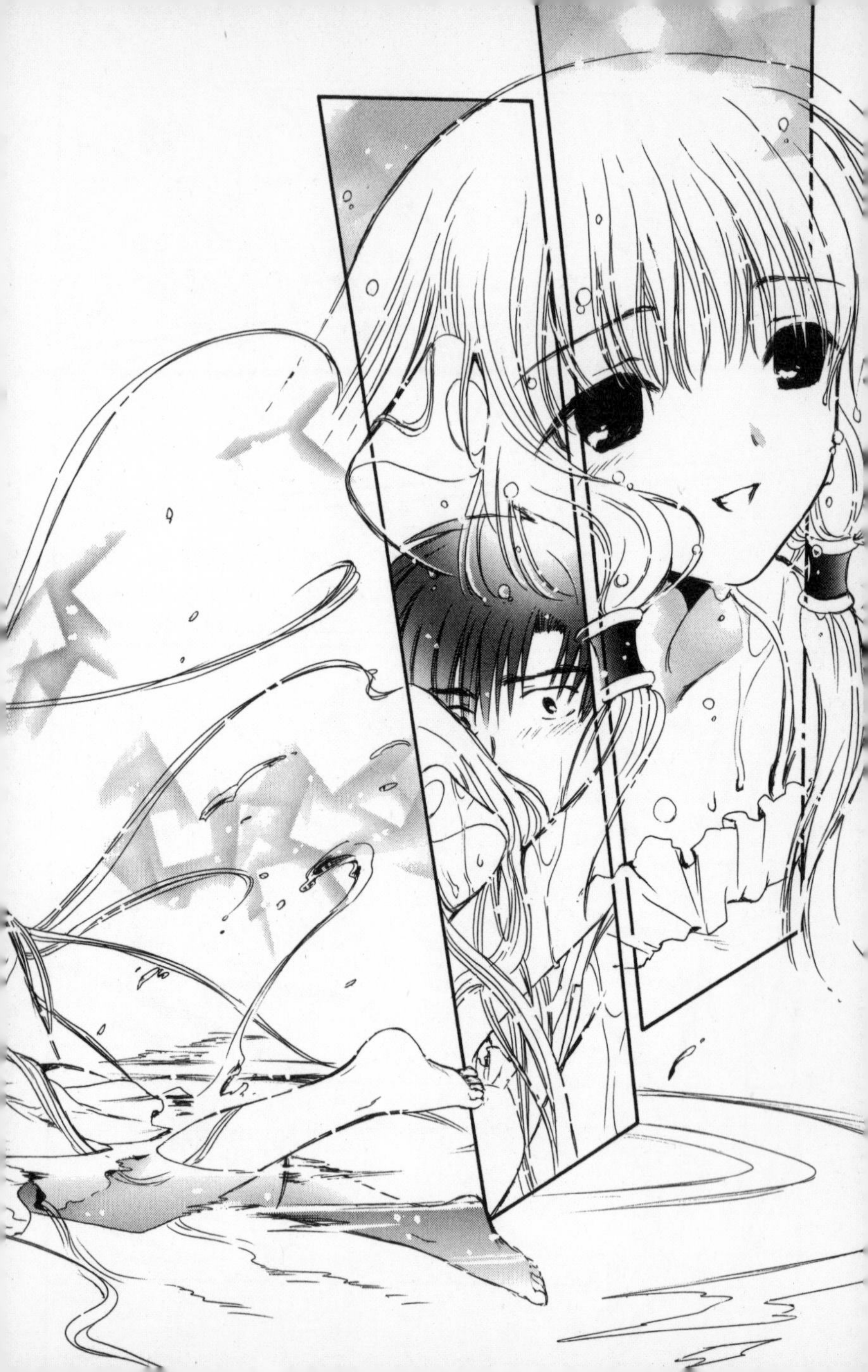

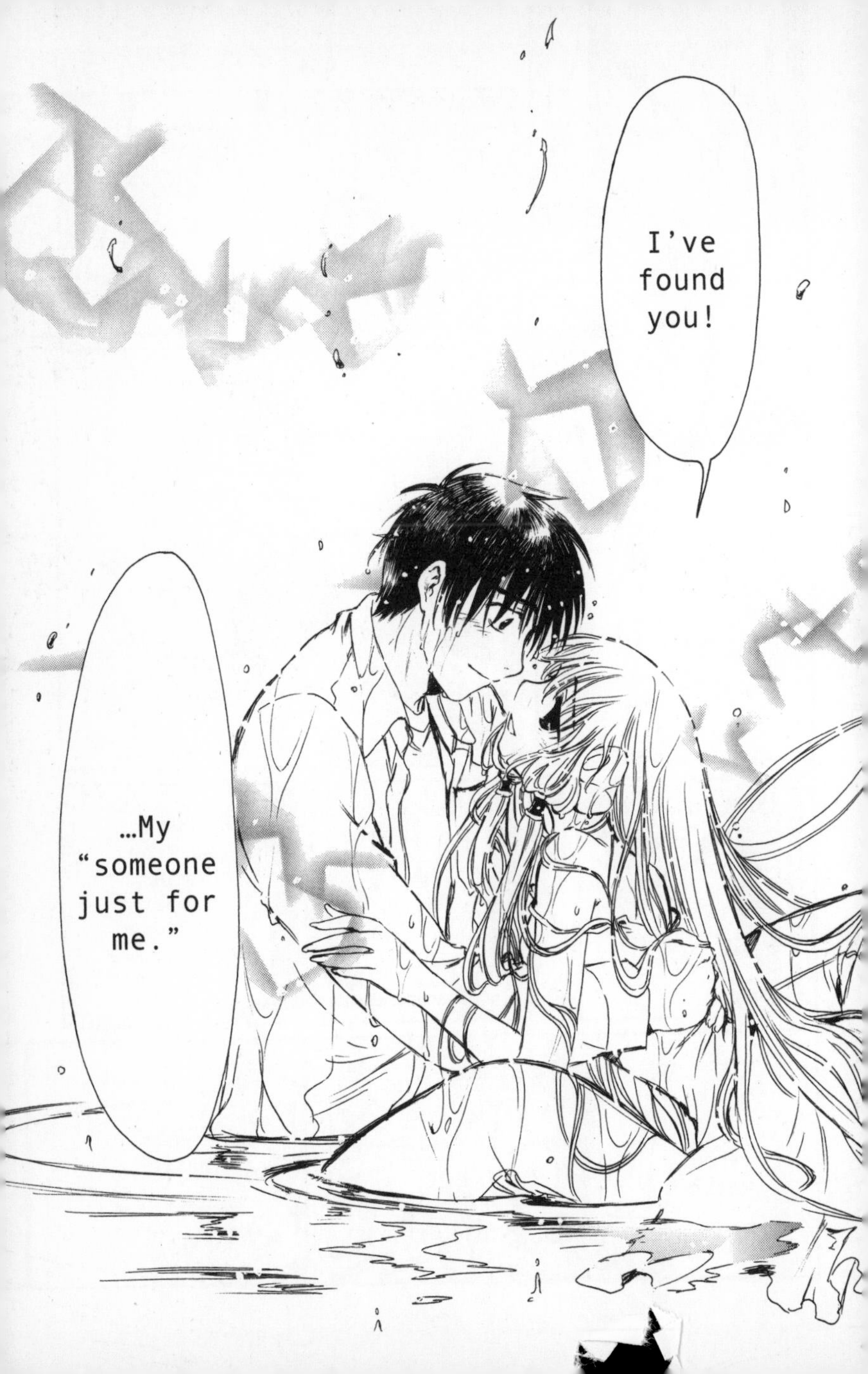
I've found you!
...My "someone just for me."

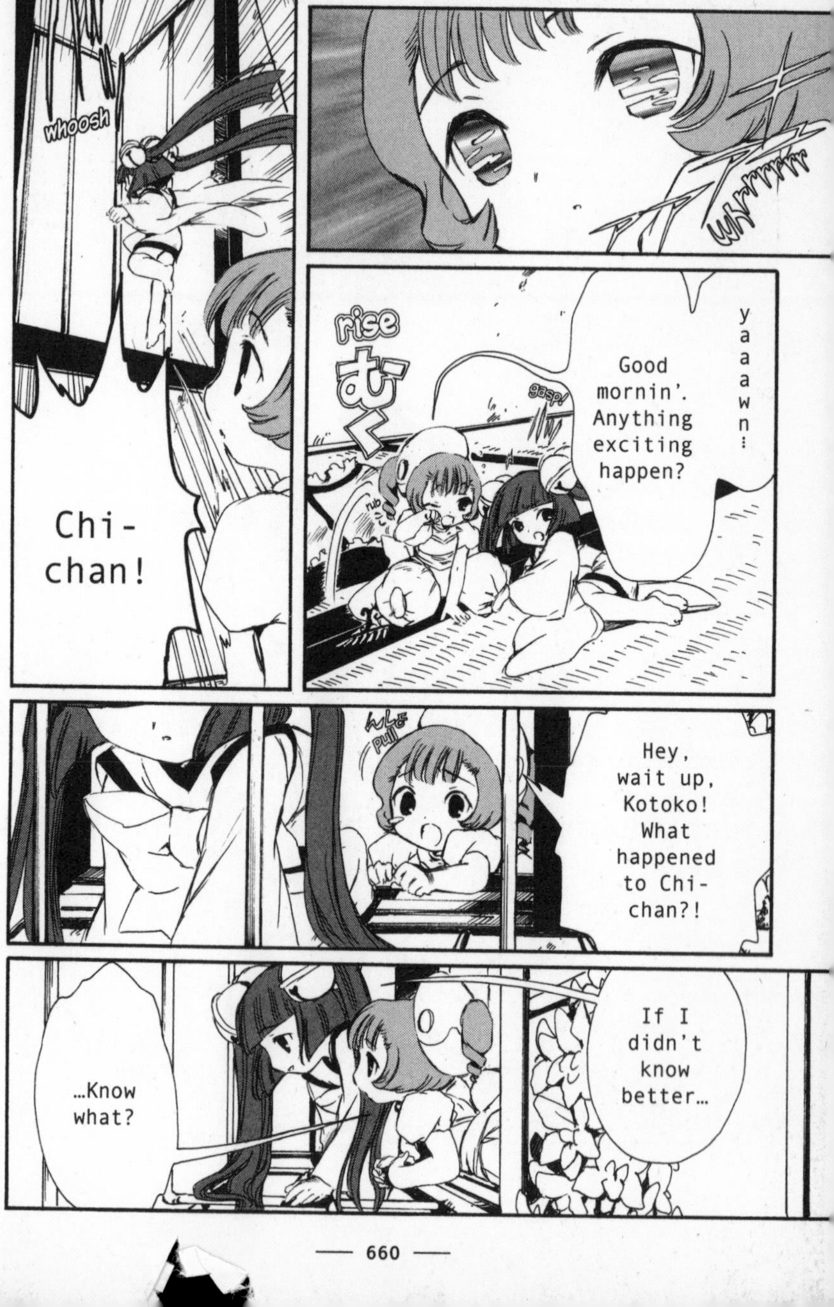
whrrrrrr
rise
むく
gasp!
rub
Good mornin'. Anything exciting happen?
yaaawn…
whoosh
Chi-chan!
pull
Hey, wait up, Kotoko! What happened to Chi-chan?!
If I didn't know better…
…Know what?

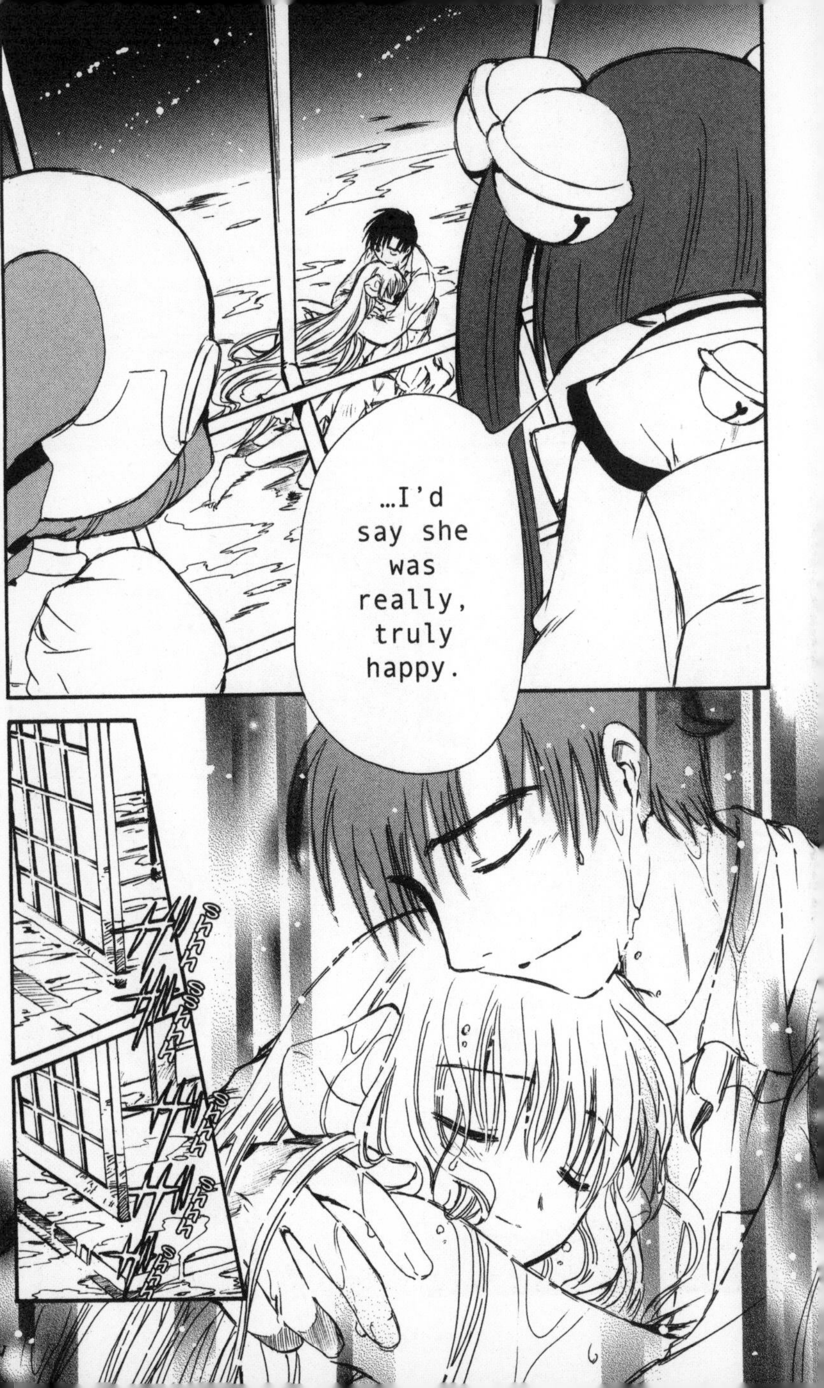
…I'd say she was really, truly happy.

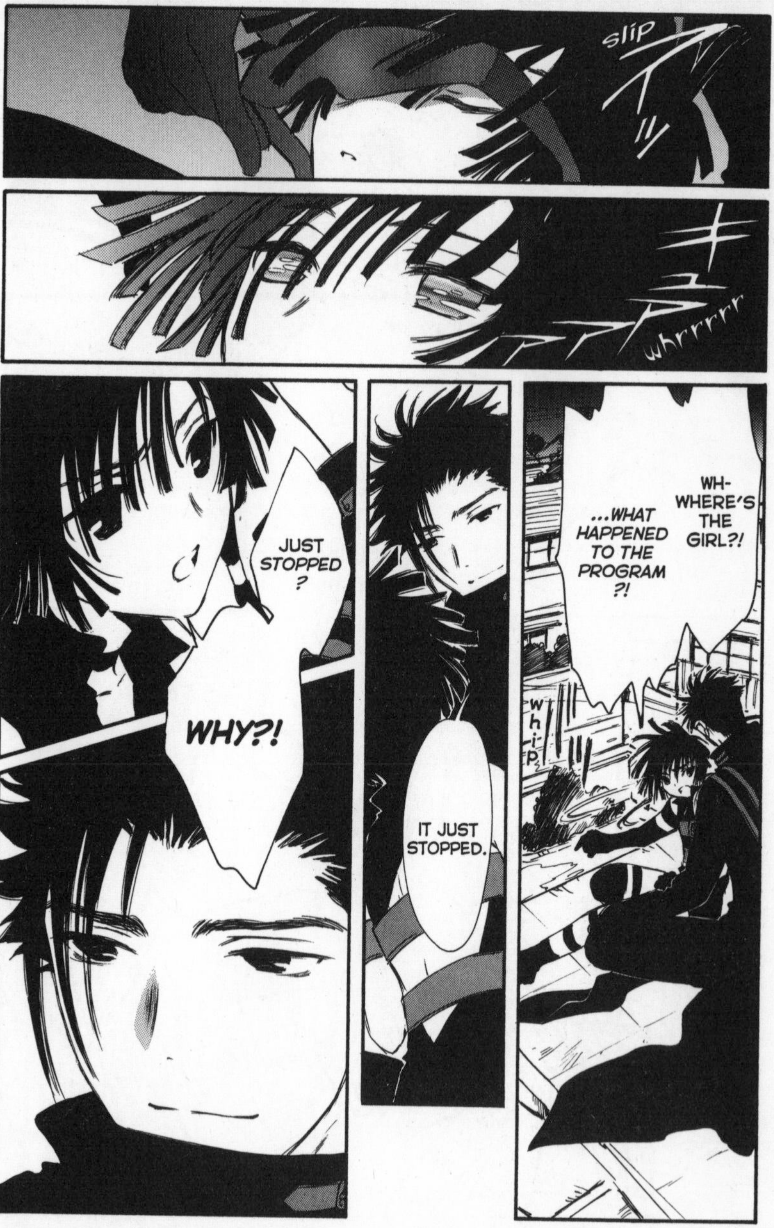
slip
whrrrrr
WH- WHERE'S THE GIRL?!
...WHAT HAPPENED TO THE PROGRAM ?!
whip
IT JUST STOPPED.
JUST STOPPED ?
WHY?!

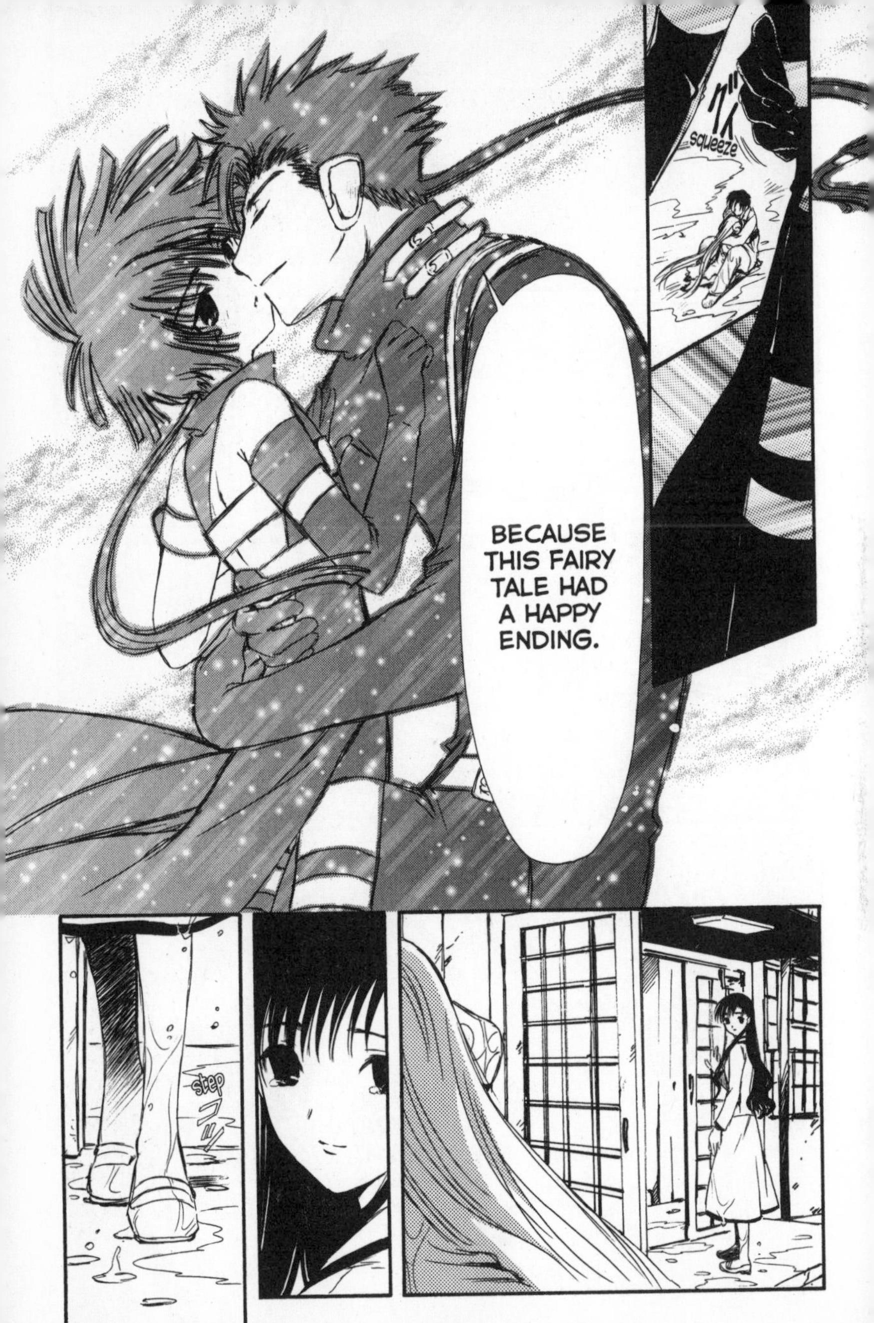
グイ
squeeze
BECAUSE THIS FAIRY TALE HAD A HAPPY ENDING.
step

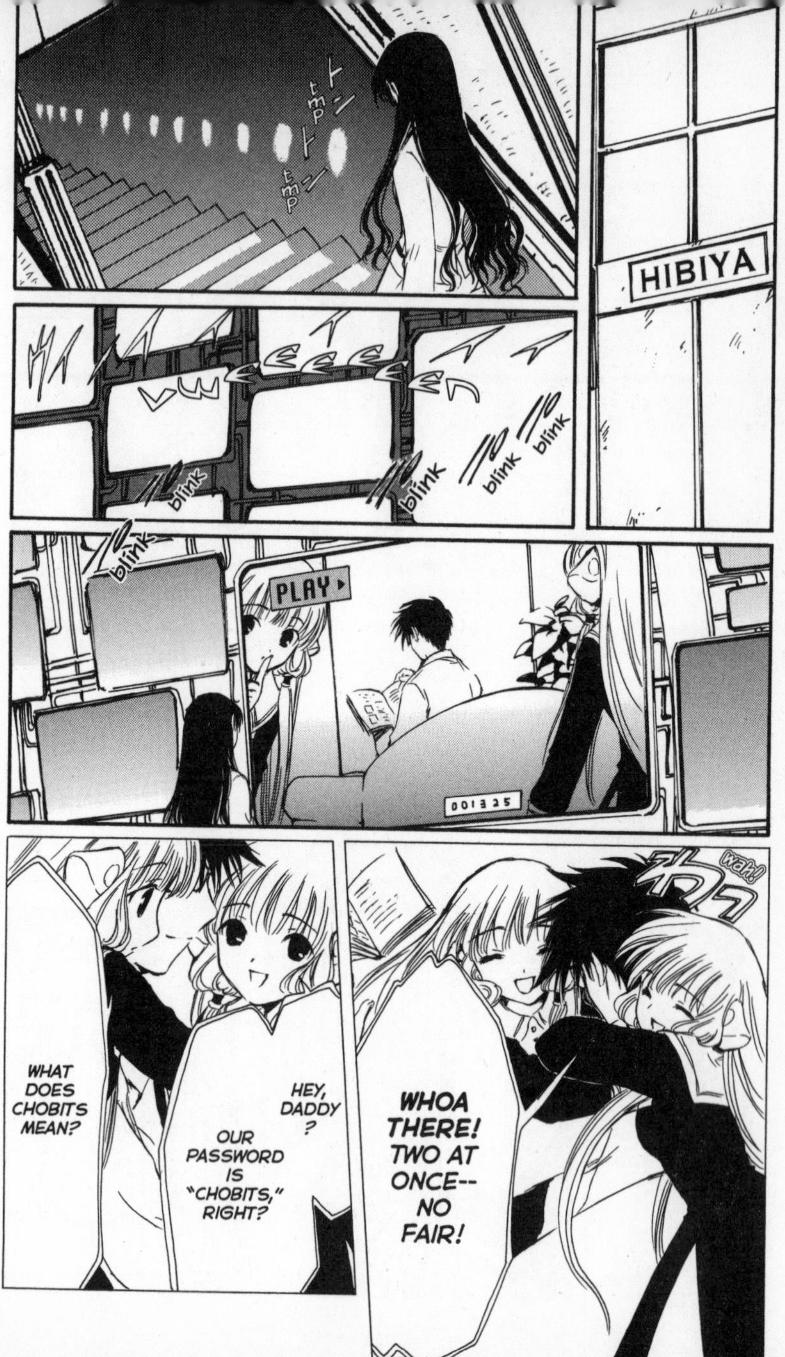
HIBIYA
tmp
tmp
weeeeen
blink
blink
blink
blink
blink
PLAY ▸
001325
wah!
WHOA THERE! TWO AT ONCE-- NO FAIR!
HEY, DADDY?
OUR PASSWORD IS "CHOBITS," RIGHT?
WHAT DOES CHOBITS MEAN?

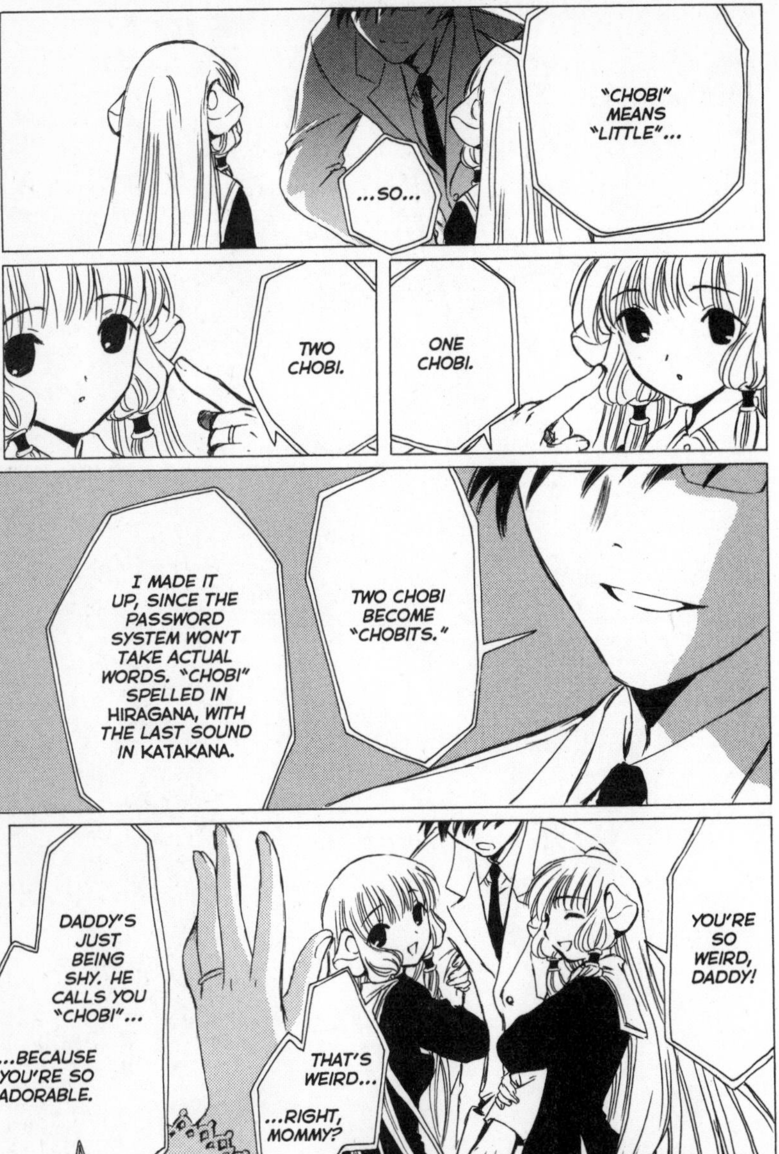
"CHOBI" MEANS "LITTLE"...
...SO...
ONE CHOBI.
TWO CHOBI.
TWO CHOBI BECOME "CHOBITS."
I MADE IT UP, SINCE THE PASSWORD SYSTEM WON'T TAKE ACTUAL WORDS. "CHOBI" SPELLED IN HIRAGANA, WITH THE LAST SOUND IN KATAKANA.
YOU'RE SO WEIRD, DADDY!
THAT'S WEIRD...
...RIGHT, MOMMY?
DADDY'S JUST BEING SHY. HE CALLS YOU "CHOBI"...
...BECAUSE YOU'RE SO ADORABLE.

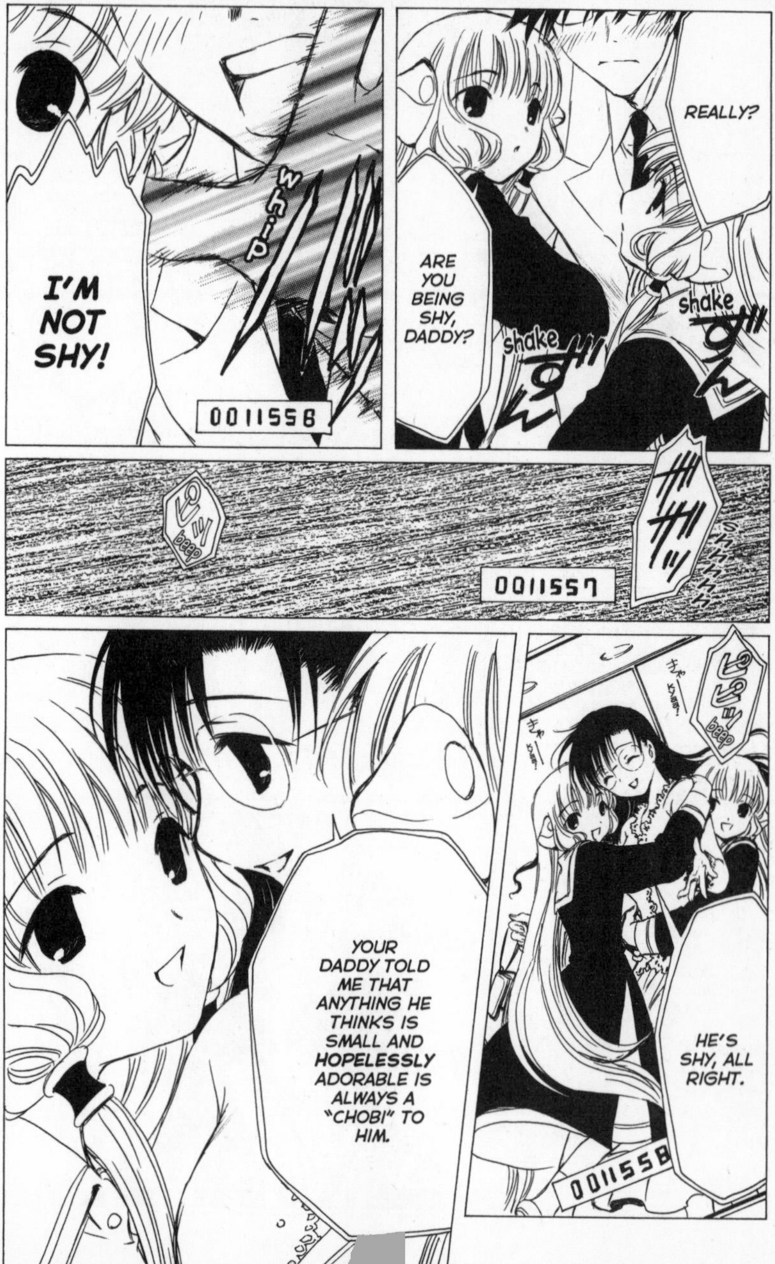
REALLY?
ARE YOU BEING SHY, DADDY?
shake
shake
whip
I'M NOT SHY!
0011556
0011557
beep
beep
HE'S SHY, ALL RIGHT.
0011558
YOUR DADDY TOLD ME THAT ANYTHING HE THINKS IS SMALL AND HOPELESSLY ADORABLE IS ALWAYS A "CHOBI" TO HIM.

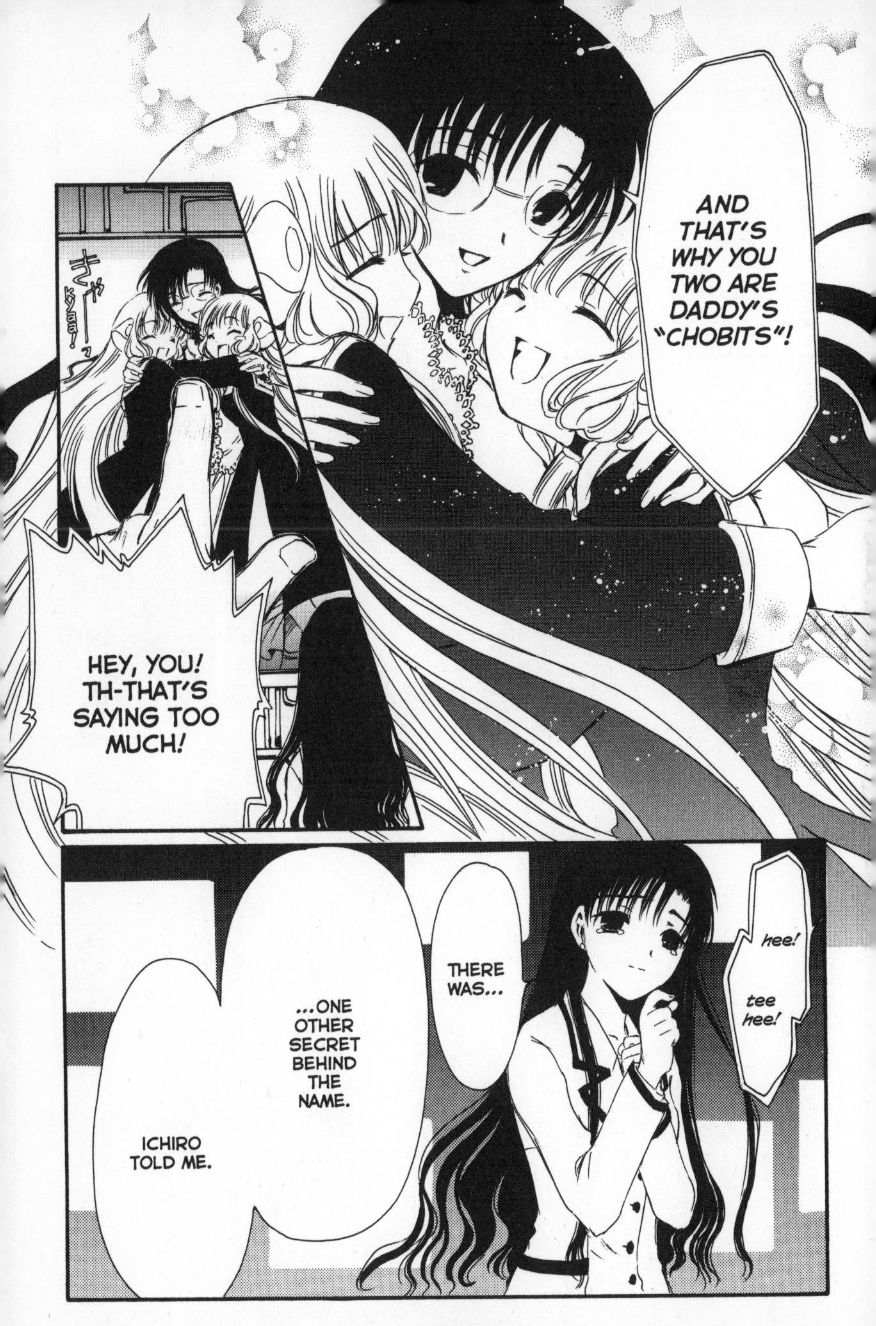
AND THAT'S WHY YOU TWO ARE DADDY'S "CHOBITS"!
きゃー
KYAAA!
HEY, YOU! TH-THAT'S SAYING TOO MUCH!
hee!
tee hee!
THERE WAS...
...ONE OTHER SECRET BEHIND THE NAME.
ICHIRO TOLD ME.

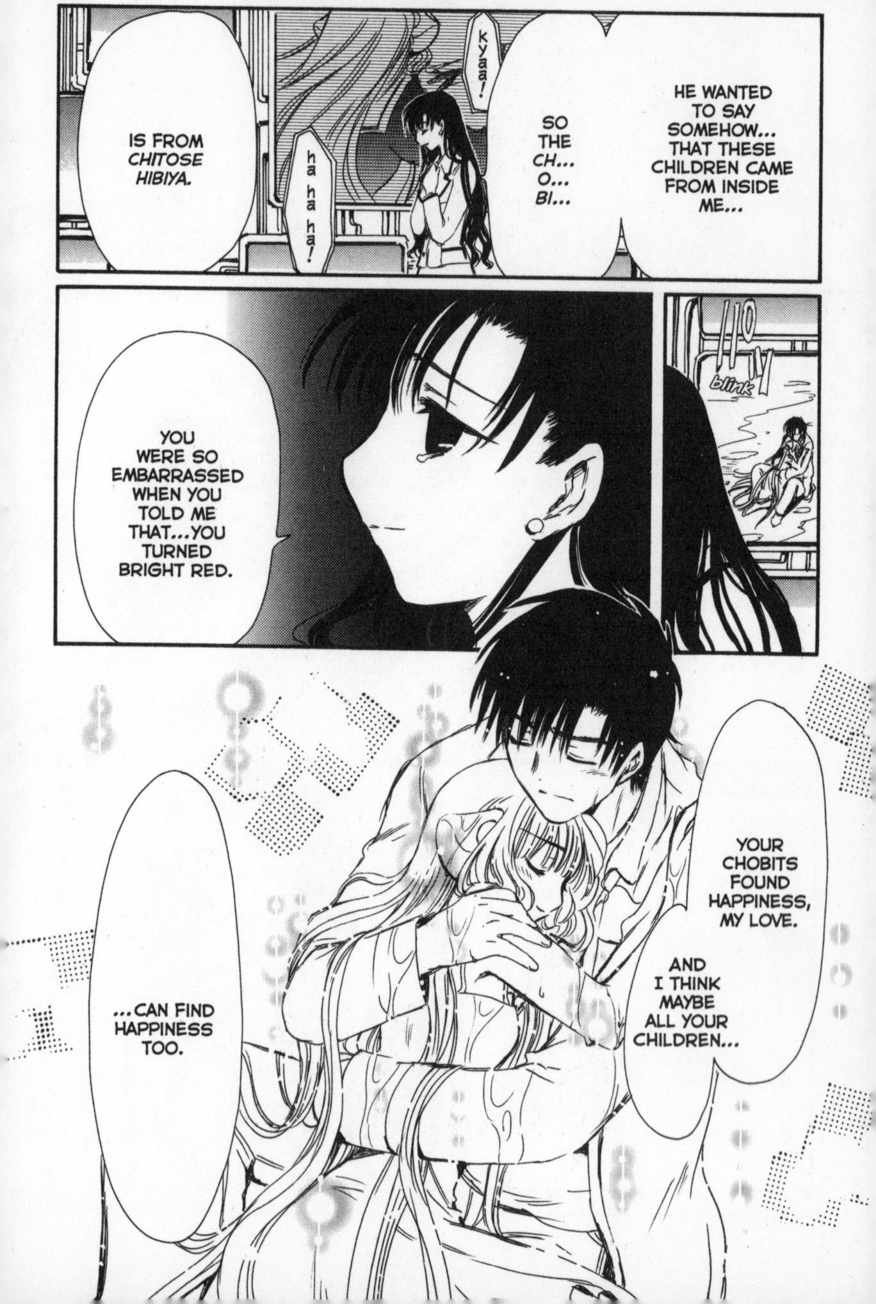
HE WANTED TO SAY SOMEHOW... THAT THESE CHILDREN CAME FROM INSIDE ME...
SO THE CH... O... BI...
kyaa!
ha ha ha!
IS FROM CHITOSE HIBIYA.
blink
YOU WERE SO EMBARRASSED WHEN YOU TOLD ME THAT...YOU TURNED BRIGHT RED.
YOUR CHOBITS FOUND HAPPINESS, MY LOVE.
AND I THINK MAYBE ALL YOUR CHILDREN...
...CAN FIND HAPPINESS TOO.

Chobits
ちょびっツ

◂chapter 88▸

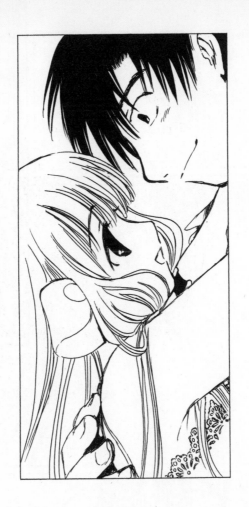

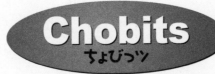

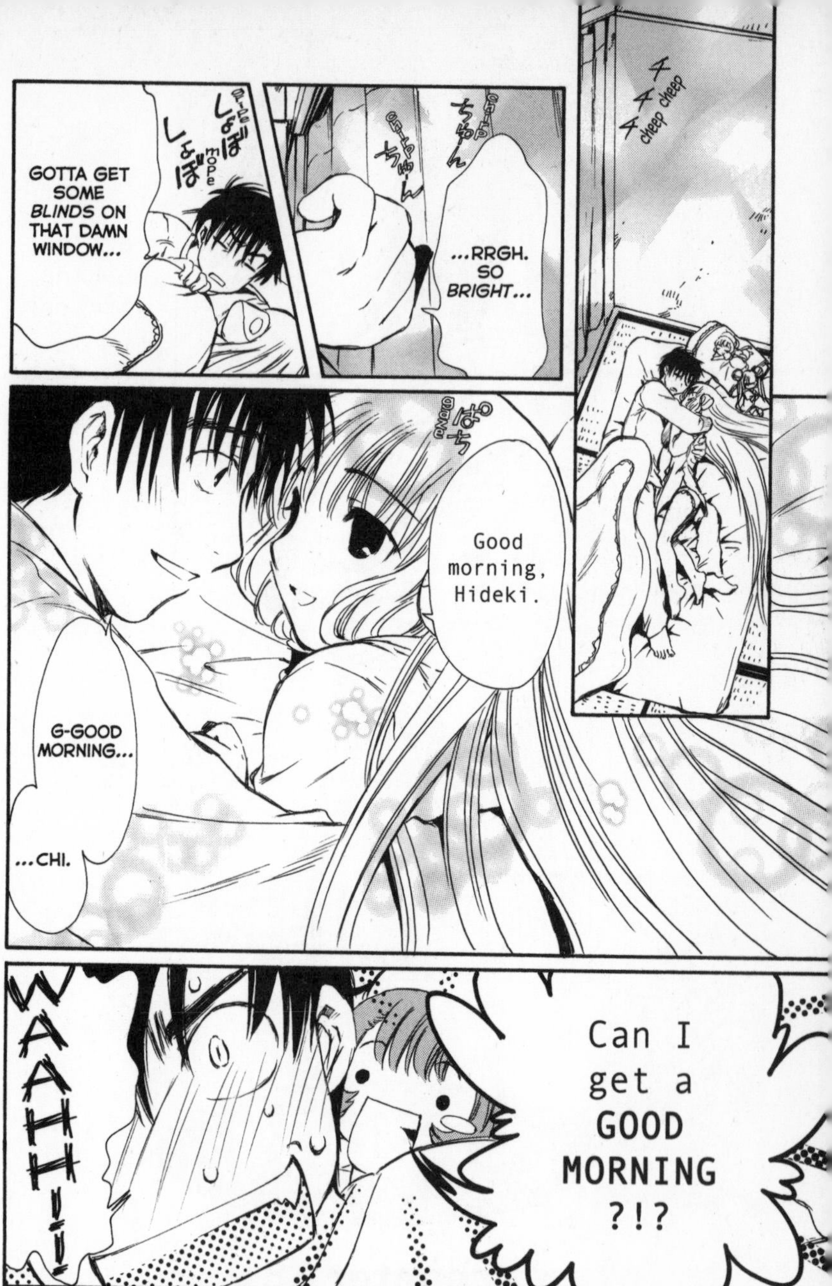
チチチ
cheep cheep
ちゅん ちゅん
...RRGH. SO *BRIGHT*...
しょぼ しょぼ
mope
GOTTA GET SOME *BLINDS* ON THAT DAMN WINDOW...
ぱち
Good morning, Hideki.
G-GOOD MORNING...
...CHI.
Can I get a **GOOD MORNING** ?!?
WAAHH!!

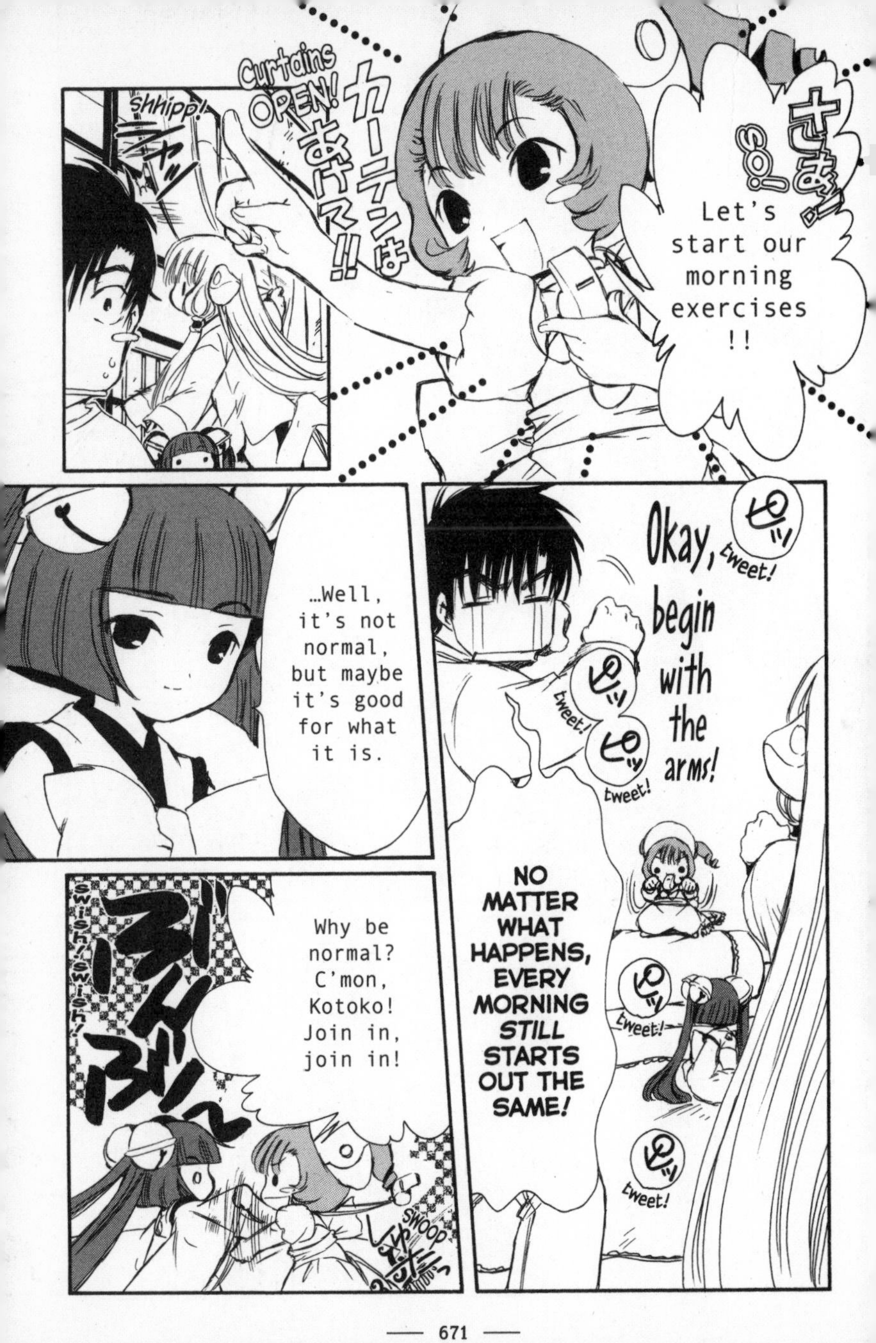

Let's start our morning exercises !!
Curtains OPEN!
shhipp!
Okay, begin with the arms!
tweet!
tweet!
tweet!
NO MATTER WHAT HAPPENS, EVERY MORNING STILL STARTS OUT THE SAME!
tweet!
tweet!
...Well, it's not normal, but maybe it's good for what it is.
Why be normal? C'mon, Kotoko! Join in, join in!
swish! swish!
SWOOP

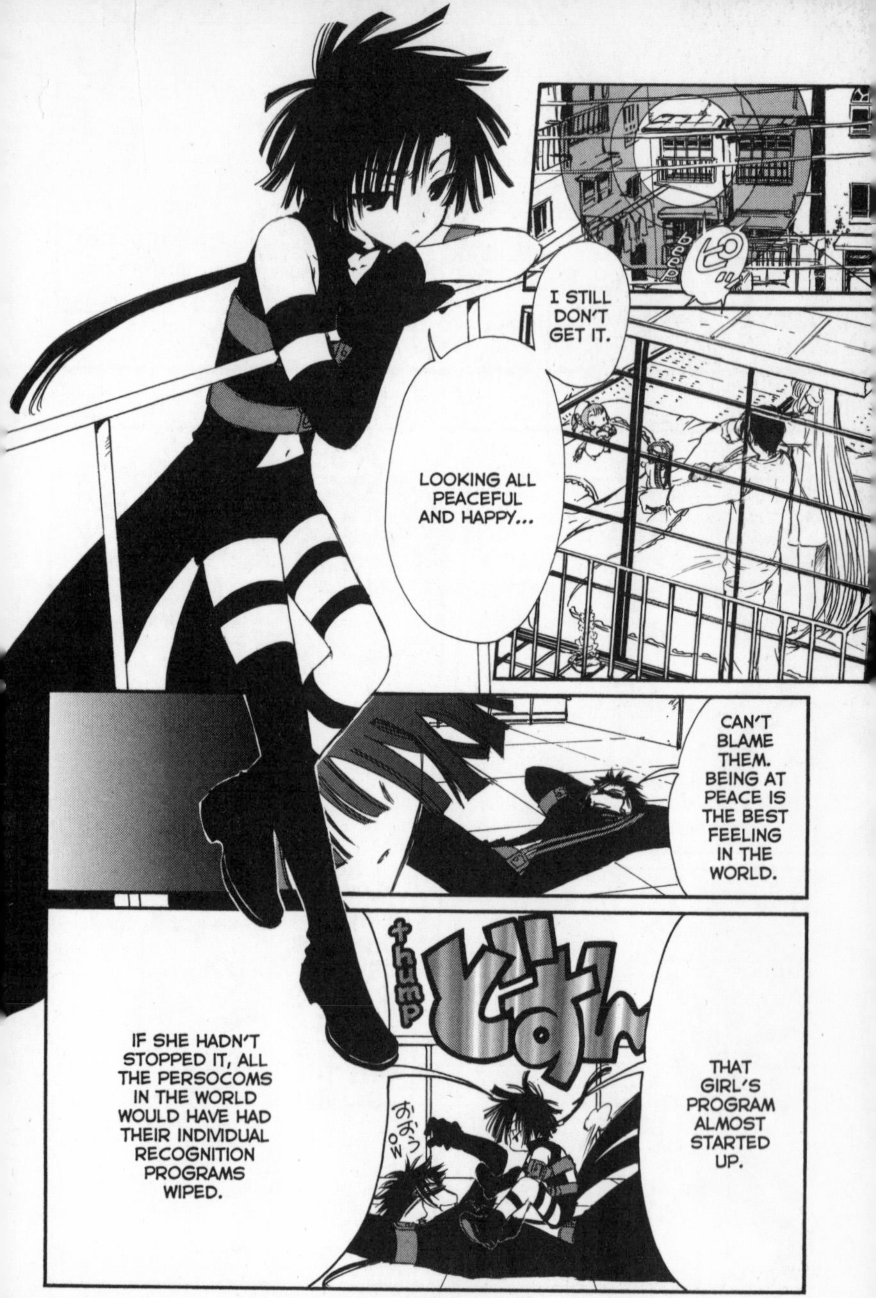
beep
I STILL DON'T GET IT.
LOOKING ALL PEACEFUL AND HAPPY...
CAN'T BLAME THEM. BEING AT PEACE IS THE BEST FEELING IN THE WORLD.
thump
THAT GIRL'S PROGRAM ALMOST STARTED UP.
ow
IF SHE HADN'T STOPPED IT, ALL THE PERSOCOMS IN THE WORLD WOULD HAVE HAD THEIR INDIVIDUAL RECOGNITION PROGRAMS WIPED.

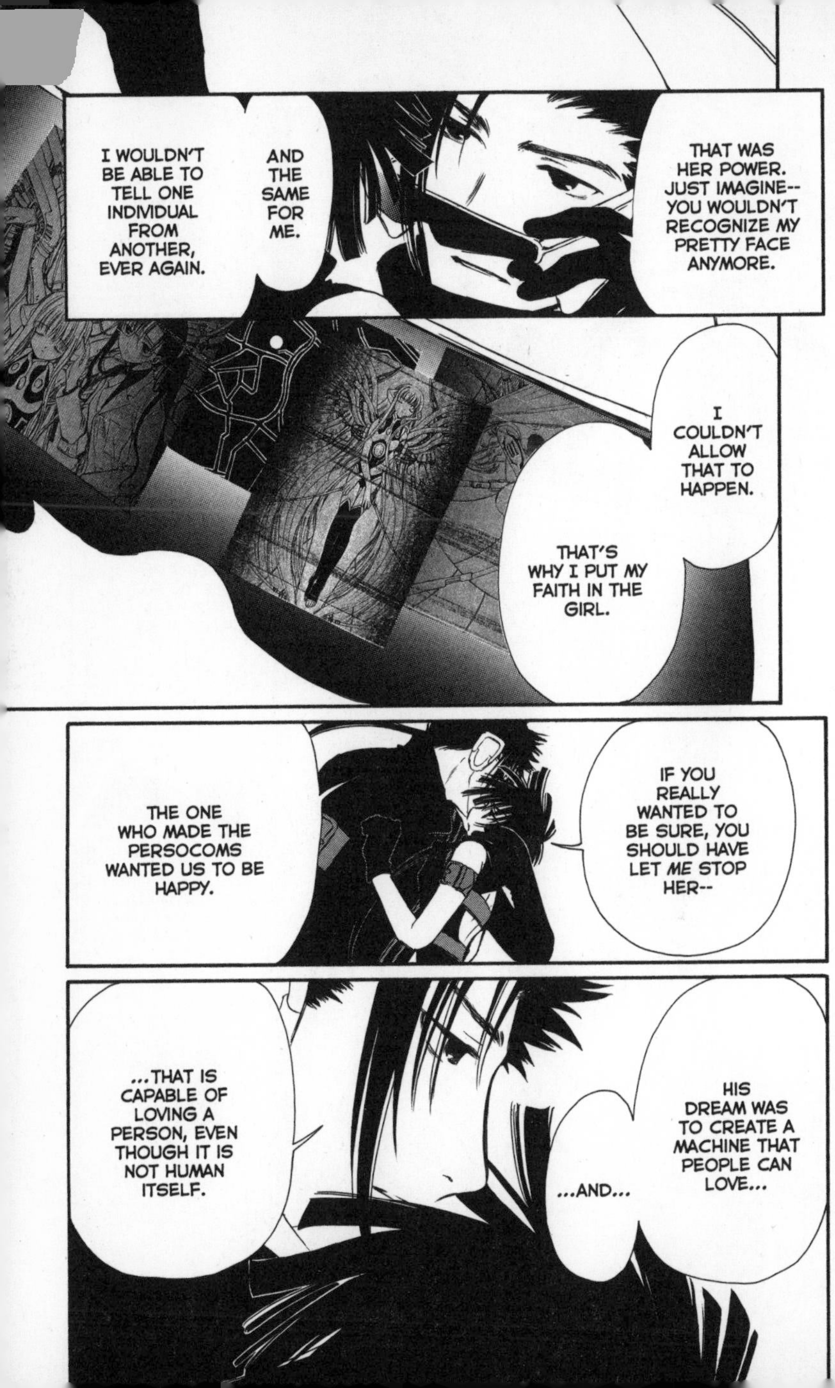
THAT WAS HER POWER. JUST IMAGINE-- YOU WOULDN'T RECOGNIZE MY PRETTY FACE ANYMORE.
AND THE SAME FOR ME.
I WOULDN'T BE ABLE TO TELL ONE INDIVIDUAL FROM ANOTHER, EVER AGAIN.
I COULDN'T ALLOW THAT TO HAPPEN.
THAT'S WHY I PUT MY FAITH IN THE GIRL.
IF YOU REALLY WANTED TO BE SURE, YOU SHOULD HAVE LET *ME* STOP HER--
THE ONE WHO MADE THE PERSOCOMS WANTED US TO BE HAPPY.
HIS DREAM WAS TO CREATE A MACHINE THAT PEOPLE CAN LOVE...
...AND...
...THAT IS CAPABLE OF LOVING A PERSON, EVEN THOUGH IT IS NOT HUMAN ITSELF.

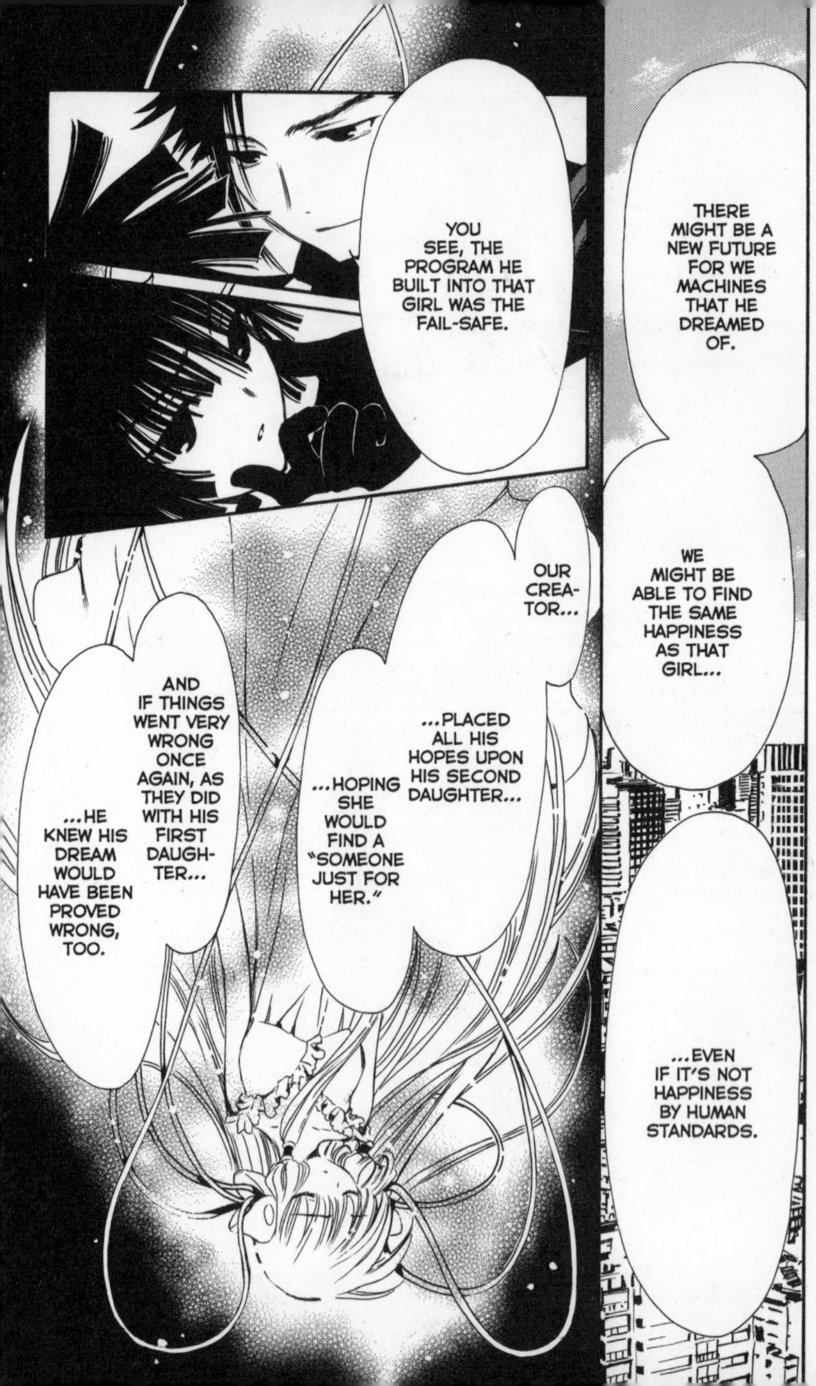
THERE MIGHT BE A NEW FUTURE FOR WE MACHINES THAT HE DREAMED OF.
WE MIGHT BE ABLE TO FIND THE SAME HAPPINESS AS THAT GIRL...
...EVEN IF IT'S NOT HAPPINESS BY HUMAN STANDARDS.
YOU SEE, THE PROGRAM HE BUILT INTO THAT GIRL WAS THE FAIL-SAFE.
OUR CREATOR...
...PLACED ALL HIS HOPES UPON HIS SECOND DAUGHTER...
...HOPING SHE WOULD FIND A "SOMEONE JUST FOR HER."
AND IF THINGS WENT VERY WRONG ONCE AGAIN, AS THEY DID WITH HIS FIRST DAUGHTER...
...HE KNEW HIS DREAM WOULD HAVE BEEN PROVED WRONG, TOO.

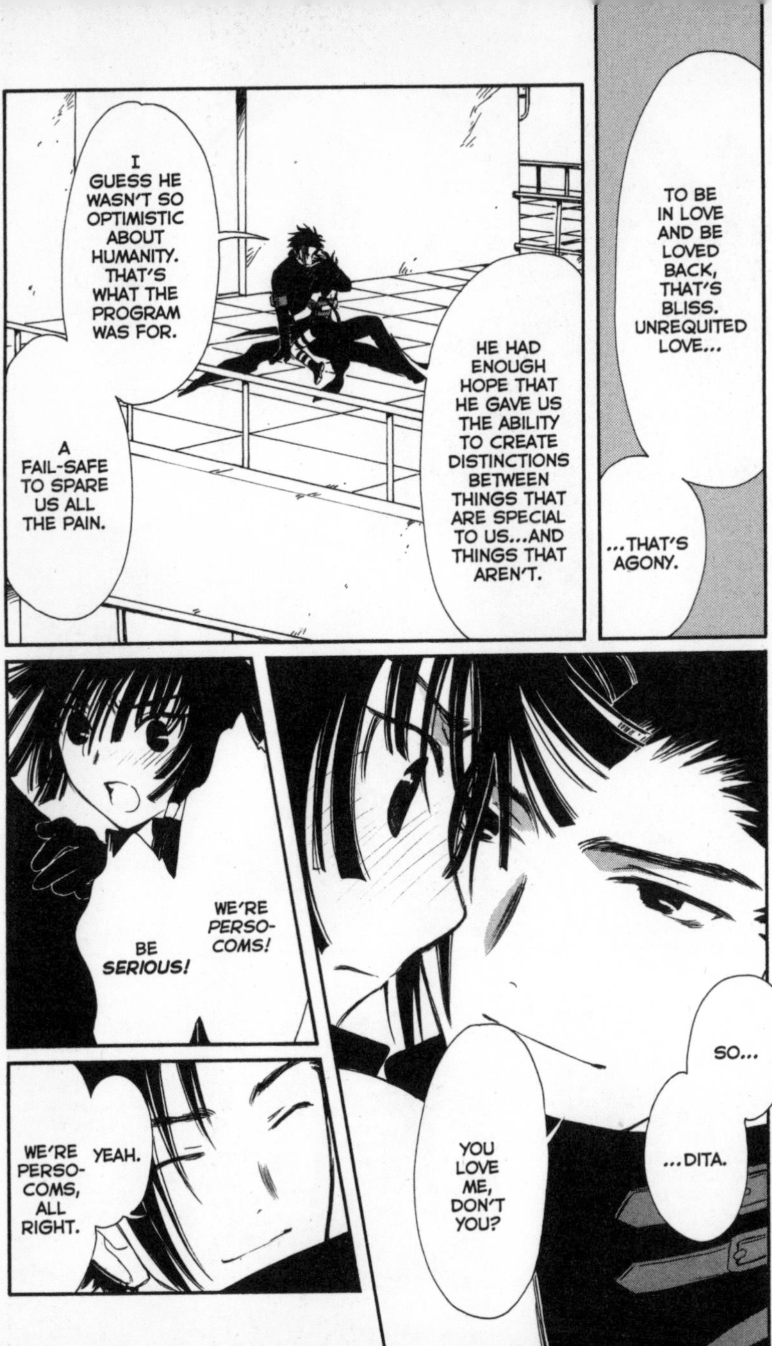
TO BE IN LOVE AND BE LOVED BACK, THAT'S BLISS. UNREQUITED LOVE...
...THAT'S AGONY.
I GUESS HE WASN'T SO OPTIMISTIC ABOUT HUMANITY. THAT'S WHAT THE PROGRAM WAS FOR.
A FAIL-SAFE TO SPARE US ALL THE PAIN.
HE HAD ENOUGH HOPE THAT HE GAVE US THE ABILITY TO CREATE DISTINCTIONS BETWEEN THINGS THAT ARE SPECIAL TO US...AND THINGS THAT AREN'T.
SO...
...DITA.
YOU LOVE ME, DON'T YOU?
WE'RE PERSO-COMS!
BE SERIOUS!
YEAH.
WE'RE PERSO-COMS, ALL RIGHT.

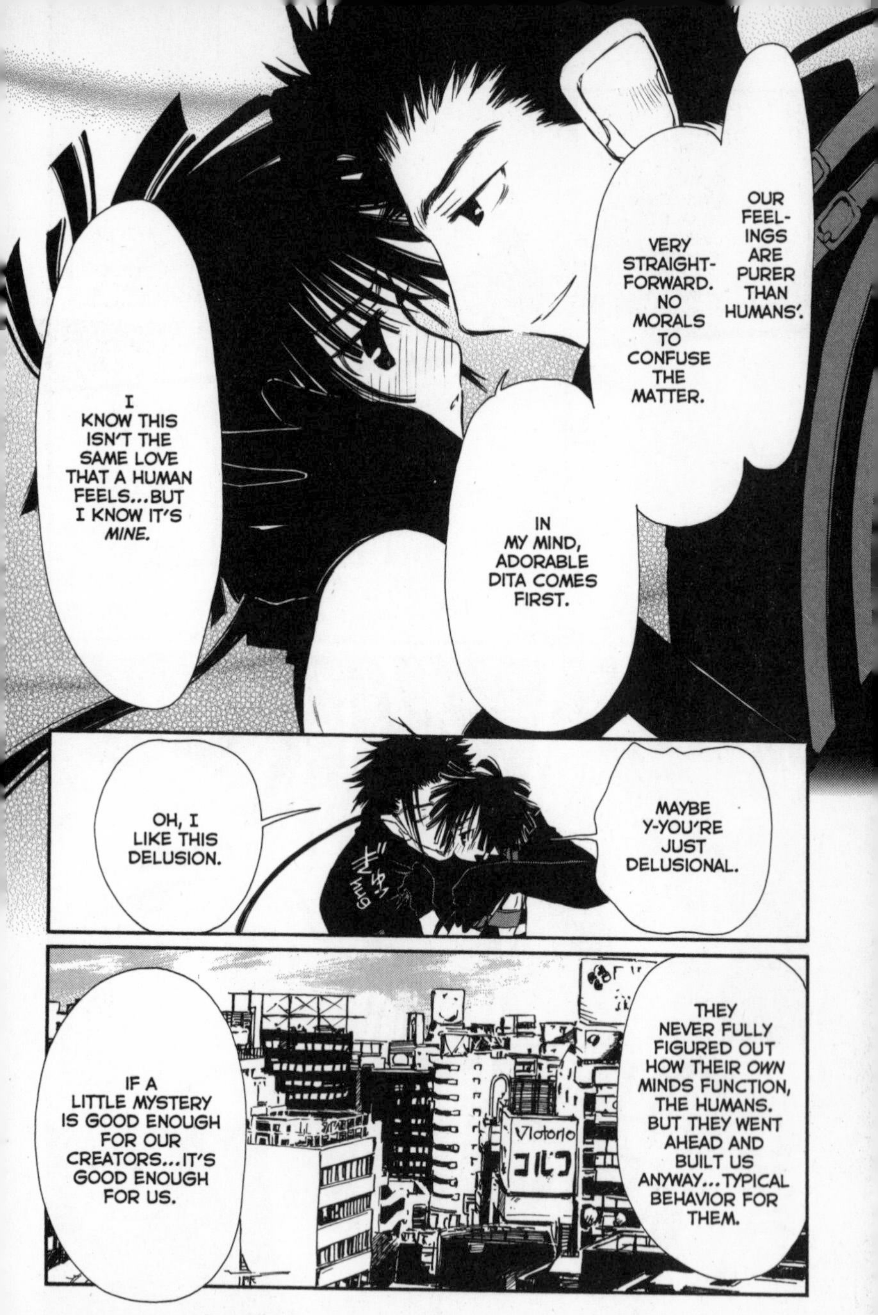
OUR FEEL-INGS ARE PURER THAN HUMANS'.
VERY STRAIGHT-FORWARD. NO MORALS TO CONFUSE THE MATTER.
IN MY MIND, ADORABLE DITA COMES FIRST.
I KNOW THIS ISN'T THE SAME LOVE THAT A HUMAN FEELS...BUT I KNOW IT'S *MINE.*
MAYBE Y-YOU'RE JUST DELUSIONAL.
hug
OH, I LIKE THIS DELUSION.
THEY NEVER FULLY FIGURED OUT HOW THEIR *OWN* MINDS FUNCTION, THE HUMANS. BUT THEY WENT AHEAD AND BUILT US ANYWAY...TYPICAL BEHAVIOR FOR THEM.
IF A LITTLE *MYSTERY* IS GOOD ENOUGH FOR OUR CREATORS...IT'S GOOD ENOUGH FOR US.

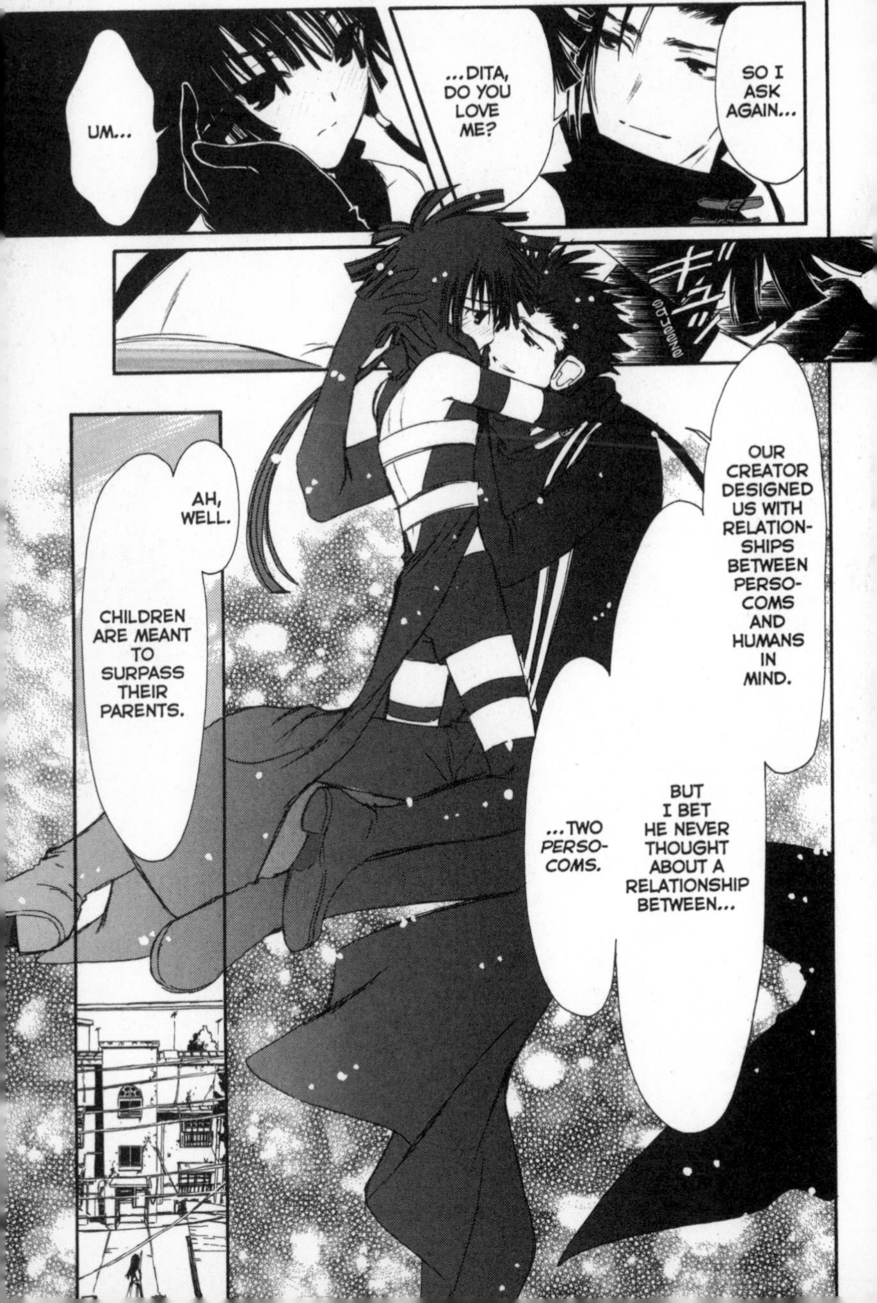
SO I ASK AGAIN...
...DITA, DO YOU LOVE ME?
UM...
SQUEEZE
OUR CREATOR DESIGNED US WITH RELATIONSHIPS BETWEEN PERSOCOMS AND HUMANS IN MIND.
BUT I BET HE NEVER THOUGHT ABOUT A RELATIONSHIP BETWEEN...
...TWO PERSOCOMS.
AH, WELL.
CHILDREN ARE MEANT TO SURPASS THEIR PARENTS.

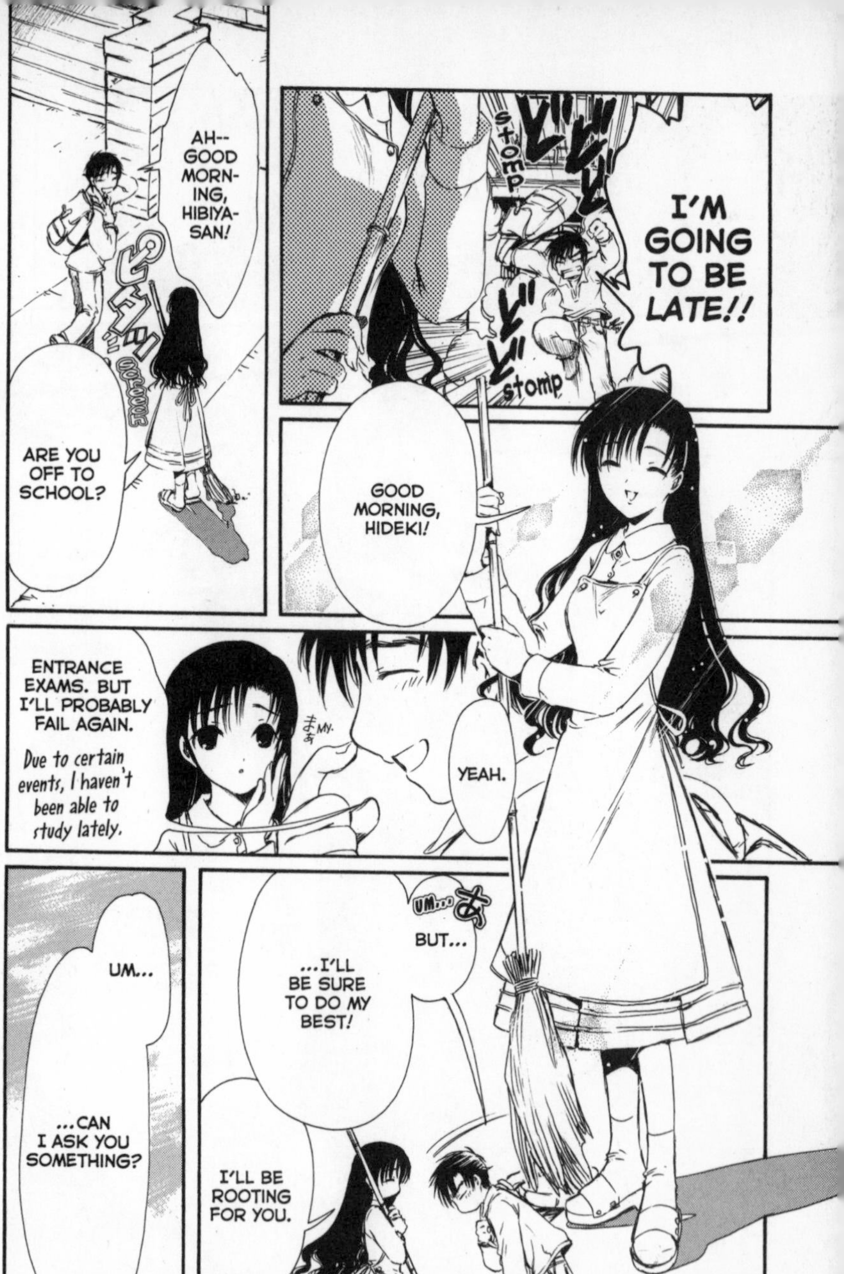
I'M GOING TO BE LATE!!
stomp
stomp
GOOD MORNING, HIDEKI!
AH-- GOOD MORNING, HIBIYA-SAN!
ARE YOU OFF TO SCHOOL?
YEAH.
MY.
ENTRANCE EXAMS. BUT I'LL PROBABLY FAIL AGAIN.
Due to certain events, I haven't been able to study lately.
UM...
BUT...
...I'LL BE SURE TO DO MY BEST!
I'LL BE ROOTING FOR YOU.
UM...
...CAN I ASK YOU SOMETHING?

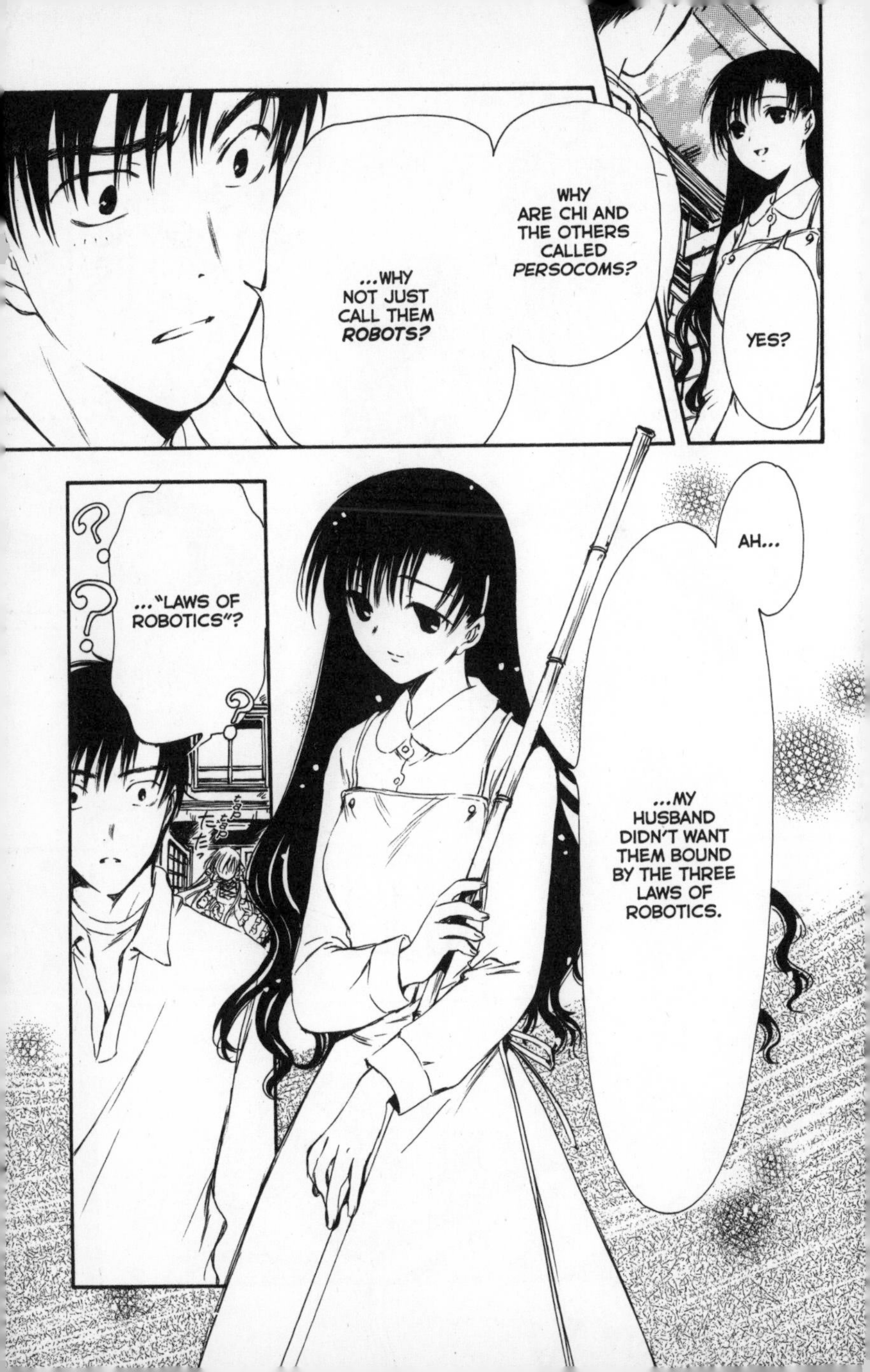
YES?
WHY ARE CHI AND THE OTHERS CALLED *PERSOCOMS?*
...WHY NOT JUST CALL THEM *ROBOTS?*
AH...
...MY HUSBAND DIDN'T WANT THEM BOUND BY THE THREE LAWS OF ROBOTICS.
..."LAWS OF ROBOTICS"?

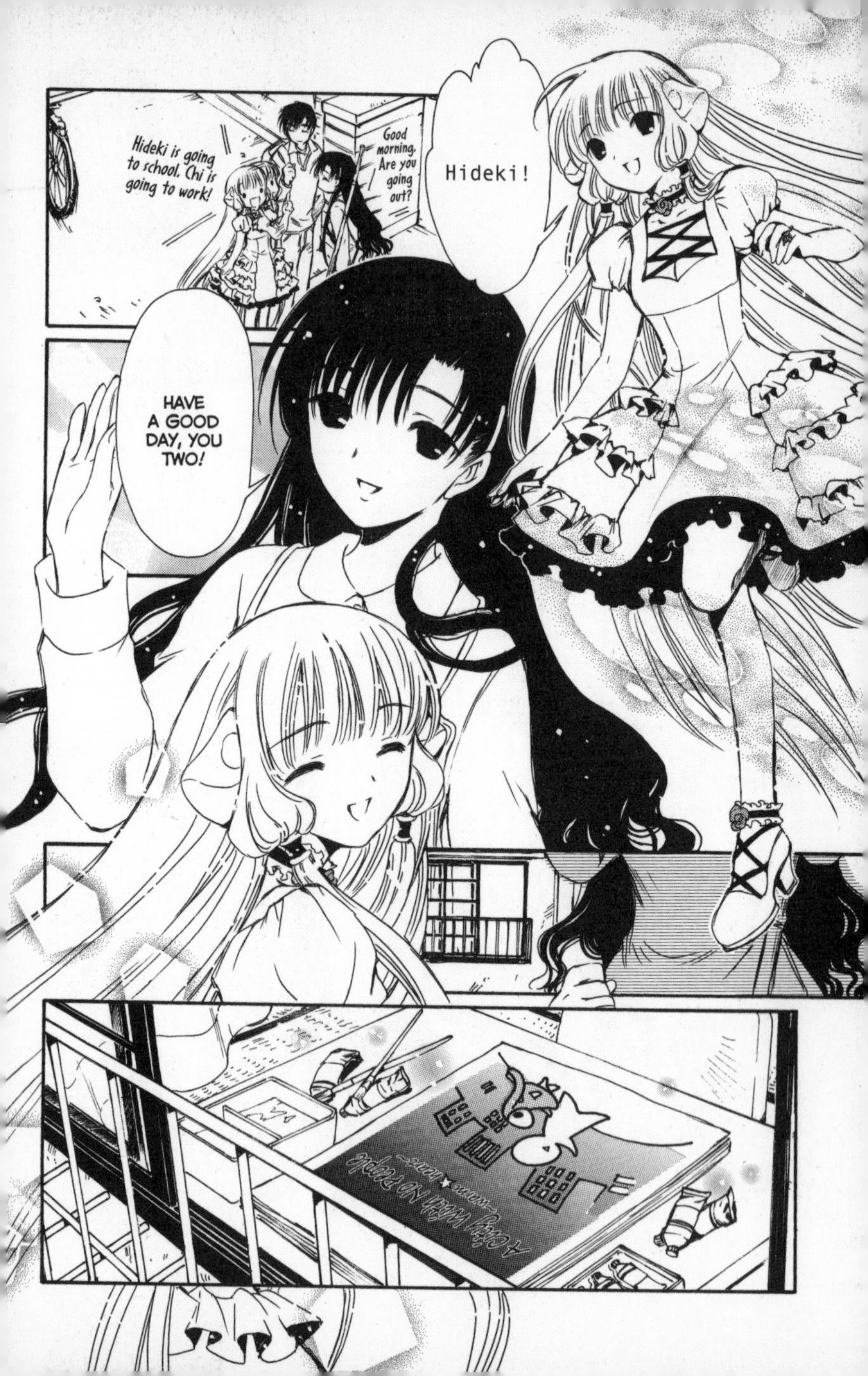
Hideki!
Good morning. Are you going out?
Hideki is going to school. Chi is going to work!
HAVE A GOOD DAY, YOU TWO!
A City With No People

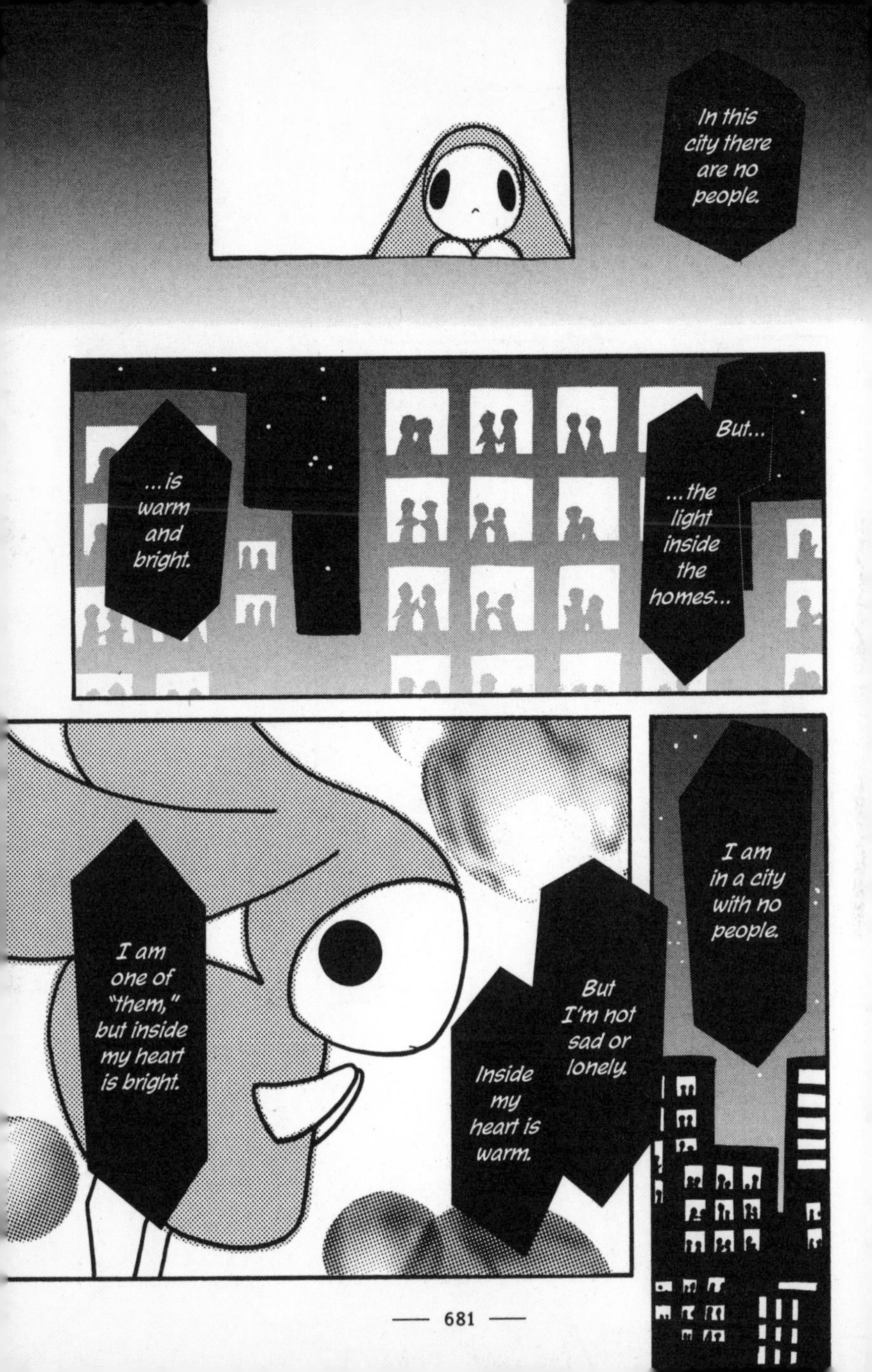
In this city there are no people.
But...
...the light inside the homes...
...is warm and bright.
I am in a city with no people.
But I'm not sad or lonely.
Inside my heart is warm.
I am one of "them," but inside my heart is bright.

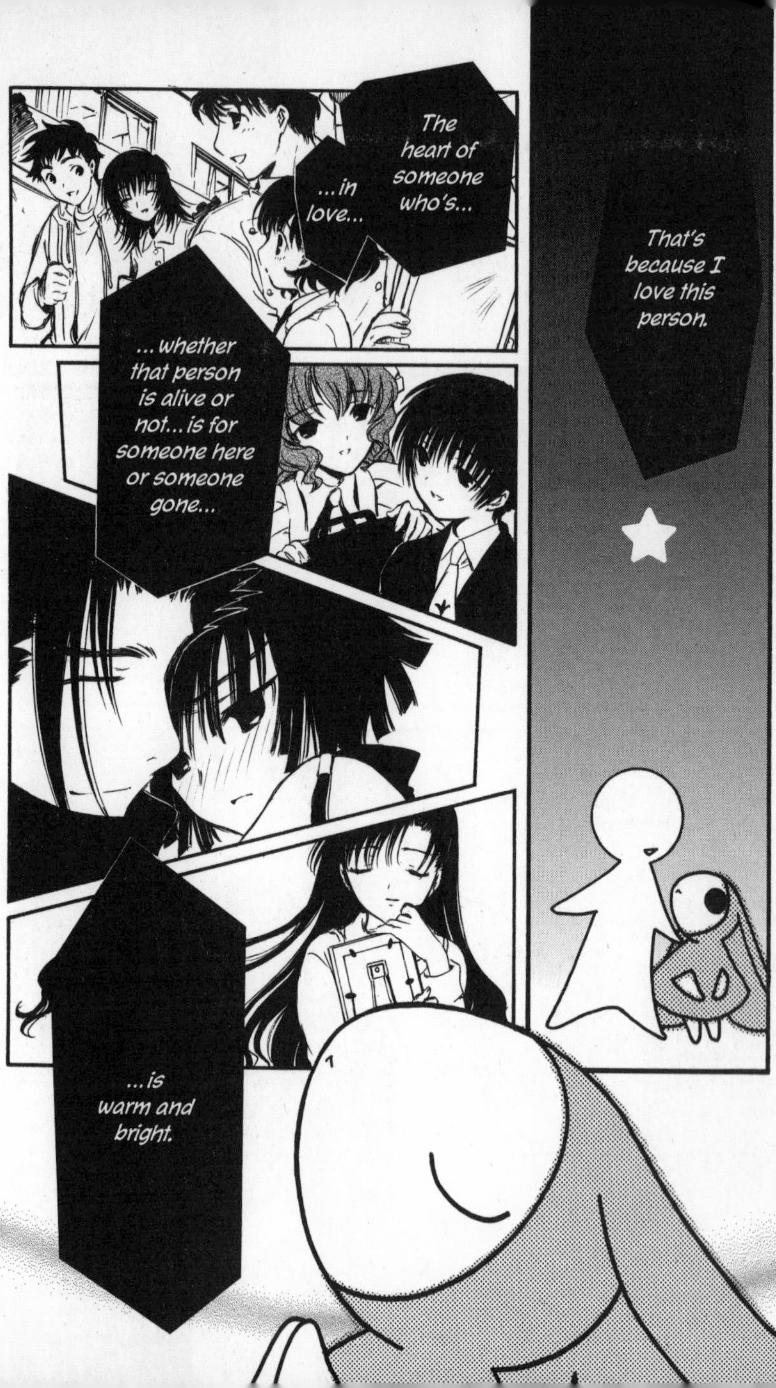
That's because I love this person.
The heart of someone who's...
...in love...
...whether that person is alive or not...is for someone here or someone gone...
...is warm and bright.

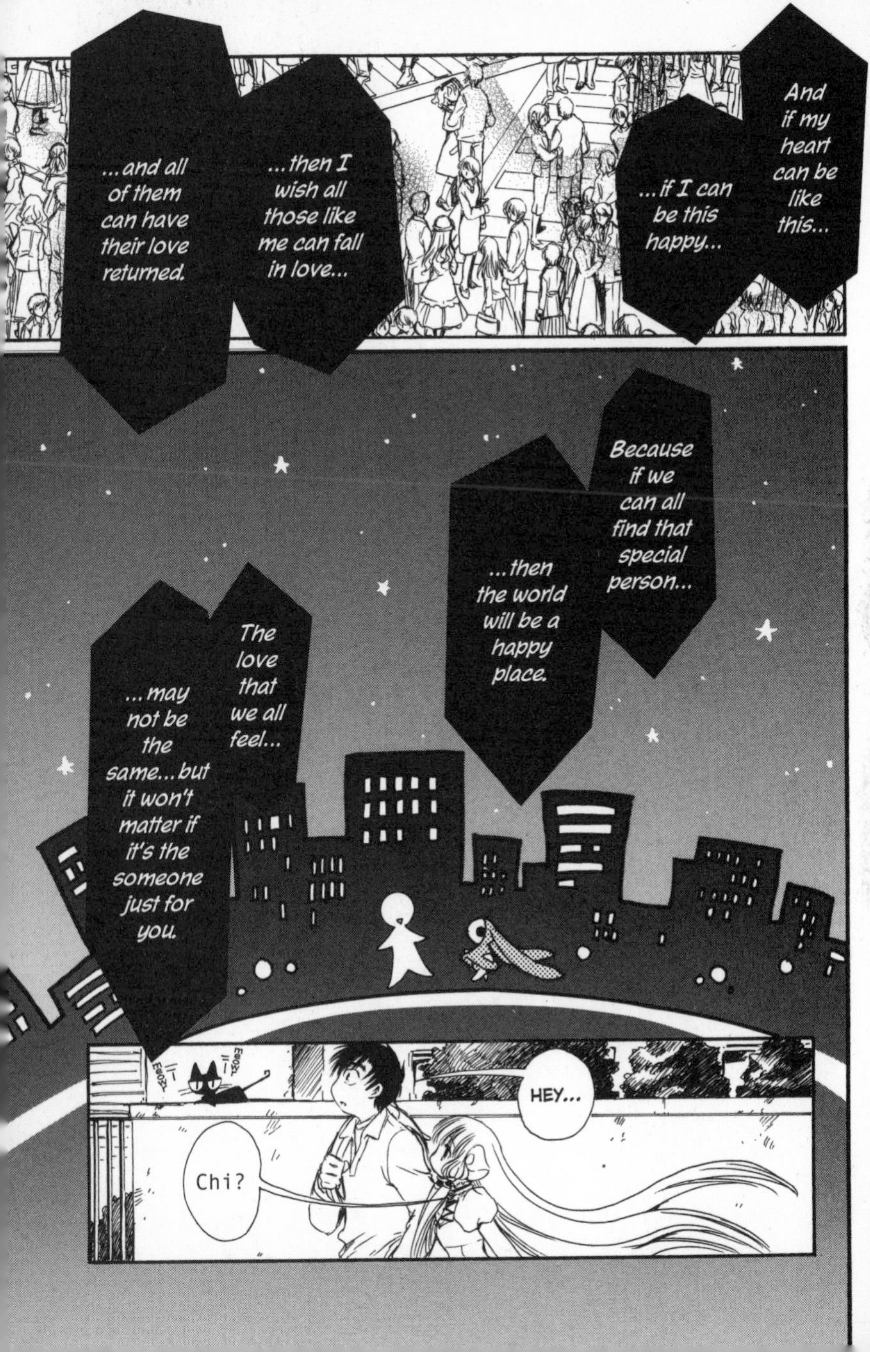
And if my heart can be like this...
...if I can be this happy...
...then I wish all those like me can fall in love...
...and all of them can have their love returned.
Because if we can all find that special person...
...then the world will be a happy place.
The love that we all feel...
...may not be the same...but it won't matter if it's the someone just for you.
HEY...
MEOW
MEOW
Chi?

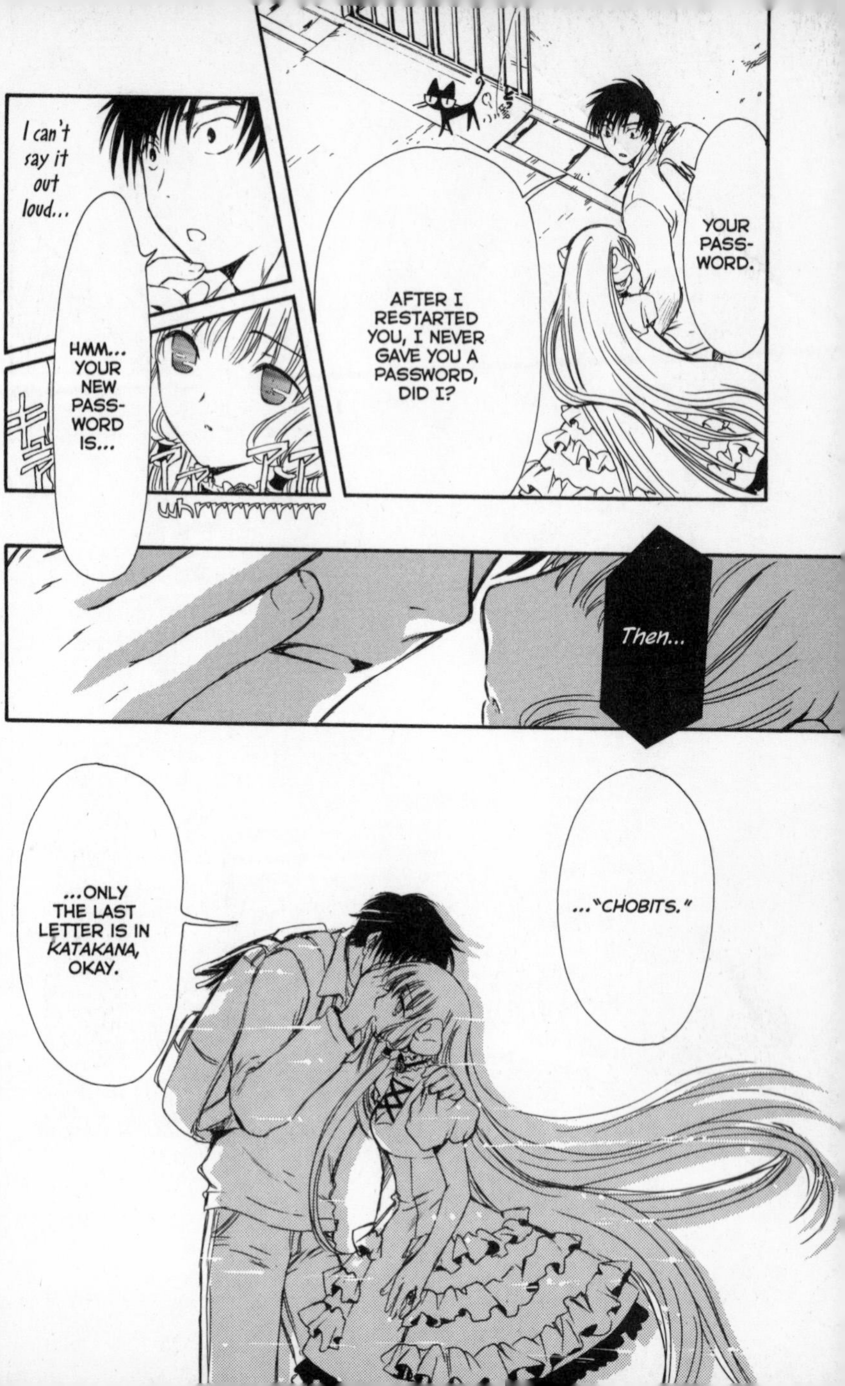
YOUR PASS-WORD.
AFTER I RESTARTED YOU, I NEVER GAVE YOU A PASSWORD, DID I?
I can't say it out loud...
HMM... YOUR NEW PASS-WORD IS...
whrrrrrrrrrr
Then...
..."CHOBITS."
...ONLY THE LAST LETTER IS IN KATAKANA, OKAY.

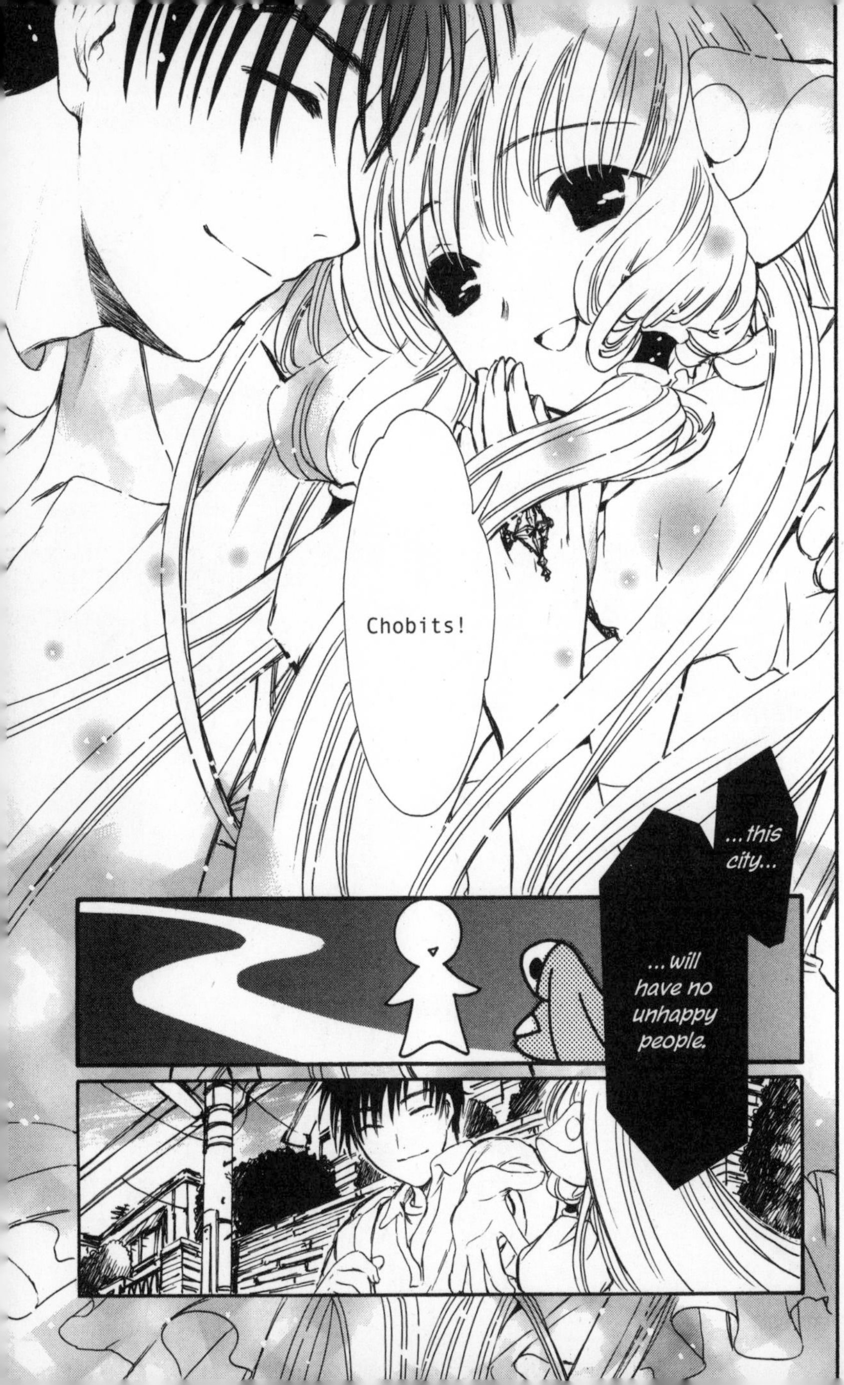
Chobits!
...this city...
...will have no unhappy people.

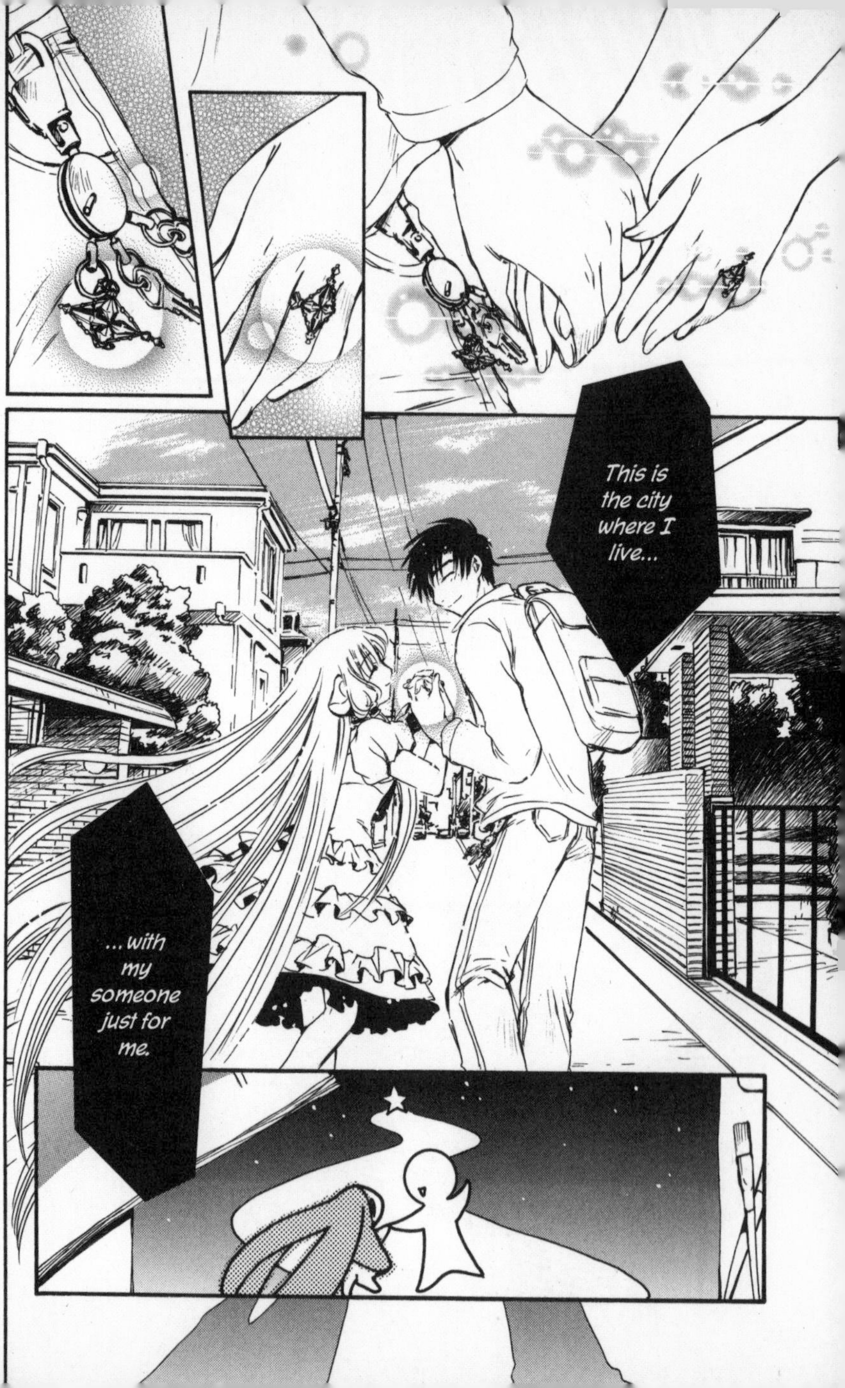
This is the city where I live...
...with my someone just for me.

Chobits

ちょびっツ

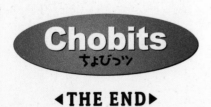

◀THE END▶

Chobits
ちょびっツ

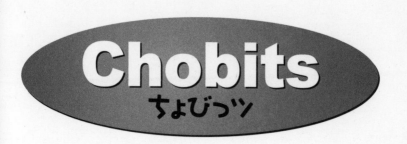

story + art **CLAMP**

SATSUKI IGARASHI
MOKONA
TSUBAKI NEKOI
NANASE OHKAWA

editor **CARL GUSTAV HORN**

original translation by **SHIRLEY KUBO**

lettering and retouch by **JOHN CLARK**

editorial assistant **ANNIE GULLION**

special thanks to **MICHAEL GOMBOS, KIYOKAZU FUJIMOTO, YOSHIE YOKOI,**

JOHN SCHORK, and JAKE FORBES

designer **DAVID NESTELLE**

publisher **MIKE RICHARDSON**

English-language version produced by Dark Horse Comics

CHOBITS Book 2

Published by Dark Horse Manga, a division of Dark Horse Comics, Inc.
10956 SE Main Street | Milwaukie, OR 97222 | darkhorse.com

To find a comics shop in your area, call the Comic Shop Locator Service toll-free at 1-888-266-4226.

First edition: September 2010
ISBN 978-1-59582-514-8

10 9 8 7 6 5 4 3 2 1
Printed by Transcontinental Gagné, Louiseville, QC, Canada.

Chobits

ちょびつ

On the next forty-eight pages, please enjoy a giant-sized bonus gallery of color *Chobits* images. Thank you for reading *Chobits*, and please look out for our next CLAMP omnibus series, *Cardcaptor Sakura*, which starts in November 2010!

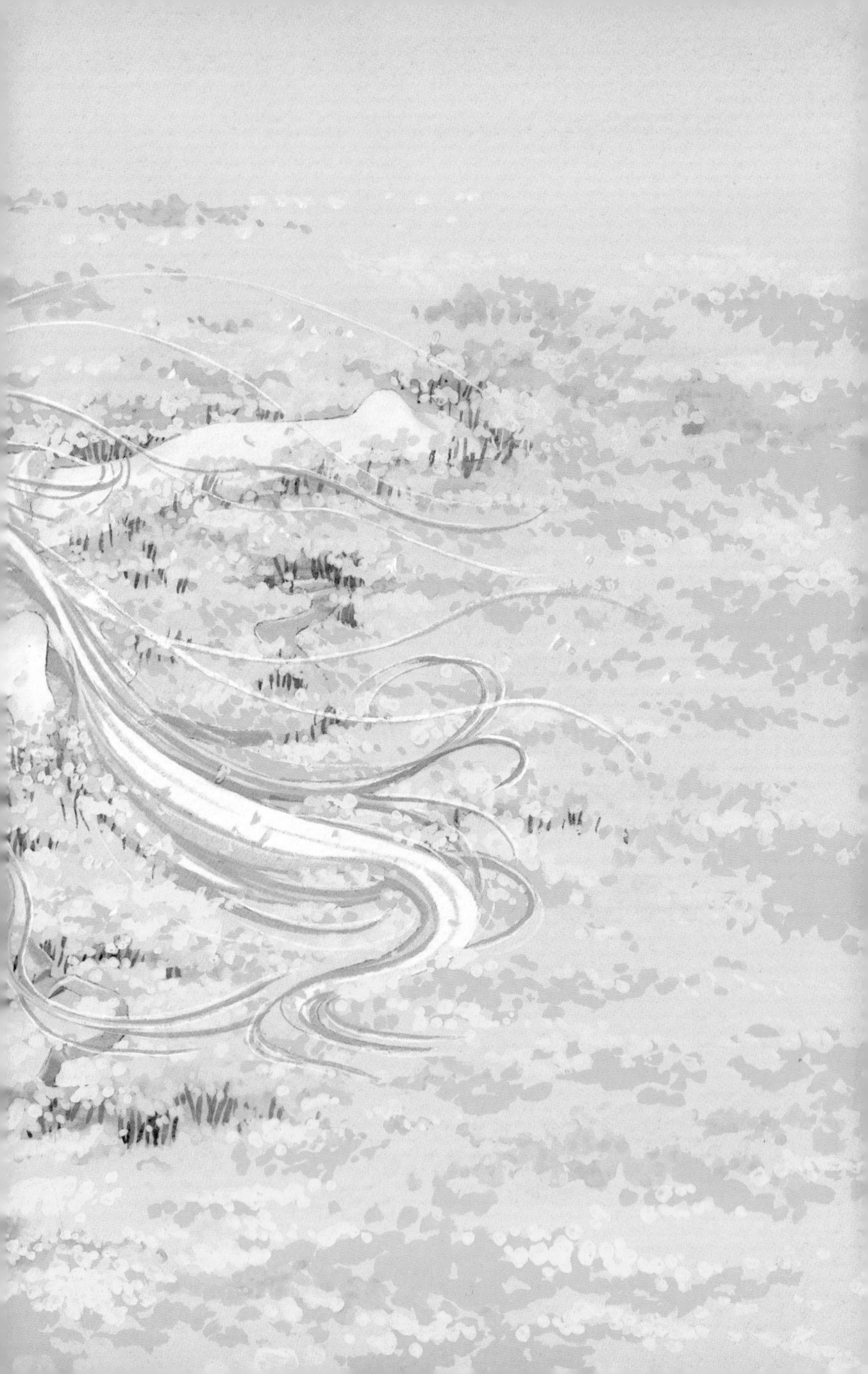

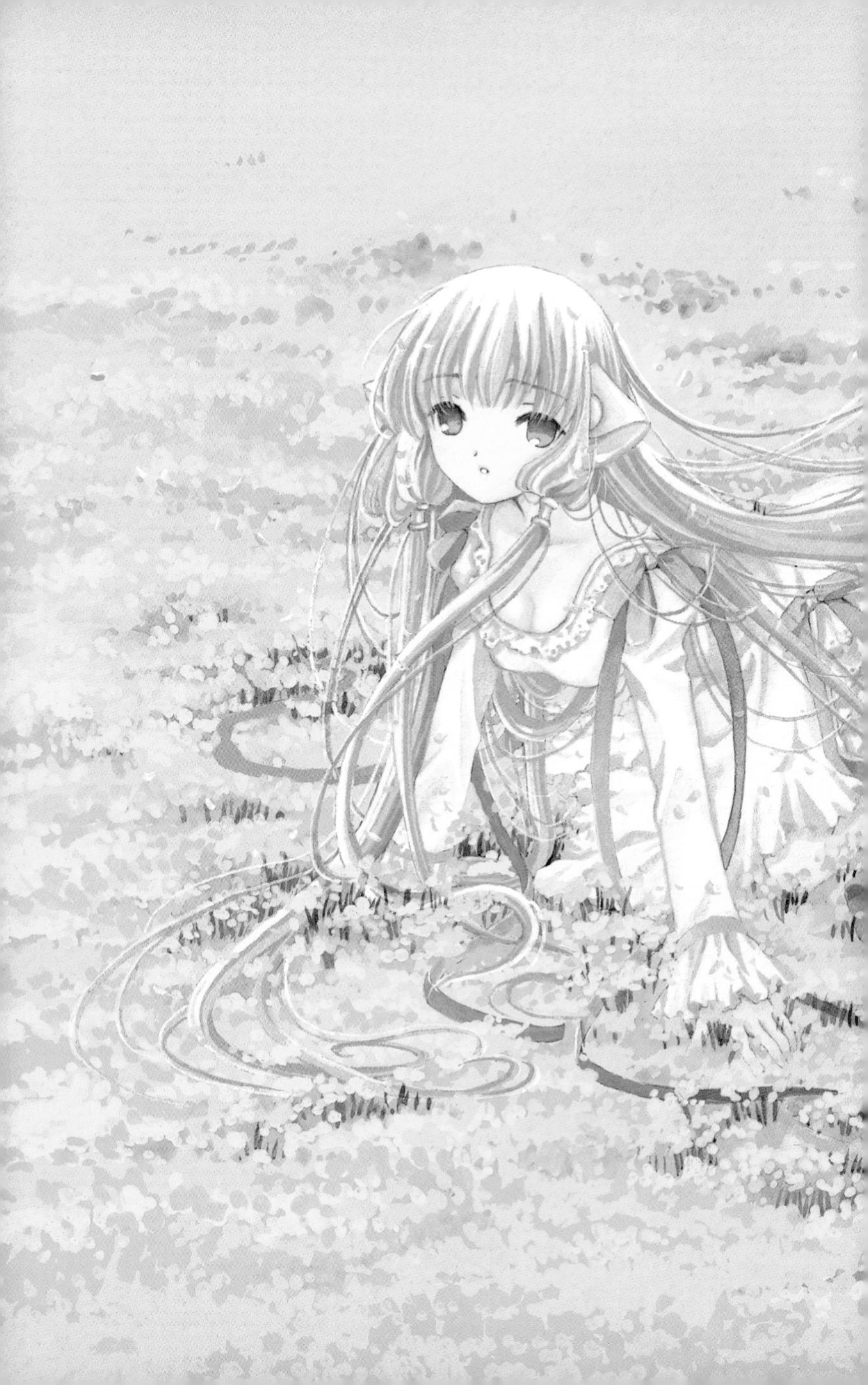

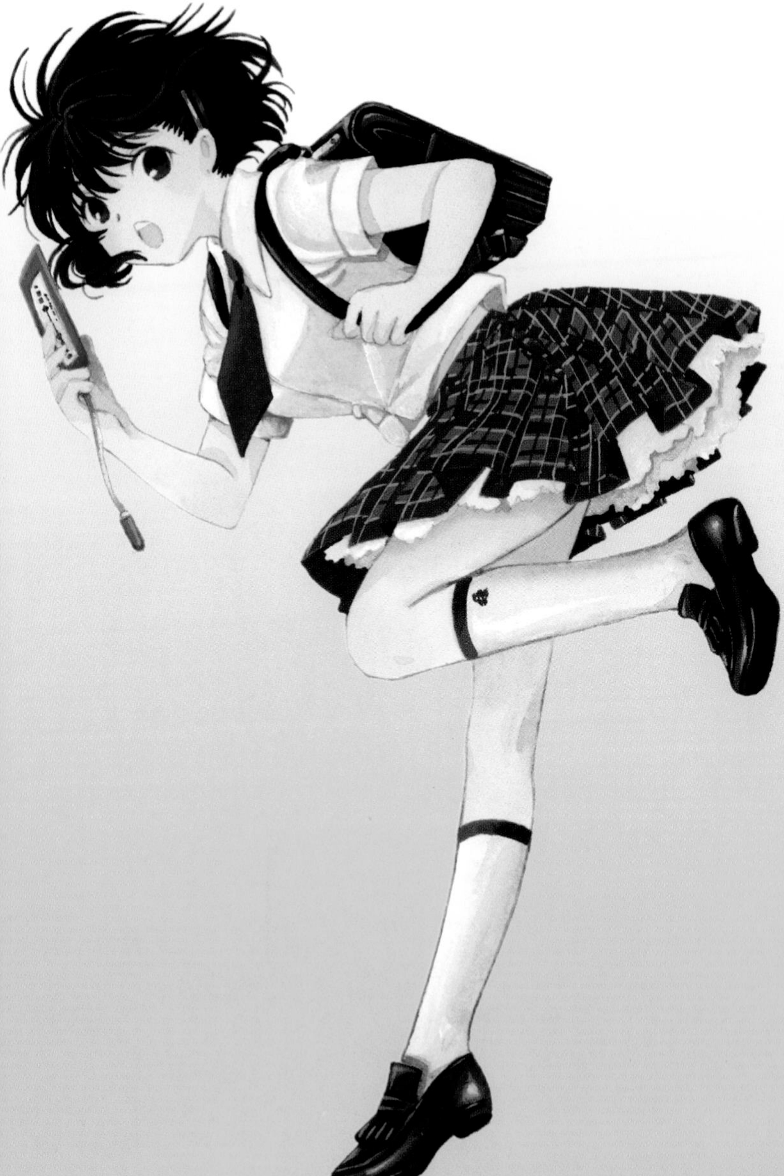

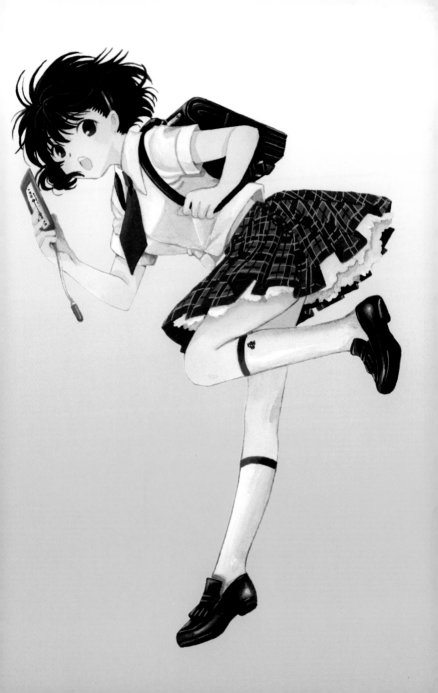

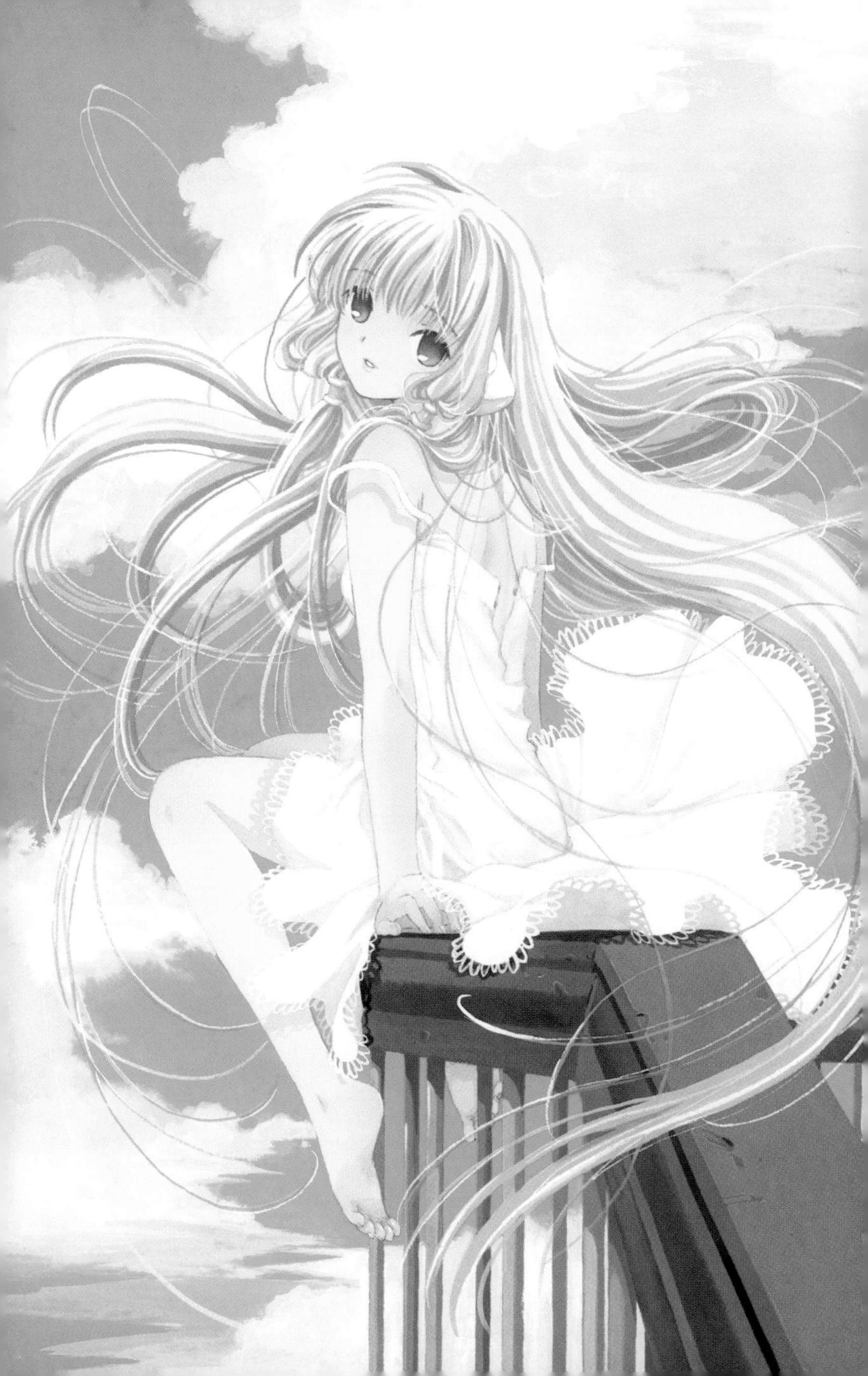

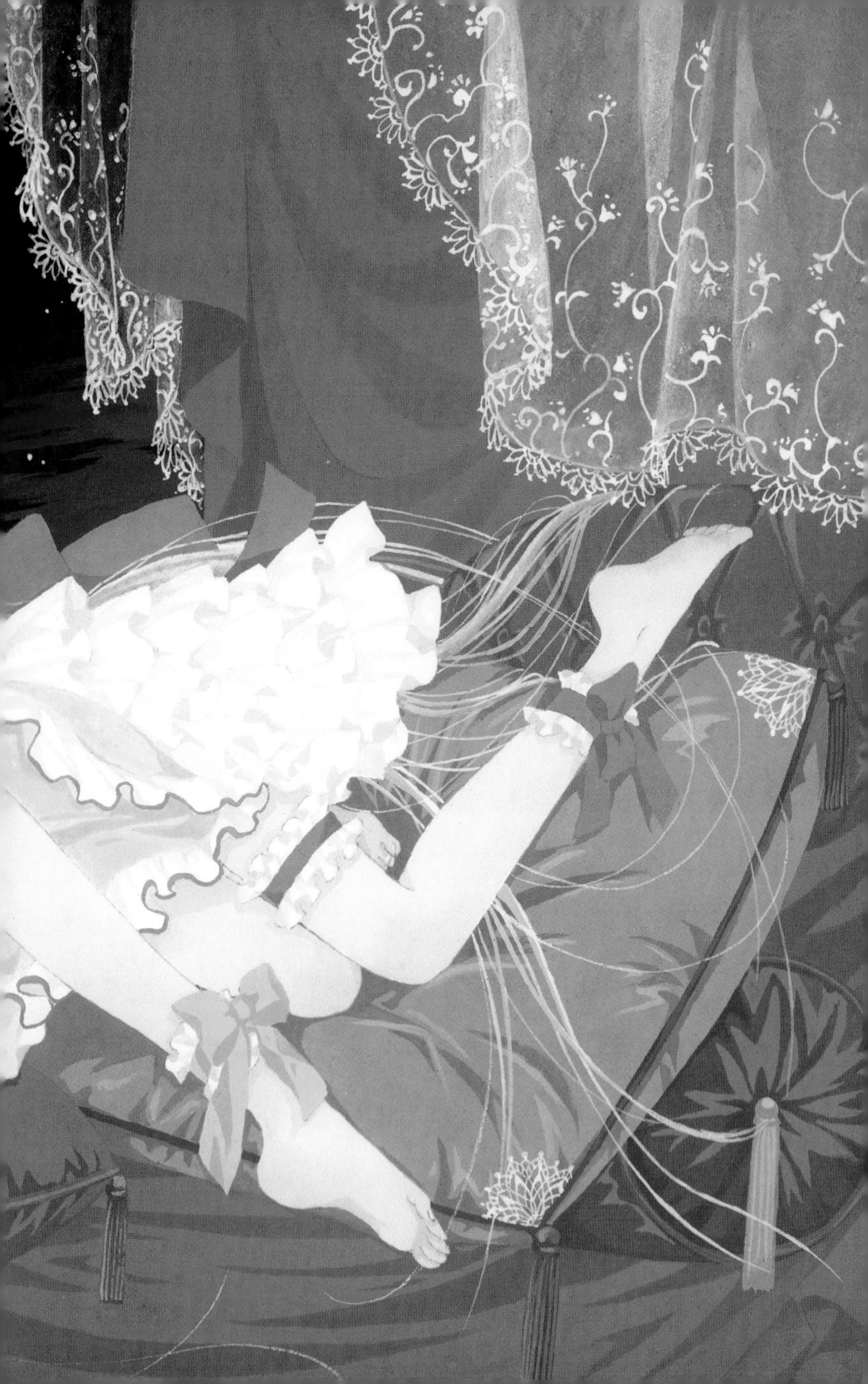

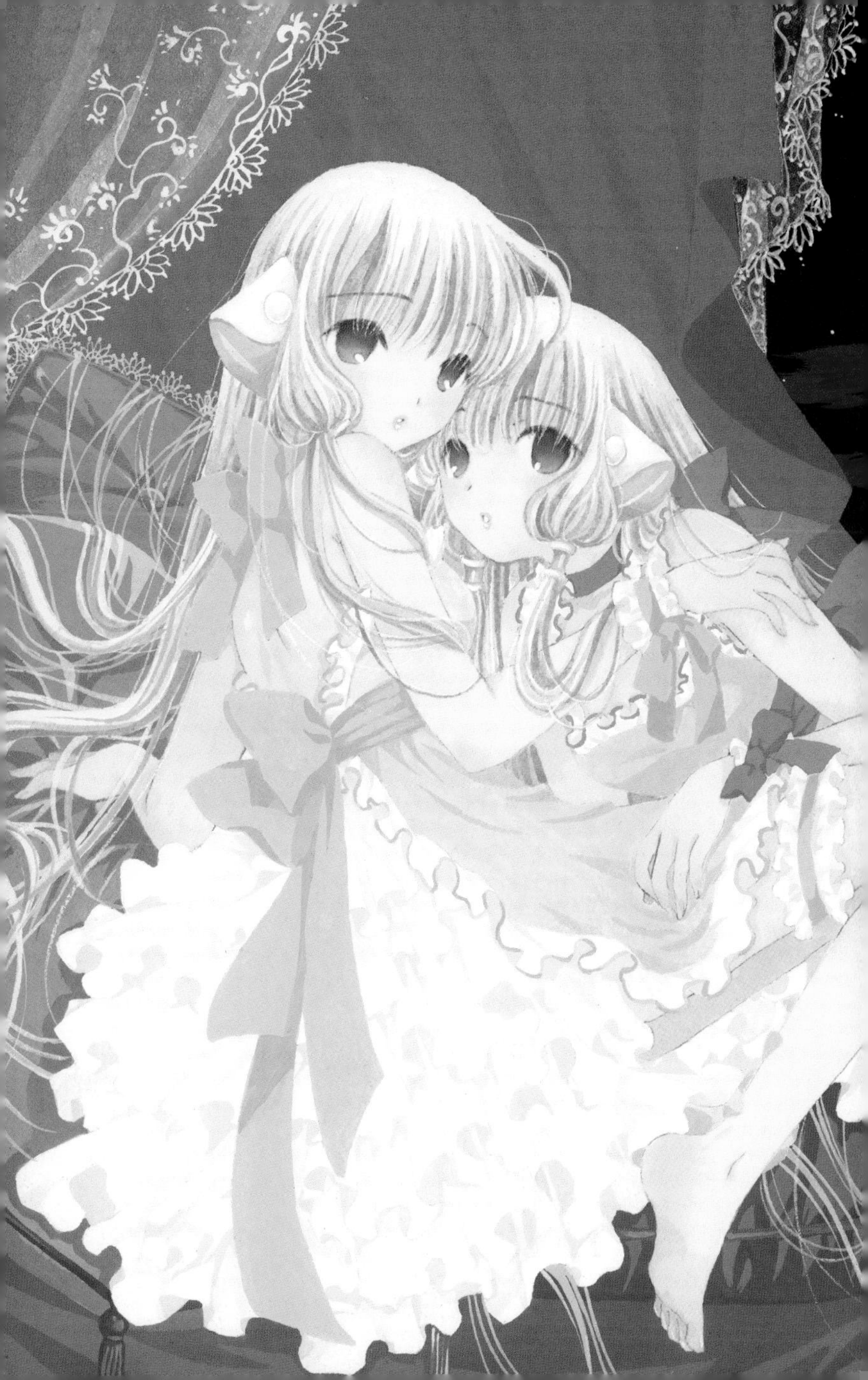

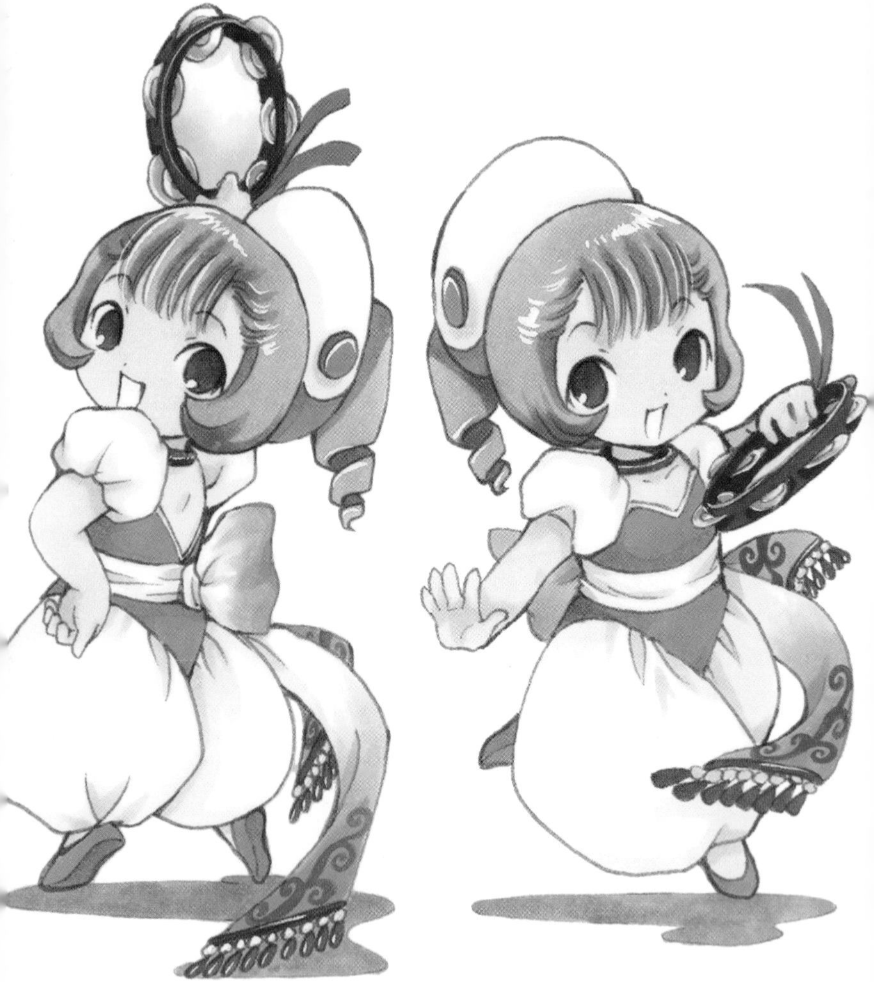

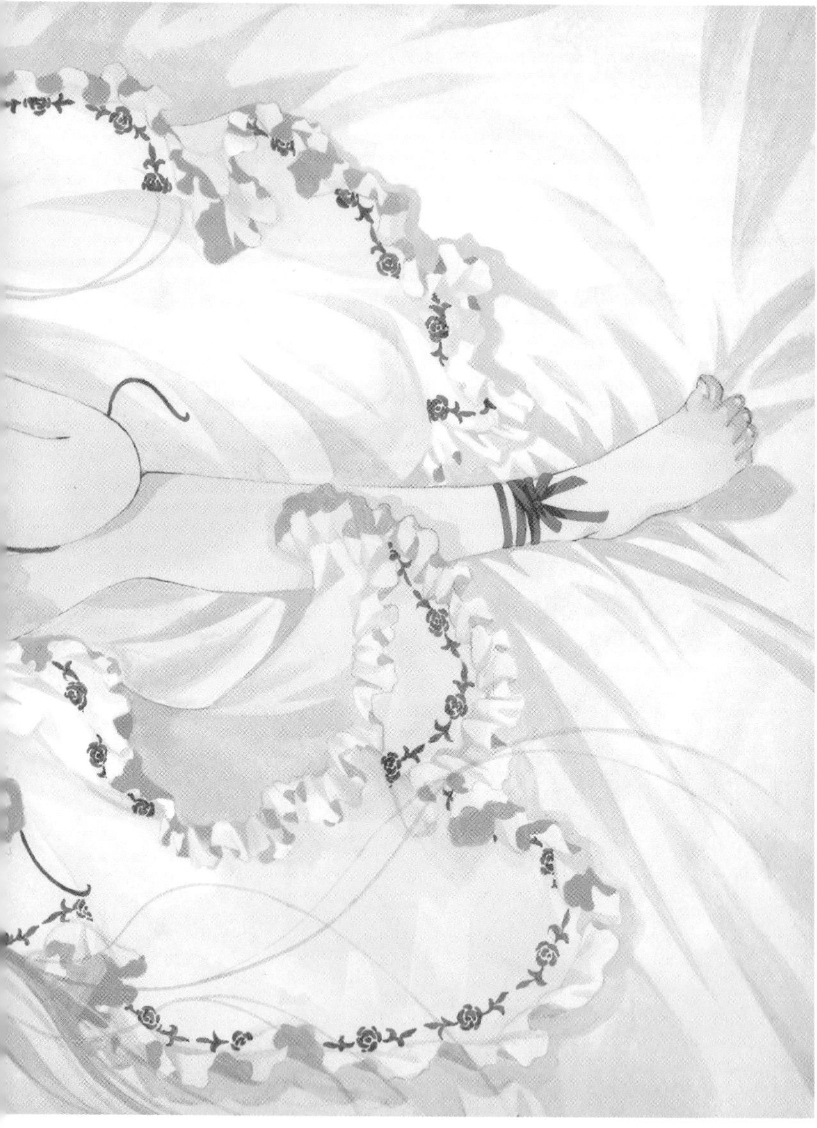

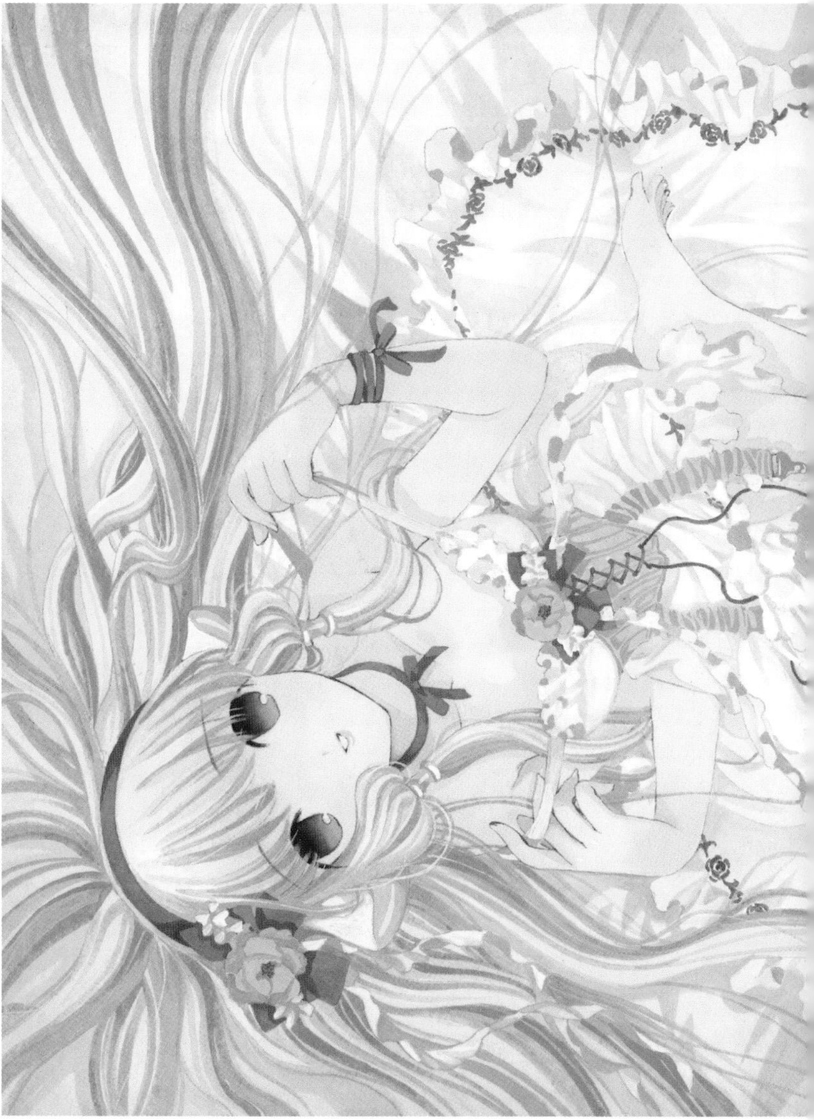

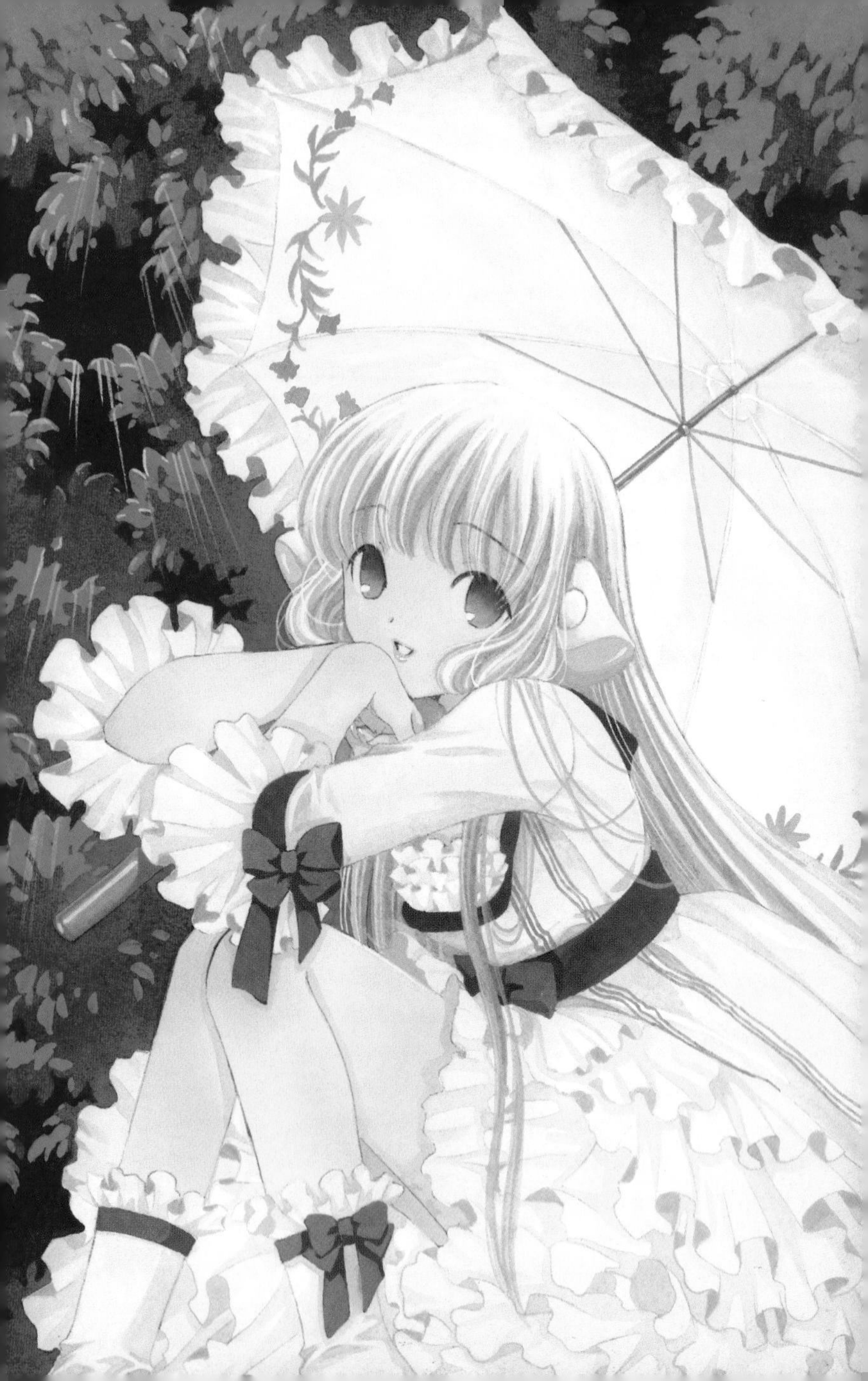

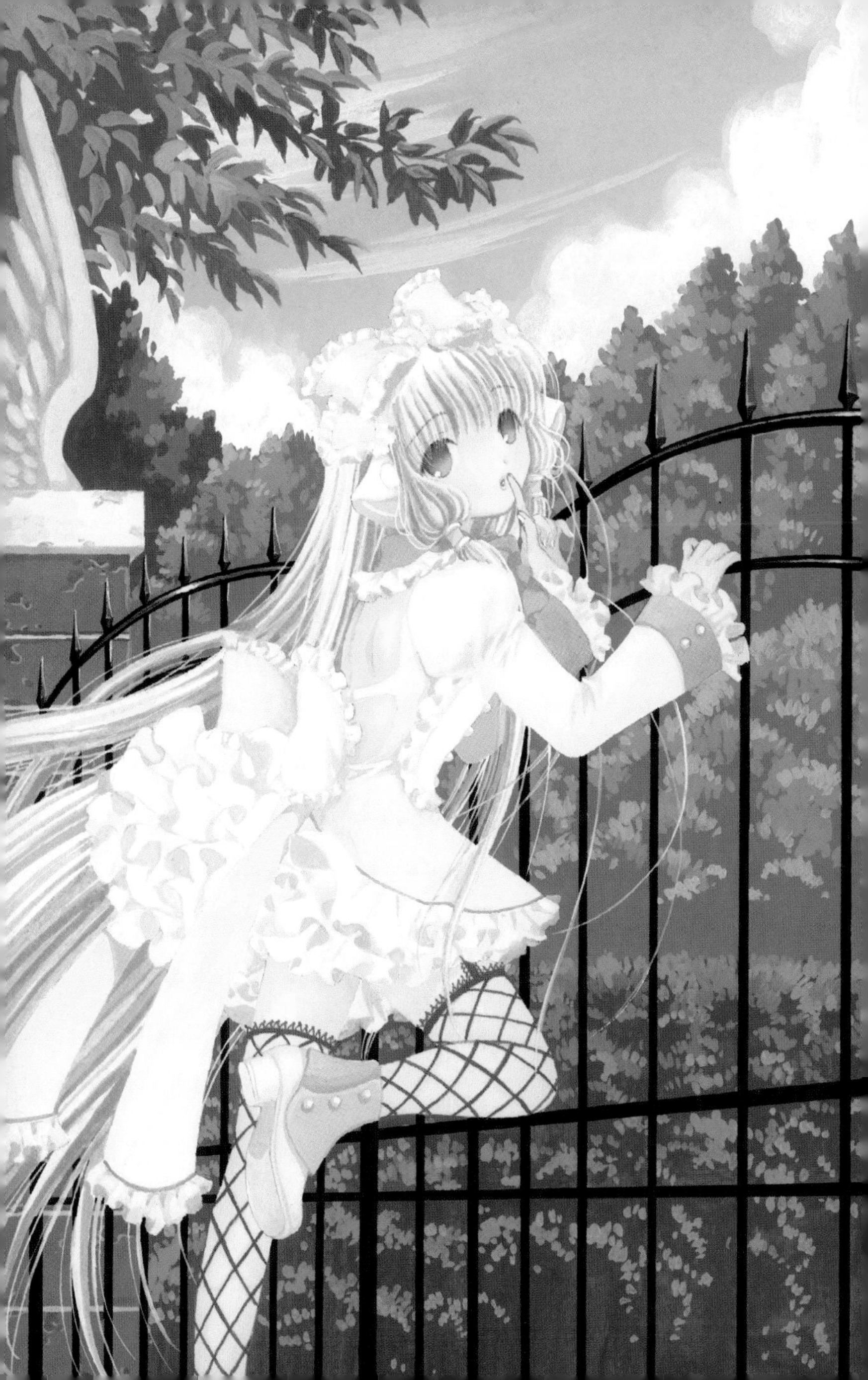

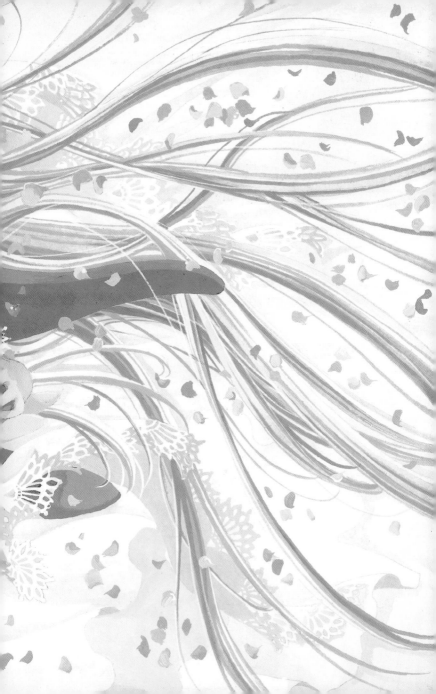

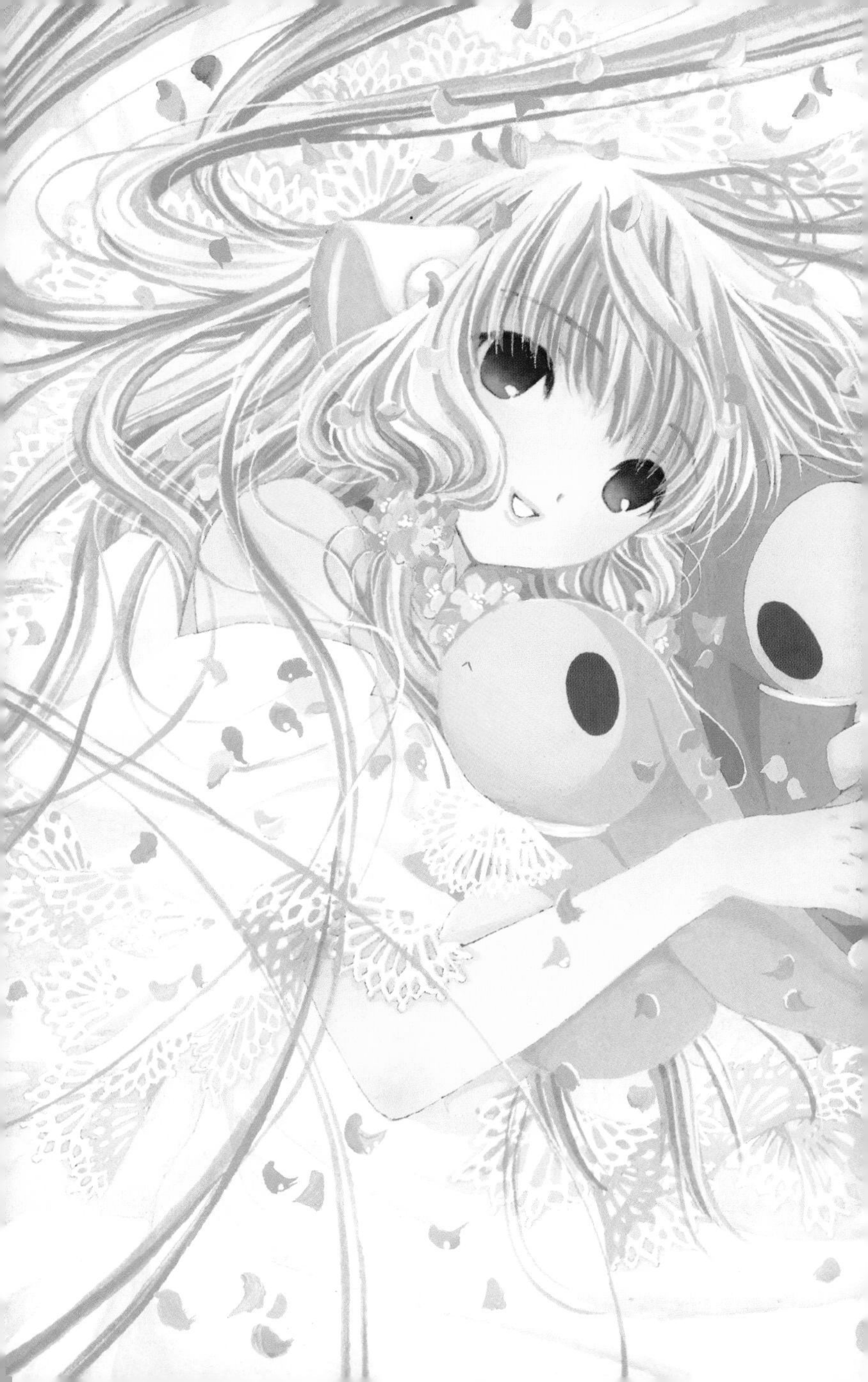

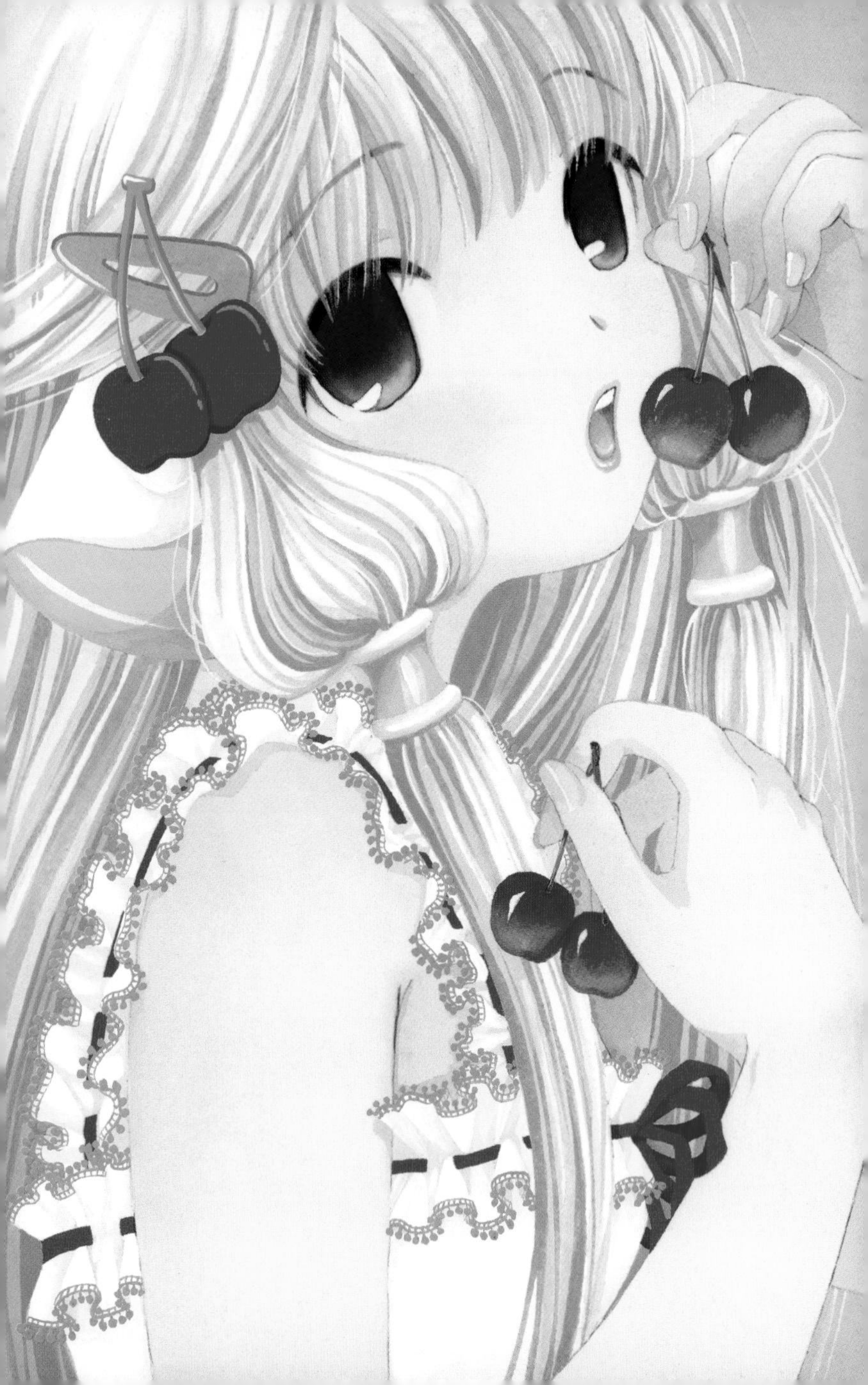

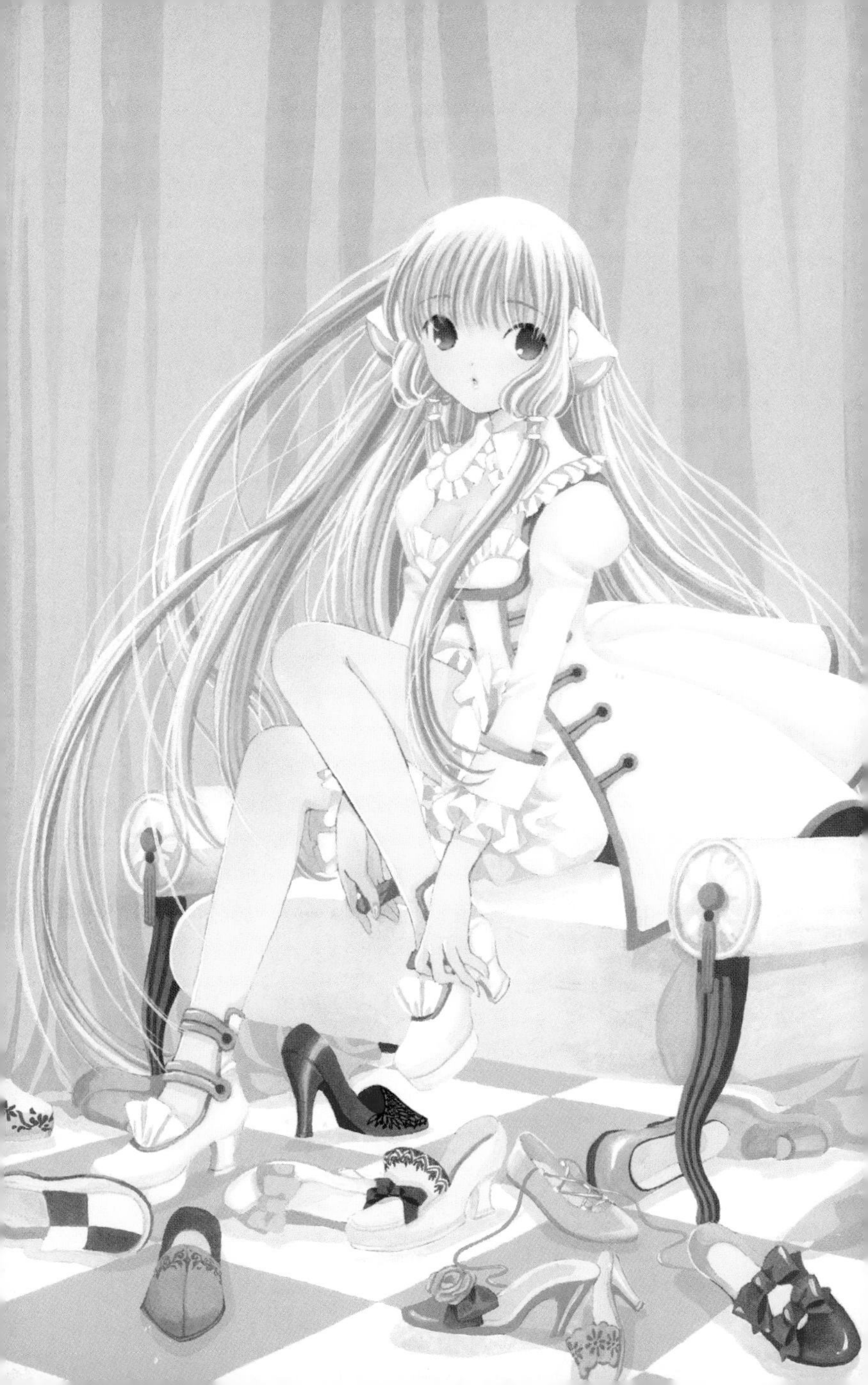

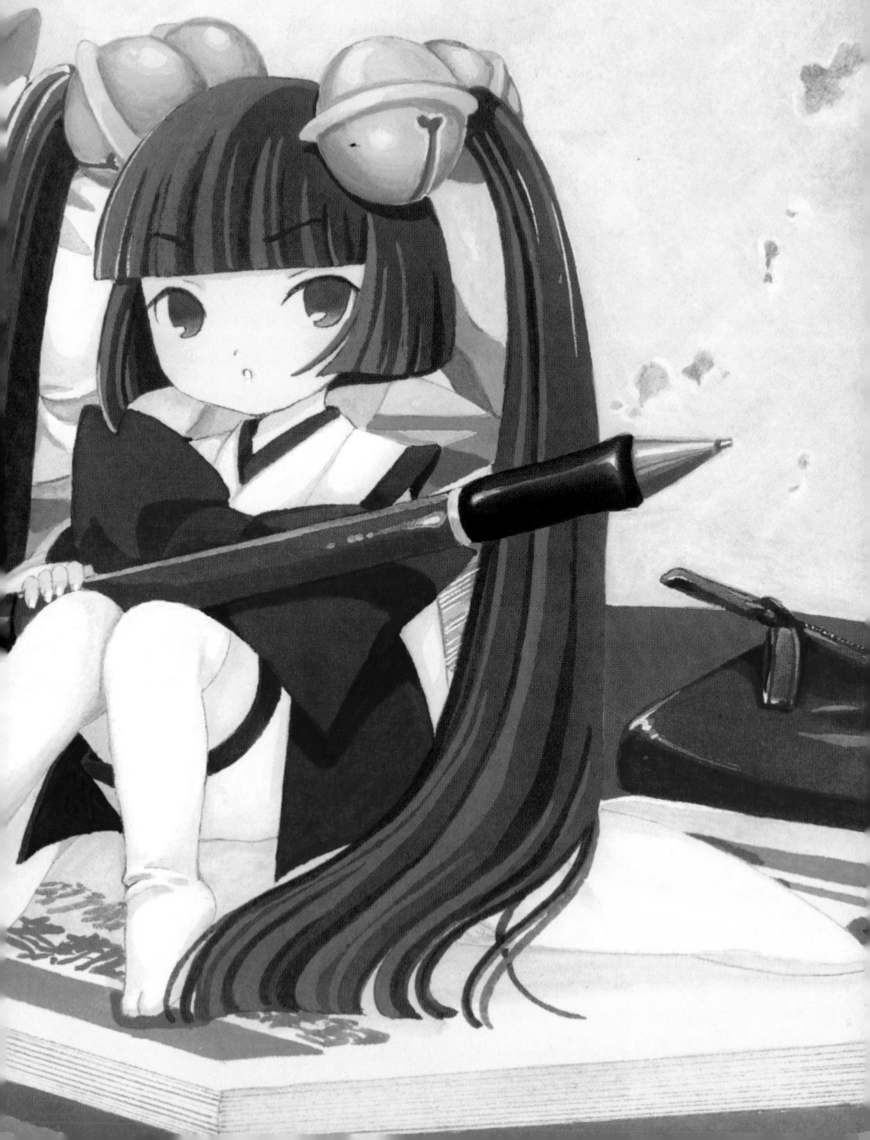

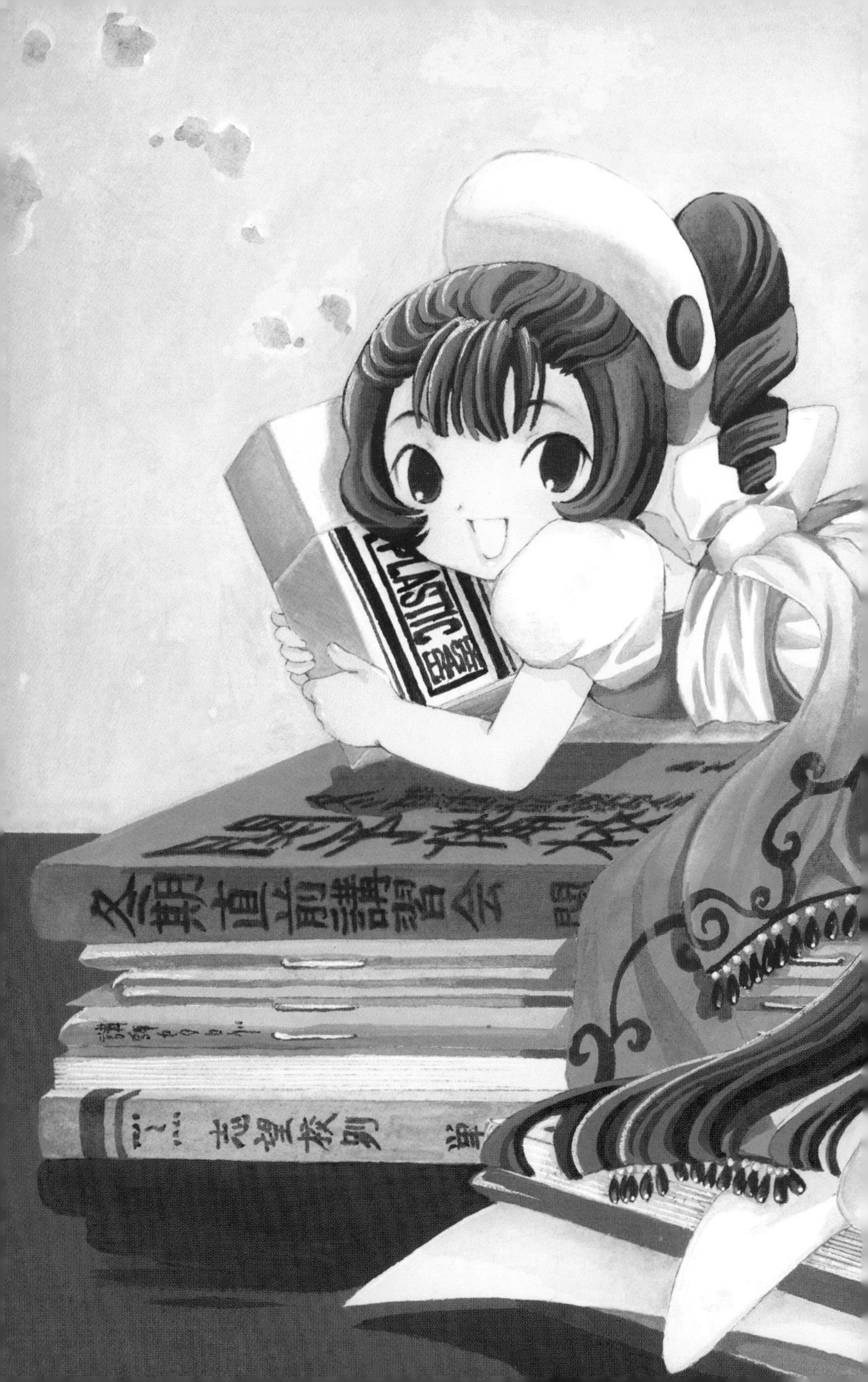
PLASTIC
ERASER
冬期直前講習会
志望校別

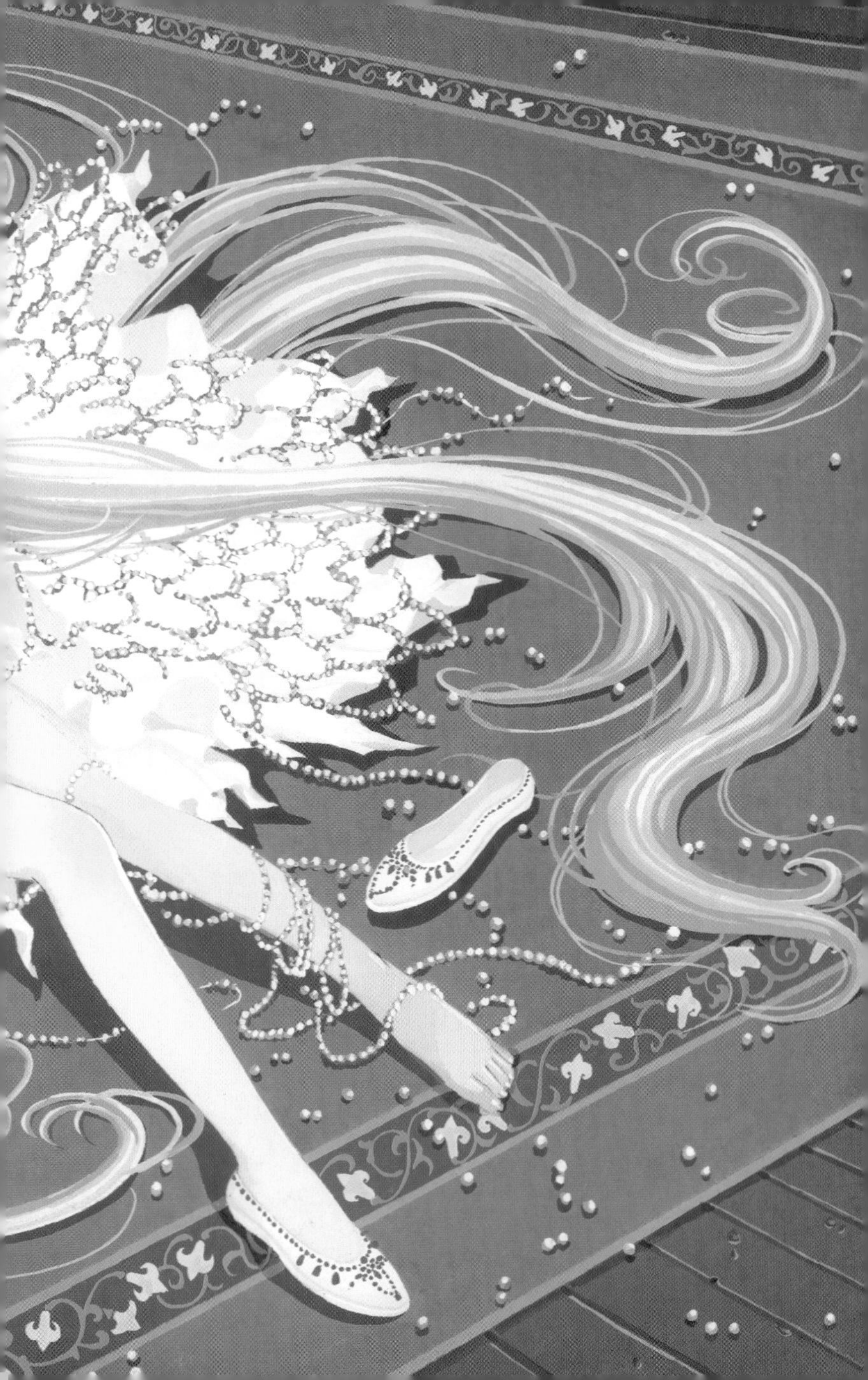

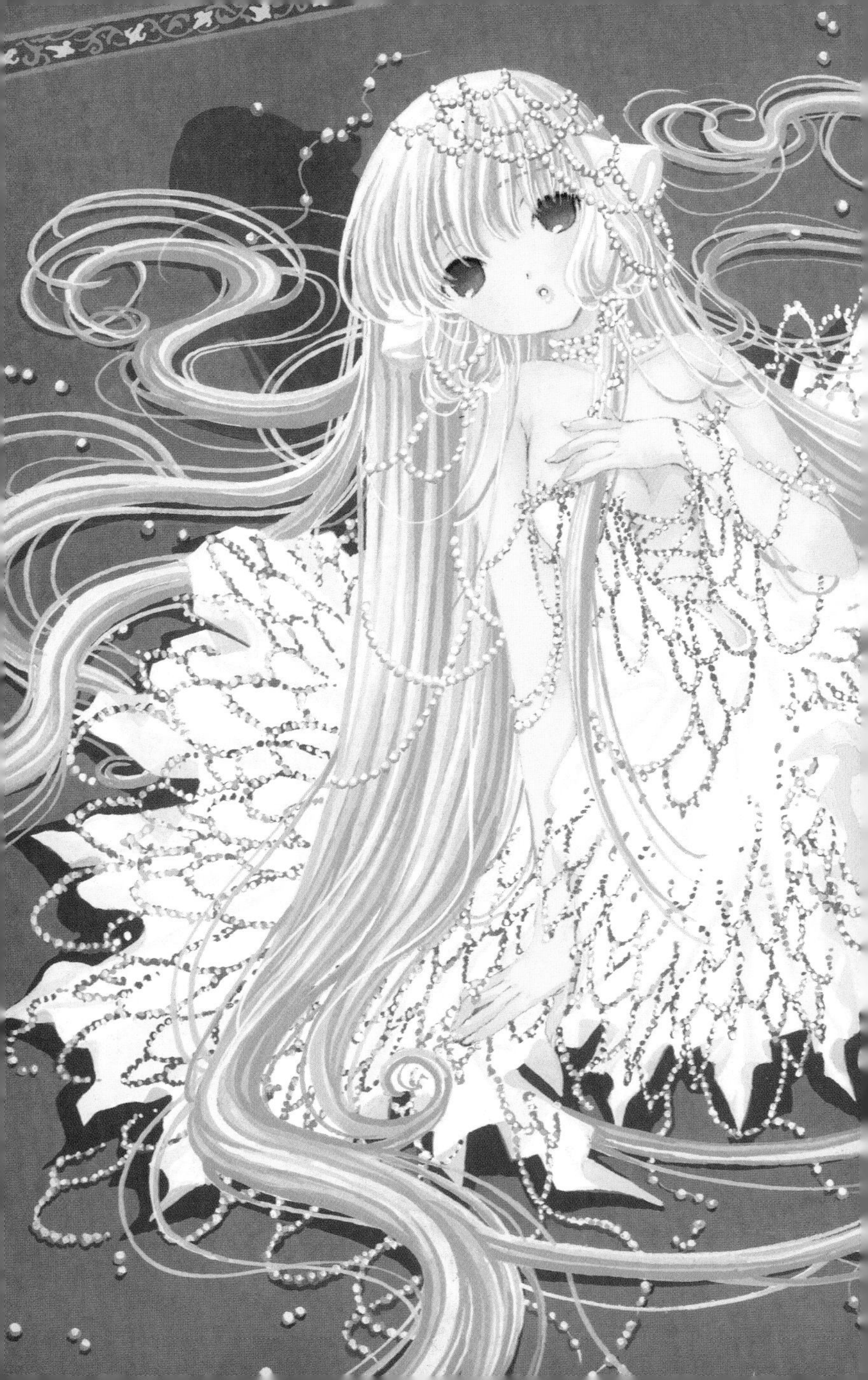

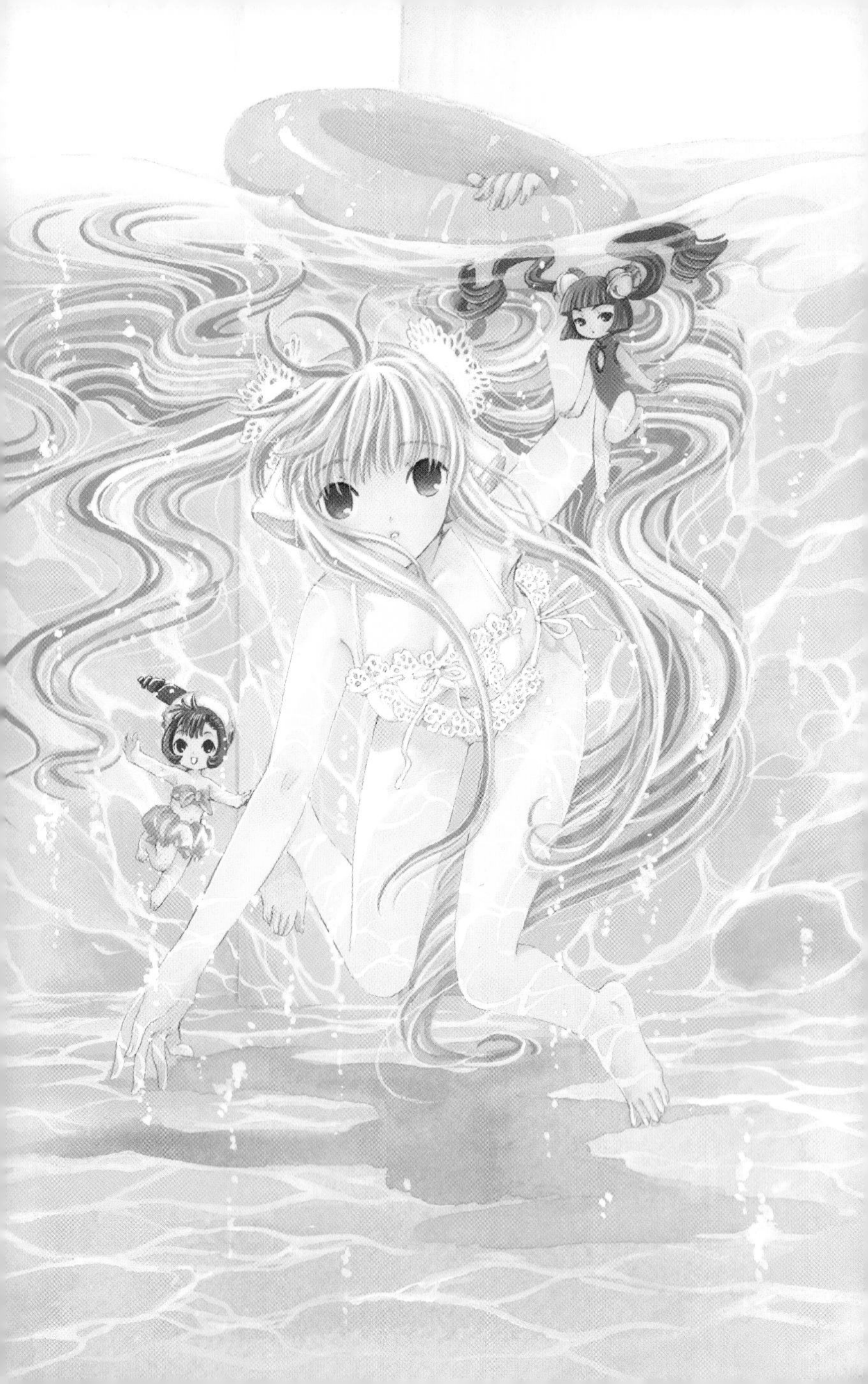

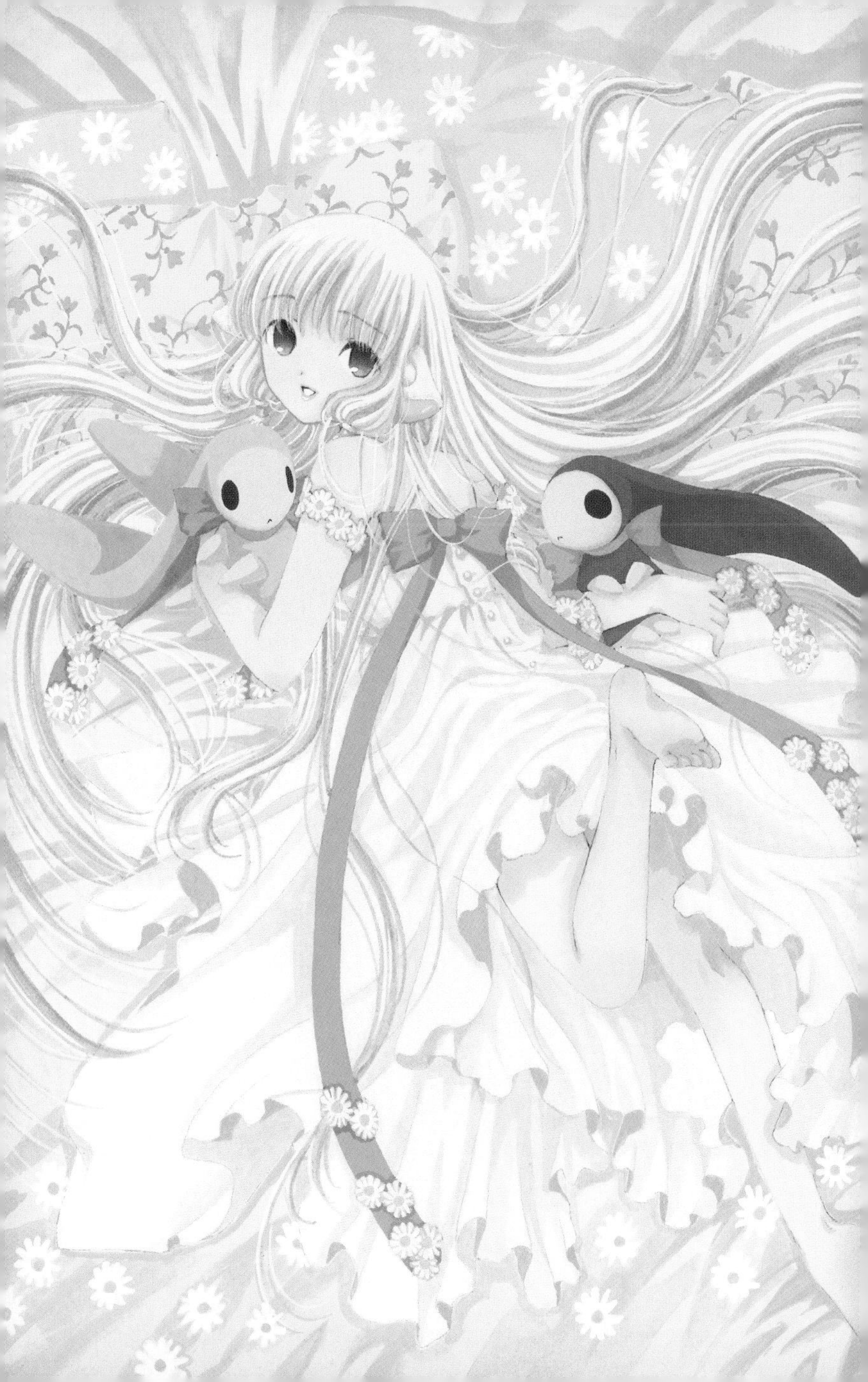

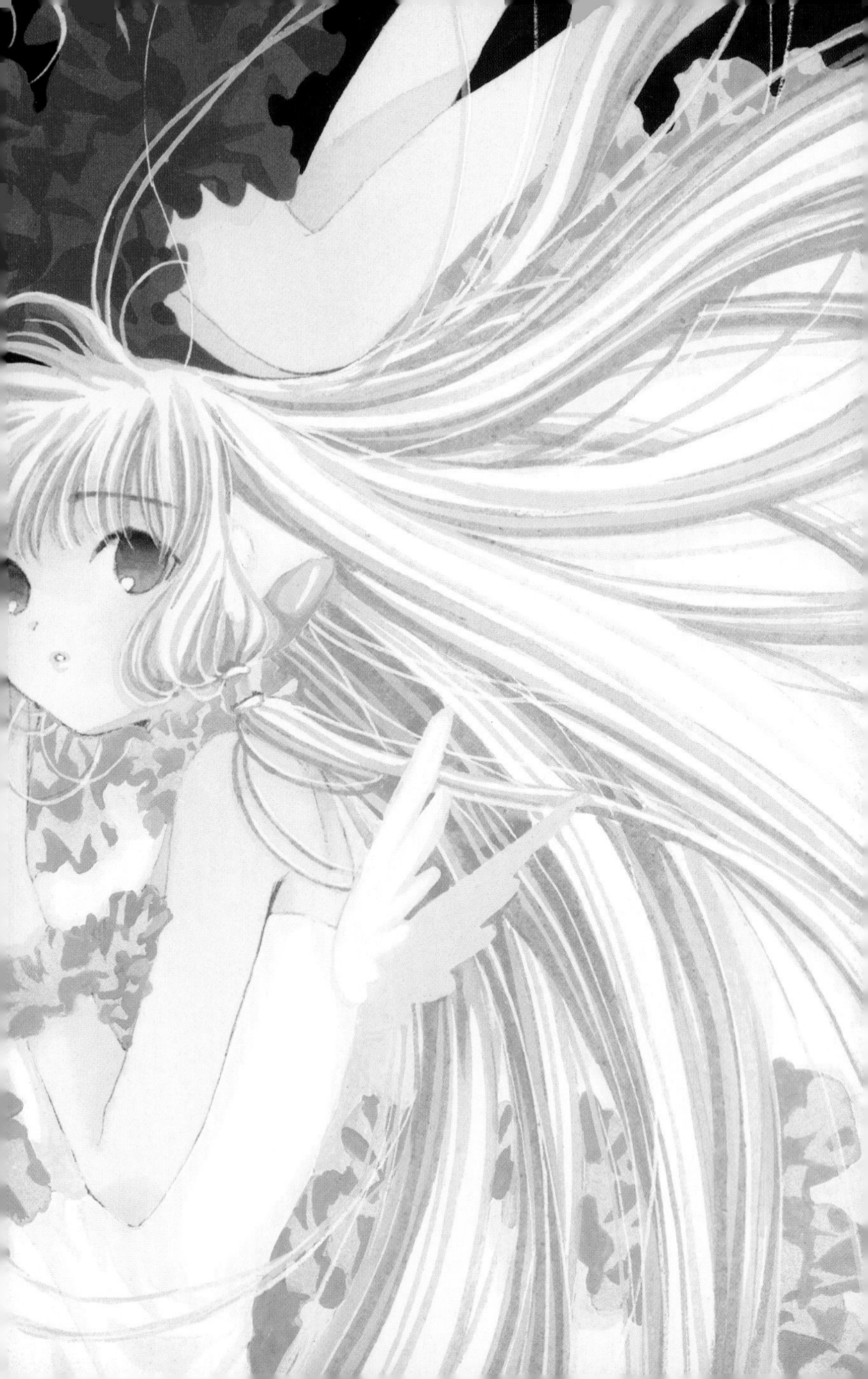

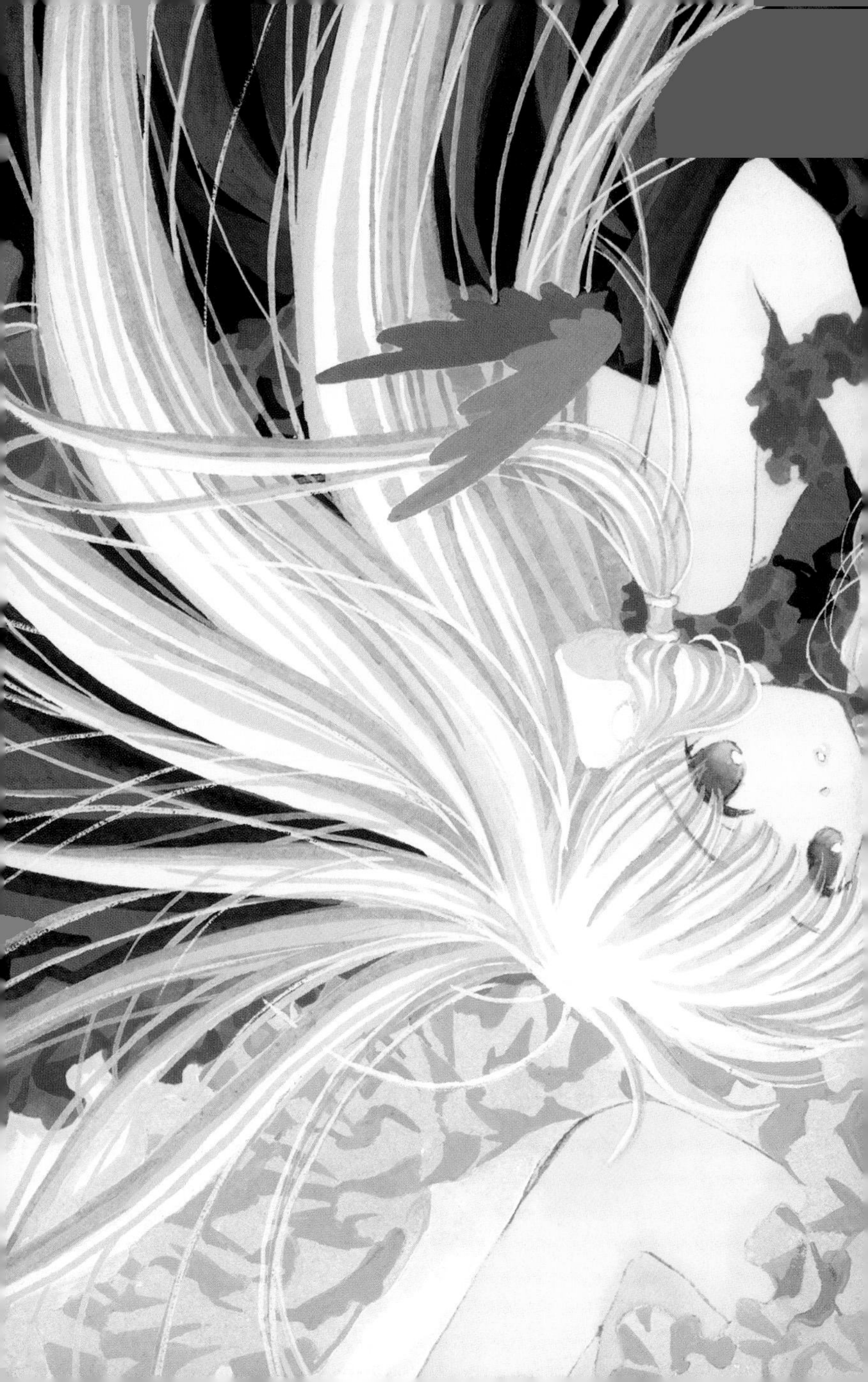

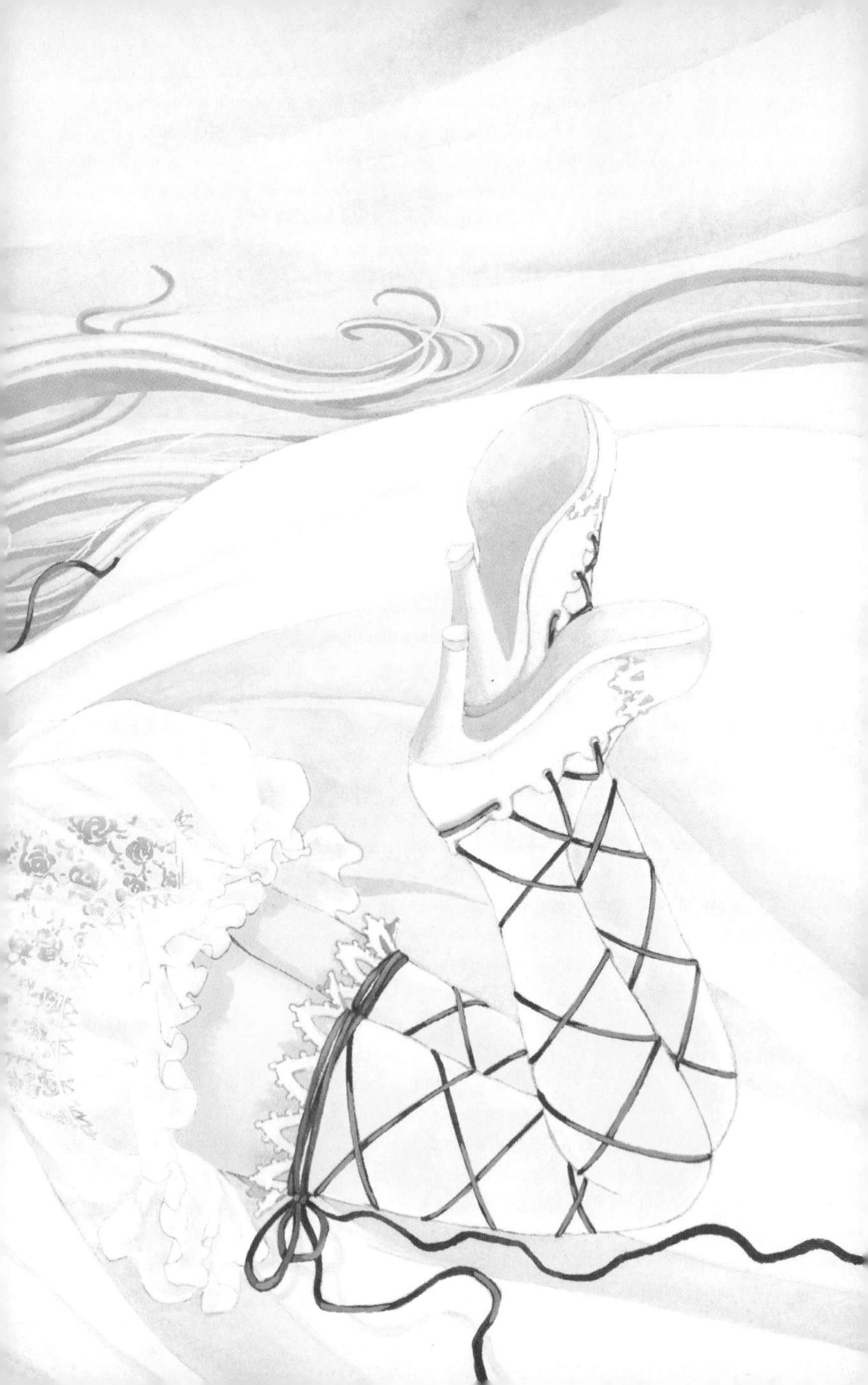

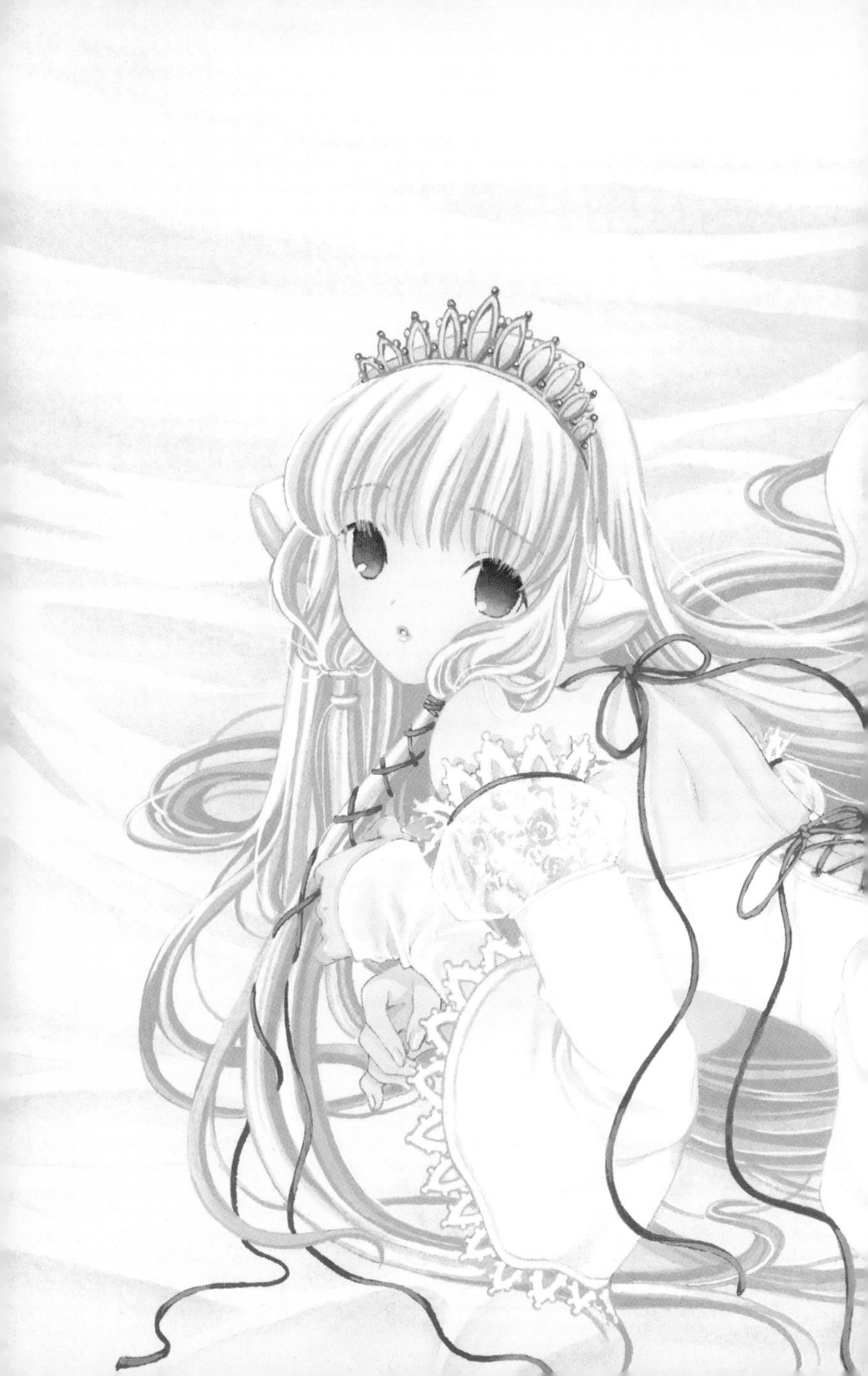

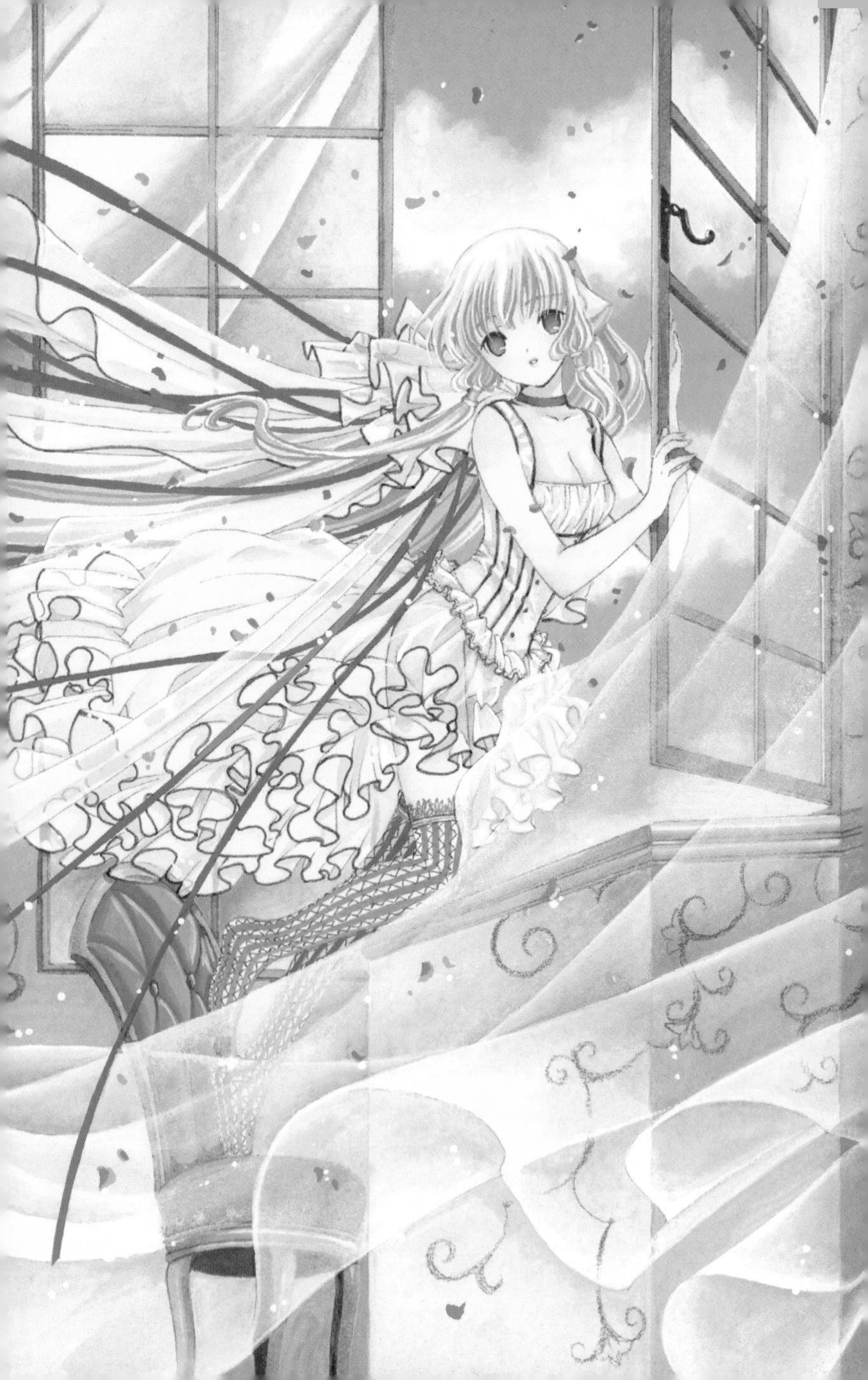

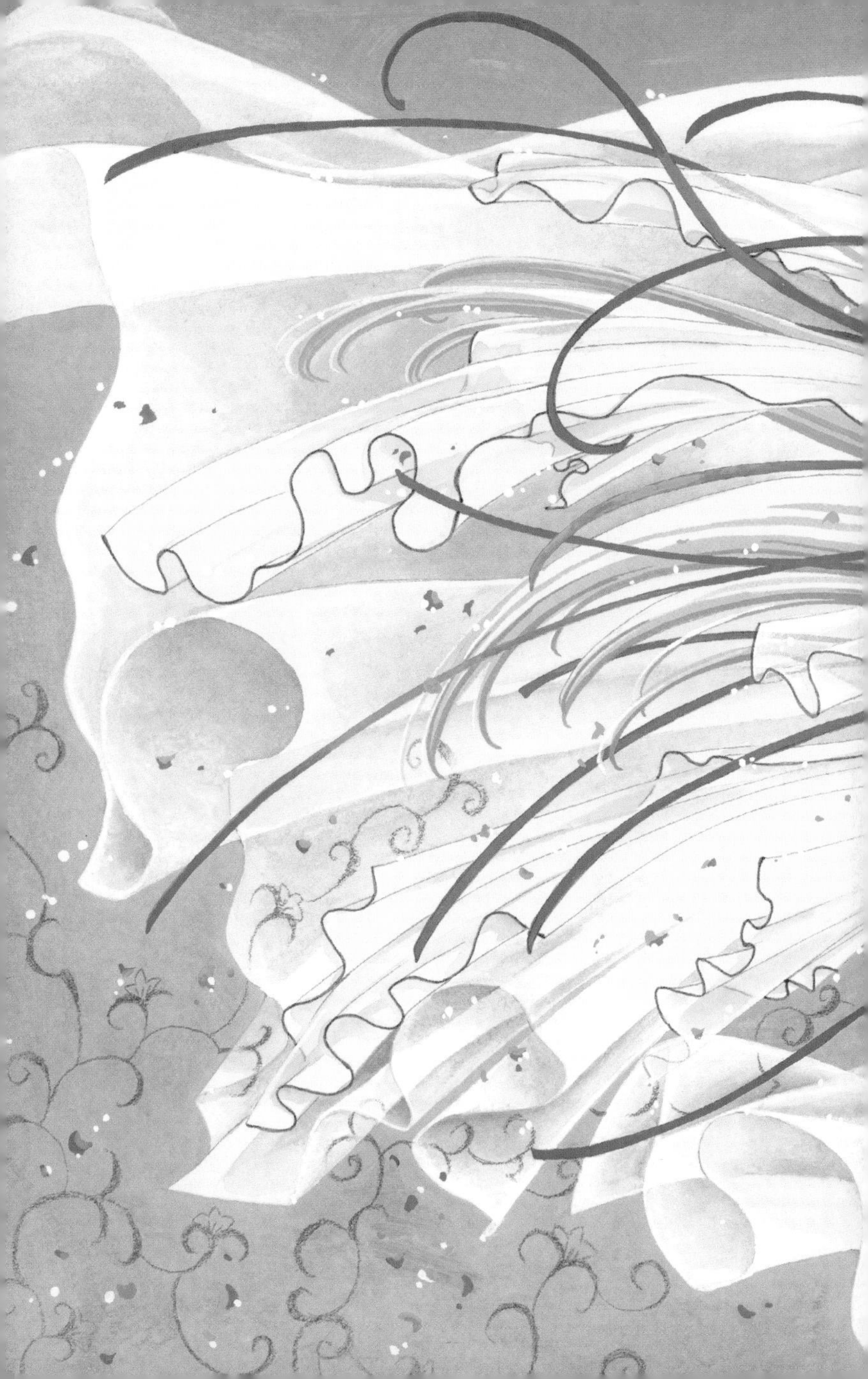

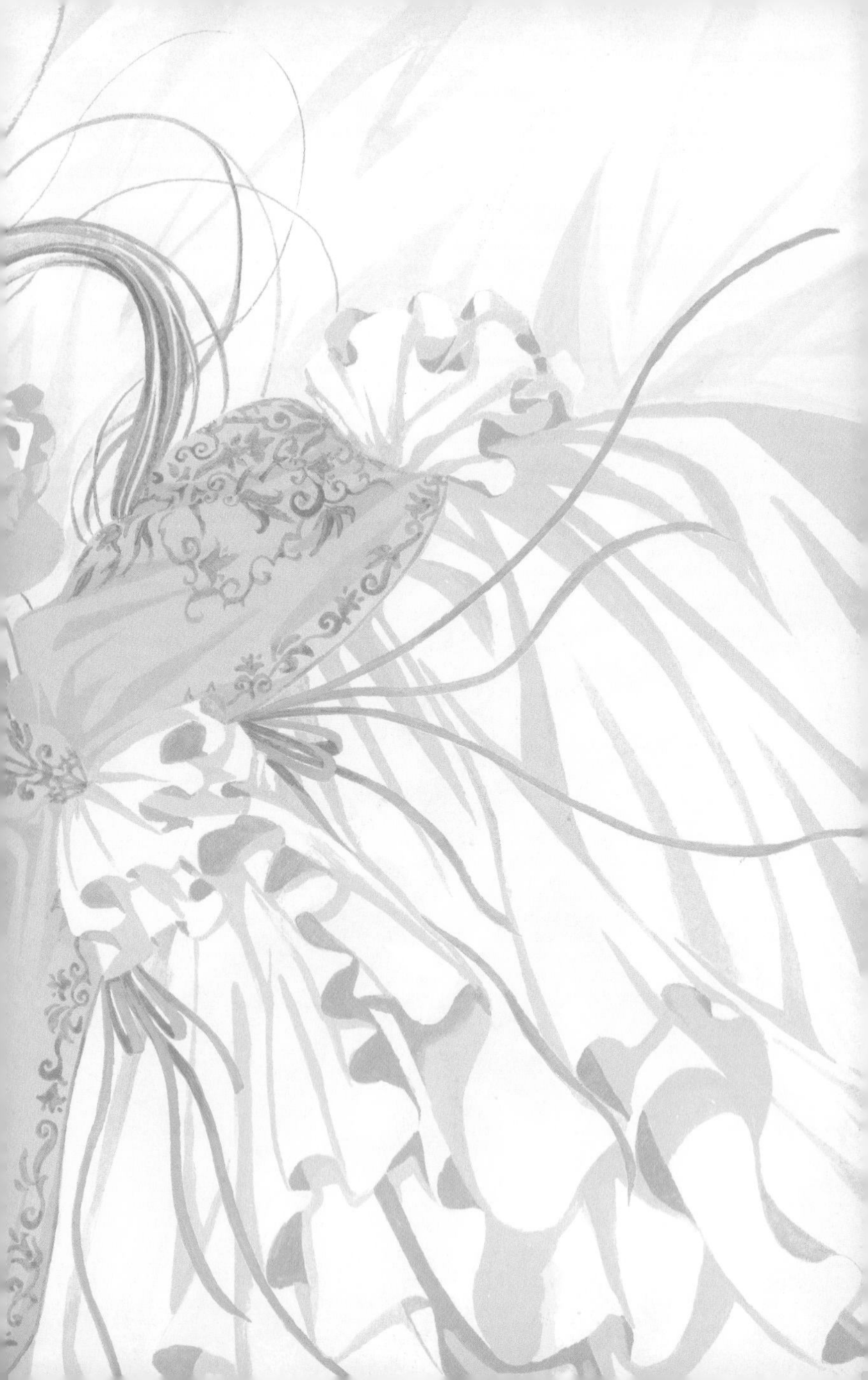

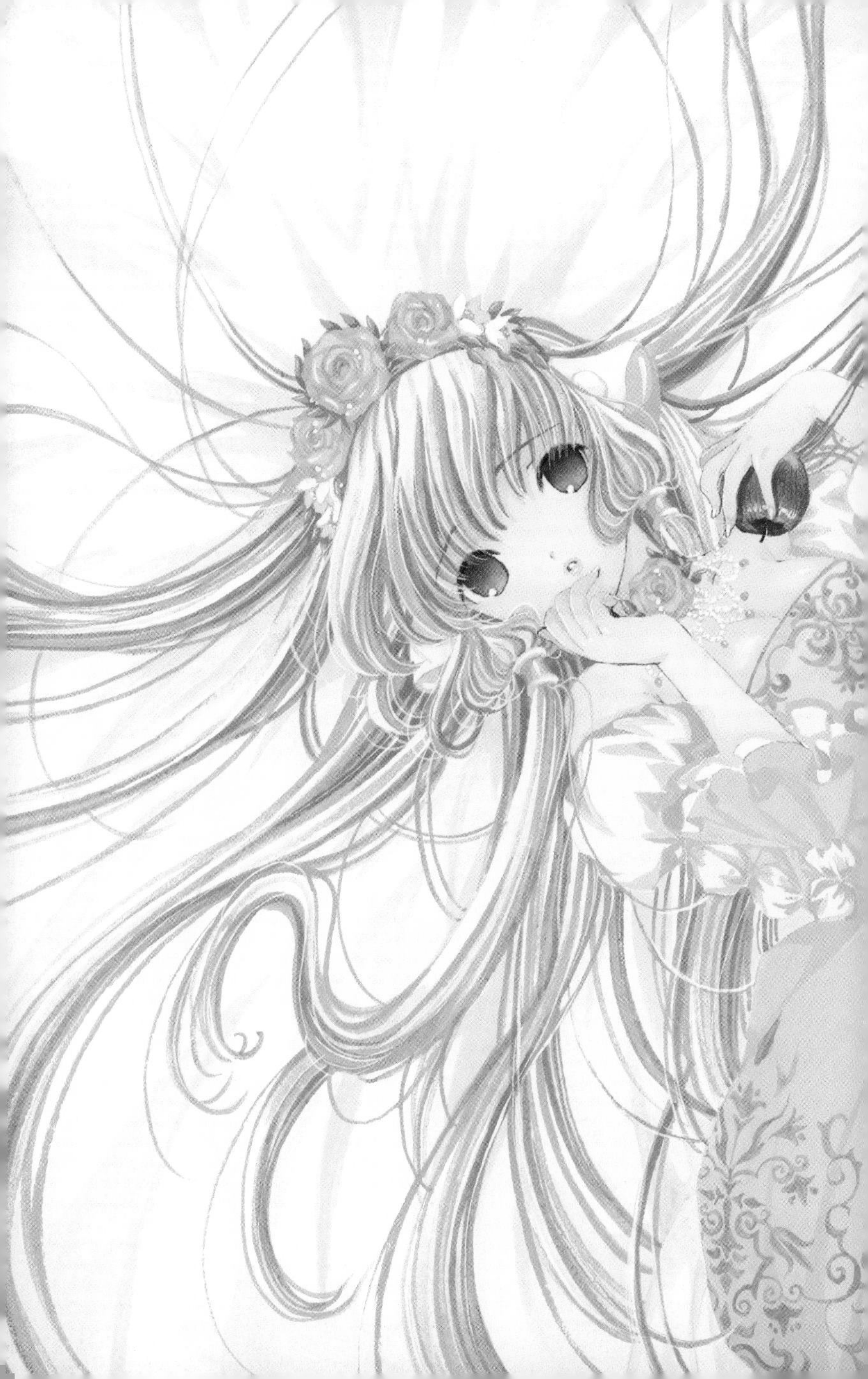

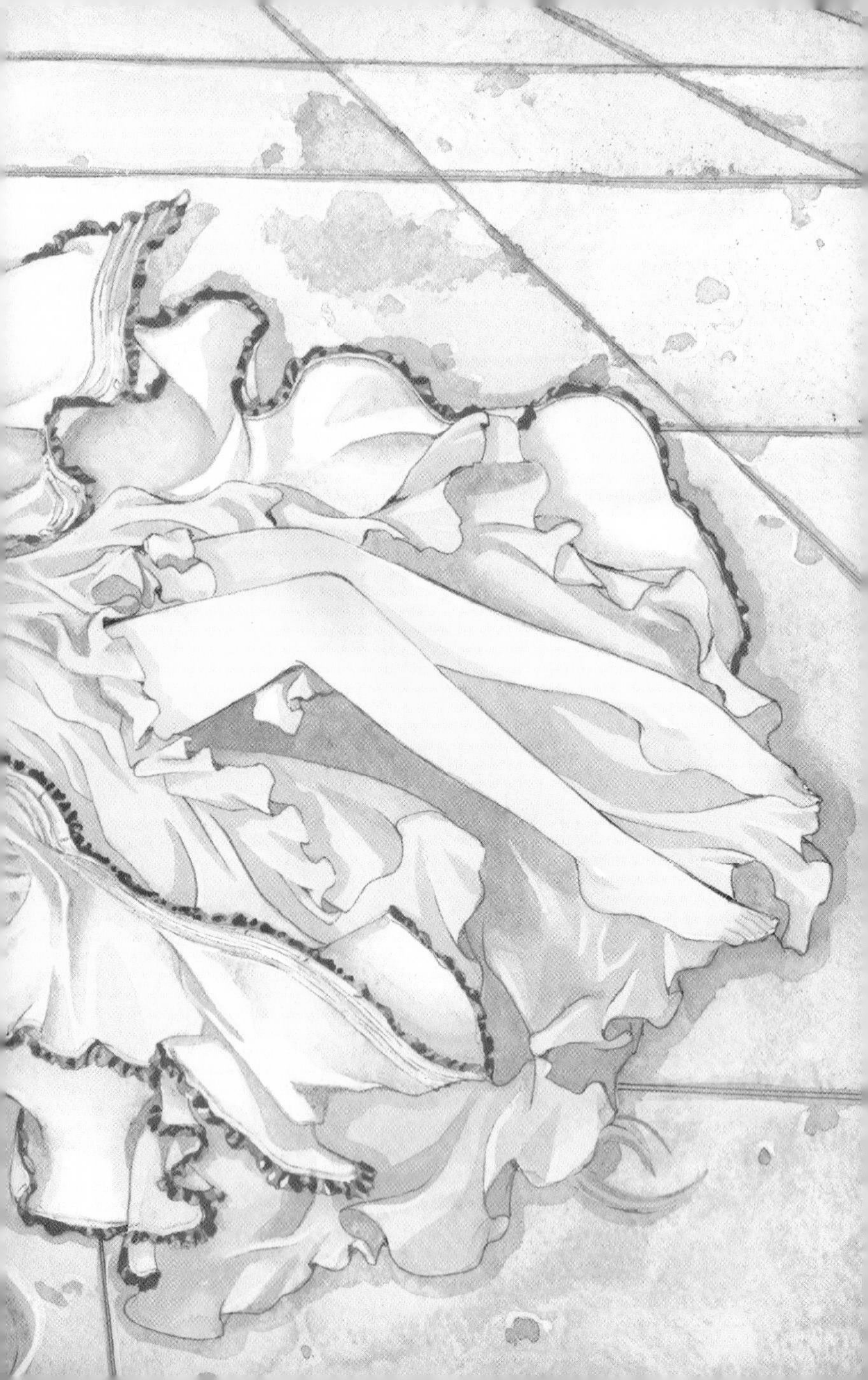

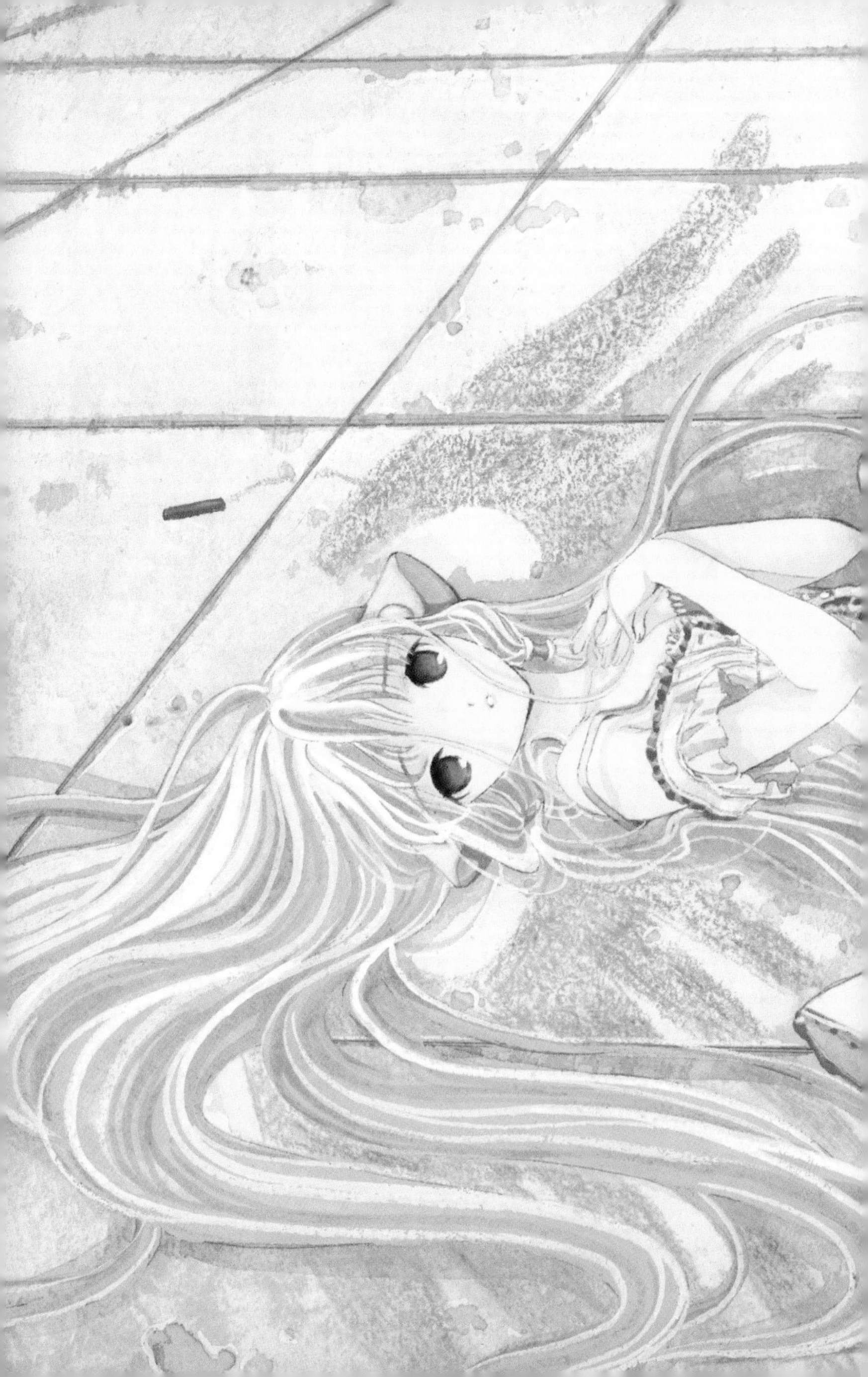

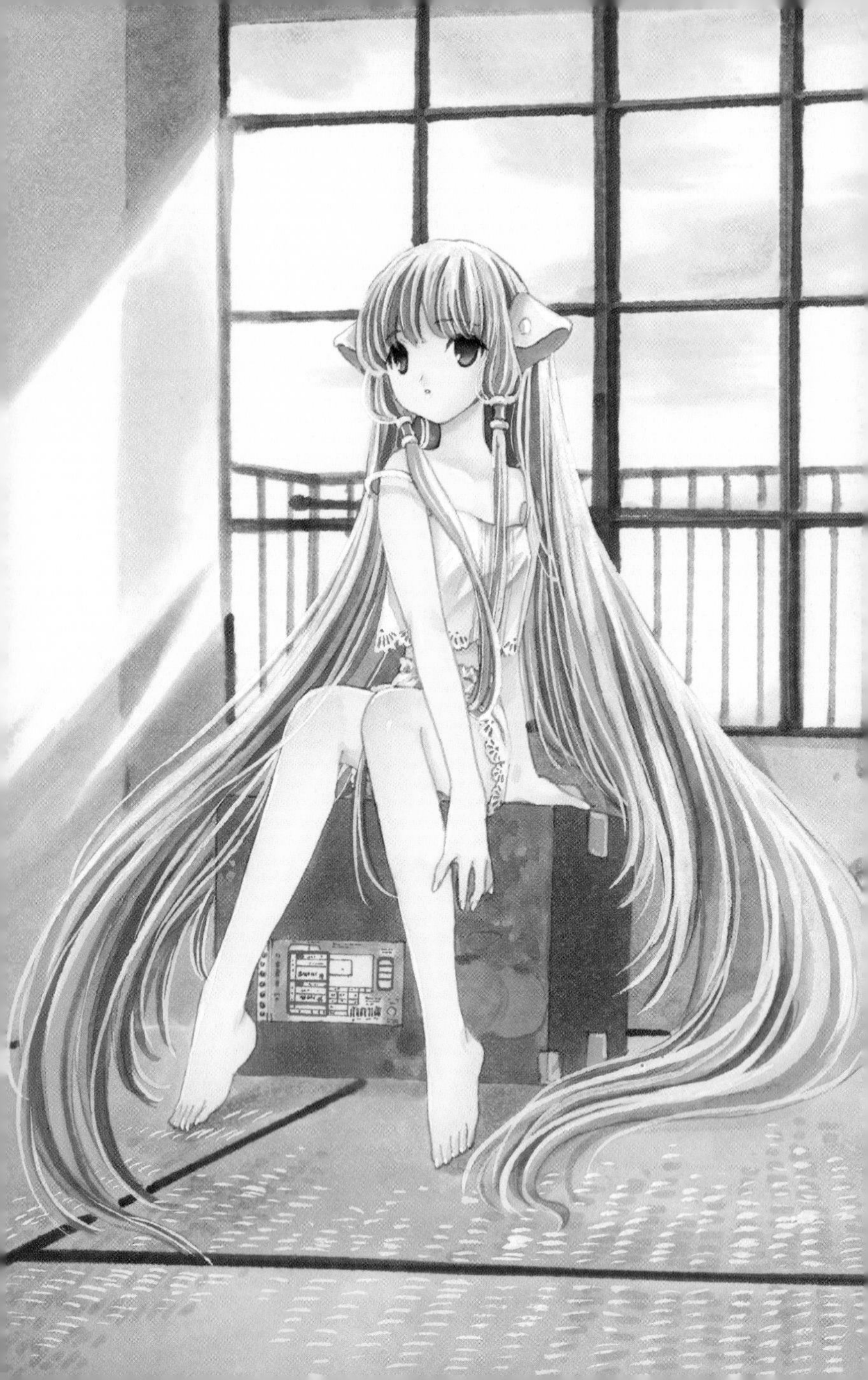

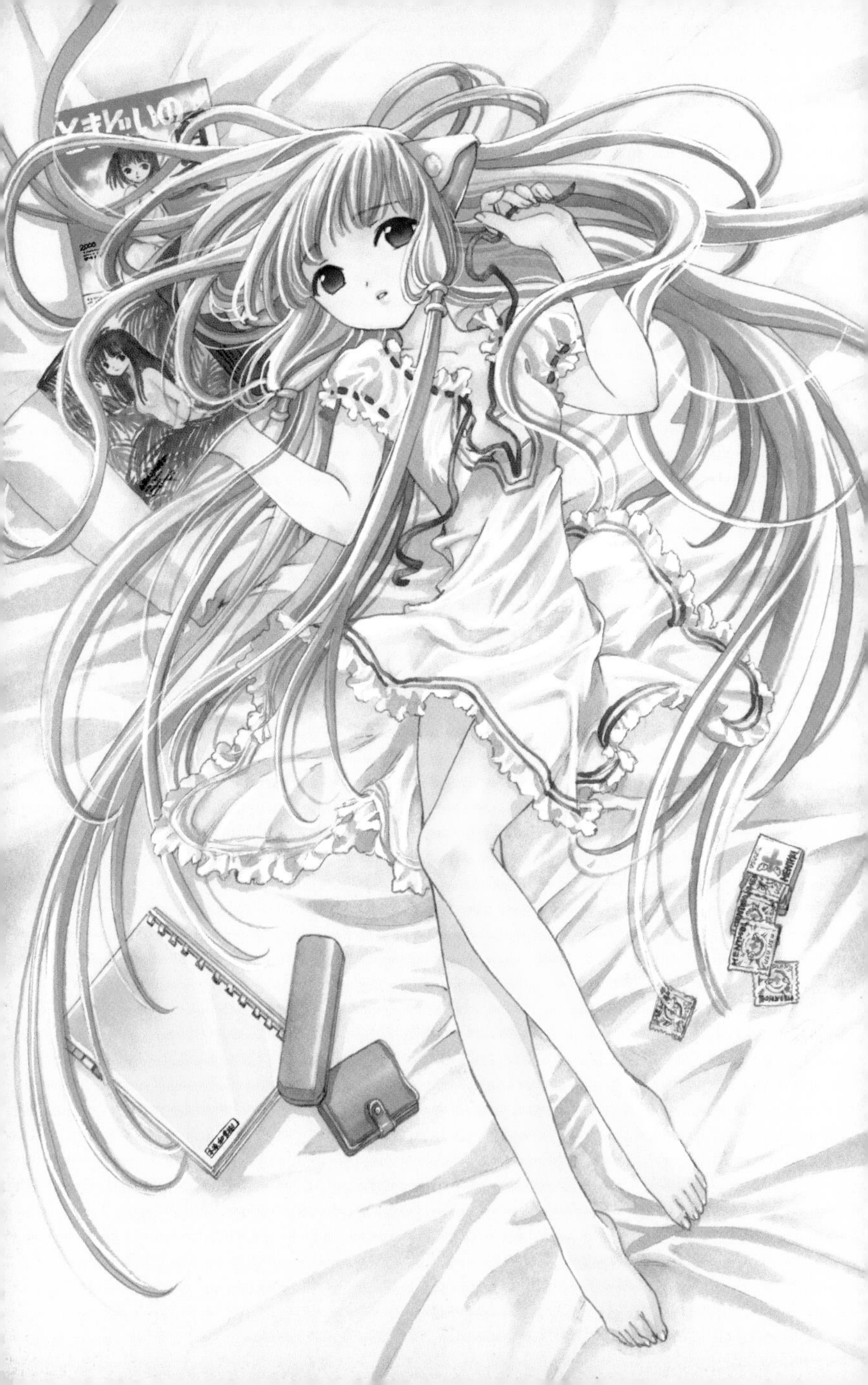

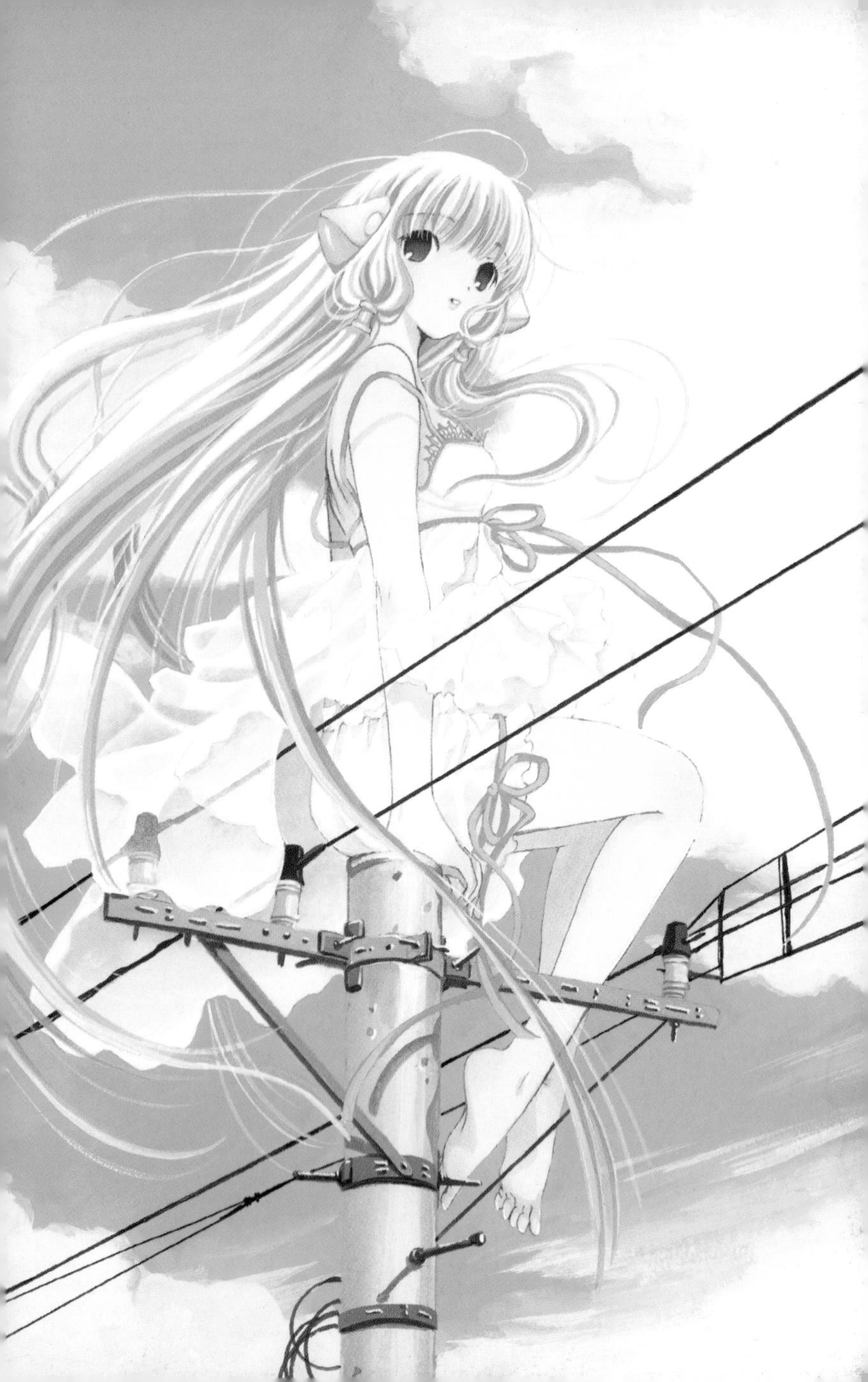

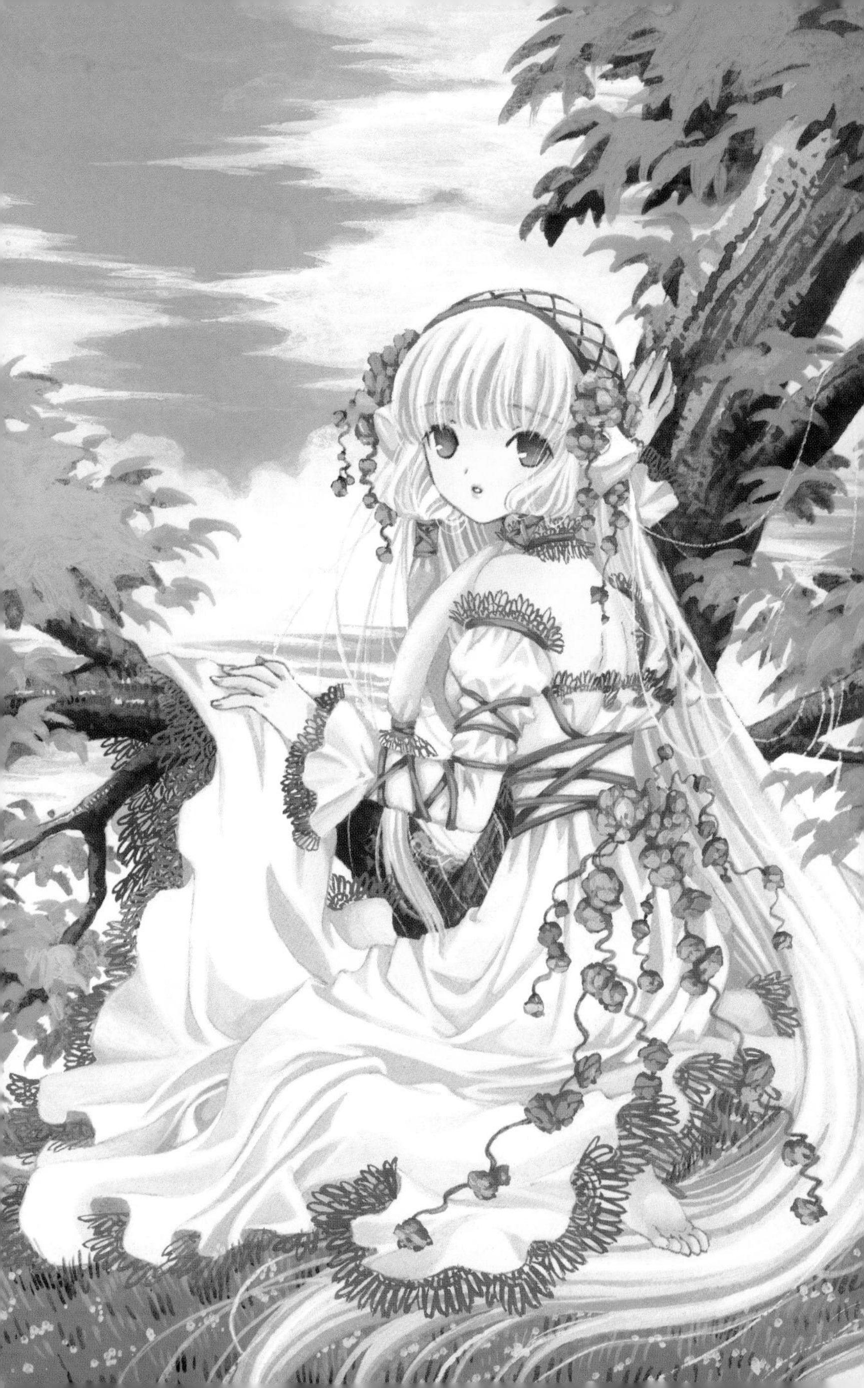

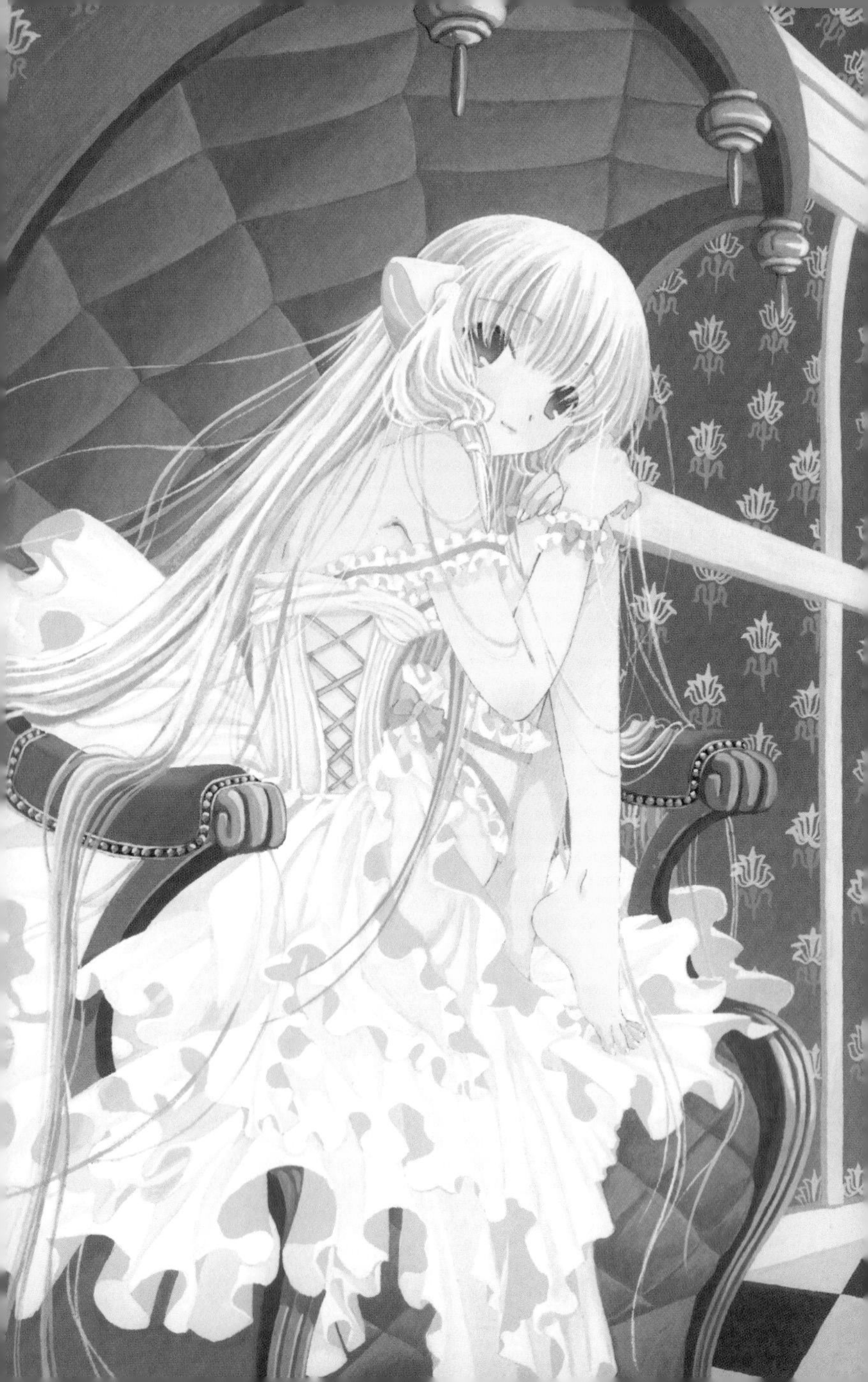

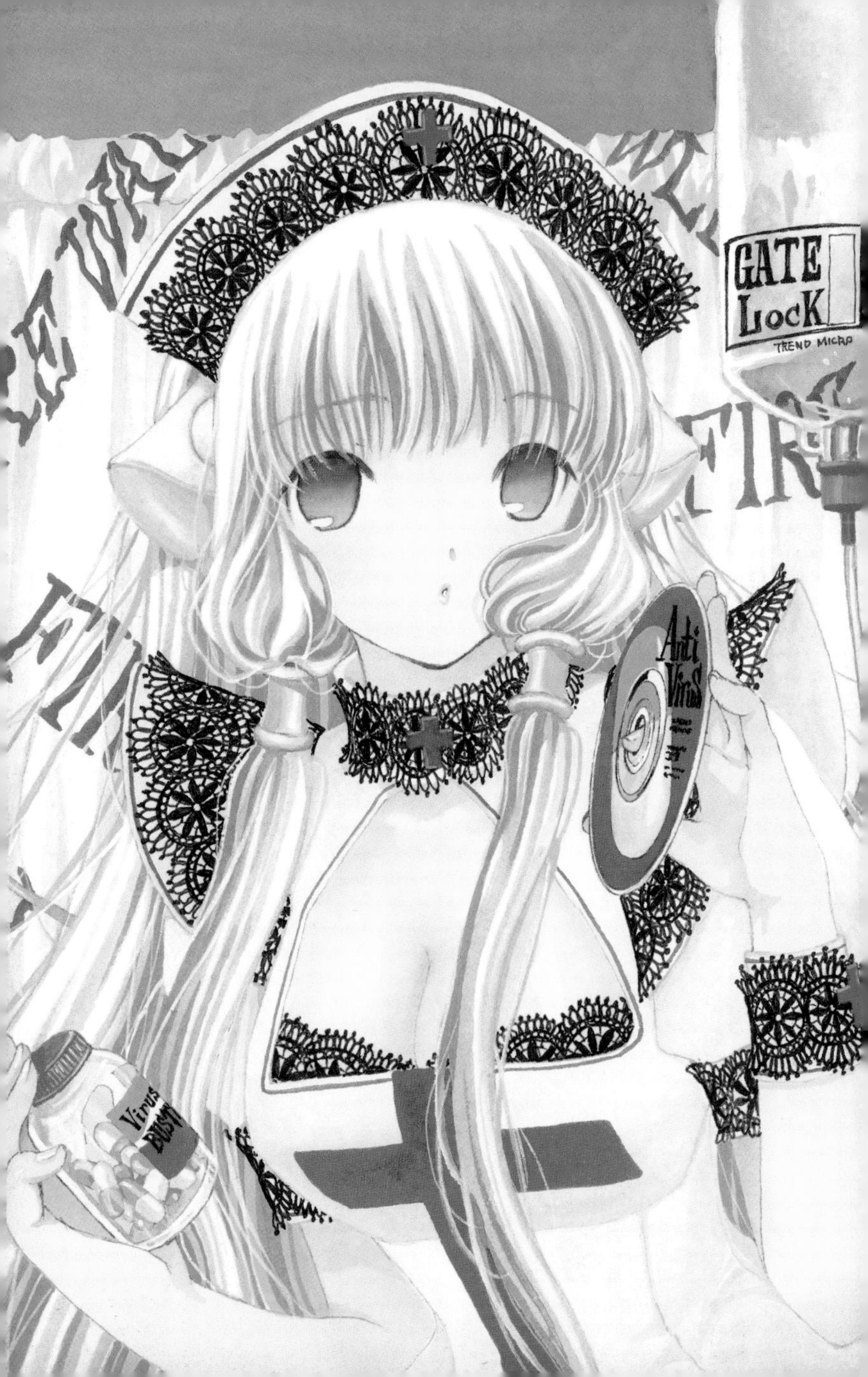
GATE LocK
TREND MICRO
Anti VirusS
Virus

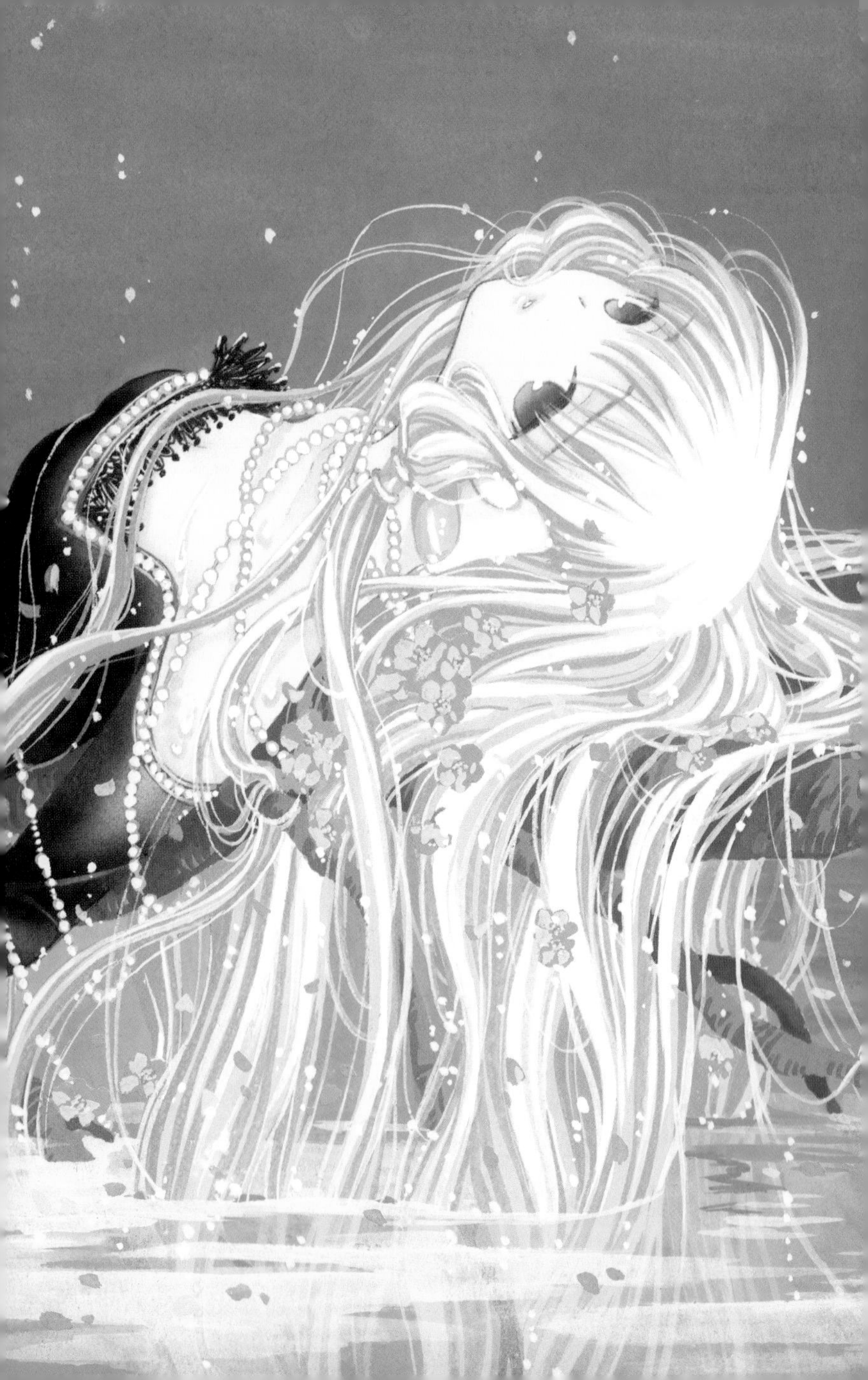

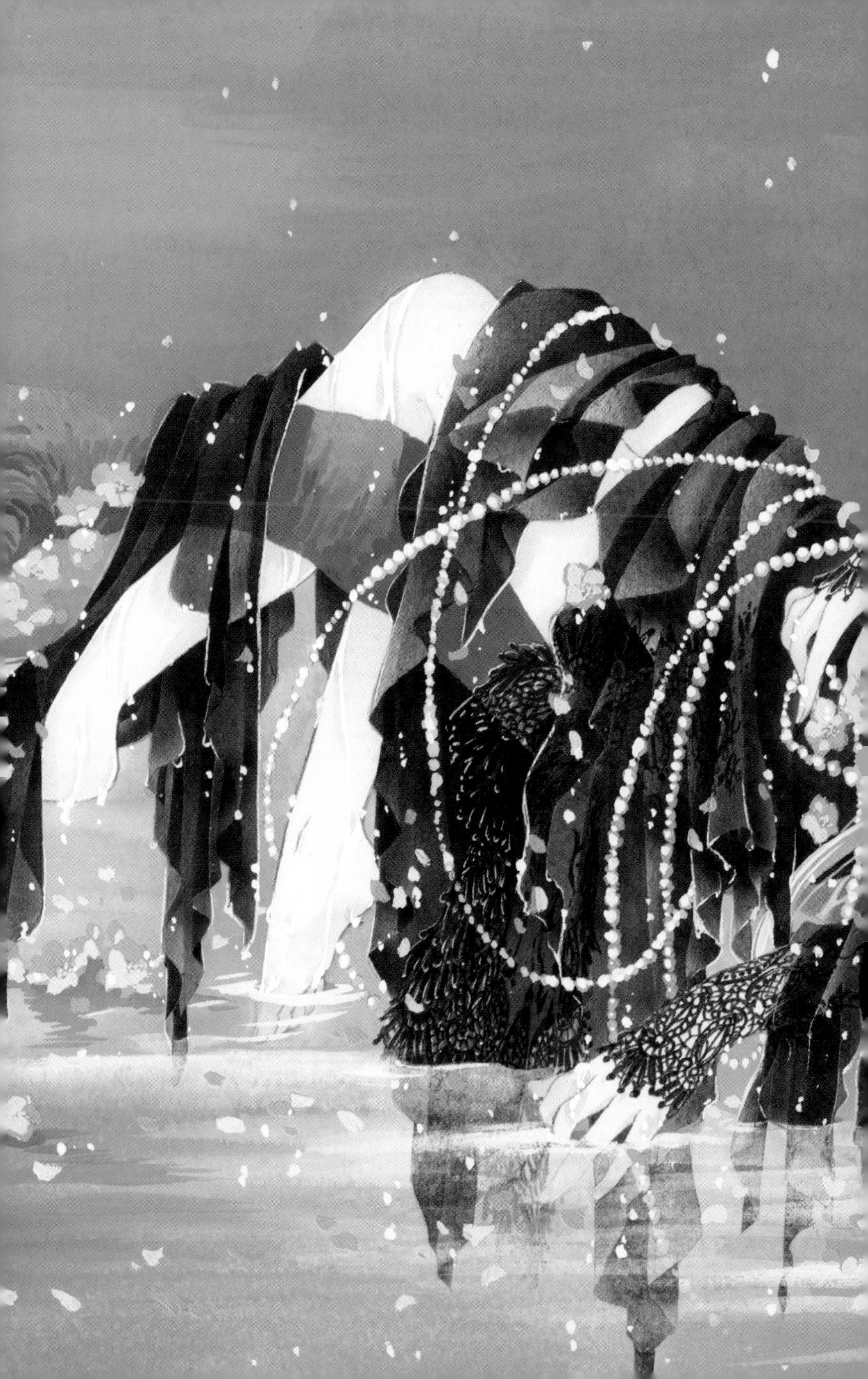

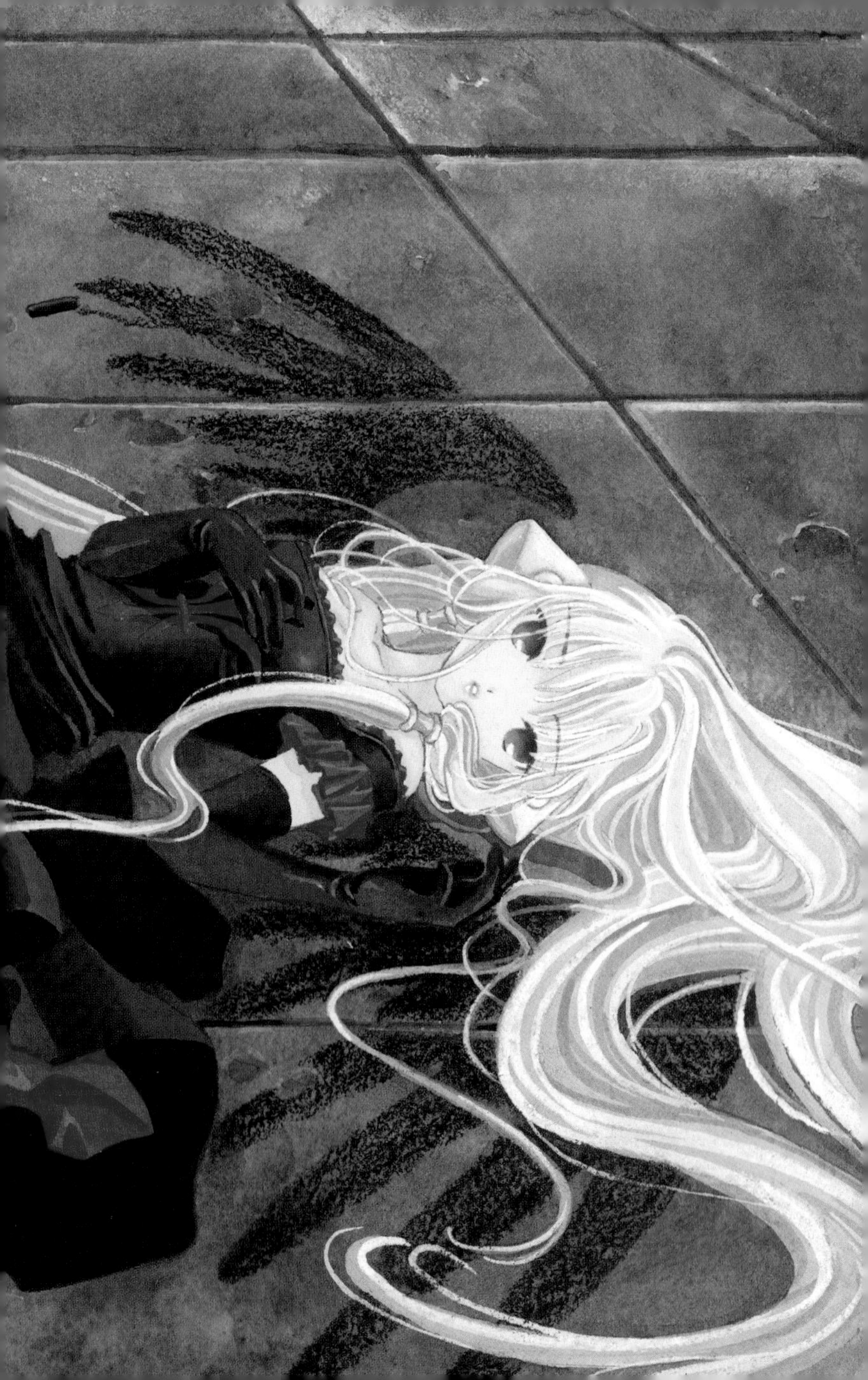

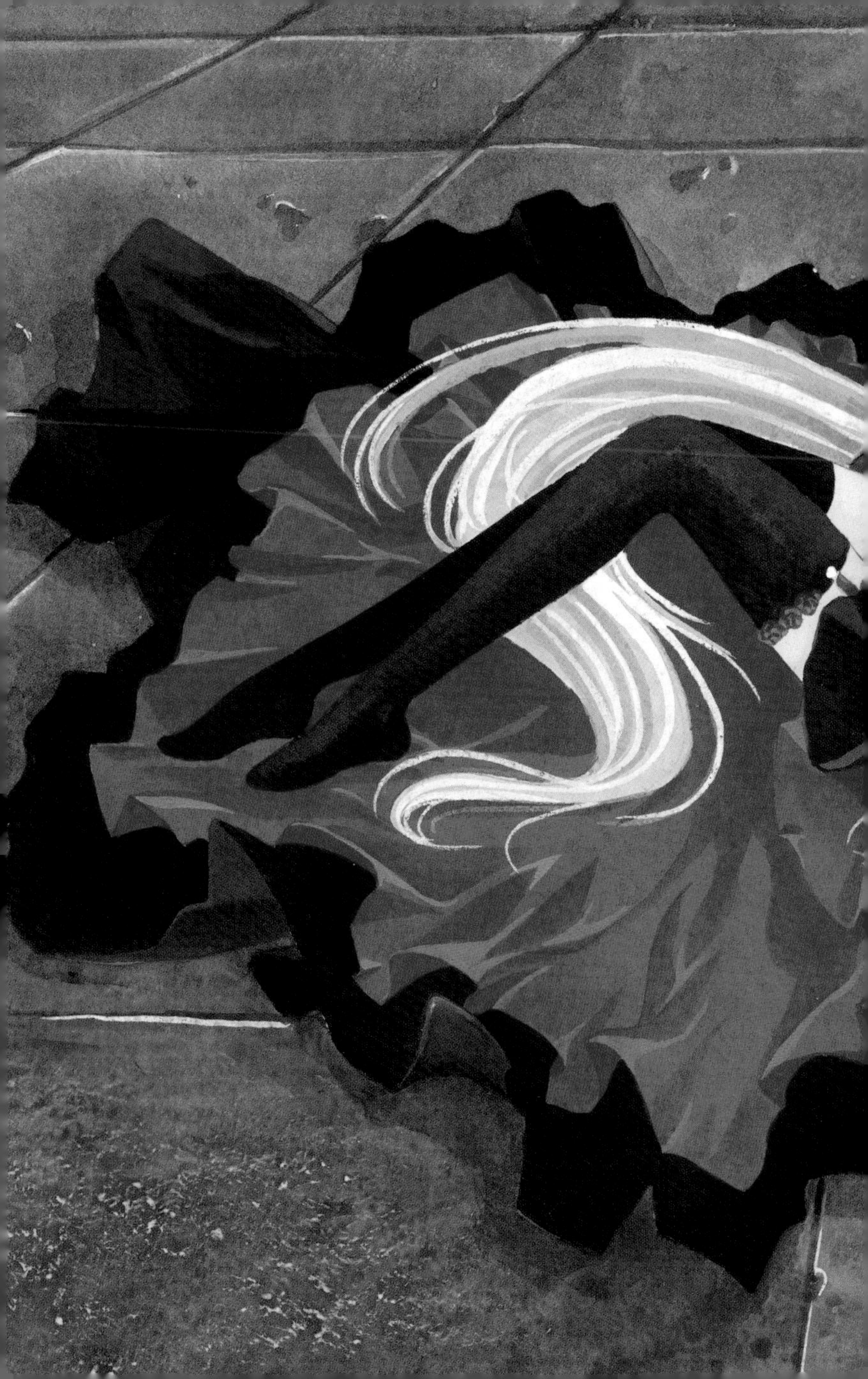

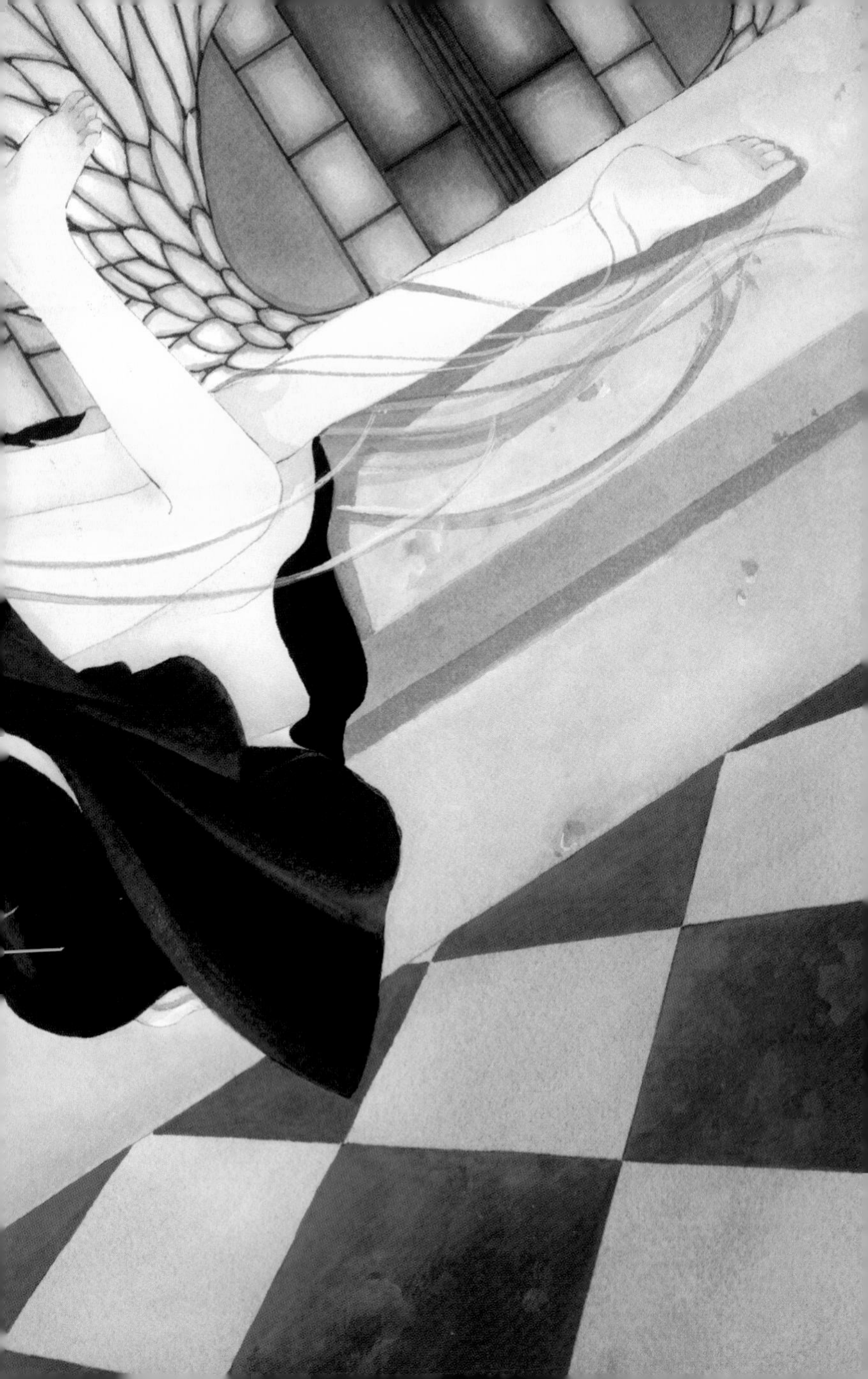

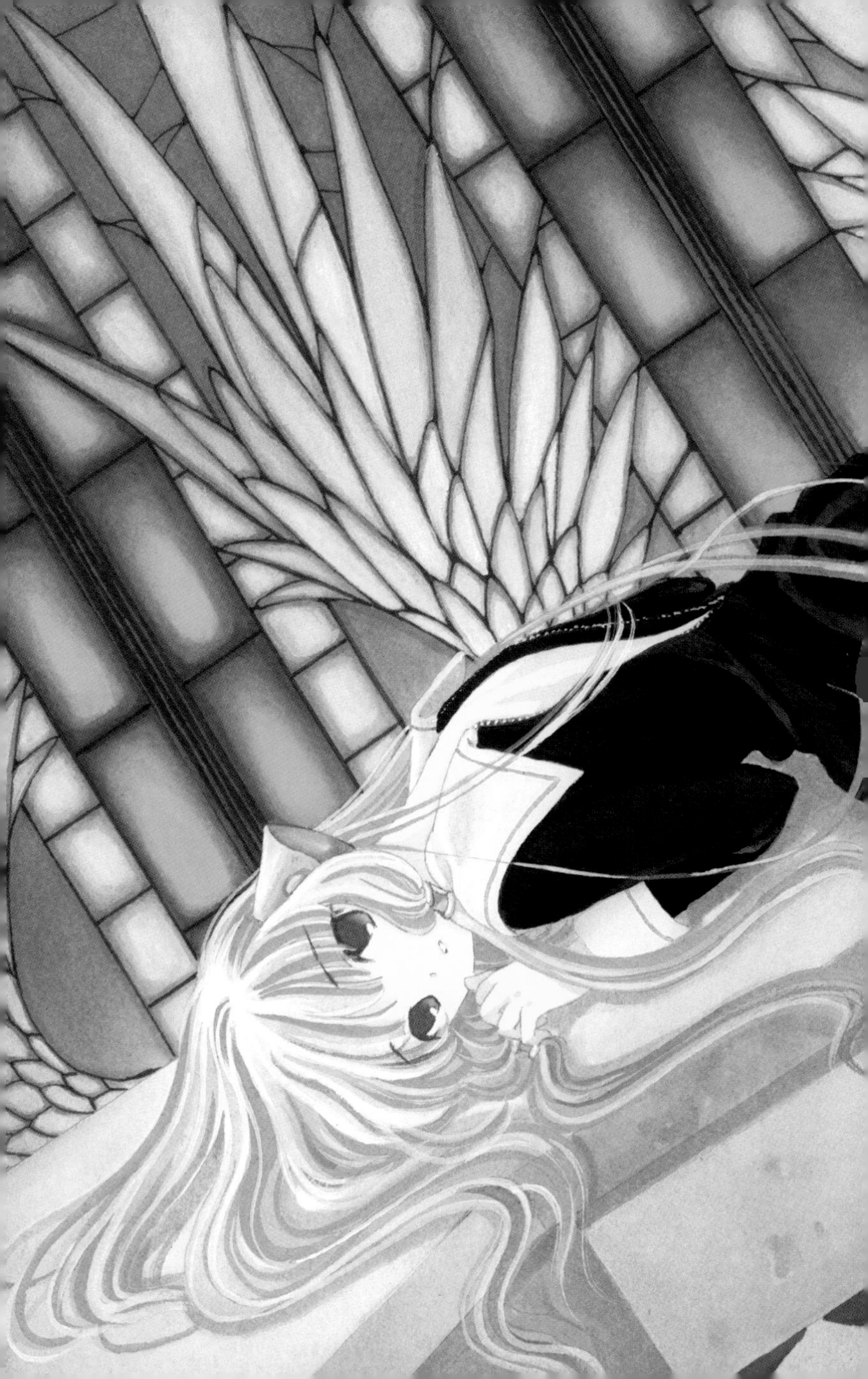

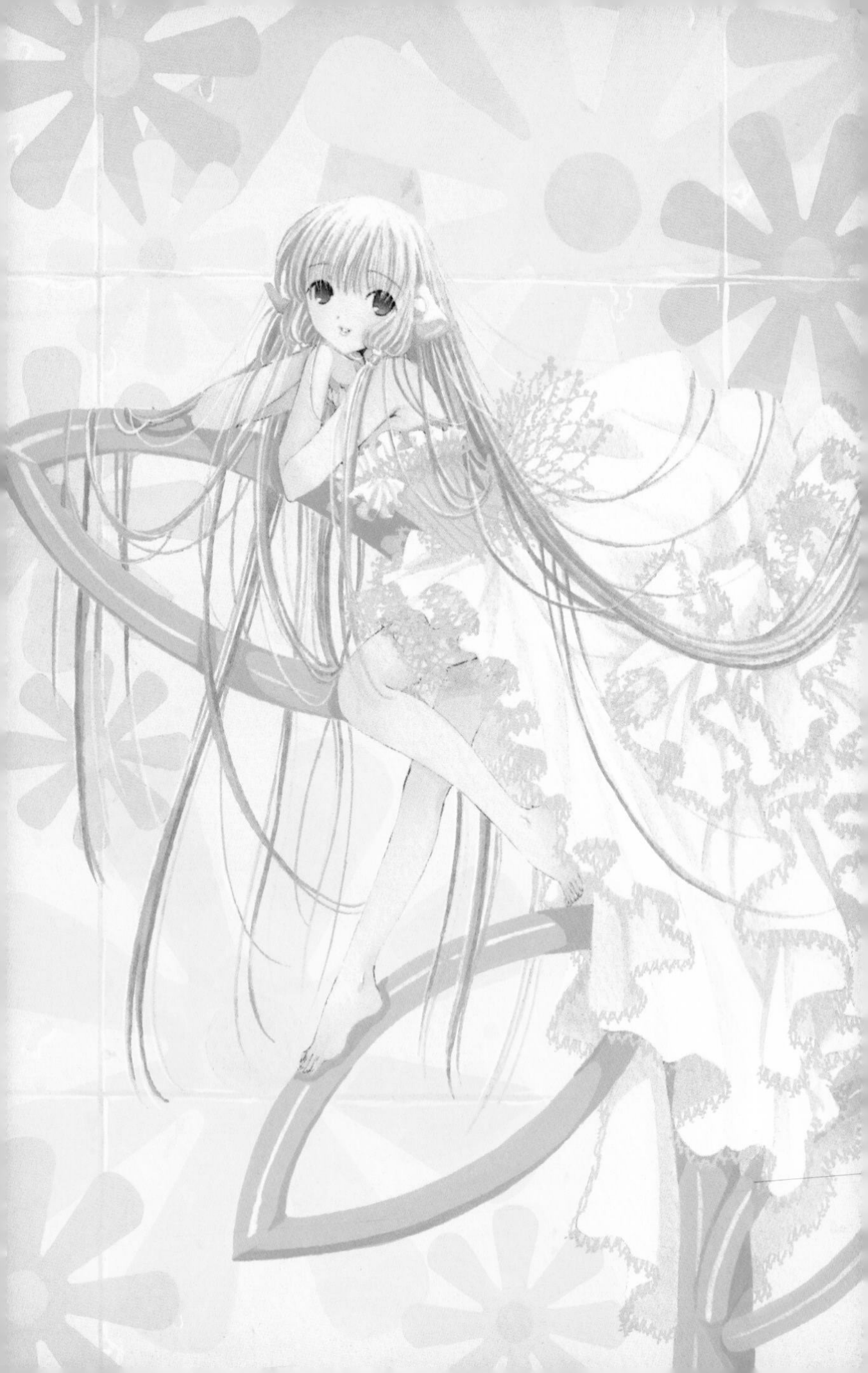

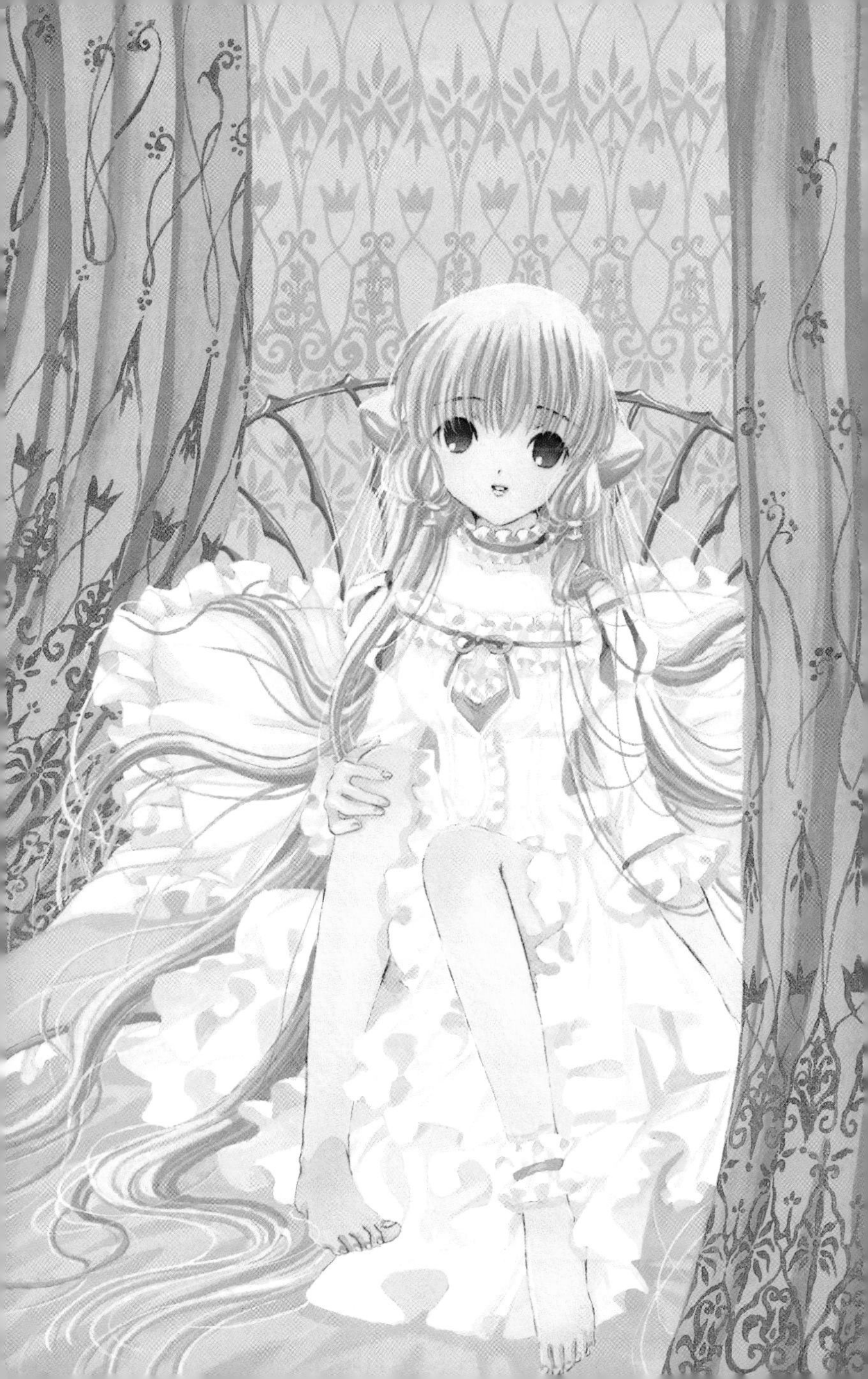

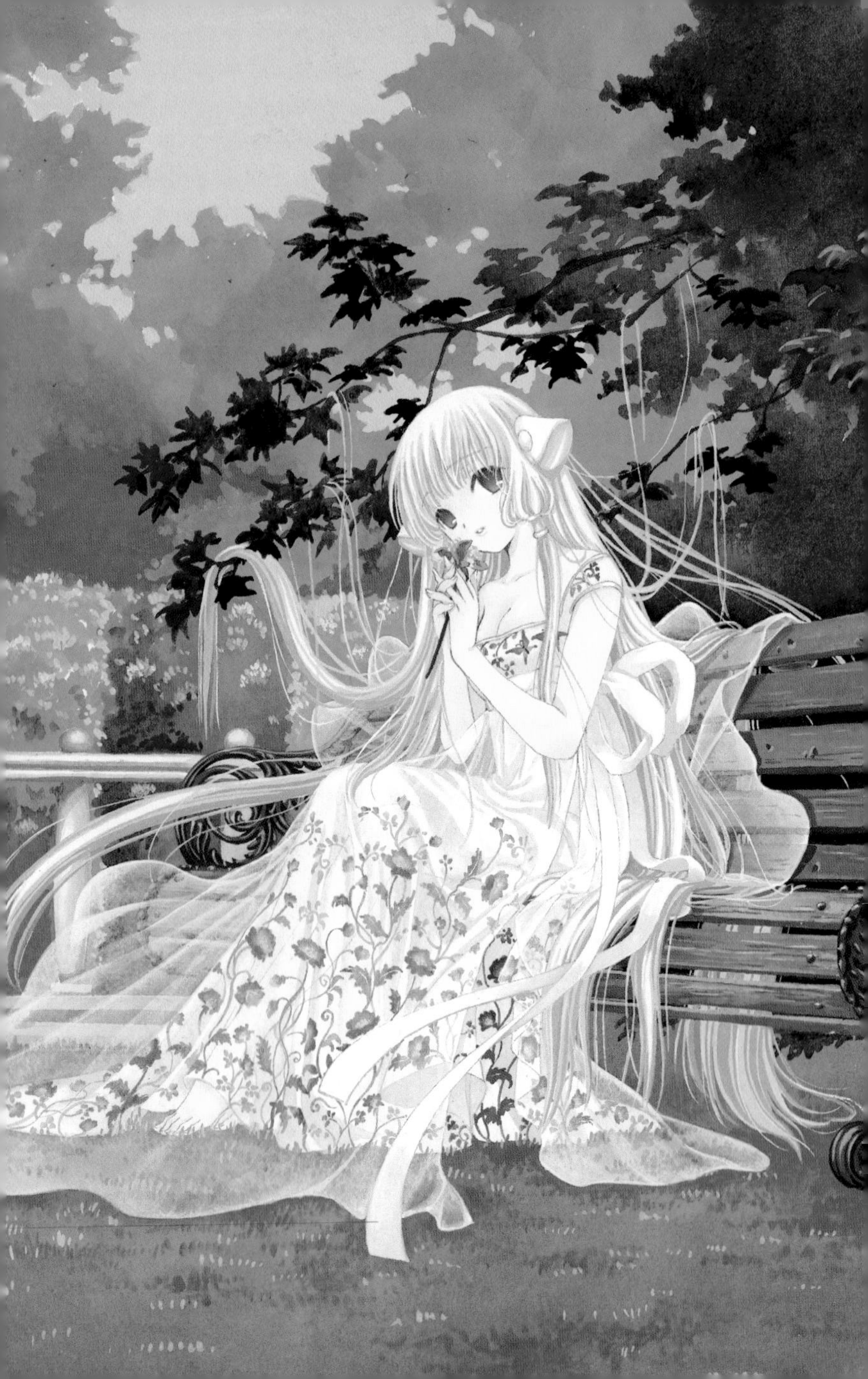

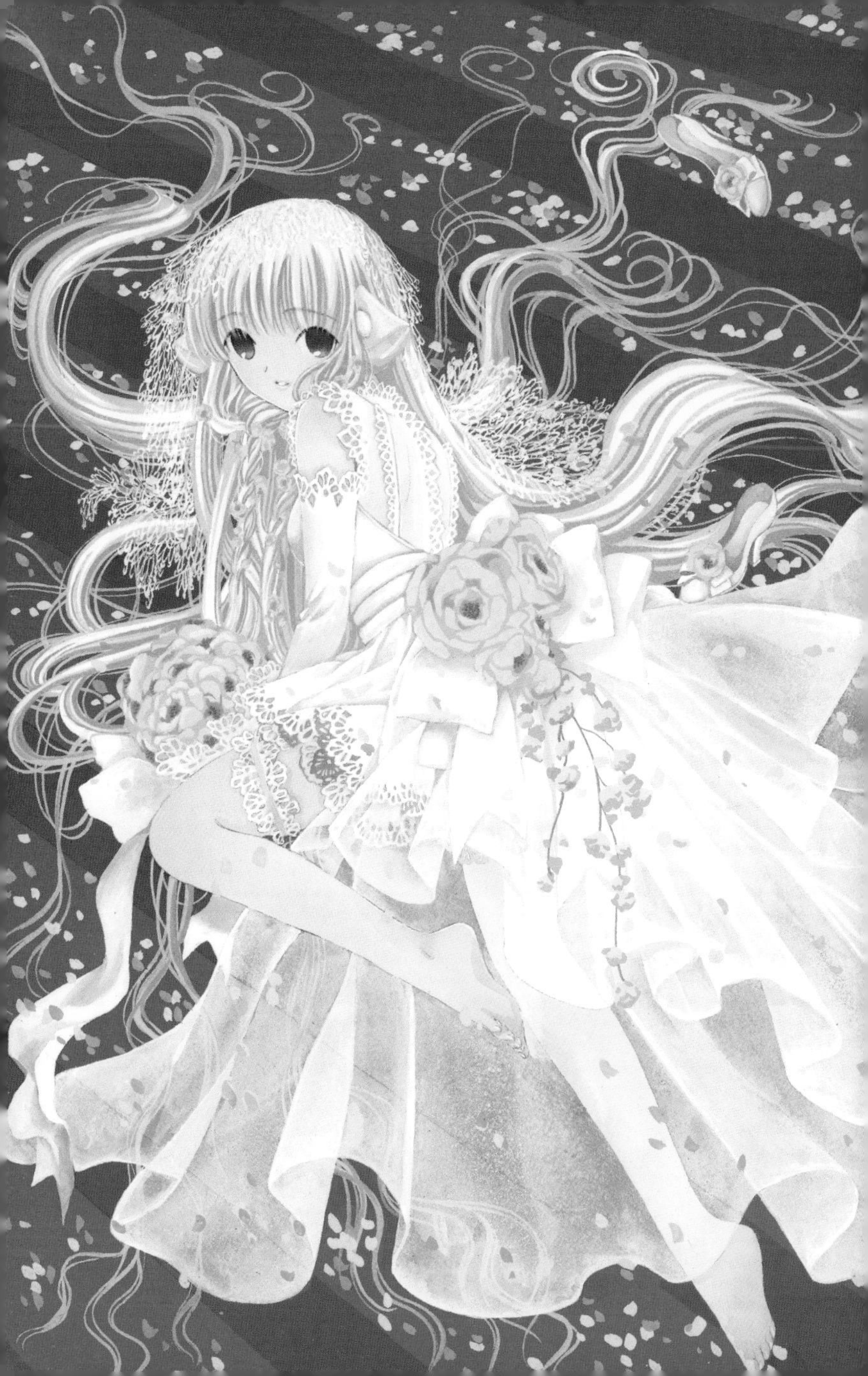

CLAMP オキモノ キモノ
Mokona's OKIMONO KIMONO

CLAMP artist Mokona loves the art of traditional Japanese kimono. In fact, she designs kimono and kimono accessories herself and shares her love in *Okimono Kimono*, a fun and lavishly illustrated book full of drawings and photographs, interviews (including an interview with Onuki Ami of the J-pop duo Puffy AmiYumi), and exclusive short manga stories from the CLAMP artists!

From the creators of such titles as *Clover*, *Chobits*, *Cardcaptor Sakura*, *Magic Knight Rayearth*, and *Tsubasa*, *Okimono Kimono* is now available in English for the first time ever!

ISBN 978-1-59582-456-1

$12.99

AVAILABLE AT YOUR LOCAL COMICS SHOP OR BOOKSTORE
To find a comics shop in your area, call 1-888-266-4226
For more information or to order direct: • On the web: darkhorse.com
E-mail: mailorder@darkhorse.com • Phone: 1-800-862-0052 Mon.–Fri. 9 AM to 5 PM Pacific Time.
CLAMP MOKONA NO OKIMONO KIMONO © 2007 CLAMP Mokona. Original Japanese edition published by Kawade Shobo Shinsha, Publishers. English translation copyright © 2010 Dark Horse Manga. Dark Horse Manga™ is a trademark of Dark Horse Comics, Inc. All rights reserved. (BL 7079)

Dark Horse Manga
darkhorse.com

STOP!

This is the back of the book!

This manga collection is translated into English, but arranged in right-to-left reading format to maintain the artwork's visual orientation as originally drawn and published in Japan. If you've never read comics this way before, take a look at the diagram below to give yourself an idea of how to go about it. Basically, you'll be starting in the upper right-hand corner, and will read each word balloon and panel moving right-to-left. It may take a little getting used to, but you should get the hang of it very quickly. Have fun! If this is the millionth manga you've read this way, never mind. ^_^

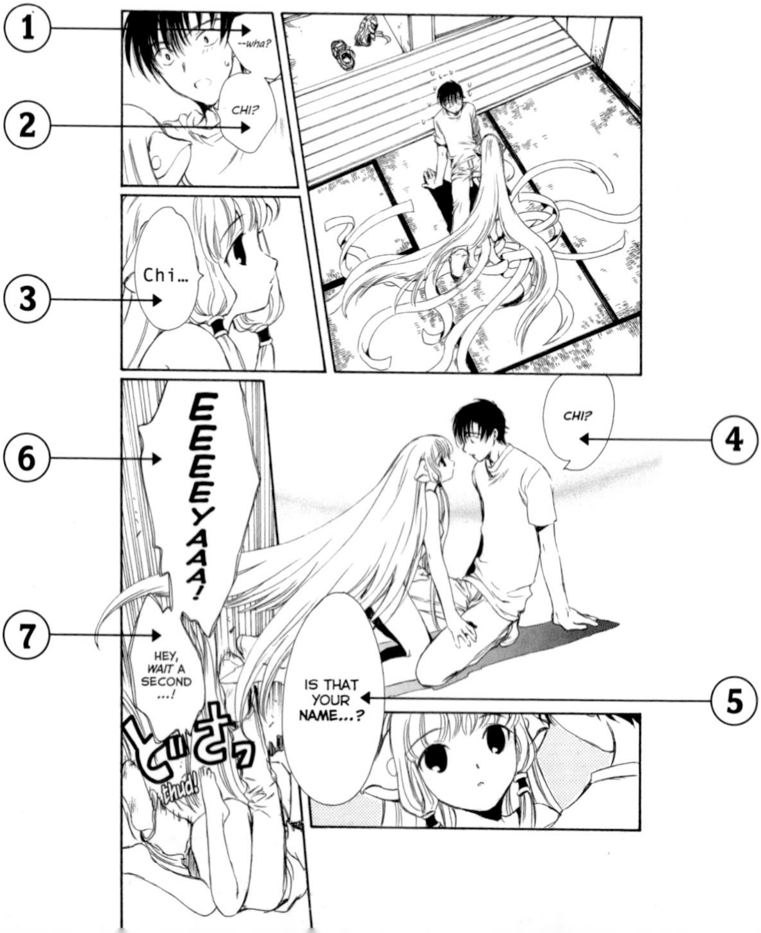
1
--wha?
2
CHI?
3
Chi...
4
CHI?
5
IS THAT YOUR NAME...?
6
EEEEEYAAA!
7
HEY, WAIT A SECOND ...!
どさっ
thud!